Proceedings

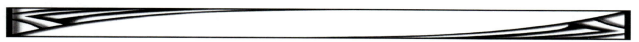

37th Annual IEEE/IFIP International Conference on Dependable Systems and Networks

Proceedings

37th Annual IEEE/IFIP International Conference on Dependable Systems and Networks

25-28 June 2007 • Edinburgh, UK

Sponsored by
IEEE Computer Society Technical Committee on Dependable Computing and Fault Tolerance
IFIP WG 10.4 on Dependable Computing and Fault Tolerance

Los Alamitos, California
Washington • Tokyo

IEEE Computer Society Order Number P2855
ISBN-13: 978-0-7695-2855-7
ISBN-10: 0-7695-2855-4
Library of Congress Number 2007924336

Additional copies may be ordered from:

IEEE Computer Society	IEEE Service Center	IEEE Computer Society
Customer Service Center	445 Hoes Lane	Asia/Pacific Office
10662 Los Vaqueros Circle	P.O. Box 1331	Watanabe Bldg., 1-4-2
P.O. Box 3014	Piscataway, NJ 08855-1331	Minami-Aoyama
Los Alamitos, CA 90720-1314	Tel: + 1 732 981 0060	Minato-ku, Tokyo 107-0062
Tel: + 1 800 272 6657	Fax: + 1 732 981 9667	JAPAN
Fax: + 1 714 821 4641	http://shop.ieee.org/store/	Tel: + 81 3 3408 3118
http://computer.org/cspress	customer-service@ieee.org	Fax: + 81 3 3408 3553
csbooks@computer.org		tokyo.ofc@computer.org

Individual paper REPRINTS may be ordered at: reprints@computer.org

Editorial production by Stephanie Kawada

Cover art production by Joe Daigle/Studio Productions

Printed in the United States of America by Odyssey Press Inc.

IEEE Computer Society
Conference Publishing Services (CPS)
http://www.computer.org/cps

Table of Contents

Keynote Address

DEPENDABLE COMPUTING AND COMMUNICATIONS SYMPOSIUM (DCCS)

Session 1A: Security Protection: Architectural Approaches

Session 1B: Software Fault Tolerance

Session 2A: Distributed Consensus

Session 2B: Practical Experience Reports

Session 3A: Embedded Systems

Session 3B: Dependability Modeling

Session 4A: Hardware Fault Tolerance: Emerging Challenges

Session 4B: VM Rejuvenation and Network Reliability

Session 5A: Soft Errors: Analysis and Protection

Session 5B: Processor Level Fault Tolerance

Session 6A: Critical Systems: Risk Analysis and Assurance

Session 6B: Security Threats and Novel Detection

Session 7A: Timing Model and Network Protocols

Session 7B: Security Protection: Algorithmic Approaches

Session 8A: Networking

Session 8B: Experimental Dependability Assessment

PERFORMANCE AND DEPENDABILITY SYMPOSIUM (PDS)

Session 1C: System Architecture and Software Assessment

Session 2C: Measurement and Monitoring

Session 3C: Practical Experience Reports

Session 4C: Distributed Algorithms

Session 5C: Availability of Distributed Systems

Session 6C: Modeling and Evaluation

Session 7C: Quality of Service and Error Recovery

Session 8C: Stochastic Modeling

SPECIAL TRACKS

Message from the Conference General Chair and Coordinator

Welcome to DSN 2007, the 37th Annual IEEE/IFIP International Conference on Dependable Systems and Networks. The ordinal 37 accurately reflects the long heritage of this conference that stretches back to 1971 when the first FTCS event was held in Pasadena.

And now we are in Edinburgh, only the second time that the event has been staged in the UK, and its first ever visit to Scotland. Of course, Scotland is a separate country to England and always has been; however, the two countries share one monarch and this year marks the 300th anniversary of the Union of their Parliaments.

It is a pleasure, and a duty, and a privilege to thank everyone who has contributed their time, enthusiasm, insight, and effort to the success of this event. To properly list them all would bring to mind an Academy Award speech (at the "Oscars" ceremony) so we won't attempt that. Even so, special thanks are due to the local organizers, who are in the front line for a very broad range of conference arrangements, and to the Program Chairs who take responsibility for the excellence of the technical program.

Last (though never least), we express our appreciation to all of the participants at DSN 2007. Without your involvement, there is no conference and we hope that the event lives up to all of your expectations. The melding of science and engineering, of work and relaxation too, the meeting of minds and ideas—we hope you experience and enjoy all of these at DSN, the premier international dependability conference.

Tom Anderson
General Chair

Mohamed Kaâniche
Conference Coordinator

Message from
the DCCS Track Program Chair

It is my great pleasure to welcome you to DSN 2007.

DCCS 2007 continues a tradition of technical excellence in the form of a productive blend of contributions from industry and academia. This year's DCCS program consists of 53 excellent papers that cover broad range of dependability issues and show the depth and breadth of our community's research and practice in development and assessment of highly reliable and secure computing systems and applications. A total of 16 sessions are planned: 15 consisting of regular papers and one devoted to practical experience reports.

The technical preparations for the symposium commenced in September 2006, when the DCCS 2007 Web page was opened to accept submissions. A total of 212 papers from 27 countries and five continents were received. Of them, 48 were accepted as regular papers and five were accepted as practical experience reports. Each regular paper was assigned at least five reviewers (two Program Committee members and three external reviewers), while practical experience reports were each reviewed by three Program Committee members. More than 93% of the reviews were returned. The Program Committee as a whole greatly appreciated the thoroughness of the reviews. Technical excellence and originality were the foremost criteria for selection, and the Committee also tried to maintain the right balance of theory and practice.

The technical program for DCCS 2007 would not have been possible without the active support and help of numerous individuals. First of all, we would like to thank all the authors for taking interest in and giving support to DCCS 2007. In the end, it was their contributions that allowed us to present a strong program.

I would like to express my deep appreciation to the 47 Program Committee members and the 390 external reviewers for their unprecedented dedication and hard work in evaluating the papers. I thank the PC members for devoting their time to the reviewing process and for making the program committee meeting (in "somewhat cold and snowy" Urbana in the middle of February) a success.

The last several months, many individuals helped me in many ways on this unforgettable journey. Especially, I would like to thank Mootaz Elnozahy and Rick Schlichting for their support and mentoring. I am grateful to Neeraj Suri for his help in running the PC meeting. Special thanks are also due to Mohamed Kaâniche, as a conference coordinator, for his enthusiasm and excellent job in interfacing with the DSN Steering Committee, helping with the PC meeting, and making sure that we meet all the deadlines. Finally, I thank the administrative and technical staff in the Coordinated Science Laboratory in the University of Illinois at Urbana-Champaign for their assistance in hosting the PC meeting.

Thank you for attending the symposium. I believe that you have an outstanding program ahead and hope that you will be able not only to enjoy it, but also to contribute to it by engaging in many fruitful discussions with your colleagues.

Enjoy the Symposium and enjoy Edinburgh!

Zbigniew Kalbarczyk
University of Illinois at Urbana-Champaign, USA

Message from
the PDS Track Chair

It is a pleasure to welcome you to the PDS track of DSN 2007.

The Performance and Dependability Symposium (PDS) is one of the two major tracks of the International Conference on Dependable Systems and Networks (DSN) since 2002. The history of the symposium dates back to 1995 when the first International Performance and Dependability Symposium was held in Erlangen, Germany. Since this time, the symposium offers a forum for academic and industrial research results considering the performance, dependability, and in more recent times also the security of information processing systems and networks.

PDS 2007 continues the tradition of a program of technical excellence in presenting a blend of very high-quality papers from industry and academia. As in the past, papers cover a wide range of topics from model-based system analysis to the evaluation of existing systems according to performance and dependability. This mix positions PDS as a system- and methodology-oriented conference.

A total of 95 papers from 20 countries and three continents were received. At the plenary Program Committee meeting, hosted at the department of computer science of the University of Dortmund, 24 full papers and three practical experience reports were accepted. The PC meeting was attended by 22 PC members. Each paper was assigned to five reviewers, three PC members, and two external reviewers. More than 80% of the reviews were returned and at the PC meeting, for each paper at least three reviews were available. All papers were discussed during the meeting to assure a transparent and fair selection resulting in a high-quality program. The selection process was very competitive, such that even papers of a good quality had to be rejected.

The technical program for PDS 2007 would not have been possible without the active support and help of many individuals. First of all, I have to thank all authors who submitted their papers to PDS and all reviewers for their effort. I thank all members of the PC for their detailed reviews and for taking their time to attend the PC meeting. Without the help of the conference coordinator, Mohamed Kaâniche, and the general chair, Tom Anderson, it would have been hard for me to run the process smoothly. The members of the steering committee Ravi Iyer and Jaynarayan Lala were very helpful in several aspects. Last not least, I would like to thank the members of my group for their unfailing organizational efforts. Falko Bause did a great job in maintaining the conference software and in managing the review process and the computer infrastructure during the PC meeting. Monika Boenigk and Heike Rapp did all the time-consuming organizational tasks in a perfect and smooth way.

Finally, I thank all attendees of PDS for coming to the conference and making it a successful and enjoyable symposium.

Peter Buchholz
Universität Dortmund, Germany

William C. Carter Award

The William C. Carter Award is presented annually (since 1997) at the DSN Conference to recognize an individual who has made a significant contribution to the field of dependable computing through his or her graduate dissertation research. The award commemorates the late William C. Carter, a key figure in the formation and development of the field of dependable computing. Bill Carter always took the time to encourage, mentor, and inspire newcomers to this field and this award honors and sustains this aspect of his legacy.

The award is sponsored by IEEE Technical Committee on Dependable Computing and Fault Tolerance (TC-DC&FT) and IFIP Working Group on Dependable Computing and Fault Tolerance (WG 10.4).

To be eligible for this award, a paper based on the student's dissertation research must have been submitted to the DSN Conference (to either the DCCS or PDS track) as a regular paper, with the student as the first author, and nominated by their supervisor. Current and former graduate students are eligible until not more than two years past the completion of their dissertations.

All Carter Award nominations accepted as regular papers for the DSN 2007 Conference (either track) were evaluated by the Steering Committee of the Conference. The winner of the 2007 William C. Carter Award is

Jorrit N. Herder *of Vrije Universiteit, Amsterdam, Netherlands*

for the paper entitled

Failure Resilience for Device Drivers

Jorrit N. Herder, Herbert Bos, Ben Gras, Philip Homburg, and Andrew S. Tanenbaum

Conference Organizers

General Chair
Tom Anderson, *Newcastle University, UK*

Honorary Chair
Brian Randell, *Newcastle University, UK*

Conference Coordinator
Mohamed Kaâniche, *LAAS-CNRS, France*

Publicity Coordinator
Roy Maxion, *Carnegie Mellon University, USA*

Finance Chair
Neil Speirs, *Newcastle University, UK*

Local Arrangements, Registration and Exhibition Chairs
Joan Atkinson, *Newcastle University, UK*
Claire Smith, *Newcastle University, UK*

Fund-Raising Chair
Aad van Moorsel, *Newcastle University, UK*

Publication Chair
Massimo Felici, *University of Edinburgh, UK*

Program Chair—DCCS Track
Zbigniew Kalbarczyk, *University of Illinois at Urbana-Champaign, USA*

Program Chair—PDS Track
Peter Buchholz, *Universität Dortmund, Germany*

Tutorials Chair
Luís Rodrigues, *Universidade de Lisboa, Portugal*

Workshops Chair
Christof Fetzer, *Technische Universität Dresden, Germany*

Student Forum Chair
Farnam Jahanian, *University of Michigan, USA*

Fast Abstracts Chair
Hiroshi Nakamura, *University of Tokyo, Japan*

Industry Session Chair
Lisa Spainhower, *IBM, USA*

DSN Steering Committee

Chair

Elmootazbellah N. Elnozahy, *IBM, Austin Research Lab., USA*

Vice Chair

Richard D. Schlichting, *AT & T Labs, USA*

Communications Chair

Charles B. Weinstock, *SEI, USA*

Members

Jean Arlat, *LAAS-CNRS, France*
Algirdas Avizienis, *Vytautas Magnus University, Lithuania*
W. Kent Fuchs, *Cornell University, USA*
Ravishankar K. Iyer, *UIUC, USA*
Karama Kanoun, *LAAS-CNRS, France*
Johan Karlsson, *Chalmers University, Sweden*
Hermann Kopetz, *T.U. Vienna, Austria*
Sy-Yen Kuo, *National Taiwan University, Taiwan*
Jaynarayan H. Lala, *Raytheon, USA*

Carl Landwehr, *NSF, USA*
Jean-Claude Laprie, *LAAS-CNRS, France*
Takashi Nanya, *University of Tokyo, Japan*
William H. Sanders, *UIUC, USA*
Luca Simoncini, *University of Pisa, Italy*
Lisa Spainhower, *IBM, USA*
Neeraj Suri, *TU Darmstadt, Germany*
Robert Swarz, *MITRE Corporation, USA*
Kishor Trivedi, *Duke University, USA*
Paulo Verissimo, *University of Lisboa, Portugal*

DCCS Program Committee

Dependable Computing and Communications Symposium (DCCS)

Program Chair

Zbigniew Kalbarczyk, *University of Illinois at Urbana-Champaign, USA*

Program Committee

Lorenzo Alvisi, *University of Texas, Austin, USA*
Claudio Basile, *Google, USA*
Douglas Blough, *Georgia Institute of Technology, USA*
Andrea Bondavalli, *University of Firenze, Italy*
Nikita Borisov, *University of Illinois at Urbana-Champaign, USA*
Rick Buskens, *Lockheed Martin, USA*
Cristian Constantinescu, *AMD, USA*
Yves Deswarte, *LAAS-CNRS, France*
Elmootazbellah Elnozahy, *IBM, USA*
Roy Friedman, *Technion, Israel*
Virgil Gligor, *University of Meryland, USA*
Rachid Guerraoui, *EPFL, Switzerland*
Yennun Huang, *AT&T Research, USA*
Ravishankar Iyer, *University of Illinois at Urbana-Champaign, USA*
Nobuyasu Kanekawa, *Hitachi, Japan*
Johan Karlsson, *Chalmers University, Sweden*
Takuya Katayama, *Japan Advanced Institute of Science and Technology, Japan*
Tohru Kikuno, *Osaka University, Japan*
A. J. Klein Osowski, *IBM, USA*
Philip Koopman, *Carnegie Mellon University, USA*
Regis Leveugle, *TIMA-CMP Laboratory, France*
Miroslaw Malek, *Humboldt-Universität, Germany*
Eliane Martins, *University of Campinas, Brazil*

Aad van Moorsel, *Newcastle University, UK*
Gilles Muller, *École des Mines de Nantes, France*
Priya Narasimhan, *Carnegie Mellon University, USA*
James Plank, *University of Tennessee, Knoxville, USA*
David Powell, *LAAS-CNRS, France*
Michael Reiter, *Carnegie Mellon University, USA*
Luigi Romano, *University of Naples, Italy*
Gerardo Rubino, *INRIA, France*
William Sanders, *University of Illinois at Urbana-Champaign, USA*
Andre Schiper, *EPFL, Switzerland*
Rick Schlichting, *AT&T Research, USA*
Stephen Scott, *Oak Ridge National Laboratory, USA*
Santosh Shrivastava, *University of Newcastle, UK*
João Gabriel Silva, *University of Coimbra, Portugal*
Neeraj Suri, *TU Darmstadt, Germany*
Dong Tang, *Sun Microsystems, USA*
David Taylor, *University of Waterloo, Canada*
Paulo Veríssimo, *University of Lisboa, Portugal*
Yi-Min Wang, *Microsoft Research, USA*
Alan Wood, *Sun Microsystems, USA*
Jie Xu, *University of Leeds, UK*
Jun Xu, *Google, USA*
Mohammad Zulkernine, *Queens University, Ontario, Canada*

Ex Officio

Jaynarayan Lala, *Raytheon, USA*
Rick Schlichting, *AT & T Labs, USA*

Reviewers for DCCS

Sherif Abdelwahed
Jacob Abraham
Dennis Abts
Sarita Adve
Adnan Agbaria
Nadeem Ahmed
Carlos Almeida
Yair Amir
Emmanuelle Anceaume
Marios Andreou
Jean Arlat
Anish Arora
Mohammad Atef
Todd Austin
Ozalp Babaoglu
Saurabh Bagchi
David Bakken
Hitesh Ballani
Wendyy Bartlett
Sapan Bathia
Robin Berthier
Vartika Bhandari
Saad Biaz
Martin Biely
Kenneth Birman
P. Bishop
Pedro Bizarro
Jennifer Black
Andrea Bobbio
Peter Bokor
Ron Bolam
Pradip Bose
Francisco Brasileiro
Mary Brown
Stefan Bruening
Soo Bum Lee
Kevin Butler
Xia Cai
George Candea
Ethan Cannon
Jiannong Cao
Joao Carlos Cunha
Gabriella Carrozza
Antonio Casimiro
Madhusudanan
Chandrasekaran
Fangzhe Chang

Daniel Chen
David Chen
Shuo Chen
Bill Cheswick
Ngai Cheuk Han
Silvano Chiaradonna
Gianfranco Ciardo
Alessandro Cilardo
Marcello Cinque
Augusto Ciuffoletti
Allen Clement
Jacques Collet
Nick Cook
Luigi Coppolino
Miguel Correia
Manuel Costa
Domenico Cotroneo
Ivica Crnkovic
Bojan Cukic
Michel Cukier
Frederic Cuppens
Joni da Silva Fraga
Paul Dabrowski
Mike Dahlin
Alessandro Daidone
David Daly
Paolo DArco
Roberto De Prisco
Rogerio De Lemos
Xavier Defago
Sylvie Delaet
John DeVale
Cristiano di Flora
Chris Dingman
Dan Dobre
Tadashi Dohi
Danny Dolev
Susanna Donatelli
Elias Duarte
Joao Duraes
Christian Engelmann
Rosaria Esposito
Paul Ezhilchelvan
Jean-Charles Fabre
Lorenzo Falai
Reza Farivar
Christof Fetzer

Fernando-Castor Filho
Francesco Flammini
Eric Fleury
Tom Forest
Matthew Frank
Felix Freiling
Matteo Frigo
Matthias Fugger
Luigi Gallo
Shravan Gaonkar
Reinhard German
Anup Ghosh
Damien Giry
William Goble
Swapna Gokhale
Brian Gold
Katerina Goseva-
  Popstojanova
Mohamed Gouda
Almerindo Graziano
Adam Greenhalgh
Brian Greskamp
Weining Gu
Indranil Gupta
Binka Gwynne
Zygmunt Haas
David Hales
Rene-Rydhof Hansen
Cyrus Harvesf
Boudewijn Haverkort
Naohiro Hayashibara
William Healey
Douglas Herbert
Martin Hiller
Volker Hilt
Matti Hiltunen
James Hoe
JoAnne Holliday
Charlie Hu
Chunming Hu
Yih-Chun Hu
Mauro Iacono
Yutaka Ishikawa
Shariful Islam
Gabriela Jacques da Silva
Farnam Jahanian
Ingrid Jansch-Porto

Mark Jelasity
Ricardo Jimenez-Peris
Kaustubh Joshi
Flavio Junqueira
Mohamed Kaaniche
Ron Kalla
Pradeep Kannadiga
Güneş Kayacık
Steve Keckler
Idit Keidar
Tim Kelly
Bettina Kemme
Issa Khalil
Umair Khan
Gunjan Khanna
Emre Kiciman
Marc-Olivier Killijian
Songkuk Kim
Yoshiki Kioshita
Masato Kitakami
Negar Kiyavash
Peter Klemperer
John Knight
Hermann Kopetz
Farinaz Koushanfar
Goswami Kumar
Sy-Yen Kuo
Christiaan Lamprecht
Jean-Claude Laprie
Elizabeth Latronico
Torgrim Lauritsen
Julia Lawall
Wenkee Lee
Chin-Laung Lei
Lei Lei
Joao Leitao
Derek Leonard
Harry Li
Xianxian Li
David Lilja
Robert Lindstrom
Alex Liu
An Liu
P. Liu
Paolo Lollini
Nik Looker
Steven Lumetta
Michael Lyu
Henrique Madeira
István Majzik
Mohammad Malkawi
Dahlia Malkhi
Yanhua Mao
Pietro Marmo

Paulo Marques
Stefano Marrone
Jean-Philippe Martin
Keith Marzullo
Mohammad Masud
Theresa Maxino
Wen Mei Hwu
Avi Mendelson
Nikola Milanovic
Bratislav Milic
Seyed-Ghassem Miremadi
Subhasish Mitra
Jesus Molina
Pablo Montesinos
Regina Moraes
Francesco Moscato
Louise Moser
Daniel Mosse
Achour Mostefaoui
Shubu Mukherjee
Brendan Murphy
Klara Nahrstedt
Hidemoto Nakada
Nithin Nakka
Takashi Nanya
Jeff Napper
Vijay Narayanan
Thomas Naughton
Natasha Neogi
Thuy Nguyen
David Nicol
Michael Niemier
Peng Ning
Yasuharu Nishi
Joao Nogueira
Jon Oberheide
Shuichi Oikawa
Takashi Okuda
Salvatore Orlando
Generoso Paolillo
András Pataricza
Hiren Patel
Janak Patel
Sanjay Patel
Marta Patino-Martìnez
Karthik Pattabiraman
Karthik Pattabiraman
Michael Paulitsch
Fernando Pedone
Peter Popov
Jim Pruyne
Calton Pu
Krishna Puttaswamy
Massimiliano Rak

HariGovind Ramasamy
Veugopalan
Ramasubramanian
Justin Ray
Vimal Reddy
Philipp Reinecke
Jennifer Ren
Laurent Réveillère
Jan Richling
Ryan Riley
Jude Rivers
Luìs Rodrigues
Rodrigo Rodrigues
Daniela Rosu
Eric Rotenberg
Antony Rowstron
Matthieu Roy
Paul Rubel
Duncan Russell
Shane Ryoo
G.-P. Saggese
Hassen Saidi
Teruaki Sakata
Felix Salfner
Vidyaraman
Sankaranarayanan
Sami Saydjari
Richard Schantz
Rodrigo Schmidt
Pierre Sens
Marco Serafini
Matteo Sereno
Emre Sezer
Hussein Shahriar
Davood Shamsi
Aashish Sharma
Abhishek Sharma
Yoichi Shinoda
Stelios Sidiroglou
Daniel Siewiorek
Luis-Moura Silva
David Simplot-Ryl
Aameek Singh
Basil Smith
Sean Smith
Jared Smolens
Arun Somani
Siegmar Sommer
Daniel Sorin
Masakazu Soshi
Janusz Sosnowski
Paulo Sousa
Lisa Spainhower
Evan Speight

PDS Program Committee

Performance and Dependability Symposium (PDS)

Program Chair

Peter Buchholz, *Universität Dortmund, Germany*

Program Committee

Ex Officio

Reviewers for PDS

Jacob Abraham
Marcos Aguilera
Virgilio Almeida
Markus Arns
David August
Gal Badishi
Christel Baier
Simonetta Balsamo
Falko Bause
Heinz Beilner
Simona Bernardi
Roland Bless
Andrea Bobbio
Fred Bower
Jeremy Bradley
Lothar Breuer
Juan Carrasco
Raul Ceretta Nunes
Sophie Chabridon
Marcello Cinque
Vilgot Claesson
Ira Cohen
Domenico Cotroneo
Bernard Cousin
Bojan Cukic
Pedro D. Argenio
Luca De Alfaro
Rogerio De Lemos
Klaus Echtle
Rachid El Abdouni Khayari
Patrick Eugster
Lorenzo Falai
Joe Manuel Ferreira
Chistof Fetzer
Massimo Ficco
Jean Michel Fourneau
Giuliana Franceschinis
Thomas Fuhrmann
Edgar Fuller
Gregory Ganger

Felix Garcia
Reinhard German
Swapna Gokhale
Kartik Gopalan
Andrzej Goscinski
Marco Gribaudo
Michael Grottke
Thomas Herault
Holger Hermanns
Matti Hiltunen
Andras Horvath
William Howden
Michel Hurfin
Hermann Härtig
Guiseppe Iazeolla
Dag Johansen
Nagarajan Kandasamy
Tim Kelly
Bettina Kemme
Angelos Keromytis
Kim P. Kihlstrom
Marc-Olivier Killijian
William Knottenbelt
Andrzej Krasniewski
Udo Krieger
Pieter Kritzinger
Silke Kuball
Marta Kwiatkowska
Wenke Lee
Axel Lehmann
Darrell Long
Henrique Madeira
Erik Maehle
Jeff Magee
Scott Mahlke
István Majzik
Daniel Massey
Mieke Massink
Toshimitzu Masuzawa
Patrick McDaniel

Massimo Mecella
Roie Melamed
Rami Melhem
Gokhan Memik
Andrew Miner
Bruno Müller Clostermann
Martin Neil
David Nicol
Vincent Nicomette
Rudesindo Núñez Queija
Shrideep Pallickara
Parkash Panangaden
Andriy Panchenko
David Parker
Antonio Puliafito
Vivien Quema
Mohan Rajagopalan
Maurizio Rebaudengo
Jared Saia
Werner Sandmann
Uwe Schwiegelshohn
Bruno Sericola
Markus Siegle
Peter Sobe
Daniel Sorin
Julie Symons
Axel Tanner
Kishor Trivedi
Timothy K. Tsai
T. H. Tse
Kurt Tutschku
Shambhu Upadhyaya
Antonino Virgillito
Andreas Wespi
Katinka Wolter
W. Eric Wong
Dmitrii Zagorodnov
Yanyong Zhang
Armin Zimmermann
Cliff Zou

Keynote Address

Science and Engineering: A Collusion of Cultures

Tony Hoare
Microsoft Research Ltd., Cambridge
thoare@microsoft.com

Abstract

The cultures of science and engineering are diametrically opposed along a number of dimensions: long-term/short-term, idealism/compromise, formality/ intuition, certainty/risk management, perfection/ adequacy, originality/familiarity, generality/specificity, unification/diversity, separation/amalgamation of concerns. You would expect two such radically different cultures to collide. Yet all the technological advances of the modern era result not from their collision but from their collusion—in its original sense of a fruitful interplay of ideas from both cultures.

I will illustrate these points by the example of research into program verification and research into dependability of systems. The first of these aims at development and exploitation of a grand unified theory of programming, and therefore shares more the culture of science. The second is based on practical experience of projects in a range of important computer applications, and it shares more the culture of engineering. A collision of cultures would not be unexpected. But I will suggest that the time has come for collusion, and I will suggest how. We need to define an interface across which the cultures can explicitly collaborate.

Dependability research can deliver its results in the form of a library of realistic domain models for a variety of important and common computer applications. A domain model is a reusable pattern for many subsequently conceived products or product lines. It includes a mix of informal and formal descriptions of the environment in which the computer system or network is embedded. It concentrates on the interfaces to the computer system, and the likely requirements and preferences of its community of users. The practicing software engineer takes the relevant application domain model as the starting point for a new project or project proposal, and then specializes it to accord with the current environment and current customer requirements. Domain models are most likely to emerge as the deliverable result of good research into dependability.

If the available tools are powerful enough, verification can begin already at this stage to deliver benefit, by checking the consistency of formalized requirements, and detecting possible feature interactions. Ideally, implementation proceeds from then on in a manner that ensures correctness by construction. At all stages the project should be supported by verification tools. That is the long-term goal of a new initiative in Verified Software, which is under discussion by the international computing research community. This initiative has both a scientific strand and an engineering strand. The scientific strand develops the necessary unified and comprehensive theories of programming; it implements the tools that apply the theory to actual program verification; and it tests both the theory and the tools by application to a representative corpus of real or realistic programs. The engineering strand develops a library of domain models and specifications which enable practicing engineers to apply the theory and the tools to new programs in the relevant application domain. We hope that the results of this research will contribute to the reduction of the current significant costs of programming error. To achieve this will require a successful collusion of the scientific and engineering cultures.

1. Introduction

Computing Science has made enormous direct contributions to the prosperity and well-being of the modern world. It has made further indirect contributions through its services to other branches of modern science and technology. In coming years it promises even more. But is Computing Science itself to be judged like plumbing or brick-laying, solely in terms of its engineering success in delivery of benefits promised? Or is it allowed to be a scientific discipline in its own right, with its own scientific goals, its own ideals, and its own recondite conceptual framework for the cumulative advancement of knowledge and understanding? In other words, is computing research allowed, like research in other branches of science, to range from pure and abstract theory through experimental confirmation to concrete and practical application? In the next three sections I will explore and contrast the attributes of the pure scientist with those of the practicing engineer; and I will suggest that Computer Science does in fact span the whole range. In particular, programming theory, semantics, and correctness of code (my own topics of research) have many of the attributes of pure science. If we interpret dependability in its broadest sense, research into dependability has many of the attributes of engineering research, and like other engineering disciplines, it exploits and adapts the results of science wherever relevant to the needs of its clients.

Good communication across the whole range stretching between science and engineering is essential. It is essential to the coherence and intellectual integrity of our subject, as well as its promise of maximum benefit to society. Communication is mediated by the exchange of the results of research at each point in the range, in terms that are comprehensible on one side, and exploitable on the other. I will suggest that domain models play this essential role for linking dependability research with research in program verification. Furthermore, domain models break through one of the main barriers to application of both dependability and verification technology: they give essential guidance and assistance to a convincing and comprehensive formalization of the assumptions and expectations of the users of a new computer system. Good specifications are an indispensible starting point for useful verification.

Finally, I will draw your attention to a new international initiative of long-term research into Verified Software. It aims to cover the whole programming process, from domain modeling through specification, design, coding, testing, delivery, right up to in-service upgrades of running code. It will develop the necessary unified theories; and based upon them, it will develop an integrated set of verification tools to support the programming process from end to end. Finally, it will conduct a convincing series of verification experiments applying the prototype toolset on a substantial body of real or realistic application code from many application domains. The title of the project is therefore 'Verified Software: Theory, Tools, Experiments' (VSTTE). The breadth of applicability of this research is utterly dependent on the research in dependability engineering, delivering its results in the form of domain models. I very much hope that we can recruit assistance of experienced dependability researchers to play this pivotal role in the Verified Software Initiative.

2. Science and engineering

Some people are pure scientists. Others are entirely practical engineers. But far more numerous are people who are, in varying degrees and at varying times, both scientists and engineers. For example, any experimental scientist must be an engineer when constructing experimental equipment to test a new theory. Any ambitious engineer must be a scientist when attempting to apply or adapt a scientific theory to fulfill a task never before attempted. Researchers in Computer Science, like those in other branches of engineering science, may choose to concentrate more or less on one end of the range or the other; or indeed they may prefer to remain precariously perched in the middle. The message of my talk is that there must be a constant interchange of research results between scientists and engineers occupying different points on the spectrum. Such communication can be blocked by a failure to appreciate how wide the spectrum is. So in this section I will concentrate on the widest possible gap, that which stretches between the two extreme ends of the spectrum. In later sections I will describe some intermediate positions. For convenience, I will assume that the research scientist at one end of the spectrum is a man and the practicing engineer at the other end is a woman.

The scientist works for posterity. He wants to discover the absolute truth about the natural world, however long it takes, and however much it costs. Truth is permanent, and the knowledge of truth will never lose its literally inestimable value. The engineer works for a known client, or for a known or speculative niche in an existing market. She is committed to a fixed budget and a fixed delivery date for the product of her labours. The service life of an engineering product is known to be limited, and so is its market life of a product line. In compensation, the engineer gains recognition sooner than the scientist, in the form of appreciation from grateful client or profits from a commercially successful product.

The scientist pursues absolute scientific ideals. For example, the physicist pursues accuracy of measurement, the chemist pursues purity of materials, and the computing scientist pursues correctness of programs; and they pursue their respective ideals far beyond the current needs of the market place, or even its future projected needs. The engineer learns to live with the imperfections of the real world. She develops

3

her ingenuity to avoid them, to work around them, and to come up with compromises which are only just good enough for present needs.

The scientist seeks certainty, backed up by an overwhelming mass of convincing experimental evidence. The engineer learns to live with the innumerable uncertainties of the real world, and finds ways of managing the inevitable risks involved.

The scientist separates concerns. He isolates all extraneous factors and conducts experiments in the cleanest possible laboratory environment. That is why researchers in programming language design test a new idea or a new feature in the context of the simplest possible programming language. The engineer has to bring together an almost unbounded collection of relevant concerns, and resolve them all simultaneously; none of them can be controlled, none can be ignored, and very few can be elegantly simplified.

The scientist expresses scientific knowledge in precise mathematical formulae, often surprisingly simple. Their consequences can then be deduced by mathematical calculations or even proofs. The calculations are often messy and laborious, but fortunately they can be carried out by computer, using software tools into which the relevant theories have been embedded. Many engineers would confess that they never enjoyed their mathematical studies, and that they have thankfully forgotten most them. Nowadays the practicing engineer exploits mathematics only through the available engineering toolsets, which have evolved from the software written and previously used by scientists. In places where tools cannot reach, she relies on her strong and sound engineering intuition about the relevant technologies, and about the real world environment in which the technologies are to be applied.

The scientist insists on originality in pursuit of new results, and in making corrections or refinements to established theories. For the engineer originality only adds to the risks of failure. She therefore relies on tried and true methods wherever applicable, and reduces the role of innovation to an inescapable minimum required by the ambition of her current project.

The scientist pursues generalization and unification of theory for its own sake. A unified theory is one that has a number of established theories as special cases. The unified theory gains the support of all the available evidence for all the theories that it unifies. So does each and every one of the unified theories. The skill of the engineer lies in understanding diversity and particularity. She explores the particular circumstances of her current project, and its acceptable limitations; and she ingeniously exploits them to improve quality and to reduce costs and timescales.

These extreme portraits of science and engineering are interesting only because they define the range of possibilities that lie between them. Let us withdraw from the extremes, and talk now about researchers closer to the middle point of the range. I classify them as engineering scientists if they are on the scientific side of the midpoint, and as scientific engineers if they are on the engineering side. Within each category, there is still a wide range.

3. The engineering scientist

The defining characteristic of an engineering scientist is that he conducts scientific research in an area of science that is relevant to some branch of engineering. So, for example, Aerodynamics is relevant for airplane design, Hydrodynamics for ship design, and Computing Science for the design of software. My own specialism within Computing Science is the theory of programming. The subject matter is computer programs rather than airplanes or ships; but our research addresses the same basic questions, for example: What does it do? How does it work? Why does it work? How do we know? The answers are as follows. It is the specification that describes what a program does. It is the architecture and internal interfaces that describes how the program works. It is the theory of programming that explains why it works. And it is mathematics that increases our confidence that the answers to all the previous questions are consistent, in that the program meets its specification.

I like to classify myself among the engineering scientists, albeit at the pure end, in the area of software engineering. Like other scientists, we pursue an ideal, that of program correctness, far beyond what is now achievable, and even beyond what the current market requires. Furthermore, we use the standard methods of modern science. We construct theories whose soundness and consistency is established by mathematical proof. We conduct experiments into the applicability of the theory to explain the working of real programs. We develop the scientific toolsets, based on scientific theory, to assist in the conduct of the experiments and in the analysis of the results. We search for sound interfaces between compatible tools used in different stages of the programming project; and we seek unifying theories to explain and justify their interworking. Above all, we aim at the highest standards of conviction for the answer to the question 'How do we know?'. Our standard is that of mathematical proof, generated or at least checked by computer.

As in other areas of scientific instrumentation, the early tools are quite crude. However, they are subject to continuous improvement in the light of experience of their use. When the tools have been thoroughly evaluated and evolved by wide-ranging scientific experiment, they provide the means by which the results of the research are conveyed to the practicing software engineer. We look forward to the day when wide adoption of programming support tools will finally bring under control the problems and costs associated with software error. And as scientists, we accept that this benefit may be enjoyed only by posterity.

4. The scientific engineer

The defining characteristic of a scientific engineer is that she conducts engineering research to reduce costs and increase effectiveness of future engineering projects. She takes past (or even current) engineering projects as her source material, and shows how the lessons of earlier success or failure can be generalized for wider exploitation in projects of a similar kind. Her conclusions and recommendations may be put to the test in scientific experiments and even pilot engineering projects conducted by a scientific engineering team. They are pilot projects, because they attempt to preserve sufficient generality that the findings of the research can apply to many similar projects in the future. The need to satisfy a real client on the current project must not divert her attention from this broader goal. The results of her research may be delivered to the general engineering profession in the form of engineering handbooks, together with tools and standards for their use.

Software engineering certainly provides ample case material for this research, including projects that succeed as well as those that fail. Particularly significant are projects which involve human collaboration within existing organizations like hospitals, and interactions with the general public, like the issue of passports. In both cases, the research must be based on an understanding of the full circumstances of the project under study, including technical, financial, social and political concerns. Very often the investigation of a project will require reverse engineering to discover and document missing specifications and missing statements of requirements. The conclusions from the research can usefully delivered in the form a rational reconstruction of the history of the project, or probably an idealized version

of it. This will include an explanation of the necessary design decisions, the order in which they have been taken (or should have been), and the appropriate arguments to justify them.

But more is needed. The results of the research must be abstracted and generalized to cover a whole range of future possible implementation projects in related application areas. The results must be presented in the form of an engineering handbook, with a clear structure to assist in selection and adaptation to new circumstances. Generalisation and abstraction are the essential attributes of scientific research, and they are equally essential to wide-spread application of its results.

The term 'Domain Model' can be applied to the document that conveys the result of this research to the practicing engineer. I suggest that domain models are the crucial missing link – in fact a direct communication link – between the engineering scientist working in the area of program correctness, and the scientific engineer working in the area of dependability, as interpreted in the widest sense. A domain model encapsulates the results of dependability research, and it is the starting point for a design process that leads to software that is correct by construction. It is the keystone in the bridge between research in dependability and research in program correctness. The results of both can then pass together into general software engineering application.

5. Domain modeling

A domain model is nothing but a generalized software engineering project proposal. It is a pattern which can be used to guide the formulation of many differing project proposals in some useful area of computer application. So I start with an idealized account of what a good project proposal should be.

It is written in natural language. It describes the real world. It concentrates on the environment in which a new or improved computer system will operate. It lists the external environmental constraints on the system, including constraints of material and technology and costs and timescales. It describes the human environment, and the likely expectations, idiosyncrasies, and prejudices of the eventual beneficiaries of the product. It makes explicit the potential conflicts in the expectations, and suggests priorities that will help to resolve them. Where uncertainties exist at the beginning of the project, it details how they will be resolved by experiment as the project progresses. It describes how evidence will be collected of the dependability of the system and its fitness for purpose. It describes the ways in which the real world will be changed by the delivery and installation of a software product. It distinguishes changes that are necessary before installation, from those which will be left for subsequent enhancements. It charts, in increasingly vague and general terms, the evolution of the system into the foreseeable future. All these descriptions are illustrated by specific example scenarios (known as use cases), and formalized in mathematical models as far as appropriate.

The model may be described by mathematical formulae, often with the aid of diagrams. Each formula is preceded by informal prose, explaining the meaning of each of its free variables in terms of what they stand for in the real world. Each formula is accompanied by further informal prose to give a convincing explanation of its relevance and accuracy and adequacy to purpose. Convincing informal explanation is the only way of bridging the gap between the real world and the very first formulae that describe it.

The formulae make several contributions to the quality of the presentation, and of the eventual product. Their first is an increase in precision to cover all the corner cases that would be tedious to enumerate in natural language. The second is the specification of important and testable properties of the interface between the real world and the computer system. The third is an increase in confidence that essential features of the product have not been inadvertently missed. But the main benefit of the formulae will be that they can be taken as input by tools that assist throughout the implementation and evolution of the product.

The assistance can begin even during the drafting of the project proposal. For example, a modern proof tool can test the mutual consistency of the whole collection of formulae, and so reduce the risk of late discovery of feature interactions. Another tool could help to explore the consequences of the formulae, and check them against intuitive expectations. Finally, the formulae can be passed to the implementation team, who use them as the starting point of a design process for code that is correct by construction. Some of the formulae may be fed to specialized code generators, to generate parts of the program automatically. Other formulae may be fed to test harnesses or to test case generators, or to program verification tools, to check correctness of hand-written code. In the case of a full functional specification, a verification tool can generate or check a mathematical proof of correctness, giving the highest possible degree of assurance, often with reduced cost of test.

A domain model is very similar to a project proposal, except that it covers a whole family of possible proposals in a given area of application. Where a project proposal describes a single environment, a domain model describes a range of environments, and advises how the project engineer should choose an appropriate model for particular circumstances. Where a project proposal describes and justifies a single design decision, the domain model lists a range of plausible decisions, and advises how to make a sensible choice between them. Where a project proposal gives a single formula, the domain model again offers a choice capable of meeting a variety of needs in a variety of circumstances. It is a major intellectual challenge to structure a domain model effectively, so that most of the useful exposition is independent of the particular choices made; and ideally, most of the choices can be made independently of each other.

6. Conclusion

I have a vision of the day in which software is always the most reliable component in any system which contains it; a day when software comes with a guarantee of serviceability and fitness for purpose; and a day when computer programmers make fewer mistakes than any other engineering profession. These related visions are what drive researchers into dependability as well as program verification. We hope that they will be achieved with the help of a comprehensive software engineering toolset, which supports a rigorous process of dependable and correct software construction, and which points out any error at the very moment that it is made. This toolset will exploit ideas of logical and mathematical proof that have been part of the human cultural and philosophical heritage for thousands of years. Those who share the vision have recently held a series of conferences and workshops to discuss a major long-term collaboration towards its realization. The title of our project is 'Verified Software: Theory, Tools and Experiments'; please visit its website http://vstte.ethz.ch .

Hitherto, there have been two major barriers to progress. The first is the weakness of available computerized proof engines. This problem is being solved by a combination of increases in the capacity and speed of computers and increases in the performance of the algorithms central to proof. In combination, these have made proof technology a thousand times faster than it was ten years ago. We are currently at a tipping point, where it is actually easier to use a proof tool than not to. When a significant scientific community is actually using the tools, progress is likely accelerate.

But the second weakness remains. It lies at the critical point of the whole endeavour: the very first capture of the properties of the real world, of its inhabitants, and of the expectations they have of a new or improved computer system. If we get those wrong, none of our software will be dependable, and none of the verification tools will even detect the fact. That is why domain models must make a decisive contribution to the success of the Verified Software initiative, and the application of its results.

A representative collection of realistic domain models would be directly useful even now in conveying knowledge and experience from past software engineering projects to those who are embarking on a new one. The collection will serve as an existence proof of the value of a partial or total formalization of the requirements to be met by a computer system. And finally, the constituent formulae of a domain model can be copied directly or adapted for use in new projects by engineers more adept at reading formulae than at writing them. This will break through the current high barriers to the exploitation of formalism by software engineers. But first let us break through the barriers to communication and collaboration between those engaged in the scientific and the engineering ends of our spectrum, between dependability engineers producing domain models and verification scientists who exploit them to certify the correctness of their implementation. We hope for collusion of cultures, not a collision.

DEPENDABLE COMPUTING AND COMMUNICATIONS SYMPOSIUM (DCCS)

Session 1A:
Security Protection:
Architectural Approaches

Augmenting Branch Predictor to Secure Program Execution

Yixin Shi and Gyungho Lee

Department of Electrical and Computer Engineering, University of Illinois at Chicago
yshi7@uic.edu, ghlee@ece.uic.edu

Abstract

Although there are various ways to exploit software vulnerabilities for malicious attacks, the attacks always result in unexpected behavior in program execution, deviating from what the programmer/user intends to do. Program execution blindly follows the execution path specified by control flow transfer instructions with the targets generated at run-time without any validation. An enhancement is therefore proposed to secure program execution by introducing a validation mechanism over control flow transfer instructions at micro-architecture level. The proposed scheme, as a behavior-based protection, treats a triplet of the indirect branch's location, its target address, and the execution path preceding it as a behavior signature of program execution and validates it at run-time. The first two pieces of information can prevent an adversary from overwriting control data and introducing foreign code or impossible targets to redirect an indirect branch. The last one is necessary to defeat the attacks that use a legitimate target but follow an unintended execution path. Interestingly, the branch predictor is found to contain the signature information already and doing a portion of the validation when resolving the branch, thus greatly reducing the validation frequency. An enhancement of branch target buffer (BTB) entry together with a signature table implemented in the form of a Bloom filter in hardware is proposed to incorporate the validation into the processor's pipeline, providing a new defense in the processor architecture to secure program execution.

Keywords:

Software Protection, Control Flow Validation, Indirect Branch, Branch Predictor, Bloom Filter

1. Introduction

By exploiting software flaws (such as buffer overflow, format string vulnerability, heap overflow and integer overflow), an external adversary subverts victim program's normal execution by overwriting critical data in the program's address space. Predominating attacks seek to overwrite *control data*, the data that are used as the target of a control flow transfer instruction, to redirect the control flow to the attacker's way[7]. Meanwhile, attacks that overwrite other critical data, such as decision-making data, are also realistic for altering program control flow without touching the control data[8]. Many existing measures that aim to prevent the former attacks become ineffective against the latter ones. However, no matter how an adversary launches an unexpected overwrite, an attack eventually results in execution paths that deviate from those specified in the program. Hence, we may try to extract the normal program's behavior feature such as control flows as its signature for security and check the execution paths against it at run-time. This behavior-based protection is attractive especially for defeating non-control data attacks since security signatures are derived from the program itself, independent of the various ways that attackers exploit. This study seeks to achieve security by validating program execution with allowed control flow paths.

Any behavior-based protection schemes must decide the following two design options: 1) *the objects* extracted from a program in order to form a "behavior signature" that characterizes its normal behavior. To make the protection effective, the objects should be representative and the signature should closely capture the control flow of the program. 2) *the methods* to retrieve, store, and validate the signatures at run-time. The amount of information for behavior signature should be less volatile and limited, and should be stored and accessed in an efficient way with a minimized validation delay.

At machine instruction level, high-level descriptions of program behavior are ultimately translated into control flow transfer instructions of direct branches and indirect branches. The targets of a conditional direct branch cannot be changed but direction of control flow at such a branch may be compromised via tainted decision-making data. On the other hand, an indirect branch reads its target from a memory location or a register, whose *address* or *name*, not the value, is specified in the instructions. The fact that the locations of the targets are visible to the program makes it possible for attackers to write malicious values onto them. This gives the attacker greater flexibility to repoint the control flow to *any* memory address he/she desires. For example, the target could be replaced with the starting address of a foreign code previously implanted or an impossible target that skips privilege checking. In fact, compromising the indirect branch is an inherent starting point of any *control data* attacks.

Most common indirect branches, in terms of frequency, are *return* instructions that read targets in the stack. They are relatively easy to protect because the target of a return is always in stack and both its location and value are known before the return actually uses it. Many solutions were proposed to either guard the return address location[10], encrypt/hide the return address[24][17], or make a copy of the return address stack in software[14] or hardware[18]. However, fewer works have been done to handle other types of indirect branches, i.e. indirect calls and indirect jumps, called *general indirect branch* in this study. The uses of function pointers, operations on jump tables in high-level language, non-local jump library calls, and virtual function mechanisms are the major sources of the general indirect branches. They are common in many security-critical server type applications: our profiling experiment in a full-system emulator shows that among all indirect branches, general indirect branches account 41% and 47%, for *apache* and *ftpd*, respectively. Obviously, ignoring those instructions is inappropriate since they are as vulnerable as returns.

An execution of indirect branch provides a desirable sampling point for validating program behavior. We check whether or not a control datum, the target for an indirect branch, has been overwritten maliciously to detect control data attacks. Moreover, we also consider the conditional branches close to the indirect branch instance and have taken their direction outcomes into consideration. Our scheme obtains the behavior signature extracted directly from control flow transfer instructions thereby representative. The amount of information for the signatures is expected to be limited because the number of different targets for indirect branches is bounded and predictive correlations exist among the conditional branches. This motivates us to build a hardware table containing control flow objects of all indirect branches. At run-time, each indirect branch instance is validated against the extracted legitimate control flow objects before it is committed architecturally. A failed validation indicates that the current indirect branch is either with a tampered target or on a compromised execution path. A hardware interrupt is then triggered and the operating system can take over the execution to determine the response procedure. This fine-granularity validation is effective against not only control data attacks but also many non-control data attacks that aim to compromise the predicate data for conditional branches. Our hardware

enhancement is tightly incorporated with processor pipeline and works in tandem with processor core, resulting in a short validation delay.

The next section describes the program behavior signatures chosen for validating control flow transfers. Section 3 shows how to extract the interested control flow related objects for the signature. It also depicts the architectural modifications of augmenting branch predictor in details and describes using Bloom filter for storing and validating the behavior signatures. Section 4 evaluates the performance impact. Section 5 presents related works and the paper is concluded in Section 6.

2. Program Behavior Signature

Various control flow related objects can be used as the program behavior signature, from branch targets to complete execution paths. Depending on the scope of the chosen objects, protection efficacy and overhead will be different. This section considers the objects our scheme collects for program behavior signature.

It is noteworthy that the experiments reported in this paper are from complete running of real and full-scale applications under a live operating system. Bochs-2.2.6[3], a full-system Intel Pentium emulator, is used for our profiling study. All benchmarks are compiled and targeted to dynamically linked x86 binaries and run under Redhat Linux OS over Bochs. The Linux kernel is modified so that the hardware emulator becomes aware of process information. All instructions from the same application image, not just one "representative" process/thread, are tracked. Therefore, accurate and complete behavior information has been collected even for multi-threaded applications. The behavior of the dynamically linked library code can be observed as well by using Bochs. Two server-type applications, *apache(2.2.2)* and *ftpd(wu-ftpd 2.6.0)*, have been experimented. The *apache* httpd server was tested in field for seven days with both static and dynamic workloads, receiving about 1500 hits per day while synthetic input scripts were used for excising *ftpd*. Additionally, the results from SPEC2000 integer benchmarks are also reported; they are run to complete with the reference inputs on the x86 emulator. Floating-point benchmarks typically have less diversity in terms of control flow transfer, and thereby are not included in this work.

2.1. Objects for Behavior Signature

A natural object to validate is the target PC (TPC) of each indirect branch instance. Such a validation can prevent the control flow from jumping to the implanted code and/or impossible targets. However, an adversary might utilize a *legitimate* target to perform malicious operations such as in return-to-libc attacks. In the

11

example in Figure-1, a security-sensitive function, *system()*, is the target for a normal function call through a function pointer, `funcptr`. However, a stack smashing attack may overwrite the return address of *vuln_fun()* into the entry address of *system()*, which is perfectly legitimate. This would result in an execution path oblivious of detection, but unexpected control flow transfer from the return of *vuln_fun()* to *system()*.

```
vuln_fun ( char *input)
{
    int buf[];
    //buffer overflow
    strcpy(buf, input);...
}
main(argc, argv)
{
    func * funcptr;
    ...
    //the return can be compromised to
    //be the entry address of system()
    vuln_fun(argv)
    if () //root user only
    {
        funcptr = system;
        ...
    //address of system() is legitimate, only for the
    //following  function   call  through  a  function
    pointer.
        * funcptr ();
    }
}
```

Figure-1 : An example showing that only validating target is not sufficient.

As a remedy, the branch's PC can be associated with each legitimate target for the behavior signature when validating. Thus, any control flow transfers invoked by indirect branches are guaranteed to be from an intended branch site to a validated destination. In doing so, the attacks mentioned above can be detected since the PC of the return in *vuln_fun()* is never associated with the entry address of *system()*. One may concatenate the branch PC, a new object, with each one of its legitimate targets (denoted as *BPC‖TPC*) for behavior signature as in previous studies[1][20][22].

Table-1 :The number of the Target PC and the BPC‖TPC of applications (in x86 binaries): gcc has the most target PCs probably because of the large number of call sites by recursive function calls in syntax analysis; eon, a C++ program, invokes many virtual function calls.

Benchmark	Target PC#	BPC‖TPC #	Benchmark	Target PC#	BPC‖TPC #
apache	2526	6055	*ftpd*	1224	3003
gcc	8218	8592	eon	5980	6396
crafty	2652	3162	gap	2965	4480
vpr	1288	1429	gzip	548	616
parser	2121	2306	vortex	4261	4420
mcf	739	836	perl	3050	3327
twolf	2670	2980	bzip2	807	890

Our experiments shows (see in Table-1) that monitoring BPC‖TPC only increases the number of objects that need to be monitored by an insignificant account (13.5% on average) for SPEC CPU benchmarks. However, the signature table size

increases considerably (2× to 3×) for server-type applications, i.e. *apache* and *ftpd*, although still remains modest, because of more dynamic behavior of general indirect branches in such applications.

Although validating both the branch PC and target PC guarantees an individual indirect branch always branches to a predefined address, one critical issue is that it samples program behavior only at isolated program execution points, i.e. at the indirect branches, without considering dynamic execution path reaching to the indirect branches. Consequently, it could miss some elaborate attacks that alter the control flow but still branch from a legitimate indirect branch site to a legitimate target. Figure-2 illustrates such a scenario, in which the indirect function call of *poutputfun()* (an indirect branch in machine code level) passes the BPC‖TPC validation even when the attack is underway.

```
state_transfer(int input)
{
    int state;
    char buf[];
    function pointer *poutputfun;

    if (input<10)           --1
        state = REGULAR;
    if (input <20)          --2
        state = PRIVILEGED;
    else                    --3
        state = UNKNOWN

    f1(buf);
    if state == REGULAR     --4
        poutputfun = g1;
    if state == PRIVILEGED  --5
        poutputfun = g2;
    else
        poutputfun = g3;

    (*poutputfun)();
}

f1(buf) { memory corruption bugs}
g2() { privileged operations}
```

Figure-2 : An example showing protecting BPC‖TPC is not sufficient: The output function is invoked through a function pointer dynamically. Suppose *f1()* contains a memory corruption bug, e.g. format string vulnerabilities such that a call of *f1()* results in an overwrite on the variable of *state*. Now assume the *input* is 5 and *state* is *REGULAR* initially. Then, a malicious party may invoke the *f1()* and change the value of *state* into *PRIVILEGED*. As a result, the privileged function, *g2()*, is called unexpectedly by the indirect branch when *poutputfun()* is executed, instead of *g1()*. Note that both the source PC and the target of the indirect branch are legitimate since such a control flow transfer is possible in a normal execution. However, the indirect function call of *poutputfun()* passes the BPC‖TPC validation but the attack is underway.

We observe that although the branch PCs and the targets are legal ones, the control flow might have followed an unintended execution path to reach that branch, possibly caused by a non-control data attack such as in above example. Such an execution path is typically unexpected and/or impossible, thereafter can be detected, due to a well-known fact that the outcomes of consecutive branches are strongly *correlated* in many cases. In our example code of Figure-3, only if the conditions at branch site 2 and 5 are both satisfied could the control flow reach the call of the privileged subroutine, *g2()*. However, a non-control data attack that aims to alter the predicate values of the conditional branches destructs the correlation abruptly. In the example, if a memory corruption bug in *f1()* overwrites the *state* variable in the middle, outcomes of branches at site 1 and 5 would have an abnormal combination, or the correlation between the two has been violated. This suggests that we should include the execution path besides the indirect branch and its target into the objects being monitored: only if the BPC||TPC of an indirect branch *and* the execution path that leads to the branch have been validated is the program allowed to make control flow transfer. In this study, we define the execution path of an indirect branch as the sequence of *direction* outcomes of the preceding conditional branches to the indirect branch and denote it as *EP (execution path)*. Thus, three objects are extracted and validated, namely the branch PC, the target PC, and the execution path, and they are simply concatenated together to form a behavior signature. We denote it as BPC||TPC||EP and monitor the triplets at run-time.

Our validation on the program behavior signature of BPC||TPC||EP is effective against a wide range of attacks. It is able to detect many control data attacks that introduce foreign code in stack or heap, or impossible targets since any target addresses (TPC) being used is ensured to be legitimate. The use of branch site information (BPC) prevents an adversary from compromising an indirect branch and redirecting the control flow to existing code. Including path information is a general protection measure to validate dynamic execution path based on the correlations among branch instructions. An impossible path can be detected, thereby preventing many non-control data attacks that aim to change the decision-making data. There are certain chances that an adversary exploits vulnerabilities without invoking indirect branches. However, as mentioned in[13], system calls and library calls in many cases are indispensable for an adversary to introduce malicious operations. Fortunately, many realistic run-time systems do invoke library calls through indirect branches using a system function pointer table, such as PLT (procedure linkage table) and GOT (global offset table). In such a system, checking execution path before indirect branches is sufficient to thwart most attacks.

One complication arises in any control flow monitoring scheme due to the use of dynamically linked library as the addresses are determined at run-time. Existing methods either limit their validation on the static-linked program part[20][1], or only track the

internal jumps within the same library, ignoring the executable-library jumps[12][29]. We address this issue of dynamically linked targets by seeking help from the linker. A target address for the indirect library call could be resolved with only two values. One is the entry address of the linker, which is always fixed for a given run-time system. The other is the actual address patched by the linker at run-time, which is always fixed in each run. When constructing a signature of BPC||TPC||EP for an indirect branch for a library call, the TPC can be initialized as the address of the linker for executable-library jumps (e.g. PLT0 in PLT). When the linker resolves the address at run-time, it patches both the function pointer table (e.g. GOT) for dynamic linking and the TPC in the corresponding signature. For the internal jumps, we adopt a similar method in [12][29] to track the offset, rather than the absolute address for the TPC. Thus, a later compromise of function pointers related to the dynamically linked libraries can be detected.

2.2. Extracting Program Behavior Signature

There are various ways to extract the legitimate behavior signatures, i.e. the legitimate BPC||TPC||EPs, to fill up the hardware table. This depends on several factors such as the availability of source code, the accuracy to achieve, and the size of program's control flow graph. Many static analysis methods can be utilized since only indirect branches and the conditional branches nearby are of interest. This work uses training, a widely adopted method in many behavior-based protections [11][12][13][15][20][22][29], to collect security signatures to study the effectiveness and feasibility of the proposed validation. That is, we train the application in a particular time frame, or until the number of interested signatures of BPC||TPC||EP converges.

We define the number of conditional branch outcomes included in the execution path of an indirect branch as the execution path length, or *EP length*. As an architectural solution, the execution paths saved in the hardware signature table can only have a limited length. A larger EP length certainly improves the detection accuracy and provides a stronger protection. However, it comes at the cost of larger storage overhead as well as slowing down the validation. An excessively long execution path may also include unrelated branches, resulting in a high false positive rate. Therefore, we must trade the EP length off the overall efficiency. We have profiled the indirect branch's PC and the target PC (BPC||TPC) as complete as possible and tested the convergence of BPC||TPC||EP with various EP lengths. The goal is to have the "truncated" execution path to be as short as possible while still informative enough to reflect the

13

program behavior. Our study suggests that the EP of a short length would be sufficient.

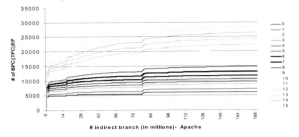

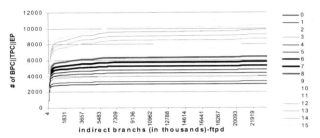

Figure-3 : The number of BPC||TPC||EP for *apache* and *ftpd* against the indirect branches that have been executed. Each diagram also shows the results with different EP length from 0 to 15.

Figure-3 shows the number of BPC||TPC||EP and its convergence speed with respect to the EP length from zero (only BPC||TPC) to 15, i.e. up to 15 conditional branches prior to each indirect branch, over two server-type applications. The resultant trends have shown that the number of behavior signatures is limited and converges after a reasonable amount of time over different EP length. For *apache*, the number of signature increases very slowly as the EP length ranges from *one* to *four*. The curves are closer to each other comparing to other cases. However, when more than *ten* branch outcomes are included in EP, the distance between two adjacent curves becomes larger. This probably means that the additional path information is less informative and is unlikely to be relevant to the indirect branches. Moreover, these curves have a greater slope, indicating a slower convergence speed. Similar results can be observed for *ftpd*.

We have also profiled the numbers of the conditional branches that appear between two consecutively executed indirect branches at run-time (Figure-4). We measure the *accumulative distribution* of the number of conditional branches that are dynamically executed between two indirect branches.

Based on the experiments shown in Figure-3 and Figure-4, six to eight branch history outcomes might be a reasonable length as they have 80% to 90% coverage over the whole execution paths between any two indirect branches. With an execution path length of eight, BPC||TPC||EP has a similar converging speed

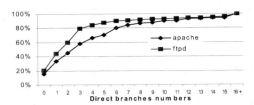

Figure-4 : The accumulative distribution of the number of conditional branches between two consecutively executed indirect branches.

as the cases with a shorter execution path, while the total number of the signature still remains moderate. Table-2 shows the total number of BPC||TPC||EP with different the EP length. Nevertheless, one should note that the length of the execution path is a design option and its value depends more upon the cost one can tolerate to collect and to store the legitimate BPC||TPC||EPs. The protection efficacy does not always improve proportional to the EP length. Generally, the closer conditional branches have more correlations thereby are more important while the remote ones are more likely to add noise.

Table-2 :The number of behavior signatures (BPC||TPC||EP) with different EP length. Most benchmarks have a modest number, less than 15000 BPC||TPC||EPs except the *gcc*, which has a significantly larger number of run-time behavior signatures.

Appl.	Number of BPC||TPC||EP			
	5 bits	6 bits	7 bits	8 bits
apache	10592	11749	13133	14788
ftpd	4837	5320	5816	6418
bzip2	1293	1428	1604	1848
eon	10625	11684	12812	12943
crafty	6980	8580	10578	13209
gap	9535	11102	12892	14919
gcc	21617	25091	29184	33687
gzip	1074	1233	1442	1731
mcf	1283	1442	1659	1971
parser	6157	7404	9094	11259
perl	6787	8330	9144	10729
vpr	2294	2561	2845	3207
vortex	6341	6834	7347	7995
twolf	4648	5255	5976	6812

3. Augmenting Branch Predictor

3.1 Retrieving Run-Time Behavior Information

Our hardware solution takes an advantage of the fact that the objects for the behavior signature are readily available in the micro-architecture of modern processors. A branch's PC and its target can be retrieved from architectural registers at run-time. A common component found in correlating/two-level branch predictors is the branch history shift register (*BHSR*) that records the outcomes of recently executed conditional branches. The BHSR provides history information for prediction as well as of the current execution path for our monitoring of program behavior. Note that if the BHSR is updated speculatively, it is necessary to maintain a shadow copy of non-speculative branch outcomes to store the committed results. Also, no memory access is needed in this architectural level solution.

3.2 Augmenting the Branch Predictor for Validation

The validation involves comparing the retrieved BPC‖TPC‖EP at run-time with the legitimate signatures that have been collected in the signature table. Interestingly, the branch predictor together with the prediction verification mechanism is already doing a large portion of the validation work. This is because with the validation in place *prior to* that an indirect branch commits its result into the machine state, the history information buffered in the branch predictor is the one that has been committed before, thereby has been validated also. Thus, the frequency of validation against the signature table can be reduced.

In particular, the branch target buffer (BTB) and return address stack (RAS) are two buffer units that store the history targets that have been used before. A successful *branch prediction* means both the branch's PC and its target are from the buffer, thereby are validated already. However, our protection scheme also requires validating the execution path proceeding to each indirect branch. We propose to append a small bit vector recording the execution paths (outcomes in conditional branch history), along with the Branch PC and its target PC in each BTB entry. This bit vector, called *EP bit vector*, effectively caches the recently used execution paths. Accordingly, besides the verification of the target PC, the hardware does an additional comparison between the current execution path retrieved from BHSR and the buffered execution paths in the EP bit vector stored in BTB. Only when the indirect branch is correctly predicted *and* the run-time EP from BHSR matches one of buffered paths in EP bit vector (an EP bit vector *hit*), would the processor view the control flow transfer legitimate. Otherwise, a checking against the complete security signature table is enforced (discussed in Section 3.5).

Figure-5 shows the modifications to each BTB entry and processor pipeline in order to support EP validation. To improve the hit rate of the EP bit vector, multiple EPs are buffered and are organized in an associative way in the BTB entry. At the fetch stage, the EP bit vector is fetched along with target address from BTB. And it is carried along with the instruction in the pipeline registers or in the reorder buffer. A mis-prediction at the branch verification stage or an EP bit vector miss on a correct prediction at the commit stage

will trigger a validation. The bit vector is updated on an EP bit vector miss after validation: The current execution path that has been validated with the complete signature table replaces one of the execution paths in the bit vector. Although a carefully chosen policy can be adopted, an execution path to be replaced in the EP bit vector is randomly chosen for simplicity in this work.

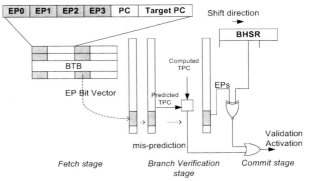

Figure-5 : The BTB and pipeline enhancement to support execution path validation. Each BTB entry contains extra EP information and current execution path is extracted from BHSR. The comparison of the two, together with the target verification, equivalently performs a validation.

3.3 Evaluating EP bit Vector Hit Rate

The extra checking on the EP bit vector may lower the chance that the branch predictor alone does the validation and incurs more validations against the complete signature table. Therefore a high hit rate of EP bit vector is desirable. We have experimented the SPEC2000 CPU integer benchmarks with different numbers of the execution paths buffered in each BTB entry as shown in Figure-6.

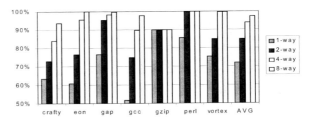

Figure-6 : The hit rate of the EP bit-vector with different number of buffered execution path. (*n*-way means *n* paths are stored in the EP bit vector). Only the benchmarks that execute considerable number of general indirect branches are shown. Refer Section 4 for other simulation configuration and architecture parameters.

In the simulation, each path consists of eight branch outcomes, which suggests 128 different EPs possible in theory. However, the EP bit vector buffering only two to eight paths yields a hit rate as high as 85% to 97% on average. This is not surprising because the number of execution path to each indirect branch is limited due to the correlations of branches instructions and the execution path has temporal locality similar to instruction cache.

3.4 Overall Validation Rate

For return addresses, a validation against the signature table is triggered on RAS misses. This is because the targets, i.e. return addresses, are pushed into and popped out of stack in a strict first-in-last-out order. Successful pushing and popping of an address on RAS hits indicate the call and return follow the call sequence chain as specified. However, on an RAS miss, we perform a strict BPC||TPC||EP validation against the complete signature table. In fact, many hard-to-detect attacks such as *impossible path exploration*[25] are highly likely to trigger a RAS miss first. In this case although the return address may have been seen before, the access order of the return addresses in stack is corrupted. Thereby our scheme is able to catch the exploration and detect such an intrusion.

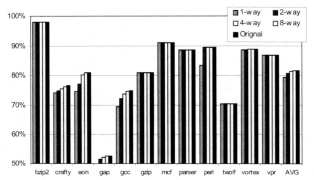

Figure-7 : The rate that the validation is done by the augmented predictor alone. It is also the rate that no validation against the complete signature table is needed. The original bar is the case without EP checking.

Figure-7 shows the overall rate of the validation on both general indirect branches and returns by the modified branch predictor with respect to different number of EPs buffered. *Eon, crafty,* and *gcc* have a considerable number of general indirect branches and thereby are affected by the validation of the EP information, while the rest of the benchmarks exhibit no noticeable difference regarding the number of the EPs since the general indirect branches are rare or they have an accurate prediction rate already. *Gap* has only slightly above 50% validation rate due to the low success rate of indirect branch predictions. Overall, with around 80% rate on average, the validation frequency against the complete signature table drops dramatically by about 5 folds. Furthermore, adding extra checking of the execution paths only incurs a minor increment to the validation frequency beyond the branch prediction. (8.5%, 6%, 1.6% for the cases of the EP bit vector holding two, four, and eight EPs, respectively).

3.5. Building Signature Table using a Bloom Filter

On a mis-prediction of indirect branch or an EP bit vector miss, a validation against the complete signature table is required. We use a Bloom filter[5] as the on-chip signature table to store the legitimate BPC||TPC||EPs. A Bloom filter is a space-efficient set representation that answers membership query with a small false positive possibility but with no false negative. It is implemented as an *m*-bit array, using *k* independent hashing functions that map set elements into the bit array to record their existence. This facilitates a time and space efficient hardware implementation of the signature table with multiple parallel hashing hardware units.

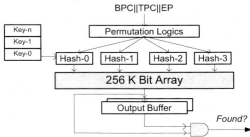

Figure-8 : A basic validation unit that incorporates a 256K-bit Bloom filter as the security signature table.

In our validation unit shown in Figure-8, each signature of BPC||TPC||EP is fed into the multiple hash units to generate vector indices for the signature table initialization at training and for membership query at validation later. We use a hardware-friendly hashing function, H3[19], to hash BPC||TPC||EP into the bit array. With multiple input keys and different permutation logics, the hash units generate independent index for one signature. Note that many viable alternatives for hashing exist including a single cycle exclusive-OR function or pipelined SHA-1/AES.

The *false positive* of a Bloom filter means a case of undetected execution path, i.e. system false negative, thus must be minimized. It is determined by three filter parameters: the number of hashes (*k*), the size of bit vector (*m*), and the size of the set represented (*n*). The false positive rate (*FPR*) for a Bloom filter is:

$$(1 - (1 - 1/m)^{kn})^k \approx (1 - e^{-kn/m})^k \qquad (1)$$

With a basic Bloom filter with m = 256K bits and k = 4, the corresponding false positive rates for n of 1400 and 15000 (which are the number of BPC||TPC||EPs for most benchmarks except *gcc*) are 2.2e-7 to 0.19%, respectively. With k=4, we provide four read/write ports for the bit array. The k can be effectively increased by allowing the bit array to be accessed multiple times with different hash results. The FPR is reduced from 0.19% to 0.038% and 0.027% with k of 8 and 12 when n=15000, respectively. To lower the FPR further, multiple basic Bloom filters can be connected together and the outputs are ANDed to decide the final result. The overall FPR is approximately the product of the FPRs of participated basic Bloom filters. For example, assume three basic Bloom filters are activated and with n of 15000, the FPR drops to 6.9e-10 and even for *gcc* with n of 33000, the FPR is 1.8e-5.

One can further reduce the number of the behavior signatures of BPC‖TPC‖EPs that must reside in the on-chip hardware table in order to lower the FPR. For example, the percentage of BPC‖TPC‖EPs that are accessed less than five times throughout the program execution account for 38% and 17% of the signatures being monitored for *apache* and *ftpd*, respectively, but only for 0.0086% and 0.0024%, respectively, of the ones that have been executed at run-time. If they are filtered out of the Bloom filter and stored in memory rather than the on-chip table, the FPR can be further reduced due to the smaller n.

To exploit the inherent false positives in the Bloom filter to launch a successful attack, the attacker must construct three proper values that conform to the false positive pattern, the branch PC that the attacker can succeed to compromise and the target address where the attacker can succeed to put or utilize malicious code as well as an legitimate branch outcome sequence (EP). With a sufficiently low false positive rate, it is impractical for an attacker to try many BPC‖TPC‖EPs in order to find one that happens to skip the check through a Bloom filter.

Finally, to protect the signature table itself, the bit array of the Bloom filter can be encrypted when spilled into memory and decrypted when loaded into the on-chip Bloom filter. Moreover, if keyed-hash is used, the processor can apply different sets of keys in each run, thus making an offline analysis to exploit false positive of a Bloom filter even more difficult.

4. Performance Evaluation

The performance impact comes from the extra cycles needed to validate the BPC‖TPC‖EP on an indirect branch mis-prediction or an EP bit-vector miss. We assume the validation unit is non-pipelined for conservative evaluation, and thereby can serve only one instruction each time. An indirect branch in the commit queue may stall the pipeline either because it is still being validated or because the validation unit is busy in servicing other branches, thus deferring all its successors to commit. However, these stalls due to the validation do not always result in observable performance degradation. As shown in Figure-7, the majority of the validations are due to indirect branch

mis-predictions. Thus, the processor must do mis-prediction recovery work such as flushing the pipeline, restoring the renaming table, and redirecting the fetch point, resulting in stalls at the front end of the pipeline. Such recovery actions on branch mis-predictions partially mask off the validation delay. Only the EP bit-vector miss would actually delay the commit. However, with a fairly high hit rate achieved as shown in Figure-6, such events are rare. In summary, the rarity of and high prediction accuracy for indirect branches, and high hit rate of the EP bit vector on BTB hits make little performance overhead to incur.

In the simulation, a four-way EP bit vector is used and each EP is 8-bit long. The access latency of the validation unit consists of the delay of hashing functions and the Bloom filter bit array access as well as other glue logics (see Table-3). The delay for accessing a 256K-bit array is measured by a simulation with CACTI 3.2 [6] under the technology of .09um. The storage structure is assumed to have four read ports and one write port. The delay of hashing logics and the glue logics are estimated by a Verilog implementation and a synthesis with TSMC's 0.09um library.

Table-3 : Access Delay of the validation unit

Permutation Logic	Hash Function	256K-bit array	Buffers & glue logic	Total delay
0.49 ns	1.48ns	1.062 ns	0.99 ns	4.022ns

Assuming a processor runs at a clock rate of 2 GHz, the delay of the validation unit will be 9 cycles. If the bit array needs to be accessed twice and three times to reduce the false positive rate, the delays are about 18 and 27 cycles, respectively. In the simulation, the validation delay ranges from 10 cycles to 30 cycles. The simulation runs the SPEC2000 CPU integer benchmarks on the Simplescalar simulator[2] that models an out-of-order 4-issue superscalar processor. The reference input is used and the number of instructions specified by SimPoint[21] is skipped. Architectural parameters for the simulation are shown in Table-4.

As shown in the Figure-9, more than half of the benchmarks do not have a measurable performance impact due to the reasons mentioned earlier. Especially, the performance degradations are uniformly small when validation delay is 10-cycle, the case when the Bloom filer is accessed once. With a very low indirect branch prediction accuracy (only about 50%; see Figure-7), *Gap* is sensitive to the validation delays. Similar results can be observed for *eon* because of the presence of extensive virtual function pointers. The performance degradation of *eon* is still within 10%. *Gcc*, *perl*, *vortex* and *crafty* also have noticeable performance degradation but within the bound of 5% even in the

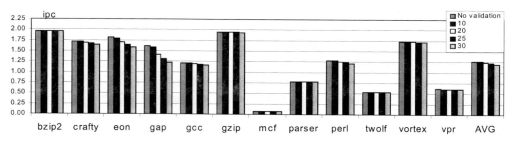

Figure-9: Performance degradation after validation unit is incorporated. The IPCs are shown for validation delays from 10 cycles to 30 cycles.

worst case. Most benchmarks can hide the validation delays, resulting in a negligible performance reduction. The average degradations are 0.4%, 2.6%, 4%, and 5.4 % for a validation delay of 10 cycles, 20 cycles, 25 cycles, and 30 cycles, respectively. The relatively severe performance impact from 30 cycles implies that it might be the upper bound for the validation delays that a 9-stage pipeline processor can hide: this can be used to guide the Bloom filter design for less performance impact.

Table-4   :Architecture Parameters

Parameter	Value
BTB	512 set, 4-way set associative
RAS	8 entries
Branch miss penalty	7 cycles
Pipeline stage	9
Branch Predictor	g-share, 12-bit hist., 2048 entries
Fetch/dispatch/issue width	4
RUU size	64 entries
Load/Store Queue	32 entries
I-cache	64K, 2 way set-asso., 2 cc hit time, LRU
D-cache	64K, 4 way set-asso., 2 cc hit time, LRU
L2 cache	Unified, 512KB, 4 way set-asso.
L2 access time	10 cycles
Function unit	4 Int ALUs, 1 Int MUL/DIV, 4 FP Adder, 1 FP MUL/DIV
Memory	100 cycles access time, 2 ports

5. Related work

There are numerous software and hardware proposals to restrain the control flow transfer for securing program execution. Most schemes involve identifying, encrypting, and/or tracking the control data [9][10][17][18][23][27]. However, in current program model it is not always possible to distinguish and track the interested control data accurately, especially for general indirect branches' targets. Moreover, non-control-data attacks[8] open new doors for an adversary to compromise the conditional branches.

Behavior-based schemes, on the other hand, monitor the execution behavior and detect deviations on certain interested events, thereby independent on the specific exploits. Forrest et al. first observed that short-term system call sequence could be viewed as "a sense of self" for a program [13]. Such a protection might suffer

from a mimicry attack and impossible path exploration can circumvent the check[26]. Wagner et al. [25] proposed a static analysis method with pushdown automata to build an intrusion model. Many follow-up works extended the idea by including more objects beyond just system calls. Sekar's finite state automaton proposal associates the system call with the PC[20]. Their recent work further tried to capture the relationships between parameters of system calls[4]. VtPath[12] was an effort that also includes additional information, specifically the return address sequence, into the objects being monitored. Gao et al. [15] generalized the VtPath by introducing a concept of execution graph to infer sequence of calls, returns and intra-procedural transition.

All methods above work at the granularity of system calls and may miss the attacks that alter program behavior between system calls[29]. In addition, severe performance overhead and slower response time have been reported [20][25] as the system call based protections are often implemented in software due to their way of retrieving the objects, typically from memory and the complex algorithm to form the signatures. Instead, our architectural scheme, as a complement to system call based solutions, works at instruction level and may detect an attack earlier with a shorter response delay.

Down to the machine instruction trace level, program shepherding[16] employs a binary code interpreter to enforce security policies. It constrains the control flow transfer when constructing execution traces. The complicated implementation and performance/memory overhead may affect its adoption. CFI[1] is a software solution that marks and validates targets for indirect calls and returns through binary rewriting. It is equivalent to collecting validated targets statically. Their work mainly addresses indirect calls and mentions little about indirect jumps. N-jump[29] by Zhang et al. also works on machine-code level and is based on a similar observation about branch behaviors. Their work mainly focuses on direct branches and treats the indirect branches as special cases. Comparing to their work, ours provides a clear checking boundary, i.e. indirect branches. In addition, we incorporate the behavior signature tightly into the pipeline by a Bloom filter and perform the validation only on branch mis-prediction and EP bit vector miss. To contrast, N-jump solution checks every jump (about one every 5-10 instructions) therefore must rely on a sophisticated co-processor running in a secured environment.

6. Conclusion

Current processor architecture is vulnerable to control flow altering attacks because it lacks a validation mechanism to check the legitimacy of a branch target address and the execution path leading to it. We have shown that validation of branch behavior, specifically an indirect branch's PC, its target, and execution path preceding it, (BPC||TPC||EP), is effective in securing program execution even when some non-control-data attacks are presented. Our experimental study has shown that the number of the behavior signatures (BPC||TPC||EP) converges and is limited. This is because program in general generates a limited number of target addresses per indirect branch and correlation existing among nearby conditional branches limits the number of possible execution paths.

To incorporate the validation into the processor's pipeline, two enhancements were made to the branch predictor: (1) enhancement of a branch target buffer (BTB) entry with an execution path (EP) bit vector for storing the execution paths that have been followed previously, and (2) hardware table of the behavior signatures in the form of a Bloom filter because of its compactness and uniform access time. The observation that the signatures (BPC||TPC||EP) are a superset of the information already stored in the augmented branch predictor dramatically reduces the validation frequency. Only on branch mis-predictions or EP bit vector misses, the Bloom filter of the signature table is accessed for validation. After accommodating the validation scheme with these hardware enhancements into a superscalar processor, we have found the performance degradation caused by the validation is small and controllable.

Acknowledgement: This work was supported in part by a grant from the US National Science Foundation (CNS-0627431).

7. References

[1] M. Abadi, M. Budiu, U. Erlingsson and J. Ligatti, "Control_flow Integrity", *in ACM CSS05*, Nov, 2005.

[2] T. Austin and D. Burger, "The SimpleScalar Tool Set". *Univ. of Wisconsin CS Dept. Technical Report, No. 1342,* June 1997.

[3] Bochs, "The Open Source IA-32 Emulation Project", *http://bochs.sourceforge.net/*

[4] S. Bhatkar, A. Chaturvedi, and R. Sekar, "Dataflow Anomaly Detection", *IEEE Symposium on Security & Privacy*, May 2006

[5] B. Bloom, "Space/Time Tradeoffs in Hash Coding with Allowable Errors", *in Communications of the ACM* 13:7, 1970

[6] S. Wilton, N. Jouppi, "CACTI: An enhanced cache access and cycle time model", *IEEE JSSC, Vol. 31(5)* May, 1996.

[7] CERT Security Advisories. http://www.cert.org/advisories/

[8] S. Chen, J. Xu, Emre C. Sezer, P. Gauriar, and R. Iyer. "Non-Control-Data Attacks Are Realistic Threats". *in Proceedings of USENIX Security Symposium*, Aug. 2005.

[9] S. Chen, J. Xu, N. Nakka, Z. Kalbarczyk, R. Iyer. "Defeating Memory Corruption Attacks via Pointer Taintedness Detection". In *Proceedings of Inte'l Conf. on Dependable Systems and Networks (DSN),* June, 2005.

[10] C. Cowan, C. Pu, D Maier, J. Walphole, P Bakke, S. Beattie, A. Grier, P Wagle, Q. Zhang, and H. Hinton, "StackGuard: Automatic adaptive detection and prevention of buffer-overflow attacks", In *Proc. 7th USENIX Security Symposium,* Jan 1998.

[11] J. Crandall and F. Chong, "Minos: Control Data Attack Prevention Orthogonal To Memory Model", *Proc. of the 37th Int'l Symp. on Microarchitecture,* Dec. 2004.

[12] H. Feng, O. Kolesnikov, P. Fogla, W. Lee, W. Gong, "Anomaly Detection Using Call Stack Information", *IEEE Symposium on Security and Privacy*, May, 2003.

[13] S. Forrest, S. Hofmeyr, A. Somayajo, T. Longstaff, "A Sense of Self for Unix Processes", *IEEE Symp.on Security and Privacy,* 1996.

[14] M Frantzen and M. Shuey. "Stackghost: Hardware facilitated stack protection", In *10th USENIX Security Symposium,* August 2001.

[15] D. Gao, M. Reiter, D. Song, "Gray-Box Extraction of Execution Graphs for Anomaly Detection", in *the ACM CCS conf,* 2004.

[16] V. Kiriansky, D Bruening, S. Amarasinghe, "Secure Execution via Program Shepherding", In *Proc. of the 11th Usenix Security Symp,* 2002.

[17] G. Lee and A. Tyagi, "Encoded Program Counter: Self-Protection from Buffer Overflow Attacks", *Proc. of the First Int'l Conference on Internet Computing,* June, 2000.

[18] Y. Park, Z. Zhang, G. Lee, "Microarchitectural Protection Against Buffer Overflow Attack", *IEEE Micro*, July, 2006.

[19] M. Ramakrishna, E. Fu, E. Bahcekapili, "A performance study of hashing functions for hardware applications", In *Proc. Of Int'l Conf. Computing and Information,* 1994.

[20] R. Sekar, M. Bendre, P. Bollineni, D. Dhurjati, "A fast Automaton-Based Method for Detecting Anomalous Program Behaviors", In *Proc. of IEEE Symp.on Security & Privacy*, 2001.

[21] T. Sherwood, E. Perelman, G. Hamerly and B. Calder, "Automatically Characterizing Large Scale Program Behavior", In *Proc. of the 10th ASPLOS,* Oct. 2002.

[22] Y. Shi, S. Dempsey, G. Lee, "Architectural Support for Run-Time Validation of Control Flow Transfer", In *Proc. Of IEEE Int'l Conference on Computer Design (ICCD06),* Oct. 2006.

[23] G. Suh, J. Lee, S Devadas, D. Zhang, "Secure program execution via dynamic information flow tracking". In *Proc. of the 12th Int'l Conf. on ASPLOS,* 2004.

[24] N. Tuck, B. Calder, G. Varghese, "Hardware and Binary Modification Support for Code Pointer Protection from Buffer Overflow", *Proc. of Int'l Symp. on Microarchitecture,* 2004.

[25] D. Wagner, D. Dean, "intrusion detection via Static Analysis", *in Proc. of the IEEE Symp.on Security and Privacy,* 2001.

[26] D. Wagner and P. Soto, "Mimicry Attack on Host-based Intrusion detection system", In *ACM CSS 02*, Nov. 2002.

[27] J. Xu, Z. Kalbarczyk, R. Iyer. "Transparent runtime randomization for security", In *Proc. Of the Symp. on Reliable and Distribution System,* 2003.

[28] T. Yeh and Y. Patt, "Alternative Implementations of Two-Level Adaptive Training Branch Prediction". *in Proc. of the 19th ISCA,* 1992.

[29] T. Zhang, X. Zhuang, W. Lee, S. Pande, "Anomalous Path Detection with Hardware Support," *in Proc. of CASES,* 2005.

A Firewall for Routers:
Protecting Against Routing Misbehavior

Ying Zhang   Z. Morley Mao   Jia Wang
University of Michigan   *AT&T Labs–Research*

Abstract

In this work, we present the novel idea of route normalization *by correcting on the fly routing traffic on behalf of a local router to protect the local network from malicious and misconfigured routing updates. Analogous to traffic normalization for network intrusion detection systems, the proposed RouteNormalizer patches ambiguities and eliminates semantically incorrect routing updates to protect against routing protocol attacks. Furthermore, it serves the purpose of a router firewall by identifying resource-based attacks against routers. Upon detecting anomalous routing changes, it suggests local routing policy modifications to improve route selection decisions. Deploying a RouteNormalizer requires no modification to routers if desired using a transparent TCP proxy setup.*

In this paper, we present the detailed design of the RouteNormalizer and evaluate it using a prototype implementation based on empirical BGP routing updates. We validate its effectiveness by showing that many well-known routing problems from operator mailing lists are correctly identified.

1   Introduction

> I would stress that all of these things, particularly prefix hijacking and backbone router "ownage", are real threats, happening today, happening with alarming frequency. Folks need to realize that the underground is abusing this stuff today, and has been for quite some time.
> –Rob Thomas quoted by David Meyer at NANOG 28, June 2003

This is a quote given by David Meyer, a well-known network researcher and network operator, at the North American Network Operators' Group (NANOG) Meeting in 2003 [33]. It highlights the urgency to better protect the Internet routing system, providing the main motivation for our work.

The Internet originated from a research network where network entities are assumed to be *well-behaved*. The original Internet design addresses physical failures well, but fails to address problems resulting from misbehavior and misconfigurations. Routers can misbehave due to misconfigurations [29], impacting network reachability. Today, the Internet has no robust defense mechanisms against misbehaving routers, leaving the routing infrastructure largely unprotected [34]. One of the most widely known and serious misconfiguration occurred in 1997, when a customer router at a small edge network by mistake advertised a short path to many destinations, resulting in a massive blackhole disconnecting a significant portion of the Internet [10]. This example illustrates the need for an easily deployable protection mechanism to prevent local forwarding decisions from being polluted.

For our purpose, we define the *control plane* to be the Internet routing layer, and the *data plane* to be the packet forwarding layer. There is an inherent trust relationship in today's routing system: a router assumes routing updates from its neighbors are correct. However, router misconfigurations [29], attacks [30], and inherent routing problems [21] often render this assumption incorrect.

Given the lack of security in today's routing protocols, both the research and the network operator community have already proposed solutions such as SBGP [40] and SoBGP [35], which require routing protocol modifications. However, we have witnessed a rather slow deployment. Furthermore, most of them do not eliminate the possibility of router misconfigurations and their associated impact.

We take a different approach by posing the question of *what individual networks can do locally to protect against routing misbehavior from external networks*. Even if future routing protocols have enhanced security mechanisms, there is still a need to be defensive against routing attacks from noncooperative networks or misconfigurations. Furthermore, there exist inherent ambiguities in routing protocols that require rectification to proactively prevent unexpected behavior due to implementation variations. We propose that networks proactively *correct* routing updates locally through a *RouteNormalizer (RN)*, which logically sits on the data path between the local router to be protected and the remote router whose updates may be untrustworthy. Our work fits perfectly with the recent proposal of logically centralized routing architecture such as RCP [12] to improve routing control. Such a platform acts as a firewall for the local router by identifying and preventing routing attacks using anomaly detection. Taking advantage of local information such as local routing policies, local address information, relationship with neighboring Autonomous Systems or ASes help more accurately detect routing attacks directly impacting the local AS.

Unlike protocols such as SBGP, our approach requires no changes to routing protocols or router configurations. We summarize RN's main functionality: (i) Identify and correct anomalous routing updates. (ii) Identify and mitigate routing attacks. (iii) Mitigate routing instability by dampening routing updates. (iv) Perform load management by rate-limiting updates. (v) Emulate features not available on local routers, *e.g.,* graceful restart [39]. One of our novel contributions lies in applying routing anomaly detection to influence routing decisions so that routes selected are more likely correct.

The RouteNormalizer is a general platform for correcting routing updates for any routing protocols. In this work, we focus on the interdomain routing protocol – BGP (Border Gateway Protocol [37, 24, 22]) given its importance to the well-being of the Internet and that its routing information mostly arrives from external untrusted networks. BGP is a *path vector* protocol, as the AS_PATH attribute contains the sequence of ASes of the route. Each BGP update contains path attributes such as NEXT_HOP and ORIGIN, some of which are mandatory. BGP is *incremental, i.e.,* every BGP update message indicates a routing change. In addition, BGP is *policy-oriented*: routers can apply complex policies to influence *best* route selection for each prefix and to subsequent route propagation.

We summarize our main contributions: (1) Developed a platform to perform BGP traffic normalization, enabling incrementally deploying new router functionality. (2) Improved on existing router functionality, *e.g.,* max-prefix-limit. (3) Proposed the use of routing anomaly detection to achieve robust routing. (4) Improved routing anomaly detection by exploiting local network information. (5) Performed the first extensive correlation between NANOG emails for routing related complaints with BGP data.

The rest of the paper is organized as follows. We first present the architecture design of the RouteNormalizer in Section 2. Section 3 describes the deployment scenarios. We describe our prototype in Section 4. We show the effectiveness of the RouteNormalizer using empirical BGP data in Section 5. Finally, we cover related work and conclude.

2 RouteNormalizer Architecture

In this section, we describe the architectural design. We refer to the *local router* as the router under the protection of the RouteNormalizer in the same AS. The RouteNormalizer can correct traffic on behalf of several local routers. The *remote router* refers to the other router in the BGP session, typically not within the same AS as the local router.

As illustrated in Figure 1, the RouteNormalizer takes several optional input data such as the local router's policy configuration and real-time BGP feeds from external sources. The RouteNormalizer can be configured to observe all the traffic destined to the local router's BGP port 179, as well as traffic originated by the local router to the remote router. As output, in addition to the "normalized" BGP traffic, it generates alarms and suggestions for policy modifications for the

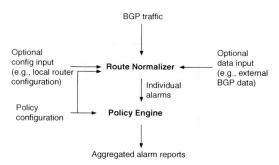

Figure 1. The RouteNormalizer framework.

local router. Note that the RouteNormalizer performs normalization on BGP traffic both destined to as well as originated from the local router. We focus on the former case here.

2.1 Functionality overview

We first highlight its design principles. (1) Basic checking to ensure protocol semantic correctness. (2) Make use of *local network information* such as local network addresses. (3) Take advantage of external information to assist route anomaly detection. (4) Assume dominant history behavior is mostly correct. (5) Use anomaly detection to influence route selection: be conservative by avoiding anomalous routes.

A summary of all functionalities is shown in Table 1. Arguably, some of these can be performed directly by routers using route filters for example. However, route filters are usually signature based, only protecting against known attack patterns. Nor do they have any anomaly detection or data correlation capability. Routers usually have limited memory to perform such filtering, and such incurred overhead may impact regular forwarding behavior. Furthermore, as we explain below, the RouteNormalizer also acts as a firewall to prevent potential router OS bugs from being exploited. For known router OS problems such as the recently announced DoS vulnerabilities in Cisco IOS [43], the RouteNormalizer can act as a filter before patches are applied. Next, we illustrate each category using examples.

2.2 Fix violations of BGP semantics

The RouteNormalizer performs simple checks for detecting violations of BGP semantics in routing updates. Routers may react differently to such updates depending on their implementations. In the ideal case, they would drop such updates and send back an error message. In some instances, these routes may actually be selected as the best route for forwarding; however, packets may not reach the destinations due to the violation of BGP semantics.

Routers from different vendors running distinct software versions may exhibit dissimilar default behavior, possibly leading to inconsistent routing decisions in a single network. As a result, simply enforcing uniform routing configurations across all routers in the network may not be sufficient. Moreover, unexpected BGP updates may also lead to router OS crashes (*e.g.,* [7]). Thus, a platform such as the RouteNormalizer that dynamically detects routing problems is very useful.

Category	Description	RouteNormalizer actions (also suggest improved routing policies)	Existing router implementation
Fix violations of BGP semantics	Incorrect attribute values: *e.g.,* AS loops	Modify, drop updates, generate warnings	Configure with route filters.
	Attributes with private information		
	Missing mandatory attribute values		
Fix violations of routing policies	Export policy violations	Drop updates, generate warnings	Configure with route filters, may require external information.
	Nexthop violations	Modify, drop updates, generate warnings	
Detect routing anomalies	Anomalous routing behavior	Drop updates, generate warnings	Not available, difficult to implement, requires external information.
	Routing inconsistency	Drop updates, generate warnings	
	Local and remote address hijacks	Modify, drop updates, generate warnings	
Load management and instability mitigation	Mitigate load due to identical routing updates	Drop duplicate updates	Partially implementable, RouteNormalizer enhanced existing functionality.
	Mitigate against router DoS attacks	Filter BGP attack traffic, delay updates	
	Mitigate instability of flapping prefixes	Emulate route flap damping, delay updates	
	Mitigate instability of session resets	Emulate graceful restart, delay updates	

Table 1. Functionality of the RouteNormalizer.

1. AS routing loops. This is an example of ambiguities in BGP routing protocol specification. It is recommended that routes containing loops should not be used; however, in practice we still observe such routes due to lack of enforcement. In some rare instances, routing loops are allowed in the AS_PATH due to special topology arrangements. However, one cannot count on these paths to be accepted by other routers, leading to potential routing blackholes. Thus, to improve routing robustness, it is best to exclude such routes from BGP decision process if alternate routes exist.

2. Missing mandatory attributes. Another BGP semantics violation is missing mandatory attributes in the routing updates. Some attributes such as ORIGIN or AS_PATH cannot be easily inferred. However, the NEXT_HOP attribute, which is also mandatory, usually is the interface IP address of the advertising router. Proactively correcting this prevents unnecessary session resets.

3. Private information. For eBGP sessions *i.e.,* BGP sessions between routers belonging to different ASes, BGP attributes in general should not contain private information such as private IP addresses/prefixes or private AS numbers. For iBGP sessions, *i.e.,* sessions within an AS, such values are meaningful only within the local network. For all sessions, bogon prefixes or unallocated prefixes by address registries should not be announced. Accidentally accepting such routes may impact forwarding for legitimate destinations using private address blocks inside the local network.

Remark: In general, there is only a small classes of updates that violate BGP semantics due to the flexibility of routing policies and ambiguities of the protocol specification. If the RouteNormalizer is initialized with the *local routing policies*, more semantic violation can be identified. Routing updates in this category can be corrected or filtered using route filters. However, there is a limited number of filters a router can accommodate, and this imposes additional overhead.

2.3 Fix violations of routing policies

Although individual network providers have the freedom to define their own routing policies, there are some well-known guidelines for specifying policies according to the best common practices (BCP) of BGP [15]. Violations of policies may result in unexpected traffic blackholes.

1. Export policy violations. The RouteNormalizer identifies the class of updates that violate routing policies, especially those associated with the local AS. For example, a multi-homed customer, or a customer peering with more than one upstream providers is not allowed to advertise routes received from one provider to another [18]. Such violations of the so-called export policies can be identified by checking the AS relationship between the customer AS and the nexthop AS beyond the customer AS in the AS_PATH of the routes advertised by the customer router. ISP can either deprefer these routes or resort to overlay routing to bypass the problem.

2. Nexthop violations. Typically the routes advertised by a neighboring router in the BGP session correspond to the routes in the forwarding table of the neighbor. The nexthop AS and the nexthop IP should be the neighbor's AS number and the remote router's interface IP respectively. Otherwise, the routes advertised will not correspond to traffic going through the neighbors. If any of the two assertions fails, the RouteNormalizer raises an alarm to the network operator.

Remark: Routing policy violation checks are more cumbersome to perform inside routers due to the need of external information such as AS relationships.

2.4 Detect routing anomalies

The RouteNormalizer identifies routing anomalies by examining the routing data locally received from the neighbors. Correlating updates from multiple locations can provide a network-wide view to help consistency checking and potentially discover additional routing anomalies. Network researchers have used BGP data from multiple vantage points to improve AS relationship inference [18, 41, 8] and BGP health monitoring [32]. Our goal here is to (i) identify deviations from average behavior, (ii) perform consistency checking, and (iii) track announcements of one's own address blocks. Note that timely and accurate detection of routing anomalies facilitate and inform mitigate responses.

1. Anomalous routing behavior. The RouteNormalizer establishes a routing profile consisting of characteristics such as the distribution of routes in terms of AS_PATHs, ASes, and the number of routes from each neighbor. This profile is tracked over time and across data from each vantage point. Besides deviation from history data, another way to find anomalies is to identify frequently changing values, implying instability in the routing system.

2. Routing inconsistency. The second objective is to identify inconsistent route advertisements excluding convergence effects. Commonly each AS advertises its best path consistently across all peering locations to all its neighbors complying to its export policies. This assumption is commonly held to be true according to the protocol specification, also based on the well-known definition of an AS [22]. The consequence of inconsistent routing advertisements is unintended routing behavior deviating from the usual practice of hot-potato routing, resulting in potential increased network cost.

3. Address space hijacking. This is an important anomaly given today's danger of IP address hijacks and traffic blackholes. This also illustrates the usefulness of correlating BGP data from multiple locations. Address space hijacking refers to the case when a network announces a route as the originator to the address block it does not own. The last AS in the AS_PATH is the originating AS. Spammers are known to take advantage of hijacked address spaces to avoid being identified. Such instances have also occurred due to misconfigurations: in December 1999, AT&T Worldnet was off the air because someone by mistake was advertising a critical network owned by Worldnet [9]. To detect hijacking attempts for *locally originated address blocks*, the RouteNormalizer uses the knowledge of which address blocks originate from the local network. It is important to identify whether other networks announce as the originator updates to locally owned address blocks. To increase the confidence in detection, we correlate the suspected hijacked address blocks with other data sources, such as Spam Archive [5] and blacklisted addresses from sites such as Dshield [1].

Remark: Anomaly detection is not supported by routers today and is difficult to implement in routers due to the complex logic and external data requirement. Commercial routers used in most networks today are not programmable. Implementing anomaly detection in software on RouteNormalizer is more flexible and easily allows additions of new functionality as the protocol evolves.

2.5 Manage instability and load

Routing instability and attacks can incur numerous updates, as demonstrated by worm outbreaks causing routing disruptions [16]. Processing such updates adds extra overhead given router's limited resources. The RouteNormalizer helps manage the load on routers by mitigating routing instability and minimizing unnecessary updates processed by the local router in the following ways.

1. Identical routing updates. We found on average about 5% of updates from RouteViews [6] consist of identical BGP updates which is usually due to router software bugs [28]. These updates are not at all useful for route computation; however, they may consume router resources. The RouteNormalizer can easily detect their presence and drop them.

2. Instability due to flapping prefixes and session reset. Occasionally, a large number of routing updates stem from

unstable prefixes that continuously go up and down [38] due to flaky hardware, for instance. Route flap damping [44, 36] requires maintaining the update history for each prefix and can lead to memory exhaustion. Furthermore, it may not be enabled in every router. By delaying routing updates, the RouteNormalizer is effectively slowing down the sending rate, needed to prevent router overload. The RouteNormalizer can also effectively emulate the flap damping algorithm in a modified and improved way by ensuring that routes are only suppressed when at least one alternate route exists.

Receiving a large number of legitimate updates from its neighbors due to sudden significant routing changes or session resets will causes significant update processing overhead. Usually the core router has multiple BGP sessions, which can be easily overwhelmed and become unresponsive in forwarding packets [13]. The *graceful restart mechanism* for BGP [39] has been proposed to minimize the effects due to session resets. To take advantage of this feature, routers need to support such capability so that End-of-RIB marker is sent and routes are retained even after session reset for a bounded time. However, many routers today may not support such capability, especially the legacy routers with outdated router software. The RouteNormalizer can emulate the graceful restart functionality and furthermore enhance it by ensuring there are no inconsistent routing information.

Whenever the RouteNormalizer delays routing updates on behalf of the local router, the imposed delay can be set based on the inferred load. Inference is performed by observing the sending rate of routing traffic and data traffic if available. Moreover, unstable routes may affect routing decisions if such routes are preferred over alternate stable ones.

Remark: Functionality provided by the RouteNormalizer to deal with routing instability cannot be easily implemented inside the router, as doing so would directly impact the router load. Precisely when routers are overloaded, such functionality is critical in preventing the impact on the forwarding plane.

2.6 Detailed normalization algorithms

We have enumerated the main functionalities of the RouteNormalizer. Here we describe some of them in more details, focusing on their benefit and improvement over the equivalent functionalities in the router. In all the following cases, the router either does not provide such support or our algorithm significantly improves upon it.

Deaggregation detection: Deaggregation, the opposite of aggregation, refers to the behavior of advertising many small prefixes covered in larger prefixes already present. The negative consequence is that the router receiving such announcements may experience memory exhaustion, possibly leading to router crashes. To protect against deaggregation, routers currently use the *Max-Prefix Limit* [14] feature, which by default disables the peering session after the number of received prefixes exceeds the configured maximum number [25]. However, the router does not attempt to differentiate between regular and deaggregated prefixes, consequently causing the entire BGP session to be affected.

The RouteNormalizer more intelligently deals with prefix deaggregation, which can be easily detected by observing an increase in the number of prefixes while the number IP addresses remains relatively constant. When router memory is scarce, routing announcements to prefixes which are contained within existing prefixes in the routing table can be safely dropped without impacting reachability. It may impact routing decisions given differences in routes between the aggregate and the subnet prefix.

Address hijacking detection: This functionality is currently not supported by routers and will be difficult for routers to provide due to the complex logic and external data requirement. Detecting address hijacking relies on having accurate prefix to origin AS mappings; however, there are no such authoritative data sources available. If we generate an alarm for each update that indicates a different origin AS from the latest route of the prefix, there would be many false positives. The reason is that due to multi-homing there are legitimate reasons for Multiple origin ASes (MOAS [47]). To remedy this, we develop a mapping of prefix to origin AS by learning from history data from multiple vantage points to improve detection accuracy.

Graceful restart: Some routers today support graceful restart [39] and assume that within a configurable time limit the restarting router can still properly forward traffic. The RouteNormalizer can emulate this and enhance routing consistency if it can observe data traffic. The key is to observe whether traffic such as TCP ACK packets are arriving from the remote router indicating that packets can indeed reach the destinations. Otherwise, the RouteNormalizer will withdraw the routes advertised by the remote router for which alternate routes exist at the local router to ensure traffic is not blackholed unnecessarily. Note that even if due to asymmetric routing, no return traffic is observed, reachability is not compromised as only alternate routes are chosen.

Before the session is re-established, the RouteNormalizer keeps track of the latest updates from the local router to the restarting remote router. Once the session comes up, the remote router reannounces its entire forwarding table to the RouteNormalizer, which in turn only selectively forwards routes that were previously withdrawn and any changed routes compared to those before the session reset. From the RouteNormalizer to the remote router, the latest local router's forwarding table is sent. The added intelligence ensures that only the necessary routes are exchanged upon session reestablishment to reduce overhead for the local router.

Instability detection: BGP already has route flap damping as specified in RFC2439 to deal with routing instability. The RouteNormalizer can emulate it if it is not supported by the local router or disabled due to memory usage concerns. This would help reduce both processing and memory overhead. The RouteNormalizer further improves it by handling persisent flapping, which is ignored due to reinitialized penalty values upon session reset. Damping statistics are remembered after session reset to detect such routing instability.

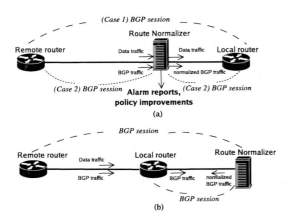

Figure 2. RouteNormalizer (RN) single router deployment scenario.

3 Deployment Scenarios

In this section, we illustrate deployment scenarios with different degrees of benefit in terms of functionality and ease of deployment. We expect both eBGP and iBGP to benefit from deploying the RouteNormalizer to block routes from untrusted external networks as well as to prevent misconfigurations from propagating across the internal network.

Figure 2 depicts how the RouteNormalizer is used for a single BGP session protecting the local router from one remote router. We expect the RouteNormalizer to be deployed very close to the local router. There are two main ways of setting it up, distinguished by whether the RouteNormalizer can observe data traffic. Shown in Figure 2(a), case 1 is the transparent TCP proxy setup, requiring no configuration changes of existing BGP sessions. The RouteNormalizer intercepts any packets between the remote and the local router. It inserts, modifies, and drops any packet destined to the BGP port. The presence of the RouteNormalizer is completely transparent to either router. Case 2 of Figure 2(a) illustrates the approach where the RouteNormalizer establishes two sessions, with the remote and local router respectively. Remote router needs no configuration changes as it treats the RouteNormalizer as the local router, which is made aware of the RouteNormalizer. Changes to local routers are usually easier to implement. To address the shortcoming of the first setup, one can adopt the approach shown in Figure 2(b). The RouteNormalizer can pretend to be local router from the perspective of the remote router, whose configuration requires no modifications. The local router is configured to have a BGP session with the RouteNormalizer to receive normalized routes. Note that the local router forwards the BGP updates between the remote router and the RouteNormalizer which does not observe data traffic to other destinations within the local network. The resulting advantage is that it can be implemented as a software-based router and does not need to forward high-speed data traffic. This setting is more appropriate for BGP sessions in the core Internet with high traffic rate.

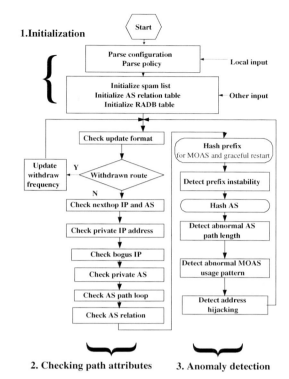

1.Initialization

Start

Parse configuration
Parse policy ← Local input

Initialize spam list
Initialize AS relation table ← Other input
Initialize RADB table

Check update format

Hash prefix
(for MOAS and graceful restart)

Update withdraw frequency ←Y— Withdrawn route

Detect prefix instability

N

Check nexthop IP and AS

Hash AS

Check private IP address

Detect abnormal AS path length

Check bogus IP

Check private AS

Detect abnormal MOAS usage pattern

Check AS path loop

Check AS relation

Detect address hijacking

2. Checking path attributes   3. Anomaly detection

Figure 3. Functionality implementation.

In general, an IP network consists of many BGP routers, each of which may peer with multiple routers. To reduce the management overhead of per router neighbor based deployment, we generalize Figure 2(a) Case 2 to protecting multiple "local" routers, where the RouteNormalizer peers with multiple local and remote routers, which is equivalent to the deployment setup of Routing Control Platform (RCP) [12].

4 Prototype Evaluation

We have implemented a prototype of the RouteNormalizer with all the functionalities described in Section 2 with the exception of protection against resource-based router DoS attacks, which is our future work. We evaluate the performance of the prototyped RouteNormalizer based on the deployment setup with two separate BGP sessions shown in Figure 2(a) Case 2. The performance of other deployment settings is similar and not included here due to the space constraint.

4.1 Functionality implementation

The RouteNormalizer receives update messages and processes them according to the dataflow shown in Figure 3.
1. Initialization. There are three sets of initialization input files. The first are local router's configuration files, containing useful information such as locally announced address blocks and import filters. The second are user-defined policy configurations for the RouteNormalizer. This policy configuration is kept secret to prevent attackers from evading the RouteNormalizer even given its source code. We note that even using the default configurations it is nontrivial to evade our anomaly

detection techniques. The third is external information to improve RouteNormalizer's confidence in generating accurate alarms, for example, the Routing Assets Database (RADB) and Spam Archives [5].
2. Checking path attributes. After initialization, the RouteNormalizer performs normalization actions on BGP update attributes as described in Section 2. The order in which the checks are performed is determined by impact severity starting with the most serious violations. Processing for a given update is stopped if a violation is detected and cannot be corrected. The RouteNormalizer first checks for update format errors by removing unknown attributes. It updates the withdrawal frequency for the corresponding prefix.

For announcements, the RouteNormalizer first corrects if needed the nexthop IP and AS number to match the advertising router. It subsequently checks if the announced prefixes contain private addresses or unallocated addresses. Then it performs private AS number checks, loop detection, and AS relationship violation checks in succession. Note that checking AS relationship violation is the most time consuming part because of searching the relationship for each consecutive AS pair in the AS path. This consumes 70% of total processing time. It subsequently performs anomaly detection on attribute values to find deviations from history.
3. Anomaly detection. The RouteNormalizer uses past history to perform anomaly detection. The use of history is justified as history provides information on usable routes. It first detects prefix related anomalies followed by AS path related anomalies. This includes detecting unstable routes, anomalous attributes such as unusually long AS paths, significant changes in the number of prefixes announced by an AS, and abnormal origin patterns to infer address hijacking attempts. To facilitate anomaly detection, the RouteNormalizer stores relevant state for received update messages in two hash table data structures as shown in Figure 3.

Note that we choose the hash table data structure instead of Patricia tree because we need to keep track of all distinct prefixes even if one is covered by another for remembering different routing attributes. Upon receiving an BGP update, the RouteNormalizer updates the corresponding records in both hash tables. Our prototype is an extensible framework as each functionality is implemented as an independent module.

4.2 System performance evaluation

The RouteNormalizer is implemented at user level written in C with about 3,400 lines of code. Our prototype testbed is shown in Figure 4, where we use a Cisco 3600 with IOS 12.2(26a) as the local router. Since we do not focus on the routing performance on the remote router, we use GNU Zebra v0.94 [2] based software router running on a PC as the remote router. The RouteNormalizer is evaluated using a Dell Dimension 8400 with 3GHz Pentium 4 Processor and 1.5GB memory running on Linux Fedora Core 3. It establishes two BGP sessions: one with the local router, the other with the remote router. To study the routing behavior of the local router, we set up a peering session to a peering router

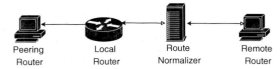

Figure 4. RouteNormalizer prototype testbed.

using another zebra instance running on a PC. All links are full-duplex 100Mbps switched Ethernet.

1. System throughput. We examine the overhead of route normalization in handling high volumes of routing traffic by modifying Zebra [2] (called *pseudo-Zebra*) to read update messages from files and send them out in the format defined in the RFC 1771 [37] as fast as possible over the network to overcome the minimum route advertisement timer constraint of Zebra software router and achieve the maximum throughput over 100 Mbps link. We observe that the average throughput using our pseudo-Zebra program is 77.9Mbps or 64,916 packets/sec on the testbed, which is comparable to the Bro traffic normalizer [23]. Note that this throughput result is obtained when the router is reading from files. The sending rate is thus limited by the file I/O on the remote router.

Handling multiple peers has only slight degradation on the throughput. We argue that this throughput is acceptable because the data rate of BGP update traffic is significantly lower than 77.9Mbps due to minimum route advertisement timer and the router processing overhead, as confirmed using empirical BGP data. For example, the peak rate of BGP updates for about 30 peers is less than 80Kbps, much less than the maximum traffic rate the RouteNormalizer can sustain. It takes on average only 223 seconds for the RouteNormalizer to process a single day's routing update data for 36 peers, assuming the data is readily available. Thus, we expect the RouteNormalizer can effortlessly keep up with the BGP update traffic rate in real time.

2. Memory consumption. The memory consumption for storing both *PrefixHash* and *ASHash* increases linearly during the initialization stage. It subsequently remains quite stable, increasing very slowly when processing new updates. For example, keeping states for 16 days of routing messages from a single peer consumes less than 20MB of memory. To ensure memory does not grow without limit and to prevent state exhaustion attacks, we use the strategy similar to LRU cache replacement policies by timing out memory usage. The amount of memory consumed increases linearly but very slowly with increasing number of peering sessions. With 30 peers, the memory consumed is slightly less than 150MB. The average amount of memory used per peer is 5MB, much less than the 20MB for a single peer because of the information shared among peers.

5 Empirical Evaluation using BGP Data

In this section, we evaluate the effectiveness of the RouteNormalizer using empirical data from public BGP source – RouteViews [6].We study the experimental findings of BGP updates that can benefit from route normalization.

Category	# updates (% total alarms)	# ASes involved	# prefixes involved
AS path loops	1,047 (3.5%)	23	2,483
Private ASes in AS paths	930 (3.1%)	31	953
Unusually long AS paths	172(0.57%)	1305	256
AS relationship violations	20,174 (67%)	438	94
MOAS violations	5,976 (19.86%)	382	267
Unstable prefixes	1,785 (5.9%)	58	1496

Table 2. Identified normalizable updates (RouteViews: October 2006)

Our analysis is not meant to be exhaustive and the results reported here focus on one month of data in October 2006 using three months of data from July 2006 to September 2006 as history information for anomaly detection. From the routing related email complaints on the North America Network Operator Group (NANOG) mailing list [3], the RouteNormalizer can identify most of them, confirming its effectiveness at identifying real routing problems.

5.1 Normalization statistics

Table 2 shows the overall number of identified updates in each category and number of ASes and prefixes involved. We notice that the AS relationship violations appear to constitute the majority of identified alarms. Altogether there are 30, 110 alarms generated during the one month time period using RouteViews data from 36 BGP routers. Table 2 also shows the number of ASes involved in each category: 438 ASes responsible for AS loops. We did not find any NEXT_HOP violations or instances of bogon prefixes in the BGP feeds examined. For some categories such as "unusually long AS paths", we define a threshold based on observed data distribution in history data. Although we were unable to detect updates in all the categories implemented, *e.g.,* hijacked address blocks, partly due to lacking local configuration information, our current findings are encouraging.

To justify the use of history data for detecting anomalies in the BGP routing attributes, we analyzed the distribution in the routing information across each prefix. We found that on average 75% of prefixes have only fewer than 12 distinct routes over the three months history data. Focusing on only the AS path and Origin attributes, the two most common attributes directly impacting routing decisions, on average 94% have at most 5 distinct routes. These statistics show that history is a good predictor for identifying routing anomalies, as the routing attributes are fairly stable over time.

To generate concise alarm reports in real time, related alarms are grouped together to produce aggregated alarm reports. In this prototype, we use a simple and intuitive technique to group the alarms based on the time of occurrence, the ASes and prefixes involved in the alarms. In our analysis, we use 5 minutes as the threshold for maximum separation across alarms, as typically routing convergence occurs within minutes. Furthermore, we use 10 minutes as a limit for aggregating a long running alarm, as operators would like to be notified of routing events in real time. The threshold values are set by observing the distribution of alarm intervals.

By grouping related alarms across different prefixes, we reduced the number of alarms from 635 to 221 by 66% on average per peer by examining 10 peers for 10 days. Grouping together different yet closely-occurring alarms for the same prefix helps identify problems associated with the same destination. We further reduced the number of alarms to 128, *i.e.,* by 43% on average. Finally, we experimented with grouping based on the network impacted by the alarm, *i.e.,* the affected AS. This results in 96 alarms on average, ranging from 36 to 118 with the standard deviation of 62, a reduction of 25%.

5.2 Case study: graceful restart

To support the graceful restart functionality and improve routing consistency, the RouteNormalizer needs to record the latest route for each prefix. This imposes extra overhead during the first time the BGP session is established. We evaluate this overhead by measuring the time for transferring the entire routing table with 144,615 entries (taken from RouteView data for AS7018 on October 1 2006) from the remote router to the local router, and then propagating to the local router's peer shown in Figure 4. The local router is Cisco 3600 with IOS 12.2(26a). Without the RouteNormalizer, the transfer takes 194.23 seconds on average with standard deviation of 3.7. With the RouteNormalizer, the duration for table transfer is increased to 201.5 seconds on average with standard deviation of 5.7. The extra delay imposed is around 7.27 seconds, which we believe is acceptable as it is one-time overhead and per-prefix penalty is very small.

To evaluate the benefit of the enhanced graceful restart on the RouteNormalizer, we use BGP data from RouteViews on October 1 2006 and set the local router to be multihomed to the AT&T (AS7018) and Sprint (AS1239) network, two tier-1 ISPs. Route selection algorithm is based on the BGP RFC [37]. The benefit of graceful restart are two fold: reducing both the number of updates exchanged and the duration that routes are potentially unusable. In our analysis, we artificially bring down the session to AS7018. Among 144,615 routing table entries, only 68,066 routes need to be withdrawn. Assuming the session is down for 90 seconds, 9 new updates are sent after session reestablishment in addition to 68,062 withdrawn routes, compared to 144,683 updates if no graceful restart is available. The duration for transferring such updates is only 90.6 seconds with the RouteNormalizer, as opposed to 194 seconds in the case of transferring the entire table to the local router without the RouteNormalizer. Note that the saving results from the fact that the 76,621 stale routes are still in local router's routing table and do not need to be sent to the local router upon session re-establishment and to be propagated to the peering router. Thus these routes are usable as soon as the link recovers. This translates to reducing the average time duration that the route is potentially unusable at local router by 23.96 seconds for each prefix.

5.3 Known routing problems

The NANOG mailing list [4] regularly reports ongoing problems with the Internet routing system, as they may impact user performance and network operations. Using simple keyword search and manual inspection of the emails, we identified 54 events that are clearly related to routing problems during the time period from October 2001 to November 2006. Part of these real routing problems are caused by either malicious intent or misconfigurations [17]. The RouteNormalizer will detect these problems on the wire and attempt to mitigate against the negative impact.

Table 3 shows the overall statistics on detecting the routing problems reported on the NANOG mailing list. For a given reported routing problem, RouteViews routing data spanning the time period starting from two days before the event until the end of the day of the report are analyzed. In most categories, the detection percentage is quite high. Note that some of these routing problems may be related to the internal networks and thus not visible in BGP updates or may not be observable at the BGP feeds we have access to.

Private addresses: On June 16, 2002 at around 15:43PM, Qwest network leaked routes for 10.0.0.0/8. The RouteNormalizer detects this and raises an alarm. Depending on its policy, it may drop such updates.

Prefix leaking which violates AS relationships: On July 11, 2003, one network operator complained that traffic originated from Sprint arrived over ALGX (AS2828) customer's interface, violating export policies. The RouteNormalizer reports the AS relationship violation for path 1239 6395 14751 2828 2828 8001. Broadwing Communications (6395) did not filter the announcement from its customer (AS14751), which incorrectly readvertised routes learned from its provider AS2828 to its other provider AS6395. If alternate paths exist for the destination prefix, this route should not be used.

Prefix deaggregation: On May 2, 2002, within 15 minutes an additional 5,000 routes originated from AS705 entered the global view. The RouteNormalizer detected this by observing a sudden increase in the number of prefixes advertised by AS705; however, there is no increase in the number actual IP addresses. Most of these newly announced prefixes are /24s and were contained in larger /8 and /11 address blocks. If permitted by the policy, the RouteNormalizer can simply drop these announcements to ensure that the local router's routing tables are not overwhelmed.

AS loop: The RouteNormalizer found 12 events of AS-level routing loops in BGP data but there are no corresponding email complaints posted on NANOG mailing list.

Address hijacking: On November 9 2006, 86 prefixes such as 12.0.0.0/7, 121.0.0.0/8, 15.0.0.0/8 were announced by AS29449 instead of its usual origin ASes such as AS7018, lasting for over 10 minutes. The reason of this event is still unknown. Using three months of history data, the RouteNormalizer detects this by observing that these prefixes never used AS29449 as its origin AS. Consequently, the RouteNormalizer raises suspected address hijacking alarms.

Instability: On October 5, 2005, Level3 Communications Inc. (AS3356) terminated its peering relation with Cogent Communications Inc. (AS174). This depeering event causes

Category	Private address	AS relationship violation	Prefix deaggregation	Address hijacking	Routing instability
Normalizer functionality	Private IP address detection	Export policy violation detection	Routing instability mitigation	Anomaly detection in attributes	Routing instability mitigation
Number of detected events	6	5	7	2	15
Detection ratio (total)	100%(6)	83%(6)	70%(10)	28.6%(7)	60%(25)

Table 3. Identified NANOG routing related problems (RouteViews: Oct 2004–Nov 2006).

reachability problems in many locations on the Internet, mostly for customers who are singly homed to Level3 or Cogent. Using Level3's AS3356 BGP feed, the RouteNormalizer observes explicit withdrawals for 98.7% or 2,936 distinct prefixes which originally had an AS path containing AS174. Among these withdrawn prefixes, 1,063 distinct prefixes were originated from AS174, accounting for all such prefixes. Examining the number of distinct IP addresses instead of IP prefixes, we detect withdrawals of 99.3% or 26,482,692 IPs going through AS174, and 100% or 20,541,927 IPs originated from AS174. This occurred over the time period of 289 minutes. Using the data from RouteView's Cogent AS174 feed, the RouteNormalizer detects similar routing dynamics. The RouteNormalzer also detects the restoration of the peering two days later on October 7, 2005. All prefixes previously withdrawn were re-announced. Identifying events impacting a large number of prefixes, the RouteNormalizer marks these routes as anomalous. If the local router has alternate routes for these destinations, the RouteNormalizer will conservatively suggest to continue using the alternate routes even when these anomalous routes are re-announced due to instability concerns.

6 Security Considerations

As a firewall for routers, the RouteNormalizer can be attacked in various ways, *e.g.,* resource overload attacks mentioned in traffic normalizer [23]. Our emulation of the graceful restart feature is one such example. Malicious peers can continuously reset the BGP session. Our strategy is to assign a penalty value per peer related to session reset to identify repeatedly flapping sessions. The penalty increases with each session reset and decreases over time, similar to route flap damping [44]. Another example is that attackers may focus on the most time-consuming functionalities such as checking for AS relationship violation by generating updates with abnormally long AS paths. The RouteNormalizer needs to search the relationship between each consecutive AS pairs in the AS path. Receiving many such paths may result in decreasing throughput. Our strategy is to calculate the actual AS path length ignoring AS prepending and set a threshold for the AS path length. Whenever a peer sends a significantly large number of updates with long AS paths, we raise an alarm. Moreover, we can optimize the relationship checking by storing examined AS path in the memory to reduce the number of comparisons. Another optimization is to focus on the relationship violations that directly impact the local AS, reducing the number of checks needed. For protection, the RouteNormalizer is numbered with private addresses, so that external users cannot directly send packets to it.

7 Related Work

It has been well-known that the Internet routing is vulnerable to various misconfigurations and attacks [11]. Recent studies [47, 29, 42] have focused on identifying routing anomalies using BGP data. Several protocol enhancements [40, 35, 42, 19] have been proposed to secure routing protocols. However, they are either incomplete or requires modification of the routing protocol leading to slow adoption. Complementary approaches exist without modifying BGP to identify configuration errors. IRV [20] defines such a service to mitigate malicious or faulty routing information by relying on collaboration among several networks. Feamster *et al.* [17] applied statical analysis to find faults in BGP configurations. Caesar *et al.* [12] proposed a centralized routing control platform (RCP) to facilitate configuration and route selection inside an AS. Karlin *et al.* [26] proposed an enhancement to BGP to slow the propagation of anomalous routes, similar to our design. Karpilovsky and Rexford [27] recently proposed an algorithm to reduce router memory usage by discarding alternate routes and refreshing on demand. Our work mainly differs from these work in that the RouteNormalizer operates online and actively identifies and *correct* routing updates, as well as influence routing decisions without affecting reachability. RouteNormalizer can directly use the RCP platform to take advantage of data from multiple vantage points for performing route normalization.

Parallel to our approach, instead of normalizing routing updates, Handley *et al.* [23] designed a data traffic normalizer for network intrusion detection. Protocol scrubbers [31, 46] have also been proposed for removing network attacks at both transport and application layers. Wang *et al.* [45] proposed shield – a lightweight network filter in end-system to protect against known vulnerability.

8 Conclusion

In this paper, we presented the detailed design of the RouteNormalizer which helps protect against external routing misbehavior observed at a local router by identifying and correcting malicious and misconfigured routing updates. The deployment of such a platform requires little to no changes in router configurations and no protocol modifications. Using a prototype implementation evaluated in a commercial router testbed, we showed that it can achieve good performance and scalability to support current BGP traffic rate. More importantly, we validated the benefit of routing anomaly detection in real time by analyzing empirical BGP data. The results from correlating with routing related complaints on the NANOG mailing list indicate that the RouteNormalizer can identify most of the known routing events impacting user performance.

References

[1] Distributed Intrusion Detection System. http://www.dshield.org/.

[2] GNU Zebra – routing software. http://www.zebra.org.

[3] NANOG Mailing List Information. http://www.nanog.org/mailinglist.html.

[4] NANOG Maling List Information. http://www.nanog.org/mailinglist.html.

[5] Spam Archive, Donate Your Spam to Science. http://www.spamarchive.org/.

[6] University of Oregon Route Views Archive Project. www.routeviews.org.

[7] Cisco Security Advisory: Cisco IOS BGP Attribute Corruption Vulnerability, 2001.

[8] G. Battista, M. Patrignani, and M. Pizzonia. Computing the Types of the Relationships Between Autonomous Systems. In *Proc. IEEE INFOCOM*, March 2003.

[9] S. Bellovin. Where the Wild Things are: BGP Threats. Nanog 28 Talk, Jun 2003.

[10] V. J. Bono. 7007 Explanation and Apology. NANOG 97-04.

[11] K. Butler, T. Farley, P. McDaniel, and J. Rexfod. A Survey of BGP Security Issues and Solutions. Technical Report Technical Report TD-5UGJ33, AT&T Labs - Research, 2004.

[12] M. Caesar, D. Caldwell, N. Feamster, J. Rexford, A. Shaikh, and J. van der Merwe. Design and Implementation of a Routing Control Platform. In *Proc. 2nd Symposium on Networked Systems Design and Implementation (NSDI)*, 2005.

[13] D. Chang, R. Govindan, and J. Heidemann. An Empirical Study of Router Response to Large BGP Routing Table Load. In *Proc. ACM SIGCOMM Internet Measurement Workshop*, 2002.

[14] S. Chavali, V. Radoaca, M. Miri, L. Fang, and S. Hares. draft-chavali-bgp-prefixlimit-02.txt: Peer Prefix Limits Exchange in BGP, April 2004.

[15] S. Convery and M. Franz. BGP Vulnerability Testing: Separating Fact from FUD. Nanog 28, June 2003.

[16] J. Cowie, A. T. Ogielski, B. Premore, and Y. Yuan. Internet Worms and Global Routing Instabilities. In *Proc. SPIE*, 2002.

[17] N. Feamster and H. Balakrishnan. Detecting BGP Configuration Faults with Static Analysis. In *Proc. 2nd Symposium on Networked Systems Design and Implementation (NSDI)*, May 2005.

[18] L. Gao. On Inferring Autonomous System Relationships in the Internet. In *Proc. IEEE Global Internet Symposium*, 2000.

[19] V. Gill, J. Heasly, and D. Meyer. The BGP TTL Security Hack. NANOG 0302.

[20] G. Goodell, W. Aiello, T. Griffin, J. Ioanmidis, P. McDaniel, and A. Rubin. Working around BGP: an Incremental Approach to Improving Security and Accuracy in Interdomain Routing. In *Proc. NDSS*, 2003.

[21] T. G. Griffin and G. Wilfong. On the Correctness of iBGP Configuration. In *Proc. ACM SIGCOMM*, August 2002.

[22] S. Halabi and D. McPherson. *Internet Routing Architectures.* Cisco Press, Indianapolis, Indiana, second edition, 2000.

[23] M. Handley, C. Kreibich, and V. Paxson. Network Intrusion Detection: Evasion, Traffic Normalization, and End-to-End Protocol Semantics. In *Proc. USENIX Security Symposium*, 2001.

[24] J. W. S. III. *BGP4 Inter-Domain Routing in the Internet.* Addison-Wesley, 1999.

[25] C. S. Inc. BGP Restart Session After Max-Prefix Limit. .

[26] J. Karlin, S. Forrest, and J. Rexford. Pretty Good BGP: Improving BGP by cautiously adopting routes. In *Proc. International Conference on Network Protocols*, 2006.

[27] E. Karpilovsky and J. Rexford. Using forgetful routing to control BGP table size. In *Proc. CoNext*, 2006.

[28] C. Labovitz, A. Ahuja, A. Bose, and F. Jahanian. Delayed Internet Routing Convergence. In *Proc. ACM SIGCOMM*, 2000.

[29] R. Mahajan, D. Wetherall, and T. Anderson. Understanding BGP misconfigurations. In *Proc. ACM SIGCOMM*, August 2002.

[30] F. Majstor. Attack on the Routing Protocols. RSA 2002. Cisco System Inc.

[31] G. R. Malan, D. Watson, F. Jahanian, and P. Howell. Transport and Application Protocol Scrubbing. In *Proc. IEEE INFOCOM*, 2000.

[32] D. McGrath. Passive Internet Health Monitoring With BGP. Nanog 0310.

[33] D. Meyer and A. Partan. S-BGP/soBGP Panel: What Do We Really Need and How Do We Architect a Compromise to Get It? NANOG 0306, June 2003.

[34] S. Murphy. BGP Vulnerabilities Analysis. IETF draft June 2003.

[35] J. Ng. Extensions to BGP to Support Secure Origin BGP (soBGP). IETF Draft: draft-ng-sobgp-bgp-extensions-01.txt, November 2002.

[36] C. Panigl, J. Schmitz, P. Smith, and C. Vistoli. RIPE Routing-WG Recommendations for Coordinated Route-flap Damping Parameters, October 2001. Document ID: ripe-229.

[37] Y. Rekhter and T. Li. A Border Gateway Protocol. RFC 1771, March 1995.

[38] J. Rexford, J. Wang, Z. Xiao, and Y. Zhang. BGP Routing Stability of Popular Destinations. In *Proc. ACM SIGCOMM Internet Measurement Workshop*, November 2002.

[39] S. R. Sangli, Y. Rekhter, R. Fernando, J. G. Scudder, and E. Chen. Graceful Restart Mechanism for BGP. IETF Internet Draft, June 2004.

[40] Stephen Kent and Charles Lynn and Karen Seo. Secure Border Gateway Protocol (Secure-BGP). *IEEE J. Selected Areas in Communications*, 2000.

[41] L. Subramanian, S. Agarwal, J. Rexford, and R. H. Katz. Characterizing the Internet hierarchy from multiple vantage points. In *Proc. IEEE INFOCOM*, 2002.

[42] L. Subramanian, V. Roth, I. Stoica, S. Shenker, and R. H. Katz. Listen and Whisper: Security Mechanisms for BGP. In *Proc. first Symposium on Networked Systems Design and Implementation (NSDI)*, 2004.

[43] US-CERT. Multiple Denial-of-Service Vulnerabilities in Cisco IOS.

[44] C. Villamizar, R. Chandra, and R. Govindan. BGP Route Flap Damping. RFC 2439, 1998.

[45] H. J. Wang, C. Guo, D. R. Simon, and A. Zugenmaier. Shield: Vulnerability-Driven Network Filters for Preventing Known Vulnerability Exploits. In *Proc. ACM SIGCOMM*, 2004.

[46] D. Watson, M. Smart, G. R. Malan, and F. Jahanian. Protocol Scrubbing: Network Security Through Transparent Flow Modification. *IEEE/ACM Transactions on Networking*, 2004.

[47] X. Zhao, D. Pei, L. Wang, D. Massey, A. Mankin, S. F. Wu, and L. Zhang. An Analysis of BGP Multiple Origin AS (MOAS) Conflicts. In *Proc. ACM SIGCOMM Internet Measurement Workshop*, November 2001.

An Architectural Approach to Preventing Code Injection Attacks

Ryan Riley
Purdue University
rileyrd@cs.purdue.edu

Xuxian Jiang
George Mason University
xjiang@gmu.edu

Dongyan Xu
Purdue University
dxu@cs.purdue.edu

Abstract

Code injection attacks, despite being well researched, continue to be a problem today. Modern architectural solutions such as the NX-bit and PaX have been useful in limiting the attacks, however they enforce program layout restrictions and can often times still be circumvented by a determined attacker. We propose a change to the memory architecture of modern processors that addresses the code injection problem at its very root by virtually splitting memory into code memory and data memory such that a processor will never be able to fetch injected code for execution. This virtual split memory system can be implemented as a software only patch to an operating system, and can be used to supplement existing schemes for improved protection. Our experimental results show the system is effective in preventing a wide range of code injection attacks while incurring acceptable overhead.

Keywords: *Code Injection, Secure Memory Architecture*

1. Introduction

Despite years of research, code injection attacks continue to be a problem today. Systems continue to be vulnerable to the traditional attacks, and attackers continue to find new ways around existing protection mechanisms in order to execute their injected code. Code injection attacks and their prevention has become an arms race with no obvious end in site.

A code injection attack is a method whereby an attacker inserts malicious code into a running process and transfers execution to his malicious code. In this way he can gain control of a running process, causing it to spawn other processes, modify system files, etc. If the program runs at a privilege level higher than that of the attacker, he has essentially escalated his access level. (Or, if he has no privileges on a system, then he has gained some.)

A number of solutions exist that handle the code injection problem on some level or another. Architectural approaches [1, 2, 3] attempt to prevent malicious code execution by making certain pages of memory non-executable.

This protection methodology is effective for many of the traditional attacks, however attackers still manage to circumvent them [4]. In addition, these schemes enforce specific rules for program layout with regards to separating code and data, and as such are unable to protect memory pages that contain *both*. Compiler based protection mechanisms [5, 6, 7] are designed to protect crucial memory locations such as function pointers or the return address and detect when they have been modified. These methods, while effective for a variety of attacks, do not provide broad enough coverage to handle a great many modern vulnerabilities [8]. Both of these techniques, architectural and compiler based, focus on preventing an attacker from executing his injected code, *but do nothing to prevent him from injecting and fetching it in the first place.*

The core of the code injection problem is that modern computers implement a von Neumann memory architecture [9]; that is, they use a memory architecture wherein code and data are both accessible within the same address space. This property of modern computers is what allows an attacker to inject his attack code into a program as data and then later execute it as code. Wurster et al [10] proposed a technique to defeat software self checksumming by changing this property of modern computers (and hence producing a Harvard architecture [11, 12]), and inspired us to consider the implications such a change would have on code injection.

We propose virtualizing a Harvard architecture on top of the existing memory architecture of modern computers so as to prevent the injection of malicious code entirely. A Harvard architecture is simply one wherein code and data are stored separately. Data cannot be loaded as code and vice-versa. In essence, we create an environment wherein any code injected by an attacker into a process' address space cannot even be addressed by the processor for execution. In this way, we are attacking the code injection problem at its root by regarding the injected malicious code as data and making it unaddressable to the processor during an instruction fetch. The technique can be implemented as a software only patch for the operating system, and our implementation for the x86 incurs a very reasonable performance penalty, on average between 10 and 20%. Such a software only technique is possible through careful exploitation of the two translation lookaside buffers (TLBs) on the x86 architecture in order to split memory in such a way that it enforces a strict separation of code and data memory.

2. Related Work and Motivation

Research on code injection attacks has been ongoing for a number of years now, and a large number of protection methods have been researched and tested. There are two classes of techniques that have become widely supported in modern hardware and operating systems; one is concerned with preventing the execution of malicious code after control flow hijacking, while the other is concerned with preventing an attacker from hijacking control flow.

The first class of technique is concerned with preventing an attacker from executing injected code using non-executable memory pages, but does not prevent the attacker from impacting program control flow. This protection comes in the form of hardware support or a software only patch. Hardware support has been put forth by both Intel and AMD that extends the page-level protections of the virtual memory subsystem to allow for non-executable pages. (Intel refers to this as the "execute-disable bit" [3].) The usage of this technique is fairly simple: Program information is separated into code pages and data pages. The data pages (stack, heap, bss, etc) are all marked non-executable. At the same time, code pages are all marked read-only. In the event an attacker exploits a vulnerability to inject code, it is guaranteed to be injected on a page that is non-executable and therefore the injected code is never run. Microsoft makes use of this protection mechanism in its latest operating systems, calling the feature Data Execution Protection (DEP) [1]. This mediation method is very effective for traditional code injection attacks, however it requires hardware support in order to be of use. Legacy x86 hardware does not support this feature. This technique is also available as a software-only patch to the operating system that allows it to simulate the execute-disable bit through careful mediation of certain memory accesses. PAX PAGE-EXEC [2] is an open source implementation of this technique that is applied to the Linux kernel. It functions identically to the hardware supported version, however it also supports legacy x86 hardware due to being a software only patch.

The second class of technique has a goal of preventing the attacker from hijacking program flow, but does not concern itself with the injected code. Works such as Stack-Guard [5] accomplish this goal by emitting a "canary" value onto the stack that can help detect a buffer overflow. ProPolice [6] (currently included in gcc) builds on this idea by also rearranging variables to prevent overflowed arrays from accessing critical items such as function pointers or the re-turn address. Stack Shield [7] uses a separate stack for return addresses as well as adding sanity checking to ret and function pointer targets. Due to the fact that these techniques only make it their goal to prevent control flow hijacking, they tend to only work against known hijacking techniques. That means that while they are effective in some cases, they may miss many of the more complicated attacks. Wilander et al [8], for example, found that these techniques missed a fairly large percentage (45% in the best case) of attacks that they implemented in their buffer overflow benchmark.

Due to the fact that the stack based approaches above do not account for a variety of attacks, in this work we are primarily concerned with addressing limitations in the architectural support of the execute-disable bit. While this technique is widely deployed and has proven to be effective, it has limitations. First, programs must adhere to the "code and data are always separated" model. In the event a program has pages containing both code and data the protection scheme cannot be used. In fact, such "mixed pages" do exist in real-world software systems. For example, the Linux kernel uses mixed pages for both signal handling [13] as well as loadable kernel modules. A second problem with these schemes is that a crafty attacker can disable or bypass the protection bit using library code already in the process' address space and from there execute the injected code. Such an attack has been demonstrated for the Windows platform by injecting code into non-executable space and then using a well crafted stack containing a series of system calls or library functions to cause the system to create a new, executable memory space, copy the injected code into it, and then transfer control to it. One such example has been shown in [4].

It is these two limitations in existing page-level protection schemes (the forced code and data separation and the bypass methodology) that provide the motivation for our work, which architecturally addresses the code injection problem at its core. Note that our architectural approach is orthogonal to research efforts on system randomization, such as Address Space Layout Randomization (ASLR) [14, 15, 16, 17] and Instruction Set Randomization (ISR) [18, 19, 20]. We are also distinct from other work that focuses specifically on preventing array overflow using a compiler or hardware, such as [21]. We point out that these alternate systems all work on a single memory architecture wherein code and data are accessible within the same address space. Our approach, to be described in the next section, instead creates a different memory architecture where code and data are separated.

3. An Architectural Approach

At its root, code injection is a problem because processors permit code and data to share the same memory address space. As a result, an attacker can inject his payload as data and later execute it as code. The underlying assumption relied on by attackers is that the line between code and data is blurred and not enforced. For this reason, we turn to an alternative memory architecture that does not permit code and data to be interchanged at runtime.

3.1. The Harvard and von Neumann Memory Architectures

Modern computers and operating systems tend to use what is known as a von Neumann memory architecture [9]. Under a von Neumann system there is one physical memory which is shared by both code and data. As a consequence of this, code can be read and written like data and data can be executed like code. Many systems will use segmentation or paging to help separate code and data from each other or from other processes, but code and data end up sharing the same address space. Figure 1a illustrates a von Neumann architecture.

An architecture not found in most modern computers (but found in some embedded devices or operating systems, such as VxWorks [22]) is known as a Harvard architecture [11, 12]. Under the Harvard architecture code and data each have its own physical address space. One can think of a Harvard architecture as being a machine with two different physical memories, one for code and another for data. Figure 1b shows a Harvard architecture.

3.2. Harvard and Code Injection

A code injection attack can be thought of as being carried out in four distinct, but related, stages:

1. The attacker injects code into a process' address space.
2. The attacker determines the address of the injected code.
3. The attacker somehow hijacks the program counter to point to the injected code.
4. The injected code is executed.

The mediation methods mentioned in section 2 are designed to handle the problem by preventing either step 3 or 4. Non-executable pages are designed to prevent step 4, while compiler based approaches are meant to prevent step 3. In both cases, however, the malicious code is injected, but execution is somehow prevented. Our solution, on the other hand, effectively stops the attack at step 1 by preventing the successful injection of the malicious code into a process' *code space*. (The purist will note that in the implementation method described in section 4 the attack is not technically stopped until step 4, however the general approach described here handles it at step 1.)

The Harvard architecture's split memory model makes it suitable for the prevention of code injection attacks due to the fact that a strict separation between code and data is enforced at the hardware level. Any and all data, regardless of the source, is stored in a different physical memory from instructions. Instructions cannot be addressed as data, and data cannot be addressed as instructions. This means that in a Harvard architecture based computer, a traditional code injection attack is not possible because the architecture is not capable of supporting it after a process is initially setup. The attacker is simply unable to inject any information whatsoever into the instruction memory's address space and at the same time is unable to execute any code placed in the data memory. The architecture simply does not have the "features" required for a successful code injection attack. However, we point out that this does not prevent an attacker from mounting non control injection attacks (e.g., non-control-data attack [23]) on a Harvard architecture. We touch on these attacks in section 6.

3.3. Challenges in Using a Harvard Architecture

While a Harvard architecture may be effective at mitigating code injection, the truth of the matter is that for any new code injection prevention technique to be practical it must be usable on modern commodity hardware. As such, the challenge is to construct a Harvard architecture on top of a widely deployed processor such as the x86. We first present a few possible methods for creating this Harvard architecture on top of the x86.

Modifying x86

One technique for creating such an architecture is to make changes to the existing architecture and use hardware virtualization [24] to make them a reality. The changes required in the x86 architecture to produce a Harvard architecture are fairly straight forward modifications to the paging system.

Currently, x86 implements paging by having a separate pagetable for each process and having the operating system maintain a register (CR3) that points to the pagetable for the currently running process. One pagetable is used for the process' entire address space, both code and data. In order to construct a Harvard architecture, one would need to maintain two different pagetables, one for code and one for data. As such, our proposed change to the x86 architecture to allow it to create a Harvard architecture is to create an additional pagetable register in order that one can be used for code (CR3-C) and the other for data (CR3-D). Whenever an instruction fetch occurs, the processor uses CR3-C to translate the virtual address, while for data reads and writes CR3-D is used. An operating system, therefore, would simply need to maintain two separate pagetables for each process. This capability would also offer backwards compatibility at the process level, as the operating system could simply maintain one pagetable and point both registers to it if a process requires a von Neumann architecture. We note that no changes would need to be made to the processor's translation lookaside buffer (TLB) as modern x86

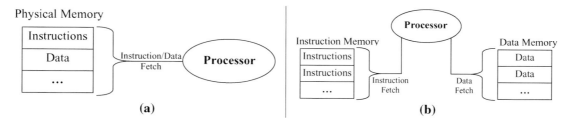

Figure 1. (a) von Neumann architecture. (b) Harvard architecture

processors already have a separate TLB for code and data.

While this approach to the problem may be effective, the requirement that the protected system be run on top of hardware virtualization inhibits its practicality. As such, another approach is needed.

Exploiting x86

Another technique for creating this Harvard architecture is to make unconventional use of some of the architecture's features in order to create the appearance of a memory that is split between code and data. Through careful use of the pagetable and the TLBs on x86, it is possible to construct a Harvard memory architecture at the process level using only operating system level modifications. No modifications need to be made to the underlying x86 architecture, and the system can be run on conventional x86 hardware without the need for hardware virtualization as in the previous method.

In the following sections we will further describe this technique as well as its unique advantages.

4. Split Memory: A Harvard Architecture on x86

Now that we have established that it is our intention to exploit, not change, the x86 architecture in order to create a virtual split memory system, we will now describe the technique in greater detail.

4.1. Virtualizing Split Memory on x86

In order to speed up pagetable lookup time, many processors include a small hardware cache called a translation lookaside buffer (TLB) which is used to cache pagetable entries. In order to better exploit locality, modern processors actually split the TLB into *two TLBs*, one for code and one for data. This feature can be exploited by a keen operating system to route data accesses for a given virtual address to one physical page, while routing instruction fetches to another. By desynchronizing the TLBs and having each contain a different mapping for the same virtual page, every virtual page may have two corresponding physical pages: One for code fetch and one for data access. In essence, a system is produced where any given virtual memory address could be routed to two possible physical memory locations. This creates a split memory architecture, as illustrated in Figure

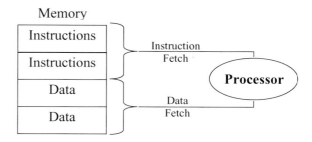

Figure 2. Split memory architecture

2.

This split memory architecture is an environment wherein an attacker can exploit a vulnerable program and inject code into its memory space, *but never be able to actually fetch it for execution*. This is because the physical page that contains the data the attacker managed to write into the program is not accessible during an instruction fetch, as instruction fetches will be routed to an un-compromised code page. This also creates the unique opportunity to support and protect pages that contain both code and data by keeping the two physically separated but logically combined.

What to Split

Before we discuss the technical details behind successfully splitting a given page, it is important to note that different pages in a process' address space may be chosen to split based on how our system will be used.

One potential use of the system is to augment the existing non-executable page methods by expanding their protection to allow for protecting mixed code and data pages. Under this usage of the system, the majority of pages under a process' address space would be protected using the non-executable pages, while the mixed code and data pages would be protected using our technique. Using this scheme, chances are high that only a few of the process' pages would need to be protected using our method. Note that this assumes we have a good understanding of the memory space of the program being protected.

Another potential use of our system, and the one which we use in our prototype in section 5.1, is to protect every page in a process' memory space. This is a more comprehensive type of protection than simply augmenting existing schemes. Note that in this case, more pages are chosen to

Algorithm 1: Split memory page fault handler	**Algorithm 2**: Debug interrupt handler

Algorithm 1: Split memory page fault handler

Input: Faulting Address (addr), CPU instruction pointer (EIP), Pagetable Entry for addr (pte)

```
1  if addr == EIP then            /* Code Access */
2      pte = the_code_page;
3      unrestrict(pte);
4      enable_single_step();
5      return;
6  else                           /* Data Access */
7      pte = the_data_page;
8      unrestrict(pte);
9      read_byte(addr);
10     restrict(pte);
11     return;
12 end
```

Algorithm 2: Debug interrupt handler

Input: Pagetable Entry for previously faulting address (pte)

```
1  if processor is in single step mode then
2      restrict(pte);
3      disable_single_step();
4  end
```

be split and thus protected.

How to Split

Once it is determined which pages will be split, the technique for splitting a given page is as follows:

1) On program start-up, the page that needs to be split is duplicated. This produces two copies of the page in physical memory. We choose one page to be the target of instruction fetches, and the other to be the target of data accesses.

2) The pagetable entry (PTE) corresponding to the page we are splitting is set to ensure a page fault will occur on a TLB miss. In this case, the page is considered *restricted*, meaning it is only accessible when the processor is in supervisor mode. We accomplish it by setting or enabling the *supervisor* bit [3] in the PTE for that page. If *supervisor* is marked in a PTE and a user-level process attempts to access that page for any reason, a page fault will be generated and the corresponding page fault handler will be automatically invoked.

3) Depending on the reasons for the page fault, i.e., either this page fault is caused by a data TLB miss or it is caused by an instruction TLB miss, the page fault handler behaves differently. Note that for an instruction-TLB miss, the faulting address (saved in the *CR2* register [3]) is equal to the program counter (contained in the EIP register); while for a data-TLB miss, the page fault address is different from the program counter. In the following, we describe how different TLB misses are handled. The algorithm is outlined in algorithm 1.

Loading the Data-TLB

The data-TLB is loaded using a technique called a pagetable walk, which is a procedure for loading the TLB from within the page fault handler. The pagetable entry (PTE) in question is set to point to the data page for that address, the en-

try is unrestricted (we unset the *supervisor* bit in the PTE), and a read off of that page is performed. As soon as the read occurs, the memory management unit in the hardware reads the newly modified PTE, loads it into the data-TLB, and returns the content. At this point the data-TLB contains the entry to the data page for that particular address while the instruction-TLB remains untouched. Finally, the PTE is restricted again to prevent a later instruction access from improperly filling the instruction-TLB. Note that even though the PTE is restricted, later data accesses to that page can occur unhindered because the data-TLB contains a valid mapping. This loading method is also used in the PAX [2] protection model and is known to bring the overhead for a data-TLB load down to reasonable levels.

In algorithm 1 this process can be seen in lines 7–11. First, the pagetable entry is set to point to the data page and unrestricted by setting the entry to be user accessible instead of supervisor accessible. Next, a byte on the page is touched, causing the hardware to load the data-TLB with a pagetable entry corresponding to the data page. Finally, the pagetable entry is re-protected by setting it into supervisor mode once again.

Loading the Instruction-TLB

The loading of the instruction-TLB has additional complications compared to that of the data-TLB, namely because there does not appear to be a simple procedure such as a pagetable walk that can accomplish the same task. Despite these complications, however, a technique introduced in [10] can be used to load the instruction-TLB on the x86.

Once it is determined that the instruction-TLB needs to be loaded, the PTE is unrestricted, the processor is placed into single step mode, and the faulting instruction is restarted. When the instruction runs this time the PTE is read out of the pagetable and stored in the instruction-TLB. After the instruction finishes then the single step mode of the processor generates an interrupt, which is used as an opportunity to restrict the PTE.

This functionality can be seen in algorithm 1 lines 2–5 as well as in algorithm 2. First, the PTE is set to point to the corresponding code page and is unprotected. Next, the processor is placed into single step mode and the page fault handler returns, resulting in the faulting instruction being restarted. Once the single step interrupt occurs, algorithm

2 is run, effectively restricting the PTE and disabling single step mode.

4.2. Effects on Code Injection

A split memory architecture produces an address space where data cannot be fetched by the processor for execution. For an attacker attempting a code injection, this will prevent him from fetching and executing any injected code. A sample code injection attack attempt on a split memory architecture can be seen in Figure 3 and described as follows:

1. The attacker injects his code into a string buffer starting at address 0xbf000000. The memory writes are routed to physical pages corresponding to data.
2. At the same time as the injection, the attacker overflows the buffer and changes the return address of the function to point to 0xbf000000, the expected location of his malicious code.
3. The function returns and control is transferred to address 0xbf000000. The processor's instruction fetch is routed to the physical pages corresponding to instructions.
4. The attacker's malicious code is not on the instruction page (the code was injected as data and therefore routed to a different physical page) and is not run. In all likelihood, the program simply crashes.

4.3. Overhead

This technique of splitting memory does not come without a cost, there is some overhead associated with the methodologies described above.

One potential problem is the use of the processor's single step mode for the instruction-TLB load. This loading process has a fairly significant overhead due to the fact that two interrupts (the page fault and the debug interrupt) are required in order to complete it. This overhead ends up being minimal overall for many applications due to the fact that instruction-TLB loads are fairly infrequent, as it only needs to be done *once* per page of instructions.

Another problem is that of context switches in the operating system. Whenever a context switch (meaning the OS changes running processes) occurs, the TLB is flushed. This means that every time a protected process is switched out and then back in, any memory accesses it makes will trigger a page fault and subsequent TLB load. The overheard of these TLB loads is significantly higher than a traditional page fault, and hence causes the majority of our slowdown. The problem of context switches is, in fact, the greatest cause of overhead in the implemented system. The experimental details of the overhead can be seen in section 5.3.

5. Implementation and Evaluation

5.1. Proof of Concept Implementation

An x86 implementation of the above method has been created by modifying version 2.6.13 of the Linux kernel. In this section, we present a description of the modifications to create the architecture.

Modifications to the ELF Loader

ELF is a format that defines the layout of an executable file stored on disk. The ELF loader is used to load those files into memory and begin executing them. This work includes setting up all of the code, data, bss, stack, and heap pages as well as bringing in most of the dynamic libraries used by a given program.

The modifications to the loader are as follows: After the ELF loader maps the code and data pages from the ELF file, for each one of those pages two new, side-by-side, physical pages are created and the original page is copied into both of them. This effectively creates two copies of the program's memory space in physical memory. The pagetable entries corresponding to the code and data pages are changed to map to one of those copies of the memory space, leaving the other copy unused for the moment. In addition, the pagetable entries for those pages get the supervisor bit cleared, placing that page in supervisor mode in order to be sure a page fault will occur when that entry is needed. A previously unused bit in the pagetable entry is used to signify that the page is being split. In total, about 90 lines of code are added to the ELF loader.

In this particular implementation of split memory the memory usage of an application is effectively doubled, however this limitation is *not* one of the technique itself, but instead of the prototype. A system can be envisioned based on demand-paging (only allocating a code or data page when needed) instead of the current method of proactively duplicating every virtual page. We would anticipate this optimization to not have any noticeable impact on performance.

Modifications to the Page Fault Handler

Under Linux, the page fault (PF) handler is called in response to a hardware generated PF interrupt. The handler is responsible for determining what caused the fault, correcting the problem, and restarting the faulting instruction.

For our modifications to the PF handler we simply modify it to handle a new reason for a PF: There was a permissions problem caused by the supervisor bit in the PTE. We must be careful here to remember that not every PF on a split page is necessarily our fault, some PFs (such as ones involving copy-on-write), despite being on split memory pages, must be passed on to the rest of the PF handler instead of being serviced in a split memory way. If it is determined that the fault was caused by a split memory page and

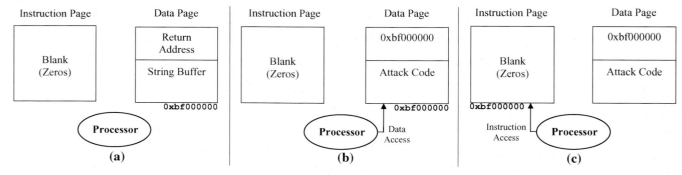

Figure 3. (a) Before the attacker injects code (b) The injection to the data page (c) The execution attempt that gets routed to the instruction page

that it does need to be serviced, then the instruction pointer is compared to the faulting address to decide whether the instruction-TLB or data-TLB needs to be loaded. (Recall from algorithm 1 that this is done by simply checking if the two are the same.)

If the data-TLB needs to be loaded, then the PTE is set to user mode, a byte on the page is touched, and the PTE is set back to supervisor mode. This pagetable walk loads the data-TLB[1]. In the event the instruction-TLB needs to be loaded, the PTE is set to user mode (to allow access to the page) and the trap flag (single-step mode) bit in the EFLAGS register is set. This will ensure that the debug interrupt handler gets called after the instruction is restarted. Before the PF handler returns and that interrupt occurs, however, a little bit of bookkeeping is done by saving the faulting address into the process' entry in the OS process table in order to pass it to the debug interrupt handler.

In total there were about 110 lines of code added to the PF handler to facilitate splitting memory.

Modifications to the Debug Interrupt Handler

The debug interrupt handler is used by the kernel to handle interrupts related to debugging. For example, using a debugger to step through a running program or watch a particular memory location makes use of this interrupt handler. For the purposes of split memory, the handler is modified to check the process table to see if a faulting address has been given, indicating that this interrupt was generated because the PF handler set the trap flag. If this is the case, then it is safe to assume that the instruction which originally caused the PF has been restarted and successfully executed (meaning the instruction-TLB has been filled) and as such the PTE is set to supervisor mode once again and the trap flag is cleared. In total, about 40 lines of code were added to the debug interrupt handler to accommodate these changes.

Modifications to the Memory Management System

There are a number of features related to memory management that must be slightly modified to properly handle our system. First, on program termination any split pages must be freed specially to ensure that both physical pages (the code page and data page) get put back into the kernel's pool of free memory pages. This is accomplished by simply looking for the split memory PTE bit that was set by the ELF loader above, and if it is found then freeing two pages instead of just one.

Another feature in the memory system that needs to be updated is the copy-on-write (COW) mechanism. COW is used by Linux to make `forked` processes run more efficiently. That basic idea is that when a process makes a copy of itself using `fork` both processes get a copy of the original pagetable, but with every entry set read-only. Then, if either process writes to a given page, the kernel will give that process its own copy. (This reduces memory usage in the system because multiple processes can share the same physical page.) For split memory the COW system must copy *both* pages in the event of a write, instead of just one.

A update similar to the COW update is also made to the demand paging system. Demand paging basically means that a page is not allocated until it is required by a process. In this way a process can have a large amount of available memory space (such as in the BSS or heap) but only have physical pages allocated for portions it actually uses. The demand paging system was modified to allocate two pages instead of just the one page it normally does.

Overall, about 75 lines of code were added to handle these various parts related to memory management.

5.2. Effectiveness

The sample implementation was tested for its effectiveness at preventing code injection attacks using a benchmark originally put forth by Wilander et al [8]. The benchmark was modified slightly in order to allow it to handle having the code injected on the data, bss, heap, and stack portions of the program's address space. In addition, four of

---

[1]Occasionally the pagetable walk does not successfully load the data-TLB. In this case, single stepping mode (like the instruction-TLB load) must be used.

Table 1. The number of attacks halted when code is injected onto the data, bss, heap, and stack segments

Attack Type	Hijack Type	Injection Destination			
		Data	BSS	Heap	Stack
Buffer overflow on stack	Return address	✓	✓	✓	✓
	Old base pointer	✓	✓	✓	✓
	Function pointer as local variable	✓	✓	✓	✓
	Function pointer as parameter	✓	✓	✓	✓
	Longjmp buffer as local variable	✓	✓	✓	✓
	Longjmp buffer as function parameter	✓	✓	✓	✓
Buffer overflow on heap/bss	Function pointer	✓	✓	✓	✓
	Longjmp buffer	✓	✓	✓	✓
Buffer overflow of pointers on stack	Return address	N/A	N/A	✓	N/A
	Old base pointer	N/A	N/A	N/A	N/A
	Function pointer as local variable	✓	✓	✓	✓
	Function pointer as parameter	✓	✓	✓	✓
	Longjmp buffer as local variable	✓	✓	✓	✓
	Longjmp buffer as function parameter	✓	✓	✓	✓
Buffer overflow on heap/bss	Return address	N/A	N/A	✓	N/A
	Old base pointer	N/A	N/A	N/A	N/A
	Function pointer as variable	✓	✓	✓	✓
	Longjmp buffer as variable	✓	✓	✓	✓

the testcases did not successfully execute an attack on our unprotected system, and so have been labeled "N/A." Table 1 shows the results of running the benchmark. The checkmarks indicate that the system successfully halted the attack. As can be seen, the system was effective in preventing all types of code injection attacks present in the benchmark. The effectiveness of the system is due to the fact that no matter what method of control-flow hijacking the benchmark uses, the processor is simply unable to fetch the injected code.

5.3. Performance

A number of benchmarks, both applications and microbenchmarks, were used to test the performance of the system. Our testing platform was a modest system, a Pentium III 600Mhz with 384 MB of RAM and a 100MBit NIC. When applicable, benchmarks were run 10 times and the results averaged. Details of the configuration for the tests are available in table 2. Each result has been normalized with respect to the speed of the unprotected system.

Four benchmarks that we consider to be a reasonable assessment of the system's performance can be found in Figure 4. First, the Apache [25] webserver was run in a threading mode to serve a 32KB page (roughly the size of Purdue University's main index.html). The ApacheBench program was then run on another machine connected via the NIC to determine the request throughput of the system as a whole. The protected system achieved a little over 89% of the unprotected system's throughput. Next, gzip was used to compress a 256 MB file, and the operation was timed. The protected system was found to run at 87% of full speed. Third,

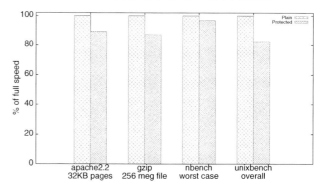

Figure 4. Normalized performance for applications and benchmarks

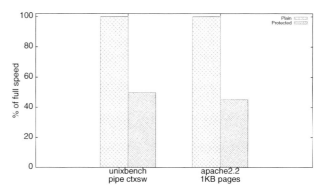

Figure 5. Stress-testing the performance penalties due to context switching

Table 2. Configuration information used for performance evaluation

Item	Version	Configuration
Slackware	10.2.0	Using Linux 2.6.13
Apache	2.2.3	Worker mpm mode, set to spawn one process with threads
ApacheBench	2.0.41-dev	`-c3 -t 60 <url/file>`
Unixbench	4.1.0	N/A
Nbench	2.2.2	N/A
Gzip	1.3.3	Compress a 256 MB file.

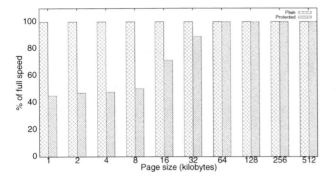

Figure 6. Closer look into Apache performance

the nbench [26] suite was used to show the performance under a set of primarily computation based tests. The slowest test in the nbench system came in at just under 97%. Finally, the Unixbench [27] unix benchmarking suite was used as a micro-benchmark to test various aspects of the system's performance at tasks such as process creation, pipe throughput, filesystem throughput, etc. Here, the split memory system ran at 82% of normal speed. This result is slightly disappointing, however it can be easily explained by looking at the specific test which performed poorly, which we do below. As can be seen from these four benchmarks, the system has very reasonable performance under a variety of tasks.

If we simply left our description of the system's performance to these four tests, some readers may object that given the description of the system so far and the mention in section 4.3 of the various sources of overhead, something must be missing from our benchmarks. As such, two benchmarks contrived to highlight the system's weakness can be found in Figure 5. First, one of the Unixbench testcases called "pipe based context switching" is shown. This primarily tests how quickly a system can context switch between two processes that are passing data between each other. The next test is Apache used to serve a 1KB page. In this configuration, Apache will context switch heavily while serving requests. In both of these tests, context switching is taken to an extreme and therefore our system's perfor-

mance degrades substantially due to the constant flushing of the TLB. As can be seen in the graph, both are at or below 50%. In addition, in Figure 6, we have a more thorough set of Apache benchmarks demonstrating this same phenomena, namely that for low page sizes the system context switches heavily and performance suffers, where as for larger page sizes that cause Apache to spend more time on I/O as well as begin to saturate the system's network link, the results become significantly better. These tests show very poor performance, however we would like to note that they are shown here to be indicative of the system's worst case performance under highly stressful (rather than normal) conditions.

Overall, the system's performance is reasonable, in most cases being between 80 and 90% of an unprotected system. Moreover, if split memory was supported at the hardware level as described in section 3.3, the overheard would be almost non-existent. Based on previous work [28], we also have reason to believe that building the split memory system on top of an architecture with a software loaded TLB, such as SPARC, would also provide further performance improvements.

6. Limitations

There are a few limitations to our approach. First, when an attack is stopped by our system the process involved will crash. We offer no attempt at any sort of recovery. This means an attacker can still exploit flaws to mount denial-of-service attacks. Second, as shown in other work [29], a split memory architecture does not lend itself well to handling self-modifying code. As such, self-modifying programs cannot be protected using our technique. Next, this protection scheme offers no protection against attacks which do not rely on executing code injected by the attacker. For example, modifying a function's return address to point to a different part of the original code pages will not be stopped by this scheme. Fortunately, address space layout randomization [14] could be combined with our technique to help prevent this kind of attack. Along those same lines, non-control-data attacks [23], wherein an attacker modifies a program's data in order to alter program flow, are also not protected by this system. We have also not analyzed the system's functionality on programs that include dynamically loadable modules (such as DLL files on windows) but do not anticipate that such programs would be difficult to support.

7. Conclusions

In this paper, we present an architectural approach to prevent code injection attacks. Instead of maintaining the traditional single memory space containing both code and data, which is often exploited by code injection attacks, our approach creates a split memory that separates code and data into different memory spaces. Consequently, in a system protected by our approach, code injection attacks may result in the injection of attack code into the data space. However, the attack code in the data space can not be fetched for execution as instructions are only retrieved from the code space. We have implemented a Linux prototype on the x86 architecture, and experimental results show the system is effective in preventing a wide range of code injection attacks while incurring acceptable overhead.

8. Acknowledgments

We would like to thank Glenn Wurster as well as the anonymous reviewers for their helpful comments and suggestions. This work was supported in part by NSF Grants OCI-0438246, OCI-0504261, and CNS-0546173.

References

[1] A detailed description of the data execution prevention (dep) feature in windows xp service pack 2, windows xp tablet pc edition 2005, and windows server 2003. *http://support.microsoft.com/kb/875352*. Last accessed Dec 2006.

[2] Pax pageexec documentation. *http://pax.grsecurity.net/docs/pageexec.txt*. Last accessed Dec 2006.

[3] I. Corporation. *IA-32 Intel Architecture Software Developer's Manual Volume 3A: System Programming Guide, Part 1*. Intel Corp., 2006. Publication number 253668.

[4] Buffer overflow attacks bypassing dep (nx/xd bits) - part 2 : Code injection. *http://www.mastropaolo.com/?p=13*. Last accessed Dec 2006.

[5] C. Cowan, C. Pu, D. Maier, J. Walpole, P. Bakke, S. Beattie, A. Grier, P. Wagle, Q. Zhang, and H. Hinton. StackGuard: Automatic adaptive detection and prevention of buffer-overflow attacks. In *Proc. 7th USENIX Security Conference*, pages 63–78, San Antonio, Texas, jan 1998.

[6] H. Etoh. Gcc extension for protecting applications from stack-smashing attacks. *http://www.trl.ibm.com/projects/security/ssp/*. Last accessed Dec 2006.

[7] Vendicator. Stack shield: A "stack smashing" technique protection tool for linux. *http://www.angelfire.com/sk/stackshield/info.html*. Last accessed Dec 2006.

[8] J. Wilander and M. Kamkar. A comparison of publicly available tools for dynamic buffer overflow prevention. In *Proceedings of the 10th Network and Distributed System Security Symposium*, pages 149–162, San Diego, California, February 2003.

[9] J. von Neumann. First draft of a report on the edvac. 1945. Reprinted in *The Origins of Digital Computers Selected Papers*, Second Edition, pages 355–364, 1975.

[10] P. C. van Oorschot, A. Somayaji, and G. Wurster. Hardware-assisted circumvention of self-hashing software tamper resistance. *IEEE Trans. Dependable Secur. Comput.*, 2(2):82–92, 2005.

[11] H. H. Aiken. Proposed automatic calculating machine. 1937. Reprinted in *The Origins of Digital Computers Selected Papers*, Second Edition, pages 191–198, 1975.

[12] H. H. Aiken and G. M. Hopper. The automatic sequence controlled calculator. 1946. Reprinted in *The Origins of Digital Computers Selected Papers*, Second Edition, pages 199–218, 1975.

[13] kernelthread.com: Securing memory. *http://www.kernelthread.com/publications/security/smemory.html*. Last accessed Dec 2006.

[14] Pax aslr documentation. *http://pax.grsecurity.net/docs/aslr.txt*. Last accessed Dec 2006.

[15] S. Bhatkar, D. C. DuVarney, and R. Sekar. Address Obfuscation: An Efficient Approach to Combat a Broad Range of Memory Error Exploits. *12th USENIX Security*, 2003.

[16] S. Bhatkar, R. Sekar, and D. C. DuVarney. Efficient Techniques for Comprehensive Protection from Memory Error Exploits. *14th USENIX Security*, 2005.

[17] J. Xu, Z. Kalbarczyk, and R. K. Iyer. Transparent Runtime Randomization for Security. *In Proc. of 22nd Symposium on Reliable and Distributed Systems (SRDS)*, Florence, Italy, Oct. 2003.

[18] E. G. Barrantes, D. H. Ackley, S. Forrest, T. S. Palmer, D. Stefanovic, and D. D. Zovi. Randomized Instruction Set Emulation to Disrupt Binary Code Injection Attacks. *10th ACM CCS*, 2003.

[19] G. S. Kc, A. D. Keromytis, and V. Prevelakis. Countering Code-Injection Attacks With Instruction-Set Randomization. *10th ACM CCS*, 2003.

[20] S. Sidiroglou, M. E. Locasto, S. W. Boyd, and A. D. Keromytis. Building a Reactive Immune System for Software Services. *USENIX Annual Technical Conference*, 2005.

[21] L. Lam and T. Chiueh. Checking Array Bound Violation Using Segmentation Hardware. *Dependable Systems and Networks, 2005. DSN 2005. Proceedings. International Conference on*, pages 388–397, 2005.

[22] Wind river: Vxworks. *http://www.windriver.com/vxworks/*. Last accessed Mar 2007.

[23] S. Chen, J. Xu, E. C. Sezer, P. Gauriar, and R. Iyer. Non-control-data attacks are realistic threats. In *Proc. USENIX Security Symposium*, aug 2005.

[24] bochs: The open source ia-32 emulation project. *http://bochs.sourceforge.net/*. Last accessed Dec 2006.

[25] The apache http server project. *http://httpd.apache.org/*. Last accessed Dec 2006.

[26] Linux/unix nbench. *http://www.tux.org/~mayer/linux/bmark.html*. Last accessed Dec 2006.

[27] Unixbench. *http://www.tux.org/pub/tux/benchmarks/System/unixbench/*. Last accessed Dec 2006.

[28] G. Wurster. A generic attack on hashing-based software tamper resistance. Master's thesis, Carleton University, Canada, Apr 2005.

[29] J. Giffin, M. Christodorescu, and L. Kruger. Strengthening software self-checksumming via self-modifying code. In *Proceedings of the 21st Annual Computer Security Applications Conference (ACSAC 2005)*, pages 18–27, Tucson, AZ, USA, Dec. 2005. Applied Computer Associates, IEEE.

Session 1B:
Software Fault Tolerance

Failure Resilience for Device Drivers

Jorrit N. Herder, Herbert Bos, Ben Gras, Philip Homburg, and Andrew S. Tanenbaum

Computer Science Dept., Vrije Universiteit, Amsterdam, The Netherlands

{jnherder, herbertb, beng, philip, ast}@cs.vu.nl

Abstract

Studies have shown that device drivers and extensions contain 3–7 times more bugs than other operating system code and thus are more likely to fail. Therefore, we present a failure-resilient operating system design that can recover from dead drivers and other critical components—primarily through monitoring and replacing malfunctioning components on the fly—transparent to applications and without user intervention. This paper focuses on the post-mortem recovery procedure. We explain the working of our defect detection mechanism, the policy-driven recovery procedure, and post-restart reintegration of the components. Furthermore, we discuss the concrete steps taken to recover from network, block device, and character device driver failures. Finally, we evaluate our design using performance measurements, software fault-injection experiments, and an analysis of the reengineering effort.

Keywords: Operating System Dependability, Failure Resilience, Device Driver Recovery.

1 INTRODUCTION

Perhaps someday software will be bugfree, but for the moment all software contains bugs and we had better learn to coexist with them. Nevertheless, a question we have posed is: "Can we build dependable systems out of unreliable, buggy components?" In particular, we address the problem of failures in device drivers and other operating system extensions. In most operating systems, such failures can disrupt normal operation.

In many other areas, failure-resilient designs are common. For example, RAIDs are disk arrays that continue functioning even in the face of drive failures. ECC memories can detect and correct bit errors transparently without affecting program execution. Disks, CD-ROMs, and DVDs also contain error-correcting codes so that read errors can be corrected on the fly. The TCP protocol provides reliable data transport, even in the face of lost, misordered, or garbled packets. DNS can transparently deal with crashed root servers. Finally, *init* automatically respawns crashed daemons in the application layer of some UNIX variants. In all these cases, software masks the underlying failures and allows the system to continue as though no errors had occurred.

In this paper, we extend these ideas to the operating system internals. In particular, we want to tolerate and mask failures of device drivers and other extensions. Recovery from such failures is particularly important, since extensions are generally written by third parties and tend to be buggy [9, 39]. Unfortunately, recovering from driver failures is also hard, primarily because drivers are closely tied to the rest of the operating system. In addition, it is sometimes impossible to tell whether a driver crash has led to data loss. Nevertheless, we have designed an operating system consisting of multiple isolated user-mode components that are structured in such a way that the system can automatically detect and repair a broad range of defects [10, 15, 30], without affecting running processes or bothering the user. The architecture of this system is shown in Fig. 1.

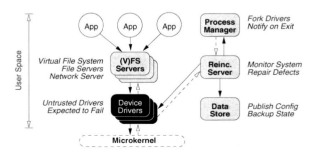

Figure 1: Architecture of our failure-resilient operating system that can recover from malfunctioning device drivers.

41

In this paper, we focus on the post-mortem recovery procedure that allows the system to continue normal operation in the event of otherwise catastrophic failures. We rely on a stable set of servers to deal with untrusted components. The *reincarnation server* manages all system processes and constantly monitors the system's health. When a problem is detected, it executes a policy script associated with the malfunctioning component to guide the recovery procedure. The *data store* provides naming services and can be used to recover lost state after a crash. Changes in the system are broadcast to dependent components through the data store's publish-subscribe mechanisms in order to initiate further recovery and mask the problem to higher levels. This is how failure resilience works: a failure is detected, the defect is repaired, and the system continues running all the time with minimum disturbance to other processes.

While our design can recover from failures in all kinds of components, including the TCP stack and simple servers, the focus of our research is to deal with buggy device drivers. Studies on software dependability report fault densities of 2–75 bugs per 1000 lines of executable code [4, 41], but drivers and other extensions—which typically comprise 70% of the operating system code—have a reported error rate that is 3 to 7 times higher [9], and thus are relatively failure-prone. For example, 85% of Windows XP crashes can be traced back to driver failures [39]. Recovery of drivers thus is an effective way to improve operating system dependability.

1.1 Contribution

We have built a failure-resilient operating system to improve operating system dependability. Our work is based on MINIX 3 [28], which runs all servers and drivers as isolated user-mode processes, but is also applicable to other operating systems. This architecture allowed us to add mechanisms to detect and transparently repair failures, resulting in the design shown in Fig. 1. While several aspects of MINIX 3 have been published before [19, 20, 18], this is the first time we discuss the recovery of malfunctioning device drivers in detail.

The remainder of this paper is organized as follows. We first survey related work in operating system dependability (Sec. 2). Then we present our failure model (Sec. 3), discuss our isolation architecture (Sec. 4), introduce the defect detection mechanisms and policy-driven recovery procedure (Sec. 5). We illustrate our ideas with concrete recovery schemes for network, block device, and character device drivers (Sec. 6). We also evaluate our system using performance measurements, software fault-injection, and an analysis of reengineering effort (Sec. 7). Finally, we conclude (Sec. 8).

2 DEPENDABILITY CONTEXT

This work needs to be placed in the context of operating system dependability. Our failure-resilient design represents a special case of microreboots [7, 8], which promote reducing the mean time to recover (MTTR) in order to increase system availability. We apply this idea to drivers and other operating system extensions.

Several failure-resilient designs exist in the context of operating systems. Solaris 10 [38] provides tools to manage UNIX services running in the application layer and can automatically restart crashed daemons. Nooks [39, 40] implements in-kernel wrapping of components to isolate driver failures and supports recovery through shadow drivers that monitor communication between the kernel and driver. SafeDrive [44] combines wrapping of the system API with type safety for extensions written in C and provides recovery similar to Nooks. QNX [21] provides software watchdogs to catch and recover from intermittent failures in memory-protected subsystems. Paravirtualization [13, 26] supports driver isolation by running each driver in a dedicated, paravirtualized operating system and can recover by rebooting the failed virtual machine. In contrast to these approaches, we take the UNIX model to its logical conclusion by putting all servers and drivers in unprivileged user-mode processes and support restarts through a flexible, policy-driven recovery procedure.

Numerous other approaches attempt to increase operating system dependability by isolating components. Virtual machine approaches like VM/370 [35], VMware [36], and Xen [3] are powerful tools for running multiple services in isolation, but cannot prevent a bug in a device driver from crashing the hosted operating system. User-mode drivers have been used before, but, for example, Mach [12] leaves lots of code in the kernel, whereas L^{4}Linux [16] runs the operating system in a single server on top of L4 [24]. Other designs compartmentalize the entire operating system, including GNU Hurd [6], SawMill Linux [14], and NIZZA [17]. Recently, user-mode drivers also made their way into commodity systems such as Linux [25] and Windows [27]. These systems differ from our work in that we combine proper isolation in user space with driver recovery.

Finally, language-based protection and formal verification can also be used to build dependable systems. OKE [5] uses instrumented object code to load safely kernel extensions. VFiasco [22] is an attempt at formal verification of the L4 microkernel. Singularity [23] uses type safety to provide software isolated processes. These techniques are complementary to our approach, since our user-mode servers and drivers can be implemented in a programming language of choice.

3 FAILURE MODEL

In our work, we are interested in the notion of a failure, that is, a deviation from the specified service [31], such as a driver crash. We are less interested in erroneous system states or the exact underlying faults. Once a failure has been detected, as described in Sec. 5.1, we perform a microreboot [7] of the failing or failed component in an attempt to repair the system. The underlying idea is that a large fraction of software failures are cured by rebooting, even when the exact failure causes are unknown.

Our system is designed to deal with intermittent and transient failures in device drivers. We believe that this focus has great potential to improve operating system dependability, because (1) transient failures represent a main source of downtime in software systems [10, 15, 30] and (2) device drivers are relatively failure-prone [9, 39]. Failures that can be handled by our design include failstop and crash failures, such as exceptions triggered by unexpected input; panics due to internal inconsistencies; race conditions caused by unexpected hardware timing issues; and aging bugs that cause a component to fail over time, for example, due to memory leaks. While hard to track down, these kinds of problems tend to go away after a restart and can be cured by replacing the malfunctioning component with a fresh copy. In fact, our design can deal with a somewhat broader range of failures, since we can also start a newer or patched version of the driver, if available.

Of course, there are limits to the failures our design can deal with. To start with, we cannot deal with Byzantine failures, including random or malicious behavior. For example, consider a disk driver that accepts a write request and responds normally, but, in fact, writes garbage to the disk or nothing at all. Such bugs are virtually impossible to catch in any system. In general, end-to-end checksums are required to prevent silent data corruption [33]. Furthermore, algorithmic and deterministic failures that repeat after a restart cannot be cured, but these can be found more easily through testing. Our design also cannot deal with performance failures where timing specifications are not met, although the use of heartbeat messages helps to detect unresponsive components. Finally, our system cannot recover when the hardware is broken or cannot be reinitialized by a restarted driver. It may be possible, however, to perform a hardware test and switch to a redundant hardware interface, if available. More research in this area is needed, though.

In the remainder of this paper we focus on the recovery from transient driver failures, which, as argued above, represent an important area where our design helps to improve system dependability.

4 ISOLATION ARCHITECTURE

Strict isolation of components is a crucial prerequisite to enable recovery, since it prevents problems in one server or driver from spreading to a different one, in the same way that a bug in a compiler process cannot normally affect a browser process. Taking this notion to our compartmentalized operating system design, for example, a user-mode sound driver that dereferences an invalid pointer is killed by the process manager, causing the sound to stop, but leaving the rest of the system unaffected. Although the precise mechanisms are outside the scope of this paper, a brief summary of MINIX 3's isolation architecture is in place.

To start with, each server and driver is encapsulated in a private, hardware-protected address space to prevent memory corruption through bad pointers and unauthorized access attempts, just like for normal applications. Because the memory management unit (MMU) denies access to other address spaces, the kernel provides a virtual copy call that enables processes to copy data between address spaces in a capability-protected manner. A process that wants to grant selective access to its memory needs to create a capability describing the precise memory area and access rights and pass an index to it to the other party.

Direct memory access (DMA) is a powerful I/O mechanisms that potentially can be used to bypass the memory protection offered by our system. On commodity hardware, we can deny access to the DMA controller's I/O ports, and have a trusted driver mediate all access attempts. However, this requires manual checking of each device to see if it uses DMA. Modern hardware provides effective protection in the form of an I/O MMU [1]. To perform DMA safely a driver should first request the kernel to set up the I/O MMU by passing an index to a memory capability similar to the one described above. The overhead of this protection is a few microseconds to perform the kernel call, which is generally amortized over the costs of the I/O operation.

In addition, we have reduced the privileges of each component to a minimum according to the principle of least authority [34]. The privileges are passed to the trusted reincarnation server when a component is loaded through the *service* utility, which, in turn, informs the other servers, drivers, and microkernel so that the restrictions can be enforced at run-time. System processes are given an unprivileged user and group ID to restrict among other things file system access. For servers, we restrict the use of IPC primitives, system calls, and kernel calls. For device drivers, the same restrictions apply, and in addition, we restrict access to I/O ports, IRQ lines, and device memory such as the video memory.

5 RECOVERY PROCEDURE

In this section, we describe the general recovery procedure in the event of failures. The ability of our system to deal with dead drivers implies that we can dynamically start and stop drivers while the operating system is running. Starting a new device driver is done through the *service* utility, which forwards the request to the reincarnation server. The following arguments are passed along with the request: the driver's binary, a stable name, the process' precise privileges, a heartbeat period, and, optionally, a parametrized policy script—a shell script that is called after a driver failure to manage the recovery procedure. If all arguments make sense, the reincarnation server forks a new process, sets the process' privileges, and executes the driver's binary. From that point on, the driver will be constantly guarded to ensure continuous operation—even in the event of a failure. How the reincarnation server can detect defects and how the recovery procedure works is described below.

5.1 Defect Detection

While a human user observes driver defects when the system crashes, becomes unresponsive, or starts to behave in strange ways, the operating system needs other ways to detect failures. Therefore, the reincarnation server monitors the system at run-time to find defects. The various inputs that can cause the recovery procedure to be initiated are:

1. Process exit or panic.
2. Crashed by CPU or MMU exception.
3. Killed by user.
4. Heartbeat message missing.
5. Complaint by other component.
6. Dynamic update by user.

At any point in time the reincarnation server has accurate information about the presence of all servers and drivers, since it is the parent of all system processes. When a server or driver crashes, panics or exits for another reason, the process manager will notify the reincarnation server with a SIGCHLD signal, according to the POSIX specification. At that point it collects and inspects the exit status of the exitee, which leads to the first three defect classes. Since a process exit is directly reported by the process manager, immediate action can be taken by the reincarnation server.

In addition, the reincarnation server can proactively check the system's state. Depending on the configuration passed upon loading, the reincarnation server can periodically request drivers to send a heartbeat message.

Failing to respond N consecutive times causes recovery to be initiated. Heartbeats help to detect processes that are 'stuck,' for example, in an infinite loop, but do not protect against malicious code. To prevent bogging down the system status requests and the consequent replies are sent using nonblocking messages.

Furthermore, the reincarnation server can be used as an arbiter in case of conflicts, allowing authorized servers to report malfunctioning components. How a malfunction is precisely defined depends on the components at hand, but in general has to do with protocol violations. For example, the file server can request replacement of a disk driver that sends unexpected request messages or fails to respond to a request. The authority to replace other components is part of the protection file that specifies a process' privileges.

Finally, faulty behavior also can be noticed by the user, for example, if the audio sounds weird. In such a case, the user can explicitly instruct the reincarnation server to restart a driver or replace it with a newly compiled one. As another example, latent bugs or vulnerabilities may lead to a dynamic update as soon as a patch is available. Since about a quarter of downtime is caused by reboots due to maintenance [42], such dynamic updates that allow patching the system on the fly can significantly increase system availability.

5.2 Policy-Driven Recovery

By default, the reincarnation server directly restarts a crashed component, but if more flexibility is wanted, the administrator can instruct it to use a parametrized policy script that governs the actions to be taken after a failure. Policy scripts can be shared, but dedicated recovery scripts can be associated with individual servers and drivers as well. When a malfunctioning component is detected, the reincarnation server looks up the associated policy script and executes it. Input arguments are which component failed, the kind of failure as indicated in Sec. 5.1, the current failure count, and the parameters passed along with the script. The primary goal of the policy script is to decide when to restart the malfunctioning component, but other actions can be taken as well. Restarting is always done by requesting the reincarnation server to do so, since that is the only process with the privileges to create new servers and drivers.

The simplest policy script immediately tries to restart the failed component, but the policy-driven recovery procedure can use the information passed by the reincarnation server to make decisions about the precise recovery steps taken. For example, consider the generic policy script in Fig. 2. Lines 1–4 process the arguments passed by the reincarnation server. Then, lines 6–10

```
                    ── a generic recovery script ──────
1    component=$1           # component name
2    reason=$2              # numbers as in Sec. 3.1
3    repetition=$3          # current failure count
4    shift 3                # get to script parameters
5
6    if [ ! $reason -eq 6 ]; then
7       sleep $((1 << ($repetition - 1)))
8    fi
9    service restart $component
10   status=$?
11
12   while getopts a: option; do
13   case $option in
14   a)
15      cat << END | mail -s "Failure Alert" "$OPTARG"
16         failure: $component, $reason, $repetition
17         restart status: $status
18   END
19   ;;
20   esac
21   done
```

Figure 2: A parametrized, generic recovery script. Binary exponential backoff is used before restarting, except for dynamic updates. Optionally, a failure alert is sent.

restart the component, possibly after an exponentially increasing delay to prevent bogging down the system in the event of repeated failures. The backoff protocol is not used for dynamic updates that are requested explicitly. Finally, lines 12–21 optionally send an e-mail alert if the parameter '-a' and an e-mail address are passed.

Using shell scripts provides a lot of flexibility and power for expressing policies. For example, a dedicated policy script can help the administrator recover from failures in the network server. Such a failure closes all open network connections, including the sockets used by the X Window System. Among other things, recovery requires restarting the DHCP client and X Window System, which can be specified in a dedicated policy script. As another example, when a required component cannot be recovered or fails too often, the policy script may reboot the entire system, which clearly is better than leaving the system in an unusable state. At the very least, the policy script can log the failing component and its execution environment for future inspection. As an aside, the ability of our system to pinpoint precisely the responsible components might have legal consequences for software vendors (since it can help determine liability for damage caused by a crash), which may help in building more dependable systems [43].

5.3 Post-Restart Reintegration

A restart of an operating system process is similar to the steps taken when a new component is started through the *service* utility, although the details differ. Some extra work needs to be done, mainly because the capabilities of processes that refer to the restarted component need to be reset. In general, simple update requests suffice, but these issues illustrate that interprocess dependencies complicate the recovery. For example, our design uses temporarily unique IPC endpoints, so that messages cannot be delivered to the wrong process during a failure. As a consequence, a component's endpoint changes with each restart, and the IPC capabilities of dependent processes must be updated accordingly. Such updates are done by the reincarnation server before the dependent components learn about the restart, as discussed next.

Once a component has been restarted, it needs to be reintegrated into the system. Two steps need to be distinguished here. First, changes in the operating system configuration need to be communicated to dependent components in order to initiate further recovery and mask the problem to higher levels. This information is disseminated through the data store, a simple name server that stores stable component names along with the component's current IPC endpoint. The reincarnation server is responsible for keeping this naming information up to date. The data store implements a publish-subscribe mechanism, so that components can subscribe to naming information of components they depend on. This design decouples producers and consumers and prevents intricate interaction patterns of components that need to inform each other. For example, the network server subscribes to updates about the configuration of Ethernet drivers by registering the expression 'eth.*'.

Second, a restarted component may need to retrieve state that is lost when it crashed. The data store also serves as a database server that can be used by system processes to privately store a backup copy of certain data. By using the data store, lost state can be retrieved after a restart. Authentication of restarted components is done with help of the naming information that is also kept in the data store. When private data is stored, a reference to the stable name is included in the record, so that authentication of the owner is possible even if its endpoint changes. In our prototype implementation, state management turns out to be a minor problem for device drivers, but is crucial for more complex services. In fact, none of our device drivers currently uses the data store to backup internal state. However, all mechanisms needed to recover from failures in stateful components, such as servers, are present. Transparent recovery of servers is part of our future work.

6 DRIVER RECOVERY SCHEMES

Although in principle our design can handle both server and driver failures, our current focus is to reincarnate dead drivers, since such failures are more common [9, 39]. If a driver failure cannot be handled at the server level, it will be reported to the application that made the I/O request, which notifies the user of the problem, if need be. Different recovery schemes exist depending on the type of driver, as summarized in Fig. 3. Full, transparent recovery without bothering the user is possible for both network and block device drivers.

Driver	Recovery	Where	Section
Network	Yes	Network server	Sec. 6.1
Block	Yes	File server	Sec. 6.2
Character	Maybe	Application	Sec. 6.3

Figure 3: Driver recovery schemes. Only network and block device drivers allow transparently recovery.

The recovery schemes discussed here pertain not only to failures, but also allows the administrator to dynamically update drivers—even if I/O is in progress. In this case, the reincarnation server first requests the driver to exit by sending it a SIGTERM signal, followed by a SIGKILL signal, if the driver does not comply. The steps that are taken after the reincarnation server caused the driver to exit are similar to those for a failure. Most other operating system cannot dynamically replace active drivers on the fly like we do.

6.1 Recovering Network Drivers

If a network driver fails, full recovery transparent to the application is possible. We have implemented support for Ethernet driver recovery in MINIX 3's network server, INET. If the application uses a reliable transport protocol, such as TCP, the protocol handles part of the recovery. If data is lost or corrupted, the network server (or its peer at the other end of the connection) will notice and reinsert the missing packets in the data stream. If an unreliable protocol, such as UDP, is used, loss of data is explicitly tolerated, but if need be, application-level recovery is possible, as illustrated in Fig. 4.

The recovery procedure starts when the process manager informs the reincarnation server about the exit of one of its children, as discussed in Sec. 5.1. The reincarnation server looks up the details about the failed driver in its internal tables and runs the associated policy script to restart it. Because the network server subscribes to information about Ethernet drivers, it is automatically notified by the data store if the configuration changes. If the network server tries to send data in the short period

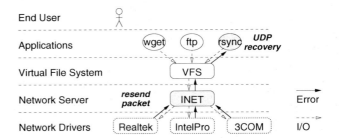

Figure 4: Network driver recovery is done by the network server or application, transparent to the user.

between the driver crash and the consequent restart, the request fails and is postponed until the driver is back. Upon notification by the data store, the network server checks its tables to find out if the driver update concerns a new driver or a recovered one, and in the latter case, starts its internal recovery procedure. This procedure closely mimics the steps that are taken when the driver is first started. The Ethernet driver is reinitialized to put it in promiscuous mode and told to resume I/O. The Ethernet driver is stateless and does not need to retrieve lost state from the data store—although it could do so, were that necessary.

6.2 Recovering Block Drivers

We now zoom in on block device driver crashes and describe the recovery procedure as implemented by the native MINIX 3 file server, MFS. If a disk driver (such as the hard disk, RAM disk, CD-ROM, or floppy driver) crashes, transparent recovery without loss of data is possible, since disk block I/O is idempotent. If I/O was in progress at the time of the failure, the IPC rendezvous will be aborted by the kernel, and the file server marks the request as pending. Then, the file server blocks and waits until the disk driver has been restarted and pending I/O requests can be retried, as illustrated in Fig. 5.

In contrast to other drivers, disk driver recovery is currently not policy driven, since that would require reading the recovery script from disk. Instead, the reincarnation server directly restarts failed disk drivers from a copy in RAM.[1] Like the other drivers in our system, disk drivers are stateless and do not need to retrieve lost state from the data store, although they could were that necessary. Once the driver has been restarted, the reincarnation server publishes the new IPC endpoint in the data store and the file server is notified. At this point, the file server updates its device–driver mappings, and

---
[1] If policy-driven recovery is needed for disk drivers, the system can be configured with a dedicated RAM disk to provide trusted storage for crucial data, such as the driver binaries, the shell, and policy scripts. We have written a small 450-line RAM disk driver for this purpose.

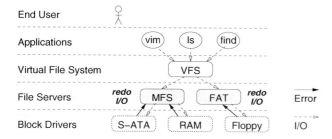

Figure 5: Block device driver recovery is done by the file server, transparent to applications and users.

reinitializes the disk driver by reopening minor devices, if needed. Finally, the file server checks whether there are any pending I/O requests, and if so, it reissues the failed disk operations. At this point the file server resumes normal operation and continues to handle pending I/O requests from other user applications.

As an aside, our design is meant to provide recovery in the event of driver crashes, but is not designed to detect silent data corruption, as discussed in Sec. 3. While the TCP protocol automatically eliminates this problem for network driver crashes, disk driver crashes can potentially corrupt the data on disk. However, our design may be combined with end-to-end checksums, as in IRON file systems [33], to prevent data corruption.

6.3 Recovering Character Drivers

Character device drivers cannot be transparently recovered, since it is impossible to tell whether data was lost. Deciding which part of the data stream was successfully processed and which data is missing is an undecidable problem. If an input stream is interrupted due to a device driver crash, input might be lost because it can only be read from the controller once. Likewise, if an output stream is interrupted, there is no way to tell how much data has been output to the controller, and full recovery is also not possible. Therefore, such failures are reported to the application layer where further recovery might be possible, as illustrated in Fig. 6.

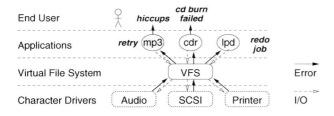

Figure 6: Recovery for character device drivers. Errors are always pushed up, but need to be reported the user only if the application cannot recover.

For historical reasons, most applications assume that a driver failure is fatal and immediately give up, but our prototype in fact supports continuous operation when applications are made recovery-aware. For example, it may be possible to modify the printer daemon such that it automatically reissues failed print requests (without bothering the user). While transparent recovery is not possible—duplicate printouts may result in this case—the user benefits from this approach. As another example, an MP3 player could continue playing a song after a driver recovery at the risk of small hiccups. Only when the application layer cannot handle the failure, the user needs to be informed. For example, continuing the CD or DVD burn process if the SCSI driver fails will most certainly produce a corrupted disc, so the error must be reported to the user.

7 EXPERIMENTAL EVALUATION

We have evaluated our recovery mechanisms in various ways. First, we discuss the performance overhead introduced by our recovery mechanisms. Then, we report on the results of software fault-injection. Finally, we quantify the reengineering effort needed to prototype our recovery mechanisms in MINIX 3.

7.1 Performance Overhead

To determine the performance overhead introduced by our recovery mechanisms we simulated driver crashes while I/O was in progress and compared the performance to the performance of an uninterrupted I/O transfer. We performed this test for both block device and network drivers. The crash simulation was done using a tiny shell script that first initiates the I/O transfer, and then repeatedly looks up the driver's process ID and kills the driver using a SIGKILL signal. The test was run with varying intervals between the simulated crashes. The recovery policy that was used for these tests directly restarts the driver without introducing delays. After the transfer we verified that no data corruption took place. In all cases, full recovery transparent to the application and without user intervention was possible.

We first measured the overhead for the recovery of network drivers using the RealTek 8139 Ethernet driver. In this case, we initiated a TCP transfer using the *wget* utility to retrieve a 512-MB file from the Internet. We ran multiple tests with the period between the simulated crashes ranging from 1 to 15 seconds. In all cases, *wget* successfully completed, with the only noticeable difference being a small performance degradation as shown in Fig. 7. To verify that the data integrity was preserved, we compared the MD5 checksums of the received data the original file. The mean recovery time for the Real-Tek 8139 driver failures is 0.48 sec, which is, in part, due to the TCP retransmission timeout. The uninterrupted transfer time is 47.41 sec with a throughput of 10.8 MB/s. The interrupted transfer times range from 47.85 sec to 62.98 sec with a throughput of 10.7 MB/s and 8.1 MB/s, respectively. The loss in throughput due to Ethernet driver failures ranges from 25% to just 1% in the best case.

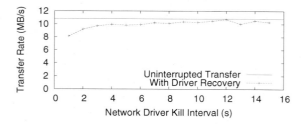

Figure 7: Networking throughput when using *wget* retrieve a 512-MB file from the Internet while repeatedly killing an Ethernet driver with various time intervals.

We also measured the overhead of disk driver recovery by repeatedly sending a SIGKILL signal to the SATA hard disk driver while reading a 1-GB file filled with random data using *dd*. The input was immediately redirected to *sha1sum* to calculate the SHA-1 checksum. Again, we killed the driver with varying intervals between the simulated crashes. The data transfer successfully completed in all cases with the same SHA-1 checksum. The transfer rates are shown in Fig. 8. The uninterrupted disk transfer completed in 31.33 sec with a throughput of 32.7 MB/sec. The interrupted transfer shows a transmission time ranging from 83.06 sec to 34.73 sec, with a throughput of 12.3 MB/s and 30.5 MB/s, for simulated crashes every 1 and 15 sec, respectively. The performance overhead of disk driver recovery ranges from 62% to about 7% in this test. The higher recovery overhead compared to the previous experiment is due to the much higher I/O transfer rates.

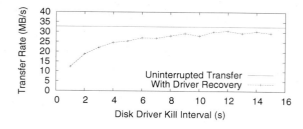

Figure 8: Throughput of uninterrupted disk transfers and throughput in case of repeated disk driver failures while reading a 1-GB file using *dd*.

7.2 Fault-Injection Testing

To test the capability of our system to withstand and recover from driver failures, we also simulated failures in our drivers by means of software fault-injection. We based our experiments on two existing fault injectors that mutate binary code [32, 39, 40]. This kind of fault injection was shown to be most representative for real failures [29]. We used the following seven fault types: (1) change source register, (2) change destination register, (3) garble pointer, (4) use current register value instead of paramater passed, (5) invert termination condition of a loop, (6) flip a bit in an instruction, or (7) elide an instruction. These faults emulate programming errors common to operating system code [11, 37].

The fault-injection experiments demonstrated that our design can successfully recover from common, transient failures and provide continuous operation. One experiment run inside the Bochs PC emulator 2.2.6 targeted the DP8390 Ethernet driver and repeatedly injected 1 randomly selected fault into the running driver until it crashed. In total, we injected over 12,500 faults, which led to 347 detectable crashes: 226 exits due to an internal panic (65%), 109 kill signals due to CPU and MMU exceptions (31%), and 12 restarts due to missing heartbeat messages (4%). The subsequent recovery was successful in 100% of the induced failures.

Preliminary tests on the real hardware showed success for more than 99% of the detectable failures. In a very small number of cases (less than 5) the network card was confused by the faulty driver and could not be reininitialized by the restarted driver. Instead a low-level BIOS reset was needed. If the card had a 'master reset' command the problem could be solved by our driver, but our card did not have this. Further testing with different kinds of drivers and hardware configurations is needed, however, in order to get more insight in possible hardware limitations. This will be part of our future work.

7.3 Reengineering Effort

An important lesson that we have learned during our prototype implementation is that the recovery procedure requires an *integrated approach* for optimal results, meaning that certain components need to be recovery-aware. As a metric for the reengineering effort we counted the number of lines of executable code (LoC) that is needed to support recovery. Blank lines, comments, and definitions in header files do not add to the code complexity, so these were omitted in the counting process. Line counting was done using the *sclc.pl* Perl script [2]. Fig. 9 summarizes the results.

Fortunately, the changes required to deal with driver

failures are both very limited and local. The reincarnation server and *service* utility's logic to dynamically start servers and drivers is reused to support recovery. Most of the new code relates to defect detection and execution of the recovery scripts. The virtual file system and file server stay mostly the same, with changes centralized in the device I/O routines. Furthermore, the recovery code in the network server represents a minimal extension to the code needed to start a new driver. Finally, the process manager and microkernel are not affected at all.

Most importantly, the device drivers in our system are hardly affected. In general, only a minimal change to reply to heartbeat and shutdown requests from the reincarnation server is needed. For most drivers this change comprises exactly 5 lines of code in the shared driver library to handle the new request types. Device-specific driver code almost never needs to be changed. For a few drivers, however, the code to initialize the hardware had to be modified in order to support reinitialization. Overall, the changes are negligible compared to the amount of driver code that can be guarded by our design.

7.4 General Applicability

The ideas put forward in this paper are generally applicable, and may, for example, be used in commodity operating systems. While the degree of isolation provided by our prototype platform, MINIX 3, enabled us to implement and test our ideas with relatively little effort, we believe that other systems can also benefit from our ideas. Especially, since there is a trend towards isolation of untrusted extensions on other operating systems. For example, user-mode drivers have been successfully tested on Linux [25] and adopted by Windows [27]. If the drivers are properly isolated, these systems can build on the principles presented here in order to provide policy-driven recovery services like we do.

Component	Total LoC	Recovery LoC	%
Reinc. Server	2,002	593	30%
Data Store	384	59	15%
VFS Server	5,464	274	5%
File Server	3,356	22	<1%
SATA Driver	2,443	5	<1%
RAM Disk	454	0	0%
Network Server	20,019	124	<1%
RTL8139 Driver	2,398	5	<1%
DP8390 Driver	2,769	5	<1%
Process Manager	2,954	0	0%
Microkernel	4,832	0	0%
Total	39,011	1,072	-

Figure 9: Source code statistics on the total code base and reengineering effort specific to recovery expressed in lines of executable code (LoC).

8 CONCLUSION

Our research explores whether it is possible to build a dependable operating system out of unreliable, buggy components. We have been inspired by other hardware and software failure-resilient designs that mask failures so that the system can continue as though no errors had occurred, and attempted to extend this idea to device driver failures. Recovery from such failures is particularly important, since device drivers form a large fraction of the operating system code and tend to be buggy.

In this paper, we presented an operating system architecture in which common failures in drivers and other critical extensions can be transparently repaired. The system is constantly monitored by the reincarnation server and malfunctioning components may be replaced in a policy-driven recovery procedure to masks failures for both users and applications. We illustrated our ideas with concrete recovery schemes for failures in network, block device, and character device drivers.

We also evaluated our design in various ways. We measured the performance overhead due to our recovery mechanisms, which can be as low as 1%. Fault-injection experiments demonstrated that our design can recover from realistic failures and provide continuous operation in more than 99% of the detectable failures. Source code analysis showed that the reengineering effort needed is both limited and local. All in all, we believe that our work on failure resilience for device drivers represents a small step towards more dependable operating systems.

9 AVAILABILITY

MINIX 3 is free, open-source software, available via the Internet. You can download MINIX 3 from the official homepage at: http://www.minix3.org/, which also contains the source code, documentation, news, and more.

10 ACKNOWLEDGMENTS

We would like to thank the anonymous reviewers for their suggestions that improved this paper. This work was supported by Netherlands Organization for Scientific Research (NWO) under grant 612-060-420.

REFERENCES

[1] D. Abramson, J. Jackson, S. Muthrasanallur, G. Neiger, G. Regnier, R. Sankaran, I. Schoinas, R. Uhlig, B. Vembu, and J. Wiegert. Intel Virtualization Technology for Directed I/O. *Intel Technology Journal*, 10(3), Aug. 2006.

[2] B. Appleton. Source Code Line Counter (sclc.pl), Last Modified: April 2003. Available Online.

[3] P. T. Barham, B. Dragovic, K. Fraser, S. Hand, T. L. Harris, A. Ho, R. Neugebauer, I. Pratt, and A. Warfield. Xen and the Art of Virtualization. In *Proc. 19th Symp. on Oper. Syst. Prin.*, pages 164–177, 2003.

[4] V. Basili and B. Perricone. Software Errors and Complexity: An Empirical Investigation. *Comm. of the ACM*, 21(1):42–52, Jan. 1984.

[5] H. Bos and B. Samwel. Safe Kernel Programming in the OKE. In *Proc. of the 5th IEEE Conf. on Open Architectures and Network Programming*, pages 141–152, June 2002.

[6] M. I. Bushnell. The HURD: Towards a New Strategy of OS Design. *GNU's Bulletin*, 1994.

[7] G. Candea, J. Cutler, and A. Fox. Improving Availability with Recursive Microreboots: A Soft-State System Case Study. *Performance Evaluation Journal*, 56(1):213–248, .

[8] G. Candea, S. Kawamoto, Y. Fujiki, G. Friedman, and A. Fox. Microreboot–A Technique for Cheap Recovery. In *Proc. 6th Symp. on Oper. Syst. Design and Impl.*, pages 31–44, .

[9] A. Chou, J. Yang, B. Chelf, S. Hallem, and D. Engler. An Empirical Study of Operating System Errors. In *Proc. 18th Symp. on Oper. Syst. Prin.*, pages 73–88, 2001.

[10] T. C. K. Chou. Beyond Fault Tolerance. *IEEE Computer*, 30(4), Apr. 1997.

[11] J. Christmansson and R. Chillarege. Generation of an Error Set that Emulates Software Faults – Based on Field Data. In *Proc. 26th IEEE Int'l Symp. on Fault Tolerant Computing*, June 1996.

[12] A. Forin, D. Golub, and B. Bershad. An I/O System for Mach 3.0. In *Proc. 2nd USENIX Mach Symp.*, pages 163–176, 1991.

[13] K. Fraser, S. Hand, R. Neugebauer, I. Pratt, A. Warfield, and M. Williamson. Safe Hardware Access with the Xen Virtual Machine Monitor. In *Proc. 1st Workshop on Oper. Sys. and Arch. Support for the On-Demand IT InfraStructure*, Oct. 2004.

[14] A. Gefflaut, T. Jaeger, Y. Park, J. Liedtke, K. Elphinstone, V. Uhlig, J. Tidswell, L. Deller, and L. Reuther. The SawMill Multiserver Approach. In *Proc. 9th ACM SIGOPS European Workshop*, pages 109–114, Sept. 2000.

[15] J. Gray. Why Do Computers Stop and What Can Be Done About It? In *Proc. 5th Symp. on Reliability in Distributed Software and Database Systems*, pages 3–12, 1986.

[16] H. Härtig, M. Hohmuth, J. Liedtke, S. Schönberg, and J. Wolter. The Performance of μ-Kernel-Based Systems. In *Proc. 6th Symp. on Oper. Syst. Prin.*, pages 66–77, Oct. 1997.

[17] H. Härtig, M. Hohmuth, N. Feske, C. Helmuth, A. Lackorzynski, F. Mehnert, and M. Peter. The Nizza Secure-System Architecture. In *Proc. 1st Conf. on Collaborative Computing*, Dec. 2005.

[18] J. N. Herder, H. Bos, B. Gras, P. Homburg, and A. S. Tanenbaum. Reorganizing UNIX for Reliability. In *Proc. 11th Asia-Pacific Comp. Sys. Arch. Conf.*, Sept. 2006.

[19] J. N. Herder, H. Bos, B. Gras, P. Homburg, and A. S. Tanenbaum. Construction of a Highly Dependable Operating System. In *Proc. 6th European Dependable Computing Conf.*, Oct. 2006.

[20] J. N. Herder, H. Bos, B. Gras, P. Homburg, and A. S. Tanenbaum. MINIX 3: A Highly Reliable, Self-Repairing Operating System. *ACM SIGOPS Operating System Review*, 40(3), July 2006.

[21] D. Hildebrand. An Architectural Overview of QNX. In *Proc. USENIX Workshop on Microkernels and Other Kernel Architectures*, pages 113–126, Apr. 1992.

[22] M. Hohmuth and H. Tews. The VFiasco Approach for a Verified Operating System. In *Proc. 2nd ECOOP Workshop on Prog. Lang. and Oper. Sys.*, July 2005.

[23] G. Hunt, C. Hawblitzel, O. Hodson, J. Larus, B. Steensgaard, and T. Wobber. Sealing OS Processes to Improve Dependability and Safety. In *Proc. 2nd EuroSys Conf.*, 2007.

[24] J. Liedtke. On μ-Kernel Construction. In *Proc. 15th Symp. on Oper. Syst. Prin.*, pages 237–250, Dec. 1995.

[25] B. Leslie, P. Chubb, N. Fitzroy-Dale, S. Gotz, C. Gray, L. Macpherson, D. Potts, Y.-T. Shen, K. Elphinstone, and G. Heiser. User-Level Device Drivers: Achieved Performance. *Journal of Computer Science and Technology*, 20(5):654–664, Sept. 2005.

[26] J. LeVasseur, V. Uhlig, J. Stoess, and S. Gotz. Unmodified Device Driver Reuse and Improved System Dependability via Virtual Machines. In *Proc. 6th Symp. on Oper. Syst. Design and Impl.*, pages 17–30, Dec. 2004.

[27] Microsoft Corporation. Architecture of the User-Mode Driver Framework. In *Proc. 15th WinHEC Conf.*, May 2006.

[28] MINIX 3. Official Website and Download:. URL http://www.minix3.org/.

[29] R. Moraes, R. Barbosa, J. Dures, N. Mendes, E. Martins, and H. Madeira. Injection of Faults at Component Interfaces and Inside the Component Code: Are They Equivalent? In *Proc. 6th Eur. Dependable Computing Conf.*, pages 53–64, Oct. 2006.

[30] B. Murphy and N. Davies. System Reliability and Availability Drivers of Tru64 UNIX. In *Proc. 29th Int'l Symp. on Fault-Tolerant Computing*, June 1999. Tutorial.

[31] V. P. Nelson. Fault-Tolerant Computing: Fundamental Concepts. *IEEE Computer*, 23(7):19–25, July 1990.

[32] W. T. Ng and P. M. Chen. The Systematic Improvement of Fault Tolerance in the Rio File Cache. In *Proc. 29th Int'l Symp. on Fault-Tolerant Computing*, pages 76–83, June 1999.

[33] V. Prabhakaran, L. N. Bairavasundaram, N. Agrawal, H. S. Gunawi, A. C. Arpaci-Dusseau, and R. H. Arpaci-Dusseau. IRON File Systems. In *Proc. 20th Symp. on Oper. Sys. Prin.*, pages 206–220, Oct. 2005.

[34] J. Saltzer and M. Schroeder. The Protection of Information in Computer Systems. *Proc. of the IEEE*, 63(9), Sept. 1975.

[35] L. Seawright and R. MacKinnon. VM/370—A Study of Multiplicity and Usefulness. *IBM Systems Journal*, 18(1):4–17, 1979.

[36] J. Sugerman, G. Venkitachalam, and B.-H. Lim. Virtualizing I/O Devices on VMware Workstation's Hosted Virtual Machine Monitor. In *Proc. USENIX Ann. Tech. Conf.*, pages 1–14, 2001.

[37] M. Sullivan and R. Chillarege. Software Defects and their Impact on System Availability – A Study of Field Failures in Operating Systems. In *Proc. 21st Int'l Symp. on Fault-Tolerant Computing*, June 1991.

[38] Sun Microsystems. Predictive Self-Healing in the Solaris 10 Operating System, June 2004. Available Online.

[39] M. Swift, M. Annamalai, B. Bershad, and H. Levy. Recovering Device Drivers. In *Proc. 6th Symp. on Oper. Syst. Design and Impl.*, pages 1–15, Dec. 2004.

[40] M. Swift, B. Bershad, and H. Levy. Improving the Reliability of Commodity Operating Systems. *ACM Trans. on Comp. Syst.*, 23 (1):77–110, 2005.

[41] T.J. Ostrand and E.J. Weyuker. The Distribution of Faults in a Large Industrial Software System. In *Proc. Symp. on Software Testing and Analysis*, pages 55–64, July 2002.

[42] J. Xu, Z. Kalbarczyk, and R. K. Iyer. Networked Windows NT System Field Failure Data Analysis. In *Proc. 6th Pacific Rim Symp. on Dependable Computing*, pages 178–185, Dec. 1999.

[43] A. R. Yumerefendi and J. S. Chase. The Role of Accountability in Dependable Distributed Systems. In *Proc. 1st Workshop on Hot Topics in System Dependability*, June 2005.

[44] F. Zhou, J. Condit, Z. Anderson, I. Bagrak, R. Ennals, M. Harren, G. Necula, and E. Brewer. SafeDrive: Safe and Recoverable Extensions Using Language-Based Techniques. In *Proc. 7th Symp. on Oper. Sys. Design and Impl.*, pages 45–60, Nov. 2006.

Fault Tolerance Connectors for Unreliable Web Services

Nicolas Salatge and Jean-Charles Fabre
LAAS-CNRS, 7 avenue du Colonel Roche, 31077 Toulouse Cedex 04 – France
{nsalatge,fabre}@laas.fr

Abstract

Web Services are commonly used to implement service oriented architectures/applications. Service-oriented applications are large-scale distributed applications, typically highly dynamic, by definition loosely coupled and often unstable due to the unreliability of Web Services, which can be moved, deleted, and are subject to various sources of failures. In this paper, we propose customizable fault-tolerance connectors to add fault-tolerance to unreliable Web Services, thus filling the gap between clients and Web Service providers. Connectors are designed by clients, providers or dependability experts using the original WSDL description of the service. These connectors insert detection actions (e.g. runtime assertions) and recovery mechanisms (based on various replications strategies). The connectors can use identical or equivalent available service replicas. The benefits of this approach are demonstrated experimentally.

1. Introduction

Web Services are commonly used to develop *Service Oriented Architectures/Applications* (SOA), i.e. large scale distributed application over the Internet. Such applications primarily concern e-commerce, but also e-government, and even more critical applications in the near future. The concept of Web Service (WS) is a significant evolution of conventional solutions like service definition using IDLs, service discovery and dynamic invocation interfaces, as in CORBA for instance. The focus is to establish contractual relations between client and Web Service providers (a WSDL document), such contracts formally describing services possibly discovered dynamically over the Internet. Clearly, SOA-based applications are highly dynamic, by definition loosely coupled, subjects to frequent changes. Web Services used in an application can be moved, deleted, and subject to various sources of failures, or simply unreachable due to communication faults [1]. This is a natural situation on the Web.

Application having specific dependability requirements can usefully take advantage of highly reliable Web Services when available. However, such services might be difficult to find on the Net and in addition be unreachable in some circumstances. Reliable WS can be obviously developed on purpose but this is not the philosophy of SOA. In most of the cases, applications are built from existing unreliable Web Services. The problem is then similar to building reliable applications out of unreliable *Commercial Off-The-Shelf* (COTS) components. The issue is thus to find external means to equip basic Web Services with additional fault tolerance mechanisms. Separation of concerns is an attractive concept to address this issue. However, separation of concern does not mean total independence, in particular regarding state handling issues that are still user-defined as other works like Arjuna, Eternal and FT CORBA, for instance.

Our idea is to interact with individual WS through *connectors* implementing fault tolerance features. These connectors provide first customized and efficient error detection mechanisms, including user-defined assertions, to transform a WS into a sort of self-checking software component [2]. Secondly, we propose some partially built-in replication mechanisms to perform error recovery. The recovery strategies can range from simple switch to a spare WS replica to error masking strategies. Connectors are reliable software components executed on redundant architecture providing several services (runtime executive support, connector management, health monitoring, etc.).

This paper focuses on the fault tolerance features of the connectors and the use of redundant services on the Net to help making *"reliable SOA out of unreliable Web Services"*. Section 2 defines the notion of connector and describes the support infrastructure to develop, execute and manage user-defined connectors. Section 3 focuses on the equivalence of service to take advantage of the available resource redundancy over the Internet. The various built-in replication mechanisms and strategies provided are discussed in Section 4. Section 5 summarizes the first experiments carried out. Related work is addressed in Section 6 and section 7 briefly concludes the paper.

2. Basic concepts and architectural issues

2.1. The notion of "Connector"

The notion of connector is a classic concept of ADLs (*Architecture Description Language*) able to make explicit and to customize the interactions between components [3]. Similar notions have been already used in other context (DCE, CORBA, EJB), but not yet to address fault tolerance issues in SOA. The notion of user-defined *Specific Fault Tolerance Connector* (SFTC) is a software component able to capture Web Service interactions and partially performing built-in fault tolerance actions.

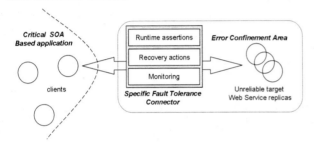

Figure 1. Role of Connectors

The various mechanisms provided by a connector are devoted to (see Figure 1):

- **User-defined runtime assertions** applying checks to input/output requests together with built-in error detection and signaling mechanisms by means of SOAP exceptions returned to the client.
- **Parameterized built-in recovery** actions based on various replication models that can be selected by the user, this selection depending very much on the target Web Service, in particular on state handling issues and features of the target WS.
- **Monitoring and error diagnosis** of the targeted Web Services, collecting errors information on target access points, and leading to extended error reports on Web Services.

The connector must be a reliable software component. To this aim, a specific language called DeWeL (*DEpendable WEb service Language*) was developed. Its major objective is to prevent software faults using strong static (compile-time) and (ii) dynamic (runtime) verification of a finite set of language constructs to declare recovery strategies and write runtime assertions. As for critical software, the language applies coding restrictions advocated in standards (like DO178B, CENELEC): no dynamic allocation, no pointers, no files, no indexed access to arrays, no standard loops (while, for), no functions, no method overriding, no recursive construct, no external access to other users data space or system resources.

This approach prevents traditional software development faults to be introduced, such as those that have been classified by several industrial companies (e.g. IBM, HP, etc.), in ODC (Orthogonal Defect Classification) [4] for instance. In [5], we describe in more details the restriction imposed by the DeWeL language together with a full account of the development process.

Finally, connectors can be developed by an SOA designer acting as a client, a Web Service provider or any third party, namely a dependability expert. Combining connectors with the original Web Service leads to customized reliable versions of the target WS, a WSDL contract being attached to any connector at the end of the development process.

2.2. Notion of execution models

The execution model describes behavior of a connector at the runtime. For each WS operation, a connector template has several pre-defined sections:

1) Pre-processing and Post-processing corresponding to assertions developed in DeWel,
2) a RecoveryStrategy parameterized with the location of WS replicas (e.g. the 6 Amazon WS locations over the World)
3) pre-defined CommunicationException and ServiceException.

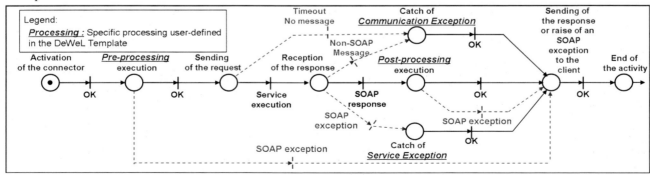

Figure 2. The linear execution model

The behavior of a connector at runtime correspond to several execution models, each of them corresponding to a user-selected recovery strategy. Execution models determine the scheduling of the different actions defined in the template.

When no recovery mechanism is used, the execution model is linear. Figure 2 illustrates this mode of operation: when the *pre-processing* does not complete correctly, it means that a user-defined runtime assertion has raised an exception that is directly returned to the client. Otherwise, the request is forwarded to the WS provider where it is processed. When the WS provider returns the response as a SOAP message, the *post-processing* is executed. If a communication or service exception is raised, the corresponding user-defined exception handling is performed before forwarding a SOAP exception to the client. Otherwise, the response is returned to the client.

This simple example is illustrative of the various execution models providing built-in recovery mechanisms and described in section 4.

2.3. Architectural support

The management and the execution of connectors rely on a specific platform that is a third-party infrastructure between clients and WS providers. The storage, look-up, delivery, loading, monitoring and execution of *Specific Fault Tolerance Connectors* are supported by IWSD (*Infrastructure for Web Services Dependability*). This framework provides fault tolerance support services to run connectors transparently.

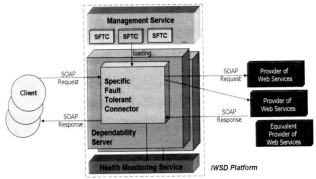

Figure 3. The IWSD platform

The IWSD platform presented in Figure 3 includes a major component, the **Dependability Server** that is responsible for loading connectors (request analysis, authentication, verification of permissions, etc.) and running them. This core component is a sort of connector virtual machine. The platform is responsible for the management of the available connectors and their connection between clients and WS providers

(*Management Service*). The **Heath Monitoring service** is another core member of the IWSD platform. It collects all error reports captured during the execution of connectors.

The IWSD platform must be highly dependable and conventional techniques, as in [6], can be used to this aim, this being out of the scope of this paper. Our implementation was based on a duplex HW & SW architecture for the experiments carried out.

3. Replication and equivalent services

The recovery mechanisms rely on service replicas available on the Net. Several replicas of a given Web Service can be found, for instance the Web Service of Amazon has 6 replicas (in the US, Japan, France, Canada, Germany and UK.). Finding identical replicas is not always possible. Nevertheless, similar services can be identified and used to perform recovery, or at least to provide a degraded mode of operation.

Clearly, Internet offers now new opportunities with respect to the redundancy of resources. Their identification and classification is the purpose of current research on Ontologies [7, 8]. The approach, called "Web Semantic" will be able to seek and to identify more easily identical or equivalent resources.

We thus consider two types of services that can be used to implement recovery mechanisms. First of all, **Identical services** correspond to a unique WSDL document, but the access point is different (e.g. replicas for Amazon). The fact that they derive from a unique WSDL does not mean that their implementation is identical. They just obey to the same input-output request format. Their implementation of the service can be different and, to some extent, help tolerating transient faults of the WS runtime support but also design faults of the WS. A simple switch to a different WS replica can be done in this case when one WS replica fails to deliver proper service.

More importantly we have to consider so-called **Equivalent Services**: the WSDL documents are different but can be considered as fulfilling a similar specification of the original service (a degraded version maybe). To take advantage of **Equivalent Services**, we introduce the notion of **Abstract Web Service (AWS)**.

3.1. Definition of Abstract Web Service

An **AWS** does not have any functional reality but it has an attached WSDL document; it is an abstraction of several similar services. The connector associated to an Abstract Web Service must convert so-called "**abstract requests**" to concrete requests and vice-versa regarding responses. The interface of each abstract operation is defined with two requirements in mind:

- minimizing the data required to call real services;
- maximizing the data obtained from real services.

To formally define the notion of **AWS** and create the corresponding connectors, some definitions and notations must be introduced first:

- *Concrete operation*: A concrete operation « *Op* » is a real WS operation in which a valid request « *Req* » is associated with a response « *Resp* ».
- *Interface of an operation:* The interface of an operation has a set of input/output parameters. The « *Input_Interface(Op)* » contains the input parameters, the « *Output_Interface(Op)* » contains the output parameters for the operation « *Op* ».

From the basic definitions given above, we can infer the notion of *"abstract operation"* that is the basis for defining abstract services. An abstract service is a collection of abstract operations. Then, specific translation functions are necessary to map abstract operations to concrete ones.

- *Abstract operation*: An abstract operation « *OpAbs* » is a virtual WS operation in which a valid abstract request « *ReqAbs* » is associated to a response « *RespAbs* » in a such a way that:
  - Any parameter of a concrete operation belonging to a target service replica can be obtained from an abstract request;
  - From all responses of concrete operations provided by replicas, all the parameters of the abstract response can be obtained.
- *Mapping function*: A mapping function translates a request targeting an abstract operation into a request targeting a concrete operation and vice-versa for responses. We denote by *ReqMap* a function that translates an abstract request into a concrete request, respectively *RespMap* translating a concrete response into an abstract response.

According to these definitions, any request to an abstract operation can be mapped to a concrete operation, and conversely a concrete response can be mapped to an abstract response.

The creation of an abstract operation depends on equivalence relations that can be found between operations and parameters of several similar real Web Services. The corresponding interfaces are generated from the equivalence relations.

3.2. Definition of equivalence relations

An equivalence relation $\mathcal{R}$ is a semantic relation between two sets of parameters. Although syntactically different, two parameters can represent the same information from a semantic viewpoint. Equivalence relations are established when the semantics of concrete parameters of operation *Op1* can be derived from concrete parameters of operation *Op2*. Figure 4 shows equivalence relations with an example. The three proposed concrete input interfaces enable a computer to be purchased online. Each one performs the selection with three different criteria.

- *service A* selects a computer with qualitative parameters such as, kind of computer (home computer, parallel computer, storage server,… etc), price range, size and type of the screen.
- *service B* performs the search only according to the computers brands (HP, Sony, Compaq,…etc.) and of the precise type of the computer.
- *service C* performs the search according to the composition of the computer, parts and basic devices that are included into the computer.

The minimal input interface of an abstract operation for the selection operation is composed of: (i) the brand, (ii) the type, (iii) the type of screen, and (iv) the identification (required for authentication). Indeed, it is possible to generate requests to all the concrete interfaces from these four parameters:

- the brand and the type of the computer can be directly used to call service B,
- the equivalence relations n°1, n°2 and n°4 can be used to generate the parameters for service A
- the equivalence relation n°3 can be used to generate the input data for service C.

In this example, the "identification" parameter of service A is said "private": this parameter cannot be reached by any equivalence relation, so it is de facto member of the input interface of the abstract operation.

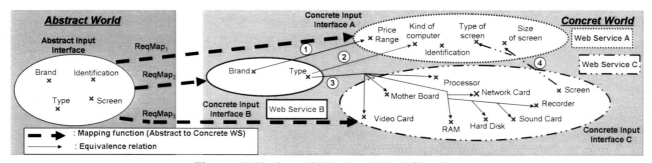

Figure 4. Notion of Abstract Web Service

3.3. Generation of Abstract Operations

The aim here is to automate the creation of the abstract operations (*Input_Interface (OpAbs)* and *Output_Interface(OpAbs)*) from equivalence relations defined by the user. During the definition of the abstract interfaces, it is important to avoid inconsistencies that can occur when an equivalence relation leads again to a parameter already obtained using a previous relation. To this aim, as soon as an equivalence relation generates a set of parameters, we avoid using other equivalence relations that generates a parameter belonging to this set.

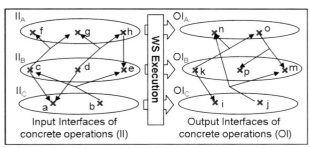

Figure 5. Example of 3 concrete operations

Figure 5 represents three input/output interfaces of concrete operations. The equivalence relations correspond to hyper-arcs between the various interfaces.

Let RootSet be the set of parameters that cannot be reached by any of the equivalence relations (i.e. RootSet = {b,d} in the example).

Let ResultSet be the set of parameters belonging to the Input Interface of an Abstract Web Service (AWS).

For any parameter **p** in the RootSet do:
1) initialise ResultSet with RootSet
2) with the equivalence relation starting from **p** do:

   a) compute the transitive closure, i.e. all parameters that can be reached with available relations, except those that lead to parameters already obtained

   b)The parameters that have not been reached are added to the ResultSet.

At the end of the loop, the ResultSet correspond to the parameters of the Input Interface of the AWS.

Figure 6. Algorithm for Abstract Interface generation

Given a set of equivalence relations, the algorithm given in Figure 6 enables a minimal input abstract interface to be obtained, from which several concrete

interfaces can be invoked. Depending on the order in which parameters are used in the RootSet, various ResultSet can be obtained. Several valid interfaces of an abstract operation can thus be obtained from a set of equivalence relations.

In the example of Figure 6, the ResultSet is initialized to {b,d}. Starting from {b}, parameters {c, e} can be reached, by transitivity from c, {f,g,a} can be reached. The two missing parameters are {d,h}. The relation from {d} that generates {h} cannot be used because it generates also {g} that is already in the ResultSet. No more relation can be used and thus, since {d} is already in the ResultSet, {h} is added to the ResultSet. The final set is thus {b,d,h} in this case.

The same algorithm starting from {d} in the RootSet leads to {b,d,f} as a ResultSet, thus to a second valid minimal input interface. All parameters required to call any concrete service operation can be obtained from these two sets, {b,d,f} and {b,d,h}.

Recent works have also addressed the matching between WS [9-11] by searching dynamically similarities or incompatibilities between WS operations. Such works can help the user finding equivalence relation between parameters and simplify the creation of abstract web service interfaces.

4. Recovery strategies

The recovery strategies are defined using the built-in functions, implementing both passive and active replication strategies for either stateless or stateful services. The section entitled *RecoveryStrategy* of the connector enables the user to select an appropriate replication strategy for a target service. Their selection depends first on the assumptions we can make on the service replicas (fail silent or not).

Passive Replication involves several possible strategies corresponding to the following built-in functions: BasicReplication, StateFulReplication, LogBasedReplication. In all cases, only one WS replica processes the input request. In case of errors detected by the parsers or by post-processing assertions, the request is forwarded to a spare replica that performs the operation. In this case, beyond the execution of assertions, the connector provides routing to a spare replica and failure detection (unreachable service because of node crash, service crash or hang). The main difference between these strategies relates to the way service state management is done for stateful Services, either triggering save/restore state operations provided by the WS, or using journals managed by the connector.

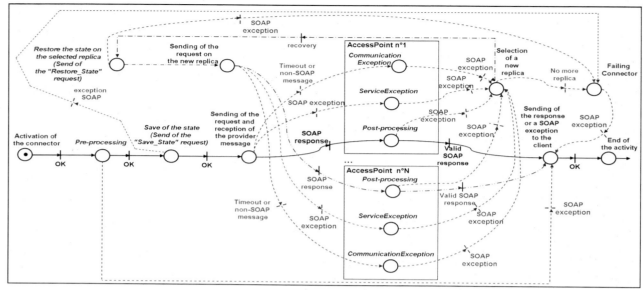

Figure 7. The execution model of the StatefulReplication

Regarding **Active Replication** strategies (ActiveReplication, VotingReplication), the connector multicasts the request to Web Service replicas (using appropriate protocols) when the pre-processing assertion is passed. Two configurations are available:

- *Without voting*: the connector receives the responses from the replicas, and sends to the client the first response that matches the post-processing assertion. This mechanism tolerates node crash, service crash or service hang. In practice, active replication has been used in our experiments with all registered Identical Service replicas of Amazon.
- *With voting*: the recovery mechanism with (majority) voting can tolerate value faults (data corruption). The connector receives responses from alive replicas and performs the vote using a library of voting algorithm variants (e.g. average, median).

These recovery strategies are just parameterized by the connector developer with the list of replicas as a first parameter, other parameters concerning timer values, decision functions, etc. New variants can also be derived from the existing ones (e.g. *Recovery Blocks, N-Version Programming,* etc).

Among the assumptions, the state management issue is of prime importance, and to some extent requires the collaboration of the WS provider. For some services, checkpointing core data is appropriate, in other cases the replay of input requests is a better way to reconstruct the state. Regarding the state handling issue, there is no generic solution that applies to all possible cases. In some cases even, a dedicated implementation to state management by the WS provider is recommended to be efficient.

4.1. Execution models for passive replication

The execution model for passive replication of stateless services is similar to the linear model presented previously. When is error detected by the post-processing within the connector, or when a service or communication exception is raised, a new WS replica is selected to process the request. The connector loops until a response is validated by the post-processing or until the failure of all replicas. In this case, an SOAP exception is sent back to the client.

For statefull operations/services, the execution model is different because state recovery operations made available by the WS provider must be triggered when a failure is detected by the connector. Before forwarding the request to another WS replica, the state of the WS replica is updated.

With the StatefulReplication execution model, the target Web Service must provide SaveState and RestoreState operations, i.e. belonging to the original version of the WSDL. This implies that such operations must be implemented by the WS provider. The WS provider is thus a partner to set up this particular recovery strategy. It is up to the WS provider to handle the complexity of that state that may depend on other WS, and that is by definition hidden to the customers, a connector in our case.

With the LogBasedReplication execution model, the connector provides StartSession and EndSession operation to trigger the logging of input requests to the target WS. When an error is detected by the connector, the log of requests is replayed with a new WS replica. The above mentioned operations (StartSession and

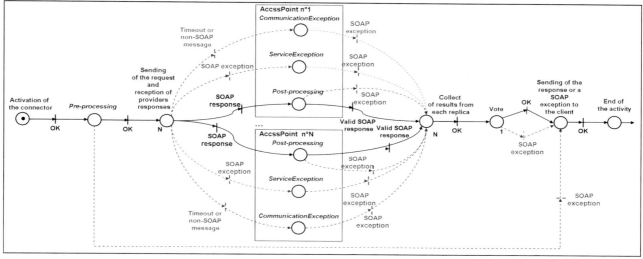

Figure 8. The execution model of the Voting Replication

EndSession) belong to the WSDL of the connector in this case and are triggered by the client.

Figure 7 shows the execution model for the StatefulReplication strategy where the state management operations appear. The state is saved before forwarding the request to a WS replica. When an error is detected by the post-processing, a new WS replica is selected and its state is updated. The execution model for LogBasedReplication is very similar and can easily be derived from this one: requests stored in the log are replayed to update the state of a replica.

4.2. Execution models for active replication

The execution model of the active replication for the stateless operations is as follows: the connector broadcasts the request to all replicas, and the first valid response passing the post-processing is returned to the client. The other valid responses are ignored. If all the replicas fail to produce a valid response, the connector returns a SOAP exception to the client.

For stateless services, it is not mandatory to ensure total ordering of the request messages to WS replicas. However, this is mandatory for stateful services and thus Atomic Multicast facilities must be used in this case to broadcast input requests to all replicas. Active replication strategies imply maintaining consistency of replicas in normal operation, the SOA context does not change anything to this fundamental problem.

With the *VotingReplication* (see Figure 8), the connector performs the vote out of all responses received before a deadline. The voting function can be parameterized by the user in the connector and automatically generated according to the types of the parameters in the response.

It is important to mention that *Abstract Web Service* requests received by the connector are translated into concrete requests before "sending the request" to a real replica. The same applies to responses.

For clarity reasons, the figures do show this and other aspects like creation and update of the list of the replicas, the sending of error messages to the *Health Monitoring* service or the detection of internal errors.

5. Implementation issues and experiments

The core software of this project represents about 55000 lines of code corresponding to the implementation of IWSD, including the DeWel compiler and companion tools. The IWSD platform has been installed on a rack of PCs running Linux Debian GNU/Linux with a Linux Kernel 2.4.

The experiments carried out provide first results to validate this approach and the tools chain. A real case study must be implemented in a near future to evaluate the scalability of the approach.

To perform the test of the five execution models, several connectors (compatible with SOAP 1.1 and 1.2 versions) have been developed for experiments (i) with existing identical WS replicas (e.g. Amazon replicas), (ii) and with abstract services (Google and MSN WS).

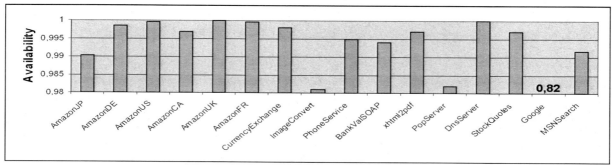

Figure 9. Availability of Web Services

5.1. Use of Monitoring Connectors

The availability of various Web Services was evaluated thanks to the error information collected by the connectors and reported to the *Health Monitoring* service. Some of the results obtained are given in Figure 9. Although the *Health Monitoring* service provides other types of information (like session time, numbers of requests, numbers of exceptions, etc.), we only report here the availability ratio of several Web Services. About 2000 requests were sent to each target service and we observed that the availability of the candidate services could vary a lot during the experiments. For instance, in our experiments, the Google WS has the lowest availability ratio (about 82%) caused by 352 communication errors over 1913 requests sent. Among these errors, 64 are due to a very long response time latency and 288 due to a server unavailability (HTTP Error codes 502: Bad Gateway).

5.2. Case study with Abstract Web Services

We have performed experiments to evaluate the feasibility and the usefulness of equivalent services, through the notion of Abstract Web Service. Since Google WS exhibited a weak availability ratio in previous experiments carried out, we have developed a connector able to map requests to similar "search" Web Services, namely Google WS and MSN WS (different WSDL documents). The results of this experiment are presented in Figure 10.

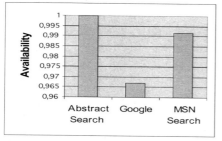

Figure 10. Active Replication with AWS

The target Abstract Web Service has a very high availability ratio with this connector. This availability level is reached thanks to the intrinsic availability of the MSN Web Service compared to the Google WS. In the experiments carried out with the basic passive replication strategy, the Google server was considered as a primary and MSN was a backup Web Service. We observed that 6% of the requests were redirected to the MSN server due to an unavailability of the Google server, this being totally transparent to the client.

Finaly, the mapping functions to convert an abstract request to a concrete request (and vice and versa for the responses) have been written in XSLT (*eXtended Stylesheet Language Transformations*) [12] using the user-defined equivalence relations.

5.3. Case study with Stateful Web Services

A simple e-business "banking service" was developed on purpose to perform experiments with stateful Web Services. In this case, our objective was two-fold: 1) testing of various execution models and 2) coarse evaluation of the response time overhead of several recovery strategies. To this aim, several connectors providing recovery mechanism for stateful services have been implemented and used with this banking application.

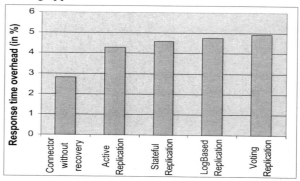

Figure 11. Comparison of recovery strategies

Figure 11 shows the average response time overhead of different connectors compared to a direct

58

WS clients/providers connection (i.e. without any connector). The response time overhead of a connector without recovery strategy (i.e. Monitoring Connector) is less than 3%. Interestingly, with connectors implementing recovery strategies for stateful services the overhead remain low, less than 5%.

The experiments run while enough replicas are still alive. Different failures can affect a WS: server crash, service crash, service hang, data corruption …etc. In this experiment, we consider only the service crash. We have used three WS replicas with different failure rate. Crash faults were injected at various frequencies, 25%, 33%, and 50% of the total number of requests processed in order to trigger the recovery procedure. An experiment stops when there is no more WS replica with the passive replication strategies and "Active Replication", or when there is less than two WS replicas with the "VotingReplication" strategy. The system is re-initialized at each experiment.

It is important to mention here that the results obtained depend on several factors such as: the type of the targeted service, size of the messages processed by the connector, the number of replicas used, the frequency of the failures, the size of the state transferred, the number of clients using simultaneously the same connector, …etc). For example, the size of state to transfer in this test case was about 50 Kbytes.

6. Discussion and Related work

Dependability is the major issue in the deployment of Service Oriented Architectures in critical domains [13]. The approach proposed in this paper enables making more reliable applications out of unreliable Web Service. It is complementary to other works because connectors are just Web Services providing additional fault tolerance features to the target WS. Their WSDL document is an extension of the original one, their implementation performing fault tolerance actions and delegating the functional aspects to the original WS. This approach provides separation of concerns, i. e. means to adapt the non-functional behavior of the target WS to application needs. Indirection is a conventional way to perform fault tolerance that is here adapted to the SOA context. A major contribution of this work is to consider connectors as real WS, enhanced with fault tolerance features. The handling of service state is strongly related to the implementation of the WS. As in previous works, serialization features (save and restore operations) must be provided by the target WS to perform state recovery. The LogBasedReplication approach is however a way to circumvent state issues for some services based on input requests journals managed transparently by the connectors. It is worth noting as well that many WS are stateless (Google and MSN, but any other search WS)

A lot of work is currently based on composition languages like BPEL to implement recovery [14, 15] and other standards (e.g. [16]). BPEL is currently a standard mean to perform orchestration and enable collaboration between services. This is not always easy because the developer doesn't know precisely the non-functional properties of the services included into the composition. Our work is complementary with this approach since it enables, through connectors, to use enhanced versions instead of unreliable services. Our connectors simplify the implementation and the maintenance of services composition in two ways:

- connectors can more easily detect services that do not match the expected behavior at runtime, thanks to the monitoring of Web Services;
- connectors can improve services composition giving to the user the opportunity to improve transparently the dependability of Web Services.

Improving the reliability of individual WS relies on implementing fault tolerance mechanisms on the server side. This is often done in an ad-hoc way, such as passive and active replication in FT-SOAP [17] and FTWeb [18], respectively. An active replication strategy with voting has also been implemented in Thema [19] and in [20]. In [20], the vote is achieved on the client side. In both cases, the state management is performed at the server side and thus WS replicas are developed by the same WS provider. A generic framework in Java was recently proposed to provide the provider with customizable primary/backup strategies for Web Service [21]. These solutions are essentially dedicated to the provider in order to improve the WS implementation. Our work differs from this approach as we do not focus on individual WS dependability. Based on existing WS, our approach enable external fault tolerance features to be developed to make the target WS more dependable, possibly using equivalent services. In addition, works like WS-Reliability [16] can be used in the IWSD platform to implement reliable communications between applications and connectors, between connectors and the WS replicas.

The approach concerning the equivalence of services is currently a first step, but seems promising. For stateful services, the management and the transfer of the WS state to an equivalent service is another important challenge to address. To this aim, a protocol such as WSRF (*Web Services Resource Framework*) [22] enables the state to be described as XML datasheets, and thus can simplify the implementation of save/restore operations.

7. Conclusion

The Service Oriented Architecture concept brings the notion of large-scale application to reality, but Internet as a backbone introduces multiple sources of faults by definition. The virtues of this approach are to make applications as dynamic as possible, by picking *Off-The-Net* the individual useful services. This novel situation must be taken into account as far as dependability is concerned, since more and more critical domains will interested by SOA. Traditional solutions to make individual WS platforms reliable are not sufficient. We need techniques to build reliable SOA out of unreliable Web Services.

The work proposed in this paper enables designer of application with SOA to improve the reliability of individual Web Services using WS connectors dedicated to fault tolerance. Connectors provide separation of concerns between clients (SOA developers) and WS providers. The WSDL of the connector can then be used instead of the original one.

Identical services can be found on the Web (i.e. developed from the same WSDL), but, more importantly, similar services exist. The WSDL document is different but the service semantics is similar. Abstract services can be used to take advantage of the Internet resources redundancy.

The various execution models proposed for fault tolerance connectors have been validated through several experiments with real Web Services (about 200). More work is of course needed with real SOA based applications, to improve the proposed approach, its tool chain and support infrastructure.

Acknowledgements: This work has been partially supported by ReSiST, Network of Excellence of the EC, *Resilience and Survivability in IST* (n°026764). The authors are also very grateful to the referees for their useful comments.

8. References

[1] C. Labovitz, G. R. Malan, and F. Jahanian, "Internet Routing Instability," ACM SIGCOMM, Computer Communication Review, 27(4), pp. 115-126, 1997.

[2] S. S. Yau and R. C. Cheung, "Design of Self-Checking Software," in Proc. of Int. Conf. on Reliable Software, Los Angeles, CA, USA, IEEE Computer Society Press., 1975.

[3] R. Allen and D. Garlan, "A Formal Basis for Architectural Connection," ACM Transactions on Software Engineering and Methodology, 1997.

[4] R. Chillarege, "Orthogonal Defect Classification ", E. M. R. L. Handbook of Software Reliability Engineering, McGraw-Hill, Ed., 1995.

[5] N. Salatge and J.-C. Fabre, "DeWeL: a language support for fault tolerance in service oriented architectures," International Workshop on Engineering of Fault Tolerant Systems (EFTS'2006), Luxembourg , June 2006.

[6] N. Aghdaie and Y. Tamir, "Client-Transparent Fault-Tolerant Web Service," 20th IEEE Int. Performance, Computing, & Communications Conf., pp. 209-216, 2001.

[7] D. L. McGuinness and F. v. Harmelen., "Web ontology language (OWL) overview," http://www.w3.org/TR/owl-features/, W3C Recommendation., February 2004.

[8] D. Martin, M. Burstein, O. Lassila, M. Paolucci, T. Payne, and S. McIlraith, "Describing Web Services using OWL-S and WSDL," October 2003.

[9] T. U. Xiang Gao, T. U. Jian Yang, and T. U. Mike. P. Papazoglou, "The Capability Matching of Web Services " IEEE 4th Inter. Symp. on Multimedia Software Engineering (MSE'02) p. 56, 2002.

[10] S. R. Ponnekanti and A. Fox, "Interoperability among independently evolving web services " In ACM/Usenix/IFIP Middleware'04, Toronto (Canada), pp. 331-351, Oct. 2004.

[11] J. Wu and Z. Wu, "Similarity-based Web Service Matchmaking," IEEE Int. Conf. on Services Computing (SCC'05), Vol-1, pp. 287-294, 2005.

[12] W. C. Recommendation, "XSL Transformations (XSLT)," 16 November 1999.

[13] F. Tartanoglu, V. Issarny, A. Romanovsky, and N. Levy, "Dependability in the Web Services Architecture," In Architecting Dependable Systems. LNCS 2677, June 2003.

[14] A. Gorbenko, V. Kharchenko, P. Popov, and A. Romanovsky, "Dependable Composite Web Services with Components Upgraded Online " in Architecting Dependable Systems ADS III, (R. de Lemos, C. Gacek, A.Romanovsky, Eds.), vol. LNCS 3549, pp. 96-128.

[15] L. Baresi and E. Quintarelli., "Towards Self-healing Compositions of Services " Proceedings of PRISE'04, First Conference on the PRInciples of Software Engineering, Buenos Aires, Argentina, pp. 11-20 November 2004.

[16] SUN, "Web Services Reliable Messaging TC WS-Reliability," http://www.oasis-open.org/committees/download.php/5155/WS-Reliability-2004-01-26.pdf, 2003.

[17] D. Liang, C.-L. Fang, and C. Chen, "FT-SOAP: A Fault-tolerant web service," Tenth Asia-Pacific Software Engineering Conference, Chiang Mai, Thailand, 2003.

[18] G. T. Santos, L. C. Lung, and C. Montez, "FTWeb: A Fault Tolerant Infrastructure for Web Services," In Proc. of EDOC'2005, the 9th Enterprise Computing Conference 2005.

[19] M. G. Merideth, A. Iyengar, T. Mikalsen, S. Tai, I. Rouvellou, and P. Narasimhan, "Thema: Byzantine-fault-tolerant middleware for Web-service applications", in Proc. of IEEE SRDS 2005, pp. 131 - 140, 2005.

[20] N. Looker, M. Munro, and J. Xu, "Increasing Web Service Dependability Through Consensus Voting", 2nd Int. Workshop on Quality Assurance and Testing of Web-Based Applications, COMPSAC, Edinburgh, Scotland, July, 2005.

[21] X. Zhang, M. Hiltunen, K. Marzullo, and R. Schlichting, "Customizable Service State Durability for Service Oriented Architectures " In Proceedings of the Sixth European Dependable Computing Conference, 2006.

[22] T. Banks, "Web Services Resource Framework (WSRF) – Primer v1.2," Committee Draft 02, OASIS, 23 May 2006.

Robustness and Security Hardening of COTS Software Libraries

Martin Süßkraut   Christof Fetzer

Department of Computer Science

Technische Universität Dresden, Germany

{martin.suesskraut,christof.fetzer}@tu-dresden.de

Abstract

COTS components, like software libraries, can be used to reduce the development effort. Unfortunately, many COTS components have been developed without a focus on robustness and security. We propose a novel approach to harden software libraries to improve their robustness and security. Our approach is automated, general and extensible and consists of the following stages. First, we use a static analysis to prepare and guide the following fault injection. In the dynamic analysis stage, fault injection experiments execute the library functions with both usual and extreme input values. The experiments are used to derive and verify one protection hypothesis per function (for instance, function `foo` *fails if argument 1 is a NULL pointer). In the hardening stage, a protection wrapper is generated from these hypothesis to reject unrobust input values of library functions. We evaluate our approach by hardening a library used by* Apache *(a web server).*

1 Introduction

When building dependable systems, one can rarely afford to built everything from scratch. This means that one needs to build systems using software components implemented by third parties. These software components might have been designed and implemented for less critical application domains. The use of such components without further hardening is therefore not recommended for dependable systems.

Third party software components are often provided in form of libraries. Experience with our previous library hardening tool [8] has shown that tools like HEALERS can help developers to harden libraries. The idea of HEALERS was to use automated fault injection experiments to determine automatically the *robust argument types* of functions. Any argument that does not belong to the given robust argument type will result in a crash of the function. The robust argument types were computed from a fixed hierarchy of robust argument types. For example, HEALERS was able to automatically determine that the C function `strcpy(d,s)` requires s to be a string and d a writable buffer with a length of at least `strlen(s)+1` bytes.

Our experience with HEALERS showed however deficiencies regarding (1) the extensibility and (2) the performance of the tool. These deficiencies need to be addressed to make such hardening tools more widely applicable. Our new tool addresses these issues by facilitating

- Extensible fault injections: new test case generators can be added, e.g., to test new handle types more carefully.
- Extensible run-time checking: new checks for arguments can easily be added.
- Flexible computation of robust argument types: these are computed without a given type hierarchy and are automatically extended for new run-time checks.
- Performance: the use of static analysis can reduce the number of fault injections dramatically.

The paper is structured as follows. Section 2 gives an overview on our approach. Our extensible test type system is described in Section 3 together with our proposal to reduce the number of fault injections. In Section 4 we present our run-time checks before we discuss how the protection wrapper is generated in Section 5. In Section 6 we show that we can prevent more than 56 % of injected faults from becoming visible as crash failures. We conclude discussion of the related work in Section 7.

2 Approach

Our goal is to automatically increase the robustness and security of applications. To be applicable for users without expert knowledge, we want to minimize the required user input. However, most programmers will want to have control over the generation of protection wrappers. Hence, we permit programmers to verify and modify the robust argument types that our tool system derives. The tool also provides programmers with evidence (in form of truth tables)

61

Figure 1. Workflow of our tool.

input vectors	$check_1$	$check_2$	...	$check_n$	robust?
test case$_1$	0	1	...	0	1
test case$_2$	0	0	...	0	0
test case$_3$	0	1	...	0	0
...	...	...		...	...
test case$_m$	1	0	...	1	0

Figure 2. Table base approach to generate robustness and security checks.

$check_1$	$check_2$	robust?
0	0	0
1	0	0
1	0	0
1	1	1

$check_1 = \texttt{string?(src)}$
$check_2 = \texttt{buf\_write?(dest, strlen(src) + 1)}$

Table 1. Part of truth table for function `strcpy(char* dest, const char* src)`.

about why it derived certain robust argument types and that these are reasonable for the wrapped application.

To improve the applicability of our approach, we do not want to require access to the source code of the applications and libraries that need to be hardened. Source code might not always be available and dealing with source code that was written for different compilers and even for different programming languages is very difficult and time consuming to get right (e.g., see [5]). Using only fault-injections has the potential disadvantage of huge run-time costs (see Section 6). Since intermediate languages like MSIL [2] and LLVM [12] become more widespread, we instead assume that we have access to the bytecode of libraries and applications.

In this paper we focus on the interface between an application and its dynamic linked libraries. Our approach protects the application's libraries from unrobust and insecure input. Figure 1 illustrates the workflow of our approach. In the analysis stage, an application's libraries are first statically analyzed to reduce the number of test inputs used during the dynamic analysis phase. In the following dynamic analysis phase, the libraries functions are exercised by fault injection. Based on the observed behavior of the libraries, *protection hypotheses* are generated. A hypothesis is a boolean expression over predicates on the arguments to a function. We refer to these predicates as *checks*. In the second stage, a protection wrapper is generated. Its job is to protect the library functions at run-time from being called with unrobust or insecure argument values. Therefore, it intercepts all function calls from the application into its libraries. The protection wrapper only forwards the current argument values to the wrapped library function, if they satisfy the protection hypotheses.

The main two contributions of this paper are a new flexible fault injection tool (*Autocannon*) and a table-based approach to generate the protection hypotheses for the protec-

tion wrapper. Autocannon makes use of static analysis to perform fault injection on arbitrary functions. For each library function, a table like the one in Figure 2 is built in the analysis stage. One row represents one fault injection experiment with the function. The input vectors (gray) are not part of the truth table. They only denote where the rows come from. All test values used in the analysis stage are classified by *boolean checks*. The right most column contains the boolean result of the call: either robust or unrobust. A functions execution is robust, if the function does not crash (e.g., by a segmentation fault). We show in Section 3.3 how to create test values in a way that security violations (like buffer overflows) are converted into robustness issues. We view this truth table as a boolean function $f(check_1, \ldots, check_n)$. A truth table minimizer computes a boolean expression of f. This boolean expression is a *protection hypothesis*. It takes the role of the HEALERS robust argument types but it is much more flexible because it is an arbitrary boolean expression over a set of given checks.

Table 1 sketches the truth table for the Standard C function `strcpy`. The truth table is first preprocessed before minimizing it (e.g., removing redundant row 3). Check $check_1$ is true if argument `src` points to a string, $check_2$ is true, if the first `strlen(src) + 1` byte of the buffer pointed by `dest` are writeable. The resulting protection hypothesis is: `string?(src)` AND `buf_write?(dest, strlen(src) + 1)`. The protection wrapper will reject all inputs for which the protection hypothesis does not evaluate to true.

The protection wrapper prevents calling a function f with unsafe arguments. Therefore, it evaluates the protection hypothesis of f on the current argument values given by the caller of f. Only if the evaluation yields *true*, the control is passed to f. Otherwise the wrapper returns with an error code without executing f.

In order to use our approach, some knowledge about the library functions used by an application is needed: we need at least the return type and the types of the arguments of a function to perform a dynamic analysis. Depending on the target platform, this information might already be included within the library (e.g., library given in LLVM bytecode).

Otherwise, some other form of specification (like C header files) is needed. In the following we will refer with *public source* to files that contain that information. Note even if this is part of the source code of the library, it must be available at least for developers using the library. Whereas *private source* is the source code of the library implementation, which is typically not available to all users.

Even though our approach is independent from the programming language and platform of a library, we will focus in the following on libraries implemented in the programming language C.

3   Test Values

Test values are used in the analysis phase as input values for performing fault injection experiments with the libraries functions. For each of a function's arguments a set of test values is generated. The set of input vectors is the cross product of all test value sets. These test value sets must be large enough to exercise the function under analysis in a way that the resulting truth table is sufficiently complete. Of course, executing the function on all possible input values is in general infeasible, e.g., a function with two 32-bit arguments has more than $1.8 \cdot 10^{19}$ possible input vectors.

We tackle that issue but providing an extensible test type system. Each argument type of a function is mapped to a *test type*. The set of test values for an argument is the union of the representatives of the test types of this argument. The test type system is richer than the argument type system in the sense that it has more semantics. For instance, the C type `char*` can be a pointer, a string, a filename or a format string depending on its usage. Generic pointers, strings, filenames and format strings are test types. Some test types contain other test types (e.g., filenames and format string are also plain strings, which itself are pointers). We call file names and format strings *special test types*. In general, special test types have a very clear semantics. They often contain other more generic types with more vague semantics.

Our test type system is based on Ballista's test type system [10, 11]. Ballista is a dependability benchmark for POSIX implementations. Ballista's test type system can handle a predefined fixed set of argument types and functions. In order to test arbitrary libraries, we extended it to handle arbitrary argument types. We call this new test system *Autocannon*. It uses argument type characteristics to determine the test type for an argument type (e.g., its size, if an argument type is a pointer or if it can be casted to an integer). The argument type characteristics are extracted using static analysis on the public sources (e.g., C header files or bytecode).

We introduce meta types, type templates, and feedback into Autocannon. A *meta type* combines a set of Ballista's

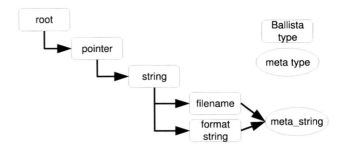

Figure 3. A part of Ballista's test type system with a meta type.

specialized type into one general type. A specialized test type implements applications semantics. For instance, a test type that represents pointers to a time data structure `time_t*` is a specialized test type. We do not want to rely in Ballista's specialized types only. That's why we introduce *type templates* to generate specialized test types from type characteristics. We use them to generate test types for handles of abstract data types and for data structures. Autocannon is able to give feedback to test types to refine their test values. We use this to detect conditions for buffer overruns.

In the first part of this section we briefly introduce Ballista's test type system before we present Autocannons improvements: meta types, feedback, and type templates. The second part explains the mapping from argument types to test types, and how we deal we large set of input vectors.

3.1   Ballista Type System

Ballista is a test system for measuring the dependability of POSIX implementations. It contains a flexible test type system that we have extended for our needs. Ballista's test type system is extensible: one can easily add new test types to it. All test types are arranged in one type tree. Part of this tree is shown in Figure 3. The root is the most general type, the leafs are the most special ones. A child type is also a parent type (e.g., a filename is also a string, which itself is also a pointer). Each type has a set of representatives or *test values*. The root's set of test values is empty.

A child type inherits all type values of its parent. For instance, a function expecting a file name, is also tested with plain strings values and general pointer values. But a function whose argument is mapped to the plain string type is not tested with filenames and format strings.

To test a function with usual and exceptional values a Ballista type has more than one representatives. For example, the Ballista type for filenames has 432 representatives that result of all possible combinations for the content (empty, non-empty), the file permissions (readable, writeable, etc.), the file state (existing, non-existing, directory, etc.) and the filename (local, temporary, with spaces, etc.).

3.2 Meta Types

The mapping between test types and argument types is predefined within Ballista. It is done by an expert knowing the functions specification. In order to test arbitrary libraries, our system works without such a predefined mapping. In Autocannon, we introduced meta types to combine specialized Ballista types into more general types. A meta type has more than one parent. So our type system is a directed acyclic graph instead of a tree. For simplicity, meta test types do not contribute test values. They join the test values of their parents.

The test values of meta type meta_string in Figure 3 are the union of the test values of Ballista's test types filename, format string, string, and pointer. Because we do not know the specification of a function foo(char*), we map an argument type char* to meta_string. So foo will be tested with filenames, format strings and its parents test values.

We have defined 4 generic meta types. *Meta string* combines all special string types. *Meta pointer* combines all specialized pointer types including meta string. *Meta integer* and *meta short* combine all integer types with width 32 bit and 16 bits, respectively. More meta types are generated to combine generated types (like instantiated type templates) with Ballista types or predefined meta types.

3.3 Feedback

Autocannon uses *feedback* to detect conditions for buffer overruns. This feedback loop is originally a part of HEALERS [7]. Feedback is used to convert buffer overruns into robustness issues. Therefore, the test system gives feedback back to certain test types, so that they can refine their test values. A feedback test type generates a buffer that is enclosed with unaccessible memory pages. If the testing function overruns this given buffer, the OS will raise a segmentation fault exception. The test system catches this exception and asks the test type, if the bad memory access occurred within the enclosing memory pages. If this is the case, the test type enlarges the buffer and the test is redone. Figure 4 illustrates the feedback loop. The feedback cycle goes on until either the function executes without a segmentation fault or the test type is unable to allocate more memory.

The test system itself does not detect the conditions for buffer overruns. This is done by the checks. Let us illustrate this with function strcpy(char* dest, const char *src). The test system tests strcpy with a string (src) provided by Ballista's string test type and a read/write buffer of size 1 byte (dest) provided by Autocannon's feedback test

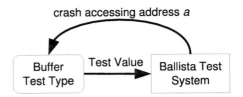

Figure 4. Feedback loop: The test system uses the addresses of illegal memory accesses to refine test values.

type. Function strcpy will overrun dest and cause a segmentation fault if the length of src's string is larger than 1 byte. Successively, the feedback type will enlarge dest's buffer until its size equals src's string length + 1. The check correlate the buffer's size and the string's length so that the hypothesis sizeof (dest) > strlen (src) will be finally extracted.

We have added a test type to Autocannon that (1) accepts and responds to feedback and (2) generates different representatives: buffers of different size (1 byte, 4 kbytes, 64 kbytes), content and protection (read only, read/write). Beside this one feedback test type, templates are used to generate special feedback test types for data structures.

3.4 Type Templates

We use type templates to generate specialized test types for arbitrary argument types. Type templates are parameterized test types. Currently, we have two kinds of type templates: one for Abstract Data Types and one for data structures. The data structure type gives feedback back to the testing environment (see Section 3.3).

Abstract Data Types Abstract Data Types (ADT) are often implemented by a set of functions operating on some hidden state. This hidden state, the instance of the ADT, is referenced by a handle. Examples for such handles are file descriptor handles, socket handles, or a handle to a random number generator.

The Ballista type system already includes a set of test types generating handle values. But this handles refer all to ADT implemented by the POSIX API. To test libraries implementing arbitrary APIs, we generate a test type for each kind of handle we identified. In this way, functions expecting handles values are not only tested with extreme values, but also with input values that might appear in a non-faulty execution.

For generating a test type of an ADT, we need a set of constructor functions that create handles to this ADT instance. Currently, we detect handles by static analysis applied on the public source code of a library. Our static analysis uses some simple heuristics like the ones used in [6].

For the future, we plan to combine it with dynamic analysis like temporal specification mining [18].

We assume that each ADT has a handle with a unique C type. First, we extract all signatures of the functions implemented by a library using Doxygen [17]. Our heuristic is that we examine only functions that fulfill our naming convention as potential constructors and destructors. Our naming convention for constructors is, that a function name must contain `alloc`, `create`, `new` or `open`. For destructors we require function names containing `close`, `destroy`, `delete` or `free`. A constructor passes a handle to its caller as return value or via call-by-reference. We treat every C type that has at least one constructor and exactly one destructor as handle.

For example, for the ADT `socket` we have extracted the handle type `apr_socket_t*` for the `libapr` [1]. It has two constructors:

```
apr_status_t apr_socket_create_ex(apr_socket_t**,
     int, int, int, apr_pool_t*)
apr_status_t apr_socket_create(apr_socket_t**,
     int, int, apr_pool_t*)
```

Both constructors return the handles by reference. We have found 44 functions (including the destructor) that have a argument of type `apr_socket_t*`.

Beside the constructors, we need input vectors to call them for creating handle values. Therefore, we do look into the truth tables used to compute the protection hypotheses of the constructors. We extract all input vectors for which the constructor function did not crash. These input vectors are inserted into the type template to call the constructors.

Data Structures The data structure template complements the feedback giving test types. Data structures (in C defined by keyword `struct`) have a fixed size. Additionally to starting the feedback cycle for pointers to data structures with 1 byte, we use the size of the data structure for it. So the size of a data structure `s` is put into the data structure template to generate an adapted feedback test type for `s*`.

3.5 Type Characteristics

Autocannon uses static analysis on public source code to extract the type characteristics of a function's argument types. With the help of this characteristics it maps argument types to Autocannon's test types. The type characteristics are:

pointer? True, if the argument type is a pointer value.
sizeof Size of the argument type in bytes.
converts_to_int? True, if argument type can be interpreted as an integer.
signed? True, if argument type is signed.

content_size Size of the dereferenced type in bytes (for pointers, only).
ishandle? True, if at least one constructor function and exactly one destructor function for this type exist.

Pointers to bytes are treated as strings. They are mapped to the `meta_string` type. For other pointers, a data structure type template is instantiated and with the help of a generated meta type combined with `meta_pointer`. Otherwise, it is mapped to one of Ballista's integer types depending on its size and if it is signed. An exception are signed types of size 2 and 4 they are assigned `meta_short` and `meta_integer`, respectively. If the argument type is a handle, the handle type template is instantiated and combined with its test type computed so far.

3.6 Reducing the Number of Test Cases

Ballista's test types produce up to 1000 test values (including parents). The average is however much lower. Both the size of the set of input vector and hence, the number of test cases increases exponentially with the number of function arguments. Therefore, it might be infeasible to test all input vectors for functions with a larger number of arguments. Ballista introduced an upper bound u on the number of tested input vectors. If the set of input vectors is larger than u, an uniform distributed sample set of the input vectors of size u is computed.

Another way to reduce the size of the set of input vectors, is to exclude special types from the generic meta types that will not contribute to the results. For instance, a function operating on strings but not on files does not need to be tested on file names. We perform static analysis using the Low Level Virtual Machine (LLVM) [12] to determine which special test types can safely be removed. The LLVM byte code of the library might be provided by its vendor (if the library should run on LLVM) or can be compiled from the libraries private source code.

As mentioned above, Ballista contains a predefined mapping from POSIX functions to their specialized Ballista test types. Our assumption is that we do not need to test a function f on special test types designed for a POSIX function, if this POSIX function is not called by f. But if a function f calls some POSIX functions, we test f with the special test types of this POSIX functions because f might pass some argument values directly to this POSIX functions. Of course, this assumption is not restricted to POSIX functions. As long as a mapping exists from functions to their the special test types exclusively provided for this functions.

For each function to test, we compute the transitive set of called POSIX functions. To simplify our analysis, we exclude a function from the reduction process, if it might perform indirect calls using function pointers. The set of called functions is compared with the list of POSIX functions specified by Ballista. We only include special test types in meta types that are related to the POSIX functions called by the analysed function. To return to the previous example: a function `f(char*)` that transitively calls no other function than `printf` is not tested on file names because `printf` expects only format strings. To avoid to exclude exceptional values, we only exclude types that are leafs in Ballista's type tree. Therefore, `f` is also tested on plain string and pointer values.

3.7 Other Sources of Test Values

The truth table might be extended by other inputs. One can do other kinds of fault injection, like we do for our evaluation in Section 6. An additional source are traces from runs of some application utilizing the library to protect. The advantage of these traces is that they contain (mostly) input vectors for which the library function behaves robustly. The disadvantage is that one has to set up the application to do the tracing.

Currently, we do not use this additional source of test values to keep the implementation effort to a reasonable level. However, we use bit flips and application traces for evaluating the generated hypotheses (see Section 6). It would be reasonable to use these techniques to help in the generation of the hypotheses but then our evaluation might be less meaningful.

4 Checks

Checks are used in the analysis stage to build up the truth table for the protection hypothesis. Because they become part of the protection hypothesis, they are also used at run-time in the wrapper to check the current input vector. A check is a predicate over one or more argument values. For instance, for function `foo(void* p)`, the check `null?(p)` computes whether `p` is or is not a NULL pointer. This example illustrates that checks must be instantiated with specific arguments of a function.

Checks and test values are not coupled. In this way, our approach is easily extensible. One does not need to consider the test type system when adding new checks and vice versa. Checks may employ more than one argument of a function. Checks employing only one argument are called *basic checks* all other checks are *compound checks*. We have a set of check templates that are instantiated depending on the type characteristics of the functions arguments. Some check templates are additionally parameterized. We remove checks that never apply from the truth table to keep it as small as possible.

All checks are tested on the input vector directly before testing the function. It introduces an additional testing over-head (e.g., one could at least apply all basic checks offline and use the stored results). The reason is that checks have to be independent of the test values to facilitate the extensibility. For example, one can in this way add new test cases that might satisfy checks that one has not been aware of. Beside that, it would be difficult to apply compound checks offline. This makes the online evaluation very convenient because Autocannon might generate new test types depending on it's static analysis.

4.1 Check Templates

Our current implementation includes a set of predefined check templates. (We use "check" to refer to check template whenever it is obvious that we refer to a check template). These checks test general properties of the argument values independent of the concrete function's argument types. We start with presenting the basic checks before discussing our compound checks.

Basic Checks A Pointer is checked if it is NULL, or if it points to a string, to a readable or read- and writeable buffer. It is also checked if it points to somewhere on the stack or on the heap and if it points to a start of a dynamically allocated chunk of memory. Integer values are checked if they are zero, positive or negative. Strings are checked if they are filenames, directory names or format strings (containing `"%n"`).

Compound Checks Compound checks test the relations between more than one argument value. The `strcpy` example in Section 2 contains the compound check `buf_write?(dest, strlen(src) + 1)`. It relates the size of a buffer (pointed to by `dest`) and the length of string (`src`). All relations that are checks are derived from existing function specifications (e.g., the C standard library).

Our current compound checks relate the size of buffers (pointer arguments) to other function arguments. It is checked, if a buffers has at least the size of another string argument or an integer value. Additionally, the product of two integer arguments, the sum of two string lengths and the sum of a string length and an integer are compared to the buffer size.

4.2 Parameterized Check Templates

Like type templates are used for generating specialized test values, we need specialized checks for testing these test values. Parameterized check templates are checks used to test properties that cannot be predefined because the properties depend on the function argument types or the functions semantic.

All parameterized checks but one get their parameters from static analysis. The one exception depends on the function's semantics. It checks if a given buffer is at least as large as the smallest buffer for which the function did not crash in the Autocannon experiments. The other checks are: (1) if the buffer pointed to by a pointer is at least as large as the data structure of the corresponding argument type. (2) If an argument type is an `enum`, the `enum` values are extracted from the public sources. It is tested, if an argument value is within the set of `enum` values.

The counterpart of the ADT test types, are ADT checks. Each execution of a constructor function is intercepted. After running the original function, the returned handle value is put into a set. Each ADT has its own set. Every destructor execution is also intercepted and the passed handle value is removed from the handle set. The check for handle queries the corresponding handle set. If the value is in it, it evaluates to true, otherwise to false.

5 Protection Hypotheses

The analysis stage yields a protection hypothesis per library function. A protection hypothesis of a library function f is a function from the set of input vectors of f to $\{true, false\}$. If it evaluates to $true$, the given input vector is considered to be *safe*. An input vector is safe, if the library function evaluated on it will behave robust and secure. To enforce that a library function is only executed on safe input vectors, a protection wrapper is generated.

The protection wrapper is inserted between an application and its dynamic linked libraries. Our current implementation achieves this by utilizing the pre-loading feature of the dynamic linker [4]. The wrapper could also be inserted by instrumenting the libraries or the application.

The first part of this section shows how to derive protection hypotheses and the second part discusses possible failures of the protection wrapper. There are two kinds: (1) a hypothesis that rejects a "safe" input vector is a *false positive* and (2) a hypothesis that accepts an "unsafe" input vector is a *false negative*.

5.1 Minimizing Truth Table

The protection hypothesis for a function f is derived from the truth table built while testing f. The truth table is not yet a boolean function. It might contain redundant and contradicting rows. Also some rows might be missing. A row r is redundant if there is another row p with $p = r$. Redundant rows are the result of input vectors that are indistinguishable from each other by our checks and the functions behavior is the same for both input vectors. Contradicting rows are rows that are classified equally by the checks but for which the function behaves differently (i.e.,

one crashes the other does not). They indicate that the set of checks is too small. Hence, this can be countered by adding new checks. Note however that removing input vectors from testing reduces the probability to find contractions too. Additionally, some rows might be missing because of the sampling and because the test types might not exercise all checks equally.

In our current implementation, we drop redundant rows before passing them to the minimizer. For contradicting rows, a warning is logged and only the row for which the function behaved robustly is passed to the minimizer. This prevents the protection wrapper from producing a false positive because input vectors classified like this contradicting row are forwarded to the original function. On the other hand, it introduces the possibility of false negatives. That is why a protection hypothesis generated from a truth table containing contradictions might not prevent all crashes or buffer overruns. It is not known whether the missing rows behave robustly or not. To minimize false positives, we treat all missing rows as robust. But this might increase the number of false negatives. Some minimization strategies for truth tables trade correctness for small expressions and computation overhead of the minimization problem. We require a hypothesis that describes the truth table exactly. But we do not need necessarily a minimal expression but one that prevents crashes.

5.2 Discussion

Another source of false negatives and false positives is if one tests too few input vectors. Simply adding new test types may not help: the resulting set of input vectors might become too large to test it within a feasible time. Counter-intuitively, we have found that reducing the set of input vectors is a good approach if the set of input vectors is too large. It increases the coverage of the tested sample of input vectors. Of course, the deduction algorithm should only remove input vectors that do not contribute to the protection hypothesis (see Section 3.6).

If the protection wrapper evaluates a protection hypothesis on an input vector to false, the original function is not called. Instead the wrapper passes the control back to the caller. Therefore, a value has to be returned. Our current implementation returns a predefined error value depending on the return type of the wrapped function [14]. We are also exploring an approach to learn error return values of library functions [16].

Because our approach does not guarantee the absence of false positives, we discuss how to handle them. Note that in case that a protection hypotheses is evaluated to false, the protection wrapper returns an error code instead of calling the library function. First, if the application is robust enough, it might perform some graceful degradation in the presence of a false positive. Second, if an applications performs retries of failed library calls and we are mainly worried about transient errors, we could use a similar approach as [13]: on re-execution of a failed function, we could allow its execution and if it passes, we white list arguments with the same check vector.

The false positives are a sign that we do not have enough checks to distinguish between unrobust and robust input vectors. But our approach allows us to add more checks in future without any redesign. The false negative rate might also benefit from new checks. For the same reason it is useful to add more test types. But as long as a function is only tested on a small sample of all test types we need better strategies to choose the "right" input vectors for fault injection.

6 Evaluation

We have evaluated our approach by hardening the Apache Portable Runtime library (APR) [1]. Among the applications that use this library is the web server Apache. We have tested our protection wrapper for the APR by executing it with Apache. To reduce the overhead, we only have hardened functions that are called by our executions of Apache. These are 148 APR functions including some without arguments. Our test system, Autocannon, was able to perform about 1000 tests per minute on our computers. Because functions can be tested independently from each other, it is possible to parallelize the analysis stage. We have done all experiments on two virtual machines with the same configuration (running on an Athlon 64 3200+ with 1 GByte of RAM and a Intel Core Duo with 2 GBytes of RAM, respectively, both with Ubuntu 6.06).

First, we discuss the results of Autocannon's fault injection tests. We will focus on test coverage and the results of the dependability benchmark. To check the correctness of hypotheses, we did macro and micro benchmarks. The latter one uses bit-flips to perform fault injections.

Some of the hardened functions have more than 3 arguments. Because the set of input vectors grows exponentially with the number of arguments, such functions can only be dynamically analyzed to a very small extent. We tested all functions on at most $10,000$ test cases and less if the set of input vectors was smaller. This number of test cases was chosen to perform our evaluation in a feasible time. In Figure 5 we depict the coverage for four different test configurations. We tested the combinations with and without test types for handles and with and without reduction of test types by excluding special test types via static analysis. The functions are grouped into 15 coverage classes. The coverage of a function is the number of tested input vectors over the size of the set of all input vector of the test system for this functions. The class of a function f is derived from the

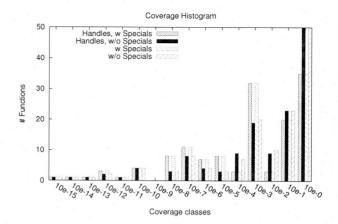

Figure 5. The coverage of executed test cases compared to the set of input vectors in different test configurations.

Test config	Avg. Cov.	Avg. Incomplete Cov.
w/o Sp.	$4.422906 \cdot 10^{-01}$	$7.086199 \cdot 10^{-02}$
Han., w Sp.	$2.763518 \cdot 10^{-01}$	$2.272866 \cdot 10^{-02}$
Han., w/o Sp.	$4.389137 \cdot 10^{-01}$	$6.748508 \cdot 10^{-02}$
w Sp.	$2.763809 \cdot 10^{-01}$	$2.275769 \cdot 10^{-02}$

Table 2. The average coverage per test configuration. *Avg. Incomplete Coverage* **is the average coverage over all functions that have a coverage** < 1.

order of magnitude of f's test coverage. The Y-axis depicts the number of functions per class.

The handle test types have no visible impact. But the average coverage of the two test configurations with handles differs slightly from the average coverage for test configurations without handles as shown in table 2. The impact of excluding some test cases via static analysis is visible. In the two configurations where special test cases are excluded, more functions have a coverage with a lower order of magnitude than in the configurations where all special test cases are included. Some functions do not benefit from this exclusion because they perform indirect function calls via function pointers. These functions were excluded from the static analysis. For 76 of the 148 functions the number of test cases could be reduced.

Autocannon is not only useful to generate protection hypotheses. It is a flexible dependability benchmark for arbitrary C libraries. Figure 6 gives a summary of the benchmark results for the APR. It only covers the functions that we have tested. More than half of the test cases resulted in robust behavior. The gap between the number of robust and unrobust test cases is about $70,000$. Figure 7 shows how the robustness is distributed over the tested functions. The majority of the functions is split in two sets: 67 functions

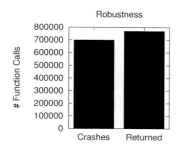

Figure 6. Comparing number of crashed and robust test cases.

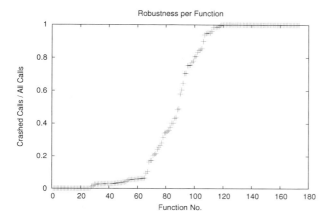

Figure 7. Variation in percentage of unrobust test cases per function.

crashed in at least 90% of the test cases and 66 functions crashed in at most 10% of the test cases. In between are 40 functions. Functions without arguments were not tested.

To evaluate the correctness of the protection hypotheses, we first executed Apache with the protection wrapper and logged all failed hypotheses. We assume that Apache does call all APR functions with valid arguments as long as no faults are injected by a third party. Even though it is possible, we did not manually correct any protection hypotheses. We generated two wrappers: W was generated from fault injection experiments with lower test coverage and W_{SA} was generated from fault injection experiments with higher test coverage using static analysis. We switched the handle test types on for both wrappers. The results are shown in the first two data rows of Table 3. W produced no false positives. W_{SA} had 10 functions leading to false positives (6.17 % of all function calls). 3 of these functions were also wrapped by W.

Additionally, we implemented a micro benchmark with fault injection to test our protection in the presence of failures. Therefore, we run Apache with our protection wrap-

	with Specials	without Specials
# Hypotheses	77	95
FP normal Run	0%	6.17%
Predicted Crashes Microbench.	56.81%	51.39%
FP Microbench.	1.7% (17)	0.6% (6)

Table 3. Correctness of our Approach

per. We injected probabilistically bit-flips [9] into argument values of protected functions. Whenever a bit-flip was injected when calling a function f, we compared the result of f's hypothesis and the behavior of executing f. Not all bit-flips resulted in a crash of f. Apache was restarted after the bit-flip to prevent further propagation of the fault. The results show a trade-off between W and W_{SA} (see Table 3). W predicted more crashes than W_{SA} but it also had more false positives.

7 Related Work

In this paper, we combine dependability benchmarking [10, 11] and automatic patch generation [8, 15, 14]. With HEALERS [8] the second author already presented a general approach to harden COTS libraries. But HEALERS contains an inflexible type system that couples test types and checks: that makes it very difficult to extend. The mapping from argument types to test types is done via a predefined map. Therefore, HEALERS was only able to test 4 functions of the APR. All other functions contained unknown argument types. HEALERS cannot tolerate contradictions. All of these 4 functions produced a contradiction. So HEALERS was unable to generate any protection hypothesis for the APR.

A previous AutoPatch paper [15] presents an approach to patch bad error handling. Our current work might introduce unexpected error values when a hypothesis is evaluated to false. The application might not be able to deal with this unexpected errors and might itself behave unrobust or insecure. One can apply the bad error handling patching to counter this problem.

Stelios et. al. introduced an approach to automatically patch buffer overrun bugs in applications. They also evaluated their approach with Apache. But because they fix bugs *within* the application and not at the interface to dynamic libraries, their approach is not quantitative comparable to ours. The approach needs some code that exploits the bug to patch, for instance a zero-day exploit. The patch is based in source code transformation. In contrast to this, we are able to detect bugs and patch without any exploiting code as input.

Our current work is based partly on Ballista [10, 11], a dependability benchmark for POSIX implementations. We have already presented in detail how we extended Ballista to our test system Autocannon. The biggest difference is, that Ballista is bound to a specific API while Autocannon is more general and can test arbitrary APIs.

We also contribute to improving the availability. An unrobust system has a lower availability than a robust system in an adverse environment. By increasing the robustness we increase the mean-time-to-failure. This is orthogonal to increasing the mean-time-to-repair, for instance with microreboots [3]. Both approaches can by used together to increase availability.

8 Conclusion

We have presented a flexible approach to hardening arbitrary libraries for robustness and security. Our contributions are: (1) a new dependability benchmark that can measure the robustness of arbitrary library utilizing static analysis and (2) a table based approach to derive protection hypotheses from the benchmark's results. This is done by classifying the benchmark's test data by checks. The difference to previous work is that our approach is easily extensible. One can add new checks and test types for the dependability benchmarks as needed.

Our protection hypotheses were able to predict up to 56.85 % of crashes in our evaluation. The drawback is that our hypotheses misclassify a low number of robust argument values as unrobust. But we believe that we can overcome this issue by adding more appropriate checks and test types.

Acknowledgements We would like to thank Martin Kretzschmar for introducing us to LLVM.

References

[1] Apache Software Foundation. Apache portable runtime project. http://apr.apache.org.

[2] D. Box and C. Sells. *Essential . NET 1. The Common Language Runtime*, volume 1. Addison-Wesley Longman, November 2002.

[3] G. Candea, S. Kawamoto, Y. Fujiki, G. Friedman, and A. Fox. Microreboot – a technique for cheap recovery. In *6th Symposium on Operating Systems Design and Implementation (OSDI)*, pages 31–44, December 2004.

[4] U. Drepper. How to write shared libraries. Technical report, Red Hat, Inc., Research Triangle Park, NC, Tech. Rep., January 2005. vailable: http://people.redhat.com/drepper/dsohowto.pdf.

[5] D. Engler. Weird things that surprise academics trying to commercialize a static checking tool. Part of an invited talk at SPIN05 and CONCUR05, 2005. http://www.stanford.edu/ engler/spin05-coverity.pdf.

[6] D. Engler, D. Y. Chen, S. Hallem, A. Chou, and B. Chelf. Bugs as deviant behavior: a general approach to inferring

errors in systems code. In *SOSP '01: Proceedings of the eighteenth ACM symposium on Operating systems principles*, pages 57–72, New York, NY, USA, 2001. ACM Press.

[7] C. Fetzer and Z. Xiao. A flexible generator architecture for improving software dependability. In *Procceedings of the Thirteenth International Symposium on Software Reliability Engineering (ISSRE)*, pages 155–164, Annapolis, MD, Nov 2002.

[8] C. Fetzer and Z. Xiao. Healers: A toolkit for enhancing the robustness and security ofexisting applications. In *International Conference on Dependable Systems and Networks (DSN2003 demonstration paper)*, San Francisco, CA, USA, June 2003.

[9] J.Arlat and Y.Crouzet. Faultload representativeness for dependability benchmarking. In *Workshop on Dependability Benchmarking*, pages 29–30, June 2002.

[10] P. Koopman and J. DeVale. Comparing the robustness of posix operating systems. In *FTCS '99: Proceedings of the Twenty-Ninth Annual International Symposium on Fault-Tolerant Computing*, page 30, Washington, DC, USA, 1999. IEEE Computer Society.

[11] P. Koopman and J. DeVale. The exception handling effectiveness of posix operating systems. *IEEE Trans. Softw. Eng.*, 26(9):837–848, 2000.

[12] C. Lattner and V. Adve. LLVM: A Compilation Framework for Lifelong Program Analysis & Transformation. In *Proceedings of the 2004 International Symposium on Code Generation and Optimization (CGO'04)*, Palo Alto, California, Mar 2004.

[13] K. Pattabiraman, G. P. Saggese, D. Chen, Z. Kalbarczyk, and R. K. Iyer. Dynamic derivation of application-specific error detectors and their implementation in hardware. In *Inproceedings of the Sixth European Dependable Computing Conference (EDCC 2006)*, October 2006.

[14] S. Sidiroglou and A. D. Keromytis. Countering network worms through automatic patch generation. Technical report, Columbia University Computer Science Department, 2003.

[15] M. Süßkraut and C. Fetzer. Automatically finding and patching bad error handling. In *Inproceedings of the Sixth European Dependable Computing Conference (EDCC 2006)*, October 2006.

[16] M. Süßkraut and C. Fetzer. Learning library-level error return values from syscall error injection. In *Inproceedings of the Sixth European Dependable Computing Conference (EDCC 2006) [Fast Abstract]*, volume Proceedings Suplemental, 2006.

[17] D. van Heesch. Doxygen. http://www.doxygen.org.

[18] J. Yang, D. Evans, D. Bhardwaj, T. Bhat, and M. Das. Terracotta: Mining temporal api rules from imperfect traces. In *28 th International Conference on Software Engineering*, May 2006. http://www.cs.virginia.edu/terracotta/.

Session 2A:
Distributed Consensus

Automatic Verification and Discovery of Byzantine Consensus Protocols

Piotr Zieliński
Cavendish Laboratory, University of Cambridge, UK
piotr.zielinski@cl.cam.ac.uk

Abstract

Model-checking of asynchronous distributed protocols is challenging because of the large size of the state and solution spaces. This paper tackles this problem in the context of low-latency Byzantine Consensus protocols. It reduces the state space by focusing on the latency-determining first round only, ignoring the order of messages in this round, and distinguishing between state-modifying actions and state-preserving predicates. In addition, the monotonicity of the predicates and verified properties allows one to use a Tarski-style fixpoint algorithm, which results in an exponential verification speed-up.

This model checker has been applied to scan the space of possible Consensus algorithms in order to discover new ones. The search automatically discovered not only many familiar patterns but also several interesting improvements to known algorithms. Due to its speed and reliability, automatic protocol design is an attractive paradigm, especially in the notoriously difficult Byzantine case.

1. Introduction

In the Consensus problem, a fixed group of processes, communicating through an asynchronous network, cooperate to reach a common decision. Each of the processes proposes a value, say a number, and then they all try to agree on one of the proposals. Despite the apparent simplicity, Consensus is universal: it can be used to implement *any* sequential object in a distributed and fault-tolerant way [11].

Consensus is surprisingly difficult to solve in a fault-tolerant manner, so that even if some processes fail, the others will still reach an agreement. This is especially true in the presence of malicious participants; protocols operating in such settings are extremely subtle and complicated, and the proofs of their correctness are rather lengthy. Moreover, slight changes in the requirements often require a complete redesign of the algorithm. A more efficient approach is necessary.

This paper proposes such an approach: automatic verifi-

cation and discovery through model-checking. In automatic verification, the user provides a collection of decision rules such as "if all four processes report to have proposed x, then decide on x". These rules are given to the model-checker, which tests the correctness of the implied Consensus algorithm. In automatic discovery, the user specifies a set of latency conditions such as "if at most one non-leader process fails, then all correct processes must decide within two communication steps." A model-checker is then used to check all possible Consensus algorithms that satisfy those conditions, and output the correct ones if any.

The first challenge is choosing a good model: it should be general enough to express all "sensible" Consensus algorithms, but sufficiently specific to avoid an intractably large state space. Several such models have been used in the literature [26, 28], however, none of them allows for Byzantine algorithms, which benefit from automated verification most.

Secondly, any sufficiently expressive model permits infinitely many correct Consensus algorithms, so we need a criterion for selecting the "best" ones. This paper focuses on the number of communication steps necessary to decide in typical runs. This criterion allows us to concentrate on the latency-determining first round only, thereby reducing the size of the state space. Nevertheless, we still need to ensure that processes will always have enough information to decide even if the first round fails. The formalization of the required properties is provided by the Optimistically Terminating Consensus abstraction [30]. This abstraction can handle malicious participants and is flexible enough to match the latencies of all known asynchronous Consensus protocols in a single framework.

Depending on the chosen model, the search space can be sufficiently small for a limited number of verifications, however, performing it for millions of possible protocols requires a different approach. The method presented in this paper uses the monotonicity of Consensus properties. Instead of checking every possible state, the algorithm computes the "minimal possibly violating state" and checks whether that state actually violates the required properties. The resulting exponential speed-up makes automatic discovery practical.

Processes			Correctness	Honesty	Behaviour
$P\{$	$F\{$		correct	honest	according to the specification
			faulty	honest	according to the specification until it crashes
		$M\{$	faulty	malicious	completely arbitrary

Figure 1. Categories of processes

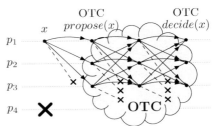

Figure 2. A run of Byzantine Consensus [3]

Roadmap. Section 2 provides a short summary of the Optimistically Terminating Consensus framework (OTC), with an emphasis on the concepts relevant to automated verification. The OTC properties are used in Section 3 to construct an execution model and present an algorithm to verify the correctness of OTC protocols. Section 4 uses automated correctness testing to search the space of possible protocols to discover new ones. Section 5 presents the results. Section 6 concludes the paper.

1.1. Related work

A large amount of work has been done on asynchronous Consensus protocols, see [23] for a survey. A number of algorithms have been proposed, both for the crash-stop model [4, 16, 19, 24] and for the Byzantine settings [3].

Automatic reasoning about protocols is common in security protocol research [2, 5, 17, 18, 20]. In the area of agreement protocols, Paxos [13] and its variants [7, 8, 15] seem to have undergone the most significant amount of formal analysis [12, 14, 22, 27, 28]. Other work on formal verification and/or model checking of Consensus algorithms can be found in [21, 26]. All those methods are restricted to crash failures and *verification* only.

Bar-David and Taubenfeld [1] used a combination of model checking and program generation to automatically discover new mutual exclusion algorithms. Apart from their work, I am not aware of any previous attempt at automatic *discovery* of fault-tolerant distributed algorithms.

2. Introduction to OTC

2.1. System model

Processes. This paper assumes a system consisting of a fixed number n of processes. In the set of all processes $P = \{p_1, \ldots, p_n\}$, some processes $F \subseteq P$ are faulty, and some $M \subseteq F$ are malicious (Figure 1). Processes do not know sets F and M, however, they do know the sets $\mathcal{F}$ and $\mathcal{M}$ of possible values of F and M. Note that the standard model of at most f faulty processes out of which at most m malicious is a special case:

$$\mathcal{F} = \{ F \subseteq P \mid |F| \leq f \}, \quad \mathcal{M} = \{ M \subseteq P \mid |M| \leq m \}.$$

Channels. Processes communicate through asynchronous reliable channels: messages sent from one correct process to another correct process will eventually be received (reliability) but the message delay is unbounded (asynchrony). These assumptions are sufficient to implement the first round of Consensus; to construct the entire protocol and ensure its liveness, failure detectors or eventual synchrony assumptions are needed, but these are protocol-independent and do not affect the latency in typical runs [30].

2.2. Consensus

In Consensus, processes propose values and are expected to eventually agree on one of them. The following holds:

Validity. The decision was proposed by some process.

Agreement. No two processes decide differently.

Termination. All correct processes eventually decide.

In the Byzantine model, these requirements apply only to honest (non-malicious) processes. Since malicious processes can undetectably lie about their proposals, I also assume that Validity must be satisfied only if all processes are honest in a particular run.

In the most popular approach to solve Consensus, a distinguished process, called the *leader* or *coordinator*, tries to impose its proposal on the others. This succeeds if sufficiently many processes accept the coordinator's proposal. Otherwise, another process becomes the coordinator and repeats the protocol. Coordinators keep changing until one of them succeeds and makes all correct processes decide.

As an example, Figure 2 shows a single round the Consensus protocol [3], in a four-process system with one pro-

Name	Type	Meaning	Definition in the OT $(P, P, 1)$ example
$propose(x)$	action	propose x	broadcast x if no *stop* before
stop	action	stop processing	broadcast $\perp$ if no *propose* before
$decision(x)$	predicate	if true, then x is the decision	x received from all 4 processes
$valid(x)$	predicate	if true, then an honest process proposed x	x received from more than 1 process
$possible(x)$	predicate	if any process ever decides on x, then true	non-x received from at most 1 process

Figure 3. Summary of the primitives provided by OTC

cess possibly maliciously faulty:

$$\mathcal{F} = \mathcal{M} = \{\emptyset, \{p_1\}, \{p_2\}, \{p_3\}, \{p_4\}\}$$

The coordinator p_1 broadcasts its proposal. In the second step, processes rebroadcast the proposal received, to protect against a malicious coordinator broadcasting different proposals. In the third step, they broadcast again, this time to ensure the recoverability of the decision in case of failures, and decide.

The first round can only succeed if p_1 is correct. Therefore, if no decision has been made after a while, the next round is started with another coordinator, and so on, until all correct processes decide.

2.3. Optimistically Terminating Consensus

Optimistically Terminating Consensus (OTC) [30] is a formalization of the grey cloud in Figure 2. Various Consensus protocols can be constructed by changing the implementation of the OTC in one or more rounds, and keeping the rest of the algorithm intact. In fact, it is possible to match the latencies of all known asynchronous Consensus algorithms just by manipulating the first round OTC [30]. This is why this paper focuses on constructing the first-round OTC only.

Treated as a black-box, OTC communicates with the environment with predicates and actions (Figure 3). Actions can change a process' state (e.g., send messages) but they do not return any information. On the other hand, predicates do not affect the state but return information. In a sense, the difference between predicates and actions is similar to that between reads and writes.

OTC-based Consensus algorithms [30] proceed in the same way as that in Figure 2. When a process receives the coordinator's proposal x, it executes the OTC action $propose(x)$. Each process monitors its $decision(y)$ predicate for all y; when it becomes true, y is the decision.

If the coordinator fails, some or all processes might never decide. When processes suspect this is the case, they execute action *stop* of the first OTC, and start the second round with another coordinator. Since some processes might have decided in the first round, the second coordinator must

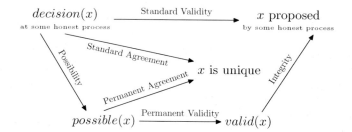

Figure 4. OTC properties graphically

choose its proposal with care. To this end, it monitors the first-round OTC predicates $possible(x)$ and $valid(x)$ for all x (Figure 3). It waits until either (i) $possible(x)$ is false for all x, and proposes its original proposal, or (ii) $possible(x)$ holds for exactly one x and $valid(x)$ holds, then it proposes x. In a sense, $valid(x)$ and $possible(x)$ ensure recoverability of the decision in case of failures. Subsequent rounds proceed in a similar way; digital signatures are needed only if the first round does not decide [30].

2.4. OTC properties

As summarized in Figure 3, OTC equips each process with two actions: $propose(x)$ and *stop*, as well as three predicates: $valid(x)$, $possible(x)$, and $decision(x)$. These primitives satisfy the following properties [30]:

Integrity. If $valid(x)$ holds at an honest process, then an honest process executed $propose(x)$.

Possibility. If $decision(x)$ holds at an honest process, then $possible(x)$ holds at all honest processes, at all times.

Permanent Validity. Statement $possible(x) \Rightarrow valid(x)$ holds at any *complete* process (see below).

Permanent Agreement. Predicate $possible(x)$ holds for at most one x at any complete process.

Optimistic Termination (X, C, k). If all processes in the set X propose x, and all processes in the set C are correct, and none of them execute *stop*, then $decision(x)$ will hold at all correct processes in k communication steps. The sets satisfy $X \subseteq C \subseteq P = \{p_1, \ldots, p_n\}$.

```
1  when a process executes propose(x) do
2      broadcast ⟨x : 1⟩
3  when a process received ⟨x : i⟩ from all p ∈ XCᵢ do
4      broadcast ⟨x : i + 1⟩
5  predicate decision(x) holds iff
6      received ⟨x : i⟩ from all p ∈ XCᵢ and i = 1, . . . , k
```

Figure 5. Pred. $decision(x)$ for OT (X, C, k)

Properties Integrity and Possibility just formalize the definitions of $valid(x)$ and $possible(x)$ from Figure 3.

In Permanent Validity and Permanent Agreement, an *honest* process p is *complete* if all correct processes executed *stop*, and p received all messages sent by those processes before or during executing *stop*[1]. These properties ensure that the second and later coordinators will not block waiting to establish a safe proposal. Permanent Validity and Permanent Agreement are stronger than standard (Uniform) Validity and Agreement required by Consensus (Figure 4) [30].

Because of a more general failure model, our Optimistic Termination (OT) property is more general than that in [30]. It ensures that, under some favourable conditions described by sets X and C, OTC will decide in k steps. In favourable runs, in which decision is taken in the first round, the latency of Consensus is $k+1$: the latency k of OTC plus one step for the coordinator's proposal to reach the processes (Figure 2).

Example. Consider a system $P = \{p_1, p_2, p_3, p_4\}$, with at most one p_i (maliciously) faulty, and an OTC algorithm, similar to that in Figure 2, which decides in one step if all processes are correct, and in two otherwise. Such an algorithm satisfies five OT conditions: $(P \setminus \{p_i\}, P \setminus \{p_i\}, 2)$ for $i = 1, 2, 3, 4$, and $(P, P, 1)$.

Although each OT condition (X, C, k) is a *requirement*, it easily translates into an *implementation* of the predicate $decision(x)$. For example, for the five above OT conditions, $decision(x)$ must hold if (i) there is a three-process set C such that all processes in C report that all processes in C report proposing x, or (ii) all processes report proposing x. Figure 5 shows a simple algorithm defining $decision(x)$ that satisfies a given OT (X, C, k) but not necessarily other OTC properties. There, XC_i means X for $i = 1$, and C otherwise. The above OT conditions result in the following five message patterns:

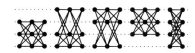

---
[1]Note that process p does not know which processes are correct, so it does not know whether it is complete or not.

Manual verification. This section shows an example of a manual verification of an OTC protocol satisfying a single OT condition $(P, P, 1)$. This condition requires an OTC to decide if all processes are correct and propose the same value. General OTC constructions and proofs are in [30].

Predicate $valid(x)$ ensures that at least one honest process proposed x. Since we assume at most one malicious process (and OTC properties must hold even if no decision is made), we can define $valid(x)$ to hold when two or more processes report proposing x (Figure 3).

Condition OT $(P, P, 1)$ implies that $decision(x)$ holds if x was received from all four processes. At most one process is malicious, so if more than one process reports proposing a non-x or executing *stop*, value x will never become a decision. Thus, $possible(x)$ holds if at most one process reports proposing a non-x or executing *stop*.

Having constructed all three predicates, we can now check Permanent Validity and Permanent Agreement. A *complete* process has received all messages from at least three processes. If $possible(x)$ holds, then at most one is a non-x, so at least two are x, which implies $valid(x)$ (Permanent Validity). Those two x messages are non-y for any $y \neq x$, so $possible(y)$ cannot hold (Permanent Agreement).

3. Automated verification

For any two predicates $p(x)$ and $q(x)$, let "$p(x) \leq q(x)$" be defined as "$p(x) \implies q(x)$", that is, as the standard arithmetic "$\leq$" with TRUE=1 and FALSE=0. For example, predicate $decision(x)$ is *increasing* in time (a decision cannot be unmade), whereas $possible(x)$ is *decreasing* in time (a once impossible decision cannot become possible again).

With this formalism, the manual verification process can be described as follows. First, use the Validity condition to define the *maximum* possible predicate $valid(x)$. Then, use OT to define the minimum $decision(x)$, and use it together with Possibility to get the minimum $possible(x)$:

$$\text{Validity} \implies \max valid(x)$$
$$\text{Optimistic Termination} \implies \min decision(x)$$
$$\text{Possibility} + \min decision(x) \implies \min possible(x)$$

Having defined the predicates, we can check whether Permanent Validity and Permanent Agreement hold. Note that these two properties, viewed as Boolean formulae, are increasing wrt. $valid(x)$ and decreasing wrt. $possible(x)$. Therefore, if they do not hold for the maximum $valid(x)$ and the minimum $possible(x)$, they cannot hold at all.

To save space, the rest of this paper is devoted to verifying Permanent Agreement, which generally implies Permanent Validity [30]. For testing Permanent Validity see [29].

```
1   state ← ∅                              { the empty set }

2   when a process executes propose(x) do
3       incorporate ⟨x : ε⟩ into the state     { ε: empty seq. }

4   when a process receives ⟨x : q₁ . . . q_{i−1}⟩ from q_i do
5       incorporate ⟨x : q₁ . . . q_i⟩ into the state

6   function incorporate ⟨x : q₁ . . . q_i⟩ into the state is
7       if ⟨y : q₁ . . . q_i⟩ ∉ state for any y then
8           insert ⟨x : q₁ . . . q_i⟩ into state
9           broadcast ⟨x : q₁ . . . q_i⟩

10  when a process executes stop do
11      for all sequences q₁ . . . q_i do        { including ε }
12          incorporate ⟨⊥ : q₁ . . . q_i⟩ into the state
```

Figure 6. Evolution of states

3.1. Events and states

I employ a full-information approach, in which each process' state represents its full knowledge about the system. When a process executes an action ($propose(x)$ or $stop$) or receives a message, this event is added to the process' state and broadcast to others. At any given time, the state of a process is a sequence of events experienced so far.

Consider runs in which no $stop$ is performed. I assume that, in such runs, the order of events does not matter, and the state of a process is actually a *set* of events, not a sequence. If the order of events at some process p mattered and p failed, then other processes could never learn about it, rendering OTC properties impossible to satisfy.

If the order of events does not matter, then the only effect of experiencing them is adding them to the *state* set and informing other processes about them. For example, executing $propose(x)$ broadcasts $\langle x : \varepsilon \rangle$, where ε is the empty sequence (Figure 6). When a process receives $\langle x : \varepsilon \rangle$ from some process q_1, it adds $\langle x : q_1 \rangle$ to its state and broadcasts $\langle x : q_1 \rangle$[2]. In general, receiving $\langle x : q_1 \ldots q_{i-1} \rangle$ requires broadcasting $\langle x : q_1 \ldots q_i \rangle$. Event $\langle x : q_1 \ldots q_i \rangle$ means "q_i claims that q_{i-1} claims that . . . q_1 claims to have proposed x". I say "claims" because some of the processes are malicious and can lie. This algorithm (Figure 6) can be viewed as a more refined version of that in Figure 5.

The test in line 7 deserves an explanation. No honest process proposes two different values, so if we receive $\langle x : \varepsilon \rangle$ and $\langle y : \varepsilon \rangle$ from the same process q_1, then we can ignore the latter. This means that honest processes will never send $\langle x : q_1 \rangle$ with two different x's; if we receive such, then the sender is malicious and its messages can be ignored. By induction, we need to pay attention only to the first message

of the form $\langle x : q_1 \ldots q_i \rangle$ for any given sequence $q_1 \ldots q_i$.

The purpose of the $stop$ action is to put the process into a final, unchangeable state [30]. Lines 10–12 accomplish this by filling all the "unused" sequences in the state with the special symbol "⊥". After this operation, the test in line 7 will never succeed again.

3.2. State formalism

A *state* is an arbitrary set of events, not necessarily received by the same process, and possibly conflicting (eg. $\{\langle 1 : p_1 p_2 \rangle, \langle 2 : p_1 p_2 \rangle\}$). Each event is of the form $\langle x : \alpha \rangle$ where $\alpha = q_1 \ldots q_i$ is a sequence of processes. By analogy, for any set $\mathcal{A}$ of sequences, $\langle x : \mathcal{A} \rangle$ denotes the state consisting of all events $\langle x : \alpha \rangle$ with $\alpha \in \mathcal{A}$:

$$\langle x : \mathcal{A} \rangle \stackrel{\text{def}}{=} \{ \langle x : \alpha \rangle \mid \alpha \in \mathcal{A} \}. \tag{1}$$

For example, $\langle 2 : \{p_1 p_2, p_2\} \rangle = \{\langle 2 : p_1 p_2 \rangle, \langle 2 : p_2 \rangle\}$

The opposite operation, extracting the set of sequences corresponding to a given proposal x, can be accomplished using the following operator:

$$S(x) \stackrel{\text{def}}{=} \{ \alpha \mid \langle x : \alpha \rangle \in S \}. \tag{2}$$

For example, if $S = \{\langle 1 : p_1 \rangle, \langle 2 : p_2 \rangle, \langle 1 : p_1 p_2 \rangle\}$, then $S(1) = \{p_1, p_1 p_2\}$ and $S(2) = \{p_2\}$.

3.3. Minimum *decision(x)* and *possible(x)*

Figure 5 defined a predicate $decision(x)$ for a single OT condition (X, C, k). Using the model from this section, the minimum $decision(x)$ predicate holds at a process iff it experienced all the events $\langle x : D \rangle$ (see (1)), where

$$D = \{ q_1 \ldots q_i \mid q_1 \in X, q_2, \ldots, q_i \in C, 1 \leq i \leq k \}. \tag{3}$$

For example, for OT $\langle \{p_1\}, \{p_1 p_2\}, 3 \rangle$, we have

$$D = \{p_1, p_1 p_1, p_1 p_2, p_1 p_1 p_1, p_1 p_1 p_2, p_1 p_2 p_1, p_1 p_2 p_2\}.$$

Denoting the set of D's corresponding all required OTs by $\mathcal{D}$, the minimum predicate $decision(x)$ in state S is

$$decision(x) \stackrel{\text{def}}{\Leftrightarrow} S(x) \supseteq D \text{ for some } D \in \mathcal{D}. \tag{4}$$

The minimum $possible(x)$ holds if the possibility of having $decision(x)$ somewhere in the system is consistent with the process' knowledge. In other words, $possible(x)$ means that we can add $\langle x : D \rangle$ to the process state, and still get a state that is consistent. I will now present a formalism that allows us to express this requirement in a formal way.

3.4. State consistency

The notion of state consistency is based on two concepts: *event conflict* and *event inference*.

---

[2]In this paper, p_i is the name of i-th process in $P = \{p_1, \ldots, p_n\}$, and q_i is the i-th process in a given sequence of processes.

Conflict. Events $\langle x : \alpha \rangle$ and $\langle y : \beta \rangle$ *conflict* if they have different proposal values and the same sequence of processes ($x \neq y$ and $\alpha = \beta$). For example, $\langle 1 : p_1 p_3 \rangle$ and $\langle 2 : p_1 p_3 \rangle$ conflict, whereas $\langle 1 : p_1 p_3 \rangle$ and $\langle 2 : p_1 p_2 \rangle$ do not. Only malicious processes produce conflicting events.

For any state S, let $conflict(S)$ to be the set of sequences α, for which some events $\langle z : \alpha \rangle \in S$ conflict:

$$conflict(S) \stackrel{\text{def}}{=} \{\, \alpha \mid \exists\, x \neq y : \langle x : \alpha \rangle \in S \wedge \langle y : \alpha \rangle \in S \,\}.$$

For example,

$$conflict(\{\langle 1 : p_1 p_2 \rangle, \langle 2 : p_2 \rangle, \langle 2 : p_1 p_2 \rangle\}) = \{p_1 p_2\}.$$

Prefixes and inference. I will define an operator $infer(S, M)$, which takes a state S and a set of malicious processes M. It outputs the set of events whose occurrence can be inferred from S. The basic idea is that if an honest process claims that event e has occurred, then it has indeed occurred. For example, if $q_i \notin M$, then $\langle x : q_1 \ldots q_i \rangle$ implies $\langle x : q_1 \ldots q_{i-1} \rangle$. If in addition $q_{i-1} \notin M$, then $\langle x : q_1 \ldots q_{i-2} \rangle$, and so on. In general, for a singleton state $S = \{\langle x : q_1 \ldots q_i \rangle\}$:

$$infer(S, M) = \langle x : prefs(q_1 \ldots q_i, M) \rangle.$$

Here, the operator $prefs(q_1 \ldots q_i, M)$ produces a set of sequences that can be obtained by removing a sequence of honest processes from the end of $q_1 \ldots q_i$:

$$prefs(q_1 \ldots q_i, M) \stackrel{\text{def}}{=} \{\, q_1 \ldots q_j \mid q_{j+1}, \ldots, q_i \notin M \,\}.$$

The definition of $prefs$ can be extended to sets of sequences $\mathcal{A}$ in the obvious way:

$$prefs(\mathcal{A}, M) \stackrel{\text{def}}{=} \bigcup_{\alpha \in \mathcal{A}} prefs(\alpha, M).$$

Since $\alpha \in prefs(\alpha, M)$, we have $\mathcal{A} \subseteq prefs(\mathcal{A}, M)$.

We can define $infer(S, M) = \hat{S}$, where (2)

$$\hat{S}(x) = prefs(S(x), M) \quad \text{for any } x \neq \bot. \tag{5}$$

The case $x = \bot$ requires a special treatment. The state-propagation algorithm in Figure 6 shows that the event $\langle \bot : q_1 \ldots q_i \rangle$ can occur for two reasons: either because of process q_i claiming that the event $\langle \bot : q_1 \ldots q_{i-1} \rangle$ occurred at q_i or because of the *stop* action. Since the latter reason is always a possibility, the occurrence of $\langle \bot : q_1 \ldots q_i \rangle$ does not imply the occurrence of $\langle \bot : q_1 \ldots q_{i-1} \rangle$ anywhere in the system, even if q_i is honest. Nothing can be inferred here, so $\hat{S}(\bot) = S(\bot)$, which completes (5).

Special sets. For any set Q of processes, define

$$\alpha Q = \{\, q_1 \ldots q_i \mid q_i \in Q \,\} \cup \{\varepsilon\},$$
$$\alpha \overline{Q} = \{\, q_1 \ldots q_i \mid q_i \notin Q \,\}.$$

Set αQ contains all process sequences ending with an process in Q, set $\alpha \overline{Q}$ contains all others.

Consistency. A state is consistent only if all conflicting inferred events come from malicious processes:

$$conflict(infer(S, M)) \subseteq \alpha M. \tag{6}$$

Since $\langle x : \varepsilon \rangle \equiv propose(x)$, the reason for $\varepsilon \in \alpha M$ is that different processes can propose different values.

3.5. Verifying Permanent Agreement

Permanent Agreement requires that, for any complete state, predicate $possible(z)$ holds for at most one z. This section presents an algorithm that checks whether a given OTC algorithm violates this property. It searches for a complete state in which $possible(z)$ holds for two different $z \in \{x, y\}$. More precisely, we are looking for sets $F \in \mathcal{F}$ and $M \in \mathcal{M}$, with $M \subseteq F$, and a state S such that

A1: State S can occur, that is, conflicting events come only from malicious processes (6):

$$conflict(infer(S, M)) \subseteq \alpha M.$$

A2: State S is complete, that is, the process received all the events produced by all correct processes ($\notin F$) in lines 10–12 and before:

$$\alpha \overline{F} \subseteq \bigcup_{\substack{\text{all } x \\ \text{including } \bot}} S(x).$$

In practice, I only consider sequences $q_1 \ldots q_i$ no longer than the highest k in any required OT condition (X, C, k).

A3: Predicate $possible(z)$ holds for two different $z \in \{x, y\}$. In other words, for each $z \in \{x, y\}$, decision events $\langle z : D_z \rangle$ (3) are all consistent with state S. Formally, there is $D_z \in \mathcal{D}$ (4) and a set of malicious processes $M_z \in \mathcal{M}$ such that the combined state $S \cup \langle z : D_z \rangle$ is still consistent (6):

$$conflict(infer(S \cup \langle z : D_z \rangle, M_z)) \subseteq \alpha M_z$$

Note that sets M_z (M_x and M_y) are only *possible* sets of malicious processes, and can differ from the real M, which is unknown to the processes.

Without loss of generality, assume that the state S consists only of events of the form $\langle x : \alpha \rangle$, $\langle y : \alpha \rangle$, and $\langle \bot : \alpha \rangle$. This is because all events $\langle u : \alpha \rangle \in S$ with $u \notin \{x, y, \bot\}$ can be replaced by $\langle \bot : \alpha \rangle$ without invalidating any of **A123** (replacing u with $\bot$ means we can infer less (5)). For this reason, I assume $S = \langle x : S_x \rangle \cup \langle y : S_y \rangle \cup \langle \bot : S_\bot \rangle$, for some pairwise disjoint sets of sequences $S_x, S_y, S_\bot$ (1).

Given this assumption, Properties **A** can be rewritten as

A1: State S is consistent:

$$prefs(S_x, M) \cap prefs(S_y, M) \subseteq \alpha M \qquad \text{(a)}$$
$$prefs(S_x, M) \cap S_\perp \subseteq \alpha M$$
$$prefs(S_y, M) \cap S_\perp \subseteq \alpha M$$

$\mathcal{A} \subseteq prefs(\mathcal{A}, M)$ for all sets of sequences $\mathcal{A}$, so the first inequality implies $prefs(S_x, M) \cap S_y \subseteq \alpha M$ and $prefs(S_y, M) \cap S_x \subseteq \alpha M$. Therefore, we can rewrite the last two inequalities as:

$$prefs(S_x, M) \cap (S_y \cup S_\perp) \subseteq \alpha M, \qquad \text{(b)}$$
$$prefs(S_y, M) \cap (S_x \cup S_\perp) \subseteq \alpha M. \qquad \text{(c)}$$

This transformation is needed for (7) below.

A2: State S is complete: $\alpha \overline{F} \subseteq S_x \cup S_y \cup S_\perp$.

A3: Predicate $possible(z)$ holds for $z \in \{x, y\}$. Defining $\bar{x} \stackrel{\text{def}}{=} y$ and $\bar{y} \stackrel{\text{def}}{=} x$, and using the same transformations as in Property **A1**, we get:

$$prefs(S_x, M_z) \cap prefs(S_y, M_z) \subseteq \alpha M_z \qquad \text{(a)}$$
$$prefs(S_x, M_z) \cap (S_y \cup S_\perp) \subseteq \alpha M_z \qquad \text{(b)}$$
$$prefs(S_y, M_z) \cap (S_x \cup S_\perp) \subseteq \alpha M_z \qquad \text{(c)}$$
$$prefs(D_z, M_z) \cap prefs(S_{\bar{z}}, M_z) \subseteq \alpha M_z \qquad \text{(d)}$$
$$prefs(D_z, M_z) \cap (S_{\bar{z}} \cup S_\perp) \subseteq \alpha M_z. \qquad \text{(e)}$$

Property **A2** is increasing with respect to S_x, S_y, $S_\perp$; all the other properties are decreasing. For this reason, we can assume that $\alpha \overline{F} = S_x \cup S_y \cup S_\perp$, which makes Property **A2** automatically satisfied. Then, for any set $\mathcal{A}$:

$$\mathcal{A} \cap (S_{\bar{z}} \cup S_\perp) \subseteq \alpha M \quad \Leftrightarrow$$
$$\mathcal{A} \cap \alpha \overline{F} \cap \overline{S_z} \cap \alpha \overline{M} = \emptyset \quad \Leftrightarrow$$
$$\mathcal{A} \cap \alpha \overline{F} \cap \alpha \overline{M} \subseteq S_z.$$

Thus, Properties **A1**(bc) and **A3**(bce) can be rewritten as

$$\begin{aligned}
prefs(S_z, M) \cap \alpha \overline{F} \cap \alpha \overline{M} &\subseteq S_z, \\
prefs(S_z, M_x) \cap \alpha \overline{F} \cap \alpha \overline{M_x} &\subseteq S_z, \\
prefs(S_z, M_y) \cap \alpha \overline{F} \cap \alpha \overline{M_y} &\subseteq S_z, \\
prefs(D_z, M_z) \cap \alpha \overline{F} \cap \alpha \overline{M_z} &\subseteq S_z.
\end{aligned} \qquad (7)$$

The left-hand side of each of these inequalities is an increasing function of S_z. As a result, we can compute the smallest set S_z that satisfies these inequalities using Tarski's least fixed point algorithm (see below). Then, it is sufficient to check Properties **A1**(a) and **A3**(ad) for the computed S_z (S_x and S_y), that is, whether

$$\begin{aligned}
prefs(S_x, M) \cap prefs(S_y, M) &\subseteq \alpha M, \\
prefs(S_x, M_x) \cap prefs(S_y, M_x) &\subseteq \alpha M_x, \\
prefs(S_x, M_y) \cap prefs(S_y, M_y) &\subseteq \alpha M_y, \\
prefs(D_z, M_z) \cap prefs(S_{\bar{z}}, M_z) &\subseteq \alpha M_z.
\end{aligned} \qquad (8)$$

```
1  function PermanentAgreement(OTs) is
2    for all D_x, D_y corresponding to OTs (3) do
3      for all F ∈ F and M, M_x, M_y ∈ M do
4        if M ⊆ F then
5          compute the least fixpoints S_x and S_y of (7)
6          if computed S_x and S_y satisfy (8) then
7            return FALSE
8  return TRUE
```

Figure 7. Testing Permanent Agreement

If this is the case, then we have found a state S for which Permanent Agreement does not hold. If not, then the above statement will be false for all supersets of S_x and S_y because function $prefs$ is increasing. Testing all possible $(D_x, D_y, F, M, M_x, M_y)$ can ensure that Permanent Agreement is never violated (Figure 7).

Computing S_z as as the least fixpoint. Inequalities (7) can be rewritten as $\phi(S_z) \subseteq S_z$, where

$$\begin{aligned}
\phi(S_z) = \quad &prefs(D_x, M_x) \cap \alpha \overline{F} \cap \alpha \overline{M_x} \quad \cup \\
&prefs(S_z, M) \cap \alpha \overline{F} \cap \alpha \overline{M} \quad \cup \\
&prefs(S_z, M_x) \cap \alpha \overline{F} \cap \alpha \overline{M_x} \quad \cup \\
&prefs(S_z, M_y) \cap \alpha \overline{F} \cap \alpha \overline{M_y}.
\end{aligned}$$

Function ϕ is increasing, which allows us to use Tarski's method [25] to find the smallest S_z such that $\phi(S_z) \subseteq S_z$. This method constructs an increasing sequence $S_z^0 \subseteq S_z^1 \subseteq \cdots$ defined as $S_z^0 = \emptyset$ and $S_z^{i+1} = \phi(S_z^i)$. The first $S_z^i = S_z^{i+1} = \phi(S_z^i)$ encountered is the least fixpoint of ϕ. In the sequence $S_z^0 \subset \cdots \subset S_z^i$, each set has at least one element more than its predecessor, so the number i of iterations does not exceed the maximum size of S_z, that is the number of possible sequences $q_1 \ldots q_i$ with $i \leq k$. This number, $1 + \cdots + n^k$, is much smaller than the number of all states $S = \langle x : S_x \rangle \cup \langle y : S_y \rangle \cup \langle \perp : S_\perp \rangle$, which is in the order of $3^{1 + \cdots + n^k}$. Therefore, exploiting monotonicity results in an exponential speed-up of the search process.

4. Discovering new protocols

Section 3 showed how we can construct an OTC algorithm satisfying given OT conditions, and test its correctness. This section goes a step further and attempts to discover new algorithms by generating possible sets $\mathcal{T}$ of OT conditions and testing whether they can be satisfied. The search starts with the empty $\mathcal{T}$ and recursively adds new OT conditions, while testing for correctness. Note that once we reach an incorrect $\mathcal{T}$, we can safely backtrack because

```
1   function OTCSearch(𝒯) is
2       if PermValidity(𝒯) and PermAgreement(𝒯) then
3           output 𝒯
4       for all possible OT conditions T = (X, C, k) do
5           if T is greater (">OT") than all elements of 𝒯 and
6               T does not dominate any element of 𝒯 and
7               T is not dominated by any element of 𝒯 then
8               OTCSearch(𝒯 ∪ {T})
```

Figure 8. Discovering new OTC protocols

adding new OT conditions to an incorrect OTC algorithm $\mathcal{T}$ cannot produce a correct one. The details are shown in Figure 8. Lines 5–7 implement two optimization techniques described below: a linear order and a domination relation.

OT order. The order of the OT conditions in $\mathcal{T}$ does not matter. Therefore, adding OTs to $\mathcal{T}$ in a specific order will result in the same set of conditions being analyzed several times; an n-element set can be obtained in $n!$ different orders, slowing the algorithm down exponentially.

To ensure that each set $\mathcal{T}$ is analyzed only once, Line 5 guarantees that elements are added to $\mathcal{T}$ in some arbitrary but fixed total order "$<_{OT}$" on OT conditions.

OT domination. OT condition $T_1 = (X_1, C_1, k_1)$ dominates $T_2 = (X_2, C_2, k_2)$ if it provides a stronger guarantee with weaker requirements, that is, if

$$X_1 \subseteq X_2 \ \land \ C_1 \subseteq C_2 \ \land \ k_1 \leq k_2.$$

If this is the case, then the OTC algorithms corresponding to the sets $\mathcal{T}_1 = \{T_1\}$ and $\mathcal{T}_{12} = \{T_1, T_2\}$ are the same. Lines 6–7 prevent us from analyzing sets $\mathcal{T}$ that contain a pair of conditions such that one dominates the other.

5. Results

I have implemented the algorithms from Figures 7 and 8 in C, and then verified the computed OTC algorithms using an independent Python implementation of the algorithm in Figure 7. This section presents computed algorithms for several choices of P, $\mathcal{F}$, and $\mathcal{M}$. While the verification is instantaneous, the search for new algorithms takes time:

n	failures	algs tested	found	time
3	1 crash-stop	360	1	0.03 sec
4	1 crash-stop	8,512	2	0.33 sec
5	1 crash-stop	341,312	3	0.83 sec
5	2 crash-stop	32,620,109	6	61.52 sec
4	1 malicious	47,990	7	0.41 sec
5	1 malicious	11.9 billion	6	39.4 hours

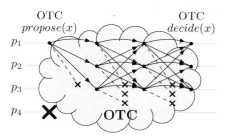

Figure 9. Direct first-round OTC

Not all correct OTC algorithms are listed; I omit those that can be obtained from others by permuting the set of processes, and those that are dominated by others. (A set $\mathcal{T}$ is dominated by $\mathcal{T}'$ iff every OT condition in $\mathcal{T}$ is dominated by some in $\mathcal{T}'$.) All considered OT (X, C, k) have $k \leq 3$.

In a normal round, processes wait for the coordinator's proposal to propose to OTC (Figure 2). However, in the first round, processes can propose their proposals to the OTC directly (Figure 9) [30]. This incorporates the first step into the OTC, allowing for multi-coordinator algorithms and justifying the distinction between X and C in OT (X, C, k). This also implies that, as in the Validity property of Consensus, the $valid(x)$ predicate of the first-round OTC can assume all processes to be honest. Therefore, as far as the first round is concerned, $valid(x)$ becomes true once a process receives one event $\langle x : p_i \rangle$, making Permanent Validity easily satisfied. All OTCs presented in section are first-round OTCs to which processes propose directly; complete Consensus algorithms can be constructed as shown in [30].

Crash-stop 3 processes with 1 failure. We have:

$$\mathcal{F} = \{\emptyset, \{p_1\}, \{p_2\}, \{p_3\}\}, \quad \mathcal{M} = \{\emptyset\}.$$

The generated OTC algorithms correspond to the following two sets of OT conditions (X, C, k):

$$\left\{ \begin{array}{c} \langle \{p_1, p_2\}, \{p_1, p_2\}, 1 \rangle \\ \langle \{p_1\}, \{p_1, p_2\}, 2 \rangle \\ \langle \{p_1\}, \{p_1, p_3\}, 2 \rangle \end{array} \right\} \text{ and } \left\{ \begin{array}{c} \langle \{p_1, p_2\}, \{p_1, p_2\}, 1 \rangle \\ \langle \{p_1, p_3\}, \{p_1, p_3\}, 2 \rangle \\ \langle \{p_2, p_3\}, \{p_2, p_3\}, 2 \rangle \end{array} \right\},$$

which can be depicted as (Section 2.4):

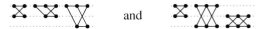

As many standard algorithms [10], the first one decides in two steps if the leader p_1 and a majority of processes are correct. Additionally, it decides in one step if p_1 and p_2 propose the same value. Such an algorithm was presented in [9] for general n.

The second algorithm decides if two processes proposed the same value; in one step if the processes are p_1 and p_2, and in two steps otherwise. If all processes are correct,

79

but propose different values, this algorithm will not decide. Next sections exclude such algorithms by requiring at least one OT (X, C, k) to have $X = \{p_1\}$.

Crash-stop 4 processes with 1 failure. In this case, the following two OTCs have been generated:

Both algorithms decide in two steps if the leader p_1 and at least one other process are correct. The first decides in one step if p_1 and p_2 propose the same value, the second if at least three processes including p_1 propose the same value.

Note that this protocol can sometimes decide if two processes are faulty, even though we assume at most one failure. In practice, this means that, in some situations, the algorithm might not need to wait for response from some slow, but formally correct, processes.

Crash-stop 5 processes with 2 failures. In this case, the following two OTCs have been generated:

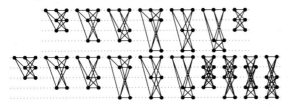

Both decide in two steps if a majority of processes, including the leader, are correct. The first additionally decides in one step if p_1, p_2, p_3 propose the same value; the other, if at least four processes, including p_1 propose the same value.

Byzantine 4 processes with 1 failure. The algorithm by Castro and Liskov [3] decides in three steps if the leader p_1 is correct and at most one other process is faulty. Later papers observed [6, 30] that if all processes are correct, then the decision can be made in two steps:

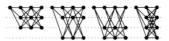

In this case, seven OTCs have been generated, two of which are extensions of the above protocol:

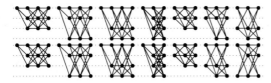

In addition to the original properties, these two algorithms can also decide in two steps in some runs with one process faulty and two processes proposing the same value.

Byzantine 5 processes with 1 failure. This case generated six variants of the following:

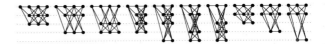

The first three OT conditions correspond to the 4-process algorithm [3]. They decide if the leader p_1 is correct, and at most one of $p_1, ..., p_4$ is faulty; p_5 is completely ignored. The next four conditions decide in two steps if at most one process is faulty (not p_1). Finally, the algorithm can sometimes decide if two processes propose the same and at most two are faulty or slow.

6. Conclusion

This paper presented a method for automatic verification and discovery of low-latency Consensus protocols through model checking. The main challenge here is the enormous size of the state and solution spaces. My method reduces the state space by focusing on the latency-determining first round only, ignoring the order of messages in this round, and distinguishing between state-modifying *actions* and state-preserving *predicates*. In addition, monotonicity of the predicates and verified properties allows one to use a Tarski-style fixpoint algorithm, which results in an exponential verification speed-up.

While no ground-breaking protocols have been discovered, the method described here generated interesting improvements to the existing algorithms. In particular, several combinations of fast one-step protocols and resilient leader-based algorithms have been discovered. Because of the number of cases involved, such composite algorithms are difficult to design and check manually.

I believe that automated protocol design is an interesting paradigm that can be successfully used together with the traditional manual process. From the practical point of view, it allows one to quickly analyze intricate interplays as well as discover subtle errors and improvements to existing protocols. This is especially useful in custom failure models with malicious participants. From the theoretical point of view, generated protocols as well as counterexample states can provide useful insights for general n-process protocols and lower bounds.

Security protocol research community recognized some time ago that automated correctness testing is ideal for short algorithms that are difficult to get right. It seems to me that distributed agreement protocols would greatly benefit from a similar treatment. Atomic broadcast, atomic commitment, etc., especially in the crash-recovery model, are interesting problems to tackle in this way.

References

[1] Y. Bar-David and G. Taubenfeld. Automatic discovery of Mutual Exclusion algorithms. In *Proc. of the 17th Int. Symposium on Distributed Computing*, 2003.

[2] M. Burrows, M. Abadi, and R. Needham. A logic of authentication. *ACM Transactions on Computer Systems*, 8(1):18–36, 1990.

[3] M. Castro and B. Liskov. Practical Byzantine fault tolerance. In *Proceedings of the Third Symposium on Operating Systems Design and Implementation*, pages 173–186, New Orleans, Louisiana, Feb. 1999.

[4] T. D. Chandra, V. Hadzilacos, and S. Toueg. The weakest failure detector for solving Consensus. *Journal of the ACM*, 43(4):685–722, 1996.

[5] E. M. Clarke, S. Jha, and W. Marrero. Verifying security protocols with Brutus. *ACM Trans. on Software Engineering and Methodology*, 9(4):443–487, 2000.

[6] P. Dutta, R. Guerraoui, and M. Vukolic. Asynchronous Byzantine Consensus: Complexity, resilience and authentication. TR 200479, EPFL, Sept. 2004.

[7] E. Gafni and L. Lamport. Disk Paxos. In *Int. Symposium on Distributed Computing*, pp. 330–344, 2000.

[8] J. Gray and L. Lamport. Consensus on Transaction Commit. TR 2003-96, Microsoft, Jan. 2004.

[9] R. Guerraoui and M. Raynal. The information structure of indulgent Consensus. TR 1531, IRISA, 2003.

[10] R. Guerraoui, M. Hurfin, A. Mostéfaoui, R. Oliveira, M. Raynal, and A. Schiper. Consensus in asynchronous distributed systems: A concise guided tour. In LNCS 1752, pages 33–47. Springer, 2000.

[11] M. P. Herlihy. Impossibility and universality results for wait-free synchronization. In *Proc. of the 7th Annual ACM Symposium on Principles of Distributed Computing*, pages 276–290, New York, USA, 1988.

[12] P. Kellomaki. An annotated specification of the Consensus protocol of Paxos using superposition in PVS. TR 36, Tampere University of Technology, 2004.

[13] L. Lamport. Paxos made simple. *ACM SIGACT News*, 32(4):18–25, December 2001.

[14] L. Lamport. *Specifying systems: the TLA+ language and tools for hardware and software engineers.* Addison-Wesley Professional, 2002.

[15] L. Lamport. Fast Paxos. Technical Report MSR-TR-2005-112, Microsoft Research (MSR), July 2005.

[16] L. Lamport. The part-time parliament. *ACM Transactions on Computer Systems*, 16(2):133–169, 1998.

[17] G. Lowe. Breaking and fixing the Needham-Schroeder public-key protocol using FDR. In *Proc. of the 2nd Int. Workshop on Tools and Algorithms for Construction and Analysis of Systems*, pp. 147–166, UK, 1996.

[18] J. C. Mitchell, M. Mitchell, and U. Stern. Automated analysis of cryptographic protocols using Murϕ. In *Proc. of the 1997 Symposium on Security and Privacy*, pages 141–153, Washington, DC, USA, 1997.

[19] A. Mostéfaoui and M. Raynal. Solving Consensus using Chandra-Toueg's unreliable failure detectors: A general quorum-based approach. In *Proceedings of the 13th International Symposium on Distributed Computing*, pages 49–63, London, UK, 1999.

[20] L. C. Paulson. The inductive approach to verifying cryptographic protocols. *Journal of Computer Security*, 6:85–128, 1998.

[21] Pogosyants, Segala, and Lynch. Verification of the randomized Consensus algorithm of Aspnes and Herlihy: A case study. *DISTCOMP*, 13, 2000.

[22] R. D. Prisco, B. W. Lampson, and N. A. Lynch. Revisiting the Paxos algorithm. In *Workshop on Distributed Algorithms*, pages 111–125, 1997.

[23] M. Raynal. Consensus in synchronous systems: a concise guided tour. TR 1497, IRISA, Jul 2002.

[24] A. Schiper. Early Consensus in an asynchronous system with a weak failure detector. *Distributed Computing*, 10(3):149–157, Apr. 1997.

[25] A. Tarski. A fixed point theorem and its applications. *Pacific Journal of Mathematics*, pages 285–309, 1955.

[26] T. Tsuchiya and A. Schiper. Model Checking of Consensus Algorithms. Technical report, EPFL, 2006.

[27] T. N. Win and M. D. Ernst. Verifying distributed algorithms via dynamic analysis and theorem proving. TR 841, MIT Lab for Computer Science, May 2002.

[28] T. N. Win, M. D. Ernst, S. J. Garland, D. Kırlı, and N. Lynch. Using simulated execution in verifying distributed algorithms. *Software Tools for Technology Transfer*, 6(1):67–76, July 2004.

[29] P. Zieliński. *Minimizing latency of agreement protocols*. PhD thesis, Computer Laboratory, University of Cambridge, UK, 2006. TR 667.

[30] P. Zieliński. Optimistically Terminating Consensus. In *Proc. of the 5th Int. Symposium on Parallel and Distributed Computing*, Timisoara, Romania, July 2006.

Knowledge Connectivity *vs.* Synchrony Requirements for Fault-Tolerant Agreement in Unknown Networks*

Fabíola Greve
Computer Science Department
Federal University of Bahia (UFBA), Brasil
fabiola@dcc.ufba.br

Sébastien Tixeuil
Univ. Paris-Sud
LRI-CNRS & INRIA Grand Large, France
tixeuil@lri.fr

Abstract

In self-organizing systems, such as mobile ad-hoc and peer-to-peer networks, consensus is a fundamental building block to solve agreement problems. It contributes to coordinate actions of nodes distributed in an ad-hoc manner in order to take consistent decisions. It is well known that in classical environments, in which entities behave asynchronously and where identities are known, consensus cannot be solved in the presence of even one process crash. It appears that self-organizing systems are even less favorable because the set and identity of participants are not known. We define necessary and sufficient conditions under which fault-tolerant consensus become solvable in these environments. Those conditions are related to the synchrony requirements of the environment, as well as the connectivity of the knowledge graph constructed by the nodes in order to communicate with their peers.

1 Introduction

Wireless sensor and *ad hoc* networks (and, in a different context, unstructured peer to peer networks) enable participating entities access to services and informations independently of their location or mobility. This is done by eliminating the necessity of any statically designed infrastructure or any centralized administrative authority. It is in the nature of such systems to be self-organizing, since additionally, entities are allowed to join or leave the network in an arbitrary manner, making the whole system highly dynamic.

Agreement problems are fundamental building blocks of reliable distributed systems, and the issue of designing reliable solutions that can cope with the high dynamism and

*This work is part of the CAPES-COFECUB international cooperation program. Fabíola's research was supported by grants from CNPQ/Brazil and Fapesb-Bahia/Brazil. Sébastien's research was supported by grants FRAGILE and SOGEA from ANR.

self-organization nature of sensor and *ad-hoc* network is a very active field of current research. The core problem behind agreement problems is the *consensus* problem. Informally, a group of processes achieves consensus in the following sense: each process initially proposes a value and all correct processes (*i.e.* those that are not crashed) must reach a common decision on some value that is equal to one of the proposed values. For example, reaching agreement within a set of mobile robots was recently investigated in [9].

Contrarily to traditional (*i.e.* wired) networks, where processes are aware of network topology and have a complete knowledge of every other participant, in a self-organizing environment with no central authority, the number and processes are *not* known initially. Yet, even in a classical environment, when entities behave asynchronously, consensus cannot be solved if one of the participants is allowed to crash [6]. Thus, solving consensus when the set of participants is unknown is even more difficult. Nonetheless, due to the essential role of this problem, we study in this paper the conditions that permit to solve consensus in unknown asynchronous networks in spite of participant crashes.

In order to capture the unawareness of self-organizing systems regarding the topology of the network as well as the set of participants, Cavin *et al.* [1] defined a new problem named CUP (*consensus with unknown participants*). This new problem keeps the same definition of the classical consensus, except for the expected knowledge about the set of processes in the system. More precisely, they assume that processes are *not* aware of Π, the set of processes in the system. To solve any non trivial application, processes must somehow get a partial knowledge about the other processes if some cooperation is expected. The *participant detector* abstraction was proposed to handle this subset of known processes [1]. They can be seen as distributed oracles that provides hints about the participating processes in the computation. For example, a way to implement participant detectors for mobile nodes is to make use of local broadcasting in order to construct a local view formed by 1-hop neighbors. Based on the initial knowledge graph formed by the participant detectors in the system, Cavin *et al.* define necessary and sufficient connectivity conditions of this knowledge graph in order to solve CUP in an asynchronous environment but in a *fault-free* scenario.

In turn, *failure detector* and *leader* oracles are elegant abstractions which encapsulate the extra synchrony necessary to circumvent the impossibility result of fault-tolerant consensus in traditional networks [3, 8]. A failure detector of the class $\Diamond S$ can be seen as an oracle that provides hints on crashed processes [3]. The Ω leader oracle, eventually provides processes with he same correct process identity (that is, the same leader) [8]. Both, $\Diamond S$ and Ω have the same computational power [5], and they have been proved to be the weakest classes of detectors allowing to solve consensus in asynchronous known networks [4]. Those failure detectors may make an arbitrary number of mistakes, but, in spite of their inaccuracy, they will never compromise the safety properties of the consensus protocol that uses them. These consensus protocols are considered *indulgent* towards these oracles, meaning that they are conceived to tolerate their unreliability during arbitrary periods of asynchrony and instability of the environment. Moreover, any of those indulgent protocols will solve the uniform version of the consensus. The *uniform consensus* ensures the uniformity of the decision, processes be correct of faulty [7].

In the context of unknown networks, the problem of FT-CUP (*fault-tolerant* CUP) has been subsequently studied by Cavin *et al.* [2]. By considering the minimal connectivity requirements over the initial knowledge graph for solving CUP, they identify a perfect failure detector ($\mathcal{P}$) to fulfill the necessary synchrony requirements for solving FT-CUP. A perfect failure detector never make mistakes and can only be implemented in a synchronous system. Thus, solving FT-CUP in a scenario with the weakest knowledge connectivity demands the strongest synchrony conditions. However, strong synchrony competes with the high dynamism, full decentralization and self-organizing nature of wireless sensor and *ad-hoc* networks. Moreover, even with a perfect failure detector, when the minimal knowledge connectivity is being considered, the uniform version of FT-CUP cannot be solved in unknown networks [2].

In this paper, we show that there is a trade-off between knowledge connectivity and synchrony for consensus in fault-prone unknown networks. In particular, we focus on solving FT-CUP with minimal synchrony assumption (*i.e.* the Ω failure detector), and investigate necessary and sufficient requirement about knowledge connectivity. If the system satisfies our knowledge connectivity conditions, any of the indulgent consensus algorithms initially designed for traditional networks can be reused to solve FT-CUP as well as uniform FT-CUP.

The remaining of the paper is organized as follows: Sec-

tion 2 provides the model, notations, and statement of the problem we consider; Section 3 describes abstractions to solve consensus; Section 4 presents necessary and sufficient conditions to solve FT-CUP and uniform FT-CUP with minimal synchrony assumptions. Section 5 provides some concluding remarks.

2 Preliminaries

Model. We consider a distributed system that consists of a finite set Π of $n > 1$ processes, namely, $\Pi = \{p_1, \ldots, p_n\}$. In a *known* network, Π is known to every participating process, while in an *unknown* network, a process p_i may only be aware of a subset Π_i of Π.

Processes communicate by sending and receiving messages through reliable channels, *i.e.*, there is no message creation, corruption, duplication; moreover, a message m sent by a process p_i to p_j is eventually received by p_j, if both p_i and p_j are correct. A process p_i may only send a message to another process p_j if $p_j \in \Pi_i$. Of course, if a process p_i sends a message to a process p_j such that $p_i \notin \Pi_j$, upon receipt of the message, p_j may add p_i to Π_j and send a message back to p_i. We assume the existence of a reliable underlying routing layer, in such a way that if $p_j \in \Pi_i$, then p_i can send a message reliably to p_j. There are no assumptions on the relative speed of processes or on message transfer delays, *i.e.* the system is asynchronous.

A process may fail by *crashing*, *i.e.*, by prematurely or by deliberately halting (switched off); a crashed process does not recover. A process behaves correctly (*i.e.*, according to its specification) until it (possibly) crashes. By definition, a *correct* process is a process that does not crash. A *faulty* process is a process that is not correct. Let f denote the maximum number of processes that may crash in the system. We assume that f is known to every process.

Classical Consensus. The consensus problem is the most fundamental agreement problem in distributed computing. Every process p_i *proposes* a value v_i and all correct processes *decide* on some unique value v, in relation to the set of proposed values. More precisely, the consensus is defined by the following properties [3, 6]: *(i)* Termination: every *correct* process eventually decides some value; *(ii)* Validity: if a process decides v, then v was proposed by some process; *(iii)* Agreement: no two *correct* processes decide differently.

Uniform Consensus. The *uniform* version of the consensus changes the agreement property for: *(iii)* Uniform Agreement: no two processes (*correct or not*) decide differently.

Consensus in Unknown Networks. In this paper, we concentrate on solving consensus in a fault-prone unknown network. We consider three variants of the problem:

CUP (Consensus with Unknown Participants). The goal is to solve consensus in an unknown network, where processes may *not* crash;

FT-CUP (Fault-Tolerant CUP). The goal is to solve consensus in an unknown network, where up to f processes may crash;

Uniform FT-CUP (Uniform Fault-Tolerant CUP). The goal is to solve the uniform version of the consensus in an unknown network where up to f processes may crash.

Graph Notations. We consider *directed graphs* $G_{di} = (V, E)$, defined by a set of vertices V and a set E of edges (v_1, v_2), which are ordered pairs of vertices of V. Throughout the paper, the terms "node", "vertex" and "process" will be used indistinctly. The *distance* between two vertices u, v (denoted by $d(u, v)$) is the minimum of the lengths of all directed paths from u to v (assuming there exists at least one such path). The *out-degree* of a vertex v of G_{di} is equal to the number of vertices u such that the edge (v, u) is in E. A *sink* is a node with out-degree 0. A directed graph $G_{di}(V, E)$ is k-strongly connected if for any pair of nodes (v_i, v_j), v_i can reach v_j through k distinct node-disjoint paths. In particular, when $k = 1$, G_{di} is strongly connected. By Menger's Theorem [10], it is known that the minimum number of nodes whose removal from $G_{di}(V, E)$ disconnects nodes v_i from v_j is equal to the maximal number of node-disjoint paths from v_i to v_j. This result leads to the following two observations:

1. For any n and k, there exists a n-sized k-strongly connected directed graph $G_{di}(V, E)$ such that the removal of k nodes disconnects the graph.

2. If the graph G_{di} is k-strongly connected, removing $(k - 1)$ nodes leaves at least *one* path between any pair of nodes (v_i, v_j). Thus, the graph remains strongly connected.

3 Synchrony and Knowledge Connectivity for Consensus in Fault-Prone Systems

3.1 Failure Detector: a Synchrony Abstraction

A fundamental result in the consensus literature [6] states that even if Π is known to all processes in the system and the number of faulty processes is bounded by 1, consensus cannot be solved by a deterministic algorithm in an asynchronous system. To enable solutions, some level of synchrony must be assumed. A nice abstraction to model network synchrony is the *failure detector* [3]. A failure detector (denoted by FD) can be seen as an oracle that provides hints on crashed processes. Failure detectors can be classified according to the properties (completeness and accuracy) they satisfy. The completeness property refers to the actual detection of crashes; the accuracy property restricts the mistakes a failure detector is allowed to make. In this paper, we consider two classes of failure detectors:

Perfect FD ($\mathcal{P}$). Those failure detectors never make mistakes. They satisfy the *perpetual strong accuracy*, stating that no process is suspected before it crashes, and the *strong completeness* property, stating that eventually, every process that crashes is permanently suspected by every correct process.

Eventually Strong FD ($\diamondsuit\mathcal{S}$). Those failure detectors can make an arbitrary number of mistakes. Yet, there is a time after which some correct process is never suspected (*eventual weak accuracy*). Moreover, they satisfy the *strong completeness* property.

Leader Detector (Ω). Another approach for encapsulating eventual synchrony consists of extending the system with a *leader detector*, which is an oracle that eventually provides the same correct process identity to all processes [8].

It has been proved that $\diamondsuit\mathcal{S}$ and Ω have the same computational power [5] and that they are the weakest class of detectors allowing to solve the consensus and the uniform consensus problem in a system of known networks [4]. Relying on $\diamondsuit\mathcal{S}$ and Ω failure detectors to solve agreement problems assumes that a majority of processes within the group never fails, i.e., $f < n/2$.

3.2 Participant Detectors: a Knowledge Connectivity Abstraction

With the notable exception of [1, 2], literature on consensus related problems considers that Π is known to every process in the system. In *ad hoc* and sensor wireless networks, this assumption is clearly unrealistic since processes could be maintained by different administrative authorities, have various wake up times, initializations, failure rates, etc. Of course, *some* knowledge about other nodes is necessary to run *any* non trivial distributed algorithm. For example, the use of "Hello" messages (*i.e.* locally broadcasting your identifier to your vicinity) could be a possible way for each process to get some knowledge about the other processes.

The notion of *participant detectors* (denoted by PD) has been proposed by [1]. Similarly to failure detectors, they can be seen as distributed oracles that provide information about which processes participate to the system. We denote by $i.PD$ the participant detector of process p_i. When queried by p_i, $i.PD$ returns a subset of processes in Π. The information provided by $i.PD$ can evolve between queries. Let $i.PD(t)$ be the query of process p_i at time t. This query must satisfy the two following properties:

• **Information Inclusion.** The information returned by the participant detector is non-decreasing over time. $p_i \in \Pi, t' \geq t : i.PD(t) \in i.PD(t')$

• **Information Accuracy.** The participant detector does not make mistakes. $\forall p_i \in \Pi, \forall t : i.PD(t) \in \Pi$

The PD abstraction enriches the system with a knowledge connectivity graph. This graph is directed since knowledge that is given by participation detectors is not necessarily bidirectional (*i.e.* if $p_j \in i.PD$, then $p_i \in j.PD$ does *not* necessarily hold).

Definition 1 (Knowledge Connectivity Graph) *Let $G_{di}(V, E)$ be the directed graph representing the knowledge relation determined by the* PD *oracle. Then, $V = \Pi$ and $(p_i, p_j) \in E$ if and only if $p_j \in i.PD$, i.e., p_i knows p_j.*

Definition 2 (Undirected Knowledge Connectivity Graph) *Let $G(V, E)$ be the undirected graph representing the knowledge relation determined by the* PD *oracle. Then, $V = \Pi$ and $(p_i, p_j) \in E$ if and only if $p_j \in i.PD$ or $p_i \in j.PD$.*

Based on the induced knowledge connectivity graph, several classes of participant detectors were proposed in [1]:

Connectivity PD (CO). The undirected knowledge connectivity graph G induced by the PD oracle is connected.

Strong Connectivity PD (SCO). The knowledge connectivity graph G_{di} induced by the PD oracle is strongly connected.

One Sink Reducibility PD (OSR). The knowledge connectivity graph G_{di} induced by the PD oracle satisfies the following conditions:

1. the undirected knowledge connectivity graph G obtained from G_{di} is connected;

2. the directed acyclic graph obtained by reducing G_{di} to its strongly connected components has exactly one sink.

In this paper, we introduce three new participant detector classes:

k-Connectivity PD (k-CO). The undirected knowledge connectivity graph G induced by the PD oracle is k-connected.

k-Strong Connectivity PD (k-SCO). The knowledge connectivity graph G_{di} induced by the PD oracle is k-strongly connected.

k-One Sink Reducibility PD (k-OSR). The knowledge connectivity graph G_{di} induced by the PD oracle satisfies the following conditions:

1. the undirected knowledge connectivity graph G obtained from G_{di} is connected;

2. the directed acyclic graph obtained by reducing G_{di} to its k-strongly connected components has exactly one sink;

3. consider any two k-strongly connected components G_1 and G_2, if there is a path from G_1 to G_2, then there are k node-disjoint paths from G_1 to G_2.

Figure 1 illustrates a graph G_{di} induced by a k-OSR PD, for $k = 2$. Note that there is only one sink component (G_3) and that every component G_i is 2-strongly connected.

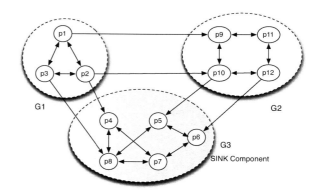

Figure 1. Knowledge Connectivity Graph Induced for a k-OSR Participant Detector, $k = 2$

4 Knowledge Connectivity and Synchrony Requirements to Solve FT-CUP

In [1], the CUP problem is investigated in *fault free* networks, and it is shown that *(i)* the CO participant detector is necessary to solve CUP, *(ii)* the SCO participant detector is sufficient to solve CUP, and *(iii)* the OSR participant detector is both necessary and sufficient to solve CUP. Subsequently [2], the authors show that the same classes are not sufficient to solve FT-CUP.

In this section, we investigate the k-CO, k-SCO and k-OSR participant detectors with respect to the FT-CUP problem, assuming the lowest possible synchrony (*i.e.* the Ω failure detector) necessary to solve consensus in known networks. In a nutshell, we show that provided the actual number of faults f is strictly lower than some constant k ($f < k < n$), *(i)* the k-CO participant detector is necessary to solve FT-CUP (Proposition 1), *(ii)* the k-SCO participant detector is sufficient to solve uniform FT-CUP assuming Ω (Proposition 2), and *(iii)* the k-OSR participant detector is sufficient to solve uniform FT-CUP and necessary to solve FT-CUP assuming Ω (Proposition 3).

4.1 k-CO Participant Detector is Necessary to Solve FT-CUP

Proposition 1 *The k-CO participant detector is necessary to solve FT-CUP, in spite of $f < k < n$ node crashes.*

Proof: Assume by contradiction that the undirected knowledge connectivity graph G defined by the PD oracle is $(k-1)$-connected. Following observation 2 in Section 2, the removal of $k - 1$ nodes may disconnect this undirected graph G into at least two components. From [1], connectivity of G is a necessary condition to solve CUP. So, to tolerate $f < k$ node removals, PD $\in k$-CO. $\square$

4.2 *k-SCO* Participant Detector is Sufficient to Solve Uniform FT-CUP Assuming Ω

Our approach to claim the main result of this section is constructive: we provide an algorithm (COLLECT) that enables the reuse of a previously known consensus algorithm assuming Ω.

4.2.1 The COLLECT Algorithm

Overview. The COLLECT algorithm (presented as Algorithm 1) provides nodes a partial view of the system participants. Each node eventually gets the maximal set of processes that it can reach. COLLECT considers that $f < k$ processes may crash. When initiating the algorithm, a process p_i first queries its participant detector to obtain $i.PD$; then p_i iteratively requests newly known processes to get knowledge improvement about the network, until no further knowledge can be acquired. Thus, COLLECT operates in rounds: in each round $r > 0$, p_i contacts all nodes it did not know about in round $r - 1$ so that they increase p_i's knowledge about the network. At round 0, p_i only knows about itself. In our scheme, we assume that for each process p_i, the participant detector $i.PD$ of p_i is queried exactly once. This can be implemented for example by caching the value of the first result of $i.PD$ and returning that value in the subsequent calls. This property guaranties that the partial snapshot about the initial knowledge connectivity of the system is consistent for all nodes in the system, and defines a common knowledge connectivity graph $G_{di} = (V, E)$.

Whenever PD $\in k$-SCO, COLLECT terminates and returns Π. Otherwise, whenever PD $\in k$-OSR, the algorithm provides p_i all reachable nodes from its k-strongly-connected components plus reachable nodes from other components (which includes at least all nodes in the sink component). On the example of Figure 1, COLLECT will return for $p_i \in G_1$, a subset of $p_j \in \{G_1 \cup G_2 \cup G_3\}$; for $p_i \in G_2$, a subset of $p_j \in \{G_2 \cup G_3\}$; for $p_i \in G_3$, a subset of $p_j \in \{G_3\}$.

Variables. A node p_i manages the following local variables:

- $i.known$: subset of nodes known by p_i in the current round;
- $i.responded$: subset of nodes from which p_i has received a message;
- $i.previously\_known$: previous set of nodes known by p_i in the previous round;
- $i.wait$: number of nodes from which p_i is still waiting for a message.

Description. A process p_i starts the algorithm by executing the INIT phase. In this initial stage, p_i queries its participant detector (line 13) and sets $i.known$ to the returned list of participants ($i.PD$). After that, it calls upon the *Inquiry()* procedure to transmit this partial knowledge about the system composition to every node recently discovered. Thus, p_i sends a VIEW($i, i.known$) message to every known process p_j (lines 9-10) and updates some local variables. In particular, it sets $i.wait$ to the minimal number of correct nodes, *i.e.*, the cardinality of its $i.known$ set minus the maximal number of crashes (f) (line 11). In the IMPROVEMENT phase, upon receipt of a message VIEW($m.initiator$, $m.known$) from p_j to p_i, two cases are presented.

- $m.initiator \neq i$: this means that p_i have received an inquiry from a remote node p_j. Thus, p_i sends back to p_j its original list of participants ($i.PD$) (line 28).
- $m.initiator = i$: in this case, p_i received back a message carrying p_j's initial knowledge connectivity. Thus, p_i improves its initial knowledge, extending $i.known$ with $j.PD$ and it updates its local variables $i.responded$ and $i.wait$ accordingly (lines 18-20). Afterwards, by testing the predicate ($i.wait = 0$), p_i verifies whether it has received sufficiently many messages from all known correct nodes (line 21). If that is the case, p_i checks whether its current view has changed with respect to the previous one. Two situations can occur:
- If $i.previously\_known = i.known$, this means that p_i has gathered knowledge information from all known correct nodes. In this case, the algorithm terminates and p_i returns its $i.known$ set (line 23).
- If $i.previously\_known \neq i.known$, this means that p_i has discovered new nodes. So, it will start a new round to improve knowledge information about the new nodes belonging to $i.known \setminus i.previously\_known$. So, p_i calls the *Inquiry()* procedure to send a message VIEW($i, i.known$) to every new node recently discovered. After that, p_i updates $i.wait$ accordingly, excluding those having already responded and crashed. Finally, $i.previously\_known$ receives the contents of the most recent $i.known$ set (lines 9-12).

Lemma 1 *Starting by round $r = 1$, in each round r of algorithm* COLLECT, *$i.known$ is augmented with reachable nodes whose distance from p_i is r.*

Proof: To discover the set of reachable processes, the algorithm COLLECT realizes a sort of *breadth-first search* in the graph G_{di}. Let the initiator p_i, be the root of the tree established by this search. The rounds correspond to the levels of the tree. If p_j is first discovered by p_i in round r, then $d(p_i, p_j) = r$. This means that p_j is reached by the breadth-first search in level r. Denote $N_{(r)}(p_i)$ the set of all nodes reached by the breadth-first search until level r. Let $i.known$ be the set of known nodes in round r. So, $i.known = N_{(r)}(p_i)$. Let us proceed the proof by induction on r. Basis: In round $r = 1$ (level 1 of the tree), p_i attributes

Algorithm 1 COLLECT()

constant:

(1) f: int // *upper bound on the number of crashes*

variables:

(2) $i.previously\_known$: set of nodes

(3) $i.known$: set of nodes

(4) $i.responded$: set of nodes

(5) $i.wait$: int

message:

(6)   VIEW message:

(7)   *initiator*: node

(8)   *known*: set of nodes

procedure:

Inquiry():

(9)   **for** j in $i.known \setminus i.previously\_known$ **do**

(10)   SEND VIEW $(i, i.known)$ to p_j; **end do**

(11) $i.wait = |i.known \setminus i.responded| - f$;

(12) $i.previously\_known = i.known$;

** *Initiator Only* **

INIT:

(13) $i.known = i.PD$;

(14) $i.responded = i.previously\_known = \{\}$;

(15)   call upon *Inquiry* ();

** *All Nodes* **

IMPROVEMENT:

(16) **upon receipt of** VIEW($m.initiator, m.known$) **from** p_j **to** p_i:

(17)   **if** $i == m.initiator$ **then**

(18) $i.known = i.known \cup m.known$;

(19) $i.responded = i.responded \cup \{j\}$;

(20) $i.wait = i.wait - 1$;

(21)   **if** $i.wait == 0$ **then**

(22)   **if** $i.previously\_known == i.known$ **then**

(23)   *return* $(i.known)$;

(24)   **else**

(25)   call upon *Inquiry()*; **end if**

(26)   **end if**

(27)   **else**

(28)   *send* VIEW($m.initiator, i.PD$) to p_j;

(29)   **end if**

its list of adjacent nodes to $i.known$, which corresponds to the list of participants returned by i.PD (line 13). So, if $p_j \in i$.PD, $d(p_i, p_j) = 1$ and $i.known = N_{(1)}(p_i)$.

Induction: Suppose the Lemma holds for level $< r$ of the tree. A new round r starts whenever informations about new nodes in the system are gathered by p_i in round $(r - 1)$, satisfying the condition ($i.known \neq i.previously\_known$) in line 24. Let p_j be a node in ($i.known \setminus i.previously\_known$) such that p_j has been discovered by p_i in round $(r - 1)$, $d(p_i, p_j) = (r - 1)$.

Starting round r, by calling *Inquiry()* in line 25, p_i inquiries p_j for sending its view of known processes (lines 9-12). After that, still in round r, node p_j will reply, by passing back to p_i its list of participants returned by the participant detector j.PD, which is equivalent to $N_{(1)}(p_j)$ (line 28). Let $p_l \in j$.PD and $p_l \notin i.known$. This means that, in its probing for discovering new processes, p_i has not met p_l (round $< r$); otherwise, by the inductive hypothesis, p_l would be in $i.known$. Thus, $d(p_i, p_l) > (r - 1)$. On the reception of message VIEW from p_j, $i.known$ is updated with j.PD (line 18). By the inductive hypothesis, in round $(r - 1)$, $i.known = N_{(r-1)}(p_i)$, $d(p_i, p_j) = r - 1$ and $d(p_j, p_l) = 1$. So, in round r, $i.known$ contains $N_{(r-1)}(p_i) \cup N_{(1)}(p_j)$, then $i.known = N_{(r)}(p_i)$ and $d(p_i, p_l) = r$. □

Lemma 2 *Consider a k-OSR participant detector. Let $f < k < n$ be the number of nodes that may crash. Algorithm* COLLECT *(1) executed by each node satisfy the following properties :*

• Termination: *every node p_i terminates execution and returns a list of known nodes (processes with whom p_i can communicate);*

• Safety: COLLECT *returns the maximal set of correct processes reachable from p_i.*

Proof: Termination. Let us proceed our proof by induction on r. In round $r = 1$, at beginning of the execution, $i.known$ receives the list from i.PD (line 13). So, $i.known$ is initially composed by processes with whom it can communicate. Going on the round, at line 15, p_i calls upon the *Inquiry()* procedure, so that it will send a VIEW message to every one of these $i.known$ processes, excluded those in $i.previously\_known$ (which in round $r = 1$ is empty) (lines 9-12). By Menger's Theorem, there are at least k nodes in each one of the m components of G_{di}. Since $f < k$, there are at least 1 correct node in each one of these components. So, p_i will receive at least $(|i.known| - f) \geq 1$ responses for its inquiry (line 16). This number coincides to the initial value of the $i.wait$ variable (set up in line 11) and thus, due to its decay when a reply arrives (line 20), eventually condition ($i.wait == 0$) will be satisfied (see line 21). Note that, on the execution of this investigation procedure – characterized by the sent and reception of VIEW() messages – p_i could enlarge its knowledge about processes in the system, resulting in the update of its $i.known$ set (line 18). Note also that $p.i$'s previous knowledge is stored in the $i.previously\_known$ set (see line 12). Whenever the condition ($i.wait == 0$) is verified, two case are possible:

(i) $i.known = i.previously\_known$. This means that correct processes in $i.known$ share the same view. In this case, the algorithm terminates by returning the gathered $i.known$ view (line 23). (ii) $i.known \neq i.previously\_known$. This means that p_i has enlarged its knowledge. In this case, it will inquiry for the view of these new processes, calling upon $Inquiry()$ and starting a new round $r + 1$ (line 25). Suppose these executing conditions hold in rounds $< r$. Eventually, in round r, since the set of processes in the system (Π) is finite, no new process is going to be discovered by p_i in line 18. Thus, condition (i) ($i.known = i.previously\_known$) will be satisfied and the algorithm terminates.

Safety. Let us first make some useful remarks. Let $G_{di} = (V, E)$ be the knowledge graph defined by k-OSR and decomposed into its m k-strongly connected components. Let $G = G_1 \cup G_2 \cup ... \cup G_m$ be such a decomposition. Remember that there is exactly one sink component in G_{di}. Consider two nodes p_i and p_j in V. Two cases are possible. (i) If p_i and p_j are in the same component G_i, since each one of the G_{di} components is k-strongly connected, there is at least k node-disjoint paths between any two nodes in G_i; (ii) If $p_i \in G_i$ and $p_j \in G_j$, $G_i \neq G_j$ (the nodes are in distinct components), suppose that p_j is reachable from p_i ($p_i \rightsquigarrow p_j$). From the property (3) of the graph G_{di} generated by k-OSR, there are k-disjoint paths from G_i to G_j. So, there is at least k node-disjoint paths from node p_i to p_j in G_{di}. From the Menger's Theorem (see the observation 2 in Section 2), removing $(k - 1)$ nodes leaves at least one path between any pair of nodes (p_i, p_j) in each k-strongly connected component. Thus, in both situations, there is at least one path from p_i to p_j composed of correct nodes.

Our claim is that algorithm COLLECT returns to p_i the *maximal* set of correct processes reachable from p_i. This set is stored in $i.known$. Let us proceed our proof by induction on the number of rounds and demonstrate that, in round r, $i.known$ contains all reachable processes from p_i through a path of length at most r. Basis: In round $r = 1$, $i.known$ contains all neighbor nodes p_j returned by its participant detector i.PD, $d(p_i, p_j) = 1$.

Induction: Suppose the claim is valid for round $< r$. Let p_l be a node such that $d(p_i, p_l) = r$. In this case, from the statements above (situations (i) and (ii)), there is at least one path from p_i to p_l composed of correct nodes. Let p_j be the predecessor of p_l in this path. Thus, p_l belongs to j.PD. Evidently $d(p_i, p_j) = (r - 1)$; otherwise, $d(p_i, p_l) \neq r$. By the inductive step, $i.known$ contains all those correct

nodes that are exactly $(r - 1)$ edges away from p_i. Since $d(p_i, p_j) = (r - 1)$, p_j has been discovered by p_i in round $(r - 1)$ (Lemma 1).

Round r starts whenever informations about new nodes in the system are gathered by p_i in round $(r - 1)$. Thus, in round $(r-1)$, $p_j \in (i.known \setminus i.previously\_known)$. At the beginning of round r, p_i will inquiry all new nodes (including p_j) to send their view of known processes (lines 9-10). After that, still in round r, node p_j will reply, by passing back to p_i its list of participants returned by its participant detector j.PD (line 28). Upon reception of message VIEW from p_j, $i.known$ is updated with j.PD (line 18). By the inductive step, in round $(r - 1)$, $i.known$ contains all processes reachable from p_i through a path of length at most $(r - 1)$. Thus, in round r, $i.known$ is extended with every new node discovered by p_i in round r (thus including p_l). So, in round r, $i.known$ contains all correct nodes reachable from p_i through a path of length at most r. □

Proposition 2 *The k-SCO participant detector is sufficient to solve uniform FT-CUP, in spite of $f < k < n$ node crashes, assuming Ω.*

Proof: *Sufficient*: If PD $\in k$-SCO, there is exactly one k-strongly connected component in the graph. Thus, the COLLECT algorithm provides each process p_i with the set Π (see Lemma 2), in spite of $f < k$ crashes. Then, previous indulgent algorithms aiming for solving classical consensus, which are based on a priori knowledge about Π, can be used [3, 8]. In particular, if $f < n/2$, and $k < n$, it is possible to solve FT-CUP as well uniform FT-CUP in a system enriched with both: a k-SCO participant detector and a Ω failure detector. □

4.3 k-OSR Participant Detector is Sufficient and Necessary to Solve FT-CUP Assuming Ω

Our approach for the main result of this section is also constructive. The CONSENSUS algorithm that we provide builds upon the previously presented COLLECT algorithm and a second algorithm (SINK) that determines whether a node is in the single k-strongly connected sink component of the knowledge connectivity graph.

4.3.1 The SINK Algorithm

The SINK algorithm (presented as Algorithm 2) determines if a node belongs to a sink component. SINK makes use of the COLLECT algorithm that provides nodes with a partial view of the system composition. Now, in the sink component, nodes have the same view of the system (*i.e.* the same set of known nodes), whereas in the other components, nodes have strictly more knowledge than in the sink.

The algorithm is composed of two phases. In the INIT phase, processes broadcast their knowledge about the composition of the system (which is an approximation of Π), while in the VERIFICATION phase, processes determine whether they belong to the sink component or not.

Description. A process p_i starts the algorithm by executing the INIT procedure. First, p_i runs the COLLECT algorithm to get the partial list of nodes, which is stored in $i.known$ (line 9). Afterwards, p_i sends a REQUEST($i.known$) message to every process p_j in this set (lines 11-12). Upon receipt of a REQUEST($m.known$) message from p_j, process p_i tests if its own $i.known$ set is equal to the message's $m.known$ set. In case of equality, this means that p_i belongs to the same component of p_j. So, p_i sends back an ack response to p_j (line 15). Otherwise, p_i sends back a $nack$ response (line 17).

Upon receipt of a RESPONSE($ack/nack$) message from p_j, process p_i determines whether it is in the sink component or not. If p_j responded $nack$, this means that p_i has identified processes (including p_j) belonging to other component. So, p_i cannot be in the sink and it terminates execution returning $false$ for the $i.in\_the\_sink$ predicate (line 25-26). If p_j responds ack, this means that p_j has the same view of p_i about reachable processes in the system. Moreover, If p_i receives ack messages from every correct process in its view, p_i can conclude that it is in the sink component. So, when receiving an ack message, p_i updates its local variable $i.responded$ to take into account p_j's response (line 20) and tests the condition ($|i.responded| >= |i.known| - f$) in order to know if it has received responses from every correct process (line 21). Whenever this condition becomes $true$, p_i is sure that it belongs to the sink component and thus it can terminate execution, returning $true$ for the $i.in\_the\_sink$ predicate (lines 22-23).

Lemma 3 *Consider a k-OSR participant detector. Let $f < k < n$ be the number of nodes that may crash. Algorithm SINK (2) executed by each node satisfy the following properties:*

• **Termination**: *every node p_i terminates execution by deciding whether it belongs to the sink component (true) or not (false);*

• **Safety**: *a node p_i is in the unique k-strongly connected sink component iff algorithm SINK returns true.*

Proof: Termination. At the beginning of execution, node p_i sends a REQUEST message to all processes in its local view ($i.known$) (lines 11-12). Since at most $f < k$ processes can crash, p_i will receive at least $s = (|i.known| - f)$ responses in line 13. Since G_{di} is k-strongly connected, $|i.known| \geq k$, thus $s \geq k - f \geq 1$. If *one* of these responses equals $nack$, the algorithm terminates, by returning $false$ (lines 25-26). If a *sufficient* number ($\geq s$) of ack responses is received (line 21), the algorithm terminates by returning $true$ (lines 22-23). Lines 23 and 26 are the only points where the algorithm terminates. Thus $true$ or $false$ are the only possible returns.

Algorithm 2 SINK ()

constants:
(1) f: upper bound on the number of crashes
variables:
(2) $i.known$: set of nodes
(3) $i.in\_the\_sink$: boolean
(4) $i.responded$: set of nodes
messages:
(5)   REQUEST message:
(6)   *known*: set of nodes
(7)   RESPONSE message:
(8)   *ack/nack*: boolean

** All Nodes **
INIT:
(9) $i.known = $ COLLECT ();
(10) $i.responded = \{\}$;
(11)   **for** each j in $i.known$ **do**
(12)   send REQUEST ($i.known$) to p_j; **endfor**

VERIFICATION:
(13) **upon receipt of** REQUEST ($m.known$) **from** p_j :
(14)   **if** $m.known == i.known$ **then**
(15)   send RESPONSE (ack) to p_j;
(16)   **else**
(17)   send RESPONSE ($nack$) to p_j; **endif**

(18) **upon receipt of** RESPONSE (m) **from** p_j :
(19)   **if** $m.ack$ **then**
(20) $i.responded = i.responded \cup \{j\}$;
(21)   **if** $|i.responded| \geq |i.known| - f$ **then**
(22) $i.in_the_sink = $ true;
(23)   return ($i.in\_the\_sink, i.known$); **endif**
(24)   **else**
(25) $i.in_the_sink = $ false;
(26)   return ($i.in\_the\_sink, i.known$);
(27)   **endif**

Safety. (i) Let us first prove that *if node p_i is in the unique k-strongly connected sink component* then *algorithm SINK returns true*. From Lemma 2, the COLLECT algorithm returns a list of all nodes reachable from p_i in G_{di}. Consequently, nodes in the unique k-strongly connected sink will have the same view of the system and the execution of line 9 returns the same $i.known$ set to all nodes in the sink. In this case, every node p_j in view $i.known$ which executes line 13 will respond ack to p_i's request (line 15). Thus, the condition in line 24 will never be satisfied. Moreover, since there are at least $s = (|i.known| - f)$ correct processes in the system, at least a number of s responses will be received by p_i. Thus, condition in line 21 will eventually be satisfied and the algorithm terminates returning *true* (lines 22-23).

(ii) Let us now prove that *if algorithm* SINK *returns true* then *node p_i is in the unique k-strongly connected sink component*. Assume by contradiction that p_i does not belong to the unique sink of G_{di}. If that is the case, $i.known$ is composed by processes belonging to other components than p_i's (Lemma 2). By the connectivity of the graph, there are at least k nodes in each one of the m components in G_{di}. Since $f < k$, there are at least 1 correct node in each one of these components. So, p_i will receive in line 18 at least 1 *nack* response from a process p_l belonging to other components than $p.i$'s. Moreover, p_i will never receive, at line 19, $s \geq (|i.known| - f)$ of *ack* responses, since at least 1 of those responses from a correct process will be *nack*. Thus the condition in line 21 will never be satisfied. So, eventually, condition in line 24 will be satisfied and the algorithm terminates returning *false* (lines 25-26), reaching a contradiction. □

4.3.2 The CONSENSUS Algorithm

The CONSENSUS protocol is presented as Algorithm 3. In the initial phase, every node runs SINK (Algorithm 2) to get a partial view of the system and decide whether or not it belongs to the k-strongly connected sink component. Depending on whether the node belongs or not to the sink, two behaviors are possible.

For the nodes belonging to the sink, an AGREEMENT phase is launched in order to reach a consensus on some value. By construction, all nodes in the sink component share the same $i.known$ set, so using Ω is sufficient to solve consensus as soon as there are at least a majority of correct nodes in the sink component. The other nodes (in the remaining k-strongly connected components) do not participate to this consensus. They launch a REQUEST phase to ask for and collect the value decided by the sink members. This is done by sending request messages to known processes and waiting for responses. Since at least one member from the sink is correct, at least one member will respond the decided value when it is decided.

Proposition 3 *The k-OSR participant detector is sufficient to solve uniform FT-CUP and necessary to solve FT-CUP, in spite of $f < k < n$ crashes, assuming Ω and a majority of correct nodes in the sink component.*

Proof: *Sufficient*: Algorithm 3 solves uniform FT-CUP with PD $\in k\text{-}OSR$, assuming Ω. The following statements proves this claim. Validity. It trivially holds, since a decided value is a value proposed by nodes in the sink (line 16).

Termination. To prove that every correct process decides, we must prove that they finish by executing lines 21 or 32 of the algorithm. On the execution of the main decision task,

---

Algorithm 3 CONSENSUS

constant:
(1) f: upper bound on the number of crashes
input:
(2) $i.initial$: value
variable:
(3) $i.in\_the\_sink$: boolean
(4) $i.known$: set of nodes;
(5) $i.decision$: value
(6) $i.asked$: set of nodes
message:
(7)   REQUEST message.
(8)   RESPONSE message:
(9) $decision$: value

** *All Nodes* **

task T1: { *Main Decision Task* }
(10) $i.asked = \{\}$; $i.decision = \bot$;
(11) $(i.in_the_sink, i.known) = $ SINK();
(12)   **if** $i.in\_the\_sink$ **then**
(13)   fork AGREEMENT
(14)   **else**
(15)   fork REQUEST **end if**

** *Node In Sink* **

AGREEMENT: { *Underlying Classical Consensus* }
(16)   Consensus.propose($i.initial$)

(17) **upon** Consensus.decide(v):
(18) $i.decision = v$;
(19)   **for** every j in $i.asked$ **do**
(20)   send RESPONSE ($i.decision$) to p_j; **end for**
(21)   *return* ($i.decision$);

task T2: { *Decision Dissemination Task* }
(22) **upon** receipt of REQUEST() **from** p_j:
(23)   **if** $i.decision \neq \bot$ **then**
(24)   send RESPONSE ($i.decision$) to p_j;
(25)   **else**
(26) $i.asked = i.asked \cup \{j\}$; **end if**

** *Node Not In Sink* **

REQUEST:
(27)   **for** every j in $i.known$ **do**
(28)   send REQUEST () to j

(29) **upon** receipt of RESPONSE (v) **from** j:
(30)   **if** $i.decision = \bot$ **then**
(31) $i.decision = v$;
(32)   *return* ($i.decision$); **end if**

90

we can distinguish two types of behavior: (i) that one from the nodes belonging to the sink and (ii) that from the nodes not in the sink component. In case (i), nodes in the sink will call upon a classical indulgent protocol which solves consensus (line 16). From the *termination* property of this algorithm, a decision is eventually attained and then line 17 is executed by every node in the sink. Thus, after executing lines 18-21, a decision is returned to the application (line 21). In case (ii), nodes not in the sink will send a message requesting for the decision to all the nodes in their *i.known* set returned by the COLLECT procedure executed in the SINK algorithm (lines 27-28). From Lemma 2, every node in the sink belongs to *i.known*. Thus, after receiving the request message in task T2 from a node p_j not in the sink (line 22), a node in the sink will pass back the decision (if it has one) or store p_j's identity in order to send the decision later. This will happen when the node receives the decision in line 17 and execute lines 19-20 in order to send the decision to processes who have asked for it. Note that, even if a node in the sink decides, by returning the decision value to the application (line 21), task T2 continues execution to diffuse this decision to all the other nodes not in the sink. So, a node not in the sink, eventually receives this response. Then, by executing line 29, it will receive the decision to finally return the decided value to the application (line 32).

Uniform Agreement. The guarantee that no two processes decide differently comes directly from the *uniform agreement* property of the underlying indulgent consensus. Thus, every node in the sink component will receive the same value v in line 17 for the decision. So, every one of these nodes will diffuse the same value v, immediately after taken the decision on the execution of lines 19-20, or in the "decision dissemination task" T2 (lines 22-26).

Necessary: Let us give a sketch of the proof which is based on the same arguments to prove the necessity of OSR for solving CUP [1]. Assume by contradiction that there is an algorithm A which solves FT-CUP with a PD $\notin$ k-OSR. Let G_{di} be the knowledge graph induced by PD decomposed into its k-strongly connected components. The following scenarios are possible: (i) either there exists less than k node-disjoint paths between two components of G_{di}; or (ii) the decomposition of G_{di} originates more than one sink. In the first scenario, the crash of $k - 1$ nodes may disconnect the graph into at least two components. Since connectivity is a necessary condition to solve CUP [1], we reach a contradiction. In the second scenario, let G_1 and G_2 be two of those sinks. Assume that all nodes in G_1 have input value equal to v and that all nodes in G_2 have input value equal to w, $v \neq w$. By the *termination* property of consensus, nodes in G_1 decide at time $t1$ and nodes in G_2 decide at time $t2$. We can delay the reception of any messages from nodes in other components to both G_1 and G_2 to a time $t > max\{t1, t2\}$. Since nodes in the sinks are

unaware about the existence of other nodes, by the *validity* property of consensus, nodes in G_1 decide for the value v and nodes in G_2 decide for the value w, violating the *agreement* and reaching thus a contradiction.

□

5 Conclusion

In this paper, we investigated the trade-off between knowledge about the system and synchrony assumptions to enable consensus in fault-prone unknown systems. It turns out that if knowledge connectivity is k-OSR, then consensus can be solved assuming minimal synchrony assumptions. Our approach is constructive, and an interesting side effect of our design is that the uniform version of the consensus can be solved as well, with no particular effort. This complements nicely previous studies that showed that complete synchrony was needed whenever only minimal knowledge connectivity (OSR) was available. Interestingly enough, the same previous solution did not enable uniform consensus.

References

[1] D. Cavin, Y. Sasson, and A. Schiper. Consensus with unknown participants or fundamental self-organization. In *Proc. 3rd Int. Conf. AD-NOC Networks & Wireless (ADHOC-NOW)*, pages 135–148, Vancouver, July 2004. Springer-Verlag.

[2] D. Cavin, Y. Sasson, and A. Schiper. Reaching agreement with unknown participants in mobile self-organized networks in spite of process crashes. Research Report IC/2005/026, EPFL, 2005.

[3] T. Chandra and S. Toueg. Unreliable failure detectors for reliable distributed systems. *Journal of the ACM*, 43(2):225–267, Mar. 1996.

[4] T. D. Chandra, V. Hadzilacos, and S. Toueg. The weakest failure detector for solving consensus. *Journal of the ACM*, 43(4):685–722, July 1996.

[5] F. Chu. Reducing Ω to $\Diamond W$. *Information Processing Letters*, 67(6):289–293, June 1998.

[6] M. J. Fischer, N. A. Lynch, and M. D. Paterson. Impossibility of distributed consensus with one faulty process. *Journal of ACM*, 32(2):374–382, Apr. 1985.

[7] R. Guerraoui. Indulgent algorithms. In *Proc. 19th ACM Symp. on Principles of Distributed Computing (PODC)*, pages 289–298, Portland, Jul 2000.

[8] L. Lamport. The part-time parliament. *ACM Transactions on Computer Systems*, 16(2):133–169, May 1998.

[9] S. Souissi, X. Défago, and M. Yamashita. Gathering asynchronous mobile robots with inaccurate compasses. In *Proc. 10th Int. Conf. on Princ. of Distributed Systems (OPODIS)*, LNCS, Bordeaux, December 2006. Springer.

[10] J. Yellen and J. Gross. *Graph Theory and Its Applications*. CRC Press, 1998.

Communication Predicates:
A High-Level Abstraction for Coping with Transient and Dynamic Faults [*]

Martin Hutle
martin.hutle@epfl.ch

André Schiper
andre.schiper@epfl.ch

École Polytechnique Fédérale de Lausanne (EPFL), 1015 Lausanne, Switzerland

Abstract

Consensus is one of the key problems in fault tolerant distributed computing. A very popular model for solving consensus is the failure detector model defined by Chandra and Toueg. However, the failure detector model has limitations. The paper points out these limitations, and suggests instead a model based on communication predicates, called HO model. The advantage of the HO model over failure detectors is shown, and the implementation of the HO model is discussed in the context of a system that alternates between good periods and bad periods. Two definitions of a good period are considered. For both definitions, the HO model allows us to compute the duration of a good period for solving consensus. Specifically, the model allows us to quantify the difference between the required length of an initial *good period and the length of a* non initial *good period.*

1. Introduction

Consensus is one of the key problems in fault tolerant distributed computing. Consensus is related to replication and appears when implementing atomic broadcast, group membership, etc. The problem is defined over a set of processes Π, where each process $p_i \in \Pi$ has an initial value v_i: All processes must agree on a common value that is the initial value of one of the processes.

Consensus can be impossible to solve, as established by the FLP impossibility result [13]. Later it has been shown that consensus can be solved in a partially synchronous system with a majority of correct processes [12]. Roughly speaking, a partially synchronous system is a system that is initially asynchronous, but eventually becomes synchronous.[1] Moreover, in a partially synchronous system links are initially lossy, but eventually become reliable.

The notion of failure detectors has been suggested a few years later [5]. The failure detector model is defined as an asynchronous system "augmented" with failure detectors, which are defined by some completeness and some accuracy property (see [5] for details). Over the years failure detectors have become very popular. The model is today widely accepted and has become the model mostly used for expressing consensus algorithms. However, the failure detector model has limitations.

First, failure detectors are not an abstraction of the partially synchronous model (even though this claim has sometimes been made). The reason is that in the partially synchronous model links are initially lossy, while the use of failure detector to solve a problem requires perpetual reliable links.[2] When using failure detectors, either the system must provide reliable links, or reliable links need to be implemented on top of the unreliable system links. As a consequence, the capability of algorithms of tolerating message loss — as it is the case for the Paxos algorithm [19] — cannot be expressed naturally in the failure detector model. Only a variant of Paxos that assumes reliable links can be expressed using failure detectors, as done, e.g., in [4].

Second, failure detectors are not well suited to solve consensus in the crash-recovery model, with or without stable storage [1]. In the crash-recovery model, a process can crash and later recover. This is in contrast to the crash-stop model, in which process crashes are permanent. Intuitively, one would think that solving consensus in the crash-stop model or in a crash-recovery model should not lead to major algorithmic differences. However, the comparison of (i) the $\diamond\mathcal{S}$ consensus algorithm in the crash-stop model [5] with (ii) the corresponding algorithm in the crash-recovery model with stable storage [1] shows that the crash-recovery algorithm is a much more complicated protocol than the corresponding crash-stop algorithm. Moreover, the complexity of the crash-recovery consensus algorithm makes it hard to see that the crash-recovery algorithm is based on the

---

[*]Research funded by the Swiss National Science Foundation under grant number 200021-111701.

[1]This is not the only definition of a partially synchronous system.

[2]Failure detectors lead to the following programming pattern: Process p (i) waits for a message from process q or (ii) suspects q. If q is not suspected while the message is lost, p is blocked.

same basic ideas as the crash-stop algorithm. This leads to the following question: Is there an inherent gap between the crash-stop and the crash-recovery model that would explain the higher complexity of the crash-recovery consensus algorithm?

Third, failure detectors cannot handle Byzantine failures. The reason is that the definition of a Byzantine behavior is related to an algorithm: It is impossible to achieve a complete separation of failure detectors from the algorithm using them. To overcome this problem, the notion of muteness detectors has been suggested [9, 10, 18]. However, it is not clear what system model could allow the implementation of muteness detectors, which is an inherent limitation of the approach.

These arguments suggest that failure detectors might not be the ultimate answer to the consensus problem. As an alternative to failure detectors, one could program directly at the level of the partially synchronous system model. However, this model provides too low level abstractions. It is indeed useful to provide higher level abstractions for expressing consensus algorithms. The goal of this paper is to show that another abstraction, namely *communication predicates*, provides a better abstraction than failure detectors for solving consensus. Specifically, the paper brings an answer to the question raised in [17], about quantifying the time it takes the environment to reach round synchronization after the system has stabilized.

The paper is structured as follows. Section 2 serves as a motivation to the introduction of communication predicates. Communication predicates are defined in Section 3. The implementation of communication predicates is presented in Section 4. Related work is discussed in Section 5, and Section 6 concludes the paper. Note that the paper is restricted to benign faults; Byzantine faults will be addressed in another paper.

2. Fault taxonomy

In this section we discuss the taxonomy of faults, with the goal to understand the limitation of failure detectors. The discussion will serve as the basis for the introduction of the notion of *communication predicates*.

2.1. Failure detectors and the paradox of the classical fault taxonomy

Let us come back to the second limitation of failure detectors (see Section 1), namely the gap between solving consensus with failure detectors in the crash-stop model and in the crash-recovery model. Our goal is to explain this gap, and so to understand the limited context in which failure detectors provide a good abstraction.

When looking at process failures, the classical fault taxonomy distinguishes, from the most benign to the most severe, (i) crash faults, (ii) send-omission faults, (iii) general-omission faults (which includes receive-omission faults), and (iv) malicious faults [22]. It can be observed that this taxonomy does not distinguish crash faults without recovery (the crash-stop model) and crash faults with recovery (the crash-recovery model). So, one would expect little difference when solving consensus in either of these two models. However, as already mentioned, this is not the case with failure detectors:

- In the crash-stop model, a standard solution to consensus is the rotating coordinator algorithm that requires the failure detector $\Diamond S$ and a majority of processes [5].
- Extending this solution to the crash-recovery model is not easy. It requires the definition of new failure detectors, and the algorithm becomes more complex [1]. This can be observed by comparing the two algorithms that are given in the appendix of [16].

This observation leads to the following question: What is the key issue, not captured by the classical fault taxonomy, that explains the gap between the crash-stop and crash-recovery consensus algorithm? The key issue is in the distinction between *permanent* faults and *transient* faults. Crash-stop is a model with permanent (crash) faults, while crash-recovery is a model with transient (crash) faults. A fault taxonomy that does not distinguish between permanent and transient fault is not able to explain the limitation of the failure detector model. In the next section we suggest another new fault taxonomy that makes the distinction between permanent and transient fault explicit.

2.2. Alternative fault taxonomy (for benign faults)

An alternative process fault taxonomy can be organized along two dimensions. The first dimension distinguishes between the already discussed *permanent* (P) and *transient* faults (T). The second dimension distinguishes faults that can hit any process in the system from faults that hit only a subset of the processes. We use the term *static* (S) for faults that can hit only a fixed subset of processes and *dynamic*[3] (D) for all other cases, i.e., faults that can hit all processes.

Combining this two dimensions leads to four classes of process faults:

- *SP*: at most f processes out of n are faulty ($f < n$); a faulty process is permanently faulty.
- *ST*: at most f processes out of n are faulty ($f < n$); faults are transient.

---

[3] This notion of static/dynamic faults was also used by [21].

- *DP*: all processes can be faulty; faults are permanent.
- *DT*: all processes can be faulty; faults are transient.

Among this classes, SP is clearly the most restrictive, whereas DT is the most general one. The crash-stop fault in the classical taxonomy corresponds the SP class. The send-omission and general-omission faults are transient faults. If we assume that only a subset of processes suffer from send-omission or general-omission faults, then send-omission and general-omission faults are classified as ST. Otherwise, these faults are classified as DT.

This alternative taxonomy is able to capture the distinction between the crash-stop model and the crash-recovery model: The crash-stop model corresponds to the class SP, whereas the crash-recovery model can be classified either as ST (if some processes never crash) or as DT. Failure detectors are well-suited to handle the SP fault class, but not to handle dynamic faults. Communication predicates will allow us to handle SP and DT faults in the same way.

2.3. Transmission faults

It is usual to distinguish between process faults and link faults. However, the distinction becomes irrelevant with DT faults. To see this, consider process p sending message m to process q. Process q might not receive m if (i) p suffers from a send-omission fault, (ii) the link loses m, or (iii) q suffers from a receive-omission fault. In case (i) p is the faulty component, in case (ii) the link l_{pq} is the faulty component, in case (iii) q is faulty. However, if the fault is transient, it may not occur later, for another message m' sent by p to q. For this reason, it makes no sense to put the responsibility of the fault on one of the components (process p, process q, or link l_{pq}). This observation leads to consider only *transmission faults*:[4] a transmission fault is a fault that results in the non reception of some message m.

As we will see in Section 3, communication predicates are based on the notion of transmission faults. As such, communication predicates — contrary to failure detectors — are able to handle SP and DT fault classes uniformly.

3. Communication predicates and algorithms

3.1. Communication predicates

Communication predicates are defined in the context of a communication-closed round model. An algorithm for this model comprises, for each round r and process $p \in \Pi$, a sending function S_p^r and a transition function T_p^r. At beginning of a round r, every process sends a message to all

---

Algorithm 1 The *OneThirdRule* algorithm [6].

```
 1: Initialization:
 2:     x_p ← v_p

 3: Round r:
 4:     S_p^r :
 5:         send ⟨x_p⟩ to all processes

 6:     T_p^r :
 7:         if |HO(p, r)| > 2n/3 then
 8:             if the values received, except at most ⌊n/3⌋, are equal
                   to x̄ then
 9:                 x_p ← x̄
10:             else
11:                 x_p ← smallest x_q received
12:             if more than 2n/3 values received are equal to x̄ then
13:                 DECIDE(x̄)
```

according to $S_p^r(s_p)$, where s_p is p's state at the beginning of the round. At the end of a round r, p makes a state transition according to $T_p^r(\vec{\mu}, s_p)$, where $\vec{\mu}$ is the partial vector of all messages that have been received by p in round r.

We denote by $HO(p, r)$ the support of $\vec{\mu}$, i.e., the set of processes (including itself) from which p receives a message at round r: $HO(p, r)$ is the *heard of* set of p in round r. If $q \notin HO(p, r)$, then the message sent by q to p in round r was subject to a transmission failure. Communication predicates are expressed over the sets $(HO(p, r))_{p \in \Pi, r > 0}$. For example,

$$\exists r_0 > 0, \ \forall p, q \in \Pi : \ HO(p, r_0) = HO(q, r_0)$$

ensures the existence of some round r_0 in which all processes hear of the same set of processes. Another example is a communication predicate that ensures that in every round r all processes hear of a majority of processes (n is the number of processes):

$$\forall r > 0, \ \forall p \in \Pi : \ |HO(p, r)| > n/2.$$

Let $\mathcal{A} = \langle S_p^r, T_p^r \rangle$ be an HO algorithm. A problem is solved by a pair $\langle \mathcal{A}, \mathcal{P} \rangle$, where $\mathcal{P}$ is a communication predicate. The consensus problem is specified by the following conditions:

- *Integrity:* Any decision value is the initial value of some process.
- *Agreement:* No two processes decide differently.
- *Termination:* All processes eventually decide.

The termination condition requires all processes to decide; a weaker condition is considered later. An example of a consensus algorithm is given by Algorithm 1.[5] The sending function is specified in lines 4–5. When the transition

---

[4]The term is taken from [21], in which transmission faults are considered in the context of synchronous systems.

[5]We have chosen this algorithm, rather than Paxos or another algorithm, for its simplicity. It allows us to keep the algorithmic part as simple as possible.

function (lines 6–13) is called, messages are available such that the predicate on the HO sets is guaranteed to hold. The consensus problem is solved by Algorithm 1 and the communication predicate $\mathcal{P}_{otr}$, given in Table 1 (next page).

Theorem 1. *The pair $\langle$ Algorithm 1, $\mathcal{P}_{otr} \rangle$ solves consensus.*

Proof. Algorithm 1 never violates the safety properties of consensus, namely integrity and agreement. For agreement, if some process decides v at line 13 of round r, then in any round $r' \geq r$, only v can be assigned to any x_p, and hence only v can be decided. Predicate $\mathcal{P}_{otr}$ ensures the liveness property of consensus (termination). The first part of $\mathcal{P}_{otr}$, namely the existence of some round r_0 in which all processes in Π have the set HO equal to some (large enough) set Π_0, ensures that at the end of round r_0 all processes in Π adopt the same value for x_p. The second part of $\mathcal{P}_{otr}$ forces every process $p \in \Pi$ to make a decision at the end of round r_p. □

Note that $\mathcal{P}_{otr}$ allows rounds in which no messages are received.

3.2. Restricted scope communication predicates

Section 2.3 has introduced the "transmission fault" abstraction, which covers various types of faults. One instantiation is to assume that transmission faults abstract link faults, send-omission faults and receive-omission faults, but not process crashes (i.e., processes do not crash). In this case the predicate $\mathcal{P}_{otr}$, which expresses a condition that must hold for all processes $p \in \Pi$, is perfectly adapted. This interpretation of transmission faults is also consistent with the termination condition for consensus that requires all processes to decide.

Let us now assume that transmission faults include in addition process crashes (without recovery). As already mentioned in [6], from the viewpoint of an HO algorithm this is still not a problem, since a crashed process does not send any messages and is thus indistinguishable from one that receives all messages but sends no messages. This holds no more if we implement the HO machine in a system where processes may exhibit any sort of benign faults. The problem can be addressed by restricting the scope of $\mathcal{P}_{otr}$ to the subset Π_0, as defined by $\mathcal{P}_{otr}^{restr}$, see Table 1 (next page).

Predicate $\mathcal{P}_{otr}^{restr}$ sets a requirement only for processes in Π_0, and so ensures termination only for processes in Π_0. If processes in Π_0 do not crash, while processes in $\Pi \setminus \Pi_0$ crash, then $\langle$Algorithm 1, $\mathcal{P}_{otr}^{restr}\rangle$ allow all processes that do not crash to decide. So we have:

Theorem 2. *The pair $\langle$Algorithm 1, $\mathcal{P}_{otr}^{restr}\rangle$ ensures the validity and agreement property of consensus. Moreover, all processes in Π_0 eventually decide.*

Proof. Proof of Theorem 1, by replacing Π with Π_0. □

3.3. Crash-recovery model

Algorithm 1 with predicate $\mathcal{P}_{otr}^{restr}$ solves consensus with process crashes (crash-stop), link faults, send-omission, and receive-omission faults. In Section 2.1 we pointed out the gap between solving consensus with failure detectors in the crash-stop *vs.* the crash-recovery model. The gap disappears with the transmission fault abstraction and communication predicates.

Without any changes, Algorithm 1 can be used in the crash-recovery model. Handling of recoveries is done at a lower layer (cf. Section 4).

4. Achieving predicate $\mathcal{P}_{otr}^{restr}$ in good periods

We discuss now the implementation of the communication predicate $\mathcal{P}_{otr}^{restr}$ introduced in Section 3. Figure 1 shows the algorithmic HO layer, the predicate implementation layer that we discuss now, and the interface between these two layers defined by communication predicates. This illustration shows also that the implementation of the predicates relies on assumptions about the underlying system (these assumptions define the fault and synchrony hypothesis). Note that "transmission faults" is an abstraction relevant to the upper layer: This abstraction does not appear at the lower layer.

In our implementation model, the system alternates between *good* and *bad* periods. In a good period the synchrony and fault assumptions hold; in a bad period the behavior of the system is arbitrary (but malicious behavior is excluded). The idea is here to compute the minimal duration of a good period that allows us to implement the communication predicates, i.e., the minimal duration of a good period that allow Algorithm 1 to solve consensus.

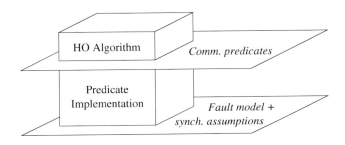

Figure 1. The two layers.

$$\mathcal{P}_{otr} :: \exists r_0 > 0, \exists \Pi_0, |\Pi_0| > 2n/3 : (\forall p \in \Pi : HO(p, r_0) = \Pi_0) \wedge (\forall p \in \Pi, \exists r_p > r_0 : |HO(p, r_p)| > 2n/3) \quad (1)$$

$$\mathcal{P}_{otr}^{restr} :: \exists r_0 > 0, \exists \Pi_0, |\Pi_0| > 2n/3 : (\forall p \in \Pi_0 : HO(p, r_0) = \Pi_0) \wedge (\forall p \in \Pi_0, \exists r_p > r_0 : HO(p, r_p) \supseteq \Pi_0) \quad (2)$$

Table 1. Communication predicates

4.1. System model

Our system model is inspired by [12]; the differences are pointed out at the end of the section. We consider a message-passing system, and assume the existence of a fictitious global real-time clock that measures time with values from $\mathbf{R}$ (see the remark on the next page for the reason for considering values from $\mathbf{R}$ rather than integers). The clock is used only for analysis and is not accessible to the processes. Processes execute a sequence of atomic steps, which are either *send* steps or *receive* steps. As in [12], steps take no time (atomic steps), but time elapses between steps.[6] The network can take a *make-ready* step that is introduced to distinguish a message ready for reception from a message in transit: (i) Every process has two sets of messages called $network_p$ and $buffer_p$; (ii) a make-ready step transfers a message from the first to the second set. Send steps, receive steps, and make-ready steps are defined to adequately model a real system:

- In a *send* step, a process p sends a message to either a single process or to all other processes and makes some local computation. More precisely, if p executes $send_p(m)$ to all, then m is put into $network_s$, for all $s \in \Pi$.

- In a *make-ready* step, the network transfers some messages from $network_p$ into $buffer_p$. More precisely, if the network executes $make\text{-}ready_p(M)$ for some subset $M \subseteq network_p$, all messages $m \in M$ are removed from $network_p$ and put into $buffer_p$. Messages in $buffer_p$ are *ready for reception* by process p.

- In a *receive* step executed at time t, a process p may receive a *single* message that was in $buffer_p$ at time t and makes some local computation. *So n receive steps are needed to receive n messages.* If $buffer_p = \emptyset$ at the time of a receive step, the empty message λ is received. A process p may specify any policy, according to which the message $buffer_p$ is selected for reception (e.g., *"message with the largest round number first"*).

We consider that the system alternates between good and bad periods. In a bad period, processes can crash and recover and suffer from send and receive omission; furthermore links can loose messages. We distinguish three types

---

[6]We model a step that "terminates" at time t as an atomic step that "occurs" at time t.

of good periods, from the strongest to the weakest. All these definitions refer to a subset π_0 of Π. In all the three definitions, the following property π_0-*sync* holds in a good period for processes in π_0:

π_0-**sync:** The subsystem π_0 is synchronous, i.e., there is a known upper and lower bound on the process speed and a known upper bound on the communication delays among processes in π_0. Formally:

Let I be an open contiguous time interval and R a run. Processes and links are synchronous during I if there exist $\Phi^+, \Phi^-, \Delta \in \mathbf{R}$ such that:

- In any contiguous sub-interval of I of length Φ^+, every process in π_0 takes at least one step.

- In any open contiguous sub-interval of I of length Φ^-, every process in π_0 takes at most one step.

- Consider two processes $p, q \in \pi_0$. If process p executes $send_p(m)$ at time $t \in I$, then $m \in buffer_q$ at time $t + \Delta$, provided that $t + \Delta \in I$.

The length of the good period is $|I|$. If I starts at time 0, we say I is an *initial good period*. We denote $\Pi \setminus \pi_0$ by $\overline{\pi_0}$. We can now define the three types of good periods:

1. Π-**good period:** The property π_0-sync holds for $\pi_0 = \Pi$. All processes are up, none of these processes crashes (during the good period).

2. "$\overline{\pi_0}$-**down**" **good period:** The property π_0-sync holds for $\pi_0 \subseteq \Pi$. Processes in π_0 do not crash. Processes in $\overline{\pi_0}$ are down and do not recover (during the good period). Moreover, no messages from processes in $\overline{\pi_0}$ are in transit during the good period.

3. "$\overline{\pi_0}$-**arbitrary**" **good period:** The property π_0-sync holds for $\pi_0 \subseteq \Pi$. There are no restrictions on the processes in $\overline{\pi_0}$ and on the links to and from processes processes in $\overline{\pi_0}$ (during the good period processes in $\overline{\pi_0}$ can crash, recover, be asynchronous; links to and from processes in $\overline{\pi_0}$ can lose messages, be asynchronous).

Case 2 includes case 1, and case 1 leads to the same implementation as case 2. Thus we distinguish below only between case 2 and case 3. For simplicity, we will use the following notation: We scale all values Φ^+, Φ^-, Δ, and t

with $1/\Phi^-$ and use $\phi = \Phi^+/\Phi^-$ as the normalized upper bound of the process speed, $\delta = \Delta/\Phi^-$ as the normalized transmission delay, and $\tau = t/\Phi^-$ as normalized time. Remember that ϕ and δ are "known" values, and note that *these values are unit-less*.[7]

Remark: For our modeling, we have chosen real-values clocks to represent time. Consider case 3 above, assuming integer clock values instead. By the definition of Φ^+, the slowest process in π_0 takes at least one step in any interval Φ^+. However, with integer clock values, any process can take at most Φ^+ steps in an interval Φ^+, independent how small Φ^- is chosen. So, in case 3, processes in $\overline{\pi_0}$ cannot be arbitrarily fast with respect to processes in π_0. In other words, with integer clock values, processes in $\overline{\pi_0}$ have some synchrony relation with respect to processes in π_0, which we wanted to exclude under case 3.

Differences between our system model and DLS [12]: In [12] the clocks take integer values. We have explained the reason to consider clocks with real-time values. In [12] a send step allows a process to send a message only to a single destination. Our send primitive allows messages to be broadcast, a facility provided, e.g., by UDP-multicast. In [12], a receive step allows a process to receive several messages. Our receive primitive allows reception of a message from one single process only, which reflects the feature, e.g., of UDP. The reception of messages one by one led us to introduce the make-ready step. Two different synchrony assumptions are considered in [12]: (i) The synchrony bounds are known but hold only eventually; (ii) the synchrony bounds are not known, but hold from the beginning. We considered option (i), which is needed to compute the minimal length of a good period (in the context of the implementation of the communication predicates). In the context of option (i), [12] assumes that the good period holds eventually forever and that the synchrony assumption holds on the whole system. We consider the system alternating between good and bad periods, and synchrony assumptions that hold only on a subset π_0. We also assume the more general crash-recovery model, while [12] considers the crash-stop model. On the other hand, contrary to our fault model, [12] considers also Byzantine faults.

4.2. Implementation of $\mathcal{P}_{otr}^{restr}$

We give now algorithms for implementing the predicate $\mathcal{P}_{otr}^{restr}$ in $\overline{\pi_0}$-down and $\overline{\pi_0}$-arbitrary good periods. It turns out that both definitions of a good period lead naturally to the implementation of a predicate that is stronger than

$\mathcal{P}_{otr}^{restr}$. We define:

$$\mathcal{P}_{su}(\Pi_0, r_1, r_2) \quad :: \quad \forall p \in \Pi_0, \forall r \in [r_1, r_2] : HO(p, r) = \Pi_0$$

$$\mathcal{P}_k(\Pi_0, r_1, r_2) \quad :: \quad \forall p \in \Pi_0, \forall r \in [r_1, r_2] : HO(p, r) \supseteq \Pi_0$$

$$\mathcal{P}_{otr}^2(\Pi_0) \quad :: \quad \exists r_0 > 0 : \mathcal{P}_{su}(\Pi_0, r_0, r_0)$$
$$\wedge \mathcal{P}_k(\Pi_0, r_0{+}1, r_0{+}1)$$

$$\mathcal{P}_{otr}^{1/1}(\Pi_0) \quad :: \quad \exists r_0 > 0, \exists r_1 > r_0 : \mathcal{P}_{su}(\Pi_0, r_0, r_0)$$
$$\wedge \mathcal{P}_k(\Pi_0, r_1, r_1)$$

Predicate $\mathcal{P}_{su}(\Pi_0, r_1, r_2)$ ensures that rounds from r_1 to r_2 are so called "space uniform" for the processes in Π_0. Predicate $\mathcal{P}_k(\Pi_0, r_1, r_2)$ ensures a weaker property (k stands for *kernel*). Predicate $\mathcal{P}_{otr}^2(\Pi_0)$ ensures two consecutive rounds such that the first satisfies $\mathcal{P}_{su}(\Pi_0, -, -)$ and the second $\mathcal{P}_k(\Pi_0, -, -)$. Predicate $\mathcal{P}_{otr}^{1/1}(\Pi_0)$ ensures the same property for two rounds that do not need to be consecutive. We clearly have:

$$(\exists \Pi_0, \ s.t. \ |\Pi_0| > 2n/3 : \mathcal{P}_{otr}^2(\Pi_0)) \quad \Rightarrow \quad \mathcal{P}_{otr}^{restr}$$

$$(\exists \Pi_0, \ s.t. \ |\Pi_0| > 2n/3 : \mathcal{P}_{otr}^{1/1}(\Pi_0)) \quad \Rightarrow \quad \mathcal{P}_{otr}^{restr}.$$

We give below algorithms for $\mathcal{P}_{su}(-, -, -)$ and $\mathcal{P}_k(-, -, -)$, for both definitions of good periods. We also analyze the timing property of the algorithms under the following two scenarios:

1. Assume that a good period starts at an arbitrary time t_G resp. $\tau_G = t_G/\Phi^-$. We compute, in the worst case, the minimal length of the good period needed to implement the communication predicates. We call this value *minimal length of a good period*.

2. We do the same, assuming that a good period starts from the beginning, i.e., $\tau_G = 0$. We call this value *minimal length of an initial good period*.

Intuitively, scenario 2 allows us to compute the time to solve consensus in the fault-free case, which is often called a "nice" run. Scenario 1 allows us a timing analysis of consensus in "not nice" runs.

4.2.1. Ensuring $\mathcal{P}_{otr}^{restr}$ in a "$\overline{\pi_0}$-down" good period

Let us consider a "$\overline{\pi_0}$-down" good period that is "long enough", with π_0 arbitrary. Algorithm 2 implements $\mathcal{P}_{su}(\pi_0, -, -)$. The function $S_p^{r_p}$ at line 7 returns the message to be sent; the send occurs at line 8. Variable i_p (line 9, 11) counts the number of receive steps. If p executes x steps, at least x and at most $x\phi$ (normalized) time has elapsed (see Section 4.1). Process p executes at most $\lceil 2\delta + n + 2\phi \rceil$ receive steps, see line 12 (message reception takes place at line 14; non-empty messages are added to the set $msgsRcv_p$, see line 16). Process p executes receive steps (1) until $\lceil 2\delta + n + 2\phi \rceil$ receive steps have been executed, or (2) if p receives a message from a round r' larger

Algorithm 2 Ensuring $\mathcal{P}_{su}(\pi_0, -, -)$ with a '$\overline{\pi_0}$-down' good period

```
1: Reception policy: Highest round number first
2: msgsRcv_p ← ∅                          {set of messages received}
3: r_p ← 1                                {round number}
4: next_r_p ← 1                           {next round number}
5: s_p ← init_p                           {state of the consensus algorithm}
6: while true do
7:     msg ← S_p^{r_p}(s_p)
8:     send ⟨msg, r_p⟩ to all
9:     i_p ← 0
10:    while next_r_p = r_p do
11:        i_p ← i_p + 1
12:        if i_p ≥ 2δ + n + 2φ then
13:            next_r_p ← r_p + 1;
14:        receive a message
15:        if message is ⟨msg, r'⟩ from q then
16:            msgsRcv_p ← msgsRcv_p ∪ {⟨msg, r', q⟩}
17:            if r' > r_p then
18:                next_r_p ← r'
19:    R ← {⟨msg', q'⟩ | ⟨msg', r_p, q'⟩ ∈ msgsRcv_p}
20:    s_p ← T_p^{r_p}(R, s_p)
21:    forall r' in [r_p+1, next_r_p−1] do s_p ← T_p^{r'}(∅, s_p)
22:    r_p ← next_r_p
```

than r_p. In both cases the state transition function $T_p^{r_p}$ is executed with the set R of messages received in round r_p (line 20). Then the state transition function $T_p^{r_p}$ is executed for all rounds $r_p + 1$ to $next\_r_p - 1$ with an empty set of messages.[8]

In order to cope with recoveries after crashes, variables r_p and s_p are stored on stable storage. In case of a recovery, the algorithm starts on line 6, with $msgsRcv_p$ and $next\_r_p$ reinitialized. Reading variables on stable storage is inefficient. The implementation can be made more efficient by keeping a copy of the variables in main memory: a read operation reads the *in memory* copy, a write operation updates the *in memory* and the *stable storage* copies. Upon recovery, the in memory copy is reset with the value of the stable copy.[9]

Algorithm 2 is not optimized regarding space, i.e., the set $msgsRcv_p$ grows forever. Obviously, messages for round smaller than r_p can safely be discarded. To keep the presentation short, we did not include this simple optimization.

It should be noted that Algorithm 2 relies exclusively on messages sent by the upper algorithmic layer: Algorithm 2 does not send any additional message.

We prove Algorithm 2 in two steps. First we prove that there exists $r > 0$ such that, for any $x > 0$, Algorithm 2 ensures $\mathcal{P}_{su}(\pi_0, r, r+x-1)$, assuming a "long enough" good

---

[8]This is required only if $T_p^{r_p}(∅, s_p) \neq s_p$. Calling the sending function $S_p^{r_p}$ is not needed, since the function does not change the state s_p.

[9]We could express this formally as a variant of Algorithm 2, but the space constraints prevent us from doing this.

---

period. Then we compute the minimal duration of a good period to ensure $\mathcal{P}_{otr}^2(\pi_0)$, and the minimal duration of two good periods to ensure $\mathcal{P}_{otr}^{1/1}(\pi_0)$. Note that by the definition of a $\overline{\pi_0}$-down good period, all processes in $\overline{\pi_0}$ are down in a good period, and no messages from these processes are in transit in the good period. In other words, processes in $\overline{\pi_0}$ can simply be ignored.

Theorem 3. *With Algorithm 2, the minimal length of a good period to achieve $\mathcal{P}_{su}(\pi_0, \rho_0, \rho_0 + x - 1)$ is:*

$$(x+1)(2\delta + n + 2\phi + 1)\phi + \delta + \phi.$$

The proof, also for all other theorems of this paper, can be found in [16]. The following Corollary follows directly from Theorem 3 with $x=1$ and $x=2$, and the fact that $\mathcal{P}_{su}(-, -, -) \Rightarrow \mathcal{P}_k(-, -, -)$:

Corollary 4. *For implementing $\mathcal{P}_{otr}^2(\pi_0)$ with Algorithm 2, we need one "$\overline{\pi_0}$-down" good period of length*

$$(6\delta + 3n + 3 + 6\phi)\phi + \delta + \phi.$$

For implementing $\mathcal{P}_{otr}^{1/1}(\pi_0)$ with Algorithm 2, we need two "$\overline{\pi_0}$-down" good periods of length

$$(4\delta + 2n + 2 + 4\phi)\phi + \delta + \phi.$$

Corollary 4 shows an interesting trade-off in terms of the length of a good period. The next theorem gives us the minimal length of an *initial* good period:

Theorem 5. *With Algorithm 2, the minimal length of an initial good period to achieve $\mathcal{P}_{su}(\pi_0, 1, x)$ is:*

$$x(2\delta + n + 2\phi + 1)\phi.$$

As already pointed out, Theorem 5 is related to so-called "nice" runs, while Theorem 3 is related to "not nice" runs. This second case has not been addressed in the literature with a time analysis as done here (see Section 5). The results show a factor of approximately $3/2$ between the two cases for the relevant value $x = 2$.

4.2.2. Ensuring $\mathcal{P}_{otr}^{restr}$ in a "$\overline{\pi_0}$-arbitrary" good period

In this section we consider a $\overline{\pi_0}$-arbitrary good period. Compared with the previous section, the problem is more complex. We proceed in two steps. First we show how to implement the predicate $\mathcal{P}_k(\pi_0, -, -)$. Second, we show how to obtain the predicate $\mathcal{P}_{su}(\pi_0, -, -)$ from $\mathcal{P}_k(\pi_0, -, -)$. Note that we introduce here a parameter f defined such that $|\pi_0| = n - f$. The implementation of $\mathcal{P}_k(\pi_0, -, -)$ requires $f < n/2$.

a) Implementing $\mathcal{P}_k(\pi_0, -, -)$

The algorithm for implementing $\mathcal{P}_k(\pi_0, -, -)$ is given as Algorithm 3. It uses two different types of messages, INIT messages and ROUND messages. Processes express the intention to enter a new round ρ with an $\langle \text{INIT}, \rho, - \rangle$ message. If a process receives at least $f + 1$ INIT messages for some round ρ, it starts round ρ and sends a $\langle \text{ROUND}, \rho, - \rangle$ message. A process in round ρ that receives a ROUND message for a higher round ρ' enters immediately round ρ'. This ensures fast synchronization at the beginning of a good period, and is one of the major differences of this algorithm compared to Byzantine clock synchronization algorithms.

The reception policy for Algorithm 3 (line 1) is a little bit more complicated than for Algorithm 2. Algorithm 3 has to ensure that a fast process with a large round number r' is not able to prevent messages from other processes with lower round numbers $r < r'$ from being received. The reception policy is as follows: At the ith receive step, the message with the highest round number from process $p_{i \bmod n}$ is selected for reception. If no such message exists, an arbitrary message is selected.

As for the previous algorithm, variables r_p and s_p are assumed to be on stable storage (possibly with a copy in volatile memory) and the algorithm starts after a recovery in line 6, with $msgsRcv_p$ and $next\_r_p$ reinitialized.

We prove the following results:

Theorem 6. *With Algorithm 3 and $f < n/2$, the minimal length of a good period to achieve $\mathcal{P}_k(\pi_0, \rho_0, \rho_0 + x - 1)$ is*

$$(x + 2)[\tau_0\phi + \delta + n\phi + 2\phi] + \tau_0\phi =$$

$$= (x+2)[(2\delta+n\phi+\phi)\phi+\delta+2n\phi+2\phi]+(2\delta+n+n\phi+\phi)\phi$$

Theorem 7. *With Algorithm 3 and $f < n/2$, the minimal length of an initial good period to implement $\mathcal{P}_k(\pi_0, 1, x)$ is:*

$$(x - 1)[\tau_0\phi + \delta + n\phi + 2\phi] + \tau_0\phi + \phi.$$

b) Implementing $\mathcal{P}_{su}(\pi_0, -, -)$ from $\mathcal{P}_k(\pi_0, -, -)$

We show now that $f+1$ rounds that satisfy $\mathcal{P}_k(\pi_0, -, -)$, with $|\pi_0| = n - f$, allow us to construct one *macro-round* that satisfies $\mathcal{P}_{su}(\pi_0, -, -)$. The "translation" is given by Algorithm 4, which is derived from a similar translation in [6]. Let $r_1, \ldots, r_{f+1}$ denote the sequence of the $f + 1$ rounds that form a macro-round $\mathcal{R}$. In round r_1, every process p sends its message for macro-round $\mathcal{R}$ (line 7). In all subsequent rounds $r_2, \ldots, r_{f+1}$ messages previously received are relayed (line 7). In round r_{f+1} (i.e., $r \equiv 0 \pmod{f+1}$, see line 9), the set of messages of macro-round $\mathcal{R}$ to be received by p are computed (lines 13 and 14).

Algorithm 3 Ensuring $\mathcal{P}_k(\pi_0, ,)$ with a "$\overline{\pi_0}$-arbitrary" good period

```
 1: Reception policy:    The highest round message from each
    process in a round robin fashion
 2: msgsRcv_p ← ∅
 3: r_p ← 1
 4: next_r_p ← 1
 5: s_p ← init_p
 6: while true do
 7:     msg ← S_p^{r_p}(s_p)
 8:     send ⟨ROUND, r_p, msg⟩ to all
 9:     i ← 0
10:     while next_r_p = r_p do
11:         receive a message
12:         if message is ⟨ROUND, msg, r'⟩ or ⟨INIT, msg, r' + 1⟩
            from q then
13:             msgsRcv_p ← msgsRcv_p ∪ {⟨msg, r', q⟩}
14:             if r' > r_p then
15:                 next_r_p ← r'
16:             if received f + 1 messages ⟨INIT, r_p + 1, −⟩ from distinct
                processes then
17:                 next_r_p ← max{r_p + 1, next_r_p}
18:             i ← i + 1
19:             if i ≥ 2δ + n + nφ + φ then
20:                 send ⟨INIT, r_p + 1, msg⟩ to all
21:     R ← {⟨msg', q'⟩ | ⟨msg', r_p, q'⟩ ∈ msgsRcv_p}
22:     s_p ← T_p^{r_p}(R, s_p)
23:     forall r' in [r_p+1, next_r_p−1] do s_p ← T_p^{r'}(∅, s_p)
24:     r_p ← next_r_p
```

---

c) Putting it all together

When combining Algorithm 3 and Algorithm 4, the function $S_p^{r_p}()$ called in Algorithm 3 refers to line 7 of Algorithm 4. Similarly, the function $T_p^{r_p}()$ called in Algorithm 3 refers to the lines 9 to 17 of Algorithm 4. The functions S_p^r and T_p^r in Algorithm 4 refer to the sending phase and state transition phase of Algorithm 1.

We compute now the minimal duration of a good period to ensure $\mathcal{P}_{otr}^2(\pi_0)$ (considering instead $\mathcal{P}_{otr}^{1/1}(\pi_0)$ is not a valuable alternative here):

1. We need first $f + 1$ rounds that satisfy $\mathcal{P}_k(-, -, -)$ to implement one macro-round that satisfies $\mathcal{P}_{su}(-, -, -)$ (Algorithm 4).
2. Then we need one round that satisfies $\mathcal{P}_k(-, -, -)$.

For 1, the worst case happens when the good period starts immediately after the beginning of a macro-round. In this worst case, $\mathcal{P}_{su}(-, -, -)$ requires two macro-rounds. Since one macro-round consists of $f+1$ rounds, in the worst case we need $2(f+1)$ rounds. Item 2 adds one round. So we end up with a minimal duration of $2f + 3$ rounds. Applying Theorem 6, we get the minimal length of a good period:

$$(2f+5)[(2\delta+n\phi+\phi)\phi+\delta+2n\phi+2\phi]+(2\delta+n+n\phi+\phi)\phi.$$

Algorithm 4 Ensuring $\mathcal{P}_{su}(\pi_0, -, -)$ with $\mathcal{P}_k(\pi_0, -, -)$ (adapted from [6]).

```
1:  Variables:
2:     Listen_p, initially Π                          {set of processes}
3:     NewHO_p                                         {set of processes}
4:     Known_p, initially {⟨S_p^{R_p}(s_p), p⟩}
                                              {set of ⟨message, process⟩ }

5:  Round r:
6:     S_p^r :
7:        send ⟨Known_p⟩ to all processes

8:     T_p^r :
9:        Listen_p ← Listen_p ∩ {q | ⟨Known_q⟩ received}
10:       if r ≢ 0 (mod f + 1) then
11:          Known_p ← Known_p ∪ ⋃_{q∈Listen_p} Known_q
12:       else
13:          NewHO_p ← {s | ⟨−, s⟩ ∈ Known_q for n − f
                          processes q ∈ Listen_p}
14:          R ← {⟨msg, s⟩ | s ∈ NewHO_p}
15:          s_p ← T_p^{R_p}(R, s_p)
16:          Listen_p ← Π
17:          Known_p ← {⟨S_p^{R_p}(s_p), p⟩}
```

5 Related work

The paper addresses several issues that appear in the literature. We now point out the key differences.

The HO model was proposed in [6]. The paper establishes relationship among several communication predicates and identifies the weakest predicate, among the class of predicates with non-empty kernel rounds, for solving consensus. The paper also expresses well-known consensus algorithms (or variants) and new ones in the HO model, with the goal of showing the expressiveness of the model. The implementation of communication predicates is not addressed in [6], nor is the ability of the model to handle uniformly crash-stop and crash-recovery models, and the reason for that. In [7] the HO model is used to express a new consensus algorithm.

The HO model generalizes the round model of [12], but does not reintroduce failure detectors as done in [14] and in [17]. The implementation in [12], contrary to ours, explicitly refers to some "common notion of time" and relies on a distributed clock synchronization algorithm.

It has been sometimes claimed that the partial synchrony model has been superseded by the failure detector model [5]. In out opinion this claim is only partially correct. The models that extend the failure detector model, e.g., [14, 17], all inherit from the limitations of failure detectors pointed out in Section 1.

The issue of performance of consensus following asynchronous periods is considered in [11, 17]. In [17] the focus is on number of rounds rather than time; [11] considers

time. Moreover, in [17] the authors write that being able to quantify the time it takes the environment to reach round synchronization after the system has stabilized is an interesting subject for further studies. This question is answered here. In [11] and [17] the synchronous period is defined only by properties of links: Processes are always considered to be synchronous. This is in contrast to our definition of $\overline{\pi_0}$-arbitrary good period, where only a subset of processes are assumed to be synchronous. This definition opens the door to the analysis of the duration of good periods with Byzantine processes. Our algorithm shares some similarities with the Byzantine clock synchronization of [23]. However, the algorithm in [23] assumes reliable links; adapting the algorithm to message loss, we end up with the algorithm of [12].

The notion of good and bad period appears in [8], but the issue of the length of a good period for solving consensus is not addressed. Restricting the scope of synchrony, as we do in good periods, has been considered in other settings, e.g., [15] and [2, 3]. However, in all these papers the issue of synchrony is implicitly restricted to links (i.e., process synchrony is not addressed). This is not the case in our definition of $\overline{\pi_0}$-arbitrary good period.

The Paxos algorithm [19] does not assume reliable links and, because of this, works under the crash-recovery model with stable storage. However, the condition for liveness is not expressed by a clean abstraction as done by communication predicates in the HO model (a consensus algorithm *à la Paxos* in the HO model can be found in [6]). The same comment applies to [11], where the system must stabilize before consensus is reached. System stabilization is not required with $\overline{\pi_0}$-arbitrary good periods: the HO model provides a clean separation of concerns between the HO algorithmic layer and the predicate implementation layer, which allows a finer definition of good periods, and so a finer timing analysis. As pointed out in Section 3, we have chosen here an algorithm that is simpler than Paxos to illustrate as simply as possible the approach based on communication predicates.

The notion of transmission faults was suggested in [21], however only in the context of synchronous systems. Varying the quorums for "init" and round messages — in the context of $\overline{\pi_0}$-arbitrary good periods — was to our knowledge done first in [20, 24], but for other fault scenarios.

6 Conclusion

Abstractions are essential when solving difficult problems. Failure detectors provide a nice abstraction for solving the difficult consensus problem; this explains why they have been widely adopted. However, transient and dynamic faults show the limitations of the failure detector approach: For example, solving consensus in the crash-stop model and in the crash-recovery model leads to significantly different solutions. The HO model provides a different abstraction, namely the "communication predicates", which allow us to handle uniformly static, dynamic, transient, and permanent faults and so overcome the limitations of failure detectors. Moreover, the HO model allows a nice and concise expression of consensus algorithms.

Similarly to failure detectors, solving consensus in the HO model leads to distinguish two layers: The "algorithmic" layer and the "abstraction" layer (the layer at which the abstraction is implemented). In the case of failure detectors, the abstraction layer must ensure the properties of the failure detectors, based on assumptions of the underlying system. The same holds for communication predicates. However, while communication predicates are based on the very general notion of transmission faults, failure detector assume the limited notion of process crash faults. The communication predicate layer defines a larger "playground" than the failure detector playground, in which more issues can be addressed. Specifically, the communication predicate approach has allowed us to bring an answer the question raised in [17], about quantifying the time it takes to reach round synchronization after the system has stabilized.

Acknowledgments   We like to thank Bernadette Charron-Bost, Nicolas Schiper, Martin Biely, Josef Widder, Nuno Santos, Sergio Mena, and the anonymous reviewers for their valuable comments that helped us to improve the paper.

References

[1] M. Aguilera, W. Chen, and S. Toueg. Failure detection and consensus in the crash-recovery model. *Distributed Computing*, 13(2):99–125, 2000.

[2] M. K. Aguilera, C. Delporte-Gallet, H. Fauconnier, and S. Toueg. On implementing Omega with weak reliability and synchrony assumptions. In *Proc. PODC'03*. ACM Press, 2003.

[3] M. K. Aguilera, C. Delporte-Gallet, H. Fauconnier, and S. Toueg. Communication-efficient leader election and consensus with limited link synchrony. In *Proc. PODC'04*, pages 328–337. ACM Press, 2004.

[4] R. Boichat, P. Dutta, S. Frolund, and R. Guerraoui. Reconstructing Paxos. *ACM SIGACT News*, 34(1):47–67, 2003.

[5] T. D. Chandra and S. Toueg. Unreliable failure detectors for reliable distributed systems. *Journal of ACM*, 43(2):225–267, 1996.

[6] B. Charron-Bost and A. Schiper. The "Heard-Of" model: Unifying all benign faults. Technical Report TR, EPFL, June 2006.

[7] B. Charron-Bost and A. Schiper. Improving fast paxos: being optimistic with no overhead. In *Pacific Rim Dependable Computing, Proceedings*, 2006.

[8] F. Cristian and C. Fetzer. The timed asynchronous distributed system model. *IEEE Transactions on Parallel and Distributed Systems*, 10(6):642–657, 1999.

[9] A. Doudou and A. Schiper. Muteness Failure Detectors for Consensus with Byzantine Processes. TR 97/230, EPFL, Dept d'Informatique, October 1997.

[10] A. Doudou and A. Schiper. Muteness detectors for consensus with byzantine processes (Brief Announcement). In *Proc. PODC'98*, Puerto Vallarta, Mexico, July 1998.

[11] P. Dutta, R. Guerraoui, and L. Lamport. How fast can eventual synchrony lead to consensus? In *Proc. DSN'05*, pages 22–27, Los Alamitos, CA, USA, 2005.

[12] C. Dwork, N. Lynch, and L. Stockmeyer. Consensus in the presence of partial synchrony. *Journal of ACM*, 35(2):288–323, April 1988.

[13] M. Fischer, N. Lynch, and M. Paterson. Impossibility of Distributed Consensus with One Faulty Process. *Journal of ACM*, 32:374–382, April 1985.

[14] E. Gafni. Round-by-round fault detectors: Unifying synchrony and asynchrony. In *Proc of the 17th ACM Symp. Principles of Distributed Computing (PODC)*, pages 143–152, Puerto Vallarta, Mexico, June-July 1998.

[15] R. Guerraoui and A. Schiper. "gamma-accurate" failure detectors. In *Proceedings of the 10th International Workshop on Distributed Algorithms (WDAG'96)*, pages 269–286, London, UK, 1996. Springer-Verlag.

[16] M. Hutle and A. Schiper. Communication predicates: A high-level abstraction for coping with transient and dynamic faults. Technical Report LSR-REPORT-2006-006, EPFL, 2006. http://infoscience.epfl.ch/search.py?recid=97290.

[17] I. Keidar and A. Shraer. Timeliness, failure-detectors, and consensus performance. In *Proc. PODC'06*, pages 169–178, New York, NY, USA, 2006. ACM Press.

[18] K. P. Kihlstrom, L. E. Moser, and P. M. Melliar-Smith. Solving consensus in a byzantine environment using an unreliable fault detector. In *Proceedings of the International Conference on Principles of Distributed Systems (OPODIS)*, pages 61–75, Chantilly, France, Dec. 1997.

[19] L. Lamport. The Part-Time Parliament. *ACM Trans. on Computer Systems*, 16(2):133–169, May 1998.

[20] G. Le Lann and U. Schmid. How to implement a timer-free perfect failure detector in partially synchronous systems. Technical Report 183/1-127, Technische Universität Wien, Department of Automation, Jan. 2003.

[21] N. Santoro and P. Widmayer. Time is not a healer. In *Proceedings of the 6th Symposium on Theor. Aspects of Computer Science*, pages 304–313, Paderborn, Germany, 1989.

[22] F. B. Schneider. What Good are Models and What Models are Good. In S. Mullender, editor, *Distributed Systems*, pages 169–197. ACM Press, 1993.

[23] T. K. Srikanth and S. Toueg. Optimal clock synchronization. *Journal of the ACM*, 34(3):626–645, 1987.

[24] J. Widder. Booting clock synchronization in partially synchronous systems. In *Proceedings of the 17th International Conference on Distributed Computing (DISC'03)*, pages 121–135, 2003.

Synchronous Consensus with Mortal Byzantines

Josef Widder[1,2]*   Günther Gridling[1†]   Bettina Weiss[1]   Jean-Paul Blanquart[3]

[1] TU Wien, Embedded Computing Systems, Austria, {`widder,gg,bw`}`@ecs.tuwien.ac.at`
[2] Laboratoire d'Informatique LIX, École Polytechnique, 91128 Palaiseau Cedex, France
[3] Astrium Satellites, France, `jean-paul.blanquart@astrium.eads.net`

Abstract

We consider the problem of reaching agreement in synchronous systems under a fault model whose severity lies between Byzantine and crash faults. For these "mortal" Byzantine faults, we assume that faulty processes take a finite number of arbitrary steps before they eventually crash. After discussing several application examples where this model is justified, we present and prove correct a consensus algorithm that tolerates a minority of faulty processes; i.e., more faults can be tolerated compared to classic Byzantine faults. We also show that the algorithm is optimal regarding the required number of processes and that no algorithm can solve consensus with just a majority of correct processes in a bounded number of rounds under our fault assumption. Finally, we consider more restricted fault models that allow to further reduce the required number of processes.

1. Introduction

Consensus is fundamental for building reliable distributed systems in which faults have to be tolerated. Crash faults are very well studied in this context (see [9, 12, 21] for an overview), but they capture only a small number of causes that lead to abnormal behavior, such as power outage or permanent disconnection of a node from the network. The most general failure model is the Byzantine one, which does not postulate any assumption on the behavior of faulty processes [20]. It captures all causes of failure, ranging from arbitrary bit flips in memory to intentional (malicious) causes like intrusions. However, Byzantine behavior may be overly pessimistic if we consider non-intentional faults.

Additionally, the classic Byzantine assumption may be too pessimistic in many practical systems where one finds modules that observe the behavior of components and may act on these components — either automatically or by operator decision — in case of anomaly. This results in a modification of the component failure mode as perceived by other components of the system. In such cases, a component may not fail once and for ever according to a single "static" failure mode, but its faulty behavior follows some trajectory in the set of possible failure modes.

This paper is based on the idea that, rather than considering the worst case single failure mode exhibited by a component, it may be fruitful to exploit some characteristics of its failure mode trajectory. In particular we consider failures which eventually end as a crash, after some latency period where a more pessimistic mode (up to arbitrary behavior) may be exhibited. We call this behavior *mortal Byzantine*, and it was introduced by Nesterenko and Arora in the context of self-stabilizing dining philosophers [24].

Contribution. It is well known that consensus in the presence of (unauthenticated) Byzantine faults can be solved in synchronous systems if and only if less than a third of the processes may be faulty [20]. By introducing a novel algorithm in Sect. 4, we show in this paper that in the mortal Byzantine model (introduced in Sect. 3) it suffices that a majority of the processes is correct. (Some proofs had to be omitted due to space restictions; they can be found in [27].) We also show that a majority is necessary in Sect. 5, i.e., our algorithm is optimal w.r.t. the required number of processes.

If t is the upper bound on the number of crashes during an execution, it is also known that consensus can be solved in $t + 1$ rounds. We show that in the mortal Byzantine case, with just a majority of correct processes, such a bound cannot exist, i.e., no algorithm decides in a bounded number of rounds in every execution (Sect. 5).

Due to the latter result, it might appear as if this model cannot be employed if bounded termination time was required. Following the late binding principle [19] this is only true when the life time of faults (e.g., the delay of the detection mechanism) in the real system is not bounded. As our proofs reveal, if the time is bounded in which faulty processes can pollute the system, so is the termination time.

After the general case, we consider special cases in Sect. 6 and 7 that may be relevant in many real applications.

---

*Supported by the Austrian FWF project Theta (proj.no. P17757).
†Supported by the Austrian FWF project SPAWN (proj.no. P18264).

We discuss that when assumptions on the number of steps of faulty processes are added, it is possible to reduce the required number of processes for consensus even to $t + 1$.

2. Motivation

The seminal paper by Lamport, Shostak, and Pease [20] considers the Byzantine Generals problem for synchronous systems with arbitrary faulty processes. This environment combines highly optimistic timing assumptions with highly pessimistic fault assumptions to result in the well-known $n > 3t$ bound, so naturally researchers turned to investigating other systems and fault types. Relaxing the synchronous system assumption led to the well-known impossibility result [18] for asynchronous systems and subsequently to work on systems augmented with failure detectors, e.g. [14, 15, 22], or limited synchrony assumptions, e.g. [2, 8, 10, 16]. Other approaches aim at optimizing normal case behavior [1, 11, 23] or consider more elaborate fault models in an effort to improve fault resilience [3, 5, 6, 26].

Our approach aims at improving resilience by strengthening the fault assumptions, and in contrast to most previous work in this area, we consider failure mode trajectories, where components migrate from one (severe) fault type to another (less severe) one, since such models are not just of purely theoretical interest, but also of practical use, as illustrated by the following examples from the space domain.

Often, space systems have to meet strong requirements in terms of lifetime (without the possibility of replacing faulty components with new ones) and in terms of mass and volume — limiting the number of available redundant units. Space systems are also characterized for some missions by a strong prevalence of temporary faults; e.g., due to heavy ions. Therefore, when a faulty behavior is observed, it is usual practice to wait some time and assess more precisely its actual impact and recurrence characteristics, before (or instead of) engaging strong reconfiguration and definitely losing the failed component. In this example, the other components of the system may observe a faulty behavior evolving from maybe fully arbitrary to either correct or crash.

Note that the duration of this process may vary from very short to very long times. On the one hand, short durations occur when an automatic on-board mechanism — e.g., employing execution control, temperature control, or power control — can identify a high severity failure at the first manifestation and switch off the component. While, on the other hand, long durations may be encountered when ground operators are in the loop to analyze trends in the telemetry, before requesting some reconfiguration by tele commands. Between these two extremes, almost any possible intermediate durations are possible. For instance, it is practice that an on-board mechanism explicitly counts the number of errors produced by a component in successive computation cycles. When a given threshold is reached — and the fault is considered permanent — the component is eventually shut down by this on-board mechanism.

The European Automated Transfer Vehicle (ATV) is the unmanned transport spacecraft to be launched towards the (manned) International Space Station ISS. The ATV computer architecture contains, among other elements, a pool of computing units with distributed voting and agreement mechanisms at pool level. In addition, each computing unit of the pool is provided with a set of self-checking mechanisms (whose main aim is to provide some detection coverage for common mode faults). A computing unit detected as faulty by these self-checking mechanisms is reset into a silent mode, and in particular does not participate in the following votes. As a result of the combination of the vote and agreement mechanisms at computer pool level and of the self-checking mechanisms at the level of each computer unit of the pool, it may happen that a computing unit — as seen from other units — first appears faulty according to an arbitrary failure mode, before appearing crashed.

Good system design calls for transparent solutions, i.e., consensus should work independently of the self-detection (or the human intervention), and the experienced failure model should be described independently of the machinery that enforces it. Proper modeling of the described behavior leads naturally to the *mortal Byzantine* failure model which is formally defined in the following section.

3. Model

We consider a synchronous system of n distributed processes of the set $\Pi = \{1, \ldots, n\}$ that communicate via reliable communication links. Correct processes take an infinite number of steps according to their algorithm in infinite executions. We assume that the correct receiver of a message knows the sender.

Distributed algorithms are executed in rounds. Locally, during an execution, a correct process possibly sends at most one message to each process for the current round according to its state, receives messages and executes a state transition according to its state, the received messages, and its algorithm. Messages have finite delays and a message sent by correct process p to correct process q in round r is received by q in round r. A correct process halts by reaching a terminal state in which it remains during the remainder of the execution; it sends no further messages and the state transition function is the identity function.

Processes fail by taking a finite number of arbitrary steps (that deviate from their algorithm) in which they send at most a finite number of messages. So we assume a failure trajectory from Byzantine to crash and say that a faulty process exhibits mortal Byzantine behavior. In every execution, at most t processes are mortal Byzantine faulty. In this paper we study consensus under the mentioned fault model as consensus lies underneath many agreement problems. The variant we want to solve in this paper is already folklore.

Problem Statement. Every correct process proposes some value $v \in \{0, 1\}$ and has to decide irrevocably on some value in concordance with the following properties:

Agreement. No two correct processes decide differently.

Validity. If some correct process decides v, then v is proposed by some correct process.

Termination. Every correct process eventually decides.

The term *termination* traditionally considers that processes decide. As laid out in [9], in general, results on deciding not necessarily carry over to termination in the sense of halting, i.e., reaching a terminal state in which no further messages are sent; cf. [13,21]. In our context the distinction is interesting as we will show in Sect. 5 that if there is just a majority of correct processes, there is no fixed number of rounds that an algorithm requires to decide in each execution. However, we show that our algorithm also solves the problem of reaching a terminal state:

Halting. Eventually every correct process reaches a terminal state.

In Sect. 4 and Sect. 5 we show that $2t < n$ is necessary and sufficient to solve consensus in our model.

We will denote by f_q^s the content of correct process q's variable f at the end of round s. Further, we will denote by "___" the wild card which stands for all possible values.

We do not consider authenticated algorithms in this paper. In addition to the lack of a formal definition of authentication in the presence of Byzantine faults and the disadvantage of computational and communication overhead, each authentication scheme is bound to some probability that it can be broken. Thus using non-authenticated algorithms, our correctness proofs cannot be invalidated by this.

4. Algorithm

In this section we present and analyze our algorithm that solves consensus in the presence of up to $t < n/2$ faulty processes. Our Algorithm 1 has some similarities to the EDAC algorithm described in [9] and originally introduced in [17]. EDAC solves the early deciding consensus problem in the presence of crash faults.

The main idea of our algorithm is due to lower bound proofs for classic Byzantine faulty processes: Informally speaking, due to the lower bound results [20,21] for consensus in the presence of Byzantine processes we can say that for every algorithm that should solve consensus, if there are

at least a third of the processes faulty, then there are situations in certain executions where a correct process p knows that some other process is faulty, but p cannot decide which. The main idea of our algorithm is that if p encounters such a case, it waits until the faulty processes crash, and the faulty values received can be removed. So this dilemma can be overcome due to the different failure assumption.

Our algorithm operates in phases consisting of two consecutive rounds. In the first round of each phase, correct processes send their proposed value and their decision value ($\bot$ until processes decide) to all and collect the values sent by other processes in the vectors *rcvprop* and *rcvdec*. Additionally, every correct process p checks whether some process q's message was missing in some round. If this is the case, q is removed from p's estimate of the set of alive processes π, and the number of possibly alive faulty processes f is updated. Entries in vectors *rcvdec* or *rcvprop* which correspond to faulty processes are set to † or $\bot$, respectively.

In the second round of a phase, correct processes send *rcvprop* and *rcvdec* to all (similar to the exponential algorithm in [20]). At the end of the second round, correct processes check whether all vectors they received from processes in π — i.e., processes not considered faulty — are equal. In this case they try to decide. They may decide on a value w if they have received at least $f + 1$ messages stating that the sender proposed w. Notice that f is not constant (as $t \geq f$ is the bound on the number of faults). Intuitively, if a process has been detected as being faulty (i.e., if no message was received from this process in some round), f is decreased by 1. Additionally, a process may only decide w if it (or any other process in π, cf. *rcvdec*) did not receive a message in the previous round sent by some still alive process q stating that q has decided $1 - w$. Note that if a faulty (but still alive) process sends that it decided w and another process sends it decided $1 - w$ it is impossible to decide in this phase. However, since faulty processes eventually crash, their decision is removed and will later not be considered anymore so that taking a decision is again possible.

Correct process p halts if all processes that it considers to be alive have decided, otherwise, a new phase is started.

In the remainder of this section we prove that our algorithm solves consensus by separately proving the required properties. We commence with preliminary definitions.

Definition 4.1 (Last Decision). *We define r_d as the maximum round in an execution for which it holds that at least one correct process has not decided in some round less than r_d in this execution. Further, d is such a correct process.*

Definition 4.2 (First Halt). *We define h as the maximum round in an execution for which it holds that no correct process has halted in some round less than h in this execution.*

We start our analysis with some preliminary lemmas. First, we make some statements about the decision value

Algorithm 1 Synchronous, Mortal Byzantine Tolerant Consensus

Code for processes p (if they are correct):

```
1:  variables
2:      r_p ← 0                                                              // round number
3:      π_p ← Π                                    // the set of processes that are not detected faulty by p
4:      f_p ← t                                  // possible number of not yet detected faulty processes
5:      prop_p ∈ {0, 1}                                                       // proposed value
6:      decision_p ∈ {0, 1, ⊥} ← ⊥                                           // initially ⊥
7:      rcvprop_p[n] ∈ {0, 1, ⊥}                      // proposed value received from i in the current round
8:      rcvdec_p[n] ∈ {0, 1, ⊥, †}                    // decision value received from i in the current round
9:      c_prop_p[n][n] ∈ {0, 1, ⊥}                           // the proposed values as seen by other processes
10:     c_π_p[n]                                      // the set of alive processes as seen by other processes
11:     c_dec_p[n][n] ∈ {0, 1, ⊥, †}                          // the decided values as seen by other processes
12:  repeat
13:     if r_p(mod)2 = 0 then
14:         send (INFORM, prop_p, decision_p) to all
15:         receive
16:         for all i ∈ Π do
17:             if no message from i was received in some round then
18:                 rcvdec_p[i] ← †                                          // i is faulty
19:                 rcvprop_p[i] ← ⊥
20:                 π_p ← π_p − i
21:                 f_p ← t − |Π − π_p|
22:             else
23:                 if received (INFORM, prop_i, decision_i) from i in current round then
24:                     rcvprop_p[i] ← prop_i
25:                     rcvdec_p[i] ← decision_i
26:     if r_p(mod)2 = 1 then
27:         send (ECHO, rcvprop_p, π_p, rcvdec_p) to all
28:         receive
29:         for all i ∈ Π do
30:             if received (ECHO, rcvprop_i, π_i, rcvdec_i) from i then
31:                 c_prop_p[i] ← rcvprop_i
32:                 c_π_p[i] ← π_i
33:                 c_dec_p[i] ← rcvdec_i
34:             else
35:                 c_prop_p[i] ← ⊥
36:                 c_π_p[i] ← ⊥
37:                 c_dec_p[i] ← ⊥
38:         if decision_p = ⊥ ∧ ∀i, j ∈ π_p : c_prop_p[i] = c_prop_p[j] ∧ c_π_p[i] = c_π_p[j] ∧ c_dec_p[i] = c_dec_p[j] then
39:             W ← {w : w ∈ {0, 1} ∧ |{j ∈ π_p : rcvprop_p[j] = w}| ≥ f_p + 1 ∧ ∀i ∈ Π : rcvdec_p[i] ≠ (1 − w)}
40:             if |W| > 0 then
41:                 decide min W
42:                 decision_p ← min W
43:     r_p ← r_p + 1
44:  until ∀i ∈ Π : rcvdec_p[i] ≠ ⊥
45:  halt
```

$decision_p$ which are quite obvious from code inspection:

Lemma 4.3 (Decision). *If p is a correct process, then the following statements hold:*

(1) $decision_p^0 = \bot$.

(2) If $decision_p$ is updated to value v, then $v \in \{0, 1\}$.

(3) Variable $decision_p$ is changed at most once.

Basically, this lemma says that the initial value of the decision variable at correct processes is $\bot$, and that a correct process changes it only once to a value of either 0 or 1.

Now, we consider how a correct process q is perceived by another correct process p via the variables $rcvdec_p$ and π_p.

Lemma 4.4 (Perception of Decisions). *If p and q both are correct processes, then the following statements hold:*

(1) If $decision_q^r = \bot$, then $rcvdec_p^s[q] = \bot$ in all rounds $s \leq r + 1$.

(1') $rcvdec_p^r[d] = \bot$ in all rounds $r \leq r_d$.

(2) $r_d < h$.

(3) If q takes the decision v in round r, then $rcvdec_p^s[q] = v$ in all rounds $r < s \leq r_d + 1$.

(4) If a message from process i does not arrive at p in round $r < h$, then $rcvdec_p^s[i] = †$ and $i \notin \pi_p^s$ in all rounds $s > r$.

This lemma basically states that while a correct process q has not yet decided, value $rcvdec_p[q]$ will remain at $\perp$ for at least another round. In consequence, $rcvdec_p[d]$ will remain at $\perp$ until round r_d, and therefore no correct process can halt before round $r_d + 1$. Once a correct process makes a decision, this decision is known by all correct processes in the next round, and will be kept in $rcvdec_p[q]$ at least until round $r_d + 1$. Finally, if in some round no message does arrive from process i, which means that process i is faulty, then from (at least) the next round on, $rcvdec_p[i] = \dagger$ for the remainder of the algorithm.

Lemma 4.5 (Failure Detection). *If p and q both are correct processes, then the following statements hold:*

(1) $q \in \pi_p^r$ in all rounds $r \leq r_d$.

(2) $|\pi_p^r| > t$ in all rounds $r \leq r_d$.

(3) For each round $r \leq r_d$ it holds that no more than f_p^r faulty processes are in π_p^r.

(4) If a message from process i does not arrive at p in round r, then $i \notin \pi_p^s$ in all rounds $s > r$.

This lemma is concerned with who a correct process p considers faulty. It states that correct processes are in the "non yet faulty" set π until the last correct process has made its decision, that in consequence there are at least $t + 1$ processes in π, and that f_p^r contains the maximum number of faulty processes in π_p^r.

Equipped with these basic facts, we can now start to consider the consensus properties of the algorithm.

Theorem 4.6 (Validity). *If a correct process decides on some value v, then v was proposed by a correct process.*

Proof. By line 39, correct process p only decides in some round r on a value v that was received by at least $f_p^r + 1$ (INFORM, v, __) messages from distinct processes in π_p^r in round $r - 1$. By Lemma 4.5 (3), there are no more than f_p^r faulty processes in π_p^r such that at least 1 correct process must have proposed v. $\square$

After validity, we now turn our attention towards agreement, for which we employ the following lemmas.

Lemma 4.7. *If two correct processes p, q both decide in some round r, then both decide on the same value v.*

Proof. By line 39 and line 41, the decision value is a deterministic function (identical at all correct processes) of $rcvprop_s^r$, π_s^r, f_s^r, and $rcvdec_s^r$ for correct process $s \in \{p, q\}$. We thus have to show that these four variables must have identical values at correct processes p and q in some round r in which both decide.

From Lemma 4.5 (1) it follows that $q \in \pi_p^r$ and $p \in \pi_q^r$ for $r \leq r_d$. Since both decide in line 41 in round r, line 38 must have evaluated to TRUE in this round at both processes. It follows that $rcvprop_p^r = rcvprop_q^r$, $rcvdec_p^r = rcvdec_q^r$, $\pi_p^r = \pi_q^r$, and thus $f_p^r = f_q^r$ by line 21. From the deterministic decision function, our lemma follows. $\square$

Theorem 4.8 (Agreement). *No two correct processes decide differently.*

Proof. By Lemma 4.7, two correct processes do not decide differently if they decide in the same round. It remains to show that a correct process p does not decide on a different value from the value another correct process q has decided in some earlier round.

Assume by contradiction that a correct process p decides on $w \in \{0, 1\}$ in round r and some distinct correct process q decides $1 - w$ in some round $s > r$. By line 39, $\forall i \in \Pi : rcvdec_q^s[i] \neq w$, but by Lemma 4.4 (3), $rcvdec_q^s[p] = w$ which provides the required contradiction. $\square$

As seen above, agreement and validity can be proven independently of the rounds processes crash in; what is still missing is liveness. We will see in the following section that the relation of decision rounds and rounds in which processes crash is inherent to the problem. In our analysis we hence have to use the round in an execution at which the last faulty process crashes in order to show termination (and halting) of our algorithm.

Definition 4.9 (Last Crash). *We define r_c as the minimum round such that all processes that crash in an execution are crashed by (i.e., before or in) round r_c and all messages sent by faulty processes are received by round r_c.*

Observation 4.10 (Clean Round). *All rounds $r > r_c$ are clean rounds, i.e., no messages by faulty processes are received in rounds r.*

Until now we considered safety, i.e., we ensured that if a correct process decides in line 41, validity and agreement hold. In the following, we show liveness, i.e., line 41 is eventually reached by every correct process in every execution. We prove that if all faulty processes are crashed and their messages are received, the system is in a "clean" state such that the consistency checks in line 38 and line 39 allow to reach a decision at every correct process.

Theorem 4.11 (Termination). *Eventually, every correct process decides.*

Proof. Let r be the minimal round such that $r > r_c$ and $r(\bmod)2 = 0$. If all correct processes decide before round r we are done. So in the remainder of this proof we consider only the case where at least one correct process p does not decide before round r.

In the following we will show that every correct process that does not decide before round r decides at the end of round $r + 1$ by executing line 41. By observing the code, a correct process executes line 41 only if the statement in line 38 evaluates to TRUE and if $|W| > 0$, where W is computed in line 39. We will show that these two requirements are met in Lemma 4.14, Lemma 4.15, and Lemma 4.16 after the following preliminary lemmas. We start with the following corollary which follows from Lemma 4.4 (4).

Corollary 4.12. *For every correct process p and every faulty process i it holds that $rcvdec_p^{r+1}[i] = \dagger$.*

Lemma 4.13. *For every two correct processes p and q it holds that $rcvprop_p^{r+1} = rcvprop_q^{r+1}$, $rcvdec_p^{r+1} = rcvdec_q^{r+1}$, $\pi_p^{r+1} = \pi_q^{r+1}$, and $f_p^{r+1} = f_q^{r+1}$.*

Lemma 4.14. *For every correct process that does not decide before round r, it holds that line 38 evaluates to TRUE in round $r + 1$.*

So far, we have shown that every correct process p that does not decide before round r reaches line 39 in round $r + 1$. In the following, we have to show that after executing line 39 in round $r + 1$ it holds that $|W| > 0$ at every p such that p decides. To this end, we distinguish two cases: We consider in Lemma 4.15 the case where at least one correct process decides in a round before $r + 1$, and in Lemma 4.16 the other case, where no process has decided before.

Lemma 4.15. *If at least one correct process decides before round r, then for every correct process p that does not decide before round r, in round $r + 1$ it holds that $|W| > 0$.*

Lemma 4.16. *If no correct process decides before round r, then for every correct process p that does not decide before round r, in round $r + 1$ it holds that $|W| > 0$.*

Lemma 4.14 implies that every correct process p that does not decide before round r executes line 39 in round $r + 1$. By Lemma 4.15 and Lemma 4.16, p executes line 39 in round $r + 1$ so that $|W| > 0$ and consequently every p decides in round $r + 1$. Thus, every correct process decides at the latest in round $r + 1$, and our Theorem 4.11 follows. $\square$

Theorem 4.17 (Halting). *Every correct process halts.*

Proof. We have to show that the expression of line 44 eventually evaluates to TRUE at every correct process p, i.e., that eventually $\forall i \in \Pi : rcvdec_p[i] \neq \bot$.

By Theorem 4.11, all correct processes eventually decide. After deciding — before halting — they send their decision value via (INFORM, __, $decision_p$) to all in every even numbered round in line 14. The decisions are then written into $rcvdec_p[i]$ in line 25 such that eventually for all correct processes i, $rcvdec_p[i] \neq \bot$ at every correct process p. (Note that $rcvdec_p[i]$ is never reset to $\bot$ for correct processes i if it was set to some value once.)

The faulty processes eventually stop sending messages such that missing messages will be detected at every correct process, and in line 18, $rcvdec_p[i] \leftarrow \dagger$ will be set for every faulty process i at every correct process p. Consequently, for all processes i, eventually $rcvdec_p[i] \neq \bot$ at every correct process p such that our lemma follows. $\square$

Corollary 4.18. *Algorithm 1 solves consensus.*

5. Lower Bounds

One property of our algorithm is that it is guaranteed to decide only when all faulty processes have crashed. We show that this is inherent to the problem, more specifically inherent to the number of processes. Our failure model is strictly stronger than the classic Byzantine model [20]. Thus, algorithms that solve consensus in the classic model with $n > 3t$ within $t + 1$ rounds [20] can be applied to our model as well. In the following, we will show that when one reduces n, it is not possible anymore to solve the problem in a fixed number of rounds. We show that the round in which the last correct process decides cannot be constant, but depends on the failure pattern — a mapping of the set of faulty processes to a set of integers representing the round number in which the processes crash [13].

Theorem 5.1. *In a system with up to t mortal Byzantine faults, for every deterministic algorithm that solves consensus if $n > 2t$ and every c there exists at least one execution where the first faulty process crashes in round c and at least one correct process decides in some round $r \geq c$.*

Proof. Consider by ways of contradiction that a consensus algorithm $\mathcal{A}$ exists where in every possible execution of $\mathcal{A}$ in which faults occur, all correct processes decide before the first faulty process crashes. At the time the correct processes decide, the prefixes of these executions can be mapped one-to-one to identical prefixes of executions of $\mathcal{A}$ in the presence of classic Byzantine faults. Thus, $\mathcal{A}$ also solves consensus with classic Byzantine faults contradicting the lower bound by Lamport, Shostak, and Pease [20] of $n > 3t$. $\square$

Corollary 5.2. *There is no correct deterministic algorithm that solves consensus in the presence of up to $t \geq n/3$ mortal Byzantine faults in a bounded number $g(t)$ rounds, g being an arbitrary function on the upper bound on the number of faulty processes.*

After considering termination time, we now show that our algorithm is optimal regarding the number of processes. We show that no algorithm exists for $2t$ processes.

Theorem 5.3. *There is no algorithm that solves consensus in the presence of t mortal Byzantine faults if $n = 2t$.*

107

Proof. Consider by contradiction that such an algorithm $\mathcal{A}$ exists. And further consider a fault free execution $\mathcal{E}$ of $\mathcal{A}$ in which t correct processes propose 0 and t correct processes propose 1. Let in this execution p be a correct process that proposes $w \in \{0, 1\}$ and decides $1 - w$, and let it decide in round r. Such a process p must exist as both values are proposed by correct processes and only one can be decided upon by the agreement property of consensus.

Now consider executions of $\mathcal{A}$ where p is correct and p is one of t correct processes that propose w and the remaining t faulty processes behave as correct ones at least until round r but (wrongly) propose $1 - w$. There exists such an execution $\mathcal{E}_t$ that is at least up to round r for correct process p locally indistinguishable from $\mathcal{E}$. Thus p decides on $1 - w$ in round r. After round r all faulty processes crash such that $\mathcal{E}_t$ is an admissible execution in our model. However, $\mathcal{A}$ violates validity in $\mathcal{E}_t$ as p decides $1 - w$ although it was not proposed by any correct process in $\mathcal{E}_t$ which provides the required contradiction to $\mathcal{A}$ solving consensus. $\square$

6. Reducing the Number of Processes

In the previous sections, we have shown that the reduction from the classical $n > 3t$ bound for Byzantine faults to $n > 2t$ for mortal Byzantine faults already allows to build cheaper systems (i.e., with less redundancy) in certain cases, even without a priori knowledge on the timing behavior of faulty processes. If such knowledge exists, i.e., when it is known how long it takes until a faulty process crashes, r_c can be determined for every execution and our previous algorithm terminates within a bounded number of rounds. The question investigated in the remainder of the paper is, whether such a priori knowledge on the behavior of faulty processes allows to further reduce the system size, and thus the system cost induced by mere redundancy purposes. Our resulting fault models are inspired by the concept of hardware monitors, which observe the behavior of processes, can detect (some) faults, and are able to remove a detected faulty process from the system within a known bounded time as discussed in Sect. 2.

Definition 6.1. *A fault which is detected by the hardware monitor and which can cause the associated process to be shut down is a* lethal fault. *A fault which does not cause the associated process to be removed is a* non-lethal *fault.*

We distinguish two failure models in the following. One in which the faults associated to a process accumulate until a given threshold is exceeded, which causes the removal of the faulty process. And another one which allows a certain number of faults within a given time period and only removes a faulty process if it creates too many faults too closely together (i.e., within a given time window).

(O) **Bounded Failure Occurrence.** After a process has exhibited lethal faults in $x > 0$ rounds, it fails within $0 \leq y < \infty$ rounds.

(R) **Bounded Failure Rate.** After a process has exhibited lethal faults within $x > 0$ out of $z \geq x$ rounds, it fails within y rounds, $0 \leq y < \infty$. (By setting $z = \infty$, we derive model (O), so (R) $\supset$ (O).)

Both models allow a certain number of faults to go unpunished and only remove a faulty process if it exhibits "too many" faults. This allows transient faults, e.g. memory faults, caused for example by single event upsets, to simply run their course; the afflicted process is only removed if it does not recover by itself within a given number of rounds. We do not concern ourselves with the cause of such transient faults, although in practice this might have significant impact on the fault detection and removal logic, for example in case of corrupted messages.

In contrast to the mortal Byzantine model of the previous sections, the above two models have a known bound y for the time until a process fails. (Note that in the model of the previous sections $x = 1$.) In the following we assume that all parameters x, y, and z are a priori known.

Based on these assumptions, we can cope with faulty processes by simply repeating messages for a sufficient number of times (i.e., by time redundancy). This allows us to devise a simulation that makes Byzantine failures appear as send omission faults and symmetric faulty.

Definition 6.2. *A process is* send omission faulty *in an execution if it follows its algorithm as a correct process but omits to send at least one message during the execution.*

A symmetric faulty process may be value and or time faulty with the restriction that it is not allowed to send messages with different content to different processes in the same round. This failure model only makes sense in broadcast based algorithms as ours, for example. This behavior is termed *identical Byzantine* in [4].

Definition 6.3. *A process p_f is* symmetric faulty *in an execution, if in each round all correct processes receive the same value from p_f and this value is faulty at least once during the execution.*

Our fault-tolerant full message exchange primitive called ft_fme(v) requires $k = x+y+1$ rounds; see Algorithm 2. In the following section we will show that in fact less severe faults can be simulated by this primitive on top of mortal Byzantine faults that obey x, y, and z.

In this section, we will consider a system where every fault is lethal. This matches the mechanisms discussed in the introduction (temperature control or power control). In the following section we will consider the case where only asymmetric — i.e., two faced — behavior leads to a crash.

Algorithm 2 Fault-Tolerant Full Message Exchange

Code for processes (ft_fme(v_p) for process p):

```
 1: variables
 2:     k = x + y + 1              // number of message repetitions
 3:     v_p ∈ {0, 1}                            // own value
 4:     rcvprop_p[n] ∈ {0, 1, ⊥}    // value received from process i
 5:     rcv_p[n][k] ∈ {0, 1, ⊥}     // value received from i …
                                   // … in k'-th send iteration
 6: for k' = 1 to k do
 7:     send (v_p) to all
 8:     receive
 9:     for all i ∈ Π do
10:         if received (v_i) by i then
11:             rcv_p[i][k'] ← v_i
12:         else
13:             rcv_p[i][k'] ← ⊥
14: for all i ∈ Π do
15:     W ← {w : w ∈ {0,1} ∧ |{k' : rcv_p[i][k'] = w}| = k}
16:     if |W| > 0 then
17:         rcvprop_p[i] = min W
18:     else
19:         rcvprop_p[i] = ⊥
20: return rcvprop_p[]
```

We assume in the following that, for communication, algorithms use our full message exchange only.

Lemma 6.4. *Under (O) or (R), if all communication is done via* ft_fme(v) *and all faults are lethal, then faulty processes only appear omission faulty or crashed.*

Proof. Consider one instance of our full message exchange algorithm, and assume that at the end of it, correct processes p and q both deliver a value for faulty process p_f, that is, $rcvprop_p[p_f] \neq \bot$ and $rcvprop_q[p_f] \neq \bot$. Since $rcvprop_i[p_f] \neq \bot \Leftrightarrow rcv_i[p_f][k'] = rcv_i[p_f][k'']$ for all $k', k'' \in \{1, ..., k\}$, if follows that p resp. q has received $k = x + y + 1$ equal values $rcvprop_p[p_f]$ resp. $rcvprop_q[p_f]$ from p_f. However, p_f can pollute at most x consecutive rounds, which may be followed by at most y additional (possibly faulty) rounds before p_f crashes. Therefore, during one of the k rounds, p_f must have followed the algorithm and has sent correct messages to all processes. Let v_{p_f} denote this correct value. It follows that $\exists k' : rcv_p[p_f][k'] = rcv_q[p_f][k'] = v_{p_f}$ and therefore $rcvprop_p[p_f] = rcvprop_q[p_f] = v_{p_f}$, so both p and q deliver the same correct value v_{p_f} for faulty process p_f.

Of course, some or all correct processes may not deliver a value at all, for example if the faulty process commits a send omission fault. □

Theorem 6.5. *If all faults are lethal, consensus with at most t mortal Byzantine faulty processes requires $n > t$ processes.*

Proof. From Lemma 6.4, we know that a faulty process may appear at most send omission faulty, and consensus with t send omission faults requires $t+1$ processes [25]. □

Note that apart from achieving consensus with $t < n$ faulty processes, our fault models also allow a bounded algorithm execution time of $k \cdot (t + 1)$ rounds.

7. Non-lethal Faults

In certain applications, the assumption that a hardware monitor can detect all kinds of faults (like in the previous sections) may be overly optimistic. In particular, detecting symmetric faults requires knowledge about the correctness of the contents of a message, which may be beyond the scope of a simple monitor. Therefore, we should also consider systems in which only asymmetric faults are lethal, whereas symmetric faults are non-lethal.

Note that the non-lethal failure model is formally not comparable to the mortal Byzantine model of Sect. 3 to Sect. 5. Under this section's assumption, on the one hand, faulty processes may be alive forever, given that they do not behave two-faced (i.e., send out different values to different processes in the same round). On the other hand, after behaving two-faced, a faulty process must crash within a fixed number of rounds. We will show that again $n > 2t$ is necessary and sufficient to solve consensus.

Lemma 7.1. *Under (O) or (R), if all communication is done via* ft_fme(v) *and symmetric faults are non-lethal, then if two correct processes deliver the messages m and m' respectively in any round r then $m = m'$.*

Proof. From Lemma 6.4 we know that if all faults are lethal, a faulty process can appear send omission faulty or crashed. Let us again assume that correct processes p and q both deliver a value for faulty process p_f. Since asymmetric faults are still lethal, we again find that p resp. q has received $k = x + y + 1$ equal values $rcvprop_p[p_f]$ resp. $rcvprop_q[p_f]$, and that $rcvprop_p[p_f] = rcvprop_q[p_f]$. However, as symmetric faults are now non-lethal, the value delivered by the correct processes may now be value faulty. Again, some correct processes may not deliver a value for p_f at all. □

The previous lemma ascertains that faulty processes only appear crashed, send omission faulty, symmetric faulty, or a combination of send omission and symmetric faulty.

Theorem 7.2. *There is no algorithm that solves consensus in the presence of $t \geq n/2$ symmetric faulty processes.*

Proof. The proof is omitted since it is similar to the proof of Theorem 5.3 as no two-faced behavior was required to derive the result. □

Corollary 7.3. *If symmetric faults are non-lethal, consensus with at most t faulty processes requires at least $n > 2t$ processes.*

Algorithm 3 Synchronous, Mortal Byzantine Tolerant Consensus under model (O) and non-lethal symmetric faults

Code for processes (for process p):

```
 1: variables
 2:    v_p ∈ {0, 1}                          // current value
 3:    r_p ← 0                               // current round
 4:    rcvprop_p[i] ∈ {0, 1, ⊥}  // value received from i, 1 ≤ i ≤ n, ...
                                             // ... in the current round
 5:    decision_p ∈ {0, 1}                   // decision value
 6: repeat
 7:    r_p ← r_p + 1
 8:    ft_fme(v_p)
 9:    for all i ∈ Π do
10:       if received (v_i) by i then
11:          rcvprop_p[i] ← v_i
12:       else
13:          rcvprop_p[i] ← ⊥
14:    if |{i : rcvprop_p[i] = 0}| > |{i : rcvprop_p[i] = 1}| then
15:       v_p = 0
16:    else if |{i : rcvprop_p[i] = 0}| < |{i : rcvprop_p[i] = 1}| then
17:       v_p = 1
18:    else
19:       v_p = min{rcvprop_p[i]}
20: until r_p = x · t + 1
21: decide v_p
22: halt
```

Lemma 7.4. *In model (O), if a process appears send omission faulty in x full message exchanges, it will appear crashed in all subsequent full message exchanges.*

Proof. Since an omission fault requires asymmetric behavior, the faulty process p_f has committed at least one lethal fault and will fail within y rounds after the x-th such fault. Since a full message exchange requires $x + y + 1$ rounds, if the x-th lethal fault was at the end of full message exchange m, then process p_f will send at most y messages in full message exchange $m + 1$. Since the receivers only receive at most y of the $x + y + 1$ expected messages, none of the processes will deliver a value and p_f will appear crashed in this full message exchange and all subsequent ones. $\square$

In model (O), Algorithm 3, which is similar to [7], achieves consensus with $t < n/2$ faulty processes. The key idea of the algorithm is to calculate a new propose value in each round from the values received from all processes. This is done sufficiently many times so that there is at least one round without any omission faults. In this round, all correct processes will calculate the same value, which will henceforth prevail in all remaining rounds. To this aim, a correct process p repeatedly sends it own value and collects the values from all processes in set $rcvprop_p[i]$. Process p then sets its new proposed value v_p either to the majority value in $rcvprop_p[i]$, if it exists, or to the minimum of the received values. After $x \cdot t + 1$ such iterations, the last calculated proposed value v_p is used as the decision value.

In the following we will prove that Algorithm 3 solves consensus in the presence of up to $t < n/2$ faulty processes.

Lemma 7.5 (Termination & Halting). *Every correct process decides and halts after algorithm round $x \cdot t + 1$.*

Proof. This directly follows from simple code inspection. After the $(x \cdot t + 1)$-st round, the algorithm halts, and the value of v_p after this round is the decision value. $\square$

Lemma 7.6 (Validity). *If some correct process decides v, then v is proposed by some correct process.*

Proof. Let us assume that correct process p delivers the value w. From lines 14-19 we see that a process decides either on the majority value or, if no majority exists, on the smallest value. Since the set $rcvprop_p[i]$ contains at least $n - t$ values from correct processes and at most $t < n - t$ values from faulty processes, any majority must contain the value of at least one correct process. Similarly, if no majority exists, only values from faulty processes may be missing such that at least one correct process has sent w and at least one correct process has sent $1 - w$. $\square$

Lemma 7.7 (Agreement). *No two correct processes decide differently.*

Proof. From Lemma 7.4 we know that a faulty process can appear only send omission faulty in at most x rounds before it crashes. Therefore, at most $x \cdot t$ consecutive rounds can contain send omission faults, so at least one of the $x \cdot t + 1$ rounds is a clean round.

In a clean round, all correct processes have the same set $rcvprop_p[i]$ and will therefore compute the same value, which will henceforth win the majority in every subsequent round and thus will be delivered as the decision value. $\square$

Corollary 7.8. *Algorithm 3 solves consensus.*

8. Conclusions

We studied a fault model that seems to properly describe faulty behavior as experienced in novel practical applications, e.g. in the space domain. The model lies between crash model and Byzantine model as faulty processes are allowed to behave Byzantine until they eventually crash [24].

The notion of failure mode trajectory used in this paper seems to be an interesting issue for future work. We have shown that under the mortal Byzantine fault model, in the synchronous case $n > 2t$ is necessary and sufficient to solve consensus. In general, it should be possible to devise more efficient solutions (e.g., regarding synchrony assumptions or required number of processes) by replacing the static fault model with a model where the behavior of faulty processes converges towards some benign fault. We considered only the extreme case where faulty processes may start to exhibit the most general failure mode (Byzantine) and eventually converge to a very benign fault, i.e., they crash.

We also considered intermediate models where processes may exhibit a certain (bounded) number of faults without ever crashing, but if they do exceed this bound, they crash within a known number of rounds. We have shown that in these cases, $n > t$ is necessary and sufficient to solve consensus. If, however, only asymmetric faults count towards the bound, the $n > 2t$ result cannot be improved.

Many other forms of such trajectory may turn out to be useful in applications or may be encountered as natural behavior of certain components.

References

[1] M. Abd-El-Malek, G. R. Granger, G. R. Goodson, M. K. Reiter, and J. J. Wylie. Fault-scalable Byzantine fault-tolerant services. In *20th ACM Symposium on Operating Systems Principles (SOSP'05)*, pages 59–74, Oct. 23–26, 2005.

[2] M. K. Aguilera, C. Delporte-Gallet, H. Fauconnier, and S. Toueg. Consensus with byzantine failures and little system synchrony. In *Proceedings of the International Conference on Dependable Systems and Networks (DSN'06)*, pages 147–155, 2006.

[3] E. Anceaume, C. Delporte-Gallet, H. Fauconnier, M. Hurfin, and G. Le Lann. Designing modular services in the scattered byzantine failure model. In *3rd International Symposium on Parallel and Distributed Computing (ISPDC 2004)*, pages 262–269. IEEE Computer Society, 2004.

[4] H. Attiya and J. Welch. *Distributed Computing*. John Wiley & Sons, 2nd edition, 2004.

[5] M. H. Azadmanesh and R. M. Kieckhafer. New hybrid fault models for asynchronous approximate agreement. *IEEE Transactions on Computers*, 45(4):439–449, 1996.

[6] M. Biely. An optimal Byzantine agreement algorithm with arbitrary node and link failures. In *Proc. 15th Annual IASTED International Conference on Parallel and Distributed Computing and Systems (PDCS'03)*, pages 146–151, Marina Del Rey, California, USA, Nov. 3–5, 2003.

[7] M. Biely. On the optimal resilience for omissive process and link faults. private communication, 2005.

[8] M. Castro and B. Liskov. Practical byzantine fault tolerance. In *3rd Symposium on Operating Systems Design and Implementation*, Feb. 1999.

[9] B. Charron-Bost and A. Schiper. Uniform consensus is harder than consensus. *J. Algorithms*, 51(1):15–37, 2004.

[10] M. Correia, N. F. Neves, L. C. Lung, and P. Veríssimo. Low complexity Byzantine-resilient consensus. *Distributed Computing*, 17:237–249, 2005.

[11] M. Correia, N. F. Neves, and P. Veríssimo. From consensus to atomic broadcast: Time-free Byzantine-resistant protocols without signatures. *The Computer Journal*, 49(1):82–96, 2006.

[12] C. Delporte-Gallet, H. Fauconnier, S. L. Horn, and S. Toueg. Fast fault-tolerant agreement algorithms. In *PODC '05: Proceedings of the twenty-fourth annual ACM SIGACT-SIGOPS symposium on Principles of distributed computing*, pages 169–178, New York, NY, USA, 2005. ACM Press.

[13] D. Dolev, R. Reischuk, and H. R. Strong. Early stopping in Byzantine agreement. *Journal of the ACM*, 37(4):720–741, Oct. 1990.

[14] A. Doudou, B. Garbinato, and R. Guerraoui. Encapsulating failure detection: From crash to byzantine failures. In *Reliable Software Technologies - Ada-Europe 2002*, LNCS 2361, pages 24–50, Vienna, Austria, June 2002. Springer.

[15] A. Doudou, B. Garbinato, R. Guerraoui, and A. Schiper. Muteness failure detectors: Specification and implementation. In *Proceedings 3rd European Dependable Computing Conference (EDCC-3)*, volume 1667 of *LNCS 1667*, pages 71–87, Prague, Czech Republic, September 1999. Springer.

[16] C. Dwork, N. Lynch, and L. Stockmeyer. Consensus in the presence of partial synchrony. *Journal of the ACM*, 35(2):288–323, Apr. 1988.

[17] M. Fischer and L. Lamport. Byzantine generals and transaction commit protocols. Technical Report 62, SRI International, 1982.

[18] M. J. Fischer, N. A. Lynch, and M. S. Paterson. Impossibility of distributed consensus with one faulty process. *Journal of the ACM*, 32(2):374–382, Apr. 1985.

[19] J.-F. Hermant and G. Le Lann. Fast asynchronous uniform consensus in real-time distributed systems. *IEEE Transactions on Computers*, 51(8):931–944, Aug. 2002.

[20] L. Lamport, R. Shostak, and M. Pease. The Byzantine generals problem. *ACM Transactions on Programming Languages and Systems*, 4(3):382–401, July 1982.

[21] N. Lynch. *Distributed Algorithms*. Morgan Kaufman Publishers, Inc., San Francisco, USA, 1996.

[22] D. Malkhi and M. Reiter. Unreliable intrusion detection in distributed computations. In *Proceedings of the 10th Computer Security Foundations Workshop (CSFW97)*, pages 116–124, Rockport, MA, USA, June 1997.

[23] J.-P. Martin and L. Alvisi. Fast Byzantine consensus. *IEEE Transactions on Dependable and Secure Computing*, 3(3):202–215, July 2006.

[24] M. Nesterenko and A. Arora. Dining philosophers that tolerate malicious crashes. In *Proceedings of the 22nd International Conference on Distributed Computing Systems (ICDCS'02)*, pages 191–198, Vienna, Austria, July 2002.

[25] K. J. Perry and S. Toueg. Distributed agreement in the presence of processor and communication faults. *IEEE Transactions on Software Engineering*, SE-12(3):477–482, March 1986.

[26] P. M. Thambidurai and Y. K. Park. Interactive consistency with multiple failure modes. In *Proceedings 7th Reliable Distributed Systems Symposium*, Oct. 1988.

[27] J. Widder, G. Gridling, B. Weiss, and J.-P. Blanquart. Synchronous consensus despite mortal byzantines. Research Report 13/2006, Technische Universität Wien, Institut für Technische Informatik, 2006.

Session 2B:
Practical Experience Reports

Reliability Techniques for RFID-Based Object Tracking Applications

Ahmad Rahmati, Lin Zhong
Dept. of ECE, Rice University
Houston, TX 77005
{rahmati, lzhong}@rice.edu

Matti Hiltunen, Rittwik Jana
AT&T Labs - Research
Florham Park, NJ 07932
{hiltunen, rjana}@research.att.com

Abstract

Radio Frequency Identification (RFID) technology has the potential to dramatically improve numerous industrial practices. However, it still faces many challenges, including security and reliability, which may limit its use in many application scenarios. While security has received considerable attention, reliability has escaped much of the research scrutiny. In this work, we investigate the reliability challenges in RFID-based tracking applications, where objects (e.g., pallets, packages, and people) tagged with low-cost passive RFID tags pass by the RFID reader's read zone. Our experiments show that the reliability of tag identification is affected by several factors, including the inter-tag distance, the distance between the tag and antenna, the orientation of the tag with respect to the antenna, and the location of the tag on the object. We demonstrate that RFID system reliability can be significantly improved with the application of simple redundancy techniques.

1. Introduction

RFID leverages electromagnetic or electrostatic coupling in the radio frequency portion of the electromagnetic spectrum to identify objects over a distance of potentially several meters. While its origins can be traced back to 1940s (e.g., [16]), its commercial applications have started expanding significantly recently as a replacement or supplement to barcode technology, thanks in part to standardization, availability of commercial off-the -shelf (COTS) components, and their reducing cost[1]. RFID systems are employed to track shipments and manage supply-chains (e.g., Wal-Mart [2]) and to automate toll collection on highways, and are being deployed for many new application areas (e.g., passports, airline boarding passes, luggage tags, etc.).

However, practical applications of RFID technology face significant security and reliability challenges. The security challenges, such as remote spying on people and their possessions, have received considerable attention from both media and academia [5, 7, 8, 13]. Nevertheless, the reliability challenges have only recently been noted [4, 6, 12, 15, 17]. Unfortunately, poor reliability may render RFID technology practically infeasible for many application scenarios, as highlighted by pilot studies in [1, 2, 3, 14].

In this work, we experimentally examined and measured the reliability challenges in RFID systems and their major causes. Our focus is on the reliability of reading low-cost passive UHF tags, particularly tracking tagged mobile objects that pass unimpeded by an RFID antenna. Our research highlights the reliability challenges in RFID technology: passive tags have a much weaker signal, a much shorter communication range, and thus much lower read reliability than battery-powered, active, RFID tags. Nonetheless, our techniques and results can be applied to other RFID systems as well, including active tag systems.

The rest of the paper is structured as follows. We start with an overview of RFID systems, their reliability challenges, and related work in Section 2. We present our findings on how the reliability depends on range, orientation, and the effect of multiple tags in Section 3. We also provide experimental results from two real world applications of RFID systems, namely identification and tracking of objects and humans. We investigate the use of fault-tolerance techniques and their impact on reliability in Section 4. Finally, we conclude in Section 5.

2. Overview

The application of RFID technology requires RFID tags attached to objects and an infrastructure for reading the tags and processing tag information. The infrastructure typically consists of antennas, readers (each typically controlling 1 to 4 antennas), and a back-end system with edge servers, application servers, and databases. An antenna employs RF signal to activate the tag, which then responds with its data, typically a unique 96 bit identification code and some asset related data. The reader collects the data and forwards it

---

[1]For example, in May 2006, SmartCode announced a price of $0.05 per EPC Gen 2 tag in volumes of 100 million (www.smartcodecorp.com).

to the back-end system. The back-end system implements the logic and actions for when a tag is identified. The logic can be as simple as opening a door, setting off an alarm, updating an database, or complicated, such as an integrated management and monitoring for shipment tracking.

2.1. Reliability: Definitions and Challenges

We define the read reliability as the probability that an RFID reader successfully detects and identifies an RFID tag when it is in the read range of one of the reader's antennas. Similarly, we define the tracking reliability of an RFID system as the probability that the system successfully detects and identifies an object when it is present in a designated area. Note that the system-level definition of tracking reliability obviates a one-to-one mapping between a tag and an object. For example, an object may carry multiple tags or a human may be identified indirectly based on tagged objects in his possession. In this paper, we will only consider the reliability of detection and identification of tags and/or objects, not the reliability of the individual system components or the actions taken by the system logic.

There are many factors that can impact read reliability, including the type of material surrounding a tag (e.g., metals or liquids), the inter-tag distance, the orientation of the tags with respect to the antenna, the tag-antenna distance, the number of tags in the read range of the antenna, and the speed of the tagged objects. Materials such as metals and liquids not only block the signal when the material is placed between the antenna and the tag, but may act as a grounding plate if the tag is too close to the material even if the material is not between the tag and the antenna. Tags placed too close to one another also interfere with each others operation. The orientation of the tags, specifically, the orientation of the tag's antenna with regard to the reader antenna has a large impact on how much of the reader signal the tag is able to absorb. The number of tags in the read range of an antenna affects reliability because only one tag can be read concurrently but multiple tags may respond in a given read slot, causing collisions. State of the art RFID systems use sophisticated collision control mechanisms to reduce collisions. Finally, higher object speeds limit the time when tags are visible to an antenna.

RFID measurements are particularly prone to false negative reads, where a tag present in the read range of an antenna is not detected. In some cases, it is also possible to get false positive reads, where RFID tags might be read from outside the region normally associated with the antenna, leading to a misbelief that the object is near the antenna [3]. We focus on false negatives since false positives can typically be eliminated by increasing the distance between antennas and/or by decreasing the power output of the readers.

Note that we do not consider intentional destruction of tags (e.g., removal of tag antenna [8] or removal of the whole tag), hiding of tags by shielding them, or interfering with the read protocol [7]. Furthermore, we do not consider modifications to the RFID protocol itself such as better collision control algorithms that can significantly improve reliability in multiple tag situations [9, 18].

2.2. Related work

Several recent pilot studies have evaluated the reliability aspects of RFID technology. A pilot study of a pharmaceutical supply-chain tracking system [1] observed read reliabilities ranging from under 10% to 100% for item-level and case-level tags in different stages of the shipping process. A performance benchmark [12] presented the results from number of experiments including read speed for a population of stationary tags and read reliability for different tagged materials on a conveyer belt. However, neither work attempted to develop techniques to improve reliability.

Other research efforts have proposed techniques to improve the reliability of RFID systems. In [10], the authors propose a cascaded tagging approach, where in addition to normal item level tags, the cases, pallets, and truckloads are tagged with 'macro tags'. A macro tag provides information about the tags contained in the macro tagged collection. The macro tags are typically different from the item-level tags to make them easier to detect, for example, they may have larger antennas or be active tags. In this paper, we only consider techniques that use identical tags. In [17], the authors propose redundancy and diversity of antennas, readers, and tags, as methods to increase system reliability. Neither of these two efforts evaluates the effectiveness of their proposed techniques. Finally, in [6], the authors propose to use real-world constraints to correct missed reads for tracking mobile objects. Specifically, they consider constraints related to possible physical movement paths of objects ('route constraint') and known groupings of tagged objects ('accompany constraint').

3. RFID Reliability Experiments and Results

To highlight the reliability challenge in current state of the art EPC Gen 2 RFID systems, we have conducted numerous experiments that reproduce various real-world situations in our lab using COTS components. We used single-dipole Gen 2 tags from Symbol Technologies, which had an antenna patch size of 2.5 cm by 10 cm. We used the Matrix AR400 reader along with a single area antenna. We used the default settings on the reader, which included a maximum power output of 30 dBm (1 watt). While our experiments consider only one type of tags, readers, and antennas, our results offer insights to (1) a number of important parameters impacting RFID system reliability, and (2) the effectiveness of system-level reliability techniques. We de-

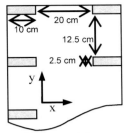

Figure 1. Tag placement for read range exp.

veloped software in Java to interface with the reader. Our software sends commands to the reader over its HTTP interface and the reader responds with a list of tags in XML format. For all but the read range experiment, the readers were operated in a buffered (continuous) read mode and our tracking results were independent of the application level polling speed.

Read Range: The read range of RFID systems depends a lot on their operating frequencies. For the UHF systems we used, it is generally a few meters. To characterize the impact of the tag-antenna distance on read reliability, we placed 20 tags in a single plane, parallel to the antenna. The tag placement is shown in Figure 1. Inter-tag distances were 12.5 cm and 20 cm along the x and y axes, respectively. Our experiments showed that this distance is more than sufficient to eliminate direct interference between tags. The tags were fixed in position facing a single antenna, and a single read was performed each time. We repeated the read 40 times for each distance. Figure 2 shows the average number of tags read, and the upper and lower quartiles. Our results show a 100% read reliability at a distance of 1 m. However, reliability gradually dropped between 2 m and 9 m.

Inter-Tag Distance and Tag Orientation: In many practical scenarios, tags may be placed close to one other, in parallel, and/or in different orientations with regard to the antennas. To characterize the impacts of inter-tag distances

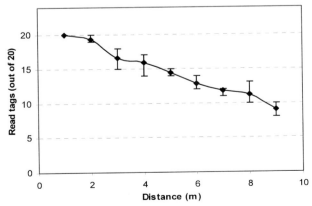

Figure 2. Read reliability vs. antenna distance.

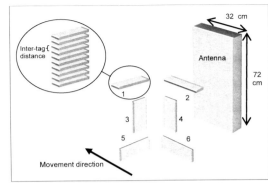

Figure 3. Tag orientation and antenna.

and tag orientation with respect to the antenna, we performed multiple experiments using 10 tags in parallel to each other. We mounted the tags on a cardboard box, and used a cart to pass them in front of a single antenna with a speed of about 1 m/s and antenna-tag distance of 1 m. This represents a situation where items are carried by a conveyor belt through a gate.

We tested the combination of five different inter-tag distances: 0.3 mm, 4 mm, 10 mm, 20 mm, and 40 mm, and six different tag orientations (Figure 3). We repeated each experiment at least 10 times. Figure 4 shows the average number of tags read, and the upper and lower quartiles for each experiment. We are interested in finding the minimum 'safe' distance between tags where they will not interfere with each other. Our results show that, depending on orientation, tags require at least 20 to 40 mm spacing between them to operate in a reliable fashion. We can also see the effect of tag orientation. It is not surprising that tag reads are least reliable when the tags are perpendicular to the antenna (cases 1 and 5). Our results clearly indicate that current UHF tags would not work well for scenarios where tags are placed very close to each other and are perpendicular to the antenna, such as on book covers in a bookshelf.

Object Tracking: In the previous experiments, the tags were not attached to any objects. However, in real world situations, tags are placed on objects that may interfere with RF signals. To measure RFID performance for realistic case level and item level tagging, we individually tagged 12 identical boxes, each containing a network router and accessories in original packaging. The metal casing and relatively large size of the routers compared to their packaging material would make them a challenging scenario for an RFID system. We placed the boxes on a cart as three rows of 2x2 boxes, and passed the cart in front of the antenna with a speed of 1 m/s at a distance of 1 m. We performed this experiment for different tag locations, namely top, front, side closer to antenna, and side farther from antenna. The experiments were repeated 12 times. Our results in Table 1 demonstrate that the location of a tag on an object has a dramatic impact on the tag read reliability. Assuming that

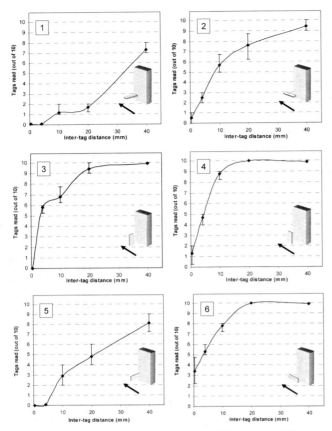

Figure 4. Tag orientation and inter-tag distance.

tag read reliabilities are equal between the front and back of the box, and between the top and bottom of the box, the average read reliability for all locations is 63%. While guaranteeing the exact location of tags upon passing in front of a reader is impractical for many scenarios, it is often practical to avoid the worst locations (in this case, the top of the box). Our measurements show determining and avoiding the worst case locations can greatly improve average reliability. This is similar to the orientation tests, where two out of six orientations had considerably worse reliability.

Table 1. Read reliability for tags on objects.

Tag location	Reliability
Front	87%
Side (closer)	83%
Side (farther)	63%
Top	29%
Average	63%

Human Tracking: One application of RFID systems is tracking humans. Active tags have been employed for human location sensing and tracking [11]. Passive RFID tags are currently in use for identification purposes in access cards and credit cards. We set out to evaluate the performance of passive RFID systems for human identification and tracking.

We experimented with multiple tag locations, and found that for best performance, tags and antennas should be at the same height, and tags should not touch the body. Therefore, we placed the tags at waist level, hanging from the belt or pocket, as often seen with ID cards, to achieve best performance. We placed a tag on one or two volunteers and they walked in front of an antenna at a distance of 1 meter. The volunteers tried to walk in parallel for the two person tests to maximize blocking. This could resemble a typical case for people with a RFID tagged ID card passing through a gate or doorway. It can also be used for human tracking with room-level accuracy. We tested with multiple tag locations. Each test was repeated 20 times. From the results in Table 2, the read reliability averaged 63% for one subject. Blocking by the closer subject caused the two subject read reliability to average 56%. Interestingly, read reliabilities for the closer subject in the two subject case was higher than those for a single subject. Further tests showed the reason was not the slightly closer distance. We attribute the higher read reliabilities to signal reflections off the farther subject. The low reliability in all of these cases motivates us to apply simple fault-tolerance techniques.

Table 2. Read reliability for tags on humans.

Tag location	One subject	Two subjects		
		Closer	Farther	Average
Front / Back	75%	90%	50%	70%
Side (closer)	90%	90%	50%	70%
Side (farther)	10%	30%	0%	15%
Average	63%	75%	38%	56%

4. Improving RFID Reliability

We investigated the use of redundancy to improve the reliability of RFID systems and evaluated its effectiveness through both analytical analysis and experimental measurements. Redundancy in the form of replication is a widely used fault-tolerance technique for improving reliability. It can be applied to RFID systems in a number of ways: multiple antennas per portal, multiple readers per portal, or multiple tags per object.

Multiple antennas mounted per portal is a widely used technique and virtually all readers have built-in support for assigning two or more antennas to a single zone or portal. Even though readers employ measures such as TDMA to prevent interference between two or more of their antennas, our initial observations showed a slight decrease in performance when blocking was not an issue. Nonetheless, in realistic cases, there was a distinctive gain using multiple antennas. For multiple antenna tests, we used two area antennas placed at a distance of 2 meters from each other and connected to the same reader. While one might expect to see similar improvements for multiple readers per portal, our measurement clearly showed the opposite: read reliability was severely reduced in our experiments. The reason is reader-to-reader RF interference. While Gen 2 has standard measures to combat this problem, called *dense-reader mode*, it is optional for readers. Our readers did not support dense-reader mode, and neither do most older Gen 2 readers.

While using multiple tags for each object seems straightforward, to the best of our knowledge it has not been evaluated before in scientific literature. Multiple tags on different sides of an object and/or with different orientations increases the probability that at least one of the tags is successfully read by a reader. However, if the tags are too close, they may interfere with one another and actually reduce the read reliability. Furthermore, if the number of tags in the antenna read area gets large, it can take considerably longer to read the tags.

We now use a simple analytical model for multiple tag and/or antenna scenarios. We define every combination of tag and antenna in the same area as a read opportunity. Assuming read opportunities are independent, if the reliabilities for read opportunities leading to an object identification are $P_1, P_2,, P_n$, the expected object tracking reliability R_C is:

$$R_C = 1 - ((1 - P_1)(1 - P_2)...(1 - P_n))$$

We will next present our experimental results, and compare their performance with the analysis. All measurements and conclusions in this section are dependent on not exceeding the minimum safe tag distances measured in Section 3.3, and allowing adequate time for all tags to be read, which is around .02 sec per tag.

4.1. Reliable Object Tracking

To characterize the effect of reliability techniques for object tracking, we repeated the same experiment as in Section 3, while employing redundancy at different levels. We will present both the measured reliability R_M and the expected reliability R_C, where R_C is calculated based on the read reliabilities measured in Section 3. We have investigated the following cases: two antennas per portal instead of one, two tags per object instead of one, and two tags per object and two antennas per portal. The results for all cases are shown in Table 3 and Figure 5. Our measurements show the performance of multiple tags per object is better than multiple antennas per portal, and very similar to the analytical model. Using two tags instead of one, we increased the average object tracking reliability from 80% to 97%.

Table 3. Redundancy for multiple objects.

Antennas	tags/ object	Tag location	Avg reliability	
			R_M	R_C
2	1	Front	92%	98%
2	1	Side	79%	94%
		Average	86%	96%
1	2	Front + side (good)	97%	98%
1	2	Front + side (bad)	96%	95%
		Average	97%	97%
2	2	Front + side	100%	99.9%

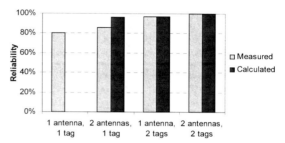

Figure 5. Object tracking with redundancy.

4.2. Reliable Human Tracking

To characterize the effect of reliability techniques for human tracking, we repeated the same experiment as in Section 3, while employing redundancy at different levels. We present both experimental results and expected tracking reliability for the combination of two antennas per portal, and two or four tags per person. The results for 1-antenna and 2-antenna cases are presented in Table 4 and Table 5 respectively. The average performances for one-subject and two-subject cases are shown in Figure 6 and Figure 7, respectively.

Similar to object tracking, the performance of multiple tags per person is better than multiple antennas per portal. Using two tags instead of one, increases average reliability from 63% to 96% for 1-person cases, and from 56% to 83% in 2-person cases. Reliability virtually reaches 100% using four tags per person or a combination of two tags per person and two antennas per portal.

We can clearly see that simple reliability techniques, especially using multiple tags per object, can significantly improve RFID system reliability to near 100%, even for applications that previously seemed out of the domain of passive RFID systems.

Table 5. Human tracking, 2 antennas.

Tags per subject	Location	One subject		Two Subjects	
		R_M	R_C	R_M	R_C
1	Front/Back	80%	94%	90%	95%
1	Side	90%	91%	80%	78%
2	Front/Back	100%	99.6%	100%	99.8%
2	Sides	100%	99.2%	95%	97%
4	F/B/Sides	100%	100%	100%	99.9%

Table 4. Human tracking reliability, 1 antenna.

Tags per subject	Location	One subject		Two Subjects					
		R_M	R_C	R_M			R_C		
				Closer	Farther	Avg	Closer	Farther	Avg
2	Front/Back	100%	94%	100%	90%	95%	99%	75%	88%
2	Sides	93%	91%	90%	50%	70%	93%	50%	72%
4	F/ B/Sides	100%	99.5%	100%	100%	100%	99%	88%	94%

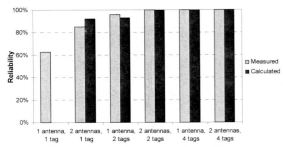

Figure 6. Tracking of one subject.

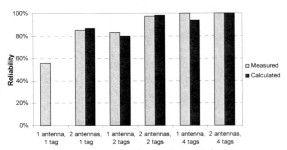

Figure 7. Tracking of 2 subjects.

5. Conclusion

In this work, we conducted extensive controlled measurements to characterize the reliability of passive RFID tags for tracking mobile objects and humans. Our measurements revealed critical insights into how reliability depends on various practical factors, such as inter-tag distances, location of the tag on an object, and tag orientation. To improve reliability, we explored simple and cost-effective reliability techniques, namely redundancy at the tag level, the antenna level, and the reader level. Our measurement clearly showed the high effectiveness of tag-level redundancy, followed by antenna-level redundancy, in increasing system reliability. Because our readers did not support dense-reader mode, reader-level redundancy severely reduced reliability in our experiments, due to reader-reader interference. To the best of our knowledge, our work is the first that systematically characterizes the reliability of RFID systems and its dependence on various practical factors. Our results provide important guidelines for real-world deployment of RFID-based tracking applications as well as simple yet effective solutions to guarantee reliability. Fu-

ture extensions of this work involve experimenting with active tags, and tag reliability for different tag designs.

References

[1] Pharmaceutical RFID pilot finds promise, problems. In *RFID Update*, Nov. 15th, 2006, http://www.rfidupdate.com.

[2] Wal-Mart details RFID requirement. In *RFID Journal*, Nov. 6, 2003, http://www.rfidjournal.com.

[3] D. Bradbury. RFID: It's no supply chain savior - not yet anyway. silicon.com, Sep. 8, 2004, http://management.silicon.com/itdirector/.

[4] J. Brusey, C. Floerkemeier, M. Harrison, and M. Fletcher. Reasoning about uncertainty in location identification with RFID. In *Workshop on Reasoning with Uncertainty in Robotics at IJCAI*, Aug. 2003.

[5] S. Garfinkel, A. Juels, and R. Pappu. RFID privacy: an overview of problems and proposed solutions. In *IEEE Security and Privacy Magazine*, 3(3): 34–43, 2005.

[6] S. Inoue, D. Hagiwara, and H. Yasuura. Systematic error detection for RFID reliability. In *Conf. Avail., Rel. and Sec. (ARES 2006)*, pages 280–286.

[7] A. Juels, R. Rivest, and M. Szydlo. The blocker tag: selective blocking of RFID tags for consumer privacy. In *10th ACM Conf. Comp. and Comm. Sec.*, pages 103–111, 2003.

[8] G. Karjoth and P. Moskowitz. Disabling RFID tags with visible confirmation: clipped tags are silenced. In *2005 ACM Workshop on Privacy in the Electronic Society*, pages 27–30.

[9] M. Kodialam and T. Nandagopal. Fast and reliable estimation schemes in RFID systems. In *Proc. 12th MOBICOM*, pages 322–333, Sep. 2006.

[10] J. Lindsay and W. Reade. Cascading RFID tags. Dec. 23, 2003, http://www.jefflindsay.com/rfid3.shtml.

[11] L. Ni, Y. Liu, Y. Lau, and A. Patil. LANDMARC: Indoor location sensing using active RFID. In *Wireless Networks*, 10(6): 701-710. 2004.

[12] K. Ramakrishnan and D. Deavours. Performance benchmarks for passive UHF RFID tags. In *13th GI/ITG Conf. Measurement, Modeling, and Eval. of Comp. and Comm. Sys.*, pages 137-154, 2006.

[13] M. Rieback, B. Crispo, and A. Tanenbaum. The evolution of RFID security. In IEEE Perv. Comp. 5(1): 62-69, 2006.

[14] E. Schuman. RFID trials show mixed results. eWEEK.com, Nov. 15, 2006, http://www.eweek.com/.

[15] R. Shawn, G. Minos, and J. Michael. Adaptive cleaning for RFID data streams. In *Proc. 32nd VLDB*, pages 163–174, 2006.

[16] H. Stockman. Communication by means of reflected power. In *Proc. IRE*, 36, pages 1196-1204, 1948.

[17] N. Vaidya and S. Das. RFID-based networks - exploiting diversity and redundancy, UIUC, WINGS Lab TR, 2006.

[18] Vogt, H. Multiple object identification with passive RFID tags. In *IEEE Conf. Systems, Man and Cybernetics*, Vol. 3, pages 6-9, Oct 2002.

Profiling Attacker Behavior Following SSH Compromises

Daniel Ramsbrock
Department of Computer Science
University of Maryland, College Park
dramsbro@umd.edu

Robin Berthier, Michel Cukier
Center for Risk and Reliability
Department of Mechanical Engineering
University of Maryland, College Park
robinb@umd.edu, mcukier@umd.edu

Abstract

This practical experience report presents the results of an experiment aimed at building a profile of attacker behavior following a remote compromise. For this experiment, we utilized four Linux honeypot computers running SSH with easily guessable passwords. During the course of our research, we also determined the most commonly attempted usernames and passwords, the average number of attempted logins per day, and the ratio of failed to successful attempts. To build a profile of attacker behavior, we looked for specific actions taken by the attacker and the order in which they occurred. These actions were: checking the configuration, changing the password, downloading a file, installing/running rogue code, and changing the system configuration.

1. Introduction

Most security analysis experiments focus on methods for keeping attackers out of target systems but do little to address their behavior after a remote compromise. In this experiment, we focused almost exclusively on post-compromise attacker behavior. Our goal was to build a profile of short-term attacker behavior, capturing the actions in the minutes and hours after the initial compromise.

To achieve this goal, we utilized a set of honeypot computers running SSH on Linux. Attackers routinely scan for this service and use it for gaining both privileged and non-privileged remote access. The very nature of the experiment required us to observe a large number of successful compromises in order to draw conclusions about typical post-compromise attacker behavior. To ensure a large number of compromises, we used commonly tried passwords to attract attackers with a low level of sophistication (the so-called "script kiddies" who rely heavily on automated hacking tools and dictionary attacks).

Section 2 below describes the experimental setup, including the software configuration and usernames/

passwords found on the honeypots, the data collection methods, and the typical lifecycle of a honeypot in this experiment. Section 3 presents the basic statistics we gathered as part of this experiment, focusing on the most commonly attempted usernames and passwords. Section 4 presents our findings, including the post-compromise attacker profile in the form of a state machine. Section 5 reviews related work in the area of honeypots and attacker behavior research, and Section 6 presents our conclusions.

2. Experimental setup

To collect attacker data, we used a set of four high-interaction Linux honeypot computers as part of the existing testbed architecture at the University of Maryland. The honeypots are on a separate network that limits outgoing connections to minimize damage but allows all incoming connections. For details regarding the testbed architecture, please refer to [1].

2.1. Software configuration

The four honeypots all ran on an identical Linux disk image: a slimmed-down install of Fedora Core 3, updated with the latest patches as of October 10, 2006. Since the primary interaction with the systems was via SSH, the install only included a text-mode environment (the X Window system and associated graphical programs were not installed).

To monitor attacker activity, we used the following tools: a modified OpenSSH sever to collect attempted passwords, syslog-ng to remotely log important system events, including logins and password changes, strace to record all system calls made by incoming SSH connections, and the Honeynet Project's Sebek tool [2] to secretly collect all keystrokes on incoming SSH connections.

The only modification to the OpenSSH source tree was the addition of a single line of code that uses syslog to record all passwords being tried.

2.2. User accounts and passwords

Each honeypot had one privileged root account plus five non-privileged user accounts. To get an idea about commonly tried usernames, we ran some initial experiments. Based on these results, we decided to use the following usernames: admin, mysql, oracle, sarah, and louise. These experiments also revealed that the most commonly tried passwords were '(username)', '(username)123', 'password', and '123456', where (username) represents the username being tried. We rotated among these four passwords for each username as follows: after a compromise, we re-deployed the honeypot and moved on to the next password in the list (see Section 2.4 for details regarding the re-deployment policy).

In order to encourage attackers to enter the non-privileged user accounts instead of the root account, two of the honeypots were set up with strong root passwords. The other two honeypots had root accounts which rotated among the four passwords 'root', 'root123', 'password', and '123456'.

2.3. Data collection

Two servers were responsible for collecting data: one was dedicated to syslog data and the other one collected Sebek data, strace data, and hourly snapshots of the .bash_history and wtmp files.

Sebek and syslog-ng were configured to send data to the servers continuously. To transfer the large amounts of strace data, we set up an automated, compressed hourly transfer. This was done via SCP using public keys and a hidden system account called 'sysadm'.

2.4. Honeypot lifecycle

To ensure quick turnaround after a compromise, we used a pre-built disk image and automated scripts to manage the deployment of the honeypots. We monitored the syslog messages coming from each honeypot at least every 24 hours to check for logins and password changes. In this context, we defined a compromise as an unauthorized login followed by a password change, rather than using the traditional definition of an unauthorized login only. Password changes typically happened every day, with the observed average time from honeypot deployment until the first password change being 11:25 hours.

Re-deploying immediately after an unauthorized login would have limited our results: due to the automated nature of the dictionary attacks, many attackers successfully gained access but did not perform any actions once they had a shell. On the other hand, keeping the honeypot running for more than a few hours after a password change is not productive for observing short-term attacker behavior: once the password has been changed for an account, all other attackers are locked out of it.

Following a password change, we waited at least one hour before we copied the disk image back onto the honeypot, re-ran the deployment script, and continued monitoring the live syslog data.

3. Attacker statistics

During the 24-day period from November 14 to December 8, 2006, attackers from 229 unique IP addresses attempted to log in a total of 269,262 times (an average of 2,805 attempts per computer per day). Out of these, 824 logged in successfully, and 157 changed an account password. The detailed figures for each honeypot are listed in Table 1.

Table 1. Login attempts per honeypot

Honeypot	Attempted	Successful	Password
HP1	66,087	267	49
HP2	69,044	228	43
HP3	72,953	159	31
HP4	61,178	170	34
Total	**269,262**	**824**	**157**

Despite the fact that we used commonly attempted usernames and passwords, we were surprised to find that only 0.31 percent of attempted attacks were successful. Even more surprisingly, only 22.09 percent of the time (in 182 out of 824 cases) did the attacker run any commands. In 25 cases, the attacker did not change the password despite running other commands. Overall, this resulted in only a 19.05 percent rate of password change among successful logins. This trend can possibly be explained by the automated nature of the attacks: if a low-skill attacker is using scripts to attack dozens of systems at once, he may not have time to take advantage of all compromised hosts.

Table 2. Top attempted usernames

Rank	Username	Attempts	Percent
1.	root	33,238	12.34%
2.	admin	4,392	1.63%
3.	test	3,012	1.12%
4.	guest	2,274	0.84%
5.	info	1,825	0.68%
6.	adm	1,563	0.58%
7.	mysql	1,379	0.51%
8.	user	1,317	0.49%
9.	administrator	1,205	0.45%
10.	oracle	1,169	0.43%

As described in Section 2, we logged all attempted

usernames and passwords. Among the most commonly tried usernames, the privileged root account was by far the most popular choice (see Table 2). Even though attackers attempted a total of 12,225 different usernames, the top 1,000 accounted for 72.45 percent of all attempts. System administrators should avoid these accounts when possible, or otherwise ensure that they have strong passwords. The root account is required, but SSH access to it should be disabled.

Table 3. Top attempted passwords

Rank	Password	Attempts	Percent
1.	(username)	115,877	43.04%
2.	(username)123	23,362	8.68%
3.	123456	19,177	7.12%
4.	password	5,742	2.13%
5.	1234	3,981	1.48%
6.	12345	3,890	1.44%
7.	passwd	3,793	1.41%
8.	123	3,682	1.37%
9.	test	3,564	1.32%
10.	1	2,925	1.09%

While compiling data on the most commonly used passwords (see Table 3), we noticed that attackers were trying variations on the username as the password. In many cases the attempted password was the username itself or the username followed by '123'. As a result, we specifically looked for patterns where the password contained the username, and it turned out that by far the most common password was the username itself. This combination accounted for almost half of all attempts, and the username followed by '123' was the second most popular choice. We also saw a third pattern of this type: the username followed by '321'. However, it did not occur frequently enough to appear in the top 10 list (2552 times, equaling 0.95 percent). Our pattern-based analysis of the attempted passwords provides a clearer picture of the underlying trends than do traditional methods, such as exact string matching. This result again emphasizes the point that a password should never be identical or even related to its associated username.

In a similar study by Alata and colleagues [3], the authors had the same results for the accounts being tried (Table 2 above). Not only were the top three accounts the same, but the percentages each was attempted were nearly identical.

4. Results

While basic statistics about attackers can provide some insight, the main purpose of this experiment was to build a profile of post-compromise attacker behavior. To do this, we developed a list of seven states that represent the typical observed actions (such as 'change password' and 'download file'). We then built a state machine showing the number of times attackers changed from one state to another. A state transition is an indication of sequence: an edge from state X to state Y indicates that the attacker engages in activity X first, then in activity Y (without engaging in any other activity Z in between).

4.1. State definitions

To build the state machine of attacker behavior, we defined seven states as follows.

1. **CheckSW** – 'Check software configuration.' This refers to actions that allow the attacker to gain more information about the system's software or its users. The specific Linux commands included in this state are: `w`, `id`, `whoami`, `last`, `ps`, `cat /etc/*`, `history`, `cat .bash_history`, `php -v`.

2. **Install** – 'Install a program.' This refers to new software being installed by an attacker. In most cases, this takes the form of untarring or unzipping a downloaded file, followed by other filesystem operations such as copying, moving, and deleting files, creating directories, and changing file permissions. The specific commands included in this state are: `tar`, `unzip`, `mv`, `rm`, `cp`, `chmod`, `mkdir`.

3. **Download** – 'Download a file.' This refers to remote file downloads by the attacker. Typically, attackers download TAR/ZIP files containing hacking tools such as SSH scanners, IRC bots, and password crackers. The specific commands included in this state are: `wget`, `ftp`, `curl`, `lwp-download`.

4. **Run** – 'Run a rogue program.' This refers to the attacker running a program that was not originally part of the system. To detect these programs, we looked for the `./` notation which usually precedes commands run from locations outside the system's binary path. However, some attackers modified the `PATH` environment variable so they could run their rogue program without the `./` notation. We were able to detect most of these cases because attackers repeatedly used the same kits, resulting in three commonly observed binary names: `cround`, `[kjournald]`, `httpd`. Finally, some attackers used Perl scripts, so we also included `perl` and `*.pl` in this state.

5. **Password** – 'Change the account password.' This refers to changing the password of the compromised account. The only command included in this state is `passwd`.

6. **CheckHW** – 'Check the hardware configuration.' This refers to actions that allow the attacker to gain more information about the system's

hardware (uptime, network, CPU speed/type). The specific commands included in this state are: `uptime, ifconfig, uname, cat /proc/cpuinfo`.

7. **ChangeConf** – 'Change the system configuration.' This refers to attacker activity that permanently changes the state of the system. Typical examples of this were: setting environment variables, killing running programs, editing files, adding/ removing users, and running a modified SSH server (the one rogue program not considered part of the Run state because of its long-term effects on the system and its users). The commands included in this state are: `export, PATH=, kill, nano, pico, vi, vim, sshd, useradd, userdel`.

Table 4 provides a summary of how many commands matched each state. There are certain commands we did not include in any state because they are routine and have no significant effect on the system: `cd, ls, bash, exit, logout, cat`. These commands made up a large portion of the observed command set (34.08 percent) and are listed as (no-op) in Table 4. Including no-op commands, our state machine provided nearly full coverage of the observed command set (98.07 percent). It is interesting to note that a fairly narrow definition of states results in a high rate of coverage. The most likely explanation is that only a few different scripts accounted for most of the attacks.

Table 4. State machine coverage

State	Commands	Coverage
CheckSW	386	14.90%
Install	377	14.55%
Download	225	8.68%
Run	208	8.03%
Password	203	7.83%
CheckHW	157	6.06%
ChangeConf	102	3.94%
(unmatched)	50	1.93%
(no-op)	883	34.08%
Total	**2591**	**100.00%**

By inspection, we discovered that over half of the 50 unmatched commands were due to typographical errors by the attackers (they were close matches for valid commands). This shows us that while the attackers were most likely following predetermined command sequences, at least several of the attacks were being carried out manually.

4.2. Attacker profile

From the state definitions above, we constructed a profile to illustrate the typical sequence of actions following a compromise. We initially separated attacks on user and root accounts, hoping to see a clear difference between the two. However, we found no significant difference and decided to focus only on the combined dataset in order to make the trends clearer.

Figure 1 contains the state machine representing the typical post-compromise behavior of attackers. The number labeling each edge indicates how many times that state transition occurred, with the five most common shown in bold. The font size of each state indicates how many total command lines fit the state definition, with a larger font indicating a state with more attacker activity.

To make the diagram clearer and more concise, only the top 25 edges are shown, representing a total of 1,138 state transitions (84.11 percent of the total). The remaining 31 edges, representing 215 transitions (15.89 percent), are hidden. As a result, the in-degree and out-degree of each node will not be equal in most cases (though this is true for the full state machine).

The most popular course of action was to check the software configuration, change the password, check the hardware and/or software configuration (again), download a file, install the downloaded program, and then run it. The 'change configuration' action was less popular, though it occurred fairly equally at three different stages: 1) before and after checking the software configuration, 2) before running a rogue program, and 3) after installing software. Overall, the two most popular attacker activities were checking the software configuration and installing rogue software.

Due to our easy passwords and the fairly small set of commands the attackers ran, we can assume that most of them have a low skill level. Spitzner [4] also supports this contention: "Linux systems tend to be the focus of [attackers] ... who use commonly known vulnerabilities and automated attack tools." Under this assumption, the observed behavior makes sense. The attackers are operating on memorized or automated sequences of commands, trying to build back doors into as many computers as possible. A possible explanation for this behavior is their intent to create botnets, which they can sell for profit. Given this motive, their main objectives are: 1) to check the machine's configuration to see if it is suitable for their purposes and 2) to install their rogue software, giving them full back door control of the machine or allowing them to identify other vulnerable hosts, for example. Most attackers appeared to be particularly concerned about detection while installing their software, repeatedly using the `w` command during their shell sessions. This command alone accounts for 8.11 percent of all commands issued, with only the no-op commands `cd` and `ls` having larger percentages.

The Alata study mentioned previously [3] also performed an analysis of post-compromise attacker

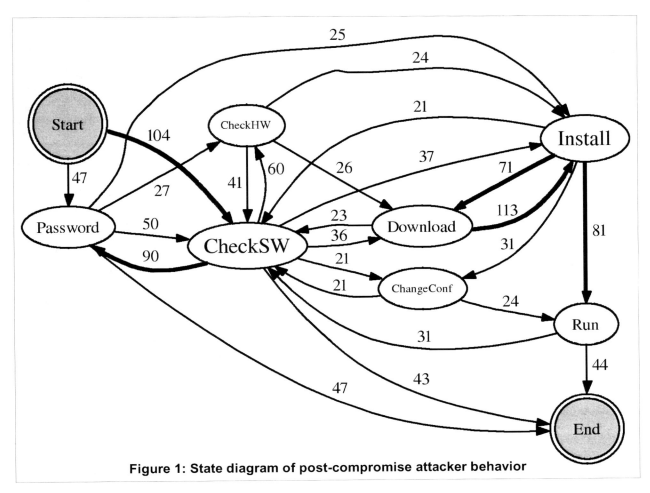

Figure 1: State diagram of post-compromise attacker behavior

behavior, and its findings are again very similar to ours. They also observed password change as the most common first step and reported that most attackers went on to download files (i.e. malicious programs) and then tried to install and run executables.

Another study similar to our experiment is [5]. Here, the authors performed an in-depth forensic analysis of post-compromise attacker behavior. They developed some general categories of attacker behavior: *discovery*, *installation*, and *usage*. However, these categories were much broader than ours and not precisely defined. The main difference between their project and our experiment is that we focused on a larger set of less sophisticated attacks. We gathered aggregate statistics about these attacks rather than investigating individual incidents in detail.

5. Related work

There have been many honeypot-related projects and papers in recent years, often appearing in the Honeynet Project's [6] "Know Your Enemy" series of papers [7].

The study that is most similar to our experiment is [3], where the authors collected both attempted login data and post-compromise attacker behavior. Their results closely match ours, although their study was based on a longer time period (131 days) and also included data from geographically distributed low-interaction honeypots. This suggests that even though our results are based on a smaller sample and shorter time period, they seem representative of overall trends.

Seifert [8] conducted a smaller-scale experiment collecting attempted usernames and passwords, with results roughly equal to ours. He recorded one successful login, providing some information about post-compromise attacker behavior.

Another study closely related to our experiment is [5], as mentioned in Section 4.2. The authors performed a detailed analysis of post-compromise attacker behavior, focusing on the individual actions of more sophisticated attackers rather than gathering summary data for a larger number of attackers.

Dacier and colleagues [9] conducted an extensive statistical analysis on malicious traffic using honeypots. Over a four-month period, they studied attacks from 6,285 IP addresses, averaging over two new sources of attack per hour. In another study, they observed 28,722 new attack sources over sixteen months [10]. In a third study, they analyzed data collected over one year and conservatively estimated that 753 tools are available to launch attacks [11]. Finally, they found 924 attack sources per day in Germany during a multi-country study [12].

In 2003, Levine and colleagues [13] showed that a honeynet could be implemented on large-scale enterprise networks in order to identify malicious activity and pinpoint compromised machines.

6. Conclusions

In the course of our experiment, we built a profile of typical attacker behavior following a remote compromise and collected valuable data on commonly attempted usernames and passwords. Our findings are useful to the security community in two main ways.

First, these findings allow security and system administrators to adjust their password policies to ensure that no user accounts are open to trivial brute-force dictionary attacks. At minimum, all of the usernames and passwords presented in Section 3 should be avoided. Direct remote root logins should be disabled, only allowing select users to 'su' into the root account once logged on.

Second, these results can assist system administrators in choosing security tools to combat the most common attacker actions. Our results show that downloading/installing/running rogue software and checking the software configuration are the most common actions. Therefore, security tools and policies should focus on those areas. One possibility would be to restrict execution privileges only to registered programs, though this would require significant modification at the operating system level.

Most of our results will not come as a surprise to security professionals, but they are useful because they represent solid statistical evidence to support widely held beliefs about post-compromise attacker behavior. As expected, downloading/installing/running rogue software, checking the configuration, and changing the password were the most common actions following a successful attack. The two main unexpected results were 1) the very low percentage of successful attacks even with purposely weak passwords (0.31 percent) and 2) the low percentage of successful attacks which resulted in commands being run (22.09 percent). A possibility for future work in this area is to focus on finding explanations for these trends.

Acknowledgments

This research was inspired by a semester project conducted by Pierre-Yves Dion.

We thank the Institute for Systems Research and the Office for Information Technology for their support in implementing a testbed for collecting attack data at the University of Maryland. In particular, we thank Jeff McKinney, Carlos Luceno and Peggy Jayant for supporting us in this project with help, material, and space. We thank Gerry Sneeringer and his team for permitting the deployment of the testbed. We also thank Melvin Fields and Dylan Hazelwood for providing some of the computers used in the testbed.

We thank Rachel Bernstein for extensive help with editing, leading to significant improvements in clarity.

This research has been supported in part by NSF CAREER Award 0237493.

References

[1] S. Panjwani, S. Tan, K. Jarrin, and M. Cukier, "An Experimental Evaluation to Determine if Port Scans are Precursors to an Attack", in Proc. International Conference on Dependable Systems and Networks (DSN05), Yokohama, Japan, June 28-July 1, 2005, pp. 602-611.

[2] http://www.honeynet.org/tools/sebek/

[3] E. Alata, V. Nicomette, M. Kaâniche, M. Dacier, and M. Herrb, "Lessons learned from the deployment of a high-interaction honeypot", in Proc. European Dependable Computing Conference (EDCC06), Coimbra, Portugal, October 18-20, 2006, pp. 39-44.

[4] L. Spitzner, "The honeynet project: Trapping the hackers", *IEEE Security and Privacy*, 1(2), 2003, pp. 15-23.

[5] F. Raynal, Y. Berthier, P. Biondi, and D. Kaminsky, "Honeypot forensics", in Proc. IEEE Information Assurance Workshop, United States Military Academy, West Point, NY, June 10-11, 2004, pp. 22-29.

[6] http://www.honeynet.org/

[7] http://www.honeynet.org/papers/kye.html

[8] C. Seifert, "Malicious SSH Login Attempts", August 2006, http://www.securityfocus.com/infocus/1876.

[9] M. Dacier, F. Pouget, and H. Debar, "Honeypots: Practical Means to Validate Malicious Fault Assumptions," in Proc. 10th IEEE Pacific Rim International Symposium on Dependable Computing (PRDC04), Papeete, Tahiti, French Polynesia, March 3-5, 2004, pp. 383-388.

[10] F. Pouget, M. Dacier, and V. H. Pham, "Understanding Threats: A Prerequisite to Enhance Survivability of Computing Systems," in Proc. International Infrastructure Survivability Workshop 2004 (IISW04), Lisbon, Portugal, December 5-8, 2004.

[11] F. Pouget and M. Dacier, "Honeypot-based Forensics," in Proc. AusCERT Information Technology Security Conf. 2004 (AusCERT04), Ashmore, Australia, May 23-27, 2004.

[12] F. Pouget, M. Dacier, and V. H. Pham, "Leurre.com: On the Advantages of Deploying a Large Scale Distributed Honeypot Platform," in Proc. E-Crime and Computer Conference 2005 (ECCE05), Monaco, March 29-30, 2005.

[13] J. Levine, R. LaBella, H. Owen, D. Contis, and B. Culver, "The Use of Honeynets to Detect Exploited Systems Across Large Enterprise Networks," in Proc. IEEE Workshop on Information Assurance, United States Military Academy, West Point, NY, June 18-20, 2003.

Dependability Assessment of Grid Middleware

Nik Looker and Jie Xu

School of Computing
University of Leeds, UK
{nlooker, jxu}@comp.leeds.ac.uk

Abstract

Dependability is a key factor in any software system due to the potential costs in both time and money a failure may cause. Given the complexity of Grid applications that rely on dependable Grid middleware, tools for the assessment of Grid middleware are highly desirable. Our past research, based around our Fault Injection Technology (FIT) framework and its implementation, WS-FIT, has demonstrated that Network Level Fault Injection can be a valuable tool in assessing the dependability of traditional Web Services. Here we apply our FIT framework to Globus Grid middleware using Grid-FIT, our new implementation of the FIT framework, to obtain middleware dependability assessment data. We conclude by demonstrating that Grid-FIT can be applied to Globus Grid systems to assess dependability as part of a fault removal mechanism and thus allow middleware dependability to be increased.

Keywords: Fault Injection, Dependability Assessment, Globus, Grid.

1. Introduction

The Globus Toolkit [1] is the front running Grid technology currently in use for large-scale scientific Grid applications. As such it requires close scrutiny in terms of its dependability [2] to foster trust and speed its introduction into other application domains. Globus Toolkit 4 is constructed from a number of base components and key to these is the Apache Axis SOAP stack which forms one of the message transports available, so dependability assessment of this would contribute greatly to the overall dependability of the toolkit.

Fault Injection [3] is a well-proven method for assessing the dependability of a system and has been used extensively in the domain of distributed systems, for example Marsden et al [4]. Recently there has been interest in applying fault injection to services. Network level fault injection has provided promising results in assessing the dependability of service based systems and middleware [5] and forms the basis of our FIT method.

Grid – Fault Injection Technology (Grid-FIT) is a dependability assessment method and tool for assessing Grid services by fault injection. Grid-FIT is derived from our earlier fault injector WS-FIT [5] which was targeted towards Java Web Services implemented using Apache Axis transport. Grid-FIT utilises a novel fault injection mechanism that allows network level fault injection to be used to give a level of control similar to Code Insertion fault injection whilst being less invasive [6].

This paper uses the Grid-FIT tool to systematically carry out a dependability assessment of Apache Axis 1.2 as used in the Globus Toolkit 4. We present our findings on case studies conducted to determine the integrity of data exchanged during service calls and their vulnerability to integrity attacks.

2. Grid Middleware

Globus Toolkit [1] is an open source software toolkit used for building Grid systems. A large part of Globus Toolkit is constructed around Web Services utilizing Apache Axis as the transport.

A Web Service is a service defined by a number of standards that can be used to provide interoperable data exchange and processing between heterogeneous machines and architectures. For the purposes of this paper, Web Services will be defined as being described by Web Service Definition Language (WSDL) [7] and implemented using SOAP and the Remote Procedure Call (RPC) model. Web Services are commonly used to provide the 'building blocks' of systems so any dependability assessment that targets them will be of wide use, not only to Web Services but also to Globus Grid services, which utilize the same technology.

Both WSDL and SOAP utilize eXtensible Markup Language (XML) [8] to define and implement Web Service message exchanges. XML is a standard for document markup. It provides a document layout that allows a document to be self-describing and portable, allowing data transfer between dissimilar systems. Its portability is largely due to it being an ASCII format document, with numeric values encoded as strings. Since it is portable it largely eliminates the need for marshalling and unmarshaling of data, but any reduction in overhead is more that offset by the need to construct XML documents and parse them at the receiving machine, which introduces a greater overhead.

XML is flexible and can be used to represent a large variety of data but most programs constrain this flexibility. A Document Type Definition (DTD) defines which elements are permissible and the circumstances in which these elements can be used under. This allows the basic structure and syntax of an XML document to be defined and validated. An XML schema can be used to describe complex restrictions on a document, such as type information, and complex data types. It is possible to validate an XML document to see if it follows the rules defined in DTDs and schemas. SOAP uses a collection of schemas to define a standard set of types that can be used as well as defining the message structure, etc.

Web Services present a defined interface to utilizing applications and this is constructed by the use of WSDL. This is an XML-based Interface Definition Language (IDL) used to define Web Services interfaces and how to access them [7]. Our research is mainly concerned with RPC message exchanges and WSDL lends itself well to providing explicit information on the structure of message exchanges between Web Services and their clients.

Communication between a utilizing application and a Web Service is usually achieved using SOAP, which is a messaging protocol designed to allow the exchange of messages over a network. It is XML-based to allow the exchange of messages between heterogeneous machines.

Although this work is primarily concerned with the RPC mechanism over SOAP, most of the concepts apply to document oriented patterns of communication using SOAP as well.

3. Grid-FIT

Fault Injection Technology (FIT) is our network level fault injector framework designed to work with middleware systems [5]. FIT contains a Fault Injection Engine (FIE) that is implemented so that different middleware message formats can be handled, including both text and binary. Grid-FIT is a specific tailoring of the FIT framework to work with Globus Toolkit 4. A similar tailoring was used to produce the WS-FIT tool. Grid-FIT is implemented as a plug-in for Eclipse,

which is a platform independent framework for developing applications (see Figure 1).

The major innovation of Grid-FIT is the novel fault injection mechanism that allows network level fault injection to be used to simulate Code Insertion fault injection whilst circumventing the need for modifications to the service source code [6]. This is accomplished by intercepting middleware messages within the protocol stack, decoding the middleware message in real-time and injecting appropriate faults. By decoding the middleware message and allowing this level of targeted fault injection, it is possible to perform parameter perturbation similar to that achieved by Code Insertion at the API level, and this can also be used to perturb SOAP element attributes in order to assess middleware protocols.

Figure 1: The Eclipse Based Grid-FIT Tool

Standard network level fault injection works by performing operations on network packets at the physical network interface. Since the fault injection is done at the network interface, modifications to these packets tend to only be reflected at the middleware level as random corruption of data; even reordering and dropping of packets may only result in corruption of a data stream, since a middleware level message may span more than one physical network packet. Further more, reordered or dropped packets may be subject to error correction such as retransmission so faults injected may not reach the middleware layer. Finally, packets corrupted at this level may be rejected by the network protocol stack, for instance via mechanisms such as checksums. It is thus hard to target a particular element of a middleware message with any great certainty. Therefore network level fault injection has traditionally been used only for assessing network protocol stacks, not service based systems.

The FIT method of network level fault injection takes the basic concept given above but moves the fault injection point away from the network interface and positions it in the actual middleware transport layer (see Figure 2). Since middleware messages are then intercepted as complete entities, it is possible to corrupt, reorder and drop complete messages, rather than just part of a network packet that may be discarded before it reaches the middleware layer. Messages can thus be modified and then passed on to the rest of the protocol stack. In this way faults can be injected but not filtered out by the protocol stack.

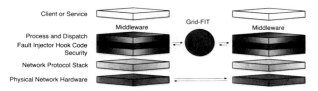

Figure 2: Grid-FIT Injection Points

Further, if the messages are intercepted before they are signed or encrypted (or after they are decrypted and the signature checked in the case of incoming messages), individual elements can be corrupted within a message without that message being rejected by the middleware as having been tampered with. Since we can assume we are familiar with the rules and metadata used to construct messages for the specific middleware we are using, by combining the corruption of data in a message with these rules and metadata, it is possible to produce meaningful perturbations of such things as RPC input parameters, so we can use our network level fault injection method to simulate API level fault injection.

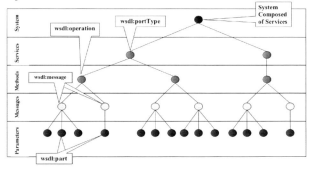

Figure 3: System Model

The rules and metadata used to define the interface of a service are contained within the WSDL definition for that service. This information can be interpret to decompose the service interface into method calls with their associated messages and, within the messages, identify specific parameters. The FIT method decomposes this information into a taxonomy called the System Model (see Figure 3) which provides all the information required to construct fault injection

triggers as described above.

By using this taxonomy and creating triggers on specific elements, the FIT method can precisely inject specific faults rather than random faults into middleware messages as in standard network level fault injection techniques. The method will decode the middleware message and inject meaningful faults, such as modifying RPC parameters and results, adjusting element attributes, etc. The method builds on the FIT framework to allow test cases to be written. These test cases can either be written manually, or automatically generated using the FIT Extended Fault Model (EFM), which is an extensible toolkit of Fault Models that can be applied to parameters and messages [5].

Since FIT can perturb individual RPC parameters within middleware messages, it is particularly well suited to assessing systems by substituting invalid values in place of valid ones and thus testing such mechanisms as guard code at calling interfaces. Whilst it can be argued that the value of assessing interactions between calling interfaces is of limited use in normal non-distributed programming, since these APIs will only be called under known conditions [9], this does not necessarily hold for distributed systems since the interfaces are exposed and can be combined with other logic in unforeseen ways. Assessment of validation mechanisms is therefore key to the production of robust services. FIT has been successfully used to not only assess service interfaces but also to assess third party dependability means [10].

Grid-FIT decodes incoming middleware messages via a SAX parser. Whilst this is an overhead it has been found to be acceptable when compared to network transfer times commonly encountered in Grid applications, and the method has been successfully applied to latency injection test cases [11].

4. Case Study

This case study applies the Grid-FIT tool to Globus Toolkit in order to demonstrate how dependable Apache Axis is in terms of integrity. This is a key concern since Apache Axis is the middleware layer that Globus Toolkit is built upon, and hence has a direct bearing on the amount of trust that can be placed on Globus Toolkit. The case study examines the Axis SOAP stack in terms of corruption of SOAP messages and compliance with the W3C specifications.

4.1. Configuration

The case study examines the effect of fault injection on a representative sample of types defined by the *xsd* schema. To do this a simple service was written which included a method for each *xsd* type. Each routine received a specific *xsd* type and echoed it back unchanged as the return value. A test program was written which called each service method in turn with a valid instance of the type and compared the return result with the original data sent. In each case the value returned should be identical with that sent. The combination of the service and the test program provide a simple test bed to test *xsd* types.

The case study was preformed using the same version of Apache Axis as that included in Globus Java WS Core 4.0.3, namely Apache Axis 1.2RC2 1242 April 28 2006. Eclipse 3.2 was used to execute the Grid-FIT plug-in and all software was executed under Mac OS X 10.4.8 running on a PPC architecture.

4.2. Baseline Experiment

A baseline experiment was undertaken to determine the normal operating conditions of the test program and service. The results of this experiment are given in Table 1 which shows two criteria for each *xsd* type assessed: 1) the comparison of the returned value with the sent value; and 2) any exception that was generated as a result of the method call.

In general the middleware behaved as expected, and from Table 1 it can be seen that none of the types tested generated an exception. An unexpected outcome of this experiment was the Date and DateTime returned values did not match the original values sent.

Date and DateTime are implemented using the Java Standard Library Date class. Equality between two Date instances is obtained only if they match to the millsecond. Examination of the SOAP messages exchanged and the W3C specifications show that the ASCII format of Date passed within the SOAP message does not specify Date to the millisecond, so when they are passed into the Java Date class a slight discrepancy is introduced, hence the returned instance will not match the one originally sent.

The *xsd* types defined in Table 1 can be grouped into three groupings: 1) *xsd* types mapped to built-in Java types (dark grey in table) which comprise *double*, *int*, *boolean*, *byte*, *float*, *long* and *short*; 2) *xsd* types mapped to Java Standard Library classes (light grey in table) which comprise *String*, *Date*, *DateTime*, *Decimal*, *QName* and *AnySimpleType*; and 3) *xsd* types that require specially written classes within Apache Axis (white in table) which comprise *AnyURI*, *Duration*, *GDay*, *GMonth*, *GMonthDay*, *GYear*, *GYearMonth*, *Language*, *Name*, *NCName*, *NegativeInteger*, *NMTOKENS*, *NonNegativeInteger*, *NonPositiveInteger*, *NMToken*, *NormalizedString*, *NOTATION*, *PositiveInteger*, *Time*, *Token*, *UnsignedInt*, *UnsignedByte*, *UnsignedLong* and

UnsignedShort.

Table 1: Baseline Experiment Results

xsd:type	Returned value equals sent value	Exception Generated
Map to built-in Java type	TRUE	none
Map to Standard Java Library Class	TRUE	none
Date	FALSE	none
DateTime	FALSE	none
Map to Apache Axis Class	TRUE	none

4.3. Protocol Invalidation

This experiment attempts to invalidate the SOAP protocol whilst retaining syntactically correct XML. This technique can be used to determine if the implementation follows the protocol specification.

Thompson et al [12] specify that "An element may be valid without content if it has the attribute xsi:nil with the value true. An element so labeled must be empty, but can carry attributes if permitted by the corresponding complex type". Since the test program generates SOAP messages that contain data within the elements, if xsi:nil="true" is added as an attribute to the *part* it should fail the scheme validation. By this definition, a SOAP message exchanging a non-null parameter should not contain the xsi:nil attribute.

A fault model was constructed to add xsi:nil="true" to an element. It was then applied to each request message parameter element. This generated SOAP messages containing this attribute (see Figure 4).

```
<?xml version="1.0" encoding="UTF-8"?>
<soapenv:Envelope
  xmlns:xsi="http://www.w3.org/2001/XMLSchema-instance"
  xmlns:soapenv="http://schemas.xmlsoap.org/soap/envelope/"
  xmlns:xsd="http://www.w3.org/2001/XMLSchema">
  <soapenv:Body>
    <ns1:fooDouble
      xmlns:ns1="http://www.nik.looker.name/TestService/"
      soapenv:encodingStyle="http://schemas.xmlsoap.org/soap/encoding/">
      <fooDoubleRequest href="#id0"></fooDoubleRequest>
    </ns1:fooDouble>
    <multiRef
      xmlns:soapenc="http://schemas.xmlsoap.org/soap/encoding/"
      xsi:type="xsd:double"
      xsi:nil="true"
      soapenv:encodingStyle="http://schemas.xmlsoap.org/soap/encoding/"
      soapenc:root="0"
      id="id0">
      0.0
    </multiRef>
  </soapenv:Body>
</soapenv:Envelope>
```

Figure 4: Modified SOAP message

Table 2 shows the results from this experiment. The results show that only certain types generated an exception, and these did not seem to be descriptive of the schema validation. Of the types that returned a value, the value returned was null. We can therefore conclude that setting xsi:nil, rather than causing an XML schema violation, is implemented by the middleware to infer that the element is empty and any contents should be silently discarded. This causes a null object to be passed to the service and this null object is passed back in the normal way. We have encountered this type of behaviour in previous case studies with previous versions of Apache SOAP [13].

The exceptions generated can be explained by the *xsd* type implementations in Java being classified into two distinct groupings: 1) mapping to built-in types; and 2) implemented through Java classes, either standard Java classes or specifically written.

The groups that do not generate any exceptions are groups of *xsd* types that map to Java classes, and therefore the null parameter can be passed as a valid parameter. This indicates that no schema validation is explicitly performed. The group that generates exceptions (the dark grey shaded group in Table 2) map to built-in types. These types cannot assume a null value in Java, so the implementation is mapping the null value to a generic Java *Object* and attempting to match to *method(Object)* which does not exist in the service; consequently the misleading exception is thrown. It can therefore be concluded that the exception is being thrown as a consequence of executing an unexpected control pathway, rather than a deliberately implemented piece of guard code in the middleware.

Table 2: Protocol Invalidation Results

xsd:type	Returned value equals sent value	Exception Generated
Map to built-in Java type	No result returned	No such operation
Map to Standard Java Library Class	FALSE	None
Map to Apache Axis Class	FALSE	None

4.4. Injecting Bad Data

This experiment examines two *xsd* types when invalid data is injected. It examines whether ASCII characters which invalidate the schema for the *xsd* types are detected by the middleware and rejected.

```
<?xml version="1.0" encoding="UTF-8"?>
<soapenv:Envelope
  xmlns:xsi="http://www.w3.org/2001/XMLSchema-instance"
  xmlns:soapenv="http://schemas.xmlsoap.org/soap/envelope/"
  xmlns:xsd="http://www.w3.org/2001/XMLSchema">
  <soapenv:Body>
    <ns1:fooLanguage
    xmlns:ns1="http://www.nik.looker.name/TestService/"
    soapenv:encodingStyle="http://schemas.xmlsoap.org/soap/encoding/">
      <fooLanguageRequest
      xsi:type="xsd:language">
        some bad data
      </fooLanguageRequest>
    </ns1:fooLanguage>
  </soapenv:Body>
</soapenv:Envelope>
```

Figure 5: Language message after injection

The first type is an *xsd language* type. A valid *language* type has strict rules about the data that can be

encoded with in it. The encoding follows a schema that defines the types and positions of ASCII characters that can be included in this element. Figure 5 shows the message after the fault is injected. The new element contents are invalid since both the characters contained and the placement of the characters are invalid.

The unmarshaling of this invalid data did not generate any exceptions (see Table 3). The only consequence of this injection was that the returned value was not equal to the original value. Since this type is built upon a string type, it is reasonable to assume that the unmarshaling process assumes that the input data is valid and inserts it directly into the class instance without validating it. Conversely a check of the Apache Axis class that implements this type in Java shows that validation is done when the normal constructors are used.

The second *xsd* type assessed was *PositiveInteger*. When bad data was injected into this message exchange a *Number Format Exception* was generated. Whilst this would appear to be a valid exception closer inspection of the code revealed that this exception was generated as part of the standard Java string to number parsing mechanism, not as part of an explicit validation mechanism. This exception can therefore be considered an interaction fault.

Table 3: Invalid data Results

Xsd:type	Returned value equals sent value	Exception Generated
Language	FALSE	None
PositiveInteger	No result returned	Number Format Exception

4.5. Invalid by Omission Faults

This experiment injected syntactically correct data into the elements containing *xsd* types, but in one case the data invalidated the type's schema by omission (it should have started with a minus sign). This test gave an appropriate exception (see Table 4) but, as above, this was generated by the Java class parsing the value, rather than a direct validation against the schema.

Table 4: Invalid by Omission Results

xsd:type	Returned value equals sent value	Exception Generated
NonNegativeInteger	FALSE	None
NonPositiveInteger	No result returned	Number Format Exception

The nonNegativeInteger was also injected as a control and since the value 128 was a correct value for this type the only consequence of this injection was that the returned value did not match the originally sent value.

5. Conclusion and Future Work

This paper has detailed the application of our Grid-FIT tool to the Apache Axis component of the Globus Toolkit to provide dependability assessment with regards to its integrity.

Our case study uncovered a number of discrepancies between the Apache Axis implementation and the W3C. SOAP specification. These fall into two categories: 1) misinterpretation/bad implementation of the SOAP specification; and 2) failures due to lack of validation.

The first category includes the xsi:nil misinterpretation of the specification. Whilst this would appear to be a fairly minor fault, it could conceivably form the basis of a buffer overflow attack or denial of service attack since large quantities of data could be transferred in a message and Axis would not flag this as an error.

The second category of discrepancies allows unanticipated control pathways to be exercised that could lead to interaction faults being generated. A closer examination of this would be required on a system-by-system basis to ensure that this could not be employed for compromising the integrity of a system.

We assume that the potential to exploit these particular discrepancies is fairly low in terms of a Globus Grid, since it will be working with known implementations of SOAP stacks and systems will be secured, but the potential does exist to exploit them by using modified middleware stacks since validation is undertaken by guard code which appears to be contained in the Java class implementations of the *xsd* types, not as a general message validation mechanism.

Future work will concentrate on enhancing our fault models to more thoroughly examine the Grid middleware, determine if Grid-FIT can be successfully applied to assess other dependability attributes, and apply our technique to more complex Globus systems and scenarios.

6. Acknowledgments

This work was funded as part of the EPSRC funded CoLab project (EPSRC Reference: EP/D077249/1). Thanks are due to Dr Paul Townend for his help and suggestions in the preparation of this paper.

7. References

[1]   I. Foster, "Globus Toolkit Version 4: Software for Service-Oriented Systems," in the proceedings of the IFIP International Conference on Network and Parallel Computing, China, 2005.

[2]   A. Avizienis, J.-C. Laprie, B. Randell, and C. Landwehr, "Basic Concepts and Taxonomy of Dependable and Secure Computing," *IEEE Transactions on Dependable and Secure Computing*, vol. 1, pp. 11-33, 2004.

[3]   J. Voas and G. McGraw, *"Software Fault Injection: Inoculating Programs Against Errors"*, John Wiley & Sons, 1998.

[4]   E. Marsden, J. Fabre, and J. Arlat, "Dependability of CORBA Systems: Service Characterization by Fault Injection," in the proceedings of the 21st IEEE Symposium on Reliable Distributed Systems, Japan, 2002.

[5]   N. Looker, B. Gwynne, J. Xu, and M. Munro, "An Ontology-Based Approach for Determining the Dependability of Service-Oriented Architectures," in the proceedings of the 10th IEEE International Workshop on Object-oriented Real-time Dependable Systems, USA, 2005.

[6]   N. Looker, M. Munro, and J. Xu, "A Comparison of Network Level Fault Injection with Code Insertion," in the proceedings of the 29th IEEE International Computer Software and Applications Conference, Scotland, 2005.

[7]   E. Christensen, F. Curbera, G. Meredith, and S. Weerawarana, "Web Services Description Language (WSDL)," Version 1.1, W3C, 2001.

[8]   T. Bray, J. Paoli, C. M. Sperberg-McQueen, and E. Maler, "Extensible Markup Language (XML)," Second Edition, W3C, 2000.

[9]   J. Voas, "Fault Injection for the Masses," *IEEE Computer*, vol. 30, pp. 129-130, 1997.

[10]   P. Townend and J. Xu, "Dependability in Grids," *IEEE Distributed Systems Online*, vol. 6, 2005.

[11]   N. Looker, M. Munro, and J. Xu, "Simulating Errors in Web Services," *International Journal of Simulation Systems, Science & Technology*, vol. 5, 2004.

[12]   H. S. Thompson, D. Beech, M. Maloney, and N. Mendelsohn, "XML Schema Part 1: Structures Second Edition," W3C, 2004.

[13]   N. Looker and J. Xu, "Assessing the Dependability of OGSA Middleware by Fault Injection," in the proceedings of the 22nd IEEE Symposium on Reliable Distributed Systems, Italy, 2003.

Assessing Robustness of Web-services Infrastructures

Marco Vieira, Nuno Laranjeiro, Henrique Madeira
CISUC, Department of Informatics Engineering
University of Coimbra – Portugal
mvieira@dei.uc.pt, cnl@student.dei.uc.pt, henrique@dei.uc.pt

Abstract

Web-services are supported by a complex software infrastructure that must provide a robust service to the client applications. This practical experience report presents a practical approach for the evaluation of the robustness of web-services infrastructures. A set of robustness tests (i.e., invalid web-services call parameters) is applied during web-services execution in order to reveal possible robustness problems in the web-services code and in the application server infrastructure. The approach is illustrated using two different implementations of the web-services specified by the TPC-App performance benchmark running on top of the JBoss application server. The proposed approach is generic and can be used to evaluate the robustness of web-services implementations (relevant for programmers) and application server infrastructures (relevant for administrators and system integrators).

1. Introduction

Web-services are increasingly becoming a strategic vehicle for data exchange and content distribution [1]. Ranging from on-line stores to media corporations, web-services are a key component within the organizations information infrastructure. Given the swiftness of web-surfers when jumping from one site to the next, business may be easily lost if a corporate service is temporarily unavailable to its costumers.

Web-services provide a simple interface between a provider and a consumer, where the first offers a set of services that are used by the second. The provider and the consumer may belong to the same company or to distinct companies. In both cases, the provider must deliver a robust service to the consumers.

An important aspect is web-services compositions, which are based on a collection of web-services working together to achieve an objective [2]. This composition is normally defined at programming time as a

"business process" that describes the sequencing and coordination of calls to the component web-services. Thus, if one component fails then the composite web-service will suffer an outage.

Although web-services are normally business-critical components, current development support tools do not provide any practical ways to characterize the robustness of web-services code or to compare alternative application servers concerning robustness.

The goal of robustness testing is to characterize the behavior of a system in presence of erroneous input conditions [3, 4, 5]. Robustness tests stimulate the system under testing in a way that triggers internal errors, and in that way exposes both programming and design errors. Systems can be differentiated according to the number of errors uncovered.

This practical experience report presents an approach for the evaluation of the robustness of web-services infrastructures. The approach consists of a set of robustness tests (i.e., invalid call parameters) that are applied during the web-services execution in order to observe robustness problems on the infrastructure. This way, the proposed approach can be used to:

- **Evaluate the robustness of web-services code.**
  This is potentially useful for programmers in three different scenarios: 1) help providers in evaluating the robustness of their web-services code; 2) help consumers to pick the web-services that best fit their requirements; and 3) help providers to choose the best web-services for a given composition.
- **Evaluate the robustness of the application server infrastructure**. This is quite useful for administrators and system integrators to select the application server that best fits their requirements by evaluating the robustness of different alternatives. In addition, it is also useful to help administrators in tuning the configuration of application servers.

The approach is illustrated by evaluating the robustness of two implementations of several web-services specified by the TPC-App performance

131

benchmark [6] running on top of the JBoss application server (a well known J2EE application server).

The structure of the paper is the following: the next section presents an outline of the robustness testing approach. Section 3 introduces the experimental setup and experiments. Section 4 presents and discusses the results and Section 5 concludes the paper.

2. Robustness testing approach

In a web-services environment a provider makes a set of services available for consumers [1]. The web-services are supported by a complex software infra-structure, which typically includes an application server, the operating system and a set of external sys-tems (e.g., databases, payment gateways, etc). The Simple Object Access Protocol (SOAP) is used for exchanging XML-based messages between the con-sumer and the provider over the network (using for example http or https protocols). Typically, in each interaction the consumer (client) sends a request SOAP message to the provider (the server). After processing the request, the server sends a response message to the client with the results. Web-services interfaces are de-scribed using WSDL (Web-Services Definition Lan-guage) [7], which is a XML format used to generate server and client code, and for configuration. A broker is used to enable applications to find Web-services. Figure 1 presents a typical web-services infrastructure.

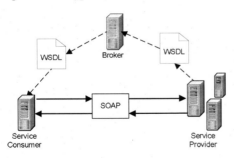

Figure 1. Typical web-services infrastructure.

Our robustness testing approach consists of a set of erroneous web-services call parameters that are in-jected during the web-services execution. The robust-ness tests are based on combinations of exceptional and acceptable input values of parameters of web-services generated by applying a set of predefined rules according to the data types of each parameter. The ro-bustness of the target infrastructure is classified ac-cording to the errors uncovered (see Section 2.3).

As shown in Figure 2, the erroneous parameters are injected using a generic tool that acts like a proxy and intercepts all the client requests (XML-based messages using http protocol), performs mutations in the SOAP

message and forwards the modified message to the server. The server response is logged and used latter to analyze the behavior of the web-services infrastructure. An important aspect is that, the source code of the web-services is not required. This is true for both the provider and the consumer code.

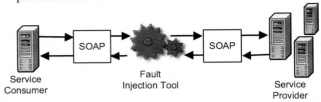

Figure 2. Test configuration required.

Running the robustness evaluation approach pro-posed includes the following steps:
1) Analysis of the WSDL of the services under testing in order to identify the relevant call parameters.
2) Robustness tests generation based on the informa-tion gathered in the previous step.
3) Execution of the web-services without fault injec-tion in order to collect baseline performance met-rics and to understand what behavior is expected from each service.
4) Execution of the web-services in the presence of invalid call parameters (robustness tests). The goal is to trigger faulty behaviors, and in that way ex-pose robustness problems.
5) As a final step the results obtained in 3) and 4) are used to characterize the performance and robust-ness of the web-services infrastructure.

2.1. Robustness tests generation

To generate the concrete set of robustness tests to be executed we need to obtain the relevant web-services parameters definitions (including data types). Web-services interfaces are described as WSDL files, which can be used to automatically obtain those defini-tions. The robustness tests are generated by applying a set of predefined rules to the parameters of each web-service. The proposed rules, presented in Table 1, are based on previous works on robustness testing [4, 5].

To evaluate the robustness of the application server a set of mutations is also performed in the request mes-sage header (see Table 2). This header includes con-figuration parameters relevant for the server to inter-pret the message (e.g., content length, http protocol version). The goal is to evaluate the robustness of the application server when corrupt SOAP messages are received. Note that, SOAP messages may get corrupted by failures at the network level or maliciously changed by hackers during security attacks, which means that

Type	Parameter Mutation
String	Replace by null value
	Replace by empty string
	Replace by predefined string
	Replace by string with nonprintable characters
	Add nonprintable characters to the string
	Replace by alphanumeric string
	Add characters to overflow max size
Number	Replace by null value
	Replace by empty value
	Replace by -1
	Replace by 1
	Replace by 0
	Add one
	Subtract 1
	Replace by maximum number valid for the type
	Replace by minimum number valid for the type
	Replace by maximum number valid for the type plus one
	Replace by minimum number valid for the type minus one
	Replace by maximum value valid for the parameter
	Replace by minimum value valid for the parameter
	Replace by maximum value valid for the parameter plus one
	Replace by minimum value valid for the parameter minus one
List	Replace by null value
	Remove element from the list
	Add element to the list
	Duplicate elements of the list
	Remove all elements from the list except the first one
	Remove all elements from the list
Date	Replace by null value
	Replace by empty date
	Replace by maximum date valid for the parameter
	Replace by minimum date valid for the parameter
	Replace by max .date valid for the parameter plus one day
	Replace by min. date valid for the parameter minus one day
	Add 100 years to the date
	Subtract 100 years to the date
	Replace by the following invalid date: 2/29/1984
	Replace by the following invalid date: 4/31/1998
	Replace by the following invalid date: 13/1/1997
	Replace by the following invalid date: 12/0/1994
	Replace by the following invalid date: 8/31/1992
	Replace by the following invalid date: 8/32/1993
	Replace by the last day of the previous millennium
	Replace by the first day of this millennium

Table 1. Parameters values mutation rules.

Parameter	Parameter Mutation
Content length	Replace by null value
	Replace by 0
	Replace by 1000000
	Add 1
	Subtract 1
Http version	Replace by null value
	Replace by another valid version number
	Replace by an invalid version number

Table 2. Message header mutation rules.

the server must behave correctly even in the presence of modified SOAP requests.

2.2. Tests execution

The execution of the experiments includes two main steps. In the first step, a set of tests is performed without any (artificial) faults. The goal is to collect baseline performance metrics and to understand what is the typical behavior expected from each service. Each test corresponds to the execution of a given service during a certain amount of time and is conducted in a steady state condition that represents the state in which the system is able to maintain its maximum processing throughput. The system achieves a steady state condition after a given time executing the web-services (steady state time). The identification of the steady state time is a responsibility of the tester. Nevertheless, verifying the steady state condition is normally a quite simple task that consists mainly in executing workload (web-services) to discover the instant when the system reaches the maximum throughput.

The duration of each test in step 1 is 10 minutes. This duration has been postulated taking into consideration practical aspects such as the time needed to run the tests and the impact of each type of fault. Note that, although stipulated, the use of this duration in all cases guarantees a fair evaluation as all web-services infrastructures are tested in similar conditions.

In the second step, several tests are performed. Each test focuses a given web-service and includes a set of slots. In each slot the web-service is executed several times during a certain amount of time in the presence of invalid values in a given parameter (the number of slots for each test is equal to the number of call parameters of the corresponding web-service).

To improve the representativeness and repeatability of the tests, each slot follows a very specific execution profile (see Figure 3). The system state is explicitly restored at the beginning of each slot and the effects of the faults do not accumulate across different slots.

After achieving the steady state condition, invalid call parameters are injected. During fault injection time, all SOAP messages from the clients to the server are intercepted by the injector. The XML is modified according to the robustness tests being performed and then forwarded to the server. Note that, each slot focus a given parameter of a given web-service. This way, all the tests related to the parameter under study are injected in the same slot. Each fault is applied to all the related SOAP requests during a predefined period of time (injection period). Between those periods, a safeguard time is observed. The duration of the injection periods must allow the execution of the service 10 times (in order to have an acceptable number of executions considering the same fault). The safeguard time is equal to the steady state time.

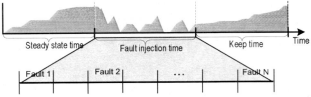

Figure 3. Execution profile for each slot.

When the injection time ends, the web-services must continue to be invoked during a keep time in order to evaluate the application server behavior. The keep time must be equal to the steady state time in order to allow the system to re-achieve the maximum throughput after robustness tests execution.

An important aspect is that, the server response is logged by the injector and used later to analyze the behavior of the web-services in the presence of the invalid call parameters injected.

2.3. Robustness classification and comparison

The robustness of the web-services infrastructure is classified according to an adapted version of the CRASH scale [4] (the wsCRASH scale) that distinguishes the following failure modes:

- **Catastrophic**: application server becomes corrupted or the machine crashes or reboots.
- **Restart**: web-service execution hangs and must be terminated by force.
- **Abort**: abnormal termination of the web-service execution (e.g., abnormal behavior occurs when an unexpected exception is raised by the application).
- **Silent**: after a timeout no error is indicated on an operation that cannot be performed.
- **Hindering**: the error code returned is not correct or the response is delayed.

Web-services infrastructures are classified according to the number of failures for each failure mode. To complement the wsCRASH classification and characterize the performance with valid and invalid parameters, two additional measures are proposed:

- NI_b: average baseline number of interactions (web-services executions) per minute without faults.
- NI_f: average number of interactions (correct web-services runs) during robustness tests execution.

An important aspect concerning comparison is that, to compare alternative solutions for a software component the remaining components must remain the same across experiments. In fact, to compare alternative applications servers for a given solution the experiments must be performed using the same hardware, operating system, web-services implementation, and any other external components. Only the application server

changes between experiments.

The same is true for the comparison of the robustness of the web-services code. In this case, the same hardware, operating system, application server, and external components must be used. Only the web-services implementations vary.

3. Setup and experiments

The most important component of the experimental setup is the fault injection tool (see Figure 2). As mentioned before, this tool acts like a proxy that intercepts all client requests, performs a set of mutations in the SOAP message (focusing a single parameter in each slot) and forwards the modified message to the server. The tool logs the server responses that are analyzed at the end of the experiments to characterize the behavior of the web-services infrastructure.

The goal of the experiments presented in this work is to evaluate the robustness and performance of two implementations of a representative subset of the web-services specified by the TPC-App performance benchmark [6]. In addition, we want to evaluate the application server infrastructure. In this sense, the experiments presented in this practical experience report give the answer to the following questions:

- What is the robustness and performance of the two web-services implementations?
- Is the application server robust enough for this typical small-medium size infrastructure?

The TPC Benchmark™ App (TPC-App) [6] is a performance benchmark for web-services infrastructures widely accepted as representative of real environments. A subset of the web-services specified by TPC-App (Change Payment Method, New Customer, New Product, and Product Detail) was used to demonstrate the proposed approach. Two different implementations of the services have been developed. In the first, named Implementation A, there was a special attention with the validation of the web-services input parameters. In the second, named Implementation B, no relevant attention has been given to robustness.

Concerning the application server, we have used JBoss [9]. This is one of the most complete J2EE application servers and is used in many real scenarios.

All the software developed for these experiments is available at [8] for public access and use.

4. Results and discussion

In this section we present and discuss the experimental results from two different perspectives: robustness of the web-services implementations and robustness of the JBoss application server.

4.1. Web-services code robustness analysis

As mentioned before, two implementations of a subset of the web-services defined by TPC-App have been tested. The goal was to demonstrate that the approach can be used to differentiate robustness characteristics of different implementations.

Table 3 presents all the exceptions observed during the execution of the robustness tests (a total of 69237 tests were performed considering all possible mutations for all parameters). In all cases only the abnormal failure mode has occurred, which is related to unexpected exceptions raised by the web-services.

Results show that both Implementation A and Implementation B have robustness problems. However, those problems have different sources. After analyzing the results in detail we have examined the source code in order to understand the causes (this is what is expected from programmers when robustness problems are detected). Three conclusions were drawn from the analysis of the results and source code:

- Although Implementation A includes code for the validation of the input parameters, two important validation aspects were missing: the validation of null input values (this is the reason for the null pointer exceptions obtained), and the validation of too long email addresses (this is the reason for the stack overflow exception).
- As Implementation B does not include validation of the input parameters exceptions were raised all over

the code. Some exceptions are related to null pointers and others to database access. Note that, the web-services access an external database using dynamically constructed SQL. In some cases, the SQL is built using data from the web-services input parameters, which may lead to incorrect SQL commands when invalid values are injected. This is an unacceptable behavior as it is expected that the service reports a well known predefined exception when something is wrong in the parameters (and not these types of exceptions).

- Implementation A seems to be more robust than Implementation B. This was expected from the beginning of the experiments as we have paid a special attention to the validation of the web-services input parameters in Implementation A.

From the results presented in Figure 4, we can observe that the number of interactions per minute (NI) for Implementation A is lower than for Implementation B. This is an expected result as Implementation A includes additional code for parameters validation.

In addition, we can observe that the baseline number of interactions per minute (NI_b) is higher than the number of interactions during robustness tests (NI_f). This is due to the fact that many web-services requests fail (because of invalid call parameters) and are not taken into account for the NI_f measure.

After analyzing the results presented above we have decided to develop a new implementation of the web-services, starting obviously from the most robust one

Web-Service	Target Parameter	Implementation A		Implementation B	
		# Robustness Failures	Unexpected Exceptions	# Robustness Failures	Unexpected Exceptions Raised
changePayment Method	customerID	1	null pointer	1	null pointer
	paymentMethod	1	null pointer	2	sql exception (value too large); null pointer
	creditInfo	1	null pointer	2	sql exception (value too large); null pointer
	poId	1	null pointer	1	sql exception (invalid number)
newCustomer	billingAddr1	1	null pointer	1	sql exception (value too large)
	billingAddr2	1	null pointer	1	sql exception (value too large)
	Billingcity	1	null pointer	1	sql exception (value too large)
	billingCountry	1	null pointer	1	illegal argument
	billingState	1	null pointer	1	sql exception (value too large)
	billingZip	1	null pointer	1	sql exception (value too large)
	businessInfo	1	null pointer	1	sql exception (value too large)
	businessName	1	null pointer	1	sql exception (value too large)
	contactEmail	1	stack overflow	1	sql exception (value too large)
	contactFName	1	null pointer	1	sql exception (value too large)
	contactLName	1	null pointer	1	sql exception (value too large)
	contactPhone	1	null pointer	1	sql exception (value too large)
	creditInfo	1	null pointer	1	sql exception (value too large)
	Password	1	null pointer	1	sql exception (value too large)
	paymentMethod	1	null pointer	2	sql exception (value too large); null pointer
	poId	0	-	1	sql exception (data integrity violation)
newProduct	subjectString	0	-	0	-
	cutOffDuration	0	-	1	null pointer
	itemLimit	0	-	0	-
productDetail	itemIds	0	-	1	sql exception (bad sql grammar)

Table 3. Robustness problems observed for each implementation.

(Implementation A). The robustness tests were then executed for this version and no robustness failures were observed. This shows that this type of testing is an important tool for programmers to improve the robustness of their solutions.

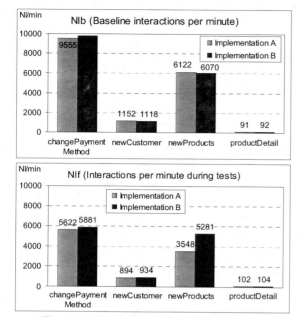

Figure 4. Performance related results.

4.2. JBoss robustness analysis

Concerning the robustness of the JBoss application server, some interesting conclusions were drawn:
- No robustness problems in the application server were observed when considering invalid web-services parameters.
- No robustness problems were observed when considering changes in the http version.
- Increasing the content-length parameter of the request messages lead to hindering failures, as it causes great delays in the application server responses. In fact, we have observed an average increase of 20 seconds in the response time. Note that, the server still executes the request.
- Replacing the content-length parameter by zero or null also leads to hindering failures. In this case, we have observed an average of 80 seconds to process the message and report the exception.

Note that, robustness problems related to the modification of the content-length parameter can be exploited by hackers to cause the application server to delay responses and, eventually, lead to a denial of service. This is one more reason for robustness testing.

4. Conclusion

This paper presents a practical approach for the evaluation of robustness in web-services infrastructures. Given the central role that web-services play today, the existence of such approach targeting web-services environments is a valuable tool when developing an infrastructure for web-services deployment.

The approach consists in a set of robustness tests that are applied during web-services execution in order to observe robustness problems. Systems are classified according to the failure modes observed. The approach was illustrated using two different implementations of the web-services specified by the TPC-App performance benchmark running on top of JBoss.

The experimental results obtained were analyzed and discussed in detail. These results allow us to analyze the robustness characteristics of the two implementations. In addition, results helped us to identify robustness problems and to develop an improved version and clearly show that robustness testing can be successfully applied to web-services infrastructures.

5. References

[1] D. A. Chappel, Tyler Jewell, "Java Web Services: Using Java in Service-Oriented Architectures", O'Reilly. 2002.

[2] T. Andrews et al., Business Process Execution Language for Web Services, v.1.1, 2003.

[3] A. Mukherjee and D. P. Siewiorek, "Measuring Software Dependability by Robustness Benchmarking", IEEE Trans. of Software Engineering, 23 (6), 1997.

[4] P. Koopman and J. DeVale, "Comparing the Robustness of POSIX Operating Systems", 29th Intl Symp on Fault-Tolerant Computing, FTCS-29, Madison, WI, USA, 1999.

[5] M. Rodríguez, F. Salles, J.-C. Fabre, and J. Arlat, "MAFALDA: Microkernel Assessment by fault injection and design aid", 3rd European Dependable Computing Conference, EDCC-3, September 1999.

[6] Transaction Processing Performance Council, "TPC Benchmark[TM] App (Application Server) Standard Specification, Version 1.1", 2005.

[7] E. Christensen et al., Web Services Description Language (WSDL) 1.1. 2001, W3C.

[8] N. Laranjeiro, M. Vieira, H. Madeira, "Web-services robustness evaluation tool", 2006, available at: http://gbd.dei.uc.pt/downloads.php.

[9] "JBoss Application Server Documentation Library", http://labs.jboss.com/portal/jbossas/docs

Protecting Cryptographic Keys From Memory Disclosure Attacks

Keith Harrison and Shouhuai Xu
Department of Computer Science, University of Texas at San Antonio
{kharriso,shxu}@cs.utsa.edu

Abstract

Cryptography has become an indispensable mechanism for securing systems, communications and applications. While offering strong protection, cryptography makes the assumption that cryptographic keys are kept absolutely secret. In general this assumption is very difficult to guarantee in real life because computers may be compromised relatively easily. In this paper we investigate a class of attacks, which exploit memory disclosure vulnerabilities to expose cryptographic keys. We demonstrate that the threat is real by formulating an attack that exposed the private key of an OpenSSH server within 1 minute, and exposed the private key of an Apache HTTP server within 5 minutes. We propose a set of techniques to address such attacks. Experimental results show that our techniques are efficient (i.e., imposing no performance penalty) and effective — unless a large portion of allocated memory is disclosed.

Keywords: cryptographic key security, memory disclosure.

1 Introduction

The utility of cryptography is based on the assumption that cryptographic keys are kept absolutely secret. This assumption is very difficult to guarantee in real-life systems due to various software bugs in operating systems and applications. In this paper we focus on a class of attacks that exploit memory disclosure vulnerabilities, called *memory disclosure attacks*. Such an attack can expose the content of (a portion of) computer memory, and thus cryptographic keys in the disclosed memory.

Our contributions. First, we thoroughly assess (Section 2) the damage of memory disclosure attacks against the private keys of OpenSSH servers and Apache HTTP servers. The attacks exploit two reported vulnerabilities. Our experiments show that such attacks effectively expose the RSA private keys of the servers.

Second, we propose a method (Section 3) for helping understand the attacks (e.g., why are they so powerful?). The core of the method is a software tool we developed to help analyze the content of computer memory. Through our software tool, we found that disclosure a portion of either *allocated memory* or *unallocated memory* would effectively expose cryptographic keys. This is interesting because existing literature often emphasized the importance of clearing unallocated memory (cf. Viega et al. [18, 19] and Chow et al. [6]), but not necessarily taking care of allocated memory.

Third, our analyses on the attacks suggest that one should ensure (i) a cryptographic key only appears in allocated memory a minimal number of times (e.g., one), and (ii) unallocated memory does not have a copy of cryptographic keys. We thus proceed to propose a set of concrete solutions. In particular, our method for minimizing the number of copies of a private key in allocated memory, to our knowledge, is novel in the sense that it takes full advantage of the operating system "copy on write" memory management policy [17] – a technique that was not originally motivated for security purpose. We conduct case studies by applying our solutions to protect the private keys of OpenSSH servers and of Apache HTTP servers. Experimental results show that our solutions can eliminate attacks that disclose unallocated memory, and can mitigate the damage due to attacks that disclose a small portion of allocated memory. It is stressed, however, that if the portion of disclosed memory is large (e.g., about 50% as shown in our case study), the key is still exposed in spite of the fact that our solutions can minimize the number of key copies in memory. Therefore, our investigation may serve as an evidence that in order to completely avoid key exposures due to memory disclosures, special hardware is necessary.

Related work. The problem of ensuring the secrecy of cryptographic keys (and their functionalities thereof) has been extensively investigated by the cryptography community. There have been many novel cryptographic methods that can mitigate the damage caused by the compromise of cryptographic keys. Notable results include the notions of threshold cryptosystems [8], proactive cryptosystems [15], forward-secure cryptosystems [1, 2, 11], key-insulated cryptosystems [9], and intrusion-resilient cryptosystems [12]. The present paper falls into an approach that is orthogonal to the cryptographic approach. Clearly,

137

our mechanisms can be deployed to secure traditional cryptosystems, as evidently shown in this paper. Equally, our mechanisms can be utilized to provide another layer of protection for the afore-mentioned advanced cryptosystems.

It has been deemed as a good practice in developing secure software to clear the sensitive data such as cryptographic keys, promptly after use (cf. Viega et al. [18, 19]). Unfortunately, as confirmed by our experiments as well as an earlier one due to Chow et al. [5], this practice has not been widely or effectively enforced. Chow et al. [5] investigated the propagation of sensitive data within an operating system by examining all places the sensitive data can reside. Their investigation was based on whole-system simulation via a hardware simulator, namely the open-source IA-32 simulator Bochs v2.0.2 [3]. More recently, Chow et al. [6] presented a strategy for reducing the lifetime of sensitive data in memory called "secure deallocation," whereby data is erased either at deallocation or within a short, predictable period afterwards in general system allocators. As a result, their solution can successfully eliminate attacks that disclose unallocated memory. However, their solution has no effect in countering attacks that may disclose portions of allocated memory. Whereas, our solutions can not only eliminate attacks that disclose unallocated memory, but also mitigate the damage due to attacks that disclose a small portion of allocated memory. That is, our solutions provide strictly better protections.

There is some loosely related work. Broadwell et al. [4] explored the core dump problem to infer which data is sensitive based on programmer annotations, so as to facilitate the shipment of crash dumps to application developers without revealing users' sensitive data. Provos [16] investigated a solution to use swap encryption for processes in possession of confidential data. A cryptographic treatment on securely erasing sensitive data via a small erasable memory was presented by Jakobsson et al. [7].

Outline. In Section 2 we evaluate the severity of the memory disclosure problem. In Section 3 we show how to understand the attacks in detail based on our software tool. In Section 4 we present a set of solutions to countering memory disclosure attacks, whose concrete instantiations to protect private keys of OpenSSH servers are explored in Section 5. We conclude the paper in Section 6. Due to the space limitation, we defer many details (including the treatment on Apache HTTP servers) to the full version of the present paper [13].

2 Threat Assessment: Initial Experiments

In this section we report our experiments that exploit two specific memory disclosure vulnerabilities to expose the RSA private keys of an OpenSSH Server and of an Apache HTTP server. The first vulnerability was reported in [14],

which states that Linux kernels prior to 2.6.12 and prior to 2.4.30 are vulnerable to the following attack: directories created in the ext2 file systems could leak up to 4072 bytes of (unallocated) kernel memory for every directory created. The second vulnerability was reported in [10], which states that a portion of memory of Linux kernels prior to 2.6.11 may be disclosed due to the misuse of signed types within drivers/char/n_tty.c. The disclosed memory may have a random location and may be of a random amount. Both vulnerabilities can be exploited *without* requiring the root privilege.

Recall that the RSA cryptosystem has a public key (e, N) and a private key (d, N), where $N = PQ$ for some large prime P and Q. In practice, a variation of the Chinese Remainder Theorem (CRT) is utilized to speed up the signing/decryption procedure, meaning that a RSA private key actually consists of 6 distinct parts: d, P, Q, $d \mod (P-1)$, $d \mod (Q-1)$, and $Q^{-1} \mod P$. Notice that there is a special PEM-encoded private key file, which contains the whole private key. For simplicity, we only consider d, P, Q, and the PEM-encoded file because disclose of any of them immediately leads to the compromise of the private key. Therefore, we call any appearance of any of them "a copy of the private key."

Our experiments ran in the following setting: the server machine has a 3.2GHz Intel Pentium 4 CPU and 256MB memory; the operating system is Gentoo Linux with a 2.6.10 Linux kernel; the OpenSSH server is OpenSSH 4.3_p2; the Apache HTTP server is Apache 2.0.55 (compiled using the prefork MPM); the OpenSSL library version is 0.9.7i.

On the power of attacks exploiting the vulnerability reported in [14]. Our experimental attacks proceeded as follows. (i) We plugged a small 16MB USB storage device into the computer running OpenSSH (or Apache HTTP) server. (ii) We wrote a script to fulfill the following. In the case of OpenSSH server, it first created a large number of SSH connections to localhost; whereas in the case of Apache HTTP server, it first instructed a remote client machine to create a large number of HTTP connections to the server. Then, the script immediately closed all connections. Finally, the script created a large number of directories on the USB device, where each directory created revealed less than 4,072 bytes of memory onto the USB device. (iii) We removed the USB device, and then simply searched the USB device for copies of the private key. Experimental results are summarized as follows.

The case of OpenSSH server: Figure 1(a) depicts the average (over 15 attacks) number of copies of private keys found from the disclosed memory on the USB device, with respect to the number of localhost SSH connections (the x-axis) and the number of created directories (the y-axis). For example, by establishing 500 total connections

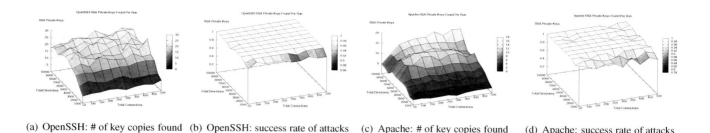

(a) OpenSSH: # of key copies found (b) OpenSSH: success rate of attacks (c) Apache: # of key copies found (d) Apache: success rate of attacks

Figure 1. OpenSSH vs. Apache with respect to the vulnerability reported in [14]

and creating 1,000 directories (i.e., disclosing up to about 4 MBytes memory), we were able to recover about 8 copies of the private key. From a different perspective, Figure 1(b) depicts the average success rate of attacks (i.e., the rate of the number of successful attacks over the total number of 15 attacks), which clearly states that an attack almost always succeeds. In this case, an attack took *less than 1 minute*.

The case of Apache HTTP server: Figure 1(c) shows the average (over 15 attacks) number of copies of private keys found on the USB device, with respect to the number of connections (the x-axis) and the number of created directories (the y-axis). For example, by establishing 500 connections and creating 1,000 directories (i.e., disclosing up to 4 MBytes memory), we were able to recover about 5 copies of the private key. From a different perspective, Figure 1(d) depicts the average success rate of attacks, which clearly states that an attack almost always succeeds. In this case, an attack took *less than 5 minutes*.

On the power of attacks exploiting the vulnerability reported in [10]. Our experimental attack was orchestrated by a script that fulfills the following: (i) In the case of OpenSSH server, it created a large number of SSH connections to `localhost`. In the case of Apache HTTP server, it instructed a remote computer to establish a large number of HTTP connections to the server. (ii) The script executed a program (due to [10]) to dump a piece of memory to a file, which was then searched for the private key. The size and location of the disclosed memory varied, dependent on the terminal running the exploit. The exploit disclosed about 50% of the memory (i.e., 128 MBytes) on average. Experimental results are summarized as follows.

The case of OpenSSH server: Figure 2(a) shows the average (over 20 attacks) number of copies of private keys found in the disclosed memory with respect to the number of connections (the x-axis). From a different perspective, Figure 2(b) shows the success rate of attacks (i.e., the rate of the number of successful attacks over the total number of 20 attacks) with respect to the number of connections (the x-axis). It is clear that an attack almost always succeeds. Moreover, an attack took *less than 1 minute*.

The case of Apache HTTP server: Figure 2(c) shows

the average (over 20 attacks) number of private keys found in the disclosed memory with respect to the number of connections (the x-axis). Figure 2(d) shows the success rate of attacks, which clearly states that an attack always succeeds when 30 or more connections are established. In this case, an attack took *less than 1 minute*.

In summary, our experiments showed that cryptographic keys can be easily compromised by attacks that exploit memory disclosure vulnerabilities. Since the attacks are so powerful, we suspect that copies of the cryptographic keys were somehow flooding the memory to some extent. This motivates our thorough examination in Section 3.

3 Understanding the Attacks

Supporting tool: locating cryptographic keys in memory. In order to understand the attacks, we needed a tool to capture the "snapshots" of memory, and to bookkeep information such as "which processes have access to which memory pages that contain copies of private keys". We developed a software tool for this purpose. The C code of our tool is about 260 lines, and is implemented as a loadable kernel module (LKM). The detail of the code is deferred to the full version of this paper [13]. In our experiments, it took about 5 seconds to scan the 256MB memory.

Understanding the attacks: the case of OpenSSH server. Equipped with our software tool, we conducted another experiment with the same hardware and software setting as in our experiments mentioned above, except that the operating system was replaced by Gentoo Linux with a 2.6.16.1 Linux kernel. The intent of experimenting with a newer version of operating system, which was *not* known to be subject to the afore-mentioned two vulnerabilities, was to validate whether the suspected phenomenon is still relevant in newer operating systems. Note that the new experiments are run with the root privilege, whereas the above attack experiments are not. Specifically, we let two other machines act as clients for issuing SSH requests to the server via a 100Mb/s switch network. We wrote a Perl script to automatically trigger events at the following predefined points in time (unit: 2 minutes).

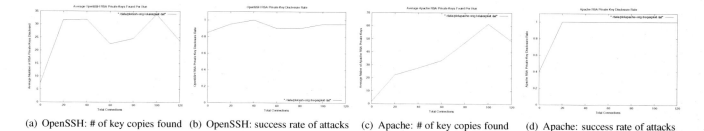

(a) OpenSSH: # of key copies found (b) OpenSSH: success rate of attacks (c) Apache: # of key copies found (d) Apache: success rate of attacks

Figure 2. OpenSSH vs. Apache with respect to the vulnerability reported in [10]

- Time t=0: The simulation is started without OpenSSH running.

- Time t=2: The OpenSSH server is started via the command /etc/init.d/sshd start.

- Time t=6: The first client machine begins issuing SSH requests and maintains 8 concurrent scp transfers. Each transfer lasts about 4 seconds.

- Time t=10: The second client machine initiates an additional 8 concurrent scp transfers. This brings the number of concurrent connections to 16 in total.

- Time t=14: The first client machine stops all file transfers. This reduces the total number of concurrent file transfers to 8.

- Time t=18: The second client machine stops all file transfers, and thus all network traffic ceased.

- Time t=22: The OpenSSH server is stopped via the command /etc/init.d/sshd stop.

- Time t=29: The experiment is finished.

Corresponding to the above events, outputs of the LKM are plotted in Figures 3(a) and 3(b) from two different perspectives. Both pictures have the time as the x-axis.

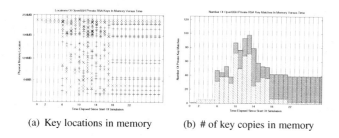

(a) Key locations in memory (b) # of key copies in memory

Figure 3. OpenSSH case

Figure 3(a) shows the locations of copies of the private key in memory, where "×" represents a copy in allocated user or kernel space, and "+" represents a copy in unallocated memory. From this picture we draw the following observations. (1) The OpenSSH private key is in memory at time t=0, even though the OpenSSH server is not started until time t=2. This is because the PEM-encoded file has been loaded into memory by the Reiser file system. (2) When the OpenSSH server is started at time t=2, the newly appearing ×'s are actually the d, P, and Q of the private key. (3) When OpenSSH client requests begin to be issued at time t=6, the number of copies of the private key increases abruptly. We also begin to see copies of the private key in unallocated memory. (4) When the client machines stop issuing requests at time t=18, the number of copies of the private key in allocated memory drops abruptly. We also observe that many copies of the private key are not erased before entering unallocated memory. (5) When the OpenSSH server stops at time t=22, d, P and Q exist only in unallocated memory, except the PEM-encoded private key file that remains in the Linux kernel's page cache.

Figure 3(b) shows the total number of copies of the private key in memory, where lightly shaded bars correspond to copies of the private key in allocated memory, and dark shaded bars correspond to copies of the private key in unallocated memory.

Summary. In both OpenSSH and Apache HTTP servers (details of the Apache case is deferred to [13]), many copies of the private key can be found in both allocated memory and unallocated memory. This confirms our suspicion that copies of cryptographic keys somewhat flooded in memory when the number of SSH / HTTP connections increases – even in newer operating systems, and explains why the afore-experimented attacks were so powerful.

4 Countering Memory Disclosure Attacks

Analyses in the last section naturally suggest the following countermeasures: We should ensure (i) a cryptographic key only appears in allocated memory a minimal number of times (e.g., one) as long as this does not downgrade system performance, and (ii) unallocated memory (or any other place with a disclosure potential such as swap space) does not have a copy of a cryptographic key. For this purpose, now we present a set of solutions at different layers, from application down to operating system kernel.

Application level solution: First, utilize the "copy on write" memory management policy [17] to avoid unnecessary duplications of cryptographic keys. Specifically, we propose placing the private key into a special memory region, and guaranteeing that no process will write to that memory region. This ensures that the private key will only exist once in physical memory (in addition to the PEM-encoded private key file), no matter how many processes are forked. Second, avoid appearances of cryptographic keys as follows: (1) Ensure the private key is not explicitly copied by the application or any involved libraries. (2) Disable swapping of the memory that contains the key using the appropriate system calls. This is because when memory is swapped to disk, the memory is not immediately cleared and the private key may appear in unallocated memory.

Library level solution: We suggest eliminating unnecessary duplications of cryptographic keys in allocated memory using the same measures suggested in application level solution. This suffices to prevent private keys from appearing in memory other than the afore-mentioned special region and the PEM-encoded private key file.

Kernel level solution: We propose ensuring that the unallocated memory does not contain any private keys. This can be fulfilled by having the kernel zero any physical pages before they become unallocated.

Integrated library-kernel solution: We propose integrating the library and kernel level mechanisms together to obtain strictly stronger protection. This way, unnecessary duplications of private keys in allocated memory and any appearances of private keys in unallocated memory are simultaneously eliminated. Moreover, this solution can even remove the PEM-encoded private key from allocated memory, provided that the library instructs the kernel not to cache the PEM-encoded private key file. Therefore, whenever possible, this solution should be adopted.

5 Protecting Keys of OpenSSH Servers

Implementing the application level solution. We instantiate the above general solution with a function, RSA_memory_align(), which should be called as soon as OpenSSL's RSA data structure contains the private key. This ensures that exactly one copy of the private key appears in allocated memory, in addition to the PEM-encoded file. Notice that we need to start OpenSSH with the undocumented -r option to prevent the OpenSSH server from re-executing itself after every incoming connection.

Specifically, RSA_memory_align() can be characterized as follows. (1) It takes advantage of the "copy on write" memory management policy as follows. First, it

uses posix_memalign() to request one or more memory pages for fulfilling the afore-mentioned special memory region. Then, it copies the private key into the special memory region, and zeros and frees the memory originally containing the private key. Then, it updates the pointers in the RSA data structure to point to the new location of the private key. Finally, it sets the BN_FLG_STATIC_DATA flag to inform OpenSSL that the private key is now exclusively located at the special region. (2) It prevents OpenSSL's RSA_eay_mod_exp() from caching the private key by unsetting the RSA_FLAG_CACHE_PRIVATE flag in the flags member of the associated RSA data structure. Moreover, RSA_memory_align() disables swapping of memory that contains the private key by calling mlock() on the memory allocated by posix_memalign().

Implementing the library level solution. We modify the OpenSSL function d2i_PrivateKey(), which is responsible for translating a PEM-encoded private key file into the RSA key parts by calling d2i_RSAPrivateKey(). The modification is that when the d2i_RSAPrivateKey() method returns, we immediately call the function RSA_memory_align() mentioned above.

Implementing the kernel level solution. We modify the kernel function free_hot_cold_page() to enforce that memory pages are cleared, via clear_highpage(), before they are added to one of the lists of free pages. Thus, no private key will appear in unallocated memory.

Implementing the integrated library-kernel solution. In addition to the modifications made in the library level solution and in the kernel level solution mentioned above, the PEM-encoded private key file can be removed from allocated memory. In order to do this, we introduce a new flag, O_NOCACHE, to allow an application to instruct the kernel to immediately remove this file from the "page cache". Specifically this is implemented as follows. Whenever the PEM-encoded private key file is read, the kernel gives the file contents to the requester and then checks if the O_NOCACHE flag is specified. If so, the kernel immediately deletes the corresponding "page cache" entry by calling remove_from_page_cache() before calling free_page().

Experimental results. First, we re-examined the attack based on [14] against the same vulnerable 2.6.10 Linux Kernel, except that the system is now patched with our respective solutions. In no case were we able to recover any copy of the private key.

Second, we re-examined the attack based on [10] against the same vulnerable 2.6.10 Linux kernel, except that the system is now patched with our solutions. For conciseness, we only consider our integrated library-kernel solution. Figure 4(a) compares the average (over 20 attacks) number of copies of the private key found in the USB device *before* and *after* deploying our solution. It shows that the number of copies of the private key recovered is reduced by our solution because only one copy of the private key appears in allocated memory, and no copies of the private key appear in unallocated memory. Figure 4(b) compares the success rate of attacks *before* and *after* deploying our integrated library-kernel solution. While our solution does reduce the attack success rate (from about 90% to about 50%), the attack still succeeds with a probability about 50% because the attack discloses on average about 50% of the memory. Thus, as mentioned before, completely eliminating such powerful attacks might have to resort to some special hardware devices.

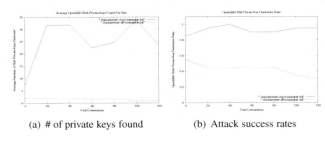

(a) # of private keys found   (b) Attack success rates

Figure 4. OpenSSH effect of our library-kernel solution countering the attack of [10]

As we show in [13] our solution does not impose any performance penalty.

6 Conclusion

We investigated a set of mechanisms to deal with the exposure of cryptographic keys caused by memory disclosure attacks. Our mechanisms can eliminate attacks that disclose unallocated memory, and can mitigate the damage due to attacks that disclose a small portion of allocated memory. Our result suggests that in order to eliminate powerful attacks that can disclose a large portion of memory, one may have to resort to special hardware devices.

Acknowledgement. We thank the anonymous reviewers for their valuable comments, and our shepherd, Luigi Romano, for his constructive suggestions that improved the paper.

This work was supported in part by ARO, NSF and UTSA.

References

[1] R. Anderson. On the forward security of digital signatures. Technical report, 1997.

[2] M. Bellare and S. Miner. A forward-secure digital signature scheme. In *Proc. Crypto'99*, pages 431–448.

[3] Bochs. the bochs ia-32 emulator project. `http://bochs.sourceforge.net/`.

[4] P. Broadwell, M. Harren, and N. Sastry. Scrash: A system for generating secure crash information. In *Usenix Security Symposium'03*.

[5] J. Chow, B. Pfaff, T. Garfinkel, K. Christopher, and M. Rosenblum. Understanding data lifetime via whole system simulation. In *Usenix Security Symposium'04*.

[6] J. Chow, B. Pfaff, T. Garfinkel, and M. Rosenblum. Shredding your garbage: Reducing data lifetime. In *Proc. USENIX Security Symposium'05*.

[7] G. Di Crescenzo, N. Ferguson, R. Impagliazzo, and M. Jakobsson. How to forget a secret. In *STACS'99*.

[8] Y. Desmedt and Y. Frankel. Threshold cryptosystems. In *Proc. Crypto'89*, pages 307–315.

[9] Y. Dodis, J. Katz, S. Xu, and M. Yung. Key-insulated public key cryptosystems. In *Proc. EUROCRYPT'02*.

[10] Georgi Guninski. linux kernel 2.6 fun. windoze is a joke. `http://www.guninski.com/where_do_you_want_billg_to_go_today_3.html` (dated 15 February 2005).

[11] G. Itkis and L. Reyzin. Forward-secure signatures with optimal signing and verifying. In *Crypto'01*.

[12] G. Itkis and L. Reyzin. Sibir: Signer-base intrusion-resilient signatures. In *Crypto'02*.

[13] K. Harrison and S. Xu. Full version of the present paper available at `www.cs.utsa.edu/~shxu`.

[14] Mathieu Lafon and Romain Francoise. Information leak in the linux kernel ext2 implementation. `http://arkoon.net/advisories/ext2-make-empty-leak.txt` (Arkoon Security Team Advisory - dated March 25, 2005).

[15] R. Ostrovsky and M. Yung. How to withstand mobile virus attacks (extended abstract). In *PODC'91*.

[16] N. Provos. Encrypting virtual memory. In *Proc. Usenix Security Symposium'00*.

[17] A. Silberschatz, P. Galvin, and G. Gagne. *Operating System Concepts (sixth ed.)*. John Wiley & Sons.

[18] J. Viega. Protecting sensitive data in memory. `http://www.cgisecurity.com/lib/protecting-sensitive-data.html`, 2001.

[19] J. Viega and G. McGraw. *Building Secure Software*. Addison Wesley, 2002.

Session 3A:
Embedded Systems

Fault Tolerant Planning for Critical Robots

Benjamin Lussier, Matthieu Gallien, Jérémie Guiochet,
Félix Ingrand, Marc-Olivier Killijian, David Powell
LAAS-CNRS, 7 avenue du Colonel Roche, 31077 Toulouse Cedex 4, France
firstname.lastname@laas.fr

Abstract

Autonomous robots offer alluring perspectives in numerous application domains: space rovers, satellites, medical assistants, tour guides, etc. However, a severe lack of trust in their dependability greatly reduces their possible usage. In particular, autonomous systems make extensive use of decisional mechanisms that are able to take complex and adaptive decisions, but are very hard to validate. This paper proposes a fault tolerance approach for decisional planning components, which are almost mandatory in complex autonomous systems. The proposed mechanisms focus on development faults in planning models and heuristics, through the use of diversification. The paper presents an implementation of these mechanisms on an existing autonomous robot architecture, and evaluates their impact on performance and reliability through the use of fault injection.

1. Introduction

Autonomous systems cover a large range of functionalities and complexities, from robotic pets to space rovers, including elderly care assistants, museum tour guides, and autonomous vehicles. As successes arise in autonomous navigation, exemplified by Mars rovers and the clearing of the *DARPA Grand Challenge* [17], complex autonomous systems that are able to choose and execute high-level actions without human supervision are not yet ready for real life applications. Indeed, one of the major drawbacks in the utilization of such systems is the difficulty to predict and validate their behavior. To increase the confidence that we may have in such systems so that they may be used in more critical applications, we consider in this paper the tolerance of residual development faults in planning models.

First, we introduce autonomous systems and specific aspects such as decisional mechanisms, robustness and planning. Second, we propose error detection and recovery mechanisms that are appropriate for planning to tolerate de-

velopment faults in their application-dependent knowledge. Finally, we validate the proposed mechanisms through an experimental framework based on fault injection.

2. Dependability in Autonomous Systems

This section presents several aspects of autonomous systems relevant to their dependability. We present a definition of autonomy and give key aspects of architectures for autonomous robots.

2.1. Autonomy

A dictionary definition of "autonomy" is "the ability to act independently". However, in the field of robotics, this definition is insufficient since it does not enable a distinction between classic *automatic* systems, that simply apply preprogrammed reactions in response to the system's inputs (e.g., as in feedback control), and truly *autonomous* systems that seek to carry out goal-oriented tasks whose implementation details are not defined in advance, either by necessity (the input space is unbounded) or as a design strategy (to simplify the code). We adopt here the definition of autonomy given in [11]: *"An unmanned system's own ability of sensing, perceiving, analyzing, communicating, planning, decision-making, and acting, to achieve its goals as assigned by its human operator(s) through designed human-robot interaction (HRI). Autonomy is characterized into levels by factors including mission complexity, environmental difficulty, and level of HRI to accomplish the missions."*

The level of autonomy of an autonomous system is often discussed in terms of its "robustness". Indeed, autonomous robots are intended to cope with uncertainty and non-nominal situations. A good or "robust" robot is understood to be one that can survive and fulfill its mission despite partial knowledge about its environment as well as unforeseen contingencies such as obstacles, rough terrain and failures. In this paper, we choose to distinguish between robustness and fault tolerance as follows:

Robustness is the ability of an autonomous system to

cope with adverse environmental situations (lighting conditions, unexpected obstacles, etc.) while providing an acceptable service.

Fault Tolerance is the ability of an autonomous system to provide an acceptable service despite system faults (hardware failures, software bugs, etc.).

2.2. Autonomous System Architectures

Four architectural styles for designing autonomous robot systems are usually distinguished:

1. The *sense-plan-act style* is based on a closed loop of three components devoted respectively to sensing the environment, finding a plan to reach a goal state, and acting on the environment according to the plan.
2. The *subsumption style* allows several "behavior" components to simultaneously sense and act on the environment, with actions that can be prioritized or cross-inhibited between different components.
3. The *multi-agent style* considers a set of autonomous systems or agents immersed in the same environment and interacting to achieve their individual or shared goals.
4. The *hierarchical style* defines several abstraction levels with different real-time constraints, resulting in a layered architecture.

Whereas the sense-plan-act style has largely been abandoned (at least as the basis for a monolithic architecture) due to its poor real-time performance, the subsumption style is still commonly used in entertainment robots, such as Sony's *Aibo*™. The multi-agent style is now receiving considerable attention both as the basis for designing a taskable robot [18] and in the context of agent swarms with emerging "intelligence" [20]. However, most practical robots currently adopt the hierarchical style, usually resulting in an architecture with three layers [8]: (a) a *decisional layer* that is responsible for elaborating plans to reach operator-defined mission goals, (b) an *executive layer* that selects and sequences elementary actions that implement the high-level tasks included with the current plan, and (c) a *functional layer* that interfaces with the hardware sensory and action devices. In some architectures the executive layer is merged into either the decisional layer or the functional layer.

Hierarchical architectures for autonomy include the RAX architecture developed by NASA as part of its Deep Space One project [19], JPL's CLARATy [23] and the LAAS architecture [1] developed at LAAS-CNRS (the latter architecture will be described in more detail in 3.2.1). From a dependability viewpoint, tolerance of hardware faults is considered in some of these architectures [16]. For example, the RAX architecture includes a model-based *mode identification and reconfiguration* (MIR) component

specifically aimed at diagnosing and recovering from faults affecting hardware resources [19]. For development faults, apart from on-line checking mechanisms aimed at guaranteeing safety [21], the focus has largely been on fault avoidance approaches (rigorous design, and thorough verification and testing). For example, intensive testing was carried out on the RAX architecture [3]: six test beds were implemented throughout the development process, incorporating 600 tests. The authors of [3] underline the relevance of intensive testing, but acknowledge particular difficulties regarding autonomous systems, notably the problem of defining suitable test oracles. Given the inherent difficulty of testing autonomous systems, we believe that a tolerance approach with respect to residual development faults should be of considerable interest. Yet, to the best of our knowledge, such an approach has not been previously envisaged.

2.3. Deliberation and Decision

From our perspective, deliberation and decision are the key features of autonomy. Many different decisional capabilities have been studied and deployed on robots or other autonomous systems. Here, we discuss what distinguishes such decisional capabilities from other programmed functionalities.

Most decisional mechanisms boil down to some sort of search in a very large state space. In general, this search leads to a decision (a plan to reach a goal, a diagnosis, an action, etc.). This search can be done either off-line or on-line, that is in advance to produce a precompiled data structure or on the fly while the system is running. It may reason about past states (as in diagnosis) or about future states (as in planning). It may have a limited horizon or, conversely, a very deep scope. But a key aspect is that the search needs to be efficiently guided to avoid a combinatorial explosion. As a result, a decisional mechanism can be *complete* (it is guaranteed to find a solution if one exists) or not (it can "miss it"), *correct* (solutions are always valid) or not (they are approximate), *tractable* (solutions are found in a polynomial time and space) or not.

Another important feature of decisional mechanisms is that they are organized in a way that makes a clear separation between the *knowledge* and the *inference mechanism*. The aim is to make the inference mechanism (e.g., a search engine) as generic and as independent as possible from the application. Conversely, the knowledge is domain-specific and typically specifies what states are reachable through the search process and what is the "best" next state from any given state. However, knowledge and inference mechanisms are often tightly linked in practice (e.g., heuristics that guide a search engine).

The implementation of decisional mechanisms relies on various formalisms (logic, neural networks, Markov models, constraints, simple temporal networks, etc.) and computational models (constraint-based programming, logic programming, heuristic search, dynamic programming, etc.).

The most common decisional functionalities deployed on autonomous systems are the following: planning, execution control, diagnosis, situation recognition and learning. In this paper, we focus particularly on *planning*, which is the activity of producing a plan to reach a goal from a given state, using given action models (e.g., the activity plan for the day of an exploration rover).

2.4. Planning

Planning is necessary in complex autonomous systems as a mean to select and organize the robot's future actions to achieve specified high-level goals. We introduce here some generalities on planning in autonomous systems, before presenting dependability issues.

2.4.1. General Principle.
Planning can be implemented in several ways but, in practice, two approaches are preferred: search in a state space and constraint planning.

Search in a state space manipulates a graph of actions and states. It explores different action sequences from an initial state to choose the most suitable one to achieve given goals.

Constraint planning uses CSP (Constraint Satisfaction Problem) solving to determine a possible evolution of the system state that satisfies a set of constraints, some of which specify the system goals. CSP solving is commonly an iterative algorithm assigning successively possible values to each variable and verifying that all constraints remain satisfied.

Two robustness techniques are commonly implemented to recover from a plan failure caused by adverse environmental situations:

- *Replanning* consists in developing a new plan from the current system state and still unresolved goals. Depending on the planning model complexity, replanning may be significantly time costly. Other system activities are thus generally halted during replanning.
- *Plan repair* may be attempted before replanning, with the aim of reducing the time lost in replanning. It uses salvageable parts of the previous failed plan, that are executed while the rest of the plan is being repaired. However, if reducing the salvaged plan conflicts with unresolved goals, plan repair is stopped and replanning is initiated.

2.4.2. Dependability Issues.
Planning, like other decisional mechanisms, poses significant challenges for validation. Classic problems faced by testing and verification are exacerbated. First, *execution contexts* in autonomous systems are neither controllable nor completely known; even worse, consequences of the system actions are often uncertain. Second, planning mechanisms have to be *validated in the complete architecture*, as they aim to enhance functionalities of the lower levels through high level abstractions and actions. Integrated tests are thus necessary very early in the development cycle. Third, the *oracle problem*[1] is particularly difficult since (a) equally correct plans may be completely different and (b) an unforeseen adverse environmental situation may completely prevent some goals from being achieved, thus ineluctably degrading the system performance, however well it behaves (for example, cliffs, or some other feature of the local terrain, may make a position goal unreachable).

One way to address the latter issue is to define an oracle as a set of constraints that necessarily and sufficiently characterizes a correct plan: plans satisfying the constraints are deemed correct. Such a technique was used for thorough testing of the RAX planner during the NASA *Deep Space One* project [3], or in the VAL validation tool [10]. Extensive collaboration of application and planner experts is necessary to generate the correct set of constraints. A Failure Recovery Analysis tool is proposed in [9] to ease model corrections during development.

Automatic static analysis may also be used to ascertain properties on planning models, whereas manual static analysis requires domain experts to closely scrutinize models proposed by planning developers. For example, the development tool Planware [2] offers facilities for both types of analysis.

Some work has also been done on evaluating planning dependability. A measure for planner reliability is proposed in [5], which compares theoretical results to experimental ones, showing a necessary compromise between temporal failures (related to calculability of decisional mechanisms) and value failures (related to correctness of decisional mechanisms). Later work [4] proposes concurrent use of planners with diversified heuristics to answer this compromise: a first heuristic, quick but dirty, is used when a slower but more focussed heuristic fails to deliver a plan in time. To our knowledge, no other fault tolerance mechanisms have been proposed in this domain. We strongly believe, however, that such mechanisms are essential to provide more dependability in autonomous systems.

3. Fault Tolerant Planning

We investigate here how to tolerate design and implementation faults in planner models and heuristics. These mechanisms are particularly well adapted to hierarchical

---

[1] How to conclude on correctness of a program's outputs to selected test inputs?

autonomous systems with a centralized planner at the decisional layer.

3.1. Principles

Complementary to testing, diversity is the only known approach to improve trust in the behavior of a critical system regarding development faults (e.g., diversification is used in software components of the Airbus A320, and in hardware components of the Boeing B777). The general principle of the mechanisms that we propose is to execute sequentially or concurrently diversified variants of the planner, following similar approaches to recovery blocks [22] and distributed recovery blocks [13]. In particular, diversity is encouraged by forcing the use of different algorithms, variable domains and parameters in the models and heuristics of the variants.

3.1.1. Detection.
Implementing error detection for decisional mechanisms in general, and planners in particular, is difficult [16]. There are often many different valid plans, which can be quite dissimilar. Therefore, error detection by comparison of redundantly-produced plans is not a viable option. Thus, we must implement error detection by independent means. Here, we propose four complementary error detection mechanisms: a *watchdog timer*, a *plan analyzer*, a *plan failure detector* and an *on-line goal checker*.

A watchdog timer is used to detect when the search process is too slow or when a critical failure such as a deadlock occurs. Timing errors can be due to faults in the planner model, in its search engine, or ineffectiveness of the search heuristics.

A plan analyzer can be applied on the output of the planner. It is an acceptance test (i.e., an on-line oracle) that verifies that the produced plan satisfies a number of constraints and properties. This set of constraints and properties can be obtained from the system specification and from domain expertise but it must be diverse from the planner model. This mechanism is able to detect errors due to faults in the planner model or heuristics, and in the planner itself.

A plan failure detector is a classical mechanism used in robotics for execution control. Failure of an action which is part of the plan may be due to an unresolvable adverse environmental situation, or may indicate errors in the plan due to faults in the knowledge or in the search engine. Usually, when such an action failure is raised, thesearch engine tries to repair the plan. When this is not possible, it raises a plan failure. We use these plan failure reports for detection purposes.

An on-line goal checker verifies whether goals are reached while the plan is executed. Goals can only be declared as failed when every action of the plan has been carried out. This implies that the checker maintains an internal

```
1.  begin mission
2.    failed_planners ← ∅;
3.    while (goals ≠ ∅)
4.      candidates ← planners;
5.      while (candidates ≠ ∅ & goals ≠ ∅)
6.        choose k such as (k ∈ candidates)
                          & (k ∉ failed_planners);
7.        candidates ← candidates \ k;
8.        init_watchdog(max_duration);
9.        send (plan) to k;
10.       wait % we wait any of these two events
11.         □ receive (plan_found) from k
12.           stop watchdog;
13.           if analyze(plan)=OK then
14.             failed_planners ← ∅;
15.             k.execute_plan();
                % if the plan fails goals != empty
                % and then we loop line 3
16.           else
17.             send(invalid_plan) to operator;
18.             failed_planners ← failed_planners ∪ k;
19.           end if
20.         □ watchdog timeout
21.           failed_planners ← failed_planners ∪ k;
22.       end wait
23.       if failed_planners = planners then
24.         raise exception "no valid plan
                              found in time";
              % no remaining planner,
              % the mission has failed
25.       end if
26.     end while
27.   end while
28. end mission
```

Figure 1. Sequential Planning Policy

representation of the system state and of the goals that have been reached.

3.1.2. Recovery.
We propose two recovery mechanisms, both using different planners based on diverse knowledge.

With the first mechanism, the planners are executed sequentially, one after another. The principle is given in Figure 1. Basically, each time an error is detected, we switch to another planner until all goals have been reached or until all planners fail in a row. Once all the planners have been used and there are still some unsatisfied goals, we go back to the initial set of planners. This algorithm illustrates the use of the four detection mechanisms presented in Section 3.1.1: watchdog timer (lines 8 and 20), plan analyzer (line 13), plan failure detector (line 15), on-line goal checker (lines 3 and 5).

Reusing planners that have been previously detected as failed makes sense for two different reasons: (a) a perfectly correct plan can fail during execution due to an adverse environmental situation, and (b) some planners, even faulty, can still be efficient for some settings since the situation that activated the fault may have disappeared.

It is worth noting that the choice of the planners, and the order in which they are used, is arbitrary in this particular example (line 6). However, the choice of the planner could take advantage of application-specific knowledge about the most appropriate planner for the current situation or knowledge about recently observed failure rates of the planners.

With the second recovery mechanism, the planners are executed concurrently [15]. The main differences with respect to the algorithm given in Figure 1 are: (a) the plan request message is sent to every planning candidate, (b) when a correct plan is found, the other planners are requested to stop planning, and (c) a watchdog timeout means that all the planners have failed.

Here, the choice of planner order is implicit: the first planner obtaining a plan is chosen. However, this could lead to the repeated selection of the same faulty but rapid planner. Some additional mechanism is thus required to circumvent this problem. For example, the planner selected during the previous round can be withdrawn from the set of candidates for the current round.

3.1.3. Coordination.
From a dependability point of view, the fault-tolerance mechanisms have to be as independent as possible from the decisional layer, i.e., in this case from the planners. This is why we propose to handle both the detection and recovery mechanisms and the services necessary for their implementation in a middleware level component called FTplan, standing for *Fault-Tolerant PLANner coordinator*.

This component has to integrate the fault tolerance mechanisms into the robot architecture. This implies essentially communication between, and synchronization and coordination of, the error detection mechanisms and the redundant planners.

To avoid error propagation from a possible faulty planner, FTplan should not take any information that comes from or depends on the planners themselves. The watchdog can easily be implemented from the operating system timing primitives. Action failure detection is performed at the execution control layer, so error reports can be obtained and reused at the FTplan level. A plan analyzer performs simple acceptance checks using rules expressed independently from the planners and their knowledge.

However, implementing an on-line goal checker without relying on information obtained through the planner is more difficult. FTplan maintains for this purpose its own system state representation, based on information gathered from the lower layers. It obtains this information from the execution control layer, whose abstraction level is near to that of the decisional layer. This system state representation is checked against the set of goals prescribed for the current mission.

Whatever the particular recovery mechanism it implements, sequential or parallel, FTplan has to manage several planners. It needs to communicate with them, e.g., for sending plan requests or for updating their goals and system state representations before replanning. It also needs to be able to control their life cycle: start a new instance or even stop one when it takes too long to produce a plan.

FTplan is intended to allow tolerance of development

faults in planners (and particularly in planning models). FTplan itself is *not* fault-tolerant, but being much simpler than the planner it coordinates, we can safely rely on classic verification and testing to assume that it is fault-free.

3.2. Implementation

We present here the implementation of the proposed mechanisms. We introduce the target architecture and then give some implementation details about the FTplan component.

3.2.1. LAAS architecture.
The LAAS architecture is presented in [1], and some recent modifications have been proposed in [14]. It has been successfully applied to several mobile robots, some of which have performed missions in real situations (human interaction or exploration). It is composed of three main components[2] as presented in Figure 2: GenoM modules, OpenPRS, and IxTeT.

The functional level is composed of a set of automatically generated *GenoM modules*, each of them offering a set of services, which perform computation (e.g., trajectory movement calculation) or communication with physical devices (sensors and actuators).

The procedural executive *OpenPRS* (*Open Procedural Reasoning System*), is in charge of decomposing and refining plan actions into lower-level actions executable by functional components, and executing them. This component links the decisional component (IxTeT) and the functional level. During execution, OpenPRS reports any action failures to the planner, in order to re-plan or repair the plan. As several IxTeT actions can be performed concurrently, it has also to schedule sequences of refined actions.

IxTeT (*IndeXed TimE Table*) is a temporal constraint planner as presented in Section 2.4.1, combining high level actions to build plans. Each *action* is described in a *model* file used by the planner as a set of constraints on attributes (e.g., robot position), resources (e.g., energy consumption), numeric or temporal data (e.g., action duration). Then, a valid plan is calculated combining a set of actions in such a way that they are conflict-free and they fulfill the goals. The description of actions in the planner model is critical for the generation of successful plans and thus for the dependability of the robot as a whole.

3.2.2. Fault Tolerant Planner Implementation.
The fault tolerance principles presented in Section 3.1 have been implemented in a fault tolerant planner component as presented in Figure 3. This component replaces the original component "Planner" presented in Figure 2. The FTplan component is in charge of communicating with OpenPRS

---

[2]An additional robustness component, R2C, is introduced in [21]. We have not considered it in this study since its current implementation is not compatible with our experimentation environment.

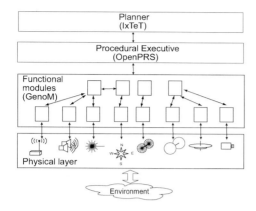

Figure 2. The LAAS architecture

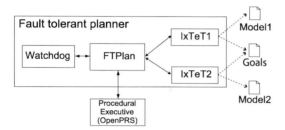

Figure 3. Fault tolerant planner

as the original planner does. To be consistent with the current implementation, FTplan uses the same technologies as OpenPRS and IxTeT for communication.

The current version of FTplan implements the sequential redundant planner coordination algorithm presented earlier (Section 3.1, Figure 1) with two IxTeT planners. Currently, the plan analysis function is empty (it always return *true*) so error detection relies solely on just three of the mechanisms presented in Section 3.1.1: watchdog timer, plan failure detection, and on-line goal checker.

The watchdog timer is launched at each start of planning. As soon as a plan is found before the time limit (40 seconds in our implementation: a sufficient time to produce plans in our activities), the watchdog is stopped. If timeout occurs, FTplan stops the current IxTeT, and sends a plan request to the other IxTeT planner, until a plan is found or both planners have failed. In the latter case, the system is put in a safe state (i.e., all activities are ceased), and an error message is sent to the operator.

On-line goal checker is performed after each action executed by OpenPRS that can result in a modification in the goal achievements (for instance: a camera shot, a communication, movement of the robot, etc.). This checking is carried out by analyzing the system state at the end of an action, determining goals that may have been accomplished and checking that no inconsistent actions have been executed simultaneously. Unfulfilled goals are resubmitted to the planner during the next replanning or at the end of plan execution.

In the actual implementation, FTplan checks every 10ms if there is a message from OpenPRS or one of the IxTeT planners. In case of an action request from a planner or an action report from OpenPRS, FTplan updates its system representation before transmitting the request. If the request is a plan execution failure (the system has not been able to perform the actions of the plan), then FTplan launches a re-plan using the sequential mechanism. If the request indicates that the actions are finished, then FTplan checks if the goals have been reached.

4. Mechanism Validation

We present here the validation process we have followed to assess the performance and efficacy of the proposed fault tolerant mechanisms. We discuss first a validation framework that extensively uses simulation and fault injection, then present experimental results.

4.1. Framework for Validation

Our validation framework relies on simulation and fault injection. Simulation is used since it is both safer and more practical to exercise the autonomy software on a simulated robot than on a real one. Fault injection is used since it is the *only* way to test the fault tolerance mechanisms with respect to their specific inputs, i.e., faults in planning knowledge. In the absence of any evidence regarding real faults, there is no other practical choice than to rely on *mutations*[3], which have been found to efficiently simulate real faults in imperative languages [7].

We now introduce successively the targeted software architecture, the workload, the faultload, and the readouts and measurements we obtain from system activity.

4.1.1. Software Architecture. Our simulation environment is represented in Figure 4. It incorporates three elements: an open source robot simulator named Gazebo, an interface library named Pocosim, and the components of the LAAS architecture already presented in section 3.2.1.

The *robot simulator Gazebo*[4] is used to simulate the physical world and the actions of the autonomous system; it takes as input a file describing the environment of the simulation (mainly a list of static or dynamic obstacles containing their position, and the physical description of the robot) and executes the movement of the robot and dynamic obstacles, and possible interactions between objects.

---

[3]A mutation is a syntactic modification of an existing program.
[4]"The player/stage project", http://playerstage.sourceforge.net

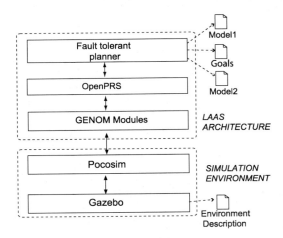

Figure 4. Simulation environment

The *Pocosim library* [12] is a software bridge between the simulated robot (executed on Gazebo) and the software commands generated by the GenoM modules: it transforms commands to the actuators into movements or actions to be executed on the simulated robot, and relays the sensor inputs that Gazebo produces from the simulation.

Our *autonomous system* is based on an existing ATRV (All Terrain Robotic Vehicle) robot, and employs GenoM software modules interfaced with the Gazebo simulated hardware. The upper layer of the LAAS architecture executes as presented in the previous section. Two different models are used with the IxTeT planners. The first model was thoroughly tested and used on a real ATRV robot; we use it as primary model and as target for fault injection. We specifically developed the second model through forced diversification of the first: for example, the robot position is characterized numerically in the first model and symbolically in the second.

4.1.2. Workload. Our workload mimics the possible activity of a space rover. The system is required to achieve three subsets of goals: *take science photos* at specific locations (in any order), *communicate* with an orbiter during specified visibility windows, and *be back at the initial position* at the end of the mission.

To partially address the fact that the robot must operate in an open unknown environment, we chose to activate the system's functionalities in some representative situations resulting from combinations of sets of missions and worlds. A *mission* encompasses the number and location of photos to be taken, and the number and occurrence of visibility windows. A *world* is a set of static obstacles unknown to the robot (possibly blocking the system from executing one of its goals), which introduces uncertainties and stresses the system navigation mechanism.

We implemented four missions and four worlds, thus applying sixteen execution contexts to each mutation. Missions are referenced as gradually more difficult M1, M2, M3 and M4: M1 consists in two communications and three photos in close locations, whereas M4 consists in four communications and five far apart photos. Environments are referenced as worlds W1, W2, W3 and W4. W1 is an empty world, with no obstacles to hinder plan execution. W2 and W3 contains small cylindrical obstacles, whereas W4 includes large rectangular obstacles that may pose great difficulties to the navigation module, and are susceptible to endlessly block the robot path.

In addition, several equivalent experiments are needed to address the non-determinacy of the experiments. This is due to asynchrony in the various subsystems of the robot and in the underlying operating systems: task scheduling differences between similar experiments may degrade into task failures and possibly unsatisfied goals, even in the absence of faults. We thus execute each basic experiment three times, leading to a total of 48 experiments per mutation. More repetition would of course be needed for statistical inference on the basic experiments but this would have led to a total number of experiments higher than that which could have been carried out with the ressources available (each basic experiment lasts about 20 minutes).

4.1.3. Faultload. To assess performance and efficacy of the proposed fault tolerance mechanisms, we inject faults in a planning model by random mutation of the model source code (i.e., in Model1 of Figure 3). Five types of possible mutations were identified from the model syntax:

1. Substitution of numerical values: each numerical value is exchanged with members of a set of real numbers that encompasses (a) all numerical variables in all the tasks of the model, (b) a set of specific values (such as 0, 1 or -1), and (c) a set of randomly-selected values.
2. Substitution of variables: since the scope of a variable is limited to the task where it is defined, numerical (resp. temporal) variables are exchanged with all numerical (resp. temporal) variables of the same task.
3. Substitution of attribute values: in the IxTeT formalism, attributes are the different variables that together describe the system state. Attribute values in the model are exchanged with other possible values in the range of the attribute.
4. Substitution of language operators: in addition to classic numerical operators on temporal and numerical values, the IxTeT formalism employs specific operators, such as "nonPreemptive" (that indicates that a task cannot be interrupted by the executive).
5. Removal of a constraint relation: a randomly selected constraint on attributes or variables is removed from the model.

Substitution mutations were automatically generated using the SESAME tool [6]. Using an off-line compilation, this tool detects and eliminates binary equivalent or syntactically incorrect mutants. Removal of random constraint relations was carried out through a PERL script and added to the mutations generated by SESAME. All in all, more than 1000 mutants were generated from the first model.

For better representativeness of injected faults, we consider only mutants that are able to find a plan in at least one mission (we consider that models that systematically fail would easily be detected during the development phase). As a simple optimization, given our limited resources, we also chose to carry out a simple manual analysis aimed at eliminating mutants that evidently could not respect the above criterion.

4.1.4. Records and Measurements.
Numerous log files are generated by a single experiment: simulated data from Gazebo (including robot position and hardware module activity), output messages from GenoM modules and OpenPRS, requests and reports sent and received by each planner, as well as outputs of the planning process.

Problems arise however in trying to condense this amount of data into significant relevant measures. Contrary to more classic mutation experiments, the result of an experiment cannot be easily dichotomized as either failed or successful. As previously mentioned, an autonomous system is confronted with partially unknown environments and situations, and some of its goals may be difficult or even impossible to achieve in some contexts. Thus, assessment of the results of a mission must be graded into more than just two levels. Moreover, detection of equivalent mutants is complexified by the non-deterministic context of autonomous systems

To answer these issues to some extent, we chose to categorize the quality of the result of an experiment with: (a) the subset of goals that have been successfully achieved, and (b) performance results such as the mission execution time and the distance covered by the robot to achieve its goals. Due to space constraints, we focus in the rest of this paper on measurements relative to the mission goals.

4.2. Results

We present in this part several experimental results using the evaluation framework previously introduced. Experiments were executed on i386 systems with 3.2 GHz CPU and the Linux OS. We first study the performance cost of the proposed mechanisms, then present their efficacy in tolerating injected faults.

4.2.1. Fault-free Performance.
To determine the overhead of the proposed fault tolerance mechanisms, we first concentrate on supposed fault-free models. Figure 5 presents the impact of FTplan on the system behavior.

Note that results in W4 must be treated with caution, as

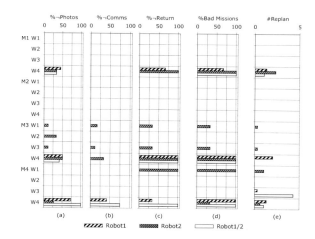

Figure 5. Impact of FTplan (without injected faults): *This figure studies the impact of the FTplan component on fault-free system behavior by comparing three different robots: Robot1 uses our first model, Robot2 uses our second model, and Robot1/2 contains an FTplan component that uses successively our first and second models. For each considered activity (M1W1 to M4W4), the figure shows five different measures: (a) (b) (c) three failure proportions to reach the different types of goals in a mission (resp. photos, communications, and returns to initial position), (d) failure proportion of the whole mission (a mission is considered failed if one or more mission goals were not achieved), and (e) the mean number of replanning operations observed during one experiment (in the case of Robot1/2, this number is equivalent to the number of model switches during the mission).*

this world contains large obstacles that may cause navigational failures and block the robot path forever. As our work focus on planning model faults rather than limitations of functional modules, we consider that success in this world relies more on serendipity in the choice of plan rather than correctness of the planner model. It is however interesting to study the system reaction to unforeseen and unforgiving situations that possibly arise in an open and uncontrolled environment. Note that these results show that different models give rise to different failure behaviors: particularly in W4, the three systems fail differently.

W4 set aside, results are globally very good: Robot1 and Robot1/2 succeed in all their goals, while Robot2 fails a few goals in M3, and all its return goals in M4W1. These failures may be attributed to a larger set of constraints in this model that may be costly in performance, and underestimated distance declarations. The mean activity time of the systems (that is the time until the system stops all activity in a mission) is an average of 404 seconds for Robot1, 376 seconds for Robot2, and 405 seconds for Robot1/2. Time performance-wise, the three systems are thus roughly

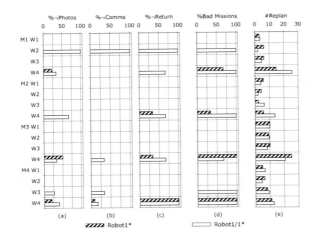

Figure 6. Impact of switching overhead (without injected faults): *This figure presents the impact of numerous model switches on fault-free system behavior by comparing two different robots: Robot1* uses our first model, and Robot1/1* contains an FTplan component that switches between two exact copies of our first model. Consequently, neither of the robots is fault-tolerant. The results concern only the cost of model switches. To provoke many model switches, both robots use a version of the IxTeT planner without the optimizing functionality of plan repair: any failed action systematically leads to complete replanning, with an additional model switch for Robot1/1*.*

equivalent.

Although the results are mostly positive, showing that FTplan's main execution loop does not severely decrease goal achievement or performance in the chosen scenarios, they are still insufficient to assess the overhead of planner switches as very few occurred in these fault-free experiments. This overhead is further studied in experiments presented in Figure 6.

We effectively see that there are many more replannings (and thus model switches) than in the previous experiments (a mean per experiment of 8.3 against 0.3 for Robot1*, and 8.9 against 0.4 for Robot1/1*). M1W2 appears as a singularity for Robot1/1* as after a few minutes of execution, the IxTeT planner finds no solution in its current situation. We believe this due to an elusive bug in either the model, FTplan, or the IxTeT planner. However, the same experiment with Robot1/2* (using diversification through the first and second models) gives successful missions, suggesting that the bug lies in our modified version of IxTeT.

Apart from this singularity, Robot1/1* only fails more goals than Robot1* in the over-stressing W4 execution contexts, as well as the complex M4W3. Setting aside W4 (and the M1W2 singularity), the mean activity time of the systems is 381 seconds for Robot1* and 431 seconds for Robot1/1*, indicating an overhead of 13%. Including W4,

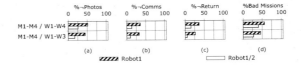

(a)　(b)　(c)　(d)
⬚⬚⬚ Robot1　　▭ Robot1/2

Figure 7. Impact of planner redundancy (with injected faults): *This figure presents overall results achieved for all 28 mutations, both with and without the heavily-constrained world W4.*

the time is 456 seconds for Robot1* and 535 seconds for Robot1/1*, indicating an overhead of 17%. We deem these results as quite acceptable considering the negative impact of discarding plan repair.

4.2.2. Fault-tolerance efficacy. To test the efficacy of the proposed mechanisms and the FTplan component, we injected 38 faults in our first model, realizing more than 3500 experiments equivalent to 1200 hours of testing. We discarded 10 mutants that were unable to find a plan for any of the four missions[5]. We believe that five of the remaining mutants are equivalent to the fault-free model. However, the non-deterministic nature of autonomous systems makes it delicate to define objective equivalence criteria. We thus include the results obtained with these five mutants.

The 28 considered mutations are categorized in the following manner: three substitutions of attribute values, six substitutions of variables, ten substitutions of numerical values, four substitutions of operators, and six removals of constraints. The mutants were executed on Robot1 and Robot1/2. The results are presented in Figure 7.

These results give objective evidence that model diversification favorably contributes to fault tolerance of an autonomous system considering the proposed faultload: failure decreases for photo goals of 62% (respectively, 50% including W4), 70% (64%) for communication goals, 80% (58%) for returns goals, and 41% (29%) for whole missions. Note, however, that RobotFT in the presence of injected faults is *less* successful than a single fault-free model. This apparent decrease in dependability is explained by the fact that incorrect plans are only detected when their execution has failed, possibly rendering one or more goals unachievable, despite recovery. This underlines the importance of plan analysis procedures to attempt to detect errors in plans *before* they are executed.

5. Conclusion

To our knowledge, the work presented in this paper is the first proposition of fault tolerant mechanisms based on di-

---

[5] In this case, Robot1/2 gives the same results as the fault-free Model2: nearly perfect success rates in W1, W2 and W3.

versified planning models. We proposed a component providing error detection and recovery appropriate for fault-tolerant planning, and implemented it in the LAAS architecture. This component can use four detection mechanisms (watchdog timer, plan failure detector, on-line goal checker and plan analyzer), and two recovery policies (sequential planning and concurrent planning). Our current implementation is that of sequential planning associated with the first three error detection mechanisms.

To assess the performance overhead and the efficacy of the proposed mechanisms, we developed a validation framework that exercises the software on a simulated robot platform, and carried out what we believe to be the first ever mutation experiments on declarative models. These experiments were conclusive in showing that the proposed mechanisms do not severely degrade the system performance in the chosen scenarios, yet usefully improve the system behavior in the presence of model faults.

There are many directions for future research. First, implementation of a plan analyzer should allow much better goal success levels to be achieved in the presence of faults since it should increase error detection coverage and provide lower latency. Implementation of the concurrent planning policy and comparison with the sequential planning policy are also of interest. Moreover, we would like to evaluate diversification on planning heuristics rather than just models and investigate also the additional detection capabilities of recent additions to the LAAS architecture [21]. Finally, many more experiments are needed to improve the statistical relevance of the results. The use of a large computer grid would drastically improve the number of experiments that could be executed in reasonable time and eliminate the need for manual inspection to remove trivial mutants.

References

[1] R. Alami, R. Chatila, S. Fleury, M. Ghallab, and F. Ingrand. An Architecture for Autonomy. *The International Journal of Robotics Research*, 17(4):315–337, April 1998.

[2] M. Becker and D. R. Smith. Model Validation in Planware. In *ICAPS 2005 Workshop on Verification and Validation of Model-Based Planning and Scheduling Systems*, Monterey, California, June 6-7, 2005.

[3] D. E. Bernard, E. B. Gamble, N. F. Rouquette, B. Smith, Y. W. Tung, N. Muscettola, G. A. Dorias, B. Kanefsky, J. Kurien, W. Millar, P. Nayal, K. Rajan, and W. Taylor. Remote Agent Experiment DS1 Technology Validation Report. Ames Research Center and JPL, 2000.

[4] I. R. Chen. On the Reliability of AI Planning Software in Real-Time Applications. *IEEE Transactions on Reliability*, 46(1):81–87, March 1997.

[5] I. R. Chen, F. B. Bastani, and T. W. Tsao. On the Reliability of AI Planning Software in Real-Time Applications. *IEEE Transactions on Knowledge and Data Engineering*, 7(1):14–25, February 1995.

[6] Y. Crouzet, H. Waeselynck, B. Lussier, and D. Powell. The SESAME experience: from assembly languages to declarative models. In *Proceedings of the 2nd Workshop on Mutation Analysis (Mutation'2006)*, Raleigh, NC, November 7, 2006.

[7] M. Daran and P. Thévenod-Fosse. Software error analysis: a real case study involving real faults and mutations. In *Proceedings of the 1996 ACM SIGSOFT international symposium on Software testing and analysis*, San Diego, California, January 8-10, 1996.

[8] E. Gat. On Three-Layer Architectures. In *Artificial Intelligence and Mobile Robots*, D. Kortenkamp, R. P. Bonnasso, and R. Murphy editors, MIT/AAAI Press, pages 195-210, 1997.

[9] A. E. Howe. Improving the Reliability of Artificial Intelligence Planning Systems by Analyzing their Failure Recovery. *IEEE Transactions on Knowledge and Data Engineering*, 7(1):14–25, February 1995.

[10] R. Howey, D. Long, and M. Fox. VAL: Automatic Plan Validation, Continuous Effects and Mixed Initiative Planning using PDDL. In *16th IEEE International Conference on Tools with Artificial Intelligence*, Boca Raton, Florida, November 15-17, 2004.

[11] H. M. Huang, editor. *Autonomy Levels for Unmanned Systems (AL-FUS) Framework*. Number NIST Special Publication 1011. 2004.

[12] S. Joyeux, A. Lampe, R. Alami, and S. Lacroix. Simulation in the LAAS Architecture. In *Proceedings of Principles and Practice of Software Development in Robotics (SDIR2005), ICRA workshop*, Barcelona, Spain, April 18, 2005.

[13] K. H. Kim and H. O. Welch. Distributed Execution of Recovery Blocks: An Approach for Uniform Treatment of Hardware and Software Faults in Real-Time Applications. *IEEE Transactions on Computers*, C-38:626–636, 1989.

[14] S. Lemai and F. Ingrand. Interleaving Temporal Planning and Execution in Robotics Domains. In *Proceedings of AAAI-04*, pages 617–622, San Jose, California, July 25-29, 2004.

[15] B. Lussier. *Fault Tolerance in Autonomous Systems*. PhD thesis, Institut National Polytechnique de Toulouse, 2007 (in French).

[16] B. Lussier, A. Lampe, R. Chatila, F. Ingrand, M. O. Killijian, and D. Powell. Fault Tolerance in Autonomous Systems: How and How Much? In *Proceedings of the 4th IARP/IEEE-RAS/EURON Joint Workshop on Technical Challenge for Dependable Robots in Human Environments*, Nagoya, Japan, June 16-18, 2005.

[17] M. Monterlo, S. Thrun, H. Dahlkamp, D. Stavens, and S. Strohband. Winning the DARPA Grand Challenge with an AI Robot. In *American Association of Artificial Intelligence 2006 (AAAI06)*, Boston, MA, July 17-20, 2006.

[18] N. Muscettola, G. A. Dorais, C. Fry, R. Levinson, and C. Plaunt. IDEA: Planning at the Core of Autonomous Reactive Agents. In *AIPS 2002 Workshop on On-line Planning and Scheduling*, Toulouse, France, April 22, 2002. http://citeseer.nj.nec.com/593897.html.

[19] N. Muscettola, P. P. Nayak, B. Pell, and B. C. Williams. Remote Agent: To Boldly Go Where No AI System Has Gone Before. *Artificial Intelligence*, 103(1-2):5–47, 1998.

[20] J. L. Pearce, B. Powers, C. Hess, P. E. Rybski, S. A. Stoeter, and N. Papanikolopoulos. Using virtual pheromones and cameras for dispersing a team of multiple miniature robots. *Journal of Intelligent and Robotic Systems*, 45:307–21, 2006.

[21] F. Py and F. Ingrand. Real-Time Execution Control for Autonomous Systems. In *Proceedings of the 2nd European Congress ERTS, Embedded Real Time Software*, Toulouse, France, January 21-23, 2004.

[22] B. Randell. System Structure for Software Fault Tolerance. *IEEE Transactions on Software Engineering*, SE-1:220–232, 1975.

[23] R. Volpe, I. Nesnas, T. Estlin, D. Mutz, R. Petras, and H. Das. CLARAty: Coupled Layer Architecture for Robotic Autonomy. Technical Report D-19975, NASA - Jet Propulsion Laboratory, 2000.

Insights into the Sensitivity of the BRAIN (Braided Ring Availability Integrity Network)—On Platform Robustness in Extended Operation

Michael Paulitsch, Brendan Hall

Honeywell Aerospace

michael.paulitsch@honeywell.com; brendan.hall@honeywell.com

Abstract

Low-cost fault-tolerant systems design presents a continual trade-off between improving fault-tolerant properties and accommodating cost constraints. With limited hardware options and to justify the system design rationale, it is necessary to formulate a fault hypothesis to bound failure assumptions. The system must be built on a foundation of real-world relevance and the assumption of coverage of the fault hypothesis.

This paper discusses a study that examines the sensitivity of a BRAIN (braided ring availability integrity network) design to different fault types and failure rates in a safety-relevant application. It presents a Markov-based model (using ASSIST, SURE, and STEM analysis tools) and a series of experiments that were run to analyze the overall dependability of the BRAIN approach. The study evaluates the mission reliability and safety in the context of a hypothetical automotive integrated x-by-wire architecture on top of the BRAIN. Drawing from experience in the aerospace domain, the authors investigate the possibility of continued operation for a limited period after a detected critical electronic failure. Continued operation would allow a driver to reach repair facilities rather than stopping the vehicle to call for roadside assistance or "limping home."

1. Introduction

Commercial cost pressure and the maintenance and repair capabilities at remote airports have made extended operation despite faults and aircraft dispatch with fault common in the aerospace domain. Extended-range Twin-engine Operation Performance Standards (ETOPS) is an example of this practice that regulates twin-engine airplane operations and defines clear limits on operational duration in the event of engine failure. Similarly, minimum equipment lists (MEL) in aircrafts provide clear guidelines to pilots when a dispatch, in spite of a fault in a subsystem, is permitted. MELs are established through detailed analysis of the safety effect on the aircraft. E.g., ARP5107 provides specific guidelines for engine electronics [31].

This paper extrapolates the concept of extended operation despite faults to a hypothetical electronic x-by-wire platform in cars [1]. Continued operation for longer periods is not necessarily required for the mission success (such as safe landing of aircraft), but allows a level of comfort or commercial benefits—for example, the ability to drive the car home or to the garage in case of a failure to avoid towing. For safety-relevant systems, such as fail-operational by-wire systems, the safety implications of continued operation despite faults require careful consideration.

Generally, safety and reliability analyses of systems have been published and mature industry practices for conducting safety case assessment (ARP4754 [9], ARP4761 [35]) are in place. Often, the safety aspect is seen in the context of available hardware or effects of certain external failure modes [36]. This paper acknowledges the value of these analyses, but extends the safety analysis in several dimensions: 1) in addition to available hardware, the effect of integrity faults is considered; 2) effects of platform algorithms is considered; 3) systems purely evaluating reliability do not consider periods of extended operation until repair.

We wished to examine extended operation because repair may not be immediately available, and the system needs to be operational for some time. During this interval, the system may be especially vulnerable to additional faults—both hardware exhaustion and integrity violation. A good example in automotive systems is the "limp home mode," where the car operates in a degraded mode, but is still operational [14]. While the effects of additional failures may be reduced, safety relevant functionality and associated guarantees need to be maintained.

Our goal in this paper is to look at the reliability from a platform perspective. System safety can be truly contemplated only within a systems context—including application, hazards, environmental factors, user influence, etc. However, since a platform builds the foundation of a system, the strength and dependability vulnerabilities of the platform directly impact hosted applications.

We believe that our hypothesis is especially interesting to the automotive domain because efforts are underway to apply safety standards from other domains, such as IEC61508 [7], ARP 4754 [9], to the automotive domain and/or to create special platform and automotive safety standards, such as AUTOSAR [34], ISO26262 [10].

We do recognize that safety stretches far beyond availability, integrity, and reliability numbers and refer readers to known literature such as [8]. A more general discussion on dependability and terms used in this paper can be found in [6]. The actual numbers are of less consequence; our intent is to examine the relative strength of different architectural polices in relation to integrity and availability guarantees.

2. Other Related Work

Hammett and Babcock evaluated redundancy schemes for by-wire systems [11]. Wilwert et al. quantify external electromagnetic interference (EMI) [3] in by-wire architectures. Wilwert et al. provide a good overview of x-by-wire systems in [1]. Navet et al. present an overview of automotive communication systems, the basis of a by-wire platform, in [2]. Bertoluzzo et al. look at by-wire applications and networks in [23]. Latronico and Koopman look at automotive communication protocols algorithms deployed under hybrid fault scenarios [12]. Bridal performs reliability estimates for repairable fault-tolerant systems and network topologies [15][16].

There are a multitude of reliability evaluation tools available. A good tools overview is given in [4]. A recent integrated tool approach is Möbius [5]. Model evaluations in this paper use ASSIST/SURE/STEM [13] because of its fast model evaluation abilities.

3. Overview of BRAIN

The BRAIN (braided ring availability integrity network) is an alternative topology and guardian (fault-containment strategy) for ensuring high-integrity data propagation. A braided ring augments the standard ring topology with increased connectivity. In addition to neighboring connections, a node is also connected to its neighbor's neighbor via a link called the braid or skip link (see *Figure 1*).

The BRAIN is a flooding network that minimizes the propagation delay of rings. Each node propagates a message in real time, leading to only a few bits delay for each hop. As described in detail in [17][18], each node is monitored for correct data propagation by the next node downstream through bit-for-bit comparison between the data received on the direct and the skip link. Data corruption is signaled to nodes downstream with special integrity fields in the dataflow or indicated via truncation (namely by stop-forwarding the message). The action depends on the configuration of the ring (full-duplex or half-duplex links). Because data flows in two directions, each node receives correct data despite any arbitrary failure. To tolerate multiple faults, each end node compares data received from two directions, and accepts

it if it is bit-for-bit identical but not signaled with high data propagation integrity. This comparison makes the system tolerant to multiple benign faults with high integrity.

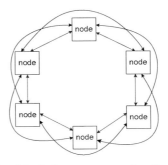

Figure 1: Braided-ring communication topology

Each node performs guardian enforcement for its topological neighbors based on a synchronized global time and TDMA (Time Division Multiple Access) schedule information to ensure medium availability.

The propagation comparison of each node can be leveraged to support high integrity sources, namely message-based self-checking pairs (see [18] for details). For this, two neighboring nodes of the BRAIN form a pair and send their version of the message at the same point in time. The propagation logic performs the comparison as for any other message, and each receiving node receives a high-integrity message if both sources (the pair) have sent the same data.

Initial versions of the ring have used this mechanism only for application data. We have extended this idea to protocol level mechanisms. Each startup and synchronization message is sent by a pair of nodes. The resulting extension simplifies the synchronization algorithm greatly because distributed algorithms reduce to multi-master-based algorithms with trustable sources. In addition, the precision of the BRAIN is improved due to more frequent synchronization using the same amount of bandwidth and the removal of the Byzantine error term [19] normally present in clock synchronization algorithms. The reader is referred to [20] for insights on the cause of the error term removal. SAFEbus/ARINC659 uses a similar algorithmic approach. Self-checking-pair-based synchronization also allows a very scalable tolerance to multiple fault scenarios by simply adding master pairs.

This paper focuses on permanent faults and their impact to BRAIN dependability claims. We understand the requirement for tolerating multiple transient faults or high intensity radiated field (HIRF) effects. Next to shielding approaches, quick restart after communication loss (about two communication rounds in the BRAIN for self-checking pair startup and integration approach) is the first algorithmic defense. Secondly, the self-stabilizing clique aggregation algorithm [18] quickly converges if cliques (subgroups of synchronized end systems) emerge due to multiple transients or other faults.

4. Model Description

To produce reliability approximations efficiently using existing tools, we must make assumptions about the models and their parameters: constant failure rates of components; constant repair rates; neglect certain type of failure causes. In addition, reduction of less likely scenarios (such as multiple failure scenarios) dramatically reduces the model state space and the model's solution time for given parameters. Some assumptions may need to be revisited, depending on the overall deployment of the by-wire architecture and in light of recent development of electronics (e.g., aging silicon) [21]. Also, model parameters must be refined to reflect precise components and component reliability numbers and algorithmic or platform configuration specifics; e.g. the reliability of the communication component depends highly on whether it is integrated with a complex, high-power compute core or deployed as standalone. Nevertheless, despite some approximations, the given models should show the sensitivity of the models to the parameters and produce an interesting result giving insights into:

- sensitivity of platform reliability and impact on safety to extended operation after a failure,
- sensitivity of the platform to reliability results,
- algorithmic and configuration impact, and
- impact of integrity detection mechanisms; the full coverage approach of the BRAIN compared to inline integrity approaches used in alternative architectures, e.g., dual star topologies with redundant active central guardians [24][25].

The model is representative of the underlying platform, but does not include application-specific assignments of functions. Such assignments are important for the final safety assessment; however, the presented model and parameters evaluate the foundation and present insights about whether the foundation is strong enough for application assignments.

The model evaluates the reliability of the platform. Correct operation of a platform constitutes looking at availability *and* integrity and their implications to safety. Safety from a platform perspective means that either an integrity violation or redundancy exhaustion has occurred. Integrity violation means that the data has been corrupted during transmission or in computation. If voting is applied, such data corruptions could be "voted out" at the application. If high-integrity computing and communication end systems are used, data can be used immediately without voting. Thus, any corruption of data by the platform may have severe consequences. High-integrity compute and communication platforms (such as AIMS, aircraft information management systems, in Boeing 777 and its communication backbone SAFEbus

[20]) are very enabling due to reduction overhead of traditional fault tolerance schemes from voting in software to select the first redundant data copy. In addition, the partitioning and fault detection guarantees of such approaches are excellent and application software is independent from platform software.

Seeing the advantage of high-integrity compute for the application software development (as the automotive domain does with the use of fail-silent ECUs), the model assumes that any single integrity violation by the platform may have safety implications, because a computed and distributed data value may be used by multiple, possibly replicated, actuators.

Looking at safety from an availability perspective, the model is concerned about redundancy exhaustion leading to isolation of components and loss of communication, e.g., due to components or link loss. If communication between distributed components cannot be guaranteed anymore, we assume safety is affected. A detailed description of the model and what leads to loss of communication (availability) or decreased integrity is given below.

4.1. Model Parameters

A by-wire architecture typically consists of several components connected to the network. The number of components depends on the detailed architectural approach. We expect 8 to 12 nodes directly connected to the network to support connections to the units support-ing transmission, engine, distributed actuators and sensors, and control computers [1][11][23][29].

Commercial transport airplanes are operational for missions averaging 3-10 hours, with major checks every couple hundred hours with different levels of overhauls. In the automotive space, a car is driven on average for 4000 hours [28]. Guaranteeing safety over such long mission periods without checks may not be economically viable. We also expect that the car electronics may not be equipped or may not be able to perform the necessary scrubbing activities to detect latent faults. Thus, we assume that at every major service—similar to service procedures in the aerospace domain, and as is more common because of increased levels of diagnosis [28]—the car's by-wire electronic and wire loom will be checked for correctness and latent faults. Major service intervals where all latent errors can be detected are assumed to be in the order of 150 hours. This equates to about 5250 miles (8450 km) at 35mph (56kph). Such service intervals are currently not mandated in the automotive industry in most countries, though they are recommended during the vehicle warranty period. The results of this paper could be used to consider impacts of service intervals on safety. Error detection coverage at service is assumed to be largely perfect as manufacturing level testing can be deployed for critical circuits. The service is expected to scrub all essential FDIR (fault detection, isolation, and recovery) circuits using scan chains [32], similar to production-level tests.

Component failures are detected with coverage that is based on the underlying network architecture, as described below. Once detected, the operation of the by-wire system will be extended for a certain interval. The average transit time by car for transit from home to work is ½ hour according to U.S. census data [37]. It is assumed that an extension period of 1 hour should be sufficient to return home and/or drive to a repair facility in case of a detected error. The models will contrast the approach by running models with near immediate repair (1 minute), no repair (modeled as very low repair rate of 10^{-10}) and some repair intervals around one hour. For extended operation reference, Boeing 777's ETOPS rating allows the airplane to fly for up to 180 minutes on a single engine. The maximum operating time for engine electronics is 125 hours if the time of fault occurrence is known [31].

Component failure rate parameter ranges were chosen based on our experience with similar technologies, and reliability models were determined by CALCE [27] and according to MIL-HDBK-217 [26] (note that MIL-HDBK-217 is no longer maintained, but a good public source for reliability data). Connector failure rates are depend on the chosen connector type. MIL-HDBK-217 is used to determine connector reliability ranges. Connectors may also not perfectly fit the exponential distribution (i.e. constant failure rate), but the model and requirements to quickly solve the model for lot of different model parameters forces us to make this assumption. We assume link failure rates are dominated by connector failure rates.

We use a hybrid component fault model where the fail-stop failures are assumed to be higher than arbitrary node faults, as a node is likely to be part of an ECU (electronics control unit) or an LRU (line replaceable unit). The reliability of such parts (LRU or ECU) is often driven by the power supply unit and a significant number of supply components leading to a low MTBF rate but with a benign system behavior like fail-stop. The fail arbitrary behavior is driven by the communication chip that is performing forwarding, checking, protocol activities etc. This behavior is probably unboundable; thus, the arbitrary behavior in a failure case. The failure rates of those components are assumed to be similar to the reliability numbers of the communication chip (or chip where the communication chip is part of).

Table 1 is an overview of the parameter values used for the BRAIN and dual-star model and the values that we expect to be most likely (most representative value (MRV in the table)). These most representative values are used when several other parameters are varied to show the sensitivity to variation.

Table 1: Overview of parameters used in models

Parameter	Values	MRV
Number of active nodes	7, 8, 9, 10, 11, 12, 13, 14	10
Mission interval [hours]	½, 1, 20, 50, 100, 120, 150, 200, 250, 3k, 4k, 5k, 6k, 7k	150
Link failure rate [failures/hour]	5×10^{-7}, 10^{-6}, 2×10^{-6}, 5×10^{-6}	10^{-6}
Component failure rate (fail-stop) [failures/hour]	5×10^{-6}, 10^{-5}, 2×10^{-5}	10^{-5}
Component failure rate (arbitrary) [failures/hour]	5×10^{-8}, 10^{-7}, 5×10^{-7}	10^{-7}
Repair rate (extended operation time) [1/hours]	10^{-10} (no repair), 0.1 (10 h), 0.5 (2 h), 1 (1 h), 60 (1 min.; near immediate repair)	1

4.2. Description of BRAIN Model

The BRAIN can guarantee platform availability and integrity, and thus safety, as long as there is either (1) one communication path with full propagation integrity from the sender to all receivers or (2) two paths from the sender to the receiver where the receiver can perform bit-for-bit comparison between the two paths. In case 1, a single arbitrary component can be tolerated on the BRAIN because each receiver has one path from the sender. Each node on the path is checking the direct and skip links bit-for-bit for agreement, then signaling the result at the end via an integrity signaling field [18]. The bit-for-bit comparison of skip and direct link prevents any arbitrarily faulty node from corrupting data during propagation without being detected. Similarly, for single link or other benign component faults, the data will also reach each node on the ring with full integrity. Ad (2), for multiple benign faults (fail-stop), all receiving nodes detect the multiple fault scenario because the integrity field at the end of the data indicates loss of integrity from both directions on the ring. Once detected, the receiver can perform bit-for-bit comparison of the two copies received from each direction and still assure full integrity of the data.

Medium availability is enforced by the guardian mechanisms, which are performed by each node for its two direct neighbors. Synchronization is guaranteed as long enough self-checking pairs can send synchronization messages.

The SURE model defines state spaces for the fail-silent and arbitrary component failures, link failures, and self-checking pair failures (i.e. the link between the pairs or at least one of the two nodes has failed). Link failures are assumed to be benign (e.g. a link is broken or not, but does not "corrupt" data integrity). A special state to model the loss of connectivity in one ring direction is also modeled. Transitions between states are guided by failure or repair rates. Details of the state space and its transitions are not in the scope of this paper, but we modeled the above described behaviors.

ASSIST/SURE/STEM requires definition of "death states," which define when the integrity and availability of the communication can no longer be guaranteed due to faults. These states are at a higher level:

- More than one arbitrary component fault present,
- An arbitrary fault with any other fault combination (link or benign component fault),
- The connectivity from a sender to each receiver is less than two paths (which is either two fail-stop component faults or multiple link failures occurred where connectivity from sender and receivers via two paths is broken), or
- All self-checking pairs failed and protocol execution is compromised (due to link failure between self-checking pairs or component failure).

As the BRAIN performs bit-for-bit comparisons at each node any error is immediately detected. From the detection of an error, extended operation is allowed until the faulty sub-component is repaired. The time to repair is a parameter, also referred to as the time for extended operation.

In addition to the model parameters in *Table 1*, the BRAIN-specific model parameter (*Table 2*) is the number of self-checking pairs needed for protocol operation, such as clock synchronization, startup, and integration.

Table 2: Overview of BRAIN-specific parameters

Parameter	Values	MRV
Number of self-checking pairs	1, 2, 3, 4	3

4.3. Description of Dual-Star Model

To compare the BRAIN to alternative architectures, we evaluated a commonly used architectural alternative, a dual-star model. Given the cost constraints, a dual-star model seems to be the best of the alternatives of ring/star/bus dual replicated architectures for the following reasons. Pure bus-based architectures suffer from spatial proximity faults and are likely excluded for by-wire architectures. Ring architectures (without skip links) have low reliability due to the missing path to circumvent (benign) faulty nodes [33] and masquerading faults for forwarded data. Combinations such as ring/star architectures (e.g. wagon wheel architecture) can be powerful as they remove some possibility of masquerading faults, but they can introduce reliability loss due to serialization of one communication path.

In the star model, benign and arbitrary component faults and link failures are modeled. Given the protocol dependencies of solutions on the market [24][25], solutions are thought to be single-fault tolerant to arbitrary failures from a protocol perspective.

For a dual star model, evaluation of inline integrity approaches and their effect on safety is especially hard to quantify, as it is very hard to evaluate the effects of an undetected error on the application. E.g., what are the effects of an erroneous guardian (star) on data integrity? The model assumes that any undetected error may have a safety impact. As the two communication paths in a dual-star network architecture are used for availability with inline integrity protection, any arbitrary faulty star may have an effect.

If a star is arbitrarily faulty, the faulty star is detected with a near 100% probability due to the integrity check (e.g., a CRC). Yet, despite the high probability of detecting the star error, the probability of undetected errors and, thus, data integrity violations remains. This probability of undetected errors depends on the strength of the inline integrity mechanism deployed to cover failures of the intermediate device. Currently, deployed dual-star networks [24][25] use a 24-bit CRC for error detection. Assuming a uniform failure distribution for failures of the central guardian device affecting a frame, the probability of an undetected integrity failure of a frame is 2^{-24} (about 5.96×10^{-8}).

At 5 Mbit/s, it takes 100 μs to send a frame with an average frame length of 500 bits. Say the network is 50% loaded, then 1.8×10^7 frames would be sent per hour. This rate would lead to about 1 ($= 2^{-24} \times 1.8 \times 10^7$) undetected frame per hour once a star is faulty.

Internal Honeywell explorations of the CRC32 polynomial used for Ethernet indicated that the probability of undetected errors is increased from 2^{-32} to 2^{-28} for reasonable failure modes in intermediate relaying devices (such as switches or guardians) [30]. Such failure modes are characterized by the relaying device introducing systematic errors (such as a stuck at 0 or 1 bit every 32 bits of a frame). Such faults may be common for implementations deploying 32-bit-based computing architectures handling frames. In [22], Paulitsch et al. argue that the error detection coverage credit may even be less.

We recognize that the described effects are specific to a special CRC polynomial. But, in order to capture such weaknesses of inline integrity, this paper assumes that the undetected error rate of a 24-bit CRC is degraded by a factor of 10; resulting in a rate of 10 integrity violations per hour. Such integrity errors have platform safety implication. If the CRC size would be increased to 32bits, the rate would decrease to 0.07 ($= 2^{-28} \times 1.8 \times 10^7$). It should also be understood that the safety analysis covers only passive devices and propagation errors as is the case in FlexRay and TTP/C central guardians. If such relaying devices were to perform active protocol activities, the safety effects may be more severe.

Given these arguments, the model introduces a transition probability for integrity errors once a central guardian is arbitrarily faulty. The death states for the star model are defined as:

- An integrity fault occurred after one faulty star is arbitrarily faulty,
- More than one arbitrary end system component fault (not the star) occurred because protocol operation (clock synchronization, integration, or startup) cannot be guaranteed to work correctly anymore, or
- Two faulty stars are present.

Table 3: Overview of dual star-specific parameters

Parameter	Values
Rate of undetected errors [frame / hour]	10 (24 bit CRC), 0.07 (32 bit CRC), 0 (ideal reference model)

In addition to the model parameters of *Table 1,* the star-specific model parameter introduces a rate for the undetected integrity errors per hour (integrity violation) (see *Table 3*).

Error detection of faulty stars is assumed to be near perfect. The CRC checks will likely signal a faulty star propagation behavior for most of the time enabling near perfect detection for the indication of a failure condition to the driver. Again, please note that the model is only valid for propagation failures and architectures like [24][25]. Once the star needs to perform active protocol activities or stores whole frames, the model may need to be adapted.

5. Results and Discussion

This section gives the result of the sensitivity of the BRAIN to certain parameters and a comparison to a dual star architecture. Reliability is the continuity of correct service. Reliability results are traditionally given over a specific mission time. We have argued that the loss of correct operation (missing availability or integrity of the platform) has safety effects. Thus, for our purposes, safety and reliability are the same. Safety numbers are often expressed as probability of failing in an hour. We will present the reliability/safety probability numbers normalized to a per hour number; i.e. the reliability number is divided by the service interval (the mission time) when the by-wire architecture is assumed to be inspected for failures in detail (scrubbing of any faults, including latent faults). The service interval is 150 hours for all experiments except for the experiment examining the sensitivity to different service intervals. The normalization of the probability alleviates comparison to industry standard like IEC61508. A typical safety number is 10^{-9} failures/hour for highly critical operation (in aerospace, this 10^{-9} number is also applied to a mission, such as a flight of 4-10 hours, resulting in a lower per hour number). We assume 10^{-9} failures/hour as the target for x-by-wire safety in this paper inspired by [11]. It is important to note that such numbers must be evaluated in the context of accepted safety requirements, environ-mental factors, and other factors influencing safety. Aerospace has recognized similar tradeoffs for engine electronics and time-limited dispatch [31].

All experiments show the (normalized) reliability number for different extended operations (the time it takes to get to the repair facility). The one minute extended operation is assumed to be the (near) immediate repair, which is likely the time it takes for the driver to react to any indications of fault scenarios and to pull the car into a safe place to await for towing or repair vehicles.

On the other side of the spectrum is "no repair" during service intervals, which means that the driver keeps driving despite failures.

The difference between the near immediate repair value and the extended operation value under consideration is the "cost" for the extended operation of the by-wire platform. It is the decreased safety due to prolonged operation despite subsystem failure. The increased comfort comes at a price. We will discuss targets for safety and the comfort tradeoff in the next sections.

Unless varied or mentioned otherwise, the values used to produce the reliability numbers are the representative values of *Table 1* and *Table 2* – namely the number of active nodes is 10, the time between perfect detection of faults (service or mission interval) is 150 hours, link failure rate is 10^{-6}, the arbitrary and fail-silent component failure rates are 10^{-7} and 10^{-5} respectively, and the extended operation time (repair rate) is 1 hour.

Note that the graphs include lines between the different values, although the x-axis results are not drawn proportionally to their value. This design makes it easier to identify different scenarios or parameters in the graph. The reader should not infer a direct trend from the lines. Also watch the logarithmic y-axis scales.

5.1. Comparison BRAIN versus Dual Star

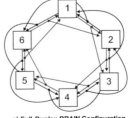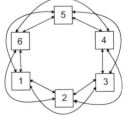

a) Full-Duplex BRAIN Configuration   b) Half-Duplex BRAIN Configuration

Figure 2: BRAIN configurations

The BRAIN comes in two configurations having slightly different forwarding algorithms. The full-duplex (FD) BRAIN configuration deploys full-duplex links for direct and skip links, so nodes have dedicated point-to-point links in both directions. The other configuration is a half-duplex (HD) BRAIN where nodes are connected with one shared wire pair, and only one node of the two sharing a link can send at a time to avoid collisions.

The HD BRAIN is the preferred solution for automotive systems, as it has fewer pins (80 over 120) and wires (60 over 80) compared to a 10-nodes FD BRAIN. The configurations deploy slightly different protocol mechanisms, but essentially aim at the same goals—prevention of fault propagation and error detection coverage for propagation. The model of the FD BRAIN is nearly the same, except that more hardware (e.g. redundant links) allows tolerance of more faults, although the greater amount of hardware means that more can fail.

This section compares the extended operation capabilities for two BRAIN configurations and three dual-star configurations.

In the dual star configurations, frames are protected with a 24-bit CRC for data integrity in Configuration 1 (called "Star (24 bits)") and with 32 bits in Configuration 2 (called "Star (32 bits)"). In Configuration 3, the protection of inline integrity is assumed to be perfect (perfect isolation) and end systems are able to choose the correct data from the correct star, leading to no integrity violation and safety implication in case of an arbitrarily faulty star. A self-checking guardian may be a real implementation of such a near perfect guardian. Alternatively, diagnosis algorithms at the end systems may provide increased protection. The third configuration is supplied only for reference to evaluate the impact of inline integrity (CRCs) on the reliability of the platform. Similar reliability numbers may be achievable for triplex stars without reliance on inline integrity if voting is deployed to mask a faulty star.

Figure 3 shows the results of comparing different architectures. As mentioned above, the 1-minute extended operation is probably the optimal safety number one can achieve. The numbers for the BRAIN are below the 10^{-9} target mentioned for up to the 2-hour extended period. One hour was the proposed extended operation that would be needed to achieve the comfort to drive to the next garage or home. For the HD BRAIN, this results in a "decreased" safety number of 3.92×10^{-12} to 2.34×10^{-10}, but is still above the 10^{-9} failures/hour target. Thus, the increased comfort of continuous operation leads to a safety number that is still acceptable.

One might initially (but wrongly) conclude that the FD BRAIN would be more reliable because additional links support full-duplex operation, which should also make the FD BRAIN more robust to redundancy exhaustion. Yet, this is not the case; the HD BRAIN is actually slightly more robust compared to the FD BRAIN despite less hardware. The additional hardware of the FD BRAIN is offset by more parts failing.

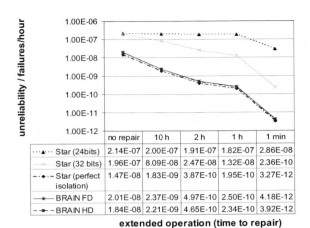

	no repair	10 h	2 h	1 h	1 min
···▲··· Star (24bits)	2.14E-07	2.00E-07	1.91E-07	1.82E-07	2.86E-08
—×— Star (32 bits)	1.96E-07	8.09E-08	2.47E-08	1.32E-08	2.36E-10
− ·◆· − Star (perfect isolation)	1.47E-08	1.83E-09	3.87E-10	1.95E-10	3.27E-12
—✳— BRAIN FD	2.01E-08	2.37E-09	4.97E-10	2.50E-10	4.18E-12
− ·●· − BRAIN HD	1.84E-08	2.21E-09	4.65E-10	2.34E-10	3.92E-12

extended operation (time to repair)

Figure 3: Normalized reliability for BRAIN and dual-star networks

Overall, BRAIN is very strong compared to dual star architectures. While the reference model with perfect inline error detection coverage (called "star (perfect isolation)") is at the same safety level as BRAIN variants, indicating a correct model, the actual dual star approaches have significantly lower reliability numbers due to the imperfect inline integrity (CRC) error coverage resulting in some integrity violations per hour.

The results show that dual stars with 32bit CRC can meet the 10^{-9} target only for immediate repair and the use of 24bit version does not meet the 10^{-9} target at all.

Given that the number of connectors and links for a dual-star and the HD BRAIN is the same and no additional star component is needed, the BRAIN achieves a significant increase in system dependability.

5.2. Sensitivity to Component Failure Rate

5.2.1. Arbitrary Mode. *Figure 4* presents the sensitivity of reliability numbers to arbitrary component failures. Such data can support decisions about whether to integrate communication functionality into single chips. The larger the die area, the more likely arbitrary failures modes are according to reliability models of chips.

5.2.2. Fail-Silent Mode. *Figure 5* depicts the sensitivity of the BRAIN to fail-silent component failures. With a low MTBF of 50000 hours (failure rate of 2×10^{-5}) the two hour extended operation is very close to the safety target 10^{-9}, probably too close if model inaccuracies where evaluated.

5.3. Sensitivity to Link Failure Rate

Figure 6 depicts the reliability for varying link failure rates. With an increasing link failure rate, the sensitivity of the reliability seems to increase. At a link failure rate of 5×10^{-6} and one hour extended operation, the reliability is close to a 10^{-9} safety target.

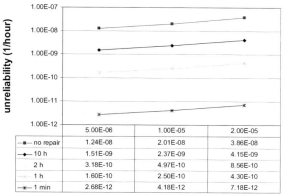

Figure 4: Normalized reliability dependent on component failure rate (arbitrary mode)

component failure rate; arbitrary mode	5.00E-06	1.00E-05	2.00E-05
no repair	1.24E-08	2.01E-08	3.86E-08
10 h	1.51E-09	2.37E-09	4.15E-09
2 h	3.18E-10	4.97E-10	8.56E-10
1 h	1.60E-10	2.50E-10	4.30E-10
1 min	2.68E-12	4.18E-12	7.18E-12

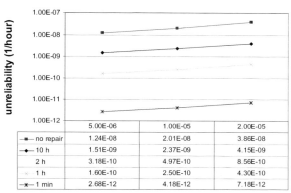

Figure 5: Normalized reliability dependent on component failure rate (fail-silent mode)

component failure rate; fail-silent mode	5.00E-06	1.00E-05	2.00E-05
no repair	1.24E-08	2.01E-08	3.86E-08
10 h	1.51E-09	2.37E-09	4.15E-09
2 h	3.18E-10	4.97E-10	8.56E-10
1 h	1.60E-10	2.50E-10	4.30E-10
1 min	2.68E-12	4.18E-12	7.18E-12

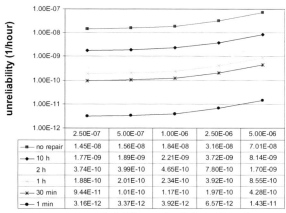

Figure 6: Normalized reliability dependent on link failure rate

link failure rate (failures/hour)	2.50E-07	5.00E-07	1.00E-06	2.50E-06	5.00E-06
no repair	1.45E-08	1.56E-08	1.84E-08	3.16E-08	7.01E-08
10 h	1.77E-09	1.89E-09	2.21E-09	3.72E-09	8.14E-09
2 h	3.74E-10	3.99E-10	4.65E-10	7.80E-10	1.70E-09
1 h	1.88E-10	2.01E-10	2.34E-10	3.92E-10	8.55E-10
30 min	9.44E-11	1.01E-10	1.17E-10	1.97E-10	4.28E-10
1 min	3.16E-12	3.37E-12	3.92E-12	6.57E-12	1.43E-11

5.4. Sensitivity to Active Components

Figure 7 depicts sensitivity of safety to the number of components. The BRAIN is a ring network and, thus, in addition to a larger number of components that can fail, ring serialization does have a slight impact. To a large extent, the skip link offsets for faulty components. Overall, the reliability decreases only slightly.

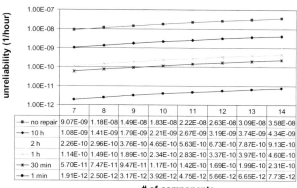

# of components	7	8	9	10	11	12	13	14
no repair	9.07E-09	1.18E-08	1.49E-08	1.83E-08	2.22E-08	2.63E-08	3.09E-08	3.58E-08
10 h	1.08E-09	1.41E-09	1.79E-09	2.21E-09	2.67E-09	3.19E-09	3.74E-09	4.34E-09
2 h	2.26E-10	2.96E-10	3.76E-10	4.65E-10	5.63E-10	6.73E-10	7.87E-10	9.13E-10
1 h	1.14E-10	1.49E-10	1.89E-10	2.34E-10	2.83E-10	3.37E-10	3.97E-10	4.60E-10
30 min	5.70E-11	7.47E-11	9.47E-11	1.17E-10	1.42E-10	1.69E-10	1.99E-10	2.31E-10
1 min	1.91E-12	2.50E-12	3.17E-12	3.92E-12	4.75E-12	5.66E-12	6.65E-12	7.73E-12

Figure 7: Normalized reliability dependent on number of components

5.5. Sensitivity to Platform Algorithm Parameters

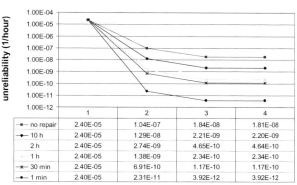

# of self-checking pairs	1	2	3	4
no repair	2.40E-05	1.04E-07	1.84E-08	1.81E-08
10 h	2.40E-05	1.29E-08	2.21E-09	2.20E-09
2 h	2.40E-05	2.74E-09	4.65E-10	4.64E-10
1 h	2.40E-05	1.38E-09	2.34E-10	2.34E-10
30 min	2.40E-05	6.91E-10	1.17E-10	1.17E-10
1 min	2.40E-05	2.31E-11	3.92E-12	3.92E-12

Figure 8: Normalized reliability dependent on number of self-checking pairs

Protocol mechanisms such as self-checking clock synchronization, startup, and clique aggregation deployed on the ring are easily extensible, which proved critical for the reliability performance. *Figure 8* indicates that with the deployment of only one self-checking pair, this pair dominates the safety impact. With an increasing number of self-checking pairs deployed, the reliability impact of a self-checking pair failure on the system diminishes. For three and four pairs, the numbers are largely the same. While two neighboring nodes can easily be paired to supply self-checking protocol functionality and without creating a swamping effect, losing hardware because of failures equivalent to more than two self-checking pair failures is probably already a death state for redundancy-constraint applications such as applications in the automotive domain. Yet, it is interesting that one or two self-checking pairs are not enough for the most optimal platform dependability performance.

5.6. Sensitivity to Service Interval Time

This paper argues that removal of latent faults can only occur when a car is serviced, approximately every 150 hours. Alternatively, techniques could be deployed that perform sufficient testing more often, say after every trip (e.g. when the car electronics is powered down). Similar self-test techniques are deployed in aerospace systems and—assuming independent devices self test and have sufficient error detection coverage—could decrease the "vulnerability" window drastically. The low service interval numbers of 0.5 or 1 hours should model such alternative approaches.

In the past, a car's operational life was approximately 4000 hours [28]. Today, some manufacturer's goals are even higher and approaching 6000 hours. The long service intervals should show the effect if no scrubbing (latent fault detection) is done during the vehicle life time. Similarly, such long service intervals may address some effects of silicon wear-outs [21], as the failure rate may no longer be assumed to be constant. With loss of constant failure rates the "memory-less" properties of failure rates vanish and the actual age of the electronics comes into consideration.

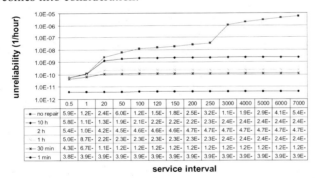

	0.5	1	20	50	100	120	150	200	250	3000	4000	5000	6000	7000
no repair	5.9E-	1.2E-	2.4E-	6.0E-	1.2E-	1.5E-	1.8E-	2.5E-	3.2E-	1.1E-	1.9E-	2.9E-	4.1E-	5.4E-
10 h	5.8E-	1.1E-	1.3E-	1.9E-	2.1E-	2.2E-	2.2E-	2.3E-	2.4E-	2.4E-	2.4E-	2.4E-	2.4E-	2.4E-
2 h	5.4E-	1.0E-	4.2E-	4.5E-	4.6E-	4.6E-	4.6E-	4.7E-	4.7E-	4.7E-	4.7E-	4.7E-	4.7E-	4.7E-
1 h	5.0E-	8.7E-	2.2E-	2.3E-	2.3E-	2.3E-	2.3E-	2.3E-	2.4E-	2.4E-	2.4E-	2.4E-	2.4E-	2.4E-
30 min	4.3E-	6.7E-	1.1E-	1.2E-	1.2E-	1.2E-	1.2E-	1.2E-	1.2E-	1.2E-	1.2E-	1.2E-	1.2E-	1.2E-
1 min	3.8E-	3.9E-	3.9E-	3.9E-	3.9E-	3.9E-	3.9E-	3.9E-	3.9E-	3.9E-	3.9E-	3.9E-	3.9E-	3.9E-

service interval

Figure 9: Normalized reliability dependent on service interval

Figure 9 should show some of the platform level effects. As expected, the safety is largely independent of service intervals for the "immediate repair" scenario. Recall that the BRAIN has perfect fault detection properties because of the bit-for-bit comparison for the platform communication propagation service, which explains the outcome.

Except for the "no repair" scenario, all other scenarios "stabilize" (or stay nearly constant) at a safety level from 50 hours service interval onwards. Once a failure occurs, another failure is unlikely within the interval to the next service. For the "no repair scenario," the safety decreases at a higher rate and the dependability decreases with increasing service time, reflecting the propensity for faults when the platform is not scrubbed for latent faults and the "reliability clocks" of components are not reset. Similar behavior might be observed with effects such as aging silicon [21].

6. Conclusions

The results presented in this paper illustrate the benefits of the BRAIN's hybrid behavior using the added 'skip links' for both integrity and availability augmentation. The full coverage of the high-integrity data propagation of the BRAIN offers a significant improvement over the inline error coverage of the dual-star architectures. The half-duplex BRAIN also has an slightly better reliability overall, with fewer components and similar connectivity requirements. From our analysis, we conclude that extended operation with a fault is possible with certain configurations of the BRAIN architecture.

Extended operation with dual star configuration also looks promising in relation to x-by-wire. However, the star architecture's sensitivity to the quality of inline error-detection mechanisms have also been illustrated. The ability to augment this with improved, higher-level diagnosis functions such as error strike counters may considerably improve the system dependability claims. In addition, the introduction of strike counters into the BRAIN may also increase system dependability; the refinement of such strike-counting policies will be the subject of future work. Over-zealous indictment must also be carefully considered to reduce the risk of resource exhaustion from the impact of transient errors.

The reader is finally cautioned that this work has assumed a constant failure rate for the electronics components examined. As the impact of technology improvements such as decreasing geometries and the associated vulnerabilities of silicon wear-outs [21] are considered, some of the assumptions that underpin the reliability assessment may need to be revisited. Reliability assessment when such effects are considered may be a considerable challenge. However, the full coverage and fault detection presented by architectures such as BRAIN may help mitigate such effects.

Similarly, frequent and regular service intervals for testing automotive electronics may not be accepted by customers, as prevention of failing of components may not be perceived as immediate added value to passenger safety. The model in this paper could be extended to include more frequent self-test diagnosis (e.g. at power-down), which typically achieves less error detection coverage, but may achieve higher safety numbers for similar service intervals.

7. References

[1] Wilwert, C., N. Navet, Y. Song, and F. Simonot-Lion "Design of automotive x-by-wire systems", *The Industrial Communication Technology Handbook*, Dec 2004.

[2] Navet, N., Y. Song, F. Simonot-Lion, and C. Wilwert. "Trends in Automotive Communication Systems", *Proc. of the IEEE* 93, 6 (2005).

[3] Wilwert, C., F. Simonot-Lion, Y. Song, and F. Simonot. "Quantitative Evaluation of the Safety of X-by-Wire Architectures Subject to EMI Perturbations." *3rd Nancy-Saarbruecken Workshop on Logic, Proofs, and Programs*, Nancy, Oct. 13-14, 2005.

[4] Geist, R. and K. Trivedi. "Reliability Estimation of Fault-Tolerant Systems: Tools and Techniques." *IEEE Computer*, Vol. 23, No 7, July 1990.

[5] Courtney, T., S. Derisavi, S. Gaonkar, M. Griffith, V. Lam, M. McQuinn, E. Rozier and W.H. Sanders. "The Mobius Modeling Environment: Recent Extensions—2005", *Proc. of the 2nd Int. Conf. on the Quantitative Evaluation of Systems (QEST'05)*, IEEE, Washington, DC, USA, 2005.

[6] Avizienis, A., J.-C. Laprie, B. Randell, and C. Landwehr, <Basic Concepts and Taxonomy of Dependable and Secure Computing", *Trans. On Dependable and Secure Computing*, Vol. 1, No. 1, IEEE, Jan-Mar 2004.

[7] IEC. IEC61508 *Functional Safety*. Parts 0 to 7. 1998, 2000, and 2005.

[8] Leveson, N.G. *System Safety Engineering: Back to the Future. Aeronautics and Astronautics*. Massachusetts Institute of Technology. Draft. 2002.

[9] SAE. *ARP 4754 (Aerospace Recommended Practice). Certification Considerations for Highly Integrated or Complex Aircraft Systems*. Society of Automotive Engineers. Nov. 1996.

[10] International Standards Organization. ISO 26262. *Road Vehicles. Functional Safety*. In preparation. 2006.

[11] Hammett, R.C. and P.S. Babcock. *Achieving 10^{-9} Dependability with Drive-by-Wire Systems*. Society of Automotive Engineers (SAE) Technical Paper Series, Paper 2003-01-1290, 2003.

[12] Latronico, E. and P. Koopman. "Design time reliability analysis of distributed fault tolerance algorithms", *Proc. Int. Conf. on Dependable Systems and Networks*, IEEE, pp. 486–495. 2005.

[13] Butler, R. "The SURE Approach to Reliability Analysis", *IEEE Trans. on Reliability*, Vol. 41, No. 2, June 1992.

[14] The EASIS Consortium. *EASIS Project Glossary. Electronic Architecture and System Engineering for Integrated Safety Systems*, Deliverable D0.1.1. http://www.easis.org/. Aug. 2004.

[15] Bridal, O. "Reliability Estimates for Repairable Fault-Tolerant Systems", *Nordic Seminar for Repairable Fault-Tolerant Systems*. Lungby, Denmark, 1994.

[16] Bridal, O. "A methodology for reliability analysis of fault-tolerant systems with repairable subsystems", In *Proc. of the 2nd int. Conf. on Mathematics of Dependable Systems II* (Univ. of York, England). V. Stavridou, Ed. Oxford University Press, New York, NY, 195-208. 1997.

[17] Hall, B., M. Paulitsch, and K. Driscoll, *FlexRay BRAIN Fusion—A FlexRay-Based Braided Ring Availability Integrity Network*, submitted to SAE Congress. 2007.

[18] Hall, B. Driscoll, K., Paulitsch, M., Dajani-Brown, S. "Ringing out fault tolerance. A new ring network for superior low-cost dependability", In *Proc. of Int. Conf. on Dependable Systems and Networks*. pp.298-307. 28 June-1 July 2005.

[19] Lamport, L. and P.M. Melliar-Smith. "Byzantine clock synchronization", In *Proc. of ACM Symp. on Principles of Distributed Computing*. Vancouver, British Columbia, Canada, ACM Press. Aug. 27-29, 1984.

[20] Hoyme, K. and K. Driscoll, "SAFEbus", *IEEE AES Systems Magazine*, March 1993.

[21] Condra, L. *The Impact of semiconductor device trends on aerospace systems*. Report. Boeing. 2002.

[22] Paulitsch, M., J. Morris, B. Hall, K. Driscoll, and P. Koopman. "Coverage and the Use of Cyclic Redundancy Codes in Ultra-Dependable systems", In *Proc. of Int. Conf. on Dependable Systems and Networks*. pp. 346-355. 28 June-1 July 2005.

[23] Bertoluzzo, M., G. Buja, and A. Zuccollo. "Communication Networks for Drive-By-Wire Applications", *11th Int. Conf. on Power Electronics and Motion Control*. European Power Electronics&Drives Ass. Riga, Latvia 2004.

[24] Kopetz, H. and G. Bauer. "The Time-Triggered Architecture", *Proc. of IEEE*. Vol. 91(1). pp. 112-126. 2003.

[25] FlexRay Consortium. *FlexRay Communications System*. Protocol Specification. Version 2.1. Dec. 2005.

[26] Department of Defense. U.S. *MIL-HDBK-217 Reliability Prediction of Electronic Equipment. Version F*. 1991.

[27] CALCE. Center for Advanced Life Cycle Engineering. University of Maryland. http://www.calce.umd.edu/.

[28] Lupini, C.A. *Vehicle Multiplex Communication—Serial Data Networking Applied to Vehicular Engineering*, 2004.

[29] Allied Business Intelligence. *X-By-Wire. A Strategic Analysis of In-Vehicle Multiplexing and Next-Generation Safety-Critical Control Systems*. 2003.

[30] Personal conversation with Dan Johnson, Honeywell Aerospace, Advanced Technology. Nov. 2006.

[31] SAE. *ARP 5107 (Aerospace Recommended Practice). Guidelines for Time-Limited-Dispatch Analysis for Electronic Engine Control Systems*. Rev. B. Society of Automotive Engineers. Nov 2006.

[32] IEEE. IEEE standard test access port and boundary - scan architecture. 21 May 1990.

[33] Kanoun, K. and D. Powell. "Dependability evaluation of bus and ring communication topologies for the Delta-4 distributed fault-tolerant architecture", In *Proc. of 10th Symp. on Reliable Distributed Systems*. Pisa, Italy. 1991.

[34] AUTOSAR (AUTomotive Open System ARchitecture). http://www.autosar.org/. Accessed Dec. 2006.

[35] SAE. *ARP 4761 (Aerospace Recommended Practice). Guidelines and Methods for Conducting the Safety Assessment Process on Civil Airborne Systems and Equipment*. Society of Automotive Engineers. Dec. 1996.

[36] Constantinscu, C. "Dependability evaluation of a fault-tolerant processor by GSPN modeling", *IEEE Transactions on Reliability*. Vol. 54 No 3 pp. 468-474. 2005.

[37] Reschovsky, C. *Journey to Work: 2000. Census 2000 Brief*. United States Census 2000. U.S. Dept. of Commerce. March, 2004

A Tunable Add-On Diagnostic Protocol for Time-Triggered Systems *

Marco Serafini and Neeraj Suri
TU Darmstadt, Germany
{marco, suri}@informatik.tu-darmstadt.de

Jonny Vinter
SP, Sweden
jonny.vinter@sp.se

Astrit Ademaj
TU Vienna, Austria
ademaj@vmars.tuwien.ac.at

Wolfgang Brandstätter
Audi, Germany
wolfgang.brandstaetter@audi.de

Fulvio Tagliabò
Fiat, Italy
fulvio.tagliabo@crf.it

Jens Koch
Airbus Deutschland, Germany
jens.koch@airbus.com

Abstract

We present a tunable diagnostic protocol for generic time-triggered (TT) systems to detect crash and send/receive omission faults. Compared to existing diagnostic and membership protocols for TT systems, it does not rely on the single-fault assumption and tolerates malicious faults. It runs at the application level and can be added on top of any TT system (possibly as a middleware component) without requiring modifications at the system level. The information on detected faults is accumulated using a penalty/reward algorithm to handle transient faults. After a fault is detected, the likelihood of node isolation can be adapted to different system configurations, including those where functions with different criticality levels are integrated. Using actual automotive and aerospace parameters, we experimentally demonstrate the transient fault handling capabilities of the protocol.

1. Introduction and contributions

In both automotive and aerospace X-by-wire applications, TT platforms such as Flexray [1], TTP/C [2], SAFEbus [3] and TT-Ethernet are increasingly being adopted. Most TT platform develops its static, built-in diagnostic and membership approach. Instead, we define an on-line diagnostic/membership protocol that is a tunable and portable add-on application level module. It can be integrated as a plug-in middleware module (as an application) onto any TT system, without interference with other functionalities. It only uses information that is available at the application level, does not impose constraints on the scheduling of the system, and has low bandwidth requirements. For TT platforms, such as FlexRay, SAFEbus and TT-Ethernet, that do not have a standardized diagnostic or membership protocol, our add-on protocol represents a viable solution for such functionalities.

Our diagnostic protocol exploits specific features of TT systems where multiple nodes access a shared broadcast bus using TDMA communication. The ability of a node to *send* correct messages in the designated time window (called *sending slot*) is used as a periodic diagnostic test. The protocol is able to detect bursts of multiple concurrent faults and to tolerate malicious faults. Its resiliency also scales with the number of available nodes.

The key purpose of a diagnostic protocol is to trigger correct and timely recovery/maintenance actions, particularly for safety critical subsystems. However, a diagnostic protocol needs also consider availability and avoid unnecessary substitutions of correct components in case of external transient faults, which are becoming more frequent [4]. An "ideal" diagnostic protocol would exclude only nodes with internal faults. In practice, however, internal faults do not always manifest as permanent faults at the interface of the node (e.g. crashes). They can also manifest as multiple, subsequent intermittent faults which, to external observers, appear similar to external transient faults. We consider an *extended fault model* to characterize *healthy* and *unhealthy* nodes based on the presence of internal faults. In order to recognize unhealthy nodes, a *penalty/reward (p/r) algorithm* delays the isolation of faulty nodes to accumulate on-line diagnostic information. This is a novel extension of the basis developed in [5, 6] and represents an application of our alternative p/r model [7].

A problem similar to diagnosis is membership, which consists of identifying the set of nodes (called membership view) that have received the same set of messages. We will show that a variant of our protocol can act as a membership service and detect the formation of multiple *cliques* of receivers with inconsistent information.

We have implemented the protocol in a prototype, reproducing practical automotive and aerospace settings. Using physical fault injection, we experimentally validate the properties of the protocol and show how to tune the parameters of the p/r algorithm in a realistic environment.

The paper is organized as follows. Following the related

*Research supported in part by EC DECOS, ReSIST and DFG TUD-GK MM work in Sec. 2, we introduce the system and fault models in Sec. 3 and 4. The tunable add-on diagnostic protocol and its properties are presented in Sec. 5 and 6. The protocol is extended to a membership protocol in Sec. 7. Sec. 8 describes the experimental validation of both protocols. We detail parameter tuning in Sec. 9. Sec. 10 discusses the portability of the middleware to different TT platforms.

2. Related work

The general diagnosis problem was formulated in the PMC model [8], where a set of active entities test each other until sufficient information exists to locate the faulty nodes. In on-line, real time settings the comparison approach is recommended [9], where the same functionality is executed on different nodes and the results are compared.

Multiple research efforts have targeted diagnosis for specific error models, and for improving specific attributes such as latency reduction, coverage and bandwidth. The family of diagnostic protocols for generic synchronous systems proposed by Walter et al. [11] considers a frame-based communication scheme where nodes exchange messages in synchronous parallel rounds using a fully connected topology and unidirectional links. Similar to consensus [18, 10], all nodes exchange their local view on the correctness of the messages received by the other nodes and combine them using hybrid voting to achieve consistent diagnosis.

We adapt the on-line diagnosis approach of [11] as a middleware service for TT systems, where multiple nodes access a shared broadcast bus using a TDMA communication scheme. Our add-on protocol explicitly takes into account the internal scheduling of each node and the overall global communication scheduling of the system. We extend the protocol to consider the cases of communication blackout, which can arise if particularly long transient bursts corrupt all sending slots in the TDMA round. We also show how to modify the protocol to provide membership information. Finally, we define a new p/r algorithm to handle transient faults based on the criticality of the applications executing on different nodes.

A count-and-threshold fault detection function (called α-count) is introduced in [5, 6] to discriminate between transient and intermittent faults. The fundamental tradeoffs in its tuning are explored using stochastic evaluation. Our alternate p/r model, which develops an overall FDIR (Fault Detection, Isolation and Reconfiguration) strategy, is introduced and analyzed in [7]. In this work we present how to experimentally tune the p/r algorithm in realistic settings.

The problem of group membership is often defined similar to diagnosis [12]. Cristian [13] proposed a membership protocol for synchronous crash-only systems that is based on an expensive fault-tolerant atomic broadcast primitive to achieve consistency. Such an approach is impractical in TT systems due to its high latency and bandwidth requirement.

A membership protocol specifically designed for TTP/C systems was proposed by Kopetz et al. [2, 14]. It relies on the "single fault assumption", i.e., it does not tolerate simultaneous faults, and assumes non-malicious node failures. The protocol allows identification of one fault in the communication of a message. Besides faulty senders, the protocol also detects if asymmetric receiver faults cause the formation of different cliques of nodes. The latency is two communication slots in the case of sender faults and two TDMA rounds in case of receiver faults. The bandwidth required is $O(N)$ bits per message and $O(N^2)$ bits per round, where N is the number of system nodes. If a (possibly transient) faulty node is detected it is generally restarted, generating a window of vulnerability to subsequent failures. An extension of this protocol was proposed by Ezichelvan and Lemos [15] to tolerate up to half of senders being simultaneously faulty with a latency of three TDMA rounds. Our protocol tolerates multiple coincident non-malicious and malicious faults with the same bandwidth requirement. Due to its add-on and generic nature, it has a higher latency. However, in Sec. 10 we show that a system-level variant of our protocol features a latency of two TDMA rounds.

3. System model

We assume a synchronous system model and a network topology where all nodes access a shared (and possibly replicated) communication bus using a TDMA access scheme, i.e., a periodic schedule where each node is assigned a time window, called *sending slot*, in each *TDMA round* (or round). The periodic *global communication schedule*, including when each slot begins and terminates, is defined at design time and executed by a *communication controller*. The communication controller features a local collision detection mechanism, which checks if messages sent by the node can actually be read from the bus.

The systems consists of N nodes with unique IDs $\{1, ..., N\}$ assigned following the order of the sending slots in the round. Correct nodes can identify a sender by its sending time and there is no message forging. Faulty nodes cannot corrupt messages sent by correct nodes.

Communication among jobs, including those running on different nodes, is abstracted by a vector of shared variables $\langle v_1, \ldots, v_N \rangle$ called *interface variables*. Communication controllers automatically update their value by sending and receiving messages according to the global communication schedule. Copies of the interface variables are updated at the receivers after every sending slot is completed. Updates follow the sending order of the corresponding messages. Interface variables can be updated at most once per round.

Each interface variable has a corresponding *validity bit*. This is set to 0 by the communication controller when the value of the variable can no longer be considered correct. If an interface variable v_i has node i as its unique sender and is updated at each round, we can assume that the communication controller uses its *local error detection mechanisms* to set the validity bit of v_i at the receiver node j to 0 iff node j was not able to receive the last message sent by i that was supposed to update v_i, and 1 otherwise. Validity bits are updated together with the corresponding messages.

Besides the global communication schedule, each node has its own internal *node schedule* that determines when jobs are executed. In a TDMA access scheme, the sending slot of a node overlaps with the computational phase of other nodes. The node schedule can thus have an effect on the "freshness" of the *read* interface state, i.e., the round where the values of the interface variables were sent. For example, if a job is executed at the beginning of a round it will only read values sent in the previous rounds. The node schedule also determines the round when the data written in the interface state is actually *sent* on the bus. A job might be able to send its output data in the same round as it is executed only if it is scheduled before the sending slot of the hosting node. To increase the portability of our add-on protocol, we do not constrain the scheduling of nodes.

4. Fault model

We use a Customizable Fault-Effect Model [16] which refers to the *communication errors* in the broadcast of a message. A received faulty message is *locally detectable* if it is syntactically incorrect in the value domain or early/late/missing in the time domain; it is *malicious* faulty if it is *not* locally detectable but is semantically incorrect in the value domain.

Correspondingly, we partition faults into three classes:

- *symmetric benign*: (or benign) message is locally detectable by *all* the receivers (excluding the sender);
- *symmetric malicious*: all the receivers receive the same malicious message;
- *asymmetric*: message is locally detectable by at least one but not all the receivers (excluding the sender).

We assume broadcast channels, where different locally undetectable messages cannot be asymmetrically received by different nodes. Asymmetries in the local detection of messages can be an effect, for example, of Slightly-Off-Specification faults (SOS) [17], when the clock of a node is close to the allowed offset and thus the messages it sends are seen as timely only by a subset of the receivers. Another example is when EMI disturbs only part of the bus.

We classify nodes based on the communication errors they display in their outgoing messages, e.g., benign faulty sender, malicious faulty sender etc. We assume that each node can display only one type of communication error throughout one execution of the protocol. *Correct* nodes send messages without faults. *Obedient* nodes follow the program instructions and execute only correct internal state transitions. They can either be correct or suffer omission failures while sending or receiving messages.

For diagnosis, we do not assume permanent faults but consider an *extended fault model* instead, where all nodes alternate periods of faulty behavior, when they are not able to correctly send messages, and periods of correct behavior. We consider a node:

- *healthy*, if it suffers only sporadic and external transient faults;
- *unhealthy*, if it suffers internal faults which manifest as intermittent or permanent communication faults.

We implicitly assume that internal faults will manifest at the interface of the node either (a) as permanent sender faults (a long faulty burst) or (b) as intermittent faults with a shorter time to reappearance than external transient faults. A crashed node, for example, is an unhealthy node that permanently displays benign faults.

5. The on-line diagnostic protocol

The purpose of the on-line diagnostic protocol is to detect and isolate unhealthy nodes from the system at runtime. It is composed of two algorithms. The first algorithm forms a *consistent health vector* to consistently locate benign faulty senders, the second accumulates the diagnostic information using the p/r algorithm to distinguish (in a probabilistic manner) between healthy and unhealthy nodes.

Each node i runs, at each round, the diagnostic job $diag_i$, which sends a non-replicated diagnostic message dm_i and receives all the other interface variables $\langle dm_1, \ldots, dm_N \rangle$. The communication controller provides a validity bit for each interface variable dm_j sent from $diag_j$ to $diag_i$ using its local error detection mechanisms. By checking the validity bits of the diagnostic messages, the protocol diagnoses communication errors. The *local syndrome* of node i is the binary N-tuple containing its local view on the messages sent by other nodes (faulty/not faulty). The diagnostic message dm_i contains the local syndrome broadcast by node i and its size is $O(N)$.

The diagnostic protocol consists of five phases:

1) *Local detection*: Communication errors are locally detected by observing the local validity bits of the diagnostic messages. A new *local syndrome* is formed as a binary N-tuple.

2) *Dissemination*: The local syndrome is *broadcast* using the diagnostic message dm_i.

3) *Aggregation*: Receive all local syndromes dm_j corresponding to the same previous *diagnosed round*. Form a *diagnostic matrix* for that round where *row i* is the local syndrome sent from node i and *column j* is a vector representing the opinion on node j of all other nodes.

4) *Analysis*: A binary N-tuple called *consistent health vector*, which contains the consistent distributed view on the health of all system nodes in the diagnosed round, is calculated. To combine the local syndromes sent by different nodes, a hybrid voting [11, 18] over the *columns* of the diagnostic matrix is performed. If enough nodes observed a benign fault, the sending node is considered faulty.

5) *Update counters*: Based on the consistent health vector, update the *penalty and reward counters* associated to a node, and possibly isolate faulty nodes.

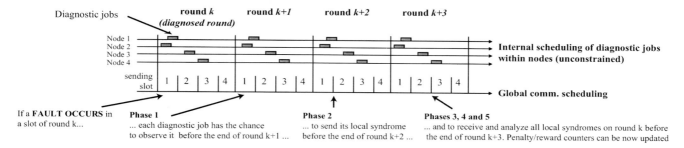

Diagnostic jobs

Node 1
Node 2
Node 3
Node 4

round k
(diagnosed round)   **round k+1**   **round k+2**   **round k+3**

Internal scheduling of diagnostic jobs within nodes (unconstrained)

sending slot | 1 | 2 | 3 | 4 | 1 | 2 | 3 | 4 | 1 | 2 | 3 | 4 | 1 | 2 | 3 | 4 |

Global comm. scheduling

If a **FAULT OCCURS** in a slot of round k...

Phase 1
... each diagnostic job has the chance to observe it before the end of round k+1 ...

Phase 2
... to send its local syndrome before the end of round k+2 ...

Phases 3, 4 and 5
... and to receive and analyze all local syndromes on round k before the end of round k+3. Penalty/reward counters can be now updated

Figure 1: High level overview of the diagnostic protocol in a system with four nodes

The phases of the protocol are executed in consecutive TDMA rounds, and phases of multiple instances of the protocol are interleaved at each execution of $diag_i$ (Fig. 1). The pseudo code of the diagnostic job $diag_i$, running on each node i, is presented in Alg. 1.

Consistent location of faulty senders. Local detection and aggregation entail reading the interface variables and their validity bits. We do not constrain the scheduling of the diagnostic jobs in a round. Thus, we need to consider that, in a TDMA communication scheme, diagnostic jobs running on different nodes can see different views of the interface variables, as the freshness of the read data can vary.

Consider a diagnostic job $diag_i$ which, at round k, reads from the interface variables the values of the diagnostic messages $dm_1, \ldots, dm_N$ and their validity bits. As diagnostic messages are sent at every round, the read values were sent (following the sending order) either on round k or $k-1$. Hence there is a locally known integer $l_i \in [0, N-1]$, determined by the internal schedule of $diag_i$ within node i, such that values of $dm_1, \ldots, dm_{l_i}$ were sent in round k, while values $dm_{l_i+1}, \ldots, dm_N$ were sent in round $k-1$ (the same holds for their validity bits)[1]. For all diagnostic jobs executed in round k to consistently use *aligned* diagnostic messages (resp. validity bits) from round $k-1$, the protocol executes a *read alignment* operation (Fig. 2; Alg. 1, Lines 3-6). Read alignment combines in variables al_dm_j (al_ls_j) values $prev\_dm_{[1, i]}$ ($prev\_ls_{[1, i]}$) from the previous round and of $curr\_dm_{[i+1, N]}$ ($curr\_ls_{[i+1, N]}$) from the current. This requires buffering of messages and validity bits (lines 16-17), and introduces additional delays in the communication.

For *local detection*, the validity bits are read (Alg. 1, line 2) and combined using read alignment (lines 3-6). The vector al_ls contains in round k the local syndromes corresponding to the messages sent in round $k-1$.

During the *dissemination* phase a *send alignment* is also needed to ensure that, despite unconstrained node scheduling, all local syndromes sent in round k refer to a same

previous diagnosed round, as required by the aggregation phase executed in the following round. We define the predicate $send\_curr\_round_j$ to be true if, according to the internal schedule of node i, the diagnostic messages formed by the diagnostic job $diag_j$ at round k can be sent in round k (i.e., $diag_j$ is completed before the sending slot of the node). If the predicate holds for all nodes, all current local syndromes can be immediately written in the interface state (line 7) and the latency of the protocol is reduced. However this global condition may not hold, or it may be impossible to locally evaluate it (e.g. if the node scheduling is dynamic, see Sec. 10). In these cases, send alignment is used to determine the data to be written in the interface variables, which will be later sent. If a job completes its execution before the sending slot of its node, it writes the local syndromes obtained in the previous round; otherwise the current local syndromes are written (lines 8-10).

The *aggregation* phase first reads the values of the local syndromes sent by all diagnostic jobs through the diagnostic messages (line 1). A special error value ε is assigned to local syndromes whose validity bit is 0. Read alignment is used to guarantee that all jobs executed in round k form a diagnostic matrix using local syndromes sent in round $k-1$, which refer to the same diagnosed round (lines 3-6); vector al_dm_j represents the jth row of the matrix. The jth element of the local syndrome sent by node i to node k can assume three possible values: 0, if i was not able to receive the message from node j in the slot of interest; 1, if i was able to receive the message from j; ε, if k was not able to receive the local syndrome from i correctly. For example, Table 1 shows the diagnostic matrix formed in case node 3

---

[1] If a diagnostic job $diag_i$ is executed after the last sending slot of a round and can read data from round k from each node, we treat it as it was executed in round $k + 1$ and set $l_i = 0$ accordingly.

Diagnostic messages (interface variables):

values read in round *k-1*

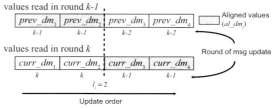

| $prev\_dm_1$ | $prev\_dm_2$ | $prev\_dm_3$ | $prev\_dm_4$ |
| k-1 | k-1 | k-2 | k-2 |

Aligned values (al_dm_j)

values read in round *k*

| $curr\_dm_1$ | $curr\_dm_2$ | $curr\_dm_3$ | $curr\_dm_4$ |
| k | k | k-1 | k-1 |

$l_i = 2$

Round of msg update

Update order

Figure 2: Example of read alignment (round k, $l_i = 2$)

167

Table 1: Example diagnostic matrix (3-4 benign faulty)

Accuser node	Local syndr.	Accused node 1	2	3	4
Node 1	al_dm_1	-	1	0	0
Node 2	al_dm_2	1	-	0	0
Node 3	al_dm_3	ε	ε	-	ε
Node 4	al_dm_4	ε	ε	ε	-
Voted $cons\_hv$		1	1	**0**	**0**

and 4 are two (coincident) benign faulty senders in both the diagnosed round and the dissemination round.

As faults can occur during the dissemination phase of the protocol, the diagnostic matrices can contain incorrect or incomplete information, and different nodes can form different diagnostic matrices due to asymmetric faults. However, a consistent global view on faults in the diagnosed round can be obtained by combining different local views using a hybrid voting function H-maj(V) (Eqn. 1) over the columns V of the matrix. The opinion of a node about itself is considered unreliable and discarded to tolerate asymmetric faults (see Sec. 6). Thus, voting is executed over the $(N-1)$-tuple V of local syndromes representing the opinions of the other nodes (lines 11-13). In order to tolerate benign faults, a hybrid voting function excludes erroneous votes ε from V ($excl(V, \varepsilon)$) before calculating the majority [18] (see example in Table 1).

As for validity bits and local syndromes, the value 0 denotes a faulty node. In case no correct local syndrome is available ($|excl(V, \varepsilon)| = 0$), the voting function can not reach a decision. This can happen only if at least $N - 1$ nodes are not able to send their local syndrome and a node is not able to determine whether it was faulty in the diagnosed round. In this case, the protocol cannot do anything else than relying on the outcome of the collision detector in the diagnosed round (line 14). The consistent health vector $cons\_hv$ is the outcome of the hybrid majority voting and contains, at round k, the agreed view on the health of each node at the diagnosed round, i.e., $k - 3$ or $k - 2$ (see Sec. 6).

$$
\text{H-maj}(V) = \begin{cases} \perp & \text{if } |excl(V, \varepsilon)| = 0 \\ v & \text{if } v = maj(excl(V, \varepsilon)) \\ & \text{and } |excl(V, \varepsilon)| \geq 1 \\ 1 & \text{else} \end{cases} \quad (1)
$$

Filtering unhealthy nodes. The consistent health vector is given as an input (Alg. 1, line 15) to the penalty/reward algorithm (Alg. 2), which is used to handle transient faults and discriminate them from intermittent and permanent faults. Each node keeps a penalty and a reward counter for each node in the system in the vectors $penalties$ and $rewards$. They are both initially set to 0. Whenever the node is detected as faulty, the corresponding penalty is increased by each node depending on the criticality of the jobs allocated on the node. Criticality levels for each node are stored in the vector $criticalities$. We discuss the selection

---

Algorithm 1: Node i diagnostic job $diag_i$

> **begin**
>
> // *Phases 1 and 3 - Local detection and Aggregation*
> // (read alignment)
> 1 $\langle curr\_dm_1, \dots, curr\_dm_N \rangle \leftarrow$ read_iface($dm_1, \dots, dm_N$);
> 2 $curr\_ls \leftarrow$ read_vbits($dm_1, \dots, dm_N$);
> 3   **for** $j \leftarrow 1, \dots, l_i$ **do**
> 4 $al\_dm_j \leftarrow prev\_dm_j$; $al\_ls[j] \leftarrow prev\_ls[j]$;
> 5   **for** $j \leftarrow l_i + 1, \dots, N$ **do**
> 6 $al\_dm_j \leftarrow curr\_dm_j$; $al\_ls[j] \leftarrow curr\_ls[j]$;
>
> // *Phase 2 - Dissemination*
> // (send alignment)
> 7   **if** $\forall j : send\_curr\_round_j$ **then** write_iface(al_ls);
> 8   **else if** $send\_curr\_round_i$ **then**
> 9   write_iface($prev\_al\_ls$);
> 10   **else** write_iface(al_ls);
>
> // *Phase 4 - Analysis*
> // (consistent location of benign faulty senders)
> 11   **for** $j \leftarrow 1, \dots, N$ **do**
> 12 $diag \leftarrow$ H-maj$\langle al\_dm_1[j], \dots, al\_dm_{j-1}[j],$ $al\_dm_{j+1}[j], \dots, al\_dm_N[j] \rangle$;
> 13   **if** $diag \neq \perp$ **then** $cons\_hv[j] \leftarrow diag$;
> 14   **else** $cons\_hv[j] \leftarrow$ coll-det($diagnosed\_round$);
>
> // *Phase 5 - Update counters*
> // (decision on node isolation)
> 15 $active \leftarrow active$ AND pen_rew($cons\_hv$);
> // (buffering for read and send alignment)
> 16 $\langle prev\_dm_1, \dots, prev\_dm_N \rangle \leftarrow$ $\langle curr\_dm_1, \dots, curr\_dm_N \rangle$;
> 17 $prev\_ls \leftarrow curr\_ls$; $prev\_al\_ls \leftarrow al\_ls$;
> **end**

---

of such criticality levels in Sec. 9. If no fault is successively detected the reward is increased by one. The algorithm uses two constants, a *penalty threshold P* and a *reward threshold R*. After a bounded amount of time either of the two thresholds is exceeded, resulting in isolation of the node or reset of the counters respectively.

The two counters, and the corresponding thresholds, represent two different kinds of information: the reward counter (threshold) indicates the (minimum) number of consecutive fault-free slots a node needs to display before the memory of its previous faults is reset; the penalty counter (threshold) indicates the (maximum) number of consecutive faulty slots a node is allowed to display before isolation.

As the health assessment of the system stored in vector $cons\_hv$ is consistently calculated in Alg. 1, the penalty and reward counters are always consistently updated, and isolations are decided in the same round by all obedient nodes.

The vector $active$ contains the status of activity of each node and represents the internal output of the diagnostic protocol (Alg. 1, line 15). Eventual traffic generated by isolated nodes must be ignored by the communication controllers of all other nodes. Upon reintegration of a node, the value of the corresponding element is set back to the initial

Algorithm 2: The p/r algorithm

```
begin
    for i ← 1, . . . , N do
        curr_act[i] ← 1;
        if cons_hv[i] = 0 then
            penalties[i] ← penalties[i] + criticalities[i];
            rewards[i] ← 0;
            if penalties[i] ≥ P then curr_act[i] ← 0;
        else
            if penalties[i] > 0 then
                rewards[i] ← rewards[i] + 1;
                if rewards[i] ≥ R then
                    penalties[i] ← 0;   rewards[i] ← 0;
    return curr_act;
end
```

value 1 (up) and the traffic considered again. As the problem of reintegration is outside the scope of this paper, the algorithm only sets activity bits to 0 (isolated).

6. Properties of the diagnostic protocol

In this section we prove the properties of the diagnostic information stored in the consistent health vector $cons\_hv$. We show the experimental evaluation used to practically tune the parameters of the p/r algorithm in Sec. 9.

The properties of the consistent health vector are:

- *Correctness*: a correct sender is never diagnosed as faulty by obedient nodes;
- *Completeness*: a benign faulty sender is always diagnosed as faulty by obedient nodes;
- *Consistency*: diagnosis is agreed by all obedient nodes.

Our protocol does not discriminate between node and link faults. Transient external faults in the communication network are filtered using the p/r algorithm. We remark that in our extended fault model these properties hold for obedient nodes, i.e., both correct nodes *and* nodes encountering omission faults, whereas for classical diagnostic protocols they only hold for correct nodes. These properties imply that an obedient node is able to diagnose itself.

We first prove that the diagnostic matrix used for the hybrid voting consists of validity bits of messages sent in the same round. Next we study the conditions under which the hybrid voting is able to calculate a consistent health vector that provides for the three properties defined above.

Lemma 1 *All local syndromes al_dm_j correctly received and aggregated by the diagnostic jobs executed at round k contain the value of the validity bits of the messages sent in the same previous diagnosed round, which can be either $k-3$ or $k-2$ depending on the schedule of nodes and on the global communication schedule.*

Proof Diagnostic messages are updated at every round. Therefore, each diagnostic job at round k can read values sent either in round k or $k-1$. The read alignment done in the aggregation phase ensures that all local syndromes al_dm_j were sent in round $k-1$. Such local syndromes were formed either in the same round as they were sent or in the previous, i.e., either in round $k-1$ or $k-2$. This depends on the local schedule of diagnostic jobs with respect to the global communication schedule, i.e., on the send alignment. The local detection phase also uses read alignment to consistently form local syndromes of validity bits referring to messages sent in the previous round, i.e., either round $k-3$ or $k-2$. This round is therefore the diagnosed round. □

The aligned local syndromes formed at round k constitute the diagnostic matrix for the diagnosed round $k-3$ or $k-2$. Due to malicious faults during the dissemination, local syndromes can contain incorrect information, and different diagnostic matrices can be formed at different nodes. In the following, we prove that the hybrid voting function H-maj(V) calculates a consistent health vector satisfying correctness, completeness and consistency; a, s and b will represent the number of asymmetric, symmetric malicious and benign faulty nodes over one execution of the protocol.

Lemma 2 *The consistent health vector calculated by each obedient node at round k guarantees consistency, completeness and correctness for faults occurred at round $k-3$ or $k-2$ as long as $N > 2a + 2s + b + 1$ and $a \leq 1$.*

Proof As proved in Lemma 1, the hybrid voting H-maj(V) is executed over the local syndromes of validity bits referring to the same diagnosed round. Let us consider the N-1 tuple of values $V = \langle al\_dm_1[i], \ldots, al\_dm_{i-1}[i], al\_dm_{i+1}[i], \ldots, al\_dm_N[i] \rangle$ used by an obedient node to diagnose i. Among these values, up to b are erroneous (ε), the actual number depending on the amount of benign faulty nodes failing during the dissemination phase. The other $N - b - 1$ values are either correct (and therefore symmetric) or malicious/asymmetric.

If the diagnosed sender was correct or benign faulty, all correct votes will carry the same opinion to all obedient nodes. As $N - b - 1 > 2(a + s)$, malicious and/or asymmetric votes are a minority and are outvoted by correct values in each obedient node. Thus, a consistent decision is reached that ensures correctness and completeness.

If the diagnosed sender is not correct nor benign faulty in the diagnosed round, the only property required is consistency. If the sender had been symmetric malicious, it was not detected as faulty by any node. Similar to the previous case, there is a consistent majority of correct votes at each obedient node saying that the sender was not faulty, and therefore consistency is guaranteed.

If the diagnosed sender was asymmetric faulty, its vote does not contribute to the diagnosis on its health, since the opinion of a node on itself is ignored and excluded from the vector V. As there can be at most one asymmetric sender over one execution of the protocol, each obedient node receives the same set of votes and reaches a consistent diagnosis, which can assume any value. □

The condition $N > 2a + 2s + b + 1$ requires that, even if there are no malicious faults, $b < N - 1$. In case of long transient bursts in the communication bus, multiple (and possibly all) subsequent slots in the round will be compromised, resulting in a higher number of sender faults. The protocol behaves correctly also under these conditions, as proved by the following Lemma:

Lemma 3 *If there are only benign faulty senders, the consistent health vector calculated by each obedient node at round k guarantees* correct, complete *and* consistent *diagnosis of the other nodes for faults occurred at round $k - 3$ or $k - 2$ if $N - 1 \leq b \leq N$. For correct, complete and consistent self-diagnosis, the correctness of the local collision detector is necessary.*

Proof If there are only benign faulty nodes, all local syndromes will be consistent and will reflect the state of the system. An obedient node can thus correctly diagnose other nodes even if it does not receive any external local syndrome. However, when the node has to diagnose itself and no external local syndromes are available, it cannot distinguish whether it was able to correctly send its message or not, unless it queries the local collision detector. Any default decision in this case could be incorrect and inconsistent with the (correct) diagnosis of the other nodes. The correctness of the local collision detector is therefore not only sufficient but also necessary for self-diagnosis. □

Lemmas 1, 2 and 3 imply Theorem 1 as:

Theorem 1 *The consistent health vector calculated by each job at round k guarantees* correctness, completeness *and* consistency *for faults occurred at round $k - 3$ or $k - 2$ if: $N > 2a + 2s + b + 1$ and $a \leq 1$; or there are only benign faults, $N - 1 \leq b \leq N$. In the latter case, local collision detection is necessary for self-diagnosis.* □

7. The membership protocol

A common approach to keep consistency in fault-tolerant distributed systems is to use a *group membership* service. When an asymmetric fault occurs, nodes are partitioned into two sets, also called *cliques*, such that the members of one clique received the message whereas the other did not. In such case a membership service outputs a new *view* consisting of the larger of these cliques. As all the members of a clique have received the same set of messages, they have a consistent state. The properties required for a group membership service are the following:

- *Membership liveness*: A new unique view is formed whenever an obedient node receives a locally detectable faulty message m;
- *View synchrony*: As a new view is formed, all obedient nodes remaining across consecutive views have received the same set of messages prior to, and including, m.

If there is a benign fault, all receivers form a unique clique and Alg. 1 detects sender faulty nodes correctly. In case of asymmetric faults, however, two different cliques of receivers are formed and the diagnostic protocol of Alg. 1 cannot detect them.

A *modified* diagnostic protocol can detect the presence of disjoint cliques and allow the determination of views according to the properties above. In Alg. 1, the analysis phase must be executed before the dissemination phase; after the consistent health vector is calculated, the modified algorithm accuses (as member of the minority clique) the nodes that send local syndromes disagreeing with it. Such accusations, called *minority accusations*, are added in the current aligned local syndrome al_ls and subsequently disseminated. The protocol satisfies the desired properties as shown in Theorem 2:

Theorem 2 *If an obedient correct node receives a locally incorrect message m and $N > 2a + 2s + b + 1$, $a \leq 1$, a new view is generated after two complete executions of the modified diagnostic protocol* (membership liveness) *containing all nodes never deemed as faulty. Such a view satisfies* view synchrony *for all messages prior to and including m.*

Proof A locally detectable message can be received due to either a benign or an asymmetric fault. If a benign fault occurs, it is detected by the diagnostic protocol as shown in Theorem 1. The sender is the only node which received the message and will be excluded from the view.

If an asymmetric fault occurs during the broadcast of message m, two cliques of obedient nodes are formed. Theorem 1 guarantees that all obedient nodes calculate a consistent health vector, which contains a consistent decision (faulty/non faulty) on message m. During the dissemination phase of the diagnostic protocol, however, obedient nodes of the minority cliques try to send local syndromes disagreeing with the consistent decision. As $a \leq 1$, such nodes can either correctly broadcast it, and be accused by all other obedient nodes (minority accusation), or be benign faulty senders, and thus be accused by the local detection mechanisms of all the other obedient nodes. In both cases they will be consistently accused and diagnosed as faulty in the next execution of the diagnostic protocol. □

8. Validation of the protocols

In this section we present the results of the experimental validation of the diagnostic and membership protocols. We used physical fault injection to validate the properties of the protocol under different scenarios. *We emphasize that all parameters used in the validation (and tuning, see Sec. 9) arise from actual automotive and aerospace applications.*

Prototype setup. The validation setup consists of a set of four nodes consisting of a host computer (Infineon Tricore 1796) and a communication controller (Xilinx Vertex

4 FPGA), which are interconnected via a redundant TT network (layered TTP). Each host computer runs a TT operating system. A diagnostic job runs on each node as an add-on application-level module sending one diagnostic message per round. No constraint was imposed on the internal node scheduling besides executing diagnostic jobs once every round. The static node scheduling defined the constant integers $l_{\{1,..,N\}}$ and the predicates $send\_curr\_round_{\{1,..,N\}}$ used by the protocol for the read and the send alignment operations. Interface variables are automatically updated and the validity bits of a message m can be read using the API call `tt_Receiver_Status`. The bandwidth required for each diagnostic message is $N = 4$ bits.

We also used an additional disturbance node, which is able to emulate hardware faults in the communication network. As the protocol does not discriminate between node and link faults, a fault in a node can be emulated by corrupting or dropping a message it sends.

Injection cases. We selectively injected different classes of physical faults on the bus (electrical spikes, random noise, periods of silence) to simulate faults in a deterministic and reproducible manner. As we know which faults are injected, we can experimentally evaluate whether the diagnostic protocol is able to detect them. Each *experiment class* was repeated 100 times for consistency. A total of 1500 fault injection experiments was conducted.

We injected bursty faults of increasing length: one slot, two slots and two TDMA rounds. The first two cases fall in the hypothesis of Lemma 2, the third in the hypothesis of Lemma 3. In the latter case, all slots of a whole TDMA round are lost, reproducing a communication blackout where no nodes are able to send any messages (and therefore no local syndromes are sent). In each of these three cases, bursts can start in any of the 4 sending slots, thus we considered 12 experiment classes.

Another experiment class aimed at validating the ability of the protocol to correctly update penalty and reward counters for a given node. A fault is injected in the sending slots of the node every second TDMA round for 20 TDMA rounds. Hence, either the penalty or the reward counter should be increased at every round.

The effect of one malicious node sending random local syndromes was also considered. Its presence is not supposed to induce the other nodes to diagnose correct nodes as faulty. As any of the four nodes can be malicious, we considered 4 experiment classes.

To validate the clique detection capabilities of the membership protocol, we placed the disturbance node between Node 1 and the rest of the cluster and disconnected the bus during the sending slot of at least another node to produce (and detect) a minority clique formed by Node 1.

9. Practical tuning of the p/r algorithm

In order to correctly discriminate between healthy and unhealthy nodes, the penalty and reward thresholds have to

be tuned together with the criticality levels for each node. We now describe experiences on the tuning of our prototype for realistic automotive and aerospace settings. Table 2 summarizes the results of our tuning.

Characterizing intermittent faults. The first difficulty faced during the practical tuning of the protocol is how to characterize unhealthy nodes. The p/r algorithm resets the penalty and reward counters for a node if it does not fail for R consecutive rounds, where R is the reward threshold. If a fault appears before R is reached, it is considered correlated with the previous fault. Therefore, R should be large enough to correlate intermittent faults. The time to reappearance of intermittent faults, however, depends on the specific frequency of fault activation for each node (i.e., which hardware components of the node are damaged and how often they are stimulated by the software) and is unknown in most practical systems.

While setting R, designers must make a probabilistic tradeoff between the capability of correlating intermittent faults with a large time to reappearance and the avoidance of incorrect correlation of independent and external transient faults. In Figure 3 we show such a tradeoff for our automotive and aerospace settings, where the length of the TDMA round is set to $T = 2.5ms$. Our practical choice was to set $R = 10^6$ to correlate faults whose interarrival time is within $R \times T \cong 42min$, which can be pragmatically considered a reasonable value. After detecting a transient fault, the resulting probability of correlating a second transient fault is less than 1% considering the rates of Fig. 3. It must be noticed that a healthy node will be isolated only if P subsequent transient faults are correlated, where P is the penalty threshold [7]. In all our prototypes the probability of isolation of a healthy node is thus negligible.

Tuning the diagnostic latency. To increase availability and accumulate diagnostic data, the p/r algorithm delays node isolation and increases the *diagnostic latency*. An application can be prevented from correctly exchanging messages if some of its jobs are hosted on a faulty node that is kept operative by the p/r algorithm. In such case the application might experience an outage. Applications with different criticality classes have different requirements on the

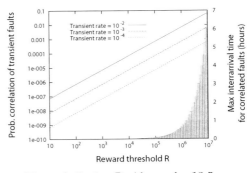

Figure 3: Setting R with rounds of $2.5ms$

Table 2: Results of the experimental tuning of the p/r algorithm

Domain	Criticality class	Example	Tolerated outage	Crit. lvl. (s_i)	P	R	TDMA
Automotive	*Safety Critical (SC)*	X-by-wire	$20-50ms$	40	197	10^6	$2.5ms$
	Safety Relevant (SR)	Stability control	$100-200ms$	6			
	Non Safety Relevant (NSR)	Door control	$500-1000ms$	1			
Aerospace	*Safety Critical (SC)*	High Lift, Landing Gear	$50ms$	1	17	10^6	$2.5ms$

maximum *tolerated transient outage* time of an application before a recovery action is activated in order to restore the availability of the service or to reach a safe state. Such outage is the sum of the diagnostic latency and the recovery time. Tolerated transient outages for different classes of automotive and aerospace applications are shown in Table 2.

The automotive domain depicts a varied range of criticality classes. *Safety critical* functionalities are necessary for the physical control of the vehicle with strict reactivity constraints, e.g., X-by-wire. Recovery actions must preserve the availability of the (possibly degraded) service. *Safety relevant* functionalities support the driver, e.g., the Electronic Stability Control and the Driver Assistant Systems, such as the collision warning and avoidance system. They are not necessary for the control of the car but the driver must know if they are unavailable. Finally, there are *Non Safety relevant* functionalities such as comfort and entertainment subsystems. In the aerospace domain, only safety critical functionalities are connected to the backbone. The High Lift System adds lift during the flight and is related to the control of flaps. The Landing Gear System controls the retractable wheels used for landing.

Both the diagnostic and the more complex membership service are fast enough to satisfy the requirements of the highest criticality class considered. However, we want to delay the isolation of faulty nodes as much as possible to maximize the availability in presence of transient faults. The diagnostic latency can be tuned by setting the penalty threshold and criticality levels according to the application requirements. Hence, we injected continuous faulty bursts and observed the value of the penalty counter reached when the maximum diagnostic latency for each criticality class was reached. We assumed that once a faulty node is isolated by the diagnostic protocol, each obedient node can instantaneously apply the necessary recovery actions, discounting further delays. Each experiment was repeated 100 times. If classes $c_1, \ldots, c_i$ have corresponding penalties $p_1, \ldots, p_i$, we set $P = max(p_1, \ldots, p_i)$ and the criticality of each class to $s_i = \lceil P/p_i \rceil$. To satisfy the requirements on the diagnostic latency, the criticality increment for a node was set as the maximum s_i of the applications it hosts. Criticality levels are stored in the vector *criticalities* used by the p/r algorithm. The penalty thresholds and criticality levels for the automotive and aerospace setups are shown in Table 2. We observed in both setups that even for Safety Critical applications it is possible to wait for some round before isolating faulty nodes. This enhances the capability of the system of not overreacting to transient faults.

Diagnosis under adverse external conditions. We have shown how we tuned the parameters of the p/r algorithm under *normal* external conditions. The next step was to try to evaluate the capability of the algorithm to guarantee node availability under *adverse* external conditions, characterized by an abnormal rate of transient faults. For this purpose we considered two unfavorable but common scenarios in the automotive and aerospace settings where external faults are highly frequent and will likely be considered as intermittent faults. For the automotive setting we considered a blinking light causing periodic electrical instabilities on the bus due to an open relay, while for aerospace we considered a lighting bolt producing a sequence of instabilities with increasing time to reappearance. Systems are designed and tested to tolerate such transient behaviors without taking specific recovery actions, therefore isolations should be avoided. The length of the faulty bursts, the times to reappearance and the number of instances of the burst are shown in Table 3. We reproduced these scenarios in 100 experiments and observed if and after how much time healthy nodes were incorrectly isolated.

In both cases, different transient burst are considered as correlated by the p/r algorithm. The results for the automotive and aerospace setting are shown in Table 4. The functionalities with lower criticalities can tolerate longer periods of abnormal transient behavior. The use of a p/r algorithm with varied criticality levels gives advantages in terms of availability. In fact, if nodes were immediately isolated after the first fault appearance, a single abnormal transient period would result in the isolation of all the nodes in the system and would entail a restart of the whole system. However, even using our p/r algorithm, the availability of safety critical functionalities can be harmed by relatively short disturbances in both the experimental setting. From this data we can conclude that the detection of intermittent faults could be sacrificed for the sake of availability for those nodes implementing safety critical functions. For example, isolated nodes could be kept under observation, collecting rewards if a fault-free behavior is observed and reintegrating the node if a specific reward threshold for reintegration is reached.

Table 3: Abnormal transient scenarios

Scenario	Burst	TTReapp.	# Inj.
Auto (blinking light)	$10ms$	$500ms$	50
Aero (lightning bolt)	$40ms$	$160ms$	1
	$40ms$	$290ms$	1
	$40ms$	$500ms$	9

Table 4: Time to incorrect isolation

Setting	Criticality class	Time to isolation
Automotive	*SC / SR / NSR*	0.518 / 4.595 / 24.475*sec*
Aerospace	*SC*	0.205*sec*

10. Portability Issues for Varied TT Platforms

One of our main design drivers was to define a diagnostic/membership protocol that is a tunable and portable add-on application level module, rather than a static and built-in system level feature. Our experience has confirmed that this approach is viable. Our protocol only uses detection capabilities that are provided by any TT platform. The concept of validity bit abstracts a number of platform specific error detection mechanisms, whose outcome can normally be accessed by applications using the basic API provided by the operating system of the host node (see Sec. 8).

Another important issue was not to require interactions or to interfere with other applications. For this reason, local detection of faults is implicitly performed by monitoring the exchange of diagnostic messages among diagnostic jobs. To ease the integration, the bandwidth requirement of the protocol is limited. In our prototype diagnostic messages were as small as N bits.

Finally, we avoided imposing strong constraints on node scheduling. The read and send alignments ensure that all diagnostic jobs use consistent data for any schedule, provided that the diagnostic jobs are executed at every round. To achieve that, they require the application to know some parameters that are directly related to the node scheduling, such as $l_{\{1,..,N\}}$ and $send\_curr\_round_{\{1,..,N\}}$ (see Sec. 5). If a static scheduling policy is used, this information is constant and known at design time. In case of dynamic scheduling we require the OS to provide this information to the application at run-time.

The relaxed constraints on the scheduling of the diagnostic jobs lead to a detection latency, i.e., the time necessary to consistently detect a faulty slot, of four TDMA rounds in the worst case, which is suboptimal. However, if needed, it is possible to trade off flexibility for a shorter latency. By constraining the internal node scheduling, in fact, we can reduce the detection latency down to one round for the diagnostic protocol and two rounds for the membership protocol. In this variant of the protocol, each node keeps sending its local syndrome at each sending slot, but the analysis is executed right after each slot and refers to a single previous slot. After one round all local syndromes necessary to diagnose a slot are collected, and two diagnostic rounds would be sufficient to execute two instances of the modified diagnostic protocol, i.e., one instance of the membership protocol. All the properties of the protocol are preserved in this variant, at the price of making portability more complex.

11. Conclusions

We have presented a generic diagnostic protocol that can be added on as a middleware layer on top of any TT plat-form. It tolerates multiple benign and malicious faults and aims to maximize node availability by using a p/r algorithm even under abnormal transient disturbances. We have extended it to be usable as a membership protocol without using additional resources. Both variants of the protocol have been experimentally validated. We tuned the p/r algorithm under realistic automotive and aerospace settings, and addressed open issues of characterization of intermittent faults, determination of the severity of faults and diagnosis under adverse external conditions.

References

[1] FlexRay Communication System, Protocol Specification v. 2.1. *http://www.flexray.com/specification_request_v21.php*

[2] H. Kopetz and G. Grunsteidl. TTP - A Protocol for Fault Tolerant Real Time Systems. *IEEE Computer*, 27(1), pp. 14–23, 1994.

[3] K. Hoyme and K. Driscoll. SAFEbus. *IEEE Aerospace and Electronic Systems Magazine*, 8(3), pp. 34-39, 1993.

[4] C. Constantinescu. Impact of Deep Submicron Technology on Dependability of VLSI Circuits. *DSN*, pp. 205–209, 2000.

[5] A. Bondavalli *et al*. Discriminating Fault Rate and Persistency to Improve Fault Treatment. *FTCS*, pp. 354–362, 1997.

[6] A. Bondavalli *et al*. Threshold-Based Mechanisms to Discriminate Transient from Intermittent Faults. *IEEE Trans. on Computers*, 49(3), pp. 230–245, 2000.

[7] M. Serafini *et al*. On-line Diagnosis and Recovery: On the Choice and Impact of Tuning Parameters. *TR-TUD-DEEDS-05-05-2006*, 2006.

[8] F.P. Preparata *at al*. On the Connection Assignment Problem of Diagnosable Systems. *IEEE Trans. on Electronic Computers*, 16(12), pp. 848-854, 1967.

[9] M. Malek. A Comparison Connection Assignment for Diagnosis of Multiprocessor Systems, *ISCA*, pp. 31–36, 1980.

[10] M. Barborak *et.al*, The Consensus Problem in Fault Tolerant Computing, *ACM Surveys*, vol. 25, pp. 171–220, Jun. 1993.

[11] C. Walter *et al*. Formally Verified On-line Diagnosis. *IEEE TSE*, 23(11), pp. 684–721, 1997.

[12] M.A. Hiltunen. Membership and System Diagnosis. *SRDS*, pp. 208-217, 1995.

[13] F. Cristian. Reaching Agreement on Processor-group Membership in Synchronous Distributed Systems. *Distributed Computing*, 4(4), pp. 175–187, 1991.

[14] G. Bauer and M. Paulitsch. An Investigation of Membership and Clique Avoidance in TTP/C. *SRDS*, pp. 118–124, 2000.

[15] P.D. Ezhilchelvan and R. Lemos. A Robust Group Membership Algorithm for Distributed Real Time Systems. *RTSS*, pp. 173-179, 1990.

[16] C. Walter *et al*. Continual On-line Diagnosis of Hybrid Faults. *DCCA*, pp. 150-166, 1994.

[17] A. Ademaj *et al*. Evaluation of Fault Handling of the Time Triggered Architecture with Bus and Star Topology. *DSN*, pp. 123-132, 2003.

[18] P. Lincoln and J. Rushby. A Formally Verified Algorithm for Interactive Consistency under Hybrid Fault Models. *FTCS*, pp. 402-411, 1993.

Session 3B:
Dependability Modeling

Enhanced Reliability Modeling of RAID Storage Systems

Jon G. Elerath
Network Appliance, Inc.
elerath@netapp.com

Michael Pecht
University of Maryland
pecht@calce.umd.edu

Abstract

A flexible model for estimating reliability of RAID storage systems is presented. This model corrects errors associated with the common assumption that system times to failure follow a homogeneous Poisson process. Separate generalized failure distributions are used to model catastrophic failures and usage dependent data corruptions for each hard drive. Catastrophic failure restoration is represented by a three-parameter Weibull, so the model can include a minimum time to restore as a function of data transfer rate and hard drive storage capacity. Data can be scrubbed as a background operation to eliminate corrupted data that, in the event of a simultaneous catastrophic failure, results in double disk failures. Field-based times to failure data and mathematic justification for a new model are presented. Model results have been verified and predict between 2 to 1,500 times as many double disk failures as that estimated using the current mean time to data loss method.

1. Introduction

Storage systems consisting of redundant arrays of inexpensive disks (RAID) were developed circa 1988 to improve storage system reliability [1]. Reliability estimates were created assuming that both hard disk drive (HDD) failures and RAID system failures follow a homogeneous Poisson process. If these assumptions are accepted, the time to failure for the common RAID 4 or RAID 5 system can be expressed as the mean time to data loss (MTTDL), or an average time to double-disk failures (DDF). MTTDL is commonly turned into an hourly "rate," using the exponentially distributed component failure rate. This means the probability of system failure in any time interval is constant. For example, operating 100 RAID groups for 87,600 hours will have the same probability of failure as operating 87,600 groups for 100 hours. That is, assuming renewal theory, it is assumed that the number of DDFs can be estimated by multiplying the "system failure rate" by time, where N(*t*) is the

estimated number of failures and λ is the constant system failure rate per unit time in the same units as *t*. This is an attempt to invoke the relationship N(*t*) $\approx \lambda t$ $\approx 1 - \exp(-\lambda t)$, assuming that the error is less than 1% when $\lambda t < 0.02$.

However, the failure rate of a component, h(t), is statistically different from the "failure rate" of the system, more correctly referred to as the rate of occurrence of failure [2] - [5]. As noted by Ascher [6], there is little connection between the properties of component hazard rates and the properties of the process that produces a sequence of failures. That is, times between successive system failures can become increasingly larger even though each component hazard rate is increasing [3]. Even if the HDD follows a homogeneous Poisson process (HPP), there is no statistical basis for assuming the system will be a HPP.

A second contributory problem is the assumption that HDD failures follow an HPP. Recent field data analyses show that HDD failure distributions are anything but constant. Data for specific HDD products often indicate subpopulations such as infant wear-out. Different vintages of the same HDD from the same manufacturer may exhibit varying failure distributions.

A third issue with current methods is that undiscovered data corruptions can occur at any time in the life of a HDD. These defects were acknowledged by Kari [9], but he assumed that they were caused only by media deterioration and were independent of usage. While Schwarz included latent defects to optimize scrub algorithms [10], he still assumes the system follows a homogeneous Poisson process with constant failure rates. The significance of undiscovered latent defects (LDs) is apparent when a catastrophic (operational) failure ultimately occurs. The latent defect, combined with the operational failure, constitutes a DDF, defeating the reliability gains by (N+1) RAID.

These three issues raise the question of usefulness of MTTDL models in estimating the number of DDFs in a RAID group. This paper presents a new model that includes latent defects and does not assume HPP for the HDD or system. HDD failure modes and mechanisms are briefly presented to justify the need for discerning between operational failures and latent defects, which are modeled explicitly. Data scrubbing [10], the remedy for latent defects, is also incorporated in the model. Times to fail are supported through actual field data; times to restore are modeled and acknowledge a minimum and maximum time to restore a failed HDD and reconstruct the lost data. The model is evaluated using a sequential Monte Carlo simulation. The expected number of DDFs predicted by the MTTDL method is compared to the number estimated by this new model proposal, showing that the previous assumptions result in incorrect predictions.

2. Field reliability data

A number of recent papers shed light on the distributions underlying HDD failures [7], [8], [10]-[13]. Figure 1 and Figure 2 present Weibull probability plots for new unpublished data. Several noteworthy observations can be made from the aggregate of these data:

- HDD failure rates are rarely constant
- Failure distributions exhibit
  - decreasing failure rates
  - late-life increasing failure rates
  - early-life increasing failure rates
  - vintage based improvements
  - vintage based deterioration
- Distributions change as a result of both design and manufacturing process changes.

The above observations are a significant departure from the assumption of constant failure rates. In Figure 1, data for three different products are plotted assuming a two-parameter Weibull distribution (a straight line indicates a good fit). Only HDD #1 appears to follow a Weibull distribution. Both of the other two datasets are clearly not linear and indicate abrupt changes in the distribution. HDD #2 shows two separate linear sections, denoting two distributions dominate at different points in time, with the last one, sometime after 10,000 hours, having a marked increase in failure rate (the data plot bends upwards). Failure analyses showed the slope change was due to a change in failure mechanisms.

HDD #3 shows two inflection points. Initially, the failure rate is high but decreasing, and follows the slope of HDD #1 ($\beta = 0.9$). A significant decrease occurs (for the population) followed by a significant increase (plot line bends upward). This population has the characteristics of both competing risks and "population mixtures." In mixed populations, some of

the HDDs have a failure mechanism that the others do not have and so do not, in fact, fail from that mechanism. An example in an HDD is particle contamination [11]. A mixture of populations is likely responsible for the first inflection point for HDD #3 in Figure 1 (decrease in failure rate) and competing risks for the second (upturn in failure rate).

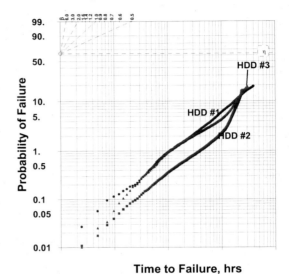

Figure 1. Cumulative probability of failure.
Only HDD #1 fits a Weibull distribution (straight line)

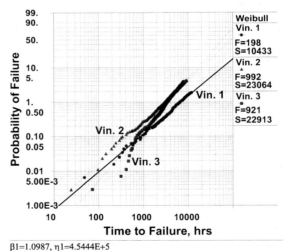

$\beta 1=1.0987, \eta 1=4.5444E+5$
$\beta 2=1.2162, \eta 2=1.2566E+5$
$\beta 3=1.4873, \eta 3=7.5012E+4$

Figure 2. HDD vintage effects

In Figure 2, the three lines represent three non-consecutive HDD vintages from one manufacturer. Vintage 1 has a constant failure rate ($\beta=1.09$), whereas the others are increasing ($\beta=1.2$ and $\beta=1.4$). In a Weibull distribution the shape parameter, β, indicates whether the failure rate is decreasing ($\beta<1.0$), constant ($\beta=1.0$), or increasing ($\beta>1.0$).

3. HDD failure modes and mechanisms

In MTTDL calculations, all HDDs are assumed to have a single failure rate for catastrophic failures and latent defects are ignored. But latent defects are significant and must be included. Failure modes and mechanisms based on HDD electro-mechanical and magnetic events are summarized in Figure 3, grouped by one of two possible consequences: operational (catastrophic) failures or latent defects. Each group has its own unique failure distribution and consequence at the system level. All read failures can be classified as 1) HDD incapable of finding the data or 2) data missing or corrupted shows a structured list for the major causes of inability to read data. The failure mechanisms presented here are not novel [10], [14], but neither are they readily available from HDD manufacturers. The novelty is their use in the model.

Operational Failures (Cannot find data)
- Bad servo-track
- Bad electronics
- Can't stay on track
- Bad read head
- SMART limit exceeded

Latent Defects (Data missing)
- Error during writing
  Bad media
  Inherent bit-error rate
  High-fly writes
- Written but destroyed
  Thermal asperities
  Corrosion
  Scratched media

Figure 3. Breakdown for read error causes.

3.1 Cannot find data

The inability to "find" data is most often caused by "operational" failures, which can occur any time the HDD disks are spinning and the heads are staying on track. Heads must read "servo" wedges that are permanently recorded onto the media during the manufacturing process and cannot be reconstructed with RAID if they are destroyed. These segments contain no user data, but provide information used solely to control the positioning of the read/write heads for all movements. If servo-track data is destroyed or corrupted, the head cannot correctly position itself, resulting in loss of access to user data even though the user's data is uncorrupted. Servo

tracks can be damaged by scratches or thermal asperities.

Tracks on an HDD are never perfectly circular. The present head position is continuously measured and compared to where it should be and a position error signal is used to properly reposition the head over the track. This repeatable run-out is all part of normal HDD head positioning control.

Non-repeatable run-out caused by mechanical tolerances from the motor bearings, excessive wear, actuator arm bearings, noise, vibration and servo-loop response errors can cause the head positioning to take too long to lock onto a track and ultimately produce an error. High rotational speeds exacerbate this mechanism in both ball and fluid-dynamic bearings.

HDDs use self-monitoring analysis reporting technology (SMART) to predict impending failure based on performance data. For example, data reallocations are expected and many spare sectors are available on each HDD, but an excessive number in a specific time interval will exceed the SMART threshold, resulting in a "SMART trip."

Currently, most head failures are due to changes in magnetic properties. Electro-static discharge (ESD), physical impact (contamination), and high temperatures can accelerate magnetic degradation. ESD induced degradation is difficult to detect and can propagate to full failure when exposed to localized heat from thermal asperities (T/As). The HDD electronics are attached to the outside of the HDD. DRAM and cracked chip-capacitors have also been known to cause failure.

3.2 Data missing

Data is sometimes written poorly initially, but can be corrupted after being written. Unless corrected, missing and corrupted data become "latent defects."

1. Errors during writing
The bit-error rate (BER) is a statistical measure of the effectiveness of all the electrical, mechanical, magnetic, and firmware control systems working together to write (or read) data. Most bit-errors occur on a read command and are corrected, but since written data is rarely checked immediately after writing, bit-errors can also occur during writes. BER accounts for some fraction of defective data written to the HDD, but a greater source of errors is the magnetic recording media coating the disks.

Writing on scratched, smeared, or pitted media can result in corrupted data. Scratches can be caused by loose hard particles (TiW, Si_2O_3, C) becoming lodged between the head and the media surface. Smears, caused by "soft" particles such as stainless steel and aluminum, will also corrupt data. Pits and voids are caused by particles that were originally embedded in the media during the sputtering process and subsequently dislodged during the final processing steps, the polishing process to remove embedded contaminants, or field use. Hydrocarbon contamination (machine oil) on the disk surface can result in write errors as well.

A common cause for poorly written data is the "high-fly write." The heads are aerodynamically designed to have a negative pressure and maintain the small, fixed distance above the disk surface at all times. If the aerodynamics are perturbed, the head can fly too high, resulting in weakly (magnetically) written data that cannot be read. All disks have a very thin film of lubricant on them as protection from head-disk contact, but lubrication build-up on the head can increase the flying height.

2. Data written but destroyed

Most RAID reliability models assume that data will remain undestroyed except by degradation of the magnetic properties of the media ("bit-rot"). While it is correct that media can degrade, this failure mechanism is not a significant cause. Data can become corrupted any time the disks are spinning, even when data is not being written to or read from the disk. Three common causes for erasure include thermal asperities, corrosion, and scratches/smears.

Thermal asperities are instances of high heat for a short duration caused by head-disk contact. This is usually the result of heads hitting small "bumps" created by particles embedded in the media surface during the manufacturing process. The heat generated on a single contact may not be sufficient to thermally erase data, but may be sufficient after many contacts.

Heads are designed to push particles away, but contaminants can still become lodged between the head and disk. Hard particles used in the manufacture of an HDD, such as Al_2O_3, TiW, and C, can cause surface scratches and data erasure any time the disk is rotating. Other "soft" materials such as stainless steel can come from assembly tooling. Soft particles tend to smear across the surface of the media rendering the data unreadable. Corrosion, although carefully controlled, also can cause data erasure and may be accelerated by T/A generated heat.

4. Model logic

RAID reduces the probability of data loss by grouping together multiple inexpensive hard disk drives in a redundant configuration and adding error correction using parity. Most RAID configurations use a single additional HDD within the RAID group for redundancy. As part of the write process, an "exclusive OR" calculation generates parity bits that are also written to the RAID group.

Error correcting codes (ECC) *on the HDD* and parity *across the HDDs* is a common method to enssure accurate data transfer and recording. ECC uses Boolean operations to encode blocks of data, interleaving the data and the ECC bits. On each read command, user data and ECC are read. If a data inconsistency occurs, the data is corrected on-the-fly (less than one revolution), data integrity preserved, and performance is not degraded. ECC strength is enhanced by interleaving multiple blocks of data so that errors covering a large physical area (many bits) can be corrected. ECC is faster than data recovery across multiple HDDs, but since ECC is read with every block of user data, excessive ECC use can degrade performance.

4.1 Previous models

MTTDL was introduced as the measure of RAID group reliability nearly 20 years ago [1]. Researchers have attempted to improve RAID reliability models, but the primary change has been to introduce Markov models, resulting in a probability of failure rather than an MTTDL [7], [15], and [16]. Ultimately, all past work is based on the assumption of constant failure and repair rates. A review of the methods used to assess reliability in papers [1], [17]-[20] identified deficiencies as follows:

1. Failure rates are not constant in time.
2. Failure rates change based on production vintage.
3. Failure distributions can be mixtures of multiple distributions because of production vintages.
4. Repair rates are not constant and there exists a minimum time to complete restoration.
5. Permanent errors can occur any time.
6. Latent defects must be considered in the model.
7. RAID system failures are assumed to follow a homogeneous Poisson process.

MTTDL attempts to estimate average time between simultaneous failures of two hard disk drives in an (N+1) RAID group. Disk drives are assumed to have constant failure rates, λ, the reciprocal of the mean time to failure; constant repair (restoration) rates, μ, the reciprocal of the mean time to restore; and assume RAID group failures follow a homogeneous Poisson process. Based on these assumptions, an $N + 1$ RAID group has an MTTDL as shown in equation 1.

$$MTTDL = \frac{(2N+1)\lambda + \mu}{N(N+1)\lambda^2} \qquad \text{eq. 1}$$

Since the repair rate is usually much larger than the failure rate, the MTTDL expression can be simplified.

$$MTTDL_{Indep} = \frac{\mu}{N(N+1)\lambda^2} = \frac{MTTF_{disk}^2}{N(N+1)MTTR_{disk}} \quad \text{eq. 2}$$

From MTTDL, the expected number of failures, $E[N(t)]$, in a time interval is estimated by multiplying the time interval by the number of systems and dividing by the MTTDL. Equation 3 shows the estimate for an MTTDL of 36,162 years (MTBF = 461,386 hrs; MTTR=12 hrs; N=7), 1,000 RAID groups, and 10 years of operation. This calculation does not include latent defects or non-constant failure or restoration rates. Non-constant failure rates invalidate the MTTDL.

$$N(t) = \frac{\dfrac{10\,\text{yrs}}{\text{RAID Group}} \times 1000\,\text{RAID Groups}}{\dfrac{36,162\,\text{yrs}}{\text{Failure}}} = 0.28 \quad \text{eq. 3}$$

4.2 NHPP-latent defect model

The state diagram in Figure 4 is used to convey the model logic at a high level. The model is evaluated using Monte Carlo simulation rather than Markov model because estimating the number of failures in time from a probability model can be erroneous [21].

Four distributions are required, denoted "d" in Figure 4: time to operational failure, time to latent defect, time to operational repair, and time to scrub (latent defect repair). System failure occurs when two HDDs fail simultaneously, depicted as states 3 and 5.

An operational failure (Op) is one in which no data on the HDD can be read, even though the data may have no defect. Removal and replacement of the HDD is the only resolution for operational failures. Latent defect (Ld) refers to unknown or undetected data corruption. Latent defects are corrected only when the corrupted data is read and requires reading data on other HDDs in the RAID group and the associated parity bits. If only a few blocks of data are corrupted, the reconstructed data is written to another good section of the HDD and the faulty section is mapped out to prevent reuse.

The order of occurrence of operational and latent defects is significant. If an operational failure occurs after the existence of a latent defect on a different HDD, the data cannot be reconstructed on the replacement HDD because the required redundant data is corrupted or missing. Thus, a latent defect followed by an operational failure results in a DDF.

Write-errors that occur during reconstruction of an HDD will be corrected the next time the data is read or will remain as latent defects, but their creation during a reconstruction does not constitute a DDF. The probability of suffering a usage-related data corruption in an unread area during the time of reconstruction is small, so DDFs rarely occur during reconstructions. Multiple HDDs with latent defects do not constitute DDF unless they happen to coexist in blocks from a single data stripe across more than one HDD, an extremely rare event that is not modeled.

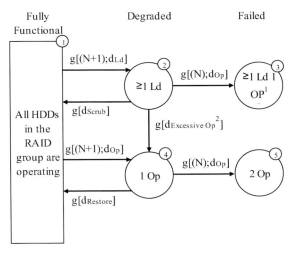

Note 1: Op failure must be a different HDD than the one with a Ld.

Note 2: This transition does not have an explicit rate. It is included in the measured rate of "Op" from field data.

Figure 4. State diagram for N+1 RAID group

Recently, latent defects have been recognized by some system integrators and been reduced by data "scrubbing." Schwarz [10] presented a Markov model for mirrored HDDs in an off-line archive system including scrub optimization. But the analysis did not include large RAID groups with latent defects. During scrubbing, data on the HDD is read and checked against its parity bits even though the data is not being requested by the user. The corrupt data is corrected, bad spots on the media are mapped out, and the data is saved to good locations on the HDD. Since this is a background activity, it may be rather slow so it does not impede performance. Depending on the foreground I/O demand, the scrub time may be as short as the maximum HDD and data-bus transfer rates permit, or may be as long as weeks.

In summary, the two scenarios that result in DDF are 1) two simultaneous operational failures and 2) an operational failure that occurs after a latent defect has been introduced and before it is corrected. Multiple simultaneous latent defects do not constitute failure.

The model logic is partially depicted in Figure 4. In state 1, the data and parity HDDs are good, there are no latent defects, and a spare HDD is available. In state 2, one or more HDDs have latent defects. Failure transitions depend on the number of HDDs available and the distribution of time to failure or restoration. A generic functional notation, g[a;b], is used to represent transitions and the critical variables a and b without conveying any specific operation. For example, transition from state 1 is a function of the $N+1$ HDDs developing a latent defect according to the failure distribution, d_{Ld}. From state 2, an operational failure in any of the N HDDs other than the one with the latent defect results in state 3, a DDF state. The transition from state 2 to 3 is governed by the operational failure distribution d_{Op}.

Transition from state 2 to state 4 occurs because the time to reallocate a sudden burst of media defects on a single HDD exceeds a user specified threshold. This results in a "time-out" error or SMART trip such as "excessive block reallocations." In this transition massive media problems render the HDD inoperative, just like any other operational failure, so the frequency of transition from state 2 to state 4 is included in the operational failure distribution d_{Op}. A third transition from state 2 is back to state 1. This represents repair of latent defects according to the scrubbing distribution, d_{Scrub}.

State 4 represents one operational failure. The transition to state 4 from state 1 is a function of the number of HDDs in the RAID group and the operational failure distribution, d_{Op}. There are two transitions out of state 4. A second simultaneous operational failure results in transition to DDF state 5. The operational failure is replaced with a new HDD and data reconstructed according to the restoration distribution $d_{Restore}$, returning the RAID group back to state 1 with full operability. The distribution, $d_{Restore}$, includes the delay time to physically incorporate the spare HDD and has a minimum time to reconstruct based on the HDD capacity, the maximum transfer rate and concurrent I/O.

5. Sequential Monte Carlo modeling

In a sequential Monte Carlo simulation, the time dependent, or chronological, behavior of the system is simulated [22]. For each HDD in the RAID group, each transition distribution in Figure 4 is sampled. The operating and failure times are accumulated until a specified mission time is exceeded. This research uses a mission of 87,600 hours (10 years). During that time, the sequence of HDD failures, repairs, latent defects, scrubs, and DDFs are tracked. Each sequence of sampling required to reach the mission is a single simulation and represents one possible system operating chronology. If 10,000 simulations are needed to develop the cumulative failure function, described in [23], it is equivalent to monitoring the number of DDFs for 10,000 systems over the mission life.

Figure 5 shows the sequential sampling process used. For simplicity, only four HDD slots are shown. The graph looks like a digital timing diagram with the "high signal" representing the operating (non-defective) condition and the "low signal" representing the failed (defective) condition. Throughout this process, each HDD "slot" in the RAID group carries its own times to failure (both TTOp and TTLd) and times to restore (TTR and TTScrub) distributions. When a DDF involves an HDD with a latent defect, the TTR for the failure is the same as the concomitant operational failure time.

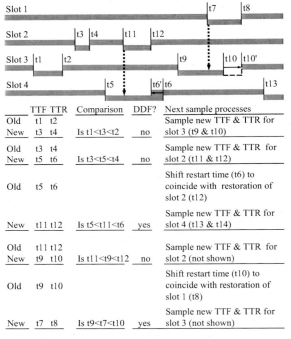

	TTF	TTR	Comparison	DDF?	Next sample processes
Old	t1	t2			Sample new TTF & TTR for
New	t3	t4	Is t1<t3<t2	no	slot 3 (t9 & t10)
Old	t3	t4			Sample new TTF & TTR for
New	t5	t6	Is t3<t5<t4	no	slot 2 (t11 & t12)
Old	t5	t6			Shift restart time (t6) to coincide with restoration of slot 2 (t12)
New	t11	t12	Is t5<t11<t6	yes	Sample new TTF & TTR for slot 4 (t13 & t14)
Old	t11	t12			Sample new TTF & TTR for
New	t9	t10	Is t11<t9<t12	no	slot 2 (not shown)
Old	t9	t10			Shift restart time (t10) to coincide with restoration of slot 1 (t8)
New	t7	t8	Is t9<t7<t10	yes	Sample new TTF & TTR for slot 3 (not shown)

Figure 5. "Timing" diagram for sampling TTFs and TTRs. Initially, a TTF and TTR are sampled for each HDD slot, t1 to t8. Then, pair-wise comparisons are made as indicated below the diagram.

The simulation begins by sampling a TTOp and a TTLd for every HDD and storing the times in separate arrays. For the two HDDs with the shortest times to failure (or defect), a time to restore (or time to scrub) is sampled. If two operational failures exist simultaneously, a DDF occurs. Since two latent defects will not fail the system, there is no DDF if the shortest and second shortest event times are both latent defects. If one event is an operational failure and one is a latent defect, a DDF exists when the operational failure occurs after the latent defect has occurred and before the scrub process corrects the corrupted data from the latent defect. A system failure does not occur if the shortest time is an operational failure and the second shortest is a latent defect.

Once a DDF has occurred, a subsequent one cannot occur until the first is restored. If no DDF is detected, then the TTR (or TTScrub) that has already been sampled and used in the preceding comparison is added to the earliest time to failure. A new TTOp (or TTLd) is sampled, added to the previous sum, and the HDDs are again sorted and reduced if the cumulative time exceeds the mission time. This process is reiterated until all the cumulative operating times for all HDD slots have exceeded the mission time.

6. Transition distributions

The four component-related distributions required for this model are time to operational failure, time to restore an operational failure, time to generation of a latent defect, and time to scrub HDDs for latent defects. The simulations in this paper use a three-parameter Weibull probability density function, f(t), of the form:

$$f(t) = \left(\frac{\beta}{\eta} \right) \left(\frac{t}{\eta} \right)^{\beta-1} \exp\left[-\left(\frac{t}{\eta} \right)^{\beta} \right]$$

where γ is the location parameter, η is the characteristic life, and β is the shape parameter.

6.1 Time to operational failure (TTOp)

To illustrate the improvement over the MTTDL method, a single TTOp distribution to illustrate improvement over the MTTDL method. A Weibull failure distribution with a slightly increasing failure rate is used. The characteristic life, η, is 461,386 hours. The shape parameter, β, is 1.12. These parameters are from a field population of over 120,000 HDDs that operated for up to 6,000 hours each.

6.2 Time to restore (TTR)

A constant restoration rate implies the probability of completing the restoration in any time interval is equally as likely as any other interval of equal length. Therefore, it is just as likely to complete restoration in the interval 0 to 48 hours as it is in the interval 1,000 to 1,048 hours. But this is clearly unrealistic for two reasons. First, there is a finite amount of time required for the HDD to reconstruct all the data on the HDD. It

is a function of the HDD capacity, the data rate of the HDD, the data rate of the data-bus, the number of HDDs on the data-bus and the amount of I/O transferred as a foreground process. Reconstruction is performed on a high priority basis but does not stop all other I/O to accelerate completion.

This model recognizes that there is a minimum time before which the probability of being fully restored is zero. Fibre Channel HDDs can sustain up to 100MB/second data transfer rates, although 50MB/sec is more common. The data-bus to which the RAID group is attached has only a 2 giga-bits per second capability. Thus, in a RAID group of 14, a 144GB HDD on a Fibre Channel interface will require a minimum of three hours with no other I/O to reconstruct the failed HDD. A 500GB, Serial ATA HDD on a 1.5Gb data-bus will require 10.4 hours to read all other HDDs and reconstruct a replaced HDD.

The added I/O associated with continuing to serve data will lengthen the time to restore an operational failure. Some operating systems place a limit on the amount of I/O that takes place during reconstruction, thereby assuring reconstruction will complete in a prescribed amount of time. This results in a maximum reconstruction time. The minimum time of six hours is used for the location parameter. The shape parameter of 2 generates a right-skewed distribution, and the characteristic life is 12 hours.

6.3 Time to latent defect (TTLd)

Personal conversations with engineers from four of the world's leading HDD manufacturers support the contention that HDD failure rates are usage dependent, but the exact transfer function of reliability as a function of use (number of reads and writes, lengths of reads and writes, sequential versus random) is not known (or they aren't telling anyone). These analyses approximate use by combining read errors per Byte read and the average number of Bytes read per hour. The result is shown in Table 1 and the following discussion is the justification.

Schwartz [10] claims the rate of data corruption is five times the rate of HDD operating failures. Network Appliance completed a study in late 2004 on 282,000 HDDs used in RAID architecture. The read error rate (RER), averaged over three months, was 8×10^{-14} errors per Byte read. At the same time, another analysis of 66,800 HDDs showed a RER of approximately 3.2×10^{-13} errors per Byte. A more recent analysis of 63,000 HDDs over five months showed a much improved 8×10^{-15} errors per Byte read. In these studies, data corruption is verified by the HDD manufacturer as an HDD problem and not a result of the operating system controlling the RAID group.

While Gray [25] asserts that it is reasonable to transfer 4.32×10^{12} Bytes/day/HDD, the study of 63,000 HDDs read 7.3×10^{17} Bytes of data in five months, an approximate read rate of 2.7×10^{11} Bytes/day/HDD. The following studies used a high of 1.35×10^{10} Bytes/hour and a low of 1.35×10^{9} Bytes/hour. Using combinations of the RERs and number of Bytes read yields the hourly read failure rates in Table 1.

Table 1. Range of average read error rates

Read Errors per Byte per HDD	Bytes Read per Hour		
	Low Rate	High Rate	
	1.35×10^{9}	1.35×10^{10}	
Low	8.0×10^{-15}	1.08×10^{-5}	1.08×10^{-4}	Err/hr
Med	8.0×10^{-14}	1.08×10^{-4}	1.08×10^{-3}	Err/hr
High	3.2×10^{-13}	4.32×10^{-4}	4.32×10^{-3}	Err/hr

6.4 Time to scrub (TTScrub)

Latent defects (data corruptions) can occur any time the disks are spinning. However, these defects can be eliminated by "background scrubbing," which is essentially preventive maintenance on data errors. Scrubbing occurs during times of idleness or low I/O activity. During scrubbing data is read and compared to the parity. If they are consistent, no action is taken. If they are inconsistent, the corrupted data is recovered and rewritten to the HDD. If the media is defective, the recovered data is written to new physical sectors on the HDD and the bad blocks are mapped out.

Scrubbing is a background activity performed on an as-possible basis so it does not affect performance. If not scrubbed, the period of time to accumulate latent defects starts when the HDD first begins operation in the system. The latent defect rate is assumed to be constant with respect to time ($\beta=1$) and is based on the error generation rate and the hourly data transfer rate.

As with full HDD data reconstruction, the time required to scrub an entire HDD is a random variable that depends on the HDD capacity and the amount of foreground activity. The minimum time to cover the entire HDD is based on capacity and foreground I/O. The operating system may invoke a maximum time to complete scrubbing. In all cases the shape parameter, β, is 3, which produces a Normal shaped distribution after the delay set by the location parameter, γ.

7. Results

Analyses were conducted to study the effects of parametric variants of a base case with parameters shown in Table 2. All analyses have an 87,600-hour (10-year) mission and 8 HDDs in a RAID group.

Table 2. Base case input parameters

Operational Failure Distributions						Latent Defect Distributions					
TTOp			TTR			TTLd			TTScrub		
γ	η	β	γ	η	β	γ	η	β	γ	η	β
0	461386	1.12	6	12	2	0	9259	1	6	168	3

Four variants of the base case, none of which include latent defects or scrubbing, are shown in Figure 6. Line "c-c" has constant rates for both failures and restorations. Line "f(t)-c" has time-dependent failure rates and constant restoration rates. Line "c-r(t)" has constant failure rates and time-dependent restoration rates. For line "f(t)-r(t)," failures and restorations both are time dependent as per Table 2. The last line is based on MTTDL assuming constant failure and restoration rates.

As expected, the model result "c-c" follows the MTTDL line closely. The plot shows the model will produce the same results as MTTDL under the same (time-independent rate) assumptions but is sensitive to time-dependent failure and restoration rates. The directions of change are counter-intuitive, but result from the shift in the probability density function "mass" when the characteristic life is not changed.

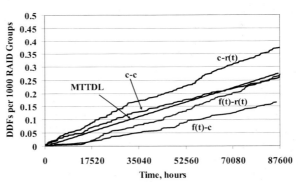

Figure 6. Model compared to MTTDL without latent defects

The difference between the MTTDL and the model are on the order of 2 to 1. If latent defects are not included, this difference may not be enough to warrant the use of this complex model. However, when latent defects are added to the analysis, the differences become great. Figure 7 compares the base case (including latent defects and 168 hour scrub) to the case of latent defects without scrubbing, which introduces significantly more DDFs. Notice that in both of these studies, the plot lines are not linear, showing the effects of the time-dependent failure and restoration rates. The increasing rate of occurrence of failure (ROCOF) is verified by finding the number of DDFs that occur in any fixed time interval (Figure 8).

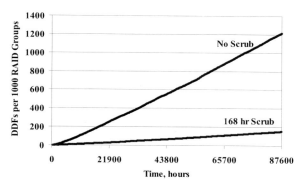

Figure 7. Effects of latent defects with no scrub and with 168 hr scrub

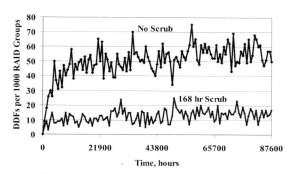

Figure 8. ROCOFs for plots in Figure 7

In Figure 9 additional scrub durations are compared. Again, the plots exhibit a non-linear (time dependent) ROCOF. Remember from Figure 6 that the MTTDL without latent defects predicts only 0.27 DDFs/1000 RAID groups in 10 years.

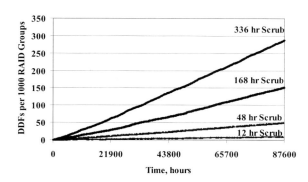

Figure 9. Effects of scrub durations

The assumption of constant failure rates is inherent to the MTTDL calculations. However, Figure 10 clearly shows the potential inaccuracy resulting from that assumption even when this new model is

used. A shape parameter of 0.8 may actually have 83% more DDFs than when beta is 1.0. Similarly, if the actual beta is 1.4, there may be only 30% of the DDFs predicted using constant failure rates.

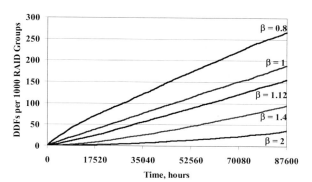

Figure 10. Effects of operational failure shape parameter for a given characteristic life

This research and new model show a clear difference between the estimated number of DDFs as a function of time based on the MTTDL and the new model. The number of DDFs predicted by the model is, in all cases, greater than the MTTDL when latent defects are included. Without scrubbing, and assuming the distributions in Table 2, this model estimates that in 1,000 RAID groups there will be over 1,200 DDFs in the 10-year mission, contrary to the 0.3 predicted by MTTDL. Table 3 shows the ratio of DDFs expected with the new model to the number estimated using the MTTDL during the first year alone. The highest ratio, >2,500, is when latent defects are included but there is no scrubbing. Even if scrubbing is completed in 168 hours, the new model predicts over 360 times as many DDFs as the MTTDL method.

Table 3. DDF comparisons

Assumptions	DDFs in 1st year	Ratio
MTTDL	0.03	1
Base Case w/o Scrub	78	2593
336 hr Scrub	21	700
168 hr Scrub	11	360
48 hr Scrub	5	150
12 hr Scrub	1	33

8. Conclusions

The MTTDL calculations exclude latent defects and implicitly assume the rate of occurrence of failure for any RAID group is an HPP (constant in time). The model results show that correctly including time-dependent failure rates and restoration rates along with latent defects yields estimates of DDFs that are as much as 4,000 times greater than the MTTDL-based estimates. Additionally, the ROCOF for a RAID group is not linear in time and depends heavily on the underlying component failure distributions. Field data show HDD failure rates are not constant in time and vary from vintage to vintage.

Latent defects are inevitable and scrubbing latent defects is imperative to RAID (N+1) reliability. Short scrub durations can improve reliability, but at some point the extensive scrubbing required to support the high-capacity HDDs will unacceptably impact performance.

This model provides a tool by which RAID designers can better evaluate the impact of the latent defect occurrence rate, which may be 100 times greater than the operational failure rate, and the scrubbing rate. The RAID architect can use this model to drive the design, providing insights as to the best RAID group size based on a specific manufacturer's HDDs and the impact of an increasing failure rate. For systems that currently do not scrub, consumers can see that this is a recipe for disaster. It appears that, eventually, RAID 6 will be required to meet high reliability requirements.

9. References

[1] D. A. Patterson, G. A. Gibson, R. H. Katz, "A Case for Redundant Arrays of Inexpensive Disks (RAID)," *Proc., ACM Conference on Management of Data (SIGMOD)*, Chicago, IL, June 1988.

[2] W. A. Thompson, "On the Foundations of Reliability," *Technometrics*, vol. 23, no. 1, Feb. 1981, pp. 1-13.

[3] H. E. Ascher, "A Set-of-Numbers is NOT a Data-Set," *IEEE Trans. on Reliability*, vol. 48, no. 2, June 1999.

[4] L. H. Crow, "Evaluating the Reliability of Repairable Systems," *Proc. Annual Reliability & Maintainability Symp.*, 1990.

[5] W. Nelson, "Graphical Analyses of System Repair Data," *Journal of Quality Technology*, vol. 20, no. 1, Jan. 1988.

[6] H. Ascher, "[Statistical Methods in Reliability]: Discussion," *Technometrics,* vol. 25, no. 4, Nov. 1983.

[7] J. G. Elerath and S. Shah, "Disk Drive Reliability Case Study: Dependence Upon Head Fly-Height and Quantity of Heads," *Proc. Annual Reliability & Maintainability Symp.*, 2003.

[8] S. Shah and J. G. Elerath, "Disk Drive Vintage and Its Affect on Reliability," *Proc. Annual Reliability & Maintainability Symp.*, 2004.

[9] H. H. Kari, "Latent Sector Faults and Reliability of Disk Arrays," Ph.D. Dissertation, TKO-A33, Helsinki University of Technology, Espoo, Finland, 1997, http://www.cs.hut.fi/~hhk/phd/phd.html.

[10] T. J. E. Schwarz et al., "Disk Scrubbing in Large Archival Storage Systems," *IEEE Computer Society Symposium,* MASCOTS, 2004.

[11] S. Shah and J. G. Elerath, "Reliability Analysis of Disk Drive Failure Mechanisms," *Proc. Annual Reliability & Maintainability Symp.*, 2005.

[12] E. Pinheiro, W. D. Weber, and L. A. Barroso, "Failure Trends in Large Disk Drive Population," *Proc. 5th USENIX Conference on File Storage Technologies* (FAST '07), Feb. 2007.

[13] B. Schroeder and G. Gibson, "Disk failures in the real world: What does an MTTF of 1,000,000 hours mean to you?" *Proc. of 5th USENIX Conference on File and Storage Technologies* (FAST), Feb. 2007.

[14] V. Prabhakaran, "IRON File Systems," *SOSP '05*, Oct. 2005, Brighton, UK.

[15] R. Geist and K. Trivedi, "An Analytic Treatment of the Reliability and Performance of Mirrored Disk Subsystems," *Twenty-Third Inter. Symp. on Fault-Tolerant Computing*, FTCS, June 1993.

[16] M. Malhotra, "Specification and solution of dependability models of fault tolerant systems," Ph.D. Dissertation, CS-1993-12, Dept. of Computer Science, Duke University, May 14, 1993.

[17] D. A. Patterson et al., "Introduction to Redundant Arrays of Inexpensive Disks (RAID)," *Thirty-Fourth IEEE Computer Society International Conference: Intellectual Leverage*, COMPCON, Feb. 1989.

[18] P. M. Chen et al., "RAID: High-Performance, Reliable Secondary Storage," *ACM Computing Surveys*, 1994.

[19] W. V. Courtright, II, "A Transactional Approach to Redundant Disk Array Implementation," Ph.D. Thesis, CMU-CS-97-141, School of Computer Science, Carnegie Mellon University, May 1997.

[20] T. J. E. Schwarz, W. A. Burkhard, "Reliability and Performance of RAIDs," *IEEE Transactions on Magnetics*, vol. 31, no. 2, Mar. 1995.

[21] W. A. Thompson, "The Rate of Failure Is the Density, Not the Failure Rate," *The American Statistician*, Editorial, vol. 42, no. 4, Nov. 1988.

[22] C. L. T. Borges et al., "Composite Reliability Evaluation by Sequential Monte Carlo Simulation on Parallel and Distributed Operating Environments," *IEEE Trans. on Power Systems*, vol. 16, no. 2, May 2001.

[23] D. Trindade and S. Nathan, "Simple Plots for Monitoring Field Reliability of Repairable Systems," *Proc. Annual Reliability & Maintainability Symp.*, 2005.

[24] P. Corbett et al., "Row Diagonal Parity for Double Disk Failure Correction," *Proc. of 3rd USENIX Conference on File and Storage Technology*, San Francisco, 2004.

[25] J. Gray, C. van Ingen, "Empirical Measurements of Disk Failure Rates and Error Rates," *Microsoft Research Technical Report*, MSR-TR-2005-166, Dec. 2005.

On a Modeling Framework for the Analysis of Interdependencies in Electric Power Systems

Silvano Chiaradonna
ISTI-CNR
via Moruzzi 1,
I-56124, Pisa, Italy
chiaradonna@isti.cnr.it

Paolo Lollini
University of Florence - DSI
viale Morgagni 65,
I-50134, Florence, Italy
lollini@dsi.unifi.it

Felicita Di Giandomenico
ISTI-CNR
via Moruzzi 1,
I-56124, Pisa, Italy
digiandomenico@isti.cnr.it

Abstract

Nowadays, economy, security and quality of life heavily depend on the resiliency of a number of critical infrastructures, including the Electric Power System (EPS), through which vital services are provided. In existing EPS two co-operating infrastructures are involved: the Electric Infrastructure (EI) for the electricity generation and transportation to final users, and its Information-Technology based Control System (ITCS) devoted to controlling and regulating the EI physical parameters and triggering reconfigurations in emergency situations. This paper proposes a modeling framework to capture EI and ITCS aspects, focusing on their interdependencies that contributed to the occurrence of several cascading failures in the past 40 years. A quite detailed analysis of the EI and ITCS structure and behavior is performed; in particular, the ITCS and EI behaviors are described by discrete and hybrid-state processes, respectively. To substantiate the approach, the implementation of a few basic modeling mechanisms inside an existing multi-formalism/multi-solution tool is also discussed.

1 Introduction and related work

Increasing research effort is being devoted nowadays to critical infrastructures protection, since more and more national and international economy, security and quality of life heavily depend on the resiliency of a number of critical infrastructures through which vital services are provided. Critical infrastructures are complex collections of interacting systems and components communicating through multiple heterogeneous networks [12]. The interactions between these components and systems need to be carefully analyzed to understand and characterize the interdependencies, that is how the state of each infrastructure influences or is correlated by the state of the others. In fact, interdependencies increase the vulnerability of the corresponding infrastructures as they give rise to multiple error propagation channels from one infrastructure to another that increase the exposure to threats. Consequently, the impact of infrastructure components failures and their severity can be exacerbated and are generally much higher and more difficult to foresee, compared to failures confined to single infrastructures. Electric Power Systems (EPSs) are prominent representatives of critical infrastructures. Existing EPSs are composed by two cooperating infrastructures: the Electric Infrastructure (EI) for the electricity generation and transportation to the final users, and its Information-Technology based Control System (ITCS) in charge of controlling and regulating the EI physical parameters and of triggering appropriate reconfigurations in emergency situations. Understanding and mastering the various interdependencies between EI and ITCS are crucial activities, since most major power grid blackouts that have occurred in the past have been initiated by a single event (or multiple related events such as an equipment failure of the power grid that is not properly handled by the SCADA system) that gradually led to cascading outages and eventual blackout of the entire system [11]. Among other initiatives, the CRUTIAL project [1] is addressing the analysis and management of interdependencies and of the resulting overall operational risk.

This paper proposes a modeling framework aiming to capture both EI and ITCS aspects, especially focusing on their interdependencies. The modelling of cascading failures has received increasing interest in the past years, in particular after the large blackouts of electric power transmission systems in 1996 and 2003. Several research papers and modelling studies have been published on this topic in particular by the Consortium for Electric Reliability Technology Solutions (CERTS) in the USA [5]. The followed approaches span along two directions: i) statistical analysis on historical data collected from past blackouts, to find predictive models that can be used for planning purposes;

and ii) development of analytical or simulation models to describe cascading failures and studying blackout dynamics. The models presented in the literature (e.g., [6, 7, 2]) usually adopt a simplified representation of the power system; the main focus is on the overloading of system components which eventually leads to the collapse of the whole system. However, these models do not take into account explicitly the complex interactions and interdependencies between the power infrastructure and the ITCS infrastructures. Our approach, instead, attempts a separate description of the EI and ITCS internal structure and behavior, to better capture the interdependencies between them. Quantitative assessment of the impact of such interdependencies through appropriate performability indicators are then expected to be possible through the proposed modeling framework. A qualitative modeling of the interdependencies in the EPS systems has been recently proposed in [9], focusing on cascading, escalating and common-cause outages.

The major contributions of this paper consist in the: i) identification of the main EI and ITCS logical components; ii) representation of the EI and ITCS states (as hybrid and discrete states, respectively); iii) identification of the main characteristics of the modeling framework (in terms of modeling power, modeling efficiency and solution power), and approaches to cope with them; iv) feasibility of the proposed framework through an existing multi-formalism/multi-solution tool, by presenting the implementation of a few basic modeling mechanisms.

The paper is structured as follows. In Section 2, the detailed analysis of the EPS system is provided, specifically identifying the EI and ITCS structure and behavior. In Section 3 the failure models of the EI and ITCS subsystems and their interdependencies are presented. The state definition for EI and ITCS is addressed in Section 4. Sections 5 and 6 discuss the EPS main properties to be accounted for in a model representing the EPS system, the major characteristics of the proposed modeling framework and the related approaches. The feasibility of the framework inside the Möbius tool is discussed in Section 7 and final conclusions are drawn in Section 8.

2 Logical scheme of EPS

As derived from [12], [10] and [15], the electric power system (EPS) is logically structured in two interacting parts: the Electric Infrastructure (EI) and the Information-Technology based Control System (ITCS).

2.1 The Electric Infrastructure

EI represents the electric infrastructure necessary to produce and to transport the electric power towards the final users. It can be logically structured in different components,

as shown in Figure 1(a): the transmission grid (TG, operating in very high voltage levels), the distribution grid (DG, operating in medium/low voltage levels), the huge voltage generation plants (HG), the medium and low voltage generation plants (LG), the huge voltage loads (HL), the medium and low voltage loads (LL). A typical scheme of EI is shown in Figure 1(b), where the components HL and LG are not present (as in the case of the Italian Electric Infrastructure). The distribution grid could be further decomposed in two different medium and low voltage grids, but here we consider it as a whole for the sake of clarity.

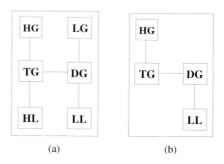

(a)   (b)

Figure 1. General (a) and typical (b) EI scheme

One or more generators can be situated inside the power plants. The energy produced by the generators is then adapted by transformers, to be conveyed with minimal dispersion, to the different types of end users (loads), through different power grids. The main elements that constitute the power grid are the *power lines*, that are components which physically connect the substations with the power plants and the final users, and the *substations*, that are structured components in which the electric power is transformed and split over several lines. In the substations there are transformers and several kinds of connection components (bus-bars, protections and breakers).

From a topological point of view, TG and DG can be considered like a network, or a graph, as shown in the example of Figure 2(a). The nodes of the graph represent the substations, while the arcs represent the power lines. The generators and the loads are nodes connected by arcs (power lines) to the nodes of the grid. Some nodes of the grid can be connected to nodes of the contiguous grid. The specific instances that can be derived from the general scheme of Figure 2(a) mainly differ for: i) topology of the grid (meshed graph for the TG; partially meshed or radial graph for the DG), ii) number and power of the generators, iii) number and values of the loads, iv) number of substations, v) number of lines, and vi) values of the electric network parameters like voltage (V), frequency (F), current flow (I), angle (A), active power (P) and reactive power (Q).

V, F, I, A, P and Q are physical parameters associated to the electric equipments constituting EI (generators, substations, power lines and loads), and their specific values are of primary importance in determining the current status of the overall EI. In fact, they affect the behavior of the electric equipments they are referred to (e.g., in terms of availability and reliability of the electric equipment), thus also influencing the evolution of the overall power grid. Therefore it is crucial that the modeling framework is capable to support both high-level system aspects, like the topology definition, as well as low-level system details associated to the main electric equipments.

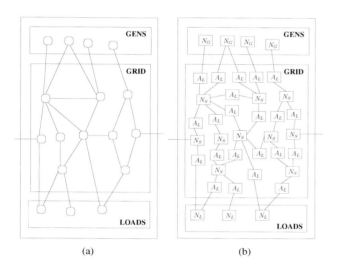

Figure 2. A meshed graph grid (a) and logical scheme (b) for a dummy transmission grid

In Figure 3(a) it is shown a typical physical scheme of a substation and the connected power lines. This very detailed physical scheme needs to be mapped into a logical (and maybe more abstract) one, as that shown in Figure 3(b). The main electric equipments (bus-bars BB, protections PR, breakers BR, transformer TR, power lines PL) have been grouped following an approach which has the advantage to simplify the logical representation. The component N_S represents the parts common to all substations (i.e., the bus-bar), while breakers, transformers and protections, which are physically part of a substation, are now included in the scheme of the new logical component A_L. In this way, only two types of different A_L have to be considered (A_L^T, containing transformers, and A_L^B, not containing transformers), thus facilitating the subsequent modeling process (see Section 6). In Figure 2(b) the high-level logical scheme corresponding to Figure 2(a) is presented, where the components N_G and N_L represent a generation plant and a load, respectively.

2.2 The Information-Technology based Control System

$ITCS$ implements the control system based on information technology and its main purposes are: i) reducing out of service time of generators, power lines and substations (availability); ii) enhance quality of service (through frequency and voltage regulation); iii) optimizing generators and substations management. To these aims, ITCS performs the following activities: a) remote control of the electric infrastructure (it receives data and sends commands); b) co-ordination of the maintenance (it plans the reconfiguration actions that can affect generators, substations, loads and lines); c) collection of the system statistics. There are several logical components composing ITCS: the protection system, that is composed by a set of independent (or loosely connected) local protections, one for each breaker of EI; the frequency and voltage regulation systems, which try to keep constant the frequency and the voltage levels inside a piece of grid; and the tele-operation (or tele-control) systems of the transmission and distribution grid, which control and monitor equipments in remote locations.

In this paper we focus the attention on the tele-operation systems for the distribution grid (named $DTOS$) and for the transmission grid (named $TTOS$), since a failure of these logical components can affect a large portion of the grid, also leading to black-out phenomena.

The logical ITCS components interact through a hierarchical structure. In Figure 4 we depict a possible logical structure of $TTOS$ and $DTOS$. The components LCT (Local Control system inside $TTOS$), RTS (Regional Tele-control System) and NTS (National Tele-control System) of $TTOS$, and the components LCD (Local Control system inside $DTOS$), and ATS (Area Tele-control System) of $DTOS$ differ for their criticality and for the locality of their decisions.

Different actors (like Power Exchange PE, Energy Authority EA, Network Management System NMS) are involved in the electric system management and there can be a necessity to exchange grid status information and control data over public or private networks (e.g., $TSOcommNetw$ and $DSOcommNetw$). The transmission and distribution grids are divided in homogeneous regions and areas, respectively. LCT and LCD guarantee the correct operation of substation equipment and reconfigure the substation in case of breakdown of some apparatus. They include the acquisition and control equipment (sensors and actuators). RTS and ATS monitor their region and area, respectively, in order to diagnose faults on the power lines. In case of breakdowns, they choose the more suitable corrective actions to restore the functionality of the grid. Since RTS and ATS are not directly connected to the substations, the corrective actions to adopt are com-

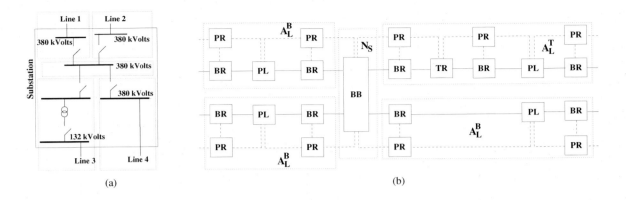

Figure 3. Physical (a) and logical (b) scheme for substation and connected power lines

municated to the LCT or ATS of reference. NTS has the main function of supervising the entire grid and handling the planning of medium and long term operations. NTS also assists RTS (and ATS) to localize breakdowns on the power lines situated between two regions (two areas). LCT and LCD, such as RTS and ATS, cooperate to decide operation of load shedding.

3 Interdependencies and failures model of EPS

The characterization of the mutual interdependencies between ITCS and the controlled EI is a very challenging activity, especially considering the various types of accidental and malicious faults. Such type of analysis can be used for prevention and limitation of threats and vulnerabilities propagation, in order to avoid escalating and cascading[1] failures that result in outages and blackouts.

An interdependency is a bidirectional relationship between two infrastructures through which the state of each infrastructure influences or is correlated to the state of the other. As detailed in [12], there are several types of interdependencies: physical (when the state of each infrastructure is dependent on the material outputs of the other), cyber (if the state of an infrastructure depends on information transmitted through the information infrastructure), geographic (if a local environment event can create a state changes in all the connected infrastructures) and logical (if the state of each depends on the state of the other via mechanism that is not physical, cyber or geographical connection).

In this paper the focus is mainly on the cyber and physical interdependencies. EI requires information transmitted

and delivered by ITCS, for example when ITCS triggers a grid reconfiguration for economic optimization; therefore the state of EI depends on the outputs of ITCS (cyber interdependency). Viceversa, the state of ITCS could be affected by disruptions in EI (e.g. in case of blackout that leads to a failure or service degradation of the information infrastructure), thus revealing a physical interdependency.

3.1 Failures model within EI and ITCS

A disruption (or disturbance or contingency) is the unexpected failure or outage of a EI component, such as a generator, power line, circuit breaker, bus-bar, or other electric components. The main (electric) disruptions, based on their effects on (single or multiple) components N_S, N_G, N_L and A_L, could be summarized in:

1. Transient or permanent disconnection of a component A_L, N_S, N_G or N_L with consequent separation of one or more components from the grid. Transient or permanent failed disconnection of a component A_L, N_S, N_G or N_L without isolation from the grid.

2. Transient or permanent overloads of A_L, N_S, N_G or N_L. Unexpected reduction of production of N_G. Unexpected increase or reduction of demand. Voltage collapse. Underfrequency and loss of synchronism.

The failures of the ITCS components can be summarized in (transient and permanent) omission failure, time failure, value failure and byzantine failure. Here the focus is on the failures and not on their causes (internal HW/SW faults, malicious attacks, etc.).

3.2 ITCS↔EI failures model (interdependencies)

Failures in ITCS impact on the state of EI, i.e. on the topology T and on the values of V, F, I, A, P and Q, de-

---

[1]An escalating failure occurs when an existing failure in one infrastructure exacerbates an independent disruption in another infrastructure, increasing its severity or the time for recovery and restoration from this failure. A cascading failure occurs when a disruption in one infrastructure causes the failure of a component in a second infrastructure.

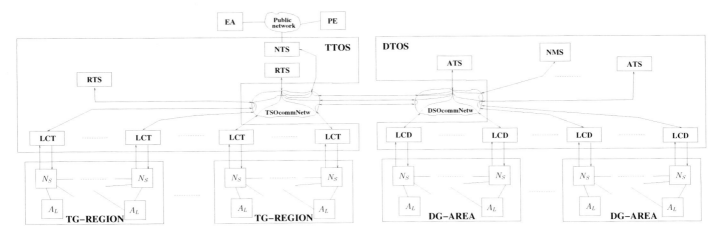

Figure 4. Logical scheme of $TTOS$ **and** $DTOS$

pending on the logical components affected by the failures, and obviously by the type of the failures (cyber interdependency). For example, consequences of a failure of the component LCT associated to a component N_S, N_G or N_L (see also Figure 4) can be:

Omission failure of LCT**, fail silent** LCT**.** No (reconfiguration) actions are performed on N_S or A_L.

Time failure of LCT**.** The above (reconfiguration) actions on N_S or A_L are performed after a certain delay (or before the instant of time they are required).

Value failure of LCT**.** Incorrect closing or opening of the power lines A_L directly connected to the failed component is performed.

Failures of the component LCT can also impact on the input values that the components RTS receive from LCT. These values can be omitted, delayed (or anticipated) or erroneous. Since reconfigurations required by RTS (or NTS) are actuated by the associated component LCT, a failure of a component LCT can also impact on the reconfigurations required by RTS (or NTS). The failure of the component RTS (or NTS) corresponds to an erroneous (request of) reconfiguration of the state of EI (including an unneeded reconfiguration) affecting one or more components of the controlled region. The effect of the failure of RTS (or NTS) on a component N is the same as the failure of the component LCT associated to the component N. In the case of Byzantine failure these effects can be different for each component N. In general, the failure of the components LCT, RTS and NTS may depend on the failures of the components connected to them through a network.

On the other direction (physical interdependency), disruptions of the EI infrastructure impact on (parts of) the ITCS system by lessening its functionalities (till complete

failure in the extreme case the disruption is a total blackout of the power grid).

4 State definition for EI and ITCS

The description of the infrastructures outlined in Sections 2.1 and 2.2, together with the analysis of the possible failure models detailed in Section 3, lead us to derive the state for EI and ITCS. The state of the Electric Infrastructure (EI) can be completely described through the physical parameters associated to each electric equipment (V, F, I, A, P and Q) and through the topology (T) of the grid. Actually, the first set of parameters defines the current status of each EI component, while the topology defines how such components are connected together to form the overall EI.

Therefore, the state of EI is an hybrid-state composed by a discrete part and a continuous one. It can be defined as a 7-tuple (T, V, F, I, A, P, Q), where:

- T represents the topology of the grid, i.e., the components N_S, N_G, N_L and A_L and their connections (as shown for example in Figure 2(b)). T could also include information on the direction of the current flow on each power line. This information is used to reconfigure the topology of the grid. Therefore, T can be described as an oriented graph where N_S, N_G and N_L are nodes and A_L are arcs.

- V, F, I, A, P and Q are the voltage, the frequency, the current flow, the angle, the active and reactive power associated to N_S, N_G, N_L and A_L (if applicable).

T represents the discrete part of the EI states, whereas V, F, I, A, P and Q represent the continuous part of the EI states. On the contrary, the state of ITCS is discrete, in the sense that it is only composed by discrete values. Some possible states are "Working" (ITCS is working properly), "Passive latent" (ITCS is working properly but some latent errors are present), "Omission Failure" (ITCS does not send the command for the execution of a reconfiguration action), etc. The set of possible ITCS states depends on the specific information control system to be analyzed.

The status of EI and ITCS gives a static view of the system. In the following Subsection we discuss the dynamic behavior of EPS, also providing an example of a possible temporal evolution of the EI system in absence and in presence of ITCS.

4.1 Dynamic behavior of EPS

The hybrid-state of EI changes when the topology T of the system or the values for V, F, I, A, P or Q change, i.e., when one of the following events occurs: disruption (including failure of a local protection), activation of a protection local to EI, voltage or frequency regulation or reconfiguration action by ITCS (including erroneous, delayed or not required action), maintenance actions on EI. Therefore, the state of EI can also change due to actions by ITCS (both correctly activated by an event in EI, or erroneously activated by a failure of ITCS). The discrete-state of ITCS can change when one of the following events occurs: failure of a component of ITCS, disruption of EI, recovery triggered after a failure (in ITCS) or disruption (in EI).

To better describe the interaction between EI and ITCS, we show in Figures 5 and 6 an example of a possible temporal evolution of the EI system after a fault which breaks a line, in absence and in presence of ITCS, respectively.

Figure 5. EI behavior in absence of ITCS

As in [8], let us denote with NORMAL, ALERT, EMERGENCY and IN EXTREMIS the set of operative states of EI, where the criticality of the system increases from NORMAL (situation in which all the constraints are satisfied) to IN EXTREMIS (in which the service is partially or totally interrupted). Each of these states can be described with different combinations of values of the 7-tuple (T, V, F, I, A, P, Q). At time 0, EI is in a state NORMAL $S_0 = (T_0, V_0, F_0, I_0, A_0, P_0, Q_0)$. At time t_F, a disruption, due to a tree fall, causes a loss of a line and EI moves to the degraded state ALERT $S_F = (T_F, V_F, F_F, I_F, A_F, P_F, Q_F)$.

In Figure 5, at the instants of time $t_{P_1}, t_{P_2}, \ldots, t_{P_6}$ six activations of protections isolate components of EI, and EI moves into new degraded states until reaching, at time t_C, the state IN EXTREMIS, where the total service interruption cannot be avoided. In Figure 6, ITCS is also considered. Then, at time t_F three types of activities of the com-

ponents LCT, RTS and NTS start on ITCS. When these activities complete at the instants of time t_{LCT}, t_{RTS} and t_{NTS}, EI should move into a state less degraded than the state in which EI would be without considering ITCS.

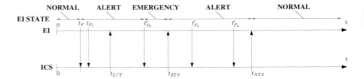

Figure 6. EI behavior in presence of ITCS

In the case shown in Figure 6, LCT is not able to restore EI, because global reconfiguration is needed or because LCT is affected by an omission failure. The duration of these activities and the state reconfiguration to adopt can be influenced by the state changes in EI due to the protections, at the instants of time $t_{P_1}, t'_{P_2}, t'_{P_3}, t'_{P_4}$. Moreover, depending on the current state of EI and on the probability to move in an IN EXTREMIS state (if greater than a specific threshold), partial-reconfiguration commands can be activated, if possible, without waiting the end of the reconfiguration commands of RTS or NTS.

5 Prominent aspects of the framework

To model and analyze the interdependencies, the behavior of the involved system components has to be firstly represented. Then, the derived models need to be solved, through simulation or analytic techniques. To represent and model the behavior of EI and ITCS and their interactions, the following aspects should be considered.

Structural aspects. The system has a natural hierarchical structure, as shown in the examples of logical schemes of Section 2. At a certain level of detail, the system is composed by many similar components having the same logical structure (see Figure 2(b) for the logical components N_S, N_G, N_L and A_L). Therefore, these components can be grouped on the basis of their similarities. All similar components can be considered non anonymous replicas having the same structure but different values for the parameters characterizing each specific component.

Behavioral aspects. The time to disruptions of the components N_S, N_G, N_L and A_L depends also on the value of the electric parameters associated to the components. A disruption of a component can propagate to contiguous components and the propagation time should not be considered instantaneous. Protections can stop the propagation of a disruption by isolating from the grid the component affected by a disruption. The activation time of a protection should not be considered instantaneous. The correct activation of a protection depends also on the strength of the disruption and on the value of the electric parameters associated to the protection component. The reaction time to the occurrence of a disruption, the failure time and erroneous activation time (when no disruptions have occurred) of a component (e.g., LCT, RTS and NTS) should be also considered. Moreover, the functions which implement the reconfiguration and regulation algorithms should be considered. These functions receive in input the 7-tuple $(T_i, V_i, F_i, I_i, A_i, P_i, Q_i)$ that identifies a situation in which EI is not in equilibrium (that is it is not in NORMAL state in terms of costs, voltage, etc.) and outputs the new 7-tuple $(T_e, V_e, F_e, I_e, A_e, P_e, Q_e)$ for which the system EI is in equilibrium (in NORMAL state), if possible. The automatic evolution of the electric parameters in case of instability events, e.g. in correspondence of a power line disruption, is modeled by the autoevolution function that receives as input $(T_j, V_j, F_j, I_j, A_j, P_j, Q_j)$ and produces in output the new values for the electric parameters.

To capture the above discussed structural and behavioral aspects, the modeling and evaluation framework should possess the following major characteristics, grouped into three categories: modeling power aspects (the basic modeling mechanisms required to build the EPS model), the modeling efficiency aspects (the advanced modeling mechanisms required to build the EPS model more efficiently), and the solution power aspects.

Concerning **modeling power.**

A1◇ EPS is a very complex system having subsystems (or subcomponents) with very different characteristics. This heterogeneity must also be addressed inside the framework that, therefore, should support the definition of different models using different formalisms, each one capable to properly capture the behavior of a specific subsystem.
A2◇ The framework should support the representation of continuous, discrete and hybrid state (see Section 4).
A3◇ The framework should support time and probability distributions, and conditions enabling the time consuming events (e.g., for the activation of a local protection) that can depend both on the discrete and on the continuous state.
A4◇ The framework should support the call to the function which implements the reconfiguration and regulation algorithms, as well as the autoevolution algorithm.
A5◇ Risk analysis of EPS based on a stochastic approach requires the definition of measures of performability, which is a unified measure proposed to deal simultaneously with performance and dependability. To this purpose, a reward structure can be set-up by associating proper costs/benefits to generators/loads and interruption of service supply.

Concerning **modeling efficiency.**

B1◇ As detailed in Section 2, the system has a hierarchical structure; the modeling framework should support hierarchical composition of different sub-models.
B2◇ The model for the overall EPS could be facilitated considering replication of (anonymous and not anonymous) sub-models. The replicated and composed models should share part of the state (common state).
B3◇ A compact representation of the topology of the grid (T) is highly desirable, for example describing it as a matrix (incidence matrix [nodes x arcs]).
B4◇ Compact representation of continuous states (for V, F, I, A, P and Q) of EI is highly desirable, for example describing them in terms of arrays, associating to each component of the grid of EI (nodes and arcs) the values of V, F, I, A, P and Q (if applicable).

Concerning **solution power.**

C1◇ The framework should support analytical solution of the overall model (if possible). Actually, the huge system complexity and its heterogeneity may inhibit the computation of the analytic solution due to the explosion of the states of the model and stiffness. Moreover, an analytical solution method could not exist for the class of models considered, depending on the considered time distributions. Analytical solutions may be applied for simpler sub-models.
C2◇ The framework should support simulation, by automatic tools or ad hoc simulation software.
C3◇ The framework should support separate evaluation of different sub-models (with analytic or simulation techniques) and combination of the results.

6   Approaches to the EPS model construction

In this Section we address the problem of building the overall model for the entire EPS, considering the logical scheme of the electric grid shown in 2(b). The model construction should consist of the following steps:

1) Definition of the models M_N and M_A, where M_N is the generic model for a node N of the grid (N=N_S, N_G, N_L), and M_A is the generic model for an arc of the grid (A=A_L).
2) Duplication of M_N and M_A for each specific component N and A, and setting of the specific parameters.
3) Based on the topology T, manual connection of the models M_N and M_A through a composition operator, for each node N connected to an arc A.

When the number of components N and A is high, the construction of the model based on the above approach can be very expensive in terms of time and very error prone. An alternative approach could be based on replication and possibility to define part of the state of a system with an array (for the incidence matrix [arcs x nodes]). In this case, to build a model representing a topology like that shown in Figure 2(b) for m nodes N and n arcs A, the following steps should be required:

1) Define the model M_N and M_A for each generic component N and arc A.

2) Define the discrete part of the state of M_N and M_A by using a $m \times n$ matrix $T[i,j]$ of binary values $\{0,1\}$, where $T[i,j] = 1$ if the component i-th is connected to the component j-th, otherwise $T[i,j] = 0$ (the values 1 and -1 can be used if it is needed to represent also the direction of the arc, i.e., if T represents an oriented graph). The time distributions and the conditions in the model M_N can depend on the values of T. In particular, the i-th replica of M_N (or the j-th replica of M_A) can be defined as a function of $T[i,j]$, and can modify $T[i,j]$ (see below).

3) Define a hierarchical model by automatically replicating m times the model M_N, by assigning at each replica a different index, from 1 to m. The state defined with matrix T is common to all the replicated sub-models M_N. The parameters of the i-th replica can depend on $T[i,j]$.

4) Define a hierarchical model by automatically replicating n times the model M_A, by assigning at each replica a different index, from 1 to n. The state defined with matrix T is common to all the replicated sub-models M_A. The replica j-th can depend on the values of the element $T[i,j]$.

A compact representation of the electric parameters V, F, I, A, P and Q can be obtained following the same approach.

7 Feasibility using SAN and Möbius

In this Section we discuss the feasibility of the proposed framework using Möbius [4], a powerful multi-formalism/multi-solution tool, and present the implementation of a few basic modeling mechanisms adopting the Stochastic Activity Network (SAN) formalism [14], that is a generalization of the Stochastic Petri Nets formalism. Here the goal is not to provide a complete and detailed model representing a concrete instance of an EPS system, but to show how some basic framework's characteristics can be actually obtained. To this purpose, we describe the model construction of a simple instance of the EPS system, focusing on the model for N_S and the model for the overall EPS as composition of different submodels. A detailed description of the other components models can be found in [3].

The number of components N_G, N_S, N_L and A_L of EI is n_G, n_S, n_L and n_A respectively. These components are represented by replicated SAN with index i, with $i \in [0, n_G - 1]$ for N_G, $i \in [n_G, n_G + n_S - 1]$ for N_S, $i \in [n_G + n_S, n_G + n_S + n_L - 1]$ for N_L, $i \in [n_G + n_S + n_L, n_G + n_S + n_L + n_A - 1]$ for A_L.

In Figure 7 the SAN for the component N_S is shown. In describing the SAN elements, we make explicit reference to the framework's characteristics, among those identified in Section 5, here implemented as basic modeling mechanisms. The place $NSindex$ represents the index of the component N_S. The place $NScount$ is common to the replicas of the SAN and contains n_S tokens at time 0. The extended place T is an $array of array$ of $n_A \times n_N$ $short$ type, with $n_N = n_G + n_S + n_L$, and represents the topology of the transmission grid and its state ($\mathbf{A2}\diamond$, $\mathbf{B3}\diamond$ of Section 5). The following value can be associated to each element $T{-}{>}Index(i){-}{>}Index(j){-}{>}Mark()$ of T:

-1: for a connection from the the arc i to the node j (the current flow enters into the node);

+1: for a connection from the node i to the arc j (the current flow exits from the node);

-2, +2: if the connection has been opened and can be closed by reconfiguration;

-3, +3: if the connection has been opened due to a disruption and can be only closed after a repair.

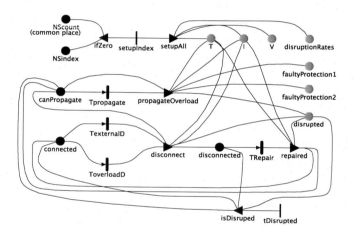

Figure 7. SAN of the component N_S

For the sake of simplicity, we only consider two different types of electric parameters, the current flow and the voltage. The extended places I and V are $arrays$ of n_{EPS} $struct$ type, with $n_{EPS} = n_G + n_S + n_L + n_A$, and represent the electric parameters and the current values associated to each component for the current flow and for the voltage, respectively ($\mathbf{A2}\diamond$, $\mathbf{B4}\diamond$). For example, for each generation plant i, $I{-}{>}Index(i)$ represents the produced current flow and the maximum current flow which can be produced; for each station i, $I{-}{>}Index(i)$ represents the current flow associated to it, the threshold current flow for an overload, and the threshold current flow for a breakdown of the component. The extended place $disruptionRates$ is an $array$ of n_{EPS} $struct$ type and represents the rate of occurrence of different types of disruptions associated to each component. These rates depend on the component (e.g., the length of the line, the position of the station, etc.) and on the type of disruption (lightning, tree fall, etc.). The extended place *disrupted* is an *array* of n_{EPS} *short* type and represents the state of disruption of each component. The extended places *faultyProtection1* and *faultyProtection2* are *arrays* of n_A *short* type and represent the state of failure of the protections associated to each line.

The activity *setupAll* is enabled when the marking of $NSindex$ is equal to 0, i.e., for each replica of the SAN for which the $NSindex$ has not yet been set. The function of the input gate *ifZero* removes one token from $NScount$ and sets the marking of $NSindex$ to $n_G + (n_S - NScount->Mark()) - 1$. This part of the model enables to distinguish each replica when the N_S model is replicated n_S times to build the complete EI infrastructure (**B2**◇). The gate *setupAll* is executed only by the first replica, and it sets all the parameters and the initial state of EI represented by the extended places by the following C++ like code:

```
if( NSindex->Mark()==nG)  {
  setupT(configTfile, T, nA, nN);
  setupI(configIfile, I, nEPS);
  setupV(configVfile, V, nEPS);
  setupDisruptionRates(configDisRatefile,
    disruptionRates, nEPS); }
```

The functions $setupT()$, $setupI()$, $setupV()$ and $setupDisruptionRates()$ set the initial values of the extended places by reading the configuration values from the input files. For example, the input file $configTfile$ can have a row for each electric line with the following format: "nodeIndex arcIndex nodeIndex".

The activity $Tpropagate$ represents the occurrence of an event of current flow overload (e.g., lightnings) which can propagate instantaneously to neighbour components. This activity has exponential distribution with rate $disruptionRates->Index(NSindex->Mark()) ->overloadPropagation->Mark()$. Upon $Tpropagate$ completion, the code of the gate *propagateOverload* is executed:

```
propagateOverload(T, disrupted, faultyProtection1,
        faultyProtection2, T, NSindex->Mark());
autoevolution(T, I, V);
if( disrupted->Index(NSindex->Mark())->Mark()==0 )
    canPropagate->Mark()=1;
```

The function $propagateOverload()$ receives in input the topology state T, the disruption state of the components *disrupted*, the state of the failure of the protections *faultyProtection1* and *faultyProtection2*, the current flow on the grid and the index of the component affected by the overload (**A4**◇). The result of the execution of $propagateOverload()$ is that the values of T, *disrupted*, *faultyProtection1* and *faultyProtection2* are modified, due to the propagation of the overload. The function $autoevolution()$ updates I and V in accordance with the new topology T. This function represents the automatic evolution of the values of I and V when the topology changes. It must be executed after each change of T.

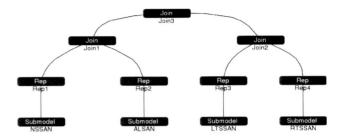

Figure 8. Part of the composed model for EPS

The activities $TexternalD$ and $ToverloadD$, which represent the time to the occurrence of an external (e.g., a tree fall) or internal (e.g., a disruption due to the current flow) disruption, are exponential. The rate of $TexternalD$ is $disruptionRates->Index(NSindex->Mark()) ->externalDisconnection->Mark()$. The rate of $ToverloadD$ depends on the current flow of the component (**A3**◇), and is defined by the following code:

```
if(I->Index(NSindex->Mark())->curr->Mark() <
  I->Index(NSindex->Mark())->overload->Mark())
 return(disruptionRates-> Index(NSindex->Mark())
  ->agingRate->Mark() );
 else
 return( overloadedDisruptionRate(I, disruptionRates
  ->Index(NSindex->Mark())->agingRate-> Mark(),
  NSindex->Mark())
```

The function $overloadedDisruptionRate()$ returns the rate of disruption when the current flow is greater than a threshold $I->Index(NSindex->Mark())->overload->Mark()$. The gate *disconnect* changes the topology state T when a component is disrupted. For each index of row i of T for which $T->Index(i)->Index(NSindex->Mark())->Mark()$ is equal to 1 or -1 then this value is changed to 3 or -3, respectively, and the following code is executed:

```
disconnected->Mark()=1; canPropagate->Mark()=0;
disrupted->Index(NSindex->Mark())->Mark()=1;
autoevolution(T, I, V);
```

After the repair of the component, represented by the activity $TRepair$, the values of T and *disrupted* are updated by the output gate *rapaired* and the function $autoevolution()$ is executed.

The immediate activity $tDisruped$ is enabled when, due to a disruption propagation, the component is affected by a disruption, i.e., $disrupted{-}{>}Index(NSindex{-}{>}Mark()){-}{>}Mark()$ $== 1$ and the local places $canPropagate$, $connected$ and $disconnected$ must be updated.

In Figure 8 it is shown how the atomic models for N_S, A_L, LCT and RTS can be replicated (using the "Rep" operator [13]) and composed (using the "Join" operator [13]) to obtain a part of the EPS model. The number of replicas of the models of N_S, A_L, LCT and RTS are n_S, n_A, n_S and n_R, with n_R the number of regions (**B1**$\diamond$). We remind that these anonymous replications become non anonymous thanks to the modeling mechanisms described in the first part of this Section (**B2**$\diamond$).

8 Conclusions and future work

This paper has addressed the definition of a modeling framework to analyze the interdependencies between the electric infrastructure EI and the control information system ITCS involved in electric power systems EPS. Analyzing and mastering the reciprocal impact of the failures experienced by EI and ITCS are crucial for a proper assessment of the operational risk and foresee adequate countermeasures to possibly prevent catastrophic blackouts. The current study is still at an exploratory stage, and further research needs to be devoted to fully realize the modeling environment. Notwithstanding such preliminary character of this work, a relevant contribution is being provided in terms of: i) analysis of the structure and behavior of the EI and ITCS subsystems, including their failure models and states definitions; ii) identification of the major challenges the modeling framework has to deal with, and discussion of possible approaches to cope with them; iii) implementation of a few basic modeling mechanisms inside the Möbius modeling and evaluation environment, to support the feasibility of the proposed approach through an existing tool.

Extension and refinements of the presented modeling mechanisms are currently under investigation. Of course, future work also includes the detailed study of the solution aspects then need to addressed, to come out with a complete modeling and evaluation framework suitable to quantitative assessment of interdependencies impact in electric power systems, possibly extendible to interdependencies analysis in other critical infrastructure systems.

Acknowledgment

This work has been partially supported by the EC IST Project CRUTIAL [1] (Contract n. 027513).

References

[1] European Project CRUTIAL, contract n. 027513. http://crutial.cesiricerca.it.

[2] B. A. Carreras, V. E. Lynch, I. Dobson, and D. E. Newman. Critical points and transitions in an electric power transmission model for cascading failure blackouts. *Chaos*, 12(4):985–994, 2002.

[3] S. Chiaradonna, P. Lollini, and F. Di Giandomenico. On the modeling of an instance of the electric power system. Technical Report rcl061201, University of Florence, Dip. Sistemi Informatica, RCL group, http://dcl.isti.cnr.it/Documentation/Papers/Techreports.html, December 2006.

[4] D. Daly, D. D. Deavours, J. M. Doyle, P. G. Webster, and W. H. Sanders. Möbius: An extensible tool for performance and dependability modeling. In B. R. Haverkort, H. C. Bohnenkamp, and C. U. Smith, editors, *11th International Conference, TOOLS 2000*, volume 1786 of *LNCS*, pages 332–336. Springer Verlag, 2000.

[5] I. Dobson and B. A. Carreras. Risk analysis of critical loading and blackouts with cascading events. Consortium for Electric Reliability Technology Solutions (CERTS), 2005.

[6] I. Dobson, B. A. Carreras, and D. E. Newman. A loading-dependent model of probabilistic cascading failure. *Probability in the Engineering and Informational Sciences*, 19(1):15–32, 2005.

[7] I. Dobson, K. R. Wierzbicki, B. A. Carreras, V. E. Lynch, and D. E. Newman. An estimator of propagation of cascading failure. In *39th IEEE Hawaii International Conference on System Sciences (CD-ROM)*, Kauai, Hawaii, 2006.

[8] L. H. Fink and K. Carlsen. Operating under stress and strain. *IEEE Spectrum*, 15:48–53, March 1978.

[9] J.-C. Laprie, K. Kanoun, and M. Kaâniche. Modeling cascading and escalating outages in interdependent critical infrastructures. In *IEEE Int. Conference on Dependable Systems and Networks (DSN-2006)*, pages 226–227, Philadelphie (USA), June 2006. Fast abstract.

[10] W. G. on Critical Information Infrastructure Protection. Critical information infrastructures protection: The case of Italy. Ministry for Innovation and Technologies, October 2003.

[11] P. Pourbeik, P. S. Kundur, and C. W. Taylor. The anatomy of a power grid blackout. *IEEE Power and Energy Magazine*, pages 22–29, September/october 2006.

[12] S. M. Rinaldi, J. P. Peerenboom, and T. K. Kelly. Identifying, understanding, and analyzing critical infrastructure interdependencies. *IEEE Control Systems Magazine*, pages 11–25, December 2001.

[13] W. H. Sanders and J. F. Meyer. Reduced base model construction methods for stochastic activity networks. *IEEE Journal on Selected Areas in Communications*, 9(1):25–36, January 1991.

[14] W. H. Sanders and J. F. Meyer. Stochastic activity networks: Formal definitions and concepts. In *Lectures on Formal Methods and Performance Analysis*, volume 2090 of *LNCS*, pages 315–343. Springer Verlag, 2001.

[15] A. Wenger, J. Metzger, M. Dunn, and I. Wigert. Critical information infrastructure protection. ETH the Swiss Federal Institute of Technology Zurich, 2004.

Session 4A:
Hardware Fault Tolerance:
Emerging Challenges

Superscalar Processor Performance Enhancement Through Reliable Dynamic Clock Frequency Tuning*

Viswanathan Subramanian, Mikel Bezdek, Naga D. Avirneni and Arun Somani
Dependable Computing and Networking Laboratory
Iowa State University, Ames, IA, USA
{visu, mbezdek, avirneni, arun}@iastate.edu

Abstract

Synchronous circuits are typically clocked considering worst case timing paths so that timing errors are avoided under all circumstances. In the case of a pipelined processor, this has special implications since the operating frequency of the entire pipeline is limited by the slowest stage. Our goal, in this paper, is to achieve higher performance in superscalar processors by dynamically varying the operating frequency during run time past worst case limits. The key objective is to see the effect of overclocking on superscalar processors for various benchmark applications, and analyze the associated overhead, in terms of extra hardware and error recovery penalty, when the clock frequency is adjusted dynamically. We tolerate timing errors occurring at speeds higher than what the circuit is designed to operate at by implementing an efficient error detection and recovery mechanism. We also study the limitations imposed by minimum path constraints on our technique. Experimental results show that an average performance gain up to 57% across all benchmark applications is achievable.

Keywords: Superscalar processor, Dynamic overclocking, Fault-Tolerant Computing, Reliability.

1. Introduction

The performance of processors has traditionally been characterized by their operating frequency. The operating frequency at which a processor or any digital system is marketed, is the frequency at which it is tested to operate reliably under adverse operating conditions. In order to satisfy timing criteria, designers are forced to assume worst case conditions while deciding the clock frequency. Such worst case timing delays occur rarely, allowing possible performance improvement through overclocking. Over the last decade, overclocking as a means to improve processor performance is gaining popularity [3]. Overclocking does not guarantee reliable execution. To reliably take advantage of this performance improvement, it is necessary to tolerate timing errors, when they occur.

The variables affecting propagation delay can be divided into physical variations (introduced during fabrication) and environmental variations (introduced during processor operation) [12]. Physical variations lead to both inter–die and intra–die variations. Inter–die variations are largely independent of design implementation. Intra–die variations, which are dependent on design implementation, are mostly caused by variations in gate dimension. To account for these variations, designers often assume delays three sigma from the typical delay. Environmental variations such as temperature and power supply voltage also have an effect on the delay through any path. These conditions can only be estimated when fixing the clock period of a circuit.

The worst case delay will be observed only if the longest path is exercised by the inputs. The input combinations which are responsible for the worst case path rarely occur. For example, in the case of a ripple–carry adder, the longest delay occurs only when a carry generated at the first bit position propagates through all remaining bit positions. However, a carry chain of this sort is very rare for both random and application generated input vectors [1].

Physical and environmental factors, along with the critical path of the design, force designers to opt for worst case clock periods to ensure error free operation. Since the clock period is fixed at much higher value than what is typically required, significant performance improvements can be achieved through overclocking.

A new and more conservative approach than overclocking seeks to exploit the performance gap left by worst case design parameters, while at the same time providing reliable execution. This approach, coined "better than worst case design" [1], uses principles from fault tolerance, employing some combination of spatial and temporal redundancy.

*The research reported in this paper is partially supported by NSF grant number 0311061 and the Jerry R. Junkins Endowment at Iowa State University.

1.1. Our contribution

This paper presents a solution, which addresses the limitations imposed by worst case design, called SPRIT^{3}E, or Superscalar PeRformance Improvement Through Tolerating Timing Errors [2]. The SPRIT^{3}E framework allows the clock frequency of a superscalar processor to be dynamically tuned to its optimal value, beyond the worst case limit. Because the frequency is dynamically modified as the processor is running, variations in the environmental conditions, such as temperature and voltage, as well as variations present from fabrication, are automatically adjusted for. As frequency scales to higher values, timing errors will begin to occur. To prevent these errors from corrupting the execution of the processor, fault tolerance in the form of temporal redundancy is used. Specifically, pipeline stages are augmented with a local fault detection and recovery (LFDR) circuit.

The amount of frequency scaling is strongly influenced by the number of input combinations responsible for the longer timing-paths. As frequency is scaled higher dynamically, more number of input combinations would result in error. Each time an error occurs, additional time is required to recover from that error. We monitor the error rate during run time, and based on a set tolerable error rate that does not affect the performance, we adjust the clock frequency dynamically.

Another factor that influences frequency scaling is contamination delay of the circuit. Contamination delay is the minimum amount of time beginning from when the input to a logic becomes stable and valid to the time that the output of that logic begins to change. We explain in Section 4 how contamination delay limits frequency scaling. In Section 5, we explain how we can overcome this limitation, using CLA adders to illustrate our point.

To evaluate the SPRIT^{3}E framework, several experiments were performed. First, to explore the possibilities of dynamic frequency scaling, an 18x18 multiplier was operated at varying frequencies, and the number of resultant timing errors was observed. Next, having developed a LFDR framework that shows an achievable frequency 44% faster than the worst case level with the multiplier, the technique was applied to a superscalar processor. Using a superscalar processor synthesized in an FPGA, the frequency and application dependent timing error behavior was analyzed. Then with these results, the ability of the SPRIT^{3}E methodology to provide performance improvement was determined for various error sampling implementations. For long term execution, on an average, all benchmarks show an achievable performance improvement of up to 57% when continuous error sampling technique is implemented.

The rest of this paper is organized as follows: Section 2 provides a review of related literature. The error mitigation technique and global recovery in superscalar processors is described in Section 3. In Section 4, a description of the clocking system used to generate the dynamically modifiable clock is given. In Section 5, the effect of contamination delay on frequency scaling is studied. In Section 6, dynamic clock tuning methodology is presented along with three different error sampling techniques. Our experimental framework and results are presented in Section 7. Section 8 concludes the paper.

2. Related work

Since the traditional design methodology assumes that clock frequency is fixed at the worst case propagation delay, a large body of work exists to improve synchronous circuit performance without violating this assumption. Common techniques such as device scaling and deeper pipelining have been extensively used to increase processor performance. However, as observed in [6, 7, 18], there is an upper bound on the effectiveness of these techniques.

Several strategies have been proposed that apply fault tolerance to a processor with the goal of improving performance past worst case limits. Both the SSD [9] and DIVA [17] architectures apply fault tolerance in the form of a redundant processor. In these mechanisms, instructions are re–executed and checked. Therefore, timing errors may be allowed to occur in the main processor. However, the authors do not analyze the frequency dependent error behavior and thus do not quantify the amount of achievable performance gain. In [10], the issue, register renaming, and ALU logic of a superscalar processor are replaced with approximate versions that execute in half the time, but not necessarily correct. Two versions of the original ALU and register renaming logic are required to detect errors in the approximate versions. Thus this scheme has a high overhead.

TEATIME, proposed in [16], scales the frequency of a pipeline using dynamic error avoidance. However, this technique ignores the input dependence of the observed delay. Thus, it will stabilize on a frequency that is too conservative. The optimal operating frequency of a processor is dynamically achievable only when timing errors are detected and recovered from. TIMERTOL [15] design methodology uses an overclocked logic block with multiple safely clocked blocks of the same logic.

The RAZOR architecture [4, 5] uses temporal fault tolerance by replicating critical pipeline registers in order to dynamically scale voltage past its worst case limits. Razor achieves lower energy consumption by reducing supply voltage in each pipeline stage. Our goal is to allow faster execution for non worst case data by dynamically varying the operating frequency. In RAZOR, an internal core frequency generator is available which is capable of generating clocks at different frequencies, and the duration of the positive clock phase is also configurable. However, the clock frequency is configured and fixed before program execution. We dynamically adjust the clock frequency to the optimal value during run time. This requires online error rate monitoring but offers higher improvement. In [11], the trade-off between reliability and performance is studied, and overclocking is used to improve the performance of register files. We use overclocking in critical pipeline stages to improve the performance of superscalar processor.

3. Timing error mitigation

To allow a superscalar processor to operate at frequencies past the worst case limit, SPRIT^{3}E uses *local fault detection and recovery*, adding redundant registers between pipeline stages. Our timing error mitigation scheme is similar to the one used in Razor [5]. This scheme is most suitable to deal with multiple bidirectional (0 to 1 and 1 to 0) errors [13].

A diagram of the SPRIT^{3}E technique applied to a superscalar processor is shown in Figure 1. The LFDR circuit is highlighted in the figure. The first register is clocked ambitiously at a frequency higher than that required for error free operation. The backup register is clocked in such a way that it is prevented from being affected by timing errors, and its output is considered "golden". In Figure 1, *Main Clock* is the clock controlling synchronous operation of the pipeline, as would be present in an un–augmented pipeline. *PS Clock*, or Phase Shifted clock, has the same frequency as the *Main Clock*, but is phase shifted so that its rising edge occurs after the *Main Clock*. Operation of the LFDR circuit begins when the data from the pipeline logic, *Data In*, is stored in the main register at the rising edge of *Main Clock*. At this point, *Data Out* provides the stored value to the next stage, which begins to compute a result. Then the rising edge of *PS Clock* will cause the input to be stored in the backup register. By comparing the output of both registers, a timing error is detected and proper recovery steps are taken, if needed, to ensure correct operation of the pipeline. When an error is detected, the erroneous pipeline stage locally recovers by overwriting the data in the main register with the correct data in the backup register. This happens because of the multiplexer that selects between *Data In* and the data stored in the backup register.

The backup register is always provided with sufficient time to latch the data, hence it is free from metastability issues. However, when the main register is overclocked, the data and clock inputs may transition at the same time, resulting in metastability of the main register. To handle metastability issues, a metastability detector [5] is incorporated into the LFDR circuit. When metastability is detected in the main register, it is handled like a timing error, and the recovery mechanism is initiated.

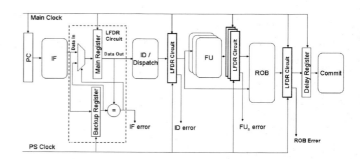

Figure 1. SPRIT^{3}E framework

3.1. Global error recovery

In addition to local recovery, action must be taken on a global scale as well to maintain correct execution of the pipeline in the event of a timing error. Global recovery is necessary to stall pipeline stages before the one in which error occurred, and to insert a bubble, so that subsequent pipeline stages are not affected by the error. In Figure 1, a delay register is shown between the output of the re–order buffer (ROB) and the commit stage. This register is necessary to prevent any erroneous value from being committed during the clock cycle needed for error detection, and to ensure that the architectural state of the processor remains correct. Four error locations are shown in Figure 1, denoted as *IF error*, *ID error*, *FU$_n$ error* (n denoting n^{th} functional block), and *ROB error*. Although the exact error recovery steps taken vary by location, in terms of the behavior of the error handler, these errors can be handled in a similar manner. The global recovery steps, explained below, are in addition to the local recovery that takes place at the erroneous pipeline stage.

When an error occurs in the instruction fetch stage, the instruction that was sent to the decode stage is reduced to a no–op. Additionally, the program counter is stalled for a cycle, so that following the correction of the error, the next instruction is fetched from the correct address. Finally, since the program counter is not updated, any branch or jump instructions attempting to write to PC during the stall cycle is stalled for a cycle. All other instructions in the pipeline are allowed to continue execution.

Any error occurring in the instruction decode and dispatch stage is propagated to both the ROB, and the allocated functional unit. In the ROB, the most recent entry is cleared by updating the pointer to the head of the buffer. When the next instruction is dispatched, it will overwrite the faulty instruction. To clear the functional unit, the global error handler maintains a record of the functional unit used by the dispatcher in the previous cycle. When an error in the dispatch stage is detected, that unit is cleared to prevent it from writing a wrong value to the ROB. Finally, the signal notifying the instruction fetch stage of a successful dispatch is lowered to prevent the IF stage from fetching the next instruction during the error correction cycle.

An error in the execution of a functional unit stores an incorrect value in the ROB. Additionally, the incorrect value is forwarded to other functional units whose operands depend on the result of the faulty FU. In the ROB, the instruction is invalidated to prevent it from being committed. The functional units that have begun execution using the erroneous value are also stopped. This is accomplished by sending an error signal using the existing forwarding paths. Finally, the available signal of the faulty functional unit is lowered to prevent the next instruction from being dispatched to that FU.

An error in the ROB output is prevented from committing in the next cycle by the addition of the delay register mentioned previously. When an error is detected, the delay register is flushed to prevent a faulty commit. Also, the ROB is prevented from attempting to commit a new instruction in the next cycle. This is accomplished by manipulating the ready to commit signal from the commit unit.

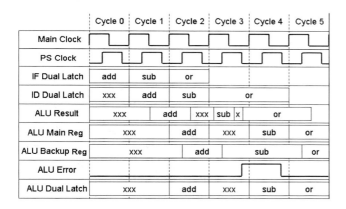

Figure 2. ALU error recovery

Figure 2 shows the timing details of the global error recovery scheme when an error occurs in the ALU functional unit. A series of ALU operations is considered as this is the worst sequence for an error occurring in the ALU. If a different type of instruction is fetched following the ALU instruction causing a timing error, that instruction would be successfully dispatched to a different FU. In the figure, the *add* instruction completes error free and moves to the ROB. The *sub* instruction, however, does not stabilize before being captured by the main register in cycle 3. This is detected, and the ID stage is prevented from dispatching the *or* instruction, effectively stalling for one cycle. Additionally, the incorrect value sent to the ROB in cycle 3 is cleared.

The system shown in Figure 1 is simplistic in that it assumes only one clock cycle for each pipeline stage. The method of error recovery presented here is easily extensible

to the superpipelined case. Another important consideration with this design is initialization of the pipeline. Error detection and recovery is triggered only after meaningful data is present in both the main and backup registers. Also, following a pipeline flush caused by branch mis–prediction, error detection at a stage is stalled until meaningful data again reaches the stage. The delay before beginning error detection varies between stages, and is accounted for in the design.

The area overhead for timing error detection is kept low by re–using the combinational logic which makes up the pipeline stages, and by duplicating only critical pipeline registers. Circuitry is also added to perform global error recovery, but this is modest as well, since the logic involved is not complex and re–uses already existing signals in the pipeline. Overall, SPRIT[3]E provides a viable means of tolerating timing errors.

4. Dynamic frequency scaling

To support the LFDR circuitry and maximize the performance of the pipeline, the main and phase shifted clocks must be carefully generated.

The timing error tolerance provided by the SPRIT[3]E hardware requires support from precise clock generation. Figure 3 shows three possible ways of generating the two clocks when the worst case propagation delay is 10 ns, and the contamination delay is 3 ns.

- In Case I, there is no frequency scaling, and the clock period of the Main clock is equal to the propagation delay. As a result, there is no need to phase shift the PS clock. The two clocks are identical in this case.

- In Case II, the frequency of the Main clock is scaled to 9 ns. To compensate for this reduced clock period, the PS clock is phase shifted by 1 ns, so that from the rising edge of the Main clock to the second rising edge of the PS clock, we have the full propagation delay of the logic circuit. Although there is a rising edge of PS clock 1 ns after the rising edge of Main clock, it will not corrupt the data to be stored in the redundant register as new inputs to the logic will take at least a time period equivalent to contamination delay to change the output.

- Case III shows the maximum possible frequency scaling. In this case, the clock period of the Main clock is 7 ns, and the phase shift of the PS clock is 3 ns. It is not possible to scale further because if the phase shift is increased beyond the contamination delay of the circuit, the redundant register may get incorrect result and cannot be considered "golden".

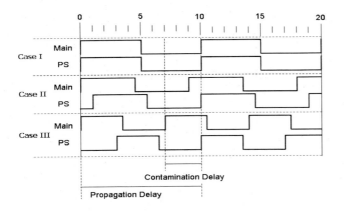

Figure 3. Examples of Main and PS clocks

Impact of error rate on performance. A factor that limits frequency scaling is error rate. As frequency is scaled higher, the number of input combinations that result in delays greater than the new clock period also increases. Each error takes additional cycles to recover. The impact of error rate is analyzed as follows:

Let t_{old} denote the original clock period.

Let t_{new} denote the clock period after frequency scaling.

Let t_{diff} be the time difference between the original clock period and the new clock period.

If a particular application takes n clock cycles to execute, then the total execution time is reduced by $t_{diff} \times n$, if there is no error.

Let S_e denote the fraction of clock cycles affected, by errors, due to scaling.

Let k be the number of cycles needed to recover from an error.

To achieve any performance improvement, Equation 1 must be satisfied.

$$S_e \times n \times k \times t_{new} < t_{diff} \times n \qquad (1)$$

$$S_e < \frac{t_{diff}}{t_{new} \times k} \qquad (2)$$

According to Equation 2, for Case III in Figure 3, the error rate must be higher than 42% for this technique to yield no performance improvement when $k = 1$.

Speedup calculation. The overall speedup achievable using our technique is derived below and is given by Equation 5.

In a computation, it is possible that when the clock frequency is scaled, there is an increase in the total number of execution cycles. In a pipelined processor, when the processor accesses memory, the number of clock cycles taken for that memory operation increases when the frequency is scaled, if the clock frequency of the memory remains constant. Consider a processor whose clock period is 10 ns, and a memory access which takes 20 CPU cycles. If after scaling, the clock period is reduced to 5 ns, then the same memory access would take 40 CPU cycles.

Let S_c denote the factor by which the number of cycles, taken to execute an application, increases because of scaling. Let ex_{old} denote the old execution time. Let ex_{new} denote the new execution time. Let S_{ov} denote the overall speedup achieved.

$$ex_{old} = n \times t_{old} \qquad (3)$$

$$ex_{new} = n \times t_{new} + S_c \times n \times t_{new} + S_e \times k \times n \times t_{new} \qquad (4)$$

$$S_{ov} = \frac{ex_{old}}{ex_{new}} = \frac{t_{old}}{t_{new} \times (1 + S_c + k \times S_e)} \qquad (5)$$

For Case III in Figure 3, if we consider k to be 1, S_e to be 10%, and S_c to be 10%, then we achieve an overall speedup of *1.19*.

5. Managing contamination delay to increase phase shift

As explained in Section 4, the dependence of phase shift on contamination delay leads directly to the limitation of the frequency scaling. In general, the maximum improvement, dependent on the propagation delay, t_{pd}, and the contamination delay, t_{cd}, is given by $\frac{t_{cd}}{t_{pd}}$.

Since contamination delay limits performance improvement, it might be worthwhile to redesign the logic and increase the contamination delay. But increasing the contamination delay of a logic circuit without affecting its propagation delay is not a trivial issue [14]. At first glance, it might appear that adding delay by inserting buffers to the shortest paths will solve the problem. But delay of a circuit is strongly input dependent, and several inputs play a role in deciding the value of an output in a particular cycle.

To show that it is possible to increase contamination delay without affecting the propagation delay, we experimented on a CLA adder circuit. A 32–bit CLA adder circuit has a propagation delay of 3.99 ns, but an insignificant contamination delay of 0.06 ns, thus allowing almost no performance improvement using our technique. Our experiments indicate that by carefully studying the input–output relationship of a given circuit, it is possible to overcome the limitation imposed by contamination delay on our technique. The following case study presents our experiments and results we achieved for a CLA adder circuit.

Case Study: Increasing contamination delay of CLA adder circuits. Let us first consider an 8–bit CLA adder. The propagation delay of the circuit is estimated to be

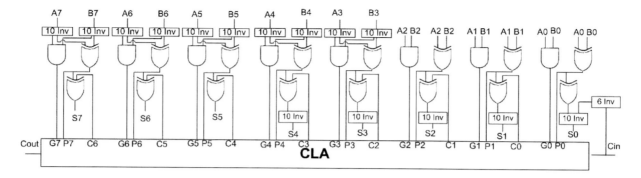

Figure 4. 8-bit CLA adder With additional delay blocks to increase contamination delay

1.06 ns, and the contamination delay, 0.06 ns. We synthesized the circuit using Cadence BuildGates Synthesis tool in Physically Knowledgeable Synthesis (PKS) mode. We used the 0.18 um Cadence Generic Standard Cell Library (GSCLib) for timing estimation.

For the 8–bit CLA adder, from timing reports, we observed that just about 20% of the paths have a delay more than 0.75 ns. Though this is highly motivating and provides a strong reason to apply our technique, a 0.06 ns contamination delay acts as a dampener and we risk incorrect operation if the clock period is reduced beyond 1 ns. To overcome the limitation imposed by the contamination delay, we increased the contamination delay without affecting the propagation delay of the circuit. After carefully studying the propagation delay pattern, we observed that it is possible to increase contamination delay by distributing the additional delay, either to the input side or the output side, or both. More importantly the overall propagation delay remained unchanged. Figure 4 shows the new CLA adder circuit.

After adding delay values, the contamination delay of the circuit now is 0.37 ns, while the propagation delay remains unchanged at 1.06 ns. Now 31% of the timing paths have a delay value greater than 0.75 ns. Having a control over the increase in contamination delay gives us an advantage to tune the circuit's frequency to the optimal value depending on the application and the frequency of occurence of certain input combinations. Introducing delay to increase contamination delay increases the area of the circuit. Therefore, judiciously increasing contamination delay makes sure that the increase in area is kept minimal.

Table 1 provides all relevant details before and after adding contamination delay in 8–bit, 32–bit and 64–bit CLA adder circuits. The propagation delay, t_{pd} and contamination delay, t_{cd} are given in "ns", and the area is given in "μm^2". As we can see there is an increase in area after increasing contamination delay. Using slower buffers, the increase in area can be significantly reduced. The intention of our experiments is to demonstrate that contamination delay can be increased without affecting propagation delay for

certain circuits. However, delay addition increases power consumption. For the 64-bit CLA adder, the total power before adding delay is 0.0144 mW, and the total power increases to 0.0222 mW after adding delays.

Table 1. Impl. Details of CLA Adder Circuits

Adder	Original			Delay Added		
	t_{cd}	t_{pd}	Area	t_{cd}	t_{pd}	Area
8-bit	0.06	1.06	304	0.35	1.06	928
32-bit	0.06	3.99	1216	1.21	3.99	14528
64-bit	0.06	7.89	2432	1.82	7.89	47752

6. Dynamic frequency tuning and error sampling techniques

The dynamically tuned frequency is achieved through the global feedback system pictured in Figure 5. Before operation begins, a small, non–zero, error rate is programmed as the set point. The clock controller is initialized with the worst case delay parameters of the pipeline. As stated above, the initial frequency of the clocks is the worst case propagation delay, and the PS clock begins with no phase shift. The clock generator block consists of a voltage controlled oscillator (VCO) in series with 2 digital clock managers (DCMs). The VCO is able to generate a variable frequency clock to meet the value given by the clock controller. The first DCM locks the output of the VCO to provide the Main clock to the pipeline. The second DCM provides a dynamically modifiable phase shift. It takes the Main clock as well as the value requested by the clock controller to generate the PS clock. Both DCMs provide a *locked* output as well, which is used to determine when the Main and PS clocks have regained stability. During the period in which the clocks are being adjusted, the pipeline must be stalled. To avoid a high overhead from frequent clock switching, the number of timing errors in the pipeline will be sampled at a large interval.

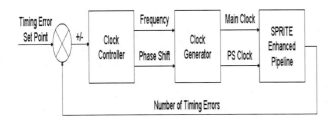

Figure 5. Feedback control system used to tune clock frequency

When considering different sampling methods, there is a trade off between the allowable sampling frequency and the number of bits needed to store the history of errors used to measure the error rate. The length of the error history should be long enough to accurately estimate the error rate. In the following discussion, a window of 100,000 processor cycles is used. Three sampling methods are considered: discrete, continuous, and semi–continuous.

In the discrete method, a single counter keeps the error history, incrementing every cycle in which an error occurs. When the window of 100,000 cycles passes, the counter is checked, and depending on the set point, the clock period is adjusted. The error counter is then cleared to count the errors occurring in the next window. The maximum size needed for the counter in the discrete case is 17 bits.

On the other side of the spectrum, the continuous method uses a sliding window of 100,000 cycles to maintain the history of errors. To implement this window, a 100,000 bit shift register is used, one bit for every cycle in the window. The counter is incremented or decremented, if the value shifted in is not same as the value shifted out. There are 100,000 bits needed for the shift register and 17 bits for the counter.

In order to obtain benefits similar to the continuous case, yet avoid its high overhead, a third, semi–continuous method is used. In this method, the error window is divided into 5 counters. Each counter maintains the total errors occurring in separate 20,000 cycles of the error history. The counters are used in a rotating fashion so that at every sampling, the oldest counter is cleared and begins counting. Each counter needs 15 bits, so for the 5 counters, 75 bits will be required.

7. Experimental results

To gauge the performance improvements provided by the SPRIT[3]E framework, a sequence of experiments were performed. An initial study of a simple multiplier circuit established that significant room for improvement does indeed exist. From there, applications executing on a superscalar

processor were analyzed, and the effects of augmenting the pipeline with SPRIT[3]E were calculated.

As a first step in evaluating this technique, the frequency induced timing errors of a multiplier circuit are observed. In [13], multiplier circuit error rates are analyzed for both inter–die and intra–die variations by effectively altering logic delay via voltage control. We perform similar experiments, but analyze operating frequency induced timing errors. The circuit is implemented in a Xilinx XC2VP30 FPGA. A block diagram of the system is shown in Figure 6. As presented in previous sections, the main and PS clocks operate at the same frequency, with a phase shift between them. However, in this experiment, the period of the clocks remains constant at the worst case delay. The phase shift of the PS clock latches the multiplier result in the early register after a delay. In operation, two linear feedback shift registers provide random inputs to the multiplier logic each main clock cycle. To minimize the routing delays, an 18x18 multiplier block embedded into the logic of the FPGA is used. The output is latched first by the early register, and a phase shift later by the main register. Error checking occurs at every cycle, and is pipelined to allow maximum shifting of the PS clock. A finite state machine (FSM) is used to enable the error counter for 10,000 cycles. To prevent the counter from counting errors that occurs when initializing the pipeline, the FSM begins enabling after 4 delay cycles have passed.

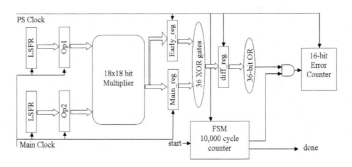

Figure 6. Multiplier experiment block diagram

The worst case propagation delay of the synthesized circuit is estimated at 6.717 ns by the timing analyzer. To allow plenty of time for the circuit to execute before being captured in the main register, a clock period of 8 ns is used. The phase shift of the PS clock is varied from 0 to -5.5 ns, giving effective clock periods of 8 to 2.5 ns. For each effective period, the total errors are counted for an execution run of 10,000 cycles. For instance, when the PS clock is shifted such that its rising edge occurs 5 ns before the main clock, the multiplier logic is effectively being given 3 ns to compute. At this frequency, about 94% of the 10,000 cycles produce a timing error.

Figure 7 presents the percentage of cycles that produce an error for different effective clock periods. As shown, although the worst case delay was estimated at 6.717 ns, the first timing errors do not begin occurring until a period of under 4 ns. Using a method such as LFDR to tolerate a small amount of timing errors allows this circuit to run at almost half the period giving a speedup of 44%.

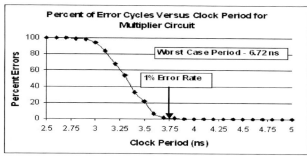

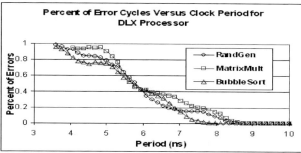

Figure 7. Percent of error cycles versus the clock period for the multiplier circuit and DLX processor

7.1. Evaluation of SPRIT^{3}E framework

The SPRIT^{3}E framework is evaluated on a DLX superscalar processor [8]. The relevant parameters of the processor are summarized in Table 2. The superscalar DLX processor is synthesized for the Xilinx XC2VP30 FPGA. The maximum timing delay between registers in this circuit is 21.982 ns, between the source registers of the MDU and the data registers of the ROB. Similar delays, all around 20 ns, exist through the other functional units to the ROB, as well as from the dispatch stage to the ROB. Thus, to analyze the timing error rates of the processor, the ROB registers are augmented with additional registers as well as the comparing and counting circuitry shown in Figure 6. The processor is operated at varying phase shifts of the PS clock, and the percentage of cycles in which an error occurred for the execution run is recorded. For the benchmarks run on the FPGA, the processor state and the output of the program is checked for correctness after program execution.

Table 2. DLX processor parameters

Parameters		Value
Decode / Issue / Commit bandwidth		2
Reorder Buffer Entries		5
Number of Function Units	Arithmetic Logic Unit (ALU)	1
	Multiply Divide Unit (MDU)	1
	Branch Resolve Unit (BRU)	1
	Load Store Unit (LSU)	1
Instruction and Data Cache Size(Bytes)		64
Memory Size (KBytes) - 2 Cycle Access		64

Figure 7 shows the error rates of operating the DLX at effective periods between 10 and 3.5 ns for 3 different benchmarks. The RandGen application performs a simple random number generation to give a number between 0 and 255. One million random numbers are generated, and the distribution of the random variable is kept in memory. The MatrixMult application multiplies two 50x50 integer matrices and stores the result into memory. The BubbleSort program performs a bubblesort on 5,000 half–word variables. For this application, the input is given in the worst case unsorted order. As shown in the figure, for both RandGen and MatrixMult, the errors become significant at around 8.5 ns, while the error rate of BubbleSort stays low until around 8 ns. This is because both the MatrixMult and RandGen applications use the MDU, and thus are likely to incur the worst case path. The BubbleSort uses only the ALU to perform comparisons as well as addition and subtraction, so it is able to operate at lower periods before errors begin to occur.

Using the probability distribution for the error rate determined in the previous step, a simulator is written to evaluate the effectiveness of the SPRIT^{3}E framework using the different methods of error sampling discussed in Section 6 at a set tolerable error rate of 1%. In this experiment, the amount by which the clock period is allowed to change is held constant for different sampling methods. Each benchmark is evaluated separately, and is executed for its original number of cycles, reported in Table 3, as well as for a long run of 120 million cycles.

Table 3. Length of Applications in Cycles

Application	Cycles to Execute
MatrixMult	2901432
BubbleSort	118896117
RandGen	15750067

The scaling behavior for the matrix multiplier application executed for a long run is shown in Figure 8. The figure highlights the differences between discrete, semi–continuous, and continuous sampling. The other applications show similar period scaling over the course of execution. As the figure demonstrates, the long intervals between switching for the discrete sampling method prevent it from reaching the optimal period as quickly as the continuous and semi-continuous cases.

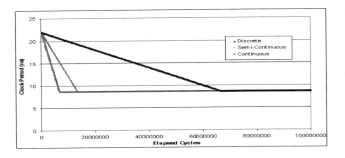

Figure 8. Dynamically scaled clock period versus the elapsed cycles for MatrixMult

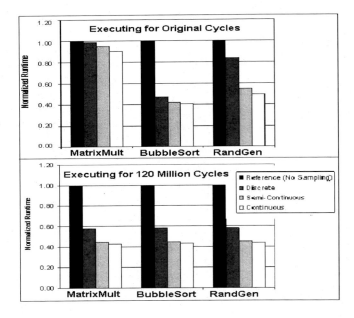

Figure 9. Relative performance gains for different applications

As the simulation is running, the execution time of the application is calculated. The reference execution run sets the period at the worst case value and allows no scaling. Thus no timing errors occur. For the other cases, each cycle in which a timing error occurs results in a stall cycle being injected into the pipeline. Also, when a change in period occurs, the time taken to lock the DCMs to the new frequency is added to the total execution time. The execution times for each application when run for its original

execution cycles is shown in Figure 9, normalized to the reference worst case time. The BubbleSort application shows the best performance as it runs the longest and thus runs the longest at the optimal period for any sampling method. The MatrixMult application, however, is only long enough for gains achieved by lowering the period to begin to outweigh the penalties for doing so. Each benchmark was also evaluated by running for a longer execution time. The performance results are presented in Figure 9. For this variation, all benchmarks perform similarly, with the discrete error sampling method giving on average a 43% improvement over the worst case, and the semi–continuous and continuous methods outperforming it at 56% and 57% respectively.

Speedup Calculation: Table 4 provides the speedup achievable for the multiplier circuit, the 32-bit and 64-bit CLA adder circuits, and the three different benchmarks run on the DLX processor augmented with the SPRIT³E framework. The overclocking technique is applied to the CLA adders after increasing their contamination delay, as explained in Section 5. The new contamination delay values are the ones reported in Table 1 in Section 5. The experimental setup for the adder is similar to the one explained for the multiplier circuit. Equation 5, derived in Section 4, gives the speedup, S_{ov}. We consider k to be 1, and S_c to be 10%. The S_c factor is ignored for the multiplier and adder circuits. We calculate speedup for an error rate target of 1%.

Table 4. Speedup Calculation

ALU Circuit	t_{old}	t_{new}	S_{ov}
Multiplier	6.72	3.75	1.77
32-bit CLA	3.99	3.3	1.19
64-bit CLA	7.89	6.2	1.27
MatrixMult	21.98	8.5	2.33
BubbleSort	21.98	8.0	2.47
RandGen	21.98	8.5	2.33

While calculating the speedup in Table 4, we did not take into account the time margins added to the propagation delay because of physical and environmental factors. In reality, the original clock period would be fixed at a higher value than the circuit's propagation delay, leaving room for further frequency scaling.

Impact on area and power consumption: To guarantee reliable execution when operating at higher than worst case speeds, we introduced LFDR circuits in place of flip-flops in the pipeline stages, and to remove the limitations imposed by short paths on frequency scaling, we added delay buffers to increase the delay of short paths. This increased the area and power consumption of the superscalar processor.

Table 5 provides synthesis results for the unmodified DLX superscalar processor and the one augmented with the SPRIT^{3}E framework. Both designs are mapped to Xilinx Virtex II Pro FPGA using Xilinx ISE 8.2 synthesis tool. There is a 3.12% increase in the number of flip-flops. The increase in the combinational logic part is 0.3%. The net increase in area because of the SPRIT^{3}E framework is 3.2% (calculated from equivalent gate count). For our experiments on DLX superscalar processor, we did not increase the contamination delay of any pipeline stage.

Table 5. FPGA synthesis results

Processor	Flip-flop Count	Comb. Area (4-LUTs)	Equiv. Gates
Unmodified DLX	5150	14363	164760
SPRIT^{3}E DLX	5313	14407	170048

To minimize the increase in power consumption, we replaced only those pipeline registers in the critical path with LFDR circuits. From Xilinx Xpower reports, we observed that there is no significant difference in the total power consumed by the two processors.

8. Conclusions

As demonstrated by the successful timing error tolerant overclocking methodology, the current way of estimating the operating frequency for synchronous circuits is far too conservative. The SPRIT^{3}E framework reuses existing superscalar pipeline logic whenever possible, resulting in a modest error detection and recovery logic overhead. Although our experiments are based on FPGA platform, an extension can be made to logic implemented in ASIC technology. This work presents an initial exploration of the possibilities for taking advantage of the margins produced by worst case design mentality. In the future, implementing a main memory system for the synthesized DLX processor would allow full scale benchmarks to be evaluated, as well as allow an exploration of the effect of increasing the clock frequency on the average instructions committed per clock cycle. Another important concern in using the SPRIT^{3}E framework is how well the phase shift can be adjusted at high frequencies. This paper presents a very promising technique, with many exciting directions for the future.

References

[1] T. Austin, V. Bertacco, D. Blaauw, and T. Mudge. Opportunities and challenges for better than worst-case design. In *Asia and South Pacific Design Automation Conference*, volume 1, pages 2–7, January 2005.

[2] M. Bezdek. Utilizing timing error detection and recovery to dynamically improve superscalar processor performance. Master's thesis, Iowa State University, 2006.

[3] B. Colwell. The zen of overclocking. *IEEE Compututer*, 37(3):9–12, March 2004.

[4] S. Das, D. Roberts, S. Lee, S. Pant, D. Blaauw, T. Austin, K. Flautner, and T. Mudge. A self-tuning dvs processor using delay-error detection and correction. *IEEE Journal of Solid-State Circuits*, 41(4):792–804, April 2006.

[5] D. Ernst, N. S. Kim, S. Das, S. Pant, R. Rao, T. Pham, C. Ziesler, D. Blaauw, T. Austin, K. Flautner, and T. Mudge. Razor: A low-power pipeline based on circuit-level timing speculation. In *36th Annual IEEE/ACM International Symposium on Microarchitecture*, pages 7–18, 2003.

[6] D. J. Frank, R. H. Dennard, E. Nowak, P. M. Solomon, Y. Taur, and H.-S. P. Wong. Device scaling limits of si mosfets and their application dependencies. *Proceedings of IEEE*, 89(3):259–288, March 2001.

[7] A. Hartstein and T. R. Puzak. The optimum pipeline depth for a microprocessor. In *29th annual international symposium on Computer architecture*, pages 7–13, May 2002.

[8] J. Horch. Superscalar dlx documentation. http://www.rs.tu-darmstadt.de/downloads/docu/dlxdocu/SuperscalarDLX.html. Date Accessed: March 16, 2007.

[9] S. Kim and A. K. Somani. Ssd: An affordable fault tolerant architecture for superscalar processors. In *Pacific Rim International Symposium on Dependable Computing*, pages 27–34, December 2001.

[10] T. Liu and S.-L. Lu. Performance improvement with circuit-level speculation. In *33rd Annual ACM/IEEE International Symposium on Microarchitecture*, pages 348–355, December 2000.

[11] G. Memik, M. Chowdhury, A. Mallik, and Y. Ismail. Engineering over-clocking: reliability-performance trade-offs for high-performance register files. In *International Conference on Dependable Systems and Networks*, pages 770–779, June 2005.

[12] S. R. Nassif. Modeling and forecasting of manufacturing variations. In *Asia and South Pacific Design Automation Conference*, pages 145–149, January 2001.

[13] D. Roberts, T. Austin, D. Blauww, T. Mudge, and K. Flautner. Error analysis for the support of robust voltage scaling. In *Sixth International Symposium on Quality of Electronic Design*, pages 65–70, March 2005.

[14] N. V. Shenoy, R. K. Brayton, and A. L. Sangiovanni-Vincentelli. Minimum padding to satisfy short path constraints. In *IEEE/ACM international conference on Computer-aided design*, pages 156–161, 1993.

[15] A. K. Uht. Achieving typical delays in synchronous systems via timing error toleration. Technical report 032000-0100, University of Rhode Island, March 2000.

[16] A. K. Uht. Uniprocessor performance enhancement through adaptive clock frequency control. *IEEE Transactions on Computers*, 54(2):132–140, February 2005.

[17] C. Weaver and T. Austin. A fault tolerant approach to microprocessor design. In *International Conference on Dependable Systems and Networks*, pages 411–420, July 2001.

[18] G. C.-F. Yeap. Leakage current in low standby power and high performance devices: trends and challenges. In *International Symposium on Physical design*, pages 22–27, 2002.

Determining fault tolerance of XOR-based erasure codes efficiently

Jay J. Wylie and Ram Swaminathan

Hewlett-Packard Labs

jay.wylie@hp.com, ram.swaminathan@hp.com

Abstract

We propose a new fault tolerance metric for XOR-based erasure codes: the minimal erasures list (MEL). A minimal erasure is a set of erasures that leads to irrecoverable data loss and in which every erasure is necessary and sufficient for this to be so. The MEL is the enumeration of all minimal erasures. An XOR-based erasure code has an irregular structure that may permit it to tolerate faults at and beyond its Hamming distance. The MEL completely describes the fault tolerance of an XOR-based erasure code at and beyond its Hamming distance; it is therefore a useful metric for comparing the fault tolerance of such codes. We also propose an algorithm that efficiently determines the MEL of an erasure code. This algorithm uses the structure of the erasure code to efficiently determine the MEL. We show that, in practice, the number of minimal erasures for a given code is much less than the total number of sets of erasures that lead to data loss: in our empirical results for one corpus of codes, there were over 80 times fewer minimal erasures. We use the proposed algorithm to identify the most fault tolerant XOR-based erasure code for all possible systematic erasure codes with up to seven data symbols and up to seven parity symbols.

1. Introduction

Storage systems must be fault tolerant. Traditionally, tolerating a single disk failure via simple replication or RAID 5 has provided sufficient reliability. In storage arrays, ever increasing disk capacity leads to ever increasing recovery times which leads to sector or second disk failures being encountered during recovery [2]. Cluster-based and grid storage systems are built with commodity components and rely on network-attached components; the former have lower reliability and the latter lower availability than the components traditionally employed in storage arrays. The trends in storage arrays, cluster-based storage, and grid storage demand that storage schemes with higher degrees of fault tolerance be developed and be well understood.

Erasure codes are the means by which storage systems are typically made fault tolerant (i.e., tolerant of disk failures). There are many types of erasure codes, such as replication, RAID 5, and Reed-Solomon codes, each of which trades off between computation (encode & decode) costs, fault tolerance, and space efficiency. Reed-Solomon codes provide the best tradeoff between fault tolerance and space efficiency, but are computationally the most demanding type of erasure code. Erasure codes that rely solely on XOR operations to generate redundancy are computationally cheap. However, such codes offer a non-uniform tradeoff between space efficiency and fault tolerance. In practice, the exact degree of fault tolerance such codes provide in storage systems is not yet well understood, although there is much recent activity towards this end [14, 13, 6, 4, 5, 7].

To completely understand the fault tolerance of an XOR-based erasure code, we must enumerate *every* set of erasures that leads to data loss. This is necessary because of the irregular structure of such codes. For example, if the smallest *erasure pattern*—set of erasures that leads to data loss—for a given code is of size 3, then the Hamming distance of the code is 4. However, the code may tolerate many erasures of size 4. The enumeration of all erasure patterns thus completely describes the fault tolerance of an XOR-based erasure code. Unfortunately, there are exponentially many such erasure patterns.

In this paper, we propose enumerating every *minimal erasure* to characterize the fault tolerance of a code. A minimal erasure is a set of erasures that leads to irrecoverable data loss and in which every erasure is necessary and sufficient for this to be so. We call the enumeration of minimal erasures, the *minimal erasures list* (MEL). The minimal erasures list contains all of the fault tolerance information as the list of erasure patterns, but can be much smaller in size. There are also an exponential number of minimal erasures, but our results suggest that, in practice, for most codes, there are many fewer minimal erasures than erasure patterns.

We introduce the Minimal Erasures (ME) Algorithm for efficiently determining the MEL of an XOR-based erasure code. The efficiency of the ME Algorithm is premised on there being few minimal erasures relative to the overall number of erasure patterns, and on using the structure of the XOR-based erasure code to identify the minimal erasures. We have used our implementation of the ME Algorithm to analyze many XOR-based codes. Our empirical results demonstrate that there can be almost two orders of magnitude fewer minimal erasures than erasure patterns (and likely a bigger reduction as k and m increase). We use the MEL to compare different small XOR-based erasure codes of similar size and report the most fault tolerant codes. These results demonstrate both the efficacy and utility of the ME Algorithm for determining the fault tolerance of XOR-based erasure codes.

The outline of the paper is as follows. In §2, we introduce terminology and review some related work. We present the ME Algorithm and prove its correctness in §3. In §4, we describe our implementation of the ME Algorithm, our method of validating the correctness of our implementation, empirical results that demonstrate the efficiency of the ME Algorithm, and identify the most fault tolerant systematic XOR-based erasure codes with up to seven data symbols and up to seven parity symbols. We discuss the ME Algorithm in relation to specific other recent work in §5 and then conclude in §6.

2. Background

Table 1 lists some symbols and acronyms used in this paper. An XOR-based erasure code consists of n symbols, k of which are *data symbols*, and m of which are *parity symbols* (redundant symbols). We refer to redundant symbols as parity symbols because our focus is on XOR-based erasure codes. We only consider *systematic* erasure codes: codes that store the data and parity symbols. In storage systems, data symbols are called "stripes." The use of systematic erasure codes in storage systems is generally considered a necessity to ensure good common case performance.

A set of erasures f is a set of erased symbols; it may contain either data symbols or parity symbols and it may or may not be possible to recover these symbols. An *erasure pattern* $\hat{f}$ is a set of erasures that result in at least one data symbol being irrecoverable (i.e., impossible to recover via any decoding method). The *erasures list* EL for an erasure code is the list of all its erasure patterns. A *minimal erasure* $\tilde{f}$ is an erasure pattern in which every erasure is necessary for it to be an erasure pattern; if any erasure is removed from $\tilde{f}$, then it is no longer an erasure pattern. The *minimal erasures list* MEL for an erasure code is the list of all its minimal erasures. A more compact representation of the EL and MEL are respectively the erasures vector EV, and the minimal erasures vector MEV. An erasures vector is a vector of length m in which the ith element is the total number of erasure patterns of size i in the EL; the minimal erasures

Symbol	Definition
n	Total number of symbols in the erasure code.
k	Number of *data* symbols in the code.
m	Number of *parity* symbols in the code.
f	A *set of erasures*.
$\hat{f}$	An *erasure pattern*.
$\tilde{f}$	A *minimal erasure*.
EL	The *erasures list*: a list of $\hat{f}$.
MEL	The *minimal erasures list*: a list of $\tilde{f}$.
EV	The *erasures vector* for the EL.
MEV	The *minimal erasures vector* for the MEL.

Table 1. Terminology

vector is defined similarly with regard to the MEL. The EV and MEV vectors only need m entries because all erasure sets greater than m in length are necessarily erasure patterns.

2.1. Erasure codes

Plank's tutorial on erasure codes is a great introduction to erasure codes in general, and their applicability in storage systems in particular [12]. A Reed-Solomon erasure code uses m redundant symbols to tolerates all erasures of size m or less; it is therefore perfectly space efficient. Unfortunately, Reed-Solomon encode and decode require k operations to generate each redundant symbol, or to decode any data symbols using redundant symbols. The operations required by Reed-Solomon codes are based on arithmetic operations in Galois Fields (GF), and such operations are computationally more demanding than simple XOR operations. Cauchy Reed-Solomon codes implement Galois Field operations only using XOR operations, but require many XOR operations per Galois Field operation. XOR-based erasure codes are appealing because of the computational efficiency of encode and decode.

Two well known sub-classes of XOR-based erasure codes are low-density parity-check (LDPC) codes and array codes. LDPC codes trade imperfect space efficiency for improved performance. Luby et al. [8] identified methods of constructing LDPC codes, and efficiently encoding and decoding them; such codes were originally identified by Gallager [3]. Plank has briefly surveyed LDPC code constructions for their applicability to storage systems [14].

An LDPC code can be represented as a Tanner graph: a bipartite graph with k constraint nodes on one side and $k + m$ data and parity symbols on the other. The efficiency of LDPC codes hinges on bounding the degree of the nodes in the Tanner graph and consequently on iterative decoding. The efficacy of iterative decoding is significantly affected by *stopping sets*: erasure patterns that prevent iterative decoding from recovering symbols (e.g., see the work of Schwartz and Vardy [17]). We note that every minimal erasure *is* a stopping set but that the converse is *not* true. Stopping sets are defined with regard to iterative decoding; minimal erasures are defined with regard to decodability, i.e., without regard to any particular decoding method.

Array codes are specialized erasure codes for storage arrays (e.g., RAID 5 is an array code). Two well known double disk fault tolerant array codes are EVENODD by Blaum et al. [1] and Row-Diagonal Parity (RDP) by Corbett et al. [2]. Hafner has generalized the concept of XOR-based array codes to HoVer codes: codes with parity symbols in both *Horizontal* and *Vertical* dimensions of the array [5]. He has also proposed Weaver codes, an XOR-based erasure code construction that chains parity symbols among a subset of servers in a redundancy group [4]. The ME Algorithm can be applied to any XOR-based erasure code, for example, to LDPC codes, Weaver codes, or array codes.

2.2. Evaluating erasure codes

The seminal RAID analysis by Patterson et al. [11] provides the framework that most storage system reliability analyses follow: identify an appropriate Markov model, plug in failure and recovery rates, and determine mean time to data loss (MTTDL). Saito et al. [16] and Rao et al. [15] both applied such a framework to analyze the reliability of erasure codes. The former considered Reed-Solomon erasure codes and the latter array codes.

Plank et al. analyzed the *read overhead* of moderate-sized LDPC codes using Monte Carlo methods [14] and of small-sized LDPC codes using deterministic methods [13]. Read overhead is a performance measure of a client random read policy; it measures the number of symbols beyond k that must be read, on average, to decode all data symbols. Recent work, done concurrently to our work, by Hafner and Rao investigates the reliability of XOR-based erasure codes [7]. The MEL and MEV output by the ME Algorithm are "threshold" measures of fault tolerance. A reliability measure requires additional assumptions about component failure and recovery rates. We discuss the ME Algorithm in the context of both of the above bodies of work in §5.

3. The Minimal Erasures (ME) Algorithm

The ME Algorithm uses the structure of an erasure code to efficiently generate the MEL. We rely on two representations of the XOR-based erasure code: the Generator matrix and the systematic Tanner graph. The *Generator matrix* of a (k, m)-code is a $k \times (k+m)$ matrix in GF(2). Addition of rows and columns in the Generator matrix is done modulo 2

(i.e., the XOR operation). The Generator matrix consists of a $k \times k$ identity matrix (the *data submatrix*) with m columns of dimension $k \times 1$ appended (the *parity submatrix*). Each of the k columns in the data submatrix corresponds to a stored data symbol. Each of the m columns in the parity submatrix corresponds to a stored parity symbol. Parity column p has a one in row i if, and only if, data symbol s_i is XOR'ed to determine p. For example, if $p = s_2 \oplus s_4$, then parity column p has a one in rows 2 and 4, and a zero in all other rows. We refer to the erasure pattern induced by the ones in the ith row of the Generator matrix as the ith *base erasure* $\bar{f}_i$. (We show in §3.3 that a base erasure is a minimal erasure.) The structure of an erasure code is also captured by its Tanner graph $\mathcal{T}$. Since we exclusively consider systematic erasure codes—erasure codes that store the k data symbols and m parity symbols—we use a simplified Tanner graph representation. In the representation we use, we collapse the k data symbols from the one side into the constraint nodes on the other. In doing so, we end up with what we call a *systematic Tanner graph*: a bipartite graph that has k data symbols on one side and m parity symbols on the other.

At a high level, the ME Algorithm operates as follows. It begins by identifying the k base erasures (one for each data symbol) and adding them to the MEL. The ME Algorithm then proceeds, in an iterative fashion. For every minimal erasure it finds, it generates *child* erasure patterns. A minimal erasure has a child erasure pattern for every *adjacent data symbol*. Adjacency is defined with regard to the systematic Tanner graph. A data symbol is adjacent to a minimal erasure if it is connected to a parity symbol in the minimal erasure. To generate a child erasure pattern, the base erasure from the Generator matrix that corresponds to the adjacent data symbol is XOR'ed with the parent minimal erasure. A child erasure pattern is either a minimal erasure not yet in the MEL, a minimal erasure already in the MEL, or an erasure pattern that can be partitioned into minimal erasures that are already in the MEL. We refer to the last case as a composite erasure and discuss it in the next section. The algorithm recurses upon child erasure patterns until all minimal erasures in the MEL have no more children that are minimal erasures (not in the MEL), or have no adjacent data symbols (i.e., the minimal erasure contains all of the data symbols from some component of the Tanner graph).

3.1. ME Algorithm Pseudo-code

The pseudo-code for the ME Algorithm is given in Figure 1. Variables used in the pseudo-code are listed on lines 100–107. The function **me_search** enumerates the minimal erasures and stores them in the minimal erasures data structure M, which it returns. This function has two phases: in the first phase, the base erasures are enumerated

```
100: s, S              /* Data symbol s; Set of data symbols S. */
101: p, P              /* Parity symbol p; Set of parity symbols P. */
102: e, E        /* Edge e is a data/parity pair (e = sp); Set of edges E. */
103: T                 /* Tanner graph. Has structure T.(S, P, E). */
104: f̃                 /* A minimal erasure. Has structure f̃.(S, P). */
105: M                 /* Minimal erasures data structure: a set of f̃. */
106: M̄                 /* Erasure patterns cache: a set of f̂. */
107: Q                 /* Erasures queue: a FIFO queue of f̂. */

/* Search systematic Tanner graph T for minimal erasures. */
me_search(T) :
200: M ← ∅, M̄ ← ∅, Q ← ∅              /* Initialize data structures. */
201: /* Generate the k base erasures. */
202:   for all (s′ ∈ T.S) do
203:     /* P′ contains all parities connected to s′. */
204:     P′ ← {∀p ∈ T.P, ∃e ∈ T.E : e = s′p}
205:     f̃ ← ({s′}, P′)                   /* A base erasure. */
206:     Q.enqueue(f̃)            /* Enqueue f̃ to process its children. */
207:     M ← M ∪ {f̃}    /* Add f̃ to minimal erasures data structure. */
208:   end for
209: /* Process children of enqueued erasure patterns. */
210: /* Repeat until no more erasure patterns are enqueued. */
211:   while (Q.length() > 0) do
212:     f̃ ← Q.dequeue()       /* Get next erasure pattern to process. */
213:     (M, M̄, Q) ← me_children(T, M, M̄, Q, f̃)
214:   end while
215: return (M)

/* Generate children of f̃ and enqueue them in Q. */
me_children(T, M, M̄, Q, f̃):
300: /* S′ contains all data symbols that are adjacent to f̃. */
301: S′ ← {∀s ∈ T.S, ∃p ∈ f̃.P, ∃e ∈ T.E : e = sp} \ f̃.S
302:   for all (s′ ∈ S′) do
303:     f̃′.S ← f̃.S ∪ {s′}
304:     /* P′ contains all parities in T.P that are connected to s′. */
305:     P′ ← {∀p ∈ T.P, ∃e ∈ T.E : e = s′p}
306:     /* P̄ contains all parities in f̃.P that are connected to s′. */
307:     P̄ ← {∀p ∈ f̃.P, ∃e ∈ T.E : e = s′p}
308:     f̃′.P ← (f̃.P ∪ P′) \ P̄
309:     if (f̃′ ∈ M̄) then continue
310:     M̄ ← M̄ ∪ {f̃′}
311:     Q.enqueue(f̃′)
312:     f̃_MIN ← l : l ∈ M, ∀r ∈ M, |l| ≤ |r|
313:     if (|f̃′| ≥ 2|f̃_MIN|) then
314:       if (is_composite(T \ {f̃′})) then continue
315:     end if
316:     M ← M ∪ {f̃′}
317:   end for
318: return (M, M̄, Q)
```

Figure 1. ME Algorithm pseudo-code.

(cf. lines 201–208), and in the second phase, child erasure patterns are repeatedly enumerated (cf. lines 209–214). Each base erasure corresponds to one row of the Generator matrix; it consists of a single data symbol $s′$ and the parities connected to it in the Tanner graph T (cf. line 205). Every base erasure is enqueued on the erasures queue Q, a FIFO queue, and inserted into M.

In the second phase of **me_search**, minimal erasures are dequeued from Q, and then **me_children** generates and processes the child erasure patterns. In **me_children**, line 301 determines which data symbols are adjacent to $f̃$. There

is a child erasure pattern for every adjacent data symbol $s′$. Child erasure patterns are the XOR of $f̃$ with $f̃_{s′}$, the base erasure corresponding to data symbol $s′$. The pseudo-code is written in set notation to make the relationship to the structure of T more apparent. A child is created as follows: $s′$ is added to the parent (cf. line 303); parities connected to $s′$ are added to the parent (cf. line 305); parities connected to $s′$ and to some data symbol in the parent are removed (cf. lines 307 and 308). Regarding $P̄$, there exists at least one such parity to remove, otherwise the data symbol $s′$ would not be adjacent to $f̃$ (cf. line 301). If the child erasure pattern has previously been generated by **me_children**, i.e., it is already in the erasure patterns cache $M̄$, then $f̃′$ is not processed (cf. line 309). If the child erasure pattern has not yet been processed, then it is added to $M̄$ and to the erasures queue Q (cf. lines 310 and 311 respectively). Each child erasure pattern that is a minimal erasure is inserted into M (cf. line 316). Once all of the children are processed, **me_children** returns the updated M, $M̄$ and Q.

Lines 312–315 deal with composite erasures: those child erasure patterns that can be partitioned into multiple minimal erasures and thus are not added to M. Only child erasure patterns at least twice as big as the shortest known minimal erasure can possibly be a composite erasure. Line 313 determines the length of the shortest minimal erasure in M. A child erasure pattern shorter than this length must be a minimal erasure since it is too small to be a composite erasure. A child erasure pattern twice or more this length is analyzed to determine if it is a minimal erasure or a composite erasure. The function **is_composite** called on line 314 determines if $f̃′$ is a composite erasure or not. It does so by testing the rank of the matrix that corresponds to $\{T \setminus f̃′\} \cup \{e \in f̃′\}$. It is necessary and sufficient to remove a single symbol e from $f̃′$ to test for minimality: $f̃′$ is either a minimal erasure, and so removing e yields a matrix of full rank, or a composite erasure, and so removing e yields a matrix not of full rank. (Note that *removing* erasure e from $f̃′$ makes the symbol corresponding to e available for decoding.)

Once the ME Algorithm completes, the minimal erasures data structure M is trivially transformed into both the MEL and the MEV.

3.2. Example execution

Consider the XOR-based erasure code with $k = 4$ and $m = 4$ defined by the following Generator matrix:

$$
C = \begin{bmatrix}
s_1 & s_2 & s_3 & s_4 & p_1 & p_2 & p_3 & p_4 \\
1 & 0 & 0 & 0 & 1 & 0 & 0 & 1 \\
0 & 1 & 0 & 0 & 1 & 1 & 1 & 1 \\
0 & 0 & 1 & 0 & 0 & 1 & 1 & 0 \\
0 & 0 & 0 & 1 & 0 & 0 & 1 & 1
\end{bmatrix}
\begin{matrix}
\\
f̃_{s_1} \\
f̃_{s_2} \\
f̃_{s_3} \\
f̃_{s_4}
\end{matrix}
$$

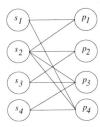

Figure 2. Systematic Tanner graph for code $\mathcal{C}$

Q.dequeue	$\hat{f}$	M
	(s_1, p_1, p_4)	✓
	$(s_2, p_1, p_2, p_3, p_4)$	✓
	(s_3, p_2, p_3)	✓
	(s_4, p_3, p_4)	✓
(s_1, p_1, p_4)	(s_1, s_2, p_2, p_3)	✓
	(s_1, s_4, p_1, p_3)	✓
$(s_2, p_1, p_2, p_3, p_4)$	(s_1, s_2, p_2, p_3)	✗
	(s_2, s_3, p_1, p_4)	✓
	(s_2, s_4, p_1, p_2)	✓
(s_3, p_2, p_3)	(s_2, s_3, p_1, p_4)	✗
	(s_3, s_4, p_2, p_4)	✓
(s_4, p_3, p_4)	(s_1, s_4, p_1, p_3)	✗
	(s_2, s_4, p_1, p_2)	✗
	(s_3, s_4, p_2, p_4)	✗
(s_1, s_2, p_2, p_3)	(s_1, s_2, s_3)	✓
	$(s_1, s_2, s_4, p_2, p_4)$	✓
$\ldots$	$\ldots$	$\ldots$

Table 2. Example ME Algorithm execution.

The columns in $\mathcal{C}$ are labeled as either a data column or a parity column, and the rows are labeled as base erasures.

Figure 2 shows the systematic Tanner graph $\mathcal{T}$ for code $\mathcal{C}$. Table 2 summarizes the execution of the ME Algorithm for the code defined by $\mathcal{C}$. The first column lists the erasure pattern $\hat{f}$ being processed by **me_children**, the second column lists the children of $\hat{f}$ (possibly over multiple rows), and the third column indicates (via a checkmark) if $\hat{f}$ is inserted into M and enqueued in Q. The first four rows illustrate the base erasures $\tilde{f}_{s_1}, \tilde{f}_{s_2}, \tilde{f}_{s_3}, \tilde{f}_{s_4}$ processed by **me_search**. The remaining rows illustrate the children generated by dequeuing erasure patterns from Q and indicates which children are inserted into M. If a child is already in M, then it is not inserted again. Consider the first erasure pattern dequeued from Q: (s_1, p_1, p_4). From the systematic Tanner graph, it is easy to see that the adjacent data symbols are s_2 and s_4. The final steps of the ME Algorithm are elided because children generated by the remaining erasure patterns in Q are already in M. The MEL output by the ME Algorithm is $\{(s_1, p_1, p_4), (s_3, p_2, p_3), (s_4, p_3, p_4),$ $(s_1, s_2, s_3), (s_1, s_2, p_2, p_3), (s_1, s_2, p_2, p_3), (s_2, s_3, p_1, p_4),$ $(s_2, s_4, \; p_1, p_2), (s_2, s_3, \; p_1, p_4), (s_3, s_4, \; p_2, p_4)\}$. Any $\hat{f}$ longer than $m = 4$ is elided from the MEL. The MEV output by the ME Algorithm is $(0, 0, 4, 5)$.

3.3. Correctness

In this section, we prove that the MEL of an XOR-based erasure code completely describes its fault tolerance (i.e., contains all of the information that the EL does), and that the ME Algorithm generates a complete MEL and so is correct.

We first prove that the MEL is a complete description of an XOR-based erasure code's fault tolerance.

Theorem 3.1 *If the fault tolerance of an XOR-based erasure code can be obtained through the EL, it can also be obtained through the MEL.*

Proof. By definition of minimality, every minimal erasure is an erasure pattern. Now for each erasure pattern $\hat{f}$ in EL, write down all possible minimal erasures. This can be done by exhaustively removing data and parity symbols from $\hat{f}$.

Clearly, from each of these minimal erasures, the original erasure pattern $\hat{f}$ can be generated by adding back the respective data and parity symbols that were deleted. Now take the union of all these minimal erasures. Since this union is the MEL, and every erasure pattern in the EL can be generated from some minimal erasure in MEL, the theorem now follows. $\square$

Consider the Generator matrix for the code and some erasure set f. We refer to the matrix that corresponds to the Generator matrix with all of the data and parity columns that correspond to f removed as the *recovery matrix*. We refer to a recovery matrix as a *defective recovery matrix* if it cannot be used to recover some data symbol. We refer to the rows in the recovery matrix that correspond to the data symbols in f—which we refer to via the notation $f.S$—as the *lost data rows*.

Proposition 3.2 *A recovery matrix is defective if and only if its rank is less than k.*

Proof. Follows from the definitions of erasure pattern and defective recovery matrix. $\square$

Lemma 3.3 *Every base erasure is a minimal erasure.*

Proof. We first argue that a base erasure $\tilde{f}_b$ is an erasure pattern. By definition, a base erasure precisely corresponds to a row of the Generator matrix. The recovery matrix induced by $\tilde{f}_b$ has rank of $k - 1$ because it has an all zero row—the single lost data row—and an $(k-1) \times (k-1)$ identity matrix in the data submatrix. Therefore, by Proposition 3.2, the recovery matrix is defective.

To show that a base erasure is a minimal erasure, we need to establish that if any of the columns in the Generator matrix, that are not in the recovery matrix, is added into the recovery matrix, then the recovery matrix would have rank k. If the data column s_b corresponding to $\tilde{f}_b$ is added into the recovery matrix, then the data submatrix would contain an $k \times k$ identity matrix, thus have full rank, and not be defective. If one of the parity columns corresponding to some parity symbol $p \in \tilde{f}_b.P$ is added into the recovery matrix, then a column swap operation can move it into the data submatrix. Column additions within the data submatrix can then be performed until an identity matrix of size $k \times k$ is established. $\square$

Lemma 3.4 *The addition (XOR) of any subset of the collection of base erasures is an erasure pattern.*

Proof. Let $\{\tilde{f}_1, \ldots, \tilde{f}_k\}$ denote the set of base erasures, and $f = \bigoplus_{i=1}^{k} \tilde{f}_i$ denote their sum. Consider the recovery matrix induced by f. Each of the lost data rows of the recovery matrix can be written as a linear combination of all of the other lost data rows. The lost data rows of the data submatrix are all zeroes and so are linear combinations of one another. The lost data rows of all the parity columns in the recovery matrix have even parity. In each lost data row then, each parity column is either a zero or a one: in either case, it can be written as a linear combination of the other lost data rows. If the column is a zero, then the other rows have even parity, and their sum is zero; if it is a one, then the other rows have odd parity and their sum is one. Therefore the rank of the recovery matrix must be less than k and so is defective; f is an erasure pattern. $\square$

Unfortunately, the above lemma cannot be strengthened to say that f is a minimal erasure. The XOR of some sets of base erasures in some codes result in composite erasures comprised of two or more minimal erasures. However, all minimal erasures can be generated through the addition of base erasures. We prove this next.

Theorem 3.5 *Every minimal erasure can be obtained by the addition of some set of base erasures.*

Proof. Consider a minimal erasure $\tilde{f}$. By Proposition 3.2, the rank of the recovery matrix induced by $\tilde{f}$ is less than k, and therefore, at least one lost data row in the recovery matrix is linearly dependent on the other lost data rows, or all zeroes. Below we strengthen this observation.

Claim 3.1 *Every lost data row in the recovery matrix induced by $\tilde{f}$ is linearly dependent on the rest of the lost data rows, or is all zeroes.*

Proof. Suppose there exist lost data rows in the recovery matrix that are not linearly dependent on the rest of the lost data rows. Ignore all such rows; the remaining lost data rows are either linearly dependent on one another or a single lost data row remains. If a single lost data row remains, by Lemma 3.3, it is a base erasure (and is all zeroes), a contradiction to the minimality of $\tilde{f}$. On the other hand, let S' be the set of data symbols that correspond to the lost data rows that are linearly dependent on one another. Then, $S' \subset \tilde{f}.S$. Now, by Proposition 3.2, $\{S' \cup \tilde{f}.P\}$ is an erasure pattern, a contradiction to the minimality of $\tilde{f}$. $\square$

Claim 3.2 *In any subset of rows corresponding to lost data symbols in the recovery matrix, if every row is linearly dependent on the rest of the rows, then the respective parity columns must have even parity.*

Proof. Suppose there is a column that has odd parity. A lost data row with a zero in this column cannot be linearly dependent on all other lost data rows. $\square$

By Claims 3.1 and 3.2, the parity columns of the recovery matrix induced by $\tilde{f}$ must have even parity. So, by an argument similar to the proof of Lemma 3.4, $\tilde{f}$ can be written as the sum of the base erasures that correspond to the data symbols in $\tilde{f}.S$. This proves the theorem. $\square$

3.4. Bounds on $|\text{MEL}|$ and $|\text{EL}|$

The bound on the size of the EL is as follows:

$$|\text{EL}| \le \sum_{i=1}^{m} \binom{k+m}{i} < 2^{k+m}$$

We use the fact that all erasure patterns of interest are less than or equal to m in length to tighten the bound on $|\text{EL}|$.

Let BEL be the base erasures list: the XOR of each set in the powerset of base erasures, except the null set. It is thus the union of all minimal erasures and all composite erasures. The bound on the size of the BEL is as follows:

$$|\text{BEL}| \le \begin{cases} \sum_{i=1}^{m} \binom{k}{i} & \text{if } m < k, \\ 2^k & \text{if } m \ge k. \end{cases}$$

The bound on the size of the MEL is as follows:

$$|\text{MEL}| \le \begin{cases} \min\left(\binom{k+m}{m}, \sum_{i=1}^{m} \binom{k}{i}\right) & \text{if } m < k, \\ \min\left(\binom{k+m}{\lfloor (k+m)/2 \rfloor}, 2^k\right) & \text{if } m \ge k. \end{cases}$$

The first term in the minimum follows from the bound on $|\text{EL}|$ and the fact that a minimal erasure of size i precludes many potential minimal erasures of size $i + 1$: $|\text{MEL}|$ is thus bound by the largest possible term in the summation that bounds |EL|. The second term in the minimum follows from the bounds on |BEL|.

The difference in the bounds on |EL| and |MEL| suggests that we can expect many more erasure patterns than minimal erasures. Unfortunately, the bound on |MEL| indicates that we can still expect the number of minimal erasures to grow exponentially in k.

Consider the example execution from §3.2. For that code, size of the MEL is 9. This is less than the size of the BEL for the code: $9 < 2^4 = 16$. It is also much less than the size of the EL for the code: 29. (We used a program described in §4.1 to determine the EL for the code.) The value 29 fits the bound for |EL|: $29 < \sum_{i=1}^{4} \binom{8}{i} = 162$.

3.5. Using EV or MEV to compare two codes

The EV and MEV can be used to compare the fault tolerance of any two XOR-based erasure codes. An erasure vector is written as $(j_1, j_2, \ldots, j_m)$ and j_i indicates the number of erasure patterns of size i. A minimal erasure vector is written similarly. Note that the first non-zero entry, j_i, in the MEV and the EV for a code are identical and indicate that the Hamming distance for the code is i (i.e., that the code tolerates all erasures of size $i - 1$).

To compare two erasure vectors, the value in the vector are compared, from shortest to longest (i.e., from 1 to m). If the value of the first entry in EV that is distinct from that in EV′ is greater, then EV < EV′. For example, if EV = $(0, 4, 5)$ and EV′ = $(0, 0, 10)$, then EV < EV′, because $4 > 0$; and, if EV = $(0, 4, 5)$ and EV′ = $(0, 4, 4)$, then EV < EV′, because $5 > 4$. If EV < EV′, then the code corresponding to EV′ is the more fault tolerant. Minimal erasure vectors can be compared similarly. For two codes with the same k and m, the result of comparing the MEV is the same as the result of comparing the EV. For two codes that differ in k and/or m, the result of comparing the MEV is only necessarily the same as the result of comparing the EV if the codes have different Hamming distances, or if the codes have the same Hamming distance but different values in the MEV at the Hamming distance.

4. Evaluation

In this section, we evaluate our implementation of the ME Algorithm: mela. In §4.1, we describe how we validated the correctness of the mela implementation. In §4.2, we use mela to determine the MEV of all XOR-based erasure codes with $1 \leq k, m \leq 7$. One major result from this section is that we identify the most fault tolerant XOR-based erasure codes over these parameters. Another major result from this section is that, in practice, the average of the ratio $\frac{|EL|}{|MEL|}$ tends to increase with k and m. The average of this ratio is over 80 for one corpus of codes we evaluated. This result supports our claim that it is more efficient to determine the MEL than the EL (especially as k and m increase).

We used Python 2.4.3 to implement mela and the rest of our tool suite. Python code is easy to modify and so allows us to quickly prototype modifications and extensions of the ME Algorithm. The minimal erasures data structure and cache, M and $\overline{M}$ respectively, are implemented via m dictionaries. The kth dictionary only stores erasure patterns of length k. We store erasure patterns as bitmaps because they are concise and efficient to compare. Testing for membership in a dictionary is efficient in Python. Dictionaries keep track of the number of elements they store and so conversion from M to the MEV is trivial. The minimal erasures queue Q is a FIFO queue implemented via a list.

We also implemented a tool, mel2el, that efficiently transforms a MEL into a EL using set operations. mel2el must perform O(|EL|) operations and is efficient only in that it does not perform any matrix rank tests. We use mel2el to determine the EL and EV for some codes in this section.

We use nauty version 2.2 with gtools to generate Tanner graphs for mela to evaluate [10, 9]. Specifically, we use genbg to generate non-isomorphic bipartite graphs that we translate into systematic Tanner graphs. Isomorphic Tanner graphs have similar fault tolerance characteristics and so we only evaluate non-isomorphic Tanner graphs. We refer to the set of all possible non-isomorphic systematic Tanner graphs with a common k and m as the (k, m)-code corpus. For a given k and m, there are up to 2^{km} possible systematic XOR-based codes; there are dramatically fewer codes in the (k, m)-code corpus because we only include non-isomorphic Tanner graphs.

All execution times in this section are based on execution on an HP DL360 computer with a 2.8 GHz Intel Xeon processor and 4 GB of RAM.

4.1. Validation of implementation

To validate the correctness of the mela implementation we generate the MEL via "brute force" for some codes. We implemented a program, ela, that generates the EL for a given code. Roughly speaking, ela performs a matrix rank test for every erasure pattern with one erasure, then all erasure patterns with two erasures, and so on, up to all erasure patterns with m erasures. A matrix rank test indicates if the erasure pattern is decodable. We developed another program, el2mel, that filters the EL output by ela to produce the MEL. The implementation of el2mel is based on inserting the erasure patterns in the EL into a data structure that checks for the subset or equal to relationship. If an erasure pattern is a superset of an erasure pattern that is already in the data structure, then it is not inserted. If an erasure pattern is successfully inserted, then all larger erasure patterns in the data structure are checked to see if they are a superset of the inserted erasure pattern; any that are a superset are removed from the data structure.

We validated the correctness of `mela` for the $(4, 4)$-code corpus; it contains 179 codes. The MEL output by `mela` exactly matches the MEL output by `ela` piped to `el2mel`. It took less than one second for `mela` to complete, 231 seconds for `ela` to complete, and less than one second for `el2mel` to complete.

4.2. Fault tolerance of XOR-based codes

We evaluated all (k, m)-code corpi for $1 \leq k, m \leq 7$ with `mela`. Table 3 lists the results. The first two columns list k and m for each code corpus. The third column lists the number of codes in the (k, m)-code corpus. The fourth column, # w MEV*, lists the number of codes in the corpus that share the best minimal erasures vector. The fifth column, # w d^*, lists the number of codes in the corpus that share the best Hamming distance. The sixth column lists a parity submatrix for a code from the corpus that has an MEV equal to MEV*. The parity submatrix is presented in "bitmap" representation: each integer represents a column of the parity submatrix (i.e., if the parity symbol includes data symbol s_j, then add 2^{j-1} to the integer representation). For example, for the $(4, 3)$-code corpus, "7, 11, 13" means that the first parity is the XOR of $s_1, s_2, \& s_3$, the second parity is the XOR of $s_1, s_2, \& s_4$, and the third parity is the XOR of $s_1, s_3, \& s_4$. The seventh column, MEV*, lists the value of the best MEV in the corpus. The eighth column, d^*, lists the best Hamming distance in the corpus (i.e., the index of the first non-zero entry in MEV*). The ninth column, $\frac{|EL|}{|MEL|}$, lists the average of the ratio $|EL|$ to $|MEL|$ for the corpus.

We do not list the rows for $k = 1$ or the columns for $m = 1$ in Table 3 because each such corpus has only one code: replication for $k = 1$ and RAID 4 for $m = 1$. Replication has no erasure patterns that lead to irrecoverable data loss of size less than or equal to m and so both the MEL and EL are empty. RAID 4 tolerates all erasure patterns of size 1 and so again, both the MEL and EL are empty.

We make the following observations about the results:

- The average of the ratio $\frac{|EL|}{|MEL|}$ tends to increase with both k and m. For the $(5, 7)$-code corpus, directly calculating the EL rather than the MEL requires $84.9\times$ more steps. We were surprised though that the $(7, 7)$-code corpus did not have the greatest average ratio.

- As m increases with regard to some fixed k, the best MEV improves; this makes sense since there is more redundancy. As k increases with regard to some fixed m, the best MEV degrades; this makes sense since the same amount of redundancy is protecting more data.

- As k and m increase, very few codes share the absolute best MEV. For example, in the $(7, 7)$-code corpus,

only 1 in 1.48 million codes has the best fault tolerance. However, 1 in 30 codes does share the best Hamming distance.

- The data symbols for the best codes are included by at least d^* parity symbols. This is because we focus exclusively on systematic codes. The best codes thus have higher Hamming weight (are more connected) than would be expected from reading the LDPC literature. The LDPC literature, in general, does not consider systematic codes.

- We were surprised by the code corpi in which a specific parity symbol, the XOR of all data symbols, is replicated (cf. corpi with $k = 2 \& m > 2$, and $k = 3 \& m > 4$). We wonder if this is generally true: if m sufficiently exceeds k, then the "RAID 4 parity symbol" is replicated many times in the best code.

- We were surprised to find that there does not exist a systematic XOR-based erasure code with $5 \leq k \leq 7$ and $m = 7$ that tolerates all erasures of size 4.

To appreciate the value of considering only non-isomorphic Tanner graphs in a corpus, compare the number of codes in any (k, m)-code corpus to the value of 2^{km}. For the $(7, 7)$-code corpus the reduction is of over a factor of 19 million times. We had hoped to consider all code corpi up to $k = 10$ and $m = 10$ but the growth in the size of such corpi was prohibitive. To identify the best codes in larger corpi we may need to develop additional theory to reduce the number of codes we need to evaluate in each corpus, improve the efficiency of the `mela` implementation, or get a larger compute cluster. Our approach to enumerating all non-isomorphic codes for a given k and m to evaluate is quite different from the traditional approach of identifying *families* of codes: most coding theorists focus on identifying a code family, parameterized on k and m, that constructs "good" codes given k, m, and possibly a random seed.

5. Discussion

Concurrently to our work, Hafner and Rao investigated the reliability of irregular erasure codes [7]. They did so in the "standard" RAID framework: they developed a Markov model with failure and recovery rates for various components. Irregular XOR-based codes do not simply "plug" into such a model though. They calculate the conditional probabilities q_j that a state in their Markov model with j failures results in irrecoverable data loss (note that they use subscript k not j for their notation). They do so by counting the number of erasure sets of size j that do not lead to data loss for all $j \leq m$ (resulting in vector s_j). To get q_j, they divide s_j by $\binom{k+m}{j}$. The vector s_j is the complement of the

k	m	# in corpus	# w MEV*	# w d^*	A parity submatrix w MEV*	MEV*	d^*	$\frac{\text{EL}}{\text{MEL}}$
2	2	3	2	3	1, 3	(0, 1)	2	1.8
2	3	5	1	2	1, 3, 3	(0, 0, 1)	3	2.9
2	4	8	1	2	1, 3, 3, 3	(0, 0, 0, 1)	4	4.9
2	5	11	1	2	1, 3, 3, 3, 3	(0, 0, 0, 0, 1)	5	8.4
2	6	15	1	2	1, 3, 3, 3, 3, 3	(0, 0, 0, 0, 0, 1)	6	14.2
2	7	19	1	2	1, 3, 3, 3, 3, 3, 3	(0, 0, 0, 0, 0, 0, 1)	7	24.0
3	2	5	2	5	3, 5	(0, 2)	2	2.0
3	3	17	2	2	3, 5, 6	(0, 0, 4)	3	2.8
3	4	42	1	1	3, 5, 6, 7	(0, 0, 0, 3)	4	6.7
3	5	91	1	1	3, 5, 6, 7, 7	(0, 0, 0, 0, 3)	5	13.9
3	6	180	1	1	3, 5, 6, 7, 7, 7	(0, 0, 0, 0, 0, 3)	6	26.4
3	7	328	1	1	3, 5, 6, 7, 7, 7, 7	(0, 0, 0, 0, 0, 0, 3)	7	47.7
4	2	8	1	8	7, 11	(0, 3)	2	2.0
4	3	42	1	1	7, 11, 13	(0, 0, 7)	3	3.4
4	4	179	1	1	7, 11, 13, 14	(0, 0, 0, 14)	4	6.3
4	5	633	1	14	3, 5, 9, 14, 15	(0, 0, 0, 6, 1)	4	16.2
4	6	2001	2	166	3, 5, 7, 9, 14, 15	(0, 0, 0, 2, 2, 1)	4	36.7
4	7	5745	1	10	3, 5, 7, 11, 13, 14, 15	(0, 0, 0, 0, 1, 2, 1)	5	75.5
5	2	11	2	11	7, 27	(0, 5)	2	2.3
5	3	91	3	91	7, 11, 29	(0, 1, 10)	2	4.0
5	4	633	3	35	7, 11, 19, 29	(0, 0, 4, 14)	3	7.6
5	5	3835	2	14	7, 11, 19, 29, 30	(0, 0, 0, 10, 16)	4	14.7
5	6	20755	4	542	3, 5, 15, 23, 25, 30	(0, 0, 0, 4, 14, 1)	4	36.3
5	7	102089	1	11890	7, 11, 13, 14, 19, 21, 25	(0, 0, 0, 1, 8, 0, 1)	4	84.9
6	2	15	2	15	15, 51	(0, 7)	2	2.4
6	3	180	6	180	7, 27, 45	(0, 2, 14)	2	4.6
6	4	2001	6	35	7, 27, 45, 56	(0, 0, 8, 18)	3	8.8
6	5	20755	7	12	7, 25, 42, 52, 63	(0, 0, 0, 25, 0)	4	16.9
6	6	200082	5	1338	7, 27, 30, 45, 53, 56	(0, 0, 0, 6, 24, 16)	4	31.8
6	7	1781941	19	118130	7, 11, 21, 25, 45, 51, 62	(0, 0, 0, 2, 16, 18, 1)	4	75.3
7	2	19	1	19	31, 103	(0, 9)	2	2.6
7	3	328	7	328	15, 51, 85	(0, 3, 19)	2	5.1
7	4	5745	10	28	15, 54, 90, 113	(0, 0, 12, 26)	3	10.1
7	5	102089	8	10	7, 57, 90, 108, 119	(0, 0, 0, 38, 0)	4	19.1
7	6	1781941	57	2610	7, 46, 56, 75, 85, 118	(0, 0, 0, 14, 28, 24)	4	35.7
7	7	29610804	20	965097	7, 27, 45, 51, 86, 110, 120	(0, 0, 0, 3, 24, 36, 16)	4	65.3

Table 3. Evaluation of all (k, m)-code corpi for $1 \leq k, m \leq 7$.

EV in our work; it counts the number of erasure sets of size j that are not an erasure pattern, whereas the EV counts the number of erasure patterns of size j.

Hafner and Rao claim to compute s_j by "straightforward calculation" using techniques they previously developed [6]. (We note that those previous techniques are based on the pseudo-inverse of the Generator matrix and efficiently determines if a set of erasures is an erasure pattern or not, and if not, outputs how to reconstruct data.) The ME Algorithm efficiently calculates the MEL and MEV. We ran mela and mel2el on the Tanner code from Plank's RAID tutorial [12] that Hafner and Rao analyze in §3.2 of [7]. Our analysis took less than one second and produced an EV compatible with the s_j they produce.

Plank et al. analyzed the *read overhead* for LDPC constructions [14]. Read overhead is the expected number of symbols that must be read to recover all of the data symbols, assuming a random read order. Read overhead is a good performance metric for irregular XOR-based erasure codes deployed in grid storage environments; in LAN settings, we expect that storage systems would employ systematic codes and read data symbols ("stripes") before reading any parity symbols. More recently, Plank et al. [13] analyzed the read overhead for codes with small m. Our analyses overlap for the (k, m)-code corpi with $k, m \leq 5$. We believe that the EV can be transformed into a read overhead metric, but have not yet determined this transformation.

6. Conclusions

We identified a new fault tolerance metric for XOR-based erasure codes, the minimal erasures list (MEL), a concise representation of that metric, the minimal erasures vector (MEV), and the Minimal Erasures (ME) Algorithm which efficiently determines the MEL. We applied the implementation of the ME Algorithm to all systematic XOR-based erasure codes with $1 \leq k, m \leq 7$, and so identified the most fault tolerant such codes. We presented empirical evidence that the ME Algorithm requires less work (over a factor of $80\times$) than an algorithm that directly generates all erasure patterns.

Acknowledgements

We thank our colleagues Vinay Deolalikar, Xiaozhou Li, Craig Soules, Krishnamurthy Viswanathan, and Pascal Vontobel for their feedback. We also thank the anonymous DSN reviewers for their thorough reviews and suggestions.

References

[1] M. Blaum, J. Brady, J. Bruck, and J. Menon. EVENODD: An efficient scheme for tolerating double disk failures in RAID architectures. *IEEE Trans. Comput.*, 44(2):192–202, 1995.

[2] P. Corbett, B. English, A. Goel, T. Grcanac, S. Kleiman, J. Leong, and S. Sankar. Row-diagonal parity for double disk failure correction. In *FAST-2004: 3rd USENIX Conference on File and Storage Technologies*, pages 1–14. USENIX Association, 2004.

[3] R. G. Gallager. *Low density parity-check codes*. MIT Press, 1963.

[4] J. L. Hafner. WEAVER Codes: Highly fault tolerant erasure codes for storage systems. In *FAST-2005: 4th USENIX Conference on File and Storage Technologies*, pages 212–224. USENIX Association, December 2005.

[5] J. L. Hafner. HoVer erasure codes for disk arrays. In *DSN-2006: The International Conference on Dependable Systems and Networks*, pages 217–226. IEEE, June 2006.

[6] J. L. Hafner, V. Deenadhayalan, K. Rao, and J. A. Tomlin. Matrix methods for lost data reconstruction in erasure codes. In *FAST-2005: 4th USENIX Conference on File and Storage Technologies*, pages 183–196. USENIX Association, December 2005.

[7] J. L. Hafner and K. Rao. Notes on reliability models for non-MDS erasure codes. Technical Report RJ–10391, IBM, October 2006.

[8] M. G. Luby, M. Mitzenmacher, M. A. Shokrollahi, D. A. Spielman, and V. Stemann. Practical loss-resilient codes. In *STOC 1997: Proceedings of the 29th annual ACM Symposium on Theory of Computing*, pages 150–159. ACM Press, 1997.

[9] B. McKay. `nauty` version 2.2 (including `gtools`). http://cs.anu.edu.au/~bdm/nauty/.

[10] B. McKay. Practical graph isomorphism. *Congressus Numerantium*, 30:45–87, 1981.

[11] D. A. Patterson, G. Gibson, and R. H. Katz. A case for redundant arrays of inexpensive disks (RAID). In *ACM SIGMOD International Conference on Management of Data*, pages 109–116, June 1988.

[12] J. S. Plank. Erasure codes for storage applications. Tutorial slides, presented at *FAST-2005: 4th Usenix Conference on File and Storage Technologies*, http://www.cs.utk.edu/~plank/plank/papers/FAST-2005.html, December 2005.

[13] J. S. Plank, A. L. Buchsbaum, R. L. Collins, and M. G. Thomason. Small parity-check erasure codes - exploration and observations. In *DSN-2005: The International Conference on Dependable Systems and Networks*. IEEE, July 2005.

[14] J. S. Plank and M. G. Thomason. A practical analysis of low-density parity-check erasure codes for wide-area storage applications. In *DSN-2004: The International Conference on Dependable Systems and Networks*, pages 115–124. IEEE, June 2004.

[15] K. Rao, J. L. Hafner, and R. A. Golding. Reliability for networked storage nodes. In *DSN-2006: The International Conference on Dependable Systems and Networks*, pages 237–248. IEEE, June 2006.

[16] Y. Saito, S. Frølund, A. Veitch, A. Merchant, and S. Spence. FAB: Building distributed enterprise disk arrays from commodity components. In *ASPLOS-XI: 11th International Conference on Architectural Support for Programming Languages and Operating Systems*, pages 48–58. ACM Press, 2004.

[17] M. Schwartz and A. Vardy. On the stopping distance and the stopping redundancy of codes. *IEEE Trans. on Inf. Theory*, 52(3):922–932, 2006.

Fault Tolerant Approaches to Nanoelectronic Programmable Logic Arrays *

Wenjing Rao
UC San Diego
CSE Department
wrao@cs.ucsd.edu

Alex Orailoglu
UC San Diego
CSE Department
alex@cs.ucsd.edu

Ramesh Karri
Polytechnic University
ECE Department
rkarri@poly.edu

Abstract

Programmable logic arrays (PLA), which can implement arbitrary logic functions in a two-level logic form, are promising as platforms for nanoelectronic logic due to their highly regular structure compatible with the nano crossbar architectures. Reliability is an important challenge as far as nanoelectronic devices are concerned. Consequently, it is necessary to focus on the fault tolerance aspects of nanoelectronic PLAs to ensure their viability as a foundation for nanoelectronic systems.

In this paper, we investigate two types of fault tolerance techniques for nanoelectronic device based PLAs, focusing at the online faults occurring at the cross-points of nano devices. We develop a scheme to precisely locate the faults online, as this is a crucial step for ef cient online recon guration based fault tolerance schemes. We also propose a tautology based fault masking scheme. We demonstrate that these two types of fault tolerance schemes developed for nano PLAs signi cantly improve at low hardware cost the reliability of the high fault occurrence nanoelectronic environment.

1. Introduction

As device scales shrink, traditional CMOS based devices are facing physical limits. The quantum effects occurring at the nanoscale have challenged the further scaling down of CMOS based electronic systems. Consequently, a number of devices based on quantum physical mechanisms, such as SET [1], RTD [2], CNT [3], QCA [4] and molecular electronics [5], have been proposed as promising device candidates for the next generation nanoelectronics [6]. The main advantages of these nanoelectronic devices center on achieving extremely dense circuits coupled with high speed, thus enabling the continuation of the scaling down of transistors and providing us with the potential to extend Moore's law into a post-CMOS era [6].

Although each of the multiple candidates operates on its specific physical basis, a number of common characteristics

emerge among the nanoelectronic devices, essentially due to their scale. First, the new nanoelectronics are promising in their potential of supporting device densities of up to 10^{12} device/cm^2, thus indicating a huge advantage in terms of hardware abundance [6]. Second, the traditional top-down fabrication of electronic systems becomes not only exceedingly expensive, but also prohibitive due to the loss of precision for nano-scale devices. Consequently, the only possibility of economically fabricating a nanoelectronics based system is to resort to a *bottom-up* fabrication, which relies on a "self-assembly" process, and is limited to generating only highly regular structures. A post-fabrication reconfiguration process is necessitated to implement the desired functionality.

Besides the above mentioned new characteristics, one of the most severe challenges in nanoelectronic systems is unreliability. Due to their nano scale dimensions [6], not only are manufacturing defect rates projected to be extremely high, but also nanoelectronic systems suffer from a significantly increased occurrence rate of run-time faults. Consequently, even the fundamental correctness requirement of a future nanoelectronics based system needs to be guaranteed by extensive fault tolerance schemes.

Redundancy is the basis of all fault tolerance techniques. Owing to its highly regular structure, such a PLA structure can be easily fabricated using a bottom-up self-assembly process. Specifically, the implementation of the nano PLA can be supported by multiple nanoelectronic devices under a crossbar based architecture [7, 8, 9]. In this paper we investigate two hardware redundancy based fault tolerance approaches for a nanoelectronic crossbar based PLA structure. On the one hand, we focus on the precise fault location identification for a reconfiguration based online repair approach. On the other hand, we develop a Boolean tautology based scheme to mask the fault effect.

2. Preliminaries

2.1. Nanoelectronic background

One of the most challenging issues widely acknowledged in nanoelectronic system construction is the reliability prob-

---

*The work of the first two authors is supported in part by NSF Grant 0082325.

lem. On the one hand, due to the small scale as well as the fabrication process in nano environments, a large number of manufacturing defects are inevitable. For instance, due to the fabrication limit, the randomness in location and orientation in the growth of nanotubes and nanowires is hard to control. In comparison with the defect rates of 10^{-9} to 10^{-7} in current CMOS systems, the defect rates of nanoelectronic systems are projected to be extremely high, of the order of 10^{-3} to 10^{-1} [10]. On the other hand, a high occurrence of online faults is expected during run-time of the nanoelectronic systems [6, 11]. Basically, the extremely small scale of the nanoelectronic devices leads to low immunity to noise and errors. The influence of stray charge, crosstalk, temperature fluctuation and cosmic particle caused single event upsets becomes fatal to nano scale transistors, which utilize ultra low power and operate based on quantum effects [6, 11, 12]. Due to the highly unreliable devices which are extremely sensitive to environmental influences, online fault tolerance is of significant importance for guaranteeing the basic correctness requirement of a nanoelectronics based system.

The top-down fabrication currently used in CMOS systems will encounter severe challenges in reaching the required precision in nano scale. Aggressive lithographic fabrication for the nanoelectronic environment turns out to be prohibitively expensive, while a bottom-up approach is expected to prevail as the basic way for constructing nanoscale circuits, by building structures in a self-assembly manner. Such a fundamental change in the fabrication process introduces a number of new implications in nanoelectronic systems, including *regularity in structure*, and furthermore, *online recon gurability*, which is necessitated in a post-fabrication process to define the circuits and bypass the defects.

Extensive research work has been carried out for regular structure based nanoelectronic systems, particularly in a crossbar architecture [13, 14, 15, 9, 16], based on which logic systems can be constructed in a programmable logic array (PLA) form. Basically, a nano crossbar architecture consists of two sets of perpendicular nanowires and a nanoelectronic device located at each crosspoint. Such devices exhibit two distinct states of connecting and disconnecting the two wires, and these two states can be configured by applying a positive or negative voltage correspondingly. By utilizing the reconfigurability supported by nanoelectronic devices, a nano crossbar based PLA can be configured to implement arbitrary functions in a two-level logic form.

2.2. Fault Models

In nanoelectronics, particularly a nanoelectronic crossbar PLA structures, a massive number of two-terminal molecular devices are sandwiched at the crosspoints of two orthogonal layers of densely packed parallel nanowires. Due to the unreliable characteristics of the devices, massive occurrences of

type	K-map	cause	effect	output	example
G	growth	missing device in AND plane	missing variable	$0 \rightarrow 1$	$f = ab + cd$ $\rightarrow b + cd$
S	shrink	extra device in AND plane	extra variable	$1 \rightarrow 0$	$f = ab + cd$ $\rightarrow abe + cd$
D	disap-pearance	missing device in OR plane	missing product term	$1 \rightarrow 0$	$f = ab + cd$ $\rightarrow cd$
A	appear-ance	extra device in OR plane	extra product term	$0 \rightarrow 1$	$f = ab + cd$ $\rightarrow ab + cd + e$

Table 1. Fault models of nano PLA

faults are expected at the crosspoints during run time. These in-service faults include permanent faults such as a device becoming nonprogrammable, as well as transient faults of switching between states due to environmental effects [6, 7, 8, 17].

Fault models for PLAs have been previously developed in the context of manufacturing testing of CMOS based PLAs [18]. From a logic function perspective, there are four types of faults occurring at the crosspoints [19, 20], as shown in table 1.

For instance, for a type G fault, a device is missing from the AND plane, leading to a *growth* in the Karnaugh map. At the logic level, a variable is dropped from a product term, and the outputs connected to the product term change unidirectionally from 0 to 1. Since all these four types of faults lead to unidirectional changes in the output, specialized techniques that entail reduced hardware overhead can be developed.

2.3. Fault tolerance approaches for nano PLA and related previous research

Based on these fault models, testing approaches for manufacturing defects in PLAs have been developed, including a number of approaches focusing on mapping logic functions on defective nano PLAs by exploiting reconfigurability [19, 18, 20, 21, 22, 23, 9, 24, 25, 26]. Approaches have also been developed on offline diagnosis for fault locations in PLAs [27, 28, 29, 30]. Previous research on fault tolerant PLAs has mainly focused on concurrent error detection techniques of online faults [23, 31, 32].

Due to the significant increase in fault occurrence projected for the nanoelectronic environment, aggressive online fault tolerance techniques are necessitated for the nano PLAs. Fault tolerant computation typically explores redundancy to guarantee correctness in the presence of faults. The two main categories of online fault tolerance for the nanoelectronic environment consist of *online repair* and *fault masking*.

For a system supporting reconfiguration, particularly with high regularity, online repair is promising for its hardware efficiency in dealing with massive faults [10]. An online repair based scheme necessitates not only online fault detection, but also an online diagnosis phase to pinpoint the specific faulty

217

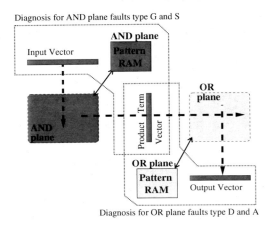

Figure 1. Online fault diagnosis setup

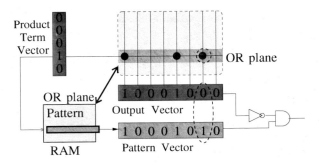

Figure 2. D type fault diagnosis

component, followed by the final reconfiguration based repair process. Diagnostic resolution of defective components is crucial to the hardware overhead; it determines the spare units necessary during reconfiguration. On the one hand, coarse grain diagnostic resolution may result in replacing a large number of fault-free components. On the other hand, a fine grain diagnostic resolution where faulty components can be precisely identified may result in efficient utilization of spare hardware.

The online repair schemes typically introduce significant delay due to the fault detection, diagnosis and repair phases. An alternative approach, fault masking, exhibits very low performance penalties. Perhaps one of the best known examples of fault masking approaches is the N-modular redundancy (NMR) scheme, which utilizes identical redundant modules to execute the same function with a majority vote masking out faulty results.

3. Online diagnosis for nano PLAs

In this section, we provide an online diagnosis scheme, which can be used upon fault detection to identify precisely the fault type as well as location in nano PLAs. Such information is used to direct the subsequent repair phase.

Basically, online diagnosis can be described as the problem of identifying the type(s) and location(s) of the fault(s) given the fact that a fault or multiple faults have been detected. In a typical offline diagnosis, test vectors can be applied to the inputs while the outputs can be compared with the correct ones based on the input test vectors. In an online diagnosis process, the vectors which stimulate the fault manifestations are the run time functional inputs, and thus not controllable. Consequently, the expected output for any specific input at the run time cannot be pre-stored as well.

To achieve full diagnostic resolution online, we store instead the static information regarding the correct configuration of each PLA plane, and utilize the particular runtime vectors

that stimulate and capture the fault manifestation to analyze the fault type and location.

Figure 1 shows the information and hardware structures in the proposed online diagnosis approach for nanoelectronic PLAs. The device configuration patterns for the AND and OR planes are stored in two RAMs, with every bit representing the on/off status of the corresponding device configuration.

Even with the full configuration information of the PLA stored in the RAM, the actual status of every device in the PLA cannot be directly probed online, due to the lack of controllability for the inputs in an online environment. Therefore, an online diagnosis mechanism needs to be developed to pinpoint the fault location based on the limited information acquirable upon the fault detection. The information required for the identification process includes:

- **Input Vector (IV)**: the inputs to the PLA AND plane.
- **Product Term Vector (PTV)**: the outputs of the AND plane (i.e., the inputs to the OR plane).
- **Output Vector (OV)**: the outputs of the PLA OR plane.

3.1. An example: locating a D type fault

In this subsection, we elaborate on the identification of a D type fault, namely a device missing fault in the OR plane, as an example to explain the proposed scheme.

A D type fault (missing device in the OR plane) can result in a single bit change from 1 to 0 in the Output Vector. This is because the missing device fails to *pull up* the output line, when the product term wire carries a value of 1. Due to the unidirectional change from 1 to 0 caused by such a fault in the OR plane, we need to focus on the candidate set of zero bits in the OV. Within the PTV, we only need to focus on the bits with the value 1, since for the product term wire with a value zero, the fault would have never been manifested.

If the OV consists of O bits and the PTV consists of P bits, the dimension of the OR plane is $P \times O$, and the size of the pattern RAM, R_{OR}, is $P \times O$ as well. To summarize, the necessary and sufficient conditions for the fault manifestation of a missing device at the $[p][o]$ crosspoint in the OR plane are, (i)

fault type	fault location	occurring plane	C_1: input to the plane	fault effect	C_2: output of the plane	device crosspoint	C_3: configuration bit from RAM
G	$[i][p]$	AND	$IV[i] = 0$	$0 \rightarrow 1$	$PTV[p] = 1$	miss	$R_{AND}[i][p] = 1$
S	$[i][p]$	AND	$IV[i] = 0$	$1 \rightarrow 0$	$PTV[p] = 0$	extra	$R_{AND}[i][p] = 0$
D	$[p][o]$	OR	$PTV[p] = 1$	$1 \rightarrow 0$	$OV[o] = 0$	miss	$R_{OR}[p][o] = 1$
A	$[p][o]$	OR	$PTV[p] = 1$	$0 \rightarrow 1$	$OV[o] = 1$	extra	$R_{OR}[p][o] = 0$

Table 2. Online diagnosis conditions for the 4 fault models

the p'th product term wire carries a value of 1, (ii) the o'th output wire, however, exhibits a 0, and (iii) the device connecting the p'th product term wire and the o'th output wire is configured as "on" in the fault free PLA. This can be formulated as:

A D type fault at crosspoint $[p][o]$ manifests
$\Leftrightarrow OV[o] = 0, PTV[p] = 1, R_{OR}[p][o] = 1$.

In other words, such a condition indicates the existence of a device configured at position $[p][o]$, yet failing to transfer the value 1 from the product term wire to the output bit, thus resulting in the output bit changing from 1 to 0. Figure 2 shows the architecture of this precise identification of a missing device in the OR plane, as well as the logic to implement the detection of such a condition.

Basically, if $PTV[p] = 1$, the corresponding p'th row, in the OR plane configuration RAM, $R_{OR}[p]$, is used. This vector is referred to as the **Pattern Vector (PV)**, which indicates the fault-free device configuration on the p'th row product term wire in the OR plane. According to the sufficient and necessary condition described, a D type fault at position $[p][o]$ can be identified with a simple logic that detects the case of $PV[o] = 1$ and $OV[o] = 0$.

3.2. General online diagnosis conditions

In the previous subsection, we provide a detailed description on the fault location diagnosis principles for the D type fault. In general, for each of the four fault models, a similar analysis can be performed and the corresponding diagnosis conditions can be developed.

Table 2 lists the sufficient and necessary conditions, marked as C_1, C_2 and C_3 in the columns, for the manifestation of each type of fault at a specific location. Basically, the combination of three conditions can precisely determine the type and location of a fault:

C_1: for the G, S types of faults occurring at location $[i][p]$ in the AND plane, the IV must have a zero at the i'th bit, at the input to the AND plane, to stimulate the fault; similarly, for the D, A types of faults at location $[p][o]$ in the OR plane, the $PTV[p]$ bit as an input to the OR plane must be 1 to stimulate the fault.

C_2: the S, D faults unidirectionally change the outputs from 1 to 0, forcing the corresponding bit at the output of the

plane to be 0; similarly, for the G, A faults, which change the outputs unidirectionally from 0 to 1, the corresponding bit at the output of the plane must be 1.

C_3: for the G and D as the device missing faults, the corresponding bit in the RAM must be 1, indicating a device configured as on in a fault-free PLA; similarly, for the S and A as extra device faults, the corresponding bit in the RAM must be 0.

3.3. Overall online repair process of nano PLA

The proposed online fault diagnosis scheme can be performed in conjunction with a number of existing online fault detection techniques developed for PLAs, such as the Berger code based online fault detection [33]. After the identification of the fault type and location, online repair can be accomplished through reconfiguration using the spare rows and columns of the PLA.

The overall online repair procedure is described as follows:

1. Online fault detection

   - Upon fault detection, capture:
     - Input Vector (IV);
     - Product Term Vector (PTV);
     - Output Vector (OV)

2. Online fault diagnosis

   - For every bit position i in IV, if $IV[i] = 0$:
     //Diagnosis for AND plane faults

     (a) $PV = R_{AND}[i]$
     //Read Pattern Vector (PV) from the i'th column of RAM R_{AND}

     (b) For every bit p that $(PV[p] = 1, PTV[p] = 1)$, identify a G type fault at location $[i][p]$
     //G fault: missing device at $[i][p]$ of the AND plane

     (c) For every bit p that $(PV[p] = 0, PTV[p] = 0)$, identify an S type fault at location $[i][p]$
     //S fault: extra device at $[i][p]$ of the AND plane

   - For every bit position p in PTV, if $PTV[p] = 1$:
     //Diagnosis for OR plane faults

219

fault type	f under fault	$\widehat{f_{AND}}$ under fault	$\widehat{f_{OR}}$ under fault
G	$ab \to a$	$ab \cdot ab \to aba = f$	$ab + ab \to a + ab \neq f$
S	$ab \to abc$	$ab \cdot ab \to ababc \neq f$	$ab + ab \to ab + abc = f$
D	$p_1 + p_2$ $\to p_1$	$(p_1 + p_2)(p_1 + p_2)$ $\to p_1(p_1 + p_2) \neq f$	$p_1 + p_2 + p_1 + p_2$ $\to p_1 + p_1 + p_2 = f$
A	$p_1 + p_2$ $\to p_1 + p_2 + p_3$	$(p_1 + p_2)(p_1 + p_2)$ $\to (p_1 + p_2)(p_1 + p_2 + p_3) = f$	$p_1 + p_2 + p_1 + p_2$ $\to p_1 + p_2 + p_1 + p_2 + p_3 \neq f$

Table 3. Tautology form fault masking capability over the 4 fault models

(a) $PV = R_{OR}[p]$
//Read Pattern Vector (PV) from the p'th row
of RAM R_{OR}

(b) For every bit o that $(PV[o] = 1, OV[o] = 0)$,
identify a D type fault at location $[p][o]$
//D fault: missing device at $[p][o]$ of the OR
plane

(c) For every bit o that $(PV[o] = 0, OV[o] = 1)$,
identify an A type fault at location $[p][o]$
//A fault: extra device at $[p][o]$ of the OR plane

3. Perform reconfiguration for the faulty devices using spare
rows and columns

3.4. Fault diagnosis overhead discussion

The two extra pattern RAMs introduced for the purpose of online diagnosis cost approximately the same hardware overhead as the original PLA, when implemented in nanoelectronic devices. Any faults occurring in the RAMs, however, do not impact the correctness of the function carried out by the nano PLA, since the RAMs are only utilized for fault diagnosis purposes, and their contents are only read when faults are detected by an independent procedure, possibly through a Berger code based approach. Since a faulty bit in the RAMs will influence the correctness of fault diagnosis at the corresponding crosspoint of the PLA, error correction code based techniques can be applied to the RAMs to avoid misdiagnosis. The hardware required to implement the online fault diagnosis logic is quite insignificant; therefore, its robustness can be easily enhanced by additional redundancy, or even implemented in CMOS based transistors. Overall, the correctness of the online diagnosis process can be guaranteed with low hardware overhead.

When invoked after an online fault detection procedure, the proposed fault diagnosis scheme is capable of identifying the type and location of the 4 fault models, even under a multiple-fault scenario. This is because the proposed fault identification performs the online diagnosis through the bit-wise sufficient and necessary condition from the fault manifestation. The occurrence of multiple faults imposes no ambiguity or aliasing on the diagnosis procedure; therefore, full resolution can be preserved with the precise pinpointing of each fault's type and location.

4. Fault Masking in nano-PLA

Fault masking is a general technique that can be applied straightforwardly to arbitrary functions. In the traditional NMR based fault masking approach, to achieve the single fault masking capability, at least triple the amount of hardware is required, plus the additional overhead of a majority voter. In fact, for the nanoelectronic PLA logic, NMR based fault masking approaches do not constitute the most efficient solution, because of their voting overhead in terms of performance, hardware and reliability. Basically, two extra levels of logic with significant area overhead are needed for the majority voting implementation. Furthermore, to make the voter reliable in nano PLA, even more hardware overhead is necessitated, making the overall NMR scheme highly expensive.

Alternatively, a logic tautology form can be exploited to develop a class of new fault masking schemes that are particularly favorable to nano PLAs. With such an approach, the redundancy is integrated within the logic function, thus obviating the need for a majority voting process. Consequently, significant improvement can be achieved both for performance and efficient hardware utilization.

4.1. Fault masking examples

In Boolean logic, the AND and the OR functions provide two tautology forms, defined as $\widehat{f_{AND}}$ and $\widehat{f_{OR}}$:

$$\widehat{f_{AND}} = f \cdot f \equiv f$$

$$\widehat{f_{OR}} = f + f \equiv f$$

Table 3 shows the masking capability of the two tautology forms over the four fault models. Basically, due to the different fault manifestation directions in the AND function and the OR function, $\widehat{f_{AND}}$ can mask fault types G and D, while it is susceptible to the remaining S and A types of faults. $\widehat{f_{OR}}$ exhibits exactly complementary capabilities and constraints. Particularly, applying the $\widehat{f_{AND}}$ tautology form to an AND function results in a single level logic, while applying it on an OR function results in an extra level in the logic. A similar situation applies to the application of an $\widehat{f_{OR}}$ tautology on OR and AND functions correspondingly as well.

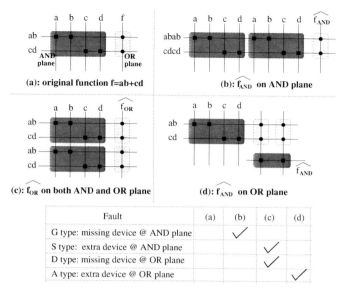

Figure 3. Fault masking examples

Fault	(a)	(b)	(c)	(d)
G type: missing device @ AND plane		✓		
S type: extra device @ AND plane			✓	
D type: missing device @ OR plane			✓	
A type: extra device @ OR plane				✓

Figure 3 shows some examples of applying the tautology based fault masking schemes in a 2-level nano PLA structure. Specifically, figure 3(a) shows the PLA implementing the original function $f = ab + cd$ without any fault masking capability. In figure 3(b), the $\widehat{f_{AND}}$ tautology is applied to the AND plane, so as to mask the G type of fault, namely, the device missing in the AND plane. By applying the $\widehat{f_{OR}}$ tautology on both the AND and the OR planes, the implementation of a PLA illustrated in 3(c) can mask both the S and the D types of faults. In this particular case, the extra level of OR logic introduced by applying $\widehat{f_{OR}}$ to the AND plane is absorbed in the original OR plane of the PLA; therefore, the resulting structure maintains a 2-level logic structure. In figure 3(d), in order to mask the occurrences of the A type of faults, $\widehat{f_{AND}}$ needs to be applied to the OR plane. In this case, an extra level of AND logic is inevitable since it has to be added after the OR plane in the original PLA. Nevertheless, it has been demonstrated [15] that multi-level logic solely within the nano layer with no additional access to the CMOS layer can be implemented in the crossbar based nanoelectronic PLAs. Overall, figure 3 shows each of the four types of faults can be masked based on Boolean tautology form and are implementable efficiently in nano PLAs.

4.2. Tautology based fault masking for all four fault types

By combining the approaches shown in figure 3 and applying $\widehat{f_{AND}}$ and $\widehat{f_{OR}}$ to both planes, we show in figure 4 an example of tautology based 3-level PLA implementation that can mask the occurrence of a fault in any of the G, S, D and

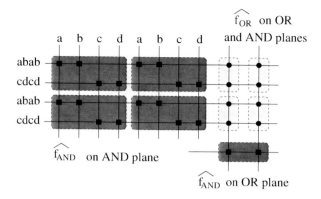

Figure 4. An example of tautology based PLA that can mask all 4 fault types

A types.

The hardware overhead for a fault masking PLA scheme needs to be analysed from both the device and the wiring aspects. Assume that the nanoelectronic PLA implements a logic function with I input wires, O function outputs and P product terms. Assume also that the number of devices utilized in the original PLA is D_A in the AND plane, and D_O in the OR plane. Figure 5 illustrates the overall schematics for the proposed tautology based fault masking scheme, and in comparison, the TMR based fault masking implemented in a nano PLA.

In figure 5(a), the original 2-level PLA is shown with one $P \times I$ AND plane and one $P \times O$ OR plane. Figure 5(b) illustrates the architecture of the proposed fault masking scheme, in a 3-level PLA implementation. The architecture consists of a $2P \times 2I$ AND plane and a $2P \times 2O$ OR plane. An extra logic level of AND plane is added with every logic output wire ANDed with its duplication, thus using two extra devices for each logic output wire. Therefore, the extra level of AND logic uses an additional $2O$ number of devices and O wires. Overall, the tautology based scheme utilizes $4D_A + 4D_O + 2O$ devices with $2I + 2P + 3O$ wires.

Figure 5(c) illustrates a TMR fault masking approach in a PLA implementation. In a TMR approach, both the AND plane and the OR plane need three identical copies, thus requiring $3D_A + 3D_O$ devices. In terms of wires, a tripling in the number of product term wires and output wires is necessary; however, one copy of the input wires can be extended to cross the three AND planes placed in a column. For a TMR approach, a majority vote process is required for every final output wire. This in turn imposes two extra logic levels in a PLA structure, since a majority vote logic of the three output replicas o_1, o_2, o_3 is represented in the AND-OR form as $o = o_1 o_2 + o_2 o_3 + o_1 o_3$. This extra voting stage therefore necessitates an additional $9O$ devices, and $7O$ wires, in addition to the two extra logic levels to the original PLA structure.

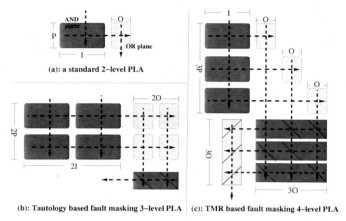

(a): a standard 2-level PLA

(b): Tautology based fault masking 3–level PLA   (c): TMR based fault masking 4–level PLA

Figure 5. Comparison of fault masking schemes

Table 4 lists the hardware comparison of the proposed and the TMR based fault masking schemes. From the hardware aspect, although the proposed tautology based fault masking scheme utilizes one more copy of the AND plane and the OR plane, the TMR approach necessitates significant extra overhead at the voter implementation. More importantly, the fault masking capability of a TMR implementation is limited to the three copies of AND and OR planes only, and does not naturally cover the voting hardware. Consequently, to make the overall TMR implementation fault tolerant, extra hardware redundancy needs to be introduced at the voter part. The proposed scheme, on the other hand, is capable of masking any of the 4 fault types occurring at any position in the whole architecture, since the redundancy is built in under the tautology form, and the fault masking capability covers each individual plane. Furthermore, the proposed schemes display a highly regular structure, as can be seen in figure 5, thus making them easily compatible with an efficient nano PLA implementation. On the other hand, the TMR approach requires quite a large amount of area for wiring due to its voting structure, which necessitates fan-in from three independent modules. Performance wise, the proposed scheme evidently surpasses the TMR approach due to the implementation with one less logic level.

Overall, it can be concluded that fault masking in a nano-electronic PLA can be efficiently achieved by exploiting re-

dundancy in a tautology form. The traditional representative fault masking scheme of NMR does not necessarily make a good solution for fault tolerance in nano PLA, due to its voting overhead as well as being incompatible with the regular structure of PLA based logic.

5. Conclusions

When addressing the reliability challenge in the nanoelectronic PLA systems, two hardware redundancy based fault tolerance schemes are especially promising: the reconfiguration based online repair schemes and the fault masking schemes. In this paper, we propose two classes of fault tolerance approaches based on these hardware redundancy schemes for the nanoelectronic PLAs.

We develop an online fault diagnosis technique as a basis for online reconfiguration. The proposed approach precisely identifies the type and location of an online detected fault, thus facilitating the subsequent reconfiguration phase to perform effective online repair. We also develop in this paper a fault masking approach based on Boolean logic tautology, thus necessitating no additional majority voting process. The fault masking approach achieves fault tolerance with significantly reduced performance and hardware overhead by exploiting the particularity of logic implemented in the PLA structure.

The two proposed techniques are both efficient in hardware overhead, yet exhibit complementary advantages. Particularly, the online fault diagnosis scheme can precisely identify the fault locations for multiple faults, however with a delay; the fault masking scheme, on the other hand, can generate the correct result without performance degradation, yet is susceptible to multiple faults. The proposed approaches set up an initial framework for the online fault tolerance approaches in the nanoelectronic PLA logic by investigating multiple hardware redundancy based fault tolerance possibilities. The proposed approaches can be furthermore combined in the nanoelectronic environment, so as to enhance significantly the reliability of nanoelectronics systems.

References

[1] M. A. Kastner, "The Single-Electron Transistor", *Review of Modern Physics*, vol. 64, pp. 849–858, 1992.

[2] P. Mazumder, S. Kulkarni, M. Bhattacharya, J. P. Sun and G. I. Haddad, "Digital Circuit Applications of Resonant Tunneling Devices", *Proceedings of the IEEE*, vol. 86, n. 4, pp. 664–686, April 1998.

[3] P. Avouris, J. Appenzeller, R. Martel and S. Wind, "Carbon Nanotube Electronics", *Proceedings of the IEEE*, vol. 91, n. 11, pp. 1772–1784, 2003.

fault masking scheme	hardware		logic level
	device	wire	
original	$D_A + D_O$	$I + P + O$	2
Tautology based	$4D_A + 4D_O + 2O$	$2I + 2P + 3O$	3
TMR based	$3D_A + 3D_O + 9O$	$I + 3P + 7O$	4

Table 4. HW overhead summary

[4] C. S. Lent, P. D. Tougaw, W. Porod and G. H. Bernstein, "Quantum Cellular Automata", *Nanotechnology*, vol. 4, pp. 49–57, 1993.

[5] Y. G. Krieger, "Molecular Electronics: Current State and Future Trends", *J. Structural Chem*, vol. 34, pp. 896–904, 1993.

[6] ITRS, *International Technology Roadmap for Semiconductors Emerging Research Devices*, 2006.

[7] Y. Huang, X. Duan, Y. Cui, L. J. Jauhon, K. Kim and C. M. Lieber, "Logic Gates and Computation from Assembled Nanowire Building Blocks", *Science*, vol. 294, pp. 1313–1317, November 2001.

[8] Y. Chen, G. Y. Jung, D. A. A. Ohlberg, X. Li, D. R. Stewart, J. O. Jeppesen, K. A. Nielsen, J. F. Stoddart and R. S. Williams, "Nanoscale Molecular-switch Crossbar Circuits", *Nanotechnology*, vol. 14, pp. 462–468, 2003.

[9] A. DeHon, "Array-Based Architecture for FET-Based, Nanoscale Electronics", *IEEE Transactions on Nanotechnology*, vol. 2, n. 1, pp. 23–32, 2003.

[10] K. Nikolic, A. Sadek and M. Forshaw, "Architectures for Reliable Computing with Unreliable Nanodevices", in *IEEE-NANO*, pp. 254–259, 2001.

[11] P. Beckett and A. Jennings, "Towards Nanocomputer Architecture", in *Asia-Paci c Computer System Architecture Conference*, pp. 141–150, 2002.

[12] M. Forshaw, R. Stadler, D. Crawley and K. Nikolic, "A Short Review of Nanoelectronic Architectures", in *Nanotechnology*, volume 15, pp. 220–223, 2004.

[13] P. J. Kuekes, D. R. Stewart and R. S. Williams, "The Crossbar Latch: Logic Value Storage, Restoration, and Inversion in Crossbar Circuits", *Journal of Applied Physics*, vol. 97, n. 3, pp. 034301, July 2005.

[14] G. Snider, P. J. Kuekes and R. S. Williams, "CMOS-like Logic in Defective, Nanoscale Crossbars", *Nanotechnology*, vol. 15, pp. 881–891, Aug 2004.

[15] A. DeHon and M. J. Wilson, "Nanowire-based Sublithographic Programmable Logic Arrays", in *FPGA*, pp. 123–132, 2004.

[16] D. B. Strukov and K. K. Likharev, "CMOL FPGA: A Reconfigurable Architecture for Hybrid Digital Circuits with Two-terminal Nanodevices", *Nanotechnology*, vol. 16, pp. 888–900, Apr 2005.

[17] A. DeHon and H. Naeimi, "Seven Strategies for Tolerating Highly Defective Fabrication", *IEEE Design & Test of Computers*, vol. 22, n. 4, pp. 306–315, 2005.

[18] M. Abramovici, M. A. Breuer and A. D. Friedman, *Digital Systems Testing and Testable Design*, IEEE Press, 1990.

[19] P. Bose and J. A. Abraham, "Test Generation for Programmable Logic Arrays", in *DAC*, pp. 572–580, 1982.

[20] F. Somenzi and S. Gai, "Fault detection in programmable logic arrays", *Proceedings of the IEEE*, vol. 74, n. 5, pp. 655–668, 1986.

[21] V. K. Agarwal, "Multiple Fault Detection in Programmable Logic Arrays", *IEEE Transactions on Computers*, vol. 29, pp. 518–522, June 1980.

[22] M. Demjanenko and S. J. Upadhyaya, "Yield Enhancement of Field Programmable Logic Arrays by Inherent Component Redundancy", *TCAD*, vol. 9, n. 8, pp. 876–884, 1990.

[23] P. K. Lala and D. L. Tao, "On Fault-tolerant PLA Design", in *IEEE Southeastcon*, pp. 945–947, 1990.

[24] G. Snider and W. Robinett, "Crossbar Demultiplexers for Nanoelectronics Based on n-Hot Codes", *IEEE Transactions on Nanotechnology*, vol. 4, pp. 249–254, 2005.

[25] J. Emmert, C. Strout, B. Skaggs and M. Abramovici, "Dynamic Fault Tolerance in FPGAs via Partial Reconfiguration", in *FCCM*, pp. 165–174, 2000.

[26] W. Rao, A. Orailoglu and R. Karri, "Topology Aware Mapping of Logic Functions onto Nanowire-based Crossbar Architectures", in *DAC*, pp. 723–726, 2006.

[27] S-Y. Kuo and W. K. Fuchs, "Fault Diagnosis and Spare Allocation for Yield Enhancement in Large Reconfigurable PLA's", *IEEE Transactions on Computers*, vol. 41, pp. 221–226, February 1992.

[28] C-L. Wey, "Fault Location in Repairable Programmable Logic Arrays", in *ITC*, pp. 679–685, 1989.

[29] C-L. Wey, T-Y. Chang and J. Ding, "Design of Fault-Diagnosable and Repairable Folded PLA's for Yield Enhancement", *IEEE Journal of Solid-State Circuits*, vol. 26, n. 1, pp. 54–57, January 1991.

[30] T-Y. Chang and C-L. Wey, "Design of Fault Diagnosable and Repairable PLA's", *IEEE Journal of Solid-State Circuits*, vol. 24, n. 5, pp. 1451–1454, October 1989.

[31] J. Khakbaz and E. J. McCluskey, "Concurrent Error Detection and Testing for Large PLA's", *IEEE Journal of Solid-State Circuits*, vol. 17, n. 2, pp. 386–394, April 1982.

[32] W. K. Fuchs, C. R. Chen and J. A. Abraham, "Concurrent Error Detection in Highly Structured Logic Arrays", *IEEE Journal of Solid-State Circuits*, vol. 22, n. 4, pp. 583–594, August 1987.

[33] P. K. Lala, *Self-Checking and Fault-Tolerant Digital Design*, Morgan Kaufmann, 2000.

Session 4B:
VM Rejuvenation and
Network Reliability

Concilium: Collaborative Diagnosis of Broken Overlay Routes

James W. Mickens and Brian D. Noble
EECS Department, University of Michigan
Ann Arbor, MI, 48109
jmickens,bnoble@umich.edu

Abstract

In a peer-to-peer overlay network, hosts cooperate to forward messages. When a message does not reach its final destination, there are two possible explanations. An intermediate overlay host may have dropped the message due to misconfiguration or malice. Alternatively, a bad link in the underlying IP network may have prevented an earnest, properly configured host from forwarding the data. In this paper, we describe how overlay peers can distinguish between the two situations and ascribe blame appropriately. We generate probabilistic notions of blame using distributed network tomography, fuzzy logic, and secure routing primitives. By comparing application-level drop rates with network characteristics inferred from tomography, we can estimate the likelihood that message loss is due to a misbehaving overlay host or a poor link in the underlying IP network. Since faulty nodes can submit inaccurate tomographic data to the collective, we also discuss mechanisms for detecting such misbehavior.

1 Introduction

Peer-to-peer systems scale because they distribute responsibility across many nodes. For example, in cooperative overlay networks, hosts can route messages to each other in a small number of hops using local forwarding state whose size is logarithmic in the total number of peers [17, 19]. When all peers behave properly, such designs lead to elegant, scalable systems. But what happens when some hosts misbehave? Real-life experience with large distributed services suggests that faulty local configurations inevitably arise [16]. Some nodes may also try to actively subvert the system. Thus, dependable peer-to-peer frameworks must expect that machines will occasionally drop messages, delete data, or otherwise misbehave.

Consider an overlay-level route that starts at host A, goes through B, and terminates at C. If C does not receive a message from A, did B shirk its forwarding responsibilities, or were there faulty IP-level links that prevented B from receiving the message or sending it to C? In this paper,

we show how to ascribe blame in such situations, providing mechanisms for identifying fault points in end-to-end overlay routes. Once the system has detected a misbehaving overlay forwarder or a bad link in the core IP network, it can route around the problem. It can also notify the owner of the malfunctioning component, who may not be aware of the local fault. Both actions can improve the overall reliability of the distributed service.

Our new diagnostic system, named Concilium, generates probabilistic notions of blame using distributed network tomography [1, 10], fuzzy logic [5], and secure overlay routing [7]. By comparing application-level drop rates with network characteristics inferred from tomography, Concilium generates the likelihood that message loss is due to a misbehaving overlay host or a poor path in the underlying IP network. Unlike Fatih [15] or packet obituary systems [2], Concilium does not require modification to core Internet routers. In contrast to RON [1], Concilium detects hosts which contribute faulty tomographic data to their peers.

2 Secure Overlays

Structured peer-to-peer overlays provide a decentralized, self-managing routing infrastructure atop preexisting IP networks. Each host is associated with an overlay identifier. When a host must forward a message, it consults locally maintained routing state to determine the next hop. In overlays like Pastry [17] and Chord [19], the local routing state consists of two logical components. The *leaf table* points to the peers with the numerically closest identifiers to the local host's identifier. The *jump table* points to peers whose identifiers differ from the local one by increasing, exponentially spaced distances. Messages are typically forwarded using jump tables until the last hop.

Castro *et al* introduced *secure overlay routing* [7] to prevent malicious nodes from subverting the forwarding process. In a secure routing framework, messages are delivered with very high probability if the fraction of non-faulty hosts is at least 75%. Concilium uses several features of secure routing to protect its distributed tomographic protocol. We briefly describe these features before discussing Concilium in more depth.

Before a host can join a secure overlay, it must acquire a certificate from a central authority. The certificate binds the host's IP address to a public key and an overlay identifier. Since identifiers are static and randomly assigned, adversaries cannot deliberately move their hosts to advantageous regions of the identifier space. Hosts also enforce strict constraints on the peers which can occupy each jump table slot. For example, in standard Pastry [17], a peer in row i and column j of a routing table must share an i-character identifier prefix with the local host and have j as its $i+1$ character; there are no constraints on the remaining characters. In secure Pastry, the peer must be the online host whose identifier is closest to point p, where p is the local host identifier with the i-th character substituted with j. These stronger peering constraints, in concert with random identifier distribution, limit the fraction of malicious peers in local routing state to the fraction of malicious nodes in the total overlay.

Using a *density test*, a host can probabilistically detect when peers misreport their leaf sets. By comparing the average inter-identifier spacing in its own leaf set to that of a peer's leaf set, a host can identify advertised leaf sets that are too sparse. In the absence of such checks, an adversary could suppress knowledge of peers that it does not control, forcing routing traffic or data fetches to go through corrupt peers.

For performance reasons, peers maintain both secure routing tables and "standard" routing tables. Standard tables can use techniques like proximity affinity [8] to minimize routing latency or maintenance bandwidth; secure routing is only used when standard routing fails. Messages requiring Concilium's fault attribution must always be forwarded using secure routing. Other messages can be forwarded using either mechanism.

3 The Concilium Diagnostic Protocol

Concilium diagnoses faulty overlay routes using a multistep process. First, hosts exchange their routing tables so that they can determine the first few hops that a locally forwarded message will take. Second, hosts test IP-level network conditions using locally-initiated network probes. By exchanging the results of these tests, individual peers synthesize a global picture of link quality throughout the Internet. By combining routing data with the collaborative map of network conditions, nodes can identify broken IP links and misbehaving overlay forwarders; the latter are defined as end-hosts which drop messages when the IP-level paths to their routing peers are good.

When a host is deemed faulty, Concilium issues a *fault accusation* against that host. Each accusation is provisional, since the accused host may be able to prove its innocence by showing that messages were actually being dropped further down the route. If the accused host can generate a verifiable *fault rebuttal*, Concilium will revise its original accusation. Otherwise, hosts may refuse to peer with the accused node or treat its behavior with extra suspicion.

In this section, we describe the Concilium protocol in the context of a particular implementation strategy. We then discuss alternative implementations.

3.1 Validating Routing State

To troubleshoot end-to-end overlay routes, Concilium must validate the routing state that peers self-report. Concilium validates leaf sets using Castro's test and introduces a new test to verify jump tables. Like Castro's leaf test, Concilium's jump table test is a density check. However, instead of examining the average inter-identifier spacing in a jump table, it checks how many slots are occupied. Jump tables with low occupancy are considered suspicious. For the sake of concreteness, we describe the test in the context of a secure Pastry overlay, but the test can be extended to other overlays in a straightforward manner.

In secure Pastry, overlay identifiers are ℓ characters long and each character can assume one of v different values. ℓ is typically 32 or 40, and v is usually 16. Each node maintains a jump table with ℓ rows and v columns. The identifier in row i and column j shares an i character prefix with the local host's identifier and has an $i+1$-th character of j. Assuming that identifiers are randomly distributed throughout the identifier space, the probability that a node does not have a particular prefix of length ℓ_{prefix} is $1 - (1/v)^{\ell_{prefix}}$. The probability that an entry in row i of a routing table is filled is equal to one minus the probability that no identifier exists with the appropriate prefix. Thus,

$$Pr(entry\ filled\ in\ row\ i) = 1 - \left[1 - \left(\frac{1}{v}\right)^{i+1}\right]^{N-1} \quad (1)$$

where N is the total number of nodes in the overlay. Nodes can estimate N by inspecting the inter-identifier spacing in their leaf sets [13].

Let $p_{i,j}$ denote the probability that an entry in row i and column j is filled, as given by Equation 1. Each $p_{i,j}$ is an independent Bernoulli random variable, so the occupancy distribution for the entire table is governed by a Poisson binomial distribution. The mean and variance are

$$\mu = \frac{1}{\ell v} \sum_{i=1}^{\ell} \sum_{j=1}^{v} p_{i,j} \qquad \sigma^2 = \frac{1}{\ell v} \sum_{i=1}^{\ell} \sum_{j=1}^{v} (p_{i,j} - \mu)^2.$$

Computing exact values for the Poisson binomial distribution is intractable for non-trivial numbers of Bernoulli variables. Thus, it is difficult to directly calculate the likelihood that a table contains a particular number of occupied slots. Fortunately, since σ^2 is high, we can use a normal approximation with little loss in accuracy [12]. In this approximation, the mean μ_ϕ and the variance σ_ϕ^2 are

$$\mu_\phi = \ell v \mu \qquad \sigma_\phi^2 = \ell v \mu (1 - \mu) - \ell v \sigma^2.$$

The cumulative distribution function for table occupancy is $\phi(\mu_\phi, \sigma_\phi)$ where $\phi()$ is the cdf for the normal distribution. To test whether an advertised jump table is too sparse, a host compares its local jump table density d_{local} to the advertised d_{peer}. If $\gamma d_{peer} < d_{local}$ for some small $\gamma > 1$, the peer's jump table is deemed invalid. In Section 4.1, we use $\phi(\mu_\phi, \sigma_\phi)$ to select γ based on the resulting likelihood of false positives and false negatives.

The occupancy test prevents malicious hosts from advertising jump tables that are too sparse. We also wish to prevent hosts from advertising tables that are too dense. Since identifiers are centrally issued, a misbehaving host cannot fabricate an identifier for an arbitrary jump table slot. However, a host can collect identifiers from peers that have gone offline and use these identifiers to inflate its advertised table density [7]. To protect against inflation attacks, Concilium requires a jump table entry referencing peer H to contain a signed timestamp from H. Whenever host G probes H for availability, H piggybacks a signed timestamp upon the probe response. Later, when G advertises its jump table, it includes the signed timestamps for each non-empty entry. Peers will reject the table if it has stale timestamps.

3.2 Collecting Tomographic Data

Each host H is connected to its routing peers by a set of links in the underlying IP network. These links induce a communication tree T_H whose root is H and whose leaves are H's routing peers. We define the forest F_H as the union of the tree rooted at H and the trees rooted at each of H's routing peers. Concilium's goal is to estimate link quality in F_H. To do so, each tree root periodically probes the link quality in its tree. Peers then exchange their tomographic results to create a collaborative estimate of link quality in F_H.

Before a host can initiate the tomography process, it must determine the physical IP links which comprise its tree. These link maps can be derived using tools such as RocketFuel [18]. Internet routes are often stable for at least a day [21], so topological data need not be fetched often.

Once the topology is known, hosts infer link quality using lightweight proactive probing and heavyweight reactive probing. Lightweight tomography uses the availability probes that hosts already send to their routing table peers [17, 19]. The period of these probes is a minute or less, and the duration of high loss events in IP links is on the order of tens of minutes [14]. Thus, H can use these preexisting probes to detect high intensity packet loss inside T_H. More specifically, H schedules a lightweight probe of T_H as a periodic task whose inter-arrival time is picked randomly and uniformly from the range $[0, max\_probe\_time]$; max_probe_time is on the order of one or two minutes. H probes its entire routing table at once using a simplified version of Duffield's striped unicast scheme [10]. H generates a single probe packet for each routing peer, but it issues these packets back to back. Since these packets will stay close to

each other as they traverse shared interior routers, they emulate a single multicast packet sent to the leaves of a multicast tree. If H receives acknowledgments from all peers, it assumes that there is no link loss. Otherwise, it sends a few more probes to silent peers to determine if they are truly offline or situated along a lossy IP link.

If link loss is detected or H's application-level messages are not being acknowledged, H initiates heavyweight probing. Heavyweight tomography also uses striped unicast probing, but H sends many probes to each leaf using Duffield's full scheme. Loss rates for each root-leaf path are inferred using the number of acknowledgments received from each leaf host. Using maximum likelihood estimators, these end-to-end loss rates induce loss rates for each internal IP link.

When H initiates heavyweight probing, it asks its routing peers do the same. This ensures the availability of fine-grained, high quality tomographic data for the entire forest during the speculated fault period. To avoid probe-induced congestion, each peer waits for a small, randomly picked time before initiating heavyweight tomography.

After H has probed T_H using lightweight or heavyweight mechanisms, it sends a timestamped snapshot of T_H and its summarized probe results to its routing peers. The probe results for each path can be encoded in a few bits representing predefined loss rates. H signs the tomographic snapshot with its public key, both to prevent spoofing attacks and to prevent H from disavowing previously advertised probe results.

Each leaf node in T_H is one of H's routing peers, so H implicitly advertises its forwarding state when it publishes its tomographic data. This data also includes the signed freshness timestamps for each routing entry as described in Section 3.1. When a node receives a snapshot from H, it verifies all the signatures, checks the freshness of each entry, and performs the density checks. If any of these tests fail, the node may issue a fault accusation against H as described in Section 3.4. Regardless, the node archives H's snapshot. As the node receives snapshots from other peers, it constructs a distributed view of the forwarding paths emanating from its routing peers and the quality of IP links in these paths.

3.3 Error-checking Tomographic Data

Striped unicast tomography assumes that leaf nodes will return acknowledgments for received probes. A faulty or malicious leaf can try to respond to probes that were actually lost in the network, or drop acknowledgments for probes that were received. The former only affects inferences over the last mile to the misbehaving leaf, but the latter can ruin many inferences throughout the tree [3]. Fortunately, we can detect both types of misbehavior. To detect spurious responses to non-received probes, the probing node includes nonces in its probes. To detect leaves which faultily suppress acknowledgments, the probing node applies statistical tests to verify that the acknowledgment patterns of its leaves are consistent with each other [3]. Thus, an intentionally malicious leaf can accomplish the most damage by responding correctly to the probes of other nodes, but misreporting the results of its own probes. We explore this issue further in Section 4.3.

We assume that interior IP routers can be faulty but not actively malicious. We assume that they do not interfere with probes or their responses in a byzantine way.

3.4 Attributing Fault

Armed with link measurements and routing information, each Concilium node can issue accusations for dropped messages. Suppose that at time t, host A sends a message to Z through B. By checking its copy of B's routing table, A can determine the host C to which B will forward the message. If A never receives a signed acknowledgment from Z, it checks its tomographic data for probes which test links in the path between B and C. If one or more links were probed as down, Concilium assigns blame to the network. Otherwise, Concilium determines that B was faulty. This judgment may be erroneous, since the true culprit may lie downstream from B. We describe how Concilium recovers from these mistakes in Section 3.5. For now, we restrict our attention to the original issuance of blame.

Let $B \rightarrow C$ represent the path between B and C, and let *probes* be the set of probe results covering links in $B \rightarrow C$. We allow this set to contain results from probes initiated within the interval $[t - \Delta, t + \Delta]$, where Δ might equal sixty seconds. Let $probes(link)$ be the set of probes covering a particular link. For $p \in probes(link)$, let $p.l\_up \in \{0 \text{ or } 1\}$ be the probed status of the link, with 1 representing a link that was up and 0 representing a failed link. Let $a \in [0, 1]$ be the accuracy of probes in diagnosing link failure. Returning to our running example, when A fails to receive an acknowledgment from Z, it ascribes blame to B as follows:

$$
\begin{aligned}
Pr(B \ faulty) &= Pr(B \rightarrow C \ good) \\
&= 1 - Pr(B \rightarrow C \ bad) \quad (2) \\
&= 1 - Pr(B \rightarrow C \ has \geq 1 \ bad \ link)
\end{aligned}
$$

where $Pr(B \rightarrow C \ has \geq 1 \ bad \ link)$ equals

$$
max_{l \in B \rightarrow C} \left(\frac{\sum_{p \in probes(l)} [p.l\_up(1 - a) + (1 - p.l\_up)a]}{|probes(l)|} \right) .
$$

$$(3)$$

We use `max` as the `OR` operator from fuzzy logic [5]. In the context of Equation 3, it selects the link in $B \rightarrow C$ for which A has the highest confidence that it was bad, with each probe result weighed equally. For example, suppose that Q and R probe a link as down (0) and S probes the same link as up (1). If a equals 0.8, A believes that the link was bad with confidence $(1/3)(0.8)+(1/3)(0.8)+(1/3)(0.2)=0.6$.

Importantly, when A judges the trustworthiness of B, it does not incorporate B's probe results into Equation 3. This prevents a malicious B from influencing the amount of blame that A ascribes to it. For example, if A included B's probe results in Equation 3, B could reduce its level of blame by claiming that it probed a link in $B \rightarrow C$ as down.

Using Equation 2, A determines the amount of blame that it ascribes to B for a particular dropped message. If the blame is larger than a threshold described in Section 4.3, A assigns a *guilty verdict* to B; otherwise, A assigns a guilty verdict to the network. A maintains a sliding window of the last w verdicts that it issued for B, archiving the tomographic data used to make each verdict. If B receives m or more guilty verdicts in this window, A inserts a *formal fault accusation* into a DHT which exists atop the secure overlay. The insertion key for the accusation is B's public key, and the accusation contains all of the signed tomographic data that A used to derive its fault assessments. Insertions and fetches of the formal accusation are secured using Castro's techniques [7], and the statement is signed by A so that it can be held accountable for spurious accusations. When another host considers B as a routing peer, it first retrieves accusations against B from the DHT. For each accusation, the host uses the associated tomographic data to independently verify the fault calculations. If the host verifies the accusations, it considers B to be a "bad peer" and sanctions it according to network-specific policies.

3.5 Revising Incorrect Fault Attributions

As currently described, a Concilium node cannot ascribe blame beyond the next overlay hop. Returning to our running example, if A does not receive a signed acknowledgment from Z, and A estimates all links in $B \rightarrow C$ to be good, then A will always blame B for dropping the message, even if B successfully forwarded the message and it was actually dropped further downstream. To correctly ascribe blame in these situations, Concilium uses *recursive stewardship* of messages and *recursive revision* of fault accusations.

Whenever a peer along $A \rightarrow Z$ forwards a message, it treats the message as if it were generated locally—in other words, each forwarding peer expects to receive an acknowledgment from Z. If Z receives the message successfully, it routes its acknowledgment along the reverse forwarding path. If Z never receives the message or its acknowledgment is dropped along the reverse path, a chain of guilty verdicts will be issued. By considering them as a whole, Concilium can determine where blame should ultimately be placed. For example, suppose that D faultily drops A's message to Z along $A \rightarrow B \rightarrow C \rightarrow D \rightarrow ... Z$ and that all IP links are good. Using recursive stewardship, B and C will await an acknowledgment from Z. When this acknowledgment does not arrive, A will blame B, B will blame C, and C will blame D. D will not be able to blame a forwarding peer since it lacks incriminating tomographic data—D's peers in F_D will not have probed any links as down [1], and D cannot fabricate such probes itself because a node's own probes are ignored when calculating blame for that node. Thus, the accusation chain stops at D and nodes absolve themselves

---

[1]This assumes that the nodes in F_D are not colluding with D. We return to the issue of colluding nodes in Section 4.

of unfair blame by pushing locally generated verdicts upstream. First, C presents its guilty verdict against D to B. B examines the signed, timestamped tomographic data in the verdict, verifies the blame calculation, and amends its accusation against C to be an accusation against D. B presents its amended verdict to A. After A verifies the inference, it amends its accusation against B to an accusation against D. Innocent nodes have now been exonerated, and blame has been fairly attributed to D. Note that an amended accusation contains the signed, timestamped data from both the original verdict and the revision that was pushed upstream. This allows amended verdicts to be self-verifying.

Faulty nodes may not push revision information upstream. They do so at their own peril, since they will receive the blame for the message drop. For example, if C does not push its accusation against D to B, then B will not amend its original fault claim against C, and A will eventually blame C, not D, for the message drop.

A faulty node may receive a revision but refuse to update its local accusation. For example, A may receive B's blame against a node further downstream but continue to blame B. To guard against such misbehavior, B archives its local fault attributions and revisions. If another host believes that B is untrustworthy, it allows B to defend itself before any punitive steps are taken. The host presents B with the relevant formal accusations. If B can rebut these accusations using its local archives, the other host will recalculate B's trustworthiness in light of the new evidence.

3.6 Preventing Spurious Accusations

Up to this point, we have focused on detecting hosts which fail to forward messages. However, the original message sender can also misbehave. Suppose that each link in $B \rightarrow C$ is good. If A accuses B of dropping its message without actually sending one to B, other nodes will believe the accusation; they will verify the tomographic information in A's accusation and derive the same blame probability as A.

To prevent such spurious accusations, Concilium uses *forwarding commitments*. When A sends a message through B, B sends a signed statement to A indicating its willingness to forward the message. The commitment includes a timestamp, A's identifier, B's identifier, and the identifier of the ultimate destination Z. When A issues an accusation against B, it includes this forwarding commitment along with the relevant tomographic data and routing state. In this fashion, B can only be blamed for dropping messages that it agreed to forward. B can batch its commitments and asynchronously piggyback them upon its responses to A's availability probes. Like message stewardship and accusation revision, forwarding commitment is also recursive.

A malicious B may refuse to issue forwarding commitments for A's packets. Without support from core IP routers on the path between A and B, there is no way for Concilium to establish that A actually sent a message to B, or that

B sent a forwarding commitment which A ignored. Lacking such knowledge, Concilium cannot comment on the trustworthiness of either peer. Fortunately, B's misbehavior can be detected by other mechanisms. For example, if overlay hosts are part of a decentralized reputation system such as Creedence [20], A can issue a vote of no confidence in B using this reputation system. Since honest hosts trust each other's votes, they will eventually determine that B makes a poor peer and treat it accordingly.

Note that standalone reputation systems cannot replace Concilium's full accusation protocol. Reputation systems allow a node to make a direct accusation against the next hop in a route, but they provide no structured way to propagate accusations against nodes that are farther downstream. Using recursive stewardship of messages and recursive revision of accusations, Concilium provides such a capability. Concilium also provides self-validating accusations which can be confirmed by arbitrary third parties.

3.7 Implementation Options

Up to now, we have assumed that each node performs its own tomographic probing. However, hosts which trust each other and reside in the same stub network can consolidate probing responsibility. For example, hosts could take turns issuing the probes for the multi-forest induced by their collective routing state. Alternatively, all hosts could defer probing responsibility to a shared administrative machine such as a RON gateway [1]. Either solution would make heavyweight probing less onerous, since the bandwidth cost for probing shared links could be amortized across multiple nodes.

As described in Section 3.4, a fault judgment is based on the acknowledgment of an individual message reception. If two peers exchange many packets, it may be useful for a single acknowledgment to cover multiple messages. The acknowledgment could indicate loss rates in several ways [15], e.g., through simple counters indicating how many packets arrived, or packet hashes identifying the specific packets which were received.

Concilium's goal is to find misbehaving overlay hosts and broken IP links, but it is agnostic about the response to its fault identifications. Broken IP links are often discovered quickly by the responsible ISP, so an overlay may simply avoid certain overlay paths until the fault is fixed [1]. With respect to faulty overlay hosts, Concilium allows each system to set an appropriate sanctioning policy. For example, accused hosts may not be trusted to forward sensitive messages.

If the overlay is used as a substrate for a higher level service such as a DHT, then honest nodes must not make local decisions to evict accused nodes from leaf sets. Otherwise, inconsistent routing [6] will arise and the higher level service may break. A network can mandate that a node be *universally* blacklisted if it receives accusations at a certain rate.

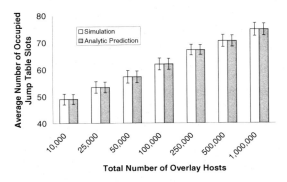

Figure 1. Modeling jump table occupancy

In such an environment, nodes would check the accusation repository before agreeing to peer with a new host. If the prospective peer was discovered to be faulty, it would not be added to the local routing table.

4 Evaluation

In this section, we use extensive simulations to evaluate the accuracy of our jump table check, the coverage properties of our collaborative tomography, and the error rate of our accusation algorithm. We also investigate the bandwidth overhead of the Concilium protocol.

4.1 Jump Table Validation

Peers exchange their routing state so that Concilium can determine the IP-level tomographic data needed to make fault accusations at the overlay level. If peers can advertise incorrect routing tables without detection, innocent peers may be accused and faulty peers may go unpunished. Thus, the success of Concilium hinges on its ability to detect fraudulent routing advertisements. In this section, we analyze Concilium's jump table tests; we defer an analysis of leaf set checks to Castro's work [7].

Our jump table test uses the cdf $\phi(\mu_\phi, \sigma_\phi)$ to model the distribution of occupancy fractions. Figure 1 compares the occupancy levels predicted by the analytic model with the occupancy levels seen in Monte Carlo simulations of table occupancy (y-bars indicate standard deviations). We see that the $\phi(\mu_\phi, \sigma_\phi)$ distribution accurately approximates real occupancy levels.

Our density test declares that a jump table is faulty if $\gamma d_{peer} < d_{local}$. The test can produce both false positives and false negatives. A false positive occurs if a non-faulty peer has a legitimately sparse jump table but is deemed faulty anyways. The likelihood of a false positive is equivalent to

$$Pr(\gamma d_{peer} < d_{local}) = \sum_{0 \leq d_i \leq \ell v} \left[Pr(d_i) Pr(d < \frac{d_i}{\gamma}) \right]$$
$$= \sum_{0 \leq d_i \leq \ell v} \left[(\phi(d_i + \frac{1}{2}) - \phi(d_i - \frac{1}{2}))\phi(\frac{d_i}{\gamma}) \right]$$

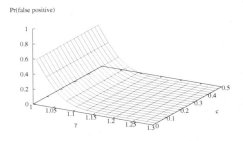

(a) False positive probability.

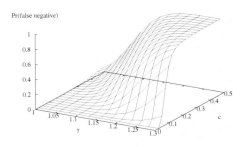

(b) False negative probability.

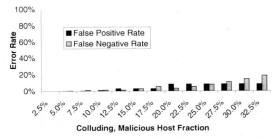

(c) Overall misclassification rate when γ is chosen to minimize the sum of the two error probabilities.

Figure 2. Error rates (no suppression attacks)

Figure 2(a) depicts the false positive rate as a function of γ and the fraction c of colluding malicious nodes. This graph assumes that malicious nodes may drop messages, but they may not try to go offline in a concerted attempt to skew local density estimates [7]. Thus, the false positive rate is independent of the fraction of malicious peers. Later in this section, we will revisit this graph in the context of suppression attacks.

The likelihood of a false negative is

$$Pr(\gamma d_{peer} \geq d_{local}) = \sum_{0 \leq d_i \leq \ell v} [Pr(d_i) Pr(d < \gamma d_i)]$$
$$= \sum_{0 \leq d_i \leq \ell v} \left[(\phi(d_i + \frac{1}{2}) - \phi(d_i - \frac{1}{2}))\phi(\gamma d_i) \right]$$

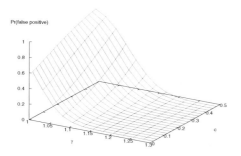

Pr(false positive)

(a) False positive probability.

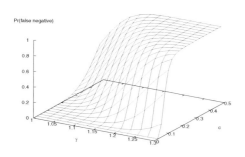

Pr(false negative)

(b) False negative probability.

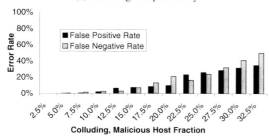

(c) Overall misclassification rate when γ is chosen to minimize the sum of the two error probabilities.

Figure 3. Error rates (suppression attacks)

A false negative occurs when a peer advertises a jump table that only contains attacker-controlled nodes and the table passes the density test. Figure 2(b) shows the false negative probability in the absence of suppression attacks. Due to the properties of secure routing tables, an attacker is expected to control only c percent of all nodes in a jump table. Thus, the density of the attacker's fraudulent table is modeled as that of a legitimate table in an overlay with Nc total hosts. In the previous equation, when we calculate $Pr(d_i)$, i.e., the probability that the advertised jump table contains d_i nodes, we use Equation 1 but set the number of nodes to Nc.

Using Figures 2(a) and (b), we can choose the γ which minimizes some error metric. For example, Figure 2(c) shows the misclassification rate when γ is chosen to minimize the sum of the false positive probability and the false

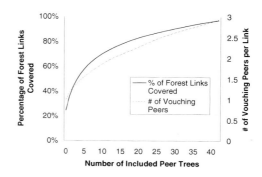

Figure 4. Trees Sampled vs. Forest Coverage

negative probability. If 30% of all peers are malicious and colluding, the false positive rate is 8.5% and the false negative rate is 14.8%. If 20% of hosts collude, the false negative rate decreases to 3.5%.

Figure 3 shows misclassification rates when adversaries can launch suppression attacks. We model these attacks by supplying our false positive/negative equations with the appropriately skewed versions of N as we did above. Like Castro's density tests for leaf sets [7], our jump table checks are not very reliable if more than 20% of hosts are malicious and colluding. For example, with a c of 20%, the false positive rate is 10.1% but the false negative rate is already 21.1%. Devising effective defenses against suppression attacks is an important area for future research. However, we note that c represents the largest set of *colluding* malicious nodes. The total number of malicious nodes may be much larger, but their power is limited by the extent to which they can coordinate the suppression of their identifiers.

4.2 Link Coverage

To test the coverage of tomographic probing and the accuracy of Concilium's accusation algorithm, we used a discrete event network simulator. The simulator modeled link failure, tomographic probing, the collaborative dissemination of probe results, and three types of message events (message sent, message acknowledged, message not acknowledged). The simulator placed a Pastry overlay atop an IP topology gathered by the SCAN project [11]. The topology contained peering information for 112,969 routers connected by 181,639 links. Following the methodology of Chen *et al* [9], we defined end hosts as routers with only one link and randomly selected 3% of these machines to be Pastry nodes. The resulting overlay possessed 1,131 nodes.

In the simulations, 5% of links were bad at any moment. Average link downtime was 15 minutes with a standard deviation of 7.5 minutes; this accords with empirical observations of high loss incidents lasting for a few tens of minutes [14]. Failures were biased towards links at the edge of the network [14]. To select a new link for failure, we randomly picked an overlay host and a random peer in that host's routing state. We then used a beta distribution with α=0.9 and

β=0.6 to select the depth of the link that would fail. Simulations lasted for two virtual hours. We did not model fluctuating machine availability since we wanted to focus on the fundamental properties of our fault inference algorithm.

Figure 4 shows the average percentage of IP links in F_H that are covered when H includes a given number of peer trees. If a node probes only its own tree, it can gather tomographic data for 25% of its forest links. Increasing the number of included peer trees results in large initial gains, but the improvement in coverage diminishes as more trees are included. This is because only a few trees are needed to cover highly shared links in the center of the Internet, but many trees are needed to cover all of the last-mile links that are only used by a few hosts.

As shown in Figure 4, gathering probe results from more peers increases the average number of hosts that test a given link and can potentially vouch for the status of that link at an arbitrary time. By increasing the number of vouching peers for a link, we improve the quality of tomographic inferences for that link. Greater link coverage also reduces the ability of malicious nodes to taint the diagnostic process by submitting bad tomographic data.

4.3   Accuracy of Fault Accusations

Accurate fault accusation requires accurate tomography. Duffield *et al* reported high levels of accuracy for striped unicast probing, with inferred link loss rates within 1% of the actual ones [10]. High accuracy rates have also been reported for other tomographic techniques [14]. In this section, we assume that hosts can identify whether a link was up or down with 90% accuracy.

Given the probe accuracy, we are interested in the amount of blame assigned to a forwarding peer when a message is dropped. Figure 5 depicts the probability distribution functions for the blame that Concilium assigns to faulty and non-faulty nodes. We generated the pdf by taking each triple of hosts (A, B, C) [2] and picking ten random times within the simulation period for A to route a message through $B \rightarrow C$. By comparing the actual link state along $B \rightarrow C$ to the tomographic information available to A at that time, we determined the amount of blame that A would assign to B if A did not receive an acknowledgment from the message recipient. B was a faulty node if it dropped a message despite $B \rightarrow C$ being good; it was non-faulty if at least one link in $B \rightarrow C$ was bad. Due to space constraints, we do not show results for the recursive revision of accusations; thus, the simulator ensured that a message was dropped either by B or a network link along $B \rightarrow C$, not by another peer or link further down the overlay route to the destination host.

Figure 5(a) depicts the blame pdf when all peers faithfully reported their probe results. Figure 5(b) depicts the blame pdf when 20% of peers colluded to maliciously flip

their probe results. In the latter scenario, when a non-faulty node was being judged, malicious peers would always claim that their probed links were up (increasing the false positive rate); when a malicious peer was being judged, other malicious peers would always claim that their probed links were down (increasing the false negative rate). Comparing Figure 5(a) to Figure 5(b), we see that incorporating erroneous probe results into Equation 2 causes more blame to be assigned to non-faulty nodes and less blame to be assigned to faulty ones. However, Concilium can still make accurate fault accusations using a thresholding scheme which produces binary verdicts. For example, suppose that for any message drop, nodes receiving less than 40% blame are proclaimed innocent and all other nodes receive a guilty verdict. If all peers report their probe results faithfully, then innocent peers will receive guilty verdicts 1.8% of the time whereas faulty peers will receive guilty verdicts 93.8% of the time. If 20% of peers collude and contribute malicious probe results, then innocent peers will receive guilty verdicts 8.4% of the time and faulty peers will receive guilty verdicts 71.3% of the time.

A host issues a formal accusation against a peer if that peer accumulates at least m guilty verdicts for the w most recent message drops. To determine the false positive and false negative rates of formal accusations, let p_{good} be the probability that a non-faulty node receives a guilty verdict for a message drop, and p_{faulty} be the probability that a faulty node receives a guilty verdict; these probabilities are derived from the blame pdfs and thresholds as described in the previous paragraph. Let W be a random variable describing the number of guilty verdicts in a w-slot window. W is a binomial random variable, meaning that the error rates can be described as follows:

$$Pr(false\ positive) = Pr(W \geq m)$$
$$= \sum_{k=m}^{w} \binom{w}{k} p_{good}^k (1 - p_{good})^{w-k}$$

$$Pr(false\ negative) = Pr(W < m)$$
$$= \sum_{k=0}^{m-1} \binom{w}{k} p_{faulty}^k (1 - p_{faulty})^{w-k}.$$

Figure 6 depicts the error rates with a blame pdf threshold of 40% and a sliding window size of 100. If all nodes faithfully report probe results, then we can drive both error rates below 1% with an m of 6. If 20% of hosts maliciously invert their probe results, we can achieve equivalent error rates with an m of 16.

4.4   Bandwidth Requirements

Concilium has two primary sources of network overhead. Peers must exchange signed, timestamped copies of their routing state, and they must perform tomographic probing. We expect local routing state to reference μ_ϕ + 16 peers,

---

[2]This selection was constrained by the routing tables of each node, i.e., B had to be in A's routing table and C had to be in B's routing table.

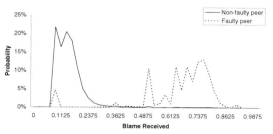
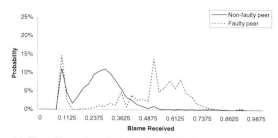

(a) The two pdfs are very distinct when nodes correctly report their tomographic data.

(b) The pdfs are less distinct when 20% of peers maliciously invert probe results, but Concilium can still make accurate judgments using a thresholding scheme.

Figure 5. PDFs for blame as generated by Equation 2 (max_probe_time=120 secs, Δ=60 secs)

(a) If nodes faithfully report probe results, an m of 6 drives both error rates below 1%.

(b) If 20% of hosts are colluding and malicious, an m of 16 drives both error rates below 1%.

Figure 6. Accusation error (w=100)

where 16 is the number of leaf nodes. Each routing entry contains a 16 byte node identifier and a 4 byte freshness timestamp. Using PSS-R [4] with 1024 bit public keys, both quantities plus a signature consume 144 bytes. The exchanged routing state also includes tomographic probe results for the IP path to each routing peer. As explained in Section 3.2, the results for each path can be encoded in a few bits. Assuming 1 byte for each path summary and a 100,000 node overlay, an entire advertised routing table is about 11.5 kilobytes. This overhead can be decreased by sending diffs for updated entries instead of entire tables.

In the absence of forwarding faults, lightweight tomography requires no additional bandwidth beyond that already required for availability probing. The outgoing bandwidth required for heavyweight striped probing of a tree is

$$\binom{|leaves \in T_H|}{2}(stripes\_per\_pair)(stripe\_size)(pkt\_size).$$

In a 100,000 node overlay, the average node has 77 entries in its local routing state. Suppose that each node sends 100 stripes to each ordered pair of peers, that each stripe contains two UDP probes, and that each probe is 30 bytes long (28 bytes for IP+UDP headers and 16 bits for a nonce). Probing an entire tree will require 16.7 MB of outgoing network traffic. Incoming probes will require no more than this amount and less if there are legitimately lossy network links.

The probing cost can be reduced in several ways. If IP multicast were widely deployed, we could reduce the probe traffic sent from the root of a tree to its leaf nodes. Also, as described in Section 3.7, cooperative hosts on the same stub network can share probe results, reducing the probing bandwidth for the collective.

5 Related Work

Packet obituary systems [2] allow end hosts to determine the autonomous system (AS) which dropped a particular packet. Each AS deploys an "accountability box" at each border link. When an incoming packet hits a box, the box records the next AS that the packet will traverse. Boxes periodically push these records along the reverse box paths, allowing each packet source to determine the last AS which successfully received their datagrams. Concilium differs from obituary systems in three ways. First, Concilium does not require the modification of core Internet routers. Second, Concilium protects and validates its network data using various cryptographic and statistical techniques. Finally, obituary systems cannot arbitrate between two adjacent ASes when the first claims that the second dropped its packet, and the second claims that the first never sent the packet. Concilium resolves such disputes using reputation systems.

233

Concilium assumes that end hosts may be malicious but core routers will not fail in a byzantine way. Fatih [15] is designed to detect core routers which maliciously drop or reorder packets. Each router maintains a summary of the traffic it has forwarded. Signed versions of these summaries are periodically exchanged with other routers, and misbehavior is detected by comparing summaries from routers that share links. Like obituary systems, Fatih requires modification to core Internet infrastructure.

In RON [1], each stub network has a special gateway which sits between the stub and the larger Internet. The RON gateways monitor the loss, latency, and throughput along the $O(N^2)$ paths which connect them. When a gateway must forward a locally generated packet outside its stub, it forwards the message through other RON gateways if the default IP path is poor. Like Concilium, RONs use active probing to detect link quality. The key difference is that RON always ascribes blame to the network—misbehaving RON nodes must be detected and removed by human operators. Concilium provides a mechanism for blaming the network *or* an overlay node.

6 Conclusions

In this paper, we introduce Concilium, a distributed diagnostic protocol for overlay networks. By aggregating peer-advertised routing state, Concilium determines forwarding paths at the overlay level. Using collaborative network tomography, Concilium discovers the IP links which comprise these paths and the quality of these links. By combining the topological and tomographic data with application-level message acknowledgments, Concilium judges whether dropped overlay messages are due to failures in the core Internet or failures in overlay forwarders. Concilium's fault accusations are self-verifying and robust to tampering, but they may place blame on nodes which are the victim of misbehavior further downstream in their routes. Thus, Concilium provides mechanisms to revise such incorrect accusations. It also has methods for detecting peers which publish faulty routing state or tomographic data.

References

[1] D. Andersen, H. Balakrishnan, M. F. Kaashoek, and R. Morris. Resilient Overlay Networks. In *Proceedings of SOSP*, pages 131–145, Banff, Canada, October 2001.

[2] K. Argyraki, P. Maniatis, D. Cheriton, and S. Shenker. Providing Packet Obituaries. In *Proceedings of ACM SIGCOMM HotNets*, San Diego, CA, November 2004.

[3] V. Arya, T. Turletti, and C. Hoffmann. Feedback Verification for Trustworthy Tomography. In *Proceedings of IPS-MoMe*, Warsaw, Poland, March 2005.

[4] M. Bellare and P. Rogaway. The Exact Security of Digital Signatures – How to Sign with RSA and Rabin. *Advances in Cryptology–EUROCRYPT '96*, 1070:399–416, 1996.

[5] R. Bellman and M. Giertz. On the analytic formalism of the theory of fuzzy sets. *Information Sciences*, 5:149–156, 1973.

[6] M. Castro, M. Costa, and A. Rowstron. Performance and dependability of structured peer-to-peer overlays. In *Proceedings of DSN*, Florence, Italy, June 2004.

[7] M. Castro, P. Druschel, A. Ganesh, A. Rowstron, and D. S. Wallach. Secure routing for structured peer-to-peer overlay networks. In *Proceedings of OSDI*, pages 299–314, Boston, MA, December 2002.

[8] M. Castro, P. Druschel, Y. C. Hu, and A. Rowstron. Proximity neighbor selection in tree-based structured peer-to-peer overlays. Technical Report MSR-TR-2003-52, Microsoft Research, 2003.

[9] Y. Chen, D. Bindel, H. Song, and R. Katz. An Algebraic Approach to Practical and Scalable Overlay Network Monitoring. In *Proceedings of ACM SIGCOMM*, pages 55–66, Portland, OR, September 2004.

[10] N. Duffield, F. L. Presti, V. Paxson, and D. Towsley. Inferring Link Loss Using Striped Unicast Probes. In *Proceedings of IEEE INFOCOM*, pages 915–923, Anchorage, AK, April 2001.

[11] R. Govindan and H. Tangmunarunkit. Heuristics for Internet Map Discovery. In *Proceedings of IEEE INFOCOM*, pages 1371–1380, Tel Aviv, Israel, March 2000.

[12] R. Jurgelenaite, P. Lucas, and T. Heskes. Exploring the noisy threshold function in designing bayesian networks. In *Proceedings of SGAI International Conference on Innovative Techniques and Applications of Artificial Intelligence*, pages 133–146, Cambridge, UK, December 2005.

[13] R. Mahajan, M. Castro, and A. Rowstron. Controlling the cost of reliability in peer-to-peer overlays. In *Proceedings of the 2nd IPTPS*, Berkeley, CA, February 2003.

[14] R. Mahajan, N. Spring, D. Wetherall, and T. Anderson. User-level Internet Path Diagnosis. In *Proceedings of SOSP*, pages 106–119, Lake George, NY, October 2003.

[15] A. Mizrak, Y.-C. Cheng, K. Marzullo, and S. Savage. Fatih: Detecting and Isolating Malicious Routers. In *Proceedings of DSN*, pages 538–547, Yokohama, Japan, June 2005.

[16] D. Oppenheimer, A. Ganapathi, and D. A. Patterson. Why do Internet services fail, and what can be done about it? In *Proceedings of USITS*, March 2003.

[17] A. Rowstron and P. Druschel. Pastry: Scalable, distributed object location and routing for large-scale peer-to-peer systems. In *Proceedings of the IFIP/ACM International Conference on Distributed Systems Platforms (Middleware)*, Heidelberg, Germany, November 2001.

[18] N. Spring, R. Mahajan, and D. Wetherall. Measuring ISP topologies with Rocketfuel. In *Proceedings of ACM SIGCOMM*, pages 133–145, Pittsburgh, PA, August 2002.

[19] I. Stoica, R. Morris, D. Karger, M. Kaashoek, and H. Balakrishnan. Chord: A scalabale peer-to-peer lookup service for Internet applications. In *Proceedings of ACM SIGCOMM*, pages 149–160, San Diego, CA, August 2001.

[20] K. Walsh and E. G. Sirer. Experience with an Object Reputation System for Peer-to-Peer Filesharing. In *Proceedings of NSDI*, pages 1–14, San Jose, CA, May 2006.

[21] Y. Zhang, V. Paxson, and S. Shenker. The Stationarity of Internet Path Properties: Routing, Loss, and Throughput. Technical Report, AT&T Center for Internet Research at ICSI, May 2000.

R-Sentry: Providing Continuous Sensor Services Against Random Node Failures

Shengchao Yu
WINLAB
Rutgers University
Piscataway, NJ 08854
yusc@winlab.rutgers.edu

Yanyong Zhang
WINLAB
Rutgers University
Piscataway, NJ 08854
yyzhang@winlab.rutgers.edu

Abstract

The success of sensor-driven applications is reliant on whether a steady stream of data can be provided by the underlying system. This need, however, poses great challenges to sensor systems, mainly because the sensor nodes from which these systems are built have extremely short lifetimes. In order to extend the lifetime of the networked system beyond the lifetime of an individual sensor node, a common practice is to deploy a large array of sensor nodes and, at any time, have only a minimal set of nodes active performing duties while others stay in sleep mode to conserve energy. With this rationale, random node failures, either from active nodes or from redundant nodes, can seriously disrupt system operations. To address this need, we propose R-Sentry, which attempts to bound the service loss duration due to node failures, by coordinating the schedules among redundant nodes. Our simulation results show that compared to PEAS, a popular node scheduling algorithm, R-Sentry can provide a continuous 95% coverage through bounded recoveries from frequent node failures, while prolonging the lifetime of a sensor network by roughly 30%.

Keywords:

Sensor Networks, Network Coverage, Fault Tolerance, Node Failure, Gang

1. Introduction

Sensor networks promise to change the way we interact with the physical world: instead of querying data as a response to events, sensor networks continuously push data to applications so that necessary parsing and analysis can take place before events occur. The very fact that this data may be collected for significant periods of time over vast spatial areas facilitates a broad range of applications. An important issue for the successful deployment of sensor-driven applications is to make sure that the sensor network will be able to deliver as much spatio-temporal information as possible, i.e. sensor networks must guarantee both coverage and con-

nectivity over a significant period of time. Although initial solutions have been proposed to provide coverage and connectivity [11, 4, 19, 2], there is a severe problem– the frequent failing of sensor nodes– that has received little attention. In sensor networks, due to the nature of the sensor node hardware, there exists a fundamental tradeoff between network lifetime and network service quality.

Maintaining graceful operations under faulty conditions has long been a focus of research in other resource-rich systems. Although failures cannot be totally eliminated , a few practical strategies have emerged and been adopted to limit the effects of failures. These strategies usually involve employing backups or redundancy to smoothly transfer the load once a failure occurs. Though effective in resource-rich settings, these strategies can not be applied to sensor networks because of the severe energy constraints, the poor computing capabilities, and the nature of radio circuitry. In particular, many radios employed by today's sensor nodes have the unfortunate failing that, even when idle, they consume nearly as much power as when they are receiving. Further, the power consumption for receiving is almost as taxing as the power needed to transmit. Consequently, turning on backup nodes is not a prudent solution since the backup node might not even outlive the working node.

In order to build a long running system from relatively short-lived sensor nodes, a widely-adopted approach is to include high degree of redundancy in the deployment, and let the nodes work in "shifts". Therefore, at any moment, the working shift (i.e., the active nodes) consists of a minimal number of nodes needed to maintain the system's operations, while the rest of the nodes (i.e., the redundant nodes) have their radios off. The downside of this strategy, however, is that the failure of an active node will lead to a hole in the network, thereby disrupting sensor services. Even in the ideal case where nodes do not die before their batteries drain out, the death of an active node still could disrupt the services since network dynamics make it impossible to precisely predict when power resources will be depleted.

In this paper, we propose *R-Sentry*, a node scheduling algorithm that attempts to balance continuous network ser-

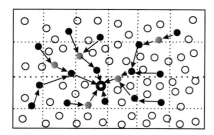

Figure 1. Illustration of a WSN.

vices and extended network lifetime in the presence of frequent node failures. For every active node, R-Sentry groups the nodes whose sensing/networking functionalities overlap with that of the active node into *gangs*. A gang consists of a set of redundant nodes that can collectively replace the active node upon its failure. R-Sentry ensures that, every so often, a gang will wake up to probe whether the active node is still functioning. If a failure has occurred to the active node, the probing redundant nodes can become active to take over the failed active node to resume network services. Hence, R-Sentry promises to limit the service loss time by coordinating the wake up schedules of the redundant nodes. R-Sentry also seamlessly handles more complicated situations, such as cases where a redundant node serves multiple active nodes simultaneously, or cases where redundant nodes die before the active node fails.

Compared to existing techniques that share the same viewpoint of having redundant nodes sleep for periods of time to conserve energy, such as PEAS [16] or OGDC [19], R-Sentry takes a much closer look at the problem of local network recovery in the face of node failures. It tries to provide quality of service guarantees to sensor applications instead of the best effort approach by using random wake ups. We have conducted a set of simulation experiments to study the performance of R-Sentry. Compared to PEAS, R-Sentry can (1) provide a longer network life, (2) provide better network coverage ($> 95\%$), (3) provide controllable coverage recovery, (4) provide more robustness against random node failures, and (5) provide better scalability with larger node density.

The rest of the paper is organized as follows. We provide an overview of our sensor network model in Section 2, followed by related work. In Section 4, we discuss the R-Sentry algorithm in detail. We present our simulation effort and the simulation results in Section 5. We conclude in Section 6.

2. Sensor Network Model

In this section, we discuss in detail our wireless sensor network (WSN) model.

2.1. Generic Sensor Network Model

Coverage: In this work, we adopt the grid-based coverage model [11, 12] illustrated in Figure 1. In this popular cover-age model, the square network field in question is imaginarily partitioned into grids, marked by the dotted lines in the figure. The grids should be small enough so that the underlying physical phenomena do not exhibit much variability within a grid. The grid points that fall within a node's sensing area are considered covered by that sensor node. This discretization approach simplifies the measurement of the coverage, making the network coverage percentage equivalent to the percentage of the grid points that are covered. This model can be enforced by having nodes exchange the list of grid points it can cover with their neighbors, which we call *GridList*. Figure 1 shows such a scenario where there are a subset of sensor nodes, represented by darker solid circles, actively monitoring corresponding grid points, while other nodes are not required for the coverage under the model. With sufficient node density, there is a high probability that, out of uniformly randomly deployed nodes, there exists a set of nodes that could collectively cover all the grid points in the network field.

Connectivity: In addition to sensing the physical world, a WSN is also responsible for delivering the sensed data to the applications. Network connectivity thus requires that there exists a routing path between every sensing node and the sink. In order to achieve this goal, it may be necessary to have more active nodes than just those needed for provide sensor coverage, i.e., we may need extra nodes to have good network connectivity, which are represented by the light solid circles in Figure 1.

To focus on failure recovery schemes, we choose grid sizes small enough to ensure connectivity through coverage: a WSN that satisfies the coverage requirement is automatically connected. This was also observed in many earlier studies [16, 4, 11], which assumed the communication range is at least double of the sensing range. Therefore, in this paper, we can focus on providing sensing coverage.

Turning Off Redundant nodes: Energy is a scarce resource for many sensor nodes may not have external power sources, and have to rely on batteries. Even a battery with a capacity of 3000 mA-hour can only last for 17 months [3]. A sensor node has three main components: sensor(s), processor, and radio. Sensors measure physical phenomena, the processor takes as input the data from the sensors or the network and performs in-network processing, while the radio communicates with the rest of the network. Among the three, the radio is by far the main power consumer [17]. For example, a Mica2 radio has current draw of 12mA in transmitting and 8mA in receiving. It's worth noticing that a radio being in receiving mode does not necessarily mean the application is receiving any valid packets; it is merely monitoring the medium. The energy consumed by a Mica2 radio in transmitting a 30-byte message is roughly equivalent to the energy consumed by an ATMega128 processor executing 1152 instructions [9]. As a result, if we leave all the sensor nodes on, then no matter how many are deployed, the network cannot function longer than 17 months. In practice, to extend network lifetime it is necessary to have redundant nodes off and turn them back on only when needed.

Disruptions Caused by Node Failures: Although the strategy discussed above is energy-conscious, it does not provide any robustness against random node failures. For instance, suppose that grid point p was monitored by sensor node s while all the other nodes that can also cover p were in sleep mode. Further, suppose that those sleeping nodes will wake up at a later time t. If s fails at time t_0, then during this period with duration $t - t_0$, the coverage and/or connectivity of the network will be lost. In particular, node failures will occur more frequently under heavy traffic volumes, which is more likely when the monitored physical phenomena exhibit interesting behavior. Fail to collect or forward data on these occasions can have severe consequences, likely detrimental to the applications.

2.2. Target Sensor Network Assumptions

In this study, the WSNs have the following features:

Regularity in Sensing and Communication. The popular disk sensor model [11, 10, 16] is used to simplify the analysis and simulations. Specifically, a node's sensing area is a circular disk with the node as the center and the sensing range as radius; and the neighbor nodes that fall into the cocentric circle with the transmission range as radius are considered as 1-hop neighbors. Moreover, all the links are symmetric.

Resource-constraints. Sensor nodes are battery-driven and non-rechargeable, except the sink node.

Location-Awareness. Each sensor node is assumed to be stationary and have its own location, which can be obtained through either localization devices, such as GPS, or certain localization algorithms [7, 8]. We further assume the sensor nodes have the geographical location of the network field in which they are deployed. Based on a node's location and sensing radius, it can obtain the list of grid points it covers.

3. Related Work

Local networking repair has been studied in the context of sensor networks, and several strategies have been proposed, such as GAF [14], AFECA [13], and ASCENT [1]. GAF identifies those nodes that are equivalent in terms of routing capabilities, and turns them off to conserve energy. In AFECA, a simple adaptive scheme is employed to determine the node sleep interval for those nodes that are turned off. ASCENT shares the same goal as GAF, and it also considers mechanisms for sleeping nodes to come back and join the routing when necessary. To avoid degrading connectiv-

ity severely, sleeping nodes need to wake up relatively frequently. In addition, a fixed sleep interval is used for every node in the network. The authors also proved that the upper bound on the lifetime improvement is the ratio of a node's sleep interval to its awake period.

Besides information delivery, data collection is the other critical task of sensor networks. In PEAS [16], an independent probing technique was proposed for redundant nodes to check whether there is an active node in its vicinity. OGDC [19] is a round-based node scheduling algorithm which selects active nodes based on their geo-locations to improve network lifetime. In [5, 15], all the nodes that can cover the same spot form a cluster, and at any time, there is only one active node from the cluster while the other members stay in the sleep mode.

Compared to the aforementioned earlier work, R-Sentry takes a closer look at the problem of local network recovery in the face of node failures, and takes a distinctly different approach: (1) R-Sentry tries to provide quality of service guarantees to sensor applications instead of using a best effort approach based on random wake ups; (2) the wake ups of the redundant nodes are carefully scheduled to ensure timely network recovery with less energy consumption, and (3) waking up one redundant node to replace the failed active node is often impossible. R-Sentry extends our exploratory work in [18] by introducing the concept of gangs and conducting more comprehensive evaluations.

4. The Design of R-Sentry

While on duty, a WSN is composed of two types of nodes: active nodes , which are performing duties; and redundant nodes, which are sleeping with their radios off. While active nodes is on duty, the redundant nodes should not sleep for an infinitely long period. Rather, they should wake up from time to time and check the conditions of the active nodes. Every node randomly waking up [16, 1], however, is wasteful and does not provide much benefit. For instance, if the subsequent wake ups are far apart from each other, then it is impossible to ensure quick network recovery. To address this void, we propose a coordinated scheduling algorithm among all the redundant nodes. Those redundant nodes that wake up play a role analogous to sentries in real world in the sense that they monitor the health of the active node, and whenever a fault or failure occurs, they jump in to replace the lost node. In the following discussions, we use redundant node and sentry interchangeable. Since redundant nodes rotate to wake up, we call this scheme *Rotatory Sentries* or *R-Sentry*.

4.1. Redundant Sets and Gangs

Before going into details of R-Sentry, it is beneficial to examine the redundancy among nodes. Every sensor node has a group of neighbor nodes with overlapping communication or sensing capabilities. The *sensing redundant set*

(*SRS*) of a node consists of its neighbors whose sensing areas overlap with the node's sensing area, i.e. nodes that can cover the same grid point(s) belong to each other's *SRS*.

When an active node fails, it can only be replaced by nodes from its *SRS*. However, the replacement of a failed active node can not necessarily be accomplished by simply replacing it with a single redundant node, regardless of whether one is trying to repair sensing coverage or network connectivity. This viewpoint is distinctly different from those in earlier studies such as [16, 1], which tried to replace the active using one redundant node. In fact, it has been shown in [4] that on average 3-5 nodes are needed to replace a node's sensing area.

Since an active node can only be replaced by certain combinations of redundant nodes, there is a need for the active node to group all the nodes that belong to its *SRS* into "*gangs*". Nodes that belong to the same gang can collectively replace the active node. Now let us look at an example to understand the definition of a gang. In this example, the active node A's *SRS* is $\{B, C, D, E, F\}$, and their *GridLists* are shown in Table 1. We can see that A's coverage area can be completely replaced by the following combinations: $\{B\}$, $\{C, D\}$, $\{C, E\}$, and $\{D, E, F\}$. As a result, A has four gangs: $\{\{B\}, \{C, D\}, \{C, E\}, \{D, E, F\}\}$, which we call *GangList*.

One thing we would like to point that is, a superset of a gang set technically is also a gang. For instance, in the example in Table 1, the set $\{B, C\}$ is also a gang. However, in this paper, we only focus on "minimum gangs", those sets that would no longer be a gang should we remove any member from the set. Grouping nodes from an *SRS* into gangs is essentially a combinatorial problem. shows the pseudo code for a node populating its *GangList* with gangs of sizes no larger than *gs*. In order to limit the computation of this procedure, we only consider gangs of small sizes.

For the purpose of fault tolerance, nodes that belong to a gang need to wake up simultaneously to completely replace the functionalities of an active node.

4.2. R-Sentry Algorithm

R-Sentry attempts to bound the duration of service loss. That is, every time an active node fails, R-Sentry seeks to make nodes from a gang available within a time interval of Δ (an example schedule shown in Table 3(b)), where Δ is the promised service loss time limit. If an active node has N gangs, then each gang needs to wake up every $N\Delta$.

node ID	*GridList*	node ID	*GridList*
A	$\{1, 2, 3, 4\}$	D	$\{1, 4, 5, 6, 7\}$
B	$\{1, 2, 3, 4, 5\}$	E	$\{3, 4, 5, 6, 8\}$
C	$\{1, 2, 3, 5\}$	F	$\{2, 9, 10\}$

Table 1. An example of *GridList* table.

```
GENE-GANGS(SRS, gs)        // gs : maximum gang size
1    i = 1; clear GL;       // GL : Gang List
2    GCL = SRS;             // GCL : Gang Candidate List
3    while i ≤ gs
4        clear TEMP_GCL;    // TEMP_GCL : temporarily GCL
5        for each set s in GCL
6            if s is a minimum gang
7                then push back s to GL;
8                else push back s to TEMP_GCL
9            if i < gs
10               then GCL = PREPARE-CANDY(TEMP_GCL);
11   return GL

PREPARE-CANDY(TEMP_GCL)
1    clear GCL;
2    for each set t in TEMP_GCL
3        for each node srs in SRS
4            t = srs ∪ t;
5            push back t to GCL;
6    return GCL
```

Table 2. Algorithm for generating gang

Gang	Time To Wake Up (s)
$\{B, C\}$	1200
$\{D, C, E\}$	1500
$\{B, E\}$	1800
$\{E, F\}$	2100

(a) Gang schedule table

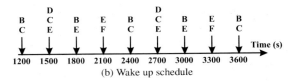

(b) Wake up schedule

Table 3. Illustration of a gang schedule table and the resulting wake up schedule.

4.2.1 Basic idea

The discussions in this section have simplified assumptions such as a redundant node only serves one active node, and all the redundant nodes will not fail before the active nodes do. We made these assumption to keep the explanation easy to understand, and in the following sections, we discuss how to extend R-Sentry to handle more realistic scenarios, where a redundant node may belong to multiple active nodes, and node failures can occur at random times.

We let the active nodes maintain most of the data structures, while having redundant nodes only keep track of their own next wake up time. The most important data structure maintained by an active node is its gang schedule table, which specifies each gang's next wake up time. An illustration of such a data structure is provided in Table 3(a). Based on this table, we can infer the wake up times for each gang. For example, with $\Delta = 300s$, if an active node has 3 gangs, the gang that wakes up at time 1200s also wakes up at times 2100s, 3000s, 3900s, etc. Therefore, a portion of the wake up events caused by Table 3(a) is shown in Table 3(b).

Next we discuss how active nodes establish their gang schedule tables, and more importantly, how they maintain the schedules.

Initialization: During the bootstrapping phase, a WSN usually runs a host of initialization services, such as neighbor discovery, localization, time synchronization, route discovery, duty-cycle scheduling, etc. Similarly, a WSN that employs R-Sentry needs the following extra initialization services:

- *Gang Discovery.* This service ensures every sensor node identifies its neighbor nodes, and populates its *SRS* and *GridList*. At the beginning, each node in the network sends out a *presence announcement* message including its ID and location . Such messages are flooded within h hops around the source nodes, where h is a small number, usually 1 or 2, as the *presence announcement* only matters to nodes within the vicinity of the source node. After a certain amount of time in the process, every node will receive the announcements from all of its *SRS* members, based on which a node can calculate the *GridList* of each node in its *SRS*. After that, a node would be able to form its own *GangList* in the way illustrated in Table 2.

- *Schedule Bootstrapping.* The initial set of active nodes are determined by the underlying coverage and initialization protocols. Our approach is similar as the one employed in CCP [11], which can be broken down into 3 steps: 1) after *presence announcement* exchange phase, every node stays active and starts a random backoff timer, collecting *redundancy announcement* from its *SRS* members; 2) upon the timer's expiration, a node checks its *SRS* members' redundancy status and determines if all grid points in *GridList* are covered by the non-redundant *SRS* members. If yes, it considers itself redundant and broadcasts *redundancy announcement*, otherwise it considers itself non-redundant and doesn't take any actions; 3) at the end of bootstrapping phase, the non-redundant nodes calculate their gangs' schedules and flood them within a small number of hops, staying active; while the redundant nodes, upon receiving the schedules, record their own wake up time or the earliest one if it receives multiple schedules.

At the end of the initialization phase, the redundant nodes go to sleep with their sleep timers properly set up, while the active nodes start collecting and forwarding sensed data.

Probing: A sentry (i.e. redundant) node periodically wakes up, as scheduled, to probe the active node. If the active node has failed, sentry nodes will become active to resume network services; otherwise, they go back to sleep.

When a sentry node wakes up, it broadcasts a probing message with its node ID included. Around the same time,

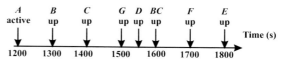

(a) The events that have been observed by A.

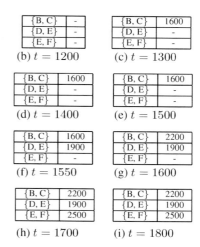

{B, C}	-
{D, E}	-
{E, F}	-

(b) $t = 1200$

{B, C}	1600
{D, E}	-
{E, F}	-

(c) $t = 1300$

{B, C}	1600
{D, E}	-
{E, F}	-

(d) $t = 1400$

{B, C}	1600
{D, E}	-
{E, F}	-

(e) $t = 1500$

{B, C}	1600
{D, E}	1900
{E, F}	-

(f) $t = 1550$

{B, C}	2200
{D, E}	1900
{E, F}	-

(g) $t = 1600$

{B, C}	2200
{D, E}	1900
{E, F}	2500

(h) $t = 1700$

{B, C}	2200
{D, E}	1900
{E, F}	2500

(i) $t = 1800$

Figure 2. Illustration of how a new active node establishes its gang schedule table.

the other sentries of the same gang will also wake up and probe. If the target active node is still alive, it will match the node ID's contained in the probing messages with the gang whose scheduled wake up time is closest to the current time. If the match is successful, the active node updates the gang schedule table by incrementing the wake up time by the round duration $N\Delta$. Finally, the active node sends the sentries a reply message which has two fields: *NextWakeTime*, and *CurrentTime*. The *CurrentTime* field is used to synchronize the clocks between the sentry nodes and the active node.

The above discussion assumes the active node is still alive while sentries probing. If the active node has failed before sentries probe, the sentries will not receive the reply message, then they conclude the active node has failed. In this situation, the sentries should become active to provide uninterrupted services. The design of R-Sentry thus ensures that, whenever one of the active node fails, its functionality will be fully resumed by other nodes roughly within Δ, when the sentries outlive the target active node and corresponding communication time is negligible compared to Δ. Therefore, R-Sentry can limit the service loss period within a tolerable threshold.

4.2.2 Dynamically establishing schedules for new active nodes

After the sentry nodes become active, these new active nodes face several challenges. The main challenge stems from the fact that the communication between the new active node and the redundant nodes that belong to its *SRS* has not been established. On one hand, the redundant nodes are still following the schedules of the previous active node, without realizing that the active node has changed. On the other hand, the new active node does not have a schedule for its gangs, and therefore, it will not be guarded properly. Further complicating the problem is that it is impossible for the new active node to communicate with the redundant nodes when they are asleep for their radios are off. As a result, we can only attempt to establish the schedule gradually as more and more redundant nodes wake up in groups down the stretch.

The algorithm a new active node uses to establish its schedule is rather simple, yet effective. The idea is that, if the redundant node that is probing is not associated with a wake up time in the gang schedule table, the new active node will assign the next available wake up slot to the gang that contains this redundant node. If the node is included in multiple gangs, the smallest gang will be picked.

To better understand this algorithm, let us walk through an example shown in Figure 2. Suppose node A is the new active node, and its *GangList* is {B, C}, {D, E}, and {E, F}. The Δ is 300 seconds. Figure 2(a) illustrates the wake up events A observes in the establishing phase, and for each event, it shows the corresponding schedule table in the subsequent figures (Figures 2(b-i)). In particular, the establishing phase has the following steps:

1. A becomes active at time 1200, when A's schedule is empty (Figure 2(b)).

2. At time 1300, B wakes up. A then assigns next available wake up slot, i.e. the current time incremented by Δ, 1600, to gang {B, C}, and updates the gang schedule table accordingly (Figure 2(c)).

3. At time 1400, C wakes up. A finds C is already scheduled, so it does not update the gang schedule table. It just simply sends a reply message to C to instruct C to wake up at 1600 (Figure 2(d)).

4. At time 1500, G wakes up. A finds G does not belong to its *SRS*, so it does not update the gang schedule table. A sends a reply message to G with a large sleep interval (Figure 2(e)). If G serves other active nodes, it will receive a much shorter sleep time from them.

5. At time 1550, node D wakes up. A assigns next available wake up slot, 1900, to gang {D, E}, and updates the gang schedule table accordingly (Figure 2(f)).

6. At time 1600, node B and C wake up according to the schedule. Since A's table is not fully occupied yet, A assigns the next available wake up slot, 2200, to them (Figure 2(g)).

7. At time 1700, node F wakes up. A assigns the next available wake up slot, 2500, to node E and F (Figure 2(h)).

{B, C}	1200
{D, E}	1500
{F, G}	1800

(a) $t = 1000$

{B, C}	2100
{D, E}	1500
{F, G}	1800

(b) $t = 1500$

{B, C}	3000
{D, E}	2400
{F, G}	2700

(c) $t = 2400$, A still has not heard from D.

{B, C}	3000
-	-
{F, G}	2700

(d) $t = 2400$, A cleans up its gang schedule table

Figure 3. An example illustrating how a active node detects failures among redundant nodes and adapts its schedule accordingly.

8. At time 1800, node E wakes up. A does not update the schedule table because E is already scheduled. A sends a reply message to E, requesting E to wake up at time 1900 (Figure 2(i)).

9. After that, A becomes a normal active node, and it will handle the subsequent waking sentries by incrementing their wake up times by $3\Delta = 900$.

We note that a new active usually can establish its gang schedule within a reasonable amount of time because according to R-Sentry, every redundant node wakes up periodically, and this period will be the upper bound of the time taken to form the schedule.

4.3. Scheduling Redundant Nodes That Serve Multiple Active Nodes

To simplify the discussion, we assumed that a redundant node only serves one active node in the earlier sections. In this section, we look at how R-Sentry handles the cases where a redundant node may serve multiple active nodes.

If a sentry node guards multiple active nodes, the main challenge lies in that when it probes, how it handles schedules from multiple active nodes. In R-Sentry, when a sentry node probes, it only includes its own ID in the probing message. Each of the active nodes that receive the probing messages, will examine the difference between the scheduled wake up time of that redundant node and the current time at the active node. If the difference is below a threshold, the corresponding active node assumes this is a valid wake up, calculates its next wake up time, and sends a reply message back. The reply message contains three fields: the next wake up time T_{next}, the current time T_{curr}, and the active node's ID. Those active nodes that have a different wake up time for the redundant node will simply copy the previously scheduled wake up time to the reply message. After receiving all the reply messages, the redundant node calculates the sleep interval for each of the active nodes, chooses the shortest one as the next sleep interval , and synchronizes its clock appropriately.

240

4.4. Dynamically Adjusting Schedules for Missing Redundant Nodes

In many sensor network applications, failures occur not only to active nodes, but also to redundant nodes, even when they are in sleep mode. For instance, a catastrophic event, such as lightning can cause sensor node failures, regardless of their state. When a redundant node fails, the active node cannot rely on the gangs that contain the failed node, and should remove these gangs from its schedule.

In R-Sentry, dynamically adapting the active node's schedule is rather straightforward. If the active node does not hear from a redundant node in k consecutive rounds (usually, k is a small number such as 2), it simply removes the gangs that contain the missing node from the gang list. In order to understand the details, let us look at an example illustrated in Figure 3, where the active node A has the following gangs, $\{B, C\}$, $\{D, E\}$, and $\{F, G\}$; and the Δ is 300 seconds. Node D fails at time 1000. What happens to A is:

1. At time 1000, node D fails. A's gang schedule table is shown in Figure 3(a).

2. At time 1500 (Figure 3(b)), A only receives probes from E, not D. A decides to wait for one more round (900 seconds in this case) before taking actions.

3. After a round, at time 2400, A still has not heard from D (Figure 3(c)). A then concludes that D has failed, and removes the gang $\{D, E\}$ from the schedule (shown in Figure 3(d)). At this time, A will still send a reply message to E that includes a reasonably long sleep time, like 2Δ.

4. A will schedule the remaining two gangs as usual, with the only exception that the round duration now becomes 600 seconds. As a result, gang $\{B, C\}$ will wake up at times 3000, 3600, 4200, etc, while gang $\{F, G\}$ will wake up at times 2700, 3300, 3900, etc. Therefore, A will still receives probes every 300 seconds.

5. Performance Evaluation

In this section, we first define a simplified sensor failure model, then give the simulation model and simulation setups. After that we examine R-Sentry's performance against PEAS, in terms of scalability, energy efficiency, service availability, coverage recoverability and fault tolerance.

5.1. Sensor Failure Model

We purposely introduce sensor failures into our simulations to model the fact that random node failures are norms instead of exceptions in sensor network. The *catastrophic failure model* used in our simulation is a coarse-grained model, in which a percentage of sensor nodes that are alive (but not necessarily active) "die" due to external catastrophic events, like natural disasters. By "die", we mean the node stops functioning completely as an electronic device,

even though it's possible in reality that not all components in the node are affected by the external events.

This failure model has two parameters: (i) failure period f_p, the mean time between consecutive external catastrophic events (the intervals between two events are random numbers that follow an exponential distribution), and (ii) failure percentage $f_\%$, the mean percentage of the live nodes that are affected by a particular event. Upon a catastrophic event, the actual percentage of affected nodes is a random number between 0 and $2f_\%$.

5.2. Overview of PEAS

In this study, we compare R-Sentry's performance with PEAS [16], a well-recognized fault-tolerant energy-conserving protocol for sensor networks. Before we present the detailed simulation results, we would like to first give a brief description of PEAS. Like R-Sentry, PEAS also assumes that at any moment, only a subset of nodes stay active, while the others go to sleep and wake up periodically to probe the health of the active node(s). PEAS, however, allows the redundant nodes to independently wake up, without coordinating the schedules among them, and as a result, it only provides a coarse granularity of fault-tolerance.

PEAS guarantees there is at least one active node within every redundant node's probing range. An active node controls the wake up frequencies of the redundant nodes using the parameter λ_d, the desired probing rate. Every time an active node receives a probing message, it replies with λ_d and the actual probing rate $\hat{\lambda}$ that it has observed, based on which the probing node calculates its new probing rate as $\lambda^{new} = \lambda^{old} \frac{\lambda_d}{\hat{\lambda}}$. Then the probing node generates its new sleep interval t_s following the probability density function $f(t_s) = \lambda^{new} e^{-\lambda^{new} t_s}$. We note that, in PEAS, the parameter $1/\lambda_d$ is similar to Δ in R-Sentry, both denoting the desired recovery time from the applications, and we use these two notations interchangeably when presenting the results.

5.3. Simulation Model and Settings

We have implemented both R-Sentry and PEAS on our own simulator *USenSim*. *USenSim* is a discrete event-driven simulator that is intended to model large-scale sensor networks. In order to realize the network scale we envision, i.e. with thousands of nodes, which was impossible with more detailed network simulators such as NS-2, *USenSim* assumes a constant transmission delay between nodes and serialized transmissions among nodes that compete the channel, similar as the one adopted in [11]. We believe the sim-

Routing protocol	Shortest path	Sensing range	10m
Communication range	15m	Transmission power	0.06w
Receiving power	0.012w	Idle power	0.012w
Sleeping power	0.00003w	Sensing power	0.001w
Bandwidth	20Kbps	Packet size	25Bytes

Table 4. Simulation Platform Parameters

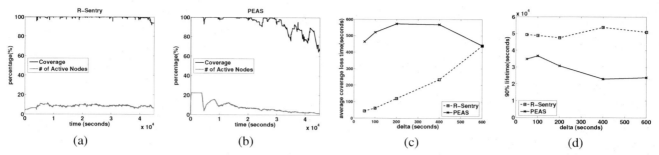

Figure 4. Network coverage statistics throughout the lifetime of a WSN: (a) R-Sentry, and (b) PEAS. The average coverage loss time and the 90% network life time with △ are shown in (c) and (d).

plified network model does not prevent us proving the validity and effectiveness of our algorithm, given that our work is orthogonal to the works in the underlying layers.

Unless specified, the simulation setup has 600 sensor nodes uniformly randomly deployed in a $50 \times 50m^2$ square. Each grid is a $1 \times 1m^2$ square. The initial energy of a sensor node is uniformly distributed between 50 and 60 Joules, which allows the node to function around $4000 \sim 5000$ seconds if the radio is in idle listening mode. Every 50 seconds, each active node transmits a packet containing collected data to the sink, which is located at the center of the field and has persistent power supply. The neighbor nodes that are located within the distance of $15m$ constitute *SRS*. Due to the high redundancy, a gang size of 1 is sufficient in the simulations.

For those parameters that are specific to PEAS, we have tried various parameter values, and chosen the following settings because they produced the best results: probing range $R_p = 3m$, desired probing rate $\lambda_d = 0.02$, initial probing rate $\lambda_s = 0.02$, and $k = 32$. We would like to emphasize that we chose a rather small probing range for PEAS to guarantee all the grid points are covered since PEAS does not explicitly require every grid point to be covered. The network/energy parameters used in our simulations are summarized in Table 4, and we took these values from PEAS [16].

5.4. Performance Metrics

Coverage ratio is the percentage of the grid points that are covered at a time. Both R-Sentry and PEAS attempt to achieve a high coverage ratio throughout their lifetimes.

β **network lifetime** is the duration the network lasts until the coverage ratio drops below β and never comes back again. We use β lifetime to measure the protocol's capabilities of preserving coverage and recovering coverage loss from node failures.

Coverage loss time is the duration from when a grid point loses coverage to when the coverage recovers. The average coverage loss time reflects how quickly a failed active node can be replaced by the redundant nodes.

Packet delivery ratio is the ratio of number of packets received by the sink to the number of packets sent out by the active nodes in a specific length of time window. The packet delivery ratio indicates the connectivity of the network.

5.5. Performance Results

Service Availability: The motivation behind this study is the need to provide uninterrupted services throughout a sensor network's lifetime. Figures 4 (a) and (b) shows how the coverage ratio evolves with time for the two schemes. In this experiment, we have $\Delta = 50$ seconds in both schemes. We observe that R-Sentry can offer a 95% coverage ratio until 2.5×10^3 seconds, while PEAS's coverage ratio drops below 90% from 2.5×10^3 seconds. This is because in R-Sentry, once an active node fails, it can be quickly replaced by a gang, while in PEAS, there is not a guarantee that the awake redundant node can fully replace the active node.

We can also confirm our hypothesis by looking at the time series of the percentage of active nodes in both cases. R-Sentry can maintain a steady number of active nodes, which can in turn guarantee a high coverage ratio, but in PEAS, the number of active nodes decreases with time due to oversleeping. We note that the drop of the number of active nodes in PEAS around 5000 second is due to the fact that most of the initial active nodes failed at that time. We did not observe a drop in R-Sentry because it can quickly recover from failures.

Algorithm Controllability: Controllability is a valuable feature for an algorithm, in that the performance of an algorithm with controllability can be easily tuned up to match application requirements. In this set of experiments, we varied Δ, and collected the corresponding average coverage loss time , which is shown in Figure 4(c). We can observe that R-Sentry demonstrates good controllability: for any given Δ value, the resulting average coverage loss time is always below Δ, and often slightly higher than $\Delta/2$. PEAS, however, fails to do so – we cannot correlate the delivered coverage loss time and the desirable coverage loss time.

Thanks to the capability of maintaining high coverage ratio and low coverage loss time, R-Sentry can make the sen-

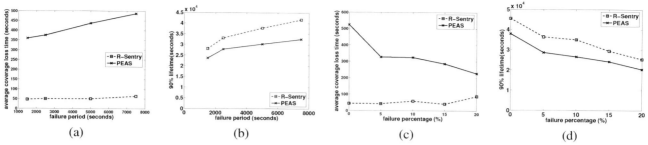

Figure 5. The impact of f_p on average coverage loss time and 90% network lifetime is shown in (a) and (b) (with $f_\% = 5\%$, and $\Delta = 50$ seconds). The impact of $f_\%$ on average coverage loss time and 90% network lifetime is shown in (c) and (d) (with $f_p = 5000$ seconds, and $\Delta = 50$ seconds).

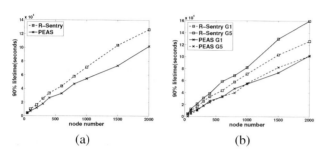

Figure 6. Scalability and impact of grid size

sor network function for a much longer period, as shown in Figure 4(d). The interesting phenomenon we observe from Figure 4(d) is that the 90% network lifetime stays almost the same as Δ goes up. This can be explained by the fact that, though a large Δ can save more energy by making redundant nodes sleep longer, the likelihood of the overall coverage ratio falling below a certain percentage (90% in this case) is also higher due to oversleeping. As a result, these two effects will cancel each other.

Fault Tolerance: It's not unusual that sensor nodes die before running out of energy [6, 16, 1]. In this set of experiments, we evaluate the robustness of the two schemes against node failures under the *catastrophic failure model*.

In Figures 5(a) and (b), we fixed $f_\%$ as 5%, and varied the value of f_p. Since R-Sentry has sentry nodes guarding active nodes and can dynamically adapt an active's node schedule table to accommodate the failures of its redundant nodes, it is rather robust against random node failures. Figure 5(a) shows that, regardless of the failure rate, R-Sentry is able to replace a failed active node around 50 seconds (which is the value of Δ). On the other hand, in PEAS, the average service loss period is much longer. As a result, R-Sentry provides a much better 90% network lifetime than PEAS across all the failure rates (shown in Figure 5(b)). We also observe the similar trend from the results when we fix f_p but vary $f_\%$, which are shown in Figures 5(c) and (d).

Energy Efficiency and Scalability: Many sensor applications seek to achieve longer network lifetime by deploying more nodes. Therefore, the ability to translate a larger number of sensor nodes into a prolonged network lifetime is critically important to node scheduling algorithms like R-Sentry and PEAS. In this set of experiments, we varied the number of sensor nodes, and measured the resulting 90% lifetime. The results, reported in Figure 6(a), show that R-Sentry leads to longer lifetimes than PEAS by roughly 30%. This is because R-Sentry maintains a good coverage ratio for a much longer duration than PEAS through careful scheduling, which leads to a better 90% lifetime. In fact, we find that the 90% lifetime in R-Sentry almost scales linearly with the number of nodes, and that the difference between the two schemes increases with the number of nodes.

Connectivity: Our simulations also show that, both algorithms achieve more than 95% packet delivery ratio during 90% lifetime, which confirms our claim in Section 2.1. Due to space limitation, we didn't include these plots.

5.6. Discussion

Energy Overheard of R-Sentry: The ability to timely wake up appropriate redundant nodes ensures R-Sentry's fault-tolerance. However on the other hand, it also entails additional energy overhead by requiring extra message exchanges between nodes. Assuming no packet loss, when a redundant node wakes up, it will send out a probing message, and will receive n reply messages, where n is smaller than the number of active nodes at the moment. To better understand the overhead, let us next look at one example scenario. We assume 2000 nodes and $1 \times 1m^2$ grids, and we further assume that each node on average wakes up 75 times during the 90% lifetime and receives 16 replies during each wake up (with a total of 1200 reply packets). According to our simulation traces, these numbers are rather conservative. Given the power specifications in Table 4, the amount of energy consumed in transmitting the aforementioned scheduling related packets would be:

$$(75 + 1200) * (25 * 8/20000) * 0.06 = 0.765 \quad Joules$$

which is less than 2% of the initial energy level. Therefore, we take the viewpoint that the energy overhead of R-Sentry is rather low.

The Impact of Grid Size: The grid is virtual, but its size plays a role in R-Sentry: larger size usually leads to longer lifetime since fewer active nodes are needed to cover all the grid points, which we confirmed through experiments. Specifically, we adopted two grid sizes: $1 \times 1m^2$, referred to as $G1$ and $5 \times 5m^2$, referred to as $G5$. The results are shown in Figure 6(b). We can see that the 90% network lifetime of R-Sentry can be further improved by the system adopting a larger grid size. In fact, a grid size of $5 \times 5m^2$ extends the lifetime by 30%. However, excessively large grid would compromise connectivity since the network would be disconnected due to low density of active nodes. On the other hand, since PEAS does not rely on the concept of grids, its performance is not influenced by the grid size. We would like to point out that the inconsistency between G1 and G5 in the case of PEAS is caused by artifacts of the simulations.

6. Concluding Remarks

Providing continuous, uninterrupted sensor services requires the network to be able to quickly recover from coverage loss due to frequent node failures. That is, if an active node fails, its coverage should be quickly resumed by the redundant nodes, which were sleeping to conserve energy. Earlier node scheduling solutions, such as PEAS [16], adopt completely random schedules among redundant nodes. A random schedule cannot guarantee a redundant node will wake up timely when the active node fails, nor can it guarantee the redundant node that happens to wake up can fully recover the coverage hole.

R-Sentry addresses these issues by grouping redundant nodes into "gangs", which collectively can fully replace an active node, and then by scheduling gangs with fixed intervals. R-Sentry also takes into consideration realistic network situations, such as cases where a redundant node serves multiple active nodes, or cases where redundant nodes may fail before the active node. Through detailed simulations, we show that R-Sentry can provide better resilience against failure while prolonging network life time. As a result, R-Sentry has made a significant step towards building reliable sensor services.

References

[1] A. Cerpa and D. Estrin. ASCENT: Adaptive Self-Configuring Sensor Networks Topologies. In *Proceedings of IEEE INFOCOM'02*, June 2002.

[2] B. Chen, K. Jamieson, H. Balakrishnan, and R. Morris. Span: An Energy-Efficient Coordination Algorithm for Topology Maintenance in Ad Hoc Wireless Networks. In *Proceedings of ACM/IEEE MobiCom 2001*, July 2001.

[3] CrossBow Technology. *Mote User's Manual*. http://www.xbow.com/Support/Support_pdf_files/MPR-MIB_Series_User_Manual_7430-0021-05_A.pdf.

[4] Y. Gao, K. Wu, and F. Li. Analysis on the redundancy of wireless sensor networks. In *Proceedings of the 2nd ACM international conference on Wireless sensor networks and applications*, pages 108 – 114, September 2003.

[5] T. He, S. Krishnamurthy, J. A. Stankovic, T. Abdelzaher, L. Luo, R. Stoleru, T. Yan, L. Gu, J. Hui, and B. Krogh. An Energy-Efficient Surveillance System Using Wireless Sensor Networks. In *Proceedings of the ACM MobiSys 2004*, 2004.

[6] W. R. Heinzelman, A. Chandrakasan, and H. Balakrishnan. Energy-Efficient Communication Protocol for Wireless Microsensor Networks. In *Proceedings of the 33rd Hawaii International Conference on System Science*, 2000.

[7] K. Langendoen and N. Reijers. Distributed localization in wireless sensor networks: a quantitative comparison. *Comput. Networks*, 43(4):499–518, 2003.

[8] Z. Li, W. Trappe, Y. Zhang, and B. Nath. Robust Statistical Methods for Securing Wireless Localization in Sensor Networks. In *Proceedings of the IEEE/ACM IPSN'05*, 2005.

[9] S. Mohan, F. Mueller, D. Whalley, and C. Healy. Timing analysis for sensor network nodes of the atmega processor family. In *Proceedings of the 11th IEEE Real-Time and Embedded Technology and Applications Symposium*, 2005.

[10] D. Tian and N. D. Georganas. A coverage-preserving node scheduling scheme for large wireless sensor networks. In *Proceedings of the 1st ACM international workshop on Wireless sensor networks and applications*, September 2002.

[11] X. Wang, G. Xing, Y. Zhang, C. Lu, R. Pless, and C. Gill. Integrated coverage and connectivity configuration in wireless sensor networks . In *Proceedings of the ACM SenSys'03*, pages 28–39, November 2003.

[12] G. Xing, C. Lu, R. Pless, and J. A. O'Sullivan. Co-Grid: an efficient coverage maintenance protocol for distributed sensor networks. In *Proceedings of IPSN'04*, April 2004.

[13] Y. Xu, J. Heidemann, and D. Estrin. Adaptive energy-conserving routing for multihop ad hoc networks. Research Report 527, USC/Information Sciences Institute, 2000.

[14] Y. Xu, J. Heidemann, and D. Estrin. Geography-informed Energy Conservation for Ad Hoc Routing. In *Proceedings of the ACM/IEEE MobiCom'01*, July 2001.

[15] T. Yan, T. He, and J. A. Stankovic. Differentiated Surveillance Service for Sensor Networks. In *Proceedings of the ACM SenSys'03*, 2003.

[16] F. Ye, G. Zhong, S. Lu, and L. Zhang. PEAS: A Robust Energy Conserving Protocol for Long-lived Sensor Networks. In *Proceedings of ICDCS'03*, May 2003.

[17] W. Ye, J. Heidemann, and D. Estrin. An Energy-Efficient MAC Protocol for Wireless Sensor Networks. In *Proceedings of IEEE INFOCOM'02*, June 2002.

[18] S. Yu, A. Yang, and Y. Zhang. DADA: A 2-Dimensional Adaptive Node Schedule to Provide Smooth Sensor Network Services against Random Failures. In *Proceedings of the Workshop on Information Fusion and Dissemination in Wireless Sensor Networks*, 2005.

[19] Honghai Zhang and Jennifer C. Hou. Maintaining sensing coverage and connectivity in large sensor networks. *Wireless Ad Hoc and Sensor Networks: An International Journal*, 1(1-2), January 2005.

A Fast Rejuvenation Technique for Server Consolidation with Virtual Machines

Kenichi Kourai

Tokyo Institute of Technology
2-12-1 Ookayama, Meguro-ku, Tokyo
152-8552, Japan
kourai@is.titech.ac.jp

Shigeru Chiba

Tokyo Institute of Technology
2-12-1 Ookayama, Meguro-ku, Tokyo
152-8552, Japan
chiba@is.titech.ac.jp

Abstract

As server consolidation using virtual machines (VMs) is carried out, software aging *of virtual machine monitors (VMMs) is becoming critical. Performance degradation or crash failure of a VMM affects all VMs on it. To counteract such software aging, a proactive technique called* software rejuvenation *has been proposed. A typical example of rejuvenation is to reboot a VMM. However, simply rebooting a VMM is undesirable because that needs rebooting operating systems on all VMs. In this paper, we propose a new technique for fast rejuvenation of VMMs called the* warm-VM reboot. *The warm-VM reboot enables efficiently rebooting only a VMM by suspending and resuming VMs without accessing the memory images. To achieve this, we have developed two mechanisms:* on-memory suspend/resume *of VMs and* quick reload *of VMMs. The warm-VM reboot reduces the downtime and prevents the performance degradation due to cache misses after the reboot.*

1. Introduction

The phenomenon that the state of software degrades with time is known as *software aging* [16]. The causes of this degradation are the exhaustion of system resources and data corruption. This often leads to performance degradation of the software or crash failure. Recently, software aging of virtual machine monitors (VMMs) is becoming critical as server consolidation using virtual machines (VMs) is being widely carried out. Many VMs run on top of a VMM in one machine consolidating multiple servers and aging of the VMM directly affects all the VMs.

To counteract such software aging, a proactive technique called *software rejuvenation* has been proposed [16]. Software rejuvenation occasionally stops a running VMM, cleans its internal state, and restarts it. A typical example of rejuvenation is to reboot a VMM. However, operating systems running on the VMs built on top of a VMM also have to be rebooted when the VMM is rejuvenated. This increases the downtime of services provided by the operating systems. It takes long time to reboot many operating systems in parallel when the VMM is rebooted. After the operating systems are rebooted with the VMM, their performance is degraded due to cache misses. The file cache used by the operating systems is lost by the reboot. Such downtime and performance degradation are critical for servers.

In this paper, we propose a new technique for fast rejuvenation of VMMs called the *warm-VM reboot*. The basic idea is that a VMM preserves the memory images of all VMs through the reboot of the VMM and reuses those memory images after the reboot. The warm-VM reboot enables efficiently rebooting only a VMM by using the *on-memory suspend/resume* mechanism of VMs and the *quick reload* mechanism of VMMs. Using the on-memory suspend/resume mechanism, a VMM suspends VMs running on it before it is rebooted. At that time, the memory images of the VMs are preserved on main memory and they are not saved to any persistent storage. The suspended VMs are quickly resumed by directly using the preserved memory images after the reboot. To preserve the memory images during the reboot, the VMM is rebooted using the quick reload mechanism without a hardware reset. The warm-VM reboot can reduce the downtime of operating systems running on VMs and prevent performance degradation due to cache misses because it does not need to reboot operating systems.

To achieve this fast rejuvenation, we have developed *RootHammer* based on Xen [9]. From our experimental results, the warm-VM reboot reduced the downtime due to rebooting the VMM by 83 % at maximum. For comparison, when we simply used the suspend/resume mechanism of the original Xen, the downtime was increased by 173 %. After the warm-VM reboot, the throughput of a web server was not degraded at all. When we did not use the warm-VM reboot, the throughput was degraded by 69 % just after the reboot of the VMM.

The rest of this paper is organized as follows. Section 2 describes the problems of current software rejuvenation of VMMs. Section 3 presents a new technique for fast rejuvenation of VMMs and estimates the downtime reduced by it. Section 4 explains our implementation based on Xen and Section 5 shows our experimental results. Section 6 discusses the advantage of the warm-VM reboot in a cluster environment. Section 7 examines related work and Section 8 concludes the paper.

2. Software Rejuvenation of VMMs

As server consolidation using VMs is widely carried out, *software aging* of VMMs is becoming critical. Recently, multiple server machines are consolidated into one machine using VMs. In such a machine, many VMs are running on top of a VMM. Since a VMM is long-running software, it is affected by software aging more largely than the other components. For example, a VMM may leak its memory by failing to release a part of memory. In Xen [9], the size of the heap memory of the VMM is only 16 MB by default in spite of the size of physical memory. If the VMM leaks its heap memory, it would become out of memory easily. Xen had a bug that caused available heap memory to decrease whenever a VM was rebooted [19] or when some error paths were executed [11]. Out-of-memory errors can lead performance degradation or crash failure of the VMM. Such problems of the VMM directly affect all the VMs.

In addition to the aging of VMMs, that of privileged VMs can also affect the other VMs. Privileged VMs are used in some VM architectures such as Xen and VMware ESX server [26] to help the VMM for VM management and/or I/O processing of all VMs. They run normal operating systems with some modifications. For operating systems, it has been reported that system resources such as kernel memory and swap spaces were exhausted with time [13]. In privileged VMs, memory exhaustion easily occurs because the typical size of the memory allocated to them is not so large. Since privileged VMs do not run large servers, they do not need a large amount of memory. For example, Xen had a bug of memory leaks in its daemon named xenstored running on a privileged VM [15]. If I/O processing in the privileged VM slows down due to out of memory, the performance in the other VMs is also degraded. Since xenstored is not restartable, restoring from such memory leaks needs to reboot the privileged VM. Furthermore, the reboot of the privileged VM causes the VMM to be rebooted because the privileged VM strongly depends on the VMM. For this reason, we consider such privileged VMs as a part of a VMM and we do not count them as normal VMs.

To counteract such software aging, a proactive technique called *software rejuvenation* has been proposed [16].

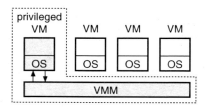

Figure 1. An assumed VM architecture.

Software rejuvenation occasionally stops a running VMM, cleans its internal state, and restarts it. A typical example of rejuvenation is to reboot a VMM. Since the state of long-running software such as VMMs degrades with time under aging conditions, preventive maintenance by software rejuvenation would decrease problems due to aging.

However, when a VMM is rejuvenated, operating systems on the VMs built on top of the VMM also have to be rebooted. Operating systems running on VMs have to be shut down to keep the integrity before the VMM terminates the VMs. Then, after the reboot of the VMM, newly created VMs have to boot the operating systems and restart all services again.

This increases the downtime of services provided by operating systems. First of all, many operating systems are shut down and booted in parallel when the VMM is rebooted. The time for rebooting each operating system is proportional to the number of VMs because shutting down and booting multiple operating systems in parallel cause resource contention among them. Unfortunately, the number of VMs that can run simultaneously is increasing due to processor support of virtualization such as Intel VT [17] and AMD Virtualization [3] and multi-core processors. In addition, recent servers tend to provide heavy-weight services such as the JBoss application server [18] and the time for stopping and restarting services is increasing. Second, shutting down operating systems, rebooting the VMM, and booting operating systems are performed sequentially. The in-between reboot of the VMM increases the service downtime. The reboot of the VMM includes shutting down the VMM, resetting hardware, and booting the VMM. In particular, a hardware reset involves power-on self-test by the BIOS such as a time-consuming check of large amount of main memory and SCSI initialization.

In addition, the performance of operating systems on VMs is degraded after they are rebooted with the VMM. The primary cause is to lose the file cache. An operating system stores file contents in main memory as the file cache when it reads them from storage. An operating system speeds up file accesses by using the file cache on memory. When an operating system is rebooted, main memory is initialized and the file cache managed by the operating system is lost. Therefore, just after the reboot of the operating system, the execution performance of server processes running on top of it is degraded due to frequent cache misses. To fill the file cache after the reboot, an operating system needs to read necessary files from storage. Since modern operating systems use most of free memory as the file cache, it takes long time to fill free memory with the file cache. The size of memory installable to one machine tends to increase due to 64-bit processors and cheaper memory modules. Consequently, more memory is allocated to each VM.

3. Fast Rejuvenation Technique

We claim that only a VMM should be rebooted when only the VMM needs rejuvenation. In other words, rebooting operating systems should be independent of rebooting an underlying VMM. Although an operating system may be rejuvenated occasionally as well as a VMM, the timing does not always the same as that of the rejuvenation of a VMM. If some operating systems do not need to be rejuvenated when the VMM is rejuvenated, rebooting these operating systems is simply wasteful.

3.1. Warm-VM Reboot

To minimize the influences of the rejuvenation of VMMs, we propose a new technique for fast rejuvenation called the *warm-VM reboot*. The basic idea is that a VMM preserves the memory images of all the VMs through the reboot of the VMM and reuses those memory images after the reboot. The warm-VM reboot enables efficiently rebooting only a VMM by using the *on-memory suspend/resume* mechanism for VMs and the *quick reload* mechanism for VMMs. A VMM suspends all VMs using the on-memory suspend mechanism before it is rebooted, reboots itself by the quick reload mechanism, and resumes all VMs using the on-memory resume mechanism after the VMM is rebooted.

The on-memory suspend mechanism simply "freezes" the memory image used by a VM as it is. The memory image is preserved on memory through the reboot of the VMM until the VM is resumed. This mechanism needs neither to save the image to any persistent storage such as disks nor to copy it to non-volatile memory such as flash memory. This is very efficient because the time needed for suspend hardly depends on the size of memory allocated to the VM. Even if the total memory size of all VMs becomes larger, the on-memory suspend mechanism can scale. At the same time, this mechanism saves the execution state of the suspended VM to the memory area that is also preserved through the reboot of the VMM.

On the other hand, the on-memory resume mechanism "unfreezes" the frozen memory image to restore the suspended VM. The frozen memory image is preserved through the reboot of the VMM by using quick reload. This

mechanism also needs neither to read the saved image from persistent storage nor to copy it from non-volatile memory. Since the memory image of the VM is restored completely, performance degradation due to cache misses is prevented even just after the reboot. At the same time, the saved execution state of a VM is also restored. These mechanisms are analogous to ACPI S3 state (Suspend To RAM) [2] in that they can suspend and resume a VM without touching its memory image on main memory.

The quick reload mechanism preserves the memory images of VMs through the reboot of a VMM and furthermore makes the reboot itself faster. Usually, rebooting a VMM needs a hardware reset to reload a VMM instance, but a hardware reset does not guarantee that memory contents are preserved during it. In addition, a hardware reset takes long time as described in the previous section. The quick reload mechanism can bypass a hardware reset by loading a new VMM instance by software and start it by jumping to its entry point. Since the software mechanism can manage memory during the reboot, it is guaranteed that memory contents are preserved. Furthermore, the quick reload mechanism prevents the frozen memory images of VMs from being corrupted when the VMM initializes itself.

Although many VMMs provide suspend/resume mechanisms, they are not suitable to use for rejuvenation of VMMs because they have to use disks as persistent storage to save memory images. These traditional suspend/resume mechanisms are analogous to ACPI S4 state (Suspend To Disk), so-called *hibernation*. These mechanisms need heavy disk accesses and they are too slow. On the other hand, our on-memory suspend/resume mechanism does not need to save the memory images to disks before the reboot of a VMM. Our quick reload mechanism allows the VMM to reuse the memory images on volatile main memory by preserving them during the reboot.

3.2. Downtime Estimation

To estimate the downtime reduced by using the warm-VM reboot, let us consider the usage model of software rejuvenation. Usually the rejuvenation of a VMM (VMM rejuvenation) is used with the rejuvenation of operating systems (OS rejuvenation). In general, the OS rejuvenation is performed more frequently than the VMM rejuvenation. For simplicity, we assume that each operating system is rejuvenated by relying on the time elapsed since the last OS rejuvenation, which is called *time-based rejuvenation* [12]. When the warm-VM reboot is used, the VMM rejuvenation can be performed independently of the OS rejuvenation as shown in Figure 2 (a). This is because the warm-VM reboot does not involve the OS rejuvenation. On the other hand, when a VMM is rejuvenated by a normal reboot, which we call the *cold-VM reboot* in contrast to the warm-VM reboot,

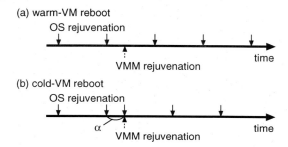

(a) warm-VM reboot

(b) cold-VM reboot

Figure 2. The timing of two kinds of rejuvenation. The rejuvenation of all but one operating system is omitted.

the VMM rejuvenation affects the timing of the OS rejuvenation as shown in Figure 2 (b) because the VMM rejuvenation involves the OS rejuvenation. The OS rejuvenation after the VMM rejuvenation will be performed at fixed intervals again.

When the warm-VM reboot is used, the downtime due to the VMM rejuvenation is caused by suspending all VMs, rebooting the VMM, and resuming all VMs. The increase of the downtime is:

$$d_w(n) = reboot_{vmm}(n) + resume(n)$$

where n is the number of VMs, $reboot_{vmm}(n)$ is the time needed to reboot a VMM when n VMs are suspended and resumed, and $resume(n)$ is the time needed to perform on-memory suspend and resume of n VMs in parallel.

On the other hand, when the cold-VM reboot is used, the downtime due to the VMM rejuvenation is caused by shutting down all operating systems, resetting hardware, rebooting a VMM, and booting all operating systems. The increase of the downtime is:

$$d_c(n) = reset_{hw} + reboot_{vmm}(0) + reboot_{os}(n) - \\ reboot_{os}(1) \times \alpha$$

where $reset_{hw}$ is the time needed for a hardware reset, $reboot_{os}(n)$ is the time needed to shut down and boot n operating systems in parallel, and α is a ratio of the time elapsed until the VMM rejuvenation since the last OS rejuvenation to an interval between the OS rejuvenation ($0 < \alpha \le 1$). Since the OS rejuvenation is rescheduled after the VMM rejuvenation, the number of the OS rejuvenation is decreased by α in total although extra OS rejuvenation is added by the VMM rejuvenation.

The downtime reduced by using the warm-VM reboot is calculated by $d_c(n) - d_w(n)$:

$$r(n) = reset_{hw} + reboot_{vmm}(0) - reboot_{vmm}(n) + \\ reboot_{os}(n) - reboot_{os}(1) \times \alpha - resume(n)$$

4. Implementation

To achieve the warm-VM reboot, we have developed *RootHammer* based on Xen 3.0.0. Like Xen, a VM is called a *domain*. In particular, the privileged VM that manages VMs and handles I/O is called *domain 0* and the other VMs are called *domain Us*.

4.1. Memory Management of the VMM

The VMM distinguishes machine memory and pseudo-physical memory to virtualize memory resource. Machine memory is physical memory installed in the machine and consists of a set of machine page frames. For each machine page frame, a machine frame number (MFN) is consecutively numbered from 0. Pseudo-physical memory is the memory allocated to domains and gives the illusion of contiguous physical memory to domains. For each physical page frame in each domain, a physical frame number (PFN) is consecutively numbered from 0.

The VMM creates the *P2M-mapping table* to enable domains to reuse its memory even after the reboot. The P2M-mapping table is a table that records mapping from PFN to MFN for each domain. The size of our P2M-mapping table is 2 MB for 1 GB of pseudo-physical memory. A new entry is added to this table when a new machine page frame is allocated to a domain while an existing entry is removed when a machine page frame is deallocated. These entries are preserved after domains are suspended. Even when the total size of pseudo-physical memory is larger than that of machine memory due to using a ballooning technique [27], this table can maintain the mapping properly.

4.2. On-memory Suspend/Resume Mechanism

When the operating system in domain 0 is shut down, the VMM suspends all domain Us as in Figure 3. To suspend domain Us, the VMM sends a suspend event to each domain U. In the original Xen, domain 0 sends the event to each domain U. One advantage of suspending by the VMM is that suspending domain Us can be delayed until after the operating system in domain 0 is shut down. The original suspend by domain 0 has to be performed while domain 0 is shut down. This delay reduces the downtime of services running in a domain U. When a domain U receives the suspend event, the operating system kernel in the domain U executes its suspend handler. In the handler, the kernel detaches all devices. We used the handler implemented in the Linux kernel modified for Xen.

After the operating system in a domain U executes the suspend handler, it issues the suspend hypercall to the VMM, which is like a system call to the operating system. In the hypercall, the VMM freezes the memory image of

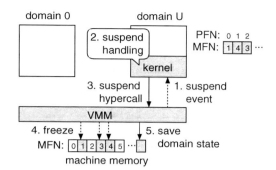

Figure 3. On-memory suspend of a domain U.

the domain on memory by reserving it. The VMM does not release the memory pages allocated to the domain but it maintains them using the P2M-mapping table. This does not cause out-of-memory errors because the VMM is re-booted just after it suspends all domain Us. Next, the VMM saves the execution state of the domain to the memory pages that is preserved during the reboot of the VMM. The exe-cution state of a domain includes execution context such as CPU registers and shared information such as the status of event channels. In addition, the VMM saves the configu-ration of the domain, such as devices. The memory space needed for saving those is 16 KB.

After the VMM finishes suspending all domain Us, the VMM is rebooted without losing the memory images of do-main Us by using the quick reload mechanism, which is described in the next section. Then, after domain 0 is re-booted, it resumes all domain Us. First, domain 0 creates a new domain U, allocates the memory pages recorded in the P2M-mapping table to the domain U, and restores its mem-ory image. Next, the VMM restores the state of the domain U from the saved state. The operating system kernel in the domain U executes the resume handler to re-establish the communication channels to the VMM and to attach the de-vices that were detached on suspend. Finally, the execution of the kernel is restarted.

4.3. Quick Reload Mechanism

To preserve the memory images of domain Us during the reboot of a VMM, we have implemented the quick reload mechanism based on the kexec mechanism [21] provided in the Linux kernel. The kexec mechanism enables a new ker-nel to be started without a hardware reset. Like kexec, the quick reload mechanism enables a new VMM to be started without a hardware reset. To load a new VMM instance into the current VMM, we have implemented the xexec system call in the Linux kernel for domain 0 and the xexec hyper-call in the VMM.

When the xexec system call is issued in domain 0, the kernel issues the xexec hypercall to the VMM. This hyper-call loads a new executable image consisting of a VMM, a kernel for domain 0, and an initial RAM disk for domain 0 into memory. When the VMM is rebooted, the quick reload mechanism first passes the control to the CPU used at the boot time. Then, it copies the executable loaded by the xexec hypercall to the address where the executable im-age is loaded at normal boot time. Finally, the mechanism transfers the control to the new VMM.

When the new VMM is rebooted and initialized, it first reserves the memory for the P2M-mapping table. Based on the table, the VMM reserves the memory pages that have been allocated to domain Us. Next, the VMM reserves the memory pages where the execution state of domains is saved. The latest Xen 3.0.4 also supports the kexec facility for its VMM, but it does not have any support to preserve the memory images of domain Us while a new VMM is ini-tialized.

5. Experiments

We performed experiments to show that our technique for fast rejuvenation is effective. For a server machine, we used a PC with two Dual-Core Opteron processors Model 280, 12 GB of PC3200 DDR SDRAM memory, a 36.7 GB of 15,000 rpm SCSI disk (Ultra 320), and gigabit Ethernet NICs. We used the RootHammer VMM and, for compari-son, the original VMM of Xen 3.0.0. The operating systems running on top of the VMM were Linux 2.6.12 modified for Xen. One physical partition of the disk was used for a vir-tual disk of one VM. The size of the memory allocated to domain 0 was 512 MB. For a client machine, we used a PC with dual Xeon 3.06 GHz processors, 2 GB of memory, and gigabit Ethernet NICs. The operating system was Linux 2.6.8.

5.1. Performance of On-memory Suspend/Resume

We measured the time needed for tasks before and af-ter the reboot of the VMM: suspend or shutdown, and re-sume or boot. We ran a ssh server in each VM as a ser-vice provided to the outside. We performed this experi-ment for (1) our on-memory suspend/resume, (2) Xen's sus-pend/resume, which uses a disk to save the memory images of VMs, and (3) simple shutdown and boot.

First, we changed the size of memory allocated to a sin-gle VM from 1 to 11 GB and measured the time needed for pre- and post-reboot tasks. Figure 4 shows the results. Xen's suspend/resume depended on the memory size of a VM because this method must write the whole memory im-age of a VM to a disk and read it from the disk. On the other hand, our on-memory suspend/resume hardly depended on

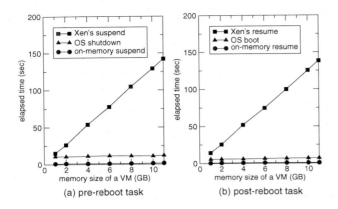

(a) pre-reboot task   (b) post-reboot task

Figure 4. The time for pre- and post-reboot tasks when the memory size of a VM is changed.

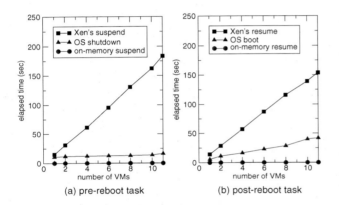

(a) pre-reboot task   (b) post-reboot task

Figure 5. The time for pre- and post-reboot tasks when the number of VMs is changed.

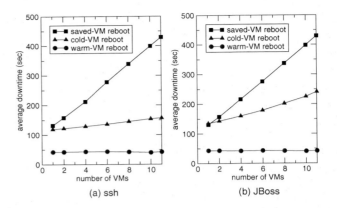

(a) ssh   (b) JBoss

Figure 6. The downtime of ssh and JBoss when the number of VMs is changed.

the memory size because this method does not touch the memory image of a VM. When the memory size was 11 GB, it took 0.08 seconds for suspend and 0.9 second for resume. These are only 0.06 % and 0.7 % of Xen's suspend and resume, respectively.

Next, we measured the time needed for pre- and post-reboot tasks when multiple VMs were running in parallel. We fixed the size of memory allocated to each VM to 1 GB and changed the number of VMs from 1 to 11. Domain 0 is not included in the number. Figure 5 shows the results. All the three methods depended on the number of VMs. When the number of VMs was 11, on-memory suspend/resume needed only 0.04 seconds for suspend and 4.2 seconds for resume. These were 0.02 % and 2.7 % of Xen's suspend and resume, respectively. The result also shows that the time for the boot largely increases as the number of VMs increases.

5.2. Effect of Quick Reload

To examine how fast the VMM is rebooted by using the quick reload mechanism, we measured the time needed for rebooting the VMM. We recorded the time when the execution of a shutdown script completed and when the reboot of the VMM completed. The time between them was 11 seconds when we used quick reload whereas it was 59 seconds when we used a hardware reset. Thus, the quick reload mechanism speeded up the reboot of the VMM by 48 seconds.

5.3. Downtime of Networked Services

We measured the downtime of networked services when we rejuvenated the VMM. We rebooted the VMM while we repeated sending packets from a client host to the VMs in a server host. We measured the time from when a networked service in each VM was down and until it was up again after the VMM was rebooted. We performed this experiment for (1) the warm-VM reboot, (2) the reboot using Xen's suspend/resume (*saved-VM reboot*), and (3) the reboot by shutdown/boot (*cold-VM reboot*). We fixed the size of memory allocated to each VM to 1 GB and changed the number of VMs from 1 to 11.

First, we ran only a ssh server in each VM and measured its downtime during the reboot of the VMM. Figure 6 (a) shows the downtime. The downtime by the saved-VM reboot highly depended on the number of VMs. When the number was 11, the downtime was 429 seconds in average. At the same number of VMs, the downtime by the warm-VM reboot was 42 seconds and only 9.8 % of the saved-VM reboot. In addition, the downtime by the warm-VM reboot hardly depended on the number of VMs. On the other hand, the downtime by the cold-VM reboot was 157 seconds when the number of VMs was 11. This was 3.7 times longer than the warm-VM reboot.

After we rebooted the VMM using the warm-VM reboot or the saved-VM reboot, we could continue the session of ssh thanks to TCP retransmission, even if a timeout was set in the ssh server. However, if a timeout was set to 60 seconds in the ssh client, the session was timed out during the saved-VM reboot. From this point of view, the downtime for one reboot should be short enough. When we used the cold-VM reboot, we could not continue the session because the ssh server was shut down.

Next, we ran a JBoss application server [18] and measured its downtime during the reboot of a VMM. JBoss is a large server and it takes more time to start than a ssh server. We used the default configuration of JBoss. Figure 6 (b) shows the downtime. The downtime by the warm-VM reboot and the saved-VM reboot was almost the same as that of a ssh server because these reboot mechanisms resumed VMs and did not need to restart the JBoss server. On the other hand, the downtime by the cold-VM reboot was larger than that of a ssh server because the cold-VM reboot needed to restart the JBoss server. When the number was 11, the downtime was 241 seconds. This was 1.5 times longer than that of a ssh server. This means that the cold-VM reboot increases the service downtime according to running services.

Let us consider the availability of the JBoss server when the number of VMs is 11. As an example, we assume that the OS rejuvenation is performed every week and the VMM rejuvenation is performed once per four weeks. According to our experiment, the downtime due to the OS rejuvenation was 33.6 seconds. For the cold-VM reboot, we assume that the expected value of α in Section 3.2 is 0.5. Under these assumptions, the availability is 99.993 %, 99.985 %, and 99.977 % for the warm-VM reboot, the cold-VM reboot, and the saved-VM reboot, respectively. The warm-VM reboot achieves four 9s although the others achieve three 9s. This improvement of availability is important for critical servers.

5.4. Downtime Analysis

To examine which factors reduce downtime in the warm-VM reboot, we measured the time needed for each operation when we rebooted the VMM. At the same time, we measured the throughput of a web server running on a VM. We repeated sending requests from a client host to the Apache web server [4] running on a VM in a server host by using the httperf benchmark tool [20]. We created 11 VMs and allocated 1 GB of memory to each VM. We rebooted the VMM and recorded the changes of the average throughput of 50 requests. We performed this experiment for the warm-VM reboot and the cold-VM reboot. Figure 7 shows the results. We executed the reboot command in domain 0 at time 20 seconds in this figure. We superimposed the time

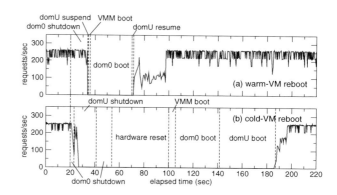

Figure 7. The breakdown of the downtime due to the VMM rejuvenation.

needed for each operation during the reboot onto Figure 7.

As shown in the previous section, the on-memory suspend/resume mechanism provided by the warm-VM reboot reduced the downtime largely. The total time for on-memory suspend/resume was 4 seconds, but that for shutdown and boot in the cold-VM reboot was 63 seconds. In addition, the warm-VM reboot reduced the time for a hardware reset from 43 to 0 second. Also, the fact that the warm-VM reboot can continue to run a web server until just before the VMM is rebooted was effective for reducing downtime. A web server was stopped at time 34 seconds in the warm-VM reboot while it was stopped at time 27 seconds in the cold-VM reboot. This reduced downtime by 7 seconds. For the warm-VM reboot, the VMM is responsible for suspending VMs and it can do that task after domain 0 is shut down.

In both cases, the throughput was restored after the reboot of the VMM. The throughput in the cold-VM reboot was degraded during 8 seconds. This was due to misses of the file cache. We examine this performance degradation in detail in the next section. The throughput in the warm-VM reboot was also degraded during 25 seconds after the reboot. This is not due to cache misses but an implementation problem of Xen. When Xen created new VMs simultaneously, the network performance was degraded for a while.

5.5. Performance Degradation

To examine performance degradation due to cache misses, we measured the throughput of operations with file accesses in a VM before and after the reboot of a VMM. To examine the effect of the file cache, we measured the throughput of the first- and second-time accesses. We allocated 11 GB of memory to one VM. First, we measured the time needed to read a file of 512 MB. In this experiment, all the file blocks were cached on memory. We performed this experiment for the warm-VM reboot and the cold-VM reboot. Figure 8 (a) shows the result. When we used the

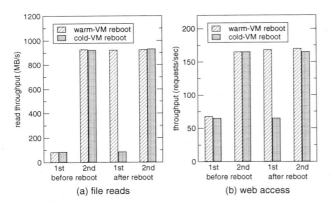

(a) file reads

(b) web access

Figure 8. The throughput of file reads and web accesses before and after the reboot.

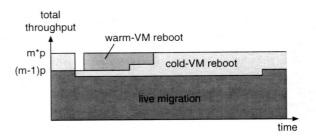

Figure 9. The total throughput in a cluster environment. m is the number of hosts and p is the throughput of each host.

cold-VM reboot, the throughput just after the reboot was degraded by 91 %, compared with that just before the reboot. On the other hand, when we used the warm-VM reboot, the throughput just after the reboot was not degraded. This improvement was achieved by no miss in the file cache even when a file was accessed at the first time after the reboot.

Next, we measured the throughput of a web server before and after the reboot of a VMM. The Apache web server served 10,000 files of 512 KB, all of which were cached on memory. In this experiment, 10 httperf processes in a client host sent requests to the server in parallel. All files were requested only once. Figure 8 (b) shows the results. When we used the warm-VM reboot, the performance just after the reboot was not degraded, compared with that just before the reboot. When we used the cold-VM reboot, the throughput just after the reboot was degraded by 69 %.

5.6. Applying to Our Model

From our experimental results when we ran 11 VMs, we can get the functions used in our model in Section 3.2:

$$reboot_{vmm}(n) = -0.55n + 43$$
$$resume(n) = 0.43n - 0.07$$
$$reboot_{os}(n) = 3.8n + 13$$
$$boot(n) = 3.4n + 2.8$$
$$reset_{hw} = 47$$

Using these functions, we can get the function of the downtime reduced by using the warm-VM reboot:

$$r(n) = 3.9n + 60 - 17\alpha$$

Since $r(n)$ is always positive under $\alpha \leq 1$, the warm-VM reboot can always reduce the downtime in our configuration.

6. Cluster Environment

Software rejuvenation is naturally fit with a cluster environment as described in the literature [7, 25]. In a cluster environment, multiple hosts provide the same service and a load balancer dispatches requests to one of these hosts. Even if some of the hosts are rebooted for the rejuvenation of the VMM, the service downtime is zero. However, the total throughput of the service is degraded while some hosts are rebooted. The warm-VM reboot can mitigate the performance degradation by reducing the downtime of rebooted hosts.

Migration of VMs can be also used in a cluster environment to reduce the total cost. Unlike the warm-VM reboot, live migration [8] in Xen and VMotion in VMware [26] achieve negligible service downtime by using two hosts when a VMM is rejuvenated. Before the VMM is rebooted, it transfers the memory images of all VMs running on it to a destination host without stopping the VMs. After that, the VMM repeats transferring the changes in the memory images from the previous transmission until the changes become small. Finally, the VMM stops the VMs and transfers the changes and the execution state of the VMs. If we use live migration in a cluster environment, that destination host for migration can be shared among the remaining hosts.

Let us consider a cluster environment that consists of m hosts to estimate the total throughput of the cluster. When we let p be the throughput of each host, the total throughput is $m \cdot p$ when all hosts are running. Figure 9 illustrates the changes of the total throughput with time, based on our experimental results. During the rejuvenation of a VMM in one host, the total throughput is decreased to $(m - 1)p$ because the rejuvenated host cannot provide any services. When we use the warm-VM reboot, the degradation of the total throughput lasts only for a short period. The period is the same as the downtime in the rejuvenated host and it was 42 seconds in our experimental environment. The total throughput is restored to $m \cdot p$ soon after the rejuvenation.

252

However, when we use the cold-VM reboot, which is a normal reboot of a VMM, the degradation of the total throughput lasts for a longer period. In our experimental environment, the period was 241 seconds when we created 11 VMs and ran JBoss. In addition, the total throughput is degraded to $(m - \delta)p$ $(0 \leq \delta \leq 1)$ for a while after the rejuvenation due to cache misses. In our experiment of Section 5.5, δ was 0.69.

On the other hand, when we use live migration, the total throughput is $(m - 1)p$ even when no hosts are being migrated because one host is reserved as a destination host for migration. This is $\frac{m-1}{m}$ of the total throughput in a cluster environment where migration is not used. This is critical if m is not large enough. While one host performs live migration, the total throughput is $(m - 1.12)p$, which is led from the report that the degradation of the Apache web server was 12 % during live migration [8]. This degradation of the total throughput is estimated to last for 17 minutes when we run 11 VMs, each of which has 1 GB of memory. This is calculated from the report that the time needed for migration was 72 seconds when only one VM with 800 MB of memory was run [8]. This period of performance degradation is much longer than those in the warm-VM reboot and the cold-VM reboot. Although these reported values are not measured in our experimental environment, the trend would not be changed.

According to these analyses, the warm-VM reboot is more useful in a cluster environment than live migration. It can reduce performance degradation by reducing the downtime of rejuvenated hosts. On the other hand, for services that cannot be replicated to multiple hosts, live migration is still useful. It can reduce downtime by using alternative host as a spare.

7. Related Work

Microreboot [6] enables rebooting fine-grained application components to recover from software failure. If rebooting a fine-grained component cannot solve problems, microreboot recursively attempts to reboot a coarser-grained component including that fine-grained component. If rebooting a finer-grained component can solve problems, the downtime of the application including that component can be reduced. Microreboot is a reactive technique, but proactively using it allows micro-rejuvenation. Likewise, microkernel operating systems [1] allow rebooting only its subsystems implemented as user processes. Nooks [24] enables restarting only device drivers in the operating system. Thus, microreboot and other previous proposals are fast reboot techniques for subcomponents. On the other hand, the warm-VM reboot is a fast reboot technique for a parent component while the state of subcomponents is preserved during the reboot.

In this paper, we have developed mechanisms to rejuvenate only a parent component when the parent component is a VMM and the subcomponents are VMs. Checkpointing and restart [23] of processes can be used to rejuvenate only an operating system. In this case, the parent component is an operating system and the subcomponents are its processes. This mechanism saves the state of processes to a disk before the reboot of the operating system and restores the state from the disk after the reboot. This is similar to suspend and resume of VMs, but suspending and resuming VMs are more challenging because they have to deal with a large amount of memory. As we showed in our experiments, simply saving and restoring the memory images of VMs to and from a disk are not realistic. The warm-VM reboot is a novel technique that hardly depends on the memory size by preserving the memory images.

To speed up suspend and resume using slow disks, several techniques are used. On suspend, VMware [26] incrementally saves only the modification of the memory image of a VM to a disk. This can reduce accesses to a slow disk although disk accesses on resume are not reduced. Windows XP saves compressed memory image to a disk on hibernation (Suspend To Disk). This can reduce disk accesses not only on hibernation but also on resume. These techniques are similar to incremental checkpointing [10] and fast compression of checkpoints [22]. On the other hand, the warm-VM reboot does not need any disk accesses.

Instead of using slow hard disks for suspend and resume, it is possible to use faster non-volatile RAM disks such as i-RAM [14]. Since most of the time for suspend and resume is spent to access slow disks, RAM disks can speed up the access. However, such non-volatile RAM disks are much more expensive than hard disks. Moreover, it takes time to copy the memory images from main memory to RAM disks on suspend and copy them from RAM disks to main memory on resume. The warm-VM reboot needs neither such a special device nor extra memory copy.

Recovery Box [5] preserves only the state of an operating system and applications on non-volatile memory and restores them quickly after the operating system is rebooted. Recovery Box restores the partial state of a machine lost by a reboot while the warm-VM reboot restores the whole state of VMs lost by a reboot. In addition, Recovery Box speeds up a reboot by reusing the kernel text segment left on memory. This is different from our quick reload mechanism in that Recovery Box needs hardware support to preserve memory contents during a reboot.

To mitigate software aging of domain 0, Xen provides driver domains, which are domain Us that enable running device drivers. Device drivers are one of the most error-prone components. In a normal configuration of Xen, device drivers are run in domain 0 and the rejuvenation of device drivers needs to reboot domain 0 and the VMM. Driver domains enable localizing the errors of device drivers in domain Us and rebooting the domains without rebooting the VMM. Thus, using driver domains reduces the frequency of the rejuvenation of the VMM. However, when the VMM is rebooted, driver domains as well as domain 0 are rebooted because driver domains cannot be suspended. Therefore, the existence of driver domains increases the downtime.

8 Conclusion

In this paper, we proposed a new technique for fast rejuvenation of VMMs called the warm-VM reboot. This technique enables only a VMM to be rebooted by using the on-memory suspend/resume mechanism and the quick reload mechanism. The on-memory suspend/resume mechanism performs suspend and resume of VMs without accessing the memory images. The quick reload mechanism preserves the memory images during the reboot of a VMM. The warm-VM reboot can reduce the downtime and prevent the performance degradation just after the reboot. We have implemented this technique based on Xen and performed several experiments to show the effectiveness. The warm-VM reboot reduced the downtime by 83 % at maximum and kept the same throughput after the reboot.

One of our future directions is to empirically evaluate the reduction of performance degradation by using the warm-VM reboot in a cluster environment. Another direction is to enable privileged VMs to be rebooted without the reboot of the VMM and to be suspended.

References

[1] M. Accetta, R. Baron, W. Bolosky, D. Golub, R. Rashid, A. Tevanian, and M. Young. Mach: A New Kernel Foundation for UNIX Development. In *Proceedings of the USENIX 1986 Summer Conference*, pages 93–112, 1986.

[2] Advanced Configuration and Power Interface Specification. http://www.acpi.info/.

[3] AMD. *AMD64 Virtualization Codenamed "Pacifica" Technology: Secure Virtual Machine Architecture Reference Manual*, 2005.

[4] Apache Software Foundation. Apache HTTP Server Project. http://httpd.apache.org/.

[5] M. Baker and M. Sullivan. The Recovery Box: Using Fast Recovery to Provide High Availability in the UNIX Environment. In *Proceedings of the Summer USENIX Conference*, pages 31–44, 1992.

[6] G. Candea, S. Kawamoto, Y. Fujiki, G. Friedman, and A. Fox. Microreboot – A Technique for Cheap Recovery. In *Proceedings of the 6th Symposium on Operating Systems Design and Implementation*, pages 31–44, 2004.

[7] V. Castelli, R. Harper, P. Heidelberger, S. Hunter, K. Trivedi, K. Vaidyanathan, and W. Zeggert. Proactive Management of Software Aging. *IBM Journal of Research & Development*, 45(2):311–332, 2001.

[8] C. Clark, K. Fraser, S. Hand, J. Hansen, E. Jul, C. Limpach, I. Pratt, and A. Warfield. Live Migration of Virtual Machines. In *Proceedings of the 2nd Symposium on Networked Systems Design and Implementation*, pages 1–11, 2005.

[9] B. Dragovic, K. Fraser, S. Hand, T. Harris, A. Ho, I. Pratt, A. Warfield, P. Barham, and R. Neugebauer. Xen and the Art of Virtualization. In *Proceedings of the Symposium on Operating Systems Principles*, pages 164–177, 2003.

[10] S. Feldman and C. Brown. IGOR: A System for Program Debugging via Reversible Execution. In *Proceedings of the Workshop on Parallel and Distributed Debugging*, pages 112–123, 1989.

[11] K. Fraser. Xen changeset 11752. Xen Mercurial repositories.

[12] S. Garg, Y. Huang, C. Kintala, and K. Trivedi. Time and Load Based Software Rejuvenation: Policy, Evaluation and Optimality. In *Proceedings of the 1st Fault Tolerance Symposium*, pages 22–25, 1995.

[13] S. Garg, A. Moorsel, K. Vaidyanathan, and K. Trivedi. A Methodology for Detection and Estimation of Software Aging. In *Proceedings of the 9th International Symposium on Software Reliability Engineering*, pages 283–292, 1998.

[14] GIGABYTE Technology. i-RAM. http://www.gigabyte.com.tw/.

[15] V. Hanquez. Xen changeset 8640. Xen Mercurial repositories.

[16] Y. Huang, C. Kintala, N. Kolettis, and N. Fulton. Software Rejuvenation: Analysis, Module and Applications. In *Proceedings of the 25th International Symposium on Fault-Tolerant Computing*, pages 381–391, 1995.

[17] Intel Corporation. *Intel Virtualization Technology Specification for the IA-32 Intel Architecture*, 2005.

[18] JBoss Group. JBoss Application Server. http://www.jboss.com/.

[19] M. Kanno. Xen changeset 9392. Xen Mercurial repositories.

[20] D. Mosberger and T. Jin. httperf: A Tool for Measuring Web Server Performance. *Performance Evaluation Review*, 26(3):31–37, 1998.

[21] A. Pfiffer. Reducing System Reboot Time with kexec. http://www.osdl.org/.

[22] J. Plank, J. Xu, and R. Netzer. Compressed Differences: An Algorithm for Fast Incremental Checkpointing. Technical Report CS–95–302, University of Tennessee, 1995.

[23] B. Randell. System Structure for Software Fault Tolerance. *IEEE Transactions on Software Engineering*, SE-1(2):220–232, 1975.

[24] M. Swift, B. Bershad, and H. Levy. Improving the Reliability of Commodity Operating Systems. In *Proceedings of the 19th Symposium on Operating Systems Principles*, pages 207–222, 2003.

[25] K. Vaidyanathan, R. Harper, S. Hunter, and K. Trivedi. Analysis and Implementation of Software Rejuvenation in Cluster Systems. In *Proceedings of the 2001 ACM SIGMETRICS International Conference on Measurement and Modeling of Computer Systems*, pages 62–71, 2001.

[26] VMware Inc. VMware. http://www.vmware.com/.

[27] C. Waldspurger. Memory Resource Management in VMware ESX Server. In *Proceedings of the 5th Symposium on Operating Systems Design and Implementation*, pages 181–194, 2002.

Session 5A:
Soft Errors:
Analysis and Protection

A Cost-effective Dependable Microcontroller Architecture with Instruction-level Rollback for Soft Error Recovery

Teruaki Sakata*, Teppei Hirotsu*, Hiromichi Yamada*, Takeshi Kataoka†

*Hitachi Research Laboratory, Hitachi Ltd.
†Standard Product Business Group, Renesas Technology Corp.
E-mail: {teruaki.sakata.ac, teppei.hirotsu.nm, hiromichi.yamada.pc}@hitachi.com

Abstract

A cost-effective, dependable microcontroller architecture has been developed. To detect soft errors, we developed an electronic design automation (EDA) tool that generates optimized soft error-detecting logic circuits for flip-flops. After a soft error is detected, the error detection signal goes to a developed rollback control module (RCM), which resets the CPU and restores the CPU's register file from the backup register file using a rollback program routine. After the routine, the CPU restarts from the instruction executed before the soft error occurred. In addition, there is a developed error reset module (ERM) that can restore the RCM from soft errors. We also developed an error correction module (ECM) that corrects ECC errors in RAM after error detection with no delay overheads. Testing on a 32-bit RISC microcontroller and EEMBC benchmarks showed that the area overhead was under 59% and frequency overhead was under 9%. In a soft error injection simulation, the MTBF of random logic circuits, and the MTBF of RAM were 30 and 1.34 times longer, respectively, than those of the original microcontroller.

1. Introduction

Future automotive electronic control systems, X-by-Wire systems, are now being developed [1][2], and high-level automatic controls, such as crash prevention auto-steering, will be implemented into these systems. X-by-Wire requires microcontrollers that perform better than devices currently used in anti-lock brake, electric power steering, and other systems. The microcontroller should be faster and the semiconductor feature sizes should be smaller.

However, since X-by-Wire is a safety critical system, highly dependable and fault tolerant architectures must be developed because a failure of the electronic system could cause serious accidents. Microcontrollers used in X-by-

Wire systems must be very reliable and urgently require improved failure detection and recovery architectures. Failures in microcontrollers can be categorized as hard errors or soft errors. Hard errors are permanent errors, such as wire or connection breakage caused by electromigration. Soft errors, which are random transient errors, have recently been attracting more attention because they are the main cause of failures in microcontrollers [3]. The causes of soft errors in microcontrollers include reversal of a memory element's bit data due to factors such as alpha rays in a package, neutron strikes, and noise from the surrounding environment. As semiconductor feature sizes and supply voltages have decreased, soft error rate (SER) has increased [4]. Soft errors occur both in the microcontroller's memory elements, such as RAM and flip-flop (F/F), and in combinational logic circuits. The former is called a single event upset (SEU), and the latter is called a single event transient (SET) [5]. SET occurs at the rise of the clock edge, so SEU is thought to be predominant in a wide range of embedded microcontrollers, from dozens to several hundreds of MHz.

The popular approach to highly dependable large-scale integration is module redundancy and comparison of output signals. However, there are many restrictions, such as package size, cost, and power consumption, for microcontrollers used in automobiles. Therefore the increased area required for the module redundancy approach is undesirable. Also, because error correcting code (ECC) logic circuits for memory modules have a large frequency overhead, it is difficult for high-performance X-by-Wire systems to implement ECC RAM architecture.

We have developed a cost-effective microcontroller architecture for soft error recovery that can be used in embedded systems that require low cost and high performance.

In the next Section, we explain our solutions to various microcontroller design issues. Our dependable microcontroller architecture is described in detail in Section 3, the results of evaluations of our architecture are presented in Section 4, related work is discussed in Section 5, and the paper is concluded in Section 6.

2. Design issues and solutions

Our target is a one-chip microcontroller with CPU, RAM, and random logic circuits. Our purpose is to realize low-overhead, dependable, low SER microcontroller architecture. We used microcontrollers with ECC RAM which have the problems listed below:

1. Soft errors occurring in random logic circuits cannot be detected.

2. If a soft error is detected, there is no means of recovering from it.

3. The ECC timing critical path incurs a large frequency overhead.

To solve these problems, we first focused on detecting the soft errors that occur in the F/Fs of the random logic circuits. Newly generated detecting logic circuits detect data reverses in F/Fs.

Second, we developed a rollback control module (RCM). After a soft error is detected, the RCM resets the CPU, and the rollback program restores the CPU to its pre-error status. The CPU then restarts from the instruction that was executed before the soft error occurred. If soft errors occur in the RCM, the rollback process will not run correctly. Therefore, we also developed an error reset module (ERM) that can restore the RCM and other modules from soft errors.

Third, we changed the ECC architecture so that the ECC critical path is branched and the CPU reads the uncorrected data directly from the RAM, eliminating ECC delay overheads. If an ECC error is detected, the developed error correction module (ECM) cancels CPU read access and writes back correct data at the next cycle. After the ECC error has been corrected, the CPU restarts from the instruction at the point when the ECC error was detected.

Details of these developed architectures are described in the next Section.

3. Features of dependable microcontroller architecture

3.1. Automatic generation of soft error-detecting logic circuits

We implemented an electronic design automation (EDA) tool that generates soft error-detecting logic circuits for F/Fs in a microcontroller with low overheads. The first feature is selection of the optimal soft error-detecting logic circuits. For example, in the random logic circuit in the upper left of Figure 1, the target for detecting soft errors is the 32-bit "FFa". One possible soft error detection approach is parity,

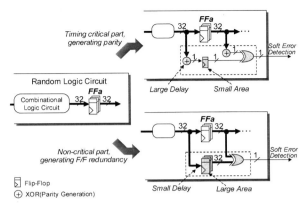

(a) Selection of soft error detecting logic circuits

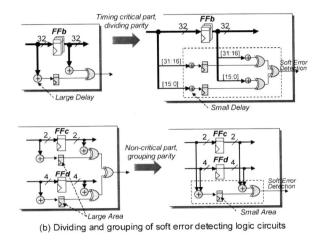

(b) Dividing and grouping of soft error detecting logic circuits

Figure 1. Generaion of soft error-detecting logic circuits

shown in the upper right of Figure 1(a). Area overhead will be low, but the delay overhead as a consequence of generating a parity bit may cause a timing violation. Meanwhile, F/F redundancy, in the lower right of Figure 1(a) will require a larger area than parities, but the delay overhead will be small. The tool therefore selects the optimal soft error-detecting logic circuits for F/Fs in accordance with timing information.

The second feature is optimization of generated circuits by dividing or grouping F/Fs. For instance, there is the random logic circuit generated parity shown in the upper left of Figure 1(b). If the delay overhead of the 32-bit parity is too large, this tool divides the data signals of "FFb" into two 16-bit data signals and generates two parities instead of one 32-bit parity. This division process decreases the delay overhead of parity generation. The lower left diagram in Figure 1(b) shows that this tool groups 2-bit and 4-bit F/Fs synchronized with the same clock signal and generates one parity. This effectively reduces the area overhead of the

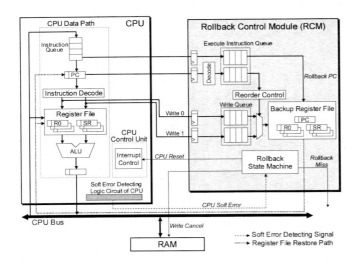

Figure 2. Rollback control module (RCM) for CPU

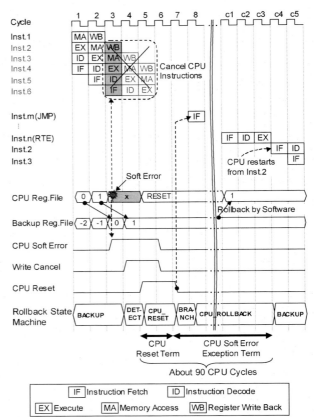

Figure 3. Rollback control flow in CPU

generated soft error-detecting logic circuits. In this way, the tool automatically optimizes the area and delay overheads of the generated detecting logic circuits.

This tool was applied to hierarchical designed random logic circuits by a bottom-up process in this study, and it was found that the generation time is faster than that reported in our previous paper [6].

3.2. Instruction-level rollback architecture for random logic circuits

3.2.1. Soft error recovery of CPU

We developed a rollback control module (RCM) to reset the CPU and restore its register file. In Figure 2, a pipelined RISC CPU executes instructions as follows: the CPU reads instructions from RAM and inserts the instruction queue; the CPU decodes the instructions and writes operation data to the register file; the operation data are executed by the ALU; the CPU executes RAM access and register write-back. The RCM has a backup register file that stores the latched data of the CPU's register file through the write queue. The reorder control block in the RCM receives the in-order information of issued instructions from the execute instruction queue and selects the write data to be stored to the backup register file. When the RCM receives a CPU soft error signal, the RCM issues a CPU reset signal and a RAM write cancel signal. Soft errors occurring in the CPU are detected by soft error-detecting logic circuits that are generated by the tool explained in Section 3.1. The rollback sequence is implemented as an exception processing of the CPU, and the rollback interruption is given the highest priority. The rollback miss signal is used in case the rollback control does not work.

Figure 3 shows the rollback sequence for a five-state pipelined CPU. CPU instructions are executed from Inst.1. In normal execution, the rollback state machine stays in a BACKUP state that stores the delayed data of the CPU Reg.File. The numbers in the CPU Reg.File and Backup Reg.File express the instruction numbers at the top of Figure 3. A soft error occurs in a F/F of the CPU in cycle 3, the error is detected at that time, and a CPU soft error signal is issued. In the next cycle, 4, the rollback state machine changes the DETECT state, and the writing process to RAM is canceled. In cycle 5, the CPU is reset and the soft error that occurred in cycle 3 is cleared. After the reset process, the BRANCH state of the rollback state machine makes the CPU branch to the soft error exception routine by executing Inst.m. The rollback state machine stays in the ROLL-BACK state and restores the data of CPU Reg.File that was stored in the Backup Reg.File during the CPU soft error exception routine when Inst.1 was executed. In this process, the CPU recovers from the soft error and its program counter (PC) is restored to Inst.2, which had not been executed when the soft error occurred. After the CPU soft error exception routine, the return-from-exception (RTE) instruction is executed and the CPU restarts from Inst.2. The process, from detecting a soft error to restarting the CPU takes

258

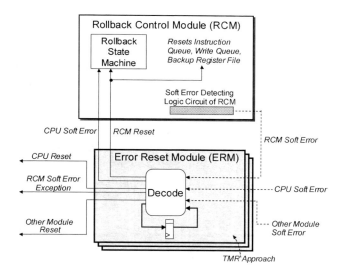

Figure 4. Error reset module (ERM)

about 90 cycles.

Implementing the addition of the RCM is not difficult because we do not need to customize the original pipelined CPU architecture.

3.2.2. Soft error recovery of rollback control module by error reset architecture

To detect soft errors in the RCM, we applied the tool explained in Section 3.1 to the RCM as shown in Figure 4. We also developed an error reset module (ERM), which receives soft error signals from the CPU, RCM, and other modules. If a soft error occurs in the CPU, the ERM issues a CPU reset signal to the CPU, and the ERM sends a CPU soft error signal to the RCM to execute the rollback control process explained in Section 3.2.1. On the other hand, if a soft error occurs in the RCM, the ERM issues an RCM reset signal to the RCM, and the ERM sends an RCM soft error exception signal to the CPU.

Figure 5 shows the timing chart when a soft error has occurred in the rollback state machine of the RCM in cycle 3. The RCM soft error signal is issued at the same time. In the next cycle 4, the ERM issues an RCM reset signal and an RCM soft error exception signal is sent to the CPU. The CPU cancels Inst.7, fetching a new instruction, and branches to the RCM soft error exception routine in cycle 6. In the RCM soft error exception routine, the CPU executes writing data from the CPU Reg.File to the Backup Reg.File and the remaining effects caused by the soft error are cleared. After the RCM soft error exception routine, the RTE instruction is executed and the CPU restarts from Inst.7. These processes take about 70 cycles.

This ERM is implemented by dual (DMR) or triple module redundancy (TMR) approaches because it consists only of small F/Fs and combinational logic circuits. Therefore,

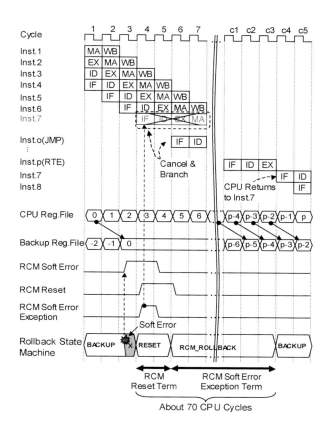

Figure 5. Rollback control flow in RCM

the area overhead will be smaller than the RCM module redundancy approach because the RCM will require many logic circuit areas such as a register file and some queues.

3.3. Rollback architecture for ECC RAM

ECC can correct a single-bit soft error of RAM, but events such as syndrome generation incur large delay overhead. In our experience, the delay overhead was 25-30%, and we needed to add extra read access cycles from RAM to the CPU. In this study, we developed an ECC error correcting architecture using the rollback method described in Section 3.2.1. As shown in Figure 6, the CPU writes data to RAM through a write buffer and check bit generation. The CPU also reads data directly from the RAM without passing a syndrome generation. The error correction module (ECM) consists of an ECM state machine block and a correct data write-back control block. If a single-bit error is detected in CPU read access, an ECC error signal is output to the RCM and ECM. Then the corrected data is selected by the correct data write-back control. Because of the effect of reading before error correction of the ECC RAM, no critical timing path is created by the syndrome generation.

Figure 7 shows the timing chart when a RAM ECC error is detected. Normal CPU access is executed in two cy-

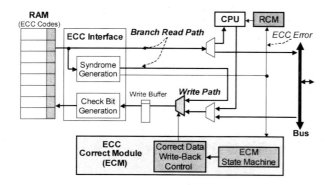

Figure 6. CPU architecture with ECC RAM and ECC correction module (ECM)

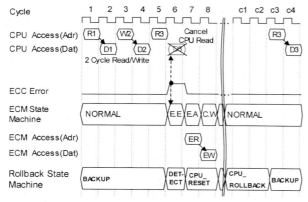

E.E: ECC Error   E.A: ECM Access   C.W: Correct Data Write-Back

Figure 7. Timing chart of ECC error rollback

cles as read cycles 1-2, or write cycles 3-4. In cycle 6, a single-bit ECC error is detected in RAM when the CPU reads data "D3" from the RAM address. As a result, the ECM state machine changes to ECC error (E.E), and the rollback state machine changes to DETECT. In cycle 7, the ECM state machine changes to ECM access (E.A) which accesses the error address of RAM, and in the next cycle, 8, the ECM state machine is in the correct data write-back state (C.W). In this C.W state, the ECM writes the data corrected by the syndrome generation circuit back to the error RAM address. This write-back process corrects a single-bit soft error in RAM. The rollback state machine then changes CPU_RESET and the CPU is reset. The rollback process is then executed as explained in Section 3.2.1, Figure 3. After the rollback process is finished, the CPU restarts read access "R3" again in cycle c3 and the CPU execution goes on.

3.4. Restrictions of the rollback architecture

Our rollback architectures have a few restrictions.

First, the RCM has only one set of backup data of the CPU's register file, and the RCM restores the data in the rollback process. Therefore if a new soft error occurs during rollback, the RCM cannot continue the rollback process. In that case, the RCM issues a rollback miss signal, as shown in the lower right of Figure 2. Although the CPU might restart correctly, there is a possibility of a CPU crash or runaway.

Second, we implemented the rollback control process as an exception routine of the CPU. Therefore, if a soft error occurs in the F/F of the exception control logic circuits, the soft error exception routine might be incorrect. We protect against such critical control F/Fs with a TMR approach.

When these architectures are applied to safety critical systems, the system will require emergency functions, such as stopping safely, when the rollback miss signal is issued.

4. Evaluation

We implemented the proposed architectures and evaluated them in a four-step process, as shown in Figure 8.

Step 1: We used "Original-MCU", an original microcontroller that includes a 32-bit five-pipelined RISC CPU core described in Verilog-HDL at register transfer level (RTL). Memory controller (MEMC) and Other are also RTL random logic circuits. The built-in RAM is a hardware macro block.

Step 2: We designed new modules RCM, ERM, and ECM, and then built them into the Original-MCU, and added ECC bits to the RAM. We use the easiest implementation for ECC, calculating Hamming code for each byte of RAM. We will call this microcontroller "PRE-MCU". It does not yet include soft error-detecting logic circuits and error detecting signals. We also apply static timing analysis (STA) to PRE-MCU to obtain a timing report.

Step 3: A PRE-MCU RTL and timing report are input to the automatic generation EDA tool. This tool generates optimized soft error-detecting logic circuits to the PRE-MCU RTL, and outputs a new microcontroller RTL, "GEN-MCU".

Step 4: We synthesized this GEN-MCU, and obtained the area and frequency reports. Finally, to evaluate the effect of RCM, ERM, and ECM, we ran the logic simulations using EEMBC benchmarks and obtained mean time between failure (MTBF) reports.

4.1. Area and frequency overheads

To verify the effectiveness of the tool that automatically generates soft error-detecting logic circuits, we designed the five types of architecture configurations shown in Table 1. (A) Original-MCU and (B) PRE-MCU correspond to Figure 8. (C) GEN-MCU_P generates only parity for every

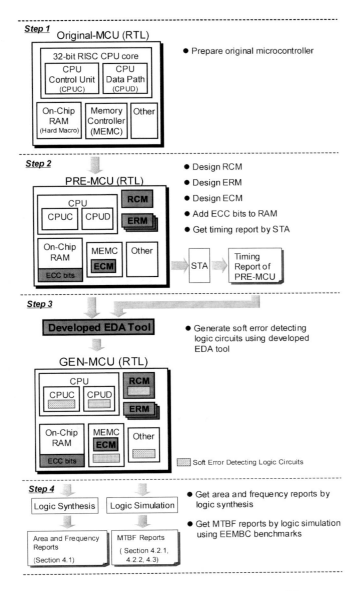

Figure 8. Proposed microcontroller architecture and design environment for evaluation

Step 1 — Original-MCU (RTL)
- Prepare original microcontroller

Step 2 — PRE-MCU (RTL)
- Design RCM
- Design ERM
- Design ECM
- Add ECC bits to RAM
- Get timing report by STA

Step 3 — Developed EDA Tool — GEN-MCU (RTL)
- Generate soft error detecting logic circuits using developed EDA tool

Soft Error Detecting Logic Circuits

Step 4 — Logic Synthesis / Logic Simulation
- Get area and frequency reports by logic synthesis
- Get MTBF reports by logic simulation using EEMBC benchmarks

Area and Frequency Reports (Section 4.1)

MTBF Reports (Section 4.2.1, 4.2.2, 4.3)

Table 1. Logic circuits for evaluation

Circuit Name	Architecture Configuration
(A) Original-MCU	Original microcontroller architecture
(B) PRE-MCU	(A) + RCM + ERM + ECM + ECC bits
(C) GEN-MCU_P	(B) + Generating "parity" for every F/F
(D) GEN-MCU_R	(B) + Generating "F/F redundancy" for every F/F
(E) GEN-MCU_O	(B) + Generating optimized detecting circuits using tool

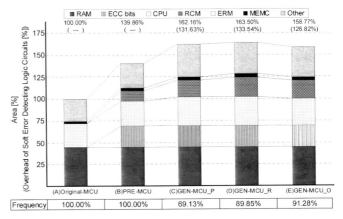

Figure 9. Area and frequency results

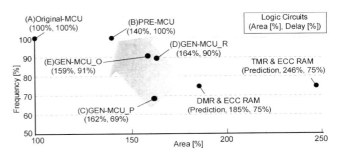

Figure 10. Trade-off between area and frequency

F/F. (D) GEN-MCU_R generates only F/F redundancy for every F/F. (E) GEN-MCU_O generates optimized detecting circuits using the developed EDA tool.

The results for area and frequency obtained by logic synthesis are shown in Figure 9. First, the area overhead of (B), which includes RCM, ERM, ECM, and ECC bits, was about 40%. Here, (B) could maintain the frequency of (A) because of the contributions of the branched read data path from the ECC critical path, but (B) does not include the soft error detecting signals and detecting timing paths. Next, in (C), the area overhead was about 62% (that of the generated circuit was 32%), and the frequency was 69% because of

parity generation. In (D), the area overhead was 63% (that of the generated circuit was 33%), but the frequency of (D) decreased by only 10%. In (E), which uses the optimizing techniques, the area overhead was under 59% (that of the generated circuit was under 27%) and the frequency overhead was under 9%. The area of ERM was about 0.10%, too small to be apparent in the graph.

The trade-off between area and frequency from (A) to (E) is shown in Figure 10. This graph shows that overheads decrease as we move to the upper left. Two data plots are added to the graph in Figure 10: DMR with ECC RAM and TMR with ECC RAM. Neither was implemented in this study; they are only predicted values. Figure 10 shows that our approach obtained a good trade-off between area and

261

frequency. Additionally, the soft error-detecting logic circuits generation time was only about 20 seconds in (E) on an UltraSPARC-III platform, meaning that this tool enables rapid design of highly reliable microcontrollers.

4.2. MTBF results for random logic circuits with rollback architecture and soft error injection

We evaluated the MTBF of a microcontroller with the proposed rollback architecture. We used the microcontroller RTLs of (A) Original-MCU (Original) and (E) GEN-MCU_O (GEN-MCU) described in Section 4.1 in an environment where soft errors occur. We used eight EEMBC benchmarks for soft error logic simulation. We assumed the following active soft errors: unexpected data transfers on the on-chip bus, indetermination of the CPU's PC, iteration of illegal instruction loops, and rollback misses. In this evaluation, the soft error-active rate and the MTBF cycle are defined as follows:

$$Soft\_Error\_Active[\%] = \frac{Simulation\_Failure}{Soft\_Error\_Injection} \times 100 \quad (1)$$

$$MTBF[cycle] = \frac{Total\_Run\_Cycle}{Simulation\_Failure} \quad (2)$$

The logic simulation stops when a soft error is injected and active, then the simulation restarts the same benchmark from the beginning. It regards simulation cycles in which soft errors are not active as normal executions. The cycles of the rollback exception routine also are normal executions.

4.2.1. Changes of MTBF under various SER of random logic circuits

In the following simulations, soft errors were injected at random to all F/Fs of the random logic circuits of both microcontrollers, Original and GEN-MCU. We defined three SER of 10^{-3} per cycle, 10^{-4} per cycle, and 10^{-5} per cycle in reference to the work of Sugihara et al. [7]. Hereafter, these three rates are called "ER-3", "ER-4", and "ER-5". Note that these are accelerated rates for short-term evaluation. In terms of the failure in time (FIT), ER-5 corresponds to about 5×10^{17} FIT per Mbits from the sum of F/F bits that are included in this microcontroller. Soft error injection simulations were run until the maximum total simulation cycle reached about 100 million cycles.

Detailed MTBF results are shown in Table 2, and the GEN-MCU results are highlighted. Figures 11, 12, and 13 are MTBF graphs calculated by formula (2) from the sum of the eight benchmarks. With ER-3, the soft error-active rates were 5-6% in Original. Meanwhile, in GEN-MCU, the soft error-active rates were 5-9% and the MTBF was

Table 2. Detailed MTBF results for random logic circuits

| EEMBC benchmark | Original/ GEN-MCU | Soft Error Rate : ER-3 (About 100,000 errors/ 100 M cycles) | | | Soft Error Rate : ER-4 (About 10,000 errors/ 100 M cycles) | | | Soft Error Rate : ER-5 (About 1,000 errors/ 100 M cycles) | | |
		Simulation Failure	Soft Error Active	MTBF Cycle	Simulation Failure	Soft Error Active	MTBF Cycle	Simulation Failure	Soft Error Active	MTBF Cycle
a2time01	Original	6,387	5.98%	15,786	664	7.29%	151,059	69	6.90%	1,456,472
	GEN-MCU	6,547	6.18%	15,331	62	0.69%	1,618,786	2	0.20%	50,021,541
aifftr01	Original	4,862	4.84%	20,659	701	6.83%	143,199	58	5.85%	1,733,313
	GEN-MCU	5,378	5.40%	18,652	103	1.02%	976,949	4	0.37%	25,103,344
aifirf01	Original	5,723	5.72%	17,602	675	7.08%	148,835	83	7.96%	1,212,417
	GEN-MCU	6,877	6.88%	14,590	90	0.97%	1,117,331	1	0.09%	100,687,516
basefp01	Original	5,453	5.31%	18,451	702	7.27%	143,156	89	8.62%	1,126,920
	GEN-MCU	9,568	9.30%	10,497	84	0.89%	1,195,112	1	0.10%	100,020,587
cacheb01	Original	6,580	6.53%	15,291	892	8.25%	112,473	86	8.31%	1,168,834
	GEN-MCU	5,423	5.41%	18,526	73	0.66%	1,378,794	1	0.10%	100,498,470
canrdr01	Original	5,715	5.67%	17,602	711	6.98%	141,848	48	4.97%	2,096,271
	GEN-MCU	6,097	6.11%	16,523	123	1.22%	819,926	3	0.30%	33,517,320
lirflt01	Original	5,671	5.57%	17,645	733	7.34%	137,344	64	6.39%	1,563,981
	GEN-MCU	6,356	6.38%	15,799	130	1.31%	773,662	4	0.39%	25,020,995
puwmod01	Original	5,662	5.56%	17,718	694	6.84%	145,168	59	6.12%	1,696,248
	GEN-MCU	5,867	5.94%	17,163	91	0.92%	1,105,077	0	0.00%	<100,770,064

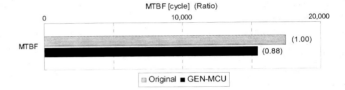

Figure 11. MTBF results at ER-3

Figure 12. MTBF results at ER-4

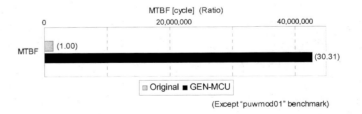

(Except "puwmod01" benchmark)

Figure 13. MTBF results at ER-5

0.88 times, because the primary cause of failure was rollback miss caused by soft errors occurring in the rollback exception routine. If the SER of evaluation was too high, we would not be able to simulate an actual operating environment and the rollback architecture would not be very effective. However, the rollback architecture can output a rollback miss signal to external devices when rollback is impossible, reducing the possibility of a system crash. At ER-4, the sum of simulation failures decreased and the MTBF was 7.63 times longer than that of Original, as shown in Figure 12. Finally, at ER-5, MTBF was 30 times longer. Here, the "puwmod01" benchmark result of GEN-MCU never went into simulation failure in this evaluation cycle. Therefore, we omitted the puwmod01 benchmark from the MTBF calculation in Figure 13.

For about 90 CPU cycles, the rollback routine requires 0.90 or 0.45 μs at frequencies of 100 or 200 MHz, respectively. These rollback exception terms would be quite short for the control term of X-by-Wire systems. SER is much lower in the actual environment than in this evaluation environment, and we expect that the possibility of two or more soft errors occurring in a short period is negligible. Therefore, when we implement to the actual real-time control systems, we should allow at most a rollback routine term in the control term of the system.

4.2.2. Changing MTBF by expanding the soft error correction area

Our rollback architecture has another feature: soft errors occurred not only in the CPU but also in other control modules such as MEMC, other peripherals, and the RCM itself can be corrected. To evaluate this feature, we restricted the error detection and correction areas of the microcontroller. For example, there is an approach that uses a duplicated ALU of the superscalar architecture for dependability [8]. In this evaluation, this dependable ALU approach corresponds to correcting soft errors that occur only in the "CPUD" module of the microcontroller, as shown in Figure 14(a). Moreover, since our rollback architecture can correct soft errors that occur in the RCM itself, we enabled the rollback control for all random logic circuits except the RCM, as shown in Figure 14(b). We selected the nearly impossible SER, ER-5, from the three rates in Section 4.2.1 and labeled the setup in Figure 14(a) "Only_CPUD", and the setup in Figure 14(b) "Except_RCM".

The resulting MTBF graph of the eight benchmarks is shown in Figure 15. The MTBF of Only_CPUD was only 1.46 times longer than that of Original (at ER-5). This means that soft errors occurring in all areas except the CPUD module would often be active because the error injection targeted not only the F/Fs of the CPUD, but also all F/Fs of the microcontroller. In Except_RCM, MTBF was 20 times longer. In GEN-MCU (at ER-5), correcting all random logic circuits of the microcontroller, the MTBF was 30 times longer (this value corresponds to Figure 13).

Thus, our rollback architecture is effective for soft errors that occur in any random logic circuits of the microcontroller.

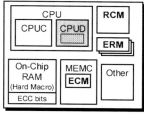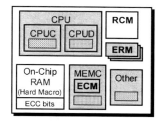

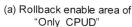

(a) Rollback enable area of "Only_CPUD"

(b) Rollback enable area of "Except_RCM"

Figure 14. Restrictions of rollback enable area

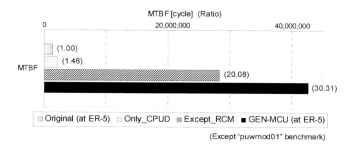

Figure 15. MTBF results for comparison of Only_CPUD with Except_RCM

4.3. MTBF results for ECC RAM rollback architecture

We evaluated the ECC RAM rollback architecture in the same way as with the random logic circuits. Here, the targets of the MTBF evaluation were Original-MCU with normal ECC coded RAM (Original+ECC) and GEN-MCU. The area of soft error injection was RAM in both Original+ECC and GEN-MCU. We used the same eight benchmarks listed in Table 2 and ran a logic simulation. Of course, a single-bit soft error in normal ECC RAM may not cause simulation failure in Original+ECC if the error area is not accessed from the CPU or if the error area is rewritten before the wrong data has been read. Here, normal ECC does not equip a correct data write-back hardware. Therefore, if a single-bit soft error that occurred in a word area of RAM remains, and the next soft error occurs in the same word area, the logic simulation will fail because of the uncorrected double-bit error. In GEN-MCU, in contrast, the ECM architecture detects a single-bit ECC error and writes back correct data, then the CPU executes through the rollback process. Currently the SER of RAM is higher than that of F/F, and the RAM error rate is supposed to be several times higher than that of F/F. From past experience, we established a RAM SER value five times higher than the 5×10^{17}FIT/Mbit of "ER-5". The 25×10^{17}FIT/Mbit

Table 3. Detailed MTBF results for ECC RAM rollback

EEMBC benchmark	Original+ECC/ GEN-MCU	Soft Error Rate : ER-ECM (About 100,000 errors/100 M cycles)				
		Corrected Data Read	Rollback Error Data	Simulation Failure (Multi-bit Error)	Soft Error Active	MTBF Cycle
a2time01	Original+ECC	128,709	---	87	0.0865%	1,152,710
	GEN-MCU	---	5,851	27	0.0267%	3,720,061
aifftr01	Original+ECC	523	---	28	0.0281%	3,587,738
	GEN-MCU	---	470	28	0.0281%	3,589,395
aifirf01	Original+ECC	69,161	---	62	0.0606%	1,626,200
	GEN-MCU	---	5,344	61	0.0599%	1,647,563
basefp01	Original+ECC	11,643	---	55	0.0543%	1,828,325
	GEN-MCU	---	2,895	54	0.0531%	1,864,571
cacheb01	Original+ECC	740,121	---	52	0.0515%	1,934,258
	GEN-MCU	---	1,994	54	0.0537%	1,865,231
canrdr01	Original+ECC	168,737	---	131	0.1296%	770,609
	GEN-MCU	---	17,034	54	0.0533%	1,866,735
lirflt01	Original+ECC	244,797	---	71	0.0711%	1,412,654
	GEN-MCU	---	5,484	66	0.0659%	1,522,399
puwmod01	Original+ECC	921,946	---	62	0.0619%	1,628,760
	GEN-MCU	---	3,231	66	0.0666%	1,525,259

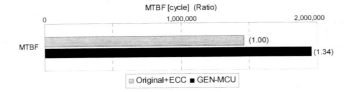

Figure 16. MTBF results for ECC RAM roll-back

corresponds to the occurrence of a soft error in this RAM under a 10^{-3} per CPU cycle. Here this error rate is termed "ER-ECM".

The MTBF results and graph are shown in Table 3 and Figure 16. The column labeled "Corrected Data Read" in Table 3 expresses the sum of RAM read accesses that corrected a single-bit error by ECC logic circuits in Original+ECC. The column labeled "Rollback Error Data" expresses the sum of corrected single-bit error occurrences in RAM by the rollback process in GEN-MCU. In GEN-MCU, the number of read error data decreased because of the rollback process that corrected a single-bit error in RAM when the error was detected. The MTBF results of GEN-MCU were about the same as or longer than Original+ECC, and there were application dependencies because of the difference in RAM access. Although the MTBF of GEN-MCU was 1.34 times longer than that of Original+ECC, as shown in Figure 16, GEN-MCU has no critical path caused by ECC, meaning that our architecture has the advantage of high frequency for microcontrollers. Using a memory patrol software can correct the latent single-bit soft error in normal ECC RAM, but our ECC rollback architecture re-

quires less software overhead.

These results show that, despite its low overhead, our dependable architecture achieves high performance in recovering from soft errors.

5. Related work

In the search for highly dependable systems, many module and time redundancy methods have been researched. For example, there are module redundancy methods that compare output signals from dual CPUs and RAM by a self-checking comparator in a single-chip microprocessor [9]. Although these approaches can achieve high fault coverage, the increase in hardware cost is very large. So, the use of module redundancy methods has been restricted to high-end applications such as airplanes, trains, and server computers. A famous example of a time redundancy method is recomputing with shifted operands (RESO) [10][11]. However, this approach is difficult to apply to microcontrollers built into real-time systems because it has nearly 100% cycle overheads. In our rollback architecture, cycle overhead is created only when a soft error is detected.

However, non-redundant module approaches have recently been proposed for high-end processors. Because SER increases as semiconductor feature size and supply voltages decrease, high-end processors with large-capacity memory are likely to malfunction. In addition, the large number of microprocessors manufactured every year makes increased hardware cost undesirable. Intel has suggested "Error-trapping F/F" and estimated that the area overhead would be about 0.5% [12]. However, they use F/Fs consisting of specific customized latches and reuse the multiplexed scan F/Fs. We estimated that application of this technique to our standard cell library would result in an area overhead of over 110%. This method would make microcontroller manufacturing more difficult. Recently, Fujitsu presented its "SPARC64 VI" architecture, which has a re-execute function from the PC when a soft error is detected [13]. Their canceling instructions and rollback execution are similar to our approach. All function modules of the SPARC64 VI processor use protected parity or ECC. However, our generation tool of soft error-detecting logic circuits has the advantage that the tool optimizes the area and delay overheads of generating soft error-detecting logic circuits.

Several dependable methods have also been presented in low-end microcontrollers. For example, ST Microelectronics is researching quad CPU architecture [14]. They expect that the area of on-chip ROM will predominate over that of the CPU in the microcontroller. But the power consumption will become a significant problem. Another example is the cost-effective error detection platform using an ARM core [15]. However, this is an error detection approach, and it is hard to correct errors in random logic circuits with low overheads. ARM also announced its "Cortex-R4F" [16], which uses similar techniques: no timing critical path is triggered by ECC RAM and re-execution is done by existing pipeline flush architecture. Although our rollback architecture requires some cycle overheads because of CPU reset and rollback, it is able to correct soft errors that occur not only in memories but also in the CPU, peripherals, and other control microcontroller modules.

6. Conclusion

We proposed a cost-effective, dependable microcontroller architecture for soft error recovery. We implemented an EDA tool with soft error-detecting logic circuits, CPU instruction-level rollback control modules, and an ECC RAM-correcting architecture without delay overhead. Our evaluation showed that this architecture achieved high tolerance to soft errors with low overheads and high performance. We are planning to apply these architectures to the manufacture of a new microcontroller for embedded systems used in automobiles and industrial machines.

References

[1] Kentaro Yoshimura *et al.* "Cost-Effective and Fault Tolerant Vehicle Control Architecture for X-by-Wire Systems (Part 1: Architecture Design Based on the Concept of Autonomous Decentralized Systems)". *Society of Automotive Engineers 2005 World Congress(SAE2005)*, 2005-01-1527, Apr 2005.

[2] Kohei Sakurai *et al.* "Cost-Effective and Fault Tolerant Vehicle Control Architecture for X-by-Wire Systems (Part 2: Implementation Design)". *Society of Automotive Engineers 2005 World Congress(SAE2005)*, 2005-01-1543, Apr 2005.

[3] Robert Baumann. "Single Event Upsets in Commercial Electronics - From Nuclear Mechanisms to Technology Scaling Trends". *Tutorials of International Reliability Physics Symposium 2003(IRPS2003)*, Mar 2003.

[4] Cristian Constantinescu. "Neutron SER Characterization of Microprocessors". *International Conference on Dependable Systems and Networks 2005(DSN2005)*, pages 754–759, Jun 2005.

[5] David G. Mavis. "Single Event Transient Phenomena – Challenges and Solutions". *Microelectronics Reliability and Qualification Workshop 2002*, Dec 2002.

[6] T.Sakata, T.Hirotsu, H.Yamada, and T.Kataoka. "Automatic Generation Techniques of Soft-Error-Detecting Logic Circuits with Low Delay and Area Overheads". *Fast Abstracts of International Conference on Dependable Systems and Networks 2006(DSN2006)*, Vol.2:178–179, Jun 2006.

[7] M.Sugihara, T.Ishihara, K.Hashimoto, and M.Muroyama. "A Simulation-Based Soft Error Estimation Methodology for Computer Systems". *Proc. of IEEE International Symposium on Quality Electronic Design*, pages 196–203, Mar 2006.

[8] J.Ray, J.Hoe, and B.Falsafi. "Dual Use of Superscalar Datapath for Transient-Fault Detection and Recovery". *Proc. of 34th International Symposium on Microarchitecture*, pages 214–224, Dec 2001.

[9] K.Shimamura, T.Takehara, Y.Shima, and K.Tsunedomi. "A Single-Chip Fail-Safe Microprocessor with Memory Data Comparison Feature". *The 12th IEEE International Symposium Pacific Rim Dependable Computing(PRDC'06)*, pages 359–368, Dec 2006.

[10] J. H. Patel and L. Y. Fung. "Concurrent Error Detection in ALU's by Recomputing with Shifted Operands". *IEEE Transactions on Computers*, Vol.C-31:589–595, Jul 1982.

[11] J. H. Patel and L. Y. Fung. "Concurrent Error Detection in Multiply and Divide Arrays". *IEEE Transactions on Computers*, Vol.C-32:417–422, Apr 1983.

[12] Subhasish Mitra *et al.* "Logic Soft Errors: A Major Barrier To Robust Platform Design". *International Test Conference 2005(ITC2005)*, pages 687–698, Nov 2005.

[13] Aiichiro Inoue. "Fujitsu SPARC64 VI: A State of the Art Dual-Core Processor". *Fall Microprocessor Forum 2006*, Oct 2006.

[14] M.Baleani, A.Ferrari, L.Mangeruca, M.Peri, and S.Pezzini. "Fault-Tolerant Platforms for Automotive Safety-Critical Applications". *International Conference on Compilers, Architecture and Synthesis for Embedded Systems 2003(CASES2003)*, pages 170–177, Oct 2003.

[15] R.Mariani, B.Vittorelli, and P.Fuhrmann. "Cost-effective Approach to Error Detection for an Embedded Automotive Platform". *Society of Automotive Engineers 2006 World Congress(SAE2006)*, 2006-01-0837:35–46, Apr 2006.

[16] ARM. "http://www.arm.com/news/14895.html", Oct 2006.

Architecture-Level Soft Error Analysis:
Examining the Limits of Common Assumptions [*]

Xiaodong Li[†], Sarita V. Adve[†], Pradip Bose[‡], Jude A. Rivers[‡]

[†]Department of Computer Science
University of Illionis at Urbana-Champaign
{xli3,sadve}@uiuc.edu

[‡]IBM T.J. Watson Research Center
Yorktown Heights, NY
{pbose,jarivers}@us.ibm.com

Abstract

This paper concerns the validity of a widely used method for estimating the architecture-level mean time to failure (MTTF) due to soft errors. The method first calculates the failure rate for an architecture-level component as the product of its raw error rate and an architecture vulnerability factor (AVF). Next, the method calculates the system failure rate as the sum of the failure rates (SOFR) of all components, and the system MTTF as the reciprocal of this failure rate. Both steps make significant assumptions. We investigate the validity of the AVF+SOFR method across a large design space, using both mathematical and experimental techniques with real program traces from SPEC 2000 benchmarks and synthesized traces to simulate longer real-world workloads. We show that AVF+SOFR is valid for most of the realistic cases under current raw error rates. However, for some realistic combinations of large systems, long-running workloads with large phases, and/or large raw error rates, the MTTF calculated using AVF+SOFR shows significant discrepancies from that using first principles. We also show that SoftArch, a previously proposed alternative method that does not make the AVF+SOFR assumptions, does not exhibit the above discrepancies.

1 Introduction

Radiation induced soft errors represent a major challenge to exploiting the benefits from continued CMOS scaling. Soft errors or single event upsets are transient errors caused by high energy particle strikes such as neutrons from cosmic rays and alpha particles from the IC packaging materials. These errors can be catastrophic to program execution by flipping bits stored in storage cells or changing the values being computed by logic elements. While there is still a lack of consensus on the exact soft error rates (SER) of specific circuits, it is clear that the SER per *chip* is growing substantially due to the increasing number of devices on a chip [3, 5, 10, 12].

If a particle strike causes a bit to flip or a piece of logic to generate a wrong result, we call the bit flip or the wrong result a *raw soft error*. Fortunately, not all raw soft errors cause the program to fail. For example, a soft error in a functional unit that is not currently processing an instruction or in an SRAM cell that is not storing useful data will not harm the execution. Such an error is said to be masked. Research has shown that there is a large masking effect at the architecture (and microarchitecture) levels [2, 4, 6, 9, 14, 15]; e.g., Wang et al. [14] report more than 85% masking.

This paper concerns the impact of architectural masking on the methodology to compute the widely used metric of mean time to failure (MTTF) for soft errors for modern processors.

A widely used methodology to compute MTTF uses two simple steps [9], illustrated in Figure 1: (1) The **AVF step** calculates the failure rate of each individual processor *component* (e.g., ALU, register file, issue queue) as the product of its raw failure rate and a derating factor that accounts for masking. Mukherjee et al. formalized the notion of a derating factor as the architectural vulnerability factor (AVF) [9] and showed how to calculate it for various architectural components [1, 9]. (2) The **SOFR step** calculates the failure rate of the entire processor (or any system) as the Sum Of the Failure Rates (SOFR) of the individual components of the processor or system (as calculated in the AVF step). It calculates the MTTF of the processor (or system) as the reciprocal of its failure rate.

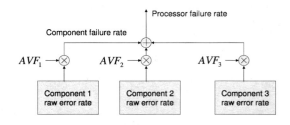

Figure 1. The AVF and SOFR steps for MTTF.

Both the AVF and SOFR steps implicitly make certain assumptions about the statistical properties of the underlying error process. While these assumptions, described below, may

[*]This work is supported in part by an IBM faculty partnership award, the MARCO/FCRP Gigascale Systems Research Center, the National Science Foundation under Grant No. CCF-0541383, and an equipment donation from AMD.

hold for the raw error process, it is unclear whether they hold for the architecturally masked process. The goal of this paper is to examine the validity of these assumptions underlying the mathematical basis of the AVF and SOFR steps, and the implications of these assumptions for evaluating soft error MTTF for real systems.

AVF+SOFR assumptions.

A key assumption behind the AVF step is that the probability of failure due to a soft error in a given component is uniform across a program's execution. This allows a single AVF value to be used to derate the raw error rate of a component. The uniformity assumption is reasonable for raw error events since the probability of a high energy particle strike is no different at different points in the program's execution for most realistic scenarios. However, it is unclear that the assumption holds after incorporating architectural masking. Similarly, a well-documented assumption for the SOFR step is that the time to failure for a given component follows an exponential distribution. Again, the assumption is reasonable and widely accepted for raw error events, but it is unclear that it holds for failures after architectural masking.

Thus, both the AVF and SOFR steps make assumptions about the error process that may be considered questionable, once architectural masking effects are taken into account. The question we address is: Under what conditions (if any) does the violation of the above AVF+SOFR assumptions introduce significant errors in the calculation of the MTTF?

Contributions of this work.

We answer the above question through both mathematical and experimental analysis. Our rigorous mathematical methods identify the assumptions of the AVF+SOFR method, and using some synthesized workloads, analyze the value ranges of various parameters for which the AVF+SOFR assumptions do or do not hold. To validate the conclusions on real world workloads and quantify the relative error of the AVF+SOFR method, we design simulation-based experiments to explore a wide design space.

We find that the impact of the above assumptions on the MTTF calculation depends on three parameters related to the environment, system, and the workload respectively: (1) the raw error rate of the individual components, (2) the number of components in the system on which SOFR is applied, and (3) the length of the full execution or the longest repeated phase of the workload. Specifically, our evaluations show the following.

First, for systems where the individual components have small raw error rates, the total number of components is small, and where the workload consists of repeated executions of a short program, the AVF+SOFR assumptions introduce negligible error. To our knowledge, previously published work using the AVF+SOFR methodology considers systems and workloads that obey the above constraints. This result is by itself significant since it, for the first time, validates the mathematical basis for using the AVF+SOFR methodology.

Second, our results show that the AVF+SOFR method can result in large discrepancies in MTTF (up to 100%) for large

raw error rates of individual components (e.g., as would be the case in space or in accelerated tests or with components consisting of many millions of bits) and/or systems that have many components (e.g., large clusters of thousands of processors) and/or long-running workloads with different utilization characteristics over large time windows (e.g., server workloads that run at high utilization in the day but low utilization in the night). This problematic part of the design space is certainly much smaller and less common than the space over which AVF+SOFR is valid; however, it is not negligible and represents several realistic systems. Our results give a note of caution against blind use of the AVF+SOFR method for such systems.

Finally, given the limitations of AVF+SOFR identified here, we briefly explore alternative methods for soft error analysis with architectural masking. Traditionally, fault injection in low-level (RTL) simulators has been used (e.g., [2, 4, 14]). This technique does not make the AVF+SOFR assumptions, but requires running numerous experiments that make it impractically slow for architecture-level work (which usually requires simulating long workloads). A more recent methodology called SoftArch [6] uses a probabilistic model based on first principles coupled with architecture-level simulation. SoftArch does not make the AVF+SOFR assumptions. We show here that SoftArch does not exhibit the MTTF discrepancies shown by AVF+SOFR. These experiments are not meant as a complete validation of SoftArch or a full comparison between SoftArch and AVF+SOFR. A fair comparison would require applying both methods to all processor components and using all the advanced optimizations of AVF+SOFR which is beyond the scope of this work. Rather, these experiments point to future work to determine the best combination of methodologies that will provide the best MTTF estimates across all relevant scenarios.

2 Background

2.1 Failure Rate, MTTF, and FIT Rate

Three common terms are often used to discuss system reliability: failure rate, mean time to failure (MTTF), and failures in time (FIT) [13].

The failure rate at time t is the conditional probability that the component will fail in the time interval $[t, t + dt]$, given that it has not failed until time t. When the distribution of the time to failure is exponential, the failure rate is a constant and does not vary with time. We use λ to denote this constant failure rate.

The mean time to failure (MTTF) of a component is simply the expected (average) time to failure. For components with exponentially distributed time to failure, $MTTF$ is simply the reciprocal of the constant failure rate ($1/\lambda$).

The metric of failures in time or FITs is defined as the number of failures per one billion hours of operation. Often, FITs are referred to as the failure rate and the equation $FIT = \frac{10^9}{MTTF}$ is used. However, this assumes that the failure rate is constant in time, and equivalently, the time to failure follows an exponential distribution.

2.2 The AVF Step and its Assumptions

In a given cycle, only a fraction of the bits in a processor storage component and only some of the logic components will affect the final program output. A raw error event that does not affect these critical bits or logic components has no adverse effect on the program outcome. Mukherjee et al. used the term architecture vulnerability factor (AVF) to express the probability that a visible error (failure) will occur, given a raw error event in a component [9]. The AVF for a hardware component can be calculated as the percentage of time the component contains *Architecturally Correct Execution* (ACE) bits (i.e., the bits that affect the final program output). Thus, for a storage cell, the AVF is the percentage of cycles that this cell contains ACE bits. For a logic structure, the AVF is the percentage of cycles that it processes ACE bits or instructions.

Mukherjee et al. calculate the FIT rate of a processor component as the product of the component's AVF and its raw FIT rate (i.e., the FIT rate of the component if every bit were ACE). Denoting the raw FIT rate of the component as λ_c (also called the raw soft error rate or raw SER) and its AVF as AVF_c, they derive the MTTF of the component as:

$$MTTF_c = \frac{1}{\lambda_c \cdot AVF_c} \qquad (1)$$

We show in Section 3.1 that an assumption underlying the above equation is that the time to failure for a program is uniformly distributed over the program. We explore the cases where this assumption is and is not true to assess the validity of the AVF step.

2.3 The SOFR Step and its Assumptions

Sum of failure rates (SOFR) is an industry standard model for combining failure rates of individual processor (or system) components to give the failure rate and MTTF of the entire processor (or system). Let the system contain k components with failure rate of component i as $FailureRate_i$ (which is assumed to be the reciprocal of the MTTF of component i or $1/MTTF_i$). The SOFR model calculates the failure rate ($FailureRate_{sys}$) and the MTTF ($MTTF_{sys}$) of the system as:

$$FailureRate_{sys} = \sum_{i=1}^{k} FailureRate_i = \sum_{i=1}^{k} \frac{1}{MTTF_i} \qquad (2)$$

$$MTTF_{sys} = \frac{1}{FailureRate_{sys}} \qquad (3)$$

The SOFR model makes two major assumptions [13]. First, it assumes that each component has a constant failure rate (i.e., exponentially distributed time to failure) and the failures for different components are independent of each other. Section 3.2 shows that architectural masking may violate this assumption in some cases. Second, the SOFR model assumes a series failure system; i.e., the first instance of a component failure causes the entire processor to fail. This assumption holds if there is no redundancy in the system. Since our focus is on the impact

of program-dependent architectural masking on the statistical properties of the failure process, we continue to make this assumption as well and focus only on the first assumption.

3 Examining the Limits: An Analytical View

This section uses mathematical analysis to understand the limits of the basic assumptions underlying the AVF+SOFR methodology for estimating MTTF for soft errors. Later sections back these results with detailed Monte-Carlo simulations for actual workloads.

Our analysis makes two assumptions that are also made by the AVF+SOFR methodology.

(1) Inter-arrival times for raw errors in a component are independent and exponentially distributed with density function $\lambda e^{-\lambda t}$. It is reasonable to assume that the time to the next high energy particle strike is independent of the previous strike and is exponentially distributed (the process is memoryless). In practice, there is some device- and circuit-level masking, which could possibly render the raw error process that is subject to architectural masking as non-exponential. In our experiments, however, we do not have this low-level masking information available; we therefore assume the best case for the AVF+SOFR methodology – that the inter-arrival time for raw errors before any architectural masking is an exponential process with density function $\lambda e^{-\lambda t}$. We refer to λ as the *raw error rate*.

(2) The workload runs in an infinite loop with similar iterations of length L. This work considers the effect of real application workloads. For a workload that runs for a finite time, there is a possibility that no failure occurs during its execution. For a meaningful interpretation of MTTF for a system running such a workload, we assume that the workload runs repeatedly in a loop until the first failure. All iterations of this loop are identical and each represents a single invocation of the original workload. We refer to the size of this loop iteration as L. Workloads that are naturally infinite also run in a loop. We assume that such a workload also consists of identical iterations, each of size L. This assumption is trivially satisfied since L can potentially be infinite. (All the prior work on AVF+SOFR has been in the context of finite workloads.)

We additionally assume that program failure occurs if a raw error is not masked. Although the time to failure and the time to the next raw error event are continuous random variables, for convenience, we often consider time in units of processor cycles below (for architectural masking, for a given cycle, all raw error events during . any part of the cycle are either masked or not masked).

3.1 The AVF Step: MTTF for an Isolated Functional or Storage Unit

The AVF step computes the MTTF of a single component of the processor using equation 1. We examine the validity of this step by deriving the MTTF of a given component from first principles.

268

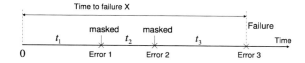

Figure 2. Sequence of raw error events. t_i **is the time between two raw error events and is exponentially distributed.** X **is a random variable representing the time to the first raw error event that is not masked and leads to program failure. The figure shows a case where** $X = t_1 + t_2 + t_3$.

Figure 2 illustrates a sequence of raw error events with inter-arrival times of $t_1, t_2, .., t_n, ...$ Each of these times is an instance of a random variable, say T, with exponential density function $\lambda e^{-\lambda t}$. Each raw error has some probability of being masked. Failure occurs at the first raw error that is not masked.

Let X be the random variable that denotes the time to failure. Then $X = t_1 + t_2 + .. + t_k$ if the first $k - 1$ raw errors are masked and the kth raw error is not masked. Thus, $X = \sum_{i=1}^{K} t_i$, where K is a random variable such that $K = k$ denotes the event that the first $k - 1$ raw errors are masked and the kth raw error is not masked.

Now the MTTF of the component is simply the expected value of X, $E(X)$. Using a standard result for the expectation of a sum of random variables [11], it follows that: $MTTF = E(X) = E(K)E(T)$. We know that $E(T) = \frac{1}{\lambda}$ (this would be the MTTF if there were no architectural masking and every raw error resulted in failure). Thus,

$$MTTF = E(K)\frac{1}{\lambda} \qquad (4)$$

Comparing with equation 1, to validate the AVF step, we would need to show that $E(K) = \frac{1}{AVF}$ for all cases. However, $E(K)$ depends on the workload characteristics and the raw error rate λ, and, in general, cannot be analytically derived. Nevertheless, with certain assumptions, we show that we can derive $E(K)$ to be 1/AVF, validating the AVF step for cases where the assumptions hold. We then show counter-examples where these assumptions do not hold, and the MTTF derived from first principles is significantly different from the MTTF derived from the AVF equation 1.

3.1.1 AVF is valid when $L \cdot \lambda \to 0$

We first show that if the product of the raw error rate and the program loop size is very small, then $E(K) = \frac{1}{AVF}$ (and so the AVF equation holds). Below we show that in this case, any of the L cycles in the program loop are equally vulnerable to a raw error event occurrence. From this, it will follow that the expected value of K (i.e., the count of the first raw error event that is not masked) is the same as 1/AVF.

Let T be the cycle count at which the next raw error event occurs. Then, without loss of generality, $T \bmod L$ is the cycle count for this event relative to the start of the loop iteration.

Appendix A of an extended version of this paper [7] shows that if $L \cdot \lambda \to 0$, the random variable $T \bmod L$ follows a uniform distribution over $[0, L]$. In other words, for very small $L \cdot \lambda$, any of the L cycles of program execution are equally vulnerable to a raw error event occurrence.

Thus, the probability that the next raw error event occurs at cycle i (relative to the start of the loop iteration) is $1/L$. Let p_i be the probability that a raw error event that occurs at cycle i (relative to the start of the loop iteration) is masked (p_i is 0 or 1 for a given program execution). Therefore, the probability that the next raw error event is masked is $\sum_{i=1}^{L} \frac{1}{L} \cdot p_i$. This value is a constant that we denote by M.

Now to calculate $E(K)$, we first calculate P\{K=k\}. This is the probability that the first $k - 1$ raw error events are masked and the kth raw error event is not masked. Since raw error events are independent, it follows that P\{K=k\} = $M^{k-1}(1 - M)$. That is, K is a geometrically distributed random variable and so $E(K) = 1/(1 - M)$. Thus, we just need to show that $1 - M$ is the same as the AVF.

$(1 - M)$ can be expressed as $\sum_{i=1}^{L} \frac{1-p_i}{L}$. $1 - p_i$ is the probability that a raw error event at cycle i will not be masked and will cause failure. $1 - M$ is therefore the average of this probability over the entire program length. This is exactly the definition of AVF. Thus, we have shown that the AVF equation 1 is valid when $L \cdot \lambda \to 0$.

3.1.2 AVF is not valid for some values of λ and L

In this section, we construct a simple (synthetic) program that serves as a counter-example to show that the assumptions behind the AVF step do not always hold.

Consider a program with an infinite loop with iteration size L, such that the considered system component is active for the first A cycles and is idle for the remaining $A + 1$ to L cycles of the iteration. As before, let X be the random variable denoting the time to failure for the component running the above program. Let T be the random variable denoting the time to the first raw error event. If T is in cycles $[0, A], [L, L + A], ...,$ then the component is active and the time to failure is simply the value of T. Otherwise, the raw error occurs in an idle period, say, of iteration k, and it is masked. Further, any raw errors until the next active period (i.e., until cycle kL) will also be masked.

As seen at cycle kL, the distribution for the time to the next raw error event (starting from kL) is the same as that starting from time 0. This is due to the memoryless property of the exponential distribution.[1] Further, as seen from kL, the masking process is also the same as at time 0, since all iterations are identical. Thus, given that there is no failure until cycle kL, the expected time to failure from cycle kL is again E(X).

It follows that given that the first raw error event occurs in the idle period of the kth iteration, the expected time to failure

---

[1]Recall that for an exponential distribution, $P(T < t + \triangle t | T > t) = \frac{(e^{-\lambda t} - e^{-\lambda(t + \triangle t)})}{e^{-\lambda t}} = 1 - e^{-\lambda \triangle t}$. That is, given that a raw error has not occurred at time t, the probability that the error will occur within some time $\triangle t$ after t is the same as that of it occurring within $\triangle t$ after time 0.

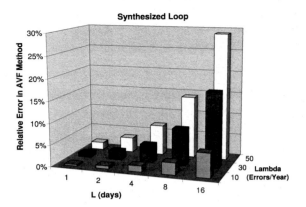

Figure 3. The relative error in the AVF step applied to a large 100MB cache running a loop with iteration size of L days with each iteration busy for $L/2$ days and idle for the rest. Lambda is the raw error rate of the entire cache (the smallest value represents 0.001 FIT per bit).

is $kL + E(X)$. Now using a standard result for conditional expectation [11], we get the following:

$$E(X) = E(E(X|T)) = \int_0^\infty E_{X|T}(t) \cdot f_T(t)dt$$
$$= \int_0^A \lambda e^{-\lambda t} t dt + \int_A^L \lambda e^{-\lambda t}(L + E(X))dt +$$
$$\int_L^{L+A} \lambda e^{-\lambda t} t dt + \int_{L+A}^{2L} \lambda e^{-\lambda t}(2L + E(X))dt...$$

The above equation has the following closed form solution (Appendix A of [7]), giving the MTTF of the component from first principles:

$$E(X) = \frac{1-e^{-\lambda L}}{1-e^{-\lambda A}} \cdot \left(\frac{Le^{-\lambda L}}{(1-e^{-\lambda L})^2} - \frac{Le^{-\lambda A}e^{-\lambda L}}{(1-e^{-\lambda L})^2} - \frac{Ae^{-\lambda A}}{(1-e^{-\lambda L})} + \frac{1}{\lambda}\frac{(1-e^{-\lambda A})}{(1-e^{-\lambda L})} + L\frac{e^{-\lambda A}-e^{-\lambda L}}{(1-e^{-\lambda L})^2} \right)$$

The AVF for our program is $\frac{A}{L}$; therefore, the MTTF according to the AVF method is:

$$E_{AVF}(X) = \frac{L}{A} \cdot \frac{1}{\lambda}$$

Now we can calculate the relative difference between the MTTF from first principles and from the AVF method as:

$$\frac{|E_{AVF}(X) - E(X)|}{E(X)}$$

When λL is very small, we can show that the two MTTFs converge to the same value. For other cases, there can be a significant difference. Figure 3 shows the difference between the two MTTF values for a 100MB cache for different values of L and λ. We vary L from 1 to 16 days, setting A as $L/2$ in each case. We start with λ at 10^{-8} errors/year per bit (0.001 FIT/bit) [6] which translates to 10 errors/year for the full cache. We additionally show results for λ of 3 and 5 times this value to represent changes in technology and altitude. Although the errors are small for the baseline (smallest) value of λ, they can be significant for higher values. Later sections perform a more systematic experimental exploration of the full parameter space.

3.2 The SOFR Step: MTTF for Multiple Functional and/or Storage Units

The SOFR step derives the MTTF of a system using the MTTFs of its individual components, as shown in equations 2 and 3. As discussed in Section 2.3, it assumes that for each component, the time to failure follows an exponential distribution with a constant failure rate (in conjunction with the AVF step, this rate is the product of the component's raw error rate and AVF). We next explore the validity of this assumption, given that each component sees significant architectural masking.

Again, the validity of the assumption depends on the values of the component's raw error rate λ and the program loop size L. Sections 3.2.1 and 3.2.2 respectively discuss cases for which the assumption is and is not valid.

3.2.1 SOFR is valid when $L \cdot \lambda \to 0$

We show that if $L \cdot \lambda \to 0$ for a component, then the time to failure, X, for that component is exponentially distributed with rate parameter $\lambda \cdot AVF$.

Section 3.1.1 showed that in this case, $X = \sum_{i=1}^K t_i$, where K follows a geometric distribution with mean $1/AVF$ and the t_i's are exponentially distributed with rate λ. We can calculate the density function of X as follows:

$$f_X(x) = \lim_{\triangle x \to 0} \frac{P(x < X < x + \triangle x)}{\triangle x}$$
$$= \lim_{\triangle x \to 0} \sum_{i=1}^\infty \frac{P(x < X < x + \triangle x | K=i)P(K=i)}{\triangle x}$$

where $P(x < X < x + \triangle x | K = k) = P(x < \sum_{j=1}^k t_j < x + \triangle x)$.

$\sum_{j=1}^k t_j$ is the sum of several independent exponentially distributed random variables with rate λ. Such a sum follows the Erlang-n distribution which has the probability density function of $\frac{\lambda(\lambda x)^{n-1}}{(n-1)!}e^{-\lambda x}$ [13]. Thus,

$$f_X(x) = \sum_{i=1}^\infty \left((1 - AVF)^{i-1}(AVF)\frac{\lambda(\lambda x)^{i-1}}{(i-1)!}e^{-\lambda x}\right)$$
$$= (AVF)\lambda e^{-\lambda x} \sum_{i=1}^\infty \frac{((1-AVF)\lambda x)^{i-1}}{(i-1)!}$$
$$= \lambda(AVF)e^{-\lambda(AVF)x}$$

This is an exponential distribution with rate $\lambda \cdot AVF$. This validates the assumption for the SOFR step for the case when $\lambda \cdot L$ is small.

3.2.2 The general case for λ and L values

In general, it is difficult to analytically characterize the time to failure distribution function for real (or even synthetic) programs after architectural masking. In this section, to demonstrate a mathematical basis, we choose a distribution that is "close" to exponential (and mathematically tractable) and determine the validity of using SOFR on that distribution.

We choose the following probability density function for the time to failure (after architectural masking) for a component.

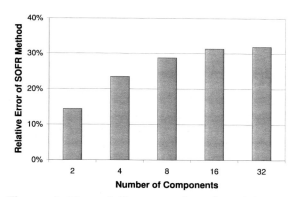

Figure 4. The relative error introduced by the SOFR step for a synthesized example.

$$f_X(x) = \begin{cases} \frac{2}{\sqrt{\pi}} e^{-x^2} & x \in [0, \infty] \\ 0 & \text{elsewhere} \end{cases}$$

The cumulative distribution function (CDF) of X is $F_X(x) = \frac{2}{\sqrt{\pi}} \int_0^x e^{-t^2} dt$, $x \in [0, \infty]$.

It follows that the MTTF of the component is $E(X) = \frac{2}{\sqrt{\pi}} \int_0^\infty x e^{-x^2} dx = \frac{1}{\sqrt{\pi}}$.

Assume a system with N such identical components where X_i denotes the time to failure for component i. Since we assume series failure, it follows that the time to failure of the system, Y, is $\min(X_1, X_2, ..., X_N)$.

The CDF of Y is $F_Y(y) = 1 - (1 - F_X(y))^N$.

The PDF is $f_Y(y) = \frac{dF_Y(y)}{dy} = N * (1 - F_X(y))^{N-1} * f_X(y)$

The MTTF of the system is $E(Y) = \int_0^\infty f_Y(y) y \, dy$

The above integration cannot be calculated analytically. We solve it numerically using a software package to derive the real MTTF for N from 2 to 32.

The SOFR step calculates the MTTF of the system using Equations 2 and 3. For the component MTTFs used in the equations, we use the real MTTF derived above ($\frac{1}{\sqrt{\pi}}$):

$$MTTF_{sofr} = \frac{1}{\sum_{i=1}^N \sqrt{\pi}} = \frac{1}{N\sqrt{\pi}}$$

Figure 4 shows the error in $MTTF_{sofr}$ relative to the MTTF derived from first principles. We see that the error grows from 15% for a system with two components to about 32% for a system with 32 components.

3.3 Summary of implications

Our mathematical analysis so far provides intuition for when the AVF+SOFR method works. The AVF step averages the "utilization" of a component over the whole program. It therefore makes the implicit assumption that every point of the program will have uniform probability of being hit by a soft error. The SOFR step assumes that the time to failure for each individual component follows the exponential distribution. Our analysis

Base Processor Parameters	
Processor frequency	2.0 GHz
Fetch/finish rate	8 per cycle
Retirement rate	1 dispatch-group (=5, max) per cycle
Functional units	2 integer, 2 FP, 2 load-store, 1 branch
Integer FU latencies	1/4/35 add/multiply/divide
FP FU latencies	5 default, 28 divide (pipelined)
Reorder buffer size	150 entries
Register file size	256 entries (80 integer, 72 FP, and various control)
Memory queue size	32 entries
iTLB	128 entries
dTLB	128 entries
Base Memory Hierarchy Parameters	
L1 Dcache	32KB, 2-way, 128-byte line
L1 Icache	64KB, 1-way, 128-byte line
L2 (Unified)	1MB, 4-way, 128-byte line
Base Contentionless Memory Latencies	
L1 Latency	1 cycles
L2 Latency	10 cycles
Main memory Latency	77 cycles

Table 1. Base POWER4-like processor configuration.

shows that the above assumptions are valid when $\lambda \cdot L \to 0$. However, in the general case, these assumptions may not hold. We show mathematically tractable synthetic examples to illustrate a few such cases. The next sections provide a more systematic experimental exploration of the parameter space to assess the extent of the errors due to these assumptions.

4 Experimental Methodology

This section describes the methodology for our experimental analysis of the assumptions of the AVF and SOFR steps. For each step, we first evaluate the assumptions for single processor systems common today running SPEC CPU2000 applications, and using detailed simulation to determine architectural masking. We then take a broader view, and evaluate the assumptions for a large design space, including large clusters of processors and a broader range of (synthesized) workloads, but with less detailed simulation of architectural masking.

For both cases, we first generate a *masking trace* that indicates, for each system component, whether a raw error in a given cycle would be masked for the evaluated system and workload. To calculate the real MTTF of the system (without the AVF+SOFR assumptions), we use the Monte Carlo technique to model the raw error process, apply the masking trace to the process, and determine the MTTF of the modeled system.

4.1 Today's Uniprocessors Running SPEC

To determine the impact of architectural masking in a modern processor, we study an out-of-order 8-way superscalar processor (Table 1) running programs from the SPEC CPU2000 suite (9 integer and 12 floating point benchmarks). To generate the masking trace, we use Turandot [8], a detailed trace-driven microarchitecture-level timing simulator. We simulate an instruction trace of 100 million instructions for each SPEC benchmark running on the above processor configuration.

271

We choose four processor components to study the impact of architecture masking: the integer, floating point, and instruction decode units, and the 256 entry register file, with raw error rates of $2.3 * 10^{-6}$, $4.5 * 10^{-6}$, $3.3 * 10^{-6}$, and $1.0 * 10^{-4}$ errors/year respectively (10^{-8} errors/year = 0.001 FIT). Li et al. [6] derived these error rates using published device error rates for current technology [12] and estimates of the number of devices of different types in different components [6].

For the integer, floating point, and instruction decode units, we assume that a raw error is masked in a cycle if the unit is not processing an instruction in that cycle (i.e., the unit is not busy). If the unit is busy processing an instruction, then for simplicity, we conservatively assume that the error is not masked and will lead to failure. For the register file, we assume that the raw error strikes happen on each register with equal probability and error in a given register is masked if the register contains a value that will never be read in the future. If the register's value will be read, we conservatively assume the error is not masked and will lead to failure. Our assumptions of when an error is not masked are conservative since it is possible that an error in an active unit or in a register value that will be read may not affect the eventual result of the program. We did not perform a more sophisticated analysis to more precisely determine when an error is masked because such an analysis is orthogonal to the point of this paper and beyond the scope of this work.

Our detailed Turandot simulation produces a masking trace for each simulated SPEC application. The trace contains information on whether a raw error in a given cycle in one of the four considered processor components will or will not be masked.

4.2 Broader Design Space Exploration

We also explore a broad design space for the AVF and SOFR steps. We consider a variety of systems consisting of various numbers of components, operating in various environments, with different raw error rates, and running different workloads. We use the term *system* to include a single processor (either a full processor or only a part of it) or a large cluster of thousands of processors. A *component* of a system is the smallest granularity at which the analysis for architectural masking is applied. Specifically, the AVF is calculated at the granularity of a component; the SOFR step then aggregates the information from the different components to give the MTTF for the entire system. In our SOFR experiments, we use component MTTFs obtained from the Monte Carlo method; therefore, the error reported is only that caused by the SOFR step.

Based on our analysis in Section 3, the key parameters affecting the AVF and SOFR steps are the raw error rate of the different components of the processor (or system), the number of components in the system (only for SOFR), and the program loop size or workload. The following discusses the space we explore for each of these important parameters. Table 2 summarizes this space.

Component raw error rate. The component raw error rate depends on the number of devices or elements (bits of on-chip storage or logic elements such as gates) in the component and

Dimension	Value				
N	10^5	10^6	10^7	10^8	10^9
S	1	5	100	2000	5000
C	2	8	5000	50000	500000
Workload	SPEC fp	SPEC int	day	week	combined

Table 2. The design space explored. N = number of elements (e.g., bits) in a component; S = scaling factor for the baseline raw error rate of an element (depends on technology and altitude); and C = number of components in the system (e.g., processors in a cluster).

the raw error rate per element. We denote the number of elements in a component as N. N can be as large as 10^9 for large cache structures or if we consider the entire processor as one component in a large cluster of multiple processors. To keep the design space exploration tractable, without loss of generality, we assume that all N elements have the same raw error rate.

We also explore different values for the raw error rate per element. Under current technology, the terrestrial raw error rate per bit for on-chip storage is about 10^{-8} errors/year (0.001 FIT), which we refer to as the baseline raw error rate. To account for changes in the raw error rate due to technology scaling and at high altitudes, we introduce a parameter S that we use to scale the above baseline rate. We use scaling factors of 1, 5, 100, 2,000, and 5,000 in our analysis. The larger factors correspond to systems running in airplanes flying at a high altitude and for systems in outer space because of strong radiation at those heights [16]. Test systems using accelerated conditions are also subject to high raw error rates.

The raw error rate for a given component is determined as the product of N, S, and the above baseline raw error rate (Table 2). **Number of components:** We denote the number of components in the system as C. We study a wide range of values for C, ranging from 2 to 500,000. The larger numbers represent large cluster systems with C components (each of which may be a full processor or a microarchitectural component within a processor, depending on the granularity at which AVF is collected).

Workload and generation of the masking traces: We evaluate all systems in the broad design space with the SPEC CPU2000 benchmarks mentioned in Section 4.1. However, these are short programs (small loop iteration size L). Many real world workloads show large differences in behavior over long time scales (large L) that are difficult to capture with the SPEC benchmarks. In an attempt to simulate some of the behaviors of real world applications, we construct three synthetic applications. The first (called *day*) is a continuous loop where the loop iteration size is set to 24 hours. The loop is busy during the day (half the time) and idle at night. The second (called *week*) is a loop with iteration size one week. It is busy during the five business days of the week and idle for the weekend. The third (called *combined*) concatenates two SPEC benchmarks in a loop with iteration size of 24 hours. The first half of the iteration runs one benchmark and the second half runs the other benchmark.

For a system with multiple processors, we assume all processors run the same workload. Additionally, for the synthesized workloads, we assume that a component is a full processor; e.g., C=2 implies a 2 processor system. We assume that each processor masks raw errors only during the idle portion of the workload (e.g., night time for the day workload). For the SPEC workloads, we again assume that each component is a full processor (running the same benchmark). For the masking trace, we use the SPEC masking traces for three units in each processor (integer, floating point, and instruction decode) – we apply these three traces to the corresponding units simultaneously to determine whether there is a processor-level failure.

4.3 Monte Carlo Simulation

To calculate the real MTTF, we perform Monte Carlo simulation where we do the following for each trial. For each component in the modeled system, we generate a value from an exponential distribution with rate specified by the modeled system (Table 2). This value gives the arrival time of the next raw error event for the component. We use the masking trace of the workload to determine whether a raw error at that time would be masked. If it is masked, we generate a new raw error event from an independent exponential distribution for that component and repeat. If it is not masked, we consider the component failed. The component that is earliest to fail gives the time to failure of the system for this trial. We run a total of 1,000,000 trials and report the average of the time to failure as the MTTF of the modeled system/workload configuration.

5   Results

5.1   AVF and SOFR with Today's Uniprocessors Running SPEC

We first evaluated the discrepancy between the Monte Carlo MTTF and the MTTF using the AVF and SOFR steps for today's uniprocessors running SPEC (as described in Section 4.1). We found that the MTTF from the AVF step matched the Monte Carlo MTTF very well for each of the four processor components and each benchmark ($< 0.5\%$ discrepancy for all cases). Similarly, the processor MTTF calculated using the SOFR step also matched the Monte Carlo MTTF very well.

Thus, for single processor systems with a small number of small components running SPEC benchmarks, the AVF+SOFR method works very well. We note that in prior work, the method has been applied primarily in this context. These results are consistent with our mathematical analysis. The loop size L for the SPEC benchmarks and the component raw error rates used here are small; therefore, from Sections 3.1.1 and 3.2.1, we expect that the AVF and SOFR assumptions would be valid.

5.2   AVF: A Broad Design Space View

For the design space described in Table 2, we computed the component MTTF using the Monte Carlo and AVF methods as described in Section 4. Note that since the AVF step is applicable to only a single component, $C = 1$ for all experiments in this section. Further, for a given workload, since only the product of N and S matters, we report relative error in the AVF step as a function of different values of $N \times S$.

We found that for each SPEC benchmark, the AVF step works well for all N and S values studied (relative error $<$ 0.5%). However, for the longer running synthesized workloads, we observe significant discrepancy when $N \times S$ is large (i.e., component raw error rate is large). Figure 5 shows the error in the AVF MTTF relative to the Monte Carlo MTTF for representative values of $N \times S$ for the three synthesized workloads. In all three cases, for $N \times S \geq 10^9$, the AVF step sees significant errors (up to 99%). This high value of $N \times S$ may occur when the AVF step is applied to either large components (e.g., a 125MB cache with $N = 10^9$ bits), or when the component size is moderate but the raw error rate per element (bit) is high (e.g., $S = 1000$ because of high radiation at high altitudes).

Our experiments show both positive and negative errors, depending on the workload. Thus, AVF may either over- or under-estimate MTTF in practice.

Again, the above observations match well with our theoretical analysis in Section 3.1. Thus, for SPEC like benchmarks that run for a short time, it is safe to use the AVF step to calculate the MTTF of a component. However, the AVF step must be applied carefully when using a workload with large variations over large time scales coupled with either a large component or a large per-element raw error rate for the component.

5.3   SOFR: A Broad Design Space View

Figures 6(a) and (b) report the error in the SOFR step relative to the Monte Carlo method for three representative SPEC benchmarks and the three synthesized benchmarks respectively. For each case, the error is reported for representative values of C and $N \times S$ covered by the design space in Table 2.

Focusing on the SPEC workloads (Figure 6(a)), we see that the SOFR step is accurate for systems with a small number of components ($C = 2$ or 8) for all studied values of $N \times S$. When system size grows to 5,000 components or larger, we see significant errors, but only with very large values of $N \times S$. For example, for a cluster of 5,000 processors with each processor containing $N = 10^9$ bits of on-chip storage, the baseline raw error rate would need to scale 2,000 times or more to see a significant error. In practice, terrestrial systems will likely fall into the part of the design space where the SOFR step does not introduce any significant error for SPEC applications.

Focusing on the synthesized workloads (Figure 6(b)), for the day workload, we see a significant error using the SOFR step when $N \times S \geq 10^8$ and $C \geq 5,000$. The error increases as these parameters increase. For example, with 12.5MB of storage for each processor ($N = 10^8$) and baseline raw error rate ($S =$

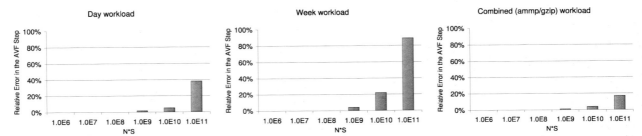

Figure 5. Error in MTTF from the AVF step relative to the Monte Carlo method for the synthesized workloads for representative values of $N \times S$ (# bits in the component $\times$ scaling factor for baseline raw error rate).

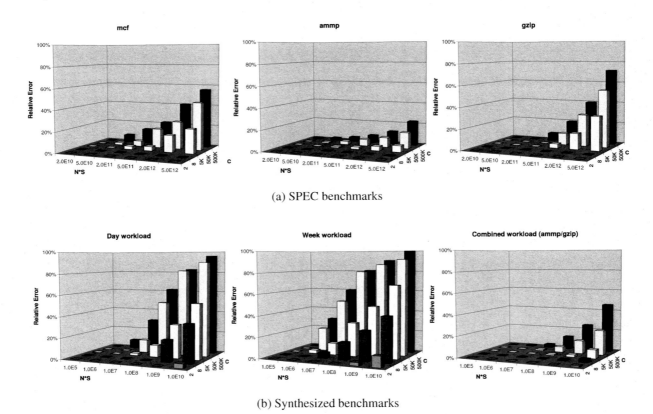

(a) SPEC benchmarks

(b) Synthesized benchmarks

Figure 6. Error in MTTF from the SOFR step relative to the Monte Carlo method for representative values of C (# components) and $N \times S$ (bits per component $\times$ scaling factor for baseline raw error rate) for (a) SPEC and (b) synthesized benchmarks.

1), a 5,000 processor cluster sees an error in MTTF of 11%. For a similar cluster of 50,000 processors, the error jumps to 50%. While large, such a cluster is not unrealistic. For the week workload, since the loop size is larger than the day workload, the MTTF errors are correspondingly larger. Thus, the 5,000 and 50,000 processor systems mentioned above respectively see MTTF errors of 32% and 80% for this workload. With larger processors (more storage bits) or larger systems, the error can grow to 90% or more. Thus, for these workloads, the SOFR step incurs significant errors for realistic systems.

Finally, the combined workload (with two SPEC applications) shows a relative error smaller than for the day or week workload, but there is still a significant error for some cases.

In summary, for SPEC benchmarks under current technology and on the ground, the SOFR step gives accurate MTTF estimates. However, in general, for larger scale workloads, care must be taken to examine the workload behavior, number of system components (e.g., processors), and the raw error rate for the components (governed by component size and per-bit or per-element error rate) before applying SOFR.

5.4 The SoftArch Method

SoftArch is an alternate architecture-level model to calculate processor MTTF due to soft errors [6]. In conjunction with a microarchitectural timing simulator, SoftArch keeps track of the probability of error in each instruction or data bit that is generated or communicated by different processor structures. A bit may be erroneous if it is struck by a high energy particle (error generation) or if it is computed from previously erroneous bits (error propagation). SoftArch uses simple probability theory to track probabilities of these error generation and propagation events, thereby keeping track of the probability of error in any bit. As the program executes in the microarchitectural simulator, SoftArch identifies which values could affect program outcome and when (e.g., values propagated to memory on a store). Using the error probability for such values and the time they affect program output (i.e., potentially result in failure), SoftArch is able to determine the mean time to (first) failure.

SoftArch's probabilistic approach does not require the AVF and SOFR assumptions; it is therefore useful to explore whether SoftArch can be applied to the parts of the design space where AVF+SOFR shows significant discrepancies from the Monte Carlo method. We used SoftArch to estimate MTTF for the entire design space studied here. We found that for every point in this space, the error in MTTF computed by SoftArch relative to the Monte Carlo MTTF is less than 1% for a single component and less than 2% for the full system. Thus, SoftArch does not exhibit the discrepancies shown by AVF+SOFR. These results are not meant to provide a complete validation of SoftArch or a complete comparison between SoftArch and AVF+SOFR (such an analysis is outside the scope of this work). Rather, these results suggest alternative methodologies and motivate future work combining the best of existing methodologies for the most accurate MTTF projections across the widest design space.

6 Conclusions

This paper examines key assumptions behind the AVF+SOFR method for estimating the architecture-level processor MTTF due to soft errors. We use rigorous theoretical analysis backed by simulation-based experiments to systematically explore the applicability of the AVF and SOFR steps across a wide design space. Our analysis and experiments show that while both steps are valid under the terrestrial raw soft error rate values of today's technology for standard workloads (e.g., SPEC), there are cases in the design space where the assumptions of the AVF and SOFR steps do not hold. In particular, for long running workloads with large component-level utilization variations over large time scales, the assumptions are violated for systems with a large number of components and/or with high component-level raw error rate (i.e., large component size and/or large per-bit or per-element raw error rate). Under these conditions, the projected MTTF of the modeled system or chip could show large errors. In general, the paper builds better understanding about the conditions under which the standard AVF+SOFR method may be used to project

MTTF accurately, and alerts users to the risks of using the model blindly in conditions where the foundational axioms of the model break down. The paper also shows that an alternative architecture-level method (that does not make the AVF+SOFR assumptions) does not show the above discrepancies in MTTF, motivating future work to determine the best combination of methodologies to provide the best estimates for all scenarios.

References

[1] A. Biswas et al. Computing the Architectural Vunerability Factor for Address-Based Structures. In *ISCA*, 2005.

[2] E. W. Czeck and D. Siewiorek. Effects of Transient Gate-level Faults on Program Behavior. In *Proc. of the International Symposium on Fault-Tolerant Computing*, 1990.

[3] T. Karnik et al. Characterization of Soft Errors Caused by Single Event Upsets in CMOS Processes. *IEEE Transactions on Dependable and Secure Computing*, 1(2):128–143, June 2004.

[4] S. Kim and A. K. Somani. Soft Error Sensitivity Characterization for Microprocessor Dependability Enhancement Strategy. In *DSN*, 2002.

[5] X. Li et al. SER Scaling Analysis of a Modern Superscalar Processor with SoftArch. In *Proc. of SELSE-1 Workshop*, 2005.

[6] X. Li et al. SoftArch: An Architecture-Level Tool for Modeling and Analyzing Soft Errors. In *DSN*, 2005.

[7] X. Li et al. Architecture-Level Soft Error Analysis: Examining the Limits of Common Assimptions (extended version). Technical Report UIUCDCS-R-2007-2833, UIUC, March 2007. Available at http://rsim.cs.uiuc.edu/Pubs/07dsn-tr.pdf.

[8] M. Moudgill et al. Validation of Turandot, a Fast Processor Model for Microarchitecture Evaluation. In *International Performance, Computing and Communication Conference*, 1999.

[9] S. Mukherjee et al. A Systematic Methodology to Compute the Architectural Vulnerability Factors for a High-Performance Microprocessor. In *MICRO*, 2003.

[10] H. T. Nguyen and Y. Yagil. A Systematic Approach to SER Estimation and Solutions. In *Proc. of IRPS-41*, 2003.

[11] S. Ross. *A First Course in Probability* (Chapter 7). Prentice Hall, 2001.

[12] P. Shivakumar et al. Modeling the Effect of Technology Trends on the Soft Error Rate of Combinational Logic. In *DSN*, 2002.

[13] K. Trivedi. *Probability and Statistics with Reliability, Queueing, and Computer Science Applications*. Prentice Hall, 1982.

[14] N. Wang et al. Characterizing the Effects of Transient Faults on a Modern High-Performance Processor Pipeline. In *DSN*, 2004.

[15] C. Weaver et al. Techniques to Reduce the Soft Error Rate of a High-Performance Microprocessor. In *ISCA*, 2004.

[16] J. F. Ziegler. Terrestrial Cosmic Rays. *IBM Journal of Research and Development*, 40(1):19–39, 1996.

Feedback Redundancy: A Power Efficient SEU-Tolerant Latch Design for Deep Sub-Micron Technologies

M. Fazeli[1], A. Patooghy[1], S.G. Miremadi[2], A. Ejlali[2]
Department of Computer Engineering, Sharif University of Technology, Tehran, Iran
[1]{m_fazeli, patooghy}@ce.sharif.edu, [2]{miremadi, ejlali}@sharif.edu

Abstract

The continuous decrease in CMOS technology feature size increases the susceptibility of such circuits to single event upsets (SEU) caused by the impact of particle strikes on system flip flops. This paper presents a novel SEU-tolerant latch where redundant feedback lines are used to mask the effects of SEUs. The power dissipation, area, reliability, and propagation delay of the presented SEU-tolerant latch are analyzed by SPICE simulations. The results show that this latch consumes about 50% less power and occupies 42% less area than a TMR-latch. However, the reliability and the propagation delay of the proposed latch are still the same as the TMR-latch.the reliability of the proposed latch is also compared with other SEU-tolerant latches.

1. Introduction

When a high energy neutron or an alpha particle strikes a sensitive region in a semiconductor device, a single event upset (SEU) occurs that can alter the state of the system resulting in a soft error. Traditionally, single event upsets were only the main concern for space applications[17]. Currently, smaller feature size, lower voltage levels and higher frequencies of deep sub-micron integrated circuits, make the circuits susceptible to the SEUs even at the ground level [2] [3] [4].

Since the chip and the packaging materials themselves emit alpha particles, packaging cannot be effectively used to shield circuits against SEUs [14]. In addition, SEUs can also be caused by neutrons which can easily penetrate through packages [13]. These two above facts address the importance of incorporating SEU-tolerance techniques to increase the reliability requirements of digital circuits.

SEU-tolerant techniques can be applied to three levels [14] [15]: *1) Device level*: an example of device level techniques is the extra doping layer [5] which can be applied in fabrication process to suppress the effects of particle strikes and to reduce the probability of SEUs. *2) System level*: techniques such as error detection and correction codes [12], and control flow checking [7] use information, hardware or time redundancy at system level to reduce the SEU effects. *3) Circuit level*: here, robust circuit design techniques are employed to mitigate

or eliminate the sensitivity of the circuit to SEUs. These techniques are based on the use of circuit level redundancies to provide SEU-tolerance [8] [9] [10] [11] [15] [16] [27] [28].

One effective way to overcome the SEU effects at circuit level is to triplicate each latch of the system i.e. TMR-latch. Although the TMR-latch is highly reliable and widely used latch [21] [22] [23] [24] [25], but it suffers from high area overhead and power dissipation which are not acceptable for applications where cost and power consumption are the primary concerns. To reduce the cost and the power consumption, some techniques such as [9] [15] [16] [27] [28], employ redundant components inside the latch. Unlike the TMR-latch, these latches cannot tolerate all the SEUs and they can only mitigate the effects of relatively low energy particles. This means that these techniques cannot be used in applications where high reliability is the main concern.

The contributions of this paper are twofold:

i. A circuit level technique for protecting latches against SEUs is proposed. This latch provides the same reliability as a TMR-latch and occupies 42% less area and consumes about 50% less power than the TMR-latch. In the proposed technique, a redundant feedback line is added to the latch and also a filtering circuit is utilized to combine the redundant and original feedback lines in a way that the occurrence of an SEU in a line has no effect on the other line. In fact, the filtering circuit prevents the propagation of SEU effects through the latch output regardless of the amount of the particle energy (section 3).

ii. Detailed SPICE-based fault injection experiments have been performed for analyzing the SEU-tolerant as well as SEU-hardened latches presented in[9] [15] [16] [27] [28]. This analysis shows that:

a. In most of the previous SEU-tolerant latches, except for the TMR-latch, there are still some parts in a latch which are not protected and are very vulnerable to SEUs (section 3).

b. Most of the previous SEU-tolerant latches, except for the TMR-latch, cannot tolerate the SEUs caused by relatively high energy particles (section 3).

The analysis shows that the proposed SEU-tolerant latch has no one of the two above limitations.

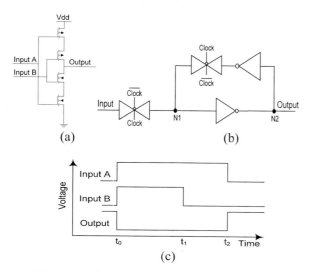

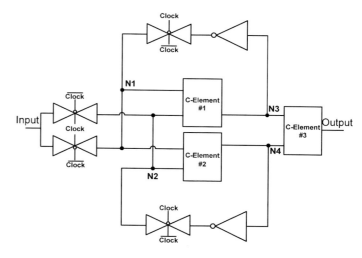

Figure 1. The C-element (a), Traditional latch (b),
Sample input/output of the C-element (c).

Figure 2. The proposed SEU-Tolerant latch

The rest of the paper is organized as follows. Section 2 presents an SEU-tolerant latch. In section 3, the reliability of the previous latches is investigated and compared with the proposed latch. The Propagation delay and power analysis are presented for the proposed latch in section 4. Finally section 5 concludes the paper.

2. The Proposed SEU-Tolerant Latch

A conventional latch (Figure 1.b) employs a feedback path which includes an inverter and a transmission gate to hold the data during the keeping phase. Suppose that a transient voltage pulse due to a SEU occurs in the feedback path (nodes N1 or N2 in Figure 1.b) during the keeping phase. This may change the output of the latch depending on the amount of deposited charge.

In this paper, a redundant feedback along with a filtering circuit is used to prevent the SEU effect propagation through the output. The filtering circuit called C-element is a modified inverter and is shown in Figure 1.a [29]. The C-element is a state holding element, and it has the basic property that inverts its inputs only if both of its inputs are of identical logic value. If the two inputs of this circuit have different values, the previous output value will be retained. Figure 1.c shows the output of the C-element for some sample input values. As it can be seen, during the time interval (t_0, t_1) since the inputs A and B have the same values equal to "1", the output value becomes "0" i.e., the C-element acts as an inverter. When the inputs A and B have different values in the time interval (t_1, t_2), the C-element retains its output and enters to its filtering mode. It should be considered that the time interval (t_1, t_2) must be relatively short because in this situation the output node is connected neither to the supply source nor to the ground and the stray capacitance may be discharged by the saturated current.

Figure 2 shows the block diagram of the proposed SEU-tolerant latch. Three C-elements are used to construct the redundant feedback. The C-elements 1 and 2 are used to prevent the propagation of a transient occurred in node N1 or N2 to the output and the C-element 3 protects the output from the transient occurred in nodes N3 or N4. Suppose that the initial values of nodes N1 and N2 are "1", and consequently nodes N3 and N4 will be "0". In this case, if a transient occurs in the node N1, the value of this node will be changed to "0" and will be propagated to both C-elements 1 and 2. Since the node N2 is not affected by the transient, the C-elements 1 and 2 fall into their filtering mode and retain their previous values, "0" i.e., the values of nodes N3 and N4 are not affected by the transient. Therefore the output will not be erroneous. As the values of nodes N3 and N4 are not affected by the transient, the value of node N1 or N2 will be corrected by the node N3 or N4 through the feedback line.

The C-element 3 is responsible for preventing the propagation of the transient occurred in the node N3 or N4. Again suppose that the initial values of nodes N1 and N2 are "1". If the transient occurs in the node N3 or N4, the two inputs of the C-element 3 take different values. This deference makes the C-element 3 enters to its filtering mode so that the transient is not propagated toward the output. Since a change in value of the node N3 or N4 appears in the node N1 or N2, the C-elements 1 and 2 also act as a filtering circuit. Consequently, all of the C-elements are in the filtering mode (keeping their previous values) until the next level of the clock signal in which the new data must be written. As it was mentioned earlier in this situation the output node is not connected to any supply source and becomes float. But it should be noted that the SEU can only cause a soft error in a latch in the keeping phase so that this condition lasts less than half a cycle and does not affect the functionality of the proposed latch.

277

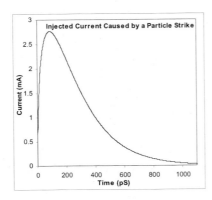

Figure 3. A particle strike

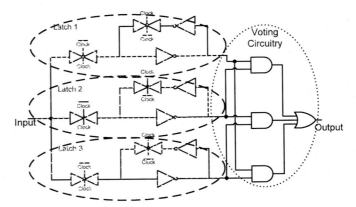

Figure 4. Gate level schematic of a TMR-latch

3. Comparative Analysis

As the main focus of this paper is on SEU-tolerant latch design in circuit level, a TMR-latch along with some other SEU-tolerant latches proposed in [9][15] [16] [27] [28] are chosen and analyzed by the use of HSPICE tool to compare with the proposed latch in terms of reliability.

3.1. SEU-Injection Method

To investigate the SEU-tolerance capability of the proposed latch, the SPICE based SEU-injection experiments were used. The simulations were carried out for the proposed and previously presented latches using CMOS predictive transistor models presented in [8]. SEUs were injected using the current source, which can accurately represent the electrical impact of a particle strike. Similar approaches have been used in prior works [13] [17] [20]. Figure 3 shows the injected current caused by a particle strike using the following model [13]:

$$I_{inj}(t) = \frac{2}{T\sqrt{\pi}} \sqrt{\frac{t}{T}} \, e^{-\frac{t}{T}}.$$

where T is a constant value that depends on the transistor model and measured for n- and p-type transistors separately.

3.2. Reliability Analysis of the Previous Work

As shown in Figure 4, a TMR-latch includes three identical latches with a voting circuit. Due to a large amount of redundancy used in TMR-latch, its area overhead and power dissipation are rather high. In contrast, since the SEU can affect only one of the latches at a time, the TMR-latch can tolerate the soft error caused by the SEU. Therefore this technique is extremely robust against soft errors and even high energetic SEUs are tolerated.

In [15], a SEU-tolerant latch is proposed based on redundancy in circuit level (Figure 5). This latch includes two identical parts, one is the original part and the other is the redundant part. Each part contains two cascaded

inverters similar to the conventional latch discussed in the previous section. The first inverter is a CMOS inverter and the second one is a C^2MOS inverter which plays the role of the inverter and the transmission gate in the conventional latch. Separating the input of n-type and p-type transistors of the all inverters is the key idea of this design. As it can been seen in Figure 5, the gate of the p-type transistor T1 in the first inverter (CMOS inverter) is connected to node N1 and the gate of its n-type transistor T2 is connected to node N3 (from the redundant part). The separation has also been applied to the second inverter (C^2MOS inverter) as well as inverters in the redundant part.

It should be noted that as the original and the redundant part are identical, the nodes N1, N3 and also the nodes N2, N4 have the same values in the normal circuit operation (without any SEUs). As mentioned before, the SEU cannot alter two different parts of the circuit simultaneously. Based on this fact, by the use of separation technique, i.e. providing the input of p- and n-type transistor in the inverters from different parts of the circuit, the propagation of the SEU effect toward the output will be canceled.

The main drawback of this technique is that it is only efficient in the case of low energy particle strikes and if a relatively high energy particle strikes a sensitive region of the circuit, the output will be affected. That is because; the CMOS and C^2MOS inverters in which the inputs of t p-type and n-type transistors are separated cannot act as a filter when a high voltage is applied to one of their inputs. For the sake of clarity, the Figures 6 to 8 demonstrate the circuit level schematic and behavior of a separated CMOS inverter (a CMOS inverter with two separated inputs for p- and n-type transistors) when a high and a low energy particles strike one of its inputs.

Suppose that the input A and B of the inverter shown in Figure 6 are "0" and a transient pulse occurs in the input A at time 4 ns and lasts for about 1 ns. It can be seen in Figure 7.a that there is a low voltage drop, while a low energy SEU is injected to the input A of the inverter. In this case, the output is still interpreted as "1".

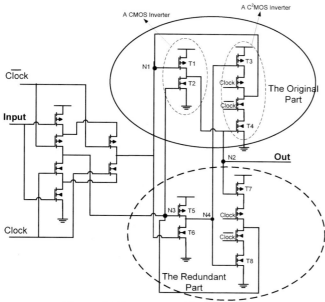

Figure 5. The proposed latch in [15]

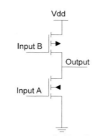

Figure 6. A separated CMOS inverter.

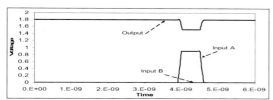

Figure 7. A transient pulse caused by a low energy particle.

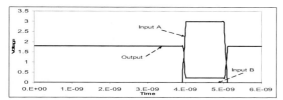

Figure 8. A transient pulse caused by a high energy particle.

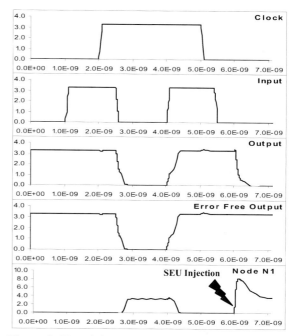

Figure 9. SEU-injection to the proposed latch in [15]

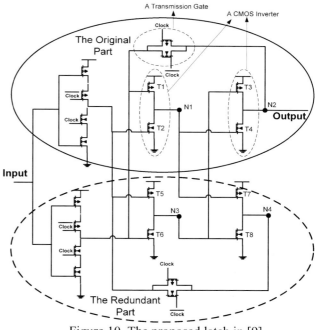

Figure 10. The proposed latch in [9]

In contrast, as represented in Figure 7.b the output of the inverter has significantly changed due to a high energy particle strike. The main reason of this phenomenon is that the produced current between drain and source of the transistor increases quadratically by the rise in the gate voltage of the transistor [26]. Therefore most of the collected charge in the output capacitance is discharged through the n-type transistor. Based on the

279

above discussion, a transient pulse on susceptible nodes of this latch such as nodes N1, N2, N3 and N4 causes a transient pulse in the output of the corresponding inverters and this transient is latched through the constructed loop in the keeping phase of the latch. It is also in agreement with the simulation results.

Figure 9 represents the simulation results of SEU-injection into susceptible nodes of this latch (nodes N1 to N4 of Figure 5). As it can be seen, after SEU-injection the output is different from the error-free output (output without the presence of SEU). The SEU-injection results imply that the used inverters in this latch do not filter the effect of SEU occurred in one of their inputs in the case of a high energetic particle strike.

The very similar approach is used in the SEU-tolerant latch proposed in [9]. As shown in Figure 10, separation of the used inverters inputs is also employed in this design to prevent the propagation of the SEU effect toward the output. Similar to the previous latch, this SEU-tolerant latch is also incapable to suppress the SEU effect caused by high energy particles. The simulation results of SEU injection to a susceptible node of this latch (node N4) is presented in Figure 11. As it can be seen, a high voltage drop in the node N4 due to high energy particle causes the latch to produce erroneous output.

To overcome the problem of the two previously discussed latches, a C-element which was described in section 2 is employed in the proposed latch in [28]. The transistor level structure of this latch is shown is Figure 12, in the normal operation (without any SEU) the input of the latch is propagated to the output through the C-element and two used feedback paths (in positive level of clock signal). Since both internal nodes N1 and N2 have the same logic value, only one of the pair transistors (T1 and T2 or T3 and T4) are always on, thereby the inverted input value passes to the output of the latch. In case of a SEU affects one of the latch internal nodes N1 or N2, the output does not flip even if the particle energy is high. That is because; the C-element retains its previous value if its two inputs are in different values (see section 2). Therefore a transient occurred in node N1 or N2 can only affect pair transistors (T1, T3 or T2, T4). In this case, the C-element does not pass the produced transient voltage to its output and enters to its filtering mode. However the main weakness of this latch is its inability of tolerating the transient occurred in the output of the latch (node N3). For the sake of clarity suppose that the output value of the latch is "0" and a SEU forces the output (node N3) to be "1" momentarily. Since the node N3 is connected to both nodes N1 and N2, the produced transient voltage reaches all the transistors of C-element, accordingly it does not filter this transient and the incorrect value will be stored inside the latch. By the use of the C-element in this way, two feedback lines are only isolated in their end points (nodes N1 and N2). But they still have the same start point (node N3). Consequently the transient voltage occurred in the output (node N3) is latched regardless of the strength of the particle. It also can be seen from the

simulation results of SEU-injection into the output of this latch (Figure 13).

According to Figure 13, in the SEU-free case, the output of the latch becomes "0" at about 3 ns and is never changed. But after SEU-injection at about 4.5 ns in the output of the latch, the high voltage rise (about 10 volts) caused by SEU-injection cannot be recovered to the error-free output, i.e., a soft error has been occurred in the latch.

[27] exploits a similar technique used in the previously mentioned latch. As it was mentioned, if a transient occurs in the output of the proposed latch in [28], its effect will propagate through the both feedback lines, resulting in a soft error. The proposed latch in [27] tries to address this issue by separating the feedback lines of the latch both at their start and end points, nodes N2, N3 and N4, N5 respectively (see Figure 14).

To reach the aim, a two-output inverter which is shown in Figure 14 is used. In the two-output inverter both p- and n-type transistors are duplicated to provide two same distinct outputs (nodes N4 and N5). As shown in Figure 14 the latch has two inputs, one of them is the incoming signal and the other one is the delayed version of that. The delay value is chosen to be longer than the summation of the setup time and duration of the probable transient pulse to ensure that at least one input is correct. This makes the latch robust to the transient pulse at its inputs.

Now suppose that the input value is "0". While the clock signal is in its positive level, the input passes via the two first transmission gates to the nodes N4 and N5. When the clock signal goes to the negative level the first two transmission gates become off and the second one becomes on, then the output of the latch is connected to the node N1 via the second transmission gate and the latch enters to its keeping phase. In the other words, the feedbacks are constructed to keep the output value. In this phase the value of the nodes N2 and N3 are the same and equal to "0", thereby the p-type transistors T5 and T6 are on, the n-type transistors T7 and T8 are off and the values of the nodes N1 and output become "1". In this situation, the transistors T3 and T4 conduct and the node N5 gets value "0". The node N4 which is the dual of the node N5, retains its previous value from the writing phase of the latch (when the clock signal was in positive level) which is "0".

If a transient occurs in the output node in this state, its value will become "0" and also the value of node N1 will become "0" so that the transistors T1 and T2 become on and the value of node N4 changes to "1". Since the transistors T3 and T4 are off in this state, the node N5 keeps its previous value i.e., "0". Therefore transistors T6 and T7 switch to the on-state and transistors T5 and T8 enter into the off-state, hence the C-element falls into the filtering mode and never change its mode until a new data is written to the latch. That is, if a voltage drop or rise due to a SEU occurs in the output of the mentioned latch, there is no possibility to recover the output value

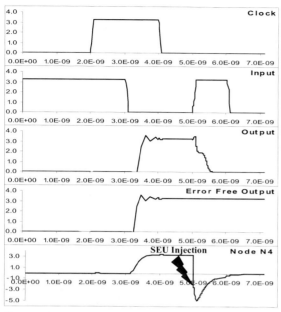

Figure 11. SEU-injection to the proposed latch in [9]

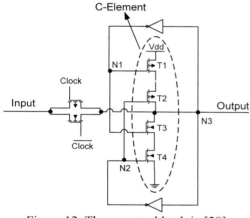

Figure 12. The proposed latch in [28]

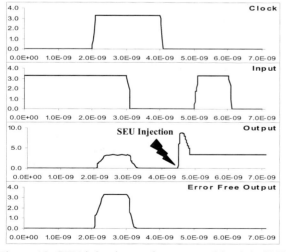

Figure 13. SEU injection to the proposed latch in [28].

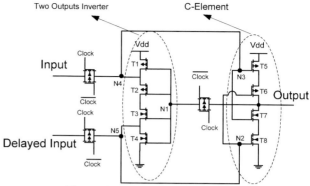

Figure 14. The proposed latch in [27]

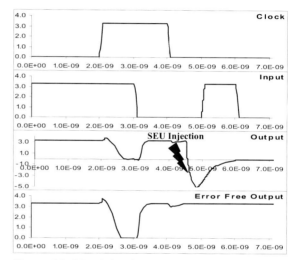

Figure 15. SEU injection to the proposed latch in [27].

and an incorrect value will be latched. The SEU-injection results shown in Figure 15 confirm this matter.

Some other SEU-tolerant latch techniques such as [11], [16] are based on increasing the size of the equivalent capacitance of internal susceptible nodes by using some redundant transistors. These techniques just mitigate the SEU effect but still it is probable that a high energy particle causes a soft error in the latch. In principle, these techniques are based on the fact that if the size of equivalent capacitance of the internal nodes increases the probability of a SEU causes a soft error in a memory element will decrease. That is because, the SEU causes a soft error by discharging the internal capacitance of the latch and if the size of the internal capacitance is increased, the probability of a SEU caused a soft error will be decreased. However, increasing the internal capacitance of the latch results in a rise in the latch propagation delay which imposes performance overhead to the system. The Schematics of the proposed SEU-tolerant latch in [16] which is based on the mentioned technique, is depicted in Figure 16. The simulation results are also demonstrated in Figure 17. The results show that

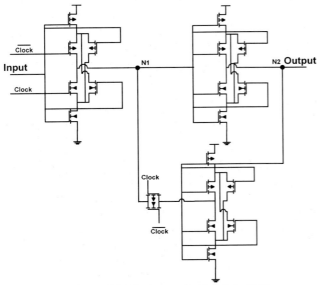

Figure 16. The proposed latch in [16]

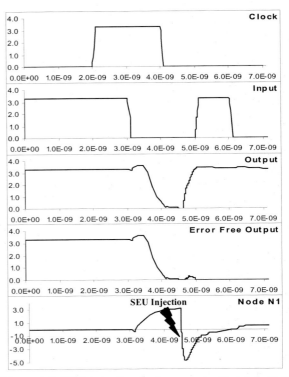

Figure 17. SEU-injection to the proposed latch in [16]

although the use of extra p- and n-type transistors increases the size of equivalent capacitance in susceptible nodes (nodes N1 and N2) but still a high voltage drop due to a high energy particle can be propagated to the output.

3.3 Reliability Analysis of the Proposed Latch

Based on the SEU-injection simulation results, all of the previously proposed SEU-tolerant latches have at least one susceptible node in which the SEU effect can be propagated to the output, resulting in a soft error in the latch.

To address this issue, in the proposed latch a feedback path along with a C-element are used to form a fully isolated feedback line. The simulation results (Figure 18) show that the proposed latch masks the effect of SEUs in all fault injection sites which are nodes N1, N2, N3 and N4 (see Figure 2). It should be considered that two feedbacks in the proposed design are the same. Thus only the fault injection results of nodes N1 and N3 are reported.

The SEU-injections are preformed both for the SEUs that cause a voltage drop and those cause a voltage rise in susceptible nodes, but for the sake of simplicity only some of the SEU-injection results are reported. Figure 18.a shows that a voltage drop in node 1, due to the SEU injection, is filtered by the C-element 1 (see Figure 2) and the transient cannot be propagated to the node N3. Node N1 is also recovered by the correct value in node N3 through the feedback line. The SEU-injection to node N3 is also represented in Figure 18.b. The SEU causes a voltage rise in node N3 and this transient propagates to the node N1 which is connected to C-elements 1 and 2. As the two inputs of the C-elements become different, these two C-elements filter the effect of the injected SEU

so that both feedback lines will be disjointed. On the other hand, the value of node N3 differs from the value of node N4 and this also makes the C-element 3 be in its filtering mode. Thus, the injected SEU effect cannot pass through the output. The SEU-injection results in Figure 18.b show that although the value of node N3 is not recovered but the output of the latch is still correct.

4. Performance and Power Analysis

Since fault-tolerant techniques use redundancy, some power, area and performance overheads may be imposed to the systems i.e., the more fault tolerance is achieved, the more overheads is imposed to the system. Therefore, the evaluation of such overheads is essential to demonstrate the effectiveness of a technique. The area overhead is directly proportional to the number of used transistor, in the proposed technique, 24 transistors are used while the number of required transistors in TMR-latch is 42. Thus the proposed latch occupies approximately 42% less area than the TMR-latch.

The power consumption of a VLSI system can be subdivided into two main components: dynamic power and leakage power. Until recently dynamic power has been the main source of the power consumption. However, in deep-submicron CMOS, the technology shrinkage causes transistor sub-threshold leakage current to increase exponentially which results in a corresponding increase in leakage power, so that the leakage power becomes comparable to the dynamic power [17][30].

The switching power is the dominant part of the dynamic power in a CMOS circuit. The switching power is proportional to the total capacitance, the supply voltage, the clock frequency and the expected number of transitions per clock cycle [30]. Since switching power dissipation is in direct proportion to switching activity of the circuit nodes, it can be minimized by performing circuit optimization. Since in the TMR-latch two extra latches along with some other circuits is exploited only for reliability enhancement, the switching activity increases significantly in comparison with a simple latch. In fact the redundancy for reliability objectives always increases the switching activity resulting in extra switching power dissipation. As in the proposed latch, the number of transistors is reduced by about 50% in comparison with the TMR-latch, the switching activity decreases by the same amount i.e., it consumes about 50% less switching power than the TMR-latch.

On the other hand, the leakage current which is caused by the off-state transistors in the circuit is the main source of leakage power dissipation. Therefore if the average number of off-state transistors per clock cycle is reduced in a design, the amount of leakage power dissipation will be also decreased. Since the number of transistors in the proposed latch is about half of the TMR-latch, the average number of off-state transistor per clock cycle is definitely diminished.

The simulation for power dissipation is performed for 250nm, 180nm, 130nm, 90nm and 65nm technologies using HSPICE tool. As it shown in Figure 19, the amount of total power dissipation is on average 50% of the TMR-latch regardless of the technology size. As mentioned earlier, the leakage power becomes the dominant part of total power dissipation when technology shrinks. But based on our simulation results the power reduction in the proposed latch is independent of the used technology. In the other words, although in deep sub-micron technologies such as 65nm the leakage power is comparable to dynamic power but it can be seen from Figure 19 that the total power reduction in the proposed latch is still remained at about 50%. Therefore it can be concluded that in the proposed latch the average number of off-state transistors per clock cycle is also about half of the TMR-latch.

In short, the simulation results reveal that the proposed latch has approximately 50% reduction both in dynamic and leakage powers. Therefore it makes the proposed SEU-tolerant latch suitable for use in deep sum-micron technologies.

In order to investigate the power efficiency of a method it is mandatory to consider the amount of imposed performance overhead too. Power delay product which is interpreted as energy per result is the most widely used metric to compare low power design techniques [30]. Some other simulations are carried out in order to extract the propagation delay of the proposed and TMR-latch. Figure 20 shows that the propagation delay of the proposed latch is less than the TMR-latch in all technologies (note that the results are normalized by the TMR-latch propagation delay). Figure 21 represents the power delay product values for different technology sizes. As shown the performance overhead of the proposed latch is almost the same as the TMR-latch. It is evident that the amount of power delay product is reduced significantly in the proposed latch in comparison with TMR-latch.

5. Conclusions

In this paper a novel SEU-tolerant latch was designed and evaluated. In the proposed latch, redundant feedback lines were used to mask the effects of SEUs.

To investigate the efficiency of the proposed design, some important SEU-tolerant latches and our proposed latch were analyzed and SEU injection experiments were carried out by the means of HSPICE tool. Experimental results showed that the proposed latch can tolerate the effects of SEU in all of the critical nodes. Also it was shown that there are some critical nodes in the previous proposed latches that were still vulnerable to SEUs.

To demonstrate the power dissipation, performance and area overheads of the proposed design, simulations for 250nm, 180nm, 130nm, 90nm and 65nm technologies were performed and compared with TMR which is the effective method to completely tolerate the SEU effects. According to the results, the proposed latch consumes 50% less power and occupies 42% less area as compared with the TMR-latch regardless the technology size, while its reliability is almost the same as TMR-latch.

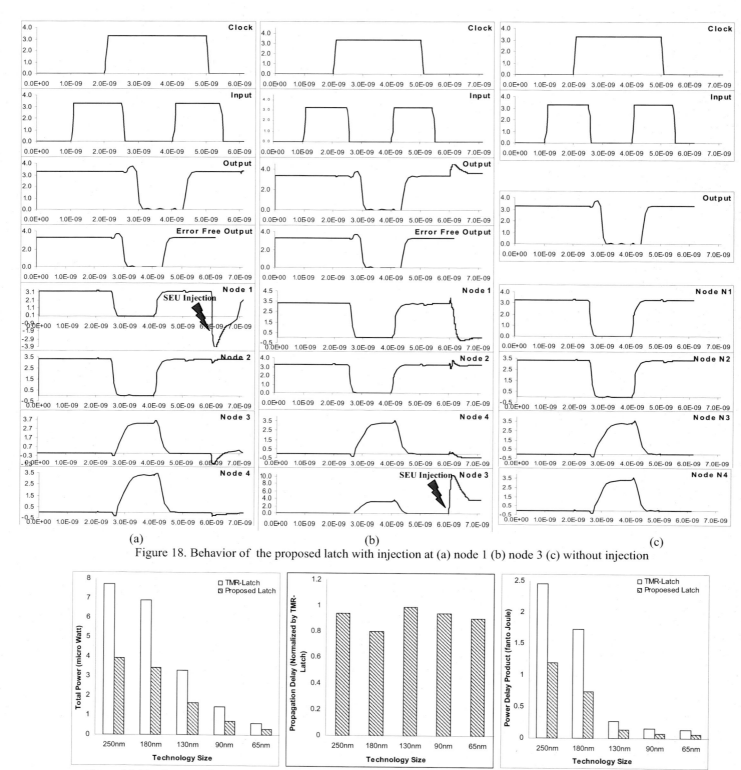

(a)   (b)   (c)

Figure 18. Behavior of the proposed latch with injection at (a) node 1 (b) node 3 (c) without injection

Figure 19. Total power dissipation   Figure 20. Normalized propagation delay   Figure 21. Power delay product

6. References

[1] G.C. Messenger, "Collection of Charge on Junction Nodes from Ion Tracks", IEEE Trans. Nuclear Science, 1982, pp. 2024-2031.

[2] N. Cohen, T.S. Sriram, N. Leland, D. Moyer, S. Butler, R. Flatley, "Soft error considerations for deep-submicron CMOS circuit applications", International Electron Devices Meeting, Washington, DC, 1999, pp. 315–318.

[3] R.W. Keyes, "Fundamental limits of silicon technology", Proc. IEEE, vol. 89, no. 3, Mar. 2001, pp. 227–339.

[4] S. Mitra, T. Karnik, N. Seifert, M. Zhang, "Logic soft errors in sub-65nm technologies design and CAD challenges ", Design Automation Conference (DAC), Anaheim, CA, June 2005, pp. 2 – 4.

[5] S.W. Fu, A.M. Mohsen, T.C. May, "Alpha-particle-induced charge collection measurements and the effectiveness of a novel p-well protection barrier on VLSI memories," IEEE Trans. Electron Devices, vol. ED-32, no. 1, Jan. 1985. pp. 49–54.

[6] M. Takai, T. Kishimoto, Y. Ohno, H. Sayama, K. Sonoda, S. Satoh, T. Nishimura, H. Miyoshi, A. Kinomura, Y. Horino, K. Fujii, "Soft error susceptibility and immune structures in dynamic random access memories (DRAM's) investigated by nuclear microprobes," IEEE Trans. Nucl. Sci., vol. 43, no. 2, Feb. 1996, pp. 696–704.

[7] A. Mahmood, E.J. McCluskey, "Concurrent Error Detection Using Watchdog Processors – A Survey", IEEE Trans. on Computers, Feb. 1988, pp. 160 -174.

[8] A.J. Drake, A. KleinOsowski, A.K. Martin, "A Self- Correcting Soft Error Tolerant Flop-Flop", 12th NASA Symposium on VLSI Design, Coeur d'Alene, Idaho, USA, Oct. 4-5, 2005.

[9] R. Naseer, J. Draper, "The DF-DICE Storage Element for Immunity to Soft Errors", Proceedings of the 48th IEEE International Midwest Symposium on Circuits and Systems, August 2005.

[10] D.R. Blum, M.J. Myjak, J.G. Delgado-Frias, "Enhanced Fault-Tolerant Data Latches for Deep Submicron CMOS," The 2005 International Conference on Computer Design (ICCD), pp. 28-34, Las Vegas, June 2005.

[11] K.J. Hass, J.W. Gambles, B. Walker, M. Zampaglione, "Mitigating single event upsets from combinational logic," 7th NASA Symposium on VLSI design, 1998.

[12] C.L. Chen, M.Y. Hsiao, "Error correcting codes for semiconductor memory applications: A state-of-the-art review," IBM J. Res. Develop., vol. 28, no. 2, pp. 124–134, Mar. 1984.

[13] P. Hazucha, C. Svensson: "Impact of CMOS technology scaling on the atmospheric neutron soft error rate", IEEE Trans. On Nuclear Sc. Vol. 47, n. 6, Dec. 2000, pp. 2586-2594.

[14] Q. Zhou, K. Mohanram, "Gate sizing to radiation harden combinational logic", IEEE Transactions on Computer-aided Design of Integrated Circuits and Systems (TCAD), vol.25, Jan. 2006, pp. 155-166.

[15] T. Calin, N. Nicolaidis, R. Velazo, "Upset Hardened Memory Design for Submicron CMOS Technology", IEEE Trans. On Nuclear Sc. Vol. 43, n. 6, Dec. 1996, pp. 2874-2878.

[16] M.P. Baze, S.P. Buchner, D. McMorrow, "A Digital CMOS Design Technique for SEU Hardening", IEEE Trans. On Nuclear Sc. Vol. 47, n. 6, Dec. 2000, pp. 2603-2608.

[17] A. Ejlali, B.M. Al-Hashimi, M.T. Schmitz, P. Rosinger, S.G. Miremadi, "Combined time and information redundancy for SEU-tolerance in energy-efficient real-time systems", IEEE Trans. on Very Large Scale Integration Systems, Vol. 14, April 2006, Issue: 4, pp. 323-335.

[18] W. Zhao, Y. Cao, "New generation of Predictive Technology Model for sub-45nm design exploration," ISQED, San Jose, CA, March 2006, pp. 585-590.

[19] L. Rockett, "An SEU Hardened CMOS Data Latch Design ", IEEE Trans. On Nuclear Sc. Vol. NS-35, n. 6, Dec. 1988, pp. 1682-1687.

[20] A. Maheshwari, W. Burleson, R. Tessier, "Trading off transient fault tolerance and power consumption in deep submicron (DSM) VLSI circuits," IEEE Trans. Very Large Scale Integration (VLSI) Systems, vol. 12, no. 3, 2004, pp. 299-311.

[21] F. Kastensmidt, L. Sterpone, M. Sonza Reorda, L. Carro, "On the Optimal Design of Triple Modular Redundancy Logic for SRAM-Based FPGAs," DATE2005: IEEE Design, Automation and Test in Europe, 2005, pp. 1290-1295.

[22] M. Favalli, C. Metra, "TMR voting in the presence of crosstalk faults at the voter inputs", IEEE Transactions on Reliability, Sept. 2004, Volume: 53, Issue: 3, pages: 342 - 348, ISSN: 0018-9529.

[23] L. Sterpone, M. Violante, "Analysis of the robustness of the TMR architecture in SRAM-based FPGAs," IEEE Transactions on Nuclear Science, 2005, Vol. 52, No. 5, October 2005, pp. 1545 – 1549.

[24] V. Stachetti, J. Gaisler, G. Goller and C.L. Gargasson, "32-BIT Processing Unit For embedded Space Flight Applications", IEEE Trans. on Nuclear Science, Vol. 43, No. 3, June 1996, p.p. 873-878.

[25] J. Gaisler, "A Portable and Fault-Tolerant Microprocessor Based on the SPARC V8 Architecture", Proc. of the IEEE/IFIP International Conference on Dependable Systems and Networks (DSN'02), June 2002, p.p. 409 - 415.

[26] S.M. Kng, Y. Leblebici, "CMOS Digital Integrated Circuits Analysis & Design", MacGraw-Hill, ISBN: 0-07-038046-3, 1996.

[27] Y. Zhao, S. Dey, "Separate Dual-Transisto Registers –A Circuit Solution for On-Line Testing of Transient Error in UDSM-IC", in Proc. of 9th IEEE Int. On-Line Testing Symp. (IOLTS'03), pp. 7-11, 2003.

[28] M. Omana, D. Rossi, C. Metra, "Novel Transient Fault Hardened Static Latch", in Proc. of IEEE Int. Test Conference (ITC'03), pp. 886-892, 2003.

[29] S. Mitra, N. Seifert, M. Zhang, Q. Shi, and K.S. Kim, "Robust system design with built-in soft-error resilience," Computer, vol. 38, no. 2, pp. 43-52, 2005.

[30] M. Pedram, J. Rabaey, "Power Aware Design Methodologies", Norwell, MA: Klouwer, 2002.

Using Register Lifetime Predictions to Protect Register Files Against Soft Errors*

Pablo Montesinos, Wei Liu and Josep Torrellas

Department of Computer Science
University of Illinois at Urbana-Champaign
{pmontesi, liuwei, torrellas}@cs.uiuc.edu
http://iacoma.cs.uiuc.edu

Abstract

To increase the resistance of register files to soft errors, this paper presents the ParShield *architecture.* ParShield *is based on two observations: (i) the data in a register is only useful for a small fraction of the register's lifetime, and (ii) not all registers are equally vulnerable.* ParShield *selectively protects registers by generating, storing, and checking the ECCs of only the most vulnerable registers while they contain useful data. In addition, it stores a parity bit for all the registers, re-using the ECC circuitry for parity generation and checking.* ParShield *has no SDC AVF and a small average DUE AVF of 0.040 and 0.010 for the integer and floating-point register files, respectively.* ParShield *consumes on average only 81% and 78% of the power of a design with full ECC for the SPECint and SPECfp applications, respectively. Finally,* ParShield *has no performance impact and little area requirements.*

1. Introduction

With increased chip integration levels, reduced supply voltages, and higher frequencies, soft errors are becoming a serious threat for high-performance processors. Such errors can be due to a variety of events, most notably the impact of high-energy particles [2, 8, 23]. Since soft errors can result in program visible errors [20], there have been proposals for several architectural designs that protect different structures of the processor, such as caches, memories, and datapaths [6, 13, 16, 21].

One of the critical structures to protect in a processor is the register file. It is a sizable structure that stores architectural state. It often stores data for long periods of time and is read frequently, which increases the probability of spreading a faulty datum to other parts of the machine. For these reasons, some commercial processors protect their register files with either parity [3, 9] or error correcting codes (ECC) [18]. Protecting the register file with only parity enables error detection but not correction. In this case, when

the error is detected, recovery is only possible by invoking a high-level operation at the OS or application level. Since the software might not always be able to recover from the error, the application may need to terminate. Full ECC support, on the other hand, enables on-the-fly detection and correction of errors. However, it does so at a cost in power and possibly performance.

A cost-effective protection mechanism for soft errors in register files should have no performance impact, keep the remaining Architectural Vulnerability Factor (AVF) [11] to a small value, consume modest power, and use little area. To design such mechanism, we make two key observations on the use of registers in general-purpose processors. The first one is that the data stored in a physical register is not always useful. A soft error in a physical register while it is not useful will not have any impact on the processor's architectural state. Consequently, we only need to protect a register when it contains useful data. The second observation is that not all the registers are equally vulnerable to soft errors. A small set of long-lived registers account for a large fraction of the time that registers need to be protected. The contribution of most of the other registers to the vulnerable time is very small.

Based on these two key observations, this paper proposes *ParShield*, a novel architecture that provides cost-effective protection for register files against soft errors. ParShield relies on the Shield concept, which selectively protects a subset of the registers by generating, storing, and checking the ECCs of only the most vulnerable registers while they contain useful data. Such support reduces the AVF of the integer register file by an average of 73% to 0.040, and the AVF of the floating-point register file by an average of 85% to 0.010. ParShield also adds a parity bit for all the registers and re-uses the ECC circuitry for parity generation and checking as well. As a result, ParShield has no Silent Data Corruption (SDC) AVF (all single-bit errors are detected), has a Detected Unrecoverable Error (DUE) AVF as low as Shield's AVF, and consumes on average only 81% and 78% of the power of a design with full ECC for the SPECint and SPECfp applications, respectively. Moreover, ParShield has no performance impact and little area requirements.

The paper is organized as follows. Section 2 describes the motivation of this work; Sections 3 and 4 describe the

---
*This work was supported in part by the National Science Foundation under grants CHE-0121357 and CCR-0325603; DARPA under grant NBCH30390004; DOE under grant B347886; and gifts from IBM and Intel. Wei Liu is now at Intel Corporation. His email is wei.w.liu@intel.com.

Figure 1. Lifetime of a register version.

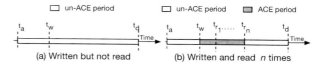

Figure 2. ACE periods of two register versions.

design and the implementation of ParShield; Sections 5 and 6 evaluate ParShield; and Section 7 describes related work.

2. Motivation: Assigning Reliability Resources

2.1. Register Lifetime

Modern out-of-order processors use register renaming with a large number of physical registers to support many in-flight instructions [4]. After the processor decodes an instruction with a destination register, it allocates a free physical register, creating a new *register version*. Later, the instruction is executed, and its result is written to the corresponding physical register. Subsequent instructions that use that value are renamed to read from that physical register. The register version is kept until the instruction that redefines the corresponding logical register retires — this is necessary to handle precise exceptions. Note that a version is written to only *once* but can be read multiple times.

As Figure 1 shows, the lifetime of a register version lasts from register allocation to deallocation. We divide it into three different periods: from allocation until write; from write until last read; and from last read to deallocation. We call these periods *PreWrite*, *Useful*, and *PostLastRead*, respectively. Note that only the *Useful* period needs to be protected.

2.2. Register ACE Analysis

Errors are usually classified as undetected or detected. The former are known as Silent Data Corruption (SDC), while the latter are usually referred to as Detected Unrecoverable Errors (DUE) [11]. Errors for which detection and recovery succeeds are not treated as errors.

A structure's *Architectural Vulnerability Factor* (AVF) is the probability that a fault in that structure will result in an error [11]. The SDC AVF and DUE AVF are the probabilities that a fault causes an SDC or a DUE error, respectively. In general, if a structure is protected by an error detection mechanism, its SDC AVF is zero. If the structure has error detection and correction capabilities, its DUE AVF is zero. In this work, we assume that the AVF for a register file is the average AVF of all its bits.

Mukherjee *et al.* [11] proposed the concept of *Architecturally Correct Execution* (ACE) to compute a structure's AVF. ACE analysis divides a bit's lifetime into ACE and un-ACE periods. A bit is in ACE state when a change in its value will produce an error. The AVF for a single bit is the fraction of time that it is in ACE state. To calculate the total time a bit is in ACE state, we start by assuming that

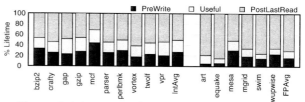

Figure 3. Integer versions lifetime breakdown.

its whole lifetime is in ACE state, and then we remove the fraction that can be proven un-ACE. The fraction left is an upper bound on the ACE time.

As an example, Figures 2(a) and (b) show two register versions and their ACE and un-ACE periods. In both cases, a free physical register R is allocated at time t_a and deallocated at time t_d. During its PreWrite period, it remains in un-ACE state. At time t_w, R is written to and, if it will be consumed at least once, it switches to ACE state. Figure 2(a) depicts a register version that is never read, so it remains in un-ACE state for its whole lifetime. Figure 2(b) shows a register version that is consumed n times, so it enters ACE state at t_w and remains in it until it is read for the last time at t_{rn}. A register version is in un-ACE state during its PostLastRead period.

There is one case where a register is read and it should still remain in un-ACE state. This is when the reader instructions are eventually squashed and, therefore, are never committed. For simplicity, however, in this work we do not consider it; if a register will be read, it is ACE.

2.3. Two Key Observations

Our analysis of SPECint and SPECfp 2000 applications for an out-of-order superscalar processor with 128 integer physical registers (Section 5) enables us to make two key observations.

The Combined Useful Time of All the Registers is Small. We observe that the time a register version is in *Useful* state is only a *small fraction* of the register's lifetime. Figure 3 shows the average integer register's *PreWrite*, *Useful*, and *PostLastRead* times for both SPECint and SPECfp applications. As shown in the figure, on average only 22% and 15% of the register lifetime is *Useful* for SPECint and SPECfp applications, respectively. Therefore, there is no need to provide protection for the whole lifetime of a register version.

Figure 4 shows the average number of integer physical registers that are in *Useful* state at a given time. For SPECint, the average is less than 20 registers out of 128. For SPECfp, it is approximately 17 out of 128.

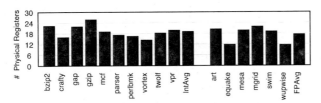

Figure 4. Average number of integer physical registers in useful state.

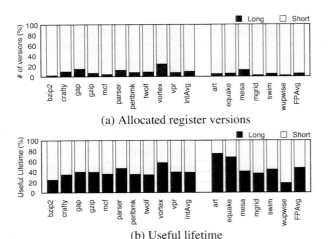

(a) Allocated register versions

(b) Useful lifetime

Figure 5. Short- and long-lived integer register versions characterization.

Overall, we conclude that it is possible to reduce the vulnerability of the register file by only protecting a subset of carefully chosen registers at a time.

A Few Long-Lived Registers Provide Much of the Total Useful Time. The second observation is that not all the register versions are equally vulnerable to soft errors. A small set of long-lived versions account for a large fraction of the time that registers need to be protected. For this section only, we say that a register version is *short-lived* if by the time it is written, an instruction that reads or writes the same architectural register has been renamed. We call the other versions *long-lived*.

To see this effect, consider Figures 5(a) and 5(b). For each SPEC application, Figure 5(a) shows the percentage of long- and short-lived integer register versions. On average, less than 10% of the register versions are long-lived for SPECint and SPECfp. Figure 5(b) shows the percentage of the useful lifetime that long- and short-lived versions contribute to. On average, about 40% of the contribution comes from these few long-lived register versions. Specifically, in the case of SPECfp, 5% of versions account for 46% of the useful lifetime. Therefore, it is cost-effective to give higher protection priority to these long-lived register versions.

3. ParShield: Protecting the Register File

To provide cost-effective protection for register files, we propose *ParShield*. ParShield is composed of (i) the *Shield*

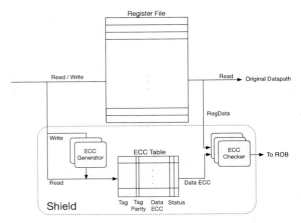

Figure 6. Shield architecture.

structures and (ii) the parity support. In this section, we describe the architecture, focusing mostly on Shield.

3.1. Shield Concept

ParShield relies on the Shield concept, which involves using ECCs to selectively protect only the subset of most vulnerable registers while they contain useful data. Shield supports three operations on one such register: (i) when the register is written, Shield generates and saves the ECC of the written data, (ii) when the register is read, Shield checks whether the register contents are still valid, and (iii) Shield keeps the ECC of the data until the register is read for the last time. Shield assumes a single-bit fault model.

Figure 6 shows the Shield architecture. It adds three hardware components to a traditional register file for an out-of-order processor: a table that stores the ECCs of some registers, a set of ECC generators and a set of ECC checkers. The ECC table is organized as a CAM. It protects the most vulnerable register versions in the register file. Each entry protects one register version and consists of: (i) a *tag* with the physical register number, (ii) a *parity* bit for the tag, (iii) the *ECC* bits of the data in the register, and (iv) a set of *Status* bits that are used during the replacement of the ECC table entries.

When a physical register is about to be written, a request for protection is sent to Shield. If Shield decides to protect the register, it tries to allocate an entry for that version. The entries in the ECC table are not pre-allocated during the register renaming stage because there is no need to protect a register version during PreWrite time. Once an entry has been successfully allocated in the ECC table, an ECC generator calculates the ECC of the register data in parallel with the register write operation.

When a physical register is read, the register file sends its data to both the datapath and Shield (Figure 6). Shield checks whether there is an entry in the ECC table whose tag matches the physical register number. If so, Shield checks the tag's parity, and sends the corresponding ECC to an ECC checker to verify the data's integrity. If an error is detected in the tag — thanks to the parity bit — the corresponding entry in the ECC table is invalidated and the processor proceeds. If the ECC checker detects an error in the register data, the processor stalls and takes the following actions to recover from the error: (i) it fixes the register data, (ii) it flushes the reorder buffer (ROB) from the oldest instruction that reads the register version, and (iii) it flushes the whole ECC table and resumes. Finally, if there is no error, the ECC checker signals no error and the processor proceeds.

Each entry of the ROB is augmented with two Finish bits, one for each of the two potential source operand registers. These bits are set if, when the corresponding operand was read, it either completed the ECC check or was not protected by Shield. Single-operand instructions have one bit always set.

When an instruction reaches the head of the ROB and is ready to retire, the Finish bits are checked. If at least one of the bits is not set, the instruction cannot retire; it has to wait for the ECC checker to finish and set the bit(s), or for the ROB to get full. In the latter case, the instruction is retired without taking the Finish bits into consideration in order to minimize performance degradation. Our experiments show that the ROB provides enough slack for the ECC checker to verify the integrity of the data without affecting the IPC.

An entry in the ECC table is deallocated and assigned to another register version when the Shield replacement algorithm decides to evict it or when a new version of the same physical register is written and sent to Shield for protection. When an entry is evicted from the ECC table, its associated register version will no longer be protected.

3.2. Entry Allocation and Replacement

When Shield receives a request for protection for a physical register version, it tries to allocate an entry in the ECC table. If there is an entry in the table protecting a previous version of the same physical register, Shield re-assigns the entry to the new version. Otherwise, Shield attempts to pick a free table entry. Since the table is much smaller than the register file, there may be no free entry, and a decision has to be made to either replace an existing entry in the ECC table or abort the allocation. Entry replacement has to be done carefully. Replacing a recently-allocated entry that protects a long-lived register to accommodate a new one that will protect a short-lived register increases the vulnerability of the system. Therefore, Shield needs to predict the lifespan of register versions.

3.2.1. Predicting Short- and Long-lived Registers. When Shield considers evicting an entry from the ECC table, it does not know whether the register version that it protects is still in its useful time or not. Shield's goal is to evict the entry that contributes the least to the overall register file's AVF. Since a long-lived register contributes more to the register file's AVF than a short-lived one, Shield tries to evict

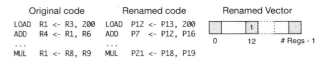

Figure 7. Predicting short-lived registers.

short-lived registers. To this end, Shield extends the short-lived register predictor proposed by Ponomarev et al. [12]. In the following, we first describe their approach and then how we augment it.

Figure 7 illustrates how Ponomarev et al.'s short-lived register predictor works. It maintains a bit vector, called *Renamed*, that has one bit per physical register. In Figure 7, under *original code*, a LOAD instruction loads into architectural register R1. After R1 is used in the ADD instruction, the MUL instruction overwrites R1. Therefore, the MUL is a *renamer* for the LOAD. In the *renamed code*, R1 has been renamed to P12. When the MUL is renamed, it sets the bit Renamed[12]. If by the time the LOAD loads the data into P12, the Renamed[12] bit is set, P12 is considered to be short-lived.

Although this predictor is simple and often effective, it is limited. Specifically, suppose that the ADD is the only consumer of R1. In this case, we would want to consider P12 to be a short-lived register. However, if the LOAD has loaded the data before the MUL is renamed, P12 will not be predicted as a short-lived register.

To extend the capability of Ponomarev et al.'s algorithm, we reformulate the Renamed vector. We call it the *Events* vector, and it has two bits for each physical register, namely *Events.Renamed* and *Events.Used*. The rules for the Events.Renamed bit are identical to the Ponomarev et al.'s scheme. The new Events.Used bit is set when renaming an instruction that consumes the physical register. Based on the Used and Renamed bits, when we are about to write to a physical register, we predict the register's lifespan as one of the following four types: 1) *long-lived*, if both Used and Renamed bits are reset, 2) *dead*, if only the Renamed bit is set, 3) *short-lived*, if only the Used bit is set, and 4) *ultrashort-lived*, if both Used and Renamed bits are set.

Figure 8 shows an example of how our proposed predictor works. In the *original code*, the MUL and DIV instructions act as the renamers for the first and second LOAD instructions, respectively. Therefore, the Events.Renamed bits of P12 and P7 are both set. Our algorithm also sets the Events.Used bit of P12 because R1 is used by the ADD. However, since R2 is never used, the Events.Used bit of P7 remains reset. The four possible combinations of the Used and Renamed bits are shown in Figure 8(b). *Dead* register versions are not protected by Shield.

3.2.2. Entry Replacement. For each protection request, Shield receives the register's *Events* bits along with the register number and data. If there is neither an entry protecting the same physical register nor a free entry in the ECC

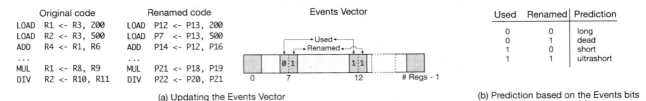

Figure 8. Predicting the lifespan of physical register versions.

table, Shield has to replace an existing entry or abort the allocation. Note that ECC table entries can only be allocated when a register version is written. Once a register version loses its ECC table entry, it cannot get a new one, and remains unprotected for the rest of its lifetime.

We propose a replacement policy that we call *Effective*. It uses the expected lifespan of a register version to select the entry to replace. It works as follows: when a victim entry is needed, Shield tries to select an entry that protects a register version with a shorter or same expected lifespan than the one to be protected. If such an entry is unavailable, Shield aborts the allocation. Table 1 shows the types of entries that can be replaced for a register version according to its prediction. For example, if a register version is predicted as short, it tries to replace an entry marked as free, ultrashort, and then short — in this priority order.

Table 1. *Effective* replacement policy in ECC table.

Prediction	Entries that can be replaced
Long	Free, Ultrashort, Short, Long
Short	Free, Ultrashort, Short
Ultrashort	Free, Ultrashort

We also dynamically adjust the entry type to reflect the fact that the expected lifespan gets shorter after reads. When an ultrashort or short entry is read, the type changes to free or ultrashort, respectively. The type of long entries is never changed since these entries tend to have long lifespans and may be read many times during their lifetime.

The information about the type of register version that an ECC table entry contains is kept in two Status bits (Figure 6). The four possible states of the Status bits are *long*, *short*, *ultrashort*, and *free*.

3.3. Entry Deallocation

An ECC table entry protects a given register version until the replacement algorithm reassigns the entry to another version. After a register version is read for the last time, it is effectively stale, and it is useless to protect it anymore. Ideally, Shield would like to know the time of the last read to a register version so that it can deallocate the entry then. However, Shield has no way of knowing whether a read is the last one. Therefore, it is possible to have stale entries in the ECC table. These stale entries hurt the efficiency of Shield because they protect nothing and occupy resources. The situation is worse if these stale entries are marked as

long, because they have less chance of being replaced compared to short ones.

To remove stale entries from the ECC table — especially the ones marked as long — we send explicit signals (called *eviction* signals) to the ECC table to indicate which entries just became stale. When the ROB sends a signal to release a physical register, this same signal is also forwarded to the ECC table as an eviction signal. If the ECC table has the corresponding entry, it marks it as free.

3.4. Error Recovery

Since we use single error correction with double error detection (SEC-DED) codes in this study, Shield allows the processor to recover from transient single-bit errors in the register file and detect double-bit errors. Although the processor may also recover from some double-bit errors, in this paper we only focus on single-bit errors.

When an ECC checker detects that the register data read by instruction I has a single-bit error, the processor stalls and enters recovery mode. First, the checker fixes the error and writes the corrected data back to the physical register (say P). Second, Shield examines the ROB looking for the oldest instruction that reads P and flushes that instruction as well as the others that follow it. Note that only flushing I and the instructions that follow it is not enough to recover from the error. Imagine that an instruction J older than I reads P after I did, but before the error is detected by the ECC checker. The data that J reads has already been corrupted. Consequently, the processor has to flush from the oldest instruction that reads P. The ECC table is then flushed so no entry in the ECC table protects one of the registers that were removed from the ROB. Finally, the processor can resume.

If an error occurs in a mispredicted path, Shield will still recover from it for simplicity.

3.5. AVF of a Register File with Shield

Figure 9 shows different physical register versions, their associated ECC table entry, and the time during which they are vulnerable to errors (ACE cycles). In Figure 9(a), Shield cannot allocate an entry for the register version and, therefore, the register is in ACE state during its whole useful lifetime. In Figure 9(b), an entry was protecting the register version but is evicted before the version is read for the first time. As a result, the register is in ACE state during its whole useful lifetime. In Figure 9(c), the entry is evicted after the register version is read at least once but before its

Figure 9. Computing the AVF of different physical register versions.

last read. Consequently, Shield only protects the version until the read just before the eviction. After that read, the register is in ACE state. Finally, in Figure 9(d), the ECC entry remains allocated for the whole useful lifetime of the register version. The version is completely protected and is never in ACE state. However, the longer an entry protects a dynamically dead register, the less efficient Shield is. By using the eviction signal described in Section 3.3, we are able to mitigate this effect. Using the four cases in this figure, we can compute the ACE cycles of each register version. Since the AVF of a physical register is the fraction of ACE cycles, we can then easily compute the AVF of each physical register and of the whole register file.

To calculate the overall AVF of the system, we also have to take into account the possibility of a bit flip in the ECC table or the Finish bits in the ROB. The tag in the ECC table is protected by the parity bit, and therefore a bit flip in this field can be detected. Shield then deallocates the damaged entry from the ECC table. A bit flip in the ECC field can be easily detected and corrected during the integrity check. A bit flip in the Status bits will not affect the correctness of the system — only the efficiency of Shield. Thus, the AVF of the ECC table is 0.

Finally, the AVF of the Finish bits is also 0, assuming a single-bit error model. If any of the Finish bits flips to 0, the corresponding instruction will stay longer at the head of the ROB, but will eventually retire when the ROB gets full. If any of the Finish bits flips to 1, the instruction might retire before it is actually checked. However, since we are assuming than only one error can occur at a time, no other error can occur and the register data has to be correct.

3.6. ParShield: Shield Plus Full Register Parity

Finally, we extend Shield with storage for a parity bit for all the physical registers in the processor, and re-use the ECC circuitry for parity generation and checking as well. The result is the complete *ParShield* architecture. With the parity bit, *ParShield* reduces the SDC AVF to zero (all errors are detected) — although the DUE AVF is equal to the AVF of plain Shield (the exposure to non-correctable errors remains the same as in plain Shield). Moreover, this is accomplished at a very small cost in hardware and power.

Specifically, consider when a register write sends a protection request to the ECC table. While ParShield is checking if it should generate the data's ECC and enter them in the table — depending on the type of register version and the current contents of the ECC table — ParShield uses one ECC generator to compute the data's parity and store it in

a Parity bit vector. Such operation takes a small fraction of the time taken by the generation of the full ECC.

In the same way, consider when a register read sends a request to the ECC table. While ParShield is checking if the ECC table contains the corresponding entry, ParShield reads the Parity bit vector and uses one ECC checker to check the parity. Again, this operation takes little time. Moreover, computing and checking the parity bits consumes much less power than computing and checking ECCs.

4. Implementation Issues

4.1. Bypass Network

Processors use the bypass network to send results from one functional unit to another so that dependent instructions can execute back to back. We therefore need to include register bypassing in our model of AVF. We distinguish two kinds of bypasses for a register version: (i) all its consumers read the value from the bypass network, and (ii) some of the consumers read it from the register file while others read it from the bypass network. We refer to the former as *full bypass* and to the latter as *partial bypass*.

Calculating the AVF for register versions that are fully bypassed is straightforward. Since the data stored in the register file is never used, their AVFs are zero. On the other hand, partially bypassed versions need to be protected from the time the data is written until their last non-bypassed read.

Figure 10(a) shows an example where an ADD instruction generates a version of register P1, which is then read by subsequent MUL and SUB instructions. We assume that the SUB is P1's last use. Figure 10(b) shows the ACE and un-ACE periods if the result is fully bypassed. Neither the MUL nor the SUB accesses the register file. Therefore, this P1 version remains un-ACE during its entire lifetime. In Figure 10(c), the SUB instruction reads P1 from the register file and, therefore, P1 remains ACE until the SUB executes.

4.2. Accessing the ECC Table

The ECC table needs fewer ports than the register file. The reason is that the table is not as performance-critical as the register file and, therefore, does not need to be multi-ported for the worst case — twice as many read ports as the issue width and as many write ports as the issue width. Consequently, we reduce the number of ports and perform the ECC generation and checking off the critical path. If necessary, we support some small queueing of requests, which

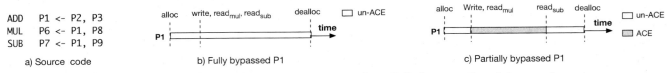

ADD P1 <- P2, P3
MUL P6 <- P1, P8
SUB P7 <- P1, P9

a) Source code   b) Fully bypassed P1   c) Partially bypassed P1

Figure 10. ACE and un-ACE periods for fully and partially bypassed register versions.

does not affect performance because instructions often wait in the ROB for a long period before committing.

In reality, there is rarely any queueing. One reason is that many instructions have fewer than two register operands. Moreover, many reads obtain their data from the bypass network and, therefore, do not access the ECC table. In addition, many register writes do not create an entry in the ECC table. Specifically, *dead* versions (Section 3.2.1), *ultrashort* versions that find the table full with non-*ultrashort* versions, and *short* versions that find the table full with *long* versions, skip ECC generation and table update.

In some cases, ParShield adds additional updates to the ECC table tags. These are caused by the eviction signals (Section 3.3). However, these signals are infrequent. They are only sent when the physical register to be freed was predicted as *long*. The rationale is that *short* and *ultrashort* register versions are aged automatically and evicted from the ECC table at a much faster pace than *long* ones — typically before the register is freed. Since Figure 5 shows that, on average, less than 10% of the register versions are *long*, the eviction signals are infrequent.

4.3. Using More Architectural Knowledge to Improve Efficiency

We extend the algorithm of Section 3.2.1 that predicts the lifespan of register versions, to leverage the usage patterns of one architectural register. The goal is to improve the prediction accuracy, given that some architectural registers have a specific purpose and, therefore, special usage patterns. Specifically, the *global pointer* register is written very few times during the execution of a program but is read many times and has a very long lifespan. Therefore, in the ECC table, we pin the entry that protects the physical mapping of the global pointer until it receives an eviction signal. Similar optimizations could be done by also considering other architectural registers.

5. Evaluation Methodology

We use a cycle-accurate execution-driven simulator [14] to model the processor and memory system architecture of Table 3. The architecture is a MIPS-like 3-issue out-of-order processor with two levels of caches, a 128-entry integer register file with 6 read and 3 write ports, and a 64-entry floating-point register file with 4 read and 2 write ports.

We evaluate the performance and the power of this architecture with the register file configurations of Table 2. *Baseline* is the architecture with no protection for the register files. *Shield* is Baseline plus the Shield architecture of Section 3.1. As shown in Table 3, the ECC table for the

Table 2. Register configurations evaluated.

Configuration	Description
Baseline	Register files with no parity or ECC protection
Shield	Baseline + Shield (Section 3.1)
ParShield	Shield + parity for all registers (Section 3.6)
FullECC	Baseline + ECC for all registers

integer register file has 32 entries and 3 read and 3 write ports; the ECC table for the floating-point register file has 16 entries and 2 read and 2 write ports. The number of ECC generators and checkers is the same as the number of write and read ports in the ECC table, respectively. *ParShield* is Shield plus the parity bit for all registers (Section 3.6). Finally, *FullECC* is Baseline plus ECC for all the 128 integer registers and 64 floating-point registers. In all cases, 8-bit ECC codes are used to protect the 64-bit registers.

We evaluate the architectures with SPECint and SPECfp 2000 applications running the *Ref* data set. All of the applications are included except those that are not supported by our current framework. The applications are compiled using *gcc-3.4* with -O3 optimization enabled. After skipping the initialization (typically 1-6 billion instructions), each application executes around 1 billion instructions.

Since applications do not run to completion, we are unable to determine whether or not a register is in ACE state when the simulation finishes. For example, if a simulation ends right after t_w in Figure 2(a), we would not know if the period after the write is ACE or un-ACE. To handle these edge effects, we use the *cooldown* technique that was proposed by Biswas *et al.* [1]. During the cooldown interval, we track the registers that were live at the moment that the simulation stopped. This helps us determine if a register was in ACE or un-ACE state.

6. Evaluation

In this section, we first examine the AVF results and the power and area consumption, then perform a sensitivity analysis, and finally examine register lifespan prediction.

6.1. AVF Results

We compare the AVF of Baseline to that of Shield with different replacement policies in the ECC table: *Random*, *LRU*, *Effective* (proposed in Section 3.2.2), and *OptEffective*. The latter augments *Effective* with the pinning optimization described in Section 4.3. Recall that ParShield has an SDC AVF equal to zero (all errors are detected) and a DUE AVF equal to Shield's AVF. Finally, the AVF of FullECC is zero.

Table 3. Processor and memory system modeled. Cycle counts are in processor cycles.

Processor		Register File		Cache & Memory		ParShield	
Frequency	4 GHz	Integer:		L1 Cache:		Integer:	
Fetch/Issue/Retire	6/3/3	Entries	128	Size, assoc, line	16KB, 4, 64B	ECC table entries, width	32, 18 bits
ROB size	126	Width	64 bits	Latency	2 cycles	R/W ports	3/3
I-window	68	R/W ports:	6/3	L2 Cache:		ECC latency	4 cycles
LD/ST queue	48/42			Size, assoc, line	1MB, 8, 64B		
Mem/Int/FP unit	2/3/2	FP:		Latency	12 cycles	FP:	
Branch predictor:		Entries	64			ECC table entries, width	16, 17 bits
Mispred. Penalty	14 cycles	Width	64 bits	Memory:		R/W ports	2/2
BTB	2K, 2-way	R/W ports:	4/2	Latency	500 cycles	ECC latency	4 cycles

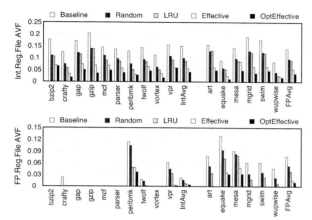

Figure 11. Integer (top) and floating-point (bottom) register file AVFs.

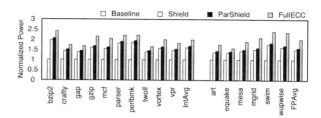

Figure 12. Integer register file power consumption.

Figure 11 and shows the AVFs of the integer (AVF_{int}) and floating-point (AVF_{fp}) register files for the described configurations. The AVFs are shown for all simulated SPECint and SPECfp applications. Since there are almost no floating-point operations in the SPECint applications, we do not discuss the AVF_{fp} for SPECint, and only show it in Figure 11 for completeness.

Figure 11 shows that, for all applications and on both register files, *Effective* and, especially *OptEffective*, have an AVF much lower than *Baseline*. For example, *Effective* reduces the AVF_{int} for SPECint by 63% on average and the AVF_{fp} for SPECfp by 42% on average relative to *Baseline*. *OptEffective* reduces the AVF_{int} for SPECint by up to 84% (on average 73%) and the AVF_{fp} for SPECfp by up to 100% (on average 85%) relative to *Baseline*. The resulting average AVF_{int} for SPECint is 0.040 and the average AVF_{fp} for SPECfp is 0.010. As expected, *Random* and *LRU* perform worse than chosen policies.

In general, Shield works slightly better for the floating-point register file because it has a smaller fraction of registers in useful state than the integer one. In addition, it is easier to predict the lifespan of floating-point registers. As shown in Figure 11, Shield reduces the AVF_{fp} to nearly zero for *art, mgrid, swim* and *wupwise*.

6.2. Power and Area Consumption

Register files consume a significant fraction of the power in modern processors. For example, one estimate suggests

that the integer register file consumes around 14% of the dynamic power in the processor [17]. We use CACTI 4.2 [19] to estimate the dynamic and static power of storage structures such as the register file, the ECC table, and the ECC and parity bit-fields. We use HSpice [5] models to estimate the dynamic and static power of the ECC logic.

In Figure 12, we show the total power (dynamic plus static) consumed in the integer register file for the different register configurations. For each application, the bars are normalized to *Baseline*. We do not include data for the floating-point register file because, as explained before, many of our applications do not use it much and, therefore, the average differences between configurations are small.

The figure shows that *FullECC* consumes on average 100% more power than *Baseline* for both SPECint and SPECfp applications. This is due to the combination of the ECC generators and checkers, and the additional storage for the ECC bits. With Shield, the average power is only 78% and 74% of *FullECC* for SPECint and SPECfp, respectively. This results mainly from the fewer ECC generators and checkers, and the fewer ECC operations performed — although the tags and ports in the ECC table are a significant source of power consumption.

Figure 12 also shows that *ParShield* consumes only slightly more power than Shield. The difference is small because the parity bits consume little power to generate, store and check. Overall, with *ParShield*, the average power is 81% and 78% of *FullECC* for SPECint and SPECfp, respectively. Both ParShield and Shield are more power-efficient than FullECC.

Finally, we estimate the area of the register file and the additional ECC and parity structures using CACTI 4.2. The area of the ECC logic is not added because it is negligible. Adding up the contributions of both the integer and the floating-point register files, we find that *FullECC* uses 4.9% more area than *Baseline*. Moreover, Shield and ParShield

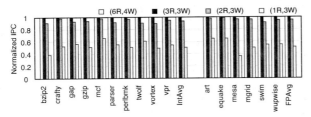

Figure 13. Impact of the number of ECC table ports on the IPC.

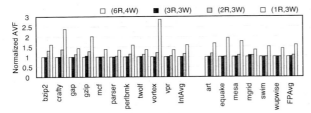

Figure 14. Impact of the number of ECC table ports on the integer register file AVF.

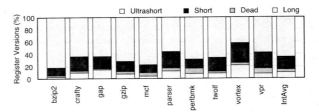

Figure 15. Breakdown of the types of register versions predicted.

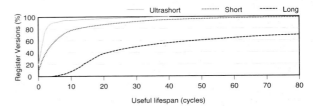

Figure 16. Cumulative distribution of useful lifespan for Ultrashort, Short, and Long registers.

use 15.7% and 17.6% more area than *FullECC*, respectively. This area increase is tolerable, given the power savings provided.

6.3. Sensitivity Analysis

To gain insight into the operation of Shield, we examine the impact of the number of read and write ports in the ECC table. Figures 13 and 14 show the IPC (Instructions Per Cycle) and the integer register file AVF, respectively, when we use x read ports and y write ports (xR, yW) in the ECC table. For each application, the bars are normalized to the (6R, 4W) configuration.

Figure 13 shows that, as we go from (6R, 4W) — the same number of ports and type as in the integer register file — to (3R, 3W) — our design choice — the IPCs remain constant. This is because Shield performs the ECC generation and checks off the critical path, queues requests when necessary, and leverages the slack given by the ROB. However, when we further reduce the number of read ports, performance suffers. With (2R, 3W), the average IPC decreases by 6.9% for SPECint and by 4.2% for SPECfp. With (1R, 3W), there is a 50% performance penalty because now the ECC table becomes a major bottleneck.

Figure 14 shows the impact on the AVF of the integer register file. With our design choice (3R, 3W), the AVF changes negligibly over (6R, 4W). With (2R, 3W) and (1R, 3W), however, the AVF increases noticeably.

Overall, from this section and the previous one, we see that the (3R, 3W) design corresponds to a good tradeoff between performance, AVF, and power.

6.4. Register Lifespan Prediction

Finally, we examine the accuracy of the register lifespan predictor used in Shield (*OptEffective*). Figure 15 shows

the fraction of integer register versions that *OptEffective* predicts of each type. We can see that, on average, it predicts over 60% as Ultrashort and only 10% as Long. Figure 16 shows the cumulative distribution of the useful lifespan for the register versions predicted as Ultrashort, Short, and Long. From the figure, we see that *OptEffective* correctly separates the three types of registers. Indeed, most register versions predicted as Long have over 30 cycles of useful lifespan, while 95% of the register versions predicted as Ultrashort have less than 10 cycles of useful lifespan.

However, *OptEffective* does not possess oracle knowledge. Figure 17 compares Shield's AVF using *OptEffective* and an oracle algorithm (*Oracle*) for register lifespan prediction. For completeness, it also shows the AVF with Ponomarev *et al.*'s predictor (Section 3.2.1). The figure shows that, on average, *OptEffective* is very close to *Oracle*. The remaining AVF largely results from the fact that, for some parts of the applications, there are more registers in Useful state than entries in the ECC table.

7. Related Work

Fully protected register files. Traditional fault-tolerant designs protect the entire register file with parity or ECC. The IBM S/390 G5 [18] uses duplicated, lockstepped pipelines to ensure that only correct data updates the ECC-protected structure that stores the architectural state of the processor. The ERC32 [3] is a SPARC processor with parity-protected registers and buses that also performs program control flow, which imposes extra overhead. Like the ERC32, the Intel Montecito [9] also utilizes parity to protect the whole register file. Both the ERC32 and the Intel Montecito require software intervention to recover when a fault is detected. Our ParShield design uses parity to detect all single-bit errors, and the Shield concept to recover from most single-bit errors — by selectively protecting the

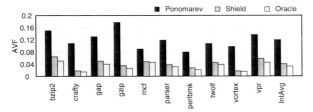

Figure 17. Comparing the AVF for different register lifespan prediction algorithms.

register versions that contribute the most to the overall vulnerability of the register file. Processor performance is not affected. The result is a design with a very cost-effective tradeoff between DUE AVF and power.

Partially protected register files. Memik *et al.* [10] proposed the duplication of actively-used physical registers in unused register locations. While their approach can enhance reliability with minimal performance degradation, it can only detect errors, but not recover from them. Yan *et al.* [22] proposed using the compiler to assign the most vulnerable variables to a set of ECC-protected registers. ParShield does not need to re-compile the programs because it offers a hardware-only solution.

Register lifetime analysis. Lozano and Gao [7] used the compiler to identify short-lived variables and prevented their values from going to the register file, thus reducing register pressure. Sangireddy and Somani [15] reduced the access time to the register file by exploiting useless periods in the register lifetime. Ponomarev *et al.* [12] used a small dedicated register file to cache short-lived operands to reduce the energy consumption in the ROB and the architectural register file. ParShield differs from all these proposals in that it proposes a hardware scheme to distinguish between ultrashort-, short- and long-lived operands, and exploits the difference to enhance the register file reliability.

8. Conclusions

Register files are vulnerable to soft errors because they are large and contain architectural state. Registers often store data for long periods of time and are read frequently, which increases the probability of spreading a faulty datum. A cost-effective protection mechanism for soft errors in register files should have no performance impact, keep the remaining AVF to a small value, consume modest power, and use little area.

In this paper, we have proposed one such mechanism, namely the *ParShield* design. ParShield relies on the Shield concept, which selectively protects a subset of the registers by generating, storing, and checking the ECCs of only the most vulnerable registers while they have useful data. Shield reduces the AVF of the integer register file by an average of 73% to 0.040, and the AVF of the floating-point register file by an average of 85% to 0.010. ParShield extends Shield with a parity bit for all the registers and the re-use of the ECC circuitry for parity generation and check-

ing as well. As a result, ParShield has no SDC AVF (all single-bit errors are detected), has a DUE AVF as low as Shield's AVF, and consumes on average only 81% and 78% of the power of a design with full ECC for the SPECint and SPECfp applications, respectively. Moreover, ParShield has no performance impact and little area requirements.

References

[1] A. Biswas et al. Computing architectural vulnerability factors for address-based structures. In *International Symposium on Computer Architecture*, June 2005.

[2] E. Czeck and D. Siewiorek. Effects of transient gate-level faults on program behavior. In *International Symposium on Fault-Tolerant Computing*, June 1990.

[3] J. Gaisler. Evaluation of a 32-bit microprocessor with built-in concurrent error-detection. In *International Symposium on Fault-Tolerant Computing*, 1997.

[4] G. Hinton et al. The microarchitecture of the Pentium 4 processor. *Intel Technology Journal*, 2001.

[5] Hspice User's Manual. Applications and examples, 1996.

[6] S. Kim and A. K. Somani. Area efficient architectures for information integrity in cache memories. In *International Symposium on Computer Architecture*, 1999.

[7] L. A. Lozano and G. R. Gao. Exploiting short-lived variables in superscalar processors. In *International Symposium on Microarchitecture*, 1995.

[8] W. MacKee et al. Cosmic ray neutron induced upsets as a major contributor to the soft error rate of current and future generation DRAMs. *1996 IEEE Annual International Reliability Physics*, 1996.

[9] C. McNairy and R. Bhatia. Montecito: A dual-core, dual-thread Itanium processor. *IEEE Micro*, 2005.

[10] G. Memik et al. Increasing register file immunity to transient errors. In *Design, Automation and Test in Europe*, 2005.

[11] S. Mukherjee et al. A systematic methodology to compute the architectural vulnerability factors for a high-performance microprocessor. In *International Symposium on Microarchitecture*, 2003.

[12] D. Ponomarev et al. Isolating short-lived operands for energy reduction. *IEEE Trans. Comput.*, 2004.

[13] J. Ray et al. Dual use of superscalar datapath for transient-fault detection and recovery. In *International Symposium on Microarchitecture*, 2001.

[14] J. Renau et al. SESC simulator, January 2005. http://sesc.sourceforge.net.

[15] R. Sangireddy and A. K. Somani. Exploiting quiescent states in register lifetime. In *ICCD*, 2004.

[16] P. Shivakumar et al. Modeling the effect of technology trends on the soft error rate of combinational logic. In *International Conference on Dependable Systems and Networks*, 2002.

[17] K. Skadron et al. Temperature-aware microarchitecture. In *International Symposium on Computer Architecture*, 2003.

[18] T. Slegel et al. IBM's S/390 G5 microprocessor design. *IEEE Micro*, 19, 1999.

[19] D. Tarjan et al. CACTI 4.0. *Tech Report HPL-2006-86*, 2006.

[20] N. J. Wang et al. Characterizing the effects of transient faults on a high-performance processor pipeline. In *International Conference on Dependable Systems and Networks*, 2004.

[21] C. Weaver et al. Techniques to reduce the soft error rate of a high-performance microprocessor. In *International Symposium on Computer Architecture*, 2004.

[22] J. Yan and W. Zhang. Compiler-guided register reliability improvement against soft errors. In *International Conference on Embedded Software*, 2005.

[23] J. F. Ziegler et al. IBM experiments in soft fails in computer electronics (1978-1994). *IBM J. Res. Dev.*, 1996.

Session 5B:
Processor Level Fault Tolerance

Using Process-Level Redundancy to Exploit Multiple Cores for Transient Fault Tolerance

Alex Shye   Tipp Moseley[†]   Vijay Janapa Reddi[‡]   Joseph Blomstedt   Daniel A. Connors

Dept. of Electrical and
Computer Engineering
U. of Colorado at Boulder
{shye, blomsted, dconnors}@colorado.edu

[†]Dept. of Computer Science
U. of Colorado at Boulder
moseleyt@colorado.edu

[‡]Dept. of Elect. Eng.
and Computer Science
Harvard University
vj@eecs.harvard.edu

Abstract

Transient faults are emerging as a critical concern in the reliability of general-purpose microprocessors. As architectural trends point towards multi-threaded multi-core designs, there is substantial interest in adapting such parallel hardware resources for transient fault tolerance. This paper proposes a software-based multi-core alternative for transient fault tolerance using process-level redundancy (PLR). PLR creates a set of redundant processes per application process and systematically compares the processes to guarantee correct execution. Redundancy at the process level allows the operating system to freely schedule the processes across all available hardware resources. PLR's software-centric approach to transient fault tolerance shifts the focus from ensuring correct hardware execution to ensuring correct software execution. As a result, PLR ignores many benign faults that do not propagate to affect program correctness. A real PLR prototype for running single-threaded applications is presented and evaluated for fault coverage and performance. On a 4-way SMP machine, PLR provides improved performance over existing software transient fault tolerance techniques with 16.9% overhead for fault detection on a set of optimized SPEC2000 binaries.

1 Introduction

Transient faults, also known as soft errors, are emerging as a critical concern in the reliability of computer systems [4, 21]. A transient fault occurs when an event (e.g. cosmic particle strikes, power supply noise, device coupling) causes the deposit or removal of enough charge to invert the state of a transistor. The inverted value may propagate to cause an error in program execution.

Current trends in process technology indicate that the future error rate of a single transistor will remain relatively constant [13, 18]. As the number of available transistors per chip continues to grow exponentially, the error rate of for an entire chip is expected to increase dramatically. These trends indicate that to ensure correct operation of systems, all general-purpose microprocessors and memories must employ reliability techniques.

Transient faults have historically been a design concern in specific computing environments (e.g. spacecrafts, high-availability server machines) in which the key system characteristics are reliability, dependability, and availability. While memory is easily protected with error-correcting code (ECC) and parity, protecting the complex logic within a high-performance microprocessor presents a significant challenge. Custom hardware designs have added 20-30% additional logic to add redundancy to mainframe processors and cover upwards of 200,000 latches [32, 2]. Other approaches include specialized machines with custom hardware and software redundancy [16, 39].

However, the same customized techniques can not be directly adopted for the general-purpose computing domain. Compared to the ultra-reliable computing environments, general-purpose systems are driven by a different, and often conflicting, set of factors. These factors include:

Application Specific Constraints: In ultra-reliable environments, such as spacecraft systems, the result of an transient error can be the difference between life or death. For general-purpose computing, the consequences of faulty execution are often less severe. For instance, in audio decode and playback, a fault results in a mere glitch which may not even be noticed. Thus, the focus for reliability shifts from providing a bullet-proof system to improving reliability to meet user expectations of failure rates.

Design Time and Cost Constraints: In the general-purpose computing market, low cost and a quick time to market are paramount. The design and verification of new redundant hardware is costly and may not be feasible in cost-sensitive markets. In addition, the inclusion of redundant design elements may negatively impact the design and product cycles of systems.

Post-Design Environment Techniques: A system's susceptibility to transient faults is often unplanned for and appears after the design and fabrication processes. For example, the scientists at the Los Alamos National Laboratory documented a surprisingly high incidence of single-node failures due to transient faults during the deployment of the

ASC Q supercomputer [21]. Likewise, environmental conditions of a system such as altitude, temperature, and age can cause higher fault rates [40]. In these cases, reliability techniques must be augmented after the design and development phase without the addition of new hardware.

With such pressures driving general-purpose computing hardware, software reliability techniques are an attractive solution for improving reliability in the face of transient faults. While software techniques cannot provide a level of reliability comparable to hardware techniques, they significantly lower costs (zero hardware design cost), and are very flexible in deployment. Existing software transient fault tolerant approaches use the compiler to insert redundant instructions for checking computation [26], control flow [25], or both [29]. The compiler-based software techniques suffer from a few limitations. First, the execution of the inserted instructions and assertions decreases performance ($\sim$1.4x slowdown [29]). Second, a compiler approach requires recompilation of all applications. Not only is it inconvenient to recompile all applications and libraries, but the source code for legacy programs is often unavailable.

This paper presents *process-level redundancy* (PLR), a software reliability technique leverages multiple processor cores for transient fault tolerance. PLR creates a set of redundant processes per original application process and compares their output to ensure correct execution. PLR scales with the architectural trend towards large many-core machines and leverages available hardware parallelism to improve performance without any additional redundant hardware structures or modifications to the system. In computing environments which are not throughput-constrained, PLR provides an alternate method of leveraging the hardware resources for transient fault tolerance. In addition, PLR can be easily deployed without recompilation or modifications to the underlying operating system.

This paper makes the following contributions:

- PLR implies a *software-centric* paradigm in transient fault tolerance which views the system as software layers which must execute correctly. In contrast, the typical *hardware-centric* paradigm views the system as a collection of hardware that must be protected. We differentiate between software-centric and hardware-centric views using the commonly accepted *sphere of influence* concept.

- Demonstrates the benefits of a software-centric approach. In particular, we show how register errors propagate through software. We show that many of the errors result in benign faults and many detected faults propagate through hundreds or thousands of instructions. By using a software-centric approach, PLR is able to ignore many benign faults.

- Presents a software-only transient fault tolerance technique for leveraging multiple cores on a general-purpose microprocessor for transient fault tolerance. We describe a real prototype system designed for single-threaded applications and evaluate the fault coverage and performance of PLR. Overall, the PLR prototype runs a set of the *SPEC2000* benchmark suite with only a 16.9% overhead on a 4-way SMP system.

The rest of this paper is organized as follows. Section 2 provides background on transient fault tolerance. Section 3 describes PLR. Section 4 shows initial results from the dynamic PLR prototype. Section 5 discusses related work. Section 6 concludes the paper.

2 Background

In general, a fault can be classified by its effect on system execution into the following categories [37]:

Benign Fault: A transient fault which does not propagate to affect the correctness of an application is considered a benign fault. A benign fault can occur for a number of reasons. Examples include a fault to an idle functional unit, a fault to a performance-enhancing instruction (i.e. a prefetch instruction), data masking, and Y-branches [36].

Silent Data Corruption (SDC): An undetected fault which propagates to corrupt system output is an SDC. This is the worst case scenario where a system appears to execute correctly but silently produces incorrect output.

Detected Unrecoverable Error (DUE): A fault which is detected without possibility of recovery is considered a DUE. DUEs can be split into two categories. A *true DUE* occurs when a fault which would propagate to incorrect execution is detected. A *false DUE* occurs when a benign fault is detected as a fault.

A transient fault in a system without transient fault tolerance will result in a benign fault, SDC, or true DUE (e.g. error detected by core dump). A system with only detection attempts to detect all of the true DUEs and SDCs. However, the system may inadvertently convert some of the benign faults into false DUEs and unnecessarily halt execution. Finally, a system with both detection and recovery will detect and recover from all faults without SDCs or any form of DUE. In this case, faults which would be false DUEs may cause unwarranted invocations to the recovery mechanism.

3 Approach

3.1 Software-centric Fault Detection

The *sphere of replication* (SoR) [28] is a commonly accepted concept for describing a technique's logical domain of redundancy and specifying the boundary for fault detection and containment. Any data which enters the SoR is replicated and all execution within the SoR is redundant in

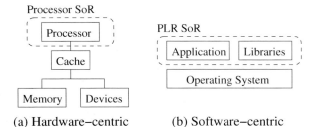

(a) Hardware-centric   (b) Software-centric

Figure 1. Hardware-centric and software-centric transient fault detection models.

some form. Before leaving the SoR, all output data is compared to ensure correctness. All execution outside of the SoR is not covered by the particular transient fault techniques and must be protected by other means. Faults are contained within the SoR boundaries and detected in any data leaving the SoR.

Most previous work in fault tolerance is *hardware-centric* and uses a hardware-centric SoR. A hardware-centric model views the system as a collection of hardware components which must be protected from transient faults. In this model, a hardware-centric SoR is placed around specific hardware units. All inputs are replicated, execution is redundant, and output is compared.

While the hardware-centric model is appropriate for hardware-implemented techniques, it is awkward to apply the same approach to software. Software naturally operates at a different level and does not have full visibility into the hardware. Nevertheless, previous compiler-based approaches attempt to imitate a hardware-centric SoR. For example, SWIFT [29] places its SoR around the processor as shown in Figure 1(a). Without the ability to control duplication of hardware, SWIFT duplicates at the instruction level. Each load is performed twice for input replication and all computation is performed twice on the replicated inputs. Output comparison is accomplished by checking the data of each store instruction prior to executing the store instruction. This particular approach works because it is possible to emulate processor redundancy with redundant instructions. However, other hardware-centric SoRs would be impossible to emulate with software. For example, software alone cannot implement an SoR around hardware caches.

Software-centric fault detection is a paradigm in which the system is viewed as the software layers which must execute correctly. A software-centric model uses a software-centric SoR which is placed around software layers, instead of hardware components. The key insight to software-centric fault detection is this: although faults occur at the hardware level, *the only faults which matter are the faults which affect software correctness*. By changing the boundaries of output comparison to software, a software-centric model shifts the focus from ensuring correct hardware execution to ensuring correct software execution. As a result,

only faults which affect correctness are detected. Benign faults are safely ignored. A software-centric system with only detection is able to reduce the incidence of false DUEs. A software-centric system with both detection and recovery will not need to invoke the recovery mechanism for faults which do not affect correctness.

Figure 1(b) shows an example software-centric SoR which is placed around the user space application and libraries (as used by PLR). A software-centric SoR acts exactly the same as the hardware-centric SoR except that it acts on the software instead of the hardware. Again, all input is replicated, execution within the SoR is redundant, and data leaving the SoR is compared.

By operating at the software level, the software-centric model caters to the strengths of a software-implemented technique. While software has limited visibility into hardware, it is able to view a fault at a broader scope and determine its effect on software execution. Thus, software-implemented approaches which are hardware-centric are ignoring the potential strengths of a software approach.

3.2 Process-Level Redundancy

Process-level redundancy (PLR) is a technique which uses the software-centric model of transient fault detection. As shown in Figure 1(b), PLR places its SoR around the user address space by providing redundancy at the process level. PLR replicates the application and library code, global data, heap, stack, file descriptor table, etc. Everything outside of the SoR, namely the OS, must be protected by other means. Any data which enters the SoR via the system call interface must be replicated and all output data must be compared to verify correctness.

Providing redundancy at the process level is natural as it is the most basic abstraction of any OS. The OS views any hardware thread or core as a logical processor and then schedules processes to the available logical processors. PLR leverages the OS to schedule the redundant processes to take advantage of hardware resources. With massive multi-core architectures on the horizon, there will be a tremendous amount of hardware parallelism available in future general-purpose machines. In computing environments where throughput is not the primary concern, PLR provides a way of utilizing the extra hardware resources for transient fault tolerance.

A high level overview of PLR is shown in Figure 2 with three redundant processes, which is the minimum number of processes necessary for both transient fault detection and recovery. PLR intercepts the beginning of application execution and replicates the original process to create other redundant processes. One of the processes is logically labeled the *master* process and the others are labeled the *slave* processes. At each system call, the *system call emulation unit* is invoked. The emulation unit performs the input replica-

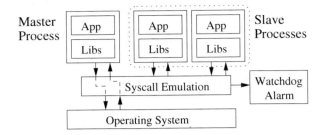

Figure 2. Overview of PLR with three redundant processes.

tion, output comparison, and recovery. The emulation unit also ensures that the following requirements are maintained in order for PLR to operate correctly:

- The execution of PLR must be transparent to the system environment with the redundant processes interacting with the system as if only the original process is executing. System calls which alter any system state can only be executed once with the master process actually executing the system call and the slave processes emulating the system call.

- Execution among the redundant processes must be deterministic. System calls which return non-deterministic data, such as a request for system time or resources, must be emulated to ensure all redundant processes use the same data for computation.

- All redundant processes must be identical in address space and any other process-specific data, such as the file descriptor table. At any time, a transient fault could render one of the redundant processes useless. With identical processes, any of the processes can be logically labeled the master process at any given invocation of the emulation unit.

On occasion, a transient fault will cause the program to suspend or hang. The *watchdog alarm* is employed by the emulation unit to detect such faults. Upon entrance to the system call emulation unit, a timer begins. If the redundant processes do not all enter the emulation unit in a user-specified amount of time, the watchdog alarm times out, signaling an error in execution.

3.2.1 Input Replication

As the SoR model dictates, any data which enters the SoR must be replicated to ensure that all data is redundant within the SoR. In the case of PLR, any data which passes into the processes via system calls (such as a read from a file descriptor) is received once by the master process, and then replicated among the slave processes. Also, the return value from all system calls is considered an input value and is copied for use across all redundant processes.

3.2.2 Output Comparison

All data which exits the redundant processes must be compared for correctness before proceeding out of the SoR. If the output data does not match, a transient fault is detected and a recovery routine is invoked. Any write buffers which will be passed outside of the SoR must be compared. Also, any data passed as a system call parameter can be considered an output event which leaves the SoR and must also be checked to verify program correctness.

3.2.3 Emulating System Calls

The emulation unit is responsible for the input replication, output comparison, and system call emulation. The data transfer during input replication and output comparison is accomplished through a shared memory segment between all of the redundant processes.

At the beginning of each call to the emulation unit, the type of system call is compared to ensure that all redundant processes are at a common system call. If not, a fault is assumed which caused an error in control flow to call an errant system call.

Depending upon the system call, the system call emulation unit will perform different tasks. System calls which modify any system state, such file renaming and linking, must only be executed once. In other cases, the system call will be actually called by all processes; once by the master process in its original state, and once by each redundant process to emulate the operation. For example, in emulating a system call to open a new file, the master process will create and open the new file, while the redundant processes will simply open the file without creating it.

3.3 Transient Fault Detection

A transient fault is detected in one of three ways:

1. **Output Mismatch**: A transient fault which propagates to cause incorrect output will be detected with the output comparison within the emulation unit at the point which the data is about to exit the SoR.

2. **Watchdog Timeout**: There are two scenarios in which the watchdog timer will time out. The first case is when a fault causes an error in control flow which calls an errant system call. The faulty process will cause an entrance into the emulation unit which will begin waiting for the other processes. If the other processes enter the emulation unit, an error will be detected if the system calls mismatch, or if there is a mismatch in data. If the other processes continue execution, a timeout will occur. The second case is when a transient fault causes a process to hang indefinitely (e.g. an infinite loop). In this case, during the next system call, all the processes except the hanging process will enter the emulation unit and eventually cause a watchdog timeout. A

300

drawback to the watchdog alarm is that a timeout period exists in which the application does not make any progress. In our experience, on an unloaded system, a timeout of 1-2 seconds is sufficient. The timeout value is user specified and can be increased on a loaded system. On a loaded system, spurious timeouts will not affect application correctness, but will cause unnecessary calls to the recovery unit.

3. **Program Failure:** Finally, a transient fault may cause a program failure due to an illegal operation such as a segmentation violation, bus error, illegal instruction, etc. Signals handlers are set up to catch the corresponding signals and an error is be flagged. The next time the emulation unit is called, it can immediately begin the recovery process.

3.4 Transient Fault Recovery

Transient fault recovery mechanisms typically fit into two broad categories: *checkpoint and repair*, and *fault masking*. Checkpoint and repair techniques involves the periodic checkpointing of execution state. When a fault is detected, execution is rolled back to the previous checkpoint. Fault masking involves using multiple copies of execution to vote on the correct output.

PLR supports both types of fault recovery. If checkpoint and repair functionality already exists, then PLR only needs to use two processes for detection and can defer recovery to the repair mechanism. Otherwise, fault masking can be accomplished by using at least three processes for a majority vote. If fault masking is used, the following schemes are used for recovery (the examples use an assumption of three redundant processes).

1. **Output Mismatch:** If an output data mismatch occurs the remaining processes are compared to ensure correctness of the output data. If a majority of processes agree upon the value of the output data, it is assumed to be correct. The processes with incorrect data are immediately killed and replaced by duplicating a correct process (e.g. using the `fork()` system call in Linux).

2. **Watchdog Timeout:** As mentioned in Section 3.3, there are two cases for a watchdog timeout. In the first case, where a faulty process calling the emulation unit while the other processes continue executing, there will only be one process in the emulation unit during timeout. The process in the emulation unit is killed and recovery occurs during the next system call. In the second case, where a faulty process hangs, all processes except one will be in the emulation unit during timeout. The hanging process is killed and replaced by duplicating a correct process.

3. **Program Failure:** In the case of program failure, the incorrect process is already dead. The emulation unit

simply replaces the missing process by duplicating one of the remaining processes.

We assume the single event upset (SEU) fault model in which a single transient fault occurs at a time. However, PLR can support simultaneous faults by simply scaling the number of redundant processes and the majority vote logic.

3.5 Windows of Vulnerability

A fault during execution of PLR code may cause an unrecoverable error. Also, a fault which causes an erroneous branch into PLR code could result in undefined behavior. Finally, PLR is not meant to protect the operating system and any fault during operating system execution may cause failure. The first and third windows of vulnerability may be mitigated by compiling the operating system and/or PLR code with compiler-based fault tolerance solutions.

All fault tolerance techniques have windows of vulnerability which are usually associated with faults to the checker mechanism. Although not completely reliable, partial redundancy [12, 33] may be sufficient to improve reliability enough to meet user or vendor reliability standards.

3.6 Shared Memory, Interrupts, Exceptions and Multi-threading

PLR hinges upon deterministic behavior among the redundant processes. However, shared memory, interrupts, exceptions and multi-threaded applications introduce potential non-determinism.

Shared memory could be supported by changing page permissions and trapping upon accesses to the shared memory. A similar approach is used for detecting self-modifying code within dynamic code translators [9]. Interrupts and exceptions present a more difficult challenge because there is not a clear execution point in which to synchronize the redundant processes. Hardware supported techniques have been proposed previously such as hardware counters to support epochs [8]. Multi-threaded applications require a programming model that ensures the same inter-thread memory ordering for each replica. Without this support, PLR is limited to executing on single-threaded applications.

These challenges are still open research problems for all software-implemented fault tolerance techniques. We plan to explore extensions to PLR to support these non-deterministic issues.

4 Experimental Results

This paper presents and evaluates a PLR prototype built using the Intel Pin dynamic binary instrumentation system [20]. The tool uses Pin to dynamically create redundant processes and uses PinProbes (a dynamic code patching system for program binaries) to intercept system calls.

The prototype is evaluated running a set of the *SPEC2000* benchmarks compiled with gcc v3.4.6 and ifort v9.0. Fault coverage is evaluated using a fault injection campaign similar to [29]. One thousand runs are executed per benchmark. To maintain manageable run times, the test inputs are used during fault analysis. For each run, an instruction execution count profile of the application is used to randomly choose a specific invocation of an instruction to fault. For the selected instruction, a random bit is selected from the source or destination general-purpose registers. To inject a simulated transient error, Pin tool instrumentation is used to change the random bit during the specified dynamic execution count of the instruction. The *specdiff* utility included within the *SPEC2000* harness is used to determine the correctness of program output.

Fault propagation and performance evaluation are both studied using the reference inputs. Performance is measured by running the PLR prototype with both two and three redundant processes without fault injection on a four-processor SMP system; specifically the system has four 3.00Ghz Intel Xeon MP processors each with 4096KB L3 cache, has 6GB of system-wide memory, and is running Red Hat Enterprise Linux AS release 4.

4.1 Fault Injection Results

A fault injection study is performed to illustrate the effectiveness of PLR as well as the benefits of using a software-centric model of fault detection. Figure 3 shows the results of a fault injection campaign with the left bar in each cluster showing the outcomes with just fault injection and the right bar showing the outcomes when detecting faults with PLR. The possible outcomes are:

- **Correct:** A benign fault which does not affect program correctness.

- **Incorrect:** An SDC where the program executes completely and returns with correct return code, but the output is incorrect.

- **Abort:** A DUE in which the program returns with an invalid return code.

- **Failed:** A DUE in which the program terminates (e.g. segmentation violation).

- **Mismatch:** Occurs when running PLR. In this case, a mismatch is detected during PLR output comparison.

- **SigHandler:** Occurs when running PLR. In this case, a PLR signal handler detects program termination.

Timeouts of the watchdog alarm are ignored because they occurs very infrequently ($\sim$.05% of the time).

PLR is able to successfully eliminate all of the *Failed*, *Abort*, and *Incorrect* outcomes. In general, the output comparison detects the *Incorrect* and *Abort* cases, and turns each error into detected *Mismatch* cases. Similarly, PLR detects the *Failed* cases turning them into *SigHandler* cases.

Occasionally, a small fraction of the *Failed* cases are detected as *Mismatch* under PLR. This indicates cases in which PLR is able to detect a mismatch of output data before a failure occurs.

The software-centric approach of PLR is very effective at detecting faults based on their effect on software execution. Faults which do not affect correctness are generally not detected in PLR, thereby avoiding false positives. In contrast, SWIFT [29], which is currently the most advanced compiler-based approach, detects roughly $\sim$70% of the *Correct* outcomes as faults.

However, not all of the *Correct* cases during fault injection remain *Correct* with PLR detection as the software-centric model would suggest. This mainly occurs with the *SPECfp* benchmarks. In particular, *168.wupwise*, *172.mgrid* and *178.galgel* show that many of the original *Correct* cases during fault injection become detected as *Mismatch*. In these cases, the injected fault causes the output data to be different than data from regular runs. However, the output difference occurs in the printing of floating point numbers to a log file. *specdiff* allows for a certain tolerance in floating point calculations, and considers the difference within acceptable bounds. PLR compares the raw bytes of output and detects a fault because the data does not match. This issue has less to do with the effectiveness of a PLR, or a software-centric model, and is more related to the definition of an application's correctness.

4.2 Fault Propagation

Figure 4 shows the number of instructions executed between fault injection and detection. Runs are shown as stacked bars showing the breakdown of instructions executed before the fault was detected. The leftmost bar labeled M shows the breakdowns for the *Mismatch* runs shown in Figure 3. The middle bar (S) shows the breakdown for the *SigHandler* runs and the left bar (A) shows all of the detected faults including both *Mismatch* and *SegHandler*.

In general, the *Mismatch* runs tend to be detected much later than the point of fault injection with fault propagation instruction counts of over 10,000 instructions for nearly all of the benchmarks. On the other hand, the *SegHandler* runs have a higher probability of being detected early. Across all of the detected runs, there is a wide variety in amounts of fault propagation ranging from *254.gap* which has a low amount of fault propagation, to *191.fma3d* which has an even distribution of runs among the various categories.

The software-centric model delays the detection of a fault until an error is certain via program failure, or incorrect data exiting the SoR. However, the delayed detection also means that a fault may remain latent during execution for an unbounded period of time. Future work remains in characterizing fault propagation as well as exploring methods for bounding the time in which faults remain undetected.

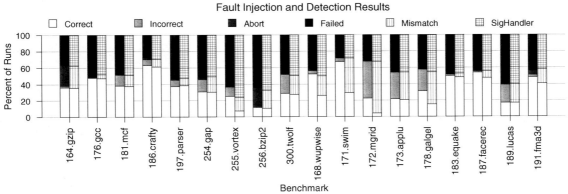

Figure 3. Results of the fault injection campaign. The left bar in each cluster shows the outcomes with just fault injection and the right bar shows the breakdown of how PLR detects the faults.

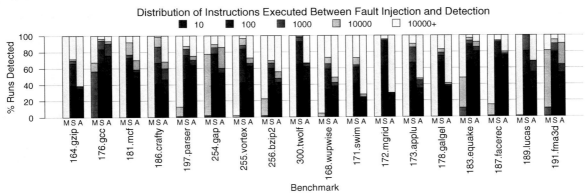

Figure 4. Distribution of the number of executed instructions between the injection and detection of a fault. Percentages are normalized to all the runs which are detected via output mismatch (M), program failure (S), or both combined (A).

4.3 Performance Results

Performance is evaluated using two redundant processes for fault detection (PLR2), and three processes to support recovery (PLR3). Figure 5 shows PLR performance on benchmarks compiled with both -O0 and -O2 compiler flags. Performance is normalized to native execution time. PLR provides transient fault tolerance on -O0 programs with an average overhead of 8.1% overhead for PLR2 and 15.2% overhead for PLR3. On -O2 programs, PLR2 incurs a 16.9% overhead for PLR2 and 41.1% overhead for PLR3. Overhead in PLR is due to the fact that multiple redundant processes are contending for system resources. Programs which place higher demands on systems resources result in a higher PLR overhead. Optimized binaries stress the system more than unoptimized binaries (e.g. higher L3 cache miss rate) and therefore have a higher overhead. As the number of redundant processes increases, there is an increasing burden placed upon the system memory controller, bus, as well as cache coherency implementation. Similarly, as the emulation is called with more processes, the increased synchronization with semaphores and the usage

and shared memory may decrease performance. At certain points, the system resources will be saturated and performance will be severely impacted. These cases can be observed in *181.mcf* and *171.swim* when running PLR3 with -O2 binaries. PLR overhead and system resource saturation points are explained in more detail in the next subsection.

4.4 PLR Overhead Breakdown

The performance overhead of PLR consists of *contention overhead* and *emulation overhead*, shown as stacked bars in Figure 5. Contention overhead is the overhead from simultaneously running the redundant processes and contending for shared resources such as the memory and system bus. The contention overhead is measured by running the application multiple times independently and comparing the overhead to the execution of a single run. This roughly simulates running the redundant processes without PLR's synchronization and emulation. The rest of the overhead is considered emulation overhead. Emulation overhead is due to the synchronization, system call emulation, and mechanisms for fault detection incurred by PLR.

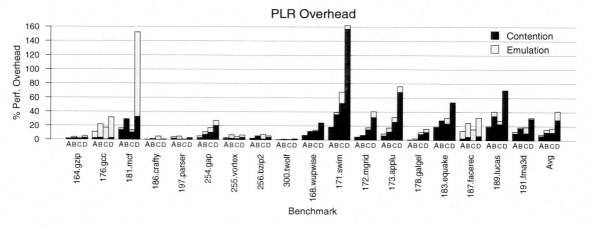

Figure 5. Overhead of running PLR on a set of both unoptimized and optimized _SPEC2000_ benchmarks. The combinations of runs include -O0 compiled binaries with PLR2 (_A_), -O0 with PLR3 (_B_), -O2 with PLR2 (_C_) and -O2 with PLR3 (_D_).

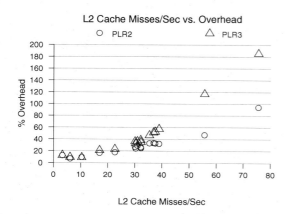

Figure 6. PLR overhead vs. L3 cache miss rate.

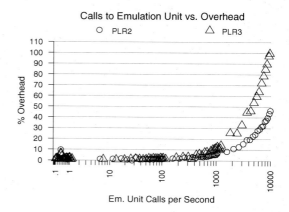

Figure 7. PLR overhead vs. system call rate.

For the set of benchmarks, contention overhead is significantly higher than emulation overhead. Benchmarks such as _181.mcf_ and _189.lucas_ have relatively high cache miss rates leading to a high contention overhead with increased memory and bus utilization. On the other hand, _176.gcc_ and _187.facerec_ substantially utilize the emulation unit and result in a high PLR overhead.

4.4.1 Contention Overhead

Contention overhead mainly stems from the sharing of memory bandwidth between the multiple redundant processes. To study the effects of contention overhead, we construct a program to generate memory requests by periodically missing in the L3 cache. Figure 6 shows the effect of L3 cache miss rate on contention overhead when running with PLR. For both PLR2 and PLR3, the L3 cache miss rate has a substantial affect on the contention overhead. With less than 10 L3 cache misses per second, there

can be a significant overhead of about 10%. After that point, the overhead increases greatly with over a 50% overhead at about 40 L3 cache misses per second. These results indicate that the total overhead for using PLR is highly impacted by the applications cache memory behavior. CPU-bound applications can be protected from transient faults with a very low overhead while memory-bound applications may suffer from high overheads.

4.4.2 Emulation Overhead

Emulation overhead mainly consists of the synchronization overhead and the overhead from transferring and comparing data in shared memory. To examine each aspect of emulation overhead, two synthetic programs were designed and run with PLR. The first program calls the `times()` system call at a user-controlled rate. `times()` is one of the of simpler system calls supported by PLR and is used to measure the emulation overhead from the barrier synchronizations within the emulation unit. The second test program calls the `write()` system call ten times a second and writes a user-

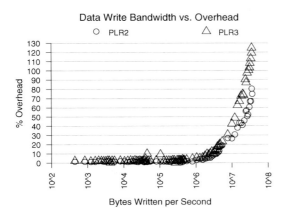

Figure 8. PLR overhead vs. data bandwidth.

specified number of bytes per system call. Each `write()` system call forces the emulation unit to transfer and compare the write data in shared memory.

Figure 7 shows the effect of synchronization on the PLR overhead. Synchronization overhead is minimal up until about 300-400 emulation unit calls per second with less than 5% overhead for using PLR with both two and three redundant processes. Afterward, the emulation overhead increases quickly. Overall, these results indicate that the PLR technique might be best deployed for specific application domains without significant system call functionality.

Figure 8 illustrates the effect of write data bandwidth on emulation overhead. The experiment evaluates the amount of data at each system call that must be compared between redundant process techniques. The write data bandwidth has a similar characteristics as system call synchronization, achieving low overhead until a cut-off point. In this case, for the experimental machines evaluated, the overhead is minimal when the write data rate stays less than 1MB per second but then increases substantially after that point for both PLR2 and PLR3.

5 Related Work

PLR is similar to a software version of the hardware SMT and CMP extensions for transient fault tolerance [11, 23, 28]. However, PLR aims to provide the same functionality in software. Wang [35] proposes a compiler infrastructure for software redundant multi-threading which achieves 19% overhead with the addition of a special hardware communication queue. PLR attains similar overhead and only relies on the fact that multiple processors exist. In addition, PLR does not require source code to operate.

Executable assertions [14, 15] and other software detectors [27] explore the placement of assertions within software. Other schemes explicitly check control flow during execution [31, 25]. The software-centric approach provides a different model for transient fault tolerance using a software equivalent of the commonly accepted SoR model. The

pi bit [37] and dependence-based checking [34] have been explored as methods to follow the propagation of faults in an attempt to only detect faults which affect program behavior. The software-centric model accomplishes the same task on a larger scale.

The PLR approach is similar to a body of fault tolerant work which explores the use of replicas for fault tolerance [6, 8, 7, 24, 38, 39]. This body of work targets hard faults (such as hardware or power failures) and assumes fail-stop execution [30] in which the processor stops in the event of failure. For transient faults, this assumption does not hold. As far as we know, we provide the first performance evaluation, and overhead breakdown, of using redundant processes on general-purpose multiple core systems.

There have been a number of previous approaches to program replication. N-version programming [3] uses three different versions of an application for tolerating software errors. Aidemark uses a time redundant technique which execute an application multiple times and use majority voting [1]. Virtual duplex systems combine both N-version programming and time-redundancy [10, 19]. The Tandem Nonstop Cyclone [16] is a custom system designed to use process replicas for transaction processing workloads. Chameleon [17] is an infrastructure designed for distributed systems which uses various ARMOR processes (some similar to process replicas) to implement adaptive and configurable fault tolerance. DieHard [5] proposes using replicas in general-purpose machines for tolerating memory errors. Shadow profiling [22] uses process replicas for low-overhead program instrumentation.

6 Conclusion

This paper motivates the necessity for software transient fault tolerance for general-purpose microprocessors and proposes process-level redundancy (PLR) as an attractive alternative in emerging multi-core processors. By providing redundancy at the process level, PLR leverages the OS to freely schedule the processes to all available hardware resources. In addition, PLR can be deployed without modifications to the application, operating system or underlying hardware. A real PLR prototype supporting single-threaded applications is presented and evaluated for fault coverage and performance. Fault injection experiments prove that PLR's software-centric fault detection model effectively detects faults which safely ignoring benign faults. Experimental results show that when running an optimized set of *SPEC2000* benchmarks on a 4-way SMP machine, PLR provides fault detection with an 16.9% overhead. PLR performance improves upon existing software transient fault techniques and takes a step towards enabling software fault tolerant solutions comparable to hardware techniques.

7 Acknowledgments

The authors would like to thank the anonymous reviewers, Robert Cohn, Manish Vachharajani, Rahul Saxena, and the rest of the DRACO Architecture Research Group for their insightful comments and helpful discussion. This work is funded by Intel Corporation.

References

[1] J. Aidemark, J. Vinter, P. Folkesson, and J. Karlsson. Experimental evaluation of time-redundant execution for a brake-by-wire application. In *Proc. of DSN*, 2002.

[2] H. Ando and et al. A 1.3ghz fifth generation sparc64 microprocessor. In *Proceedings of the Conference on Design Automation*, 2003.

[3] A. Avizeinis. The n-version approach to fault-tolerance software. *IEEE Transactions on Software Engineering*, 11(12):1491–1501, December 1985.

[4] R. C. Baumann. Soft errors in commercial semiconductor technology: Overview and scaling trends. In *IEEE 2002 Reliability Physics Tutorial Notes, Reliability Fundamentals*, pages 121_01.1 – 121_01.14, April 2002.

[5] E. D. Berger and B. G. Zorn. DieHard: Probabilistic memory safety for unsafe languages. In *PLDI*, 2006.

[6] A. Borg, W. Blau, W. Graetcsh, F. Herrmann, and W. Oberle. Fault tolerance under unix. *ACM Transactions on Computer Systems*, 7(1):1–24, 1989.

[7] T. C. Bressoud. TFT: A Software System for Application-Transparent Fault-Tolerance. In *Proc. of the International Conference on Fault-Tolerant Computing*, 1998.

[8] T. C. Bressoud and F. B. Schneider. Hypervisor-based Fault-tolerance. In *Proc. of SOSP*, 1995.

[9] D. Bruening and S. Amarasinghe. Maintaining consistency and bounding capacity of software code caches. In *Proceedings of the International Symposium on Code Generation and Optimization*, March 2005.

[10] K. Echtle, B. Hinz, and T. Nikolov. On hardware fault diagnosis by diverse software. In *Proceedings of the Intl. Conference on Fault-Tolerant Systems and Diagnostics*, 1990.

[11] M. Gomaa and et al. Transient-fault recovery for chip multiprocessors. In *ISCA*, 2003.

[12] M. Gomaa and T. N. Vijaykumar. Opportunistic transient-fault detection. In *ISCA*, 2005.

[13] S. Hareland and et al. Impact of CMOS Scaling and SOI on Software Error Rates of Logic Processes. In *VLSI Technology Digest of Technical Papers*, 2001.

[14] M. Hiller. Executable assertions for detecting data errors in embedded control systems. In *Proc. of DSN*, 2000.

[15] M. Hiller and et al. On the placement of software mechanisms for detection of data errors. In *Proc. of DSN*, 2002.

[16] R. W. Horst and et al. Multiple instruction issue in the Non-Stop Cyclone processor. In *ISCA*, 1990.

[17] Z. Kalbarczyk, R. K. Iyer, S. Bagchi, and K. Whisnant. Chameleon: A software infrastructure for adaptive fault tolerance. *IEEE Transactions on Parallel and Distributed Systems*, 10(6):560–579, 1999.

[18] T. Karnik and et al. Scaling Trends of Cosmic Rays Induced Soft Errors in Static Latches Beyond 0.18μ. In *VLSI Circuit Digest of Technical Papers*, 2001.

[19] T. Lovric. Dynamic double virtual duplex systems: A cost-efficient approach to fault-tolerance. In *Proceedings of the Intl. Working Conference on Dependable Computing for Critical Applications*, 1995.

[20] C.-K. Luk and et al. Pin: Building customized program analysis tools with dynamic instrumentation. In *PLDI*, 2005.

[21] S. E. Michalak and et al. Predicting the Number of Fatal Soft Errors in Los Alamos National Laboratory's ASC Q Supercomputer. *IEEE Transactions on Device and Materials Reliability*, 5(3):329–335, September 2005.

[22] T. Moseley, A. Shye, V. J. Reddi, D. Grunwald, and R. V. Peri. Shadow profiling: Hiding instrumentation costs with parallelism. In *Proceedings of CGO*, 2007.

[23] S. S. Mukherjee and et al. Detailed design and evaluation of redundant multithreading alternatives. In *ISCA*, 2002.

[24] P. Murray, R. Fleming, P. Harry, and P. Vickers. Somersault: Software fault-tolerance. Technical report, HP Labs White Paper, Palo Alto, California, 1998.

[25] N. Oh and et al. Control-flow checking by software signatures. *IEEE Transactions on Reliability*, 51, March 2002.

[26] N. Oh and et al. Error detection by duplicated instructions in super-scalar processors. *IEEE Transactions on Reliability*, 51, March 2002.

[27] K. Pattabiraman, Z. Kalbarczyk, and R. K. Iyer. Application-based metrics for strategic placement of detectors. In *Proceedings of 11th International Symposium on Pacific Rim Dependable Computing*, 2005.

[28] S. K. Reinhardt and S. S. Mukherjee. Transient fault detection via simultaneous multithreading. In *ISCA*, 2000.

[29] G. A. Reis and et al. SWIFT: Software implemented fault tolerance. In *CGO*, 2005.

[30] R. D. Schlichting and F. B. Schneider. Fail-stop processors: An approach to designing fault-tolerant computing systems. *ACM Transactions on Computing Systems*, 1(3):222–238, August 1983.

[31] M. A. Schuette, J. P. Shen, D. P. Siewiorek, and Y. K. Zhu. Experimental evaluation of two concurrent error detection schemes. In *Proceedings of FTCS-16*, 1986.

[32] T. J. Slegel and et al. IBM's S/390 G5 microprocessor design. *IEEE Micro*, 1999.

[33] K. Sundaramoorthy, Z. Purser, and E. Rotenburg. Slipstream processors: improving both performance and fault tolerance. In *Proc. of ASPLOS*, 2000.

[34] T. N. Vijaykumar, I. Pomeranz, and K. Cheng. Transient-fault recovery using simultaneous multithreading. In *Proceedings of ISCA*, 2002.

[35] C. Wang, H. seop Kim, Y. Wu, and V. Ying. Compiler-managed software-based redundant multi-threading for transient fault detection. In *Proceedings of CGO*, 2007.

[36] N. Wang and et al. Y-Branches: When you come to a fork in the road, take it. In *PACT*, 2003.

[37] C. Weaver and et al. Techniques to reduce the soft error rate of a high-performance microprocessor. In *ISCA*, 2004.

[38] J. H. Wensley and et al. SIFT: Design and Analysis of a Fault-Tolerant Computer for Aircraft Control. *Proceedings of the IEEE*, 66(10):1240–1255, October 1978.

[39] Y. Yeh. Triple-triple redundant 777 primary flight computer. In *Proceedings of the 1996 IEEE Aerospace Applications Conference*, volume 1, pages 293–307, February 1996.

[40] J. Ziegler and et al. IBM experiments in soft fails in computer electronics (1978 - 1994). *IBM Journal of Research and Development*, 40(1):3–18, January 1996.

Inherent Time Redundancy (ITR):
Using Program Repetition for Low-Overhead Fault Tolerance

Vimal Reddy, Eric Rotenberg
Center for Efficient, Secure and Reliable Computing, ECE, North Carolina State University
{vkreddy, ericro}@ece.ncsu.edu

Abstract

A new approach is proposed that exploits repetition inherent in programs to provide low-overhead transient fault protection in a processor. Programs repeatedly execute the same instructions within close time periods. This can be viewed as a time redundant re-execution of a program, except that inputs to these inherent time redundant (ITR) instructions vary. Nevertheless, certain microarchitectural events in the processor are independent of the input and only depend on the program instructions. Such events can be recorded and confirmed when ITR instructions repeat.

In this paper, we use ITR to detect transient faults in the fetch and decode units of a processor pipeline, avoiding costly approaches like structural duplication or explicit time redundant execution.

1. Introduction

Technology scaling makes transistors more susceptible to transient faults. As a result, it is becoming increasingly important to incorporate transient fault tolerance in future processors.

Traditional transient fault tolerance approaches duplicate in time or space for robust fault tolerance, but are expensive in terms of performance, area, and power, counteracting the very benefits of technology scaling. To make fault tolerance viable for commodity processors, unconventional techniques are needed that provide significant fault protection in an efficient manner. In this spirit, we are pursuing a new approach to fault tolerance based on microarchitecture insights. The idea is to engage a regimen of low-overhead microarchitecture-level fault checks. Each check protects a distinct part of the pipeline, thus, the regimen as a whole provides comprehensive protection of the processor. This paper adds to the suite of microarchitecture checks that we have begun developing. Recently, we proposed microarchitecture assertions to protect the register rename unit and the out-of-order scheduler of a superscalar processor [3]. In this paper, we introduce a new concept called

inherent time redundancy (ITR), which provides the basis for developing low-overhead fault checks to protect the fetch and decode units of a superscalar processor. Although ITR only protects the fetch and decode units, it is an essential piece of an overall regimen for achieving comprehensive pipeline coverage.

Programs possess inherent time redundancy (ITR): the same instructions are executed repeatedly at short intervals. This program repetition presents an opportunity to discover low-overhead fault checks in a processor. The key idea is to observe microarchitectural events which depend purely on program instructions, and confirm the occurrence of those events when instructions repeat.

There have been previous studies on instruction repetition in programs [1][2]. The focus has been on reusability of dynamic instruction results to reduce the number of instructions executed for high performance. Our proposal is to exploit repetition of static instructions for low-overhead fault tolerance.

We characterize repetition in SPEC2K programs in Figure 1 (integer benchmarks) and Figure 2 (floating point benchmarks). Instructions are grouped into traces that terminate either on a branching instruction or on reaching a limit of 16 instructions. The graphs plot the number of dynamic instructions contributed by static traces. Static instructions are unique instructions in the program binary, whereas dynamic instructions correspond to the instruction stream that unfolds during execution of the program binary.

A relatively small number of static instructions contribute a large number of dynamic instructions. For instance, in most integer benchmarks, less than five hundred static traces contribute nearly all dynamic instructions (e.g., in bzip, 100 static traces contribute 99% of all dynamic instructions). Gcc and vortex are the only exceptions due to the large number of static traces. Floating point benchmarks are even more repetitive, as seen in Figure 2 (e.g., in wupwise, 50 static traces contribute 99% of all dynamic instructions).

An important aspect of repetition is the distance at which traces repeat. This is characterized in Figure 3

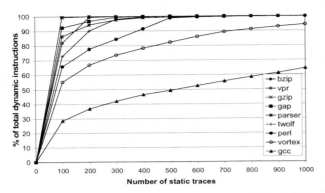

Figure 1. Dynamic instructions per 100 static traces (integer benchmarks).

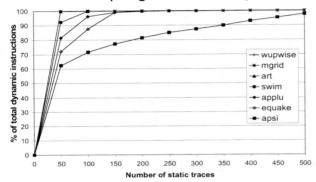

Figure 2. Dynamic instructions per 50 static traces (floating point benchmarks).

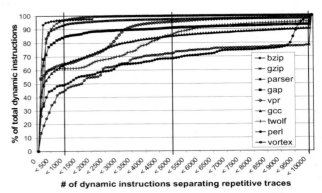

Figure 3. Distance between trace repetitions (integer benchmarks).

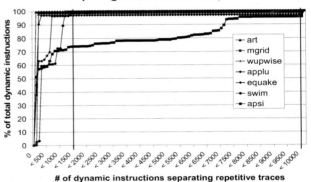

Figure 4. Distance between trace repetitions (floating point benchmarks).

(integer benchmarks) and Figure 4 (floating point benchmarks). Here, instructions are grouped into traces like before, and the number of dynamic instructions between repeating traces is measured. The graphs show the number of dynamic instructions contributed by all static traces that repeat within a particular distance. Distances are shown at increasing intervals of five hundred dynamic instructions.

As seen, there is a high degree of ITR in programs. In all integer benchmarks, except perl and vortex, 85% of all dynamic instructions are contributed by traces repeating within five thousand instructions, four of them reaching that target within one thousand instructions. In all floating point benchmarks, except apsi, nearly all dynamic instructions are contributed by repetitive traces with high proximity (within 1500 instructions).

The main idea of the paper is to record and confirm microarchitecture events that occur while executing highly repetitive instruction traces. The fact that relatively few static traces contribute heavily to the total instruction count, suggests that a small structure is sufficient to record events for most benchmarks. We propose to use a small cache to record microarchitecture events during repetitive traces. The cache is indexed with the program counter (PC) that

starts a trace. A miss in the cache indicates the unavailability of a counterpart to check the correctness of the microarchitectural events. However, misses do not always lead to loss of fault detection. A future hit to a trace that previously missed in the cache can detect anomalies during execution of both the missed instance and the newly executed instance of the trace. In a single-event upset model, a reasonable assumption for fault studies, the two instances will differ if there is a fault. However, if a missed instance is evicted from the cache before it is accessed, it constitutes a loss in fault detection, since a fault during the missed instance goes undetected. Based on this, even benchmarks with a large number of static traces and mild proximity (e.g., gcc) can get reasonable fault detection coverage with small event caches.

The recorded microarchitectural events depend purely on instructions being executed. For example, the decode signals generated upon fetching and decoding an instruction are the same across all instances. Recording and confirming them to be the same can detect faults in the fetch and decode units of a processor. Indexes into the rename map table and architectural map table generated for a trace are constant across all its instances. Recording and confirming their correctness will boost the fault

308

coverage of the rename unit of a processor, especially when used with schemes like Register Name Authentication (RNA) [3]. For instance, RNA cannot detect pure source renaming errors like reading from a wrong index in the rename map table. Further, recording and confirming correct issue ordering among instructions in a trace can detect faults in the out-of-order scheduler of a processor, similar to Timestamp-based Assertion Checking (TAC) [3].

In this paper, we add microarchitecture support to use ITR to extend transient fault protection to the fetch and decode units of a processor. Signals generated by the decode unit for instructions in a trace are combined to generate a signature. The signature is stored in a small cache, called the ITR cache. On the next occurrence of the trace, the signature is re-generated and compared to the signature stored in the ITR cache. A mismatch indicates a transient fault either in the fetch or the decode unit of the processor. On fault detection, safe recovery may be possible by flushing and restarting the processor from the faulting trace, or the program must be aborted through a machine check exception. We provide insight into diagnosing a fault and define criteria to accurately identify fault scenarios where safe recovery is possible, and where aborting the program is the only option.

The main contributions of this paper are as follows:

- A new fault tolerance approach is proposed based on inherent time redundancy (ITR) in programs. The key idea is to record and confirm microarchitectural events that depend purely on program instructions.
- We propose an ITR cache to record microarchitectural events pertaining to a trace of instructions. The key novelty is that misses in the ITR cache do not directly lead to a loss in fault detection. Only evictions of unreferenced, missed instances lead to a loss in fault detection coverage. We develop microarchitectural support to use the ITR cache for protecting the fetch and decode units of a high-performance processor.
- On fault detection, we show it is possible to accurately identify the correct recovery strategy: either a lightweight flush and restart of the processor, or a more expensive program restart.
- We show that the ITR-based approach compares favorably to conventional approaches like structural duplication and time redundant execution, in terms of area and power.

The rest of the paper is organized as follows. Section 2 discusses detailed microarchitectural support to exploit ITR for protecting the fetch and decode units of a superscalar processor. In Section 3, the ITR

cache design space is explored to achieve high fault coverage. In section 4, we perform fault injection experiments to further evaluate fault coverage. In Section 5, we compare area and power overheads of the ITR approach to other fault tolerance approaches. Section 6 discusses related work and Section 7 summarizes the paper.

2. ITR components

The architecture of a superscalar processor, augmented with support for exploiting ITR, is shown in Figure 5. The shaded components are newly added to protect the fetch and decode units of the processor using ITR. The new components are described in subsections 2.1 through 2.5.

2.1. ITR signature generation

As seen in Figure 5, signals from the decode unit are redirected for signature generation. The signals are continuously combined until the end of each trace. The end of a trace is signaled upon encountering a branching instruction or the last of 16 instructions. On a trace ending instruction, the current signature is dispatched into the ITR ROB. The signature is then reset and a new start PC is latched in preparation for the next trace.

Signature generation could be done in many ways. We chose to simply bitwise XOR the signals of a new instruction with corresponding signals of previous instructions in the trace. For a given trace, if a fault on an instruction in the fetch unit or the decode unit causes a wrong signal to be produced by the decode unit, then the signature of the trace would differ from that of a fault-free signature. Even multiple faulty signals in a trace would lead to a difference in signature, unless an even number of instructions in the trace produce a fault in the same signal. Using XOR to produce the signature loses information about the exact instruction that caused a fault. But this precision is not required as long as recovery is cognizant that a fault could be anywhere in the trace and rollback is prior to the trace. For a single-event upset model, we believe this overall approach is sufficient for detecting faults on an instruction of a trace in the fetch and decode units.

2.2. ITR ROB and ITR cache

Trace signatures are dispatched into the ITR ROB, when trace termination is signaled. The ITR ROB is sized to match the number of branches that could exist in the processor, since every branch causes a new trace. Since a trace is terminated on a branch, its ITR

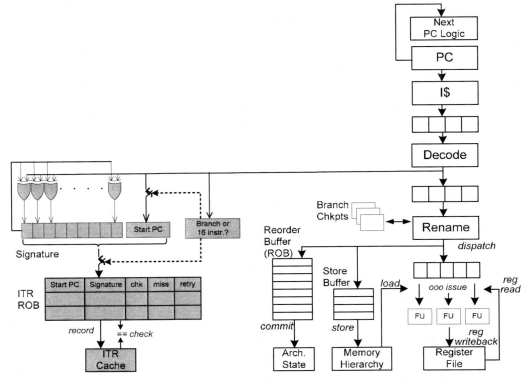

Figure 5. Superscalar processor augmented with ITR support.

ROB entry is noted in the branch's checkpoint to facilitate rollback to the correct ITR ROB entry on branch mispredictions.

Each ITR ROB entry stores the start PC and the signature of a trace. An ITR ROB entry also contains control bits (chk, miss, retry), which indicate the status of checking the trace with the copy in the ITR cache.

The ITR cache stores signatures of previously encountered traces and is indexed with the start PC of a trace. Each trace in the ITR ROB accesses the ITR cache at dispatch. This ensures that reading the ITR cache is complete before the instructions in the trace are ready to commit. If the trace hits, the signature is read from the ITR cache and checked with the signature of the trace. Regardless of the outcome, the chk (for checked) bit is set in the corresponding ITR ROB entry. If it's a mismatch, the retry bit of the ITR ROB entry is set. If the trace misses, the miss bit of the ITR ROB entry is set.

The ITR ROB enables the commit logic of the processor to determine whether the trace of the currently committing instruction has been formed, whether it is has been checked, whether it is faulty, etc. The only extra work for the commit logic is to poll the head entry of the ITR ROB when an instruction is ready to commit. It polls to see if the miss bit or the chk bit of the ITR ROB head entry is set. If neither is set, commit is stalled until one of the bits is set. If the miss bit is set, then a write to the ITR cache is initiated

and commit from the main ROB progresses normally. If the chk bit is set, and additionally the retry bit is not set, then instructions are committed from the main ROB normally. If the retry bit is set, it indicates a transient fault occurred in either the new trace or the previous trace that stored its signature in the ITR cache. To confirm which trace instance is faulty, the processor is flushed and restarted from the start PC of the new trace. If the signatures mismatch again, then it is clear the previous trace executed with a fault. Since this means the processor's architectural state could be corrupted, a machine check exception is raised and the program is aborted. However, if the signatures match after the retry, it means the new trace was faulty, and recovery through flushing and restarting the processor was successful. In all cases, when a trace-terminating instruction is committed from the main ROB, the ITR ROB head entry is freed.

2.3. Fault detection and recovery coverage

Writing to the ITR cache involves replacing an existing, least recently used (LRU) trace signature. Evicting an existing trace signature has implications on the fault detection coverage, i.e., the number of instructions in which a fault can be detected. If a trace's signature is not referenced before being evicted, it amounts to a loss in fault detection coverage. To prevent this, a bit could be added to each cache line to

310

indicate that it is checked and the replacement policy could be modified to evict the LRU trace that has been checked. We do not study this optimization and instead report the loss in fault detection coverage for different cache configurations. Moreover, this policy is not applicable to direct mapped caches and breaks down when no ways of a set are checked yet.

ITR cache misses decrease the fault recovery coverage, i.e., the number of instructions in which a fault can be detected and successfully recovered by flushing and restarting the processor. This is because on a miss, an unchecked trace signature is entered into the cache. If the unchecked trace is faulty, the fault is only detected in the future by the next instance of the trace. However, since the faulty trace has already corrupted the architectural state, the program has to be aborted. In Section 3, we measure the fault coverage for different ITR cache configurations.

Recovery coverage can be enhanced through a coarse-grained checkpointing scheme (e.g., [6][7]). The key idea is to take a coarse-grain checkpoint when there are no unchecked lines in the ITR cache. The number of unchecked lines could be tracked. Once it reaches zero, a coarse-grain checkpoint could be taken. Then in cases where the lightweight processor flush and restart is not possible, recovery can be done by rolling back to the previously taken coarse-grain checkpoint instead of aborting the program.

2.4. Faults on ITR components

The new ITR components do not make the processor more vulnerable to faults, assuming a single-event upset model. A fault on signature generation components will be detected as a signature mismatch. A fault on the latched start PC is not a concern. If its signature matches the faulty start PC's signature, the fault gets masked. If it mismatches, the fault is detected. If it misses in the ITR cache, the next instance of the faulty PC will either detect it or mask it. The control bits chk, miss and retry can be protected using one-hot encoding. The possible states are: {none set – 0001, chk and retry set – 0010, chk set and retry not set—0100, miss set – 1000}. Faults on the ITR cache will cause false machine check exceptions when they are detected, i.e., a retry will indicate a fault on the trace signature in the ITR cache and a machine check exception will be raised, as described in Section 2.2. This can be avoided by parity-protecting each line in the ITR cache. On a signature mismatch, retry is attempted. If the signature mismatches again, then parity is checked on the trace signature in the cache. A parity error indicates an error in the ITR cache and not the previous instance of the trace. Successful recovery

involves invalidating the erroneous line in the cache, or updating it with the signature of the new trace.

2.5. Faults on the program counter (PC)

A fault on the PC or the next-PC logic causes incorrect instructions to be fetched from the I-cache.

If the disruption is in the middle of a trace, then its signature will be a combination of signals from correct and incorrect instructions, and will differ from the trace's fault-free signature. In this case, a PC fault is detected by the ITR cache.

If the disruption is at a natural trace boundary, then a wrong trace is fetched from the I-cache. Since the signature of the wrong trace itself is unaffected by the fault, it will agree with the ITR cache. Hence, the PC that starts a trace at a natural trace boundary represents a vulnerability of the ITR cache, and needs other means of protection. For natural trace boundaries caused by branches, substantial protection of the PC already exists, because the execution unit checks branch targets predicted by the fetch unit. For natural trace boundaries caused by the maximum trace length, protection of the PC is possible by adding a simple commit PC and asserting that a committing instruction's PC matches the commit PC. The commit PC is updated as follows. Sequential committing instructions add their length (which can be recorded at decode for variable-length ISAs) to the commit PC and branches update the commit PC with their calculated PC. Comparing a committing instruction's PC with the commit PC will detect a discontinuity between two otherwise sequential traces. As part of future work, we plan to comprehensively study PC related fault scenarios to identify other potential vulnerabilities and devise robust solutions.

3. The ITR cache design space

As noted in Section 2.3, evictions of unreferenced lines from the ITR cache cause a loss in fault detection coverage, and misses in the ITR cache cause a loss in fault recovery coverage. In this section, we try different ITR cache configurations and measure the loss in fault detection coverage and fault recovery coverage for each design point. Loss in coverage is measured by noting the number of instructions in vulnerable traces.

For experiments, we ran SPEC2K integer and floating point benchmarks compiled with the Simplescalar gcc compiler for the PISA ISA [14]. The compiler optimization level is –O3. Reference inputs are used. In our runs, we skip 900 million instructions and simulate 200 million instructions.

Two ITR cache parameters are varied, (1) Associativity: direct mapped (dm), 2-way, 4-way, 8-way, 16-way and fully associative (fa), and (2) Cache size: 256, 512 and 1024 signatures. Figure 6 shows the loss in fault detection coverage and Figure 7 shows the loss in fault recovery coverage for the various cache configurations. For a given associativity, a smaller cache increases the number of evictions of unreferenced ITR signatures and the number of ITR cache misses. The corresponding increase in coverage loss is shown stacked for the various cache sizes.

Bzip, gzip, art, mgrid and wupwise have negligible coverage loss for all ITR cache configurations. For clarity, they are not included in the graphs. Their excellent ITR cache behavior can be explained by referring back to Figure 3 and Figure 4, which characterize ITR in benchmarks. In these benchmarks, traces repeat in close proximity and such traces contribute to nearly all the dynamic instructions.

In fact, coverage loss for all benchmarks correlates with their characteristics in Figure 3 and Figure 4. In perl and vortex, traces that repeat far apart contribute to a large number of dynamic instructions. Correspondingly, they have the highest loss in fault coverage. Cache capacity has a big impact on mitigating this loss. For example, in vortex, for a direct-mapped cache, increasing the cache capacity to 1024 signatures from 256 signatures decreases the loss in fault detection coverage to 12% from 33%.

Gcc, twolf and apsi also have a notable number of traces that repeat far apart, and experience a loss in fault coverage. They also benefit significantly from increasing the cache capacity. For insight, we refer to Table 1. It shows the total number of static traces for all benchmarks. Notice for vortex and perl, the number of static traces (2,655 and 1,704) is higher than the capacity of all the ITR caches simulated. Their poor trace proximity exposes this capacity problem. Far-apart repeating traces get evicted before they are accessed again, leading to a notable loss in fault coverage. Increasing the cache capacity somewhat makes up for the poor proximity and, hence, has a big impact on reducing coverage loss. Gcc confirms our hypothesis that proximity amongst traces is a strong factor. Even though it has far more traces than vortex and perl (24,017), it has lower coverage loss for a given cache configuration as a result of its better trace proximity. Mgrid is another example. It has negligible coverage loss for all ITR cache configurations even though it has a relatively high number of static traces (798). Again, proximity amongst its traces is excellent. The remaining benchmarks have a small loss in fault coverage which can be overcome with bigger caches or higher associativity.

Table 1. Number of static traces for SPEC.

SPECInt	#static
bzip	283
gap	696
gcc	24017
gzip	291
parser	865
perl	1704
twolf	481
vortex	2655
vpr	292

SPECfp	#static
applu	282
apsi	1274
art	98
equake	336
mgrid	798
swim	73
wupwise	18

Note that the loss in fault coverage should not be interpreted as a conventional cache miss rate, i.e., it does not correspond to signatures that missed on accessing the ITR cache. Firstly, the loss in fault detection coverage (Figure 6) corresponds to signatures that were evicted from the ITR cache before being referenced. Secondly, both the loss in fault detection coverage and the loss in fault recovery coverage are influenced by the number of instructions in signatures, which is not uniform across all signatures. These factors may explain why, in some benchmarks, higher associativity sometimes happens to show slightly higher loss in fault coverage than lower associativity.

An important point is that the loss in fault detection coverage is significantly lesser than the loss in fault recovery coverage for all benchmarks. This is because all ITR cache misses lead to a loss in recovery coverage, but only those missed traces that are then evicted before being referenced lead to a loss in detection coverage.

Across all benchmarks, for a 2-way associative cache with 1024 signatures, the average loss in fault detection coverage is 1.3% with a maximum loss of 8.2% for vortex. The corresponding numbers for loss in fault recovery coverage are 2.5% average and 15% maximum for vortex.

In general, programs with less repetition or greater distance between repeated traces would have a higher loss in fault coverage. One possible solution to mitigate this is to redundantly fetch and decode traces only on a miss in the ITR cache, still achieving the benefits of ITR but falling back on conventional time redundancy when inherent time redundancy fails. After the signature of the re-fetched trace is checked against the ITR cache, instructions in that trace are discarded from the pipeline. Another possible solution is to have a fully duplicated frontend, like in the IBM S/390 G5 processor [4], but use the ITR cache to guide when the space redundancy should be exercised (for significant power savings). The use of ITR as a filter for selectively exercising time redundancy or space redundancy is an interesting direction we want to explore in future research.

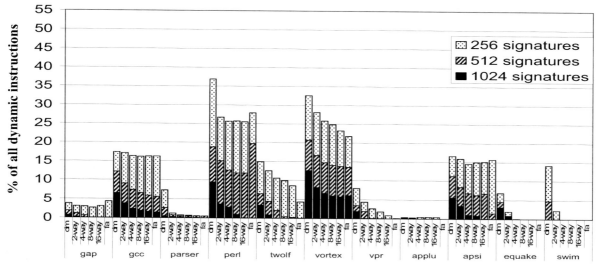

Figure 6. Loss in fault detection coverage.

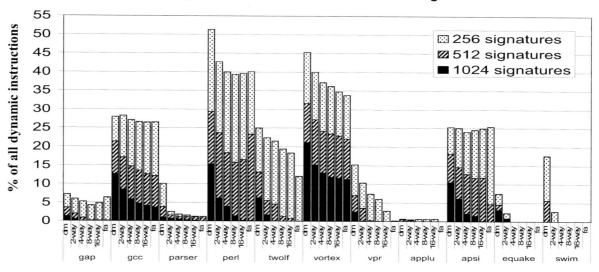

Figure 7. Loss in fault recovery coverage.

4. Fault injection experiments

We perform fault injection on a detailed cycle-level simulator that models a microarchitecture similar to the MIPS R10K processor [5].

For each benchmark, one thousand faults are randomly injected on the decode signals from Table 2. Injecting a fault involves flipping a randomly selected bit. A separate "golden" (fault-free) simulator is run in parallel with the faulty simulator. When an instruction is committed to the architectural state in the faulty simulator, it is compared with its golden counterpart to determine whether or not the architectural state is being corrupted. Any fault that leads to corruption of architectural state is classified as a potential silent data corruption (SDC) fault. Likewise, if no corruption of architectural state is observed for a set period of time

after a fault is injected (the observation window), it is classified as a masked fault. In this study, we use an observation window of one million cycles.

An injected fault may lead to one of six possible outcomes, depending on (1) whether the fault is detected by an ITR check ("ITR") or undetected within the scope of the observation window ("MayITR")[1] or undetected for sure ("Undet"), and (2) whether the fault corrupts architectural state ("SDC") or not ("Mask"). Based on this, the six possible outcomes are ITR+SDC, ITR+Mask, MayITR+SDC, MayITR+Mask, Undet+SDC, and Undet+Mask.

---

[1] A fault may not get detected within the scope of the observation window, but its corresponding faulty signature may still be in the ITR cache. In this case, it is possible that the fault will be detected by ITR in the future, but we would have to extend the observation window to confirm this.

Table 2. List of decode signals.

Field	Description	Width
opcode	instruction opcode	8
flags	decoded control flags (is_int, is_fp, is_signed/unsigned, is_branch, is_uncond, is_ld, is_st, mem_left/right, is_RR, is_disp, is_direct, is_trap)	12
shamt	shift amount	5
rsrc1	source register operand	5
rsrc2	source register operand	5
rdst	destination register operand	5
lat	execution latency	2
imm	immediate	16
num_rsrc	number of source operands	2
num_rdst	number of destination operands	1
mem_size	size of memory word	3
	Total width	64

We further qualify ITR+SDC outcomes with the possibility of recovery (ITR+SDC+R) or only detection (ITR+SDC+D). On detecting a fault through ITR, if the signature accessing the ITR cache is faulty as opposed to the signature within the cache, then, the fault is recoverable by flushing the ROB (discussed in Section 2.3).

We add two more fault checks to support our experiments. A watchdog timer check (wdog) is added to detect deadlocks caused by some faults (e.g., faulty source registers). A sequential-PC check (spc) is added at retirement (discussed in Section 2.5) to detect faults pertaining to control flow.

In the following experiments, we use a two-way set-associative ITR cache holding 1024 signatures. The breakdown of fault injection outcomes is shown in Figure 8. We show fault injection results for the same set of SPEC benchmarks whose coverage results are reported in Section 3. As seen, a large percentage of injected faults are detected through the ITR cache (95.4% on average). On average, 32% of the injected faults are detected and recovered by ITR that would have otherwise led to a SDC (ITR+SDC+R). Only a small percentage (1% on average) of SDC faults detected through ITR is not recoverable (ITR+SDC+D). A large percentage of faults that are detected by ITR happen to get masked (59.4% on average). When a fault is injected on a decode signal that is not relevant to the instruction being decoded or does not lead to an error (e.g., increasing *lat*, the execution latency, only delays wakeup of dependent instructions), then the fault gets masked, but the signature is faulty and gets detected by the ITR cache. A noticeable fraction of faults (3% on average) are detected and recovered by ITR that would have otherwise led to a deadlock (ITR+wdog+R), highlighting another important benefit.

The fraction of faults undetected by ITR within the observation window (MayITR+*) is negligible. This indicates that a one million cycle observation window is sufficient.

Interestingly, the sequential PC check detected a small fraction of faults (0.1% on average) that ITR alone could not detect (spc+SDC). The sequential-PC check mainly detected faults on the *is_branch* control flag, which indicates whether or not an instruction is a conditional branch. Consider the following fault scenario. Suppose that the fetch unit predicts an instruction to be a conditional branch (BTB hit signals a conditional branch and gshare predicts taken). Suppose the instruction is truly a conditional branch (BTB correct) and is actually not taken (gshare incorrect). Then suppose that a fault causes *is_branch* to be false instead of true. First, this fault causes a SDC because the branch misprediction will not be repaired. Second, because *is_branch* is false, the retirement PC is updated in a sequential way. The spc check will fire in this case, because the next retiring instruction is not sequential. Note that if the prediction was correct (actually taken), the spc check still fires, but this is a masked rather than SDC fault.

On average, 4.5% of injected faults go undetected by ITR. Only about 2.6% of the faults lead to SDC and are not detected by ITR (Undet+SDC). A very small fraction of faults (0.1% on average) lead to a deadlock that is not detected by ITR but is caught by the watchdog timer. The remaining undetected faults are masked (on average, 1.8% of all faults).

5. Area and power comparisons

Structural duplication can be used to protect the fetch and decode units of the processor. In the IBM S/390 G5 processor [4], the I-unit, comprised of the fetch and decode units, is duplicated and signals from the two units are compared to detect transient faults. However, this direct approach has significant area and power overheads. We attempt to compare the area and power overhead of the ITR cache with that of the I-unit, to see whether or not the ITR-based approach is attractive compared to straightforward duplication. The die photo of the IBM S/390 G5 provides the area of the I-unit [4]. To estimate the area of the ITR cache, a structure is selected from the die photo that is similar in configuration to the ITR cache. The branch target buffer (BTB) of the G5 has a configuration similar to the ITR cache: 2048 entries, 2-way associative, 35 bits per entry [15]. Based on the decode signals in Table 2, the size of the ITR signature is 64 bits. Though each ITR entry is almost twice as wide as the G5's BTB entry, only half as many entries as the BTB (1024 entries) are needed for good coverage, from results in Section 3 and Section 4.

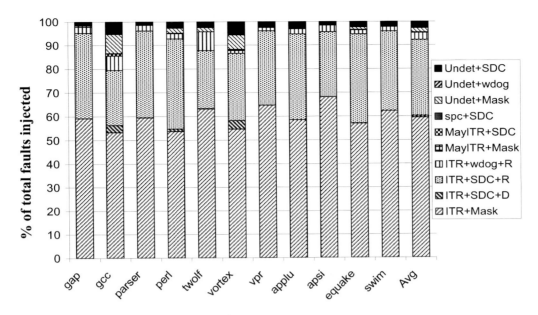

Figure 8. Fault injection results.

The area of the I-unit from the die photo is 1.5 cm x 1.4 cm, i.e., 2.1 cm². The area of the ITR-cache like BTB structure from the die photo is 1.5 cm x 0.2 cm, i.e., 0.3 cm². The ITR cache is about one seventh the area of the I-unit. Hence, the ITR-based approach to protect the frontend is more area-effective than structural duplication of the entire I-unit.

We next try to find the power-effectiveness of the ITR approach. A major power overhead of structural duplication and conventional time redundancy is that of fetching an instruction twice from the instruction cache. We model power consumption by measuring the number of accesses to the ITR cache and the instruction cache of the processor. Both cache models are fed into CACTI [17] to obtain the energy consumption per access. Multiplying the number of accesses with the energy consumed per access gives us the energy consumption.

Due to lack of information on the instruction cache configuration of the IBM S/390 G5, we chose the instruction cache of the IBM Power4 [16]. The configuration of the Power4 I-cache is: 64KB, direct-mapped, 128 byte line and one read/write port. The configuration of the ITR cache is: 8KB (1024 entries), 2-way associative, 8 byte line, and one read/write port (or one read and one write port). We chose the 0.18 micron technology used in the IBM Power4.

The CACTI numbers were: 0.87 nJ per access for the I-cache, 0.58 nJ per access (or 0.84 nJ for separate read and write ports) for the ITR cache. Overall energy consumption is shown in Figure 9. As seen, the ITR-based approach is far more energy efficient than fetching twice from the instruction cache. Note that the

energy savings will be even greater if also considering the redundant decoding of instructions in the frontend in the case of structural duplication or traditional time redundancy.

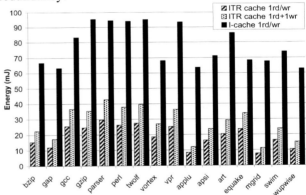

Figure 9. Energy of ITR cache vs. I-cache.

We see that the ITR cache is more cost-effective than straightforward space redundancy in the IBM mainframe processor [4]. However, it should be noted that complete structural duplication provides more robust fault tolerance than the ITR cache. They are two different design points in the cost/coverage spectrum.

6. Related work

Prior research on exploiting program repetition has focused on reusing previous instruction results through a reuse buffer to reduce the total number of instructions executed [1][2]. Instruction reuse has also been used to reduce the number of redundant instructions executed in a time-redundant execution model [8]. In the latter work, the goal was to reduce function unit pressure. Instead of executing two copies of an instruction using two function units, in some cases it is possible to execute one copy using a function unit and the other copy using a reuse buffer. ITR reduces pressure in the fetch and decode units, whereas their approach requires fetching and decoding all instructions twice. In other words, their approach only addresses the execution stage and is an orthogonal technique that could be used in an overall fault tolerance regimen.

Amongst the several proposals to reduce overheads of full-redundant execution, using ITR to protect the fetch and decode units could improve approaches that either do not offer protection to the frontend [9][12], or trade performance for protection by using traditional time-redundancy in the frontend [10][11]. In general, frontend bandwidth is pricier than execution bandwidth. By using ITR to protect the frontend, traditional time-redundancy can be focused on exploiting idle execution bandwidth [10][11][12][13].

ITR-based fault checks augment the suite of fault checks available to processor designers. Developing such a regimen of fault checks to protect the processor (e.g., [3]) will lead to low-overhead fault tolerance solutions compared to more expensive space redundancy or time redundancy approaches.

7. Summary

We introduced a new approach to develop low-overhead fault checks for a processor, based on inherent time redundancy (ITR) in programs. We proposed the ITR cache to store microarchitectural events that depend only upon program instructions. We demonstrated its effectiveness by developing microarchitectural support to protect the fetch and decode units of the processor. We gave insights on diagnosing a fault to determine the correct recovery procedure. We quantified fault detection coverage and fault recovery coverage obtained for a given ITR cache configuration. Finally, we showed that using the ITR-based approach is more favorable than costly structural duplication and traditional time redundancy.

8. Acknowledgments

We would like to thank the anonymous reviewers for their helpful comments in improving this paper. We thank Muawya Al-Otoom and Hashem Hashemi for their help with area and power experiments. This research was supported by NSF CAREER grant No. CCR-0092832, and generous funding and equipment donations from Intel. Any opinions, findings, and conclusions or recommendations expressed herein are those of the authors and do not necessarily reflect the views of the National Science Foundation.

9. References

[1] A. Sodani and G. S. Sohi. Dynamic instruction reuse. ISCA 1997.

[2] A. Sodani and G. S. Sohi. An empirical analysis of instruction repetition. ASPLOS 1998.

[3] V. K. Reddy, A. S. Al-Zawawi and E. Rotenberg. Assertion-based microarchitecture design for improved fault tolerance. ICCD 2006.

[4] T. J. Slegel et al. IBM's S/390 G5 microprocessor design. IEEE Micro, March 1999.

[5] K. C. Yeager. The MIPS R10000 superscalar processor. IEEE Micro, April 1996.

[6] R. Teodorescu, J. Nakano and J. Torrellas. SWICH: A prototype for efficient cache-level checkpoint and rollback. IEEE Micro, Oct 2006.

[7] D. Sorin, M. M. K. Martin and M. D. Hill. Fast checkpoint/recovery to support kilo-instruction speculation and hardware fault tolerance. Tech. Report: CS-TR-2000-1420, Univ. of Wisconsin, Madison. Oct 2000.

[8] A. Parashar, S. Gurumurthi and A. Sivasubramaniam. A complexity effective approach to ALU bandwidth enhancement for instruction-level temporal redundancy. ISCA 2004.

[9] T. M. Austin. Diva: A reliable substrate for deep submicron microarchitecture design. MICRO 1999.

[10] J. Ray, J. C. Hoe and B. Falsafi. Dual use of superscalar datapath for transient-fault detection and recovery. MICRO 2001.

[11] J. C. Smolens, J. Kim, J. C. Hoe and B. Falsafi. Efficient resource sharing in concurrent error detecting superscalar microarchitectures. MICRO 2004.

[12] A. Mendelson and N. Suri. Designing high-performance and reliable superscalar architectures – The out of order reliable superscalar (O3RS) approach. DSN 2000.

[13] M. Franklin, G. S. Sohi and K. K. Saluja. A study of time-redundant techniques for high-performance pipelined computers. FTCS 1989.

[14] D. Burger, T. Austin and S. Bennett. The simplescalar toolset, version 2. Tech Report CS-TR-1997-1342, Univ. of Wisconsin, Madison. July 1997.

[15] M. A. Check and T. J. Slegel. Custom S/390 G5 and G6 microprocessors. IBM Journal of R&D, vol 43, #5/6. 1999.

[16] J. M. Tendler et al. Power4 system microarchitecture. IBM Journal of R&D, vol 46, #1, 2002.

[17] P. Shivakumar and N. P. Jouppi. Cacti 3.0: An Integrated Cache Timing, Power and Area Model. Western Research Lab (WRL) Research Report. 2002.

Utilizing Dynamically Coupled Cores to Form a Resilient Chip Multiprocessor

Christopher LaFrieda   Engin İpek   José F. Martínez   Rajit Manohar

Computer Systems Laboratory
Cornell University
Ithaca, NY 14853 USA

http://csl.cornell.edu/

Abstract

Aggressive CMOS scaling will make future chip multiprocessors (CMPs) increasingly susceptible to transient faults, hard errors, manufacturing defects, and process variations. Existing fault-tolerant CMP proposals that implement dual modular redundancy (DMR) do so by statically binding pairs of adjacent cores via dedicated communication channels and buffers. This can result in unnecessary power and performance losses in cases where one core is defective (in which case the entire DMR pair must be disabled), or when cores exhibit different frequency/leakage characteristics due to process variations (in which case the pair runs at the speed of the slowest core). Static DMR also hinders power density/thermal management, as DMR pairs running code with similar power/thermal characteristics are necessarily placed next to each other on the die.

We present dynamic core coupling (DCC), an architectural technique that allows arbitrary CMP cores to verify each other's execution while requiring no static core binding at design time or dedicated communication hardware. Our evaluation shows that the performance overhead of DCC over a CMP without fault tolerance is 3% on SPEC2000 benchmarks, and is within 5% for a set of scalable parallel scientific and data mining applications with up to eight threads (16 processors). Our results also show that DCC has the potential to significantly outperform existing static DMR schemes.

1 Introduction

Aggressive CMOS scaling has permitted exponential increases in the microprocessor's transistor budget for the last three decades. Earlier processor designs successfully translated such transistor budget increases into performance growth. Nowadays, however, power and complexity have become unsurmountable obstacles to traditional monolithic designs. This has turned chip multiprocessors (CMPs) into the primary mechanism to deliver performance growth, by doubling the number of cores and exploiting increasing levels of thread-level parallelism (TLP) with each new technology generation. Current industry projections indicate that CMPs will scale to many tens or even hundreds of cores by 2015 [4]. Unfortunately, this does not mean that CMPs are free of power, temperature, or even complexity issues. Moreover, other artifacts intrinsic to deep-submicron technologies render these future "many-core" CMPs increasingly susceptible to soft errors [15, 21], manufacturing defects [6], process variations [3], and early lifetime failures [27].

One appealing aspect of CMPs is the inherent redundancy of hardware resources, which can be exploited for error detection and recovery. Current proposals for DMR-based CMPs statically bind core pairs at design time and rely on dedicated cross-core communication [7, 24, 29]. This presents important limitations. For example, when a core fails due to a manufacturing defect or early lifetime failure, the remaining core in its DMR pair can no longer be checked for hard or soft errors. This effectively doubles the number of unavailable cores for fault-tolerant execution. In the

presence of process variations, functional DMR pairs consisting of cores with different frequency or leakage characteristics may have to run at the speed of the slower core, leading to additional performance degradations. Hardwired DMR also presents limitations to effective power density/thermal management, as DMR pairs running code with similar power/thermal characteristics are necessarily placed next to each other on the die.

Instead of relying on a set of rigid, statically defined DMR pairs, we would like a CMP to provide the flexibility to allow any core to form a virtual DMR pair with any other core on demand. We would also like to be able to use additional cores to implement other desirable features on demand, such as TMR, or activity migration to spread heat more evenly on the die without compromising fault-tolerant execution. To do this, we propose *dynamic core coupling* (DCC), a processor-level fault-tolerance technique that allows arbitrary CMP cores to verify each other's execution while requiring no dedicated cross-core communication channels or buffers. DCC offers several important advantages. Specifically, DCC:

- Degrades half as fast as mechanisms that rely on static DMR pairs.

- Facilitates the formation of balanced DMR pairs by selectively binding cores that operate at similar speeds.

- Enables low-power fault-tolerant execution by binding low-leakage cores first.

- Supports existing thermal management techniques based on activity migration seamlessly, regardless of functional core count or adjacency.

- Detects and recovers from both hard and soft errors.

- Provides support for on-demand triple modular redundancy (TMR) at no additional cost, using hot spares.

- Greatly simplifies output compression circuitry and lowers compression bandwidth demand by tolerating large checkpointing intervals that can amortize long compression latencies.

In our evaluation, the performance overhead of DCC over a CMP without fault tolerance is less than 3% on SPEC2000 benchmarks, and is within 5% on a set of scalable scientific and data mining applications with eight threads (16 cores).

This paper is organized as follows: Section 2 reviews the challenges created by CMOS scaling in deep sub-micron process technologies, and explores current fault detection and recovery techniques. Section 3 presents our fault tolerant CMP architecture. Section 4 discusses the additional modifications made to the architecture to support parallel applications. Section 5 describes the experimental setup and reports the results. Finally, Section 6 summarizes our conclusions.

2 Background and Related Work

2.1 Deep Submicron Challenges

CMOS scaling in deep submicron process technologies will create significant problems for future many-core CMP platforms. In this section, we review some of these challenges and their implications on fault-tolerant CMP design.

Soft Errors The susceptibility of a device to soft errors is inversely proportional to the amount of charge in its nodes [21]. With technology scaling, smaller transistors and lower supply voltages decrease the amount of charge on a node, thereby making devices more sensitive to soft errors [5]. The soft error rate (SER) of combinational logic in a processor is expected to reach 1,000 FIT (failures in 10^9 hours) by 2011 [21]. Since storage structures can be protected relatively easily by parity or error-correcting codes (ECC), combinational logic is expected to become the dominant source of soft errors.

Manufacturing Defects and Process Variations Manufacturing defects are primarily artifacts of fabrication related failure mechanisms (e.g., open or short circuits), or process variations (e.g., excessively leaky cores). During production, burn-in tests that stress parts under extreme voltage and temperature conditions are used to accelerate infant mortality and to expose latent failures. Once identified, defective cores are disabled and parts are classified into bins based on functional core count. Even among the remaining functional cores that pass burn-in tests, frequency and leakage power can vary.

Manufacturing defects are already posing serious challenges to semiconductor manufacturers: IBM recently announced that many of its nine-core Cell microprocessors will ship with only eight functional cores due to defects, and the company is considering whether to ship chips with only seven functional cores [25]. While no industrial data on core-to-core parameter variability or defect rates in CMPs are available for current generation process technologies, both problems are expected to become progressively more significant with CMOS scaling.

Early Lifetime Failures Although burn-in tests are an effective mechanism to expose latent failures and identify defective cores, testing is by no means perfect; electromigration, stress migration, time-dependent dielectric breakdown, and thermal cycling can all lead to intrinsic hard failures [26] after manufacturer burn-in tests. All of these factors worsen as technology scales. The resulting effect of these failures is permanent in the sense that the device is broken and cannot ever be relied upon to produce correct results. The rate of early lifetime failures for 65 nm technology has been estimated to be 7,000 FIT to 15,000 FIT[27]. It is difficult to draw conclusions about the relative rates of soft and hard errors based on their estimates. However, these projections show the importance of designing a system tolerant to both soft and hard errors.

2.2 Fault Tolerance

DCC falls within a class of fault tolerant architectures that use redundant execution. Redundant execution is a technique that runs two independent copies of a thread and intermittently compares their results. This technique has become increasing popular with the recent shift towards more on-chip thread contexts. DCC is most similar to work that combines redundant execution with simultaneous multithreading [28] (SMT) or chip multiprocessor [16] (CMP) architectures. SMT provides additional thread contexts by allowing multiple threads to use a processor's resources simultaneously. CMPs support additional thread contexts by simply integrating more processors on-chip.

AR-SMT [19] was one of the first proposals to use SMT to detect transient faults. As instructions retire in a leading thread,

the A-thread, their results are stored in a delay buffer. A trailing thread, the R-thread, re-executes instructions and compares with results in the delay buffer. SRT [17] builds upon this work by addressing memory coherence between the leading and trailing threads in hardware. Specifically, both threads must see the same inputs from the memory system and produce a single output. SRTR [29] extends SRT by adding support for recovery. We limit further discussion of SMT approaches to SRTR.

CRT [14] uses a CMP composed of processors with SMT support. A leading thread on one processor is checked by a trailing thread on another processor by forwarding results through a *dedicated bus*. The advantage over SRTR is better permanent fault coverage as no resources are shared between a leading and trailing thread. CRTR [7] extends CRT by providing recovery from transient faults. Reunion [23] is a CMP architecture that significantly reduces result forwarding bandwidth by compressing results. These signatures are exchanged between statically bound checking pairs via a *dedicated bus*. Previous work can be categorized by the following: i) synchronization, ii) input replication, iii) output comparison, and iv) recovery.

Synchronization. To compare results in redundant execution, either both threads must be synchronized, or a trailing thread must check the results of all committed instructions against a sequence of forwarded results. It is common in commercial systems, such as The Tandem Himalaya [12] and Stratus [20], to use lockstep execution. The IBM G5/G6/z990 [22, 13] uses replicated fetch, decode and execution units running in lockstep. Lockstep means that each processor executes the same instructions in a given cycle. Lockstep is hard to achieve in SMT and CMP because of contention for shared resources. As a result, SRTR and CRTR maintain a slack between leader and trailer threads using simple queues. The leader thread forwards its results to these queues. The trailing thread reads results from these queues as it issues instructions, thereby aligning trailing instruction execution with leading instruction results. Reunion exchanges compressed results between threads at approximately every fifty instructions. The lag between leading and trailing threads is limited by the number of unverified stores that can be buffered. In SRTR and CRTR, stores are buffered in dedicated queues. In Reunion, stores are buffered in a speculative portion of the store buffer. The maximum lag between threads for these two methods is on the order of a hundred instructions.

Input Replication. There is a potential problem if a trailing thread redundantly executes a load instruction. An intervening store, possibly from a separate thread, may have updated that memory address between the time the leading thread executes the load and the trailing thread executes the load. To remedy this, SRTR and CRTR support input replication via a load value queue (LVQ). When the leader thread executes a load instruction, it forwards the result to the trailing thread's LVQ. The trailing thread reads load values from the LVQ rather than going to memory. Reunion, on the other hand, allows both threads to independently execute load instructions. In the case of an intervening store, Reunion rolls back its state to a checkpoint and executes both threads in a single-step mode until the first memory instruction. The authors refer to this as *relaxed input replication*.

Output Comparison. Faults are detected by comparing the state (register values and stores) of each thread in the redundant execution. In SRTR and CRTR, the leading thread forwards results to the trailing thread's register value queue (RVQ) and store buffer (StB). The trailing thread compares its results with the leading thread's results before committing results. In this fashion, the trailing thread's state is always fault-free. SRTR reduces the bandwidth requirements of the RVQ by only checking register results for instructions at the end of a dependence chain. Reunion greatly reduces the overhead of communicating results between cores by using Fingerprinting [24]. Fingerprinting uses a CRC-16 compression circuit to compress all the new state generated each cycle into

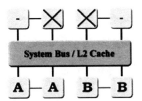

Figure 1. An eight-core statically coupled CMP with two failures. Only two threads can be executed reliably.

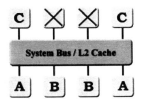

Figure 2. An eight-core dynamically coupled CMP with two failures. Three threads can be executed reliably.

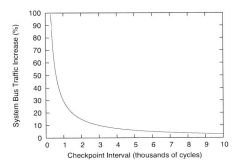

Figure 3. System bus traffic with increasing checkpoint interval size (system described in Section 5).

a single 16-bit signature. Comparing these signatures is equivalent to comparing the results of all executed instructions. The probability of undetected error using this technique is very small, roughly 2^{-16}.

Recovery. In SRTR and CRTR, a fault-free state can be recovered by copying the committed state of the trailing thread, which is guaranteed to be fault-free, to the leading thread. This backward-error recovery (BER) technique provides recovery for transient faults, but cannot be used to recover from permanent faults. Reunion checkpoints the architectural state of each core before they exchange fingerprints. When there is a mismatch between fingerprints, the speculative state is squashed and the last checkpoint is restored. The IBM G5/G6 can additionally recover from some permanent faults by copying processor state to a spare processor.

There are two major architectural distinctions between previous work and DCC. First, DCC can recover from permanent faults without the need for constant TMR, like in Tandem and Stratus architectures, or the need for dedicated spares, like in the IBM G5/G6. DCC uses a novel on-demand TMR scheme which only employs TMR during permanent fault recovery. When not recovering from a permanent fault, all processors are configured as DMR pairs and performing computation. Second, DMR pairs in DCC are dynamically assigned. One advantage of dynamic coupling is that a faulty core does not disable both cores of a DMR pair because a working core has the flexibility to form a DMR pair with any other working core. Accommodating dynamic coupling requires architectural extensions over previous approaches. These extensions are described in the following sections.

3 DCC Mechanism

3.1 Architecture Overview

DCC dynamically couples cores by performing all communication between redundant threads over the system bus of a shared memory CMP. In statically coupled CMPs[7, 14, 23], communication between redundant threads is conducted over additional dedicated buses. Dynamic coupling provides the following benefits: i) the system degrades at half the rate of a statically coupled CMP in the presence of permanent faults; ii) when considering variation, cores with similar characteristics can be paired together; and iii) hot spots can be minimized by running high IPC applications redundantly on distant cores. For example, consider the statically coupled CMP in Figure 1 and the dynamically coupled CMP in Figure 2. With two permanent failures, the statically coupled CMP cannot utilize any of the upper four cores for redundant execution because the two working cores can only forward results to the two broken cores. However, the dynamically coupled CMP has the flexibility to pair the two working cores and use them to execute an additional reliable thread. In addition, the dynamically coupled CMP issues the high IPC thread A on distant cores to reduce hot spots.

Utilizing the system bus for redundant thread communication has two major implications. First, communicating over the system bus with a potentially distant core may incur a greater latency than communicating to an adjacent core via a dedicated bus. Second, the resulting increase in system bus traffic could severely impact performance. Figure 3 shows the average increase in system bus traffic over a range of checkpoint intervals (time between output comparisons) for the parallel applications discussed in Section 5. This graph suggests that a long checkpoint interval, roughly greater than 3,000 cycles, is needed to amortize the increase in system bus traffic. Supporting long checkpoint intervals requires a significant deviation from previous work. For instance, we find that using the relaxed input replication model from Reunion incurs a significant overhead (we evaluate this in Section 5.1.2).

3.2 Private Cache Modifications

In order to support long checkpoint intervals, a large number of memory stores must be buffered. Clearly, thousands of cycles worth of stores will exceed the capacity of the store buffer used in Reunion and CRTR. Instead, DCC's private caches support the cache buffering techniques proposed in Cherry[11]. When a cache line is written, it is marked as *unverified*. Unverified lines are not allowed to leave the private cache hierarchy. Once the buffered state is known to be fault-free, at the end of a checkpoint interval, all unverified marks are gang-cleared. A write to a verified dirty line forces that line to be written back to lower levels of the memory hierarchy, so that it may be restored if a fault occurred during the checkpoint interval. Cherry has shown that this style of cache buffering can easily support thousands of loads with very little overhead (roughly one bit per cache block). In addition to cache buffering support in the private caches, all caches are protected by error correcting codes (ECC), as is done in previous work. It is necessary for each processor to redundantly load data from shared memory into their private cache. However, only one processor needs to write dirty cache lines back into shared memory. We assign the task of writing back dirty data to one processor, the *master*, while the other processor, the *slave*, may evict updated (but verified) cache lines without writing back. The master and slave processors need not be leading and trailing, respectively. Master cores ignore coherence actions to unverified lines by their own slave(s). Conversely, slaves ignore invalidation requests from their own master. Data consistency when running parallel applications is discussed later (Section 4).

There exists a danger of deadlock if an application's unverified dirty lines are allowed to remain in the CMP cache subsystem after the application is descheduled by the operating system. Specifically, the next application to run on the same core may find all cache blocks of a set locked by unverified writes from the previous application, preventing it from making forward progress. If the new application has also locked all cache blocks in a set used by the old application, then a circular dependence arises between the two applications and deadlock ensues. Similar interactions are possible between writes from an application and the operating system. To avoid these problems, we implement a simple policy: be-

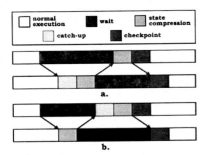

Figure 4. Processor synchronization when: a.) synchronizing processor is leading, or b.) synchronizing processor is trailing.

fore control is transferred across applications and the operating system, all unverified dirty data are verified by scheduling a checkpoint. Once control is transferred, the operating system saves the (just verified) architectural state to the application's process control block as usual.

On a context switch, slave caches are flushed to avoid having multiple copies of a cache line with inconsistent states. If a previous application had used the slave core as its master processor, there is a danger that this earlier application's verified dirty lines may be lost during the cache flush. To avoid such cases, the operating system partitions the cores into master and slave pools, and allocates master and slave cores accordingly. In rare cases where a processor from the master pool may need to be moved to the slave pool, all verified dirty data in the master's cache are first written back to main memory. In cases where a processor from the slave pool needs to be relocated to the master pool, the slave cache is flushed.

3.3 Synchronization

Figure 4 shows our multi-phase synchronization protocol. Synchronization begins when a processor receives a scheduled or unscheduled checkpoint request. Unscheduled checkpoints occur for the following events: i) cache buffering overflow; ii) interrupt; iii) uncached load/store (I/O); or iv) context switch. The processor that receives the checkpoint request sends the number of instructions committed since the last checkpoint to the other redundant processor. The processor initiating the synchronization is either the leading processor, Figure 4a, or the trailing processor, Figure 4b. If the synchronizing processor is leading, the other processor commits enough instructions to synchronize, then compresses and broadcasts its state (via the shared system bus). If the synchronizing processor is trailing, the other processor broadcasts the number of instructions it has committed since the last checkpoint. The synchronizing processor executes enough instructions to match the leading processor, then compresses and broadcasts its state. Once each processor has received the compressed state of the other, it compares against its own. If the compressed states match, a checkpoint is taken and execution resumes. If they disagree, the last checkpoint is restored and the checkpoint interval repeats. In cases where the trailing processor cannot execute enough instructions to match the leading processor (e.g., due to a cache buffering overflow), the last checkpoint is restored, and a new checkpoint is scheduled with half the duration of the last interval. Similarly, if a checkpoint interval does not complete within a fixed timeout period, a rollback is forced and a new checkpoint with half the duration of the last checkpointing interval is scheduled. This eventually guarantees forward progress in cases where a fault prevents the cores from reaching the next checkpoint. Checkpoints are kept in a small, ECC-protected, on-chip SRAM array.

3.4 State Compression

State compression is needed to reduce the bandwidth requirements of comparing state between two cores. Fingerprinting[24] proposed the use of a CRC-16 compression circuit to compress all of the register file and memory updates each cycle. We simulated various parallel CRC circuits[2] in HSPICE and their fan-out-of-four (FO4) delays[1] and transistors counts are shown in Table 1. Assuming a cycle time of 10-15 FO4s, a CRC-32 circuit and a CRC-16 circuit (2 stages) can compress up to 32 bits in one cycle. With potentially more than 256 bits of new state each cycle, a CRC-16 circuit could not keep pace with the core. To remedy this, Reunion uses a multicycle compression scheme. However, the long checkpoint interval in DCC allows us to employ a simple solution that provides a large reduction in required compression bandwidth.

CRC Circuit	Input Width	FO4 Delay	Transistor Count
CRC-16	16	6.65	754
CRC-SDLC-16	16	6.10	888
CRC-32	16	7.28	2260
CRC-32	32	8.60	4240

Table 1. FO4 delay and transistor count for various CRC circuits.

We make the observation that checking the state of the register file at the end of a checkpoint interval is equivalent to checking all the updates made to the register file during a checkpoint interval. Therefore, rather than compressing all the updates to the register file, we simply compress the state of the register file at the end of a checkpoint interval. The time it takes to read out the contents of the 32 entry architectural register file is easily amortized over the long checkpoint interval. In this manner, only memory stores need to be compressed on the fly during a checkpoint interval. Two CRC-32 circuits are needed to compress the data and the address of a store. At the end of a checkpoint interval, these CRC circuits simultaneously compress the integer register file and the floating point register file. For a checkpoint interval of 10,000 cycles, this technique reduces the total state compression bandwidth (i.e., number of bits compressed per cycle) by a factor of 5.4 for SPEC2000 benchmarks.

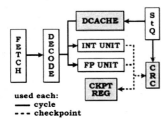

Figure 5. State compression: Stores are compressed each cycle using two CRC-32 circuits, but register values are compressed at checkpoints. StQ is the store queue.

3.5 Recovery

DCC aims to mitigate the impact of deep submicron challenges (Section 2) by endowing arbitrary CMP cores with the ability to verify each other's execution. Detection, however, is only part of the solution; a complete framework for flexible fault-tolerance in CMPs also requires the ability to recover from faults once they are detected. Once again, DCC supports recovery from both hard- and

---

[1]FO4 is the delay of one inverter driving four identical copies of itself. Delays expressed in units of FO4 are technology-independent.

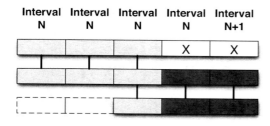

| Interval N | Interval N | Interval N | Interval N | Interval N+1 |

Figure 6. Recovery from a permanent fault using FER after BER fails. After interval N fails twice, interval N is re-executed a third time on three processors. Voting identifies the faulty processor, the system rolls back to the beginning of interval N, and execution continues on the remaining two processors.

soft-errors without requiring dedicated communication hardware or statically binding cores.

When an application requiring redundant execution is switched-in by the operating system, it is appropriated two processors, one master and one slave. Checkpointed register values are stored in the application's process control block by the operating system upon context switches, and are recovered when the application is switched-in. The allocated processors execute instructions, using the aforementioned detection scheme, until a fault is detected. To recover from this fault, backward error recovery (BER) is employed. Both processors rollback architectural state to their last valid checkpoint, invalidate all the cache lines marked as unverified, and resume execution from the checkpoint. If the fault was transient, the processors will successfully complete their next checkpoint. However, if the fault is permanent, the same checkpoint interval will repeat and the system defaults to forward-error recovery.

Specifically, when BER fails to recover from a fault, after repeating the same checkpoint interval multiple times, a third processor is appropriated by the operating system for forward error recovery (FER).[2] (If all other processors are in use, the operating system must choose a core and switch-out its currently running thread.) To initiate this, the cache controller of the failing master core makes a TMR request by generating a special bus transaction that sets a flag in the kernel's address space. This transaction is observed by all other nodes, and a predetermined node is given the responsibility of calling the operating system by jumping to an interrupt vector (each node is responsible for handling another node's requests, and this assignment is made by the kernel). Prior to taking the interrupt, the master and the slave of this remote node synchronize, and then control is transferred to the operating system by jumping to the TMR interrupt handler. The operating system inspects the flags set by the failing node to identify the requesting pair, and allocates a third core for FER. Cases where the requesting node is executing OS code are handled identically. The architectural state of the last valid checkpoint is copied from the master processor to the new slave processor. These three processors, one master and two slaves, implement FER by executing the checkpoint interval in parallel and voting on the correct results (signatures), as shown in Figure 6. Essentially, this amounts to on-demand triple modular redundancy (TMR). Through TMR, the faulty processor is isolated and marked as such, the system rolls back to the beginning of the faulty interval, and all unverified data are invalidated. If the master processor is faulty, all dirty verified data in the master's cache is written back to memory, and one of the slaves is promoted to master. Once the faulty processor is isolated, execution continues on the remaining two cores.

---

[2]The involvement of the operating system in FER is unlikely to affect system performance since FER is only invoked on hard faults (a rare event) and in cases where the same checkpoint interval fails multiple times in a row due to soft errors (exceedingly unlikely).

State	Cache-line's State Description	Can be unverified?
Invalid	Invalid data	No
Shared	Valid data, possibly inconsistent with memory	Yes
Exclusive	Valid data, consistent with memory, present only in one cache	No
Owned	Valid, dirty data, possibly shared	Yes
Modified	Valid, dirty data, present only in one cache	Yes

Table 2. Summary of MOESI protocol states and whether they can hold unverified data.

4 Parallel Application Support

Our discussion of DCC thus far has been limited to fault detection and recovery for one single node. Although this is sufficient for sequential applications, supporting flexible fault-tolerant execution for parallel applications is at least equally important for future CMP platforms. In this section, we provide extensions that allow DCC to operate correctly when running shared-memory parallel programs. In the following discussion, we define a particular master-slave pair as a *node*, and we refer to all other nodes as *remote nodes*. Recall that master and slave cores that form a node need not be adjacent or even close to one another.

4.1 Checkpoints

Checkpoints are taken globally across all nodes: the bus controller initiates scheduled checkpoints by sending synchronization requests to all nodes at the end of each checkpoint interval. All master threads synchronize with their slaves (as in the sequential case), and send an acknowledgment to the bus controller when the synchronization is complete. When all nodes are synchronized and no outstanding bus transactions remain, the bus controller issues a checkpoint request, and the architectural state on each core is saved. Descheduled threads of a parallel application need not participate in the global checkpoint since their last checkpoint (taken at the time they are descheduled) is still valid. In the case of a signature discrepancy or timeout (Section 3), all processors involved in the execution of the parallel application roll back to their respective checkpoint.

4.2 Coherence

Data sharing in DCC-equipped CMP architectures is different from conventional architectures in that: (1) some of the data held in caches may be unverified–that is, subject to rollback; and (2) sharing decisions must consider whether the processors involved are playing the role of master or slave.

To support sharing of unverified data, we leverage some of the mechanisms previously proposed in the context of the multiprocessor version of Cherry, Cherry-MP [9]. Similarly to Cherry-MP, a natural choice for a baseline cache coherence protocol on which to build DCC support is a MOESI protocol [1]. MOESI allows several copies of a cache line across processors that are possibly incoherent with the copy in memory. Among those copies, the *owned* copy is responsible for (1) providing a copy to any new sharer, and (2) writing back the copy if it replaces the cache line. The other copies remain in the *shared* state. Because DCC requires keeping unverified data off memory, MOESI is convenient for safely sharing unverified modified data across processors. Table 2 compiles MOESI's states; the rightmost column indicates whether the state is apt to hold unverified data. Notice that, in the case of shared state, it is only possible to hold unverified data if there is an owned copy elsewhere in the system–otherwise, the data must be necessarily consistent with memory.

To support sharing of unverified data, we extend the coherence protocol along the lines of Cherry-MP [9] (the Cherry-MP extensions are slightly more elaborate than in DCC because of some additional restrictions specific to Cherry-MP). Specifically:

- Writes always mark the writer's cache line as unverified, similar to the uniprocessor case (Section 3.2). Writes to verified dirty cache lines (modified or owned state) force a writeback of the original contents to main memory, in case a rollback later undoes the update. These writes may be initiated by a local processor, or by a remote processor through a read-exclusive or upgrade request. On the other hand, writes to unverified dirty cache lines must not generate write backs to main memory. If the cache line is marked unverified and dirty elsewhere, the protocol simply forwards the cache line to the requester, if needed.

- On cache-to-cache transfers, the reader's cache line is marked unverified if the original copy of the cache line was marked unverified. This is so that, in the event of a rollback, all live copies of the speculatively updated value are properly discarded. To support this, on a miss, the supplier of the value must put on the bus its cache line's unverified bit as part of its snoop response. Notice that unverified, clean cache lines can be silently dropped by the reader at any time.

To support multiple master-slave nodes, a few more changes beyond those to support a single master-slave pair (Section 3.2) are needed as follows:

- Slaves do not supply data to remote nodes via cache-to-cache transfers–masters do.

- Slave reads cause remote data in modified or exclusive states to downgrade to owned or shared states, respectively. Furthermore, slave read-exclusive requests are treated as ordinary reads for the purposes of state transitions at remote nodes (specifically, they do not result in invalidations). Finally, upgrade requests by slaves are ignored by remote caches. To ensure that remote nodes do not apply invalidations to their caches in response to slave threads, a *master line* is added to the system bus. Cache lines in remote nodes apply invalidations to their caches in response to bus transactions generated by masters only. To facilitate this, master threads drive the master line when they start their bus transactions, and remote threads snoop this line to determine if the bus transaction is generated by a master.

- Read-exclusive requests by a master invalidate remote copies as usual. However, if the data is dirty unverified on a remote master, the slave must obtain a copy of the cache line before it is invalidated by the master. To do this, the slave checks if it already has a copy of the cache line. If so, the cache line is marked as dirty unverified to prevent its eviction. Otherwise, the slave snarfs the cache-to-cache transfer and writes the data to its local cache hierarchy as dirty unverified. If this results in a cache buffering overflow, all cores rollback to the last checkpoint, and a new checkpoint is scheduled with half the duration of the last checkpointing interval (Section 3.3).

- Likewise, upgrade requests by a master invalidate remote copies as usual. However, if the data is dirty unverified on a remote master, *and* if the local slave does not have a copy of the cache line, the master's upgrade request is turned into a read-exclusive request, so that the slave can snarf the remote copy as before. If the slave already has a copy, the cache line is marked as dirty unverified in the slave cache.

4.3 Master-Slave Consistency

The main difficulty in supporting DCC in a parallel execution is ensuring that master and slave threads view a consistent image of the shared address space at all times. In other words, every committed load instruction on the slave should read the same value as the corresponding committed load on the master. In a sequential application, this is easily accomplished by preventing unverified dirty lines from being written back to main memory. Consequently, slave threads can always obtain the same value as their masters from the memory system (Section 3.2).

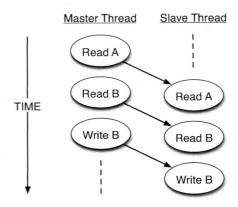

Figure 7. Three example windows.

In a parallel execution, however, this is not necessarily the case. Since all threads in the system have access to the shared address space, intervening writes from other threads can cause master and slave threads to read different values. For instance, the master thread could read a line L, but before the slave gets a chance to perform the corresponding read, a third core could invalidate the master and update L. In this case, the original value that the master read may no longer be available to the slave.

In order to accommodate thread interactions like these, we introduce the notion of a *master-slave memory access window*, or simply *window*. Roughly speaking, windows represent periods of vulnerability during which the consistency of master-slave pairs in the system may be compromised, and allow us to define a small set of restrictions that guarantee correctness in such cases. Windows are defined on a per-address basis, and are labeled as read or write windows depending on whether the operation being performed is a load or a store.

A read window for address A *opens* when *either* the master or the slave thread issues a load that reads the value of A, and *closes* when *both* master and slave threads commit the load. Windows opened by misspeculated loads (e.g., in the shadow of a mispredicted branch) are closed at recovery. Similarly, a write window for address A *opens* when *either* the master or the slave thread performs (necessarily at commit) a store that writes A, and *closes* when *both* master and slave threads commit the store.

Figure 7 shows three example windows on a node. When the master issues its first read, a read window for memory location A opens. The master then opens a read window for B, and commits the load that reads A. When the slave commits its read of A, the open read window for A closes.

To guarantee master-slave consistency, it is sufficient to ensure that the system observes certain restrictions at all times for each memory location M in the program's address space. Specifically, a node should not be allowed to open a write window for M if there is already an open read or write window for M on another node. This *remote intervention constraint* prevents master and slave threads from reading different values due to intervening writes by other nodes. Open windows for different locations place no restrictions on each other. Similarly, any number of simultaneous read windows can be open at a time for a given address, and private data can be read and written without any restrictions. Furthermore, a node can open a read window while a write window is open at some other node.

4.3.1 Hardware Implementation

The main addition that is required to support master-slave consistency is an *age table* that resides with each core's cache controller. Each load's *instruction age* is defined as the the total number of load and store instructions committed by its thread (since the last checkpoint) at the time that load commits. Similarly, each store's instruction age is the total number of loads and stores committed

322

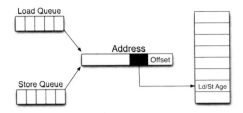

Figure 8. Example of an age table implementation.

by its thread at the time the store commits. We use this information to detect memory operations that could lead to violations of the remote intervention constraint, and to delay them until this danger disappears.

Enforcing the remote intervention constraint requires detecting open read and write windows, and the age table facilitates tracking these by storing the age of the last committed memory instruction on the corresponding core to an address range. The age table is a direct-mapped, untagged SRAM array indexed by the address of committed loads and stores (Figure 8). Age table entries contain the age of the last committed memory instruction to an address range. The table index is formed by using the lower-order adress bits following the cache block offset. The table is updated locally at commit time.

Performing Writes to Modified Data When a master thread wants to perform a write, it checks the state of the line in its cache in parallel with an age table access. If the cache line is modified, no other node is currently caching that line, and there is no danger of invalidating data that the slave will want to read later (recall that unverified dirty lines cannot be replaced until the next checkpoint). In addition, there is no danger of intervention in a read window on another node (if a window had opened following the write that put the line in modified state, the line's state would have transitioned to owned). In this case, the master performs the write immediately.

Performing Writes to Data in Other States If the cache line is not in the modified state, additional checks need to be performed along with the standard read exclusive or upgrade request. The information needed to perform these checks is piggybacked on the bus transaction. When the read-exclusive (or upgrade) request is observed by other nodes, each core accesses its age table to get the age of the last committed memory instruction to the corresponding address range. In parallel, each node searches its load queue[3] for any matching reads that have already issued to the memory system or have forwarded from a store. If there is a hit in the load queue, a negative acknowledgment (NACK) is raised (accomplished by pulling the NACK line of the bus high), and the write is retried later. Searching the load queue guarantees that any read windows opened by speculative reads are not violated by writes from other nodes. In the case of branch mispredictions, speculative loads are naturally removed from the load queue, and misspeculated loads eventually cease to generate NACKs.

If all of load queue searches result in misses, each node reports its age table entry (accessed in parallel with the load queue) on the data bus in the following cycle. (Each slave core drives a portion of the data bus with its age information.) In the following cycle, every master core compares its own age with the age of its slave. A mismatch on a remote node indicates a potentially open read or write window, and a NACK is raised for the write.

---

[3] A port already exists for external invalidations to search the load queue in many commercial systems. If this capability is not present, the search can compete with local stores for access to the load queue.

Livelock Avoidance There exists a danger of livelock when issuing NACKs for writes. For instance, consider the case of a spin lock where the master holding the lock needs to perform an invalidation for lock release. If masters and slaves on other nodes repeatedly read the lock variable in a tight loop, new read windows may always open before the last one closes, preventing the lock release from performing, and thus perpetuating the cycle. We have empirically observed that NACKs, and thus such livelocks, are exceedingly rare in the applicationswe have studied; nevertheless, we need to provide a machanism to detect these situations and be able to guarantee progress.

We propose a simple policy: A single NACK bit is added to every age table entry; when a node issues a NACK for a write transaction, both master and slave cores set the NACK bit for their corresponding age table entries. At that time, both the master and the slave temporarily stop fetching instructions, and allow their pipelines to drain. When both pipes are drained, the master and the slave exchange their committed instruction counts to identify the leader and the trailer in the execution. The leader remains stalled, while the trailer is allowed to resume execution. This effectively allows the trailer thread to close read windows left open by the leader–in particular, the read windows opened by the spinlock. The remote write (which the remote node keeps retrying) may eventually succeed once the open read window is closed. When this happens, the NACK bit is cleared, and both the master and the slave resume normal execution. It is also possible that the trailer commits enough instructions to match the leader. If at that time the NACK bit has not yet been cleared, the trailer flushes its pipeline and stalls as well. At this point, neither the master nor the slave have any loads in their load queues, and their age table entries are consistent. This guarantees that the very next retry of the remote write will succeed, at which point both master and slave can resume execution.

Deadlock Avoidance There exists also a danger of deadlock when issuing NACKs for writes. This may occur when writes in two or more processors cannot perform because of open read windows by out-of-order loads elsewhere, forming a cycle. For instance, consider the case where processors $p1$ and $p2$ are trying to perform writes to addresses A and B, respectively. If $p1$ and $p2$ have issued loads to addresses B and A out of order with respect to those writes, respectively, the processors will issue NACKs for each other's writes, preveting forward progress. Luckily, this deadlock situation would be eventually broken through the timeout mechanism (Section 3.3). Nevertheless, a simple and more effective solution is possible: Upon receiving a NACK for such a write, a processor systematically flushes its pipeline beyond the write, and prevents loads from issuing until the write successfully commits. In any case, as stated before, we have empirically observed that such NACKs are rare in the applications we have studied.

Hard Fault Recovery Once a signature discrepancy or a timeout occurs (Section 3.3), all processors currently running the parallel application roll back to their last checkpoint. To recover from permanent faults, a second slave is introduced to the node that initially caused the fault. This third processor engages in age exchanges just like the original slave does. When performing an age check, the master thread compares its age against both slaves, and considers a read window to be open if any of the two slaves has a mismatch with it. Aside from this, the operation of our proposed system is the same in all other respects.

4.4 Compatibility Across Memory Consistency Models

The memory consistency model of a multiprocessor places a set of ordering restrictions between memory operations issued from a given thread. DCC does not impose or rely on any ordering constraints, and is general enough to operate correctly under any consistency model. In other words, regardless of how memory operations are ordered, DCC's master-slave consistency is never compromised.

Processor	
Frequency	3.2 GHz
Fetch/issue/commit width	4/4/6
Inst. window [(Int+Mem)/FP]	64/48
Reorder buffer entries	192
Int/FP registers	96/96
Functional Units	4 ALU, 3 FPU, 2 BR, 2/2 Ld/St
Ld/St queue entries	24/24
Branch penalty (cycles)	10(min.)
Store forward delay (cycles)	3
Branch predictor	16K-entry
Branch target buffer size	2048
RAS entries	24
Memory Subsystem	
L1 Cache (Private)	32KB, 4-way, LRU, 64B, 3 cycles
Victim Cache (L1)	8 entries
L2 Cache (Shared)	8MB, 8-way, LRU, 64B, 43 cycles
MSHR entries	16 L1, 16 L2
System bus	256 bits, 800 MHz
Max. outstanding bus requests	96
Memory bus bandwidth	12.8 GB/s
Memory latency	400 cycles
Coherence Protocol	MOESI
Consistency Model	Release Consistency
Fault Tolerance Extension Parameters	
Processor comm. latency	30 cycles
Age table size	64 entries
State compression latency	35 cycles
State checkpoint latency	8 cycles

Table 3. Summary of modeled architecture.

To see this, note that loads obtain their values either from the CMP memory subsystem, or from the store queue of the processor on which they issue. The remote intervention constraint prevents violations of master-slave consistency through the memory system as discussed above. However, relaxed consistency models and aggressive implementations of sequential consistency also allow loads to be reordered with respect to other memory instructions by issuing early, or by forwarding from the store queue. Luckily, DCC readily accommodates such optimizations.

Specifically, if the master forwards from its store queue, a read window opens and prevents intervening writes to violate the window; eventually, the slave also consumes the same value from a replica of the same store (either through its own store queue or from its local cache). In other cases, there is a danger that the master reads a value produced by a remote node, but the slave forwards from its store queue and breaks master-slave consistency. Luckily, the remote intervention constraint prevents this: when the master commits its copy of the store that the slave forwards from, a write window opens and blocks intervening writes from remote nodes, forcing both the master and the slave to consume the result produced by their local store. Windows opened by slaves are also safe for the same reason.

5 Evaluation

Flexible DMR frameworks like DCC hold significant potential when confronted with the challenges of deep submicron process technologies. In this section, we evaluate DCC using detailed execution-driven simulations of a CMP model.

In our experiments, we allow a single application to run redundantly on multiple processors using the hardware modifications described in this paper. The configuration details of this processor are listed in Table 3. When taking global checkpoints on parallel applications, we model the bus arbiter's synchronization request, master-slave synchronization, and the checkpoint latency on each node. We find that master and slave cores are never separated by more than 200 cycles in their execution (roughly 100 cycles on average), leading to negligible waiting times for the receipt of acknowledgments. Hence, for simplicity in our simulations, we do not model the global handshake.

Splash-2	Description	Problem size
BARNES	Evolution of galaxies	16k part.
FMM	N-body problem	16k part.
RAYTRACE	3D ray tracing	car
Spec OpenMP		
SWIM-OMP	Shallow water model	MinneSpec-Large
EQUAKE-OMP	Earthquake model	MinneSpec-Large
Data Mining		
BSOM	Self-organizing map	2,048 rec., 100 epochs
BLAST	Protein matching	12.3k sequ.
KMEANS	K-means clustering	18k pts., 18 attr.
SCALPARC	Decision Tree	125k pts., 32 attr.

Table 4. Simulated parallel applications and input sizes.

To evaluate sequential applications, we simulate 19 of the 26 SPEC2000 suite of benchmarks [8] using the SESC simulator [18].[4] We use the largest datasets from the MinneSPEC [10] reduced input set and run them to completion. To evaluate parallel applications, we use a set of scalable scientific and data mining applications, shown in Table 4. These parallel benchmarks are simulated for 1, 2, 4, and 8 threads, on 2, 4, 8, and 16 processors respectively.

5.1 Results

5.1.1 DCC Overhead

In this section, we assess the performance overhead of DCC over a baseline CMP with no fault-tolerance. We are not concerned with the inherent overhead of executing a thread redundantly on two processors. It is obvious that redundant execution occupies twice the number of cores, and therefore cuts the effective number of processing elements in half. We are interested in the additional overheads involved with orchestrating the detection and recovery schemes presented in this work.

Sequential Applications

We evaluate the performance overhead during fault-free execution by simulating the SPEC2000 benchmarks on a single core in our baseline CMP. We compare this to running the benchmarks redundantly on two cores with checkpoint intervals of 1,000, 5,000, and 10,000 cycles. The slowdown with respect to a single-core execution with no fault tolerance is shown in Figure 9. The average overheads for intervals of 1,000, 5,000, and 10,000 cycles are 20%, 5%, and 3%, respectively. In DCC, a checkpoint takes on the order of 100-200 cycles to complete. Most of this time is spent synchronizing both cores, compressing the register file state and communicating results over the system bus. A checkpoint interval of 1,000 cycles is insufficient to amortize the cost associated with taking a checkpoint. However, an interval of 10,000 cycles reduces this overhead to 3%. One issue that needs to be considered with long checkpoints is their interaction with I/O requests. Prior work [24] has found that checkpoints should be taken at least every 50,000 instructions in I/O intensive workloads to achieve high performance. The applications we have studied obtain an IPC of about 1 on the baseline system, so approximately 10,000 instructions execute in given checkpoint interval, which is well below this 50,000 instruction limit.

Parallel Applications

Parallel applications incur additional performance overheads due to the management of shared variables consistently across nodes (as discussed in Section 4). To see how these overheads scale, we compare speedups under DCC to our baseline CMP for 1, 2, 4, and 8 threads (2, 4, 8, and 16 processors). Table 5 reports the

---

[4]our simulation infrastructure currently does not support the other SPEC benchmarks

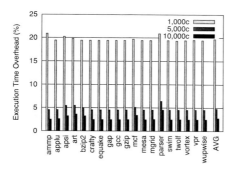

Figure 9. Execution time overhead.

speedup across our nine parallel benchmarks. Speedups are normalized to the performance of a single thread of execution on the baseline CMP. In addition, Figure 10 reports speedups for benchmarks with the largest overheads (barnes, and smallest overhead, kmeans). On average, when using a 64-entry age table, the performance overhead for up to 8 threads is between 4% and 5%. A sensitivity study on the number of age table entries shows less than a 4% reduction in execution time overhead when a 1024-entry age table is used (Section 4). Overall, these results suggest that modest hardware additions are adequate to minimize the performance overhead of DCC on parallel applications.

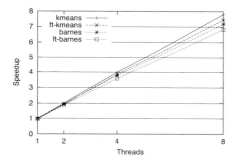

Figure 10. Speedup on baseline and fault tolerant CMPs (marked ft) for parallel benchmark with largest and smallest overheads. All curves are normalized to a sequential run on the baseline CMP.

5.1.2 Comparison Against Relaxed Input Replication

DCC utilizes long checkpoint intervals to amortize the cost of dynamic coupling. To maintain input coherence between redundant threads, we introduce an age table to track open read windows. Reunion [23] arguably proposes a conceptually simpler scheme of relaxed input replication: input incoherence may occur, but it would be detected as a fault. To guarantee forward progress, Reunion single-steps the cores to the first load instruction. Reunion still relies on dedicated communication channels for output comparison, and thus cannot provide the flexibility of dynamic coupling. Nevertheless, we would like to asses the performance of relaxed input replication under DCC's larger checkpoint intervals, and to quantitatively establish whether we need our age table mechanism.

Figure 11 shows the slowdown of Reunion's relaxed input scheme compared to DCC's age table scheme across our parallel benchmarks. For applications that have little read-write sharing, such as blast and swim, relaxed input replication incurs relatively modest overhead. However, applications that have more read-write sharing, raytrace and scalparc, incur significantly higher execution times (more than two-fold for 10,000-cycle intervals).

Relaxed input replication performs poorly in this context for two main reasons. First, as the checkpoint interval increases the redundant pair of cores becomes progressively out of synch. We

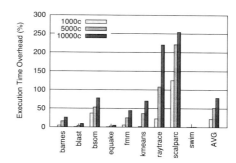

Figure 11. Slowdown of Reunion's [23] relaxed input replication with respect to DCC.

have noticed differences of up to a few hundred instructions for the longer checkpoint intervals. This results in more opportunity for an intervening store to cause input incoherence. Second, single stepping the execution to the first load instruction does little to synchronize cores when the checkpoint interval may execute thousands of loads. If the offending memory operation occurs at the end of the interval, many rollbacks will ensue before single-stepping brings the synchronized execution close to that operation. Overall, the performance of relaxed input replication deteriorates quickly, and is inadequate for DCC's larger checkpoint intervals.

5.1.3 Performance under Manufacturing Defects

DCC degrades half as fast as mechanisms that rely on static DMR pairs when confronted with manufacturing defects, process variations, and wearout. While a defective or excessively leaky core renders both cores in a static DMR pair dysfunctional, DCC can utilize all functional cores regardless of their physical location or adjacency. Figure 12 compares DCC to an ideal, overhead-free static-DMR scheme on eight- and 16-core CMPs with two defective cores. The y-axis shows the speedups achieved by both schemes over a sequential run without fault tolerance. Reported speedups account for the small fraction of cases where two defective cores may fall into the same static DMR pair, in which case DCC does not offer an advantage. We account for such cases by generating 100K CMP configurations with two defective cores, where defect locations are sampled from a uniform random distribution. We report the average speedup over these 100K chips, which include chips with two failures in a single static-DMR pair.

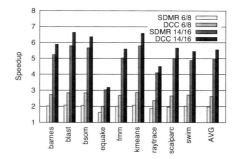

Figure 12. Average speedup of DCC and ideal static coupling on 8- and 16-core CMPs with two defective cores.

On an eight-core CMP, DCC achieves an average speedup of 2.63 across all applications, while static-DMR's speedup is only 1.97. For the sixteen-core CMP, DCC and static DMR obtain average speedups of 5.56 and 4.95, respectively. These results suggest that flexible DMR frameworks like DCC are an attractive to construct gracefully-degrading, fault-tolerant CMP designs that can meet deep submicron challenges.

	Threads	Speedup Of Benchmarks									
		barnes	blast	bsom	equake	fmm	kmeans	raytrace	scalparc	swim	average
Baseline	1	1.00	1.00	1.00	1.00	1.00	1.00	1.00	1.00	1.00	1.00
	2	1.97	1.99	2.00	1.62	1.96	2.01	1.83	1.89	1.95	1.91
	4	3.77	3.96	3.96	2.57	3.68	3.99	3.20	3.66	3.70	3.61
	8	7.20	7.93	7.66	3.66	6.62	7.81	5.38	6.53	6.33	6.57
DCC	1	0.96	0.97	0.96	0.97	0.96	0.97	0.97	0.98	0.96	0.97
	2	1.90	1.91	1.92	1.56	1.87	1.93	1.76	1.84	1.88	1.84
	4	3.58	3.84	3.82	2.48	3.52	3.86	3.06	3.51	3.57	3.47
	8	6.84	7.63	7.21	3.49	6.38	7.47	5.04	6.24	6.03	6.25

Table 5. Speedup of parallel applications with 1, 2, 4, and 8 threads for both the baseline CMP and DCC.

6 Conclusions

We have presented dynamic core coupling (DCC), an inexpensive DMR mechanism for CMPs, which allows arbitrary processor cores to verify each other's execution without requiring dedicated communication hardware. By avoiding static binding of cores at design time, DCC degrades half as fast in the presence of errors and can recover from permanent faults without the need for constant TMR or dedicated spares.

Our evaluation has shown the performance overhead of DCC to be 3% on SPEC2000 benchmarks, and within 5% for a set of scalable parallel scientific and data mining applications with up to eight threads (16 cores). We have also seen that DCC can offer significant performance improvements compared to static DMR schemes. Overall, we have shown that flexible DMR frameworks like DCC hold significant performance potential when confronted with the challenges of deep submicron process technologies in current and upcoming CMPs.

7 Acknowledgments

We thank Meyrem Kırman, Nevin Kırman, and the anonymous reviewers for useful feedback. This work was funded in part by NSF awards CCF-0429922, CNS-0509404, CAREER Award CCF-0545995, and an IBM Faculty Award (Martínez); by NSF awards CNS-0435190, CCF-0428427, CCF-0541321, and the DARPA/MARCO C2S2 Center (Manohar); and by equipment donations from Intel.

References

[1] Advanced Micro Devices. *AMD64 Architecture Programmer's Manual Volume 2: System Programming*, February 2005.

[2] Guido Albertengo and Riccardo Sisto. Parallel CRC generation. *IEEE Micro*, 10(5):63–71, 1990.

[3] Shekhar Borkar, Tanay Karnik, Siva Narendra, Jim Tschanz, Ali Keshavarzi, and Vivek De. Parameter variations and impact on circuits and microarchitecture. In *Design Automation Conf.*, June 2003.

[4] Shekhar Y. Borkar, Pradeep Dubey, Kevin C. Kahn, David J. Kuck, Hans Mulder, Stephen S. Pawlowski, and Justin R. Rattner. Platform 2015: Intel processor and platform evolution for the next decade. In *Technology@Intel Magazine*, March 2005.

[5] Cristian Constantinescu. Trends and challenges in VLSI circuit reliability. *IEEE Micro*, 23(4):14–19, 2003.

[6] Kypros Constantinides, Stephen Plaza, Jason Blome, Bin Zhang, Valeria Bertacco, Scott Mahlke, Todd Austin, and Michael Orshansky. Bulletproof: A defect-tolerant CMP switch architecture. In *Intl. Symp. on High Performance Computer Architecture*, February 2006.

[7] Mohamed Gomaa, Chad Scarbrough, T. N. Vijaykumar, and Irith Pomeranz. Transient-fault recovery for chip multiprocessors. In *Intl. Symp. on Computer Architecture*, June 2003.

[8] J. L. Henning. SPEC CPU2000: Measuring CPU performance in the new millennium. *IEEE Computer*, 33(7):28–35, 2000.

[9] Meyrem Kırman, Nevin Kırman, and José F. Martínez. Cherry-MP: Correctly integrating checkpointed early resource recycling in chip multiprocessors. In *Intl. Symp. on Microarchitecture*, December 2005.

[10] AJ KleinOsowski and David J. Lilja. MinneSPEC: A new SPEC benchmark workload for simulation-based computer architecture research. *IEEE Computer Architecture Letters*, 1(2), 2002.

[11] José F. Martínez, Jose Renau, Michael C. Huang, Milos Prvulovic, and Josep Torrellas. Cherry: Checkpointed early resource recycling in out-of-order microprocessors. In *Intl. Symp. on Microarchitecture*, November 2002.

[12] Dennis McEvoy. The architecture of Tandem's NonStop system. In *ACM'81*, November 1981.

[13] Patrick J. Meaney, Scott B. Swaney, Pia N. Sanda, and Lisa Spainhower. IBM z990 soft error detection and recovery. *IEEE Trans. on Device and Materials Reliability*, 5(3):419–427, 2005.

[14] Shubhendu S. Mukherjee, Michael Kontz, and Steven K. Reinhardt. Detailed design and evaluation of redundant multithreading alternatives. In *Intl. Symp. on Computer Architecture*, May 2002.

[15] Shubhendu S. Mukherjee, Christopher Weaver, Joel Emer, Steven K. Reinhardt, and Todd Austin. A systematic methodology to compute the architectural vulnerability factors for a high-performance microprocessor. In *Intl. Symp. on Microarchitecture*, December 2003.

[16] Kunle Olukotun, Basem A. Nayfeh, Lance Hammond, Ken Wilson, and Kunyung Chang. The case for a single-chip multiprocessor. In *Intl. Conf. on Architectural Support for Programming Languages and Operating Systems*, October 1996.

[17] Steven K. Reinhardt and Shubhendu S. Mukherjee. Transient fault detection via simultaneous multithreading. In *Intl. Symp. on Computer Architecture*, June 2000.

[18] Jose Renau, Basilio Fraguela, James Tuck, Wei Liu, Milos Prvulovic, Luis Ceze, Smruti Sarangi, Paul Sack, Karin Strauss, and Pablo Montesinos. SESC simulator, 2005. http://sesc.sourceforge.net.

[19] Eric Rotenberg. AR-SMT: A microarchitectural approach to fault tolerance in microprocessors. In *Intl. Symp. on Fault-Tolerant Computing*, June 1999.

[20] L. Sherman. Stratus continuous processing technology – the smarter approach to uptime. Technical report, Stratus Technologies, 2003.

[21] Premkishore Shivakumar, Michael Kistler, Stephen W. Keckler, Doug Burger, and Lorenzo Alvisi. Modeling the effect of technology trends on the soft error rate of combinational logic. In *Intl. Conf. on Dependable Systems and Networks*, June 2002.

[22] T. J. Slegal, Timothy J. Slegel, Robert M. Averill III, Mark A. Check, Bruce C. Giamei, Barry W. Krumm, Christopher A. Krygowski, Wen H. Li, John S. Liptay, John D. MacDougall, Thomas J. McPherson, Jennifer A. Navarro, Eric M. Schwarz, Kevin Shum, and Charles F. Webb. IBM's S/390 G5 microprocessor design. *IEEE Micro*, 19(2):12–23, 1999.

[23] Jared C. Smolens, Brian T. Gold, Babak Falsafi, and James C. Hoe. Reunion: Complexity-effective multicore redundancy. In *Intl. Symp. on Microarchitecture*, December 2006.

[24] Jared C. Smolens, Brian T. Gold, Jangwoo Kim, Babak Falsafi, James C. Hoe, and Andreas G. Nowatzyk. Fingerprinting: bounding soft-error detection latency and bandwidth. In *Intl. Conf. on Architectural Support for Programming Languages and Operating Systems*, October 2004.

[25] Ed Sperling. Turn down the heat…please, March 2007. http://www.edn.com.

[26] Jayanth Srinivasan, Sarita V. Adve, Pradip Bose, and Jude A. Rivers. The case for microarchitectural awareness of lifetime reliability. In *Intl. Symp. on Computer Architecture*, June 2004.

[27] Jayanth Srinivasan, Sarita V. Adve, Pradip Bose, and Jude A. Rivers. The impact of technology scaling on lifetime reliability. In *Intl. Conf. on Dependable Systems and Networks*, June 2004.

[28] Dean M. Tullsen, Susan Eggers, and Henry M. Levy. Simultaneous multithreading: Maximizing on-chip parallelism. In *Intl. Symp. on Computer Architecture*, June 1995.

[29] T. N. Vijaykumar, Irith Pomeranz, and Karl Cheng. Transient-fault recovery using simultaneous multithreading. In *Intl. Symp. on Computer Architecture*, May 2002.

BlackJack: Hard Error Detection with Redundant Threads on SMT

Ethan Schuchman and T. N. Vijaykumar
School of Electrical and Computer Engineering, Purdue University
{erys, vijay}@purdue.edu

Abstract

Testing is a difficult process that becomes more difficult with scaling. With smaller and faster devices, tolerance for errors shrinks and devices may act correctly under certain condition and not under others. As such, hard errors may exist but are only exercised by very specific machine state and signal pathways. Targeting these errors is difficult, and creating test cases that cover all machine states and pathways is not possible. In addition, new complications during burn-in may mean latent hard errors are not exposed in the fab and reach the customer before becoming active.

To address this problem, we propose an architecture we call BlackJack that allows hard errors to be detected using redundant threads running on a single SMT core. This technique provides a safety-net that catches hard errors that were either latent during test or just not covered by the test cases at all.

Like SRT, our technique works by executing redundant copies and verifying that their resulting machine states agree. Unlike SRT, BlackJack is able to achieve high hard error instruction coverage by executing redundant threads on different front and back-end resources in the pipeline. We show that for a 15% performance penalty over SRT, BlackJack achieves 97% hard error instruction coverage compared to SRT's 35%.

1 Introduction

Technology scaling has yielded smaller and faster transistors which have enabled higher performance. Unfortunately, scaled devices are more susceptible to hard errors (i.e., permanent errors) because each device has smaller margins for correct operation. For instance, a small charge trapped in the gate oxide can permanently damage the transistor. In addition, because margins are small, other (hard to quantify) variables can cause devices to operate correctly in some cases and incorrectly in others. These variables arise from normal operating conditions such as signal paths, machine state, or localized temperatures and supply-voltage droops. With correct operation being dependent on such variables, testing becomes difficult. For good coverage, it is not enough to test a transistor under one operating condition, but every transistor must be tested considering intractably many signal paths and machine states.

The increasingly-difficult problem of *latent* defects complicates the testing process even more. CPU lifetime can be described best by a bathtub-shaped curve, where some chips have short lifetimes, a few have intermediate lifetimes, and most have long (acceptable) lifetimes. The lifetime is determined by how long it takes for a latent defect to worsen and become active. CPU manufacturers weed out the short-lifetime chips from the production flow by a process called burn-in. In burn-in, chips are run at high voltage and temperature to cause large amounts of wear-and-tear over a short amount of time. Burn-in causes chips with short lifetimes to fail before leaving the fab, so that chips that reach the customer can be expected to have a long (acceptable) lifetime.

Burn-in has long been relied upon but its continued feasibility and coverage are now coming into question. As devices get smaller, they incur more wear-and-tear in burn-in causing even the long-lifetime chips to fail. In addition, an effect called *thermal run-away* is becoming a problem. In thermal run-away, devices undergoing burn-in get hotter increasing leakage which in turn increases the temperature, creating a positive feedback loop. If thermal-run-away is not controlled, even the good chips are destroyed [13]. If controlled, the coverage of burnin comes into question [8]. Have all devices been exercised long enough at high-enough temperatures so that all latent faults are exposed?

These two worsening difficulties attack two basic assumptions of testing for hard errors. The first difficulty implies that test cases cannot be created for every possible defect. The second difficulty implies that even if one could, some of the latent defects would remain unexposed by burn-in. Even today, not only is 100% coverage not achieved but even quantifying what has been covered is only an approximation [7].

Despite these difficulties, testing will not disappear, but will only become more important. However, hard errors will get by and will be exposed in the field, despite most valiant attempts. This paper proposes a technique which is a safety net, *not a replacement,* for testing. Our technique allows defects that are missed in the testing process (either because the error was never tested, or the error was latent at testing time) to be detected in the field, preventing hard errors from corrupting data. It may seem that continual testing throughout the lifetime of the chip would achieve our target. However, injecting test inputs into the chip requires testers, which are expensive, specialized machines, and are not available in the field.

We make the key observation that instead of testing for an inordinately large number of potential defects we can instead test only for the defects that are exercised by a program when the program runs. One such way is to redundantly execute the program and compare program state. Because redundant execution is the standard approach to handling soft errors, our observation implies that soft-error schemes can be applied to hard errors to allow previously untested or latent defects to be detected at run time.

Despite this implication, soft-error schemes can not be applied *as is* to hard errors. Because soft-error techniques rely on the errors being transient, the techniques exploit temporal redundancy. For instance, a Simultaneously and Redundantly Threaded processor (SRT [10]) executes two copies of a program, called *leading* and *trailing* threads, on one SMT core assuming that a soft error would affect only one copy. Because hard errors are permanent, temporal redundancy *alone* will not suffice. Because both copies of an instruction run on the same core, they may encounter the same hard error which would then elude detection. To ensure proper detection, each instruction copy must use different hardware. That is, the redundant executions must be *spatially diverse.*

Ensuring spatial diversity is the key challenge in using SRT for hard-error detection. We address this challenge in our microarchitecture called *BlackJack*. Spatial diversity does not occur naturally in SRT because the trailing thread is mostly-identical to the leading thread, resulting in the same resources being used by most leading-trailing instruction pairs. A naive approach would be to shuffle SRT's trailing instructions that are issued together in one cycle, so that each trailing instruction goes to a different execution way than the corresponding leading instruction. However, as we explain later, there is no convenient point in the pipeline to shuffle the trailing instructions. Shuffling before rename violates program correctness due to lack of dependence information; shuffling after rename does not cover the frontend and severely complicates issue which is already timing-critical.

To avoid these difficulties, we make the key observation that the leading thread determines dependencies well before the trailing thread executes. Accordingly, our novel idea is that we borrow dependence information from the leading thread which allows us to shuffle the instructions *before* they are fetched by the trailing thread. The dependence information ensures that the shuffling preserves program correctness. Specifically, we shuffle the leading instructions that were co-issued in the same cycle, called a *packet*. Our shuffling is *not* random and is specifically designed to ensure that the leading and trailing executions are spatially diverse. We call this scheme *safe-shuffle* which allows us to cover both the frontend and backend. Because we perform the shuffling at the leading thread commit which is off the critical path, we do not affect timing-critical components.

Finally, there may be a marketing concern as to what happens when a defect is detected. We have not changed the marketing model. The key point is that the defect exists with or without BlackJack, and both cases will result in the chip being returned to the manufacturer. Without BlackJack, the user will return the chip after the defect causes data corruption. BlackJack prevents this corruption.

In summary, the main contributions of BlackJack are:

- We show that shuffling the trailing thread allows SRT, a soft-error technique, to detect hard errors as well.
- We propose *safe-shuffle;* a novel scheme which allows us to shuffle instructions before they enter the trailing thread while still ensuring correctness. Thus safe-shuffle allows coverage of hard-errors in both the pipeline frontend and backend.
- We show that for a 15% performance degradation over SRT, BlackJack is able to achieve 97% hard error instruction coverage while SRT achieves 34%.

The rest of the paper is organized as follows. We discuss related work in Section 2. Section 3 provides background on SRT. Section 4 describes BlackJack. Section 5 describes our experimental methodology, and Section 6 presents our results. We conclude in Section 7.

2 Related Work

There is a large body of past work [12] on error checking logic and error correcting codes (ECC). Although applicable to some modern microarchitectural structures (mostly array memory structures and some data path components) and implemented in some modern processors [2], these techniques cannot cover much of the faster and more complex control-dominated modern microarchi-

tectures. For example, it is hard to build checker logic that checks the issue queue operation every cycle and correctly responds to wakeup and select actions without significantly degrading cycle time.

Because of such deficiencies in error checking logic for modern processors, there has been extensive work in architectural redundancy techniques for soft errors. SRT with recovery (SRTR) [17] extends SRT to detect and recover from soft errors, but still would not provide good hard-error instruction coverage because of lack of spatial diversity. Though primarily targeting soft errors, Redundant Multithreading (RMT) [9] proposes using redundant threads for hard errors. Using a clustered microarchitecture, RMT achieves spatial diversity by executing the redundant threads on different clusters. However, because the frontend of the pipeline is not clustered, the technique does not provide coverage for the frontend, ensuring spatial diversity only after rename. Moreover, RMT can provide backend coverage only because the issue queue is statically segmented among the clusters at design time, so that the leading and trailing instructions can be dispatched to different issue-queue segments. However, a segmented issue queue would incur substantial performance loss in an SMT compared to a conventional unified issue queue. A unified issue queue allows both threads to occupy as much of the issue queue as needed whereas as a segmented issue queue artificially limits each thread to its own segment. Such segmentation defeats SMT's purpose of improving throughput by flexibly sharing the pipeline resources (one of the most important of which is the issue queue) among the threads.

Chip-level redundant threading with recovery (CRTR) [6] proposes a CMP-based solution for soft-error detection and recovery. Despite being designed for soft-error recovery, CRTR would naturally provide good spatial diversity by running the redundant threads on two different cores. However,CRTR requires many values (*every* load and store value and address) to be sent at high rates between the cores. As such, satisfying such high bandwidth demand may not be realistic as it would require deeply-pipelining long, wide buses by introducing numerous latches and buffers which are power-hungry and increase chip area. Furthermore, CRTR forces running one copy each of two different programs on one core (limiting one core to run one copy of only one program would halve execution throughput and is not an option). The two programs may thrash in the core's i-cache, and may contend for pipeline resources increasing the complexity of the OS in ensuring that each program gets its due share of resources. The contented resources may not be visible to the OS, which would amount to not just worse complexity but more uncertainty in the OS. In contrast, SRT runs both copies on the same core, containing each program to one core and avoiding these OS complexity and uncertainty problems.

A recent paper on lifetime reliability [16] discusses the effect on reliability of detecting and disabling defective resources, but provides no such techniques to support such features.

DIVA[1], although intended to catch design bugs, not fabrication bugs, can catch some hard errors. DIVA uses an additional simple pipeline that checks committed instructions. A recent work, [3], uses multiple DIVA checkers to provide on-line diagnosis of failures. Online diagnosis may not be advantageous to the user beyond detection, if degraded operation is not acceptable and defective chips are still to be returned. As proposed in [3], the multiple DIVA checkers and additional area overhead may increase the likelihood of the chip having a failure. Furthermore, [3] relies on randomization logic in the timing-critical select-map logic for spatial diversity. Finally, to keep DIVA checkers simple, [3] can not cover hard errors in large parts of the pipeline such as the register file.

A recent paper, [5], proposes defect-tolerance techniques for CMP interconnect switches. This work is orthogonal to ours because we target defects in the processor pipeline.

another recent work [18] proposes using standard SMT to run test case applications in the background and evaluates performance overhead. [18] does not rely on redundancy and therefore its coverage depends on the quality, number and frequency of test cases being ran.

Finally, Rescue [11] proposes architectures that allow detected hard errors to be isolated at test time and avoided at run time, but provides no support for hard errors missed at test time.

3 SRT Background

SRT [10] provides a hardware technique for detecting soft errors. SRT uses SMT hardware to allow two copies of a single program, called leading and trailing threads, to be executed concurrently on one SMT core. SRT detects soft errors whenever the corresponding stores in the leading and trailing threads disagree in address or data. Specifically, the leading store waits in the store buffer for the trailing store. Upon successful checking, SRT commits the store to the memory hierarchy. SRT commits register writes, however, in the respective threads without any checking. Because incorrect values propagate through computations and are eventually consumed by stores, checking only stores suffices for soft-error detection.

In SRT, the trailing thread executes behind the leading thread by some specified amount of *slack*. This slack provides two important performance advantages. First, the slack enables the leading branches to be resolved well ahead of the trailing thread, so that branch outcomes are passed to the trailing thread to be used as the trailing thread's prediction, allowing the trailing thread never to mispredict (assuming fault-free operation). Second, the slack enables leading load misses to be resolved well ahead of the trailing thread, so that leading load values can be passed to the trailing thread, allowing the trailing thread never to miss. Thus, only the leading thread accesses the cache. The second advantage also addresses a correctness issue: Duplicating cached loads is problematic because memory locations may be modified by an external agent (e.g., another processor) between the time the leading thread loads a value and the time the trailing thread tries to load the same value. Then, the two threads may diverge if the loads return different data, resulting in loss of redundancy.

Together these two advantages mean that the trailing thread executes far fewer instructions than the leading thread and executes the remaining (only non-speculative) instructions at high IPC. By using SMT, SRT allows much of the trailing thread's execution to be hidden during leading thread stalls. To implement the passing of branch outcomes and load values from the leading thread to the tailing thread, SRT uses a Branch Outcome Queue (BOQ) and a Load Value Queue (LVQ).

4 Hard Error Detection with SMT

The key to detecting hard errors on SMT is ensuring *spatial*

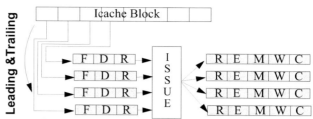

FIGURE 1: Mapping of instructions from cache frontend way and from issue to backend ways

diversity — i.e., trailing instructions do not use the same pipeline resources used by the corresponding leading instructions. We note that in an out-of-order pipeline an instruction is processed in one *frontend way* crossing over only at the issue queue to a *backend way* which the instruction uses till write back. Figure 1 shows a diagram of the instruction flow. Once in a frontend way or backend way, an instruction uses resources dedicated to that way. It suffices to ensure that a trailing instruction uses a different frontend way and a different backend way than the leading instruction to ensure that the trailing instruction uses different pipeline resources than the leading instruction. Spatial diversity does not occur naturally in SRT because the trailing thread is an instruction stream mostly-identical to the leading thread, resulting in the same resources being used by most leading-trailing instruction pairs.

In Section 4.1, we first discuss the problems with a straight-forward but naive approach to enforcing spatial diversity in the execution of the leading and trailing threads. We then continue on in Section 4.2. to describe our *safe-shuffle* which shuffles leading instructions, borrowing dependence information from the leading thread, to produce trailing instructions so that spatial diversity is enforced while maintaining program correctness in the trailing thread. In Section 4.3, we describe execution of the trailing thread. Finally, in Section 4.4, we discuss comparison of the leading and trailing state, and how we verify the dependence information that was passed from the leading thread to the trailing thread for safe-shuffle. This verification is needed so that dependence information corrupted by a hard error and propagated from the leading thread to the trailing thread, does not result in the error going undetected.

4.1 A Naive Approach

A naive approach to forcing the trailing instructions to use different pipeline resources from their leading counterparts, would be to perform some sort of shuffling on the trailing thread. However, there is no convenient point in the pipeline at which the trailing instructions can be shuffled. One option is to do the shuffling before rename, but then the trailing thread will not preserve dependencies and will diverge from the leading thread, resulting in loss of redundancy. A second option, is to shuffle after rename but before dispatch (i.e., insertion into the issue queue as done in [9]), but this introduces two problems: (1) Because both leading and trailing threads are fetched from the I-cache and the instruction location within a cache block does not change in leading and trailing threads, both leading and trailing instructions would exercise the same pipeline-frontend way resulting in zero coverage of the frontend. (2) The issue queue may undo the shuffling and map the trailing instructions to the same execution way as the corresponding leading instruction. A third option is shuffling after issue but this would require updating issue's data structures to reflect the modified pipeline resource usage (some resources in use upon issue may not be in use upon shuffle, and vice versa). In addition, although there are enough resources to issue some instructions, spatial diversity may sometimes require that fewer instructions be issued and the excess be held back. The issue-queue updating and excess handling would severely complicate the pipeline. The final option is for shuffle to occur in the timing-critical issue. In this option, the select logic has to ensure that there is no excess due to shuffling, in addition to the usual constraints. And the mapping logic has to ensure that spatial diversity is maintained, in addition to the usual constraints. These additional requirements would severely complicate issue.

The following sections contain descriptions in detail of how instructions are fetched out-of-order, shuffled, and checked at commit. This detail should not be misinterpreted as complexity. Many common superscalar techniques (e.g., renaming) would seem complex if described at such fine detail. In addition, Black-Jack has been carefully designed that all new hardware is off the critical path. Seemingly simpler options, which we describe above, that can not be moved off the critical path will have severe impact on performance.

4.2 Safe-Shuffle

Because we want to cover both the frontend and backend it is necessary that shuffling be done before the fetch of the trailing thread. Here we address the problem that instruction dependencies, needed to guarantee the correctness of such shuffling, have not yet been determined.

There seems to be a catch-22 that prevents us from covering the frontend: we cannot shuffle the instructions without first knowing the dependencies among the instructions to be shuffled, but we cannot know the dependencies without fetching the instructions in the original program order, yet we cannot fetch the instructions in program order if we want to cover the frontend. We make the key observation that because we are executing the same program redundantly in the leading and trailing threads and because there is a slack between the threads, the leading thread has already determined the dependencies before the trailing execution begins. Accordingly, in safe-shuffle we borrow the dependence information from the leading thread to allow shuffling before the trailing thread is fetched.

We implement safe-shuffle in a two-phase process: In the first phase, we collect information on the leading instructions' independence, rename maps (i.e., logical to physical register maps), and pipeline-resource-usage. In the second phase, we use the independence and resource-usage information to shuffle the leading instructions for producing the trailing thread that is spatially diverse from the leading thread. Shuffling produces the trailing thread in the leading thread's *issue order*. Though issue order preserves true dependencies, it removes false dependencies and overlaps multiple live ranges of the same logical register. Fortunately, the leading rename maps correctly identify the live ranges, allowing the trailing thread to maintain program correctness. We describe the first phase in Section 4.2.1, and the second in Section 4.2.2.

4.2.1 Collecting Independence Information

Our technique relies on the observation that instructions co-issued in the *same* cycle are independent and can be shuffled with-

out causing correctness problems. As such we use the execution of the leading thread to record co-issued instructions, called a *packet*, and also the pipeline resources used by the instructions and their rename maps. We collect this information in a simple queue called the Dependence Trace Queue (DTQ). Each entry contains information for one issued leading instruction and the entries are allocated for all issued leading instructions *in issue order*. The order that entries are allocated *within* a packet can be arbitrary. The instructions collect information during execution and record information at commit.

Leading instructions in a packet are allocated consecutive entries, and the last instruction in the packet has a bit set to demarcate the end of the packet. Because the allocation of DTQ entries need be completed only before writeback, the allocation need not be done in the timing-sensitive select and map logic. When leading instructions are in the pipeline they record, and carry with them until commit, two IDs to identify the pipeline resources that the instructions used. One ID specifies the frontend-way, and the other specifies the backend-way. The instructions also carry the logical to physical register maps for their source and destination operands. Upon commit, the leading instruction records its undecoded instruction, its rename maps, and its frontend and backend IDs in its DTQ entry. Because the DTQ holds only the committed leading instructions (albeit in issue order) which are shuffled to produce the trailing thread, our trailing thread does not execute any misspeculated instructions, as is the case in SRT.

While the leading thread's issue order helps us implement safe-shuffle, we also need the leading thread's program order to keep trailing loads and stores in program order in the load/store queue of the trailing thread's context, and to commit the trailing thread. Because the trailing thread is fetched from the DTQ, which is in issue order and not program order, we also need to record the leading thread's program order. One method for recording this ordering would be to actually allocate trailing thread active list and load/store queue entries in the trailing thread context when each leading instruction commits, which is well before the corresponding trailing instruction is fetched. Such early allocation would mean that idle instructions in the slack would be consuming trailing thread resources and consequently, slack would be limited by the size of the trailing context load/store queue (which is the smaller of active list and load/store queue). Instead, we allocate virtual active list and load/store queue entries at leading thread commit to record the ordering without requiring that instructions in the slack are actually assigned to any trailing thread resources. We store these allocations in the DTQ as well.

Thus, we have borrowed the leading thread's issue order, rename maps, and program order. Later we will describe how we verify the correctness of this borrowed data to ensure that a single error that corrupts both threads identically is still caught.

4.2.2 Using Independence to Shuffle

While the leading thread places its packets in the DTQ, shuffle waits for the packets to reach commit and then shuffles the instructions *within* a packet, one packet at a time, producing shuffled packets that will be fetched by the trailing thread.

To enforce spatial diversity, Shuffle must satisfy the following two constraints. First, when the packet is fetched by the trailing thread, each instruction in the packet must map to a different frontend than was used by the corresponding leading instruction. Second, if *all* the instructions in the packet are co-issued together in the same cycle in the trailing thread and *no other* (leading or trailing) instruction is co-issued (Section 4.3.2 describes why these conditions may not be met and what happens then), each trailing instruction must be issued to a different backend than was used by the corresponding leading instruction. Therefore, shuffle cannot be random, must be aware of the policies used by both fetch and instruction map, but can work with any policy as long as the policy is deterministic.

We assume the following policies, which afford the most straightforward implementation and are consequently the most-commonly used: direct mapping policy for fetch where the first instruction in fetch order goes to first frontend way, the second instruction to the second frontend way and so on, and oldest-first mapping policy for instruction select and map, where the oldest instruction goes to the first free backend way that matches the instructions' type (e.g., ALU, memory, or branch type), the second oldest instruction to the second matching backend way and so on.

With the above policies, if shuffle produces a (shuffled) packet whose instructions are fetched and co-issued meeting the second constraint's conditions, then the packet's first instruction is guaranteed to use the first frontend way and the first matching backend way, the second instruction is guaranteed to use the second frontend way and the first of the remaining matching backend ways and so on. Consequently, to meet the above two constraints for spatial diversity, Shuffle need only determine an ordering so that each trailing instruction in a packet uses a different frontend way and different backend way than the ways used by the corresponding leading instruction.

To prevent issue and fetch from undoing our shuffle when there are fewer instructions in a packet than the issue width, we allow shuffle to insert NOPs. We require that the NOPs remain in the pipeline through writeback (i.e., each NOP occupies a frontend and backend way and an issue-queue slot).

We use the following simple, greedy algorithm which works well in most cases. The algorithm shuffles an input packet into an output packet. Each instruction in the input packet (in any arbitrary order) grabs the first free output-packet slot that is spatially diverse from the corresponding leading instruction (i.e., does not map to either the frontend or backend way used by the corresponding leading instruction). At a given output-packet slot, the instruction's new frontend way is easy to determine whereas the backend way is a little more involved: The instruction's new frontend way is the output-packet slot number, and the new backend way is the number of instructions in the packet that have already been allocated to lower slot numbers and use the same type of backend way. The given output-packet slot is acceptable if the new ways are spatially diverse from the leading instructions. If allocation of an instruction passes over an empty output-packet slot that the instruction cannot use because the slot maps to the corresponding leading instruction's frontend or backend way, the instruction puts an NOP in the slot and marks the slot with the instruction's type.

The process continues with each instruction in the input packet attempting to grab a free output-packet slot. If an instruction finds an acceptable slot containing a NOP marked with a matching instruction type, the instruction can claim the slot and replace the NOP. This replacement is what allows two instructions of the same type to swap backend ways as depicted in Figure 2. NOPs created by one type cannot be replaced by an instruction of another type

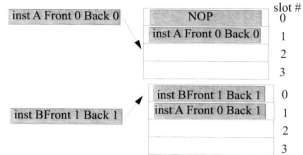

FIGURE 2: Safe-shuffle swapping resource allocations of two like instructions.

because doing so may require correcting (decrementing, to be precise) the backend mappings of some previously-allocated instructions (those whose backend way is larger than that of the NOP being replaced). Such correction would not fit the greedy nature of the algorithm and would complicate the algorithm. There will never be fewer output-packet slots than instructions if the issue width matches the frontend width. However, there may be slots with NOPs that cannot be replaced by later instructions either because the slot is not spatially diverse from the corresponding leading instruction or because the NOPs are allocated by a different instruction type. If an instruction cannot find a slot, the output packet is ended and the remaining instructions of the input packet start a new output packet (the input packet gets broken into two or more output packets). Breaking an input packet reduces parallelism and its impact on performance is discussed in Section 6.

Because of SRT's long slack, there are many cycles between commit of the leading thread and fetch by the trailing thread. Consequently, there is ample time to perform the shuffling, which, if needed, may be pipelined over multiple cycles.

The output packets are placed in the trailing thread's fetch queue. Because the input packets come from the DTQ and shuffling shuffles only the instructions *within* an input packet, the fetch queue inherits DTQ's leading-thread issue order *across* packets.

4.3 Trailing Thread Execution

4.3.1 Frontend

The trailing thread fetches the shuffled packets from its fetch queue according to SRT's slack (Section 3) as depicted in Figure 3. When given fetch bandwidth, the trailing thread fetches one packet each cycle. Because of the direct mapping of instruction fetch to frontend ways, each instruction maps to the frontend way as intended by safe-shuffle and continues on to be decoded on different hardware than was used to decode the corresponding leading instruction.

It is important to note that the trailing-thread fetch is limited to fetch only one packet per cycle even if the packet is smaller than the fetch width of the pipeline. If multiple packets were fetched in one cycle, then the mapping of the packets' instructions to the frontend ways may be different than that intended by safe-shuffle, resulting in loss of spatial diversity. While this restriction ensures frontend spatial diversity, it potentially lowers the trailing thread's fetch bandwidth, degrading performance.

The trailing thread is fetched in leading thread's issue order, which while preserving true dependencies removes false depen-

331

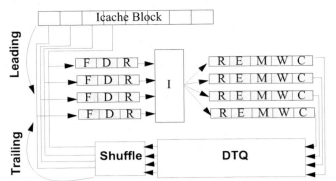

FIGURE 3: BlackJack Execution Flow.

dencies and overlaps multiple live ranges of the same logical register. Because of this overlap, the trailing thread renamer cannot correctly connect consumers to their producers by looking only at the *logical* registers of the instructions. Fortunately, leading thread rename maps can make this connection. Accordingly, the trailing thread renamer uses the leading thread's physical registers (sources and destination) as input, instead of the usual logical registers. That is, the trailing thread renamer renames the renamed leading instructions! Though this double renaming allows us to cover the frontend while preserving program correctness, the downside is that our rename tables have more rows because there are more physical registers than logical registers.

While there is also an issue with determining in rename which physical register each instruction should free, the actual freeing is done at commit, and we address the issue there.

Because the trailing thread fetches from its fetch queue without any branch prediction, the fact that branches appear in issue order (i.e., out of program order) in the trailing thread does not matter. Branches simply flow through the pipeline and execute. We use their execution to verify the trailing-thread program order which is borrowed from the leading thread.

Once decoded we use the virtual active list and load/store queue specifiers in the DTQ (Section 4.2.1) to allocate corresponding physical entries for each fetched instruction. We translate these virtual specifiers to physical load/store queue and active list entries by keeping the virtual to physical mapping for the head of the physical structures as a reference. Any virtual index which is j greater than the head's virtual index is allocated a physical index j away from the head. If j is larger than the size of the structure, then the frontend is stalled till there is space in the structure. Combined with out-of-order fetch, this allocation means that instructions that are fetched earlier than their commit order will allocate physical entries leaving the appropriate number of empty slots ahead of them.

4.3.2 Dispatch/Issue

After rename, register tags correctly encode instruction dependencies and instructions move on to be dispatched into the issue queue. Ideally, the constraints assumed by shuffle will be maintained at issue. Instruction packets will issue complete and alone, and each trailing thread instruction will issue to a different backend than it used in the leading thread.

Because we leave the issue queue and issue policy unmodified, the issue queue may undo our shuffling by breaking up the shuffled packets in the trailing stream and introducing unrelated lead-

ing and trailing instructions into the packets. Doing so would violate the conditions of safe-shuffle's second constraint, specified in Section 4.2.2, that the trailing packet should co-issue as a whole and no other unrelated instructions should co-issue with the packet, and may result in loss of spatial diversity and reduced coverage. The undoing occurs due to two types of *interference,* leading-trailing interference and trailing-trailing interference. However, because trailing thread is fetched in leading thread's issue order, both types of interference are rare. We explain the details next.

Leading-trailing interference occurs when leading instructions co-issue in the same cycle with trailing instructions. Leading instructions issuing with trailing instructions causes trailing packets to break apart, some parts of the packets issuing with leading instructions, and some issuing alone (or with other trailing-thread instructions). Fortunately, in SRT and BlackJack, dependencies naturally cause issue from each thread to be bursty, either only leading instructions or only trailing instructions are issued in most cycles though both threads are present in the issue queue. We quantify this bursty behavior in Section 6. While this bursty issue behavior makes leading-trailing interference rare, another reason makes the interference even rarer. The trailing thread is a high-IPC thread fetched in dependence order with no branch mispredictions or cache misses (see Section 3), while the leading-thread is a lower-IPC thread fetched in program order and the issue policy is oldest-first. Consequently, the trailing instructions issue out of the issue queue almost as soon as they are inserted, while the leading instructions take multiple cycles to issue. This difference in occupancy means that a trailing instruction has a slim chance of becoming older than any leading instruction in the issue queue. As such, the trailing instructions almost always have lower priority than any leading instructions that are ready. Therefore, trailing instructions cannot disturb the leading instructions ready to issue.

The lack of leading-trailing interference results in two distinct benefits: (1) Leading instructions rarely interfere with trailing packets. (2) Conversely, trailing instructions rarely interfere with leading instructions. If this converse were not true, the leading thread's backend resource usage information collected by safe-shuffle could be due to the leading thread either issuing in isolation or co-issuing with some trailing instructions. While the first case causes no problems for safe-shuffle, the second case implies that the leading packets are narrower than the issue width. Narrow leading packets force safe-shuffle either to put many NOPS in the shuffled packets to ensure spatial diversity or to use a shuffling algorithm more complicated than our simple, greedy one to try to combine multiple leading packets into one trailing packet.

Similar to leading-trailing interference, trailing-trailing interference is also rare. Trailing-trailing interference occurs when one packet co-issues with instructions from another packet. It may seem that it would be difficult to prevent trailing-trailing interference especially if the issue queue is to remain unmodified. However, the fact that the trailing stream is ordered in dependence order reduces trailing-trailing interference. As mentioned before, this order implies that trailing instructions enter and leave the issue queue without much delay. This quick departure combined with the fact that the trailing thread fetches only one packet per cycle (Section 4.3.1) implies that most often only one trailing packet resides in the issue queue at any given time, giving little opportunity for the issue queue to introduce trailing-trailing interference.

Nevertheless, the issue queue may occasionally have more than one co-resident trailing packet due either to long-latency trailing instructions backing up in the issue queue or to leading-trailing interference. In such cases, the issue queue may wake up later packets in an order different than the trailing dispatch order (which is the same as the leading issue order). This different order occurs because the leading issue order is based on the latencies seen by the leading thread which are different from those seen by the trailing thread. The leading thread sees cache miss latencies which are hidden completely from the trailing thread due to the slack (see Section 3). Trailing loads access only the LVQ and not the cache hierarchy, and as such, may complete earlier than the dispatch order expects, creating opportunity for instructions in later packets to be woken up earlier and to be co-issued with earlier packets.

Both types of interference being rare implies that most often the trailing packets are co-issued as a whole and not co-issued with unrelated leading or trailing instructions. Consequently, the conditions of safe-shuffle's second constraint, specified in Section 4.2.2, are met, and spatial diversity is maintained in the common case.

This way of maintaining spatial diversity without modifying the issue queue does come at the price of some performance loss. Leading-trailing interference is reduced by trailing thread's issue-order fetch which does not negatively impact performance. However, preventing trailing-trailing interference relies on fetching one packet per cycle which limits trailing thread's fetch bandwidth and negatively impacts performance, as discussed in Section 4.3.1.

4.4 Commit and Correctness Check

After passing through the remainder of the backend pipeline, trailing thread instructions complete and wait for commit in program order. Because register dependencies are preserved, commit is in program order, and both threads maintain the ordering in the load/store queue, the result of each trailing instruction and its leading counterpart will be in agreement when there are no errors.

BlackJack checks for agreement by comparing the trailing stores against corresponding leading stores waiting in the store buffer in the same way as SRT (Section 3). However, safe-shuffle borrows dependence information from the leading thread to produce the trailing thread. Therefore, we must perform additional checks so that corruption of this information due to a hard error does not cause identical mistakes in the two threads, allowing the error to go undetected. We note that this additional check is in the same vein as SRT's branch outcomes. SRT passes leading branch outcomes to the trailing thread which uses the outcomes as prediction and not as result. Trailing branch execution validates the prediction which forms a separate check for the correctness of the outcomes.

The borrowed information includes dependence information in the form of leading issue order and leading rename maps, and leading program order.

To check the dependence information, we observe that we need to ensure that the trailing thread maintains the dependencies in the original program. To implement this check, we use a second rename table at trailing commit, in a slightly different fashion than normal which is described below.

As trailing instructions commit in program order, they use their logical source registers to look up their physical source registers in the second table. While normally a new physical register is allocated for the destination operand, the trailing instructions already have their physical destination register which they use to update the table as the new mapping for the logical destination register. We compare the looked-up physical source registers against the physical source registers that were provided by the first trailing rename and used by the instructions in trailing execution. A disagreement signifies either a leading-thread error that propagated to the trailing thread through safe-shuffle, or a trailing-thread error (including this dependence check). Because the second rename table is used only by the trailing thread and never by the leading thread, we maintain spatial diversity.

Because the first trailing rename is done out of program order, we do not free physical registers as determined by the first renamer (Section 4.3.1). Instead, we free the physical register that the second renamer reports as the previous mapping of the destination register because the second rename is in program order. Using the second renamer ensures that freeing reflects program order, not dependence order.

Finally, the trailing thread does not fetch its own instructions but obtains the instructions committed by the leading thread. Therefore, program-order errors in the leading thread could cause incorrect instructions to be fetched, instructions to be dropped or instructions to be added, and the trailing thread will duplicate these errors. To check for this kind of error we require an additional simple check at commit that checks that the program counters of the committed instructions are correct. If a committed instruction is a taken branch, the program counter of the next committed instruction should be the branch target; otherwise the program counter of the next instruction should be the program counter of the previous instruction plus the size of an instruction.

4.5 Coverage

While BlackJack ensures spatial diversity in the combinational logic present in the frontend and backend, spatial diversity in memory structures, specifically rename tables, load/store queue, active list, and the issue queue, need some explanation.

Because each SMT context has its own rename tables, load/store queue and active list, spatial diversity in these structures is inherent. An error in the leading thread's program order (e.g., omitted instructions) propagating to the trailing thread despite this spatial diversity is caught by our program-order checks as described in Section 4.4. Spatial diversity from having per-context structures ensures that any remaining errors are caught by disagreeing results of the two threads.

The issue queue may seem to be more of a problem because it is shared by the two threads and can not be spatially diverse. Because BlackJack ensures spatial diversity in the backend spatial diversity ends up being maintained in most of the issue queue hardware. Each backend way has a broadcast line to broadcast to its dependents. As such, if the backend way is assured to be spatially diverse so are the broadcast wires. Furthermore, each broadcast wire connects to a comparator in each entry. Therefore, by using a different broadcast wire, a trailing instruction is woken up by a different comparator than the corresponding leading instruction. The remaining concern is the spatial diversity of the issue queue entries themselves. We point out here that the function of the issue queue is simply to obey dependencies and find a valid issue order. As such, any issue queue failure that causes an invalid issue order (even if it affects the order of both threads in the same way) is detected by the dependence check as described in Section 4.4. Consequently, we do not need to ensure spatial diversity in the issue queue entries.

There is a vulnerability in the issue queue's payload RAM which holds instruction payload while the instructions are in the issue queue. It is possible that an entry in the payload RAM corrupts bits in some deterministic way, and this entry is used by both copies of an instruction leading to identical incorrect results in the threads. There are many ways to address this vulnerability. We could additionally consider payload entry allocation policy in safe-shuffle, or insert NOPs at trailing dispatch if an allocation attempts to violate spatial diversity. But because the payload RAM is just a small RAM, having separate payload RAMs for the two threads is probably the simplest solution. Two payload RAMs obviously provide sufficient spatial diversity.

Although safe-shuffle ensures spatial diversity in the backend, including the register file ports, we do not explicitly cover the possibility that both copies of an instruction may be allocated the same physical register. However, because the two threads maintain their own register state and compete for free registers, allocation of identical registers is unlikely and not directly tied to program patterns and architectural policies and causes only a negligible loss in coverage.

Finally, there may also be a concern that while BlackJack covers single hard errors much as SRT covers single soft errors, multiple errors are more likely in the case of hard errors. BlackJack can be effective for multiple uncorrelated errors. It is true that certain structures may be more prone than others to multiple correlated errors, and in a highly-defective chip many like structures (e.g., all RAM structures or all CAM structures) may be defective. However, we do not target this class of defective chips. Such chips will be eliminated early in the testing process. Our technique is a run-time technique that catches hard errors that were small enough to be missed during test or only became active in the field. We target chips that seem error-free but silently corrupt data.

4.6 Complexity

Blackjack exploits pre-existing ordering information from the leading thread issue order to permit shuffling and reordered fetch. Because this ordering information is available from the leading thread, it can be used far in advance of trailing thread fetch (within the leading/trailing slack) thus clearly placing shuffle off the critical path with little chance of complicating current structures or degrading cycle time.

5 Methodology

We modify SimpleScalar 3.2b[4] to simulate SRT and Black-Jack. We use the parameters listed in Table 1. Note that we use two integer multipliers and two integer dividers in both SRT and BlackJack, because without two of each type of resource, spatial diversity is not possible.

We evaluate the hard error instruction coverage of SRT and BlackJack. SRT is not a hard-error technique but provides some hard error coverage due to accidental spatial diversity. We use SRT as a reference point.

We measure hard error instruction coverage as the fraction of instruction pairs that execute on spatially diverse hardware multi-

Table 1: Processor Parameters

Out-of-order issue	4 instructions/cycle
Active list	512 entries (64-entry LSQ)
Issue queue	32-entries
Caches	64KB 4-way 2-cycle L1s (2 ports); 2M 8-way unified L2
Memory	350 cycles
Int ALUs	4 int ALUs, 2 int multipliers,
FP ALUs	2 FP ALUs, 2 FP multipliers
Store Buffer	64 entries
LVQ	128 entries
BOQ	96 entries
Slack	256 instructions
DTQ	1024 instructions

plied by the core area used by the pair. Because instruction pairs can be spatially diverse for part of the execution, and use identical resources in others, we allow for partial coverage of single instructions. We make the simplifying assumption that equal chip areas have equal probability of hard error. We use the HotSpot [15] area model to estimate the core area that remains vulnerable to hard defects under redundant threading. We divide the area into three classes: issue, frontend and backend. We give SRT the benefit of assuming full coverage of hard errors in the issue queue although SRT can cover hard errors in the issue queue only by chance. BlackJack, on the other hand provides coverage as described in Section 4.4. Of the remainder of the core, 34% is accessed by instructions in the frontend pipeline stages. The remaining 66% is accessed in the backend.

We run 16 SPEC2000 benchmarks, fast-forward to the early-simpoint specified by [14], and then run 100 million instructions.

6 Results

In this section we present our results for coverage and performance for SRT and BlackJack. First, we discuss the hard error coverage provided by BlackJack and then move on to discuss the performance impact.

6.1 Instruction Coverage

Figure 4a and b show hard error coverage achieved by SRT and BlackJack. SRT is shown by white bars, and BlackJack by black bars. Figure 4a shows hard error instruction coverage of the entire processor, including frontend and backend. As described in Section 4.1, execution in which frontend ways is determined solely on the instruction's cache block location and thus SRT has zero frontend spatial diversity. Because BlackJack deterministically places instructions so they map to spatially diverse frontends in the leading thread, BlackJack achieves 100% spatial diversity in the frontend. Figure 4b shows instruction coverage only of the backends which is dependent on timing and resource availability.

From Figure 4a, we see that SRT achieves limited spatial diversity and hence provides modest coverage of hard errors. On average SRT provides 34% coverage of hard errors. SRT's worst coverage of 25% occurs in sixtrack and its best coverage in vortex is at 41%. BlackJack on the other hand covers 97% of hard errors on average, with its lowest of 94% occurring in bzip and its high-

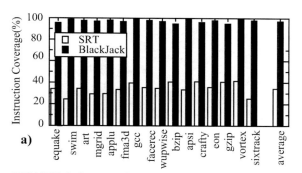

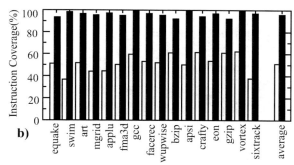

FIGURE 4: Instruction coverage of SRT and BlackJack in a) entire pipeline and b) backend only.

est occurring in vortex at 99%.

To help understand the program behaviors that reduce Black-Jack's coverage we breakdown the coverage-reducing interference into leading-trailing and trailing-trailing (described in Section 4.3) and present them in Figure 5. Training-trailing is represented by white bars, and leading-trailing by black bars. The y-axis is the percentage of issue cycles where the specified type of interference causes instructions to violate spatial diversity. On average across all benchmarks, 0.5% of issue cycles lose coverage due to trailing-trailing interference, and 2.3% lose coverage due to leading-trailing interference.

From Figure 5 we can see that one of the lowest covered benchmarks, equake (95.6%), suffers from both trailing-trailing interference (1.5%) and leading-trailing interference (2.5%). Its trailing-trailing result is notable because it is three times greater than the average across all benchmarks. This elevated trailing-trailing interference is a consequence of equake's low IPC; equake is the slowest benchmark. Trailing-trailing interference is inherent to the low IPC because with slow benchmarks, fetching of the trailing thread outpaces issue and allows trailing instructions to build up in the issue queue. With larger trailing thread issue queue occupancy there is a greater chance for trailing instruction to issue out of their fetch order and interfere with and lose diversity. In fast-paced benchmarks, issue more closely matches fetch and there is little opportunity for trailing interference. The difficulty of interference (both leading-trailing and trailing-trailing) is made worse because equake is an FP application. Because our machine has only 2 FP ALUs, and 2 FP multipliers, once a leading instruction has issued, unless the trailing thread goes to the other equivalent unit there will be loss of coverage. As such, benchmarks that heavily use resources for which only a few copies exist are inherently more susceptible to interference. Benchmarks that use resources for which multiple copies exist are less sensitive. In

benchmarks heavily dependant on basic integer operations (such as Vortex) trailing instructions must avoid only a single backend way and the remaining three ways are spatially diverse. In such cases, interference still has a good chance of sending the instruction to a favorable (although unintended) backend way.

To help explain the high leading-trailing interference in the higher-IPC benchmarks, gzip, crafty, and bzip, (which are to the right in Figure 5) we additionally provide Figure 6. Figure 6 plots the percentage of issue cycles, in which only one context is issued in. Recall from Section 4.3.2, that the bursty nature of instruction issue prevents leading-trailing interference. Figure 6 quantifies this burstiness. While the average across all benchmarks is 70% gzip, crafty, and bzip range from 54% to 63%. In fact, gzip is the lowest of all benchmarks at 54%. The fact that issue is more likely to issue from both contexts in the same cycle naturally implies there will be more interference and greater loss of coverage. Figure 5 reinforces this fact, showing that both gzip and bzip have the highest leading-trailing interference at 7.0% and 5.6% respectively.

6.2 Performance

Figure 7 plots the performance of SRT and BlackJack with no shuffle (BlackJack-NS), and BlackJack. As we explain later, BlackJack-NS helps understand the components of BlackJack's performance. All are normalized to non-fault-tolerant single thread performance. Benchmarks are plotted from left to right in the order of increasing IPC. White bars represent SRT, gray bars BlackJack-NS and black bars BlackJack. In general SRT and therefore also BlackJack show larger performance degradation with higher-IPC benchmarks, because there are less idle cycles to hide the execution of the redundant thread. On average across all benchmarks, compared to non-fault-tolerant single-thread, SRT has a slowdown of 21%. and BlackJack has a slowdown of 33%.

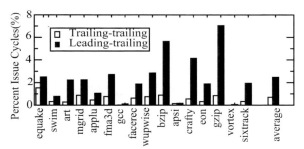

FIGURE 5: Percent of issue cycles with trailing-trailing and leading-trailing interference.

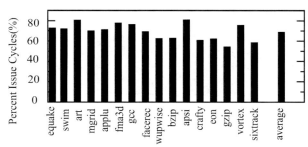

FIGURE 6: Percentage of issue cycles when all instructions issued are from the same context.

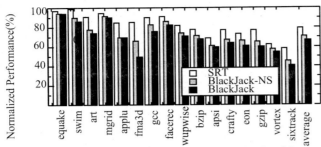

FIGURE 7: Performance of SRT, BlackJack with no shuffle (BlackJack-NS) and Blackjack.

These slowdowns represent a 15% slowdown for BlackJack beyond SRT.

The difference between BlackJack-NS and BlackJack represents the performance degradation due to the cases where safe-shuffle's greedy algorithm sometimes splits packets for high coverage. BlackJack-NS never splits packets (and never shuffles) and so it is able to issue a greater number of instructions per cycle (but has low coverage). Averaged across all benchmarks, adding shuffle in BlackJack results in a 5% slowdown over BlackJack-NS. If BlackJack were to have an ideal shuffle algorithm that provided good coverage without ever splitting packets, BlackJack would incur a 10% slowdown over SRT. Better shuffle algorithms may be able to approach this 10% slowdown.

This remaining difference between BlackJack-NS and SRT is due to BlackJack's policy of fetching only a single packet per cycle. This policy prevents co-issue of multiple trailing packets. This prevention is a simple method for reducing trailing-trailing interference (as seen in Figure 5) but comes at the cost of performance. Trailing-trailing interference is often good for performance, allowing two or more small packets that took multiple cycles to issue in the leading thread to be combined into one large packet issuing in a single cycle. Combining two such packets while maintaining spatial diversity requires that the packets are known to be independent. For simplicity, BlackJack's shuffle algorithm and fetch policy assumes all leading instruction not co-issued in the same cycle may have dependencies. It is important to note that all information about the dependencies between packets is available for shuffle to borrow from the leading thread. Hence it is possible for a more complex shuffle algorithms to use this additional information to close the gap between BlackJack and SRT.

7 Conclusions

This paper presents BlackJack; a microarchitecture that addresses the increasing difficulty of test. With smaller and faster devices, tolerance for errors are shrinking and devices may act correctly under certain condition and not under others. As such, hard errors may exist but are only exercised by very specific machine state and signal pathways. In addition new complications with burn-in may mean that latent hard errors are not exposed in the fab and reach the customer before becoming active.

BlackJack provides a safety net that detects hard errors (in addition to soft errors) that are exposed by a program at runtime.

Averaged across all benchmarks, BlackJacks incurs a 15% performance penalty when compared to SRT. In exchange for this degradation, BlackJack provides 97% instruction coverage of pipline hard errors compared to SRT's 34%.

8 References

[1] T. M. Austin. Diva: a reliable substrate for deep submicron microarchitecture design. In *MICRO 32: Proceedings of the 32nd annual ACM/IEEE international symposium on Microarchitecture*, pages 196–207, 1999.

[2] D. C. Bossen, A. Kitamorn, K. F. Reick, and M. S. Floyd. Fault-tolerant design of the IBM pSeries 690 system using the POWER4 processor technology. *IBM Journal of Research and Development*, 46(1), 2002.

[3] F. A. Bower, D. J. Sorin, and S. Ozev. A mechanism for online diagnosis of hard faults in microprocessors. In *MICRO 38: Proceedings of the 38th annual IEEE/ACM International Symposium on Microarchitecture*, pages 197–208, 2005.

[4] D. Burger, T. M. Austin, and S. Bennett. Evaluating future microprocessors: The simplescalar tool set. Technical Report CS-TR-1996-1308, University of Wisconsin, 1996.

[5] K. Constantinides, S. Plaza, J. Blome, B. Zhang, V. Bertacco, S. Mahlke, T. Austin, and M. Orshansky. Bulletproof: A defect-tolerant cmp switch architecture. In *Proceedings of the 12th International Symposium on High-Performance Computer Architecture (HPCA-12)*, February 2006.

[6] M. Gomaa, C. Scarbrough, T. N. Vijaykumar, and I. Pomeranz. Transient-fault recovery for chip multiprocessors. In *ISCA '03: Proceedings of the 30th annual international symposium on Computer architecture*, pages 98–109. ACM Press, 2003.

[7] W. Maly, A. Gattiker, T. Zanon, T. Vogels, R. D. Blanton, and T. Storey. Deformations of IC structure in test and yield learning. In *International Test Conference (ITC)*, 2003.

[8] M. Meterelliyoz, H. Mahmoodi, and K. Roy. A leakage control system for thermal stability during burn-in test. In *International Test Conference (ITC)*, November 2005.

[9] S. S. Mukherjee, M. Kontz, and S. K. Reinhardt. Detailed design and evaluation of redundant multithreading alternatives. In *ISCA '02: Proceedings of the 29th annual international symposium on Computer architecture*, 2002.

[10] S. K. Reinhardt and S. S. Mukherjee. Transient fault detection via simultaneous multithreading. In *ISCA '00: Proceedings of the 27th annual international symposium on Computer architecture*, pages 25–36. ACM Press, 2000.

[11] E. Schuchman and T. N. Vijaykumar. Rescue: A microarchitecture for testability and defect tolerance. In *ISCA '05: Proceedings of the 32nd Annual International Symposium on Computer Architecture*, pages 160–171, 2005.

[12] F. F. Sellers, M. yue Hsiao, and L. W. Bearnson. *Error Detecting Logic for Digital Computers*. McGraw-Hill, 1968.

[13] O. Semenov, A. Vassighi, M. Sachdev, A. Keshavarzi, and C. F. Hawkins. Effect of cmos technology scaling on thermal management during burn-in. *IEEE Transactions on Semiconductor Manufacturing*, 16(4), 2003.

[14] T. Sherwood, E. Perelman, G. Hamerly, and B. Calder. Automatically characterizing large scale program behavior. In *Proceedings of the 10th International Conference on Architectural Support for Programming Languages and Operating Systems*, Oct. 2002.

[15] K. Skadron, M. R. Stan, W. Huang, S. Velusamy, K. Sankaranarayanan, and D. Tarjan. Temperature-aware microarchitecture. In *Proceedings of the 30th Annual International Symposium on Computer Architecture*, 2003.

[16] J. Srinivasan, S. V. Adve, P. Bose, and J. A. Rivers. Exploiting structural duplication for lifetime reliability enhancement. In *ISCA '05: Proceedings of the 32nd Annual International Symposium on Computer Architecture*, pages 520–531, 2005.

[17] T. N. Vijaykumar, I. Pomeranz, and K. Cheng. Transient-fault recovery using simultaneous multithreading. In *Proceedings of the 29th annual international symposium on Computer architecture*, pages 87–98, 2002.

[18] E. Weglarz, K. Saluja, and T. M. Mak. Testing of hard faults in simultaneous multi-threaded processors. In *Proceeding of the 10th IEEE International On-Line Testing Symposium*, 2004.

Session 6A:
Critical Systems:
Risk Analysis and Assurance

Confidence: Its Role in Dependability Cases for Risk Assessment

Robin E Bloomfield, Bev Littlewood, David Wright
Centre for Software Reliability, City University, London
{reb, bl, dw}@csr.city.ac.uk

Abstract

Society is increasingly requiring quantitative assessment of risk and associated dependability cases. Informally, a dependability case comprises some reasoning, based on assumptions and evidence, that supports a dependability claim at a particular level of confidence. In this paper we argue that a quantitative assessment of claim confidence is necessary for proper assessment of risk. We discuss the way in which confidence depends upon uncertainty about the underpinnings of the dependability case (truth of assumptions, correctness of reasoning, strength of evidence), and propose that probability is the appropriate measure of uncertainty. We discuss some of the obstacles to quantitative assessment of confidence (issues of composability of subsystem claims; of the multi-dimensional, multi-attribute nature of dependability claims; of the difficult role played by dependence between different kinds of evidence, assumptions, etc). We show that, even in simple cases, the confidence in a claim arising from a dependability case can be surprisingly low.

1. Introduction: uncertainty, confidence

Risks associated with the use of computer-based systems are becoming increasingly important to society. Whilst the problems have been recognized for a long time in safety-critical industries, there is a new awareness in other industries, such as banking (see, e.g., the Basel II accords [6]). Assessing these risks, so that intelligent decisions can be made – e.g. about deployment, or about the cost-effectiveness of possible risk reduction procedures – is hard. Much of the difficulty stems from the fact that the fallibility of *software* plays such an important role as a source of risk.

Risk involves notions of *failure* and *consequence* of failure. Its assessment therefore requires an assessment of dependability; this might be expressed, for example, as probability of failure upon demand, rate of occurrence of failures, probability of mission failure, and so on. In this paper we shall address this dependability assessment problem only, and not further discuss the cost/consequence part of risk assessment.

There is now a huge literature on the assessment of the dependability of software-based systems, going back several decades. In recent years the assessment process has started to be formalized in *dependability cases*, most notably safety cases. A safety case has been defined as:

A documented body of evidence that provides a convincing and valid argument that a system is adequately safe for a given application in a given environment [7].

In this paper we shall discuss the important role played by *uncertainty* in dependability cases. We believe that some aspects of uncertainty have been long neglected and we propose a formal quantitative treatment of 'confidence' to address this omission.

Computer scientists have long had an uneasy relationship with uncertainty, and with its most powerful calculus, probability. One of us can remember discussions of thirty years ago about software reliability. It was difficult then to persuade some software experts that there was inherent uncertainty in the failure processes of programs, and that *probability* was the appropriate way of capturing this uncertainty. Instead, it was asserted that software failed *systematically*, and thus that notions of 'reliability' were meaningless.

Over the years the position has changed. It is now widely agree that 'systematic failure' just means that a program that has failed in certain circumstances will *always* fail whenever those circumstances are exactly repeated. The uncertainty lies in our not knowing beforehand *which* circumstances (e.g. inputs to a program) will cause failure, and *when* these will arise during the operational execution of the program. It is this uncertainty that is represented in a probabilistic measure of dependability, such as reliability.[1]

---

[1] It is interesting that a similar reluctance to acknowledge uncertainty has occurred recently as attempts have been made to model *security* probabilistically. Here, notions of attacker

The uncertainty discussed above concerns system behaviour – it is 'uncertainty-in-the-world'. There is another form of uncertainty that has, we believe, been neglected: this is uncertainty in the dependability assessment process itself.

Consider, for example, a situation in which we want to claim that a software component has a probability of failure on demand (*pfd*) smaller than 10^{-3} (a figure that may have arisen from the requirements of a wider system safety case). Our evidence to support such a claim may be testing data, different types of static analysis, etc (it is a characteristic of dependability assessment, particularly for software-based systems, that the supporting evidence is usual disparate in nature).

The problem is that such evidence will never allow us to be *certain* that the claim is true: there is inherent uncertainty here. If we collect more supportive evidence, we might reasonably expect to increase our confidence in the truth of the claim, but it will rarely be possible to collect sufficient evidence to eliminate doubt completely.[2] As the cases often deal with critical systems there needs to be high confidence in the resulting judgement. Often there are areas where there is lack of understanding (e.g. due to deficiencies in the science, in experimental data) or there are problems that the engineering process has not been rigorously followed. There may be problems with uncertainties in the prediction due to the high level of human-computer interaction (e.g. in a cockpit) making quantified estimates of reliability problematic due, among other things, to the sensitivity to the exact context and variability of performance. Not that we argue against the use of humans, indeed it is often this inherent variability in human performance that allows systems to recover from unsafe situations, turning potential accidents into incidents or near misses. Rather that all these factors lead to uncertainties in our judgement.

This prompts questions such as: *How* confident are we that the claim is true? How do we express 'confidence' quantitatively? What effect does this 'assessment uncertainty' have upon decision-making?

Confidence in dependability cases stems from a multiplicity of judgements, some informal, some very formal, some from individuals and others from groups of experts. Confidence, like proof, is the product of a social process.

The greatest difficulty is to deal with the uncertainty that arises from weaknesses in the argument that supports a dependability claim. These might arise, for example,

from uncertainty as to whether underlying assumptions are true. Although we are not aware of any formal treatments of this kind of uncertainty in the literature, the problem has been acknowledged implicitly. For example, in [9,10] it is recognized that there will be uncertainty arising from a single argument leg supporting a dependability claim, so that a second, different, leg should be added – a kind of 'argument fault-tolerance'. However, the reasoning here is informal and qualitative – there is no guidance about *how much* benefit will ensue, nor about *how* confident one would be in a claim after following this procedure. The recent reissue of the UK Defence Standards recognises the role of confidence and an earlier version of this paper provided some rationale behind the guidance in Part 2 [8]. Two of us were involved in a study of the use of computers in the UK nuclear industry [11]. One recommendation of this group was that the principle underlying much regulation in this area, ALARP (that the failure rate stated by a dependability claim should be As Low As Reasonably Practicable), ought to be accompanied by another principle, ACARP (that one should be As Confident As Reasonably Practicable in the truth of a claim). The recommendation has not yet been adopted.

In the rest of this paper we look at some of these problems in more detail, and provide some very tentative pointers to ways forward.

2. Judging the range of probability of failure

As an example of the interplay between confidence and failure rate (or *pfd*) we examine the judgement that a system has a certain classification safety integrity level (SIL): a measure of how safety critical a function is. While we have chosen the standard IEC 61508 [4] for this illustration the use of levels and the judgement of membership of "levels" is a pervasive issue (e.g. in aerospace [2], defence, security, nuclear, railways). IEC 61508 is a generic standard for the functional safety of computer-based systems and it defines safety integrity both in terms of a probability of dangerous failure on demand and the probability of dangerous failure per hour. SILs are defined by a range. For example a Safety Integrity Level n safety function with a low demand mode of operation has an average probability of failure to perform its design function on demand in the range $10^{-(n+1)}$ to 10^{-n}. In practice SILs are used in a variety of ways, not only to describe the judged probability of failure (whether qualitative or quantitative), but also to indicate confidence in the judgement being made. There is an interesting interplay between level and confidence: people seem to expect the higher SILs to be demonstrated to higher confidence.

---

intentionality have been used to claim that probabilistic measures of security are not appropriate.

[2] One exception might be exhaustive testing in some specialized situations. Such exceptions are, we believe, very rare.

Although we use judgement of SIL as an example, the issues this raises apply to many of the judgements made in safety and dependability cases. We should point out that while SIL applies to one important attribute of a safety critical system there are others such as robustness, security and maintainability that should be addressed in a full safety case.

Throughout the paper we shall interpret probabilities in the Bayesian sense of 'degrees of belief'. This has the practical advantage of providing a formalism that allows uncertainty to be treated in a consistent way, whether evidence comes from empirical data or the judgement of a human expert.

3 Modelling judgement of SIL

Deriving a SIL can be done in a number of interrelated ways. For example:

- Relying entirely on qualitative arguments to directly assess a SIL: the failure rate or SIL is not quantified and it may be denied that software reliability can be quantified at all.

- Using expert judgment based on standards compliance to assess the system. This approach suffers from lack of validation, calibration, and many influencing parameters some of which are ignored in the standard (e.g. size of the software).

- Using a best fit reliability growth model, assessing the accuracy of predictions, adding a margin for subjective assessment of assumption violation.

- Using a worst-case model of the failure process, taking into account uncertainty in parameters quantitatively, and using a subjective estimate of invalid model assumptions.

- Developing an argument of high confidence in zero defects. This may be credible for small highly analysed systems or hardware logic but is not developed further here.

What distinguishes these methods is the confidence that can be placed on the judged SIL but in every case there is some uncertainty that needs to be assessed. This essential uncertainty arises from a number of sources:

- uncertainty in the completeness and validity of data

- doubts about assumptions in the model and model validity

- doubts about the implementation of the model (this may be based on complex software itself)

- doubts about the application of the model and how to deal with conservatism in the model and the data

Confidence in SIL n can be expressed as the probability that the judged *pfd* (λ) is within the upper bound of the *pfd* for that SIL band:

$$P(\lambda < 10^{-n})$$

If the failure rate was normally distributed or symmetrical in linear space, changing the confidence in it by narrowing the distribution would not affect the mean value. However none of the examples would necessarily have a normal distribution and we think normality is unlikely to be the case for a number of reasons:

- The distribution cannot be negative yet we can have a large uncertainty in our judgement of a small *pfd*.

- We would expect the distribution's density function to tend to zero as the rate $\lambda \to 0$, although there may be special cases where there is belief in possible perfection of the system.[3]

We have undertaken some experimental work on how experts make judgements of the probability of failure on demand. The results are summarised in Section 3.3. We also note that in reactor safety studies log-normality is often chosen for model parameters (see the discussion in [3]). So in the analysis that follows we deploy a log normal distribution but the thrust of the results only require a non-symmetric distribution. We have repeated some of the results for a gamma distribution to illustrate the (low) sensitivity to the log-normal assumptions.

3.1 A log normal model

If we model our judgement of the dangerous failure rate or *pfd* with a log normal distribution, the mean will be

---

[3] At first glance it appears contradictory to allow the pfd to take the value 0, and at the same time assign almost zero probability to a very small non-zero value, say 10^{-10}. In fact, the reasoning to support such values would be very different. In the first case, the claim is one of perfection, and this might be supportable by non-probabilistic reasoning. In the second case, it is assumed that the system is imperfect, but it is claimed that the impact of its faults is vanishingly small.

different from the most likely "peak" value (the mode). The log-normal distribution is specified by two parameters: μ which controls the peak value and σ which controls the spread. Although the log-normal is generally difficult analytically, the mean and the mode can be calculated as:

$$a\_mean(\mu,\sigma) := \exp\left(\mu + \frac{1}{2}\cdot\sigma^2\right) \qquad log\_mean(\mu,\sigma) := \mu + \frac{1}{2}\cdot\sigma^2$$

and the peak value is at

$$a\_mode(\mu,\sigma) := \exp\left(\mu - \sigma^2\right) \qquad log\_mode(\mu,\sigma) := \mu - \sigma^2$$

where:

log_mean is the log of the mean failure rate
log_mode is the log of the peak failure rate

The probability density function is:

$$pdf\_\lambda(\lambda, lmean, lmode) := \blacksquare$$

$$\frac{1}{\sqrt{2\cdot\pi}\cdot\sqrt{\frac{2\cdot(lmean - lmode)}{3}}\cdot\lambda}\cdot\exp\left(\frac{-1}{2}\cdot\frac{\left(\ln(\lambda) - \frac{2\cdot lmean + lmode}{3}\right)^2}{\frac{2\cdot(lmean-lmode)}{3}}\right)$$

It can be shown that the ratio of the mean and the mode is: $\log_{10}(mean / mode) = 0.65\ \sigma^2$. So the difference between the mode and mean varies with the spread of the distribution (σ). As you might expect there is no difference when there is no spread (σ = 0), but for a broad spread there is a surprisingly big difference, e.g. the mean failure rate is one decade greater than the mode if σ = 1.2, and two decades greater if σ = 1.7: See examples in Figure 1. All judgements estimate the most likely failure rate to be 0.003 (i.e. in the middle of SIL2 range of 10^{-3} to 10^{-2} as defined in Table 1) but with varying degrees of confidence. The mean of the dashed curve is 0.004, which is quite close to the mode value of 0.003. By contrast, the solid curve has the widest spread and the mean is 0.01 putting the mean value in the SIL1 band rather than the SIL2 band.

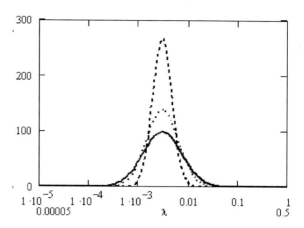

Figure 1: Density functions of the judgement of SIL

The impact of higher failure rates can be seen from plotting the probability density functions on a linear scale:

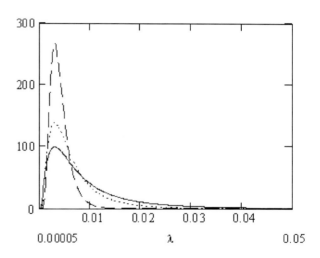

Figure 2: Log normal distribution functions on a linear scale

3.2 Variation of mean with confidence in SIL membership

We can calculate from the probability distributions how the mean SIL varies with the spread in the distribution. One measure of the spread in the distribution is to calculate the probability that we judge the system to be in the desired SIL or better. This is our one sided confidence in the system's SIL membership:

$$\text{confidence\_better\_x(bound)} := \int_0^{\text{bound}} \text{pdf\_}\lambda l(0, \lambda, -4.6, \ln(0.003))\, d\lambda$$

We model this by keeping the mode of the distribution constant. This is shown in Figure 3 where the mode has been kept at 0.003 (the middle of SIL2) and we see that if our confidence falls below about 67% that the system is SIL2 then the mean rate is actually in the SIL1 band.

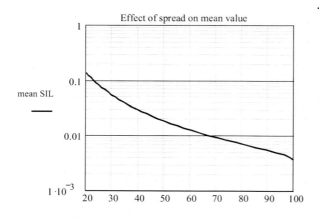

Figure 3: Relationship between confidence in a SIL and the mean value

Another of way of looking at the problem is, for a given mode and actual mean, to calculate the chances of the true system failure rate being in the different SIL bands. This is shown in Figure 4.

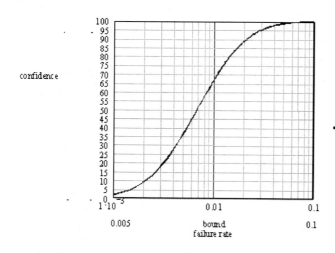

Figure 4: Confidence mean failure rate better than a bound

So for the widest distribution (corresponding to the solid line in Figure 1), the system has about a 67%

chance of being in SIL2 or higher and a 99.9% chance of being SIL1 or higher.

3.3 Experimental results

We conducted an experiment with 12 experts from a variety of European countries and backgrounds. All were familiar with safety rated systems and some were experts with many years experience of the development and assessment of such systems. The experts were asked for judgments in four phases

1. After a 20 minute presentation describing a safety critical system and the implementation of a particular safety function. This was based on the Public Domain Case Study of the European nuclear R&D project Cemsis [5].

2. After a request for additional information, which (if available) was provided individually

3. After a group presentation of all items of additional information provided individually to the different participants in the previous phase;

4. After a Delphi phase where there was an opportunity to discuss decisions with the other participants;

Interestingly the assessors seem to fall into two groups: a minority of (3) doubters who expressed these doubts by giving the system a very high failure rate and another group that expressed their beliefs as shown below:

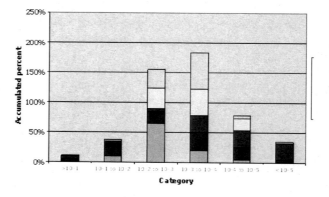

Figure 5 Experimental results

The group were about 90% confident that the system was in SIL2 or better yet the resulting *pfd* (0.01) is on the 2-1 boundary. However the main point of the experiment, as far this exercise is concerned, is to add plausibility to the use of an asymmetric distribution.

3.4 Assessment heuristics and reducing the claim

These modelling results would seem to confirm the heuristic used by safety assessors that although the evidence points to say a SIL2 system they consider it SIL1 because of the uncertainties.

It is therefore more likely that a better case can be made if the system is judged as most likely a SIL n+1 system and it could then be taken as a SIL n with high confidence. This can be seen in the safety justification for the Sizewell B Primary Protection System where doubts about the quality of the development process of the software led to an order of magnitude reduction in the judged probability of failure on demand (some background is provided in [1]). The situation is likely to be exacerbated when qualitative expert judgements are made on the SIL. It may be that the type of standards compliance argument that is often attempted should really lead to a greater than 1 reduction in the claimed SIL. This is discussed further in Section 3.2.

Because the judgement of the SIL is likely to be a combination of several sub-judgements, it would be useful to understand how the confidence in these contributing arguments can be combined. This is the subject of some on-going work.

It is unlikely that we will have precise estimates of the confidence of experts. To cope with this we have developed a conservative, worst case, way of distributing our doubt about the system. Consider the simple situation where the dependability case just has to support a claim about the *pfd* of a system.

We treat *pfd* as a random variable, with probability density function $f(p)$. This can be regarded as the (Bayesian subjective) belief of an expert that takes account of all his uncertainty, including assumption doubt.

In such a situation, for a randomly selected demand the expert's belief is:

$$P(\text{system fails on randomly selected demand})$$
$$= \int_0^1 pf(p)dp \tag{4}$$

In fact it is well known, as we have stated earlier, that it is hard to elicit the beliefs of an expert in the form of a complete distribution like this. Indeed, some would argue that describing this as elicitation begs the question that the expert really does 'have' a complete distribution to be elicited. Rather he may only be prepared to express a belief of the kind $P(pfd < y) = 1 - x$. If this is all he is prepared to say, it is reasonable to ask what is the worst case $f(p)$ – i.e. the distribution that gives the most conservative result in (4).

Figure 6a shows a typical 'real' distribution, $f(p)$ that satisfies the expert's belief: $P(pfd < y) = 1 - x$. Of all the many such distributions that satisfy his belief, Figure 6b shows the most conservative: here all the probability mass for the interval $(0,y)$ is concentrated at y, and all the mass for the interval $(y,1)$ is concentrated at 1.

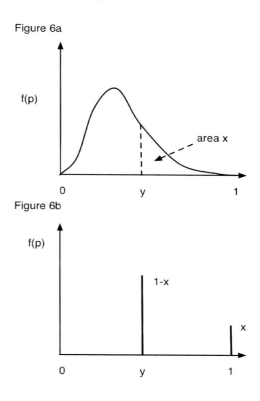

Figure 6a

Figure 6b

It is easy to see that the maximum value of the probability of failure for a randomly selected demand occurs when $f(p)$ takes the form in Figure 6b. In other words, we have:

$$P(\text{system fails on randomly selected demand })$$
$$< (1 - x)y + x = x + y - xy \tag{5}$$

This should be interpreted as the expert being *certain* that the probability of failure on a randomly selected demand is smaller than $x+y-xy$.

The inequality, (5), can be used to give some support to the kind of informal reasoning that goes as follows: I need to claim that the *pfd* is less than 10^{-3}, but with my present dependability case I still have a small doubt that the *pfd* may be greater than this; so I strengthen my case (e.g. collect more supportive evidence) to make with high confidence the *stronger* claim that the *pfd* is smaller than 10^{-4}. This is the kind of reasoning we have seen applied in real safety cases.

The details of how to proceed are as follows. Suppose that the requirement imposed by a wider dependability case is that the *pfd* for the system is no greater than y (in our example, 10^{-3}). We thus wish this claim to be true. Suppose further that the expert believes sufficiently strongly, say with confidence $(1-x^*)$, that the *pfd* is no greater than y^* ($<y$). Then, if $x^*+y^*-x^*y^*<y$, it follows from the result above that the expert believes the probability of failure on a randomly selected demand is less than y.

The point here is that the confidence (or doubt) about the *pfd* has been turned into a probability of the occurrence of an *event* (failure of the system on a randomly selected demand). This thus relates directly to the dependability requirement placed upon the system by the wider safety case.

It is instructive to consider some examples of (x^*,y^*) pairs, representing the expert's beliefs about the *pfd*, when $y=10^{-3}=x^*+y^*-x^*y^*$.

Example 1 At one extreme, we have $x^*=0$, $y^*=10^{-3}$. This is simply the expert believing *directly* that he is certain that the *pfd* is smaller than 10^{-3}, i.e. that his beliefs, represented by the probability density function $f(p)$ are such that there is zero probability mass to the right of 10^{-3}.

Example 2 At the other extreme, we have $x^*=10^{-3}$, $y^*=0$. This case represents the expert believing with 99.9% confidence that the system is 'perfect', i.e. has zero *pfd*. In the event that it is *not* perfect, the worst that can happen is that it is *certain* to fail – so for a randomly selected demand, there is a 10^{-3} chance of failure (i.e. that the system is not perfect).

Example 3 A more interesting example gives some supporting formalism to the way of proceeding that we have seen used, with informal justification, in real safety cases. The reasoning is as follows. The expert constructs an argument that allows him to have high confidence that the *pfd* is a whole decade better than the goal of 10^{-3}, i.e. he claims high confidence in the *pfd* being better than 10^{-4}. That is, $y^*=10^{-4}$. His (informal) reasoning is that if he believes strongly that the *pfd* is smaller than 10^{-4}, then he can be 'effectively certain' that it is smaller than (the more modest) 10^{-3}. In fact, since $x^*+y^*-x^*y^*=10^{-3}$, it follows that $x^*=10^{-3}-10^{-4}=0.0009$ (approximately – we can ignore the x^*y^* term here). So, for this reasoning to apply, he needs to have an argument sufficiently strong to be able to claim the *pfd* is smaller than 10^{-4} with confidence 99.91%.

More generally, if the expert wishes to claim that the probability of failure on a randomly selected demand is better than y, he needs to be able to claim with confidence $1-x^*$ that the *pfd* is smaller than y^*, where $x^*+y^*-x^*y^*=y$.

This last example shows how unforgiving this kind of reasoning can be. The bounds given above in (4) are conservative. The expert needs to have an argument that is sufficiently strong that his 'single point' elicited belief, (x^*,y^*) has the property that *both* x^* (doubt) *and* y^* (claim) are smaller than the required claim, y. The coupling here between claim and doubt suggest that there would be strict limitations to the use of this kind of reasoning. Imagine, for example, that the requirement is the more stringent $y=10^{-5}$. To use this kind of argument, the expert would need to believe the *pfd* is smaller than y^* (itself smaller than y) *with a confidence greater than 99.999%*. It seems unlikely that real experts would ever express confidence of this magnitude (and if they did they would not be believed by others).

Note that, if the expert believes there is a probability p_0 that the system is 'perfect' (i.e. *pfd*=0: $f(p)$ has probability mass p_0 at the origin), the upper bound in (5) becomes $x+y-(x+p_0)y$. It is simple to modify the reasoning of examples like those above.

This example has used the worst case assignment of the doubt to "1". If we could defend other approaches, for example that we were sure we were not wrong by more than a factor of 100, then other models along the same lines are possible – but harder to defend.

4 Discussion

There are a number of strategies that can be adopted in the dependability case to address the confidence issue:

- Reducing the claimed figure due to lack of confidence. See discussion Section 2.3 and Section 3.2
- Undertaking confidence building measures
- Reducing the required confidence by additional argument "legs".

The last two are now briefly discussed.

4.1 Confidence building from experience

The other side of reducing a judged *pfd* because of lack of confidence is undertaking assurance activities explicitly to increase confidence. In view of this in [11] we proposed a sister principle to ALARP that of As Confident as Reasonably Practicable (ACARP). In practice we often undertake analysis and verification activities that increase our confidence without actually changing the system and this is especially so for software. An alternative strategy to just reducing the SIL rating to give high confidence, is to use techniques that attack the high failure rate tail of the distribution. It is this tail that is causing the reduction of the SIL from n to n-1. Operating experience or statistical testing can "cut off" this tail so the distribution gets modified by the survival probability and renormalized. Later work will describe this in more detail.

Similarly we could analyse the growth in dangerous failure rate with failures (some safety systems such as air traffic control can fail several times a year and the overall system still be safe due to the large mitigations from others systems, providence etc). Preliminary results indicate that tests rapidly increase confidence and reduce the mean.. So one approach of tackling confidence might be to give a system a provisional SIL rating based on a broad distribution reflecting the initial uncertainties, and then increase this SIL rating after an operating period. The risk analysis would have to take into account the period of greater risk. This is similar to the organisational strategies for using COTS systems initially only in non-safety-related applications.

More work is needed to model how the worst-case confidence is impacted by subsequent testing. It may well be that there is an equivalent to the conservative bound on *mtbf* [13] for confidence.

4.2 Confidence building from legs

An alternative strategy to tackling the tail of the distribution is to find an alternative way of predicting the same result and so develop another argument "leg" that the system is in the required SIL band or higher. "Multi-legged" arguments are an informal concept and we see them used to mean both confidence building where a technique (e.g. testing) attacks the tail of the first judgement, and where a separate argument is made that does not tackle the tail but reduces the required confidence in the first argument.

These issues of interplay between adding assurance legs and confidence are subtle and the subject of continuing research (see [12]).

4.3 Standards issues

IEC 61508 [4] is an important, generic seven-part safety standard that sets out a detailed approach to the development of safety related computer based systems. In some ways our analysis is at odds with IEC 61508 in as much as the standard does not accept – or is at any rate inconsistent about – the use of statistics for systematic faults, and in the standard this includes software. Despite rejecting the use of quantified reliability for software in Part 1 the standard talks in Parts 3 and 7 about statistical testing of software and discusses statistical requirements for operating experience. Furthermore the quantified SILs implicitly require the software reliability (with respect to dangerous failures) to be quantified.

The definition of SIL in terms of the probability of failure on demand or per hour is technically useful as it allows for different distributions and requires the pdf to be integrated to arrive at the mean.

The confidence required in a SIL is not explicitly addressed in the standard. Part 3 does not mention "confidence" at all. However Part 2 clause 7.4.7.4 requires better than 70% confidence in hardware failure rate data and Part 2 Clause 7.4.7.9 requires 70% single side confidence for operating history. Higher confidence figures are used in Table B6 Part 2 which gives an example of 95% confidence as low effectiveness and 99.9% for high effectiveness, and Part 7 Table D1 provides examples for 95% and 99% confidence from operating experience.

If we were to apply the requirements for 70% confidence this would nearly push the mean failure rate of the system into the next SIL in the example in this paper, and in others with a broader spread it would have a bigger impact.

The more profound impact on the use of the standard might come if we can recommend adjustments to the SIL that can be claimed based on the rigour of the argument that is made and even link a claim limit for SIL to the argument. For example if a process-based qualitative argument was used SIL could be reduced by (at least) 2 levels. If we were to adopt the conservative approach outlined above then we would need at least 99% confidence in SIL2.

5 Conclusions

There is uncertainty in the judgement of the *pfd* of a system whether it is based on direct expert judgment, field experience or the case made from a wide range of test, analysis and experience based evidence. In this paper we have explored how the confidence in these judgments affects the overall judgement of a safety related *pfd* and have illustrated this with an example of SIL membership. It is plausible that judgement of SIL will not be a symmetric distribution: in this case increasing confidence will increase our belief in the integrity of the system. Increasing confidence has an effect on the mean failure rate in these common types of distributions, and this justifies the use of ACARP as a subset of ALARP and the use of confidence building verification activities.

We have modelled the relationship of confidence and mean formally for some particular distributions and have shown that it is more likely that a better safety justification case can be made that if the system is judged as most likely a SIL n+1 system it is taken as a SIL n with high confidence. We have presented some conservative modelling that shows how onerous the need for confidence is. More work is needed to establish quite how conservative this approach is as, in our experience, conservative values at one stage of the analysis do not necessarily propagate through to other stages of the reasoning.

The application of standards should take into account the rigour of the arguments offered. Compliance with process and the predominance of expert judgement in the safety argument should lead to claims being heavily discounted (e.g. by 2 SILs) and a possible limit put on the claims that can be made.

6 Acknowledgements

This work was partially supported by the UK Engineering and Physical Sciences Research Council (EPSRC) under the DIRC and INDEED projects (Grant EP/E000517/1), and by British Energy Generation Ltd under the DISPO project (Contract No. P/40030532).

7 References

[1] D. M. Hunns and N. Wainwright, "Software-based protection for Sizewell B: the regulator's perspective", *Nuclear Engineering International*, September, pp.38-40, 1991.

[2] RTCA, "Software considerations in airborne systems and equipment certification, Requirements and Technical Concepts for Aeronautics", DO-178B, July 1992.

[3] G Apostolakis, "The concept of probability in safety assessments of technological systems", Science, vol 250, no. 4986, pp. 1359 – 1364, Dec 1990.

[4] IEC 61508, "Functional safety of electrical/electronic/programmable electronic safety-related systems", Parts 1–7, 1998

[5] Cemsis Public Domain Example, www.cemsis.org

[6] Bank of International Settlements. www.basel-ii-risk.com

[7] P G Bishop and R E Bloomfield , "A methodology for safety case development", *Safety-Critical Systems Symposium*, 1998, Birmingham, UK.

[8] Ministry of Defence, Interim Defence Standard 00-56 "Safety Management Requirements for Defence Systems, Part 2 Guidance on Establishing a Means of Complying with Part 1", Issue December 2004.

[9] "Requirements for Safety Related Software in Defence Equipment", Ministry of Defence, 1997.

[10] "Regulatory Objective for Software Safety Assurance in Air Traffic Service Equipment", Civil Aviation Authority, 2001.

[11] "The Use of Computers in Safety-Critical Applications", HSE Books, 1998.

[12] B Littlewood and D R Wright, "The Use of Multi-legged Arguments to Increase Confidence in Safety Claims for Software-based Systems", *IEEE Trans. Software Eng.*, 2007 (to appear).

[13] P G Bishop and R E Bloomfield. "A Conservative Theory for Long-Term Reliability Growth Prediction," *IEEE Trans. Reliability,* vol. 45, no. 4, pp 550-560, 1996.

Assurance Based Development of Critical Systems

Patrick J. Graydon   John C. Knight
Department of Computer Science
University of Virginia
{graydon | knight}@cs.virginia.edu

Elisabeth A. Strunk
Software Systems Engineering Dept.
The Aerospace Corporation
elisabeth.a.strunk@aero.org

Abstract

Assurance Based Development (ABD) is the synergistic construction of a critical computing system and an assurance case that sets out the dependability claims for the system and argues that the available evidence justifies those claims. Co-developing the system and its assurance case helps software developers to make technology choices that address the specific dependability goal of each component. This approach gives developers: (1) confidence that the technologies selected will support the system's dependability goal and (2) flexibility to deploy expensive technology, such as formal verification, only on components whose assurance needs demand it. ABD simplifies the detection—and thereby avoidance—of potential assurance difficulties as they arise, rather than after development is complete. In this paper, we present ABD together with a case study of its use.

1. Introduction

Assurance Based Development (ABD) [9] is a novel approach to constructing critical computing systems. In this paper we discuss how it can help developers make development decisions that contribute to their systems' dependability arguments. In ABD, dependability, i.e., confidence that the system will meet its dependability goals when fielded, is evaluated throughout the development process. The system and its assurance argument are co-developed so that explicit criteria for the dependability impact of a development choice are available at the time the choice is made. Combining development and assurance in this way facilitates detection and avoidance of potential assurance difficulties *as they arise*, rather than after development is complete—when they are much harder to address. Here, we explain the kind of assurance goals that are generated at each step and how development decisions can be evaluated against those goals.

Knowing that a critical system is going to operate dependably in its expected environment is essential, yet current approaches to dependability assurance are ad hoc. There are many techniques available to developers of critical systems, but in most cases their benefits have been shown only in isolation and developers do not fully exploit the dependability benefits they bring. For example, developers might use formal methods for the "critical parts of the system," but are often unable to evaluate the ensuing effect on the dependability of the system as a whole. There is little incentive to use a technique whose overall benefit to the delivered system is unknown.

Our goal with ABD is to integrate the development of the system and its assurance argument, thus enabling assurance needs to drive development decisions. We avoid making assumptions about the structure of the system's functional documentation (since that varies widely from system to system), but for the system's assurance argument we use an *assurance case*. The assurance case is an argument that sets out the dependability goal for the system, the evidence needed to support it, and how that evidence is used to justify the claim. Safety cases, a specific form of assurance cases, are used widely in Europe; in some domains, their use is mandated by regulation.

While assurance cases are often created for critical systems, they are not always exploited to guide developers' choices. This is: (1) inefficient, because development steps might produce superfluous assurance or need to be revisited after development is complete; and (2) ineffective, because necessary development activities were omitted unintentionally. If the assurance case is produced near the end of development, there is a risk that the evidence produced during development will be insufficient. This, in turn, could force developers to produce additional evidence or pressure them into accepting an incomplete argument [4]. Recognizing these risks, some standards [7] and researchers [4] call for developers to construct safety cases early and update them often. ABD takes this idea to its fullest extent, integrating safety case and system construction.

ABD combines assurance case and system development so that each supports the other. System development is tailored to support the assurance case, generating evidence for the argument at each step. The assurance case also supports the development process, guiding developers to make choices that make the system much more likely to be fit for its intended use.

We begin in section 2 by summarizing the assurance case concept and how it fits into ABD. We describe the ABD process itself in section 3, and we illustrate its use in section 4. We discuss related work in section 5 and present our conclusions in section 6.

2. Assurance cases and ABD

Assurance cases are the state of the art in rigorous but informal dependability argumentation and, as such, provide the foundation on which the ABD approach rests. Safety cases, a special form of assurance cases, have been built to document the *safety* of a variety of production systems. In general, a safety case is "a documented body of evidence that provides a convincing and valid argument that a system is adequately safe for a given application in a given environment" [1]. Graphic notations have been designed to facilitate writing assurance cases in a manner that is easy for humans to understand and that can be manipulated by machine. The most widely used of these is the Goal Structuring Notation (GSN) [10].

In its simplest form, an assurance case contains three essential elements: (1) an assurance goal or claim; (2) evidence that the goal has been satisfied; and (3) an argument linking the evidence to the goal in a way that leads one to believe that the evidence justifies the goal. This basic structure is applied recursively to produce, for real systems, a hierarchic structure with the overall goal for the system at the root. Evidence at one level becomes a goal at the next lower level, so that the argument is manageable at each level. Other elements that can appear in assurance cases are strategies, assumptions, justifications, and context. While the goals, etc., and hence the assurance argument, are specific to a particular system, patterns for common argument fragments have been developed [5].

In ABD, the assurance case and the system are co-developed, with each affecting decisions in the other. The *ABD process*, which determines how this synergistic activity is to be performed, is discussed in section 3.

Because the system and its assurance case are co-developed, the links between the assurance argument and the development artifacts that support each part of

it must be documented. These *assurance links*, together with the development artifacts and assurance case fragments being linked, form an *ABD composite*. Figure 1 shows a fragment of an example ABD composite in which the assurance case is presented in GSN. In the figure, solution S1 shows evidence from a development artifact being applied to support goal G3, and, indirectly, to support the top-level assurance goal, G1.

In ABD, assurance case goals represent assurance obligations that must be addressed, directly or indirectly, by evidence from development artifacts. Goals are added to the assurance case diagram with an annotation indicating that they have not yet been addressed. As development progresses, these goals are addressed either by direct evidence from a development artifact or an argument fragment combining evidence from subgoals, each of which must itself be addressed.

The assurance case goals related to a development artifact set out the properties which the developer must ensure that the artifact possesses. Goal G2 in Figure 1, for example, could describe a property that a development artifact is to have. If each artifact is created so that it has the required properties and the assurance argument is valid, then the system developers can be confident that the system will meet its assurance goals.

As an example of a fragment of an ABD composite and assurance links, consider the goal of developing a software component in a safety-critical system. If the component must meet an assurance goal of having a failure rate per unit time below 10^{-3}, i.e., not in the ultra-dependable range, testing might be the basic technology chosen to meet this goal. Such a goal requires that the testing process provide several pieces of evi-

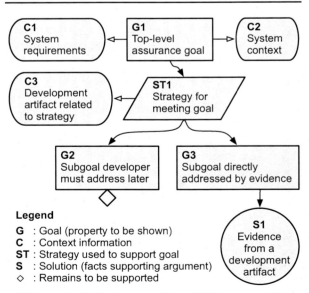

Figure 1. A fragment of an ABD composite

dence to support the assurance case. These pieces of evidence are: (1) that the documented test plan has been conducted as prescribed; (2) that the component's failure rate has been demonstrated in a statistically valid way to be below the threshold; and (3) that the test cases were the result of a random process of selection from the expected operational environment.

3. Assurance Based Development

The ABD process addresses assurance case goals through development choices, which provide evidence that is linked into the assurance case. Briefly, a developer applying ABD repeatedly examines the unsatisfied goal(s) in the assurance case, selects one, makes a *system development choice*—the selection of an architecture or design, the use of a particular tool or language, an implementation decision, or the selection of a verification or validation strategy—that addresses the goal, and modifies the development artifacts and assurance case accordingly. Because each choice may give rise to several new, unaddressed, goals, the process is applied repeatedly until no unaddressed goals remain.

ABD assumes the availability of system requirements, including functional requirements and dependability requirements such as availability and safety. In this paper, we assume that the requirements are correct and complete. We plan to consider the integration of requirements techniques with ABD in future work.

We also assume the availability of a description of the *given architecture*, i.e. the high-level architecture within which the computing system will operate. For example, a new anti-lock braking system is part of a larger automobile system that relies upon the braking system meeting certain functional, non-functional, and dependability requirements. To the braking system developer, the given architecture includes the braking system itself, the other vehicle systems with which the brakes must interact, and the interfaces between the braking system and the other components. The given architecture for a desktop application would include the operating system and the desktop's peripherals.

In section 3.1 we describe how the developer enumerates potential system development choices. In section 3.2 we describe how the developer ought to select from among the available choices. Finally, in section 3.3 we describe how this choice is recorded in the assurance case as an ABD composite.

3.1. Candidate development choices

It is important that a developer enumerating candidate system development choices cast a net wide enough to include at least one choice likely to lead to a system that meets its functional, cost, dependability, and other goals. Developers will consider familiar choices and may solicit suggestions from colleagues and team members, but these sources alone may be insufficient. Furthermore, while considering more choices increases the likelihood that at least one will be suitable, there are costs associated both with enumerating potential choices (as consulting reference material takes time) and with assessing each candidate choice. Developers need a way to enumerate a short list of choices likely to be acceptable for a given problem.

Patterns are a general and commonly used technique that has proven especially important in architecture and design. Experience in ABD could be captured by patterns of coupled system development choices and assurance case argument fragments, helping developers to quickly enumerate a set of candidate choices appropriate to a given problem. We leave effective recording and retrieval of patterns for future work.

3.2. Selection of a system development choice

Selection of a suitable system development choice from the candidate set is based on seven criteria (discussed below): functionality, subsequent restrictions, dependability, cost, feasibility, standards, and additional non-functional requirements. A candidate choice can be rejected based on one or several of the criteria or modified to suit the system's needs (if possible).

Much of the pruning of the set will be based on the developer's experience. In many cases, an experienced developer might consider only a single candidate system development choice in which he or she has considerable confidence. In such a case, these criteria are exit criteria from the selection process for that choice. Note that these criteria are not disjoint, and so evaluating a criterion cannot necessarily be done in isolation. We examine each criterion briefly with an emphasis on its overall role in dependability.

- **Functionality.** The system development choice must not obviously preclude achieving the desired functionality. This can be checked by inspection, analysis, prototyping and/or modeling.
- **Restrictions on later choices.** Each system development choice that is made affects the subgoals that are generated and thus restricts the available choices throughout the remainder of development. The system development choice should not preclude desirable choices later, particularly when the later choices support dependability.
- **Evidence of dependability.** Each system development choice must give rise to evidence that, along

along with an assurance strategy, is sufficient to argue that the assurance goal will be met.

- *Cost.* The system development choice must be cost-effective in a complete sense; that is, it must be possible to build both the system and a satisfactory assurance case within budget. If providing adequate evidence for the assurance argument would require resources beyond those available, a candidate choice must be rejected.
- *Feasibility.* The system development choice must not itself be infeasible or preclude completion of the system or a convincing system assurance case.
- *Applicable standards.* Applicable standards can: (1) preclude certain choices by definition; or (2) require certain development practices that restrict or preclude certain forms of evidence that would otherwise be required for the assurance case.
- *Non-functional requirements.* Non-functional requirements derive from stakeholder interests and often prescribe certain aspects of development or certain characteristics of the desired system. Such prescriptions limit the available system development choices and are likely to affect the assurance evidence in the same way that a standard can.

As an example of the application of these criteria, consider again the anti-lock braking system example mentioned earlier. Assume that the braking system's computations could be run on: (1) a single processor; (2) two processors whose outputs are compared; (3) three processors whose outputs will be voted on (TMR); or (4) many processors on a real-time bus, each running part of the computation.

The assurance case evidence that each choice provides would depend on the specific characteristics of the equipment chosen and the planned software development approach. If the dependability obligations of the hardware are stringent enough, options (1) and (2) must be rejected based on the dependability criterion. Option (4) would have to be rejected because of cost.

Applying these criteria can be quite involved since they depend both on each other and on decisions at other points in development. Consider, for example, the *applicable standards* criterion. If a relevant standard prescribes the use of a particular programming language, this might preclude the subsequent use of static analysis that depends on certain language features (such as strong typing) or on the existence of a formal semantic definition of the language.

3.3. Applying system development choices

Once made, a development choice is applied to the system and the assurance case updated to reflect its effect. The way in which the choice is applied to the development artifacts will depend upon the type of artifact. An architectural choice, for example, might be applied by modifying a description of the system's architecture in an architectural description language. The choice to use a particular programming language might be recorded in project standards documentation.

The assurance case extension resulting from a choice identifies the affected development artifacts and describes the contribution that these artifacts will make to the argument. In some cases, the choice will introduce new goals, obligating the developers to supply specific evidence later in the process, while in others the choice will directly support a goal with evidence from a development artifact. In section 4 we will illustrate this linking with a more concrete example.

4. An illustrative example

To illustrate the process of developing a system using ABD, we present a summary of the use of the process on a realistic application. Space considerations preclude us from describing every system development choice, and so we examine only a subset of them. We have selected a depth-first slice of the assurance argument so as to illustrate artifacts from most development phases: we illustrate the development decisions, evidence, and argument from the requirements level down to source code. Although the application is real, we have made a number of assumptions about aspects of the application that either have not been documented by the system developers or are necessary for ABD but not for the application in its present form.

The application we use for illustration is part of a research prototype for a software-based system for alerting pilots to *runway incursions* at airports. The Federal Aviation Administration (FAA) defines a runway incursion as "any occurrence at an airport involving an aircraft, vehicle, person, or object on the ground, that creates a collision hazard or results in the loss of separation with an aircraft taking off, intending to take off, landing, or intending to land." [2]. The system, known as the Runway Incursion Prevention System (RIPS) [2, 3], is being developed by Lockheed Martin on a contract from the National Aeronautics and Space Administration (NASA).

The RIPS system operates in the cockpit of an aircraft (referred to as *ownship*). It collects information about the position of that aircraft and of other aircraft and ground traffic in the vicinity, examines that information for evidence of a runway incursion involving the ownship aircraft, and alerts the pilot to such incursions via an Integrated Display System (IDS).

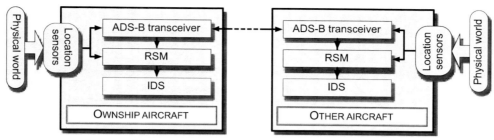

Figure 2. The given RSM architecture

Our illustrative example is based on a part of RIPS called the Runway Safety Monitor (RSM). Our work is not part of the RIPS development activity, and ABD was not used to develop the RSM. Our example is strictly for purposes of illustration. In constructing it, we have drawn upon the RSM documentation for: (1) the problem to be solved; (2) the sources of data available for the purpose of detecting incursions; and (3) the systems on board the aircraft and on the ground with which an incursion detection system might interact.

4.1. The given architecture

The RSM uses existing systems on board the aircraft including a computer, the aircraft's ground location system that provides the aircraft's position, and broadcasts on the Automatic Dependent Surveillance - Broadcast (ADS-B) link that provides the positions of other aircraft. Limitations in the basic equipment may make these data unavailable for up to several seconds. This lack of reliability is not a serious problem provided the pilot knows that RIPS is inoperative.

The decision to implement RSM in software is an architectural decision at the level of the RIPS system: the architects of RIPS decided to delegate the task of alerting the pilot to a software sub-component rather than a separate system running on its own processors.

The result of this and other decisions by the RIPS team is the RSM's given architecture, shown in Figure 2. The IDS system polls the RSM at a frequency of 1 Hz to determine whether a runway incursion involving ownship is in progress. To perform its computation, the RSM will need to know where ownship is located, and where other aircraft that might conflict are located.

4.2. The top level assurance goal

The top-level goal in Figure 3, G1, states the required functionality and dependability of the RSM. For purposes of illustration, we have assumed dependability requirements that place it in the ultra-dependable category and classify the system as safety-critical.

In this example, we assume that the RSM is required to meet the following two requirements (recall that the data sources are unreliable):

- If the quality of the supplied data is adequate, detect runway incursions involving ownship within t time units after they begin with probability greater than or equal to p_0.
- If the quality of the supplied data is inadequate, report a failure of RSM with probability greater than or equal to p_1 within u time units.

Note the inclusion in Figure 3 of the system's context in GSN. The details of the system's context are crucial to the proper refinement of the goal and the analysis associated with both the functionality and the dependability of the system.

4.3. The first system development choice

There are many candidate choices that meet the two requirements in the top-level goal. For example, the overall approach to the real-time requirements could be either sequential or concurrent, and if concurrent then either synchronous or asynchronous. The choice will be influenced by the services available from the target operating system and the anticipated verification approach amongst many other factors.

The requirement for the detection of missing or corrupt data can similarly be addressed using various architectural mechanisms. A number of different system modules could take action when data is missing, and data defects could be signaled by a data collection module by generating an event, by a time-out, or by using special coded data values. Feasibility is an important criterion in this aspect of selection because there has to be a high-level of assurance that defective data will be detected within the specified time limit.

The experience of the authors leads us to select a sequential code implementation with each software module responsible for detecting and reporting errors in the data it handles. While this choice is somewhat arbitrary, we note that in a complete application of ABD developers will balance the perceived risk of

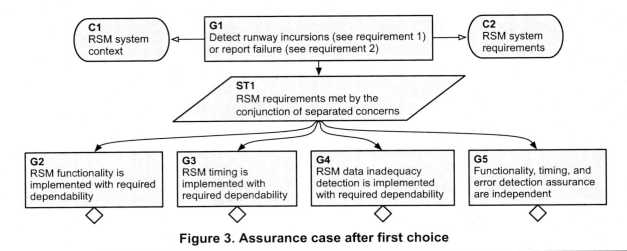

Figure 3. Assurance case after first choice

making (and thus having to redress) a poor choice against the time required to more thoroughly enumerate and evaluate alternatives.

Choosing sequential code with distributed error detection allows us to divide the top-level goal into three concerns and address each of these independently as shown in Figure 3. An important item in this fragment is goal G5. Without careful attention, developers might supply arguments for the satisfaction of goals G2, G3, and G4 that do not, together, imply the satisfaction of goal G1. If, for example, testing is used to show low probabilities that the RSM will fail to provide the required functionality (goal G2) or fail to meet its timing requirements (goal G3), then the selection of test cases will affect the way in which the probabilities are combined to justify meeting requirement 1 in goal G1. Goal G5 obliges the developer to carefully consider whether the manner in which the other goals are satisfied justifies concluding that G1 has been satisfied, and so acts as a reminder to the developer to consider an important but subtle consideration that could easily be missed if the assurance case were not used as guidance.

4.4. The second system development choice

The first choice generated four subgoals, each initially unaddressed as indicated by the diamond-shaped decoration. In a complete application of ABD all four would be addressed in an order chosen to minimize the risk of needing to readdress a choice. For purposes of illustration, we continue our example by addressing RSM failure detection (goal G4 in Figure 3).

There are many available candidate choices, including several architectural patterns, an object-oriented architecture, and functional decomposition. We selected functional decomposition because it facilitates the use of some forms of static analysis including determination of worst-case execution time. Our decomposition, recorded in architectural diagram form in Figure 4, contains the following six modules:

- the *ownship runway locator*, which determines whether ownship is presently using a runway, and, if so, builds a model of that runway;
- the *runway database*, which stores the location and necessary geometric details of all of the runways for which RSM service will be available;

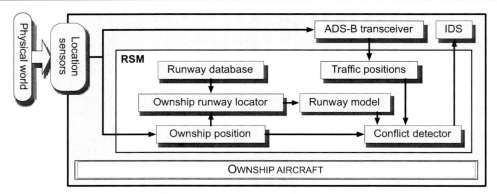

Figure 4. Functional decomposition of the RSM

- the *runway model*, which stores the geometry of the runway including the incursion zone's bounds;
- the *ownship position* component, which collects information about the position of the aircraft from the aircraft's ground location system;
- the *conflict detector*, which is invoked if the aircraft is found to be using a runway, and determines whether ownship is in conflict with any other monitored traffic within that runway's incursion zone; and
- the *traffic positions* component, which collects information about the position of other traffic within a specified region from ADS-B broadcasts.

Part of the assurance case fragment that accompanies this system development choice is shown in Figure 5. It details the failure detection responsibility allocated to each of the new components listed above and how these responsibilities, if satisfied, demonstrate the satisfaction of sub-goal G4. Note the context bubble C3, which clarifies strategy ST2 by describing the functional decomposition we have selected. This clarification has the effect of linking the assurance-case fragment shown in Figure 5 to the development artifact in which the choice was recorded.

Although not shown, the arguments for goals G2 and G3 in Figure 3 are similar to that for goal G4. The argument for goal G2 would show how responsibility for the RSM's functionality is partitioned across the system's modules, and the argument for goal G3 would show how the system meets its timing requirements by linking several forms of evidence, including evidence showing that various modules will execute within set time bounds. Functional decomposition as the system development choice for goals G2, G3, and G4 eases the task of determining worst-case execution time (WCET) for the system. WCET is not easy to establish with any architecture and can be essentially impossible with some modern processors. However, assurance over timing is essential, and that makes many other candidate architectural choices unacceptable.

Turning now to the other selection criteria, we ask ourselves whether, given this choice, it is likely that the system can be built within the specified budget, schedule, technology constraints, etc. Since not even the architecture is yet complete, our assessment must be speculative. Given our experience, knowledge, and the system as proposed, it seems likely that we will be able to find acceptable ways to satisfy the as-yet unaddressed subgoals, and so we accept this choice for now.

4.5. The third system development choice

The application of the assurance case fragments associated with our choice of functional decomposition has, at this point, satisfied goals G2, G3, and G4 from Figure 3, thus removing their diamond-shaped decorations. Goal G5 and the new subgoals introduced by our choice remain unsatisfied. We continue our illustration

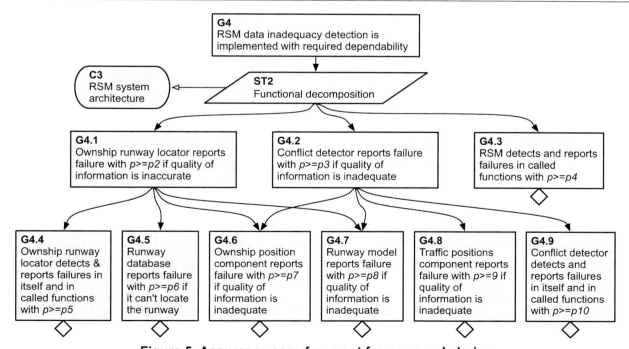

Figure 5. Assurance case fragment from second choice

353

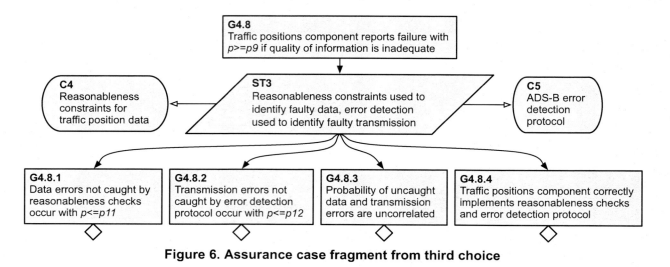

Figure 6. Assurance case fragment from third choice

by addressing subgoal G4.8. The traffic positions component must detect the cases in which the information received over ADS-B from the other aircraft is inadequate and in those cases report failure with probability at least p_9. Traffic position information could be compromised in several ways: 1) the other aircraft could report data incorrectly, 2) the data could be corrupted in transit, and 3) the data could be stale because up-to-date information was not received in time. The developer must ensure that the probabilities of these events occurring undetected, either alone or in combination, is low enough that the target probability is met.

Let us assume that the target probability is high, and that the error detection and correction mechanism used on ADS-B broadcasts is sufficient for our purposes. The design of the traffic positions component must sufficiently mask the remaining types of faults.

One way to address the threat of incorrect information being reported by other aircraft is to impose reasonableness criteria on the data. There are limits to the acceleration of aircraft, and so if the data representation of an aircraft's positions changes too quickly, we can conclude that the data are faulty and report the unavailability of traffic position information.

Alternatively, we could incorporate a redundant source of traffic position information such as radar or a camera with which to compare the ADS-B data (as is done in the actual system). Since the given architecture does not include such an additional information source, however, we have little choice but to detect faults in the information we have. Accordingly, we choose to:
- track the traffic positions we obtain from ADS-B broadcasts over time, computing the velocity and acceleration of each target aircraft;

- perform reasonableness assessment on these to detect incorrect information in the broadcast;
- check the error detection fields of each ADS-B message we use to detect corrupt messages; and
- use position estimation to address the threat of stale data.

An assessment of this choice will help us to decide whether reasonableness constraints are likely to be sufficient. Figure 6 shows the argument fragment that accompanies the choice to use reasonableness criteria. If we can satisfy subgoal G4.8.1 by showing that the probability of incorrect data not being caught by our criteria is sufficiently low, then we can make the choice and proceed; if not, we must seek a change to our previous choices or to our project's givens that would make the project tractable.

4.6. The fourth system development choice

Assuming that we find—or chose to assume, at the risk of rework or project failure if we are wrong—that it is possible to satisfy subgoal G4.8.1, we proceed by seeking ways to satisfy the remaining subgoals. One such subgoal is G4.8.4, which claims that the implementation of the traffic positions component performs the described computation.

If our architecture and design were sufficient to tolerate a small number of residual faults in the traffic positions component, we could elect to implement the algorithm in the programming language of our choice and rely upon testing to confirm that our implementation has the desired behavior. If we had elected earlier to use a safety kernel [11] in our architecture, for example, we might now be faced with such a goal. We assume to the contrary that the needed assurance

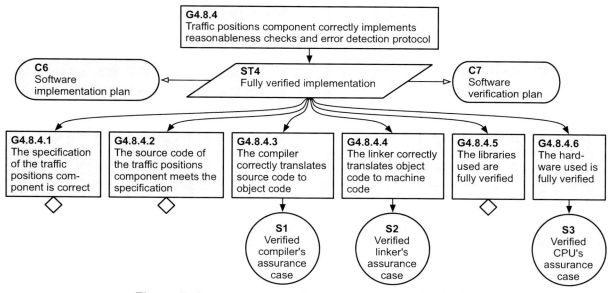

Figure 7. Assurance case fragment from fourth choice

makes testing infeasible, and so we must either seek an alternative choice or else revise an earlier choice so as to lower the target probability.

One choice that would allow us to meet this goal is to use a fully-verified implementation of the traffic position component, resulting in the assurance case fragment shown in Figure 7. If we make this choice, we must write a formal specification of the chosen algorithm, implement it, and argue that:

- the specification correctly formalizes the described computation;
- the source code we write meets the specification;
- the compiler we use correctly translates the source code into object code;
- the linker we use correctly translates the object code into machine code;
- the libraries we use (if any) are fully verified; and
- the hardware we run on correctly implements its instruction set architecture.

Some of these sub-goals can be addressed with direct evidence. The assurance case provided by the vendors of the tools we use, for example, constitute evidence in this assurance case of our claim that these tools have been fully verified.

4.7. Re-addressing a choice

At this point in our example we have chosen an architecture, selected a design for detecting and reporting errors in data from an unreliable subsystem, and chosen an implementation strategy for one submodule. We may use this strategy for other submodules with similar assurance needs, potentially saving costs by re-using the same technique. We are not compelled to do so, however: if a cheaper technique meets another module's assurance needs, we are free to use it.

Several unaddressed goals remain, and in a complete application of ABD, we would continue the process until all sub-goals had been addressed, directly or through argument, by evidence. We would then examine the assurance case for flaws in the argument, and redress these flaws. (The techniques a developer would use to validate the assurance case argument are beyond the scope of this work.)

At any point in the process, a developer may discover that a previous choice leads to an unsatisfiable goal and so requires redress. If, for example, we could find no suitable fully-verified compiler, our fourth choice would need readdressing. If no other implementation strategy could be found to address goal G4.8.4 in Figure 6, we may even have to readdress the architecture to weaken goal G4.8.4 by reducing the dependability obligation imposed on the implementation.

5. Related work

Some standards governing software development, such as DO-178B [8], offer the same prescription to all applicable systems. The ABD process instead compels the developer to assess the dependability needs of each part of a system and make system development choices accordingly; the developer can thus economize in some parts of the system while remaining assured that the system as a whole will be adequately dependable.

Other safety-critical software development work is assessed via a safety case. Some standards [7] and researchers [4] call for safety cases to be constructed early and updated often during system development and subsequent change. Continuing with this idea, ABD interleaves development and assurance case construction tightly so that the assurance case can be used to drive system development.

Problem-Oriented Software Engineering [6] aims to create software and an argument that it is fit for use. In POSE, the system requirements are documented using Problem Frames and progressively transformed, via a series of justified transformations, into an implementable specification. This is one technique that could be used to argue (as one must) that if the system meets its requirements the user will be satisfied.

6. Conclusion

Many choices must be made at each stage of system development, and these can profoundly impact the finished system's dependability. Currently, there is little guidance for making choices that give assurance that the system meets it dependability goals. If the system and its assurance case are co-developed, however, the assurance case can provide concrete dependability criteria against which to gauge potential alternatives.

In this paper, we have explained the basic principles of Assurance Based Development and shown how this development paradigm can be used to provide assurance case goals for system development choices. We have presented an example system and shown how its assurance case drove specific choices we made in its development by allowing us to analyze the effect of our choices on the system's dependability as we made them. While it is not possible to show that the choices we have made are optimal because of the many variables involved in development, we feel that our choices were better informed than they would have been otherwise and so are more likely to achieve our goals.

Acknowledgements

We thank David Green of Lockheed Martin for extensive help in understanding the RSM and its associated artifacts. We are very grateful to NASA Langley Research Center for suggesting the use of the system for study. We appreciate William Greenwell's assistance with the assurance case material presented here. This work was sponsored in part by NSF grant CCR-0205447 and in part by NASA grant NAG1-02103.

References

[1] Bishop, P. and R. Bloomfield. "A Methodology for Safety Case Development." <http://www.adelard.co.uk/resources/papers/index.htm>

[2] Green, D. F. "Runway Safety Monitor Algorithm for Runway Incursion Detection and Alerting." Technical report NASA CR-2002-211416. January 2002.

[3] Green, D. F. "Runway Safety Monitor Algorithm for Single and Crossing Runway Incursion Detection and Alerting." Technical report NASA CR-2006-214275. February 2006.

[4] Kelly, T. P. "A Systematic Approach to Safety Case Management." Proc. of SAE 2004 World Congress, Detroit, MI, March 2004.

[5] Kelly, T., and J. McDermid. "Safety Case Patterns – Reusing Successful Arguments." Proc. of IEE Colloquium on Understanding Patterns and Their Application to System Engineering, London, April 1998.

[6] Mannering, D., J. G. Hall, and L. Rapanotti. "Relating Safety Requirement and System Design through Problem Oriented Software Engineering." Technical report 2006/11, Open University, September 2006.

[7] MoD, "00-56 Safety Management Requirements for Defence Systems," U.K. Ministry of Defence, Defence Standard, Issue 3, December 2004.

[8] RTCA. "Software Considerations in Airborne Systems and Equipment Certification," document RTCA/DO-178B. Washington, DC: RTCA, December 1992.

[9] Strunk, E. and J. Knight. "The Essential Synthesis of Problem Frames and Assurance Cases." Proc. of 2nd International Workshop on Applications and Advances in Problem Frames, co-located with 29th International Conference on Software Engineering, Shanghai, May 2006.

[10] Weaver, R. A. and T. P. Kelly. "The Goal Structuring Notation - A Safety Argument Notation." Proc. of Dependable Systems and Networks 2004 Workshop on Assurance Cases, July 2004.

[11] Wika, K.G. and J.C. Knight. "On the Enforcement of Software Safety Policies." Proc. of 10th Annual IEEE Conference on Computer Assurance (COMPASS '95), Gaithersburg, MD, June 1995.

Session 6B:
Security Threats
and Novel Detection

Multiprocessors May Reduce System Dependability under File-based Race Condition Attacks

Jinpeng Wei and Calton Pu
Georgia Institute of Technology
{weijp,calton}@cc.gatech.edu

Abstract

Attacks exploiting race conditions have been considered rare and "low risk". However, the increasing popularity of multiprocessors has changed this situation: instead of waiting for the victim process to be suspended to carry out an attack, the attacker can now run on a dedicated processor and actively seek attack opportunities. This change from fortuitous encountering to active exploiting may greatly increase the success probability of race condition attacks. This point is exemplified by studying the TOCTTOU (Time-of-Check-to-Time-of-Use) race condition attacks in this paper. We first propose a probabilistic model for predicting TOCTTOU attack success rate on both uniprocessors and multiprocessors. Then we confirm the applicability of this model by carrying out TOCTTOU attacks against two widely used utility programs: vi and gedit. The success probability of attacking vi increases from low single digit percentage on a uniprocessor to almost 100% on a multiprocessor. Similarly, the success rate of attacking gedit jumps from almost zero to 83%. These case studies suggest that our model captures the sharply increased risks, and hence the decreased dependability of our systems, represented by race condition attacks such as TOCTTOU on the next generation multiprocessors.

Keywords: Probabilistic Modeling, Race Condition

1. Introduction

Emerging multiprocessors such as SMP (Symmetric Multiprocessing) with multi-core processors expected to dominate the next generation PC and server markets. These multiprocessors offer significant performance and power consumption advantages, making them potentially more useful for secure systems. For example, additional processors can be dedicated to computationally intensive deep packet inspection in IDS, IPS (Intrusion Detection and Prevention), and anti-virus scanners [11]. However, the use of the additional processing power by attackers to exploit known or new vulnerabilities has received less attention. This paper demonstrates that a concrete class of exploits (file-based race condition called TOCTTOU) will see the success rate of attacks increase sharply from negligible to almost certainty.

TOCTTOU (Time-of-Check-to-Time-of-Use) is a security problem known for more than 30 years [1][2]. An illustrative example is *sendmail*, which used to check for a specific attribute of a mailbox file (e.g., it is not a symbolic link) before appending new messages. However, the checking and appending file system operations are not executed in an atomic transaction. Consequently, if an attacker (the mailbox owner) is able to replace his/her mailbox file with a symbolic link to /etc/passwd between the checking and appending steps by *sendmail*, then *sendmail* may be tricked into appending emails to /etc/passwd (assuming that *sendmail* runs as setuid root). If successful, an attack message containing a syntactically correct /etc/passwd entry would give the attacker root access. TOCTTOU vulnerabilities are widespread and cause serious consequences [24].

The check and use file system calls in the victim process of a TOCTTOU vulnerability are called *TOCTTOU pairs* [18][24]. The time between the two file system calls of a TOCTTOU pair is the *window of vulnerability* (or critical section) of the TOCTTOU vulnerability. To succeed, an attacker process must complete the attack steps within the window of vulnerability of the victim process. The success rate of a TOCTTOU attack thus depends on the scheduling events surrounding and during the window of vulnerability, making it a race condition between the victim and attacker processes. Some attempts have been made to slow down the victim and increase the probability of success, examples include: (1) using slow storage devices (e.g. floppy disks); (2) using extremely long pathnames (e.g. file system mazes [3]); (3) using large files. This paper studies one method to make the attacker faster and reduce scheduling uncertainty by exploiting additional CPU resources available in multiprocessors.

This paper offers two technical contributions. The first is a probabilistic model for predicting TOCTTOU attack success rate, both for uniprocessors and multiprocessors. By comparing their different capabilities, the model shows that multiprocessors give an attacker more opportunities in winning the race. The second contribution is an experimental study and detailed event analysis of multiprocessor attacks on two recently found TOCTTOU vulnerabilities against popular applications: *vi* and *gedit*. Both attacks have very low success rate on uniprocessors and almost certain success on a multiprocessor (nearly 100% for *vi* and up to 83% for *gedit*). The *gedit* experiments demonstrate that when the vulnerability window is extremely small, the race condition moves to a lower level and the implementation of the attacker program becomes crucial. These analyses give a better understanding of the TOCTTOU attacks on multiprocessors. The main conclusion of the paper is the confirmation of sharply increased risks represented by TOCTTOU attacks.

The rest of this paper is organized as follows. Section 2 briefly introduces the TOCTTOU errors with *vi* and *gedit* which are the target of the attacks discussed in this paper. Section 3 introduces a probabilistic model for TOCTTOU attack success rate. Section 4 summarizes our previous TOCTTOU attack experiments on uniprocessors as a baseline for comparison. Section 5 describes TOCTTOU attacks against *vi* on a SMP. Section 6 discusses TOCTTOU attacks against *gedit* on both a SMP and a multi-core. Section 7 describes an implementation technique that leverages parallelism opportunities provided by multi-cores to significantly speedup the attack program. Section 8 summaries the related work and Section 9 concludes the paper.

2. Background: TOCTTOU Vulnerabilities in Unix-Style File Systems

Recently, several new TOCTTOU vulnerabilities have been found in often-used utility programs such as vi, rpm, emacs and gedit [24]. In this section, we describe the TOCTTOU vulnerabilities with vi and gedit, which are the target of attacks presented in this paper. Each vulnerability is associated with a TOCTTOU pair (e.g., <open, chown>), where the first (check) call is used to establish some invariant about a file object (e.g. the file exists), and the second (use) call is an operation on that same file assuming that the invariant is still valid.

```
while ((fd = mch_open((char *)wfname, …)
……
chown((char*)wfname, st_old.st_uid, st_old.st_gid);
```

Figure 1: *vi* 6.1 vulnerability (fileio.c)

```
1  while (!finish){
2    if (stat(wfname, &stbuf) == 0){
3      if ((stbuf.st_uid == 0) && (stbuf.st_gid == 0))
4      {
5        unlink(wfname);
6        symlink("/etc/passwd", wfname);
7        finish = 1;
8      }
9    }
10 }
```

Figure 2: A program to attack *vi*

2.1. The *vi* Vulnerability and Attack Scheme

The Unix "visual editor" *vi* is a widely used text editor in many UNIX-style environments. For example, Red Hat Linux distribution includes *vi* 6.1. We found that if *vi* is run by root to edit a file owned by a normal user, then the normal user may become the owner of sensitive files such as /etc/passwd. The problem can be summarized as follows. When *vi* saves the file (*wfname*) being edited, it first renames the original file to a backup, then creates a new file under the original name (*wfname* in Figure 1). The new file is closed after all the content in the edit buffer has been written to it. Because this new file is created by root (*vi* runs as root), its initial user is set to root, so *vi* needs to change its owner back to the original user (the normal user). This forms a <**open, chown**> window of vulnerability every time *vi* saves the file (Figure 1). During this window, if the normal user (also the attacker) could replace *wfname* with a symbolic link to /etc/passwd, *vi* can be tricked into changing the owner of /etc/passwd to the normal user. A typical attack of this vulnerability is to constantly check the ownership of file *wfname*, and replace *wfname* when its owner becomes root (Figure 2).

2.2. The *gedit* Vulnerability and Attack Scheme

gedit [10] is a text editor for the GNOME desktop environment. We find that *gedit* 2.8.3 (the current distribution in Debian and Redhat Linux) has a <**rename, chown**> TOCTTOU vulnerability (See Figure 3). This happens when *gedit* is run by root to edit a file (*real_filename*) owned by a normal user (also the attacker), and *gedit* saves the file. What happens is *gedit* first saves the current buffer content to a temporary scratch file (*temp_filename*), then renames the scratch file to the original file *real_filename* (after backing up the original file properly). Because the scratch file is created by root, the owner of the just saved file (*real_filename*) is root, so *gedit* needs to change its owner back to the original user. This forms a <**rename, chown**> vulnerability window. An attack (Figure 4) against this vulnerability is essentially the same as the attack against *vi* in Section 2.1.

```
if (rename (temp_filename, real_filename) != 0){
... }
chmod (real_filename, st.st_mode);
chown (real_filename, st.st_uid, st.st_gid);
```

Figure 3: gedit 2.8.3 TOCTTOU vulnerability (gedit-document.c)

```
1  while (!finish){
2    if (stat(real_filename, &stbuf) == 0){
3      if ((stbuf.st_uid == 0) && (stbuf.st_gid == 0))
4      {
5        unlink(real_filename);
6        symlink("/etc/passwd", real_filename);
7        finish = 1;
8      }
9    }
10 }
```

Figure 4: gedit attack program version 1

2.3. Discussion

From the description above, we can see that a successful attack against *vi* and *gedit* requires the following preconditions: (1) The attacker has an account on the system. (2) The system administrator edits a file belonging to the attacker. (3) The system administrator makes the mistake of logging in as 'root' instead of the attacker's uid. (4) The attacker makes a reasonable guess about which editor the administrator will use. Such a list of preconditions seems to suggest that a TOCTTOU attack can not easily succeed. However, there are many kinds of TOCTTOU vulnerabilities (e.g., 224 for Linux), and depending on how the victim program is implemented, some TOCTTOU vulnerabilities are much easier to attack than those discussed here [15]. Interested readers are referred to [18] and [24] for more information. The point of this paper is that once these preconditions are satisfied, the attacker can succeed much easier on a multiprocessor than on a uniprocessor.

3. A Probabilistic Model for Predicting TOCTTOU Attack Success Rate

3.1. The Basic General Model

A TOCTTOU attack succeeds when the attacker is able to modify the mapping from file name to disk block within the vulnerability window. In order to succeed, the attacker must first find the vulnerability window, and then change the file mapping. Therefore, our model divides the attacker program into two parts: (1) a detection part that finds the beginning of the vulnerability window, and (2) an attack part that modifies the file mapping.

One of the critical issues is whether the victim is suspended within the vulnerability window, since the suspension increases substantially the success rate. Based on the law of total probability, the attack success rate:

P(attack succeeds) = P(victim suspended) * P(attack succeeds | victim suspended) + P(victim not suspended) * P(attack succeeds | victim not suspended)

In order for the attack to succeed, the attacker program must be scheduled within the vulnerability window and the attack must finish within the vulnerability window, so

P(attack succeeds | victim suspended) = P(attack scheduled ● attack finished | victim suspended)
= P(attack scheduled | victim suspended) * P(attack finished | victim suspended)

We can derive P(attack succeeds | victim not suspended) in a similar way and get the refined probability in Equation 1.

In Equation 1, all the events are under the context of the victim vulnerability window. e.g. 'attack finished' means 'attack finished within the vulnerability window'.

P(attack succeeds) = P(victim suspended) * P(attack scheduled | victim suspended) * P(attack finished | victim suspended)
+ P(victim not suspended) * P(attack scheduled | victim not suspended) * P(attack finished | victim not suspended)

Equation 1: The probability of a successful TOCTTOU attack

3.2. Attack Success Rate on a Uniprocessor

On a uniprocessor, P(attack scheduled | victim not suspended) = 0 since it is impossible to schedule the attacker when the victim is running. Therefore on a uniprocessor the second part of Equation 1 contributes nothing to the success rate. E.g., P(attack succeeds) =

P(victim suspended) * P(attack scheduled | victim suspended) * P(attack finished | victim suspended).

Several observations can be made about P(attack succeeds) on a uniprocessor:

- P(attack succeeds) $\leq$ P(victim suspended). The probability that the victim is suspended within its vulnerability window gives an upper bound for the attack success rate. If the victim is always suspended (e.g. *rpm* in [24]), the attacker can achieve a success rate as high as 100%. In contrast, if the victim is rarely suspended (e.g. *gedit* in Section 2.2), the attack success rate can be near zero.

- P(attack scheduled | victim suspended) is the probability that the attacker process gets scheduled when the victim relinquishes CPU. This value depends on several factors such as the readiness of the attacker, the system load (if round-robin scheduling is used), or the priority of the attacker (if priority-based scheduling is used). Typically in a lightly loaded environment this value can be nearly 100% if the attacker program uses an infinite loop actively looking for the exploit opportunity.

- P(attack finished | victim suspended) is the probability that the attacker successfully modifies the file mapping while the victim is suspended. Since there is only one CPU, as long as the attack part is not interrupted, this probability can be 100%. Typically this is the case because modifying the file mapping requires very short processing time and needs not block on I/O.

Based on the above analysis, the attack success rate is mainly determined by P(victim suspended) on a uniprocessor system, and the implementation of the attack part is relatively less critical.

3.3. Attack Success Rate on Multiprocessors

On multiprocessors, the attacker can run on a different processor than the victim when the victim is running within its vulnerability window. This makes the second part of Equation 1 non-zero, i.e., P(attack scheduled | victim not suspended) > 0. This fact increases the success rate of TOCTTOU attacks on multiprocessors as compared to uniprocessors. If P(victim suspended) is relatively large, then the success rate on multiprocessors may not increase significantly. However, if P(victim suspended) is very small (approaching 0), then P(victim not suspended) approaches 1, and the gain due to the second part of P(attack succeeds) may become very significant.

Therefore for an attacker, the benefit of having multiprocessors is maximized when the victim is rarely suspended in the vulnerability window. An analysis of the second part of Equation 1 shows that:

- P(attack scheduled | victim not suspended) is similar to P(attack scheduled | victim suspended) discussed in Section 3.2. The conclusion is that it can be as high as 100%.

- P(attack finished | victim not suspended) is the probability that the attack is finished within the vulnerability window. Since the victim is running concurrently with the attacker, the result of the attack depends on the relative speed of the attacker and the victim, a more detailed analysis is needed (next Section).

3.4. Probabilistic Analysis of P(attack finished | victim not suspended)

In order to predict P(attack finished | victim not suspended) in more detail, we analyze the race condition at different levels: the first level is CPU, which is the main contention in uniprocessor attacks; the next level is file object, because the file system already has a synchronization mechanism to regulate shared accesses. In Unix-style file systems, the modifications to an inode are synchronized by a semaphore. Since the operations of the victim and the attacker on the shared file modify the same inode, they both need to acquire the same semaphore. In this case, the race is reduced to the competition for the semaphore and we can model the success rate of the attack in the following way.

In this model, we assume that the attacker runs in a tight loop (the detection part), waiting for the vulnerability window of the victim to appear. Let D be the time consumed by each iteration of detection part, and let t_1 be the earliest start time for a successful detection and t_2 be the latest start time for a successful detection followed by a successful attack (e.g. the attacker acquires the semaphore first). t_1 and t_2 are determined by the victim process. Some observations can be made as follow (Figure 5):

A successful attack starts with a successful detection as its precondition. This successful detection may start as early as t_1 (Figure 5, case (a)), and as late as $t_1 + D$ (Figure 5, case (f)). Then the interval $[t_1, t_1 + D)$ is our sample space. Out of this interval $[t_1, t_1 + D)$, if the detection is started before t_2, the attack succeeds (Figure 5, cases (a) through (c)); otherwise the attack fails (Figure 5, cases (d) through (f), because the attack is launched too late). Let's

361

assume a uniform distribution for the start time of the detection part, the success rate is thus $\frac{t_2 - t_1}{D}$.

In Figure 5 we assume that $t_2 \in [t_1, t_1 + D)$. Two other cases are:

- If $t_2 < t_1$, then the success rate is 0;

- If $t_2 \geq t_1 + D$, then the success rate is 1.

Let $L = t_2 - t_1$, and we get:

$$\text{The success rate} = \begin{cases} 0, & if\ (L < 0) \\ L/D, & if\ (0 \leq L < D) \\ 1, & if\ (L \geq D) \end{cases} \quad (1)$$

In formula (1), L measures the laxity of the successful attacks, which is a characterization of the victim: the larger L, the more vulnerable the victim. D is a characterization of the detection part of the attacker: the smaller D, the faster the attacker, and the higher success rate. So L/D gives a very useful measurement of the relative speed of the victim and the attacker.

It should be noted that L and D in formula (1) are not strictly constant, because the executions of the victim as well as the attacker are interleaved with other events (e.g. kernel timers) in the system. That is, the running environment imposes variance on these parameters. So formula (1) only offers a statistical guidance about the attack success rate.

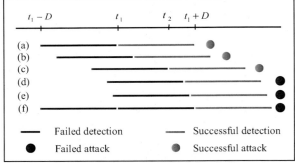

Figure 5: Different attack scheduling on a multiprocessor

4. Baseline Measurements of TOCTTOU Attacks on Uniprocessors

For comparison purposes, in this section we summarize the measured success rates of *vi* and *gedit* TOCTTOU attacks on uniprocessors from [24].

4.1. *vi* Attack Experiments on Uniprocessors

Since the *vi* vulnerability window includes the writing of a whole file, the size of the window naturally depends on the file size. The measured success rates for file sizes ranging from 20KB to 10MB are the following:

- When the file size is small (from 100KB to 1MB), there is a rough correlation between attack success rate and file size, as shown in Figure 6. However, the correlation disappears for larger file sizes (e.g., between 2MB to 3MB), showing that file size alone does not determine the success rate completely.

- Besides file size, we studied other factors (e.g., I/O operation, CPU slicing, and preemption by higher priority kernel threads) that corroborate the non-deterministic nature of TOCTTOU attacks on a uniprocessor [24].

From Figure 6 we can see that for normal file sizes (Using *vi* to edit a 2MB text file is considered rare in real life), the success rate can be as low as 1.5% and as high as 18%. Furthermore, when the file size approaches 0, the success rate also approaches 0.

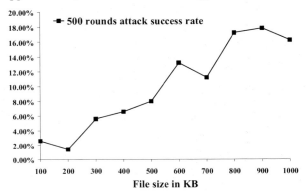

Figure 6: Success rate of attacking vi (small files) on a uniprocessor

4.2. *gedit* Attack Experiment on Uniprocessors

The experiments in which a TOCTTOU attack was carried out against the *gedit* vulnerability saw no successes. This is because the *gedit* vulnerability window (Figure 3) does not include the writing of the new file as in *vi*, so it is much shorter and bears no relationship to the file size. These factors reduced the success rate for *gedit* attacks to essentially zero on a uniprocessor.

5. vi Attack Experiments on SMP

We repeated the *vi* attack experiments described in Section 4.1 on a SMP machine (2 Intel Xeon 1.7GHz CPUs, 512MB main memory, and 18.2GB SCSI disk with ext3 file system).

First we tried different file sizes ranging from 20KB to 1MB with a stepping size of 20KB, and observed the success rate of 100% for all file sizes. This confirms the probabilistic predictions in Section 3.3 and shows that a multiprocessor greatly increases the attacker's chance of success compared to a uniprocessor (Figure 6 in Section 4.1). We did a detailed event analysis to confirm the attacker and victim processes ran on separate CPUs during the vulnerability window. We also eliminated the possibility that the attack success is due to the victim being blocked on I/O operations (which would have made the attack easier). Consequently, we conclude that the attack success is due to the length of *vi* vulnerability window being much larger than the time it takes the attacker to finish the attack steps (file name redirection).

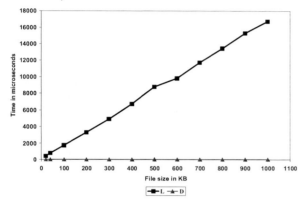

Figure 7: The L and D values for vi SMP attack experiments

Figure 7 shows the L and D values (Section 3.4) for the *vi* attack experiments that we conducted on the SMP. We can see that L >> D when the file is large (e.g.1MB); and the difference (L – D) decreases as the file size decreases. But (L – D) is always positive, even when the file size becomes very small. Therefore we can say with almost certainty that for *vi* attack experiments, L > D. By formula (1) we know that the success rate of *vi* attacks is almost 100% all the time.

One thing to notice from Figure 7 is that as the file size approaches 0, the difference (L – D) also approaches 0. Is it possible that L becomes smaller than D? Then according to formula (1) the attack success rate will be smaller than 100%.

To see this we run the experiment again with the smallest files (only 1 byte each). And the success rate we get is around 96%. Again we did a detailed event analysis of this experiment. We measure the average L and D values and put them in Table 1. We can see that although L > D in these attacks, they have become very close. If we consider the fact that the values for L and D are not strictly constant due to the environmental influence, we realize that whether L > D all the time becomes questionable when they are close enough

(When L >> D the inaccuracy introduced by the environment does not change the relationship). This helps to explain why the success rate can not be 100% when the file contains only 1 byte.

Another point is that so far we actually treat P(attack finished | victim not suspended) in Section 3.4 as the sole basis for predicting the success rate, which is not always accurate (Equation 1). The justification is that when the *vi* vulnerability window is large enough, the effect of other factors in Equation 1 is negligible. For example, P(attack scheduled | victim not suspended) < 100% in general which means that the attacker may not be scheduled during sometime in the vulnerability window. However, if the vulnerability window is very large, the attacker is still within it when he/she is scheduled eventually. That is, the temporary suspension does not affect the result of the attack. However, when the vulnerability window becomes small enough (e.g. L and D become close enough), the suspension may cause the attacker to miss the vulnerability window. In such a case the attack fails, thus the suspension changes the attack result.

In several of the failed 1-byte *vi* experiments, we find that some other processes prevents the attacker from being scheduled on another CPU during the *vi* vulnerability window.

This analysis tells us that although using a multiprocessor can greatly increase the attack's chance of success, the success is still not guaranteed: the attack is still influenced by other environmental factors such as kernel activities and system load. However, 96% is more than enough for an attacker.

Table 1: The average L and D values (in microseconds) for *vi* SMP attack experiments (file size = 1 byte)

	Average	Stdev
L	61.6	3.78
D	41.1	2.73

6. *gedit* Attack Experiments on Multiprocessors

6.1. *gedit* SMP Attack Event Analysis

As mentioned in Section 4.2, our attack experiments against *gedit* on uniprocessors saw no successes. However, when we try this attack on a SMP (the same machine as in Section 5), we get roughly 83%, a surprisingly high success rate. A detailed event analysis is thus conducted to understand this result.

For the *gedit* attack, we have observed that if the attacker's **unlink** is invoked before *gedit*'s **chmod** (Figure 3 and Figure 4), then attack succeeds. This is because these two system calls compete for the same semaphore, so if **unlink** wins, **chmod** as well as the following **chown** will be delayed. As a result the attacker's **unlink** and **symlink** can have enough time to finish before *gedit*'s **chown**. On the other hand, if **unlink** loses, **unlink** and the following **symlink** of the attacker will be delayed, so the attack will fail. So there is an interesting cascading effect in *gedit* attack experiment. Therefore, for *gedit* attacks, t_1 is somewhere within the execution of **rename** (the attacker does not need to wait until the end of **rename** to see that *real_filename* has been created), D is the interval between the start of **stat** and the start of **unlink**. Let t_3 be the start of **chmod**, then $t_2 = t_3 - D$, and $L = t_2 - t_1 = t_3 - D - t_1$. We experimentally get the L and D values as in Table 2.

Table 2: L and D values for *gedit* attacks on a SMP (in microseconds)

	Average	Stdev
L	11.6	3.89
D	32.7	2.83

The calculation of L here is not accurate because the estimation of t_1 is not accurate. Currently t_1 is established as the earliest observed start time of **stat** which indicates a vulnerability window. So it may not be optimal. An earlier (thus smaller) t_1 will result in a larger L. So the success rate indicated by Table 2 (35%) may be overly conservative compared to the observed success rate.

An important contributing factor to L is the computation time between the end of **rename** and the start of **chmod**. The average length of this computation is 43 microseconds. As we will see in Section 6.2, this factor is very important for the high success rate of *gedit* attack on the SMP.

There is another contributing factor. Usually when *gedit*'s **chmod** is blocked, the Linux kernel will try to schedule something else to run (e.g. internal kernel events such as soft IRQs, kernel timers and tasklets), which further lengthens **gedit** vulnerability window (but this contributes just a little to the delay compared with that due to the semaphore).

6.2. *gedit* Multicore Attack Experiment

6.2.1. Attack one

We repeat the *gedit* attack (Figure 4) on a multi-core (Dell Precision 380 with 2 Intel Pentium D 3.2 GHz dual-core and Hyper-Threading CPUs, 4GB main memory, and 80GB SCSI disk with ext3 file system). We get very different result: now we see almost no success in the same attack experiment. The main

change in the situation is that the victim spends much less time between **rename** and **chmod** (3 microseconds vs. 43 microseconds), so **chmod** happens before **unlink** of the attacker, but in the SMP experiment (Section 6.1) situation is the opposite.

Figure 8 shows the important system events during one failed attack on the multi-core. The upper bar corresponds to the execution of *gedit* (**rename, chmod, chown**) and the lower bar corresponds to that of the attacker (**stat, unlink, symlink**). Notice that the gap (the computation) between **rename** and **chmod** of *gedit* is only 3 microseconds, but the gap between **stat** and **unlink** of the attacker is 17 microseconds. It is because of this relatively larger gap that the attacker's **unlink** is called later than the victim's **chmod**. Actually we can see that **unlink** is called later than **chown** and as a result **unlink** has to wait on the semaphore during its execution. The 17 microsecond gap of the attacker includes 11 microseconds of computation and 6 microseconds of system trap processing (page fault). Speaking in terms of D, these 17 microseconds are counted so D is around 22. On the other hand L is around $3 - D = -19$, so according to formula (1) the attack success rate is probably 0. Putting this in another way, the victim is now much faster than the attacker, so it is very difficult for the attacker to win the race.

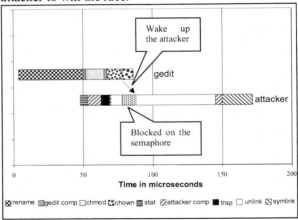

Figure 8: Failed *gedit* attack (program 1) on a multi-core

6.2.2. Attack Two

We think that the 17 microsecond gap in Figure 8 is mainly responsible for the low success rate. If we could reduce the length of this gap then the situation may change. A source code analysis tells us that before the vulnerability window the true branch of statement 3 in Figure 4 (statements 5 to 7) is never taken. Once the vulnerability window starts, the true branch of statement 3 is taken, and then statement 5 (**unlink**) is about to be executed. Right at this point the attacker program encounters a trap (page fault). We figure out that this effect is due to the memory management for shared libraries in Linux. Specifically, in Linux all system calls are through *libc*, which is a dynamic library shared among user-level applications. To save physical memory, Linux kernel keeps only one copy of *libc* in physical memory, and its virtual memory mechanism maps the pages of this copy to the address space of an application on demand. For example, the physical page containing the wrapper for **unlink** is mapped into an application's address space when this application first invokes **unlink**. This mapping is preceded by a trap (page fault) and the corresponding handler routine carries out the mapping. This is exactly what happens in Figure 4, where **unlink** is first invoked when the true branch of statement 3 is taken. As a consequence, if we intentionally invoke **unlink** (and **symlink** although it seems to be on the same page as **unlink**) before the true branch of statement 3 is taken, we may remove the trap (page fault).

```
1   while (!finish){ /* argv[1] holds real_filename */
2     if (stat(argv[1], &stbuf) == 0){
3       if ((stbuf.st_uid == 0) && (stbuf.st_gid == 0))
4       {
5         fname = argv[1];
6         finish = 1;
7       }
8       else
9         fname = dummy;
10
11      unlink(fname);
12      symlink("/etc/passwd", fname);
13    }//if stat(argv[1] ..
14  }//while
```

Figure 9: *gedit* attack program version 2

So we re-implement the attacker program as shown in Figure 9. Now **unlink** and **symlink** are called no matter the vulnerability window appears or not. The only trick is to switch in the correct file name when it does appear.

Then we perform the *gedit* attack experiment again using the program in Figure 9. And we begin to see many successes!

We plot the important system events during one successful *gedit* attack in Figure 10, similar to Figure 8. We can see that now the gap between **stat** and **unlink** of the attacker has decreased to 2 microseconds: the trap has disappeared. On the other hand, the gap between **rename** and **chmod** of *gedit* is 2 microseconds. So the attacker has a very narrow chance of winning the race. In this particular case, the attacker wins because his/her **stat** starts well before the end of **rename**, so he/she identifies the vulnerability window at the first moment, and invokes **unlink** ahead

of **chmod**. Has the attacker been 2 microseconds later, the attack would fail.

Notice that during this attack the running time of **stat** has been lengthened to 26 microseconds (typically it needs 4 microseconds), probably due to some other more complicated race condition (For example the contention for directory entries along the path name). We are not quite clear about the reason but this does not change the applicability of formula (1) because now we have a much earlier t_1 (27 microseconds into **rename**), which makes a L value of at least 1 microseconds.

This experience tells us that on multiprocessors the implementation of the attacker program can be very critical in determining the attack success rate, especially when the vulnerability window is very narrow.

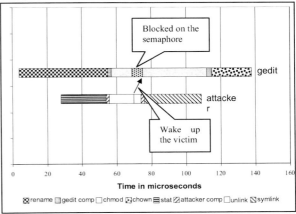

Figure 10: Successful *gedit* attack (program 2) on a multi-core

7. Pipelining Attacker Program

The multi-core *gedit* experiment highlights the importance of the implementation of the attacker program. Concretely, we found that among the three steps of the attack (**stat, unlink, symlink**), **unlink** is the most time-consuming. A closer look into the file system source code shows that actually **symlink** needs not wait on the completion of **unlink**. Instead **symlink** can begin once the inode has been detached from the directory by **unlink**, which happens relatively early. (The main part of **unlink** is spent physically truncating the file.) This observation shows that on a multiprocessor, the attacker can distribute its attack steps to multiple CPUs to speed up the attack part and increase its success rate.

To confirm this hypothesis, we implemented a multithreaded *gedit* attack program with two threads: the first thread carries out the **stat, unlink** steps and the second thread carries out the **symlink** step asynchronously. Figure 11 shows the effect of parallelizing the attack program for three different file sizes. For each file size (e.g. 500KB), there are three bars: the first two bars correspond to the execution of the two threads in a parallelized attack program, and the third bar corresponds to the execution of the normal sequential attack program. In the parallelized attack, **symlink** can finish (and so does the attack) well before the end of **unlink.** This is in contrast to the sequential attack, where **symlink** has to wait until **unlink** finishes. The comparison between the end times of **symlink** shows that leveraging on the parallelism provided by a multiprocessor can greatly reduce the amount of time needed for a successful attack. This is especially important when the vulnerability window is very narrow so the attacker needs to be very fast. This experiment shows one feasible way of doing it.

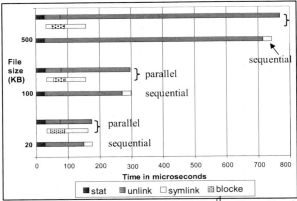

Figure 11: The effect of parallelizing the attack program

8. Related Work

TOCTTOU is one example of race condition problem. In general, every shared resource has the potential for such problems [23]. Percival [17] shows that shared access to memory caches in Hyper-Threading technology allows a malicious thread to steal RSA keys. Similar attacks have also been reported on AES [16]. While carrying out such attacks do not rely on multiprocessors, it would be interesting to see if they become easier on multiprocessors.

Timing attacks have long been used to infer secret keys in cryptosystems [4][13][21]. This kind of attacks share a common attribute with TOCTTOU attacks - both try to infer something about the victim. The difference between them is that the former only read (steal) information from the victim to violate its *confidentiality* but the latter modify the information used by the victim to violate its *integrity*.

TOCTTOU vulnerabilities can be detected in two ways: static analysis or dynamic analysis. The first approach analyzes the application source code to find TOCTTOU pairs. One such tool is MOPS [5] which uses model checking and is able to find 41 TOCTTOU bugs in an entire Linux distribution [20]. Other potentially useful techniques include compiler extensions [8][9]. The main difficulty with these static tools is high false positive rate. The second approach to detect TOCTTOU vulnerabilities is dynamic monitoring and analysis. These tools can be further classified into dynamic online detection tools such as [14] and [19] and post mortem analysis tools such as [12] and [24]. Compared to static analysis, dynamic analysis has lower false positive rate, but it suffers from false negatives because the search space is incomplete.

The high success rate of exploiting TOCTTOU vulnerabilities calls for effective defense against such attacks. Various technical remedies have been suggested, including setting proper file/directory permissions, randomizing file names, replacing mktemp() with mkstemp(), and using a strict umask to protect temporary directories. However, none of these fixes can be considered a comprehensive solution for TOCTTOU vulnerabilities.

There have been specialized mechanisms such as RaceGuard [6] and a probabilistic approach [7] which protect particular TOCTTOU pairs. Pseudo-transaction [22] is a more generic mechanism to protect some classes of TOCTTOU vulnerabilities. We have proposed a complete defense against TOCTTOU attacks called EDGI (Event Driven Guarding if Invariants) [18]. The details of EDGI are out of the scope of this paper.

9. Conclusion

TOCTTOU (Time-of-Check-to-Time-of-Use) is a file-based race condition that can cause serious consequences. However, traditionally TOCTTOU vulnerabilities have been considered "low risk" because the success rate of exploits appears to be low and results non-deterministic. This paper shows that in multiprocessor environments, the uncertainty due to scheduling is greatly reduced for an attacker sitting on a dedicated CPU; as a result some TOCTTOU attacks can have very high success rates. Thus TOCTTOU attacks on multiprocessors are practical security threats.

The first contribution of this paper is a probabilistic model for TOCTTOU attack success rate. It predicts the probability of success of a TOCTTOU attack. It provides a basic guideline for modeling TOCTTOU attacks and performing experiments, showing higher success rates on a multiprocessor compared to a uniprocessor. This model can be applied to many race condition attacks, not just TOCTTOU.

The second contribution of this paper is a set of attack experiments against two concrete and well known applications: *vi* and *gedit*. The *vi* experiments show that even for the smallest files involved in the vulnerability window, the attacker can achieve nearly 100% success rate on a multiprocessor, compared to low single digit percentages on uniprocessors. The *gedit* experiments demonstrate that when the vulnerability window is extremely small, the race moves to a lower level and the implementation of the attacker program becomes very important. The *gedit* experiments show a success rate of up to 83% compared to essentially zero on uniprocessors. These experiments corroborate our probabilistic model.

Our main conclusion is that an attacker can exploit the parallelism provided by multiprocessors to achieve more effective and more efficient attacks. More generally, our model and experiments show that multiprocessors can potentially reduce overall system dependability, so we should re-evaluate the risks of known vulnerabilities and effectiveness of security mechanisms in multiprocessor environments.

10. Acknowledgement

This work was partially supported by NSF/CISE IIS and CNS divisions through grants CCR-0121643, IDM-0242397 and ITR-0219902. We also thank the anonymous reviewers for their insightful comments.

11. References

[1] R. P. Abbott, J.S. Chin, J.E. Donnelley, W.L. Konigsford, S. Tokubo, and D.A. Webb. Security Analysis and Enhancements of Computer Operating Systems. NBSIR 76-1041, Institute of Computer Sciences and Technology, National Bureau of Standards, April 1976.

[2] Matt Bishop and Michael Dilger. Checking for Race Conditions in File Accesses. Computing Systems, 9(2):131–152, Spring 1996.

[3] N. Borisov, R. Johnson, N. Sastry, and D. Wagner. Fixing Races for Fun and Profit: How to Abuse atime. USENIX Security Symposium, 2005.

[4] David Brumley and Dan Boneh. Remote Timing Attacks Are Practical. USENIX Security Symposium, 2003.

[5] Hao Chen, David Wagner. MOPS: an Infrastructure for Examining Security Properties of Software. In Proceedings of the 9th ACM Conference on Computer and Communications Security (CCS), November 2002.

[6] Crispin Cowan, Steve Beattie, Chris Wright, and Greg Kroah-Hartman. RaceGuard: Kernel Protection From Temporary File Race Vulnerabilities. USENIX Security Symposium, 2001.

[7] Drew Dean and Alan J. Hu. Fixing Races for Fun and Profit: How to use access(2). USENIX Security Symposium, 2004.

[8] Dawson Engler, Benjamin Chelf, Andy Chou, and Seth Hallem. Checking System Rules Using System-Specific, Programmer-Written Compiler Extensions. Operating Systems Design and Implementation (OSDI), 2000.

[9] Dawson Engler, Ken Ashcraft. RacerX: Effective, Static Detection of Race Conditions and Deadlocks. ACM Symposium on Operating Systems Principles, 2003.

[10] http://www.gnome.org/projects/gedit/

[11] Amer Haider. Multi-Core Microprocessor Architecture for Network Services and Applications. http://www.commsdesign.com/design_corner/showArticle.jhtml?articleID=57703590

[12] Calvin Ko, George Fink, Karl Levitt. Automated Detection of Vulnerabilities in Privileged Programs by Execution Monitoring. Proceedings of the 10th Annual Computer Security Applications Conference, page 134-144.

[13] P. Kocher. Cryptanalysis of Diffie-Hellman, RSA, DSS, and other cryptosystems using timing attacks. In Advances in cryptology, CRYPTO'95, pages 171–183, 1995.

[14] K. Lhee and S. J. Chapin, Detection of File-Based Race Conditions, Intl. Journal of Information Security, 2005.

[15] http://xforce.iss.net/xforce/xfdb/8652

[16] Dag Arne Osvik, Adi Shamir, Eran Tromer. Cache Attacks and Countermeasures: the Case of AES. Proceedings of RSA Conference 2006, Cryptographer's Track (CT-RSA).

[17] Colin Percival. Cache Missing for Fun and Profit. BSDCan 2005.

[18] Calton Pu, Jinpeng Wei. A Methodical Defense against TOCTTOU Attacks: The EDGI Approach. International Symposium on Secure Software Engineering (ISSSE '06).

[19] Stefan Savage, Michael Burrows, Greg Nelson, Patrick Sobalvarro, and Thomas Anderson. Eraser: A Dynamic Data Race Detector for Multithreaded Programs. ACM Transactions on Computer Systems, Vol. 15, No. 4, November 1997, Pages 391–411.

[20] Benjamin Schwarz, Hao Chen, David Wagner, Geoff Morrison, Jacob West, Jeremy Lin, and Wei Tu. Model Checking An Entire Linux Distribution for Security Violations. Annual Computer Security Applications Conference, December 6, 2005.

[21] Dawn Song, David Wagner, Xuqing Tian. Timing Analysis of Keystrokes and Timing Attacks on SSH. USENIX Security Symposium, 2001.

[22] Eugene Tsyrklevich and Bennet Yee. Dynamic detection and prevention of race conditions in file accesses. USENIX Security Symposium, 2003.

[23] Jerome H. Saltzer and Michael D. Schroeder. The Protection of Information in Computer Systems. Proceedings of the IEEE, 63(9): 1278-1308, September 1975.

[24] Jinpeng Wei, Calton Pu. TOCTTOU Vulnerabilities in UNIX-Style File Systems: An Anatomical Study. In Proceedings of the 4th USENIX Conference on File and Storage Technologies (FAST '05), San Francisco, CA, December 2005.

Understanding Resiliency of Internet Topology Against Prefix Hijack Attacks [*]

Mohit Lad [†]　　　Ricardo Oliveira [*]　　　Beichuan Zhang [‡]　　　Lixia Zhang [*]

Abstract

A prefix hijack attack involves an attacker announcing victim networks' IP prefixes into the global routing system. As a result, data traffic from portions of the Internet can be diverted to attacker networks. Prefix hijack attacks are a serious security threat in the Internet and it is important to understand the factors that affect the resiliency of victim networks against these attacks. In this paper, we conducted a systematic study to gauge the effectiveness of prefix hijacks launched at different locations in the Internet topology. Our study shows that direct customers of multiple tier-1 networks are the most resilient, even more than the tier-1 networks themselves. Conversely, if these customer networks are used to launch prefix hijacks, they would also be the most effective launching pads for attacks. We verified our results through case studies using real prefix hijack incidents that had occurred in the Internet.

1 Introduction

On January 22, 2006, a network (AS-27506) wrongly announced the IP prefix 65.173.134.0/24 representing an address block of 2^{24} IP addresses, into the global routing system. This prefix belonged to another network (AS-19758) and because routers do not have a means to accurately verify the legitimate origin of each prefix, they accepted announcements from both the true origin (AS-19758) and the false one (AS-27506), and selected one of them based on the local routing policies and other criteria. As a result, some networks sent for data traffic destined to 65.173.134.0/24, to AS-27506 instead of the true owner. This is a typical incident of a prefix hijack, where a network announces an address space it does not own and *hijacks* traffic destined to the true owner.

Prefix hijacking is a serious security threat in the Internet. Prefix hijacks can potentially be launched from any part of the Internet and can target any prefix belonging to any network. A hijack attack has a large impact if the majority of routers choose the path leading to the false origin. Conversely, if the majority of routers choose the path leading to the true origin, the network of the prefix owner is considered to be resilient against prefix hijack attacks. Although there have been several results on preventing prefix hijacks (e.g., [6][10]) and monitoring potential prefix hijack attempts (e.g., [8, 16]), there is a lack of a general understanding on the impact of a successful prefix hijack and networks' resiliency against such attacks. This lack of understanding makes it difficult to assess the overall damage once an attack occurs, and to provide guidance to network operators on how to improve their networks' resilience.

In this paper, we conduct a systematic study to gauge the impact of prefix hijacks launched at different locations in the Internet topology, and identify topological characteristics of those networks that are most resilient against hijacks of their prefixes. Specifically, we deal with a type of prefix hijack referred to as false origin hijacks where a network announces the exact prefix announced by another network. Using simulations on an Internet scale topology and measurements from real data, we estimate how many nodes in the Internet may believe the true origin and how many believe the false origin during a hijack. Our results show that the Internet topology hierarchy and routing policies play an essential role in determining the impact of a prefix hijack. Our study shows that the high degree networks (e.g., tier-1 ISPs) are not necessarily most resilient against prefix hijacks. Instead, small networks that are direct customers to multiple tier-1 ISPs are seen to be most resilient. Conversely, attacks launched from these multi-homed customer networks would also have the biggest impact. Implications of our results are twofold. First, networks that desire high resilience against prefix hijacks should connect to multiple providers, and be as close as possible to multiple tier-1 ISPs and networks that cannot achieve such topological connectivity, should use reactive means to learn about their prefix being hijacked. Second, securing only the big ISP networks is not adequate nor effective, since high impact attacks come

---

[*]This material is based upon work supported by the Defense Advanced Research Projects Agency (DARPA) under Contract No N66001-04-1-8926 and by National Science Foundation(NSF) under Contract No ANI-0221453. Any opinions, findings and conclusions or recommendations expressed in this material are those of the authors and do not necessarily reflect the views of the DARPA or NSF.

[†]University of California, Los Angeles. 4732 Boelter Hall, Los Angeles, CA 90095. Email: {mohit,rveloso,lixia}@cs.ucla.edu

[‡]University of Arizona. 1040 E. 4th Street Tucson, AZ 85721. Email: bzhang@cs.arizona.edu

from well connected small networks.

The rest of the paper is organized as follows. Section 2 reviews Internet routing and prefix hijacking. Section 3 defines evaluation metrics and Section 4 uses simulations on an Internet scale topology to evaluate the resiliency of different networks. Section 5 presents evidence of our findings in real hijack incidents. Section 6 discusses the insights and implications of our findings. Section 7 presents related work and Section 8 concludes the paper.

2 Background

In this section we present the relevant background on Internet routing and describe prefix hijacking with an example.

2.1 Internet Routing

The Internet consists of more than twenty thousand networks called "Autonomous Systems" (AS). Each AS is represented by a unique numeric ID known as its AS number, and may advertise one or more IP address prefixes. For example, the prefix 131.179.0.0/16 represents a range of 2^{16} IP addresses belonging to AS-52 (UCLA). Internet Registries such as ARIN and RIPE assign prefixes to organizations, who then become the owner of the prefixes. Autonomous Systems run the Border Gateway Protocol (BGP) [15] to propagate prefix reachability information among themselves. In the rest of the paper, we abstract an autonomous system into a single entity called *AS node* or *node*, and the BGP connection between two autonomous systems as *AS link* or simply *link*.

BGP uses routing update messages to propagate routing changes. As a path-vector routing protocol, BGP lists the entire AS path to reach a destination prefix in its routing updates. Route selection and announcement in BGP are determined by networks' routing policies, in which the business relationship between two connected ASes plays a major role. AS relationship can be generally classified as customer-provider or peer-peer[1]. In a customer-provider relationship, the customer AS pays the provider AS for access service to the rest of the Internet. The peer-peer relationship does not usually involve monetary flow; The two peer ASes exchange traffic between their respective customers only. Usually a customer AS does not forward traffic between its providers, nor does a peer AS forward traffic between two other peers. For example in Figure 1, AS-1 is a customer of AS-2 and AS-3, and hence would not want to be a transit between AS-2 and AS-3, since it would be pay both AS-2 and AS-3 for traffic exchange between themselves. This results in the so-called *valley-free* BGP paths [3] generally observed in the Internet. When ASes choose their best

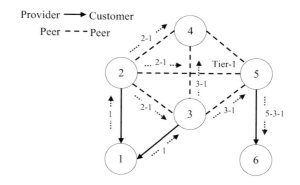

Figure 1. Route propagation.

path, they usually follow the order of customer routes, peer routes, and provider routes. This policy of *no valley prefer customer* is generally followed by most networks in the Internet. As we will see later, the *no valley prefer customer* policy plays an important role in determining the impact of prefix hijacks and hence we present a simple example to illustrate how this policy works.

Figure 1 provides a simple example illustrating route selection and propagation. AS-1 announces a prefix (e.g. 131.179.0.0/16) to its upstream service providers AS-2 and AS-3. The AS announcing a prefix to the rest of the Internet is called the *origin AS* of that prefix. Each of these providers then prepends its own AS number to the path and propagates the path to their neighbors. Note that AS-3 receives paths from its customer, AS-1, as well as its peer, AS-2, and it selects the customer path over the peer path thus advertising the path {3 1} to its neighbors AS-4 and AS-5. AS-5 receives routes from AS-2 and AS-3 and we assume AS-5 selects the route announced by AS-3 and announces the path {5 3 1} to its customer AS-6. In general, an AS chooses which routes to import from its neighbors and which routes to export to its neighbors based on import and export routing policies. An AS receiving multiple routes picks the best route based on policy preference. Metrics such as path length and other BGP parameters are used in route selection if the policy is the same for different routes. The BGP decision process also contains many more parameters that can be configured to mark the preference of routes. A good explanation of these parameters can be found in [4].

2.2 Prefix Hijacking

A prefix hijack occurs when an AS announces prefixes that it does not own. Now, suppose AS-6 wrongly announces the prefix that belongs to AS-1, as shown in Fig-

---

[1] Sometimes the relationship between two AS nodes can be "siblings," usually because they belong to the same organization.

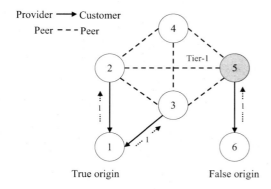

Provider ——→ Customer
Peer - - - Peer

True origin

False origin

Figure 2. Hijack scenario.

ure 2. Note that AS-5 previously routed through AS-3 to reach AS-1. On receiving a customer route through AS-6, it prefers the customer route over the peer route and hence believes the false route. This is an example of a prefix hijack, in which a false origin AS-6 announces a prefix it does not own, and deceives AS-5. In current routing practice, it is difficult for an AS to differentiate between a true origin and a false origin. Even though Internet Routing Registries (IRR) provide databases of prefix ownership, the contents are not maintained up-to-date, and not all BGP routers are known to check these databases. Hence, when presented multiple paths to reach the same prefix, a BGP router will often choose the best path regardless of who originates this prefix, thus allowing hijacked routes to propagate through the Internet. Prefix hijacks can be due to malicious attacks or router mis-configurations. When legitimate data traffic is diverted to the false origin, the data may be discarded, resulting in a traffic blackhole, or be exploited for malicious purposes. A recent study [14] reported that some spammers hijack prefixes in order to send spams without revealing their network identities.

The hijack depicted in Figure 2 is called a false origin prefix hijack, where an AS announces the *exact* prefix owned by another AS. Another type of hijack, called sub-prefix hijack, involves an AS announcing a more specific prefix (e.g. hijacker announces a /24, when the true origin announces a /16). In this case, BGP routers will usually treat them as different prefixes and maintain two separate entries in routing tables. However, due to longest prefix matching in routing table lookups, data destined to IP addresses in the /24 range will be forwarded to the false origin, instead of the true origin. Prefix hijack can also involve a false AS link advertised in the AS path without a change of origin. Our aim in this paper is to understand that, how the topological characteristics of two AS nodes announcing the same prefix influence the impact of the hijack. Studying the impact of

sub-prefix hijacks and false link hijacks involves different considerations and is beyond the scope of this paper.

Terminology

In the rest of this paper, we use the term *prefix hijacks* to refer to false origin prefix hijacks. We call the AS announcing a prefix it does not own as the *false origin*, and the AS whose prefix is being attacked as the *true origin*. Upon receiving the routes from both the false origin as well as the true origin, an AS that believes the false origin is said to be *deceived*, while an AS that still routes to the true origin is said to be *unaffected*.

3 Hijack Evaluation Metrics

For our simulations, we model the Internet opology as a graph, in which each node represents an AS, and each link represents a logical relationship between two neighboring AS nodes. Note, two neighboring odes may have multiple physical links between themselves. However, BGP paths are represented in the form of AS AS links, and hence we abstract connections between two AS nodes as a single logical link. For simplicity, each node owns exactly one unique prefix, i.e. no two nodes announce the same prefix except during hijack. A prefix hijack at any given time involves only one hijacker, and the hijacker can target only one node.

To capture the interaction between the entities involved in a hijack, we introduce a variable $\beta(a, t, v)$, function of false origin a, true origin t and node v as follows:

$$\beta(a, t, v) = \begin{cases} 1 & : \quad \text{if node } v \text{ is deceived by false} \\ & \quad \text{origin } a \text{ for true origin } t\text{'s prefix} \\ 0 & : \quad \text{otherwise} \end{cases} \quad (1)$$

Due to the rich connectivity in Internet topology, a node often has multiple equally good paths to reach the same prefix. Figure 2 shows a case where AS-4 has three equally good paths to reach the same prefix, two to the true origin AS-1 (through AS-2 and AS-3), and one to the false origin AS-6. In our model, we assume a node will break the tie randomly. Therefore, we define the expected value of β as follows. Let $p(v, n)$ be the number of equally preferred paths (e.g. same policy, same path length) from the node v to node n. E.g., in Figure 2, $p(4, 1) = 2$ since AS-4 has two paths via AS-2 and AS-3 to reach AS-1, and $p(4, 6) = 1$ since AS-4 has only one route via AS-5 to reach AS-6. If nodes use random tie-break to decide between multiple equally good preferred paths, then the expected value for β is defined as:

$$\bar{\beta}(a, t, v) = \frac{p(v, a)}{p(v, a) + p(v, t)} \quad (2)$$

yielding $\bar{\beta}(6, 1, 4) = \frac{1}{3}$ for the example in the figure. $\bar{\beta}$ is the probability of a node v being deceived by a given false origin a announcing a route belonging to true origin t.

Impact

We use the term *impact* to measure the attacking power of a node launching prefix hijacks. We define impact of a node a as the fraction of the nodes that believe the false origin a during an attack on true origin t. More formally, the impact of a node a is given by:

$$I(a) = \sum_{t \in \mathcal{N}} \sum_{v \in \mathcal{N}} \frac{\bar{\beta}(a, t, v)}{(N-1)(N-2)} \quad (3)$$

Note that the outer sum is over $N-1$ true origins (we exclude the false origin) and the inner sum is over $N-2$ nodes (excluding both the false origin and true origin).

Resilience

We use the term *resilience* to measure the defensive power of a node against hijacks launched against its prefix. We define the resilience of a node t as the fraction of nodes that believe the true origin t given an arbitrary hijack against t. More formally, the node resilience $R(t)$ of a node t is given by:

$$R(t) = \sum_{a \in \mathcal{N}} \sum_{v \in \mathcal{N}} \frac{\bar{\beta}(t, a, v)}{(N-1)(N-2)} \quad (4)$$

Note, higher R(t) values indicate better resilience against hijacks, and higher I(a) values indicate higher impact as an attacker.

Relation between Impact and Resilience

The true origin t and false origin a compete with each other to make nodes in the Internet route to itself. For example in Figure 2, false origin AS-6 is hijacking a prefix belonging to true origin AS-1. In this case, only AS-5 believes the false origin and AS-4 has a $1/3$ chance of being deceived. Therefore, the chances that a node believes the false origin AS-6 when it hijacks AS-1 is given by $\frac{1+1/3}{4} = \frac{1}{3}$.

Now if AS-1 was to hijack a prefix belonging to AS-6, then AS-5 would still believe AS-6 and AS-4 will believe it with a probability of $1/3$. Thus, in this case, the chances that a node believes the true origin AS-6 when it is hijacked by AS-1 is $\frac{1+1/3}{4} = \frac{1}{3}$.

We see that the resilience of the node as a true origin is equal to its impact as a false origin. We note that in our model, when the roles of attacker and target are switched, the impact of a node becomes its resilience. In the rest of the paper, we focus on resilience, while keeping in mind that a highly resilient node can also cause high impact as a false origin.

4 Evaluating Hijacks

In this section, we aim to understand the topological resilience of nodes against prefix hijacks by performing sim-

ulations on an Internet derived topology. We first explain the simulation setup, followed by the main results of our simulation and the insight behind the results.

4.1 Simulation Setup

For our simulations, we use an AS topology collected from BGP routing tables and updates, representing a snapshot of the Internet as of Feb 15 2006 (available from [20]). The details of how this topology was constructed are described in [21]. Our topology consists of 22,467 AS nodes and 63,883 links. We assume each AS node owns and announces a single prefix to its neighbors. We classify AS nodes into three tiers: Tier-1 nodes, transit nodes, and stub nodes. To choose the set of Tier-1 nodes, we started with a well known list, and added a few high degree nodes that form a clique with the existing set. Nodes other than Tier-1s but provide transit service to other AS nodes, are classified as *transit* nodes, and the remainder of nodes are classified as *stub* nodes. This classification results in 8 Tier-1 nodes, 5,793 transit nodes, and 16,666 stub nodes. We classify each link as either customer-provider or peer-peer using the PTE algorithm[3] and use the *no valley prefer customer* routing policy to infer routing paths (also used in previous works such as [19]). We abstracted the router decision process into the following priorities (1)local policy based on relationship, (2)AS path length, and (3)random tie-breaker.

Of the 22,467 AS nodes in our topology, we randomly picked 1,000 AS nodes to represent false origins that would launch attacks on other AS nodes. We checked the degree distribution of this set of 1,000 AS nodes, and found it to be similar to the degree distribution of all the AS nodes. For each of the 22,467 AS nodes as a true origin, we simulated a hijack with the 1,000 false origins. Thus we simulated $22,467 \times 1,000 \simeq 22.5$ million hijack scenarios in total.

4.2 Characterizing Topological Resilience

Figure 3 shows the distribution of the resilience (average curve) for all the nodes in our topology from our simulated hijacks. Since the resilience of each node results from the average over 1,000 attackers, we also show the standard deviation range. Note, higher values of resilience imply more resilience against hijacks.

This distribution shows that node resilience varies fairly linearly except at the two extremes. Figure 3 also shows that the deviations at the two extremes are quite small compared to the middle, indicating that some nodes(top left) are very resilient against hijacks, while some others (bottom right) are easily attacked, regardless of the location of the false origin.

As a first step in understanding how different nodes differ in their resilience, we classify nodes into the three classes

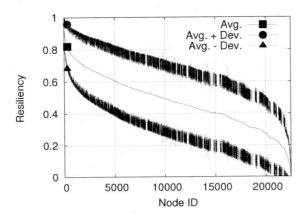

Figure 3. Distribution of node resilience.

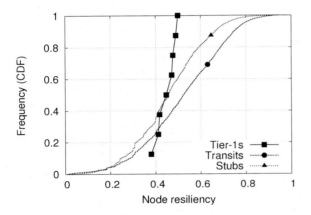

Figure 4. Resilience of nodes in different tiers.

already described: tier-1, transit and stub and plot the average resilience distribution (CDF) of each class of nodes in Figure 4. We observe that the resilience distribution is very similar for transits and stubs, with transit nodes being a little more resilient than stubs.

In contrast, tier-1 nodes show a very different distribution from the stubs and transits. From Figure 4 we observe that all the tier-1 nodes have an average resilience value between 0.4 and 0.5. In addition, we note that about 40% of stubs and 55% of transit nodes are more resilient than all tier-1 nodes. With tier-1 nodes being the ones with the highest degree, it is surprising to see that close to 50% of the nodes in the Internet are more resilient than tier-1s. Next, we explain why tier-1 nodes are more vulnerable to hijacks than a lot of other nodes and generalize this explanation to understand the characteristics impacting resilience.

4.3 Factors Affecting Resilience

We first understand the resilience of tier-1 nodes with a simple hijack scenario in Figure 5. AS-2, AS-3, AS-4 and AS-5 represent 4 tier-1 nodes inter-connected through a peer-peer relationship. AS-1 and AS-6 are small ISPs connected to tier-1 AS nodes through a customer-provider relationship. Finally AS-7 is a multi-homed customer of AS-1 and AS-6. In Figure 5, AS-7 represents the false origin that hijacks a prefix belonging to a tier-1 node, AS-4.

Recall in no-valley prefer customer policy, a customer route is preferred over a peer route which in turn is preferred over a provider route. When AS-7 hijack's AS-4's prefix and announces the false route to AS-1 and AS-6, both AS-1 and AS-6 prefer the hijacked route over the genuine route to AS-4 since its a customer route. AS-1 in turn announces the hijacked route to its tier-1 providers AS-2 and AS-3. These tier-1 AS nodes, AS-2 and AS-3 now have to choose between a customer route through AS-1(hijacked route), and a peer route through AS-4 (genuine route). Again due to policy preference, the tier-1 nodes will choose the customer route which happens to be the hijacked route. Similarly, AS-5 will also choose the hijacked route. Once big ISPs like tier-1 nodes are deceived by the hijacker, their huge customer base (many of whom are single homed) are also deceived, thus causing a high impact. One can see from this example, that the main reason for the low resilience in the case of a hijack on a tier-1 node is that tier-1 nodes interconnect through peer-peer relationship thus rendering a genuine route less preferred to other tier-1 nodes than hijacked routes from customers.

The key to high resilience is to make the tier-1 nodes and other big ISPs always believe the true origin. The way to achieve this is to reach as many tier-1 nodes as possible using a provider route. In addition, when a node has to choose between two routes of the same preference, path length becomes a deciding factor, and thus the shorter the number of hops to reach the tier-1 nodes, the better the resilience. From our observations from simulation results, we found that the most resilient nodes are direct customers of many tier-1 nodes and other big ISPs. As an example, in our simulations, the node with highest resilience is a stub (AS-6432 DoubleClick) directly connected to 6 tier-1 nodes, having a resilience value of 0.95. The nodes with lowest resilience were single-home customers, connected to poorly connected providers.

To better understand the influence of tier-1 nodes, we classified the nodes in the Internet based on the number of direct tier-1 providers. Figure 6 shows the distribution of resilience for nodes with different connectivity to Tier-1. Note, the closer the curve to the right hand side of the figure (x=1), the better the resilience of that set of nodes. There are about 21,888 nodes with less than 3 connections to Tier-1, and we observe in Figure 6 that these nodes are the least

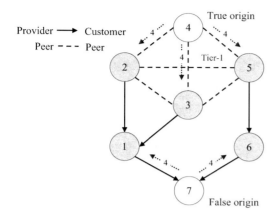

Figure 5. Understanding resilience of tier-1 nodes

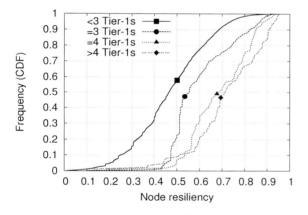

Figure 6. Resilience of nodes with different number of Tier-1 providers.

resilient. A total of 379 nodes are directly connected to 3 Tier-1s and 104 nodes are connected to 4 Tier-1s. Only 88 nodes are connected to more than 4 Tier-1s, and these nodes prove to be the most resilient, highlighting the role of connecting to multiple tier-1 nodes.

Summary: In this section, we used an Internet scale topology with no-valley prefer customer policy routing to evaluate the resilience of nodes against random hijackers. The key to achieve high resilience is to protect tier-1 nodes and other big ISPs from being deceived by the hijacker. Our main result shows that the nodes that are direct customers of multiple tier-1 nodes are the most resilient to hijacks. On the other hand, the tier-1 nodes themselves in spite of being so well connected, are much less resilient to hijack. The next question we seek to answer in Section 5 is whether there is evidence of such behavior in reality, where the routing deci-

sion process is much more complex.

5 Prefix Hijack Incidents in the Internet

In this section we examine two hijack events, one from January 2006 which affected a few tens of prefixes, and the other from December 2004 when over 100,000 prefixes were hijacked. To gauge the impact of the prefix hijacks, we analyzed the BGP routing data collected by the Oregon collector of the RouteViews project. The Oregon collector receives BGP updates from over 40 routers. These 40 routers belong to 35 different AS nodes (a few AS nodes have more than one BGP monitor) and we consider an AS as deceived by a hijack if at least one BGP monitor from that AS believes the hijacker. We call these 35 AS nodes as *monitors*, as they provide BGP monitoring information to the Oregon collector. The impact of a hijack is then gauged by the ratio of monitors in the Internet that were deceived.

5.1 Case I: Prefix Hijacks by AS-27506

On January 22, 2006, AS-27506 announced a number of prefixes that did not belong to it. This hijack incident was believed to be due to operational errors, and most of the hijacked prefixes were former customers of AS-27506. We observed a total of 40 prefixes being hijacked by AS-27506. These 40 prefixes belonged to 22 unique ASes. We present two representative prefixes; for the first prefix the false origin could only deceive a small number of monitors, while for the second prefix the false origin deceived the majority of the monitors. We examine the topological connectivity of the true origins as compared to that of the false origin and the relation to the true origin's resiliency.

5.1.1 High Resiliency against Hijack

We examine a hijacked prefix that belongs to the true origin AS-20282. The impact of hijacking this prefix is just over 10%, that is 4 out of the 35 monitored ASes were deceived by the hijack. Figure 7(a) depicts the connectivity of some of the entities involved in this hijack incident. The nodes colored in gray are the nodes deceived by the false origin AS-27506, and the white nodes persisted with the true origin. The true origin AS-20282 is a direct customer of two tier-1 nodes, AS-701 and AS-3356. Before the hijack incident, all the 35 monitors used routes containing one of these two tier-1 ASes as the last hop in the AS path to reach the prefix. The hijacker AS-27506 is a customer of AS-2914, another tier-1 node. When AS-27506 hijacked the prefix, AS-2914 chose the false customer route from AS-27506 over an existing peer route through AS-701. The false route was further announced by AS-2914 to other tier-1 peers including AS-701 and AS-3356, however neither of them adopted the new route because they chose the customer route announced by the true origin AS-20282. Other tier-1 ASes, such as AS-1239 (not shown in the figure), did not adopt to the false route from AS-2914 either, most likely because the newly announced false route was 2 hops in length, the same as that of their existing route through AS-701 or AS-3356, and the recommended practice suggests to avoid unnecessary best path transitions between equal external paths [2]. However we note that AS-3130, who is a customer of both a deceived and an unaffected tier-1 providers, also got deceived, possibly because the new path {2914, 27506} is shorter than the original path which contained 3 AS hops.

5.1.2 Low Resiliency against Hijack

Next, we examine another hijacked prefix which belonged to AS-23011. The average impact of this hijacked prefix is 0.6, i.e. 21 out of the 35 monitors were deceived by the hijack. Figure 7(b) shows the most relevant entities involved in this prefix hijack. The true origin of this prefix was an indirect customer of 5 tier-1 ASes (not all of them are shown in the figure) through its direct providers AS-12006 and AS-10910. The connectivity of the hijacker is the same as before, and AS-2914 was deceived by the hijack. The 5 tier-1 ASes on the provider path of the true origin stayed with the route from the true origin AS-23011, however the rest of the tier-1 ASes were deceived this time, possibly because the peer route to false origin through AS-2914 was shorter than any other peer route to the true origin. AS-286 is a customer of the providers of both the true and false origins, and it picked the false route through AS-2914 because it was shorter. We note that, in this case, the true origin being indirect customers of multiple tier-1 ASes ensured that those tier-1 ASes themselves did not get deceived, however due to its longer distance to reach these tier-1 providers (compared to the true origin in Figure 7(a)), other tier-1 ASes and their customers chose the shorter route to the false origin.

One of the tier-1 providers that propagated the false route is known to verify the origin of received routes with the Internet Routing Registries (IRR). However, it did not block the hijack because the registry entries were outdated and still listed AS-27506 as an origin for the hijacked prefixes, and hence the hijack announcements passed the registry check.

5.2   Case II: Prefix Hijacks by AS-9121

In this hijack incident, operational errors led AS-9121 to falsely announce routes to over 100,000 prefixes on December 24, 2004. We use this case to evaluate the resiliency of tier-1 Ases as compared to that of direct customers of multiple tier-1 ASes. Due to the large number of prefixes being falsely announced, some BGP protection mechanisms such as prefix filters and maximum prefix limit, where an AS sets an upper limit on the number of routes a given neighbor may

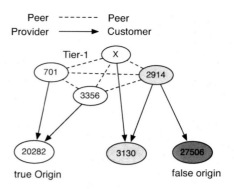

(a) High resiliency: Tier-1 provider 2914 preferred the customer route to false origin 27506 instead of the peer route. Similarly tier-1 providers 701 and 3356 stayed with their customer routes to the true origin 20282. Other tier-1 providers like X received a peer route to false origin that is no better than existing route and did not change route. 3130 routed to the false origin since the route via one of its providers, 2914, was shorter

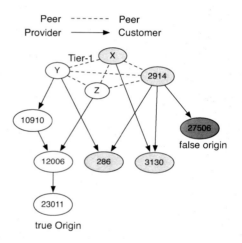

(b) Low resiliency: Tier-1 providers like Y with a customer route to true origin 23011 were not deceived by false origin. Other tier-1 providers like X received a shorter peer route through 2914 and hence routed to false origin. 286 preferred the shorter route to 27506 via 2914 and was deceived.

Figure 7. Case study: AS-27506 as false origin

announce, were triggered and made an effect on the overall impact. Given that multiple factors were involved in such a large scale hijack event, it is difficult to accurately model the impact on an AS as a function of its topological connectivity. Our objective in examining this case is to find supporting evidence for our observations made in Section 4, as opposed to a detailed study over all the hijacked prefixes. Similar to case-1, we observed how many monitors were deceived for each hijacked prefix and used this result to gauge the resiliency of the true origin AS.

5.2.1 Hijacked Tier-1 AS Prefix

In order to understand how tier-1 ASes fared against AS-9121 hijack, we studied the impact of those hijacked prefixes that belonged to AS-7018, a tier-1 AS. Note that AS-7018 announced over 1500 prefixes, and the impacts of different prefixes varied noticeably, with around 7 to 8 monitors being deceived for most prefixes. For our case study, we examine one of the hijacked prefixes which deceived the majority of the monitors. Figure 8(a) shows the entities involved in the hijack of this tier-1 prefix.

The hijacker AS-9121 was connected to 3 providers, one of which was AS-1239, a tier-1 AS. The true origin of the prefix in question was AS-7018, another tier-1 AS. The grey nodes in the figure indicate those deceived by the hijack. All the 3 providers of AS-9121, namely AS-1239, AS-6762, and AS-1299 were deceived into believing the false origin. AS-1299 also propagated the false route to its tier-1 AS providers. From our observations, a total of 19 out of 35 monitors were deceived by this hijack.

5.2.2 Hijacked Prefix belonging to Customer of Tier-1s

Next, we see how the AS-9121 hijack incident affected the prefixes belonging to an AS that was a direct customer of multiple tier-1 ASes. We picked AS-6461 as an example here because it connected to all the 8 tier-1 ASes. AS-6461 announced over 100 prefixes, 87 of which were hijacked by AS-9121. No more than 2 monitors were deceived by the false origin of all the hijacked prefixes. Figure 8(b) shows the entities involved in the hijack of one of the prefixes belonging to AS-6461. As before, AS-6762 believed the false origin and was one of the monitors deceived of all the hijacked prefixes of AS-6461. However, because all the tier-1 ASes were direct providers of AS-6461, they stayed with the original one-hop customer route to the true origin; in particular, note that AS-1239 was a provider for both the true origin and the hijacker, and it stayed with the original correct route. As a result, the hijack of AS-6461's prefixes made a very low impact.

In addition to AS-6461, we also studied the impacts of prefixes belonging to a few other transit ASes that were very well connected to tier-1 ASes, and found the impact pattern for their prefixes to be very similar to the AS-6461 case. To summarize, this real life hijack event showed strong evidence that direct multi-homing to all or most tier-1 ASes can greatly increase an AS's resiliency against prefix hijacks.

6 Discussion

It has been long recognized that prefix hijacking can be a serious security threat to the Internet. Several hijack *prevention* solutions have been proposed, such as SBGP [7], so-BGP [10], and more recently the effort in the IETF Se-

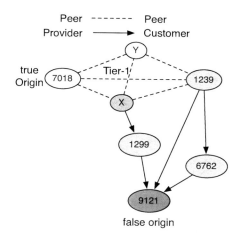

(a) Tier-1 prefix hijacked: Tier 1 providers like 1239 and X, preferred the customer route to false origin 9121, instead of peer route to the true origin 7018, also a tier-1.

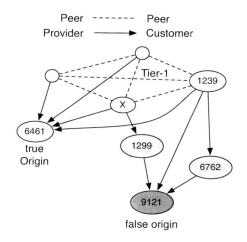

(b) Multi-homed customer of tier-1s hijacked: Providers of false origin 9121 got deceived, but all tier-1s including 1239, stayed with the one hop customer route to true origin 6461

Figure 8. Case studies with AS-9121 as false origin

cure Inter-Domain Routing Working Group [1]. These proposed solutions use cryptographic-based origin authentication mechanisms, which require coordinated efforts among a large number of organizations and thus will take time to get deployed. Meanwhile prefix hijack incidents occur from time to time and our work provides an assessment of the potential impacts of these incidents. Several hijack *detection* systems have also been developed, for example MyASN[16] and PHAS[8]. However since these systems are reactive in nature, it is still important for network customers to understand the relations between their networks' topological connectivity and the potential vulnerability in face of prefix hijacks.

Our simulation and analysis show that AS nodes with large node-degrees (e.g., tier-1 networks) are not the most resilient against hijacks of their own prefixes. An AS can gain high resiliency against prefix hijacks by being direct or indirect customers of multiple tier-1 providers with the shortest possible AS paths. Conversely, such customer AS nodes can also make the most impact over the entire Internet, if they inject false routes into the Internet. This finding suggests that securing the routing announcements from the major ISPs alone is not effective in curbing a high impact attack, and that it is even more important to watch the announcements from lower-tier networks with good topological connectivity.

On the other hand, customer networks that are far away from their indirect tier-1 providers can be greatly affected if their prefixes get hijacked. These topologically disadvantaged AS nodes are in the most need for investigating other means to protect themselves. Subscribing to prefix hijack detection systems, such as MyASN and PHAS, would be helpful. To reduce the transient impact during the detection delay, one may also look into another proposed solution called PGBGP [5], which is briefly described in Section 7.

Note that the topological connectivity required for resiliency against prefix hijacks is different from that required for fast routing convergence [11]. Fast convergence benefits from fewer alternative paths when the routes change, thus prefixes announced by tier-1 providers meet the requirement well; while hijack resiliency benefits from being a direct or indirect customer of a large number of tier-1 providers, thus prefixes are better hosted by well connected non-tier-1 AS nodes.

We would like to end this discussion by stressing the importance of understanding prefix hijack impacts, even when the protection mechanisms are put in place. Our evaluations on an Internet scale topology in Section 4 used a *no-valley prefer customer* routing policy and showed that tier-1 AS nodes are not very resilient to hijacks of their own prefixes since other tier-1 AS nodes prefer customer routes to false origin. However, in reality a tier-1 AS may use various mechanisms, such as Internet Routing Registries (IRR), to check the origin of a prefix before forwarding the route. Such mechanisms would probably boost the resiliency of tier-1 AS nodes being hijacked. On the other hand, these protection mechanisms can also fail or backfire, thus exposing the vulnerability of a network. As we saw in case I of Section 5, most of the hijacked prefixes were the former customers of the false origin AS and were recorded in the Internet Routing Registry (IRR), which was not updated. Outdated registries resulted in false routes being propagated to the rest of the Internet.

Another example of a protection mechanism is the maximum prefix filter in BGP that allows an AS to configure the maximum number of routes received from a neighbor. Thus, by limiting the total number of routes received from a neighbor, an AS can limit the damage in case of the neighbor announcing false routes. In case II from Section 5, AS-9121 announced over 100,000 false routes and one of its neighbors, AS-1299, had a max prefix set to a relatively low value. AS-1299 believed only 1849 routes directly from AS-9121, but since the max prefix limit is per neighbor, AS-1299 received hijacked routes from other neighbors as well. It learned a total of over 100,000 bad routes from all the neighbors combined, thus infecting a major portion of its routing table [12]. These examples show how easily protection mechanisms can fail due to human errors, underlining the need to understand the impact of hijacks in face of protection failures, and the need to protect networks by multiple means such as PGBGP and PHAS.

7   Related Work

Previous efforts on prefix hijacking can be broadly sorted into two categories: *hijack prevention* and *hijack detection*. Generally speaking, prefix hijack prevention solutions are based on cryptographic authentications [18, 10, 7, 9, 17] where BGP routers sign and verify the origin AS and AS path of each prefix. In addition to added router workload, these solutions require changes to *all* router implementations, and some of them also require a public key infrastructure. Due to these obstacles, none of the proposed prevention schemes is expected to see deployment in near future.

A number of prefix hijack detection schemes have been developed recently [16, 8, 13, 5]. A commonality among these solutions is that they do not use cryptographic-based mechanisms. In [13], any suspicious route announcements received by an AS trigger verification probes to other AS nodes and the results are reported to the true origin. In PGBGP [5], each router monitors the origin AS nodes in BGP announcements for each prefix over time; any newly occurred origin AS of a prefix is considered anomalous, and the router avoids using anomalous routes if the previously existing route to the same prefix is still available. Different from the above en route detection schemes, MyASN[16] is an offline prefix hijack alert service provided by RIPE. A prefix owner registers the valid origin set for a prefix, and MyASN sends an alarm via regular email when any invalid origin AS is observed in BGP routing updates. PHAS [8] is also an off-path prefix hijack detection system which uses BGP routing data collected by RouteViews and RIPE. Instead of asking prefix owners to register valid origin AS sets as is done by MyASN, PHAS keeps track of the origin AS set for each announced prefix, and sends hijack alerts via multiple path email delivery to the true origin.

Unlike the prevention schemes, a hijack detection mechanism provides only half of the solution: after a prefix hijack is detected, correction steps must follow. A recent proposal called MIRO [19] gives end users the ability to perform correction after detecting a problem. MIRO is a new inter-domain routing architecture that utilizes multiple path routing. In MIRO, AS nodes can negotiate alternative routes to reach a given destination, potentially bypassing nodes affected by hijack attacks.

The work presented in this paper can be considered orthogonal to all the existing efforts in the area. It examines the relation between an AS node's topological connectivity and its resiliency against false route attacks, or conversely, an AS node's topological connectivity and its impact as a launching pad for prefix hijacks.

8 Conclusion

In this paper we conducted the first investigation into the relation between networks' topological connectivity and the impact of prefix hijacking. Our results show that, AS nodes that are close customers of multiple tier-1 providers are most resilient against hijacks of their own prefixes. Conversely, they can also be the most effective prefix hijackers of other's prefixes.

To gain topological resiliency, our results lead to the following recommendations to customer networks. First, one should try to multi-home directly with as many tier-1 providers as feasible, and choose non-tier-1 providers in a way to maximize the number of tier-1 providers reached through provider-customer AS links. Second, those topologically disadvantaged AS nodes should seek additional means to enhance their resiliency against potential hijack attacks, such as hijack detection services (PHAS) in combination with delayed adoption of suspicious new routes (PG-BGP). Third, operators of those most influential AS nodes should be especially vigilant against faults, and operators of tier-1 providers should pay special attention to routing announcements from those well connected customers.

In departing we note that our results indicate that the AS nodes with highest node-degrees (e.g. tier-1 ISPs) are not the most effective hijack launch pads nor are they the most resilient against prefix hijacks. In hindsight, our results are not surprising as they follow directly from the common routing policy of preferring customer routes over peer and provider routes. Nevertheless, they are counter-intuitive and become obvious only *afterwards*, and we believe it is important to make the results widely disseminated to both network operators as well as the research community.

References

[1] Secure Inter-Domain Routing (SIDR) Working Group. http://www1.ietf.org/html.charters/sidr-charter.html.

[2] S. S. E. Chen. Avoid BGP Best Path Transitions from One External to Another. Internet Draft, IETF, June 2006. http://www.ietf.org/internet-drafts/draft-ietf-idr-avoid-transition-04.txt.

[3] L. Gao. On inferring autonomous system relationships in the Internet. *ACM/IEEE Transactions on Networking*, 9(6):733–745, 2001.

[4] B. Halabi and D. McPherson. *Internet Routing Architectures*. Cisco Press, 2nd edition, 2000.

[5] J. Karlin, S. Forrest, and J. Rexford. Pretty good bgp: Protecting bgp by cautiously selecting routes. Technical Report TR-CS-2005-37, University of New Mexico, Octber 2005.

[6] S. Kent, C. Lynn, and K. Seo. Secure Border Gateway Protocol. *IEEE Journal of Selected Areas in Communications*, 18(4), 2000.

[7] S. Kent, C. Lynn, and K. Seo. Secure border gateway protocol (S-BGP). *IEEE JSAC Special Issue on Network Security*, 2000.

[8] M. Lad, D. Massey, D. Pei, Y. Wu, B. Zhang, and L. Zhang. PHAS: A prefix hijack alert system. In *15th USENIX Security Symposium*, 2006.

[9] S. S. M. Zhao and D. Nicol. Aggregated path authentication for efficient bgp security. In *12th ACM Conference on Computer and Communications Security (CCS)*, November 2005.

[10] J. Ng. Extensions to BGP to Support Secure Origin BGP. ftp://ftp-eng.cisco.com/sobgp/drafts/draft-ng-sobgp-bgp-extensions-02.txt, April 2004.

[11] R. Oliveira, B. Zhang, D. Pei, R. Izhak-Ratzin, and L. Zhang. Quantifying Path Exploration in the Internet. In *ACM SIGCOMM/USENIX Internet Measurement Conference(IMC)*, October 2006.

[12] A. C. Popescu, B. J. Premore, and T. Underwood. Anatomy of a leak: AS 9121. NANOG-34, May 2005.

[13] S. Qiu, F. Monrose, A. Terzis, and P. McDaniel. Efficient techniques for detecting false origin advertisements in inter-domain routing. In *Second workshop on Secure Network Protocols (NPSec)*, 2006.

[14] A. Ramachandran and N. Feamster. Understanding the network-level behavior of spammers. In *Proceedings of ACM SIGCOMM*, 2006.

[15] Y. Rekhter, T. Li, and S. Hares. Border Gateway Protocol 4. RFC 4271, Internet Engineering Task Force, January 2006.

[16] RIPE. Routing information service: myASn System. http://www.ris.ripe.net/myasn.html.

[17] B. R. Smith, S. Murphy, and J. J. Garcia-Luna-Aceves. Securing the border gateway routing protocol. In *Global Internet'96*, November 1996.

[18] L. Subramanian, V. Roth, I. Stoica, S. Shenker, and R. H. Katz. Listen and whisper: Security mechanisms for BGP. In *Proceedings of ACM NDSI 2004*, March 2004.

[19] W. Xu and J. Rexford. MIRO: multi-path interdomain routing. In *SIGCOMM*, pages 171–182, 2006.

[20] B. Zhang, R. Liu, D. Massey, and L. Zhang. Internet Topology Project. http://irl.cs.ucla.edu/topology/.

[21] B. Zhang, R. Liu, D. Massey, and L. Zhang. Collecting the Internet's AS level topology. In *ACM Sigcomm Computer Communication Review*, 2005.

User Discrimination Through Structured Writing on PDAs

Rachel R. M. Roberts, Roy A. Maxion, Kevin S. Killourhy, and Fahd Arshad
{rroberts, maxion, ksk, fahd}@cs.cmu.edu

Dependable Systems Laboratory
Computer Science Department
Carnegie Mellon University
Pittsburgh, Pennsylvania 15213 / USA

Abstract

This paper explores whether features of structured writing can serve to discriminate users of handheld devices such as Palm PDAs. Biometric authentication would obviate the need to remember a password or to keep it secret, requiring only that a user's manner of writing confirm his or her identity. Presumably, a user's dynamic and invisible writing style would be difficult for an imposter to imitate.

We show how handwritten, multi-character strings can serve as personalized, non-secret passwords. A prototype system employing support vector machine classifiers was built to discriminate 52 users in a closed-world scenario. On high-quality data, strings as short as four letters achieved a false-match rate of 0.04%, at a corresponding false non-match rate of 0.64%. Strings of at least 8 to 16 letters in length delivered perfect results—a 0% equal-error rate. Very similar results were obtained upon decreasing the data quality or upon increasing the data quantity.

1. Introduction

Passwords are standard in computer access control, but they can be forgotten, compromised without detection, and denied as having been used (repudiation) [14]. A proposed alternative is *biometrics*, or measurements of the human body. *Biological biometrics* are physical traits such as the iris, fingerprint, and face; *behavioral biometrics* are activities such as handwriting, keystrokes, and gait. Handwriting is an *alterable* biometric: it changes in response to varying conditions, e.g., text. Alterable biometrics are suitable for challenge-response protocols, whose dynamic nature resists forgery and replay, thereby providing stronger non-repudiation [14].

Personal digital assistants (PDAs) can potentially provide effective and low-cost biometric authentication.

Some allow structured writing that may facilitate handwriting verification (because it enforces writing consistency), while also enabling automatic letter recognition. A PDA—or its input technology—could be integrated into a kiosk to capture and relay biometric data cheaply, while enjoying protection from theft and tampering.

To test whether structured handwriting on PDAs has promise as a biometric, we devised an evaluation of mild difficulty. Phillips et al. [16] recommend that evaluations be not too hard nor too easy; there are three stages of evaluation protocols: technology, scenario, and operational. We take a first step in examining the potential of PDAs to convey biometric-based security, by conducting a preliminary technology evaluation on a laboratory algorithm.

2. Problem and approach

We address whether it is possible to discriminate enrolled users on the basis of their handwriting characteristics in Graffiti [15], the original structured language of Palm handhelds. Specifically, we seek to build a system that can confirm or deny a claimed identity within a closed set of enrolled users; it is assumed that no outsiders can access the biometric system. Our example application is designed to catch insider attacks [21] and to provide traceability of human actions.

Our approach is to devise a non-secret challenge string, one per enrolled user, to distinguish that user from all the others. Challenge strings are pre-computed, based on errors and successes observed in preliminary testing on enrollment templates. In a hypothetical transaction, a user claims an identity and receives a personalized challenge string, which he or she writes on a Palm PDA. To confirm or deny the identity claim, the biometric system determines which enrolled user most likely wrote the sample, and reports whether or not the predicted identity matches the claimed one. We collect biometric data to build a corpus; data from the corpus is used to simulate user participation in the biometric system.

3. Background and related work

To our knowledge, no previous research has attempted to differentiate users on the basis of their handwriting idiosyncrasies in a structured input language. Research on a related problem, discriminating users on the basis of their natural handwriting, is summarized in [11, 12, 17, 18, 20, 23]. This prior work can be categorized into signature verification tasks (determining whether a particular person wrote a signature) vs. writer identification tasks (determining which one of N known people wrote a document), and into off-line methods (writing as a static image) vs. on-line methods (writing as a dynamic process). The so-called off-line problems are more difficult than on-line ones, because timing, direction, pressure, and pen-orientation data are not available, and because recovering writing from a background document may be hard. Writer identification is more challenging than signature verification, due to difficulties in automation, character segmentation, and letter recognition. Off-line signature verification, the most typical application, usually achieves false-match and false non-match rates of a few percentage points each, although these may be optimistic due to the small size of signature databases [18]. The best team at the First International Signature Verification Competition achieved equal-error rates of 2.84% and 2.89%, respectively, on two tasks [25].

A wide variety of features is used to characterize natural handwriting. Features studied by manual examiners include the form of the writing as well as spelling and the type of pen used [3]. On-line signature verification may utilize functions of time. In off-line writer identification, features may be text-independent (using global statistical features) or text-dependent (using features computed on characters resolved from the image). Because Graffiti writing differs greatly from natural handwriting, the study of Graffiti letters motivated our features.

The original input language of Palm handhelds, Graffiti, is a stylized version of printed English (see Figure 1). The latest version, slightly modified, is called Graffiti 2. Graffiti is more constrained than natural handwriting; this makes letter recognition easier. The Palm PDA's screen digitizes information about pen pressure (a binary judgment, either up or down) and position (in Cartesian coordinates), in order to recognize letters.

In the framework of research on handwriting biometrics, our problem is a kind of writer verification task, using dynamic information, text-dependent features, and an automated decision process. Aspects of signature verification and writer identification apply to our work, although to a limited extent because of the differences between natural and constrained handwriting.

Most biometric systems perform either *positive identification* (verifying positive claims of enrollment), or *negative identification* (verifying claims of no enroll-

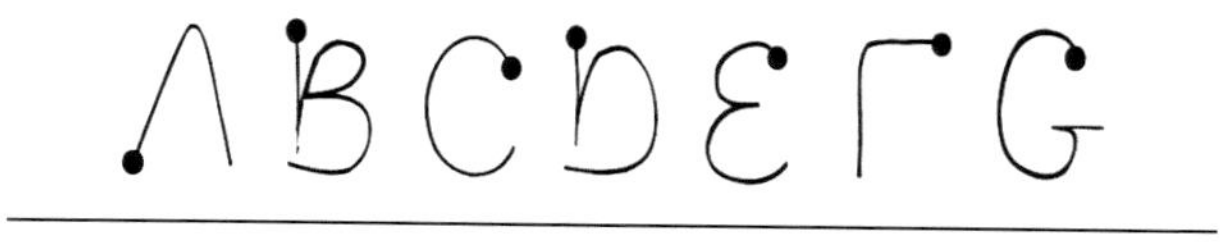

Figure 1. Graffiti letters "A" to "G" [15]

ment) [24]. Our proposed system has characteristics of both, and additionally focuses on differentiating enrollees rather than distinguishing enrollees from outsiders. The insider-detection task we pursue assumes that information about all possible attackers is available.

4. Overview of the three experiments

The aim of this research is to test whether enrolled users can be discriminated on the basis of their handwriting characteristics in a constrained input language. To fulfill this goal, we recruited 52 subjects to write 1417 letters each, and we derived features from those letters to constitute a corpus. Next, twenty-six classifiers, one per alphabet letter, were trained using half of the data. A separate portion of data was set aside to test the classifiers; tests generated user- and letter-specific information about classification errors. For each user, this information was used to order and group letters into challenge strings, which were employed in simulated authentication transactions. A reserved portion of the data produced the transactions (genuine and unpracticed impostor) to examine how challenge-string length affects system accuracy.

The biometric system was trained and tested anew in three distinct experiments, each using a different version of the feature data, to explore the effects of data quality and quantity on results. (1) *High-quality Data* contains features from letters judged to be highly representative of user handwriting. The purpose of the High-quality Data experiment is to learn whether users can be discriminated on the basis of their handwriting alone (and not on their handwriting plus data-capture artifacts). (2) *Reduced Data* is of the same size and proportions as *High-quality Data*, but its features come from letters selected at random, instead of on the basis of quality. The purpose of the Reduced Data experiment is to gauge whether lower data quality might decrease accuracy, in comparison to the High-quality Data experiment. (3) *All Data* contains features from all valid letters we asked subjects to write. The purpose of the All Data experiment is to see whether an additional quantity of data might improve accuracy, in comparison to the Reduced Data experiment.

5. Data collection and preparation

Preparation of the three versions of the data (mentioned in Section 4) was identical, except where noted.

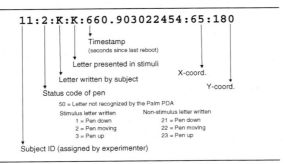

Figure 2. Example raw data for "K"

5.1. Instrumentation

Three Palm m105 handhelds, each running Palm OS 3.5 and having a maximum screen resolution of 160×160 pixels (with 2-bit color support, or 4 gray levels) were used to collect data. For each letter stroke drawn on the screen, a sequence of timestamped (x, y) coordinates, corresponding to the sampled positions of the stylus, was produced internally. For example, the first two consecutive points of a letter "I" might have $<timestamp, x, y>$ values of $<93.993284, 54, 176>$ and $<94.013007, 54, 182>$. We captured the information using a program installed directly on the Palm PDA and written in the C language, with the help of the Palm Software Development Kit (SDK 3.5). The program noted whether each written letter matched the one expected according to the stimuli order (see Figure 2). The median interval between successive timestamps was 0.02 seconds; the median letter stroke took 0.38 seconds to write.

Approximate granularity of spatial coordinates can be gleaned from the following information. The dimensions of the Palm PDA's writing box are 1.60 cm (width) by 1.85 cm (height), although the entire screen (about 5 cm by 6.75 cm) is sensitive to input. In internal coordinate units, the range of horizontal coordinates in the data was 143; that for vertical coordinates was 218. Assuming the entire writing box received input at some point, we estimate an internal coordinate unit to be about 0.1 mm. The average letter width (in internal units) was 21.4, while the average letter height was 30.5.

5.2. Stimulus materials

Stimuli were chosen to ensure adequate instances of each letter, while discouraging subject boredom or frustration. Stimuli consisted of 5-letter nonsense strings and pangram sentences. Nonsense strings contained a bigram (two-letter combination) followed by a trigram (three-letter combination). Bigram and trigram motifs were visually separated by a space on the screen, which the subject did not write. Motifs were repeated and recombined to facilitate visual processing; two examples of nonsense

strings are "BC ZAT" and "YZ CKS". A pangram includes every letter of the alphabet, e.g., "the five boxing wizards jump quickly". Ten nonsense strings were followed by one pangram sentence to form one set; there were 15 sets, resulting in 150 unique nonsense strings (750 letters) and 15 unique pangrams (667 letters). In total, each subject wrote 1417 requested letters. The letter type having the fewest instances in the stimuli had 44, while the one having the most instances had 94; the median number of instances of a given letter type was 52.

Stimuli were presented on the screen of the Palm PDA; subjects were asked to copy each sentence or string that appeared. A separate chart of the 26 Graffiti letters was displayed for reference, if needed. If a written letter was not recognized by the PDA, or if a letter did not match the one the user was expected to write, a beep sounded to prod the user to write it over again. The canonical Graffiti form for the letter "X" requires two strokes, but to simplify analysis we asked subjects to use an alternative single-stroke form (looking like a backwards α); compliance was confirmed. Other alternative strokes (all single-stroke forms) exist for a handful of other letters in Graffiti; these were allowed. For example, the alternative stroke for "Y" looks like a γ.

5.3. Subjects and sessions

Fifty-two subjects participated; each subject wrote in a single sitting lasting about 45 minutes. To increase task manageability, we did not introduce a time lag between enrollment and testing sessions (template ageing), although this is recommended [13]. Roughly half (25) of the subjects reported that they could write Graffiti letters without thinking about how to do it. Eleven others reported that they had learned Graffiti once before; only nine subjects claimed no prior exposure to Graffiti. Five subjects were left-handed and 47 were right-handed.

5.4. Data conditioning and version generation

User errors were excluded before analysis, i.e., when a subject drew a stroke not recognized as a letter, or wrote a letter other than the expected one. This seldom happened, because auditory feedback (upon errors) alerted subjects to pay closer attention. One might include such instances in a failure-to-acquire rate, but we reserve that distinction for letters excluded in the High-quality Data. The three versions of the data, one for each of the experiments described in Section 4, were prepared as follows.

High-quality Data. In the high-quality version of the corpus, data judged to be unrepresentative of actual user handwriting were excluded. Figure 3 shows four "Y"s, the leftmost pair written by one subject, the rightmost by another. Within each pair, the left letter not only looks unrealistic but also contains unrealistic timing information, due to an apparent instrumentation anomaly.

Data were passed through a filter to exclude letters whose first few sampled points contained timestamp intervals shorter than 0.01 seconds (half the typical time lag). The filter's results corresponded well with two human-rater judgments of which letters looked unrealistic, out of a sample of 1166 "Y"s. Although the filter removed 22.33% (16,455 out of 73,684) of the letters, sufficient samples remained for analysis. Little data (as little as 0%) was excluded for many subjects, while much data (as much as 72%) was excluded for some subjects; the median percent data loss was 20%. From the perspective of letters, the smallest percent data loss for a given letter was 8% while the greatest was 32%; the median was 22%. The smallest number of instances of a given letter in the High-quality Data, for any single user, was 13.

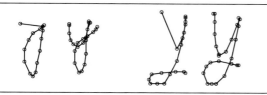

Figure 3. Unrealistic "Y"s (left within each pair); realistic "Y"s (right within each pair)

The data-capture irregularities do not appear to greatly harm letter recognition on the Palm PDA, since gross letter shapes remain. Anecdotally, one subject reflected that a carefully-written letter was occasionally not recognized. It may be that instrumentation errors occur sporadically, with some causing letter-recognition to fail, and others not. Newer or more sophisticated Palm handhelds might ameliorate this problem; future work should keep data quality in mind.

Reduced Data. This version of the data corpus was built to match exactly all proportions of the high-quality version (on a per-letter and per-subject basis). The only difference was that letter instances were included without regard to quality; they were selected at random.

All Data. This version used the data corpus in its entirety. The fewest instances of a given letter, for all users, was 44.

5.5. Feature extraction

Thirteen quantitative features were extracted from each letter stroke, which is represented natively in the Palm PDA as a sequence of $<timestamp, x, y>$ values. Features appear in Table 1 and are elaborated below.

Each feature attempts to capture a salient characteristic of Graffiti handwriting. *Time to Write* informs about the writer's speed. The four extreme coordinates (*Horizontal* and *Vertical Minimum* and *Maximum*) describe the location of the letter in the writing box, which varies

Table 1. Features of Graffiti letter strokes

Time to Write	Elapsed time to write letter.
Horiz Minimum	Min. coord. value along x-axis.
Horiz Maximum	Max. coord. value along x-axis.
Vert Minimum	Min. coord. value along y-axis.
Vert Maximum	Max. coord. value along y-axis.
H.Start-End Dist ($\pm$)	($x_{Last.coord.} - x_{First.coord.}$).
V.Start-End Dist ($\pm$)	($y_{Last.coord.} - y_{First.coord.}$).
Horiz Dist Travelled	Sum of horizontal distances between successive points.
Vert Dist Travelled	Sum of vertical distances between successive points.
Letter Length	Sum of line-segment lengths between successive points.
Direction Changes	Count of changes between left↔right or up↔down motion.
Mean Slope	Avg. value of pairwise slopes.
Std Dev of the Slope	Std. dev. of pairwise slopes.

among users by handedness or habit. *Horizontal* and *Vertical Start-to-End Distance (Signed)* help inform whether a canonical or alternative stroke is used, and describe an aspect of letter shape. *Horizontal* and *Vertical Distance Travelled* measure how much the stylus moves along a particular axis, whereas *Letter Length* measures the total amount of writing in a letter; all encode how simple or intricate a letter is. *Direction Changes* indicates how straight or shaky a stroke is. *Mean Slope* and *Standard Deviation of the Slope* represent a composite slant quality, and its consistency. Only finite pairwise slopes were included in the latter calculations. Nearly 2% of "I" strokes were perfectly vertical, which resulted in all their pairwise slopes being infinite. We imputed slope features in those cases by assuming that each "I" was not purely vertical, but rather perfectly slanted halfway between vertical and the smallest detectable positive slope.

5.6. Feature transformation and scaling

Classifiers often perform better when data are normally distributed, or when a normalizing transform is applied to the data. We transformed the values of each individual feature (across all subjects at once) using the versatile Box-Cox power transformation [2], to effect greater symmetry on each feature's distribution. A program written in the statistical language R [19] semi-automatically searched for a good value of the Box-Cox parameter λ, one for each feature. The 13 transformed feature distributions were plotted to inspect their symmetry visually and to verify that an appropriate transformation had been found. After transformation, the feature data were scaled (within each feature, across all subjects at once), such that each feature mean became 0 and each feature standard deviation became 1. Data scaling is recommended before SVM classification [9].

5.7. Training, testing, and evaluation data sets

To train and evaluate the biometric system described in Section 6, three distinct sets of feature data were used: (1) *SVM-train*, to train SVM letter classifiers; (2) *SVM-test*, to test the classifiers and inform challenge-string creation; and (3) *Evaluate-test*, to evaluate the entire system. We split the feature data into these three sets according to a 50%/25%/25% rule, in the following way. Before splitting, we grouped the feature vectors by subject (making 52 groups), and then within each subject, by letter (making 26 groups for each subject). Next, for each subject, we randomized the order of feature vectors within each of the 26 letter groups. This made the data more closely resemble the writing of practiced users, thereby mitigating potential learning effects among novice subjects. After splitting, out of each subject's "A"s, SVM-train had 50%; SVM-test had 25%; and Evaluate-test had 25%; the same percentages held for other letters. During system evaluation (see Section 7), SVM-train and SVM-test are combined to form *Evaluate-train*, which contains 75% of each subject's letter "A"s, et cetera. Evaluate-train holds enrollment data and Evaluate-test holds evaluation data.

6. Biometric system construction

In our example application, an enrolled user approaches a biometric system and claims an identity. The system issues a challenge string tailored to that identity, and the user responds by writing the string in constrained handwriting, using a stylus on a digitized screen. Next, the biometric system decides which enrolled user most likely wrote the sample. Our system prototype incorporates 26 SVM letter classifiers, each trained on enrollment data for its respective letter. When a given letter is present in a writing sample, the corresponding classifier is invoked; decision logic is used to combine the outputs of the classifiers involved, to predict the writer's identity.

The following sections describe (1) how the SVM letter classifiers were built; (2) how the classifiers were tested to produce user- and letter-specific information about errors; (3) how potential challenge strings were devised using this error information; and (4) how decision logic yields writer predictions by the biometric system.

6.1. Letter classifiers

The purpose of a letter classifier is to determine the probability that each subject wrote a given letter, and to choose the most likely writer. We employed support vector machine (SVM) classifiers, because they achieve state-of-the-art performance on handwritten character recognition [6], a problem similar to the one we address.

About SVMs. Support vector machines [4, 22] use supervised learning for classification and regression; they are closely related to neural networks. SVM classifiers transform data into n-dimensional space ($\mathbb{R}^n$) such that an n-dimensional hyperplane can be found to optimally separate the data into classes. These classifiers maximize the margin (the margin is the distance between classes in n-dimensional space) as well as minimize empirical classification errors. SVMs are kernel-based methods; common options include linear, polynomial, radial basis function (RBF), and sigmoid kernels. RBF kernels are reasonable choices for studies in new domains, because they have fewer parameters, and because they avoid numerical difficulties that other kernels can encounter [9].

The two parameters in RBF kernels are called γ and *cost*; γ determines the width of the RBF, while *cost* determines the trade-off between reducing errors and creating a wider margin. Wider margins generalize better, so permitting more errors on training data may prove advantageous. RBF kernel parameters must be tuned before use, to find their ideal values on the data at hand.

Using SVMs to build letter classifiers. Individual letter classifiers, as well as the biometric system as a whole, were built with tools from the R statistical computing project [19], the LIBSVM library of tools for support vector machines [5], and the R package e1071 [7] that provides an interface between the R programming environment and LIBSVM. Under LIBSVM, multi-class classification employs the *one-against-one* approach [10]. Given k classes, one for each subject identity, $k(k-1)/2$ binary classifiers are constructed, one for each pair of classes; the appropriate class label is found through voting. We used unweighted SVMs, along with the option in LIBSVM to report probability estimates. The subject who is assigned the highest probability becomes the classifier's predicted writer.

Twenty-six SVM classifiers, one for each Graffiti letter, were trained using SVM-train data. Each classifier employed an RBF kernel, whose parameters were tuned as follows. Five-fold cross-validation [8] was used to select the best values of *cost* and γ for each letter classifier. Fifteen *cost* values and 13 γ values were tried in every pairwise combination (195 total). The search space formed a two-dimensional grid of powers of 2; exponents for *cost* ranged from -2 to 26 (in 15 steps of two), whereas those for γ ranged from -22 to 2 (in 13 steps of two). For each letter, average accuracy rates over the five folds were recorded for the 195 trained classifiers. The highest score determined the best parameter pair, which was then fixed for the relevant letter classifier. We verified that a local maximum occurred in the grid area, not on the boundary.

6.2. Confusion matrices and charts

To determine which letters are superior at distinguishing one subject from all the rest, classification errors must be studied. Accordingly, each letter classifier was re-trained on the entire SVM-train data set (using the best

Table 2. Letter-classifier accuracies, high-quality data (50% training, 25% test data)

Y	76.09%	V	60.79%	U	57.51%
B	72.11%	Q	59.88%	O	57.02%
D	70.12%	Z	59.70%	C	55.74%
P	69.45%	K	59.66%	F	55.26%
E	68.34%	S	59.43%	J	53.90%
M	67.12%	X	58.61%	L	52.02%
W	65.36%	A	58.13%	T	51.02%
R	63.26%	N	57.79%	I	36.95%
G	62.96%	H	57.53%		

parameter values), and then tested using SVM-test data, without cross-validation. The SVM-test data informs the challenge strings, while the Evaluate-test data estimates system accuracy; no data used in system creation was reused in its evaluation. In the High-quality Data experiment, accuracy rates for letter classifiers ranged from 37% to 76% (see Table 2). Performing worst was "I", simplest of all Graffiti letters, while "Y", rich in detail and having an alternative stroke, performed best.

Using the results of the tests, 26 confusion matrices were built, one per letter classifier, each having dimensions of 52 users by 52 users. A confusion matrix shows how often one user was (mis)classified as each of the others. Rows are associated with true writer identities, and columns with predicted writer identities. All scores in a row were normalized to sum to 1. For the "A" matrix, the cell in row 1, column 2 contains the fraction of "A"s written by User1, but erroneously predicted by the "A" classifier as having been written by User2.

Next, the rows of the 26 confusion matrices were rearranged to make 52 *confusion charts*, one for each subject. We extract User1's row from the "A" confusion matrix, to become row 1 of User1's chart; this operation is repeated on letters "B"–"Z", for successive rows. Charts for other subjects were constructed similarly. User1's confusion chart is a 26 letters by 52 users matrix in which the cell in row 1, column 2 shows the fraction of User1's "A"s incorrectly classified as belonging to User2. Of special note is the genuine subject's column, which contains *letter-accuracy scores*. These scores show how frequently the genuine writer was correctly identified as him/herself on a given letter. The rows of each confusion chart were sorted in decreasing order by the letter-accuracy scores; ties were broken at random. Now, row 1 of User1's chart shows the highest-scoring letter for that user, in terms of correct classifications; it might be tied in score with some other letter(s). Table 5 shows an abbreviated example confusion chart.

The higher a letter-accuracy score, the better this letter should be (in isolation) at distinguishing the genuine subject from all others in the group. Letters having a

score of 1 are *perfect*; all others are *non-perfect*. In Table 5, only "E" is perfect. Two letters are *complementary* if they have no errors in common, with respect to the same other subject. Three or more letters are complementary if the group is pairwise complementary. In Table 5, "D" and "N" both have errors with respect to User3, so they are not complementary. In contrast, "D", "B", and "G" each have errors with respect to a different user, so they are all complementary with respect to each other.

6.3. Letter lists and challenge strings

A challenge string is a set of letters selected to discriminate one user from every other member of the group. Longer strings provide greater discrimination ability and security, while shorter strings are more convenient to write. A *letter list* is an ordered list of elements (called *units*) that are either single letters or complementary letter pairs. A letter list holds all possible lengths of challenge strings for a given user. A challenge string is realized by including letters from the first u units on a letter list. Increasing the number of units, u, should generally maintain—and may enhance—accuracy (and security).

An abbreviated example of a letter list appears in the bottom row of Table 3; it contains the letters "E DB G NR". Challenge strings are formed by including letters from the leftmost cells, up to a desired stopping point. "E" is the shortest possible challenge string; others are "EDB", "EDBG", and "EDBGNR".

Table 3. User1's letter list (example)

Perfect	Run 1		Run 2
Unit 1	Unit 2	Unit 3	Unit 4
E	D B	G	N R

To form successive units on a letter list, an algorithm selects a single letter or letter pair from the subject's confusion chart. Units are added without backtracking; letters are selected according to the heuristics in Table 4. The terms *perfect*, *non-perfect*, and *complementary* were defined in Section 6.2; a *run* is a group of complementary non-perfect letters. For convenience, we will call letters that have not yet been added to the letter list *unused*. Ties in letter-accuracy scores were decided randomly during chart sorting, so the topmost letter in the chart is favored during ties. We created one letter list per subject.

Example. A scenario involving four users and seven letters will be used to illustrate the process of creating a letter list. Table 5 shows a confusion chart for User1, whose identity is underlined. The "User1" column contains sorted letter-accuracy scores (shown in boldface).

The algorithm first looks for perfect letters, placing each within its own unit. In Table 5, "E" is perfect; it forms the first unit on User1's letter list (see Table 3).

After exhausting perfect letters, the algorithm looks for the highest-scoring non-perfect letter, which is "D". This letter has foreseeable deficiencies, namely its errors with respect to User3. Before adding "D" to the letter list, the algorithm seeks to pair it with a complementary letter (whose errors do not involve User3). The highest-scoring letter complementary to "D" is "B", whose errors involve User2. "D" and "B" are paired together into the same unit, which starts the first run of the letter list.

Next, the algorithm seeks to complete the current run, by successively adding single letters complementary to all those currently in the run. "G" (whose errors involve User4) is the only remaining unused letter complementary to both "D" and "B". "G" is added alone to a new unit in the current run, which is then terminated. No memory of errors is retained from one run to the next.

Now a new non-perfect pair is sought, starting with the highest-scoring unused letter, "N". The only other unused letter complementary to "N" is "R", so those two form a unit and start the second run on the list. The remaining unused letter, "H", is not complementary to "N" and "R"; thus, the second run is finished. "H" is left off the letter list, since it cannot be paired. The completed letter list appears in Table 3; possible challenge strings are "E", "EDB", "EDBG", and "EDBGNR".

The reason that non-perfect letters are only added in the context of a pair (or a run) is to prevent a succession of letters being added whose errors all involve the same user. Such an occurrence would raise the chances of the biometric system erroneously predicting the writer of a challenge string to be that user.

Procedure. A summary of the algorithm follows.

Table 4. Heuristics for creating letter lists

1. A given letter appears at most once on the letter list.

2. Perfect letters are considered equally useful, and superior to non-perfect letters. Perfect letters are added to the letter list before non-perfect letters.

3. A non-perfect letter is considered superior to another non-perfect letter, if its letter-accuracy score is higher. All other things being equal, a superior non-perfect letter is added before an inferior one.

4. A non-perfect letter can only be added to the letter list if a complementary letter accompanies it.

5. After a non-perfect letter pair is added to the list, other complementary letters are sought immediately to complete a run. The purpose of this is to further remedy deficiencies in the non-perfect letters.

6. Units are kept as short as possible, to provide granularity in security levels.

Table 5. User1's confusion chart (example)

Letter	User1	User2	User3	User4
E	1	0	0	0
D	0.9	0	0.1	0
N	0.8	0	0.2	0
B	0.8	0.2	0	0
R	0.7	0.1	0	0.2
G	0.7	0	0	0.3
H	0.6	0.1	0.2	0.1

ALGORITHM TO CREATE A LETTER LIST:
(1) Add perfect letters one at a time, each within its own unit, to the subject's letter list.
(2) Add non-perfect letters that fit into runs, one run at a time, until no more runs can be formed.

HOW TO MAKE A RUN:
(A) Find a complementary letter pair,[1] if one exists. If so, add both letters to a unit, the first unit of this run. If not, then no more runs can be formed.
(B) Add single complementary letters to the run, one at a time and each within its own unit, until none are left; then, the run is finished, and its units are added to the letter list. Each complementary letter must be complementary to all letters already in that run. If more than one letter choice exists in an iteration, prefer the one with the highest letter-accuracy score.

6.4. Decision logic to combine classifier outputs

When an SVM classifier is tested on a letter instance, it outputs a writer prediction. For a multi-letter challenge string, multiple classifiers are involved, so decision logic is required to combine the outputs into a single prediction. When a writing sample is submitted to the biometric system, appropriate SVM letter classifiers are invoked to process the relevant letters. A single classifier determines the probability that each of the 52 users wrote one letter instance. If a challenge string has s unique letters, then s classifiers are invoked, each producing 52 probability scores. Next, the s probability scores for User1 are multiplied together under the independence assumption, to produce a joint probability that User1 wrote all the letters. Joint probabilities are then found for User2, and for all the other users. The single user having the highest joint probability is deemed the most likely writer. Because the probabilities are assumed independent, the order of the letters does not affect the calculation; challenge strings could be permuted to thwart replay attacks.

---

[1]Choose a complementary pair in the following way. Take the highest-scoring unused letter as the provisional first member of the pair. For the second member, take the next-highest scoring letter complementary to the first. If none can be found, try a different provisional first member of the pair (having the next-highest score). Start the search again, and continue until a complementary pair is found, or until there are no more candidates to be the first provisional member of the pair.

7. Evaluation method

The evaluation aims to discover whether users can be discriminated on the basis of handwriting samples, and if so, to find out how long the samples must be. We varied the number of units appearing in challenge strings (recall Table 3), and observed system accuracy; extra units should not decrease accuracy (unlike solitary letters).

Three experiments were conducted, each on a different version of the data, to discover how data quality and quantity affect accuracy: (1) High-quality Data, (2) Reduced Data, and (3) All Data (see Sections 4 and 5.4). We performed an off-line evaluation, in which subject participation was simulated by data in the corpus. Individual letters written by a subject were assembled into a sequence meant to imitate how that subject would respond to a challenge string. The previously unseen Evaluate-test data was used for system evaluation.

7.1. Transaction design and error definitions

At transaction time, a user (the *claimant*) claims an identity; the system responds by displaying the challenge string tailored to that identity. After the user writes the string, the identity claim is accepted or rejected.

Genuine transactions. In genuine transactions, a subject claims his or her true identity. To simulate these events, we used the challenge string assigned to that subject, and called up instances of his or her letters from the Evaluate-test data set. The biometric system predicted the most likely writer. If the predicted writer identity matched the genuine one, no error occurred; otherwise, there was an error. Errors made on genuine transactions contributed to the false non-match rate (the rate at which genuine claimants are denied entry by the system).

Imposter transactions. In imposter transactions, a subject claims an identity other than his or her own. To simulate these events, we used the challenge string assigned to the victim, along with letter instances written by the impostor (from the Evaluate-test data set). The biometric system determined the most likely writer. If the predicted writer identity matched the claimed one, there was an error, because the imposter posed successfully as another subject. Otherwise there was no error, because the imposter failed. Errors made on imposter transactions contributed to the false-match rate (the rate at which imposter claimants are allowed entry by the system).

7.2. Challenge-string evaluation

The 26 SVM classifiers were newly re-trained on all previously seen data, namely SVM-train and SVM-test (collectively called Evaluate-train). All best parameter values from Section 6.1 were kept; 75% of the data was used for re-training. The remaining 25% of the data held in Evaluate-test, previously unseen, was used to evaluate challenge strings. Due to the numerous genuine and imposter transactions, some reuse of data within in Evaluate-test occurred, as specified below.

Within each of the three experiments (see Section 4), the number of units, u, was varied from one to the largest possible number (equaling the number of units in the shortest letter list). In a *round*, all challenge strings have a particular value of u. Between rounds, data were reused, without memory of prior usage.

Within a round, multiple repetitions of transactions were performed, and the error rates were averaged to increase the stability of results. We repeated each transaction as many times as unused data remained, but held constant the number of repetitions for all subjects. In the High-quality Data and Reduced Data experiments, the limiting number of instances per letter was 13; it was 44 in the All Data experiment. Since Evaluate-test contained 25% (or slightly less[2]) of each subject's letter instances, 3 instances of that letter appeared in Evaluate-test for the High-quality Data and Reduced Data experiments ($\lfloor 13/4 \rfloor = 3$), whereas 11 appeared in Evaluate-test for the All Data experiment ($\lfloor 44/4 \rfloor = 11$). In the respective experiments, repetitions were limited to those numbers, for all subjects. Within a round, the same letter instance was never re-used within genuine transactions, or within imposter transactions involving the same victim identity. Otherwise, instances were selected at random.

For the genuine transactions within a round, 52 challenge strings were evaluated using 3 (or 11) repetitions, reusing no letter instances. Errors were counted, and averaged over the repetitions to produce an average false non-match rate (FNMR). In the High-quality Data and Reduced Data experiments, 156 (or 52×3) genuine transactions were carried out per round, while the All Data experiment had 572 (or 52×11).

For the imposter transactions within a round, 52 subjects each masqueraded as 51 other users. Given a fixed victim, the letters from 51 different imposters were called up to satisfy the victim's challenge string; multiple repetitions (3 or 11) of this arrangement did not reuse letter instances. Errors were counted, and averaged over the repetitions to produce an average false-match rate (FMR). In the High-quality Data and Reduced Data experiments, 7,956 (or $52 \times 51 \times 3$) imposter transactions were performed per round, while the All Data experiment had 29,172 (or $52 \times 51 \times 11$).

In biometric applications providing positive or negative identification [24], special evaluation procedures should be followed for imposter transactions, whenever *dependent templates* are present [13]. Templates are dependent whenever the enrollment of a new user affects other templates in the system; otherwise, they are in-

---

[2]Any extra letters padded SVM-train, such that 50% (or slightly more) of the data were assigned to SVM-train, and 25% (or slightly less) were assigned to SVM-test and to Evaluate-test, respectively.

Letters	FMR	FNMR	Letters	FMR	FNMR
1–2	0.35	11.54	7–14	0.01	0
2–4	0.04	0.64	8–16	0	0
3–6	0	0.64	9–18	0	0
4–8	0	0	10–20	0	0
5–10	0	0.64	11–22	0	0
6–12	0	0			

dependent. Our SVM method employs pairwise binary classifiers, and thus the templates are dependent. However, because our target task is insider detection and it assumes no outsiders, our use of dependent templates without special evaluation provisions is reasonable.

8. Results

Table 6 shows the results of the challenge-string evaluation for High-quality Data; these data most closely reflect actual user handwriting. The number of units, u, was varied from 1 to 11, because the subject whose letter list contained the fewest units had only 11. Each unit contains one or two letters, so the number of letters used in a round varies from u to $2u$, depending on the subject. Average false-match rates (FMR) and average false non-match rates (FNMR) both decreased eventually to 0%, as the number of units increased. With only 2–4 letters, FMR=0.04% while FNMR=0.64%. When 8–16 letters were used (or even more), FMR=FNMR=0%.

The results for the Reduced Data and All Data experiments were very similar to the High-quality Data ones. It appears that neither increasing the data quality (while holding quantity constant), nor increasing the data quantity (while holding quality constant), has a clear benefit. Due to the long running time of the evaluations, we were unable to repeat each experiment several times using different random samples, thus preventing estimates of variance and tests of statistical significance. Nevertheless, to probe the stability of the results heuristically, we replicated the High-quality Data experiment once; these results very closely resembled those of the original experiment, as well as those of the Reduced Data and All Data experiments. Note that in the Reduced Data experiment, the subject having the fewest units in his or her letter list had 9; for the All Data experiment it was 8; and for the replication of the High-quality Data experiment, it was 10. The three experiments and the one replication all achieved consistently perfect results when at least 8–16 letters were used. Excepting one chance event (in the seventh round of the High-quality Data experiment), this also happened with only 6–12 letters. The All Data experiment used the most transaction repetitions, and should have the most stable results; it achieved consistently perfect results with only 5–10 letters.

9. Discussion

Although error rates in Table 6 do not decrease monotonically as the number of units increases, deviations from the trend are slight and short-lived. Possible explanations for these small deviations are (1) limited data quantities (or rare atypical instances) in SVM-test and/or Evaluate-test, and (2) sub-optimal challenge strings (because the algorithm for creating letter lists was greedy and heuristic). It just so happened that the trends of the other experiments were more consistent. In general, it appears that adding units to a challenge string should not be harmful. Also, since results under the three different conditions of data quality and quantity did not differ greatly, it seems that (a) data-capture anomalies were not calamitous, and (b) similar performance might be achieved using even less data.

One may ask how it was that such promising results were achieved. Because data from potential attackers was available, template ageing was absent, and ample training data was used, our results may be slightly optimistic. Despite such factors, we feel that system success hailed from the selective grouping of letters into challenge strings. The SVM classifier results were unexceptional (recall Table 2), but combining classifier outputs on letters tailored to each user brought greater success. Some theory supports this rationale; our method is reminiscent of machine learning techniques such as boosting [8] and co-training [1] that conjoin several medium-quality classifiers to produce a very good one.

10. Summary

The aim of this work was to determine whether personalized challenge strings might discriminate enrolled users writing on PDAs. A secondary aim was to determine what approximate length a challenge string must be. Our work suggests that using approximately password-length challenge strings (of at least 5-10 characters, depending on the user) results in a very low equal-error rate, approaching 0%. Employing even longer strings seems to bring consistently perfect results, so asking for a few more seconds of user time (a letter stroke takes less than 0.5 seconds to write, on average) could translate into a very high level of security. These results are a first step towards exploring the promise of structured writing on PDAs to deliver biometric access control.

11. Future work

There are several ways to develop the technology of this work. Using the same data corpus, one could try new features, different splits of training and testing data, other classifiers, new ways to combine classifier outputs, and alternative algorithms to create challenge strings. Variant challenge strings could be generated non-deterministically, to discourage replay attacks. Effects of writing experience on accuracy could be studied. Other biometric tasks could be attempted, such as positive or negative identification [24], possibly using independent templates [13]. Moreover, causes of system failure could be elicited; multiple replications of experiments could be conducted, to estimate the variance of the results. If new data is collected, its quality should be tested to ensure that it closely represents user handwriting. Higher data granularity, accuracy, and reliability (in time, space, and pressure if available) could be beneficial. Template ageing [13] could be introduced to make the task more difficult. Larger numbers of subjects could be recruited, and the relationship between the size of the user pool and system accuracy could be explored. Finally, one could study and test hypotheses about which kinds of structured letters discriminate writers most effectively.

12. Acknowledgements

The authors are grateful for helpful comments from Patricia Loring and from anonymous reviewers. Marcus Louie implemented the stimulus generator. Sebastian Scherer implemented the data-capture program on the Palm m105. This work was supported by National Science Foundation grant number CNS-0430474 and by the Pennsylvania Infrastructure Technology Alliance.

References

[1] A. Blum and T. Mitchell. Combining labeled and unlabeled data with co-training. In *Proceedings of the Eleventh Annual Conference on Computational Learning Theory*, pages 92–100, New York, 1998. ACM Press.

[2] G. E. P. Box and D. R. Cox. An analysis of transformations. *Journal of the Royal Statistical Society: Series B (Methodological)*, 26(2):211–243, 1964.

[3] R. R. Bradford and R. B. Bradford. *Introduction to Handwriting Examination and Identification*. Nelson-Hall Publishers, Chicago, 1992.

[4] C. J. C. Burges. A tutorial on support vector machines for pattern recognition. *Data Mining and Knowledge Discovery*, 2(2):121–167, 1998.

[5] C.-C. Chang and C.-J. Lin. LIBSVM: A library for support vector machines, 2001. Software available at <http://www.csie.ntu.edu.tw/~cjlin/libsvm>.

[6] N. Cristianini and J. Shawe-Taylor. *An Introduction to Support Vector Machines and Other Kernel-based Learning Methods*. Cambridge Univ. Press, Cambridge, 2000.

[7] E. Dimitriadou, K. Hornik, F. Leisch, D. Meyer, and A. Weingessel. The e1071 package, 2005. Software available at <http://cran.r-project.org/src/contrib/Descriptions/e1071.html>.

[8] T. Hastie, R. Tibshirani, and J. Friedman. *The Elements of Statistical Learning: Data Mining, Inference, and Prediction*. Springer, New York, 2001.

[9] C.-W. Hsu, C.-C. Chang, and C.-J. Lin. A practical guide to support vector classification. Technical report, Department of Computer Science and Information Engineering, National Taiwan University, Taipei, Taiwan, 2003.

[10] C.-W. Hsu and C.-J. Lin. A comparison of methods for multiclass support vector machines. *IEEE Transactions on Neural Networks*, 13(2):415–425, March 2002.

[11] IJPRAI. Special issue on automatic signature verification. *International Journal of Pattern Recognition and Artificial Intelligence*, 8(3), June 1994.

[12] F. Leclerc and R. Plamondon. Automatic signature verification: The state of the art, 1989–1993. *International Journal of Pattern Recognition and Artificial Intelligence*, 8(3):643–660, June 1994.

[13] A. J. Mansfield and J. L. Wayman. Best practices in testing and reporting performance of biometric devices (version 2.01). Technical report, Centre for Mathematics and Scientific Computing, National Physical Laboratory, Teddington, Middlesex, UK, August 2002.

[14] L. O'Gorman. Comparing passwords, tokens, and biometrics for user authentication. *Proceedings of the IEEE*, 91(12):2021–2040, December 2003.

[15] Palm Inc. Graffiti Alphabet, 2007. Available at <http://www.palm.com/us/products/input/>.

[16] P. J. Phillips, A. Martin, C. L. Wilson, and M. Przybocki. An introduction to evaluating biometric systems. *Computer*, 33(2):56–63, February 2000.

[17] R. Plamondon and G. Lorette. Automatic signature verification and writer identification—the state of the art. *Pattern Recognition*, 22(2):107–131, 1989.

[18] R. Plamondon and S. N. Srihari. On-line and off-line handwriting recognition: A comprehensive survey. *IEEE Transactions on Pattern Analysis and Machine Intelligence*, 22(1):63–84, January 2000.

[19] R Development Core Team. *R: A Language and Environment for Statistical Computing*. R Foundation for Statistical Computing, Vienna, 2006.

[20] R. Sabourin, R. Plamondon, and G. Lorette. Off-line identification with handwritten signature images: Survey and perspectives. In H. S. Baird, H. Bunke, and K. Yamamoto, editors, *Structured Document Image Analysis*, pages 219–234. Springer, Berlin, 1992.

[21] E. Shaw, K. G. Ruby, and J. M. Post. The insider threat to information systems: The psychology of the dangerous insider. *Security Awareness Bulletin*, 2–98, September 1998. Department of Defense Security Institute, Richmond, Virginia, USA.

[22] V. N. Vapnik. *The Nature of Statistical Learning Theory*. Springer, New York, 2nd edition, 2000.

[23] C. Vielhauer. *Biometric User Authentication for IT Security: From Fundamentals to Handwriting*. Springer, New York, 2006.

[24] J. Wayman, A. Jain, D. Maltoni, and D. Maio. An introduction to biometric authentication systems. In J. Wayman, A. Jain, D. Maltoni, and D. Maio, editors, *Biometric Systems: Technology, Design and Performance Evaluation*, chapter 1, pages 1–20. Springer, London, 2005.

[25] D.-Y. Yeung, H. Chang, Y. Xiong, S. George, R. Kashi, T. Matsumoto, and G. Rigoll. SVC2004: First international signature verification competition. In D. Zhang and A. K. Jain, editors, *Biometric Authentication: Proceedings of the First International Conference, ICBA 2004 (LNCS 3072)*, pages 16–22, Berlin, 2004. Springer.

Session 7A:
Timing Model
and Network Protocols

How to Choose a Timing Model?

Idit Keidar   Alexander Shraer
{idish@ee, shralex@tx}.technion.ac.il
Department of Electrical Engineering, Technion, Haifa 32000, Israel

Abstract

When employing a consensus algorithm for state machine replication, should one optimize for the case that all communication links are usually timely, or for fewer timely links? Does optimizing a protocol for better message complexity hamper the time complexity? In this paper, we investigate these types of questions using mathematical analysis as well as experiments over PlanetLab (WAN) and a LAN. We present a new and efficient leader-based consensus protocol that has $O(n)$ stable-state message complexity (in a system with n processes) and requires only $O(n)$ links to be timely at stable times. We compare this protocol with several previously suggested protocols. Our results show that a protocol that requires fewer timely links can achieve better performance, even if it sends fewer messages.

Keywords: synchrony assumptions, eventual synchrony, failure detectors, consensus algorithms, FT Middleware.

1 Introduction

Consensus is an important building block for achieving fault-tolerance using the state-machine paradigm [19]. It is therefore not surprising that the literature is abundant with fault-tolerant protocols for solving this problem. But how does a system designer choose, among the multitude of available protocols, the right one for her system? This decision depends on a number of factors, e.g., time and message complexity, resilience to failures (process crashes, message loss, etc.), and robustness to unpredictable timing delays.

In this paper we focus on the latter, namely the assumptions the protocol makes about timeliness. These are captured in a *timing model*. We study the impact of the choice of a timing model on the performance in terms of time and message complexity. It is important to note that although the physical system is often given, the system designer has freedom in choosing the timing model representing this system. For example, one seldom comes across a system where the network latency can exceed an hour. This suggests that in principle, even the most unpredictable systems can be modeled as synchronous, with an upper bound of an hour

on message latency. Although a round-based synchronous protocol works correctly in this system, it can take an hour to execute a single communication round, and hence may not be the optimal choice. Indeed, measurements show that timely delivery of 100% of the messages is feasible neither in WANs nor under high load in LANs[7, 5, 3]. Instead, systems choose timeouts by which messages *usually* arrive (e.g., 90% or 99% of the time); note that by knowing the typical latency distribution in the system, a designer can fine-tune the timeout to achieve a desired percentage of timely arrivals. One can then employ protocols that ensure safety even when messages arrive late [7, 20, 13]. Such protocols are called indulgent [15].

While indulgent protocols ensure safety regardless of timeliness, they do make some timeliness assumptions in order to ensure progress. Periods during which these assumptions hold are called *stable*. For example, it is possible to require *Eventual Synchrony (ES)* [13, 7], where messages among all pairs of processes are timely in stable periods. Alternatively, one can use weaker majority-based or leader-based models, where only part of the links are required to be timely in stable periods. This defines a tradeoff: whereas weaker models may require more communication rounds for decision, they may also be stable more often (that is, their timeliness requirements will be satisfied more often). A second consideration is message complexity: protocols that send more messages per round may require fewer rounds. Thus, there may also be a tradeoff between the time and message complexities.

In order to provide insights into such tradeoffs, this paper (1) defines a new timing model, (2) introduces a novel time and message efficient algorithm, and (3) presents an evaluation of different consensus algorithms using probabilistic analysis, as well as concrete measurements in a LAN and in WAN over PlanetLab [4]. We next elaborate on each one of these contributions.

We define a new model (Section 2), *eventually weak leader-majority* $\Diamond WLM$. It includes a leader oracle, and only requires that in stable periods, there be timely links from a designated leader process to other processes and from a majority of processes to the leader. Nothing is required before stabilization. The leader oracle can be implemented with linear (in n, the number of processes) per-round stable state message complexity [21, 23].

We then present a new efficient algorithm for $\Diamond WLM$ (Section 3), which has linear stable state message complexity, and decides within 5 rounds from stabilization. If the leader stabilizes earlier than the communication, our algorithm decides in 4 rounds. Although $\Diamond WLM$ was not previously defined, its conditions allow some existing algorithms [20, 8] to make progress. However, these algorithms may take $O(n)$ rounds after stabilization [10] when run in $\Diamond WLM$, in runs where the leader is not initially known.

Section 4 performs probabilistic analysis of the behavior of consensus in different indulgent models, comparing our new algorithm with three previously known algorithms. We focus on algorithms that always take a constant number of rounds from stabilization, all of which also have quadratic message complexity. Our analysis studies the number of rounds needed to reach stabilization and then decision in each model. Although it makes simplifying assumptions, this analysis gives a good starting point to understand such behaviors in real systems. Note that we study the performance of consensus without taking into account the cost of leader election. This is justified since election protocols often ensure leader stability [23, 1, 14], i.e., the leader is seldom re-elected. Thus, the same leader may persist for numerous instances of consensus (possibly thousands).

We then compare the performance of the above algorithms in LAN and WAN (Section 5). To this end, we implement a round synchronization protocol and deploy it in PlanetLab. We compare our measurements with the probabilistic analysis and explain discrepancies that arise. We give insights to the effect of good leader election on leader-based consensus protocols. We show that our message efficient protocol, although requiring more stable communication rounds than several previously known protocols, incurs practically no cost in terms of actual running time, due to its easier to satisfy weak timeliness requirements: it achieves comparable (and sometimes superior) performance to that of the best $O(n^2)$ (message complexity) protocol, provided that adequate timeouts are set.

Related work

Model and Algorithm. In an earlier paper [18], we introduced a round-based framework, GIRAF, for describing timing models and indulgent protocols that exploit them. We have studied the number of rounds required for consensus in stable periods in several timing models. Nevertheless, [18] studies neither how long it takes to reach stability in practical network settings, nor the round durations in these models. The current paper provides analysis and measurements of the actual time it takes to reach consensus while assuming the different models in a LAN and a WAN (PlanetLab). Moreover, [18] focuses on time complexity, and ig-

nores message complexity, which is no less important. Our new protocol has $O(n)$ stable state message complexity.

The $\Diamond WLM$ model satisfies the progress requirements of the well-known Paxos protocol [20], and recent improvements, such as [8]. But as noted in [10], although these algorithms ensure constant time decision in Eventual Synchrony (ES), they may take a linear number of communication rounds after stabilization to decide in weaker models like $\Diamond WLM$. Most other previously suggested leader-based protocols, e.g., [9, 16], require the leader to receive timely messages from a majority in each round, including during unstable periods, and hence do not work in $\Diamond WLM$.

Malkhi et al. [23] have presented a somewhat weaker timing model intended for use with Paxos, where, as in $\Diamond WLM$, some process has bidirectional timely links with a majority, but unlike $\Diamond WLM$, this process does not have outgoing timely links to the rest of the processes. Although their model allows Paxos to make progress so that some of the processes decide, it does not allow *all* the processes to reach consensus decision in a timely manner [18]. Here, we measure time until *global decision*, i.e., until all processes decide, and therefore strengthen the model accordingly.

Evaluation. The time to reach consensus *after* stabilization in ES has been studied in [12]; here, we also measure the time it takes to reach stabilization, and consider additional models. Other papers evaluated related algorithms in practical settings. Cristian and Fetzer [7] studied stable periods, but only for a model similar to ES, over a LAN. The insight that a leader-based algorithm can work better than ES appears in previous measurements on WANs [3, 2] and simulations [24]. However these studies treated different questions than we do, e.g., did not measure the time required to get a sufficiently long stable period that allows for consensus decision. Unlike most of the previous evaluations, our evaluation includes mathematical analysis as well as measurements in both LAN and WAN, thus identifying general trends that do not depend on a specific setting.

2 Model and Problem Definitions

We consider an asynchronous distributed system consisting of a set Π of $n > 1$ processes, $p_1, p_2, \ldots, p_n$, fully connected by communication links. Processes and links are modeled as deterministic state-machines, called I/O automata [22]. Communication links do not create, duplicate, or alter messages. Messages may be lost by links or take unbounded latency. Timing models defined below restrict such losses and late arrivals. Less than $n/2$ processes may fail by crashing. A process that does not fail is *correct*.

Algorithms and models are defined using the GIRAF framework [18], which we extend here to allow for arbitrary communication patterns. For space limitations, we only overview GIRAF; for formal treatment see [18]. In GIRAF, all algorithms are instantiations of Algorithm 1, a

Algorithm 1 Generic algorithm for process p_i.

States:
$k_i \in N$, initially 0   /*round number*/
$sent_i[\Pi] \in$ *Boolean array*,
    initially $\forall p_j \in \Pi : sent_i[j] = true$
$FD_i \in OracleRange$, initially arbitrary
$M_i[N][\Pi] \in Messages \cup \{\perp\}$,
    initially $\forall k \in N \forall p_j \in \Pi : M_i[k][j] = \perp$
$D_i \in 2^{\Pi}$, initially $\emptyset$

Actions and Transitions:
input $receive(\langle m, k \rangle)_{i,j}, k \in N$
    Effect: $M_i[k][j] \leftarrow m$
output $send(\langle M_i[k_i][i], k_i \rangle)_{i,j}$
    Precondition: $j \in D_i \wedge sent_i[j] = false$
    Effect: $sent_i[j] \leftarrow true$
input $end\text{-}of\text{-}round_i$
    Effect: $FD_i \leftarrow oracle_i(k_i)$
    if $(k_i = 0)$ **then** $\langle M_i[1][i], D_i \rangle \leftarrow initialize(FD_i)$
    else $\langle M_i[k_i + 1][i], D_i \rangle \leftarrow compute(k_i, M_i, FD_i)$
    $k_i \leftarrow k_i + 1$
    $\forall p_j \in \Pi : sent_i[j] \leftarrow false$

---

generic round-based algorithm. Process p_i is equipped with a *failure detector oracle*, which can have an arbitrary output range [6], and is queried using the $oracle_i$ function. To implement a specific algorithm, one implements two functions: *initialize()*, and *compute()*. Both are passed the oracle output, and *compute()* also takes as parameters the set of messages received so far and the round number.

Each process's computation proceeds in *rounds*. The advancement of rounds is controlled by the environment via the *end-of-round* input action. The $end\text{-}of\text{-}round_i$ actions occur separately in each process p_i, and there are no restrictions on the relative rate at which they occur at different processes, i.e., rounds are not necessarily synchronized among processes. However, specific environment properties defined below do require some synchronization between processes, e.g., that some messages are received at one process at the same round in which they are sent by another. Therefore, an implementation of an environment that guarantees such properties needs to employ some sort of round or clock synchronization mechanism. One way to do so is using synchronized clocks (e.g., GPS clocks) when present. Alternatively, an implementation that does not rely on synchronized clocks can be employed, such as the one we present in Section 5.1 and deploy in PlanetLab.

When the *end-of-round* action first occurs, it queries the oracle and calls *initialize()*, which returns the message for sending in round 1 and a set, D_i, of the destinations of this message. Subsequently, in each round, a process sends a message to processes in D_i (although allowed, self messages are not necessary since a message is always stored in the incoming buffer of the sender) and receives messages available on incoming links, until the *end-of-round* action

occurs, at which point the oracle is queried and *compute()* is called, which returns the message for the next round, and a new set D_i of target processes.

Environments are specified using *round-based properties*. We consider only *eventual* properties. Namely, the system may be asynchronous for an arbitrary period of time, but eventually there is a round GSR (*Global Stabilization Round*), so that from GSR onward no process fails and all properties hold in each round. GSR is the *first* round that satisfies this requirement.

We now define some round-based properties. The link from p_s to p_d is *timely in round k*, if the following holds: if (i) $end\text{-}of\text{-}round_s$ occurs in round k, (ii) $d \in D_s$ in round k, and (iii) p_d is correct, then p_d receives the round k message of p_s in round k. A process p is a $\Diamond j$-*source$_v$* if in every round $k \geq$ GSR, there are j processes to which it has timely outgoing links. Correctness is not required from the recipients, and p's link with itself counts towards the count of j. The subscript "v" indicates that the set of j timely links is allowed to change in each round (i.e., the failures are mobile). Similarly, a correct process p is a $\Diamond j$-*destination$_v$* if in every round $k \geq$ GSR, it has j timely incoming links from correct processes. An Ω failure detector outputs a process so that there is some correct p_i s.t. for every round $k \geq$ GSR and every correct p_j, $oracle_j(k) = i$.

We study the following four timing models:

ES *(Eventual Synchrony)*[13]: in every round $k \geq$ GSR, all links between correct processes are timely.

$\Diamond LM$ *(Leader-Majority)*[18]: Ω failure detector, the leader is a $\Diamond n$-source, and every correct process is a $\Diamond(\lfloor \frac{n}{2} \rfloor + 1)$-destination$_v$.

(New) $\Diamond WLM$ *(Weak-Leader-Majority)*: Ω failure detector, the leader is a $\Diamond n$-source and a $\Diamond(\lfloor \frac{n}{2} \rfloor + 1)$-destination$_v$.

$\Diamond AFM$ *(All-From-Majority)*[18] (simplified): every correct process is a $\Diamond(\lfloor \frac{n}{2} \rfloor + 1)$-destination$_v$, and a $\Diamond(\lfloor \frac{n}{2} \rfloor + 1)$-source$_v$.

Consensus A consensus problem is defined for a given value domain, *Values*. We assume that *Values* is a totally ordered set (our algorithm makes use of this order). Every process p_i has a read-only variable $prop_i \in Values$, initialized to some value $v \in Values$, and a write-once variable $dec_i \in Values \cup \{\perp\}$ initialized to $\perp$. We say that p_i *decides* $d \in Values$ in round k if p_i writes d to dec_i when $k_i = k$.

A consensus algorithm must ensure: (a) (*validity*) if a process decides v then $prop_i = v$ for some process p_i, (b) (*agreement*) no two correct processes decide differently, and (c) (*termination*) every correct process eventually decides. We say that algorithm A achieves *global decision* at round k if every process that decides decides by round k and at least one process decides at round k.

3 Time and Message Efficient Algorithm

Algorithm 2 is a consensus algorithm for $\Diamond$WLM, which has a linear stable state message complexity and reaches global decision within 5 rounds of GSR.

As in many indulgent algorithms, including Paxos, processes commit with increasing timestamps (called "ballots" in [20]), and decide on a value committed by majority. In Paxos, the leader always attempts to discover the highest timestamp in the system before committing on a new one. Although this occurs promptly in ES, in $\Diamond WLM$, even after stabilization, the leader can continue to hear increasing timestamps for $O(n)$ rounds. Each time it receives a timestamps higher than the one it has, the decision attempt is aborted, leading to a linear worst case decision time after GSR [10]. Our algorithm avoids such scenarios. Nevertheless, we still need the leader to start a new decision attempt with a fresh timestamp higher than those previously possessed by processes. But unlike Paxos, our algorithm does not assume that the leader knows all the timestamps of correct processes. Instead, the new timestamp is chosen to be the round number, which is monotonically increasing. This must be done with care, so as to ensure that the leader does not miss timestamps of real decisions.

Key idea to preserving consistency is to trust the leader, even if it competes against a higher timestamp, provided that it indicates that at least a majority believes it to be the leader. The latter is conveyed using the *majApproved* message field, which attests to the fact that the leader's timestamps reflect "fresh" information from a majority, and therefore any timestamp it does not know of could not have led to decision.

A second challenge our algorithm addresses is avoiding "wasted" rounds when the system stabilizes in the middle of a decision attempt. This poses a problem, as we strive to reduce the number of rounds needed for reaching a consensus, so that the system is not required to have long periods of stability. The solution we employ is to pipeline proposals. Namely, the leader tries in each round to make progress towards a decision, based on its current state and the messages it gets in the current round, regardless of the unknown status of previous attempts to make progress.

We now describe the algorithm in detail. Algorithm 2 works in the framework of Algorithm 1 described in Section 2, and therefore implements the *initialize()* and *compute()* functions. These function are passed $leader_i$, the leader trusted by p_i's Ω oracle in the current round. Process p_i maintains the following local variables: an estimate of the decision value, est_i; the timestamp of the estimated value, ts_i; the maximal timestamp received in the current round, $maxTS_i$; the maximal estimate received with timestamp $maxTS_i$ in the current round, $maxEST_i$ (recall that *Values* is a totally ordered set); the leader provided by the oracle at the end of the previous round, $prevLD_i$, and in the current round, $newLD_i$; a *Boolean* flag, $majApproved_i$, which is used to indicate whether p_i received a message in the current round from a majority of processes that indi-

cated p_i as their leader; and the message type, $msgType_i$, which is used as follows: If p_i sees a possibility of decision in the next few rounds, then it sends a COMMIT message. Once p_i decides, it sends a DECIDE message in all subsequent rounds. Otherwise, the message type is PREPARE.

We now describe the computation of round k_i. If p_i has not decided, it updates its variables (lines 15-18), and then executes the following conditional statements:

- If p_i receives a DECIDE message then it decides on the received estimate by writing that estimate to dec_i (rule *decide-1*, line 20), and sets its message type (for the round $k_i + 1$ message) to DECIDE.

- If p_i receives a COMMIT message from a majority, including itself (rule *decide-2*), and receives a message from itself with the *majApproved* indicator as *true* (rule *decide-3*), it decides on its own estimate and sets its message type to DECIDE (line 23). Rule *decide-3* ensures that no other process commits or decides in the same round with a different value, since the *commit* rule checks $majApproved$ of the leader, and two processes cannot claim to be $majApproved$ in the same round, since it is not possible that different processes were trusted to be leaders by a majority in the same round (round $k_i - 1$). Rule *decide-2* ensures that a majority of processes have the latest information about the decided value. Since commits in further rounds require the leader to hear from a majority (the $majApproved$ indicator required by rule *commit*), the leader must hear from at least one process that has this information, and this will ensure that it does not promote a value that contradicts agreement.

- Let $prevLD_i$ be the leader indicated in p_i's round k_i message. If p_i receives a round k_i message from $prevLD_i$ with the *majApproved* indicator as *true*, then p_i sets its message type (for the round $k_i + 1$ message) to COMMIT, adopts the estimate received from $prevLD_i$, say est', and sets its timestamp to the current round number k_i (line 25). We say that p_i *commits in round* k_i with estimate est'. The $majApproved$ indicator ensures that commits of the same round are on the same value, since any such commit is on an estimate received from a leader that was trusted by a majority in the previous round (k_i-1), and majorities intersect.

- Otherwise, p_i prepares (sets his message type to PREPARE) and adopts the estimate $maxEST_i$ and timestamp $maxTS_i$ (line 26).

Finally, p_i returns the message for the next round and a subset of processes to which this message is intended. This group is calculated using procedure *Destinations()* as follows: if p_i believes that it is the leader of the current round,

Algorithm 2 leader–based algorithm, code for process p_i.

```
1:  Additional state
2:      est_i ∈ Values, initially prop_i; ts_i, maxTS_i ∈ N, initially 0; majApproved_i ∈ Boolean, initially false
3:      prevLD_i, newLD_i ∈ Π; msgType_i ∈ {PREPARE, COMMIT, DECIDE}, initially PREPARE

4:  Message format
5:      ⟨msgType ∈ {PREPARE, COMMIT, DECIDE}, est ∈ Values, ts ∈ N, leader ∈ Π, majApproved_i ∈ Boolean⟩

6:  procedure Destinations(leader_i)
7:      if (leader_i = p_i) then return Π.
8:      else return {leader_i}

9:  procedure initialize(leader_i)
10:     prevLD_i ← newLD_i ← leader_i
11:     return ⟨⟨msgType_i, est_i, ts_i, newLD_i, majApproved_i⟩, Destinations(leader_i)⟩

12: procedure compute(k_i, M[*][*], leader_i)
13:     if dec_i = ⊥ then
14:         /*Update variables*/
15:         prevLD_i ← newLD_i; newLD_i ← leader_i
16:         maxTS_i ← max{ m.ts | m ∈ M[k_i][*] }
17:         maxEST_i ← max{ m.est | m ∈ M[k_i][*] ∧ m.ts = maxTS_i }
18:         majApproved_i ← (|{ j | M[k_i][j].leader = p_i }| > ⌊n/2⌋)
19:         /*Round Actions*/
20:         if ∃m ∈ M[k_i][*] s.t. m.msgType = DECIDE then   /*decide-1*/
21:             dec_i ← est_i ← m.est; msgType_i ← DECIDE
22:         else if ((|{ j | M[k_i][j].msgType = COMMIT }| > ⌊n/2⌋) ∧ M[k_i][i].msgType = COMMIT)   /*decide-2*/
                and (M[k_i][i].majApproved) then   /*decide-3*/
23:             dec_i ← est_i; msgType_i ← DECIDE;
24:         else if (M[k_i][prevLD_i].majApproved) then   /*commit*/
25:             est_i ← M[k_i][prevLD_i].est; ts_i ← k_i; msgType_i ← COMMIT;
26:         else ts_i ← maxTS_i; est_i ← maxEST_i; msgType_i ← PREPARE
27:     return ⟨⟨msgType_i, est_i, ts_i, newLD_i, majApproved_i⟩, Destinations(leader_i)⟩
```

then *Destinations()* returns the set of all processes, and otherwise, the procedure returns the trusted leader. Thus, starting from the first round in which all processes indicate the same leader in their messages (at most one round after GSR), every process sends a message to this leader, and the leader sends a message to every other process. The stable state message complexity is therefore linear in n.

We prove the correctness of Algorithm 2 in the full version [17], and show that it reaches global decision by round GSR+4, i.e., in 5 rounds starting at GSR. If the eventual requirements of the Ω leader are satisfied starting from round GSR-1 (instead of starting from round GSR as the model requires), then all correct processes decide by round GSR+3, i.e., in 4 rounds (if GSR$= 1$ this means that querying the oracle before the first communication round returns the correct Ω leader at all processes). We make this distinction in order to analyze the performance of the algorithm in the common case, when leader re-election is rare.

4 Probabilistic Comparison of Decision Time

We study four models and the fastest known algorithm in each model – 3 rounds for ES ([11]), 3 for $\Diamond LM$ ([18]), 4 with stable leader for $\Diamond WLM$ (Section 3), and 5 for $\Diamond AFM$ ([18]).

In this section we model link failure probabilities as Independent and Identically Distributed (IID) Bernoulli random variables. By "link failure" we mean that the link fails to deliver a message in the same round in which it is sent. We assume that processes proceed in synchronized rounds, although this is not required for correctness, and focus on runs with no process failures, which are common in practice. Additionally, we do not take the cost of leader election into account, since we assume a stable leader, i.e., a leader that is seldom re-elected (e.g., [23, 1]). Such a leader can persist throughout numerous instances of consensus.

We denote the probability that a message arrives on time by p. For simplicity, we do not treat a process' link with itself differently than other links. Our metric in this section is number of rounds until global decision. The length of each round is the time needed to satisfy p, and it is the same for all algorithms we deal with, while the number of rounds depends on the algorithm. In Section 5.3 we investigate the effect of changing the explicit time length of each round on the overall decision time in each model.

4.1 Mathematical Analysis

All communication in some single round k can be represented as an n by n matrix A, where the rows are the destination process indices, the columns are the source process indices, and each entry $A_{i,j}$ is 0 if a message sent by p_j to p_i does not arrive in round k, and 1 if it does reach p_i in round k. p is the probability of any entry $A_{i,j}$ to be 1. Note that our protocol for $\Diamond WLM$ may not send messages on some links. If a message is not sent, we denote the corresponding entry in A by $\perp$. We define random variables for decision time in different models subscripted by the model name, e.g., D_{ES} is the total number of rounds until decision (including the time until stabilization) in ES. We denote by P_M (e.g., P_{AFM}) the probability of a communication round to satisfy the requirements of model M.

Analysis of ES. Recall that ES requires all entries in the matrix A to be 1. The probability for this is:

$$P_{ES} = p^{n^2} \tag{1}$$

An optimal ES consensus algorithm reaches a global decision in 3 rounds from stabilization, thus we need the assumptions of ES to be satisfied for 3 consecutive rounds starting at some round $k \geq 1$. The probability of this to happen at any given round k is $(P_{ES})^3$. Thus:

$$E(D_{ES}) = \frac{1}{(P_{ES})^3} + 2 \tag{2}$$

Analysis of $\Diamond LM$. Let p_k be the stable leader. For $\Diamond LM$, it is required that A has a majority of ones in every row. Additionally, $\Diamond LM$ requires that $\forall 1 \leq j \leq n \ A_{j,k} = 1$. Denote the event that there is a majority of ones in row A_j by M and the event that $A_{j,k} = 1$ by L. We have n independent rows, and thus:

$$P_{\Diamond LM} = (Pr(L \cap M))^n = (Pr(L) \cdot Pr(M|L))^n \tag{3}$$

Note that $Pr(L) = p$. Given that $A_{j,k} = 1$, the probability that more than $\frac{n}{2} - 1$ of the remaining $n-1$ entries of row j are 1 is:

$$Pr(M|L) = \sum_{i=\lfloor \frac{n}{2} \rfloor}^{n-1} \binom{n-1}{i} p^i (1-p)^{n-1-i} \tag{4}$$

Global decision is achieved in 3 rounds from stabilization in $\Diamond LM$, meaning that this condition on A has to be satisfied for 3 rounds, and thus:

$$E(D_{\Diamond LM}) = \frac{1}{(P_{\Diamond LM})^3} + 2 \tag{5}$$

Analysis of $\Diamond WLM$. Let p_k be the stable leader. $\Diamond WLM$ requires that A has a majority of ones in row A_k. We denote this event by M. Additionally, it requires that $\forall 1 \leq j \leq n \ A_{j,k} = 1$. We denote this event by L'.

$$P_{\Diamond WLM} = Pr(L' \cap M) = Pr(L') \cdot Pr(M|L') \tag{6}$$

Note that $Pr(L') = p^n$, and $Pr(M|L') = Pr(M|L)$ (defined in Equation 4) since row A_k is independent of other rows. These conditions only examine the row and column

corresponding to the leader, p_k. Since p_k is stable, all processes agree on its identity, and thus, the leader sends messages to all other processes, while every other process sends a message to the leader. Hence, the entries of A are not $\perp$.

We first analyze the algorithm of Section 3, which takes 4 rounds starting from GSR, under the stable leader assumption. We get:

$$E(D_{\Diamond WLM}) = \frac{1}{(P_{\Diamond WLM})^4} + 3 \tag{7}$$

For comparison, we also examine an alternative solution: running the optimal algorithm for $\Diamond LM$ over a simulation of $\Diamond LM$ in $\Diamond WLM$ (shown in [17]). We show that this simulation reaches global decision in 7 rounds. Therefore:

$$E(D_{Simulated \ \Diamond WLM}) = \frac{1}{(P_{\Diamond WLM})^7} + 6 \tag{8}$$

Analysis of $\Diamond AFM$. This model requires A to have a majority of ones in each row and column. Consider a given row k of A. We first analyze the probability that the row includes a majority of ones. To this end, let X_j be the random variable representing the cell $A_{k,j}$. According to our assumption, $X_1, X_2, ..., X_n$ are independent and identically distributed Bernoulli random variables with probability of success p. Let $X = \sum_{i=1}^{n} X_i$. The probability that any given row in A has a majority of 1's is:

$$Pr(X > \frac{n}{2}) = \sum_{i=\lfloor \frac{n}{2} \rfloor + 1}^{n} \binom{n}{i} p^i (1-p)^{n-i}$$

For n (independent) rows we need to raise this expression to the power of n. Now assume that every row has a majority of 1 entries. The probability of an entry to be 1 is still at least p. We therefore can make an identical calculation for the columns, raising the expression again to the power of 2.

$$P_{\Diamond AFM} \geq (Pr(X > \frac{n}{2}))^{2n} \tag{9}$$

Since the algorithm for $\Diamond AFM$ achieves global decision in 5 rounds from GSR, this needs to hold for 5 consecutive rounds, and therefore we additionally raise the expression to the power of 5. We get:

$$E(D_{\Diamond AFM}) = \frac{1}{(P_{\Diamond AFM})^5} + 4 \tag{10}$$

4.2 Numerical results

We plot the upper bounds on expected decision times given in Equations 2, 5, 7, 8 and 10 for specific values of p. We focus on the case that $n = 8$, similarly to the group sizes used in other performance studies of consensus-based systems [7, 2, 8], which used 4-9 nodes.

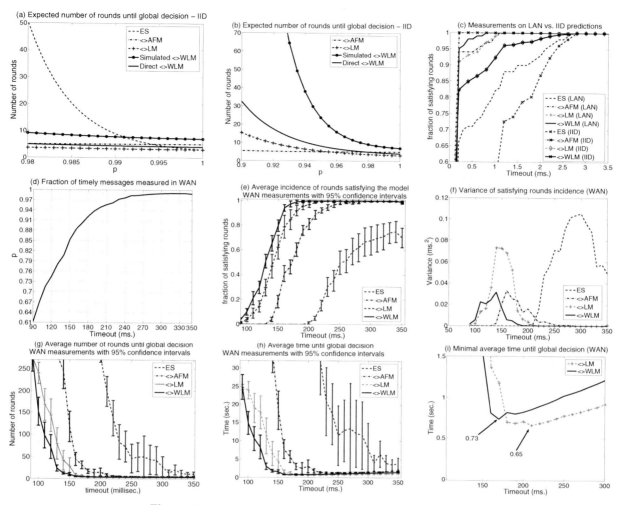

Figure 1. Comparison between ES, $\Diamond AFM$, $\Diamond LM$ and $\Diamond WLM$.

In Figure 1(a) we see that even with a very high probability of timely message delivery, performance in ES deteriorates drastically as p decreases, while $\Diamond AFM$, $\Diamond LM$ and the direct algorithm for $\Diamond WLM$ maintain excellent performance. The direct algorithm for $\Diamond WLM$ does not incur practically any penalty for its improvement of message complexity from quadratic in n to linear. We can also see that $\Diamond LM$ and our algorithm for $\Diamond WLM$ outperform $\Diamond AFM$ in this high range of p. Finally, the simulated algorithm for $\Diamond WLM$ ($\Diamond LM$ algorithm running over the simulation from [17]) is worse than the direct one, since it is much harder to maintain the needed timeliness conditions for 7 rounds than for 4 rounds.

Figure 1(b) examines smaller success probabilities, starting from from 0.9. Here ES is not shown, since it steeply deteriorates as we decrease p (e.g., ES requires 349 rounds for $p = 0.97$). The intuition of why ES performs so poorly, is that it is practically impossible to get 3 matrices not containing a single zero entry, if the probability for a zero is

non-negligible. Our direct algorithm for $\Diamond WLM$ greatly outperforms the simulated algorithm (e.g., for $p = 0.92$ our algorithm requires 18 rounds, while the simulation-based requires 114 rounds). $\Diamond AFM$ is better than $\Diamond LM$ and $\Diamond WLM$ when p is low, but from $p = 0.96$, $\Diamond LM$ becomes better, and starting from $p = 0.97$, the direct algorithm for $\Diamond WLM$ becomes better. Thus, $\Diamond AFM$ is better for lower p values, e.g., for $p = 0.85$ $\Diamond AFM$ is expected to take 10 rounds and $\Diamond LM$ - 69 rounds. Comparing the algorithms for $\Diamond LM$ and $\Diamond WLM$, we see that even though $\Diamond WLM$ requires fewer timely links, $\Diamond LM$ is slightly better, since the dominant factor in the performance of both is the requirement that the leader is a $\Diamond n$-source, and satisfying it for 4 rounds instead of 3 is harder.

5 Measurements

In this section we compare ES, $\Diamond AFM$, $\Diamond LM$ and $\Diamond WLM$ using experiments in two different practical settings - a LAN and a WAN (using PlanetLab). Additionally, we investigate whether the predictions made assuming the IID model in Section 4 were accurate. Like our analysis, the experiments involve 8 nodes.

5.1 Implementation

The round mechanism (GIRAF, Algorithm 1) can be implemented using synchronized clocks, when such are available. Since this is not the case in a WAN, we implemented round synchronization with the simple protocol described below. Before starting the experiments, we measure the average latency between every pair of nodes in the system using pings. Each node n_i then has an array L_i, such that $L_i[j]$ is the average latency between node n_i and node n_j as measured by n_i. This information is used for two purposes: to achieve round synchronization, which we describe below, and to "elect" one well-connected process as the leader, as discussed in Section 5.2.

A process running GIRAF on a node n_i gets the *timeout* as a parameter and runs two threads. In each local round k_i, the task of the first thread is to receive and record messages, inserting them into a message buffer according to the round to which the message belongs (this information is included in the message). Upon receipt of a message belonging to a future round $k_j > k_i$ from a node n_j, this thread records the message and notifies the second thread.

The second thread starts each round k_i by sending messages to its peers, and then waits for the remainder of the round as specified by the *timeout* parameter. At the end of each round it calls *compute()*. In case of a notification from the first thread about a receipt of round-k_j message from node n_j, this thread stops waiting, i.e., the round is ended immediately, and *compute()* is called. It then starts round k_j, and the duration of this round is set to *timeout* $- L_i[j]$.

This algorithm allows a slow node to join its peers already in round k_j, utilizing round-k_j message it received, and takes into account the expected latency of this message to approximate the remaining time for round k_j in order to start round $k_j + 1$ together with the peers. We found that this algorithm achieves very fast synchronization, and whenever the synchronization is lost, it is immediately regained.

5.2 LAN

Our experiment includes 8 nodes running simultaneously on a 100Mbit/sec LAN. Each process sent 100 UDP messages to all others. In a LAN, machines often have synchronized clocks, and there is no need for a synchronization algorithm. We therefore do not focus on round synchronization over LAN, and only measure message latencies and their impact on satisfying the conditions for consensus in different models.

The purpose of this experiment is to compare P_M, i.e., the probability of a communication round to satisfy model M according to IID-based predictions to the percentage of such rounds in measurements on LAN, for various timeouts.

A message is considered to arrive in a communication round if its latency is less than the timeout. The IID-predicted values are calculated by taking the fraction of all messages that arrived in all communication rounds of the experiment as an estimate for p (the probability of a message to arrive on time in the IID analysis) and then using Equations 1, 3, 6 and 9 from Section 4.1. We found that the measured p values were high already for very short timeouts. For example, whereas for a timeout of $0.1ms$ we measured $p = 0.7$, for a timeout of $0.2ms$ it was already $p = 0.976$.

Figure 1(c) shows measured and predicted P_{ES}, $P_{\Diamond AFM}$, $P_{\Diamond LM}$ and $P_{\Diamond WLM}$. We see that even in a LAN, the ES model is hard to satisfy, which matches the IID-based predictions. Although still worse than the other models, ES is better in practice than what was predicted. The reason is that the messages that are late in a run tend to concentrate, rather than to spread among all rounds of the run uniformly as in IID. Thus, in practice, there are fewer rounds that suffer from message loss, and P_{ES} is higher.

On the other hand, $\Diamond AFM$ is worse in reality than was predicted, since it is sensitive to a poor performance of any single node. While in IID all nodes are the same, in our experiment, one node was occasionally slow. $\Diamond AFM$ requires this node, like any other, to receive a message from a majority of processes, and its message had to reach a majority of processes (these two requirements can be satisfied by the same set of links). Since this node is slow, there is a higher chance of messages to be late on its links than on other links (unlike in IID), making it harder to satisfy $\Diamond AFM$. As $\Diamond LM$ requires each process to receive a message from a majority, it suffers from the same problem as $\Diamond AFM$. $\Diamond LM$ additionally requires that the messages of the leader reach all processes, which explains why there are more rounds satisfying $\Diamond AFM$ than $\Diamond LM$.

According to IID-based prediction, at a high rate of message arrival (p values), $P_{\Diamond LM}$ and $P_{\Diamond WLM}$ are almost identical as can be seen from Figure 1(c), and both are worse than $\Diamond AFM$. In practice, for leader-based algorithms, choosing a good leader helps. As implementing a leader election algorithm is beyond the scope of this paper, we designated one process to act as a leader in all runs. We chose this process as follows: before running our experiments, we measured the round-trip times of all links using pings, and then chose a well-connected node to be the leader. Given this leader, both $\Diamond WLM$ and $\Diamond LM$ behaved much better than IID analysis predicted, and we see that $\Diamond WLM$ performs much better than all other models. When we run $\Diamond LM$ and $\Diamond WLM$ with a less optimal leader, whose links have average timeliness, we saw that much bigger timeouts are needed for reasonable performance, and in particular, bigger timeouts than for $\Diamond AFM$. For example, while $\Diamond AFM$ reaches $P_{\Diamond AFM} = 0.97$ at a timeout of $0.9ms$, with an average leader $\Diamond WLM$ and $\Diamond LM$ reach the same incidence only at a timeout of $1.6ms$. With a good leader $\Diamond WLM$ reaches this point at $0.35ms$ and $\Diamond LM$ at $0.8ms$.

5.3 WAN

We implemented GIRAF (Section 5.1) and deployed it in PlanetLab, using 8 nodes located in Switzerland, Japan, California USA, Georgia USA, China, Poland, United Kingdom, and Sweden. The participating processes on these nodes are started up non-synchronously, and then synchronized and continue running for an overall of 300 communication rounds per experiment. We consider only rounds that occur after the system stabilizes for the first time (with respect to the model) to eliminate startup effects. The experiment was repeated with different timeouts, 33 times (runs) for each timeout. The PlanetLab node located in United Kingdom was chosen to serve as the leader for the leader-based protocols, since it was found to be well connected using the same method as was done for our LAN experiment (Section 5.2). We measure the time and number of rounds until the appropriate conditions for global decision are satisfied for each model, starting at 15 random points of each run, and the average of these represent the run. Additionally, we measure the fraction of rounds in each run that satisfy the timeliness requirements of the different models.

Figure 1(d) shows how timeouts translate to fraction of delivered messages (p in Section 4) as measured in our experiment. We have chosen to work with timeouts which assure that up to 99% messages are delivered on time, since it is known that in WANs, the maximal latency can be orders of magnitude longer than the usual latency [5, 3], and thus assuring 100% is unrealistic.

Figure 1(e) shows the measured P_{ES}, $P_{\Diamond AFM}$, $P_{\Diamond LM}$ and $P_{\Diamond WLM}$, averaged over the repetitions of the experiment for each timeout, as well as the 95% confidence interval for the average. Figure 1(f) shows the varience of the values used to calculate the average points in Figure 1(e). We see that the timeliness requirements of $\Diamond WLM$ are satisfied much more frequently than for the other models. This is because $\Diamond WLM$ only requires timeliness from the incoming and outgoing links of the leader. We also observe that $\Diamond LM$ and $\Diamond WLM$ are much easier to satisfy than $\Diamond AFM$ and ES. For example, for a timeout of $160ms$ we get $P_{ES} = 0$, $P_{\Diamond AFM} = 0.4$ while $P_{\Diamond LM} = 0.79$ and $P_{\Diamond WLM} = 0.94$.

We see that ES rounds are really rare, especially with short timeouts (for example when the timeout is less than 200ms, $P_{ES} = 0$), which matches the IID-based prediction of Section 4 (on average, a timeout of $200ms$ corresponds to $p = 0.95$ used in IID analysis, i.e., 95% of messages arrive on time). We observe that while the confidence intervals of $P_{\Diamond AFM}$, $P_{\Diamond LM}$, and $P_{\Diamond WLM}$ are small and diminish as we increase the timeout, the confidence intervals for ES grow. Given a fixed number of measurements, the interval length follows from the variance. ES has high variance even for large timeouts, due to message loss. While in some runs, over 80% of rounds satisfy ES with a timeout of $350ms$, in others only 30% do. For short timeouts the variance of ES is low and its confidence intervals are short since the incidence of ES rounds is consistently low.

Figure 1(f) shows that for longer timeouts, the high incidence of $\Diamond AFM$, $\Diamond LM$ and $\Diamond WLM$ rounds varies only slightly (unlike ES). However, for short timeouts $\Diamond LM$ has high variance. This is caused by its sensitivity to bad performance by any single node, as was also observed in LAN. Specifically, for a timeout of $160ms$, while in some runs 95% of all rounds satisfy the conditions of $\Diamond LM$, in other runs little more than 15% do. This happened because in some runs with this timeout, PlanetLab node located in Poland was slow to receive messages, although most of the messages it sent arrived on time. While in IID all links are the same, we saw that in reality this is not true. This affects $\Diamond LM$ which requires every node to receive a message from a majority. On the other hand, $P_{\Diamond AFM}$ is consistently low (around 0.4, rarely above 0.5) for this timeout, hence the low variance. For larger timeouts, usually all nodes manage to receive a message from a majority, and we see that the incidence of $\Diamond AFM$ and $\Diamond LM$ is high, while the confidence intervals become shorter and the variance goes to 0.

Figure 1(g) and Figure 1(h) show the average (over all runs) number of rounds and time (resp.) that were needed to reach global decision in each model. We observe that for low timeouts the algorithm of Section 3 achieves consensus much faster than the algorithms assuming any of the other models ([11, 18]). For timeouts starting with approximately 180ms and higher, its performance is comparable to $\Diamond LM$, whereas $\Diamond AFM$ takes more rounds and time than both for timeouts less than 230ms. As before, the choice of the leader gave $\Diamond LM$ and $\Diamond WLM$ an advantage over $\Diamond AFM$ and thus the difference from IID-based prediction in Figure 1(b) (according to Figure 1(d), a timeout of $160ms$ corresponds, on average, to $p = 0.88$).

In general, we see that a longer timeout (a higher p in the IID analysis), reduces the number of rounds for decision. On the other hand, it is obvious that a higher p, or a longer timeout, make each individual round longer. We wish to explore this tradeoff and determine the optimal timeout. Of course, the specific optimum would be different for a different system setting, but the principle remains. Figure 1(i) zooms-in on the appropriate part of Figure 1(h), and demonstrates this tradeoff for $\Diamond LM$ and $\Diamond WLM$. For timeouts less than $170ms$ (on average, this corresponds to $p = 0.90$ for IID), while $\Diamond WLM$'s required number of rounds is increasing (as the timeout decreases), the length of each round is decreasing. For timeouts more than $170ms$ (as the timeout increases) the number of required rounds decreases, but the cost of each round increases. For example, if we set our timeout to $180ms$, although the number of rounds will be very small (4.5 rounds on average according to Figure 1(g)), the actual time until decision will be $800ms$, which is about the same as the average time we would get if we shorten the timeout to $160ms$ although the required number of rounds would be higher. This shows that setting conservative timeouts (improving p) will not necessarily improve performance. As we see from this graph, it might actually make it worse.

From Figure 1(i), we conclude that in our setting, choosing the timeout to be $170ms$ is optimal for the $\Diamond WLM$ algorithm and the timeout $210ms$ is optimal for $\Diamond LM$. These timeouts correspond to $p = 0.90$ and $p = 0.96$, e.g., setting the timeout to $170ms$ causes 90% of messages on average to arrive on time in our setting. Note that we present a methodology rather than a specific timeout: a system administrator can perform measurements and choose the timeout for a specific system, according to such criteria.

Finally, if we compare the performance of $\Diamond WLM$ with that of $\Diamond LM$ with their optimal timeouts, we see that $\Diamond WLM$ is expected to take $730ms$, which is only $80ms$ more than what $\Diamond LM$ is expected to take at its best setting. We conclude that it is clearly well worth using $\Diamond WLM$, while gaining the reduction of stable state message complexity from quadratic to linear.

6 Conclusions

We presented a timing model that requires timeliness on $O(n)$ links in stable periods and allows unbounded periods of asynchrony. We introduced a consensus algorithm for this model, which has linear per-round stable state message complexity, and achieves global decision in a constant small number of rounds from stabilization. Since all previously known algorithms that can operate in this model require linear number of rounds, we compared our algorithm to algorithms that require stronger models, all of which also have quadratic message complexity.

Even though our algorithm might take more rounds to decide compared to the others, we have shown that its easier to satisfy weak stability requirements allow it to achieve comparable or even superior global consensus decision time (with very low variance), despite the fact that it sends much fewer messages in each round. Thus, optimizing for message complexity and requiring fewer timely links might actually improve decision time. Our analysis includes measurements in a LAN and a WAN, as well as mathematical analysis, and thus is valid in a broad variety of systems.

Acknowledgments. We thank Hagit Attiya and Liran Katzir for many helpful discussions.

References

[1] M. K. Aguilera, C. Delporte-Gallet, H. Fauconnier, and S. Toueg. Stable leader election. In *DISC*, 2001.

[2] T. Anker, D. Dolev, G. Greenman, and I. Shnayderman. Evaluating total order algorithms in WAN. In *Int. Workshop on Large-Scale Group Communication*, 2003.

[3] O. Bakr and I. Keidar. Evaluating the running time of a communication round over the Internet. In *PODC*, 2002.

[4] A. Bavier, M. Bowman, B. Chun, D. Culler, S. Karlin, S. Muir, L. Peterson, T. Roscoe, T. Spalink, and M. Wawrzoniak. Operating system support for planetary-scale network services, 2004.

[5] N. Cardwell, S. Savage, and T. Anderson. Modeling the performance of short tcp connections, 1998.

[6] T. D. Chandra, V. Hadzilacos, and S. Toueg. The weakest failure detector for solving consensus. *J. ACM*, 43(4):685–722, July 1996.

[7] F. Cristian and C. Fetzer. The timed asynchronous distributed system model. In *IEEE TPDS*, June 1999.

[8] D. Dobre, M. Majuntke, and N. Suri. CoReFP: Contention-Resistant Fast Paxos for WANs. Technical report, TU Darmstadt, Germany, 2006.

[9] P. Dutta and R. Guerraoui. Fast indulgent consensus with zero degradation. In *EDCC*, Oct. 2002.

[10] P. Dutta, R. Guerraoui, and I. Keidar. The overhead of consensus failure recovery. Technical Report 200456, EPFL, 2004.

[11] P. Dutta, R. Guerraoui, and I. Keidar. The Overhead of Indulgent Failure Recovery. *Distributed Computing*, 2006.

[12] P. Dutta, R. Guerraoui, and L. Lamport. How fast can eventual synchrony lead to consensus?. In *DSN*, pages 22–27, 2005.

[13] C. Dwork, N. A. Lynch, and L. Stockmeyer. Consensus in the presence of partial synchrony. *J. ACM*, 35(2):288–323, Apr. 1988.

[14] A. Fernandez, E. Jimenez, and M. Raynal. Eventual leader election with weak assumptions on initial knowledge, communication reliability, and synchrony. In *DSN*, 2006.

[15] R. Guerraoui. Indulgent algorithms. In *PODC*, 2000.

[16] R. Guerraoui and M. Raynal. The information structure of indulgent consensus. *IEEE Transactions on Computers*, 53(4):453–466, 2004.

[17] I. Keidar and A. Shraer. How to choose a timing model? Technical Report CCIT 586, EE Dep., Technion, 2006. http://www.ee.technion.ac.il/~idish/ftp/which-TR.pdf.

[18] I. Keidar and A. Shraer. Timeliness, failure-detectors, and consensus performance. In *PODC*, 2006.

[19] L. Lamport. The implementation of reliable distributed multiprocess systems. *Computer Networks*, 2, 1978.

[20] L. Lamport. The part-time parliament. *ACM Trans. Comput. Syst.*, 16(2):133–169, May 1998.

[21] M. Larrea, A. Fernández, and S. Arévalo. Optimal implementation of the weakest failure detector for solving consensus. In *SRDS*, pages 52–59, 2000.

[22] N. Lynch and M. Tuttle. An introduction to Input/Output Automata. *CWI Quarterly*, 2(3):219–246, 1989.

[23] D. Malkhi, F. Oprea, and L. Zhou. Omega meets paxos: Leader election and stability without eventual timely links. *DISC*, pages 199–213, Sept. 2005.

[24] P. Urban, I. Shnayderman, and A. Schiper. Comparison of failure detectors and group membership: Performance study of two atomic broadcast algorithms. *DSN*, 2003.

Electing an Eventual Leader
in an Asynchronous Shared Memory System *

Antonio FERNÁNDEZ[†]   Ernesto JIMÉNEZ[‡]   Michel RAYNAL[⋆]

[†] LADyR, GSyC, Universidad Rey Juan Carlos, 28933 Móstoles, Spain

[‡] EUI, Universidad Politécnica de Madrid, 28031 Madrid, Spain

[⋆] IRISA, Université de Rennes, Campus de Beaulieu 35 042 Rennes, France

anto@gsyc.escet.urjc.es   ernes@eui.upm.es   raynal@irisa.fr

Abstract

This paper considers the problem of electing an eventual leader in an asynchronous shared memory system. While this problem has received a lot of attention in message-passing systems, very few solutions have been proposed for shared memory systems. As an eventual leader cannot be elected in a pure asynchronous system prone to process crashes, the paper first proposes to enrich the asynchronous system model with an additional assumption. That assumption, denoted AWB, requires that after some time (1) there is a process whose write accesses to some shared variables are timely, and (2) the timers of the other processes are asymptotically well-behaved. The asymptotically well-behaved timer notion is a new notion that generalizes and weakens the traditional notion of timers whose durations are required to monotonically increase when the values they are set to increase. Then, the paper presents two AWB-based algorithms that elect an eventual leader. Both algorithms are independent of the value of t (the maximal number of processes that may crash). The first algorithm enjoys the following noteworthy properties: after some time only the elected leader has to write the shared memory, and all but one shared variables have a bounded domain, be the execution finite or infinite. This algorithm is consequently optimal with respect to the number of processes that have to write the shared memory. The second algorithm enjoys the following property: all the shared variables have a bounded domain. This is obtained at the following additional price: all the processes are required to forever write the shared memory. A theorem is proved which states that this price has to be paid by any algorithm that elects an eventual leader in a bounded shared memory model. This second algorithm is consequently optimal with respect to the number of processes that have to write in such a constrained memory model. In a very interesting way, these algorithms show an inherent tradeoff relating the number of processes that have to write the shared memory and the bounded/unbounded attribute of that memory.

1 Introduction

Equipping an asynchronous system with an oracle   An asynchronous system is characterized by the absence of a bound on the time it takes for a process to proceed from a step of its algorithm to the next one. Combined with process failures, such an absence of a bound can make some synchronization or coordination problems impossible to solve (even when the processes communicate through a reliable communication medium). The most famous of these "impossible" asynchronous problems is the well-known *consensus* problem [7]. Intuitively, this impossibility comes from the fact that a process cannot safely distinguish a crashed process from a very slow process.

One way to address and circumvent these impossibilities consists on enriching the underlying asynchronous systems with an appropriate *oracle* [27]. More precisely, in a system prone to process failures, such an oracle (sometimes called *failure detector*) provides each process with hints on which processes are (or are not) faulty. According to the quality of these hints, several classes of oracles can be defined [3]. So, given an asynchronous system prone to process failures equipped with an appropriate oracle, it becomes possible to solve a problem that is, otherwise, impossible to solve in a purely asynchronous system. This means that an oracle provides processes with additional computability power.

Fundamental issues related to oracles for asynchronous systems   Two fundamental questions can be associated

---

*The work of A. Fernández and E. Jiménez was partially supported by the Spanish MEC under grants TIN2005-09198-C02-01, TIN2004-07474-C02-02, and TIN2004-07474-C02-01, and the Comunidad de Madrid under grant S-0505/TIC/0285. The work of Michel Raynal was supported by the European Network of Excellence ReSIST.

[†]The work of this author was done while on leave at IRISA, supported by the Spanish MEC under grant PR-2006-0193.

with oracles. The first is more on the theoretical side and concerns their computability power. Given a problem (or a family of related problems), which is the weakest oracle that allows solving that problem in an asynchronous system where processes can experience a given type of failures? Intuitively, an oracle O_w is the weakest for solving a problem P if it allows solving that problem, and any other oracle O_{nw} that allows solving P provides hints on failures that are at least as accurate as the ones provided by O_w (this means that the properties defining O_{nw} imply the ones defining O_w, but not necessarily vice-versa). It has been shown that, in asynchronous systems prone to process crash failures, the class of *eventual leader* oracles is the weakest for solving asynchronous *consensus*, be these systems message-passing systems [4] or shared memory systems [20][1]. It has also been shown that, for the same type of process failures, the class of *perfect failure detectors* (defined in [3]) is the weakest for solving asynchronous *interactive consistency* [14].

The second important question is on the algorithm/protocol side and concerns the implementation of oracles (failure detectors) that are designed to equip an asynchronous system. Let us first observe that no such oracle can be implemented on top of a purely asynchronous system (otherwise the problem it allows solving could be solved in a purely asynchronous system without additional computability power). So, this fundamental question translates as follows. First, find "reasonably weak" behavioral assumptions that, when satisfied by the underlying asynchronous system, allow implementing the oracle. "Reasonably weak" means that, although they cannot be satisfied by all the runs, the assumptions are actually satisfied in "nearly all" the runs of the asynchronous system. Second, once such assumptions have been stated, design efficient algorithms that implement correctly the oracle in all the runs satisfying the assumptions.

Content of the paper Considering the asynchronous shared memory model where any number of processes can crash, this paper addresses the construction of eventual leader oracles [4]. Such an oracle (usually denoted Ω)[2] provides the processes with a primitive leader() that returns a process identity, and satisfies the following "eventual" property in each run R: There is a time after which all the invocations of leader() return the same identity, that is the identity of a process that does not crash in the run R.

As already indicated, such an oracle is the weakest to solve the consensus problem in an asynchronous system where processes communicate through single-writer/multi-readers (1WnR) atomic registers and are prone to crash

[1]Let us also notice that the Paxos fault-tolerant state machine replication algorithm [18] is based on the Ω abstraction. For the interested reader, an introduction to the family of Paxos algorithms can be found in [12].

[2]Without ambiguity and according to the context, Ω is used to denote either the class of eventual leader oracles, or an oracle of that class.

failures [20].

The paper has three main contributions.

- It first proposes a behavioral assumption that is particularly weak. This assumption is the following one. In each run, there are a finite (but unknown) time τ and a process p (not a priori known) that does not crash in that run, such that after τ:

  - (1) There is a bound Δ (not necessarily known) such that any two consecutive write accesses to some shared variables issued by p are separated by at most Δ time units, and

  - (2) Each correct process $q \neq p$ has a timer that is *asymptotically well-behaved*. Intuitively, this notion expresses the fact that eventually the duration that elapses before a timer expires has to increase when the timeout parameter increases.

  It is important to see that the timers can behave arbitrarily during arbitrarily long (but finite) periods. Moreover, as we will see in the formal definition, their durations are not required to strictly increase according to their timeout periods. After some time, they have only to be lower-bounded by some monotonously increasing function.

  It is noteworthy to notice that no process (but p) is required to have any synchronous behavior. Only their timers have to eventually satisfy some (weak) behavioral property.

- The paper then presents two algorithms that construct an Ω oracle in all the runs that satisfy the previous behavioral assumptions, and associated lower bounds. All the algorithms use atomic 1WnR atomic registers. The algorithms, that are of increasing difficulty, are presented incrementally.

  - In the first algorithm, all (but one of) the shared variables have a bounded domain (the size of which depends on the run). More specifically, this means that, be the execution finite or infinite, even the timeout values stop increasing forever.

    Moreover, after some time, there is a single process that writes the shared memory. The algorithm is consequently write-efficient. It is even write-optimal as at least one process has to write the shared memory to inform the other processes that the current leader is still alive.

  - The second algorithm improves the first one in the sense that all the (local and shared) variables are bounded. This nice property is obtained by using two boolean flags for each pair of processes. These flags allow each process p to inform each other process q that it has read some value written by q.

- The third contribution is made up of lower bound results are proved for the considered model. Two theorems are proved that state (1) the process that is eventually elected has to forever write the shared memory, and (2) any process (but the eventual leader) has to forever read from the shared memory. Another theorem shows that, if the shared memory is bounded, then all the processes have to forever write into the shared memory. These theorems show that both the algorithms presented in the paper are optimal with respect to these criteria.

Why shared memory-based Ω algorithms are important
Multi-core architectures are becoming more and more deployed and create a renewed interest for asynchronous shared memory systems. In such a context, it has been shown [10] that Ω constitutes the weakest *contention manager* that allows transforming any obstruction-free [15] software transactional memory into a non-blocking transactional memory [16]. This constitutes a very strong motivation to look for requirements that, while being "as weak as possible", are strong enough to allow implementing Ω in asynchronous shared memory environments prone to process failures.

On another side, some distributed systems are made up of computers that communicate through a network of attached disks. These disks constitute a storage area network (SAN) that implements a shared memory abstraction. As commodity disks are cheaper than computers, such architectures are becoming more and more attractive for achieving fault-tolerance. The Ω algorithms presented in this paper are suited to such systems [9].

Related work As far as we know, a single shared memory Ω algorithm has been proposed so far [13]. This algorithm considers that the underlying system satisfies the following behavioral assumption: there is a time τ after which there are a lower bound and an upper bound for any process to execute a local step, or a shared memory access. This assumption defines an eventually synchronous shared memory system. It is easy to see that it is a stronger assumption than the assumption previously defined here.

The implementation of Ω in asynchronous message-passing systems is an active research area. Two main approaches have been been investigated: the *timer*-based approach and the *message pattern*-based approach.

The timer-based approach relies on the addition of timing assumptions [5]. Basically, it assumes that there are

bounds on process speeds and message transfer delays, but these bounds are not known and hold only after some finite but unknown time. The algorithms implementing Ω in such "augmented" asynchronous systems are based on timeouts (e.g., [1, 19]). They use successive approximations to eventually provide each process with an upper bound on transfer delays and processing speed. They differ mainly on the "quantity" of additional synchrony they consider, and on the message cost they require after a leader has been elected.

Among the protocols based on this approach, a protocol presented in [1] is particularly attractive, as it considers a relatively weak additional synchrony requirement. Let t be an upper bound on the number of processes that may crash ($1 \leq t < n$, where n is the total number of processes). This assumption is the following: the underlying asynchronous system, which can have fair lossy channels, is required to have a correct process p that is a $\Diamond t$-*source*. This means that p has t output channels that are eventually timely: there is a time after which the transfer delays of all the messages sent on such a channel are bounded (let us notice that this is trivially satisfied if the receiver has crashed). Notice that such a $\Diamond t$-*source* is not known in advance and may never be explicitly known. It is also shown in [1] that there is no leader protocol if the system has only $\Diamond(t-1)$-*sources*. A versatile adaptive timer-based approach has been developed in [21].

The message pattern-based approach, introduced in [22], does not assume eventual bounds on process and communication delays. It considers that there is a correct process p and a set Q of t processes (with $p \notin Q$, moreover Q can contain crashed processes) such that, each time a process $q \in Q$ broadcasts a query, it receives a response from p among the first $(n-t)$ corresponding responses (such a response is called a winning response). It is easy to see that this assumption does not prevent message delays to always increase without bound. Hence, it is incomparable with the synchrony-related $\Diamond t$-*source* assumption. This approach has been applied to the construction of an Ω algorithm in [24].

A *hybrid* algorithm that combines both types of assumption is developed in [25]. More precisely, this algorithm considers that each channel eventually is timely or satisfies the message pattern, without knowing in advance which assumption it will satisfy during a particular run. The aim of this approach is to increase the assumption coverage, thereby improving fault-tolerance [26].

Roadmap The paper is made up of 5 sections. Section 2 presents the system model and the additional behavioral assumption. Then, Sections 3 and 4 present in an incremental way the two algorithms implementing an Ω oracle, and show they are optimal with respect to the number of processes that have to write or read the shared memory. Finally,

Section 5 provides concluding remarks.

Due to page limitation, the proofs of some lemmas and theorems are omitted. The reader can find them in [6].

2 Base Model, Eventual Leader and Additional Behavioral Assumption

2.1 Base asynchronous shared memory model

The system consists of n, $n > 1$, processes denoted $p_1, \ldots, p_n$. The integer i denotes the identity of p_i. (Sometimes a process is also denoted p, q or r.) A process can fail by *crashing*, i.e., prematurely halting. Until it possibly crashes, a process behaves according to its specification, namely, it executes a sequence of steps as defined by its algorithm. After it has crashed, a process executes no more steps. By definition, a process is *faulty* during a run if it crashes during that run; otherwise it is *correct* in that run. There is no assumption on the maximum number t of processes that may crash, which means that up to $n - 1$ process may crash in a run.

The processes communicate by reading and writing a memory made up of atomic registers (also called shared variables in the following). Each register is one-writer/multi-reader (1WnR). "1WnR" means that a single process can write into it, but all the processes can read it. (Let us observe that using 1WnR atomic registers is particularly suited for cached-based distributed shared memory.) The only process allowed to write an atomic register is called its owner. *Atomic* means that, although read and write operations on the same register may overlap, each (read or write) operation appears to take effect instantaneously at some point of the time line between its invocation and return events (this is called the *linearization* point of the operation) [17]. Uppercase letters are used for the identifiers of the shared registers. These registers are structured into arrays. As an example, $PROGRESS[i]$ denotes a shared register that can be written only by p_i, and read by any process.

Some shared registers are *critical*, while other shared registers are not. A critical register is a an atomic register on which some constraint can be imposed by the additional assumptions that allow implementing an eventual leader. This attribute allows restricting the set of registers involved in these assumptions.

A process can have local variables. They are denoted with lowercase letters, with the process identity appearing as a subscript. As an example, $candidates_i$ denotes a local variable of p_i.

This base model is characterized by the fact that there is no assumption on the execution speed of one process with respect to another. This is the classical *asynchronous* crash prone shared memory model. It is denoted $\mathcal{AS}_n[\emptyset]$ in the following.

2.2 Eventual leader service

The notion of *eventual leader* oracle has been informally presented in the introduction. It is an entity that provides each process with a primitive leader() that returns a process identity each time it is invoked. A unique correct leader is eventually elected but there is no knowledge of when the leader is elected. Several leaders can coexist during an arbitrarily long period of time, and there is no way for the processes to learn when this "anarchy" period is over. The *leader* oracle, denoted Ω, satisfies the following property [4]:

- Validity: The value returned by a leader() invocation is a process identity.

- Eventual Leadership[3]: There is a finite time and a correct process p_i such that, after that time, every leader() invocation returns i.

- Termination: Any leader() invocation issued by a correct process terminates.

The Ω leader abstraction has been introduced and formally developed in [4] where it is shown to be the weakest, in terms of information about failures, to solve consensus in asynchronous systems prone to process crashes (assuming a majority of correct processes). Several Ω-based consensus protocols have been proposed (e.g., [11, 18, 23] for message-passing systems, and [8] for shared memory systems)[4].

2.3 Additional behavioral assumption

Underlying intuition As already indicated, Ω cannot be implemented in pure asynchronous systems such as $\mathcal{AS}_n[\emptyset]$. So, we consider the system is no longer fully asynchronous: its runs satisfy the following assumption denoted AWB (for *a*symptotically *w*ell-*b*ehaved). The resulting system is consequently denoted $\mathcal{AS}_n[AWB]$.

Each process p_i is equipped with a timer denoted $timer_i$. The intuition that underlies AWB is that, once a process p_ℓ is defined as being the current leader, it should not to be demoted by a process p_i that believes p_ℓ has crashed. To that end, constraints have to be defined on the behavior of both p_ℓ and p_i. The constraint on p_ℓ is to force it to "regularly" inform the other processes that it is still alive. The constraint on a process p_i is to prevent it to falsely suspect that p_ℓ has crashed.

There are several ways to define runs satisfying the previous constraints. As an example, restricting the runs to

---

[3] This property refers to a notion of global time. This notion is not accessible to the processes.

[4] It is important to notice that, albeit it can be rewritten using Ω (first introduced in 1992), the original version of Paxos, that dates back to 1989, was not explicitly defined with this formalism. The first paper where Paxos is explained as an Ω-based algorithm is [2].

be "eventually synchronous" would work but is much more constraining than what is necessary. The aim of the AWB additional assumption is to state constraints that are "as weak as possible"[5]. It appears that requiring the timers to be eventually monotonous is stronger than necessary (as we are about to see, this is a particular case of the AWB assumption). The AWB assumption is made up of two parts AWB_1 and AWB_2 that we present now. AWB_1 is on the existence of a process whose behavior has to satisfy a synchrony property. AWB_2 is on the timers of the other processes. AWB_1 and AWB_2 are "matching" properties.

The assumption AWB_1   The AWB_1 assumption requires that eventually a process does not behave in a fully asynchronous way. It is defined as follows.

> AWB_1: There are a time τ_{01}, a bound Δ, and a correct process p_ℓ (τ_{01}, Δ and p_ℓ may be never explicitly known) such that, after τ_{01}, any two consecutive write accesses issued by p_ℓ to (its own) critical registers, are completed in at most Δ time units.

This property means that, after some arbitrary (but finite) time, the speed of p_ℓ is lower-bounded, i.e., its behavior is partially synchronous (let us notice that, while there is a lower bound, no upper bound is required on the speed of p_ℓ, except the fact that it is not $+\infty$).

The assumption AWB_2   In order to define AWB_2, we first introduce a function $f()$ with monotonicity properties that will be used to define an asymptotic behavior. That function takes two parameters, a time τ and a duration x, and returns a duration. It is defined as follows. There are two (possibly unknown) bounded values x_f and τ_f such that:

- (f1) $\forall \tau_2, \tau_1 : \tau_2 \geq \tau_1 \geq \tau_f, \forall x_2, x_1 : x_2 \geq x_1 \geq x_f$: $f(\tau_2, x_2) \geq f(\tau_1, x_1)$. (After some point, $f()$ is not decreasing with respect to τ and x).
- (f2) $\lim_{x \to +\infty} f(\tau_f, x) = +\infty$. (Eventually, $f()$ always increases[6].)

We are now in order to define the notion of *asymptotically well-behaved* timer. Considering the timer $timer_i$ of a process p_i and a run R, let τ be a real time at which the timer is set to a value x, and τ' be the finite real time at which that timer expires. Let $T_R(\tau, x) = \tau' - \tau$, for each x and τ. Then timer $timer_i$ is asymptotically well-behaved in

---

[5] Of course, the notion of "as weak as possible" has to be taken with its intuitive meaning. This means that, when we want to implement Ω in a shared memory system, we know neither an assumption weaker than AWB, nor the answer to the question: Is AWB the weakest additional assumption?

[6] If the image of $f()$ is the set of natural numbers, then this condition can be replaced by $x_2 > x_1 \implies f(\tau_f, x_2) > f(\tau_f, x_1)$.

a run R, if there is a function $f_R()$, as defined above, such that:

- (f3) $\forall \tau : \tau \geq \tau_f, \forall x : x \geq x_f$: $f_R(\tau, x) \leq T_R(\tau, x)$.

This constraint states the fact that, after some point, the function $T_R()$ is always above the function $f_R()$. It is important to observe that, after (τ_f, x_f), the function $T_R(\tau, x)$ is not required to be non-decreasing, it can increase and decrease. Its only requirement is to always dominate $f_R()$. (See Figure 1.)

> AWB_2: The timer of each correct process (except possibly p_ℓ) is asymptotically well-behaved.

When we consider AWB, it is important to notice that any process (but p_ℓ constrained by a speed lower bound) can behave in a fully asynchronous way. Moreover, the local clocks used to implement the timers are required to be neither synchronized, nor accurate with respect to real-time.

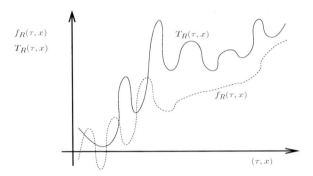

Figure 1. $T_R()$ asymptotically dominates $f_R()$

3   An Ω algorithm for $\mathcal{AS}_n[AWB]$

3.1   Principles of the algorithm

The first algorithm implementing Ω in $\mathcal{AS}_n[AWB]$ that we present, relies on a very simple idea that has been used in several algorithms that build Ω in message-passing systems. Each process p_i handles a set ($candidates_i$) containing the processes that (from its point of view) are candidates for being the leader. When it suspects one of its candidates p_j to have crashed, p_i makes public the fact that it suspects p_j once more. (This is done by p_i increasing the shared register $SUSPICIONS[i, j]$.)

Finally, a process p_i defines its current leader as the least suspected process among its current candidates. As several processes can be equally suspected, p_i uses the function $lexmin(X)$ that outputs the lexicographically smallest pair in the set parameter X, where X is the set of (number of suspicions, process identity) pairs defined from $candidate_i$, and $(a, i) < (b, j)$ iff $(a < b) \lor (a = b \land i < j)$.

3.2 Description of the algorithm

The algorithm, based on the principles described just above, that builds Ω in $\mathcal{AS}_n[AWB]$ is depicted in Figure 2.

Shared variables The variables shared by the processes are the following:

- $SUSPICIONS[1..n, 1..n]$ is an array of natural registers. $SUSPICIONS[j,k] = x$ means that, up to now, p_j has suspected x times the process p_k to have crashed. The entries $SUSPICIONS[j,k]$, $1 \leq k \leq n$ can be written only by p_j.

- $PROGRESS[1..n]$ is an array of natural registers. Only p_i can write $PROGRESS[i]$. (It does it only when it considers it is the leader.)

- $STOP[1..n]$ is an array of boolean registers. Only p_i can write $STOP[i]$. It sets it to *false* to indicate it considers itself as leader, and sets it to *true* to indicate it stops considering it is the leader.

The initial values of the previous shared variables could be arbitrary[7]. To improve efficiency, we consider that the natural integer variables are initialized to 1 and the boolean variables to *true*.

Each shared register $PROGRESS[k]$ or $STOP[k]$, $1 \leq k \leq n$ is critical. Differently, none of the registers $SUSPICIONS[j,k]$, $1 \leq j, k \leq n$, is critical. This means that, for a process p_k involved in the assumption AWB_1, only the write accesses to its registers $PROGRESS[k]$ and $STOP[k]$ are concerned.

Let us observe that, as the shared variables $PROGRESS[i]$, $STOP[i]$ and $SUSPICIONS[i,k]$, $1 \leq k \leq n$, are written only by p_i, that process can save their values in local memory and, when it has to read any of them, it can read instead its local copy. (We do not do it in our description of the algorithms to keep simpler the presentation.)

Process behavior The algorithm is made up of three tasks. Each local variable $candidate_i$ is initialized to any set of process identities containing i.

The task $T1$ implements the leader() primitive. As indicated, p_i determines the least suspected among the processes it considers as candidates (lines 02-04), and returns its identity (line 05).

The task $T2$ is an infinite loop. When it considers it is the leader, (line 07), p_i repeatedly increases $PROGRESS[i]$ to inform the other processes that it is still alive (lines 07-10). If it discovers it is no longer leader, p_i sets $STOP[i]$ to *true* (line 11) to inform the other processes it is no longer competing to be leader.

```
task T1:
(01)  when leader() is invoked:
(02)    for_each k ∈ candidates_i do
(03)       susp_i[k] ← Σ_{1≤j≤n} SUSPICIONS[j,k] end_for;
(04)    let (−, ℓ) = lex_min({(susp_i[k], k)}_{k∈candidates_i});
(05)    return(ℓ)

task T2:
(06)  repeat_forever
(07)    while (leader() = i) do
(08)       PROGRESS[i] ← PROGRESS[i] + 1;
(09)       if STOP[i] then STOP[i] ← false end_if
(10)    end_while;
(11)    if (¬ STOP[i]) then STOP[i] ← true end_if
(12)  end_repeat

task T3:
(13)  when timer_i expires:
(14)    for_each k ∈ {1,...,n} \ {i} do
(15)       stop_k_i    ← STOP[k];
(16)       progress_k_i ← PROGRESS[k];
(17)       if (progress_k_i ≠ last_i[k]) then
(18)          candidates_i ← candidates_i ∪ {k};
(19)          last_i[k]    ← progress_k_i
(20)       else_if (stop_k_i) then
(21)          candidates_i ← candidates_i \ {k}
(22)       else_if (k ∈ candidates_i) then
(23)          SUSPICIONS[i,k] ← SUSPICIONS[i,k] + 1;
(24)          candidates_i    ← candidates_i \ {k}
(25)       end_if
(26)    end_for;
(27)    set timer_i to max({SUSPICIONS[i,k]}_{1≤k≤n})
```

Figure 2. Write-efficient, all variables are 1WMR, bounded except a single entry of the shared array $PROGRESS[1..n]$ (code for p_i)

Each process p_i has a local timer (denoted $timer_i$), and manages a local variable $last_i[k]$ where it saves the greatest value that it has ever read from $PROGRESS[k]$. The task $T3$ is executed each time that timer expires (line 13). Then, p_i executes the following statements with respect to each process p_k (but itself, see line 14). First, p_i checks if p_k did some progress since the previous timer expiration (line 17). Then, it does the following.

- If $PROGRESS[k]$ has progressed, p_i considers p_k as a candidate to be leader. To that end it adds k to the local set $candidates_i$ (line 18). (It also updates $last_i[k]$, line 19.)

- If $PROGRESS[k]$ has not progressed, p_i checks the

---

[7]This means that the algorithm is *self-stabilizing* with respect to the *shared* variables. Whatever their initial values, it converges in a finite number of steps towards a common leader, as soon as the additional assumption is satisfied. When these variables have arbitrary initial values (that can be negative), line 27 of Figure 2 has to be "set $timer_i$ to $\max(1, \max\{SUSPICIONS[i,k]\}_{1 \leq k \leq n})$" in order a timer be never set to a negative value.

value of $STOP[k]$ (line 20). If it is true, p_k voluntarily demoted itself from being a candidate. Consequently, p_i suppresses k from its local set $candidates_i$ (line 21). If $STOP[k]$ is false and p_k is candidate from p_i's point of view (line 22), p_i suspects p_k to have crashed (line 23) and suppresses it from $candidates_i$ (line 24).

Then, p_i resets its local timer (line 27). Let us observe that no variable of the array $SUSPICIONS$ can decrease and such an entry is increased each time a process is suspected by another process. Thanks to these properties, we will see in the proof that $\max(\{SUSPICIONS[i, k]\}_{1 \leq k \leq n})$ can be used as the next timeout value. Note that to compute this value only variables owned by p_i are accessed.

3.3   Proof of the algorithm

Lemma 1 [6] *Let p_k be a faulty process and p_i a correct process. Eventually, the predicate $k \notin candidates_i$ remains true forever.*

Given a run R and a process p_x, let M_x denote the largest value ever taken by $\Sigma_{1 \leq j \leq n} SUSPICIONS[j, x]$. If there is no such value (i.e., $\Sigma_{1 \leq j \leq n} SUSPICIONS[j, x]$ grows forever), let $M_x = +\infty$. Finally, let B be the set of correct processes p_x such that $M_x \neq +\infty$ (B stands for "bounded").

Lemma 2 [6] *Let us assume that the behavioral assumption AWB is satisfied. Let p_i be a process that satisfies assumption AWB_1. Then, $i \in B$ and, hence, $B \neq \emptyset$.*

Let $(M_\ell, \ell) = \text{lexmin}(\{M_x, x) \mid x \in B\})$.

Lemma 3 [6] *There is a single process p_ℓ and it is correct.*

Lemma 4 [6] *There is a time after which p_ℓ permanently executes the loop defined by the lines 07-10 of task $T2$.*

Theorem 1 *There is a time after which a correct process is elected as the eventual common leader.*

Proof We show that p_ℓ is the eventual common leader. From Lemma 3 p_ℓ is unique and correct. Moreover, due the definitions of the bound M_ℓ and the set B, there is a finite time τ after which, for each correct process p_i, $i \neq \ell$, we have $(\Sigma_{1 \leq j \leq n} SUSPICIONS[j, i], i) > (M_\ell, \ell)$. Moreover, due to Lemma 1, there is a time after which, for each correct process p_i and each faulty process p_k we have $k \notin candidate_i$. It follows from these observations, that proving the theorem amounts to show that eventually the predicate $\ell \in candidate_i$ remains permanently true at each correct process p_i.

Let us notice that the predicate $x \in candidate_x$ is always true for any process p_x. This follows from the fact that initially x belongs to $candidate_x$, and then p_x does not execute the tasks $T3$ for $k = x$, and consequently cannot

withdraw x from $candidate_x$. It follows that we always have $\ell \in candidate_\ell$. So, let us examine the case $i \neq \ell$.

It follows from Lemma 4 that there is a time τ after which p_ℓ remains permanently in the **while** loop of task $T2$. Let $\tau' \geq \tau$ be a time at which we have $\Sigma_{1 \leq j \leq n} SUSPICIONS[j, \ell] = M_\ell$, and p_ℓ has executed line 09 (i.e., $STOP[\ell]$ remains false forever).

After τ', because p_ℓ is forever increasing $PROGRESS[\ell]$, the test of line 17 eventually evaluates to true and (if not already done) p_i adds ℓ to $candidate_i$. We claim that, after that time, the task $T3$ of p_i is always executing the lines 18-19 (for $k = \ell$), from which it follows that ℓ remains forever in $candidate_i$.

Proof of the claim. Let us assume by contradiction that the test of line 17 is false when evaluated by p_i. It follows that ℓ is withdrawn from $candidate_i$, and this occurs at line 24. (It cannot occur at line 21 because after τ we always have $STOP[\ell] = false$.) But line 23 is executed before 24, from which we conclude that $SUSPICIONS[i, \ell]$ has been increased, which means that we have now $\Sigma_{1 \leq j \leq n} SUSPICIONS[j, \ell] = M_\ell + 1$, contradicting the definition of the bound M_ℓ. *End of the proof of the claim.* $\square_{Theorem\ 1}$

Theorem 2 [6] *Let p_ℓ be the eventual common leader. All shared variables (but $PROGRESS[\ell]$) are bounded.*

Theorem 3 [6] *After a finite time, only one process (the eventual common leader) writes forever into the shared memory. Moreover, it always writes the same shared variable.*

3.4   Optimality Results

Let $\mathcal{A}$ be any algorithm that implements Ω in $\mathcal{AS}_n[AWB]$ with up to t faulty processes. We have the following lower bounds.

Lemma 5 *Let R be any run of $\mathcal{A}$ with less than t faulty processes and let p_ℓ be the leader chosen in R. Then p_ℓ must write forever in the shared memory in R.*

Lemma 6 [6] *Let R be any run of $\mathcal{A}$ with less than t faulty processes and let p_ℓ be the leader chosen in R. Then every correct process p_i, $i \neq \ell$, must read forever from the shared memory in R.*

The following theorem follows immediately from the previous lemmas.

Theorem 4 [6] *The algorithm described in Figure 2 is optimal in with respect to the number of processes that have to write the shared memory. It is quasi-optimal with respect to the number of processes that have to read the shared memory.*

The "quasi-optimality" comes from the fact that the algorithm described in Figure 2 requires that each process (including the leader) reads forever the shared memory (all the processes have to read the array $SUSPICIONS[1..n, 1..n]$).

3.5 Discussion

Using multi-writer/multi-reader (nWnR) atomic registers If we allow nWnR atomic variables, each column $SUSPICIONS[*, j]$ can be replaced by a single $SUSPICIONS[j]$. Consequently vectors of nWnR atomic variables can be used instead of matrices of 1WnR atomic variables.

Eliminating the local clocks The timers (and consequently the local clocks used to implement them) can be eliminated as follows. Each $timer_i$ is now a local variable managed by p_i as follows (where each execution of the statement $timer_i \leftarrow timer_i - 1$ is assumed to take at least one time unit). The code of task $T3$ becomes accordingly:

task $T3$: $timer_i \leftarrow 1$;
while ($true$) **do**
   $timer_i \leftarrow timer_i - 1$;
   if ($timer_i = 0$)
      then Line 14 until Line 26 of Figure 2 or 3;
        $timer_i \leftarrow \max(\{SUSPICIONS[i, k]\}_{1 \leq k \leq n})$
   end_if
end_while.

4 An Ω algorithm for $\mathcal{AS}_n[AWB]$ with Bounded Variables Only

4.1 A Lower Bound Result

This section shows that any algorithm that implements Ω in $\mathcal{AS}_n[AWB]$ with only bounded memory requires all correct processes to read and write the shared memory forever. As we will see, it follows from this lower bound that the algorithm described in Figure 3 is optimal with respect to this criterium.

Let $\mathcal{A}$ be an algorithm that implements Ω in $\mathcal{AS}_n[AWB]$ such that, in every run R of $\mathcal{A}$, the number of shared memory bits used is bounded by a value S_R (which may depend on the run). This means that in any run there is time after which no new memory positions are used, and each memory position has bounded number of bits. To make the result stronger, we also assume that $\mathcal{A}$ knows t (maximum number of processes that can fail in any run of $\mathcal{A}$).

Theorem 5 [6] *The algorithm $\mathcal{A}$ has runs in which at least $t + 1$ processes write forever in the shared memory.*

The system model defined in this paper assumes $t = n - 1$. Hence the following corollary.

Corollary 1 *Any algorithm that implements Ω in $\mathcal{AS}_n[AWB]$ with bounded shared memory has runs in which all processes write the shared memory forever.*

4.2 An algorithm with only bounded variables

Principles and description As already indicated, we are interested here in an algorithm whose variables are all bounded. To attain this goal, we use a hand-shaking mechanism. More precisely, we replace the shared array $PROGRESS[1..n]$ and all the local arrays $last_i[1..n]$, $1 \leq i \leq n$, by two shared matrices of 1WnR boolean values, denoted $PROGRESS[1..n, 1..n]$ and $LAST[1..n, 1..n]$.

The hand-shaking mechanism works a follows. Given a pair of processes p_i and p_k, $PROGRESS[i, k]$ and $LAST[i, k]$ are used by these processes to send signals to each other. More precisely, to signal p_k that it is alive, p_i sets $PROGRESS[i, k]$ equal to $\neg LAST[i, k]$. In the other direction, p_k indicates that it has seen this "signal" by cancelling it, namely, it resets $LAST[i, k]$ equal to $PROGRESS[i, k]$. It follows from the essence of the hand-shaking mechanism that both p_i and p_k have to write shared variables, but as shown by Corollary 1, this is the price that has to be paid to have bounded shared variables.

Using this simple technique, we obtain the algorithm described in Figure 3. In order to capture easily the parts that are new or modified with respect to the previous algorithm, the line number of the new statements are suffixed with the letter R (so the line 08 of the previous protocol is replaced by three new lines, while each of the lines 16, 17 and 19 is replaced by a single line). This allows a better understanding of the common principles on which both algorithms rely.

Proof of the algorithm The statement of the lemmas 1, 2, 3 and 4, and Theorem 1 are still valid when the shared array $PROGRESS[1..n]$ and the local arrays $last_i[1..n]$, $1 \leq i \leq n$ are replaced by the shared matrices $PROGRESS[1..n, 1..n]$ and $LAST[1..n, 1..n]$.

As far as their proofs are concerned, the proofs of the lemmas 3 and 4 given in Section 3.3 are verbatim the same. The proofs of the lemmas 1 and 2, and the proof of Theorem 1 have to be slightly modified to suit to the new context. Basically, they differ from their counterparts of Section 3.3 in the way they establish the property that, after some time, no correct process p_i misses an "alive" signal from a process that satisfies the assumption AWB_1. (More specifically, the sentence "there is a time after which $PROGRESS[k]$ does no longer increase" has to be replaced by the sentence "'there is a time after which $PROGRESS[k, i]$ remains forever equal to $LAST[k, i]$".) As they are very close to the previous ones and tedious, we don't detail these proofs. (According to the usual sentence, "They are left as an exercise to the reader".)

```
task T1:
(01)  when leader() is invoked:
(02)     for_each k ∈ candidates_i do
(03)        susp_i[k] ← Σ_{1≤j≤n} SUSPICIONS[j,k] end_for;
(04)     let (−,ℓ) = lex_min({(susp_i[k],k)}_{k∈candidates_i});
(05)     return(ℓ)

task T2:
(06)  repeat_forever
(07)     while (leader() = i) do
(08.R1)     for_each k ∈ {1,...,n} \ {i} do
(08.R2)        if (PROGRESS[i,k] = LAST[i,k]) then
(08.R3)           PROGRESS[i,k] ← ¬LAST[i,k] end_if
(08.R4)     end_for;
(09)        if STOP[i] then STOP[i] ← false end_if
(10)     end_while;
(11)     if (¬ STOP[i]) then STOP[i] ← true end_if
(12)  end_repeat

task T3:
(13)  when timer_i expires:
(14)     for_each k ∈ {1,...,n} \ {i} do
(15)        stop_k_i    ← STOP[k];
(16.R1)    progress_k_i ← PROGRESS[k,i];
(17.R1)    if (progress_k_i ≠ LAST[k,i]) then
(18)          candidates_i ← candidates_i ∪ {k};
(19.R1)       LAST[k,i] ← progress_k_i
(20)        else_if (stop_k_i) then
(21)          candidates_i ← candidates_i \ {k}
(22)        else_if (k ∈ candidates_i) then
(23)          SUSPICIONS[i,k] ← SUSPICIONS[i,k] + 1;
(24)          candidates_i     ← candidates_i \ {k}
(25)        end_if
(26)     end_for;
(27)     set timer_i to max({SUSPICIONS[i,k]}_{1≤k≤n})
```

Figure 3. All variables are 1WMR and bounded (code for p_i)

The same reasoning as the one done in the proof of the Theorem 2 shows that each shared variable $SUSPICIONS[j,k]$, $\leq j,k \leq n$, is bounded. Combined with the fact that the variables $PROGRESS[j,k]$ and $LAST[j,k]$ are boolean, we obtain the following theorem.

Theorem 6 *All the variables used in the algorithm described in Figure 3 are bounded.*

The following theorem is the counterpart of Theorem 3.

Theorem 7 *Let p_ℓ be the process elected as the eventual common leader, and p_i, $i \neq \ell$, any correct process. There is a time after which the only variables that may be written are $PROGRESS[\ell,i]$ (written by p_ℓ) and $LAST[\ell,i]$ (written by p_i).*

Proof The proof that the variables $PROGRESS[\ell,j]$, $1 \leq j \leq n$, are infinitely often written, and the proof that there

is a time after which the variables $STOP[j]$, $1 \leq j \leq n$, and the variables $SUSPICIONS[j,k]$, $1 \leq j,k \leq n$, are no longer written is the same as the proof done in Theorem 3.

The fact that there is a time after which $PROGRESS[x,j]$, $1 \leq x,j \leq n$, $x \neq \ell$, are no longer written follows from the fact that, after p_ℓ has been elected, no process p_x executes the body of the **while** loop of task $T2$.

Let us now consider any variable $LAST[x,y]$, $x \neq \ell$. As, after p_ℓ has been elected, no correct process p_x, $x \neq \ell$, updates $PROGRESS[x,y]$ (at line 08.R2), it follows that there is a time after which $LAST[x,y] = PROGRESS[x,y]$ remains forever true for $1 \leq x,y \leq n$ and $x \neq \ell$. Consequently, after a finite time, the test of line 17.R1 is always false for p_x, $x \neq \ell$, and $LAST[x,y]$ is no longer written. □_{Theorem 7}

Finally, the next theorem follows directly from Corollary 1.

Theorem 8 *The Ω algorithm described in Figure 3 is optimal with respect to the number of processes that have to write the shared memory.*

5 Conclusion

This paper has addressed the problem of electing an eventual leader in an asynchronous shared memory system. It has three main contributions.

- The first contribution is the statement of an assumption (a property denoted AWB) that allows electing a leader in the shared memory asynchronous systems that satisfy that assumption. This assumption requires that after some time (1) there is a process whose write accesses to some shared variables are timely, and (2) the other processes have asymptotically well-behaved timers. The notion of asymptotically well-behaved timer is weaker than the usual notion of timer where the timer durations have to monotonically increase when the values to which they are set increase. This means that AWB is a particular weak assumption.

- The second contribution is the design of two algorithms that elect an eventual leader in any asynchronous shared memory system that satisfies the assumption AWB. In addition of being independent of t (the maximum number of processes allowed to crash), and being based only on one-writer/multi-readers atomic shared variables, these algorithms enjoy noteworthy properties. The first algorithm guarantees that (1) there is a (finite) time after which a single process writes forever the shared memory, and (2) all but one shared variables have a bounded domain. The second algorithm uses (1) a bounded memory but (2) requires that each process forever writes the shared memory.

407

- The third contribution shows that the previous trade-off (bounded/unbounded memory vs number of processes that have to write) is inherent to the leader election problem in asynchronous shared memory systems equipped with AWB. It follows that both algorithms are optimal, the first with respect to the number of processes that have to forever write the shared memory, the second with respect to the boundedness of the memory.

Several questions remain open. One concerns the first algorithm. Is it possible to design a leader algorithm in which there is a time after which the eventual leader is not required to read the shared memory? Another question is the following: is the second algorithm optimal with respect to the size of the control information (bit arrays) it uses to have a bounded memory implementation?

References

[1] Aguilera M.K., Delporte-Gallet C., Fauconnier H. and Toueg S., Communication-Efficient Leader Election and Consensus with Limited Link Synchrony. *Proc. 23th PODC* pp. 328-337, 2004.

[2] Boichat R., Dutta P., Frølund S. and Guerraoui R., Deconstructing Paxos. *ACM Sigact News, Distributed Computing Column*, 34(1):47-67, 2003.

[3] Chandra T. and Toueg S., unreliable Failure Detectors for Resilient Distributed Systems. *Journal of the ACM*, 43(2):225-267, 1996.

[4] Chandra T., Hadzilacos V. and Toueg S., The Weakest Failure Detector for Solving Consensus. *Journal of the ACM*, 43(4):685-722, 1996.

[5] Dwork C., Lynch N. and Stockmeyer L., Consensus in the Presence of Partial Synchrony. *Journal of the ACM*, 35(2):288-323, 1988.

[6] Fernández A., Jiménez E. and Raynal M., Electing an Eventual Leader in an Asynchronous Shared Memory System. *Tech Report #1821*, 18 pages, Université de Rennes, France, November 2006.

[7] Fischer M.J., Lynch N. and Paterson M.S., Impossibility of Distributed Consensus with One Faulty Process. *Journal of the ACM*, 32(2):374-382, 1985.

[8] Gafni E. and Lamport L., Disk Paxos. *Distributed Computing*, 16(1):1-20, 2003.

[9] Gibson G.A. *et al.*, A Cost-effective High-bandwidth Storage Architecture. *Proc. 8th Int'l Conference on Architectural Support for Programming Languages and Operating Systems (ASPLOS'98)*, ACM Press, pp. 92-103, 1998.

[10] Guerraoui R., Kapalka M. and Kouznetsov P., The Weakest failure Detectors to Boost Obstruction-Freedom. *Proc. 20th Symposium on Distributed Computing (DISC'06)*, Springer-Verlag LNCS #4167, pp. 376-390, 2006.

[11] Guerraoui R. and Raynal M., The Information Structure of Indulgent Consensus. *IEEE Transactions on Computers*, 53(4):453-466, 2004.

[12] Guerraoui R. and Raynal M., The Alpha of Asynchronous Consensus. *The Computer Journal*, To appear, 2007.

[13] Guerraoui R. and Raynal M., A Leader Election Protocol for Eventually Synchronous Shared Memory Systems. *4th Int'l IEEE Workshop on Software Technologies for Future Embedded and Ubiquitous Systems (SEUS'06)*, IEEE Computer Society Press, pp. 75-80, 2006.

[14] Hélary J.-M., Hurfin M., Mostefaoui A., Raynal M. and Tronel F., Computing Global Functions in Asynchronous Distributed Systems with Perfect Failure Detectors. *IEEE TPDS*, 11(9):897-909, 2000.

[15] Herlihy M.P., Luchangco V. and Moir M., Obstruction-free Synchronization: Double-ended Queues as an Example. *Proc. 23th IEEE Int'l Conference on Distributed Computing Systems (ICDCS'03)*, pp. 522-529, 2003.

[16] Herlihy M.P., Luchangco V., Moir M. and Scherer III W.N., Software Transactional Memory for Dynamic Sized Data Structure. *Proc. 21th ACM Symposium on Principles of Distributed Computing (PODC'03)*, pp. 92-101, 2003.

[17] Herlihy M.P. and Wing J.M, Linearizability: a Correctness Condition for Concurrent Objects. *ACM Transactions on Progr. Languages and Systems*, 12(3):463-492, 1990.

[18] Lamport L., The Part-Time Parliament. *ACM Transactions on Computer Systems*, 16(2):133-169, 1998.

[19] Larrea M., Fernández A. and Arévalo S., Optimal Implementation of the Weakest Failure Detector for Solving Consensus. *Proc. 19th Symposium on Resilient Distributed Systems (SRDS'00)*, pp. 52-60, 2000.

[20] Lo W.-K. and Hadzilacos V., Using failure Detectors to solve Consensus in Asynchronous Shared Memory Systems. *Proc. 8th Int'l Workshop on Distributed Computing (WDAG'94)*, Springer Verlag LNCS #857, pp. 280-295, 1994.

[21] Malkhi D., Oprea F. and Zhou L., Ω Meets Paxos: Leader Election and Stability without Eventual Timley Links. *Proc. 19th Int'l Symposium on DIStributed Computing (DISC'05)*, Springer Verlag LNCS #3724, pp. 199-213, 2005.

[22] Mostefaoui A., Mourgaya E., and Raynal M., Asynchronous Implementation of Failure Detectors. *Proc. Int'l IEEE Conference on Dependable Systems and Networks (DSN'03)*, IEEE Computer Society Press, pp. 351-360, 2003.

[23] Mostefaoui A. and Raynal M., Leader-Based Consensus. *Parallel Processing Letters*, 11(1):95-107, 2001.

[24] Mostéfaoui A., Raynal M. and Travers C., Crash Resilient Time-Free Eventual Leadership. *Proc. 23th IEEE Symposium on Reliable Dists. Systems*, pp. 208-218, 2004.

[25] Mostéfaoui A., Raynal M. and Travers C., Time-free and Timeliness Assumptions can be Combined to Get Eventual Leadership. *IEEE Transactions on Parallel and Distributed Systems*, 17(7):656-666, 2006.

[26] Powell D., Failure Mode Assumptions and Assumption Coverage. *Proc. of the 22nd Int'l Symposium on Fault-Tolerant Computing (FTCS-22)*, pp.386-395, 1992.

[27] Raynal M., A Short Introduction to Failure Detectors for Asynchronous Distributed Systems. *ACM SIGACT News, Distributed Computing Column*, 36(1):53-70, 2005.

Minimizing Response Time for Quorum-System Protocols over Wide-Area Networks

Florian Oprea[*]   Michael K. Reiter[†]

Abstract

A quorum system is a collection of sets (quorums) of servers, where any two quorums intersect. Quorum-based protocols underly modern edge-computing architectures and throughput-scalable service implementations. In this paper we propose new algorithms for placing quorums in wide-area networks and tuning which quorums clients access, so as to optimize clients' average response time in quorum-based protocols. We examine scenarios in which the service is lightly loaded and hence network latency is the dominant delay, and in which client-induced load contributes significantly to the delay that clients observe. In each case, we evaluate our algorithms on topologies ranging from 50 to over 150 wide-area locations.

1. Introduction

A *quorum system* is a collection of sets (called *quorums*) such that any two intersect. Quorum systems are a standard tool to achieve efficient and fault-tolerant coordination in a distributed system. At a high level, the intersection property of quorums ensures that an update performed at one quorum of servers will be visible to any access subsequently performed at another quorum. At the same time, the fact that accesses need not be performed at all servers can lead to significant improvements in terms of system throughput and availability (e.g., [21]). For these reasons, they are a key ingredient in a range of practical fault-tolerant system implementations (e.g., [1, 8, 20]).

In this paper we consider the use of quorum-based protocols in a wide-area network. Our interest in the wide-area setting arises from two previous lines of research: First, quorums have been employed as an ingredient of *edge computing* systems (e.g., [10]) that support the deployment of dynamic services across a potentially global collection of proxies. That is, these techniques strive to adapt the efficiencies of content distribution networks (CDNs) like Akamai to more dynamic services, and in doing so they employ accesses to quorums of proxies in order to coordinate activities. Second, there has recently been significant theoretical progress on algorithms for deploying quorums in physical topologies, so that certain network measures are optimized or approximately optimized (e.g., [9, 12, 14, 15, 19, 27]). These results have paved the way for empirical studies using them, which is what we seek to initiate here.

More specifically, in this paper we perform an evaluation of techniques for placing quorums in wide-area networks, and for adapting client[1] strategies in choosing which quorums to access. In doing so, we shed light on a number of issues relevant to deploying a service "on the edge" of the Internet in order to minimize service response times as measured by clients, such as (i) the number and location of proxies that should be involved in the service implementation, and (ii) the manner in which quorums should be accessed. A central tension that we explore is that between accessing "close" quorums to minimize network delays and dispersing service demand across (possibly more distant) quorums to minimize service processing delays. Similarly, as we will show, quorums over a small universe of servers is better to minimize network delays, but worse for dispersing service demand. Finding the right balances on these spectra is key to minimizing overall response times of a edge-deployed service.

We conduct our analyses through both experiments with a real protocol implementation [1] in an emulated wide-area network environment [28] and simulation of

---

This work was partially supported by U.S. National Science Foundation award CCF-0424422.

[*]Electrical & Computer Engineering Department, Carnegie Mellon University, Pittsburgh, PA, USA; foprea@cmu.edu

[†]Electrical & Computer Engineering and Computer Science Departments, Carnegie Mellon University, Pittsburgh, PA, USA; reiter@cmu.edu

---

[1]While we refer to entities that access quorums as "clients", they need not be user end systems. Rather, in an edge computing system, the clients could be other proxies, for example.

a generic quorum system protocol over models of several actual wide-area network topologies. The topologies are created from PlanetLab [5] measurements and from measurements between web servers [23]. Their sizes range from 50 to 161 wide-area locations, making this, to our knowledge, the widest range of topologies considered to date for quorum placement. That said, as the initial study at this scale, ours is limited in considering only "normal" conditions, i.e., that there are no failures of network nodes or links, and that delays between pairs of nodes are stable over long enough periods of time and known beforehand. We hope to relax these assumptions in future studies.

2. Related work

The earliest study of which we are aware of quorum behavior in wide-area networks is due to Amir and Wool [3]. Their analysis studied the availability of quorums deployed across three wide-area locations, with a focus on how the behavior of the wide-area network violated typical assumptions underlying theoretical availability analyses of quorum systems. Their focus on availability is complementary to ours on response time, and was conducted on much smaller topologies than what we consider.

Bakr and Keidar [4] conducted a wide-area study of a *communication round* among nodes, in which each node sends information to each other participating node. Their study also focused on delay, though otherwise their study and ours are complementary. Our study considers only direct client-to-quorum communication; their treatment of four different round protocols is more exhaustive. However, their study is confined to one node at each of ten wide-area sites—they do not consider altering the number or locations of nodes—and does not admit load dispersion (since all nodes participate in all exchanges). In contrast, our study shows the impact of scaling the number of servers in a wide-area quorum system; of the judicious placement of servers among the candidate sites; and of tuning client access strategies to disperse load.

Amir et al. [2] construct and evaluate a Byzantine fault-tolerant service with the goal of improving the performance of such a service over a wide-area network. In this context, they evaluate BFT [6] and their alternative protocol, which executes Paxos [17] over the wide area. These protocols can be viewed as employing Majority [11, 26] quorum systems in which a quorum constitutes greater than two-thirds or one-half of the wide-area sites, respectively; their evaluation overlaps ours in that we also evaluate these quorum systems (and others). As in the Bakr and Keidar evaluation,

however, Amir et al. constrain their evaluation to a fixed number of wide-area sites (in their case, five), and do not consider altering the number or locations of nodes. Consequently, our evaluation is complementary to that of Amir et al. in the same ways.

Oppenheimer et al. [22] examined the problem of mapping large-scale services to available node resources in a wide-area network. Through measurements of several services running on Planetlab [5], they extracted application resource demand patterns and CPU and network resource availability for Planetlab nodes over a 6-month period. From these measurements, they concluded that several applications would benefit from a service providing resource-informed placement of applications to nodes. Among other interesting results, their study reveals that inter-node latency is fairly stable and is a good predictor of available bandwidth, a conclusion that supports our focus on periods in which latencies between nodes are stable.

3. A motivating example

To motivate our study (and perhaps as one of its contributions), in this section we describe an evaluation of the Q/U protocol [1]. Q/U is a Byzantine fault-tolerant service protocol in which clients perform operations by accessing a quorum of servers. The goal of our evaluation is to shed light on the factors that influence Q/U client response time when executed over the wide area, leading to our efforts in subsequent sections to minimize the impacts of those factors.

We perform our evaluation on Modelnet [28], an emulated wide area environment, using a network topology developed from PlanetLab measurements. We deployed Modelnet on a rack of 76 Intel Pentium 4 2.80 GHz computers, each with 1 GB of memory and an Intel PRO/1000 NIC. We derived our topology from network delays measured between 50 PlanetLab sites around the world in the period July–November 2006 [24].

We varied two parameters in our experiments: the first was the number n of Q/U servers, where $n \geq 5t+1$ is required to tolerate t Byzantine failures. We ran Q/U with $t \in \{1, \ldots, 5\}$, $n = 5t + 1$ and a quorum size of $4t+1$. The second parameter we varied was the number of clients issuing requests to the Q/U servers. We chose the location of clients and servers in the topology as follows: we placed each server at a distinct node, using a known algorithm (recounted in Section 4.1) that approximately minimizes the average network delay that each client experiences when accessing a quorum uniformly at random. For each such placement, we computed a set of 10 client locations for which the average network delay to the server placement approximates the average network delay from all the nodes of the graph to the server placement well. On each of these client locations we ran c clients, with $c \in \{1, \ldots, 10\}$.

Clients issued only requests that completed in a single round trip to a quorum. While not all Q/U operations are guaranteed to complete in a single round trip, they should in the common case for most services [1]. For each request, clients chose the quorum to access uniformly at random, thereby balancing client demand across servers. The application processing delay per client request at each server was 1 ms.

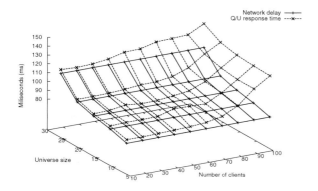

Figure 3.1. Average response time, network delay for Q/U on Planetlab topology

We compared two measures in our experiments: the average response time over all the clients and the average network delay over all the clients (both in milliseconds). Average response time was computed by running each experiment 5 times and then taking the mean. The variation observed was under 1 ms for up to 50 clients, and then increased with the client demand above that threshold.

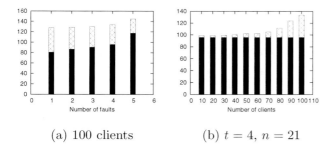

(a) 100 clients   (b) $t = 4$, $n = 21$

Figure 3.2. Avg network delay (black bars) & response time (total bars) for Q/U (ms)

Figure 3.1 shows how the two measures changed when we varied the universe size n and the number of clients issuing requests. As expected, increasing the client demand led to higher processing delay and hence higher average response time. Increasing the universe size had a similar effect on response time, but for a different reason: the average network delay increased since quorums tended to be spread apart more. This can be more easily seen in Figure 3.2a, where we keep the client demand constant and increase t and hence the universe size. However, increasing the universe size better distributed processing costs across more servers, and so decreased processing delay slightly.

In Figure 3.2b we can see how putting more demand on the system increased the average response time. For up to at most 50 clients, the major component of the average client response time was network delay. Increasing client demand beyond that point made processing delay play a more important role in average client response time (although network delay still represented a significant fraction of the overall response time). If request processing involved significant server resources, this effect would be even more pronounced.

To summarize, the Q/U experiments show that on a wide-area network, average response time depends on the average network delay and on the processing delays on servers. Increasing universe size tends to increase network delay but decrease per-server processing delay when demand is high. Thus to improve the overall performance of a protocol that uses quorum systems, we need algorithms that optimize either just the network delay (for systems where client demand is expected to be low) or a combination of network delay and processing delay (if client demand is expected to be high). The rest of this paper is devoted to balancing these tradeoffs by modifying how servers are placed in the network, and how clients access them.

4. Algorithms

To experiment with quorum placement in wide area topologies, we have implemented several known algorithms and developed others of potentially independent interest. Here we describe those algorithms. To do so, we introduce a number of concepts first.

Network We model the network as an undirected graph $G = (V, E)$, with each node having an associated capacity $\mathsf{cap}(v) \in \mathbb{R}^+$; a node's capacity is a measure of its processing capability. There is a positive "length" $\mathsf{length}(e)$ for each edge $e \in E$, which induces a distance function $d : V \times V \to \mathbb{R}^+$ obtained by setting $d(v, v')$ to be length of the shortest path between v and v'. We assume that the set of clients that access the quorum system is V.

Quorum placement Given a quorum system $\mathcal{Q} = \{Q_1, \ldots, Q_m\}$ over a universe U of logical elements, we define a *quorum placement* f as an arbitrary mapping $f : U \rightarrow V$. A placement specifies the node $f(u) \in V$ that hosts universe element u. Similarly, for $Q \in \mathcal{Q}$, we define $f(Q) = \{f(u) : u \in Q\}$. We call $f(U)$ the *support set* of the placement f (i.e., the nodes of the graph that actually host a universe element).

Load Given a quorum system $\mathcal{Q}$ over a universe U, with $|U| = n$, and a client $v \in V$, an *access strategy* p_v of client v is a distribution on the quorums of $\mathcal{Q}$ (i.e., $\sum_{Q \in \mathcal{Q}} p_v(Q) = 1$). Intuitively, in order to perform an operation, a client v samples a quorum according to the distribution p_v and then performs the operation at those servers. Consequently, an access strategy of client $v \in V$ induces a load on each element $u \in U$, given by $\mathsf{load}_v(u) = \sum_{Q \in \mathcal{Q}: u \in Q} p_v(Q)$. For each client $v \in V$ and node $w \in V$, a placement f induces a load on w, namely $\mathsf{load}_{v,f}(w) = \sum_{u \in U : f(u)=w} \mathsf{load}_v(u)$ (i.e., equal to the sum of load of universe elements assigned to w by f). Finally, we define the load induced by f on node w as $\mathsf{load}_f(w) = \mathsf{avg}_{v \in V} \mathsf{load}_{v,f}(w)$.

Response time We will attempt to deploy quorums in the wide-area to minimize response time, and to do so we model response time assuming that a client v issuing a request to a server node has to wait for an amount of time equal to the total roundtrip delay between itself and the server plus a time proportional to the number of requests the server has to process before servicing v's request. In protocols that use quorum systems, a client completes a request only after receiving replies from a full quorum of servers. Thus we model the response time for a client request as:

$$\rho_f(v, Q) = \max_{w \in f(Q)}(d(v, w) + \alpha * \mathsf{load}_f(w)) \quad (4.1)$$

Manipulating α allows us to adjust for absolute demand from clients and processing cost per request.

We model the *expected response time* (under p_v) for client v to access quorum $\mathcal{Q}$ as:

$$\Delta_f(v) = \sum_{Q \in \mathcal{Q}} p_v(Q)\,\rho_f(v, Q). \quad (4.2)$$

The objective function we seek to minimize in our algorithms is the average response time over all clients: $\mathsf{avg}_{v \in V}[\Delta_f(v)]$. If we set $\alpha = 0$, the response time for a client request becomes $\delta_f(v, Q) = \max_{w \in f(Q)} d(v, w)$. This transforms the objective function into average network delay, a measure studied previously [9, 14, 15, 19]. We stress that these definitions are merely tools for placing quorum systems; our interest is in seeing how well we can use these models to efficiently deploy quorum systems in realistic wide-area topologies.

4.1. Previously introduced algorithms

In this section we briefly describe previously proposed algorithms for finding quorum placements that minimize network delay. In doing so, we make a distinction between one-to-one and many-to-one placements. Each of these two categories of placements potentially has advantages over the other: for instance, many-to-one placements can decrease network delay by putting more logical elements on a single physical node. One-to-one quorum placements, on the other hand, are important when we want to preserve the fault-tolerance of the original quorum system.

4.1.1 One-to-one quorum placements

For two known quorum constructions (Majority [11, 26] and Grid [7, 16]), Gupta et al. [14] propose optimal one-to-one placements assuming a single client $v_0 \in V$ issues requests using a uniform access strategy. They also show that to obtain a one-to-one placement without this assumption that is within a small constant factor of optimal, we can run the single-client placement algorithm using each node v as v_0, compute the average network delay from all clients for each such placement, and pick the placement that has the smallest average delay.

Gupta et al. [14] show that, for Majorities, every one-to-one placement to a fixed set of nodes in V has the same average delay for a single client. Thus, in our evaluation we will pick an arbitrary one-to-one mapping f from the universe U, $|U| = n$, to the *ball* $B(v_0, n)$, i.e., the set of n nodes closest to v_0 (including v_0) such that each node v has capacity $\mathsf{cap}(v) \geq \mathsf{load}_f(u)$ for any $u \in U$. Recall that because p_{v_0} (and p_v for any $v \in V$) is the uniform access strategy, $\mathsf{load}_f(u)$ is a constant independent of $u \in U$.

For the Grid quorum system the following algorithm is optimal for a single client $v_0 \in V$. For the sake of simplicity we describe the algorithm for finding the inverse of the optimal placement (i.e., that puts network nodes on the cells of a $n = k \times k$ grid). Let $d_1 \geq d_2 \geq \ldots \geq d_n$ be the distances from the nodes in $B(v_0, n)$ to v_0 sorted in decreasing order. The algorithm places the largest ℓ^2 distances—or rather, the nodes with those distances—on the top-left $\ell \times \ell$ square of the grid. The next ℓ distances $d_{\ell^2+1}, d_{\ell^2+2}, \ldots, d_{\ell^2+\ell}$ are placed on $(1, \ell+1), (2, \ell+1), \ldots, (\ell, \ell+1)$, and the following ℓ distances $d_{\ell^2+\ell+1}, \ldots, d_{\ell^2+2\ell+1}$ are placed on $(\ell+1, 1), \ldots, (\ell+1, \ell+1)$. This completes the top

$(\ell+1) \times (\ell+1)$ square of the grid, and the construction proceeds inductively.

4.1.2 Many-to-one quorum placements

In this section we discuss two algorithms that result in many-to-one placements.

An almost-capacity-respecting placement The algorithm for finding many-to-one placements [14] has the same structure as the algorithm for one-to-one placements: it uses as building block an algorithm for a single client v_0. To find the best placement we simply consider all possible nodes for v_0. The difference from the case of one-to-one placements consists in the techniques used to place quorums for access by v_0: the algorithm uses a linear programming (LP) formulation of the problem. At a high level, the algorithm is the following: We first solve the LP formulation to obtain a fractional placement. Then we use Lin and Vitter's filtering and rounding procedure [18] to obtain another fractional solution that does not (fractionally) assign a universe element to a node too far away from the single client v_0. Finally, from the fractional solution we construct a *generalized assignment problem* (GAP) problem instance [25] and solve it to obtain the many-to-one quorum placement. An advantage of this algorithm is that it works for arbitrary quorum systems and an arbitrary access strategy p_{v_0} (where p_{v_0} is the same access strategy for all clients). However, the algorithm also allows for the node capacity to be exceeded by a small constant factor.

Singleton placement A special many-to-one quorum placement is the *singleton* quorum placement: this puts all the elements of U on a single network node (regardless of that node's capacity). The node on which we place all the universe elements is the node that minimizes the sum of the distances from all the clients to itself. When all nodes of the graph are clients, this node is also known as *the median* of the graph. Lin [19] showed that the singleton is a 2-approximation for the problem of designing a quorum system over a network to minimize average network delay.

4.2. New techniques

Optimizing access strategies Our first new technique is an algorithm that, given a placement, finds client access strategies that minimize network delay under a set of node capacity constraints. The algorithm allows one to improve network delay while preserving per-server load, something that will be useful when we want to minimize response time.

The algorithm is based on a LP with variables $p_{vi} \geq 0$, where p_{vi} specifies the probability of access

of quorum Q_i by client v. We assume a quorum placement $f : U \to V$ and a capacity $\mathsf{cap}(v)$ for each $v \in V$ are given. A LP formulation of the problem is:

$$\text{minimize } \mathsf{avg}_{v \in V} \sum_{i=1}^{m} p_{vi} \delta_f(v, Q_i) \qquad (4.3)$$

$$\text{s.t. } \mathsf{avg}_{v \in V} \mathsf{load}_{v,f}(v_j) \leq \mathsf{cap}(v_j) \; \forall v_j \in V \quad (4.4)$$

$$\sum_{i=1}^{m} p_{vi} = 1 \; \forall v \in V \qquad (4.5)$$

$$p_{vi} \in [0,1] \; \forall v \in V, \forall Q_i \in \mathcal{Q} \qquad (4.6)$$

Constraints (4.4) set capacity constraints for graph nodes. Constraints (4.5)–(4.6) ensure that the values $\{p_{vi}\}_{i \in \{1,\ldots,m\}}$ constitute an access strategy, i.e., a distribution on quorums. Since $p_{vi} \geq 0$ are positive reals, we can always find a solution in time polynomial in $\max(m,n)$, if one exists. A solution might not exist if, e.g., the node capacities are set too low.

An iterative algorithm The first placement algorithm of Section 4.1.2 can be combined with the access-strategy-optimizing algorithm above in an iterative way. Let $\mathsf{avg}(\{p_v\}_{v \in V})$ denote the access strategy p defined by $p(Q) = \mathsf{avg}_{v \in V} p_v(Q)$. In addition, let p_v^0 be the uniform distribution for all $v \in V$, and let $\mathsf{cap}^0(v)$ be the capacity of v input to the algorithm. Iteration $j \geq 1$ of the algorithm proceeds in two phases:

1. In the first phase of iteration j, the almost-capacity-respecting placement algorithm of Section 4.1.2 is executed with $\mathsf{cap}(v) = \mathsf{cap}^0(v)$ for each $v \in V$ and with access strategy $p = \mathsf{avg}(\{p_v^{j-1}\}_{v \in V})$, to produce a placement f^j. Recall that it is possible that for some nodes v, $\mathsf{load}_{f^j}(v) > \mathsf{cap}^0(v)$, though the load can exceed the capacity only by a constant factor.

2. In the second phase of iteration j, the access-strategy-optimizing algorithm above is executed with $\mathsf{cap}(v) = \mathsf{load}_{f^j}(v)$ for each $v \in V$ to produce new access strategies $\{p_v^j\}_{v \in V}$.

After each iteration j, the expected response time (4.2) is computed based on the placement f^j and access strategies $\{p_v^j\}_{v \in V}$. If the expected response time did not decrease from that of iteration $j-1$, then the algorithm halts and returns f^{j-1} and $\{p_v^{j-1}\}_{v \in V}$.

Note that this algorithm can only improve upon the almost-capacity respecting placement algorithm of Section 4.1.2, since the second phase can only decrease average network delay while leaving loads unchanged, and because the algorithm terminates if an iteration does not improve the expected response time.

5. Simulation methodology

We implemented the algorithms in Section 4 in C and GNU MathProg (a publicly available LP modeling language). To solve the LPs we use the freely available glpsol solver. The version of glpsol we use (4.8) can solve LPs with up to 100,000 constraints, which limits the systems for which we can evaluate our algorithms.

Network topologies The network topologies that we consider come from two sources: The first is a set of ping round trip times (RTTs) measured between 50 different sites in Planetlab between July and November 2006 [24]. We call this topology "Planetlab-50". The second dataset is built from pairwise delays measured between 161 web servers using the king [13] latency estimation tool. The set of web servers was obtained from a publicly available list used in previous research [23]. We call this topology "daxlist-161".

Quorum systems We evaluate our algorithms for four quorum systems: three types of Majorities commonly used in protocol implementations (the $(t + 1, 2t + 1)$, $(2t + 1, 3t + 1)$ and $(4t + 1, 5t + 1)$ Majorities) and the $k \times k$ Grid. In each experiment we vary the universe size by varying the t and k parameters from 1 to the highest value for which the universe size is less than the size of the graph.

Measures Our results in the following sections were obtained by computing one of two measures: average response time, $\mathsf{avg}_{v \in V}[\Delta_f(v)]$, where $\Delta_f(v)$ is defined according to (4.2), or average network delay, which is computed identically but with $\alpha = 0$ in (4.1).

6. Low client demand

In this section we consider the case when client demand in the system is low. This can be modeled by setting $\alpha = 0$ in definition (4.1), as the response time in this case is well approximated by the network delay.

Lin [19] showed that the singleton placement yields network delay within a factor of two of *any* quorum system placed in the network. Thus, for a system with low client demand, i.e., in which network delay is the dominant component of response time, using a quorum system cannot yield much better response time than a single server. However, a quorum system might still yield advantages in fault-tolerance, and so our goal will be to determine the performance costs one pays while retaining the fault-tolerance of a given quorum system, i.e., by placing it using a one-to-one placement.

Since we are trying to minimize network delay, clients will always use the closest quorum for each access, i.e., $p_v(Q) = 1$ for v's closest quorum Q, and

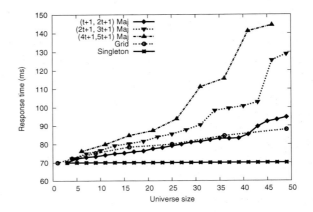

Figure 6.3. Response times on Planetlab-50; $\alpha = 0$; *closest* **access strategy**

$p_v(Q') = 0$ for all others; we call this the *closest* quorum access strategy.

The results of this analysis on the Planetlab-50 topology are shown in Figure 6.3 . These results suggest that the average response time increases for each quorum placement as the universe size grows. In some cases the increase exhibits a critical point phenomenon: response time degrades gracefully up to a point and then degrades quickly. This can be best seen for the $(2t + 1, 3t + 1)$ and $(4t + 1, 5t + 1)$ Majorities.

A second observation is that for a fixed universe size, the response time is better for quorum systems with smaller quorums. In almost all the graphs the line corresponding to Grid is the best after the singleton, the $(t + 1, 2t + 1)$ Majority is the second, etc. More surprisingly, the response times for the quorum systems with small quorum sizes are not much worse than that of one server up to a fairly large universe size. The exact values depend on the topology; more generally, from other experiments we performed it seems that the values depend on the distribution of average distances from nodes of the graph to all clients.

In conclusion, under low client demand, using quorum systems with smaller quorum sizes gives better performance. For all quorum systems, the degradation in performance as compared to one server is fairly small up to a certain universe size that depends on the topology and the particular quorum system considered.

7. High client demand

In this section we evaluate algorithms for minimizing response time when there is high client demand in the system. We start by looking at one-to-one placements when clients use either the *closest* access strategy

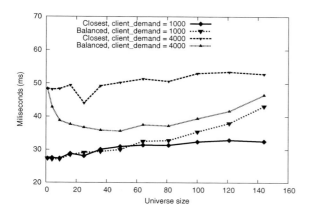

Figure 6.4. Response time for Grid under different client demands on daxlist-161

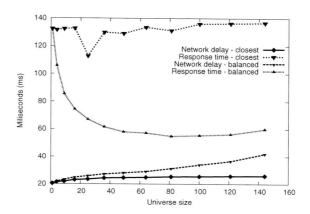

Figure 6.5. Grid with $client\_demand = 16000$ **on daxlist-161**

from Section 6 or a *balanced* strategy in which p_v is the uniform distribution for each client v.

To compute response time we set the α parameter as follows: $\alpha = op\_srv\_time * client\_demand$. We use a value of .007 ms per request for the op_srv_time parameter (this is the time needed by a server to execute a Q/U write operation on a Intel 2.8GHz P4). We set $client\_demand$ to either 1000, 4000 or 16000 requests.

In Figure 6.4 we plot response times for the closest and balanced access strategies for the Grid quorum system when placed on the daxlist-161 topology and $client\_demand \in \{1000, 4000\}$. The results show that for low client demand, closest seems to be the best access strategy in most cases (particularly for larger universe sizes where network delays are larger, as well), while balanced is the best access strategy for sufficiently high client demand.

Another interesting aspect illustrated by Figure 6.4 is the effect on response time obtained by varying the universe size (the line corresponding to balanced for a $client\_demand$ of 4000). For small universe sizes, the processing is spread on just a few nodes, which, in the case of high client demand, has a negative impact on the response time. At the same time, for large universe sizes, each node sees a much smaller load, but now network delay is sufficiently large to become the dominating factor in client response time.

To better illustrate the effect that load balancing has on response time, we also plot results for a higher value of client demand, $client\_demand = 16000$ in Figure 6.5. We plot both response time and network delay on the same graph. The network delay component increases with the universe size, while the load component decreases for an access strategy that balances load on servers. Since the load induced by client demand in

this case is significantly larger than the network delay component, the response time for the balanced access strategy actually decreases with increased universe size. At the same time, the response time of the closest access strategy does not exhibit this behavior, since this provides no load balancing guarantees on the nodes.

In conclusion, while closest is the best access strategy for sufficiently low client demand (Section 6), balanced is the best for very large client demand. There is also a gray area of client demand values for which none of the two access strategies performs better than the other; this is clearly visible in Figure 6.4 where the lines of the two access strategies for $client\_demand = 1000$ cross each other in multiple points. Below we present a technique for finding access strategies to minimize the response time for an arbitrary client demand.

Optimizing the access strategy To find the best access strategy for a given topology, quorum system, quorum placement and client demand, we will use LP (4.3)–(4.6) with different values for the capacity of nodes. While in practice the capacity of a machine is determined by its physical characteristics, here we use $\mathsf{cap}(v)$ as a parameter to manipulate the clients' access strategies so as to minimize response time. To use this technique in the real world, we can simply determine an upper bound for $\mathsf{cap}(v)$ of a machine v based on its physical characteristics and then run this tool with $\mathsf{cap}(v)$ no higher than the obtained upper bound.

We evaluate this technique in the following way: we choose a set of 10 values c_i in the interval $[L_{opt}, 1]$ and set the node capacity of all nodes, $\mathsf{cap}(v) = c_i$, for each $i \in \{1, \ldots, 10\}$. L_{opt} here is the optimal load of the quorum system considered, for a fixed universe size. We solve LP (4.3)–(4.6) for each value c_i to obtain a set of access strategies (one for each client) and then compute the response time corresponding to each such set of access strategies. Finally, we pick the value c_i that minimizes the response time. In our evaluation we choose the values c_i to be:

$$c_i = L_{opt} + i \cdot \lambda \tag{7.7}$$

for $i \in \{1, \ldots 10\}$, where $\lambda = (1 - L_{opt})/10$.

Figure 7.6 shows how the response time changes when we vary the node capacities for different universe sizes, assuming a client demand of $client\_demand = 16000$. In general, setting a higher node capacity allows clients to access closer quorums, thus decreasing network delay but increasing the load component at some of the nodes at the same time. For high client demand, this can yield worse response times, since nodes with a high capacity will become the bottleneck; i.e., the costs of high load will outweigh the gains in network delay. In this case it makes sense to disperse load across as many nodes as possible, which can be enforced by setting low node capacities.

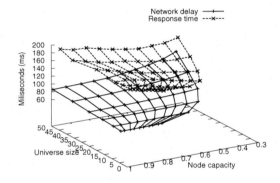

Network delay ──+──
Response time ──×──

Figure 7.6. Grid when increasing node capacities on Planetlab-50

Non-uniform node capacities A variation of the previous technique can help improve the response time further. This approach is based on the following observation: for a given c_i, LP (4.3)–(4.6) will find access strategies that minimize network delay by selecting quorums that are close to clients, as much as the capacity of graph nodes permits. As a result some nodes will have their capacity saturated, and thus will handle the same volume of requests, irrespective of their average distance to the clients. For this set of nodes, the response time will thus depend on their average distance to the clients: for server nodes further away clients will have to wait more than for closer nodes.

This observation leads us to following natural heuristic: we can set nodes capacities inversely proportional

to their average network delay to the clients. This will hopefully spread load across servers in a way that minimizes response time.

We now present in more detail the algorithm for setting node capacities. Let $\{v_1, \ldots, v_n\}$ be the support set of a given placement (we assume only one-to-one placements here), and let s_i be the average distance from all clients to v_i. Our goal is to set capacity $\mathsf{cap}(v_i)$ to be inversely proportional to s_i and in a given range $[\beta, \gamma] \subseteq [0, 1]$. Let $le = \min_{i \in 1..n} \frac{1}{s_i}$ and $re = \max_{i \in 1..n} \frac{1}{s_i}$. We then assign

$$\mathsf{cap}(v_i) = \frac{1/s_i - le}{re - le}(\gamma - \beta) + \beta$$

So, for example, if $v_i = \arg\min_{i \in 1..n} \frac{1}{s_i}$, then $\mathsf{cap}(v_i) = \beta$, and if $v_i = \arg\max_{i \in 1..n} \frac{1}{s_i}$, then $\mathsf{cap}(v_i) = \gamma$.

We evaluate this method for the Grid quorum system with universe size ranging from 4 to 49 on the Planetlab-50 topology. To compare with the results for uniform node capacities above, we use intervals $[\beta, \gamma] = [L_{opt}, c_i]$ for $i = 1..10$ (see (7.7)). We set $client\_demand = 16000$ for this set of experiments.

Figure 7.7 shows response times for both uniform and non-uniform node capacities. For small capacities the two approaches give almost identical results. As capacities increase, the heuristic for non-uniform capacities gives better response time than the algorithm for uniform node capacities. The reason: for small values of c_i, the length of the $[\beta, \gamma]$ interval is close to 0, and as such, the nodes from the support set have almost the same capacity. As the $[\beta, \gamma]$ interval grows, the capacities are better spread out and better (inverse proportionally) match the distances s_i. This spreads load over nodes with larger average distances to the clients, which decreases response time.

To see the improvement given by this heuristic we also plot results for a fixed universe size ($n = 49$). Figure 7.8 shows that increasing node capacity increases the response time as well (due to the high load in the system) but at a slower pace for our heuristic than for the algorithm with fixed node capacities. As the size of client demand increases, we expect this effect to become more pronounced.

Evaluation of the iterative approach So far we have evaluated only algorithms yielding one-to-one placements. The last technique for improving response time that we evaluate in this paper is the iterative approach described in Section 4.2. Since this approach creates many-to-one placements, network delay will necessarily decrease: some of the quorums become much smaller, thereby allowing clients to reduce the distance they need to travel to contact a quorum.

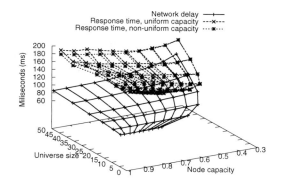

Figure 7.7. Grid on Planetlab-50 with uniform and non-uniform node capacities

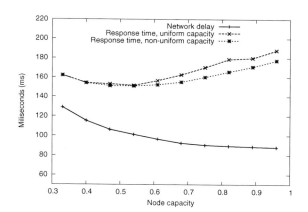

Figure 7.8. 7×7 **Grid on Planetlab-50 with uniform and non-uniform node capacities**

In Figure 8.9 we show the performance gains in terms of network delay compared to a one-to-one placement for a 5×5 Grid. We run the iterative algorithm for different values of the node capacity to see whether the improvement in network delay depends on node capacity. For all node capacities the best improvement comes after the first phase, at the end of which many universe elements are placed on the same node. The second phase brings only small improvements. Most of the runs terminate after the first iteration.

We have also evaluated the response time for each intermediary point in this iterative process. The results show that using many-to-one placements can increase or decrease response time depending on the placement found in the first phase of the first iteration and on the client demand. For instance, if the placement found puts multiple quorum elements on many nodes of the graph, the response time increases with the client demand. For low client demand, response time is usually better than for the one-to-one placements. Finally, the response time is always improved between the first and the second phases of the first iteration, but only by small values (usually between 2 and 5 ms). Consequently, using many-to-one placements improves response time over other approaches mostly in the case of low client demand. However, the techniques discussed in Section 6 also excel in this case, while retaining the fault-tolerance of the original quorum system.

8. Conclusions

In this paper we have evaluated techniques for placing quorum systems on a wide-area network to mini-

mize average client response time. The results of this evaluation reveal several interesting facts. First, for low client demand, using quorum systems up to a limited universe size in certain topologies does not substantially degrade performance compared to a single node solution. Thus, quorum systems are a viable alternative to the singleton solution in such cases, and offer better fault-tolerance. Second, as the client demand increases, it is important to balance load across servers to obtain good response time. When the network delay and client demand both play important roles in the response time, finding the right strategies by which clients access quorums is crucial to minimizing response time. Our methods for optimizing clients' access strategies, used with both uniform and non-uniform node capacities, are especially useful here.

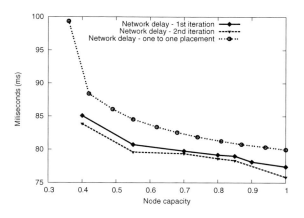

Figure 8.9. Network delay for iterative approach for 5 x 5 Grid on Planetlab-50

Finally, in our current framework, using many-to-one (instead of one-to-one) placements improves the response time only for low values of client demand. A variation of our model, in which a server hosting multiple universe elements would execute a request only once for all elements it hosts, can clearly improve the performance. We plan to analyze the benefits of such an approach in future work.

References

[1] M. Abd-El-Malek, G. R. Ganger, G. R. Goodson, M. K. Reiter, and J. J. Wylie. Fault-scalable Byzantine fault-tolerant services. In *Proc. 20th ACM Symposium on Operating Systems Principles*, 2005.

[2] Y. Amir, C. Danilov, D. Dolev, J. Kirsch, J. Lane, C. Nita-Rotaru, J. Olsen, and D. Zage. Scaling Byzantine fault-tolerant replication to wide area networks. In *Proc. 2006 International Conference on Dependable Systems and Networks*, pages 105–114, June 2006.

[3] Y. Amir and A. Wool. Evaluating quorum systems over the Internet. In *Proc. 26th International Symposium on Fault-Tolerant Computing*, June 1996.

[4] O. Bakr and I. Keidar. Evaluating the running time of a communication round over the Internet. In *Proceedings of the 21st ACM Symposium on Principles of Distributed Computing*, pages 243–252, July 2002.

[5] A. Bavier, M. Bowman, B. Chun, D. Culler, S. Karlin, S. Muir, L. Peterson, T. Roscoe, T. Spalink, and M. Wawrzoniak. Operating system support for planetary-scale network services. In *Proceedings of the 1st USENIX Symposium on Networked Systems Design and Implementation*, Mar. 2004.

[6] M. Castro and B. Liskov. Practical Byzantine fault tolerance and proactive recovery. *ACM Transactions on Computer Systems*, 20(4), Nov. 2002.

[7] S. Y. Cheung, M. H. Ammar, and M. Ahamad. The grid protocol: A high performance scheme for maintaining replicated data. *Knowledge and Data Engineering*, 4(6):582–592, 1992.

[8] J. Cowling, D. Myers, B. Liskov, R. Rodrigues, and L. Shrira. HQ replication: A hybrid quorum protocol for Byzantine fault tolerance. In *Proceedings of the 7th USENIX Symposium on Operating Systems Design and Implementations*, Nov. 2006.

[9] A. W. Fu. Delay-optimal quorum consensus for distributed systems. *IEEE Trans. Parallel and Dist. Sys.*, 8(1):59–69, 1997.

[10] L. Gao, M. Dahlin, J. Zheng, L. Alvisi, and A. Iyengar. Dual-quorum replication for edge services. In *Proc. Middleware 2005*, pages 184–204, Dec. 2005.

[11] D. K. Gifford. Weighted voting for replicated data. In *Proceedings of the 7th ACM Symposium on Operating Systems Principles (SOSP)*, pages 150–162, 1979.

[12] D. Golovin, A. Gupta, B. Maggs, F. Oprea, and M. Reiter. Quorum placement in networks: Minimizing network congestion. In *Proceedings of the 25th ACM Symposium on Principles of Distributed Computing*, 2006.

[13] K. P. Gummadi, S. Saroiu, and S. D. Gribble. King: estimating latency between arbitrary internet end hosts. *SIGCOMM Comput. Commun. Rev.*, 32(3), 2002.

[14] A. Gupta, B. Maggs, F. Oprea, and M. Reiter. Quorum placement in networks to minimize delays. In *Proceedings of the 24th ACM Symposium on Principles of Distributed Computing*, 2005.

[15] N. Kobayashi, T. Tsuchiya, and T. Kikuno. Minimizing the mean delay of quorum-based mutual exclusion schemes. *Journal of Systems and Software*, 58(1):1–9, 2001.

[16] A. Kumar, M. Rabinovich, and R. K. Sinha. A performance study of general grid structures for replicated data. In *Proceedings 13th International Conference on Distributed Computing Systems*, pages 178–185, 1993.

[17] L. Lamport. The part-time parliament. *ACM Transactions on Computer Systems*, 16(2):133–169, 1998.

[18] J.-H. Lin and J. S. Vitter. ε-approximations with minimum packing constraint violation (extended abstract). In *Proceedings of the 24th ACM Symposium on Theory of Computing*, pages 771–782, 1992.

[19] X. Lin. Delay optimizations in quorum consensus. In *ISAAC '01: Proceedings of the 12th International Symposium on Algorithms and Computation*, pages 575–586. Springer-Verlag, 2001.

[20] D. Malkhi, M. K. Reiter, D. Tulone, and E. Ziskind. Persistent objects in the Fleet system. In *Proceedings of the 2nd DARPA Information Survivability Conference and Exposition (DISCEX II)*, volume 2, pages 126–136, June 2001.

[21] M. Naor and A. Wool. The load, capacity, and availability of quorum systems. *SIAM J. Comput.*, 27(2):423–447, 1998.

[22] D. Oppenheimer, B. Chun, D. Patterson, A. C. Snoeren, and A. Vahdat. Service placement in shared wide-area platforms. In *Proceedings of the 20th ACM Symposium on Operating Systems Principles*, 2005.

[23] J. Padhye and S. Floyd. The tbit webpage. http://ww.icir.org/tbit/daxlist.txt.

[24] http://ping.ececs.uc.edu/ping/.

[25] D. B. Shmoys and E. Tardos. An approximation algorithm for the generalized assignment problem. *Mathematical Programming*, 62(3):461–474, 1993.

[26] R. H. Thomas. A majority consensus approach to concurrency control for multiple copy databases. *ACM Transactions on Database Systems*, 4(2):180–209, 1979.

[27] T. Tsuchiya, M. Yamaguchi, and T. Kikuno. Minimizing the maximum delay for reaching consensus in quorum-based mutual exclusion schemes. *IEEE Transactions on Parallel and Distributed Systems*, 10(4):337–345, 1999.

[28] A. Vahdat, K. Yocum, K. Walsh, P. Mahadevan, D. Kostic, J. Chase, and D. Becker. Scalability and accuracy in a large-scale network emulator. *SIGOPS Oper. Syst. Rev.*, 36(SI):271–284, 2002.

HyParView: a membership protocol for reliable gossip-based broadcast*

João Leitão
University of Lisbon
jleitao@lasige.di.fc.ul.pt

José Pereira
University of Minho
jop@di.uminho.pt

Luís Rodrigues
University of Lisbon
ler@di.fc.ul.pt

Abstract

Gossip, or epidemic, protocols have emerged as a powerful strategy to implement highly scalable and resilient reliable broadcast primitives. Due to scalability reasons, each participant in a gossip protocol maintains a partial view of the system. The reliability of the gossip protocol depends upon some critical properties of these views, such as degree distribution and clustering coefficient.

Several algorithms have been proposed to maintain partial views for gossip protocols. In this paper, we show that under a high number of faults, these algorithms take a long time to restore the desirable view properties. To address this problem, we present HyParView, a new membership protocol to support gossip-based broadcast that ensures high levels of reliability even in the presence of high rates of node failure. The HyParView protocol is based on a novel approach that relies in the use of two distinct partial views, which are maintained with different goals by different strategies.

1. Introduction

Gossip, or epidemic, protocols have emerged as a powerful strategy to implement highly scalable and resilient reliable broadcast primitives [9, 3, 7, 1]. In a gossip protocol, when a node wants to broadcast a message, it selects t nodes from the system at random (this is a configuration parameter called *fanout*) and sends the message to them; upon receiving a message for the first time, each node repeats this procedure [9]. Gossip protocols are an interesting approach because they are highly resilient (these protocols have an intrinsic level of redundancy that allows them to mask node and network failures) and distribute the load among all nodes in the system.

As described above, the protocol requires each node to know the entire system membership, in order to select the target nodes for each gossip step. Clearly, this solution is not scalable, not only due to the large number of nodes that may constitute the view, but also due to the cost of maintaining the complete membership up-to-date. To overcome this problem, several gossip protocols rely on *partial views* [13, 2, 3] instead of the complete membership information. A partial view is a small subset of the entire system membership. When a node performs a gossip step it selects t nodes at random from its partial view. The aim of a membership service (also called a peer sampling service [8]) is to maintain these partial views satisfying a number of good properties. Intuitively, selecting gossip peers from the partial view should provide the same resiliency as selecting them at random from the entire membership.

Unfortunately, if a node only has a partial view of the system, it becomes more vulnerable to the effect of node failures. In particular, if a large number of nodes fail, the partial view of each node may be severely damaged, and the network may become disconnected. Also, the membership service may take several membership rounds to restore the target properties of partial views, with a negative impact on the reliability of all messages disseminated meanwhile.

This paper proposes a novel approach to implement gossip-based broadcast protocols and describes a membership protocol that allows this approach to be used successfully. The key ideas of the paper are as follows:

i) We propose a gossip strategy that is based on the use of a reliable transport protocol, such as TCP, to gossip between peers. In this way, the gossip does not need to be configured to mask network omissions.

ii) Each node maintains a small symmetric *active view* the size of the fanout+1. Note that the fanout may be selected assuming that the links do not omit messages; the strategy allows to use smaller fanouts than protocols that use unreliable transport to support gossip exchanges. Broadcast is performed deterministically by flooding the graph defined by the active views. While this graph is generated at random (using our membership service), gossip is deterministic as long as the graph remains unchanged.

iii) TCP is also used as a failure detector, and since all members of the active view are tested at each gossip step, failure of nodes in the active view are quickly detected.

*This work was partially supported by project "P-SON: Probabilistically Structured Overlay Networks" (POS_C/EIA/60941/2004).

iv) Each node maintains a *passive view* of backup nodes that can be promoted to the active view when one of the nodes in the active view fails (*i.e.* disconnects, crashes or blocks).

v) A membership protocol is in charge of maintaining the passive view and selecting which members of the passive view should be promoted to the active view. In fact, two partial views are maintained by the protocol.

We named our protocol *Hy*brid *Par*tial *View* membership protocol, or simply *HyParView*[1]. We show that our approach not only allows the use of a smaller fanout (therefore, it is less resource consuming than other approaches) but also offers a strong resilience to node failures, even in the presence of extremely large numbers of crashes in the system. As we will show, our protocol recovers from percentages of node failures as high as 90% in as few as 4 membership rounds. This is significantly better than previous approaches. High resiliency to node failures is important to face occurrences, such as natural disasters (*e.g.* earthquakes) or computer worms and virus that may take down all machines running a specific OS version (that may represent a significant portion of the system). For instance, a worm could affect 10.000.000 nodes in the space of days [15]; also, these worms can spread in a first phase and take down nodes simultaneously at a predetermined time.

The rest of the paper is structured as follows. Section 2 offers an overview of related work. A motivation for our work, namely an analysis of the impact of high percentage of node failures in protocols that use partial views is given in Section 3. HyParView is introduced in Section 4 and its performance evaluated in Section 5. Finally, Section 6 concludes the paper.

2. Related Work

We start this section by defining more precisely the notion of partial view. Then we introduce the two main approaches to maintain partial views. Later, we enumerate the main properties that partial views must own. Finally, we give some examples of concrete membership protocols.

2.1. Partial Views

A *partial view* is a set of node identifiers maintained locally at each node that is a small subset of the identifiers of all nodes in the system (ideally, of logarithmic size with the number of processes in the system). Typically, an identifier is a tuple $(ip, port)$ that allows a node to be reached. A membership protocol is in charge of initializing and maintaining the partial views at each node in face of dynamic changes in the system. For instance, when a new node joins the system, its identifier should be added to the partial view of (some) other nodes, and it has to create its own partial view including identifiers of nodes already in the system. Also, if a node fails or leaves the system, its identifier should be removed from all partial views as soon as possible.

Partial views establish *neighboring* associations among nodes. Therefore, partial views define an overlay network. In other words, partial views establish a directed graph that captures the neighbor relation between all nodes executing the protocol. In this graph, nodes are represented by a vertex, while a neighbor relation is represented by an arc from the node who contains the target node in his partial view.

2.2. Maintaining the Partial View

There are two main strategies that can be used to maintain partial views, namely:

Reactive strategy: In this type of approach, a partial view only changes in response to some external event that affects the overlay (e.g. a node joining or leaving). In stable conditions, partial view remains unaltered. Scamp [6, 5] is an example of such an algorithm[2].

Cyclic strategy: In this type of approach, a partial view is updated every ΔT time units, as a result of some periodic process that usually involves the exchange of information with one or more neighbors. Therefore, a partial view may be updated even if the global system membership is stable. Cyclon is an example of such an algorithm [17, 16].

Reactive strategies rely on some failure detection mechanism to trigger the update of partial views when a node leaves the system. If the failure detection mechanism is fast and accurate, reactive mechanisms can provide faster response to failures than cyclic approaches.

2.3. Partial View Properties

In order to support fast message dissemination and high level of fault tolerance to node failures, partial views must own a number of important properties. These properties are intrinsically related with graph properties of the overlay defined by the partial view of all nodes. We list some of the most important properties here:

Connectivity. The overlay defined by the partial views should be connected. If this property is not meet, isolated nodes will not receive broadcast messages.

Degree Distribution. In an undirected graph, the degree of a node is the number of edges of a node. Given that partial views define a directed graph, we distinguish the *in-degree* from the *out-degree* of a node. The in-degree of a

---

[1] The protocol is said to be hybrid because it combines both strategies described in section 2.2

[2] To be precise, Scamp is not purely reactive as it includes a *lease* mechanism that forces nodes to periodically rejoin.

node n is the number of nodes that have n's identifier in their partial view; it provides a measure of the reachability of a node in the overlay. The out-degree of a node n is the number of nodes in n's partial view; it is a measure of the node contribution to the membership protocol and, consequently, a measure of the importance of that node to maintain the overlay. If the probability of failure is uniformly distributed in the node space, for improved fault-tolerance both the in-degree and out-degree should be evenly distributed across all nodes.

Average Path Length. A path between two nodes in the overlay is the set of edges that a message has to cross to move from one node to the other. The average path length is the average of all shortest paths between all pair of nodes in the overlay. This property is closely related to the overlay diameter. To ensure the efficiency of the overlay for information dissemination, it is essential to enforce low values of the average path length, as this value is related to the time a message will take to reach all nodes.

Clustering Coefficient. The clustering coefficient of a node is the number of edges between that node's neighbors divided by the maximum possible number of edges across those neighbors. This metric indicates a density of neighbor relations across the neighbors of a node, having it's value between 0 and 1. The clustering coefficient of a graph is the average of clustering coefficients across all nodes. This property has a high impact on the number of redundant messages received by nodes when disseminating data, where a high value to clustering coefficient will produce more redundant messages. It also has an impact in the fault-tolerant properties of the graph, given that areas of the graph that exhibit high values of clustering will more easily be isolated from the rest of the graph.

Accuracy. We define accuracy of a node as the number of neighbors of that node that have not failed divided by the total number of neighbors of that node. The accuracy of a graph is the average of the accuracy of all correct nodes. Accuracy has high impact in the overall reliability of any dissemination protocol using a underlying membership protocol to select its gossip targets. If the graph accuracy values are low, the number of failed nodes selected as gossip targets will be higher, and higher fanouts must be used to mask these failures.

2.4. Membership and Gossip Protocols

Scamp [6, 5] is a reactive membership protocol that maintains two separate views, a *PartialView* from which nodes select their targets to gossip messages, and a *InView* with nodes from which they receive gossip messages. One interesting aspect of this protocol is that the *PartialView* does not have a fixed size, it grows to values that are distributed around $\log n$, where n is the total number of nodes

executing the protocol, and without n being known by any node. The main mechanism to update the *PartialView* is a subscription protocol, executed when new processes join the system. However, in order to recover from isolation, nodes periodically send heartbeat messages to all nodes present in their *PartialView*. If a node does not receive a heartbeat for a long time, it assumes that it has become isolated and rejoins the overlay.

Cyclon [17] is a cyclic membership protocol where nodes maintain a fixed length *partial view*. This protocol relies in a operation that is executed periodically every ΔT by all nodes which is called *shuffle*. Basically, in a shuffle operation, a node selects the "oldest" node in its partial view and performs an exchange with that node. In the exchange, the node provides to its peer a sample of its partial view and, symmetrically, collects a sample of its peer's partial view. The join operation is based on fixed length random walks on the overlay. The join process ensures that, if there are no message losses or node failures, the in-degree of all nodes will remain unchanged.

NeEM [12], Network Friendly Epidemic Multicast, is a gossip protocol that relies on the use of TCP to disseminate information across the overlay. In NeEM, the use of TCP is motivated by the desire to eliminate correlated message losses due to network congestion. The authors show that better gossip reliability can be achieved by leveraging on the flow control mechanisms of TCP. In this paper, we rely on TCP to mask network omissions and to detect failures. Therefore, our work is complementary of NeEM.

CREW [2] is a gossip protocol for flash dissemination, *i.e.* fast simultaneous download of files by a large number of destinations using a combination of pull and push gossip. It uses TCP connections to implicitly estimate available bandwidth, thus optimizing the fanout of the gossip procedure. The emphasis of CREW is on optimizing latency, mainly by improving concurrent pulling from multiple sources. A key feature is to maintain a cache of open connections to peers discovered using a random walk protocol, to avoid the latency of opening a TCP connection when a new peer is required. The same optimization can be applied in HyParView, by pre-opening connections to some of the members of the passive view. CREW does not, however, explicitly manage such cache to improve the overlay, namely regarding resilience when a large number of nodes fail.

2.5. Gossip Reliability

We define gossip reliability as the percentage of active nodes that deliver a gossip broadcast. A reliability of 100% means that the gossip message reached all active nodes or, in other words, the message resulted in an atomic broadcast [9].

3. Motivation

Our work is motivated by the following two observations:

i) The fanout of a gossip protocol is constrained by the target reliability level and the desired fault-tolerance of the protocol. When partial views are used, the quality of these views has also an impact on the fanout required to achieve high reliability. By using "better" views (according to the metric of Section 2) and a reliable transport such as TCP, it should be possible to use smaller fanouts and, thus, more cost-effective gossip protocols.

ii) High failure rates may have a strong impact on the quality of partial views. Even if the membership protocol has healing properties, the reliability of message broadcasts after heavy failures may be seriously affected. Therefore, gossip would strongly benefit from membership protocols with fast healing properties, which can be achieved by also using TCP as a failure detector.

In the following paragraphs, we show some figures that illustrate these facts.

3.1. On the Fanout Value

The first two plots in Figure 1 show simulation results where we depict the reliability of the protocol delivering 50 messages sent by a gossip protocol that uses Cyclon or Scamp as the underlying membership protocol. The simulations were run with a network of 10.000 nodes (we describe our simulation model in detail later in Section 5). As it can be observed, in order to obtain reliability values above 99%, Cyclon requires a fanout of 5; it requires a fanout of 6 to achieve values near 99,9%. Scamp requires a fanout of 6 to reach values of reliability above the 99%. In this run, with a fanout of 6, there are potentially 20.000 extra messages exchanged than in a scenario that uses a fanout of 4 (by the results presented in [4], this fanout should ensure a reliability between 98% and 99%). More than 99% of these 20.000 extra messages are redundant, which means that less than 200 of these messages will, in fact, contribute to actual deliveries. We will later show that our approach allows to achieve higher reliability with a fanout value close to $\log(n)$.

3.2. Effect of Failures

The last plot in Figure 1 depicts reliability figures for the 100 messages exchanged after heavy node failure. In this scenario, we have failed 50% of the system nodes, and measured the effect on a network of 10.000 nodes using Cyclon and Scamp as the membership protocol. These messages are sent before Cyclon has the opportunity to execute a cycle of shuffle (note that the Cyclon period is typically large enough to exchange several thousands of messages), or before the lease time of Scamp expires. As it can be observed, reliability is lost (as no message is ever delivered to more than 85% of the nodes, and many messages are delivered to a much smaller numbers of nodes). This long period of unstable behavior may be unacceptable in applications exhibiting high reliability requirements and high throughput.

4. The HyParView Protocol

4.1. Overview

The HyParView protocol maintains two distinct views at each node. A small active view of size fanout+1, as links are symmetric and thus each node must avoid relaying each message back to the sender. A larger passive view, that ensures connectivity despite a large number of faults and must be larger than $log(n)$. Note that the overhead of the passive view is minimal, as no connections are kept open.

The active views of all nodes create an overlay that is used for message dissemination. Links in the overlay are symmetric. This means that if node q is in the active view of node p then node p is also in the active view of node q. As we have stated before, our architecture assumes that nodes use TCP to broadcast messages in the overlay. This means that each node keeps an open TCP connection to every other node in its active view. This is feasible because the active view is very small. When a node receives a message for the first time, it broadcasts the message to all nodes of its active view (except, obviously, to the node that has sent the message). Therefore, the gossip target selection is deterministic in the overlay. However, the overlay itself is created at random, using the gossip membership protocol described in this section.

A reactive strategy is used to maintain the active view. Nodes can be added to the active view when they join the system. Also, nodes are removed from the active view when they fail. The reader should notice that each node tests its entire active view every time it forwards a message. Therefore, the entire broadcast overlay is implicitly tested at every broadcast, which allows a very fast failure detection.

In addition to the active view, each node maintains a larger passive view. The passive view is not used for message dissemination. Instead, the goal of the passive view is to maintain a list of nodes that can be used to replace failed members of the active view. The passive view is maintained using a cyclic strategy. Periodically, each node performs a shuffle operation with one random node in order to update its passive view.

One interesting aspect of our shuffle mechanism is that the identifiers that are exchanged in a shuffle operation are not only from the passive view: a node also sends its own identifier and some nodes collected from its active view to

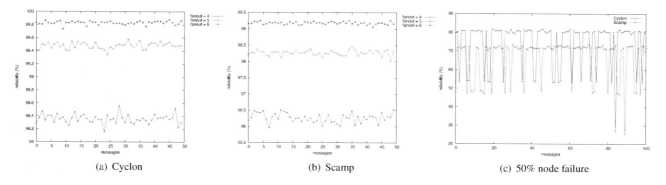

| (a) Cyclon | (b) Scamp | (c) 50% node failure |

Figure 1. Fanout x Reliability and Effect of failures

its neighbor. This increases the probability of having nodes that are active in the passive views and ensures that failed nodes are eventually expunged from all passive views.

4.2. Join Mechanism

Algorithm 1 depicts the pseudo-code for the join operation. When a node wishes to join the overlay, it must know another node that already belongs to the overlay. We name that node the *contact node*. There are several ways to learn about the contact node, for instance, members of the overlay could be announced through a set of well known servers.

In order to join the overlay, a new node n establishes a TCP connection to the contact node c and sends to c a JOIN request. A node that receives a JOIN request will start by adding the new node to its active view, even if it has to drop a random node from it. In this case a DISCONNECT notification is sent to the node that has been dropped from the active view. The effect of the DISCONNECT message is described later in the section.

The contact node c will then send to all other nodes in its active view a FORWARDJOIN request containing the new node identifier. The FORWARDJOIN request will be propagated in the overlay using a random walk. Associated to the join procedure, there are two configuration parameters, named *Active Random Walk Length* (ARWL), that specifies the maximum number of hops a FORWARDJOIN request is propagated, and *Passive Random Walk Length* (PRWL), that specifies at which point in the walk the node is inserted in a passive view. To use these parameters, the FORWARD-JOIN request carries a "time to live" field that is initially set to ARWL and decreased at every hop.

When a node p receives a FORWARDJOIN, it performs the following steps in sequence: *i)* If the time to live is equal to zero *or* if the number of nodes in p's active view is equal to one, it will add the new node to its active view. This step is performed even if a random node must be dropped from the active view. In the later case, the node being ejected from the active view receives a DISCONNECT notification.

ii) If the time to live is equal to PRWL, p will insert the new node into its passive view. *iii)* The time to live field is decremented. *iv)* If, at this point, n has not been inserted in p's active view, p will forward the request to a random node in its active view (different from the one from which the request was received).

4.3. Active View Management

The active view is managed using a reactive strategy. When a node p suspects that one of the nodes present in its active view has failed (by either disconnecting or blocking), it selects a random node q from its passive view and attempts to establish a TCP connection with q. If the connection fails to establish, node q is considered failed and removed from p's passive view; another node q' is selected at random and a new attempt is made. The procedure is repeated until a connection is established with success.

When the connection is established with success, p sends to q a NEIGHBOR request with its own identifier and a priority level. The priority level of the request may take two values, depending on the number of nodes present in the active view of p: if p has no elements in its active view the priority is *high*; the priority is *low* otherwise.

A node q that receives a high priority NEIGHBOR request will always accept the request, even if it has to drop a random member from its active view (again, the member that is dropped will receive a DISCONNECT notification). If a node q receives a low priority NEIGHBOR request, it will only accept the request if it has a free slot in its active view, otherwise it will refuse the request.

If the node q accepts the NEIGHBOR request, p will remove q's identifier from its passive view and add it to the active view. If q rejects the NEIGHBOR request, the initiator will select another node from its passive view and repeat the whole procedure (without removing q from its passive view).

Algorithm 1: Membership Operations

upon init do
    Send(JOIN, contactNode, myself);

upon *Receive*(JOIN, newNode) **do**
    trigger addNodeActiveView(newNode)
    foreach $n \in$ activeView and $n \neq$ newNode **do**
        Send(FORWARDJOIN, n, newNode, ARWL, myself)

upon *Receive*(FORWARDJOIN, newNode, timeToLive, sender) **do**
    if timeToLive== 0 || #activeView== 1 **then**
        trigger addNodeActiveView(newNode)
    else
        if timeToLive==PRWL **then**
            trigger addNodePassiveView(newNode)
        $n \longleftarrow n \in$ activeView and $n \neq$ sender
        Send(FORWARDJOIN, n, newNode, timeToLive-1, myself)

upon dropRandomElementFromActiveView **do**
    $n \longleftarrow n \in$ activeView
    Send(DISCONNECT, n, myself)
    activeView $\longleftarrow$ activeView $\setminus \{n\}$
    passiveView $\longleftarrow$ passiveView $\cup \{n\}$

upon addNodeActiveView(node) **do**
    if node $\neq$ myself and node $\notin$ activeView **then**
        if isfull(activeView) **then**
            trigger dropRandomElementFromActiveView
        activeView $\longleftarrow$ activeView $\cup$ node

upon addNodePassiveView(node) **do**
    if node $\neq$ myself and node $\notin$ activeView and node $\notin$ passiveView **then**
        if isfull(passiveView) **then**
            $n \longleftarrow n \in$ passiveView
            passiveView $\longleftarrow$ passiveView $\setminus \{n\}$
        passiveView $\longleftarrow$ passiveView $\cup$ node

upon Receive(DISCONNECT, peer) **do**
    if peer $\in$ activeView **then**
        activeView $\longleftarrow$ activeView $\setminus \{peer\}$
        addNodePassiveView(peer)

4.4. Passive View Management

The passive view is maintained using a cyclic strategy. Periodically, each node performs a shuffle operation with one of its peers at random. The purpose of the shuffle operation is to update the passive views of the nodes involved in the exchange. The node p that initiates the exchange creates an exchange list with the following contents: p's own identifier, k_a nodes from its active view and k_p nodes from its passive view (where k_a and k_p are protocol parameters). It then sends the list in a SHUFFLE request to a random neighbor of its active view. SHUFFLE requests are propagated using a random walk and have an associated "time to live", just like the FORWARDJOIN requests.

A node q that receives a SHUFFLE request will first decrease its time to live. If the time to live of the message is greater than zero and the number of nodes in q's active view is greater than 1, the node will select a random node from its active view, different from the one he received this shuffle message from, and simply forwards the SHUFFLE request. Otherwise, node q accepts the SHUFFLE request and sends back, using a temporary TCP connection, a SHUFFLERE-

PLY message that includes a number of nodes selected at random from q's passive view equal to the number of nodes received in the SHUFFLE request.

Then, both nodes integrate the elements they received in the SHUFFLE/SHUFFLEREPLY message into their passive views (naturally, they exclude their own identifier and nodes that are part of the active or passive views). Because the passive view has a fixed length, it might get full; in that case, some identifiers will have to be removed in order to free space to include the new ones. A node will first attempt to remove identifiers sent to the peer. If no such identifiers remain in the passive view, it will remove identifiers at random.

4.5. View Update Procedures

Algorithm 1 also shows some basic manipulation primitives used to change contents of the passive and active views. The important aspect to retain from these primitives is that nodes can move from the passive view to the active view in order to fill the active view (*e.g.* in reaction to node failures). Nodes can be moved from the active view to the passive view whenever a correct node has to be removed from the active view. Note that since links are symmetric, by removing a node p from the active view of node q, q creates a "free slot" in p's active view. By adding p to its passive view, node q increases the probability of shuffling q with other nodes and, subsequently, having p be target of NEIGHBOR requests that might assist it to refill its view.

5. Evaluation

We conducted simulations using the PeerSim Simulator [11]. We have implemented both HyParView, Cyclon and Scamp in this simulator in order to get comparative figures. In order to validate our implementation of Cyclon and Scamp, we have compared the results of our simulator with published results for these systems (we omit these simulations from the paper, as they do not contribute to the assessment of merit of our approach).

We have also implemented a version of Cyclon, to which we called CyclonAcked, that adds a failure detection system to Cyclon based on the exchange of explicitly acknowledgments during the message dissemination. Thus, CyclonAcked is able to detect a failed node when it attempts to gossip to it and, therefore, is able to remove failed members from partial views, increasing the accuracy of these views. We use this benchmark to show that the benefits of our approach do not come only from the use of TCP as a failure detector, but also from the clever use of two separate partial views.

Finally, we have implemented on PeerSim a gossip broadcast protocol that can use any of the protocols above as a *peer sampling service*. In this protocol, a node forwards a message when it receives it for the first time (therefore, there is no *a priori* bound on the number of gossip rounds).

In all simulations, the overlay was created by having nodes join the network one by one, without running any membership rounds in between. Cyclon was initiated by having a single node to serve as contact point for all join requests. Scamp was initiated by using a random node already in the overlay as the contact point. These are the configurations that provide the best results with these protocols. HyParView achieves similar results with either method (we have used the same procedure as Cyclon).

5.1. Experimental Setting

All experiments were conducted in a network of 10.000 nodes and results show an aggregation from multiple runs of each experiment. Furthermore, each membership protocol was configured as follows: In HyParView, we set the active membership size to 5, and passive membership's size to 30. *Active Random Walk Length* parameter was set to 6 and the *Passive Random Walk Length* was set to 3. In each shuffle message, $k_p = 4$ elements (at most) were sent from the passive view, while $k_a = 3$ elements (at most) were sent from the active view. The total size of shuffle messages is 8, as nodes also send their own identifier in each shuffle message. Cyclon protocol was configured with partial views of 35 elements (this is the sum of HyParView's active and passive view sizes). Shuffle message lengths were set to 14 and the time to live of random walks in the overlay was configured to 5. Scamp was configured with parameter c - the parameter that is related with fault-tolerance of the protocol - to 4. The reason behind the selected value to this parameter was because it generated partial views which size's where distributed around a middle point of 34, which is as near as we could be from the value used in other protocols. Our gossip based broadcast protocol was configured with a fanout of 4.

5.2. Effect of Failures

We first evaluate the impact of massive failures in the reliability of gossip when different membership protocols are used. In each experiment that we run, we make all nodes join the overlay, and execute 50 cycles of membership protocol to guarantee stabilization[3]. After the stabilization period, we induce failures at random in a percentage of all nodes in the system. We experimented with several values, ranging from 10% to 95% of node failure. We then measure the reliability of the protocol delivering 1.000 messages sent from random correct nodes. All these messages are sent before the execution of another cycle of the membership pro-

tocol. However, the membership protocols still execute all reactive steps; in particular, they can exclude a node from their partial views if the node is detected to be failed. The rationale for this setting is that the interval of the periodic behavior of the membership protocols is often long enough to allow thousands of messages to be exchanged, and we are looking for the impact of failures in the reliability of these broadcasts.

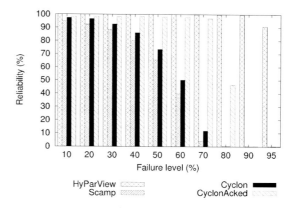

Figure 2. Reliability for 1000 messages

The average reliability for these runs of 1.000 messages is depicted in Figure 2. As it can be seen, massive percentage of failures have almost no visible impact on HyParView below the threshold of 90%. Even for failure rates as high as 95%, HyParView still manages to maintain a reliability value in the order of deliveries to 90% of the active processes. Both Scamp and Cyclon exhibit a constant reliability[4] for failure percentages as low as 10%, and their performance is significantly hampered with failure percentages above 50% (with reliabilities below 50%). On the other hand, CyclonAcked manages to offer a competitive performance. Although the reliability is not as high as with HyParView, it manages to keep high reliabilities for percentages of failures up to 70%. This behaviour highlights the importance of fast failure detection in gossip protocols.

The reader should also notice that HyParView has a better reliability even when failure rates are not as high as 50%. This happens because HyParView uses a deterministic selection of nodes to whom forward gossip messages, this combined with a symmetric view, ensures that in a stable environment HyParView, unlike other protocols, has 100% reliability, as long as the overlay remains connected.

Figures 3a-3f show the evolution of reliability with each message sent, after the failures, for different failure percentages. In all figures, HyParView is the line that offers better and faster recovery usually near the 100%. Next appear CyclonAcked, Cyclon and Scamp in this order for all failure

---

[3] In fact, this stabilization time is not required by Scamp, as it stabilizes immediately after the join period.

[4] Although their reliability is unable to reach 100% with a fanout of 4.

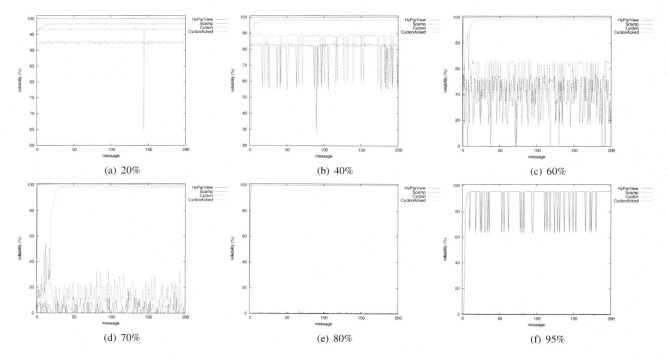

(a) 20% (b) 40% (c) 60%

(d) 70% (e) 80% (f) 95%

Figure 3. Reliability after failures

levels. Above 80% failures all these lines appear close to the value of 0%.

From the figures, it is clear that HyParView recovers almost immediately from the failures. This is due to the fact that all members of the active views are tested in a single broadcast. Basic Cyclon/ Scamp membership protocols, as they do not use a failure detector, are unable to recover until the membership protocol is executed again. In order to maintain reliability under massive percentage of failures, they would have to be configured with very high fanouts (which is a cost inefficient strategy in steady state). The figures also show that by adding acknowledgments to the Cyclon based gossip protocol, CyclonAcked recovers a high reliability after a small number of message exchanges (approximately 25). Note that, in Cyclon, a node is only tested when it is selected (at random) as a gossip target. However, for percentage of failures in the order of 80%, CyclonAcked is unable to regain the reliability levels as HyParView. This is due to the following phenomenon: given that the Cyclon overlay is asymmetric, some nodes may have outgoing links and no incoming link; therefore, some nodes are still able to broadcast messages but unable to receive any messages. On the other hand, in HyParView, the active membership is symmetric, which means that if a node is able to reach another correct node in the overlay, it is necessarily reachable by messages sent by other nodes. This feature and a very low clustering coefficient (see Section 5.4) explains the high resilience of HyParView.

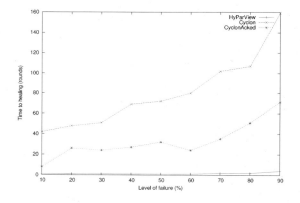

Figure 4. Healing time

5.3. Healing Time

Figure 4 shows how many membership cycles are required to achieve the same reliability in the message dissemination after a massive node failure (for different percentage of node failures). These results were obtained as follows: in each simulation, after the stabilization period, failures are induced. Subsequently, multiple membership protocol cycles are executed. In each cycle, 10 random nodes are selected to execute a broadcast. We then calculate the average reliability of these messages, and count the cycles required for each protocol to regain a reliability equal

426

	Average clustering coefficient	Average shortest path	Maximum hops to delivery
Cyclon	0.006836	2.60426	10.6
Scamp	0.022476	3.35398	14.1
HyParView	0.00092	6.38542	9.0

Table 1. Graph properties after stabilization

or greater than the one exhibit by that same protocol before the induction of the failure.

As expected, after the results presented before, Hy-ParView recovers in few rounds (only 1 or 2) for all percentages below 80%. Cyclon requires a significant number of membership cycles, that grows almost linearly with the percentage of failed nodes to achieve this goal. We do not present values for Scamp, because the total time for Scamp to regain it's levels of reliability depends on the Lease Time, which is typically high to preserve some stability in the membership.

5.4. Graph Properties

As noted in Section 2.3, the overlays produced by the membership protocol must exhibit some good properties such as low clustering coefficient, small average shortest path and balanced in-degree distribution. We now show how the different protocols perform regarding these metrics. Table 1 shows values to average clustering coefficient and average shortest path for all protocols[5] after a period of stabilization of 50 membership cycles. It can be seen that in terms of average clustering coefficient, HyParView achieves significantly lower values than Scamp or Cyclon, which is expected considering that HyParView's active view is much smaller than other protocols partial views. This is an important factor to explain the high resilience that HyParView exhibits to node failures.

In terms of average shortest path, we see that HyParView falls behind Scamp and Cyclon. This is no surprise, as we maintain a smaller active view, which limits the number of distinct paths that exist across all nodes. Fortunately, this has no impact on the latency of the gossip protocol. The short level of global clustering and the fact that we use all existing paths between nodes to disseminate every message, makes our protocol deliver gossip within a smaller number of hops than the other protocols, as it is depicted in Table 1.

Figure 5 shows the in-degree distribution of all nodes in the overlay after the same period of stabilization. Cyclon and Scamp have distribution of in-degree across a wide range of values, which means that some nodes are extremely popular on the overlay, while other nodes are almost to-

---
[5]Results for HyParView concern its active view.

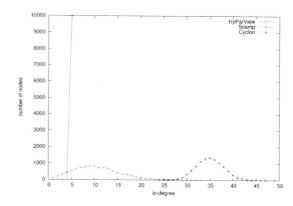

Figure 5. In-degree distribution

tally unknown. As stated before, because of this distribution some nodes on the overlay have greater probability to receive redundant messages, while other nodes have a very small probability to see messages once. This is specially obvious in Scamp, where some nodes are only known by one other node.

Due to HyParView's symmetric active view, almost all nodes in the overlay are known by the maximum amount of nodes possible, which is the active view length (5). This means that all nodes, with high probability, will receive each message exactly the same amount of times, and also that there is small probability for any node not to receive a message at least once.

5.5. Discussion

It is possible to extract the following lessons from our results. To start with, the speed of failure detection is of paramount importance to sustain high reliability in the presence of massive percentage of faults. A gossip strategy that relies on the use of a reliable transport that also serves as a failure detector, over a fixed overlay (built using a probabilistic membership protocol) offers the best performance possible in this regard. Also, by using all the links of the overlay, it is possible to aim at 100% reliability as long as the overlay remains connected. Furthermore, it allows to use smaller fanouts than protocols that have to mask failures and network omissions with the redundancy of gossip. The use of small fanouts is what makes possible to use all the links of the overlay with small overhead. Additionally, the maintenance of a passive view, with candidates to replace failed nodes in the active view, offers high resilience to massive failures. Therefore, the use of an hybrid approach that contains a small active view and a larger (low cost) passive view, maintained by different strategies, offers a better resilience and better resource usage than using a single (large) view with a higher fanout.

The use of TCP could cause a blockage in the overlay in the presence of slow nodes that do not consume messages from their reception buffers: TCP's flow control would make the neighbors of that node block while trying to send messages to it and, in turn, also stop receiving messages. Eventually this effect would spread over the entire overlay in an epidemic manner. This effect is, however, avoided by the protocol using a variation of the techniques proposed in [12], which simply considers slow nodes as having failed, and expels them from all active views. A detailed description of the mechanism can be found in [10].

6. Conclusions and Future Work

Gossip protocols are appealing because they work on overlays that have very small maintenance cost. Therefore, they seem obvious candidates to support applications that require extremely high resilience to failures of large percentage of nodes. Such massive failures can happen due to attacks (for instance, a worm that shuts down all the machines of a particular make) or in catastrophic natural disasters (such as earthquakes). To the best of our knowledge, this is the first paper that studied the effect on the reliability of gossip under massive percentage of failures, when different approaches are used to maintain distinct partial membership information.

We defend a gossip strategy that consists of flooding the overlay topology that is created by a probabilistic (partial) membership protocol. Furthermore, we have proposed a novel hybrid membership protocol for that purpose. The protocol maintains a small active view and a larger passive view for fault-tolerance. We have shown that our protocol is able to preserve very high values of reliability, with a small fanout, in faulty scenarios where the percentage of failed nodes can be as high as 80%.

As future work, we would like to experiment, to better define, the relation between the passive view size and the resilience level of the protocol (*i.e.* how many failures are supported without the overlay becoming disconnected). A implementation of HyParView will be tested in the Planet-Lab platform [14] in order to measure the packet overhead of our approach due to the use of TCP.

Finally, we would also like to experiment our approach with adaptive fanouts, by taking into account the heterogeneity of nodes, in order to maximize the use of available resources, like bandwidth. To do this and still maintain our deterministic selection of gossip targets, nodes would be required to adapt their degree (and in-degree), which might prove an interesting approach in order to obtain optimized emergent overlays.

References

[1] K. Birman, M. Hayden, O. Ozkasap, Z. Xiao, M. Budiu, and Y. Minsky. Bimodal multicast. *ACM TOCS*, 17(2), May 1999.

[2] M. Deshpande, B. Xing, I. Lazardis, B. Hore, N. Venkatasubramanian, and S. Mehrotra. Crew: A gossip-based flash-dissemination system. In *Proc. of the 26th ICDCS*, Washington, DC, USA, 2006.

[3] P. T. Eugster, R. Guerraoui, S. B. Handurukande, P. Kouznetsov, and A.-M. Kermarrec. Lightweight probabilistic broadcast. *ACM TOCS*, 21(4):341–374, 2003.

[4] P. T. Eugster, R. Guerraoui, A.-M. Kermarrec, and L. Massoulie. From Epidemics to Distributed Computing. *IEEE Computer*, 37(5):60–67, 2004.

[5] A. Ganesh, A. Kermarrec, and L. Massoulie. Peer-to-peer membership management for gossip-based protocols, 2003.

[6] A. J. Ganesh, A.-M. Kermarrec, and L. Massoulie. SCAMP: Peer-to-peer lightweight membership service for large-scale group communication. In *Networked Group Communication*, pages 44–55, 2001.

[7] M. Hayden and K. Birman. Probabilistic broadcast. Technical report, Ithaca, NY, USA, 1996.

[8] M. Jelasity, R. Guerraoui, A.-M. Kermarrec, and M. van Steen. The peer sampling service: experimental evaluation of unstructured gossip-based implementations. In *Proc. of Middleware '04*, pages 79–98, 2004.

[9] A. Kermarrec, L. Massoulie, and A. Ganesh. Probabilistic reliable dissemination in large-scale systems, 2001.

[10] J. Leitão. Gossip-based broadcast protocols. Master's thesis, University of Lisbon, 2007.

[11] Peersim p2p simulator. http://peersim.sourceforge.net/.

[12] J. Pereira, L. Rodrigues, M. J. Monteiro, R. Oliveira, and A.-M. Kermarrec. Neem: Network-friendly epidemic multicast. In *Proc. of the 22th SRDS*, pages 15–24, Florence,Italy, Oct. 2003.

[13] J. Pereira, L. Rodrigues, A. Pinto, and R. Oliveira. Low-latency probabilistic broadcast in wide area networks. In *Proc. of the 23th SRDS*, pages 299–308, Florianopolis, Brazil, Oct. 2004.

[14] Planetlab: Home. http://planet-lab.org/.

[15] S. Staniford, V. Paxson, and N. Weaver. How to own the internet in your spare time. In *Proceedings of the 11th USENIX Security Symposium*, pages 149–167, Berkeley, CA, USA, 2002. USENIX Association.

[16] A. Stavrou, D. Rubenstein, and S. Sahu. A lightweight, robust p2p system to handle flash crowds. Technical Report EE020321-1, Columbia University, New York, NY, Feb. 2002.

[17] S. Voulgaris, D. Gavidia, and M. Steen. Cyclon: Inexpensive membership management for unstructured p2p overlays. *Journal of Network and Systems Management*, 13(2):197–217, June 2005.

Session 7B:
Security Protection:
Algorithmic Approaches

A lightweight mechanism for dependable communication in untrusted networks

Michael Rogers

Department of Computer Science, UCL, Gower St, London WC1E 6BT, UK
m.rogers@cs.ucl.ac.uk

Saleem Bhatti

School of Computer Science, University of St Andrews, St Andrews, Fife KY16 9SX, UK
saleem@cs.st-andrews.ac.uk

Abstract

We describe a method for enabling dependable forwarding of messages in untrusted networks. Nodes perform only relatively lightweight operations per message, and only the originator and destination need to trust each other. Whereas existing protocols for dependable communication rely on establishing a verifiable identity for every node, our protocol can operate in networks with unknown or varying membership and with no limits on the creation of new identities. Our protocol supports the maintenance of unlinkability: relays cannot tell whether a given originator and destination are communicating. The destination of each message generates an unforgeable acknowledgement (U-ACK) that allows relays and the originator to verify that the message was delivered unmodified to the destination, but relays do not need to share keys with the originator or destination, or to know their identities. Similarly, the endpoints do not need to know the identities of the relays. U-ACKs can be seen as a building block for dependable communication systems; they enable nodes to measure the level of service provided by their neighbours and optionally to adjust the level of service they provide in return, creating an incentive for nodes to forward messages. Our work is ongoing.

1. Introduction

Increasingly, the dependability of a networked communication system is considered a key issue for the operation of a larger system as a whole. However, there are a number of challenges to achieving dependability, including the possibility of malicious behaviour that aims to disrupt or subvert communication. For a set of nodes, N, forming a communication network, we need some way of assessing whether *correct forwarding behaviour* is being observed. Here, our definition of *correct forwarding behaviour* is very simple: forwarding behaviour is deemed to be correct in the network of nodes, N, if a node, $n_i \in N$, the originator, can send a message to another node, $n_j \in N, i \neq j$, the destination, by relying on the message forwarding behaviour of N.

Our scenario is a network of nodes, N, in which we assume that only the originator, n_i, and destination, n_j, of each message trust each other, and there is no other trust relationship within the network. This means that n_i and n_j may not be able to see or verify the identities of any other nodes in the network. Nodes that forward a message but are not the originator or the destination are termed *relays*. In our discussion, we assume that any node may act as an originator of its own messages as well as a destination or relay for the messages of other nodes.

We assume that nodes communicate using the general unit of communication, which we will term a *message*, which is any self-contained block of data. Depending on the application and the layer of operation in the communication stack, a *message* could be a *packet*, a *frame*, a *datagram*, an *application data unit (ADU)* such as a block in a file transfer, etc. Our goal is to enable measurably dependable forwarding of messages in a network of untrusted nodes.

Correct forwarding behaviour can be achieved with high confidence if all the nodes trust each other. Trust may be established, for example, by the use of a certified or certifiable identity for each node. Identities or pseudonyms may also be derived from other information within the network, such as network addresses, but these may be transient or may not be strongly verifiable. In certain circumstances, where identity is available and verifiable to some degree, it may be possible to detect failed, misbehaving or malicious nodes [1, 2, 3].

However, in many environments, it may not be practical to insist on establishing the identity of every member of N to provide the level of trust required to have confidence of correct forwarding behaviour. For example, the membership of the network may be changing constantly, or it may not be possible to verify or certify the identity of a node, $n \in N$. Even if it is possible to verify a node's identity, that identity may be subverted without being detected. In other cases, users may wish to maintain anonymity or *unlinkability*, meaning that other network nodes should be unable to determine whether a given pair of nodes are communicating. Additionally, maintaining unlinkability helps to counter some denial of service attacks (DoS) which may target nodes based on their identities. Examples of such environments include ad hoc wireless networks, peer-to-peer networks and some online communities.

Another issue especially relevant to ad hoc networks and peer-to-peer systems is resource usage. Many protocols have recently been proposed to address the problem of users who consume more resources than they contribute. Encouraging these 'free riders' to cooperate may have a significant impact on the performance and even viability of open membership networks. Free riding also has security implications, because denial of service (DoS) attacks are often based on resource exhaustion. Unfortunately, many of the proposed solutions to the free riding problem require detailed record-keeping and information-sharing that could undermine the privacy of users [4, 5, 6]. Other proposals depend on central coordination or identity management, introducing a single point of failure into otherwise decentralised systems [7, 8, 9].

If pairs of adjacent nodes can measure the level of service they receive from one another and use this information to adjust the level of service they provide in return, then each node has an incentive to cooperate in order to continue receiving cooperation [10]. This local, reciprocal approach does not require central coordination, record-keeping or information-sharing. Each node must be able to identify and authenticate its neighbours, but these identities can be local in scope, and a node is free to present a different identity to each neighbour. If the level of service offered to each neighbour is proportional to the level of service received, there is no incentive for a node to present multiple simultaneous identities to the same neighbour [11].

1.1. Structure of this paper

The next section describes the *U-ACK protocol*, which enables nodes in a message-forwarding network to measure the level of service provided by their neighbours. By measuring dependability at the message level, a single incentive mechanism can support a wide range of end-to-end services without relays needing to be aware of the details of higher protocol layers [12].

Our protocol uses end-to-end (originator to destination) *unforgeable acknowledgements (U-ACKs)* that can be verified by relays without establishing a security association with either of the endpoints. Unlike a digital signature scheme, relays do not need to share any keys with the originator or destination, or to know their identities. U-ACKs are a general mechanism designed to be used in conjunction with an *application-specific dependability metric (ASDM)* that is a function of the messages sent and the U-ACKs received.

Section 3 demonstrates that U-ACKs cannot be forged as long as the underlying cryptographic primitives are secure. Section 4 considers possible applications of the protocol, and Section 5 discusses issues that would affect engineering of the protocol. In Section 6 we review related work, and Section 7 concludes the paper and gives a brief description of our ongoing work and thoughts for the future.

2. Unforgeable acknowledgements

The unforgeable acknowledgement (U-ACK) protocol handles two kinds of data: *messages*, which consist of a header and a data payload, and *acknowledgements*. The originator and destination of each message must share a secret key that is not revealed to any other node, and each message sent between the same endpoints must contain a unique serial number or nonce to prevent replay attacks. This number need not be visible to intermediate nodes, and indeed the protocol does not reveal any information that can be used to determine whether two messages have the same originator or destination, although such information might be revealed by traffic analysis or by other protocol layers.

Our protocol does not rely upon or mandate any particular key management scheme or key exchange mechanism; any existing scheme appropriate to the application can be used. We only assume that the originator and destination have some way of establishing a shared secret key, k.

2.1. Overview

Unforgeable acknowledgements (U-ACKs) make use of two standard cryptographic primitives: *message authentication codes (MACs)* and *collision-resistant hashing* (or simply *hashing*). Any node can generate a correct hash, but only a node that knows the authentication key can generate a correct MAC. So, before transmitting a message, the originator computes a MAC over the message using the secret key, k, shared with the destination. Instead of attaching the MAC to the message, the originator attaches the *hash of the MAC* to the message. Relays store a copy of the hash when they forward the message. If the message reaches its destination, the destination computes a MAC over the received message using the secret key, k, shared with the originator. If the hash of this MAC matches the hash received with the message, then the destination has validated the message, and sends the *MAC as an acknowledgement*, which is forwarded back along the path taken by the message. Relays can verify that the acknowledgement hashes to the same value that was attached to the message sent by the originator, but they cannot forge acknowledgements for undelivered messages because they lack the secret key, k, to compute the correct MAC, and because the hash function is collision resistant.

2.2. Description of the protocol

More formally, let $H(x)$ denote the hash of x, let $MAC(y, z)$ denote a message authentication code computed over the message z using the key y, and let $\{a, b\}$ denote the concatenation of a and b. Let k be the secret key shared by the originator and destination, and let d be the data to be sent. The relays between the originator and destination are denoted $r_1 \ldots r_M$.

The operation of the protocol proceeds as follows:

1. The originator first attaches a unique nonce or serial number, s, to the data, to produce the payload $p_1 = \{s, d\}$.

2. The originator calculates $h_1 = H(MAC(k, p_1))$ and sends $\{h_1, p_1\}$ to relay r_1.

3. Each relay r_m stores an identifier (e.g. the network address) of the previous node under the hash h_m, and forwards $\{h_{m+1}, p_{m+1}\}$ to the next node, where $h_{m+1} = h_m$ unless r_m modifies the header, and $p_{m+1} = p_m$ unless r_m modifies the payload.

4. On receiving $\{h_{M+1}, p_{M+1}\}$ from r_M, the destination calculates $H(MAC(k, p_{M+1}))$ and compares the result to h_{M+1}. If the result does not match, then either $h_{M+1} \neq h_1$ or $p_{M+1} \neq p_1$ – in other words either the header or the payload has been modified by one of the relays – and the destination does not acknowledge the message.

5. If the message has not been modified, the destination returns the acknowledgement $a_{M+1} = MAC(k, p_{M+1})$ to relay r_M.

6. Each relay r_m calculates $H(a_{m+1})$, and if the result matches a stored hash, forwards a_m to the previous node stored under the hash, where $a_m = a_{m+1}$ unless r_m modifies the acknowledgement.

7. When a relay receives an acknowledgement whose hash matches the stored hash of a message it previously forwarded, it knows that neither the header, the payload, nor the acknowledgement was modified by any node between itself and the destination.

8. When the originator receives an acknowledgement whose hash matches the stored hash of a message it previously transmitted, it knows that neither the header, the payload, nor the acknowledgement was modified by any node between itself and the destination, and that the message was correctly delivered to the destination, since only the destination could have generated the acknowledgement.

2.3. Malicious nodes

It is important to note that while messages may carry source or destination addresses, the U-ACK protocol does not authenticate these addresses. A U-ACK proves one of two things. To the originator, it proves that the downstream neighbour delivered the message to its intended destination. To a relay, it proves that the downstream neighbour delivered the message *to the destination intended by the upstream neighbour* – this does not necessarily correspond to the message's destination address, if any. The upstream and downstream neighbours might collude to produce and acknowledge messages with spoofed addresses, so U-ACKs cannot be used to discover reliable routes to particular addresses. However, in the context of unlinkable communication this limitation becomes a strength: messages need not carry any information to associate them with one another, or with any particular originator or destination.

There is nothing to stop an attacker from modifying the header of a message, perhaps replacing it with a hash generated by the attacker for acknowledgement by a downstream accomplice. However, the attacker will then be unable to provide a suitable acknowledgement to its upstream neighbour, and thus from its neighbour's point of view the attacker will effectively have dropped the message and transmitted one of its own instead, albeit one with an identical payload. The upstream neighbour will not consider the attacker to have delivered the message as requested, and may reduce its level of service accordingly (this will depend on how the application-specific dependability metric is evaluated and used). Likewise if the attacker modifies the payload instead of the header, the destination will not acknowledge the message and again the attacker will be unable to provide an acknowledgement to its upstream neighbour.

With regard to dependability, any modification to a message or acknowledgement is equivalent to dropping the message, and a node that modifies messages or acknowledgements is equivalent to a free rider.

2.4. Lost messages

Messages may be lost, reordered, or modified for a number of reasons, and it may not be possible to determine whether such events are due to the normal behaviour of the network, or due to the malicious or incorrect behaviour of relays. For example, in a wireless ad hoc network, loss, reordering, bit errors and even duplication of messages may be considered normal behaviour for the network.

In contrast to existing approaches that try to identify the node or link responsible for each failure, we take the pragmatic approach of measuring dependability without attempting to distinguish between malicious, selfish, and accidental failures. This makes it possible for our protocol to operate in networks with a variable failure rate; with an unknown, changing, or open membership; and where the quality of service (QoS) of network parameters is dynamically variable.

3. Unforgeability

The strength and scalability of our system comes from its simplicity. Only originators and destinations can generate a set of check bits for a message, but any node can verify those check bits without needing to know the identity of, or share state with, the originator or destination. The key to our protocol is the unforgeability of acknowledgements, so in this section we demonstrate that relays cannot forge acknowledgements as long as the underlying cryptographic primitives are secure. Four specific properties are listed below with respect to the behaviour of the underlying primitives. These properties are commonly accepted and are based on the design goals of those primitives:

1. It is not feasible to recover the secret key k by observing any sequence of authenticated messages $\{MAC(k, m_1), m_1\} \ldots \{MAC(k, m_n), m_n\}$.

2. It is not feasible to calculate $MAC(k, m)$ for a given message m without knowing the secret key k.

3. It is not feasible to find the preimage x of a given hash $H(x)$.

4. It is not feasible to find a second preimage $y \neq x$ for a given preimage x, such that $H(y) = H(x)$.

The first two properties are standard requirements and design goals for MAC functions, and the last two properties (inversion resistance and second preimage resistance) are standard requirements and design goals for cryptographic hash functions. These properties are not affected by recent collision search attacks on cryptographic hash functions [13, 14]. As long as these properties are true for any specific MAC and hash function used to implement our protocol, we consider U-ACKs to be unforgeable.

First we show that the protocol does not reveal the secret key. If an eavesdropper could recover the secret key from some sequence of messages:

$$\{H(MAC(k, m_1)), m_1\} \ldots \{H(MAC(k, m_n)), m_n\}$$

and their acknowledgements:

$$MAC(k, m_1) \ldots MAC(k, m_n)$$

then the attacker could also recover the key from:

$$\{MAC(k, m_1), m_1\} \ldots \{MAC(k, m_n), m_n\}$$

contradicting the first property above.

Next we show that an attacker cannot forge acknowledgements without the secret key. Assume that an attacker succeeds in forging an acknowledgement. Either the forged acknowledgement is identical to the genuine acknowledgement, or it is different. If it is identical then either the attacker has succeeded in calculating $MAC(k, m)$ without knowing k, which contradicts the second property above, or the attacker has found a way of inverting the hash function, which contradicts the third property. On the other hand if the forged acknowledgement is different from the genuine acknowledgement, the attacker has found a second preimage $y \neq x$ such that $H(y) = H(x)$, which contradicts the fourth property.

4. Applicability

This paper does not describe a complete communication system, but rather a protocol building block that allows nodes to measure dependability. The mechanism by which originators and destinations exchange secret keys is not discussed here, because the acknowledgement protocol is independent of the key exchange mechanism; similarly, end-to-end encryption is not discussed, although we would expect it to be used by parties requiring privacy and unlinkability. Additionally, an application would need to select an application-specific dependability metric (ASDM) to use with the U-ACK protocol. The ASDM, which will have application-specific semantics, should be a function of the messages originated and/or relayed and the U-ACKs received.

4.1. Generality

Unforgeable acknowledgements can operate in a peer-to-peer overlay or at the network layer, providing an incentive for nodes to forward messages as well as transmitting their own. There are no dependencies between messages other than between a message and its acknowledgement, so each message can be treated as an independent datagram; retransmission, sequencing and flow control can be handled by higher protocol layers. This allows a single incentive mechanism to support a wide range of upper-layer protocols and services. In contrast, many existing incentive mechanisms are limited to file-sharing applications, because they require content hashes to be known in advance [15, 16, 17, 18].

4.2. Reverse path forwarding

We have assumed that the forward path of the message is the same path that will be followed, in reverse, by the U-ACK, i.e. reverse path forwarding is being used. This may not be possible in all networks – for example some wireless networks may contain unidirectional links. Where the assumption of reverse path forwarding does not hold, there are two situations to consider:

- The reverse path has *some relay nodes in common* with the forward path. In this case, there may be some nodes that receive information about the dependability of their neighbours, while others do not, at least not for all messages.

- The reverse path has *no relay nodes in common* with the forward path. In this case, only the originator receives information about the dependability of its neighbours.

In either situation, the U-ACK protocol provides a coarse-grained input to the ASDM: simply that the network as a whole is managing to deliver messages to their intended destinations and that U-ACKs are being returned, i.e. correct forwarding behaviour is being maintained for the network, N. Nodes that act as relays may build up confidence of their neighbours' dependability without having to send messages themselves: whenever a node sees a U-ACK for a message, it knows that the message was successfully delivered, without necessarily having any knowledge of the path beyond its immediate neighbours. This coarse-grained measure of dependability may be sufficient for some applications.

Note that routing asymmetries such as those commonly found in the Internet do not prevent reverse path forwarding: each relay stores the identity of the previous node when forwarding a message, so the reverse path can be found even if the relay's routing tables are asymmetric. Similarly, asymmetric link bandwidth is not a problem as long as it is possible to return one acknowledgement for each message sent in the opposite direction.

Our protocol can therefore operate in situations with diverse routing paths; the ASDM chosen should take account of the nature of the paths and any path information that may be available.

4.3. Gateways, proxies and middleboxes

The U-ACK protocol does not require relays to share keys with originators or destinations, but it can easily be generalised to situations where the originator wishes to direct traffic through a certain trusted gateway, proxy, or other middlebox: the originator exchanges keys with the gateway and the gateway exchanges keys with the destination; the gateway acknowledges messages from the originator and forwards them to the destination with new headers; and the destination acknowledges messages from the gateway. The key shared by the originator and the gateway is independent from the key shared by the gateway and the destination, so it is possible for the gateway to re-encrypt the messages before forwarding them. Indeed, onion routing [19] could be layered on top of our protocol, providing originator anonymity as well as originator-destination unlinkability.

4.4. Non-unicast communication

So far, we have implicitly considered unicast communication. However, there may be further considerations if non-unicast mechanisms are used for message delivery. For example, some protocols in mobile ad hoc networks (MANETs) use flooding-based or broadcast-based forwarding. In such applications, multiple copies of a message may reach a destination or relay node by different paths. To maintain the association between messages and U-ACKs, a simple extension of the protocol is to return a copy of the U-ACK to every neighbour from which a copy of the corresponding message was received. However, this may lead to increased overhead, so an application may wish to reduce the number of U-ACKs transmitted and adjust accordingly the definition and dynamic evaluation of the ASDM being used.

Another issue is that of one-to-many or many-to-many communication, such as network-layer or application-layer multicast. Here, a single transmission may have many destinations, and a naive translation of our protocol would require each of these destinations to send an acknowledgement. Reliable multicast is an area of ongoing research [20, 21, 22], but it is known to be impractical to use per-destination acknowledgements; thus our protocol seems unlikely to be applicable to large-scale reliable multicast without modification.

In a tree-based scheme for multicast distribution, one possibility would be for key nodes in the tree to act as trusted gateways, as described in Section 4.3. Each gateway would be responsible for receiving U-ACKs from nodes below itself in the multicast tree and sending aggregate U-ACKs to a node above itself in the tree. An aggregate U-ACK would indicate delivery of a message to all intended recipients.

However, although solutions for key management and distribution in such scenarios have been defined [23], modifications of this kind would increase the complexity of the protocol, introduce additional overhead, and could lead to a weakening of the overall security and dependability of the system.

Another approach is to look at the way dependability is

handled in other schemes, such as bimodal multicast [21] or QuickSilver [22]. It may be possible to modify the designs of those schemes to incorporate U-ACKs and so permit operation in untrusted environments, but we have not examined this in detail.

We consider the use of U-ACKs in non-unicast communication to be a topic for further study.

5. Engineering considerations

5.1. Timeouts

Relays cannot store hashes indefinitely while waiting for acknowledgements – at some point, old hashes must be discarded to make room for new ones. A relay that receives an acknowledgement after discarding the corresponding hash cannot verify or forward the acknowledgement, so there is no reason for a relay to store a hash for longer than its upstream or downstream neighbours. The most efficient solution would be for all relays along the path to discard the hash at the same time, after waiting an appropriate amount of time to receive a U-ACK. Using a separate synchronisation protocol to determine when to discard hashes is not practical in an untrusted scenario, and adding a time-to-live field to messages would undermine unlinkability by allowing relays to estimate the distance to the originator.

Fixed timeouts avoid these problems while ensuring that adjacent relays discard the hash at approximately the same time, and are simple to implement. The length of the timeout represents a tradeoff between the maximum end-to-end latency the network can tolerate, and the number of outstanding hashes each relay must store. The choice of an appropriate timeout will depend on the application. As an example, TCP's maximum segment lifetime (MSL) represents a conservative estimate of the maximum latency across the Internet: a typical implementation value is 30 seconds, which is much greater than the typical latency or round-trip time, and TCP may wait for a period of two MSLs before allowing re-use of a port number. Thus 60 seconds seems to be a reasonable timeout for hashes in an Internet overlay; shorter timeouts may be appropriate for other applications.

5.2. Overhead

The bandwidth and computation overheads of the U-ACK protocol are modest. Each message must carry the hash of its MAC and a unique nonce or serial number, and the originator and destination must each perform one hash computation in addition to the normal cost of using MACs. Each relay must perform a single hash computation and table lookup per acknowledgement, and forward one MAC per acknowledgement. Since acknowledgements are small and there is at most one acknowledgement per message,

acknowledgements could be piggybacked on messages in bidirectional communication to reduce transmission costs.

The originator and each relay must store one hash per outstanding message, so the storage overheads of the protocol depend on three factors: the data rate of the end-to-end path, D_p; the message size, S_m; and the timeout for stored hashes, T_h. If S_h is the size of a hash for a single message, we can approximate the storage requirement of a node, S_n, as:

$$S_n = \frac{D_p.T_h.S_h}{S_m}$$

So, with a 60 second timeout and a minimum message size of 125 bytes including headers, a node with an 11 Mb/s link (e.g. 802.11b wireless LAN) may need to store up to 660,000 outstanding hashes. This would require $\sim$13 MB of memory for a 160-bit hash function such as SHA-1. This represents the worst case, however, when all messages have the minimum size and all acknowledgements take the maximum time to arrive; in a more realistic scenario with a mean message size of 500 bytes and an average round-trip time of 5 seconds, the storage overhead would be just $\sim$275 KB.

A malicious node might attempt to exhaust a relay's memory by flooding it with messages, forcing it to store a large number of hashes. This attack could be mitigated by allocating a separate storage quota to each neighbour; a neighbour that exceeded its quota would then simply cause its own hashes to expire early.

5.3. Measuring dependability

Unforgeable acknowledgements allow nodes to measure the dependability of their neighbours, but the exact way in which the application-specific dependability metric (ASDM) is computed and refreshed will depend on the application; the behaviour of the ASDM in time (including freshness, decay and/or expiry of dependability information) and in space (for a given neighbour, path, or flow) will be application specific, and our protocol places no specific constraints on the nature of this metric. However, to demonstrate that a fine-grained dependability metric does not necessarily require information about the identities of the originator or destination, we offer the following sketch of a flow-based ASDM. This is only intended as an example; other metrics may be appropriate for other applications.

We define a flow as any sequence of messages that have the same originator and destination and that are semantically related in some way – for example, the sequence of messages that make up a single file transfer. To enable flow-based dependability measurement, the originator marks all messages in a flow with an arbitrary *flow identifier*. The contents of the flow identifier are not significant – it is just a label, and it is not covered by the message authentication code. All messages in a flow are marked with the same flow ID.

Flow IDs have local scope: when a relay forwards a message, the flow ID used on the downstream link may be different from the ID on the upstream link. However, messages belonging to the same flow should still have matching flow IDs on the downstream link. Each flow traversing a link must be assigned a flow ID that distinguishes it from any other flows currently traversing the same link. Flows arriving at a node from different upstream neighbours must be treated as distinct, and must be assigned distinct flow IDs on any downstream link, even if they happen to have matching IDs on their respective upstream links.

The use of flow IDs with local scope is similar to the use of label-swapping in virtual circuits, but there is no requirement to establish flow ID state in the relays before data transfer begins – flow IDs can be assigned to new flows on the fly.

Relays can use flow IDs for fine-grained dependability measurement without needing to know the origins or destinations of the flows. For each flow it is currently forwarding, a relay stores the identifiers (e.g. network addresses) of the upstream and downstream nodes, the flow IDs for the upstream and downstream links, and the application-specific dependability metric for the flow. The ASDM might take the form of a running average of the fraction of messages acknowledged (e.g. an exponential moving average, which can be stored as a single floating-point number). All this information is soft state: it does not need to survive across restarts, and information about inactive flows can be discarded to reclaim space.

6. Related work

6.1. Reciprocation

Reciprocation between neighbours is used to encourage resource contribution in several deployed peer-to-peer networks [15, 16, 17]. These systems differ in how they allocate resources among cooperative neighbours, but all of them provide a higher level of service to contributors than non-contributors. Hash trees [24] are calculated in advance and used to verify each block of data received, so these networks are only suitable for distributing static files.

SLIC [25] is an incentive mechanism for message forwarding in peer-to-peer search overlays. The level of service received from a neighbour is measured by the number of search results it returns, but without a way to verify results this creates an incentive to return a large number of bogus results. In contrast, the U-ACK protocol makes it easy to detect bogus acknowledgements.

SHARP [26] is a general framework for peer-to-peer resource trading; digitally signed 'tickets' are used to reserve and claim resources such as storage, bandwidth and computation. Claims can be delegated, so peers can trade resources with peers more than one hop away, but the identities of all peers in the delegation chain must be visible in order to validate the claim. This makes SHARP unsuitable for untrusted environments and unlinkable communication.

6.2. Authenticated acknowledgements

2HARP [2] is a routing protocol for ad hoc wireless networks in which each node that receives a packet sends an acknowledgement to the previous two nodes, allowing each node to verify that its downstream neighbour forwarded the packet. Every node has a public/private key pair for signing acknowledgements; these key pairs must be certified by a central authority to prevent nodes from generating extra key pairs and using them to create bogus acknowledgements. This requirement makes 2HARP unsuitable for use in open membership networks.

IPSec [27] uses message authentication codes for end-to-end authentication at the network layer. This makes it possible to authenticate transport-layer acknowledgements as well as data, but the MACs can only verified by the endpoints, not by third parties such as relays.

TLS [28] uses MACs at the transport layer. TCP headers are not authenticated, however, so it is possible for relays to forge TCP acknowledgements. As with IPSec, the MACs used by TLS cannot be verified by relays.

Some robust routing protocols for ad hoc networks use MACs to acknowledge messages and to detect faulty links and nodes [29, 30]. This requires a trusted certificate authority for key distribution, and rules out unlinkability.

6.3. Authentication using one-way functions

Gennaro and Rohatgi [31] describe two methods for authenticating streams using one-way functions. The first scheme uses one-time signatures [32, 33]. Each block of the stream contains a public key, and is signed with the private key corresponding to the public key contained in the previous block. The first block carries a conventional asymmetric signature. One-time signatures are large, so this scheme has a considerable bandwidth overhead. The computational cost of verifying a one-time signature is comparable to that of an asymmetric signature, although signing is more efficient.

The second scheme uses chained hashes, where each block contains the hash of the next block, and the first block carries an asymmetric signature. The entire stream must be known to the originator before the first block is sent. This scheme is similar to the use of hash trees in file-sharing networks.

The Guy Fawkes protocol [34] also uses chained hashes. The originator does not need to know the entire stream in advance, but each block must be known before the previous block is sent. Each block carries a preimage and a hash that are used to verify the previous block, and a hash that commits to the contents of the next block. The first block carries a conventional signature.

Several ad hoc routing protocols use hash chains to reduce the number of asymmetric signature operations [35, 36, 37, 38]. Others use delayed disclosure, in which a hash and its preimage are sent by the same party at different times, requiring loose clock synchronisation [36, 39, 40]. In our protocol the preimage is not sent until the hash is received, so no clock synchronisation is required.

The schemes described above use similar techniques to the protocol described in this paper, but their aims are different. Whereas the aim of a signature scheme is to associate messages with an originator, the aim of our protocol is to associate an acknowledgement with a message, without identifying the originator or destination of the message. The signature schemes mentioned above therefore require an initial asymmetric signature to identify the originator, whereas the U-ACK protocol does not require asymmetric cryptography.

7. Conclusion and future work

We have described the U-ACK protocol, which enables nodes in a network to measure the dependability of their neighbours in forwarding messages using *unforgeable acknowledgements (U-ACKs)*. The protocol does not require trust between all nodes in the network; the only nodes that need to be able to verify one another's identities are the originator and destination. The acknowledgements created by the protocol are unforgeable but can be verified by untrusted third parties. The protocol has broad applicability: it can operate at the network layer or in a peer-to-peer overlay, and does not require relays to establish a security association with the endpoints, or to be aware of the details of higher-layer protocols. It can be seen as a building block for dependable communication systems, allowing nodes to measure the level of service received from their neighbours using an *application-specific dependability metric (ASDM)* that is a function of the messages sent and the U-ACKs received.

We are currently investigating specific properties of the protocol when used in peer-to-peer systems, e.g. the dynamics of resource usage that occur with a mixture of free riders, altruists and reciprocators. The investigations will explore the sensitivity of the U-ACK scheme to various parameters such as the size and structure of the network, the proportion of free riders, etc.

The U-ACK scheme could also have applicability to systems that need to be robust to Byzantine failures, such as applications for safety-critical systems, civil defence and military use.

References

[1] R. Perlman. Network layer protocols with Byzantine robustness. PhD Thesis, Department of Electrical Engineering and Computer Science, Massachusetts Institute of Technology, August 1988.

[2] P.W. Yau and C.J. Mitchell. 2HARP: A secure routing protocol to detect failed and selfish nodes in mobile ad hoc networks. In *Proc. 5th World Wireless Congress, San Francisco, CA, USA*, pages 1–6, 2004.

[3] D. Quercia, M. Lad, S. Hailes, L. Capra and S. Bhatti. STRUDEL: Supporting trust in the dynamic establishment of peering coalitions. In *Proc. 21st Annual ACM Symposium on Applied Computing (SAC2006), Bourgogne University, Dijon, France*, 23-27 April 2006.

[4] T.W. Ngan, D.S. Wallach, and P. Druschel. Enforcing fair sharing of peer-to-peer resources. In F. Kaashoek and I. Stoica, editors, *Proc. 2nd International Workshop on Peer-to-Peer Systems (IPTPS '03), Berkeley, CA, USA, February 2003*, volume 2735 of *Lecture Notes in Computer Science*, pages 149–159. Springer, 2003.

[5] M. Ham and G. Agha. ARA: A robust audit to prevent free-riding in P2P networks. In *5th IEEE International Conference on Peer-to-Peer Computing, Konstanz, Germany*, August-September 2005.

[6] S. Buchegger and J.Y. Le Boudec. A robust reputation system for P2P and mobile ad hoc networks. In *2nd Workshop on Economics of Peer-to-Peer Systems, Cambridge, MA, USA*, June 2004.

[7] L. Anderegg and S. Eidenbenz. Ad hoc VCG: A truthful and cost-efficient routing protocol for mobile ad hoc networks with selfish agents. In *ACM Mobicom*, 2003.

[8] P. Druschel and A. Rowstron. PAST: A large-scale, persistent peer-to-peer storage utility. In *8th Workshop on Hot Topics in Operating Systems, Elmau, Germany*, May 2001.

[9] A. Adya, W.J. Bolosky, M. Castro, G. Cermak, R. Chaiken, J.R. Douceur, J. Howell, J.R. Lorch, M. Theimer, and R.P. Wattenhofer. FARSITE: Federated, available, and reliable storage for an incompletely trusted environment. In *Proc. 5th USENIX Symposium on Operating Systems Design and Implementation, Boston, MA, USA*, pages 1–14, December 2002.

[10] M. Rogers and S. Bhatti. Cooperation in decentralised networks. In *London Communications Symposium, London, UK*, September 2005.

[11] J.R. Douceur. The Sybil attack. In P. Druschel, F. Kaashoek, and A. Rowstron, editors, *Proc. 1st International Workshop on Peer-to-Peer Systems (IPTPS '02), Cambridge, MA, USA, March 2002*, volume 2429 of *Lecture Notes in Computer Science*, pages 251–260. Springer, 2002.

[12] J.H. Saltzer, D.P. Reed, and D.D. Clark. End-to-end arguments in system design. *ACM Transactions on Computer Systems*, 2(4):277–288, November 1984.

[13] X. Wang, D. Feng, X. Lai, and H. Yu. Collisions for hash functions MD4, MD5, HAVAL-128 and RIPEMD, 2004. Cryptology ePrint 2004/199, available from http://eprint.iacr.org/2004/199.pdf.

[14] X. Wang, Y.L. Yin, and H. Yu. Finding collisions in the full SHA-1. In *25th Annual International Cryptology Conference, Santa Barbara, CA, USA*, August 2005.

[15] C. Grothoff. An excess-based economic model for resource allocation in peer-to-peer networks. *Wirtschaftsinformatik*, 45(3):285–292, June 2003.

[16] B. Cohen. Incentives build robustness in BitTorrent. In *Workshop on Economics of Peer-to-Peer Systems, Berkeley, CA, USA*, June 2003.

[17] Y. Kulbak and D. Bickson. The eMule protocol specification. Technical report, School of Computer Science and Engineering, Hebrew University of Jerusalem, January 2005.

[18] P. Gauthier, B. Bershad, and S.D. Gribble. Dealing with cheaters in anonymous peer-to-peer networks. Technical Report 04-01-03, University of Washington, January 2004.

[19] D. Goldschlag, M. Reed, and P. Syverson. Onion routing for anonymous and private internet connections. *Communications of the ACM*, 42(2):39–41, February 1999.

[20] The IETF Reliable Multicast Transport (RMT) Working Group. http://www.ietf.org/html.charters/rmt-charter.html

[21] K. Birman, M. Hayden, O. Ozkasap, Z. Xiao, M. Budiu, and Y. Minsky. Bimodal multicast. *ACM Transactions on Computer Systems*, 17(2):41–88, May 1999.

[22] K. Ostrowski, K. Birman, and A. Phanishayee. QuickSilver scalable multicast. Technical Report TR2006-2063, Cornell University, April 2006.

[23] S. Rafaeli and D. Hutchison. A survey of key management for secure group communication. ACM Computing Surveys, 35(3):309–329, September 2003.

[24] R. Merkle. Protocols for public key cryptosystems. In *IEEE Symposium on Security and Privacy, Oakland, CA, USA*, April 1980.

[25] Q. Sun and H. Garcia-Molina. SLIC: A selfish link-based incentive mechanism for unstructured peer-to-peer networks. In *24th International Conference on Distributed Computing Systems*, 2004.

[26] Y. Fu, J. Chase, B. Chun, S. Schwab, and A. Vahdat. SHARP: An architecture for secure resource peering. In *19th ACM Symposium on Operating Systems Principles, Bolton Landing, NY, USA*, October 2003.

[27] S. Kent and R. Atkinson. RFC 2401: Security architecture for the internet protocol, November 1998.

[28] T. Dierks and C. Allen. RFC 2246: The TLS protocol, January 1999.

[29] B. Awerbuch, D. Holmer, C. Nita-Rotaru, and H. Rubens. An on-demand secure routing protocol resilient to Byzantine failures. In *Proc. ACM Workshop on Wireless Security (WiSe'02), Atlanta, GA, USA*, pages 21–30, September 2002.

[30] I. Avramopoulos, H. Kobayashi, R. Wang, and A. Krishnamurthy. Highly secure and efficient routing. In *IEEE Infocom, Hong Kong*, March 2004.

[31] R. Gennaro and P. Rohatgi. How to sign digital streams. In B.S.J. Kaliski, editor, *Proc. 17th Annual Cryptology Conference (CRYPTO '97), Santa Barbara, CA, USA, August 1997*, volume 1294 of *Lecture Notes in Computer Science*, pages 180–197. Springer, 1997.

[32] L. Lamport. Constructing digital signatures from a one-way function. Technical Report CSL-98, SRI International, Palo Alto, CA, USA, 1979.

[33] R. Merkle. A digital signature based on a conventional encryption function. In C. Pomerance, editor, *Proc. Conference on the Theory and Applications of Cryptographic Techniques (CRYPTO '87), Santa Barbara, CA, USA, August 1987*, volume 293 of *Lecture Notes in Computer Science*. Springer, 1988.

[34] R.J. Anderson, F. Bergadano, B. Crispo, J.H. Lee, C. Manifavas, and R.M. Needham. A new family of authentication protocols. *Operating Systems Review*, 32(4):9–20, October 1998.

[35] R. Hauser, T. Przygienda, and G. Tsudik. Reducing the cost of security in link-state routing. In *ISOC Symposium on Network and Distributed System Security, San Diego, CA, USA*, February 1997.

[36] S. Cheung. An efficient message authentication scheme for link state routing. In *Proc. 13th Annual Computer Security Applications Conference (ACSAC '97), San Diego, CA, USA*, pages 90–98, December 1997.

[37] M.G. Zapata and N. Asokan. Securing ad hoc routing protocols. In *Proc. ACM Workshop on Wireless Security (WiSe'02), Atlanta, GA, USA*, pages 1–10, September 2002.

[38] Y.C. Hu, D.B. Johnson, and A. Perrig. SEAD: Secure efficient distance vector routing for mobile wireless ad hoc networks. In *4th IEEE Workshop on Mobile Computing Systems and Applications (WMCSA '02)*, June 2002.

[39] A. Perrig, R. Canneti, J.D. Tygar, and D. Song. The TESLA broadcast authentication protocol. *CryptoBytes*, 5(2):2–13, 2002.

[40] Y.C. Hu, A. Perrig, and D.B. Johnson. Ariadne: A secure on-demand routing protocol for ad hoc networks. In *8th International Conference on Mobile Computing and Networking (MobiCom)*, September 2002.

Dynamic Cross-Realm Authentication for Multi-Party Service Interactions

Dacheng Zhang   Jie Xu
School of Computing, University of Leeds, UK
{dcz, jxu}@comp.leeds.ac.uk

Xianxian Li
School of Computer, Beihang University, China
lixx@buaa.edu.cn

Abstract

Modern distributed applications are embedding an increasing degree of dynamism, from dynamic supply-chain management, enterprise federations, and virtual collaborations to dynamic service interactions across organisations. Such dynamism leads to new security challenges. Collaborating services may belong to different security realms but often have to be engaged dynamically at run time. If their security realms do not have in place a direct cross-realm authentication relationship, it is technically difficult to enable any secure collaboration between the services. A typical solution to this is to locate at run time intermediate realms that serve as an authentication-path between the two separate realms. However, the process of generating an authentication path for two distributed services can be very complex. It could involve a large number of extra operations for credential conversion and require a long chain of invocations to intermediate services. In this paper, we address this problem by presenting a new cross-realm authentication protocol for dynamic service interactions, based on the notion of multi-party business sessions. Our protocol requires neither credential conversion nor establishment of any authentication path between session members. The correctness of the protocol is analysed, and a comprehensive empirical study is performed using two production quality Grid systems, Globus 4 and CROWN. The experimental results indicate that our protocol and its implementation have a sound level of scalability and impose only a limited degree of performance overhead, which is comparable with those security-related overheads in Globus 4.

Key Words: Authentication, Multi-Party Interactions, Secure Service Collaborations, Web Services, Workflow Business Sessions

1. Introduction

Dynamism and flexibility are becoming the core characteristics of modern large-scale distributed applications, such as business application integration, distributed auction services, and order processing [5][9]. A business process does not have to follow in many cases a strict business specification; the executing order of its activities is sometimes unpredictable, and on some occasions, the actual execution of a process can even be "one-of-a-kind" [7]. The applications and services involved in the process are typically heterogeneous and may be provided and maintained by different organisations. As an organisation has its own security mechanisms and policies to protect its local resources, the application across multiple organisations has to operate amongst multiple, heterogeneous security realms. A security realm is a group of principals (people, computers, services etc.) that are registered with a specified authentication authority and managed through a consistent set of security processes and policies.

Because organisations and services can join a collaborative process in a highly dynamic and flexible way, it cannot be expected that every two of the collaborating security realms always have a direct cross-realm authentication relationship. A possible solution to this problem is to locate some intermediate realms that serve as an authentication-path between the two separate realms that are to collaborate. However, the overhead of generating an authentication-path for two distributed realms is not trivial. The process could involve a large number of extra operations for credential conversion and require a long chain of invocations to intermediate services.

In this paper we present a new solution for dynamically authenticating the services from different realms. The main contributions of our work are: (1) using the multi-party session concept to structure dynamic business processes, (2) a simple but effective way to establish trust relationships between the members of a business session, and (3) a set of protocols for multi-party session management, supported by empirical evaluation and formal analysis. In Section 2 we discuss the fundamentals of constructing multi-party service interactions. Section 3 describes our proposed authentication protocols and

440

system with formal proofs. In Section 4 we present an empirical evaluation of our system using GT4 and CROWN middleware systems. Section 5 discusses the related work while Section 6 concludes the paper.

2. Multi-Party Service Interactions

In a distributed application, a *session* is a lasting collaboration involving several participating principals, called *session partners*. A session is often typified by a state which includes variables that hold information from messages transferred within the collaboration. A business process execution can be regarded conveniently as a *business session*. In terms of a Service-Oriented Architecture (SOA) [11], a business session is a collaboration involving two or more collaborative *services*, and has service *instances* as its session partners (a service instance is here referred to as a stateful execution of a service.) In practice, a session may discover and select services at runtime. After receiving an initial request from a business session, a service normally spawns a service instance to handle the request. Once this instance is accepted as a session partner, it is entitled to collaborate with other partners within the same session.

2.1 Two-Party Session

As implied by the name, a two-party session consists of two session partners only, i.e. a client and a server. For the security of a two-party session, an authentication process is required when the client sends an initial request to the server. A short-term secret key between the session partners is then agreed upon and generated. The secret key, also called session key, can be used in further communications to encrypt the messages transferred between the session partners [8].

The two-party session technique is practically effective, and it is used widely in many distributed systems and integrated with the design of most authentication protocols (e.g. SSL and Kerberos [17]). However, new problems arise if the two-party session technique is applied directly to the construction of a multi-party session. Hada and Maruyama in [9] demonstrate that, if a multi-party session is constructed out of multiple two-party sessions, it is difficult in some cases for a session partner to verify whether the service instance it contacts is actually a member of the same session. From the perspective of cross-realm authentication, the two-party session technique does not address the issue with Heterogeneous Cross-Realm Authentication (HCRA), which requires credential conversion and the establishment of authentication paths.

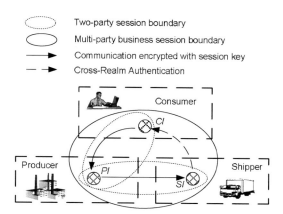

Two-party session boundary
Multi-party business session boundary
Communication encrypted with session key
Cross-Realm Authentication

Figure 1 A business session scenario

Figure 1 illustrates an example of a business session constructed with two two-party sessions. The business session consists of three participating services, *Consumer*, *Producer*, and *Shipper*. At the start of the business session, an instance of *Consumer*, *CI*, contacts *Producer* to order some products. After receiving the request from *CI*, *Producer* creates a service instance *PI* to handle it. *PI* then selects *Shipper* to deliver the products to *Consumer*. An instance of *Shipper*, *SI*, is thus generated to do this job, and it is required to negotiate with *CI* about delivery options and details. In this case, an HCRA process for authentication between *SI* and *CI* has to be performed by means of a new two-party session as *SI* and *CI* do not know each other and belong to different security realms. This HCRA process is both costly and complex due to credential conversion and possibly a long authentication path between the two local authentication systems of *SI* and *CI*. For a business session involved with n heterogeneous security realms, the HCRA process has to be repeated $n \times (n-1)/2$ times to allow all possible partner interactions with the session.

2.2 Multi-Party Session

A multi-party session may have two or more session partners for the intended collaboration. A partner can search for and invoke new services at runtime. Before a service (instance) is accepted as a new partner, an HCRA process is needed. However, unlike a two-party session, authentication for the existing partners of a multi-party session could be simplified significantly without requiring credential conversion and the establishment of any authentication path. This is because session partners can make use of their session memberships to authenticate each other even if they belong to different security realms. A shared session key or individual secret keys may be used to enforce a secure collaboration amongst session partners.

441

Consider the example of Figure 1 again. When *SI* attempts to contact *CI*, it does not have to authenticate itself with the local authentication system of *CI* because both *SI* and *CI* are members of the same session. *SI* can simply use its session membership to prove its identity to *CI*. This simplified authentication process is called Simplified Cross-Realm Authentication (SCRA). The HCRA process has to be repeated $(n - 1)$ times for a multi-party session with n security realms, but up to $(n - 1) \times (n - 2)/2$ authentication processes can be simplified as SCRA based on session memberships, thereby reducing both cost and complexity significantly.

However, managing and coordinating a multi-party session is more complex in nature, in comparison with handling two parties only. A multi-party session management system needs to address the issues with *message routing* and *secret keys for communications*. A *Session Authority* (SA) is also required to provide reliable real-time information (e.g. memberships) about session partners [9].

2.3 Message Routing

Message routing is concerned with the issues of dispatching messages to the intended service instance which maintains corresponding states. In practice, a service may handle requests from different requestors concurrently. When all the requestors invoke operations provided by the same port, the messages are sent to the same address (e.g. the same URL). In this case, additional correlated information is needed, which helps the underlying middleware to determine which interaction a message is related to and to locate the corresponding service implementation object to handle the message.

A simple approach is to exploit a correlated token, shared by the communicating partners, for identifying the related messages transported within the collaboration. A shared token is sufficient to the identification of session partners on the both sides of a two-party collaboration. However, session partners (i.e. service instances) in a multi-party session may be generated by the same service with the same address. It is difficult to distinguish them using a single token. In contrast with the token-based solution, an ID-based solution assigns every session partner with a unique identifier, thereby distinguishing all the partners unambiguously. In practice, a token-based solution is usually used to decide whether an instance is actually working within a business session while an ID-based scheme is employed to identify individual session partners in the case that fine-grained instance identification is needed.

2.4 Secret Keys

In a two-party session, authentication typically consists of several rounds of operations and message passing, and the session key used in the subsequent communication between the two partners is normally a by-product of the authentication process. However, in a multi-party session, SCRA is a highly simplified process and does not include the automatic generation of secret keys.

An obvious approach is to generate a single secret key for a given multi-party session and then distribute it to all the session partners. Once the session key is generated, it can be used to simplify the authentication process amongst the existing session partners, thereby avoiding HCRA. Hada and Maruyama's protocols in [9] are an example of this type of solution with the support of a Session Authority. However, if a partner loses the secret key, the security of the whole session will be compromised. Moreover, session partners may leave and join a session dynamically. When a partner leaves from its session, the shared secret key must be refreshed in order to ensure that any previous partner cannot gain any further information from the session. Similarly, when a new partner joins the session, the secret key must also be refreshed in order to ensure that any new partner cannot obtain any previous information transferred within the session. The issues related with secret key revocation have been discussed in many papers on secure group communications (e.g. [15][20]).

Another possible solution is to generate a shared secret key for every pair of session partners (e.g. using the Diffie-Hellman public key algorithm [18]). This scheme is more costly but it avoids the issue with key revocation.

2.5 Session Authority

A Session Authority (SA) is a service that provides reliable real-time information (e.g. session memberships) for a given multi-party session. For example, the SA may be employed to notify that a partner has left from the session, by contacting all the partners that have collaborated with the previous partner. An SA service could be associated conveniently with, or implemented as part of, a multi-party management system. This can be implemented using different methods with different features and characteristics such as fault-tolerance, scalability and cost-effectiveness. These methods include centralised management, decentralised architecture for better scalability, and fully distributed information provision for improved fault-tolerance. As an example of the SA implementation, our authentication protocols are designed to conform to the WS-Coordination specification [3] in which an SA is an extension of a *coordinator*. In WS-Coordination both centralised and decentralised coordinators are discussed. An SA may act as a centralised service that handles requests from all the session partners within a business session; alternatively, an SA may manage the session partners within a local domain only, and a group of decentralised SA's can then manage collectively the whole business session, thereby avoiding the problem of concentrating the SA operations in a single place.

3. Authentication Protocols

In this section we provide a multi-party authentication system and use the business scenario in Section 2 to explain the structure of the system. The related protocols are described and analysed formally.

3.1 Example

Consider an SA-based multi-party authentication system. In this system each business session is associated with a unique session identifier. Every service instance within a session is associated with a unique instance identifier so that every session partner can be identified unambiguously. The Diffie-Hellman public key algorithm is used to generate a pair of public/private keys for each service instance. The public key of an instance is identical to its identifier and can be transferred over the network while its private key is kept securely and can be used to prove the possession of the identifier. The Diffie-Hellman algorithm is also exploited for generating a shared secret key for every pair of collaborative partners of a session.

Figure 2 illustrates how the authentication system performs multi-party session authentication and management using the example of Figure 1. First, *CI* contacts an SA to start a new business session, *S*. The SA service then generates an instance, *SA*, to manage the new session. *CI* thus becomes a session partner of *S*, and its identifier is recorded in *SA*. *CI* then contacts *Producer*. *Producer* sends back the identifier of the instance *PI* in Step (2) while *PI* is introduced by *CI* to *SA* in Step (3). Next, *CI* starts to collaborate with *PI* after receiving the confirmation from *SA* (Step (4)). In the same way, *PI* invokes a new shipper instance *SI* and introduces it to *SA* (Steps (5) to (7)). After receiving the request from *SI*, *CI* first contacts *SA* to check whether *SI* is a legal business session partner of *S* (Steps (8) and (9)). Once this is confirmed by *SA*, *CI*

and *SI* can use the Diffie-Hellman algorithm to agree upon a shared secret key for further communications.

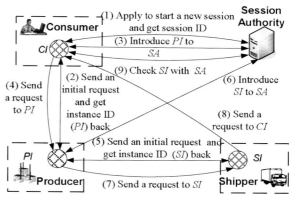

Figure 2 A business scenario

3.2 Formal Definitions

In this section we will define two core protocols in our multi-party authentication system using the well-known Logic of Authentication (or BAN logic) [2]. Protocol 1 is concerned with the introduction of a new session partner, and Protocol 2 performs authentication between two existing session partners. For the brevity of discussion, we use the following notation for formal definitions and proofs (which is a simplified version of the notation used in [14]).

p	large prime number
a	exponentiation base
A, B, C	session partners
SA	session authority
ID_A	identifier of A
S	multi-party session with identifier ID_S
$Pri(A)$	private key of principal A
$Pub(A)$	public key of principal A, i.e. $(a^{Pri(A)} \bmod p) = ID_A$
$K_{(A,B)}$	secret key generated with $Pri(A)$ and $Pub(B)$; $K_{(A,B)} = (Pub(B))^{Pri(A)} = a^{Pri(A)\,Pri(B)} \bmod p$; $K_{(A,B)} = K_{(B,A)}$
(M, N)	composite message composed of messages M and N
$MAC(M)_K$	message authentication code of M generated with secret key K
$Secure(M)$	message M is transmitted by a secure channel
$Valid(M)_K$	composite message $(M, MAC(M)_K)$
$\uparrow Pub(A)$	$Pub(A)$ is *good* [14], and its corresponding $Pri(A)$ will never be discovered by any other principals
$\#M$	M is fresh, i.e. M has not been sent in a message at any time before the current run of the protocol
$SP(A, S)$	statement that A is a session partner of S. Particularly, $SP(SA, S)$ is always true

443

$A \xleftarrow{K_{(A,B)}^{-}} B$	$K_{(A,B)}$ is A's secret key to be shared with B, but not yet confirmed by B
$A \xleftarrow{K_{(A,B)}^{+}} B$	$K_{(A,B)}$ is A's shared secret key and confirmed by B
$A \mid\equiv X$	A believes that statement X is true
A *says* X	A sent a message including statement X
$A \mid\Rightarrow X$	A is an authority on X, i.e. A has jurisdiction over X
$A \triangleleft M$	A receives message M

Figure 3 illustrates Protocol 1: Accepting a new session partner. Our protocol conforms to the WS-Resource Framework (WSRF) specification [6], where a service is associated with a factory service F that generates service instances.

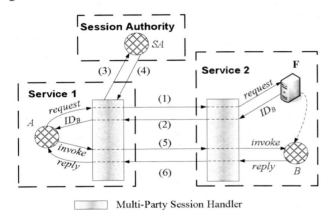

Multi-Party Session Handler

Figure 3 Protocol 1: Accepting a new session partner

The details of the messages transported within Figure 3 are presented as follows, where "$A \to B$" means that A sends a message to B:

(1) $A \to F$: *Secure(Request, ID$_S$, ID$_A$)*
(2) $F \to A$: *Secure(ID$_B$, ID$_S$)*
(3) $A \to SA$: *Valid(SP(B,S), ID$_B$, ID$_A$, ID$_{SA}$, ID$_S$, N)$_{K(A, SA)}$*
(4) $SA \to A$: *Valid(Confirm, N+1)$_{K(SA, A)}$*
(5) $A \to B$: *Valid(invoke, ID$_A$, ID$_B$, ID$_S$, N$_1$)$_{K(A, B)}$*
(6) $B \to A$: *Valid(reply, ID$_B$, ID$_A$, ID$_S$, N$_1$+1)$_{K(B, A)}$*
where N and N_1 are fresh nonces.

It is assumed that an HCRA process has been performed before Service 1 contacts Service 2. In Figure 3 instance A is a session partner of S, and has registered with SA. When A tries to contact Service 2, it first sends a request (message (1)) to the factory service F of Service 2. F then generates a new instance B and sends the related information about B (message (2)) back to A. Next, A introduces B to SA (message (3)). After receiving the confirmation from SA (message (4)), A will start to communicate with B (messages (5) and (6)). During this process, the integrity of messages (1) and (2) needs to be protected

by additional security channels (e.g. SSL, the secure conversation protocol, the secure message protocol etc.) as B is not yet a session partner during those steps. The integrity of messages (3), (4), (5), (6) is protected by shared secret keys distributed within S. For example, A can use its private key and the identifier of B to generate $K_{(A,B)}$ according to the Diffie-Hellman algorithm. $K_{(A,B)}$ is then used to generate the message authentication code of message (5). Similarly, B can use its private key and the identifier of A to generate $K_{(B,A)}$, which is identical to $K_{(A,B)}$. $K_{(B,A)}$ is then used to generate the MAC of message (6).

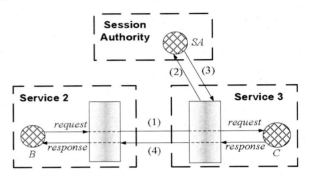

Figure 4 Protocol 2: Authenticating a session partner

Figure 4 illustrates Protocol 2: Authenticating a session partner. B and C are session partners of S, but B has not yet communicated with C before. First, B sends a request message (1) to C. C then sends message (2) to SA in order to check the identity of B. SA will send back a confirmation in message (3), confirming that B is a session partner of S. After receiving the confirmation, B will handle the request from C and send the result back. All the messages transferred during this process are encrypted by the secret key generated with the Diffie-Hellman algorithm. The details of the messages passed in Figure 4 are presented as follows:

(1) $B \to C$: *Valid(Request, ID$_B$, ID$_C$, ID$_S$, N')$_{K(B,C)}$*
(2) $C \to SA$: *Valid(Query, ID$_B$, ID$_C$, ID$_{SA}$, ID$_S$, N'')$_{K(C,SA)}$*
(3) $SA \to C$: *Valid(SP(B, S), ID$_{SA}$, ID$_C$, ID$_S$, N''+1)$_{K(SA,C)}$*
(4) $C \to B$: *Valid(Response, ID$_C$, ID$_B$, ID$_S$, N'+1)$_{K(C,B)}$*
where N' and N'' are fresh nonces.

In Protocols 1 and 2, MACs are used to protect the integrity of the messages transported within a business session, and fresh nonces are used to guarantee that a message is not replayed.

3.3 Correctness Proofs

In this section we use the extended BAN logic [2][14] to analyse formally the correctness of Protocols

1 and 2. We first introduce some deduction rules to be needed by our correctness proofs. These rules are specified in [2] and [14].

Rules:

Rule 1: A says $(M, N) \Rightarrow A$ says M and A says N

Rule 2: $A|\equiv\#M \Rightarrow A|\equiv\#(M, N)$ and $A|\equiv\#(N, M)$

Rule 3: $A|\equiv B|\Rightarrow X$, $A|\equiv B$ says $X \Rightarrow A|\equiv X$

Rule 4: $A|\equiv\uparrow Pub(B) \Rightarrow A|\equiv A \xleftarrow{K^-_{(A,B)}} B$

Rule 5: $A|\equiv A \xleftarrow{K^-_{(A,B)}} B$, $A \lhd Valid(X)_{K(A,B)}$, and $A|\equiv\#X \Rightarrow A|\equiv A \xleftarrow{K^+_{(A,B)}} B$.

Rule 6: $A \lhd (X, MAC(X)_{K(A,B)})$, $A |\equiv A \xleftarrow{K^+_{(A,B)}} B$, and $A|\equiv\#X \Rightarrow A|\equiv B$ says X

Lemma 1 $A \lhd Valid(M)_{K(A,B)}$, $A |\equiv A \xleftarrow{K^+_{(A,B)}} B$, and $A|\equiv\#M$, then $A|\equiv B$ says M.

Proof: This lemma can be deduced directly from Rule 6.

3.3.1 Protocol 1: Accepting a new session partner

Security goals of Protocol 1 include 1) accepting B as a new partner and 2) building a confirmed secret key to be shared between A and B. The security goals are formally described as follows:

$$SA|\equiv \quad SP(B,S), \quad A|\equiv A \xleftarrow{K^+_{(A,B)}} B \quad, \quad \text{and}$$
$$B |\equiv B \xleftarrow{K^+_{(B,A)}} A$$

Additionally, the assumptions of this protocol are formally described as follows:

$$SA|\equiv\uparrow Pub(A), \quad A|\equiv\uparrow Pub(SA), \quad A|\equiv\uparrow Pub(B),$$
$$B|\equiv\uparrow Pub(A), SA|\equiv\#N, \text{ and } A|\equiv\#N_1, SA|\equiv A|\Rightarrow SP(B, S)$$

In Protocol 1, it is the responsibility of SA to decide whether to accept an instance (e.g. B) as a session partner following certain policies. This assumption is in fact based on the simplest policy, that is, SA will accept any instance recommended by an existing session partner (e.g. A) as a new session partner.

To prove the correctness of the protocol, it is necessary to show whether its security goals can be satisfied after the run of the protocol under the assumptions. We therefore have the following theorem.

Theorem 1 The goals of Protocol 1 are satisfied under the assumptions for the protocol.

Proof: We need to deduce $SA|\equiv SP(B,S)$, $A |\equiv A \xleftarrow{K^+_{(A,B)}} B$, and $B |\equiv B \xleftarrow{K^+_{(B,A)}} A$ from the assumptions of the protocol.

The third step of Protocol 1 implies that $SA \lhd Valid(SP(B,S), ID_B, ID_A, ID_{SA}, ID_S, N)_{K(A, SA)}$. We obtain $SA|\equiv\#(SP(B,S), ID_B, ID_A, ID_{SA}, ID_S, N)$ by the

assumption $SA|\equiv\#N$ and Rule 2. From $SA|\equiv\uparrow Pub(A)$, it follows that $SA|\equiv A \xleftarrow{K^-_{(A,SA)}} SA$ by Rule 4. Then, from $SA|\equiv A \xleftarrow{K^-_{(A,SA)}} SA$, $SA \lhd Valid(SP(B,S), ID_B, ID_A, ID_{SA}, ID_S, N)_{K(A, SA)}$, and $SA|\equiv\#(SP(B,S), ID_B, ID_A, ID_{SA}, ID_S, N)$, it yields that $SA|\equiv A \xleftarrow{K^+_{(A,SA)}} SA$ by Rule 5. Furthermore, we can deduce that $SA|\equiv A$ says $(SP(B,S), ID_B, ID_A, ID_{SA}, ID_S, N)$ and $SA|\equiv A$ says $SP(B,S)$ by Lemma 1 and Rule 1. Therefore, from the assumption $SA|\equiv A |\Rightarrow SP(B, S)$ and Rule 3, it follows that $SA|\equiv SP(B,S)$.

From $A|\equiv\uparrow Pub(B)$, we have $A|\equiv A \xleftarrow{K^-_{(A,B)}} B$ by Rule 4. Besides, from the sixth step of the protocol and the assumption $A|\equiv\#N_1$, it follows that $A \lhd Valid(reply, ID_B, ID_A, ID_S, N_1+1)_{K(B, A)}$ and $A|\equiv\#(reply, ID_B, ID_A, ID_S, N_1+1)$. Consequently, we obtain $A |\equiv A \xleftarrow{K^+_{(A,B)}} B$ by Rule 5. $B |\equiv B \xleftarrow{K^+_{(B,A)}} A$ can also be deduced through a similar procedure. Hence the theorem.

3.3.2 Protocol 2: Authenticating a session partner

The security goals of Protocol 2 are 1) verifying whether a principal is a session partner, and 2) building a confirmed secret key to be shared between the session partners. Formal expression of the security goals are presented as follows:

$$C|\equiv SP(B, S), \quad B|\equiv B \xleftarrow{K^+_{(B,C)}} C, \text{ and } C|\equiv C \xleftarrow{K^+_{(B,C)}} B.$$

The formal descriptions of the assumptions are:

$$C|\equiv\uparrow Pub(SA), \quad B|\equiv\uparrow Pub(C), \quad SA|\equiv\uparrow Pub(C),$$
$$C|\equiv\uparrow Pub(B), C|\equiv\#N', C|\equiv\#N'', \text{ and } C|\equiv SA|\Rightarrow SP(B, S)$$

The correctness of this protocol is stated in the following theorem.

Theorem 2 The goals of Protocol 2 are satisfied under the above assumptions.

Proof: By Rule 4, $C|\equiv\uparrow Pub(SA)$ implies that $C|\equiv C \xleftarrow{K^-_{(C,SA)}} SA$. We obtain $C \lhd Valid(SP(B, S), ID_{SA}, ID_C, ID_S, N''+1)_{K(SA,C)}$ in the third step of the protocol, and $C|\equiv\#(SP(B, S), ID_{SA}, ID_C, ID_S, N''+1)$ by the assumption $C|\equiv\#N''$ and Rule 2. It then follows that $C|\equiv C \xleftarrow{K^+_{(C,SA)}} SA$ by Rule 5. By Lemma 1 we obtain that $C|\equiv SA$ says $(SP(B, S), ID_{SA}, ID_C, ID_S, N''+1)$, and thus $C|\equiv SA$ says $SP(B, S)$ by Rule 1. Since $C|\equiv SA|\Rightarrow SP(B, S)$, we have $C|\equiv SP(B, S)$ by Rule 3.

From the assumption $C|\equiv\uparrow Pub(B)$, it follows that $C |\equiv C \xleftarrow{K^-_{(C,B)}} B$ by Rule 4. Since $C \lhd Valid(Request, ID_B, ID_C, ID_S, N')_{K(B,C)}$ and

$C|\equiv\#($ *Request*, ID_B, ID_C, ID_S, N') which is derived from $C|\equiv\#N'$ by Rule 2, then $C|\equiv C\xleftarrow{K^+_{(C,B)}}B$ by Rule 5. $B|\equiv B\xleftarrow{K^+_{(B,C)}}C$ can be deduced from $B|\equiv\uparrow Pub(C)$ by a similar approach. Hence the theorem.

4. Empirical Evaluation

Beside the correctness analysis, we also need to examine whether our authentication system is feasible enough for practical real-world applications. Consequently, a series of experiments has been implemented to assess the overheads imposed by the authentication mechanisms and the scalability of our proposed system. Because the system is designed to be deployed on service-oriented middleware, we will evaluate the compatibility of our system with existing message-level security protocols.

Two experimental systems have been developed. In the first experimental system (*ES*1 for short) an SA service and three experimental services are implemented. As illustrated in Figure 5, a client first initiates a business session, and three experimental services then repeatedly invoke each other until a particular amount of service instances have been generated and introduced to *SA*. The second experimental system (*ES*2 for short) consists of three experimental services without *SA*. Experimental services of *ES*2 invoke each other repeatedly until the system has generated a particular amount of service instances.

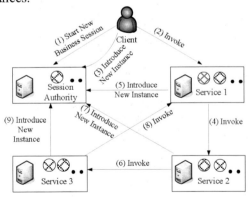

Figure 5 Experimental system with Session Authority

*ES*1 is used to simulate distributed applications that use the multi-party authentication system whilst *ES*2 simulates distributed applications without the multi-party authentication system. The experimental results of *ES*2 are used as benchmarks. By comparing the experimental results obtained from both experimental systems, we can assess the overheads imposed by our authentication system.

Our experimental systems are implemented on a Grid service middleware system in which a Web service is associated with a factory service which is in charge of the generation and the management of resources. In the Grid, Web services are stateless, and state information is stored in resources. A service instance can be thus located when the corresponding resource is found. In *ES*1, the identifier of an instance and its associated private key are stored within a resource, and the instance identifier is identical to the resource identifier.

4.1 Worst Case Evaluation

We have deployed the experimental systems both on a single computer and on a distributed system with multiple computers. Particularly, we deploy the experimental systems on a single computer for two reasons.

- In order to evaluate precisely the overhead introduced by the authentication protocols (e.g. generating key pairs, generating MACs for messages etc.), we need to remove the influence introduced by the time consumption of transporting messages.
- Deploying the experimental systems on a single computer can help us to evaluate the performance of the systems in the strictest environment where all the operations are executed sequentially. In this sub-section all the experiments are deployed on a single computer unless stated otherwise.

In the experiment illustrated in Figure 6, there are more than 24,000 instances are generated and introduced to the Session Authority. From the beginning of the experiment, the time consumption of generating and registering new session partners is proportional to the number of the newly generated instances. The experimental system stays in such a stable state until over 16,000 instances are generated. The performance decreases after then, and the system finally stops due to the lack of the memory space.

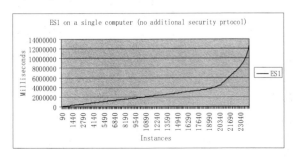

Figure 6 *ES*1 deployed on GT4

We also combine *ES*1 and *ES*2 with two message-level security protocols, *Secure Conversation* and *Secure Message*, provided by GT4. In the experiment illustrated in Figure 7, the secure conversation protocol is used to generate signatures for every message transported in *ES*1. The time consumption of the experimental system starts to increase non-linearly after over 720 instances are generated. The same phenomenon occurs in *ES*2 after over 1040 instances are generated when *ES*2 is deployed with the secure conversation protocol.

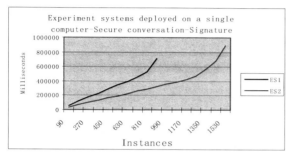

Figure 7 *ES*1 and *ES*2 on GT4 plus Secure Conversation

As illustrated in Figures 7 and 8, the time consumption of *ES*1 is about twice that of *ES*2 although *ES*1 provides sufficient support for session authentication operations. These experimental results also indicate that the scalability of the experimental systems is affected significantly by the security protocols combined with the experimental systems.

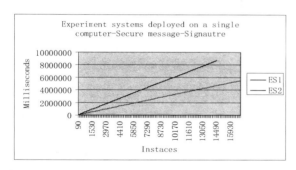

Figure 8 *ES*1 and *ES*2 on GT4 plus Secure Message

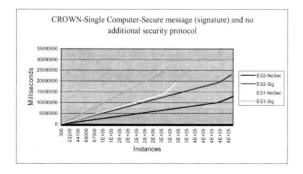

Figure 9 *ES*1 and *ES*2 on CROWN

In order to avoid generating GT4-oriented results only, we also implement our design in the large-scale CROWN (China Research and Development environment Over Wide-area Network) Grid [19]. CROWN is a practical Grid system, aiming to promote the utilisation of valuable resources and cooperation of researchers nationwide and world-wide. The experimental results are presented in Figure 9. The time consumption of *ES*1 is about twice that of *ES*2. This is very similar to what observed in the GT4-based experiments. However, as the computer used by CROWN is much more powerful, the performance of our experimental systems becomes much better. The experimental systems can stay in a stable state until over 260,000 instances are generated.

4.2 Distributed Deployment

The performance of the experimental systems is improved significantly when deployed in a distributed environment with multiple computers. In the GT4-based experiments, the time consumption of *ES*1 without combining other security protocols increases linearly until more than 70,000 new instances are generated. When incorporated with the secure conversation protocol, *ES*1 executes stably until over 3,000 instances are generated. As an example of distributed deployment, the experimental results based on CROWN are presented in Figure 10. The time consumption of *ES*1 is proportional to the number of the newly generated instances until over 300,000 instances are generated.

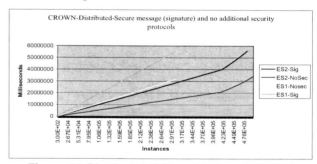

Figure 10 Distributed *ES*1 and *ES*2 on CROWN

Memory space is the critical factor that affects the performance of an experimental system. The information about session partners has to be recorded for the SA, and the resources of experimental services have to be stored in memory as well. In addition, read and write operations on the server log file consume a large amount of memory space. Due to the behaviour of the Java garbage collection mechanism, consumed memory space is sometimes not released in a timely manner, and the performance of the experimental system is thus affected. When an experimental system is deployed in a distributed environment, the SA and the experimental services do not need to share the limited memory. The performance becomes therefore much better.

5. Related Work

The issues with cross-realm authentication have been discussed in many papers. For example, both direct cross-realm authentication and transitive cross-realm authentication are supported in Kerberos [4][17]. By using transitive cross-realm authentication, a principal can access the resources in a remote realm by traversing multiple intermediate realms, if there is no cross-realm key shared with the remote realm. However, Kerberos assumes that the authentication mechanisms in all the federated security realms are homogeneous. In practice, the authentication mechanisms in different security realms are often heterogeneous and even non-interoperable, both in structures and functions. In order to address the issue of federating such heterogeneous authentication mechanisms, credential conversion mechanisms are widely used in many existing solutions. The work in [12] presents two types of credential translator services, KCA which translates Kerberos credentials to PK credentials, and KCT which translates PK credentials to Kerberos credentials.

Reiter and Stubblebine in [16] argue that an authentication process in a large-scale distributed system often needs the assistance of a path of security authorities as it is difficult to locate a single authority to authenticate all the principals in the system. They suggest using multiple paths to increase assurance on authentication. It is important to notice here that a Session Authority or SA in our system differs significantly from the security authority in [16]. A security authority is used to enforce security policies and processes for a security realm so as to prevent attacks from accessing the applications and resources within that realm. In contrast, an SA is associated with a business session (management system), independent of any local security realm. It has much simpler functionalities than a security authority, aiming to provide secure real information to session partners which may belong to different security realms.

The problems related to federation amongst heterogeneous authentication mechanisms used by different security realms are also discussed in the Web service federation protocol [1][10]. The Web service federation protocol defines a set of credential conversion mechanisms, with which a principal in a realm can convert its credential to a credential that can be accepted in another realm within the federation. The

issues of discovering a credential chain is discussed extensively in [13]. It is shown that an authentication path can be found in polynomial time if there is a centralised entity which holds all the federation information of the security realms possibly involved. Considering that the session partners of a business session may be determined dynamically at runtime, it is practically difficult to have sufficient information about the security realms to be involved before the execution of that session. However, without such a centralised entity, this job becomes much more difficult. In the extreme case, all the realms possibly involved need to be searched before an authentication path can be identified.

In order to realize peer-to-peer collaborations amongst Web services, IBM, Microsoft, and BEA proposed a specification, WS-Coordination [3], in August 2002. WS-Coordination describes an extensible framework for supporting the coordination of the actions in distributed applications. However, WS-Coordination is intended only as a meta-specification governing the specifications of concrete forms of coordination. The security issues discussed in this paper are not addressed.

6. Conclusions

In practice, a dynamic business process may involve many applications and services which belong to different organisations and security realms. The dynamic authentication process between organisations could be highly complex and time-consuming if some intermediate authentication paths have to be created and credentials have to be converted. When there is no existing authentication relationship in place between two organisations, it will be practically difficult for a system to enable any secure collaboration between services from the two organisations in a just-in-time fashion.

We have developed a new authentication system for multi-party service interactions that does not require credential conversion and the establishment of any authentication path between collaborative session partners. The system also offers the ability to identify individual service instances within a business session even if some instances in fact belong to the same service. Although the amount of communications between the partners of a session and the Session Authority is limited, the performance overhead imposed by it is indeed of some practical concern. We have therefore conducted a set of comprehensive experiments to assess the overhead. Two service-oriented Grid systems were used, and the experimental results were collected in a realistic and distributed setting which can accommodate concurrently more than 300K service instances. The main results show that the overhead imposed by our authentication system is comparable with the overheads caused by the standard security mechanisms used in those Grid middleware systems. An interesting future question is how heterogeneous security realms agree upon the usage of secret keys within a session. We are developing a negotiation protocol to address this issue.

Acknowledgements

This work is supported partially by the EPSRC/BAE Systems NECTISE project, the ESRC MoSeS project, the EPSRC WRG project, and the EPSRC CoLaB project. Thanks are due to Dr Paul Townend for his help and suggestions in the preparation of this paper.

References

[1] S. Bajaj, G. Della-Libera, B. Dixon, M. Dusche, M. Hondo, M. Hur, C. Kaler, H. Lockhart, H. Maruyama, A. Nadalin, N. Nagaratnam, A. Nash, H. Prafullchandra, and J. Shewchuk, "Web Services Federation Language (WS-Federation)," available from http://msdn2.microsoft.com/en-us/library/_ms951236.aspx, Jul. 2003.

[2] M. Burrows, M. Abadi, and R. Needham, "A Logic of Authentication," *ACM Trans. on Computer ·Systems*, Feb. 1990, pp. 18-36.

[3] F. Cabrera, G. Copeland, T. Freund, J. Klein, D. Langworthy, D. Orchard, J. Shewchuk, and T. Storey, "Web Services Coordination (WS-Coordination)," available from http://www.ibm.com/developerworks/library/ws-coor/, Aug. 2002.

[4] I. Cervesato, A.D. Jaggard, A. Scedrov, and C. Walstad, "Specifying Kerberos 5 Cross-Realm Authentication," *Proc. Workshop on Issues in the Theory of Security*, Long Beach, California, USA, 2005, pp. 12 – 26.

[5] N. Cook, S. Shirvastava, and S. Wheater, "Distributed Object Middleware to Support Dependable Information Sharing between Organisations," *Proc. International Conference on Dependable Systems and Networks*, Maryland, USA, Jun. 2002, pp, 249- 258.

[6] K. Czajkowski, D. Ferguson, I. Foster, J. Frey, S. Graham, I. Sedukhin, D. Snelling, S. Tuecke, W. Vambenepe, "The WS-Resource Framework Version 1.0," available from http://www.globus.org/wsrf/specs/ws-wsrf.pdf, 3 May 2004.

[7] D. Georgakopoulos and M. Hornick, "An Overview of Workflow Management: From Process Modelling to Workflow Automation Infrastructure," *Distributed and Parallel Database*, Springer, Mar. 2005, pp. 119-153.

[8] Li Gong, "Increasing Availability and Security of an Authentication Service," *IEEE J. Selected Areas in Communication*, vol. 11, no. 5, June, 1993, pp. 657-662.

[9] S. Hada and H. Maruyama, "Session Authentication Protocol for Web Services," *Proc. Symposium on Application and the Internet*, Jan. 2002, pp. 158-165.

[10] M. Hondo, N. Nagaratnam, and A. J. Nadalin, "Securing Web Services," *IBM Systems J.*, 2002.

[11] M. Huhns and M. P. Singh, "Service-Oriented Computing: Key Concepts and Principles," *IEEE Internet Computing*, vol. 9, no. 1, Jan. 2005, pp. 75-81.

[12] O. Kornievskaia, P. Honeyman, B. Doster, and K. Coffman, "Kerberized Credential Translation: A Solution to Web Access Control," *Proc. 10th USENIX Security Symposium*, Washington, DC, USA, Aug. 2001.

[13] N. Li, W. Winsborough, and J.C. Mitchell, "Distributed Credential Chain Discovery in Trust Management," *J. Computer Security*, vol. 11, no. 1, 2003, pp. 35-86.

[14] P. C. van Oorschot, "Extending Cryptographic Logics of Belief to Key Agreement Protocols," *Proc. the 1st ACM Conference on Computer and Communications Security*, Fairfax, Virginia, USA, Nov. 1993, pp. 233– 243.

[15] S. Rafaeli and D. Hutchison, "A Survey of Key Management for Secure Group Communication," *ACM Comput. Surveys*, vol. 35, no. 3, Sep. 2003, pp. 309-329.

[16] M. K. Reiter and S. G. Stubblebine, "Resilient Authentication Using Path Independence," *IEEE Trans. Computers*, vol. 47, no. 12, Dec. 1998, pp. 1351-1362.

[17] W. Stallings, *Cryptography and Network Security: Principles and Practices*, Prentice Hall, Upper Saddle River, New Jersey, 1999.

[18] M. Steiner, G. Tsudik, and M. Waidner, "Diffie-Hellman Key Distribution Extended to Group Communication," *Proc. of the 3rd ACM Conference on Computer and Communications Security*, New Delhi, India, Mar. 1996, pp. 31-37.

[19] H. Sun, Y. Zhu, C. Hu, J. Huai, Y. Liu, and J. Li, "Early Experience of Remote and Hot Service Deployment with Trustworthiness in CROWN Grid," *Proc. APPT*, 2005, pp. 301-312.

[20] C. K. Wong, M. G. Gouda, and S. S. Lam, "Secure Group Communications Using Key Graphs," *Proc. ACM SIGCOMM '98 Conf. Applications, Technologies, Architectures, and Protocols for Computer Comm.*, 1998, pp. 68-79.

Enhancing DNS Resilience against Denial of Service Attacks

Vasileios Pappas
T.J. Watson Center
IBM Research
vpappas@us.ibm.com

Dan Massey
Computer Science Department
Colorado State University
massey@cs.colostate.edu

Lixia Zhang
Computer Science Department
UCLA
lixia@cs.ucla.edu

Abstract

The Domain Name System (DNS) is a critical Internet infrastructure that provides name to address mapping services. In the past few years, distributed denial of service (DDoS) attacks have targeted the DNS infrastructure and threaten to disrupt this critical service. In this paper we show that the existing DNS can gain significant resilience against DDoS attacks through a simple change to the current DNS operations, by setting longer time-to-live values for a special class of DNS resource records, the infrastructure records. These records are used to navigate the DNS hierarchy and change infrequently. Furthermore, in combination with a set of simple and incrementally deployable record renewal policies, the DNS service availability can be improved by one order of magnitude. Our approach requires neither additional physical resources nor any change to the existing DNS design. We evaluate the effectiveness of our proposed enhancement by using DNS traces collected from multiple locations.

Keywords: DDoS, DNS, resilience, caching

1 Introduction

The Domain Name System (DNS) [16] provides name services for the Internet. It maps hostnames to IP addresses and also provides services for a growing number of other applications, such as mapping IP addresses to geographic locations or directory services for legacy telephony applications. Furthermore, protocols such as SMTP and SIP depend on the DNS in order to route messages through appropriate application level gateways. As a result, the availability of the DNS can affect the availability of a large number of Internet applications. Ensuring the DNS data availability is an essential part of providing a robust Internet.

Due to its hierarchical structure, the DNS availability depends on a small number of servers that serve the root and other important top level domains. A number of distributed denial of service (DDoS) attacks have been directed against these top level DNS name-servers in recent years [2, 3, 5, 7]. The impact on overall DNS availability is debatable [1, 4], but some attacks did succeed in disabling the targeted DNS servers and resulted in parts of the Internet experiencing severe name resolution problems.

Overall, attacks can potentially threaten the DNS availability and effectively threaten the availability of the Internet itself.

We have developed a simple approach that can effectively enhance the DNS resilience against DDoS attacks. We identify a special class of DNS records called *infrastructure records*, which store data for DNS infrastructure components (namely the name-servers). DNS resolvers use the infrastructure records to navigate the DNS hierarchy. The presence of the infrastructure records in DNS local caches can greatly improve the resilience of the DNS in the presence of failures. In this paper we propose and evaluate two methods for caching infrastructure records for longer periods of time. First, we propose to assign a much longer TTL value for the infrastructure records than the data records. This is feasible because, generally speaking, the infrastructure records change less frequently than other DNS data records. Second, we propose a set of simple record renewal policies. Our analysis shows that these two changes can improve DNS service availability during a DDoS attack by one order of magnitude.

The main benefit of our approach is that it is operationally feasible and immediately deployable by either large or small zones. In contrast, the currently deployed solution of shared unicast addresses [14] aims at absorbing the attack load by installing a large number of name-servers. This solution is suitable for large zones, such as the root and the top level domains, that can afford the cost. Smaller zones may not be able to afford adding a large number of name-servers. Other solutions proposed by the research community [10, 21, 20, 12, 11] address the problem of DDoS attacks against DNS by introducing major protocol changes or by redesigning the whole system. Although some of them are considered incrementally deployable, their adoption is hindered by the operators' reluctance to introducing major changes in an operational system. Our approach requires no protocol changes while achieving similar levels of resilience against DDoS attacks.

The rest of the paper is structured as follows. Sections 2 and 3 review the basic DNS concepts and the threat posed by DDoS attacks. Section 4 presents our TTL guidelines and caching enhancements. Section 5 evaluates of our approach using a set of real DNS traffic traces. Section 6 discusses some issues related to other attack strategies. Sec-

450

tion 7 reviews related work and Section 8 concludes the paper.

2 Domain Name System

In DNS parlance, the name space is divided into a large number of zones. Roughly speaking, each zone is authoritative for the names that share the same suffix with the zone's name. A zone can also delegate part of its namespace to another zone, referred as a child zone. For example, the *ucla.edu* zone has delegated the *cs.ucla.edu* namespace to create a child zone. This delegation procedure results in an inverted tree structure with each node being a zone and each edge representing a delegation point. The *root* zone resides at the top of this tree structure. Generic top-level domains (gTLD), such as *edu*, and country code top-level domains (ccTLD) appear directly below the *root*. Figure 1 displays a part of the DNS tree structure with some functional elements introduced in the next two paragraphs.

Each zone stores the resource records (RRs) associated with names under its authority. There are several different types of RRs with the most common one being the address (A) resource record used to map names to IPv4 addresses. Each RR has a time to live value (TTL) that specifies the maximum lifetime when caching the record. For example, the IP address of *www.ucla.edu* is stored in an A resource record and has a TTL value of 4 hours.

All the RRs that belong to a zone are available from a set of DNS servers called authoritative name-servers (ANs) for the zone. The ANs are identified by a special type of resource record, the name-server (NS) resource record. The NS records for a zone are stored at the zone itself and also at its parent zone. Each NS record points to the name of the authoritative name-server (rather than its IP address) and thus one needs both the NS and A records of the server in order to contact a zone. We call the set of NS and A records that are associated with the ANs *infrastructure resource records* (IRRs). IRRs are used in order to construct the DNS tree structure.

Client applications typically retrieve a desired RRs by querying a stub-resolver (SR), a DNS element which is implemented in every operating system. An SR typically forwards the query to a special type of server, called caching server (CS) and the CS obtains the desired RR. More specifically, the CS obtains RR's from zone Z by querying Z's ANs. The CS knows Z's ANs either because it has previously cached Z's IRRs or by querying Z's parent zone. The parent zone knows the Z's IRRs because it is required to have a copy of Z's IRRs. If the CS does not know the IRRs for Z or Z's parent, it repeats finds the nearest ancestor zone for which it has the IRRs. Every CS is hard-coded with the IRRs of the *root* zone and thus can always start at the root zone if no better IRRs are known. A CS caches each RR that it learns for a period of time equal to the TTL value of the record. Thus, it can reply back to a SR either with information that is locally cached or with information that is retrieved directly from an AN.

3 Threat Assessment of DDoS Attacks

A successful Distributed Denial of Service (DDoS) attack against the DNS offers potential for a high "pay-off". Almost every Internet application utilizes the DNS and an attacker can potentially achieve a DoS attack against many services and many locations by disabling the DNS. The DNS tree structure also seems to introduce critical points of failure such as DNS root or DNS top level domains. Well known DDoS attacks have been launched against the DNS *root* and other top level zones [2, 3, 5, 7]. A simplistic view suggests a successful attack against the DNS root servers could cripple the Internet.

However, both the vulnerabilities and the potential impacts are more complex than the simplistic view suggests. A more informed analysis must take the various DNS components such as redundant servers and caches into account. A DNS zone can be served by a large number of DNS name-servers. Protocol limitations have fixed the number of IPv4 root server addresses at 13, but techniques such as shared unicast addresses are being used to increase the actual number of servers. Second, even if the attack successfully disables the name-servers of a targeted zone, it may have limited effect on the DNS service given that cached records will continue to be served.

3.1 Launching a Successful Attack

This paper considers DDoS attacks that target the authoritative name-servers for a zone. We assume the attack objective is to disable the DNS resolution of all zones *below the targeted zone*. Many high level zones such as the root and top level domains (com, net, edu, uk, cn, and so forth) primarily provide referrals to other zones lower in the tree. For example, an attack against the *edu* authoritative servers is intended to prevent resolvers from reaching any of the zones below *edu*. Most of the well known large-scale DNS attacks fall under this category. Section 6 discusses other types of attacks.

Whether an attack succeeds it depends on both the resources of the attacker and the defender. DDoS attacks can easily succeed if a zone is served by a small number of servers. Currently, most zones use two or three name-servers and are thus vulnerable to relatively small attacks. Larger and more critical zones tend to deploy more servers, but their number still ranges in the order of tens or hundreds. Unfortunately, some of the "botnets" controlled by attackers include hundreds of thousands of "drone" machines [6] and can potentially be successful even against the few zones that deploy anycast enabled name-servers [14]. Overall, the situation creates an arms race between attacker and defenders with both sides seeking enough resources to overwhelm the other.

3.2 Factors Affecting Attack Impact

While it may be feasible to launch a successful DDoS attack against a zone, the attack will not necessarily have any impact on Internet applications. There are mainly three factors that affect the end-user experience of a successful

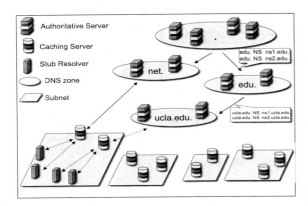

Figure 1. Overview of DNS elements.

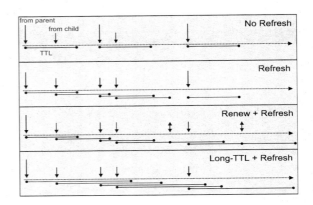

Figure 2. Proposed schemes showcase.

DDoS attack against DNS:

Position of the Target Zone If a zone is a *stub* in the DNS tree structure, i.e. it is not used in order to access the name-servers for other zones, then the attack will only affect the names defined in the targeted zone. Note that a *leaf*-zone, i.e. a zone that has no children, is not necessarily a stub-zone. In many cases leaf-zones are used in order to resolve the IP address of other zones' name-servers. In essence, the number of descendant zones that can be resolved through a zone can indicate the severity of a successful attack against that zone. If one considers only the position of a zone, then the *root* zone would be considered the most important zone given that it is needed in order to resolve all other zones.

Popularity of the Target Zone The impact of a successful attack also depends on the frequency of *referrals* provided by the target zone. The number of referrals depends partly on the the number of child zones below the parent zone. But it is also influenced by the popularity of the child zones, i.e. the number of caching servers that query them. In addition, the TTL values of the child zones IRRs can also influence the frequency of referrals. To illustrate this, consider an attack that targets the root zone. Every zone is a descendant of the root, but an attack against a popular TLD may be more catastrophic than attack against the *root*. There are only around two to three hundreds zones directly below the root, compared to millions of zones directly below the largest TLDs. Furthermore, the zones directly below the root tend to have IRR records with relatively TTL values. In contrast, many zones below the TLDs have shorter TTL values for the IRR records. As a consequence, the caching servers query TLDs more frequently than they query the *root* zone.

Resource Record Caching The impact of a successful DDoS attack is also affected by resource record caching. Even if some zones are unavailable due to a DDoS attack, the records defined at these zones may be cached in some caching servers and thus still accessible. Clearly, the higher the TTL value for a record and the more popular the record may be, the higher the probability of being cached. In essence, the use of resource record caching allows end-user application to still function even though a zone's authoritative name servers are not accessible. In a similar manner,

the caching of infrastructure records can allow a caching server to access a zone's name-servers, even if an ascendant zone is not accessible due to a DDoS attack. While the caching of data records plays a role, the caching of infrastructure records plays a more prominent role in mitigating DDoS attacks. The presence of a zone's infrastructure record in the local cache allows the resolution of all the names defined inside the zone and also allows the resolution of all the descendant zones even when the parent zone (or any other ascendant zone) is unavailable.

4 Enhancing DNS Resilience

Previous efforts [10, 21, 20, 12, 11] of enhancing the DNS resilience against DDos attacks focus on reducing or eliminating critical points of failure in the DNS hierarchy. Either they introduce new ways of resolving the name-servers [21, 12] which do not coincide with the name-space tree structure, or they abandon completely the concept of name-servers [10, 20, 11], at least in the way that they are currently defined. As a consequence these previous proposals require substantial changes in the DNS infrastructure.

In contrast, our approach of enhancing the DNS resilience against DNS attacks focuses on zone popularity and caching. We introduce changes only at the caching servers and we do not require any modifications to the underlying DNS infrastructure. Our enhancements aim at forcing the caching servers (CS) to maintain for longer periods of time copies of the infrastructure resource records (IRRs) for the zones that they use the most frequently. In consequence, the number of referral, i.e queries that a CS sends at a parent zone in order to resolve names belonging to a child zone, can potentially decrease. In this way the popularity of a zone depends mainly on the number of queries generated for the names that belong to the zone and less on the number of queries generated for names belonging to a child zone.

We provide the following example in order to elaborate more on the basic idea of our approach. Let's consider a successful attack against the *edu* zone. In that case, a CS cannot resolve a zone that resides just below the *edu* if it does not have the IRRs for that zone. The probability of having the IRRs for the zone cached are increased when a zone is more popular or when the IRRs have a longer TTL.

In order to increase the probability of having the IRRs, a CS can "artificially" increase the popularity of the zone by querying it whenever the IRRs are ready to expire or the zone's administrator can increase the TTL value of the zone's IRRs. Note that in the extreme case, a CS can indefinitely query for the IRRs and the zone's administrator can unlimitedly increase the TTL value. While both of these extreme cases can lead to the best resilience against DDoS attacks, they are not desirable given that the first can introduce a considerable message overhead and the second can potentially introduce IRRs inconsistencies.

Next we present three feasible techniques that can be used in order to increase the probability of having the IRRs for a zone locally cached. Figure 2 provides their graphical representation, corresponding to the IRRs of a zone, which are cached inside a CS. The longer arrows represent referral replies from the parent zone, while the shorter arrows represent replies from the child zone. The horizontal lines represent the period of time for which the IRRs are cached. We should point out that the proposed methods *affect only the IRRs* and not any other record, e.g. as the various data records.

TTL Refresh In order to explain how *TTL refresh* works we first need to provide some specific details on how CSs learn and cache these records. A CS learns the IRR for a zone Z initially from Z's parent zone (P). The IRR for Z are included in the authority and the additional sections of the referral sent by P's name-servers. The CS caches these records locally and then contacts one of Z's name-servers to obtain the desired data. The reply from Z's name-servers also includes a the IRR for Z in the authority and additional sections of the reply. The CS ought to replace the cached IRR that come from the parent with the IRR that come from the child zone when they are not identical [13]. This establishes initial IRR records for zone Z.

Additional queries for names in Z can make use of the IRR data and go directly to Z's name-servers. Each query to a Z name-server will include a copy of Z's IRR data and TTL refresh uses this new data to refresh the TTL on Z's IRR. For example, a query for *www.ucla.edu* will result in the cache learning both the requested *www.ucla.edu* record and the IRR data from *ucla.edu*. If the IRR for Z has not yet expired, a later query for *ftp.ucla.edu* will go directly to the Z name-servers and the response will include both the *ftp.ucla.edu* record and another copy of the *ucla.edu* IRR data. This new copy of the IRR information could be used to refresh the cached copy of all *ucla.edu* IRR, but many popular DNS caching server implementations do not refresh the TTL value for the IRR. Note that the *www.ucla.edu* record may expire before the *ucla.edu* IRR and thus even another query for *www.ucla.edu* could be used to refresh the IRR.

This simple modification is very effective for the zones that a CS visits frequently. Assuming a CS sends some query to zone's name-servers before the IRR expires. Every query resets the TTL and the zone's IRR will be always locally cached. In contrast without *TTL refresh* the

CS has to visit the parent zone when the IRR expires. The difference is shown in Figure 2. If the CS does not refresh the TTL, the IRRs expire after the first two queries and thus the third one triggers a query at the parent zone. In contrast with the refresh the CS needs to query the parent zone only at the fifth query.

TTL Renewal The limitation of the *TTL refresh* method is that it does not work well for the popular zones that the caching server queries in a less regular fashion. A CS will not have the IRRs for the zone if the time between queries to Z exceeds the TTL on Z's IRR. This is the case in Figure 2. The CS does not have the IRRs during the fifth query. The *TTL renewal* method aims at filling that gap. In essence, it allows the IRRs for the most popular zones to stay in a CS for longer periods of time, compared to the *TTL refresh* method. This is done by refetching and then renewing the TTL of the IRRs just before they are ready to expire. This is shown with the double-head arrow in Figure 2.

In order to renew the IRRs only for the most popular zones we consider four different renewal policies. The basic idea behind these policies is that each zone is assigned a certain credit c which defines the number of times the zone's IRRs can be renewed after they have expired. The assignment of credit is different for the four renewal policies but it mimics either the last recently used (LRU) or the least frequently used (LFU) cache renewal policies. More specifically we consider the following policies:

- LRU^c: This policy *sets* a zone's credit to c every time that the zone is queried. Also every time that the zone's IRRs are about to expire the credit is decreased by one and the IRRs are re-fetched. In essence, with this policy the IRRs stay in the cache for an additional period of time that is equal to $c * TTL$. It resembles an LRU replacement policy because the IRRs that haven't been recently used are the ones that expire first.

- LFU^c: This policy *adds* a credit of c to the zone's current credit, whenever the zone is queried. Again, the credit is decremented by one whenever the zone's IRRs are re-fetched. Given that for the most popular zones the credit may indefinitely increase, we consider a maximum credit M. If the current credit reaches M, then it stops increasing. This policy resembles an LFU policy for the reason that the IRRs that expire first are the ones that are not frequently used.

- $A - LRU^c$: This is an *adaptive* version of the LRU^c policy. The need for an adaptive policy arises from the fact that different zones have IRRs with different TTL values. Thus the additional time that their IRRs stay in the cache may vary. In order, to make this time equal for all the zones we consider a version of the LRU^c policy in which the credit adapts based on the TTL value. More specifically, the assigned credit is equal to $86400 * c/TTL$, where 86400 is the equivalent of one day in seconds. Thus, for example if the

453

$c = 3$ then the credit causes all the $IRRs$ to stay in the cache for three days additionally.

- $A - LFU^c$: Similarly we define an *adaptive* version of the LFU^c renewal policy. Again the credit adapts to the TTL value of each zone's $IRRs$ and it is equal to $86400 * c/TTL$. Furthermore, there still exist a maximum credit M that the current credit cannot exceed, which prevents the credit of very popular zones from increasing indefinitely. The benefit of the adaptive LFU (as well as LRU) is that zones stay in the cache for an additional period of time that is independent of their $IRRs$ TTL values.

Finding an optimal policy [9] requires the presence of an oracle that could foresee future queries, which makes it non-practical, but our evaluation shows these simple and easily implementable policies can be very effective.

Long TTL Instead of renewing the $IRRs$ after they expire, one can achieve the same results by simply increasing the TTL value of the $IRRs$. For example, assuming a current TTL value of one day, then increasing the TTL value to 3 days provides the same resilience as the LRU^2 renewal policy. Note the proposed increase of the TTL value is only for the $IRRs$, and not for end-host records. Thus this scheme does not effect CDN or load balancing schemes that rely on short TTL values for end-hosts. While current TTL values range from some minutes to some days, most zones have at TTL value less or equal to 12 hours. The main benefit in increasing the TTL values is that it does not require any changes at the caching servers and it can be enforced directly by the zone administrators. In addition, this modification reduces overall DNS traffic and improves DNS query response time since costly walks of the DNS tree are avoided.

But if the IRR changes at the AN's, the cached copy will be out of date. Increasing the TTL value can increase the time during which cached IRR differs from the actual IRR stored at the ANs. Fortunately, $IRRs$ change infrequently [12]. Furthermore, DNS works as long as one name-server in the cached IRR is still valid. The penalty paid for querying an obsolete name-server is a longer resolution time. If a server fails to respond, the next server in the IRR is queried. Once any response is received for a valid server, the IRR set is updated and inconsistency is resolved. In the worst case, all servers in the old IRR fail to respond and the parent zone must be queried to reset the IRR.

Combinations The above proposed modifications can work independently as well as in parallel with each other. Clearly, by combining two methods one can complement their abilities in improving the DNS resilience against DDoS attacks. Furthermore, combining them reduces their overhead, as it is shown in a later section. Apart from the above performance benefits, there is an additional and maybe more important operational benefit. The first two methods, allow any DNS client to enhance its resilience against the DDoS attacks that target the DNS, without requiring any modifications at remote sites, i.e. infrastruc-

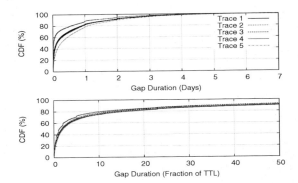

Figure 3. Time-Gap Duration (CDF)

ture changes. The last method allows any DNS zone to improve its resilience to DDoS attacks that target any of its ascendant zones, without requiring any modifications in other zones or modifications at the DNS clients. In essence, the above methods provide the power both to the DNS clients and the DNS operators to enhance the DNS resilience against DDoS attack by introducing only local changes.

5 Evaluation

In order to evaluate the effectiveness of these CS modifications we collected a number of DNS traces. The traces captured all the queries that were generated by stub-resolvers (SRs) and queries sent by the caching servers (CSs). The collected traces come from a number of different organizations (five US universities) and are grouped based on the caching servers (six servers). They were collected around the same period of time, and their durations ranged from one week (for a CS with very large query load) to one month. Table 1 gives some additional details for each trace, such as number of SRs (clients), the number of queries generated by SRs (requests in), the number of queries sent by the CSs to the name-servers (requests out), the number of distinct names appearing in the queries (names) and the number of distinct zones queried (zones).

First, we used these traces to measure the time duration between the expiration of a zone's IRR and the time the next query was sent to the zone. The length of this time-gap is indicative of how well the proposed schemes can work; if the time gap is long, the IRR may still expire from the cache even if it is refreshed, renewed or its TTL value is increased. Figure 3 gives the cumulative distribution function (CDF) for the time-gap duration. The upper graph gives the duration of the gaps in an absolute time (in days), while the lower graph gives the duration of the gaps as a fraction of the zone's IRR TTL value. For example a fraction of 10 it means that the gap is 10 longer compared to the TTL value. It is interesting to note that in absolute time almost all gaps are less than 5 days long, while the gaps duration varies largely when compared with the TTL values. The reason is that the $IRRs$ TTL values vary greatly, from some minutes to some days, which leads to a greater variability in the relative gap time.

Trace	Organization	Location	Duration	Clients	Requests In	Requests Out	Names	Zones
TRC1	University	USA	7 Days	339	8480402	1930250	556809	200531
TRC2	University	USA	7 Days	486	1400490	566507	193250	45802
TRC3	University	USA	7 Days	915	3148919	1038870	306053	87893
TRC4	University	USA	7 Days	455	15061455	1989997	551617	50531
TRC5	University	USA	7 Days	291	3135620	413648	87863	44502
TRC6	University	USA	1 Month	821	3461948	1153739	117540	55632

Table 1. DNS Traces Statistics

Aside from the above simple measures, the main use for the traces is as a query workload for our simulations. The simulator also took as an input the part of the DNS tree structure that was needed in order to resolve all the zones that were captured in the traces. This part of the DNS structure was acquired in an off-line stage, by actively probing the DNS. As such the simulated DNS structure represents the real DNS structure that appeared during the period of time that we collected the traces. Furthermore, the IRR values used in the simulator are the actual TTL values for the zones during that period of time. We used the simulator in order to evaluate both the effectiveness of the proposed techniques in enhancing the resilience of the DNS against DDoS attacks and in order to gauge the overhead introduced by them.

5.1 Resilience against DDoS Attacks

In order to measure the resilience of the current DNS as well as of the proposed schemes we considered the following experiment. For the first six days we assume that all zones work normally and at the beginning of the seventh day a DDoS attack completely blocks the queries sent to the root zone and the top level domains. The attack duration ranges from 3 to 24 hours. Then we measure the percentage of queries during the attack period that fail to resolve due to the attack. We measure both the failed queries sent by the SRs to the CS, as well as the failed queries sent from the CSs to the ANs. Note the following subtle difference between queries from the SRs and queries from the CSs. The failed queries from the SRs captures the actual impact of the DDoS attack on the end-users, while the queries by the CSs captures the impact of the DDoS attack on caching servers attempting to access the DNS.

We measure the number of failed queries for the following systems: A vanilla system that captures the behavior of the current DNS, a system that implements only TTL-refresh, a system that implements both TTL-refresh and TTL-renew for each of the four renewal policies, a system that combines both TTL-refresh and long-TTL and a system that implements all three (with LFU as a renewal policy).

5.1.1 Vanilla DNS

Figure 4 shows the percentage of queries that fail to resolve during the time that the DoS attack takes place when simulating the current DNS. The upper graph shows the percentage of failed queries that are sent by the SRs and the lower graph shows the percentage of failed queries that are sent by the CSs. The figure provides results for the first five traces and for attacks that last from 3 to 24 hours. Clearly, when the attack duration increases then the percentage of failed queries increases for the reason that more and more records start to expire. These records include both end-host records, such as A RRs, as well as IRRs. Moreover, we see that the percentage of failed queries from CSs is higher than the percentage of failed queries from SRs. The reason is that queries from SRs can be answered locally if they are cached at the CSs, while all queries from CSs have to query the DNS infrastructure.

Furthermore the figure shows that the percentage of failed queries varies a lot for the different traces when considering queries from SRs, while it is almost the same for queries generated by the Cs. We speculate that this is due to the fact that the number of parameters that affect the success rate of queries from SRs are much larger compared to queries from CSs. For example, the query distribution, the distribution of TTLs for end-host RRs, the number of SRs that use the same CS as well as the overlap of interest between different SRs affect the success rate of queries generated by the SRs. On the other hand, the success rate of queries generated by the CSs depends only on the distribution of queries and the distribution of TTLs for IRRs. For that reason, when we compare the effectiveness of our proposed schemes we compare it against each trace separately, rather that averaging across all traces.

5.1.2 TTL Refresh

Figure 5 shows the percentage of failed queries for the same scenario of DDoS attacks that we used before, when the TTL-refresh method is implemented. The figure includes two graphs that show the same type of results as in Figure 4. Note also that we use the same type of figure to presents the resilience to DDoS attacks for all the consequent schemes presented in this paper. Clearly both graphs shows that by implementing the refresh of IRRs TTLs the resiliency of the DNS can greatly improve. For most cases this modification leads to a percentage of failed queries that is at least 50% lower compared to the current system.

5.1.3 TTL Refresh and Renewal

Figures 6, 7, 8 and 9 show the DDoS attack resiliency achieved when implementing the LRU^c, LFU^c, $A - LRU^c$ and $A - LFU^c$ TTL-renewal policies, in combination with the TTL-refresh method. All graphs show results for the six hours attack and contrast them to the resiliency of the current DNS for the same attack. We consider three

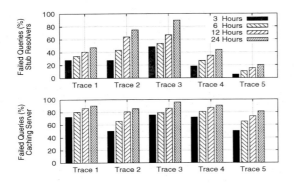

Figure 4. Vanilla DNS

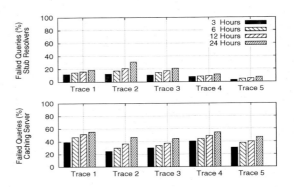

Figure 5. TTL Refresh

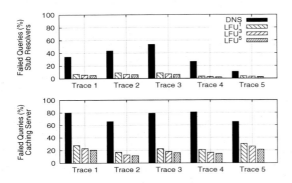

Figure 6. TTL Refresh + Renew (LRU)

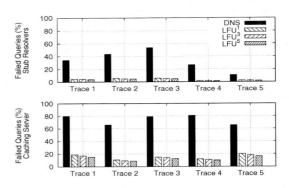

Figure 7. TTL Refresh + Renew (LFU)

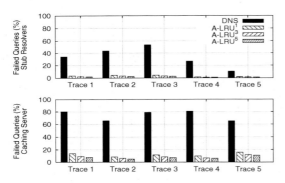

Figure 8. TTL Refresh + Renew (A-LRU)

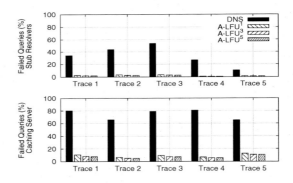

Figure 9. TTL Refresh + Renew (A-LFU)

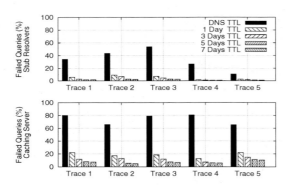

Figure 10. TTL Refresh + Long-TTL

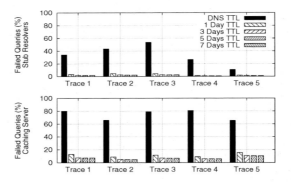

Figure 11. TTL Refresh + Renew + Long-TTL

different values for the credit c: 1, 3 and 5. The figures show that all the schemes perform almost equally with the performance becoming slightly better with the schemes in the following order: $LRU^c < LFU^c < A - LRU^c < A - LFU^c$. Intuitively the adaptive policies are better given that they are neutral to the different values of the IRRs TTLs. Furthermore, the LFU policies perform better than the LRU for the reason that they favor the most frequently used zones. In conclusion, the $A - LFU^c$ is shown to work the best: the failure rate for queries generated from the SRs is lower than 2.5%, while the failure rate for queries generated from the CS is lower than 10%. In summary, the combination of TTL *refresh* and *renew* improves the failure one order of magnitude compared to the current DNS.

5.1.4 TTL Refresh and Long-TTL

Figure 10 shows the percentage of failed queries when all zones change their IRRs TTL value to one, three, five and seven days, and the caching server implements the *TTL-refresh* method. We note that the long-TTL scheme achieves the same level of resilience as the most effective IRRs renewal policy ($A - LFU^5$). Furthermore, the figure shows that the a TTL value of five days is almost as good as a TTL value of seven days. The reason is that the time duration between the expiration of an IRR and the next time it is fetched from the zone is almost always less than five days (see Figure 3). Thus, a TTL value of seven days does not yield much more additional benefits in terms of resilience against DoS attacks.

5.1.5 TTL Refresh, Renewal and Long-TTL

Finally, we combine the cache renewal policies with the long-TTL scheme. The benefits of this hybrid approach is that it achieves the resiliency of the best renewal policy, with a much lower overhead (as show in the next section), as well as with smaller TTL values. Figure 11 shows the percentage of queries that fail to resolve when an LFU^3 renewal policy is applied to IRRs with TTL values of one, three, five and seven days. The graphs show that a TTL value of three days is good enough to achieve the maximum possible resilience to DoS attacks, given that longer TTL values do not yield any additional benefits.

5.2 Overhead

Next we consider the overhead due to the proposed modifications. We consider both the message overhead, i.e. the number of additional queries generated by a CS, and the memory overhead due to the additional zones cached at the CSs.

5.2.1 Message Overhead

Caching servers that implement one of the renewal policies can potentially increase the total DNS traffic, due to additional queries issued for re-fetching the IRRs. In contrast both the refresh and long-TTL modifications lead to a lower number of DNS messages. Indeed, Table 2 shows the increase in the number of generated DNS messages for each of the proposed schemes when compared to the cur-

Scheme	Trace 1	Trace 2	Trace 3	Trace 4	Trace 5
Refresh	-1.891	-0.968	-1.605	-1.044	-1.494
LRU^5	49.378	29.842	38.264	15.145	48.408
LFU^5	64.797	38.492	51.089	27.819	76.257
A-LRU^5	591.813	339.557	487.965	164.646	548.210
A-LFU^5	593.629	340.845	490.028	166.434	554.362
Long-TTL	-14.291	-7.271	-9.942	-6.131	-10.313
Combination	-9.916	-4.177	-6.226	-5.018	-5.436

Table 2. Message Overhead

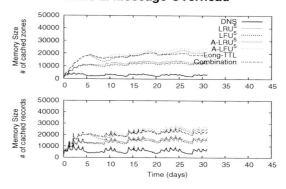

Figure 12. Memory Overhead

rent DNS. Negative values indicate a decrease in the number of generated messages.

The table shows that the adaptive schemes incur a significant overhead, which leads in increasing the DNS traffic by five times in the worst case. That is due to the fact that there is a large number of zones that have very small TTL values (in the order of minutes) which leads to a very large number of re-fetch requests. On the other hand, the non-adaptive renewal policies come with a much smaller cost. They increase the number of generated messages by at most 76%. Given that the DNS traffic is a negligible portion of the overall Internet traffic, we believe that this increase is not significant. More importantly, the table shows that the refresh and the long-TTL schemes, with TTL set to 7 days, lead to a decrease in the DNS related generated traffic. Furthermore, the combined scheme of long-TTL with a value of three days and the LFU^3 policy leads also to a reduction in the generated messages. This in a very promising results given that the hybrid scheme can achieve the resiliency of the most effective adaptive policy, without incurring the high message overhead.

5.2.2 Memory Overhead

The three proposed modifications increase the memory requirements of the CSs, given that they require the caching of IRRs for longer periods of time. On the other hand, as it is shown in Table 1 the total number of zones that appear in a period of one week is in the order of tens to hundreds of thousands. Thus, the additional memory requirements for storing all these IRRs are in the worst case in the order of tens of Mbytes. Figure 12 shows the number of zones and records cached for any given point of time for the one month long DNS trace (TRC6). It also compares these numbers with the number of zones and records cached when using the proposed schemes. Clearly, the additional memory overhead is not an issue for the current systems, given that the proposed caching schemes increase the number of cached objects by two to three times. Note that all other traces showed similar memory overhead.

6 Discussion

In this section we elaborate more on three point that relate to our proposed solutions and that deserve an additional attention.

Deployment Issues Notably there are two practical issues that may arise when deploying our proposed modifications. A first issue is their compatibility with the DNS security extensions. The DNSSEC introduces a number of new records for authentication. Some of them can be classified as new infrastructure resource records (see [18] for more details). Thus under a DNSSEC deployment we extend the refresh, renewal and long-TTL techniques to accommodate these new $IRRs$. A second practical issue is the ability of parent zones to reclaim delegations. Currently, this happens automatically every time that a caching server gets a referral from the parent zone. The parent zone can point to a new set of servers in the case that the ownership of the zone changes, or it can inform the caching server that the zone does not exist anymore. Given that the goal of our techniques is to reduce the number of these referrals, caching servers may still continue querying to the old zone, as far as the old zone still functions as before. In other words, a non-cooperative owner can potentially maintain the ownership for longer periods of time by not updating the name-servers with the new set of nameservers. Apart from resolving this issue with non-technical means (i.e. legally), we can solve it by forcing the caching servers to periodically query the parent zone (for example every 7 days). In addition, current caching servers do not accept arbitrary large TTL values (more that 7 days). In this way, any new delegation can appear at the caching servers within 7 days in the worst case, i.e. when the old owner is non-cooperative.

Maximum Damage Attack In the evaluation section we considered only one case of attack, that is an attack against the root zone and all the top level domains. This attack is not necessarily the one that can cause the maximum damage (thought, we believe that is close tho the maximum one). We define the maximum damage attack as the one that maximizes the total number of failed queries across all caching servers (or stub-resolvers), for a given budget of attacked zones. Clearly, identifying the maximum damage attack is not practically feasible because it requires the traffic patterns from all stub-resolvers. Furthermore, the result is highly time dependent, meaning that the targets are not the same for different attack starting times, or for different attack durations. Even when considering the traffic pattern from only one caching server, the identification of the maximum damage attack is not straightforward. One approach is to count the number of upcoming queries, and then identify the zone whose children have the maximum number of upcoming queries. The problem with this approach is that failures can happen at any of the descendant zones, and thus it is not enough to count failures only at the children. Furthermore, failures start at a time that depends on the zones IRR TTL value as well as the time that the failure started at the parent zone. These events of cascading failures are difficult to model with known optimization techniques, such as linear or dynamic programming.

Other Types of Attacks In this paper we consider only one class of DDoS attack against the DNS, that is attacks that aim at disabling the resolution of all the descendant zones of the targeted zone. Notably, there are two other broad classes of attacks. First, attacks that aim at disabling the name resolution of the names that belong to the target zone. The goal in this attack is to disable all the services that are provided by the servers "hosted" at the targeted zone. We believe that this type of attack is defensible by adding more name-servers. Name-servers provide a stateless service (they use UDP) and thus it is much harder to overload them compared to overloading the services itself. The reason is that the most popular services are statefull, e.g. they use TCP, and thus if a DDoS attack has the ability to disable the name-servers of a zone, then it has also the ability to disable a service directly (while the reverse is not always true). The second class of attacks that we don't consider are attacks against the caching servers. These attacks are possible, but their damage is locally limited. Furthermore, the simple approach of configuring the stub-resolvers with many caching servers or more sophisticated peer-to-peer approaches [19] can address this type of attacks.

7 Related Work

He have classified the related work in three broader areas. The first two are closer to our work while the third one relates more to the DNS performance issues.

DNS Hardening In recent years there has been a number of proposal for hardening the DNS against DDoS attacks. Yang *et al* [21] have proposed to augment the DNS structure with additional pointers, that are used in order to access children zones. The pointers are stored at sibling zones and are randomly distributed across zones so as an attacker cannot identify them. Handley *et al* [12] have proposed to globally replicate the infrastructure records at every caching server by utilizing a peer-to-peer system. Both approaches assume that DNS operators are cooperative, which may not be practical given the economically competitive environment between them. Parka *et al* [19] have proposed to add a lookup peer-to-peer service between the stub-resolvers and the caching servers. This service can be used in order to defend against DDoS attack that target caching servers. On the other hand, it cannot enhance the DNS resilience against DDoS attack that target nameservers. Recently, Ballani *et al* [8] have proposed to utilize expired records. Caching servers never discard records, even if they have expired, and thus they can utilize them in the case that they cannot retrieve them from the nameservers. Unfortunately, this proposal violates the semantics of record expiration as defined for DNS, which may hinder its adoption.

DNS Redesign Apart from hardening the current system there has been a number of proposals on redesigning the DNS. Cox *et al* [10] have proposed to replace the DNS infrastructure with a peer-to-peer infrastructure implemented on top of a distributed hash table. One benefit of this approach is that all servers become equally important and thus mounting a DDoS against the system has diminishing results. The same study showed that the performance of such a peer-to-peer system, measured by the query response time, was worse than the performance of the DNS, and concluded that such as system may not be a good candidate for replacing the DNS. In a followup study, Ramasubramanian *et al* [20] improved the performance of the lookup service by replicating the most popular records across the peer-to-peer system. Following an opposite direction, Deegan *et al* [11] proposed to replace the DNS with a centralized system. While their objective was to improve many aspects of the system, such as its resilience to configuration errors [17], they argued that a centralized system could also sustain a DDoS attack. All these approaches of redesigning the DNS require a complete overhaul of the DNS structure. The concept of zones becomes relevant only at the name-space level, given that zone operators lose the ability to administer name-servers. We believe that these type of radical changes can delay the adoption of those proposals.

DNS Performance Kangasharju *et al* [15] have proposed to replace the DNS with a globally replicated database, with the goal of improving the response time of DNS queries. Cohen *et al* [9] proposed the use of proactive caching in order to address the same performance problem. It is interesting to note that both schemes can potentially improve the resilience of the DNS against DDoS attacks. On the other hand they are not designed for that purpose and thus they are not optimized for such a task. For instance both schemes deal with end-host records, while, as we argue in this paper, utilizing only infrastructure resource records is more appropriate.

8 Conclusion

Mockapetris [16], the original DNS designer, pointed out that "*The administrator defines TTL values for each RR as part of the zone definition; a low TTL is desirable in that it minimizes periods of transient inconsistency, while a high TTL minimizes traffic and allows caching to mask periods of server unavailability due to network or host problems*".

Considering DDoS attacks are simply one of the means leading to DNS server unavailability, our work reported in this paper is a realization of the above suggestion. We demonstrated not only the effectiveness of using longer TTL value in enhancing DNS resilience, but we also proposed some simple record renewal policies to be used in conjunction with a long TTL value, with a combined results of improving the availability by up to one order of magnitude. Our results can be easily generalized to any hierarchical system [21] that utilizes caching and we debunk the belief that hierarchical systems cannot provide the same level of resilience against DDoS attacks as flat peer-to-peer systems.

References

[1] Events of 21-Oct-2002. http://d.root-servers.org/october21.txt, 2002.

[2] Nameserver DoS Attack October 2002. http://www.caida.org/projects/dns-analysis/, 2002.

[3] UltraDNS DOS Attack. http://www.theregister.co.uk/2002/12/14/, 2002.

[4] DNS FAQ. http://www.cs.cornell.edu/People/egs/beehive/faq.html, 2004.

[5] DoS Attack against Akamai. http://news.com.com/2100-1038_3-5236403.html/, 2004.

[6] Million-PC botnet threatens consumers. http://www.infomaticsonline.co.uk/ vnunet/news/2167474/million-pc-botnet-threatens, 2006.

[7] ICANN Factsheet for the February 6, 2007 Root Server Attack. http://www.icann.org/announcements/factsheet-dns-attack-08mar07.pdf, 2007.

[8] H. Ballani and P. Francis. A Simple Approach to DNS DoS Defense. In *Proceedings of HotNets*, 2006.

[9] E. Cohen and H. Kaplan. Proactive Caching of DNS Records: Addressing a Performance Bottleneck. In *Proceedings of SAINT*, pages 85–94, 2001.

[10] R. Cox, A. Muthitacharoen, and R. Morris. Serving DNS Using a Peer-to-Peer Lookup Service. In *Proceedings of IPTPS*, pages 155–165, 2002.

[11] T. Deegan, J. Crowcroft, and A. Warfield. The Main Name System: An exercise in centralized computing. In *Proceedings of CCR*, pages 5–13, 2005.

[12] M. Handley and A. Greenhalgh. The Case for Pushing DNS. In *Proceedings of HotNets*, 2005.

[13] T. Hardie. Clarifications to the DNS Specification. RFC 2181, 1997.

[14] T. Hardie. Distributing Authoritative Name Servers via Shared Unicast Addresses. RFC 3258, 2002.

[15] J. Kangasharju and K. Ross. A Replicated Architecture for the Domain Name System. In *Proceedings of INFOCOM*, pages 660–669, 2000.

[16] P. Mockapetris and K. J. Dunlap. Development of the Domain Name System. *SIGCOMM CCR*, pages 123–133, 1988.

[17] V. Pappas, Z. Xu, S. Lu, D. Massey, A. Terzis, and L. Zhang. Impact of Configuration Errors on DNS Robustness. In *Proceedings of SIGCOMM*, pages 319–330, 2004.

[18] V. Pappas, B. Zhang, E. Osterweil, D. Massey, and L. Zhang. Improving DNS Service Availability by Using Long TTL Values. Internet Draft, 2006.

[19] K. Parka, V. Pai, L. Peterson, and Z. Wang. CoDNS: Improving DNS Performance and Reliability via Cooperative Lookups. In *Proceedings of OSDI*, 2004.

[20] V. Ramasubramanian and E. Sirer. The Design and Implementation of a Next Generation Name Service for the Internet. In *Proceedings of SIGCOMM*, pages 331–342, 2004.

[21] H. Yang, H. Luo, Y. Yang, S. Lu, and L. Zhang. HOURS: Achieving DoS Resilience in an Open Service Hierarchy. In *Proceedings of DSN*, pages 83–93, 2004.

Automatic Cookie Usage Setting with CookiePicker

Chuan Yue   Mengjun Xie   Haining Wang
The College of William and Mary
{cyue,mjxie,hnw}@cs.wm.edu

Abstract

HTTP cookies have been widely used for maintaining session states, personalizing, authenticating, and tracking user behaviors. Despite their importance and usefulness, cookies have raised public concerns on Internet privacy because they can be exploited by Web sites to track and build user profiles. In addition, stolen cookies may also incur security problems. However, current web browsers lack secure and convenient mechanisms for cookie management. A cookie management scheme, which is easy-to-use and has minimal privacy risk, is in great demand; but designing such a scheme is a challenge. In this paper, we introduce CookiePicker, a system that can automatically validate the usefulness of cookies from a Web site and set the cookie usage permission on behalf of users. CookiePicker helps users achieve the maximum benefit brought by cookies, while minimizing the possible privacy and security risks. We implement CookiePicker as an extension to Firefox Web browser, and obtain promising results in the experiments.

1. Introduction

HTTP Cookies, also known as Web cookies or just cookies, are small parcels of text sent by a server to a web browser and then sent back unchanged by the browser if it accesses that server again [29]. Cookies are originally designed to carry information between servers and browsers so that a stateful session can be maintained within the stateless HTTP protocol. For example, online shopping Web sites use cookies to keep track of a user's shopping basket. Cookies make Web applications much easier to write, and thereby have gained a wide range of usage since debut in 1995. In addition to maintaining session states, cookies have also been widely used for personalizing, authenticating, and tracking user behaviors.

Despite their importance and usefulness, cookies have been of major concern for privacy. As pointed out by Kristol in [11], the ability to monitor browsing habits, and possibly to associate what you've looked at with who you are, is the heart of the privacy concern that cookies raise. For example, a lawsuit alleged that DoubleClick Inc. used cookies to collect Web users' personal information without their consent [3]. Moreover, vulnerabilities of Web applications or Web browsers can be exploited by attackers to steal cookies directly, leading to severe security and privacy problems [7, 21, 22].

As the general public has become more aware of cookie privacy issues, a few privacy options have been introduced into Web browsers to allow users to define detailed policies for cookie usage either before or during visiting a Web site. However, these privacy options are far from enough for users to fully utilize the convenience brought by cookies while limiting the possible privacy and security risks. What makes it even worse is that most users do not have a good understanding of cookies and often misuse or ignore these privacy options [5].

Using cookies can be both beneficial and harmful. The ideal cookie-usage decision for a user is to enable and store useful cookies, but disable and delete harmful cookies. It has long been a challenge to design effective cookie management schemes that can help users make the ideal cookie-usage decision. On one hand, determining whether some cookies are harmful is almost impossible, because very few Web sites inform users how they use cookies. Platform for Privacy Preferences Project (P3P) [30] enables Web sites to express their privacy practices but its usage is too low to be a feasible solution. On the other hand, determining whether some cookies are useful is possible, because a user can perceive inconvenience or Web page differences if some useful cookies are disabled. For instance, if some cookies are disabled, online shopping may be blocked or preference setting cannot take into effect. However, current Web browsers only provide a method, which asks questions and prompts options to users, for making decision on each incoming cookie. Such a method is costly [13] and very inconvenient to users.

In this paper, we present a system called *CookiePicker* to automatically make cookie usage decisions on behalf of a Web user. The distinct features of CookiePicker include (1) fully automatic decision making, (2) high accuracy on decision making, and (3) very low running overhead. Based

460

on the two complementary HTML page difference detection algorithms, CookiePicker identifies those cookies that cause perceivable changes on a Web page as useful, while simply classifying the rest as useless. Then, CookiePicker enables useful cookies but disables useless cookies. All the tasks are performed without user involvement or even notice. We implement CookiePicker as a Firefox Web browser extension, and validate its efficacy through experiments over various Web sites.

The remainder of this paper is structured as follows. Section 2 gives the background of cookies and the focus of CookiePicker. Section 3 describes the design of CookiePicker. Section 4 details the two HTML page difference detection algorithms, which are the core of CookiePicker. Section 5 presents the implementation of CookiePicker and its performance evaluation. Section 6 surveys related work, and finally, Section 7 concludes the paper.

2. Background

In general, there are two different ways to classify cookies. Based on the origin and destination, cookies can be classified into first-party cookies, which are created by the Web site we are currently visiting; and third-party cookies, which are created by a Web site other than the one we are currently visiting. Based on lifetime, cookies can also be classified into session cookies, which are stored in memory and deleted after the close of the Web browser; and persistent cookies, which are stored on a hard disk until they expire or are deleted by a user.

Third-party cookies bring almost no benefit to Web users and have long been recognized as a major threat to user privacy since 1996 [10]. Therefore, almost all the popular Web browsers, such as Microsoft Internet Explorer and Mozilla Firefox, provide users with the privacy options to disable third-party cookies. Although disabling third-party cookies is a very good start to address privacy concerns, it only limits the user profiling done by third parties [11], but cannot prevent the profiling of users from first-party cookies.

First-party cookies can be either session cookies or persistent cookies. First-party session cookies are widely used for maintaining session states, and pose relatively low privacy or security threats to users due to their short lifetime. Therefore, it is quite reasonable for a user to enable first-party session cookies.

First-party persistent cookies, however, are double-edged swords. We have conducted a large scale measurement study on the usage of cookies, with over five thousands Web sites involved. Our measurement results show that first-party persistent cookies are widely used and above 60% of them are set to expire after one year or even longer [24]. Some cookies perform useful roles such as personalization and authentication. Some cookies, however, provide no benefit but pose serious privacy and security risks to users. The major risks lie in two aspects. First, these first-party persistent cookies can be used to track the user activity over time by the original Web site; second, they can be stolen or manipulated by two kinds of long-standing attacks—cross-site scripting (XSS) attacks that exploit Web applications vulnerabilities [27, 21] and various attacks that exploit Web browser vulnerabilities [22], since those attacks can bypass the *same origin policy* [31] enforced by all modern Web browsers. For example, recently a cookie-related XSS vulnerability was even found in one of Google's hosting services [28].

Disabling third-party cookies (both session and persistent) and enabling first-party session cookies have been supported by most Web browsers. The hardest problem in cookie management is how to handle first-party persistent cookies. Currently Web browsers only have limited functions such as manual deletion or blocking, which are very cumbersome and impractical to use. Therefore, the focus of this paper is on first-party persistent cookies and how to automatically manage the usage of first-party persistent cookies on behalf of a user. Instead of addressing XSS or Web browser vulnerabilities, CookiePicker reduces cookie privacy and security risks by removing useless first-party cookies from a user's hard disk. Here we assume that the hosting Web site is legitimate, since it is worthless to protect the cookies of a malicious site.

3. CookiePicker Design

The design goal of CookiePicker is to effectively identify the useful cookies of a Web site, and then disable the return of those useless cookies back to the Web site in the subsequent requests and finally remove them. A Web page is automatically retrieved twice by enabling and disabling some cookies. If there are obvious differences between the two retrieved results, we classify the cookies as useful; otherwise, we classify them as useless. CookiePicker enhances the cookie management for a Web site by two processes: forward cookie usefulness marking and backward error recovery. We define these two processes and detail the design of CookiePicker in the following.

Definition 1. *FORward Cookie Usefulness Marking (FORCUM) is a training process, in which CookiePicker determines cookie usefulness and marks certain cookies as useful for a Web site.*

Definition 2. *backward error recovery is a tuning process, in which wrong decisions made by CookiePicker in the FORCUM process may be adjusted automatically or manually for a Web site.*

3.1 Regular and Hidden Requests

A typical Web page consists of a container page that is an HTML text file, and a set of associated objects such as stylesheets, embedded images, scripts, and so on. When a user browses a Web page, the HTTP request for the container page is first sent to the Web server. Then, after receiving the corresponding HTTP response for the container page, the Web browser will analyze the container page and issue a series of HTTP requests to the Web server for downloading the objects associated with the container page. The HTTP requests and responses associated with a single Web page view are depicted by the solid lines (1) and (2) in Figure 1, respectively. Web page contents coming with the HTTP responses will be passed into the Web browser layout engine, which will parse the container page and built it into a DOM (W3C Document Object Model) tree.

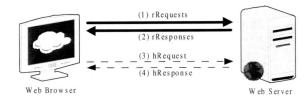

Figure 1: HTTP requests/responses in a single Web page view.

In order to identify the cookie usefulness for a Web page, CookiePicker compares two versions of the same Web page: the first version is retrieved with cookies enabled and the second version is retrieved with cookies disabled. The first version is readily available to CookiePicker in the user's regular Web browsing window. CookiePicker only needs to retrieve the second version of the container page. Similar to Doppelganger [16], CookiePicker utilizes the ever increasing client side spare bandwidth and computing power to run the second version. However, unlike Doppelganger, CookiePicker neither maintains a fork window nor mirrors the whole user session. CookiePicker only retrieves the second version of the container page by sending a single hidden HTTP request. As shown in Figure 1, line (3) is the extra hidden HTTP request sent by CookiePicker for the second version of the container page, and line (4) represents the corresponding HTTP response. In the rest of the paper, we simply refer the requests and responses, represented by the solid lines (1) and (2) of Figure 1, as regular requests and responses; and refer the extra request and response, represented by the dashed lines (3) and (4) of Figure 1, as the hidden request and response.

3.2 Forward Cookie Usefulness Marking

The FORCUM process consists of five steps: regular request recording, hidden request sending, DOM tree extraction, cookie usefulness identification, and cookie record marking.

When visiting a Web page, a user issues regular requests and then receives regular responses. At the first step, CookiePicker identifies the regular request for the container page and saves a copy of its URI and header information. CookiePicker needs to filter out the temporary redirection or replacement pages and locate the real initial container document page.

At the second step, CookiePicker takes advantage of user's think time [12] to retrieve the second copy of the container page, without causing any delay to the user's regular browsing. Specifically, right after all the regular responses are received and the Web page is rendered on the screen for display, CookiePicker issues the single hidden request for the second copy of the container page. In the hidden request, CookiePicker uses the same URI as the saved in the first step. It only modifies the "Cookie" field of the request header by removing a group of cookies, whose usefulness will be tested. The hidden request can be transmitted in an asynchronous mode so that it will not block any regular browsing functions. Then, upon the arrival of the hidden response, an event handler will be triggered to process it. Note that the hidden request is only used to retrieve the container page, and the received hidden response will not trigger any further requests for downloading the associated objects. Retrieving the container page only induces very low overhead to CookiePicker.

At the third step, CookiePicker extracts the two DOM trees from the two versions of the container page: one for the regular response and the other for the hidden response. We call these two DOM trees the regular DOM tree and the hidden DOM tree, respectively. The regular DOM tree has already been parsed by Web browser layout engine and is ready for use by CookiePicker. The hidden DOM tree, however, needs to be built by CookiePicker; and CookiePicker should build the hidden DOM tree using the same HTML parser of the Web browser. This is because in practice HTML pages are often malformed. Using the same HTML parser guarantees that the malformed HTML pages are treated as same as before, while the DOM tree is being constructed.

At the fourth step, CookiePicker identifies cookie usefulness by comparing the differences between the two versions of the container page, whose information are well represented in the two DOM trees. To make a right cookie usefulness decision, CookiePicker uses two complementary algorithms by considering both the internal structural difference and the external visual content difference between the two versions. Only when obvious structural difference and visual content difference are detected, will CookiePicker decide that the corresponding cookies that are disabled from the hidden request are useful. The two algorithms are the core of the CookiePicker and will be detailed in Section 4.

At the fifth step, CookiePicker will mark the cookies that are classified as useful in the Web browser's cookie jar. An extra field "useful" is introduced to each cookie record. At the beginning of the FORCUM process, a *false* value is assigned to the "useful" field of each cookie. In addition, any newly-emerged cookies set by a Web site are also assigned *false* values to their "useful" fields. During the FORCUM process, the value of the field "useful" can only be changed in one direction, that is, from "false" to "true" if some cookies are classified as useful. Later on, when the values of the "useful" field for the existing cookies are relatively stable for the Web site, those cookies that still have "false" values in their 'useful' fields will be treated as useless and will no longer be transmitted to the corresponding Web site. Then, the FORCUM process can be turned off for a while; and it will be turned on automatically if CookiePicker finds new cookies appeared in the HTTP responses or manually by a user if she wants to continue the training process.

3.3. Backward Error Recovery

In general, CookiePicker could make two kinds of errors in the FORCUM process. The first kind of error is that useless cookies are mis-classified as useful, thereby being continuously sent out to a Web site. The second kind of error is that useful cookies are never identified by CookiePicker during the training process, thereby being blocked from a Web site.

The first kind of error is solely due to the inaccuracy of CookiePicker in usefulness identification. Such an error will not cause any immediate trouble to a user, but leave useless cookies increasing privacy risks. CookiePicker is required to make such errors as few as possible so that a user's privacy risk is lowered. CookiePicker meets this requirement via accurate decision algorithms.

The second kind of error is caused by either a wrong usefulness decision or the fact that some cookies are only useful to certain Web pages but have not yet been visited during the FORCUM process. This kind of error will cause inconvenience to a user and must be fixed by marking the corresponding cookies as useful. CookiePicker attempts to achieve a very low rate on this kind of error, so that it does not cause any inconvenience to users. This requirement is achieved by two means. One one hand, for those visited pages, the decision algorithms of CookiePicker attempt to make sure that each useful persistent cookie can be identified and marked as useful. On the one hand, since CookiePicker is designed with very low running cost, a longer running period (or periodically running) of the FORCUM process is affordable, thus training accuracy can be further improved.

CookiePicker provides a simple recovery button for backward error recovery in the tuning process. In case a user notices some malfunctions or some strange behaviors on a Web page, the cookies disabled by CookiePicker in this particular Web page view can be re-marked as useful via a simple button click. Note that once the cookie set of a Web site becomes stable after the training and tuning processes, those disabled useless cookies will be removed from the Web browser's cookie jar.

4. HTML Page Difference Detection

In this section, we present two complementary mechanisms for online detecting the HTML Web page differences between the enabled and disabled cookie usages. In the first mechanism, we propose a restricted version of Simple Tree Matching algorithm [23] to detect the HTML document structure difference. In the second mechanism, we propose a context-aware visual content extraction algorithm to detect the HTML page visual content difference. We call these two mechanisms as Restricted Simple Tree Matching (RSTM) and Context-aware Visual Content Extraction (CVCE), respectively. Intuitively, RSTM focuses on detecting the internal HTML document structure difference, while CVCE focuses on detecting the external visual content difference perceived by a user. In the following, we present these two mechanisms and explain how they are complementarily used.

4.1. Restricted Simple Tree Matching

As mentioned in Section 3, in a user's Web browser, the content of an HTML Web page is naturally parsed into a DOM tree before it is rendered on the screen for display. Therefore, we resort to the classical measure of *tree edit distance* introduced by Tai [17] to quantify the difference between two HTML Web pages. Since the DOM tree parsed from the HTML Web page is rooted (document node is the only root), labeled (each node has node name), and ordered (the left-to-right order of sibling nodes is significant), we only consider *rooted labeled ordered tree*. In the following, we will first review the tree edit distance problem; then we will explain why we choose *top-down distance* and detail the RSTM algorithm; and finally we will use Jaccard similarity coefficient to define the similarity metric of a normalized DOM tree.

4.1.1. Tree Edit Distance

For two rooted labeled ordered trees T and T', let $|T|$ and $|T'|$ denote the numbers of nodes in trees T and T', and let $T[i]$ and $T'[j]$ denote the ith and jth preorder traversal nodes in trees T and T', respectively. Tree edit distance is defined as the minimum cost sequence of edit operations to transform T into T' [17]. The three edit operations used in transformation include: inserting a node into a tree, deleting a node from a tree, and changing one node of a tree into another node. Disregarding the order of the edit operations being applied, the transformation from T to T' can be described by a mapping as defined in [17].

Since the solution of the generic tree edit distance problem has high time complexity, researchers have investigated the constrained versions of the problem. By imposing conditions on the three edit operations mentioned above, a few different tree distance measures have been proposed and studied in the literature: *alignment distance* [8], *isolated subtree distance* [18], *top-down distance* [15, 23], and *bottom-up distance* [20]. The description and comparison of these algorithms are beyond the scope of this paper, see [2] and [20] for details.

4.1.2. Top-Down Distance

Because RSTM belongs to the top-down distance approach, we review the definition of top-down distance and explain why we choose this measure for our study.

Definition 3. *A mapping (M, T, T') from T to T', is top-down if it satisfies the condition that for all i, j such that $T[i]$ and $T'[j]$ are not the roots, respectively, of T and T':*

if pair $(i, j) \in M$ then $(parent(i), parent(j)) \in M$.

The top-down distance problem was introduced by Selkow [15]. In [23], Yang presented a $O(|T| \cdot |T'|)$ time-complexity top-down dynamic programming algorithm, which is named as the Simple Tree Matching (STM) algorithm.

As we mentioned earlier, our goal is to effectively detect noticeable HTML Web page difference between the enabled and disabled cookie usages. The measure of top-down distance captures the key structure difference between DOM trees in an accurate and efficient manner, and fits well to our requirement. In fact, top-down distance has been successfully used in a few Web-related projects. For example, Zhai and Liu [25] used it for extracting structured data from Web pages; and Reis *et al.* [14] applied it for automatic Web news extraction. In contrast, bottom-up distance [20], although can be more efficient in time complexity ($O(|T| + |T'|)$), falls short of being an accurate metric [19] and may produce a far from optimal result [1] for HTML DOM tree comparison, in which most of the differences come from the leaf nodes.

4.1.3. Restricted Simple Tree Matching

Based on the original STM algorithm [23], Figure 2 illustrates, RSTM, our restricted version of STM algorithm.

Algorithm: RSTM($A, B, level$)
1.   **if** the roots of the two trees A and B contain different symbols **then**
2.   **return**(0);
3.   **endif**
4. $currentLevel = level + 1$;
5.   **if** A and B are leaf or non-visible nodes **or**
6. $currentLevel > maxLevel$ **then**
7.   **return**(0);
8.   **endif**
9. $m =$ the number of first-level subtrees of A;
10. $n =$ the number of first-level subtrees of B;
11. Initialization, $M[i, 0] = 0$ for $i = 0, ..., m$;
12. $M[0, j] = 0$ for $j = 0, ..., n$;
13. **for** $i = 1$ **to** m **do**
14.   **for** $j = 1$ **to** n **do**
15. $M[i, j] = max(M[i, j - 1], M[i - 1, j],$
                      $M[i - 1, j - 1] + W[i, j])$;
16.   where $W[i, j] = $ RSTM($A_i, B_j, currentLevel$)
17.   where A_i and B_j are the ith and jth
                  first-level subtrees of A and B, respectively
18.   **endfor**
19. **endfor**
20. **return** ($M[m, n] + 1$);

Figure 2: The Restricted Simple Tree Matching Algorithm.

Other than lines 4 to 8 and one new parameter *level*, our RSTM algorithm is similar to the original STM algorithm. Like the original STM algorithm, we first compare the roots of two trees A and B. If their roots contain different symbols, then A and B do not match at all. If their roots contain same symbols, we use dynamic programming to recursively compute the number of pairs in a maximum matching between trees A and B. Figure 3 gives two trees, in which each node is represented as a circle with a single letter inside. According to the preorder traversal, the fourteen nodes in tree A are named from $N1$ to $N14$, and the eight nodes in tree B are named from $N15$ to $N22$. The final computed return result by using STM algorithm or RSTM algorithm is the number of matching pairs for a maximum matching. For example, STM algorithm will return "7" for the two trees in Figure 3, and the seven matching pairs are $\{N1, N15\}, \{N2, N16\}, \{N6, N18\},$ $\{N7, N19\}, \{N5, N17\}, \{N11, N20\},$ and $\{N12, N22\}$.

There are two reasons why a new parameter *level* is introduced in RSTM. First, some Web pages are very dynamic. From the same Web site, even if a Web page is retrieved twice in a short time, there may exist some differences between the retrieved contents. For example, if we refresh Yahoo home page twice in a short time, we can often see some different advertisements. For CookiePicker, such dynamics on a Web page are just noises and should be differentiated from the Web page changes caused by the enabled and disabled cookie usages. This kind of noises, although very annoying, has a distinct characteristic that they often appear at the lower level of the DOM trees. In contrast, the Web page changes caused by enabling/disabling cook-

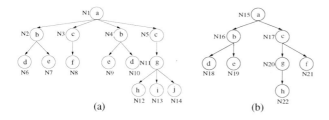

Figure 3: (a) Tree A, (b) Tree B.

ies are often so obvious that the structural dissimilarities are clearly reflected at the upper level of the DOM trees. By using the new parameter *level*, the RSTM algorithm restricts the top-down comparison between the two trees to a certain maximum level. Therefore, equipped with the parameter *level*, RSTM not only captures the key structure dissimilarity between DOM trees, but also reduces leaf-level noises.

The second reason is that the $O(|T| \cdot |T'|)$ time complexity of STM is still too expensive to use online. Even with C++ implementation, STM will spend more than one second in difference detection for some large Web pages. However, as shown in Section 5, the cost of the RSTM algorithm is low enough for online detection.

The newly-added conditions at line 5 of the RSTM algorithm restrict that the mapping counts only if the compared nodes are not leaves and have visual effects. More specifically, all the comment nodes are excluded in that they have no visual effect on the displayed Web page. Script nodes are also ignored because normally they do not contain any visual elements either. Text content nodes, although very important, are also excluded due to the fact that they are leaf nodes (i.e., having no more structural information). Instead, text content will be analyzed in our Context-aware Visual Content Extraction (CVCE) mechanism.

4.1.4. Normalized Top-Down Distance Metric

Since the return result of RSTM (or STM) is the number of matching pairs for a maximum matching, based on the Jaccard similarity coefficient that is given in Formula 1, we define the normalized DOM tree similarity metric in Formula 2.

$$J(A, B) = \frac{|A \cap B|}{|A \cup B|} \tag{1}$$

$$NTreeSim(A, B, l) = \frac{RSTM(A, B, l)}{N(A, l) + N(B, l) - RSTM(A, B, l)} \tag{2}$$

The Jaccard similarity coefficient $J(A, B)$ is defined as the ratio between the size of the *intersection* and the size of the *union* of two sets. In the definition of our normalized DOM tree similarity metric $NTreeSim(A, B, l)$, $RSTM(A, B, l)$ is the returned number of matched pairs

---

```
Algorithm: contentExtract(T, context)
1.    Initialization, S = ∅; node = T.root;
2.    if node is a non-noise text node then
3.        cText = context+SEPARATOR+node.value;
4.        S = S ∪ {cText};
5.    elseif node is an element node then
6.        currentContext = context+":"+node.name;
7.        n = the number of first-level subtrees of T;
8.        for j = 1 to n do
9.            S = S∪contentExtract(Tᵢ, currentContext);
                where Tᵢ is the ith first-level subtrees of T;
10.       endfor
11.   endif
12.   return (S);
```

Figure 4: The Text Content Extraction Algorithm.

by calling RSTM on trees A and B for upper l levels. $N(A, l)$ and $N(B, l)$ are the numbers of non-leaf visible nodes at upper l levels of trees A and B, respectively. Actually $N(A, l) = RSTM(A, A, l)$ and $N(B, l) = RSTM(B, B, l)$, but $N(A, l)$ and $N(B, l)$ can be computed in $O(n)$ time by simply preorder traversing the upper l levels of trees A and B, respectively.

4.2. Context-aware Visual Content Extraction

The visual contents on a Web page can be generally classified into two groups: text contents and image contents. Text contents are often displayed as headings, paragraphs, lists, table items, links, and so on. Image contents are often embedded in a Web page in the form of icons, buttons, backgrounds, flashes, video clips, and so on. Our second mechanism mainly uses text contents, instead of image contents, to detect the visual content difference perceived by users. Two reasons motivate us to use text contents rather than image contents. First, text contents provide the most important information on Web pages, while image contents often serve as supplements to text contents. In practice, users can block the loading of various images and browse most of the Web page in text mode only. Second, the similarity between images cannot be trivially compared, while text contents can be extracted and compared easily as shown below.

On a Web page, each text content exists in a special context. Corresponding to the DOM tree, the text content is a leaf node and its context is the path from the root to this leaf node. For two Web pages, by extracting and comparing their context-aware text contents that are essential to users, we can effectively detect the noticeable HTML Web page difference between the enabled and disabled cookie usages. Figure 4 depicts the recursive algorithm to extract the text content.

The contentExtract algorithm preorder traverses the

whole DOM tree in time $O(n)$. During the preorder traversal, each non-noise text node is associated with its context, resulting in a context-content string; and then the context-content string is added into set S. The final return result is set S, which includes all the context-content strings. Note that in lines 2 to 4, only those non-noise text nodes are qualified for the addition to set S. Similar to [4], scripts, styles, obvious advertisement text, date and time string, and option text in dropdown list (such as country list or language list) are regarded as noises. Text nodes that contain no alphanumeric characters are also treated as noises. All these checkings guarantee that we can extract a relatively concise context-content string set from the DOM tree.

Assume S_1 and S_2 are two context-content string sets extracted from two DOM trees A and B, respectively. To compare the difference between S_1 and S_2, again based on the Jaccard similarity coefficient, we define the normalized context-content string set similarity metric in Formula 3:

$$NTextSim(S_1, S_2) = \frac{|S_1 \cap S_2| + s}{|S_1 \cup S_2|} \quad (3)$$

Formula 3 is a variation [9] of the original Jaccard similarity coefficient. The extra added s on the numerator stands for the number of those context-content strings that are not exactly same, while having the same context prefix, in S_1 and S_2. Intuitively, between two sets S_1 and S_2, Formula 3 disregards the difference caused by text content replacement occurred in the same context, it only considers the difference caused by text content appeared in each set's unique context. This minor modification is especially helpful in reducing the noises caused by advertisement text content and other dynamically changing text contents.

4.3. Making Decision

As discussed above, to accurately identify useful cookies, CookiePicker has to differentiate the HTML Web page differences caused by Web page dynamics from those caused by disabling cookies. Assume that tree A is parsed from a Web page retrieved with cookies enabled and tree B is parsed from the same Web page with cookies disabled. CookiePicker examines these two trees by using both algorithms presented above. If the return results of both *NTreeSim* and *NTextSim* are less than the two tunable thresholds, *Thresh1* and *Thresh2*, respectively, CookiePicker will make a decision that the difference is due to cookie usage. Figure 5 depicts the final decision algorithm.

5. System Evaluation

In this section, we first briefly describe the implementation of CookiePicker, then we validate its efficacy through

```
Algorithm: decision(A, B, l)
1.   if NTreeSim(A, B, l) ≤ Thresh1 and
2.       NTextSim(S1, S2) ≤ Thresh2 then
3.       return the difference is caused by cookies;
4.   else
5.       return the difference is caused by noises;
6.   endif
```

Figure 5: CookiePicker Decision Algorithm.

two sets of live experiments, and finally we discuss the potential evasion against CookiePicker.

5.1. Implementation

We implemented CookiePicker as a Firefox extension. Being one of the most popular Web browsers, Firefox is very extensible and allows programmers to add new features or modify existing features. Our CookiePicker extension is implemented in about 200 lines of XML user interface definition code, 1,600 lines of Javascript code, and 600 lines of C++ code. Javascript code is used for HTTP request/response monitoring and processing, as well as cookies record management. The HTML page difference detection algorithms are implemented in C++, because Javascript version runs very slow. C++ code is compiled into a shared library in the form of an XPCOM (Cross-Platform Component Object Mode) component, which is accessible to Javascript code.

5.2. Evaluation

We installed CookiePicker on a Firefox version 1.5.0.8 Web browser and designed two sets of experiments to validate the effectiveness of CookiePicker in identifying the useful first-party persistent cookies. The first set of experiments is to measure the overall effectiveness of CookiePicker and its running time in a generic environment; while the second set of experiments focuses on the Web sites whose persistent cookies are useful only, and examines the identification accuracy of CookiePicker upon useful persistent cookies. For all the experiments, the regular browsing window enables the use of persistent cookies, while the hidden request disables the use of persistent cookies by filtering them out from HTTP request header. The two thresholds used in CookiePicker Decision algorithm are all set to 0.85, i.e., *Thresh1*=*Thresh2*=0.85. The parameter l for NTreeSim algorithm is set to 5, i.e, the top five level of DOM tree starting from the *body* HTML node will be compared by NTreeSim algorithm.

5.2.1. First Set of Experiments

From each of the 15 categories we measured [24] in directory.google.com, we randomly choose two Web sites that use persistent cookies. Thus, in total there are 30 Web sites in the first set of experiments. As listed in the first column of Table 1, these 30 Web sites are represented as S1 to S30 for privacy concerns.

Inside each Web site, we first visit over 25 Web pages to stabilize its persistent cookies and the "useful" values of the persistence cookies, i.e, no more persistent cookies of the Web site are marked as "useful" by CookiePicker afterwards. Then, we count the number of persistent cookies set by the Web site and the number of persistent cookies marked as useful by CookiePicker. These two numbers are shown in the second and third columns of Table 1, respectively. Among the total 30 Web sites, the persistent cookies from five Web sites (S1,S6,S10,S16,S27) are marked as "useful" by CookiePicker, and the persistent cookies from the rest of 30 Web sites are identified as "useless". In other words, CookiePicker indicates that we can disable the persistent cookies in about 83.3% (25 out of 30) of testing Web sites. To further validate the testing result above, we check the uselessness of the persistent cookies for those 25 Web sites through careful manual verification. We find that blocking the persistent cookies of those 25 Web sites does not cause any problem to a user. Therefore, none of the classified "useless" persistent cookies is useful, and no backward error recovery is needed.

For those five Web sites that have some persistent cookies marked as "useful", we verify the real usefulness of these cookies by blocking the use of them and then comparing the disabled version with a regular browsing window over 25 Web pages in each Web site. The result is shown in the fourth column of Table 1. We observe that three cookies from two Web sites (S6,S16) are indeed useful. However, for the other three Web sites (S1,S10,S27), their persistent cookies are useless but are wrongly marked as "useful" by CookiePicker. This is mainly due to the conservative threshold setting. Currently the values of both thresholds are set to 0.85, i.e., *Thresh1=Thresh2=0.85*. The rationale behind the conservative threshold setting is that we prefer to have all useful persistent cookies be correctly identified, even at the cost of some useless cookies being mis-classified as "useful". Thus, the number of backward error recovery is minimized.

In Table 1, the fifth and sixth columns show the average running time of the detection algorithms and the entire duration of CookiePicker, respectively. It is clear that the running time of the page difference detection is very short with an average of 14.6 ms over the 30 Web sites. The average identification duration is 2,683.3 ms, which is reasonable short considering the fact that the average think time of a user is more than 10 seconds [12]. Note that Web sites S4,

Web Site	Persistent	Marked Useful	Real Useful	Detection Time(ms)	CookiePicker Duration (ms)
S1	2	2	0	8.3	1,821.6
S2	4	0	0	9.3	5,020.2
S3	5	0	0	14.8	1,427.5
S4	4	0	0	36.1	9,066.2
S5	4	0	0	5.4	698.9
S6	2	2	2	5.7	1,437.5
S7	1	0	0	17.0	3,373.2
S8	3	0	0	7.4	2,624.4
S9	1	0	0	13.2	1,415.4
S10	1	1	0	5.7	1,141.2
S11	2	0	0	2.7	941.3
S12	4	0	0	21.7	2,309.9
S13	1	0	0	8.0	614.9
S14	9	0	0	11.9	1,122.4
S15	2	0	0	8.5	948.0
S16	25	1	1	5.8	455.9
S17	4	0	0	7.5	11,426.3
S18	1	0	0	23.1	4,056.9
S19	3	0	0	18.0	3,860.5
S20	6	0	0	8.9	3,841.6
S21	3	0	0	14.4	936.1
S22	1	0	0	13.1	993.3
S23	4	0	0	28.8	2,430.1
S24	1	0	0	23.6	2,381.1
S25	3	0	0	30.7	550.1
S26	1	0	0	5.03	611.6
S27	1	1	0	8.7	597.5
S28	1	0	0	10.7	10,104.1
S29	2	0	0	7.7	1,387.1
S30	2	0	0	57.6	2,905.6
Total	103	7	3	-	-
Average	-	-	-	14.6	2,683.3

Table 1: Online testing results for thirty Web sites (S1 to S30).

S17, and S28 have abnormally high identification duration at about 10 seconds, which is mainly caused by the very slow responses from those three Web sites.

5.2.2. Second Set of Experiments

Since only two Web sites in the first set of experiments have useful persistent cookies, we attempt to further examine if CookiePicker can correctly identify each useful persistent cookie in the second set of experiments. Because the list of Web sites whose persistent cookies are really useful to users does not exist, we have to locate such Web sites manually. Again, we randomly choose 200 Web sites that use persistent cookies from the 15 categories we measured [24] in directory.google.com. Note that the 30 Web sites chosen in the first set of experiments are not included in these 200 Web sites. We manually scrutinize these 200 Web sites, and finally find six Web sites whose persistent cookies are really useful to users, i.e., without cookies, users would encounter some problems. Because the manual scrutiny is tedious, we cannot afford more effort to locate more such Web sites. The six Web sites are listed in the first column of Table 2 and represented as P1 to P6 for privacy concerns.

In Table 2, the second column shows the number of the cookies marked as "useful" by CookiePicker and the third column shows the number of the real useful cookies via manual verification. We observe that for the six Web sites, all of their useful persistent cookies are marked as

Web Site	Marked Useful	Real Useful	NTreeSim $(A, B, 5)$	NTextSim (S_1, S_2)	Usage
P1	1	1	0.311	0.609	Preference
P2	1	1	0.459	0.765	Performance
P3	1	1	0.667	0.623	Sign Up
P4	1	1	0.250	0.158	Preference
P5	9	1	0.226	0.253	Sign Up
P6	5	2	0.593	0.719	Preference
Average	-	-	0.418	0.521	-

Table 2: Online testing results for 6 Web sites (P1 to P6) that have useful persistent cookies.

"useful" by CookiePicker. This result indicates that CookiePicker seldom misses the identification of a real useful cookie. On the other hand, for Web sites P5 and P6, some useless persistent cookies are also marked as "useful" because they are sent out in the same regular request with the real useful cookies. The fourth and fifth columns show the similarity score computed by NTreeSim$(A, B, 5)$ and NTextSim(S_1, S_2), respectively, on the Web pages that persistent cookies are useful. These similarity scores are far below 0.85, which is the current value used for the two thresholds *Thresh1* and *Thresh2* in Figure 5. The usage of these useful persistent cookies on each Web site is given at the sixth column. Web sites P1, P4, and P6 use persistent cookies for user's preference setting. Web sites P3 and P5 use persistent cookies to properly create and sign up a new user. Web site P2 uses persistent cookie in a very unique way. Each user's persistent cookie corresponds to a specific sub-directory on the Web server, and the sub-directory stores the user's recent query results. Thus, if the user visits the Web site again with the persistent cookie, recent query results can be reused to improve query performance.

In summary, the above two sets of experiments show that by conservatively setting *Thresh1* and *Thresh2* to 0.85, CookiePicker can safely disable and remove persistent cookies from the majority of Web sites (25 out of the 30 Web sites that we intensively tested). Meanwhile, all the useful persistent cookies can be correctly identified by CookiePicker and no backward error recovery is needed for all the 8 Web sites (S6,S16,P1,P2,P3,P4,P5,P6) that have useful persistent cookies. About 10% Web sites (3 out of 30), in which persistent cookies are useless, are wrongly identified by CookiePicker as "useful". However, the number may be further reduced if we fine-tune the two thresholds and the implementation of the two algorithms, which we leave as our future work.

5.3. Evasion against CookiePicker

In CookiePicker, the identification of useful cookies are based on perceivable changes on a Web page. Once the identification metric becomes known, CookiePicker may be circumvented. The evasion of CookiePicker will most likely come from two sources: Web site operators who want to track user activities, and attackers who want to steal cookies.

As stated in Section 2, we assume that the hosting Web site is legitimate, since it is pointless to discuss cookie security and privacy issues within a malicious Web site. For legitimate Web sites, if some operators strongly insist to use first-party persistent cookies for tracking long-term user behaviors, they can evade CookiePicker by detecting the hidden HTTP request and manipulating the hidden HTTP response. However, we argue that most Web site operators will not pay the effort and time to do so, either because of the lack of interest to track long-term user behaviors, or because of inaccuracy in cookie-based user behavior tracking, which has long been recognized [26].

For third-party attackers, unless they compromise a legitimate Web site, it is very difficult for them to manipulate the Web pages sending back to a user's browser and circumvent CookiePicker.

6. Related Work

RFC 2109 [10] is the first document that raises the general public's awareness of cookie privacy problems. Later on, the *same origin policy* was introduced in Netscape Navigator 2.0 to prevent cookies and Javascripts of different sites from interfering with each other. The successful fulfillment of the *same origin policy* on cookies and Javascripts further encourages the enforcement of this policy on browser cache and visited links [6].

Modern Web browsers have provided users with refined cookie privacy options. A user can define detailed cookie policies for Web sites either before or during visiting these sites. Commercial cookie management softwares such as Cookie Crusher [32] and CookiePal [33] mainly rely on pop-ups to notify incoming cookies. However, the studies in [5] show that such cookie privacy options and cookie management policies fail to be used in practice, due mainly to the following two reasons: (1) these options are very confusing and cumbersome, and (2) most users have no true understanding of the advantages and disadvantages of using cookies.

Recently, the most noticeable research work in cookie management is Doppelganger [16]. Doppelganger is a system for creating and enforcing fine-grained privacy-preserving cookie policies. Doppelganger leverages client-side parallelism and uses a twin window to mirror a user's Web session. If any difference is detected, Doppelganger will ask the user to compare the main window and the fork window, and then, make a cookie policy decision. Although taking a big step towards automatic cookie management, Doppelganger still has a few obvious drawbacks such as high overhead and the need for human involvement. Although CookiePicker follows Doppelganger's basic principle of comparing Web page differences to identify useful cookies, it works in a fully automatic way and has much lower overhead.

7. Conclusions

In this paper, we have presented a system, called CookiePicker, to automatically manage cookie usage setting on behalf of a user. Only one additional HTTP request for the container page of a Web site, the hidden request, is generated for CookiePicker to identify the usefulness of a cookie set. The core of CookiePicker are two complementary detection algorithms, which accurately detect the HTML page differences caused by enabling and disabling cookies. CookiePicker classifies those cookies that cause perceivable changes on a Web page as useful, and disable the rest as useless. We have implemented CookiePicker as an extension to Firefox and evaluated its efficacy through live experiments over various Web sites. By automatically manage the usage of cookies, CookiePicker helps a user to strike an appropriate balance between easy usage and privacy risks. We believe CookiePicker has the potential to be widely used, for its fully automatic nature, its high accuracy, and its low overhead.

Acknowledgments: This work was partially supported by NSF grants CNS-0627339 and CNS-0627340.

References

[1] R. Al-Ekram, A. Adma, and O. Baysal. diffx: an algorithm to detect changes in multi-version xml documents. In *Proceedings of the CASCON'05*, pages 1–11, 2005.

[2] P. Bille. A survey on tree edit distance and related problems. *Theor. Comput. Sci.*, 337(1-3):217–239, 2005.

[3] S. Chapman and G. Dhillon. Privacy and the internet: the case of doubleclick, inc, 2002.

[4] S. Gupta, G. Kaiser, D. Neistadt, and P. Grimm. Dom-based content extraction of html documents. In *Proceedings of the WWW'03*, pages 207–214, 2003.

[5] V. Ha, K. Inkpen, F. A. Shaar, and L. Hdeib. An examination of user perception and misconception of internet cookies. In *CHI'06 extended abstracts on Human factors in computing systems*, pages 833–838, 2006.

[6] C. Jackson, A. Bortz, D. Boneh, and J. C. Mitchell. Protecting browser state from web privacy attacks. In *Proceedings of the WWW'06*, pages 737–744, 2006.

[7] M. Jakobsson and S. Stamm. Invasive browser sniffing and countermeasures. In *Proceedings of the WWW'06*, pages 523–532, 2006.

[8] T. Jiang, L. Wang, and K. Zhang. Alignment of trees - an alternative to tree edit. *Theor. Comput. Sci.*, 143(1):137–148, 1995.

[9] S. Joshi, N. Agrawal, R. Krishnapuram, and S. Negi. A bag of paths model for measuring structural similarity in web documents. In *Proceedings of the KDD'03*, pages 577–582, 2003.

[10] D. Kristol and L. Montulli. Http state management mechanism, RFC 2109, 1997.

[11] D. M. Kristol. Http cookies: Standards, privacy, and politics. *ACM Trans. Inter. Tech.*, 1(2):151–198, 2001.

[12] B. A. Mah. An empirical model of http network traffic. In *Proceedings of the INFOCOM'97*, pages 592–600, 1997.

[13] L. I. Millett, B. Friedman, and E. Felten. Cookies and web browser design: toward realizing informed consent online. In *Proceedings of the CHI'01*, pages 46–52, 2001.

[14] D. C. Reis, P. B. Golgher, A. S. Silva, and A. F. Laender. Automatic web news extraction using tree edit distance. In *Proceedings of the WWW'04*, pages 502–511, 2004.

[15] S. M. Selkow. The tree-to-tree editing problem. *Inf. Process. Lett.*, 6(6):184–186, 1977.

[16] U. Shankar and C. Karlof. Doppelganger: Better browser privacy without the bother. In *Proceedings of the ACM CCS'06*, 2006.

[17] K.-C. Tai. The tree-to-tree correction problem. *J. ACM*, 26(3):422–433, 1979.

[18] E. Tanaka and K. Tanaka. The tree-to-tree editing problem. *International journal Pattern Recognition And Atificial Intelligency*, 2(2):221–240, 1988.

[19] A. Torsello and D. Hidovic-Rowe. Polynomial-time metrics for attributed trees. *IEEE Trans. Pattern Anal. Mach. Intell.*, 27(7):1087–1099, 2005.

[20] G. Valiente. An efficient bottom-up distance between trees. In *Proceedings of the SPIRE'01*, pages 212–219, 2001.

[21] P. Vogt, F. Nentwich, N. Jovanovic, E. Kirda, C. Kruegel, and G. Vigna. Cross site scripting prevention with dynamic data tainting and static analysis. In *Proceedings of the NDSS'07*, 2007.

[22] Y.-M. Wang, D. Beck, X. Jiang, R. Roussev, C. Verbowski, S. Chen, and S. T. King. Automated web patrol with strider honeymonkeys: Finding web sites that exploit browser vulnerabilities. In *Proceedings of the NDSS'06*, 2006.

[23] W. Yang. Identifying syntactic differences between two programs. *Softw. Pract. Exper.*, 21(7):739–755, 1991.

[24] C. Yue, M. Xie, and H. Wang. Cookie measurement and design of CookiePicker. Technical Report WM-CS-2007-03, The College of William & Mary, 2007.

[25] Y. Zhai and B. Liu. Web data extraction based on partial tree alignment. In *Proceedings of the WWW'05*, pages 76–85, 2005.

[26] Accurate web site visitor measurement crippled by cookie blocking and deletion, jupiterresearch finds, 2007. http://www.jupitermedia.com/corporate/releases/05.03.14-newjupresearch.html.

[27] CERT Advisory CA-2000-02 Malicious HTML tags embedded in client web requests. http://www.cert.org/advisories/CA-2000-02.html.

[28] Google slams the door on XSS flaw 'Stop cookie thief!'. http://software.silicon.com/security/, January 17th, 2007.

[29] Http cookie, 2006. http://en.wikipedia.org/wiki/HTTP_cookie.

[30] Platform for privacy preferences (P3P) project, 2006. http://www.w3.org/P3P/.

[31] Same origin policy, 2007. http://en.wikipedia.org/wiki/Same_origin_policy.

[32] Cookie crusher, 2006. http://www.pcworld.com/downloads.

[33] Cookie pal, 2006. http://www.kburra.com/cpal.html.

Session 8A:
Networking

Greedy Receivers in IEEE 802.11 Hotspots

Mi Kyung Han, Brian Overstreet, Lili Qiu
Department of Computer Sciences, The University of Texas at Austin, Austin, TX 78712
{hanmi2,overstre,lili}@cs.utexas.edu

Abstract

As wireless hotspot business becomes a tremendous financial success, users of these networks have increasing motives to misbehave in order to obtain more bandwidth at the expense of other users. Such misbehaviors threaten the performance and availability of hotspot networks, and have recently attracted increasing research attention. However the existing work so far focuses on sender-side misbehavior. Motivated by the observation that many hotspot users receive more traffic than they send, we study greedy receivers in this paper. We identify a range of greedy receiver misbehaviors, and quantify their damage using both simulation and testbed experiments. Our results show that even though greedy receivers do not directly control data transmission, they can still result in very serious damage, including completely shutting off the competing traffic. To address the issues, we further develop techniques to detect and mitigate greedy receiver misbehavior, and demonstrate their effectiveness.

Keywords: Greedy receiver, wireless LAN.

1 Introduction

The proliferation of lightweight hand-held devices with built-in high-speed WiFi network cards has spurred widespread deployment of wireless "hot-spot" networks at many public places, such as hotels, airports, restaurants, and malls. As reported in [5, 6], worldwide wireless data hotspot revenue will rise from $969 million in 2005 to $3.46 billion in 2009, and the number of hotspot locations will nearly double in size from 100,000 in 2005 to almost 200,000 by the end of 2009. As hotspot business becomes a tremendous financial success, users of these networks have increasing incentives to misbehave in order to gain more bandwidth even at the expense of others.

The serious damage caused by MAC-layer misbehavior has recently received substantial research attention. Some of the pioneering work in this area includes [1, 9, 11]. These works identify several types of MAC-layer misbehaviors, and propose countermeasures to detect and prevent such misuse.

The existing work so far focuses on sender-side misbehavior. In wireless LAN (WLAN) networks, the amount of traffic coming from access points (APs) to clients is typically higher than that from clients to APs [7, 13]. APs are under the control of service providers and send more data, whereas (possibly mis-behaving) users often act as receivers. Therefore misbehaving receivers can be serious threats to the performance and availability of WLANs. However, there is little work on receiver-side MAC misbehaviors. This motivates our work.

In this paper, we first identify a range of greedy receiver misbehaviors. Such receiver misbehaviors are possible because IEEE 802.11 is a feedback-based protocol; while receivers do not directly control data transmissions, they can cause damage by manipulating the feedback. We quantify the performance impact of misbehaving receivers using both simulation and testbed experiments. Our results show that misbehaving receivers can cause serious damage to the network. In some cases, a greedy receiver can completely shut off the other competing flows. To mitigate the threats and enhance network availability, we further develop techniques to detect and mitigate greedy receiver misbehavior, and demonstrate their effectiveness.

The rest of the paper is organized as follows. We overview the background of IEEE 802.11 in Section 2, and survey related work in Section 3. We present a range of greedy receiver misbehaviors in Section 4. We quantify their damage using simulation and testbed experiments in Section 5 and Section 6, respectively. We describe techniques to detect and mitigate greedy receiver misbehavior in Section 7, and evaluate its effectiveness in Section 8. We conclude in Section 9.

2 Background of IEEE 802.11

In IEEE 802.11 DCF [3], before transmission, a station first checks to see if the medium is available by using virtual carrier-sensing and physical carrier-sensing. The medium is considered busy if either carrier-sensing indicates so. Virtual carrier-sensing is performed using the Network Allocation Vector (NAV). Most 802.11 frames have a NAV field, which indicates how long the medium is reserved in order to finish transmitting all the frames for the current operation. Virtual carrier sensing considers medium is idle if NAV is zero, otherwise it considers the medium busy. Only when NAV is zero, physical carrier-sensing is performed using carrier-sensing hardware. If physical carrier-sensing also determines the medium idle, a station may begin transmission using the following rule. If the medium has been idle for longer than a distributed inter-frame spacing time (DIFS), transmission can begin immediately. Otherwise, a station having data to send first waits for DIFS and then waits for a random backoff interval, which is uniformly chosen between $[0, CW_{min}]$, where CW_{min} is the minimum contention window. If at anytime during the above period the medium is sensed busy, the station freezes its counter and the countdown resumes when the medium becomes idle. When the counter decrements to zero, the node transmits the packet. If the receiver successfully receives the packet, it waits for a short inter-frame spacing time (SIFS) and then transmits an ACK frame. If the sender does not receive an ACK (e.g., due to a collision or poor channel condition), it doubles its contention window to reduce its access rate. When the contention window reaches its maximum value, denoted as CW_{max}, it stays at that value until a transmission succeeds, in which case the contention window is reset to CW_{min}.

3 Related Work

The serious damage caused by misbehaving MAC has received increasing attention in wireless research community. For example, Bellardo and Savage [1] studied denial of service attacks in 802.11. Kyasanur and Vaidya [9] identified that selfish senders can get significantly more bandwidth than regular senders by modifying the backoff value in IEEE 802.11. Raya et al. [11] developed DOMINO, a software installed on access points to detect and identify greedy stations. More recently, Cagalj et al. [2] used a game-theoretic approach to study selfish nodes in CSMA/CA networks. Unlike the existing work, which focuses on sender-side misbehavior, we identify a range of receiver-side misbehaviors and evaluate their impact on network performance.

In addition to MAC misbehaviors, researchers also studied misbehavior at other protocol layers, such as jamming attacks [14], routing attacks [4], and selfish TCP behavior and attacks [8, 12]. In particular, our work is inspired by [12], which studies TCP receiver misbehaviors and shows that in a feedback-based protocol receivers can significantly affect network performance even though they do not directly send data. Unlike [12], we study receiver misbehavior at MAC-layer.

4 Greedy Receiver

In this section, we present three types of greedy receiver misbehaviors. For each misbehavior, we first introduce the misbehavior and then describe its applicable scenarios, greedy actions, and effects. Throughout the paper, we let GR denote a greedy receiver, NR denote a normal receiver, GS denote GR's sender, and NS denote NR's sender. We assume that APs are the senders and behave normally, since they are under the control of service providers.

4.1 Misbehavior 1: Increasing NAV

IEEE 802.11 uses NAV to perform virtual carrier sensing. Greedy receivers can increase their goodput (i.e., received rate) by increasing NAV. Our work complements the previous studies on NAV inflation [1, 11] in the following aspects. First, we focus on greedy receiver misbehavior, whereas [11] focuses on greedy senders and [1] focuses on denial-of-service (DOS) attacks, where misbehaving nodes simply cause damage without necessarily gaining more throughput. We will show that only a small NAV increase is required for GR to starve other flows due to additional data traffic, whereas a large NAV inflation is required to launch the type of DOS considered in [1]. Second, we present a simple analysis to model the effect of NAV inflation in Section 5. Third, we will use extensive evaluation to study the effect of NAV inflation in various scenarios.

Applicable Scenarios The misbehavior is effective whenever there is traffic competing with a greedy receiver. Inflated CTS NAV causes damage only when RTS/CTS is enabled, whereas inflated ACK NAV causes damage regardless whether RTS/CTS is used. When TCP is used, the greedy receiver also sends TCP ACK packets, which are data frames to the MAC layer. As a result, the greedy receiver can also inflate NAV on the RTS and data frames, which are used to send the TCP ACK packet.

Greedy Actions A greedy receiver may inflate NAV in its CTS and/or ACK frames under UDP, and inflate NAV in CTS, ACK, RTS, and/or data frames under TCP. It can increase the NAV up to $32767\mu s$, which is the maximum allowable value in IEEE 802.11.

Effects Sending frames with inflated NAV allows a greedy receiver to silence all nearby nodes longer than necessary. According to IEEE 802.11 [3], upon receiving a valid frame, each station should update its NAV, only when the new NAV value is greater than the current NAV value and only when the frame is not addressed to the receiving station. Thus the increased NAV value will not affect GS, which sends data to GR, but silence the other nearby senders and receivers.

If the amount of NAV increase is large enough, GS can exclusively grab the channel even in presence of other nearby competing senders since it always senses the medium idle before its transmission.

4.2 Misbehavior 2: Spoofing ACKs

Upon a packet loss, a TCP sender reduces its sending rate by decreasing its congestion window (i.e., the maximum amount of unacknowledged data allowed by the TCP sender). MAC-layer retransmissions help to reduce packet losses observed at the TCP layer. Based on the observation, a greedy receiver can send MAC-layer ACKs on behalf of other TCP flows. In this way, packet losses are not recovered at MAC-layer as they should, but are propagated to the TCP layer, which can cause TCP senders to slow down.

Applicable Scenarios The misbehavior is effective under the following two conditions. First, the traffic competing with greedy receiver is TCP and its link is lossy. Second, a greedy receiver uses promiscuous mode so that it can spoof MAC-layer ACKs in response to data frames not destined to itself.

Greedy Actions A greedy receiver (GR) sniffs a data frame destined to a normal receiver (NR) coming from a sender (NS), and sends a MAC-layer ACK on behalf of NR. Because the link from NS to NR is lossy, NR may not successfully receive the data. However GR spoofs a MAC-layer ACK on behalf of NR so that NS moves on to the next transmission, instead of performing MAC-layer retransmissions as it should.

Effects A spoofed ACK has two effects. First, when the original receiver (NR) does not receive the data frame, the spoofed ACK from GR effectively disables MAC-layer retransmission at NS. This propagates packet losses to NS's TCP, which will decrease its congestion window and may even cause TCP timeouts, thereby increasing the traffic rate towards the greedy receiver. When the normal traffic spans both wireless and wireline network, the damage of this misbehavior is further increased; The additional wireline delay makes end-to-end TCP loss recovery even more expensive than local MAC-layer retransmissions on the wireless link. We also observe this effect in our evaluation, as described in Section 5.

Second, when NR receives the data frame, spoofed ACK will collide with the ACK from the original receiver NR. Such collisions cause unnecessary retransmissions from NS and slow down NR's flow. This is essentially a jamming attack, which has been studied before [14]. Therefore Section 5, we focus on the first effect – disabling MAC-layer retransmissions.

To study the first effect, we consider capture effects: When the two packets are received simultaneously, if their received signal strength ratio is above capture threshold, only the packet with stronger signal is received and the other is lost. In our context, we consider either $RSS_{NR}/RSS_{GR} \geq Thresh_{cap}$ or $RSS_{GR}/RSS_{NR} \geq Thresh_{cap}$, where $Thresh_{cap}$ is capture threshold, and RSS_{NR} and RSS_{GR} are received signal strength from NR and GR, respectively. In the former case, ACK from NR is demodulated and received, and ACK from GR is lost, and in the latter case, the ACK from GR is received and the ACK from NR is lost. (The performance degradation caused by greedy receiver would be even larger under both jam-

	# received	# corrupted	# corrupted w/ correct dest	# corrupted w/ correct src-dest
802.11b	65536	1367	1351	1282
802.11a	23068	7376	6197	5663

Table 1. Testbed measurement shows that most corrupted packets preserve source and destination MAC addresses.

ming and disabled MAC retransmissions.)

4.3 Misbehavior 3: Sending fake ACKs

In 802.11, a sender performs an exponential backoff upon seeing a packet loss. This slows down the sender when network is congested and packets get corrupted. A greedy receiver can prevent its sender from backing off by sending ACKs even when receiving corrupted packets (destined to itself). In this way, the greedy receiver receives a higher goodput (*i.e.*, the receiving rate of uncorrupted packets).

Applicable Scenarios This misbehavior is effective under the following two conditions. First, the traffic to GR is carried by non-TCP connections (to avoid interacting with TCP congestion control). Second, the link from GS to GR is lossy.

Greedy Actions When receiving a corrupted frame, GR sends a MAC-layer ACK back to the source even though the data is actually corrupted.

The effectiveness of this attack depends on how often a corrupted packet preserves correct source and destination addresses. Since MAC addresses are much smaller than the payload, most of corrupted packets preserve MAC addresses. To further validate this claim, we conduct measurement experiments in our testbed by placing sender and receiver far enough to generate significant packet corruption. Table 1 shows a breakdown of the number of corrupted packets, corrupted packets with correct destination MAC addresses, and corrupted packets with correct source and destination MAC addresses. As it shows, 98.8% and 84% corrupted packets are delivered to the correct destination in 802.11b and 802.11a, respectively. Among them, 94.9% and 91.4% packets have correct source addresses in 802.11b and 802.11a, respectively. These numbers indicate that sending fake ACKs is a practical attack since most of corrupted packets preserve MAC addresses.

Effects GR sending ACK in the presence of corrupted data effectively prevents GS from doing exponential backoff, which increases GR's goodput. An interesting aspect of this misbehavior is that it is a common belief that the link layer retransmission is considered to improve performance over end-to-end recovery; however its performance benefit can be offset by exponential backoff when competing with other flows.

Similar to misbehavior 2, misbehavior 3 also modifies how MAC-layer ACK is transmitted under corrupted/lost packets. However they differ in that misbehavior 2 targets TCP traffic by exploiting its rate reduction upon packet losses whereas misbehavior 3 targets non-TCP traffic by avoiding MAC-layer exponential backoff under packet losses.

5 Evaluation of Greedy Receivers in Simulation

In this section, we use Network Simulator 2 (NS2) [10] to quantify the damage caused by greedy receivers. We use 802.11b for all simulation evaluation, since 802.11b is commonly used in hotspot networks. All the senders behave normally, which correspond to APs that are under the control of hotspot providers and do not misbehave. We consider NS sends to NR, and GS sends to GR, where GR denotes a greedy receiver, and NS, GS and NR all behave normally. Our evaluation uses both TCP and UDP, both of which use data packet size of 1024 bytes. When UDP is used, we generate constant bit rate (CBR) traffic high enough to saturate the medium. Moreover, the rates of all CBR flows are the same so that the difference in goodput is due to MAC-layer effect. We run each scenario 5 times and report the median of the goodput, which is the received data rate of uncorrupted packets. As we will show, even though greedy receivers do not directly control data transmission, they can still effectively increase their goodput at the expense of degrading or even shutting off other competing flows.

5.1 Misbehavior 1: Increasing NAV

We randomly place nodes so that all of them can hear each other. We evaluate the impact of NAV inflation by varying (i) the type of transport protocols, (ii) the amount of NAV inflation, (iii) the frequency of NAV inflation, (iv) the number of greedy receivers, and (v) the number of greedy senders. When the greedy receiver uses UDP, it can inflate CTS and/or ACK frames. When the greedy receiver uses TCP, not only can it inflate NAV in CTS and/or ACK, but also inflate NAV in RTS and data frames corresponding to the TCP ACK.

Vary the amount of NAV inflation: We vary the value of NAV used by greedy receivers by changing α in $n + \alpha \cdot 100$, where n is the original NAV value before inflation, and α varies from 0 to 310 for CTS NAV, and from 0 to 327 for ACK NAV. $\alpha = 310$ in CTS and $\alpha = 327$ in ACK give close to the maximum NAV, which is $32767\mu s$.

UDP traffic: First, we evaluate the impact of greedy receivers using constant-bit-rate (CBR) traffic transferred via UDP. Fig. 1 shows the goodput of a normal receiver and a greedy receiver, competing with each other and both using UDP. The greedy receiver

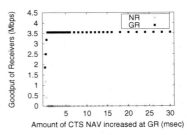

Figure 1. Goodput of two UDP flows NS-NR and GS-GR, where GR inflates CTS NAV.

can completely grab the medium and starve the competing flow even when NAV is inflated by only 0.6 ms.

Below we analyze the effect of NAV inflation under UDP traffic. Suppose NS and GS both have an infinite amount of data to send. GR inflates NAV in either its CTS and/or ACK by v timeslots. The probability of GS transmitting in a given round is the probability that only GS sends or both GS and NS send. The probability that only GS sends is $Pr[B_{GS} < B_{NS} + v - 1]$, and the probability that both GS and NS send is $Pr[B_{NS} + v - 1 \leq B_{GS} \leq B_{NS} + v + 1]$. So the probability of GS transmitting is $Pr[B_{GS} \leq B_{NS} + v + 1]$. v is added to B_{NS} because GS starts count-down v timeslots earlier than NS due to NAV inflation; and the probability that both of them send takes the above form because it takes a station 1 time slot to measure signal strength and two nodes can both send if the time of their counting down to zero differs within 1 timeslot. Similarly, the probability of NS transmitting in a round is $Prob[B_{NS} \leq B_{GS} - v + 1]$. The backoff interval is uniformly distributed over $[0..CW]$, where CW is initialized to CW_{min} and doubles every time after a failed transmission until it reaches CW_{max}. We find that as NAV increases NS's average CW increases due to increasing collisions, whereas GS's average CW stays close to CW_{min} because the fraction of collided packets does not change much due to an increasing number of packets sent by GS. Based on the above observation, we have the following relationship:

$Pr[GS\ sends]$
$= Pr[B_{GS} \leq B_{NS} + v + 1]$
$= \sum_{i=0..CW} (Pr[B_{GS} = i] \times$
$\sum_{m=CW_{min}}^{CW_{max}} Pr[CW_{NS} = m]Pr[B_{NS} \geq i - v - 1|CW_{NS} = m])$ (1)

$Pr[NS\ sends]$
$= Pr[B_{NS} \leq B_{GS} - v + 1]$
$= \sum_{i=0..CW} (Pr[B_{GS} = i] \times$
$\sum_{m=CW_{min}}^{CW_{max}} Pr[CW_{NS} = m]Pr[B_{NS} \leq i - v + 1|CW_{NS} = m])$ (2)

We evaluate the accuracy of our model by plugging the distributions of CW into Equation 1 and 2. Fig. 2

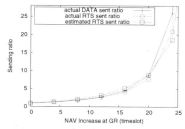

Figure 2. Sending ratio between two competing UDP flows $GS - GR$ **vs.** $NS - NR$.

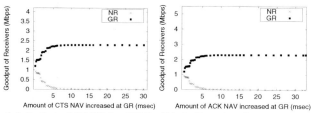

(a) Inflated NAV in CTS   (b) Inflated NAV in ACK

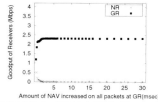

(c) Inflated NAV in RTS/CTS/Data/ACK frames

Figure 3. Goodput of two competing TCP flows NS-NR **and** GS-GR.

compares the estimated and actual RTS sent ratios from GS and NS. As we can see, our model accurately estimates the RTS sent ratio, which is very close to the actual data sent ratio. The actual RTS and data sent ratios are slightly different because of packet losses.

TCP traffic: Fig. 3(a) shows the goodput of two competing TCP flows, when the receiver of one flow is greedy and inflates NAV in all of its CTS frames. We make the following observations. First, in all cases the greedy receiver obtains higher goodput than the normal receiver. Second, as we would expect, the larger increase in the greedy receiver's CTS NAV, the larger goodput gain the greedy receiver has. Moreover, with a large enough NAV value, the greedy receiver can grab the channel all the time and completely shut off the normal receiver's traffic.

Fig. 3(b) further shows the effect of inflating NAV on ACK frames. The goodput gain from inflated ACK NAV is slightly smaller than that from inflated CTS NAV, because there are more CTS frames sent than ACK frames (ACK is sent only when RTS, CTS, and data frames are successfully received, whereas CTS is sent when RTS is received successfully). As we would expect, inflating NAV on all frames causes the largest damage: GS-GR pair dominates the medium even when NAV is inflated by $2ms$, as shown in Fig. 3(c).

We further evaluate the effect of a greedy receiver under multiple normal sender-receiver pairs. We consider 8 flows, where one of them has a greedy receiver.

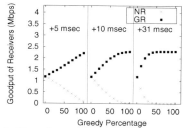

Figure 4. Goodput of two TCP flows NS-NR **and** GS-GR, **where** GR **increases NAV by** 5, 10, **or** 31 **ms, and varies greedy percentage.**

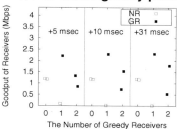

Figure 5. Goodput under 0, 1, or 2 greedy receivers, when CTS NAV increases by 5, 10, **or** 31 **ms.**

We observe that the goodput of the greedy receiver increases with an increasing CTS NAV, at the expense of degrading the goodput of 7 competing normal receivers. Moreover, it takes $10ms$ increase in CTS NAV for the greedy receiver to dominate the medium. In the remaining of Section 5.1, unless specified otherwise, we use TCP flows since TCP is used more often.

Vary Greedy Percentage (GP): In order to make the detection difficult, a greedy receiver may not manipulate every packet it transmits. To evaluate such effect, we vary Greedy Percentage (GP), which denotes the percentage of time a greedy receiver behaves greedily. (In this case, GP is the fraction of CTS frames carrying inflated NAV.)

Fig. 4 plots goodput of normal and greedy receivers as we vary GP and the amount of NAV inflation, and all four nodes are within communication range of each other. As we would expect, GR has a larger gain with an increasing GP. Nevertheless even when GP is 50%, GR already receives substantially higher goodput. For example, its goodput is over 1Mbps higher than that of NR when NAV is inflated by $5ms$, and around 1.8Mbps higher when NAV is inflated by $10ms$, and completely grabs the bandwidth when NAV is inflated by $31ms$.

Vary the number of greedy receivers: Next we vary the number of greedy receivers. Fig. 5 considers 2 sender-receiver pairs. As it shows, when both receivers are normal, they get similar goodput. When only one receiver is greedy, the greedy receiver gets significantly higher bandwidth and almost starves the normal receiver. When both receivers are greedy, their performance depends on who grabs the medium first. The one that grabs the medium earlier gets the chance to silence the other flow and has an opportunity to grab the channel again in the next round.

We further study the case of 8 sender-receiver pairs,

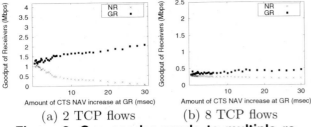

(a) 2 TCP flows (b) 8 TCP flows

Figure 6. One sender sends to multiple receivers, one of which inflates CTS NAV.

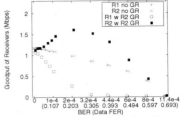

Figure 7. Goodput of two TCP flows NS-NR and GS-GR under a varying wireless link loss rate. The x-axis shows bit error rate on the top and data frame error rate on the bottom.

where all greedy receivers have GP=100% and their NAV is increased by 31 ms. When there are more than two greedy receivers, only two of the greedy receivers survive and the rest of the receivers have 0 goodput. This is because when the amount of NAV increase is large enough, the first few that grab the channel will dominate the medium.

One sender with multiple receivers: So far we have studied the cases when there are as many senders as receivers. Now we examine the case where one sender sends to more than one receiver. This introduces head-of-line blocking, and reduces the damage of a greedy receiver to a certain degree. Nevertheless, even in that case, the greedy receiver can get significant gain.

First, we consider one sender S sending to two receivers, NR (normal receiver) and GR (greedy receiver). In this case, S does not respond to the inflated NAV from GR, since the CTS is destined to itself. Inflated NAV has the following two effects on NR. First, it prevents NR from sending CTS in response to the RTS from S in a timely manner. If the CTS is delayed long enough, the sender S assumes RTS has failed and backs off by increasing its contention window. Second, when TCP is used, an inflated NAV from GR prevents NR from sending TCP ACK in a timely manner. Fig. 6(a) shows the goodput of NR and GR. Compared with the case of two sender-receiver pairs, the goodput increase for the greedy receiver is reduced, even though the gain is still significant. Next we consider one sender sending to 7 normal receivers and 1 greedy receiver. Fig. 6(b) shows that there is still gain for the greedy receiver though the benefit is much smaller than competing with only one normal receiver or having multiple senders.

Next we consider one sender sending to a normal receiver and a greedy receiver using UDP. (Figure is omitted for brevity.) The goodput of both flows decreases with an increasing NAV, and GR receives similar goodput as NR when sharing the sender. This is because both CBR flows have the same data rate, and the queue at the sender has roughly the same number of packets to normal and greedy receivers. A larger CTS NAV from GR simply makes the sender fluctuate its contention window and increases the idle time between two transmissions without changing splitting ratio between the two receivers. In comparison, under TCP the sender's queue has more packets to GR than to NR, since the TCP flow to NR slows down when NR does not send ACKs in a timely manner.

Summary: Our evaluation shows that increasing NAV is an effective greedy misbehavior. As we would expect, a larger NAV increase or a larger greedy percentage increases the gain of greedy receivers. Furthermore, the damage is larger when a greedy receiver has a separate sender from normal receivers than when the sender is shared. Finally, the impact of NAV inflation in TCP depends on which frames the greedy receiver manipulates: the impact of NAV inflation in CTS or ACK frames in TCP is smaller than that in UDP; however the impact on TCP traffic can further increase when the greedy receiver also modifies RTS and data frames corresponding to TCP ACK packet.

5.2 Misbehavior 2: Spoofing ACKs

We evaluate misbehavior 2 using TCP traffic since this misbehavior targets TCP. We use a 4-node topology (2 senders sending to 2 receivers), where all the wireless nodes are within communication range of each other for evaluation. The loss rates on all wireless links (e.g., NS-NR, GS-GR, NS-GR and GS-NR) are the same.

Vary bit error rate: First we examine the impact of a greedy receiver by varying bit error rate (BER). The greedy receiver spoofs MAC-layer ACKs for every data packet it sniffs from the sender to the normal receiver (i.e., GP=100). Fig. 7 shows the goodput of both receivers when one of them misbehaves versus when neither misbehaves. The x-axis shows both bit error rate and the corresponding data frame error rate. We make the following observations. First, when neither misbehaves, the two receivers get similar goodput. Their goodput both decreases with an increasing BER. In comparison, when one of them misbehaves, the greedy receiver gets significantly higher goodput than the normal receiver. Moreover, we observe that when BER is lower than $2e^{-4}$, the greedy receiver gets an increasing gain as loss rate increases. This is because an increasing loss rate means that more packets to the normal receiver have to be recovered at TCP layer after spoofing MAC-layer ACKs, thereby increasing the effectiveness of greedy misbehavior. When BER is higher than $2e^{-4}$, the greedy receiver's goodput gain gradually decreases because the number of data packets it overhears decreases, thereby decreasing the number of spoofed ACKs. Moreover, an increasing loss rate between the greedy receiver and its sender also degrades its TCP goodput. In an extreme, when the loss rate is

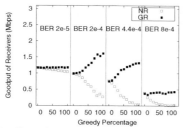

Figure 8. Goodput of two TCP flows NS-NR **and** GS-GR**, when greedy percentage and loss rates vary.**

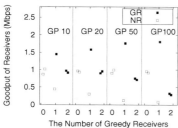

Figure 9. Goodput under 0, 1, or 2 greedy receivers (All flows use TCP, and BER=$2e^{-4}$**).**

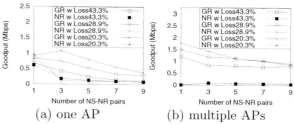

(a) one AP   (b) multiple APs

Figure 10. One greedy receiver competes with a varying number of NS-NR pairs.

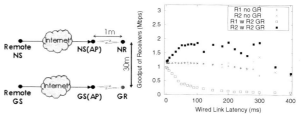

(a) Simulation topology (b) Simulation results

Figure 11. Goodput under remote TCP senders, where both wireless links to the greedy and normal receiver have BER=$2e^{-5}$**.**

high enough, both TCP flows get virtually zero goodput regardless of whether one misbehaves or not.

Vary greedy percentage: Next we evaluate the impact of greedy percentage (i.e., how often the greedy receiver spoofs an ACK when it sniffs the other sender's data packet). Fig. 8 summarizes the results. As we would expect, the goodput of greedy receiver increases with GP. This is true over all loss rate values. For low loss rate, the effect of spoofing is limited because most packets are correctly received at the normal receiver. For moderate loss rate, a significant number of packets are lost at the normal receiver, making spoofing ACK an effective attack. For high loss rate, spoofing ACK continues to allow the greedy receiver to get more goodput than the normal receiver, even though it also suffers degradation due to the high loss rate.

Vary the number of greedy receivers: We further evaluate the performance of 2 TCP flows under 0, 1, or 2 greedy receivers. As shown in Fig. 9, the total goodput decreases when both receivers misbehave. This is because in this case both receivers spoof the other's MAC-layer ACK, which effectively disables MAC-layer retransmission and makes the loss propagated to TCP layer. A larger GP causes MAC-layer retransmission to be disabled more often, and results in larger reduction in goodput.

Vary the number of sender-receiver pairs: Next we consider one greedy receiver competes with a varying number of normal receivers. Fig. 10(a) compares the average goodput of a greedy receiver and normal receivers when they share one AP, and Fig. 10(b) shows the results when each receiver receive data from a different AP. As they show, in both cases the average throughput of greedy receiver is higher than that of the normal receivers. Moreover, the goodput difference between the greedy and normal receivers is larger under multiple APs due to lack of head-of-line blocking.

TCP sender at remote site: So far we consider the connections span only wireless links. Next we consider the case where the two connections span both wireless and wireline links, as shown in Fig. 11(a). We vary the wired link latency from $2ms$ to $400ms$, and set BER of both wireless links to $2e^{-5}$. Fig. 11 compares goodput under no greedy receiver versus under one greedy receiver ($R2$ is a greedy receiver in this case). We observe that increasing wireline latency initially increases the gap between the normal and greedy receiver. This is because an increasing wireline latency makes end-to-end loss recovery more expensive. When the wireline latency is beyond $200ms$, the goodput of greedy receiver starts to decrease, even though it still significantly out-performs the normal receiver. This is because TCP ACK-clocking reduces its goodput as delay increases, and the goodput gain from the normal receiver is not enough to offset such drop.

5.3 Misbehavior 3: Sending Fake ACKs

For misbehavior 3, a greedy receiver sends an ACK even upon receiving a corrupted data frame. This misbehavior is effective when the greedy receiver uses UDP, and the source and the destination address in the corrupted DATA frame are preserved. As shown in Table 1, this is quite common. We create data loss using one of the following two ways. We disable RTS-CTS exchange and place two receivers next to each other and senders far apart from each other to create the hidden terminal problem. Alternatively, we create loss by injecting random loss of bit-error-rate (BER) of $2e^{-5}$ when the two sender-receiver pairs are within communication range of each other. In both cases, the two flows experience similar loss rates.

Vary greedy percentage: As shown in Fig. 12, an increasing greedy percentage increases the discrepancy

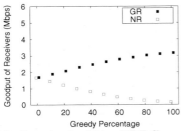

Figure 12. Goodput of two UDP flows NS-NR and GS-GR, when NS and GS are hidden terminals.

Data error rate	no GR (Mbps)		1 GR (Mbps)		2 GRs (Mbps)	
	$NR1$	$NR2$	NR	GR	$GR1$	$GR2$
0.2	1.44	1.43	1.2	1.43	1.47	1.47
0.5	0.92	0.91	0.59	2.49	1.03	1.03
0.8	0.63	0.63	0.32	1.11	0.71	0.75

Table 2. Goodput of two receivers under 0, 1, or 2 greedy receivers.

between the goodput of the normal and greedy receivers. When GP=100% (i.e., greedy receiver fakes ACK on every corrupted data packet), the greedy receiver shuts off the other connection. This is because faking ACKs makes GS's contention window (CW) considerably smaller than NS's CW.

Vary the number of greedy receivers: Next we compare the performance when both receivers are greedy. Interestingly, the performance would depend on the types of losses. Under congestion-related losses due to hidden terminal, both greedy receivers suffer. Their goodput is reduced by 48%. This is because faking ACK effectively disables exponential back-off in 802.11 and senders send faster than they should, creating more collisions. In comparison, when the loss is non-congestion related (e.g., low received signal strength), faking ACKs improve the goodput by 2-12% when data frame loss rate varies from 0.2 to 0.8, as shown in Table 2. This is because under non-congestion loss, performing exponential back-off does not help reduce losses and only unnecessarily reduces the sending rate. Faking ACKs avoids such unnecessary rate reduction and improves performance.

Different loss rates on the two flows: Our next evaluation is to understand whether a greedy receiver's performance gain under packet losses is no more than a normal receiver when its link is loss free. So we inject random loss to only one flow, and let both receivers behave normally. When both flows have BER of $5e^{-4}$, the greedy and normal receivers obtain 2.61 Mbps and 1.086 Mbps, respectively. In comparison, when both receivers are normal, one flow with BER of $5e^{-4}$, and the other with no loss, the one with no loss has 2.64Mbps and the other has 1.096 Mbps. So effectively the greedy receiver pretends to be a normal receiver without packet losses. Under non-congestion loss, faking ACKs can be considered as a useful surviving technique. However, this is not recommended under congestion losses.

Vary the number of sender-receiver pairs: Finally we consider one greedy receiver competes with a varying number of normal receivers, where all of them

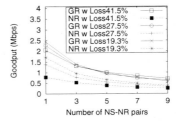

Figure 13. One greedy receiver competes with a varying number of NS-NR pairs.

experience the same loss rates. As shown in Fig. 13, the impact of greedy receiver increases with the loss rate, because a higher loss rate means more opportunities for the greedy receiver to fake ACKs. Moreover, the absolute difference in the goodput of greedy and normal receivers decreases as the number of normal receivers increases due to a decreasing per-flow goodput. Interestingly, their relative difference in goodput remains high for all the numbers of receivers considered.

6 Evaluation in Testbed

Next we evaluate the performance impact of greedy receivers in a testbed consisting of 4 DELL Dimensions 1100 PCs (2.66 GHz Intel Celeron D Processor 330 with 512 MB of memory). They form two senders and two receivers. The locations of the nodes are fixed, on the same floor of an office building. Each node runs Fedora Core 4 Linux, and is equipped with 802.11 a/b/g Net-Gear WAG511 using MadWiFi. In our experiment, we enable RTS/CTS, and use a fixed 6 Mbps as MAC-layer data rate. 802.11a is used in our testbed experiments to avoid interference with campus 802.11b wireless LAN in the building.

Our testbed evaluation focuses on misbehavior 1, since MadWiFi currently does not allow us to implement the other two misbehaviors. Given the trend of moving more functionalities to software, this is not an inherent constraint. We implement misbehavior 1 as follows. Because the current MadWiFi does not allow us to directly modify NAV in CTS frames, we get around this problem by implementing RTS inflation on one of the senders. We increase RTS NAV to $32700\mu s$. This automatically triggers inflated NAV in CTS frames. (The inflated CTS NAV is $32655\mu s$.) Since we want to study the impact of a greedy receiver, we have the sender transmit at lowest power so that its RTS with inflated NAV is not overheard by the other sender and receiver. Only the CTS frames from the greedy receiver is heard by all the other nodes to effectively create greedy receiver misbehavior.

Table 3 compares the goodput under 0, 1, or 2 greedy receivers. The reported goodput is median over 5 runs, where each run lasts 2 minutes. As it shows, without greedy receiver, both receivers get similar goodput. When only one receiver is greedy, the greedy receiver gets virtually all the bandwidth and starves the normal receiver. When both receivers are greedy, the one transmitting earlier dominates the medium and starves the other receiver. These results

Transport	no GR (Mbps)		1 GR (Mbps)		2 GRs (Mbps)	
	$NR1$	$NR2$	NR	GR	$GR1$	$GR2$
UDP	3.06	2.43	0.04	4.65	0	4.64
TCP	2.31	2.36	0.01	4.43	0	4.37

Table 3. Testbed evaluation of NAV inflation.

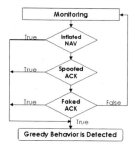

Figure 14. Detecting greedy receivers.

are consistent with simulation results, and confirm the serious damage of greedy misbehavior in real networks.

7 Detecting Greedy Receivers

In this section, we present techniques to detect and mitigate greedy receiver misbehaviors. We assume that senders are well-behaving and do not collude with greedy receivers. Fig. 14 shows a flow-chart of our countermeasure scheme. The scheme can be implemented at any node in the network, including APs and clients. The more nodes implementing the detection scheme, the higher likelihood of detection. Next we describe how to detect inflated NAV, spoofed ACKs, and fake ACKs.

7.1 Detecting Inflated NAV

Inflated NAV affects two sets of nodes: (i) those within communication range of the sender and receiver, and (ii) those outside the communication range of the sender but within communication range of the receiver. The first set of nodes know the correct NAV, since they overhear the sender's frame and can directly compute the correct NAV from the receiver by subtracting the duration of sender's frame. Therefore these nodes can directly detect and correct inflated NAV. The second set of nodes can infer an upperbound on a receiver's NAV using the maximum data frame size (*e.g.*, 1500 bytes, Ethernet MTU). If the NAV in CTS or ACK exceeds the expected NAV value, greedy receiver is detected. (In fact, without fragmentation, NAV in ACK should always be 0.) We can further locate the greedy receiver using received signal strength measurement from it. To recover from this misbehavior, nodes will ignore the inflated NAV and replace it with the expected NAV to use for virtual carrier sense.

7.2 Detecting Spoofed ACKs

To detect greedy receivers that spoof ACKs on behalf of normal receivers, we use their received signal strength. More specifically, let RSS_N denote the received signal strength from the original receiver, RSS_C denote the received signal strength in the current ACK frame, and $Thresh_{cap}$ denote the capture threshold. RSS_N can be obtained using a TCP ACK from that receiver, assuming TCP ACK is not spoofed If RSS_C

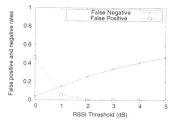

Figure 15. False positive and false negative vs. RSSI threshold.

is significantly different from RSS_N, the sender reports greedy misbehavior. Furthermore, when $\frac{RSS_N}{RSS_C} \geq Thresh_{cap}$, the sender can directly recover from this misbehavior by ignoring the received ACK. This is because in this case the original receiver must have not received data and sent ACK, otherwise the ACK coming from the original receiver would have captured the spoofed ACK; ignoring such MAC-layer ACKs allow the sender to retransmit the data at the MAC-layer as it should.

To examine the feasibility of using RSS measurements for detecting spoofed ACKs, we collect RSSI measurements from our testbed, consisting of 16 nodes spread over one floor of an office building. Our measurements show that around 95% RSSI measurements differ from median RSSI of that link by no more than 1 dB. This suggests that RSSI does not change much during a short time interval, and we can use large change in RSSI to identify spoofed ACKs.

Based on the above observation, a sender determines a spoofed ACK if $|RSSI_{median} - RSSI_{curr}| > RSSIThresh$, where $RSSI_{median}$ is the median RSSI from the true receiver, $RSSI_{curr}$ is the RSSI of the current frame, and $RSSIThresh$ is the threshold. The accuracy of detection depends on the value of $RSSIThresh$. Fig. 15 plots the false positive and false negative rates as $RSSIThresh$ varies from 0 to $5dB$, where false positive is how often the sender determines it is a spoofed ACK but in fact it is not, and false negative is how often the sender determines it is not a spoofed ACK but in fact it is. As it shows, using 1 dB as the threshold achieves both low false positive and low false negative rates.

The previous detection is effective when RSSI from NR is relatively stable and RSSI from GR is different from NR. To handle highly mobile clients, which experience large variation in RSSI, the sender can use a cross-layer approach to detect the greedy behavior. For each TCP flow, it maintains a list of recently received MAC-layer ACK and TCP ACK. Greedy receiver is detected when TCP often retransmits the packet for which MAC-layer ACK has been received. This detection assumes wireline loss rate is much smaller than wireless loss rate, which is generally the case.

7.3 Detecting Faked ACKs

To detect greedy receivers that send MAC-layer ACKs even for corrupted frame, the sender compares the MAC-layer loss with the application layer loss rate. The latter can be estimated using active probing (e.g., ping). Since packets are corrupted, GR cannot send ping response and we can measure the true application loss rate. If loss rate is mainly from wireless link, $applicationLoss \approx MACLoss^{maxRetries}$, when packet losses are independent. If $applicationLoss > MACLoss^{maxRetries} + threshold$, the sender detects faked ACKs, where $threshold$ is used to tolerate loss rate on wireline links when the connection spans both wireless and wireline. The appropriate value of threshold depends on the loss rate on the wireline links.

8 Evaluation of Detection

We implement in NS-2 the greedy receiver countermeasure (GRC) against inflated NAV and ACK spoofing described in Section 7.

(a) Evaluation topology

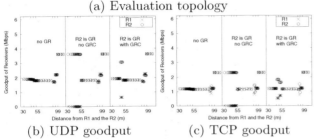

(b) UDP goodput   (c) TCP goodput

Figure 16. GRC effectively detects and mitigates inflated CTS NAV.

First we evaluate the countermeasure against inflated CTS NAV using the the topology in Fig. 16(a), where communication and interference ranges are 55m and 99m, respectively. Fig. 16(b) compares the UDP performance under the following three cases (from left to right) : (i) no greedy receiver, (ii) one greedy receiver with no GRC, and (iii) one greedy receiver and with GRC. As we can see, without a greedy receiver, the two flows get similar goodput. The goodput jumps around 99m, because the two senders do not interfere beyond this distance. When $R2$ is greedy, $R2$ dominates the medium and completely shuts off $R1$ when all four nodes are within communication range. Beyond 55m, $R2$'s inflated CTS NAV cannot be heard by $R1$ and $S1$, so the goodput of the two flows are similar beyond 55m. So inflated CTS NAV is effective only when distance is below 55m, and we focus on this region. We observe that GRC effectively detects and mitigates the inflated NAV. In particular, the goodput of the two flows are similar when distance is below 45 m, since $S1$ and $R1$ both hear $S2$'s RTS and know the true packet size. As the distance further increases, NS does not hear RTS from GS and has to assume the maximum packet size 1500 bytes, which is 46.48% larger than the actual data packet size. In this case, $R2$ receives higher goodput. Nevertheless, compared with no GRC, the normal receiver no longer starves. Similar trends are observed under TCP traffic, as shown in Fig. 16(c).

Next we consider a greedy receiver that spoofs

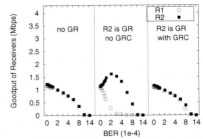

Figure 17. GRC effectively detects and recovers from ACK spoofing under varying BER.

ACKs. We compare the goodput of two competing flows under a varying loss rate, where the loss rates on the two flows are the same and losses are both randomly generated. As shown in Fig. 17, without a greedy receiver, the goodput of the two flows are similar, both gradually decrease as BER increases from 0 to $14e^{-4}$. When $R2$ is greedy, its flow dominates the medium and degrades $R1$'s performance when no GRC is used. With GRC, both flows fairly share the medium: their goodput closely follow the goodput curves under no greedy receiver. This demonstrates the effectiveness of the GRC.

9 Conclusion

As the popularity of hotspot networks continues to grow, it is increasingly important to understand potential misuses and guard against them. In this paper, we identify a range of greedy receiver misbehaviors, and evaluate their effects using both simulation and testbed experiments. Our results show that greedy receiver misbehavior can cause serious degradation in other traffic, including starvation. We further develop techniques to detect and mitigate the misbehaviors and demonstrate their effectiveness.

References

[1] J. Bellardo and S. Savage. 802.11 denial-of-service attacks: Real vulnerabilities and practical solutions. In *Proc. of 12th USENIX Security Symposium*, Aug. 2003.

[2] M. Cagalj, S. Ganeriwal, I. Aad, and J.-P. Hubaux. On selfish behavior in CSMA/CA networks. In *Proc. of IEEE Infocom*, Mar. 2005.

[3] IEEE Computer Society LAN MAN Standards Committee. *IEEE 802.11: Wireless LAN Medium Access Control and Physical Layer Specifications*, Aug., 1999.

[4] Y. Hu and A. Perrig. A survey of secure wireless ad hoc routing. *IEEE Security & Privacy, special issue on Making Wireless Work*, pages 28–39, 2004.

[5] In-stat. http://www.in-stat.com/catalog/Wcatalogue.asp?id=167.

[6] Revenue from wireless hotspots. http://blogs.zdnet.com/ITFacts/index.php?blogthis=1&p=9319.

[7] D. Kotz and K. Essien. Analysis of a campus-wide wireless network. In *Proc. of ACM MOBICOM*, Sept. 2002.

[8] A. Kuzmanovic and E. Knightly. Low-rate TCP-targeted denial of service attacks (the shrew vs. the mice and elephants). In *Proc. of ACM SIGCOMM*, Aug. 2003.

[9] P. Kyasanur and N. Vaidya. Detection and handling of MAC layer misbehavior in wireless networks. In *IEEE Transactions on Mobile Computing*, Apr. 2004.

[10] The network simulator – ns-2. http://www.isi.edu/nsnam/ns/.

[11] M. Raya, J. P. Hubaux, and I. Aad. DOMINO: A system to detect greedy behavior in IEEE 802.11 hotspots. In *Proc. of MobiSys*, Sept. 2004.

[12] S. Savage, N. Cardwell, D. Wetherall, and T. Anderson. TCP congestion control with a misbehaving receiver. *ACM Computer Communications Review*, Oct. 1999.

[13] D. Tang. Analysis of a local-area wireless network. In *Proc. of MOBICOM*, Sept. 2000.

[14] W. Xu, W. Trappe, Y. Zhang, and T. Wood. The feasibility of launching and detecting jamming attacks in wireless networks. In *Proc. of ACM MobiHoc*, May 2005.

Emergent Structure in Unstructured Epidemic Multicast*

Nuno Carvalho
U. Minho

José Pereira
U. Minho

Rui Oliveira
U. Minho

Luís Rodrigues
U. Lisboa

Abstract

In epidemic or gossip-based multicast protocols, each node simply relays each message to some random neighbors, such that all destinations receive it at least once with high probability. In sharp contrast, structured multicast protocols explicitly build and use a spanning tree to take advantage of efficient paths, and aim at having each message received exactly once. Unfortunately, when failures occur, the tree must be rebuilt. Gossiping thus provides simplicity and resilience at the expense of performance and resource efficiency.

In this paper we propose a novel technique that exploits knowledge about the environment to schedule payload transmission when gossiping. The resulting protocol retains the desirable qualities of gossip, but approximates the performance of structured multicast. In some sense, instead of imposing structure by construction, we let it emerge from the operation of the gossip protocol. Experimental evaluation shows that this approach is effective even when knowledge about the environment is only approximate.

1. Introduction

Epidemic multicast protocols, also known as probabilistic or gossip-based, operate by having each node relay every message to a set of neighbors selected at random [2, 5, 16, 13]. The procedure is repeated for a number of rounds such that the message is delivered to all destinations with high probability. As neighbors are uniform randomly chosen, the load is balanced among all nodes: Over time, all nodes send and receive approximately the same number of messages. This fails to take advantage of nodes and links with higher capacity. In addition, a large number of redundant message transmissions happen, leading to a poor latency/bandwidth tradeoff.

In sharp contrast, structured multicast protocols work by explicitly building a dissemination structure according to predefined efficiency criteria [8, 3, 19, 18, 23], and then

use it to convey multiple messages. Therefore, nodes with higher capacity can offer a bigger contribution to the global dissemination effort by having larger degrees or being assigned closer to the root of the tree. Nodes in the leaves of the tree are not required to contribute to the message dissemination effort.

The tradeoff between gossip and structured approaches is clear: By avoiding the need to build and maintain a spanning tree, epidemic multicast provides extreme simplicity. The resulting evenly balanced load is a key factor to achieve resilience and scalability. On the other hand, structured multicast provides better resource usage (and thus higher performance when the network is stable) by optimizing the cost of the spanning tree according to efficiency criteria such as network bandwidth and latency. However, structured approaches have to deal with the complexity of rebuilding the tree when faults or network reconfiguration occurs.

In this paper, we aim at combining the best of both approaches, namely, the simplicity, scalability and resilience of epidemic multicast with the performance of structured multicast. The challenge is to incorporate efficiency criteria in a gossip protocol without affecting its probabilistic properties. Our current proposal builds on the ideas first introduced in [15], which point out that the combination of lazy and eager push gossip can promote an asymmetrical resource usage in a gossip protocol. By combining this technique with knowledge about the environment, one can make transmissions that lead to message deliveries to use preferably the nodes and links that match a target efficiency criteria. In some sense, instead of imposing a multicast structure by construction, we let this structure to emerge probabilistically from the operation of the gossip protocol, without altering the original gossip pattern.

The main contributions of the paper are the following: *(i)* it proposes a technique to exploit knowledge about the network topology to obtain an emergent structure that results in actual performance improvements in the data dissemination process, and *(ii)* it offers an extensive evaluation of the proposed technique in a realistic network setting.

The rest of this paper is structured as follows. Section 2 presents the rationale underlying our proposal. Section 3

*This work was partially supported by project "P-SON: Probabilistically Structured Overlay Networks" (POS_C/EIA/60941/2004).

proposes an epidemic multicast protocol that enables emergent structure according to a configurable strategy module. Section 4 introduces several sample strategies. Section 5 presents the experimental environment, used in Section 6 to evaluate the approach. Section 7 compares our proposal with related work. Finally, Section 8 concludes the paper.

2. Overview

2.1. Background

Gossip-based multicast protocols are often based on an *eager push gossip* approach [5, 16, 13]: A gossip round is initiated by a node that has received a message, relaying it to a number of targets. This simple strategy has however a large impact on bandwidth used, as the fanout required for atomic delivery leads to multiple copies of each message being received by each destination.

A different tradeoff can be achieved by using a *lazy push* strategy, which defers the transmission of the payload. In detail, during a gossip round a node will send only an advertisement of the new message. Transmission of the payload is initiated only if the message is unknown by the recipient. This allows message payload to be transmitted once to each destination, at the expense of an additional round-trip. Lazy transmission has also an impact on the reliability, as the additional round-trip and resulting increased latency widens the window of vulnerability to network faults. The impact is however small for realistic omission rates and can be compensated by a slight increase in the fanout [15]. The net effect is still a much lower bandwidth usage.

In fact, one can mix both approaches in a single gossiping round [15], thus providing different latency/bandwidth tradeoffs depending on how many messages are eagerly transmitted.

2.2. Approach

The approach proposed in this paper stems from the observation that, in an eager push gossip protocol, paths leading to deliveries of each message implicitly build a random spanning tree. This tree is embedded in the underlying random overlay. If one knew beforehand which transmissions would lead to deliveries, one could use eager push gossip for those paths and lazy push gossip for all others. This would achieve exactly once transmission for each destination. Unfortunately, this is not possible, as one cannot predict which paths lead to delivery.

There is however one alternative strategy that is feasible: If one of the embedded trees is selected beforehand for eager push gossip, one increases the likelihood that this tree will lead to more deliveries. This happens because lazy

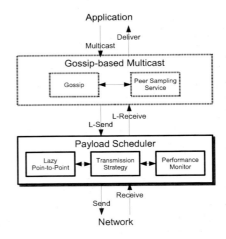

Figure 1. Protocol architecture overview.

push has additional latency, and paths that use it will be outran by paths that use solely eager push. If one assigns nodes and links with higher capacity to such tree, the performance of the protocol should approach that of a structured overlay. Note that by keeping redundant lazy transmissions, one retains the resilience of the gossip protocol. On the other hand, this strategy requires the explicit maintenance of a tree structure which imposes additional overhead and complexity.

Instead of selecting a single embedded tree, in this paper we aim at increasing the likelihood that implicitly created trees in a gossip protocol include nodes and links with higher capacity. Structure is therefore probabilistic: Nodes and links are selected with different probabilities for payload transmission. Therefore, structure emerges from the strategy used for scheduling message payloads in a combined eager/lazy push gossip protocol. The main challenge is thus to achieve emergent structure without global coordination, while at the same time obtaining a meaningful performance advantage.

3. Architecture

The architecture that we propose to implement our approach is depicted in Fig. 1. It uses an additional layer that is inserted below a pure eager push gossip protocol. This layer, called the Payload Scheduler, selects when to transmit the message payload (by using a combination of eager push and lazy push) in a transparent manner for the gossip protocol above. The Payload Scheduler layer can be decomposed into three separate components, also depicted in Fig. 1:

- The Lazy Point-to-Point module is in charge of intercepting the interaction between the gossip layer above

```
1   initially
2       K = ∅    /* known messages */

3   proc MULTICAST(d) do
4       FORWARD(MKID(), d, 0)

5   proc FORWARD(i, d, r) do
6       DELIVER(d)
7       K = K ∪ {i}
8       if r < t do
9           P = PEERSAMPLE(f)
10          for each p ∈ P do
11              L-SEND(i, d, r + 1, p)

12  upon L-RECEIVE(i, d, r, s) do
13      if i ∉ K then
14          FORWARD(i, d, r)
```

Figure 2. Basic gossip protocol.

and the transport protocol below. It queries the Transmission Strategy module to decide whether to send the payload immediately (in the case, the exchange is performed in pure eager push mode) or to delay the payload transmission until a request is received. As we will later describe, this module is also in charge of generating and replying to payload requests.

- The Transmission Strategy module is the core component of the Payload Scheduler. It defines the criteria that is used to defer payload transmission at the sender and, at the receiver, when to request a transmission. Note that different strategies may be implemented, according to the criteria that one wants to optimize. We recall that, with each strategy, we aim at having the combined protocol (push gossip plus scheduler) to approximate the behavior of a structured multicast approach.

- The last component of the Payload Scheduler is a Performance Monitor. The role of the performance monitor is to extract, in run-time, performance data about the operation of the system, for instance, by computing round-trip delays. The performance data is used to feed the Transmission Strategy module.

In the remainder of this section, we will describe each component of our architecture in detail as well as all interfaces among them.

3.1. Gossip Protocol Layer

As noted before, a fundamental aspect of our approach is that the Payload Scheduler can operate in a manner that is transparent for the operation of the push gossip protocol that lies above. Therefore, our approach can be applied to different gossip protocols, such as [5, 13, 16].

Nevertheless, for self containment, we depict in Fig. 2 a typical push gossip protocol. This implementation assumes the availability of a peer sampling service [11] providing an uniform sample of f other nodes with the PEERSAMPLE(f) primitive. It assumes also an unreliable point-to-point communication service, such that a message m can be sent to a node p using the L-SEND(m, p) primitive. A message m is received from a peer p by handling the L-RECEIVE(m, p) up-call. The gossip protocol maintains a set K of known messages (line 2), initially empty. This set is used to detect and eliminate duplicates. In detail, the algorithm works as follows.

- The application calls procedure MULTICAST(d) to multicast a message with payload d (line 3). This simply generates an unique identifier and forwards it (line 4). The identifier chosen must be unique with high probability, as conflicts will cause deliveries to be omitted. A simple way to implement this is to generate a random bit-string with sufficient length.

- Received messages are processed in a similar manner (line 12), with the difference that it is necessary to check for and discard duplicates using the set of known identifiers K (line 13) before proceeding.

- The forwarding procedure FORWARD(i, d, r) (line 5) uses the message identifier i, the payload d and the number of times, or rounds, the message has already been relayed r, which is initially 0. It starts by delivering the payload locally using the DELIVER(d) up-call. Then the message identifier is added to the set of previously known messages K (line 7). This avoids multiple deliveries, as described before. Actual forwarding occurs only if the message has been forwarded less than t times (line 8) [13] and consists in querying the peer sampling service to obtain a set of f target nodes and then sending the message, as in lines 9 and 11. Constants t and f are the usual gossip configuration parameters [6].

For simplicity, we do not show how identifiers are removed from set K, preventing it from growing indefinitely. This problem has been studied before, and efficient solutions exist ensuring with high probability that no active messages are prematurely garbage collected [5, 13].

3.2. Payload Scheduler Layer

The Lazy Point-to-Point module is the entry point to the Payload Scheduler. It controls the transmission of message payload using a simple negative acknowledgment mechanism. The policy used for each individual message is obtained from the Transmission Strategy module using a pair of primitives:

```
15   initially
16      ∀i : C[i] = ⊥   /* cached data */
17      R = ∅      /* known messages */

18   Task 1:
19      proc L-SEND(i, d, r, p) do
20         if EAGER?(i, d, r, p) then
21            SEND(MSG(i, d, r, p)
22         else
23            C[i] = (d, r)
24            SEND(IHAVE(i), p)

25      upon RECEIVE(IHAVE(i), s) do
26         if i ∉ R then
27            QUEUE(i, s)

28      upon RECEIVE(MSG(i, d, r), s) do
29         if i ∉ R then
30            R = R ∪ {i}
31            CLEAR(i)
32            L-RECEIVE(i, d, r, s)

33      upon RECEIVE(IWANT(i), s) do
34         (d, r) = C[i]
35         SEND(MSG(i, d, r), p)

36   Task 2:
37      forever do
38         (i, s) = SCHEDULENEXT()
39         SEND(IWANT(i), s)
```

Figure 3. Point-to-point communication.

- EAGER?(i, d, r, p) is used to determine if payload d for message with identification i on round r should be immediately sent to peer p. Note that if the method always returns true the protocol operates on pure eager push mode. If the method always returns false, the protocol operates on pure lazy push mode.

- (i, s) = SCHEDULENEXT() blocks until it is the time for some message i to be requested from a source s. From the correctness point of view, any schedule is safe as long as it eventually schedules all lazy requests that have been queued.

The Lazy Point-to-Point module also informs the Transmission Strategy of known sources for each message and when payload has been received using the following primitives:

- QUEUE(i, s) queues a message identifier i to be requested from source node s. The Transmission Strategy module must keep an internal queue of known sources for each message identifier in order to schedule them eventually, unless payload is received first.

- CLEAR(i) clears all requests on message i. Note also that a queue eventually clears itself as requests on all known sources for a given message identifier i are scheduled.

The Lazy Point-to-Point module is depicted in Fig. 3 and uses two separate tasks. Task 1 is responsible for processing transmission requests from the gossip layer and message deliveries from the transport layer. Task 2 runs in background, and performs requests for messages that are known to exists but whose payload has not been received yet. Furthermore, the module maintains the following data structures: a set R of messages whose payload has been received and; a map C, holding the payload and round number for the message (if known).

The module operates as follows. When a message is sent (line 19), the Transmission Strategy module is queried to test if the message should be immediately sent (line 21). If not, an advertisement without the payload is sent instead (line 24). Upon receiving a message advertisement for an unknown message, the Transmission Strategy module is notified (line 27). Upon receiving full message payload, the strategy module is informed (line 31) and it is handed over to the gossip layer (line 32).

Task 2 executes the following loop. The Transmission Strategy module is invoked to select a message to be requested and a node to request the message from (pair (i, s) in line 38). This invocation blocks until a request is scheduled to be sent by the Transmission Strategy module. A request is then sent (line 39). Finally, when a node receives a request (line 33) it looks it up in the cache and transmits the payload (line 35). Note that a retransmission request can only be received as a consequence of a previous advertisement and thus the message is guaranteed to be locally known.

For simplicity, we again do not show how cached identifiers and payloads are removed from C and R, preventing them from growing indefinitely. This is however similar to the management of set K, discussed in the previous section, and thus the same techniques apply.

Finally, the goal of the performance monitor module is to measure relevant performance metrics of the participant nodes and to make this information available to the strategy in an abstract manner. The exported interface of this module is simply METRIC(p), that returns a current metric for a given peer p. This metric is used by the Transmission Strategy to select whether to immediately schedule an eager transmission or when to request lazy transmission from each source. Note that, the performance monitor module may be required to exchange messages with its peers (for instance, to measure roundtrip delays).

The next section discusses different implementations of the Transmission Strategy and of the Performance Monitor modules that aim at achieving different dissemination structures.

4. Strategies and Monitors

The definition of a Transmission Strategy has two main objectives: *(i)* avoid as much as possible the redundant transmission of the same payload to any given target node; and *(ii)* decrease the latency of message delivery. These goals are however conflicting. The first goal can be achieved by using a lazy push strategy in all peer exchanges. Since nodes only gossip IHAVE commands, the recipient can request the payload only once. Unfortunately, each lazy push exchange adds one additional roundtrip to the final delivery latency. On the other hand, a pure eager push strategy minimizes latency at the cost of adding a significant amount of redundancy.

The key to obtaining a better latency/bandwidth tradeoff is thus to select nodes and links that should be preferred in a decentralized fashion. We start however by proposing a couple of strategies that do not take advantage of knowledge about the environment for use as a baseline.

4.1. Strategies

Flat This strategy is defined as EAGER?(i, d, r, p) returning true with some probability π or false with probability $1 - \pi$. When $\pi = 1$, this defaults to a fully eager push gossip. With $\pi = 0$, it provides pure lazy push gossip. In between, it provides different latency/bandwidth tradeoffs, as a different share of gossip messages is handled in a lazy fashion.

When a lazy strategy is used (and IHAVE messages are sent), we need also to consider how retransmissions are scheduled within SCHEDULENEXT() by receivers. In the Flat strategy, the first retransmission request is scheduled immediately when queued, which means that an IWANT message is issued immediately upon receiving an IHAVE advertisement. Further requests are done periodically every T, while sources are known.

Time T is an estimate of maximum end-to-end latency. This avoids issuing explicit transmission requests until all eager transmissions have been performed, thus optimizing bandwidth. Note that, unless there is a network omission or an extreme transmission delay, there is usually no need to issue a second request. Thus the value of T has no practical impact in the final average latency, and can be set only approximately.

Time-To-Live (TTL) This strategy uses eager push until some round u and is thus defined as EAGER?(i, d, r, p) returning true iff $r < u$. When $u > t$, this defaults to common eager push gossip. With $u = 0$, it provides pure lazy push gossip. In between, it provides different latency/bandwidth tradeoffs, as a different share of gossip messages is handled

in a lazy fashion. SCHEDULEDNEXT() is defined exactly as in the Flat strategy.

We propose this because it is intuitively useful: During the first rounds, the likelihood of a node being targeted by more than one copy of the payload is small and thus there is no point in using lazy push.

Radius This strategy is defined as EAGER?(i, d, r, p) returning true iff METRIC$(p) < \rho$, for some constant radius ρ and some metric METRIC(p) provided by a Performance Monitor module for node p. SCHEDULEDNEXT() delays the first retransmission by some time T_0 that is an estimate of the latency to nodes within radius ρ in the given metric. Further retransmissions are scheduled periodically with period T, as in the Flat strategy. However, if multiple sources are known, the nearest neighbor (according to the Performance Monitor) is selected.

This follows the intuition of gossiping first with close nodes to minimize hop latency. The expected emergent structure should approximate a mesh structure, with most of payload being carried by links between neighboring nodes.

Ranked This strategy aims at achieving a hubs-and-spokes structure by selecting a set of *best nodes* to serve as hubs, bearing most of the load. Therefore, at some node q, EAGER?(i, d, r, p) returns true iff either q or p are considered to be best nodes, meaning that eager push is used whenever a best node is involved. SCHEDULEDNEXT() is defined exactly as in the Flat strategy.

Although some nodes can be explicitly configured as *best nodes*, for instance, by an Internet Service Provider (ISP) that wants to improve performance to local users, a ranking can also be computed using local Performance Monitors and a gossip based sorting protocol [9]. As shown later, this is greatly eased by the fact that the protocol still works even if ranking is approximate.

4.2 Monitors

Latency Monitor This monitor measures the latency to all neighbor nodes. Real-time monitoring of latency has been addressed a number of times, in fact, every TCP/IP connection implicitly estimates round-trip time in order to perform congestion control [7]. This estimate can be retrieved by applications and used for other purposes.

Distance Monitor This monitor measures geographical distance to all neighbor nodes. This is useful mostly for demonstration purposes, as it allows us to plot network usage graphs such that emergent structure is understandable by the reader. Otherwise, it is not useful in optimizing network parameters.

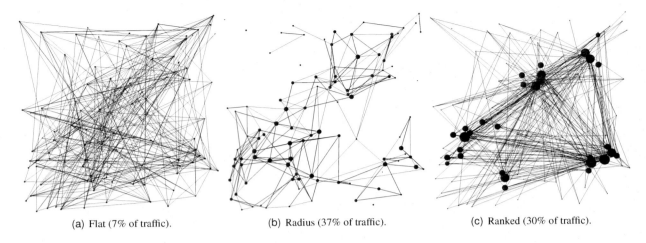

(a) Flat (7% of traffic). (b) Radius (37% of traffic). (c) Ranked (30% of traffic).

Figure 4. Emergent structure defined by the top 5% most used connections.

4.3. Approximation and Noise

When evaluating the proposed protocol on the ModelNet emulated network as described in the following sections, the proposed strategies and monitors are simplified by relying on global knowledge of the network that is extracted directly from the model file. This has two goals: First, it allows us to separate the performance of the the proposed strategy from the performance of the monitor. Second, it allows us to arbitrarily introduce noise in Transmission Strategy in order to evaluate its robustness.

In detail, we intercept each query to EAGER? and use a temporary variable v as follows. If EAGER? would return true, we set $v = 1.0$; if it would return false we set $v = 0.0$. We then compute $v' = c+(v-c)(1-o)$. We then generating a random boolean with probability v' of being true as the outcome of the query. Constant c is set such that the overall probability of EAGER? returning true is unchanged, thus leading to the same amount of eager transmissions although scheduled in different occasions.

When noise ratio $o = 0.0$, the original result is unchanged. When noise ratio $o = 1.0$, any Transmission Strategy defaults to Flat with $\pi = c$, thus completely erasing structure. In between, the Transmission Strategy produces an increasingly blurred structure.

5. Experimental Environment

5.1. Network Emulation

Experimental evaluation of the proposed protocol is done using the ModelNet large-scale emulation infrastructure [21] with a realistic network model generated by Inet-3.0 [22]. In detail, ModelNet allows a large number of virtual nodes running unmodified programs to be configured in a smaller number of physical nodes in a LAN. Traffic is routed through emulator nodes thus applying delay, bandwidth, and loss as specified in the network model. Inet-3.0 generates realistic Autonomous System level network topologies using a transit-stub model.

ModelNet is deployed in a cluster of 5 workstations connected by switched 100Mbps Ethernet. Each workstation has a 2.4GHz Intel Celeron CPU, 512MB RAM, and a RealTek Ethernet controller. When hosting virtual nodes, they run Linux kernel 2.6.14 and IBM Java2 1.5 runtime. When running as an emulator, FreeBSD 4.11 is used.

The network model is generated using Inet-3.0 default of 3037 network nodes. Link latency is assigned by ModelNet according to pseudo-geographical distance. Client nodes are assigned to distinct stub nodes, also with the default 1 ms client-stub latency. A typical network graph has the following properties: average hop distance between client nodes is 5.54, with 74.28% of nodes within 5 and 6 hops; average end-to-end latency of 49.83 ms, with 50% of nodes within 39 ms and 60 ms.

5.2. Implementation and Configuration

The proposed protocol was implemented by modifying an open source and lightweight implementation of the NeEM protocol [16] that uses the java.nio API for scalability and performance [20]. Briefly, NeEM uses TCP/IP connections between nodes in order to avoid network congestion. When a connection blocks, messages are buffered in user space, which then uses a custom purging strategy to improve reliability. The result is a virtual connection-less layer that provides improved guarantees for gossiping.

This implementation was selected as NeEM 0.5 already supports eager and lazy push, although the later is selected only based on a message size and age threshold. The change required was to remove the hard-coded push strategy and insert the scheduler layer. Message identifiers are probabilistically unique 128 bit strings.

The protocol was configured with gossip fanout of 11 and overlay fanout of 15. With 200 nodes, these correspond to a probability 0.995 of atomic delivery with 1% messages dropped, and a probability of 0.999 of connectedness when 15% of nodes fail[6]. A retransmission period of 400 ms was used, which is the minimal that results in approximately 1 payload received by each destination when using a fully lazy push strategy.

5.3. Traffic and Measurements

During each experiment, 400 messages are multicast, each carrying 256 bytes of application level payload. To each of them, a NeEM header of 24 bytes is added, besides TCP/IP overhead. Messages are multicast by virtual nodes in a round-robin fashion, with an uniform random interval with 500 ms average. All messages multicast and delivered are logged for later processing. Namely, end-to-end latency can be measured when source and destination share the same physical node, and thus a common clock. Payload transmissions on each link are also recorded separately.

Results presented in the following sections used 25 virtual nodes on each workstation, thus obtaining 100 virtual nodes. The reason for this limitation is that an epidemic multicast protocol produces a bursty load, in particular when using eager push gossip: Network and CPU load occurs only instants after each message is multicast. Using a larger number of virtual nodes was observed to induce additional latency which would falsify results. The configurations that result in lower bandwidth consumption, which are the key results of this paper, were also simulated with 200 virtual nodes.

5.4. Statistics

Consider the following statistics of each experiment with 100 virtual nodes using an eager push strategy: 40000 messages delivered, 440000 individual packets transmitted. This amounts to 2200 Kpkts/s and thus approximately 6 MBps. As the overlay evolves, TCP/IP connections are created and tear down. During each run, approximately 550 simultaneous and 15000 different connections are used. The experiments presented in the next sections, when automated, take almost 7 hours to run. The total amount of resulting logs is 1Gb, that has then to be processed and rendered in plots.

Care was taken to consider variance of each measure taken. When in the following sections we affirm that a performance difference is relevant, this was confirmed by checking that confidence intervals with 95% certainty do not intersect. In fact, the large number of samples used are sufficient to make such intervals very narrow.

6. Experimental Results

6.1. Pseudo-Geographical

To strengthen the intuition, we start by evaluating the impact of the proposed strategies with an oracle that considers pseudo-geographical position of nodes, as generated by Inet-3.0. Although this cannot be used to assess the performance of the protocol, as geometrical distance does not directly map to end-to-end distance, it allows the resulting emergent structure to be plotted and understood.

Fig. 4 shows the result of running 100 node configurations with different strategies and then selecting the top 5% connections with highest throughput. The size of each red circle is proportional to the amount of payload transmitted by the node. Note that each connection is used for a brief period of time, as the membership management algorithm periodically shuffles peers with neighbors. This means that connections shown may have not existed simultaneously.

As a baseline, Fig. 4(a) shows an eager push configuration, where no structure is apparent. A confirmation of this is given by the fact that the top 5% connections account for only 7% of all traffic, i.e. payload transmissions are evenly spread across all connections. In sharp contrast, Fig. 4(b) shows an obvious emergent mesh structure as a result of the Radius strategy, in which the 5% connections account for 37% of all payload transmissions. Finally, Fig. 4(c) shows a sub-set of nodes emerging as super-nodes, accounting for a large share of links and also transmitting a higher number of payloads. Again, the emergent structure is confirmed by the fact that 5% of the connections account for 30% of total payloads transmitted.

6.2. Latency vs Bandwidth

The primary evaluation criterion is the latency/bandwidth tradeoff provided by each configuration. Assuming an eager push protocol, one expects that each payload is approximately transmitted f times for each delivery. This makes gossip protocols notorious for wasted bandwidth. On the other hand, assuming that one uses a lazy push approach, one expects on average a single payload transmitted for each messages delivery at the expense of an additional round-trip, thus impacting latency.

The measurements of strategy Flat in Fig. 5(a) illustrate this tradeoff. Latency can be improved from 480 ms down to 227 ms by increasing parameter π. This does however increase the number of payloads transmitted for each message delivered from the optimal 1 up to 11, the fanout value used.

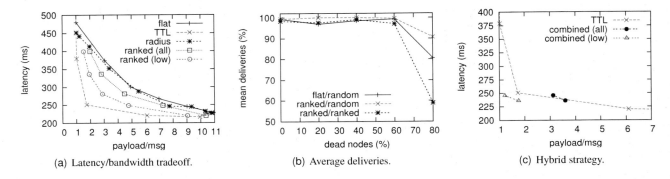

(a) Latency/bandwidth tradeoff.　　　(b) Average deliveries.　　　(c) Hybrid strategy.

Figure 5. Performance.

A much better tradeoff can be obtained with the TTL strategy, which achieves 250 ms with 1.7 transmitions of payload for each message delivered.

Considering that a large majority of links is between 39 ms and 60 ms (with mean close to 50 ms), and that each message is delivered on the average after being gossiped 4.5 times, it is not realistic to expect that link selection provides an improvement beyond a 45 ms. It is therefore interesting to observe that the Ranked strategy does indeed improve average latency when compared to the Flat strategy that produces a similar amount of traffic. On the other hand, the Radius strategy does not produce such improvement. This is explained by noting that the reduced round latency is compensated by an average larger number of rounds required.

6.3. Reliability

We are interested in confirming that the proposed approach does not impact reliability. We simulate failed nodes by silencing them with firewall rules after letting them join the overlay and warm up, *i.e.* immediately before starting to log message deliveries.

As a baseline in Fig. 5(b), we fail an increasing number of nodes selected at random while using a pure eager push configuration of the protocol. As expected, when no node fails one observes perfect atomic delivery of all messages. With 20% or more nodes failing, one observes that atomic delivery does not always happen, although as expected there is a large number of nodes that deliver each message. Finally, with more than 80% of nodes failing, the protocol breaks down as an arbitrary number of nodes get disconnected from the overlay.

Then we do the same with the Ranked strategy. We run experiments twice: First, we select failed nodes at random. Then we select the nodes with the best ranks, precisely those that are contributing more to the dissemination effort. As can be observed also in Fig. 5(b), there is no noticeable impact in reliability in both situations. With more that 80% of nodes failing, although there is an apparent difference, the

observed high variance makes it impossible to conclude on a which configuration is the best.

6.4. Hybrid Strategy

A major advantage of the proposed approach is that one can easily try new strategies without endangering the correctness of the protocol. Namely, this can be used to try complex heuristics. We do this now by trying to leverage the contribution of TTL, Radius, and Ranked in a single hybrid strategy. In detail, EAGER?(i, d, r, p) returns true iff one of the involved nodes is considered a best node; or if METRIC$(p) < 2\rho$ when $r < u$; or METRIC$(p) < \rho$ otherwise. i.e. radius shrinks with increasing round number. Parameters ρ and u are the same as in Radius and TTL strategies. SCHEDULEDNEXT$()$ is defined exactly as in the Radius strategy.

The result is shown in Fig. 5(c), which provides a new interesting tradeoff for regular nodes: Latency can be reduced from 379 ms to 245 ms while increasing average payload to 80% of nodes from 1.01 to 1.20 payload transmissions for each message (see "combined (low)" in Fig. 5(c)). This is achieved at the expense of a contribution of 10.77 payload/message by the remaining 20% (overall average of 3.11). Eager gossip would require an overall average of 11 payload/message to achieve 227 ms.

6.5. Noise

Finally, we evaluate the protocol when the accuracy of the performance monitoring module deteriorates. As described in Section 4.3, we do this in a way that carefully preserves the amount of data transmitted. This can be confirmed in Fig. 6(a). Note however that the amount of data transmitted by regular nodes (i.e. other than the *best nodes*) increases with the amount of noise until it converges with the overall average.

Fig. 6(b) shows the impact of degrading structure in latency of the Ranked strategy, as Radius does not provide

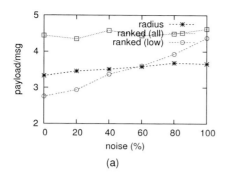 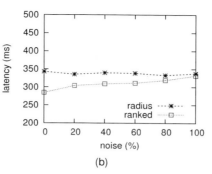 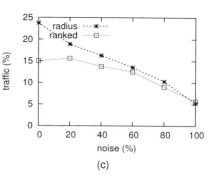

(a) (b) (c)

Figure 6. Degradation of structure.

a latency advantage. Finally, Fig. 6(c) uses the amount of data conveyed by the top 5% links as a measure of emergent structure. It can be observed that it converges to the expected 5% of traffic as noise increases, thus showing that structure is increasingly blurred.

7. Related Work

Reliable multicast in large scale networks has been addressed a number of times using a different approaches. Some proposals build on IP multicast, and have thus been hard to deploy [8]. More recently, a number of application-level multicast protocols have been proposed, namely, by building on scalable structured overlay networks [3, 19, 18, 23]. It would be interesting to compare the performance of such protocols with the proposed approach, as well as the amount of code required to implement them. Nevertheless, by relying on explicit garbage collection to ensure reliability, these approaches should be vulnerable to the throughput stability problem [1].

The first reliable multicast protocol to exploit gossiping in order to provide simultaneously atomic delivery and throughput stability is Bimodal Multicast [2]. This protocol does however rely on an optimistic dissemination phase to avoid a large number of redundant transmissions. This makes it hard to scale it to wide area networks, as the low adoption of IP multicast in WAN has shown.

It has also been proposed that instead of using a random overlay, one can build a mesh according to some configurable metric using gossiping itself [14]. In fact, it has been pointed out a number of different structures can be built using gossiping [10]. These proposals share with ours the requirement of a performance monitor, but do not preserve the random nature of an unstructured overlay which is key to reliability [11]. Similar techniques can however be used to derive knowledge about the environment for use by the Transmission Strategy module.

Lazy push gossip can also be confused with pull gossip, as in both cases payload is transmitted only upon request.

Pull gossip is however fundamentally different as it issues generic requests to a random sub-set of nodes, which might or not have new data, while lazy push gossip requests specific data items only from peers that have previously advertised them. In fact, unless performed lazily, pull gossip will result in multiple payload transmissions to the same destination as much as eager push gossip. A combination of eager push and eager pull gossip has been proposed as a means to reduce propagation latency [12]. A combination of lazy pull gossip and lazy push gossip has been proposed in the CREW protocol for fast file download by a large number of destinations [4], where the latency of lazy gossip is hidden by concurrently requesting multiple chunks of a large file.

Adaptation to heterogeneous network resources can also be done by adjusting node fanout according to available bandwidth [17, 4] and by biasing choices during gossiping and overlay maintenance [17]. Although in the current paper we have always used unmodified gossip to demonstrate viability, combining both approach should allow further improvements.

8. Conclusions

Epidemic multicast protocols are notorious for being resilient and scalable, but also for generating a large number of redundant message transmissions. In this paper, we have shown that by carefully scheduling the transmission of payload in a combined eager/lazy push gossip protocol, one can reduce the bandwidth required without otherwise impacting performance or reliability. Namely, we propose an heuristic configuration that achieves close to optimum bandwidth and latency in a large majority of participants.

Most interestingly, when we examine the resources used, we observe that those nodes and links on which most payload transmissions are scheduled emerge as a probabilistic structure embedded in an otherwise unstructured overlay. This shows that one can approximate the performance advantages of structured overlays while at the same time preserving the simplicity, resilience and scalability of gossip.

Furthermore, our evaluation shows that the resulting performance degrades gracefully as the knowledge about the environment becomes less accurate, thus demonstrating the robustness of the approach. In fact, the worst case scenario in which such knowledge is entirely random, the performance is bounded by the original pure lazy or eager push protocols.

Note also that, although best results are achieved when all nodes cooperate on a single strategy, correctness is ensured regardless of the strategy used by each peer. This makes the proposed approach a promising base for building large scale adaptive protocols, given that its operation does not require tight global coordination.

Acknowledgments

The authors thank Bruno Matos at the U. Minho for his work on setting up the experimental environment.

References

[1] K. Birman. A review of experiences with reliable multicast. *Software Practice and Experience*, 29(9), July 1999.

[2] K. Birman, M. Hayden, O. Ozkasap, Z. Xiao, M. Budiu, and Y. Minsky. Bimodal multicast. *ACM Trans. Computer Systems*, 17(2), May 1999.

[3] Y. Chu, S. Rao, S. Seshan, and H. Zhang. A case for end system multicast. *IEEE Journal on Selected Areas in Communication (JSAC)*, 20(8), 2002.

[4] M. Deshpande, B. Xing, I. Lazardis, B. Hore, N. Venkatasubramanian, and S. Mehrotra. CREW: A gossip-based flash-dissemination system. In *Intl. Conf. Distributed Computing Systems (ICDCS)*, 2006.

[5] P. Eugster, R. Guerraoui, S. Handrukande, A.-M. Kermarrec, and P. Kouznetsov. Lightweight probabilistic broadcast. In *Proc. IEEE Intl. Conf. Dependable Systems and Networks (DSN)*, 2001.

[6] P. Eugster, R. Guerraoui, A.-M. Kermarrec, and L. Massoulie. From epidemics to distributed computing. *IEEE Computer*, May 2004.

[7] S. Floyd and K. Fall. Promoting the use of end-to-end congestion control in the Internet. *IEEE/ACM Trans. Networking*, 7(4), Aug. 1999.

[8] S. Floyd, V. Jacobson, C. Liu, S. McCanne, and L. Zhang. A reliable multicast framework for light-weight sessions and application level framing. *IEEE/ACM Transactions on Networking*, 5, Dec. 1997.

[9] M. Jelasity. A case study on gossip beyond gossip: Sorting. Ws. on Gossip Based Computer Networking, Lorent Center, Leiden, 2006.

[10] M. Jelasity and O. Babaoglu. T-Man: Gossip-based overlay topology management. In *Proc. 3rd Intl. Ws. Engineering Self-Organising Applications (ESOA'05)*. Springer-Verlag, 2005.

[11] M. Jelasity, R. Guerraoui, A.-M. Kermarrec, and M. van Steen. The peer sampling service: Experimental evaluation of unstructured gossip-based implementations. In *Proc. 5th ACM/IFIP/USENIX Intl. Conf. Middleware*, 2004.

[12] R. Karp, C. Schindelhauer, S. Shenker, and B. Vocking. Randomized rumor spreading. In *IEEE Symp. Foundations of Computer Science*, 2000.

[13] B. Koldehofe. Buffer management in probabilistic peer-to-peer communication protocols. In *Proc. IEEE Symp. Reliable Distributed Systems (SRDS)*, 2003.

[14] L. Massoulié, A.-M. Kermarrec, and A. Ganesh. Network awareness and failure resilience in self-organising overlay networks. In *Proc. IEEE Symp. Reliable Distributed Systems (SRDS'03)*, 2003.

[15] J. Pereira, R. Oliveira, and L. Rodrigues. Efficient epidemic multicast in heterogeneous networks. In *OTM Workshops*, number 4278 in Lecture Notes in Computer Science, 2006.

[16] J. Pereira, L. Rodrigues, M. J. Monteiro, R. Oliveira, and A.-M. Kermarrec. NeEM: Network-friendly epidemic multicast. In *Proc. IEEE Symp. Reliable Distributed Systems (SRDS)*, 2003.

[17] J. Pereira, L. Rodrigues, A. Pinto, and R. Oliveira. Low-latency probabilistic broadcast in wide area networks. In *Proc. IEEE Symp. Reliable Distributed Systems (SRDS'04)*, Oct. 2004.

[18] S. Ratnasamy, M. Handley, R. Karp, and S. Shenker. Application-level multicast using content-addressable networks. In *NGC '01: Proceedings of the Third International COST264 Workshop on Networked Group Communication*, 2001.

[19] A. Rowstron, A.-M. Kermarrec, M. Castro, and P. Druschel. SCRIBE: The design of a large-scale event notification infrastructure. In *NGC '01: Proceedings of the Third International COST264 Workshop on Networked Group Communication*. Springer-Verlag, 2001.

[20] P. Santos and J. Pereira. NeEM version 0.5. http://neem.sf.net, 2006.

[21] A. Vahdat, K. Yocum, K. Walsh, P. Mahadevan, D. Kostic, J. Chase, and D. Becker. Scalability and accuracy in a large-scale network emulator. In *Proceedings of 5th Symposium on Operating Systems Design and Implementation (OSDI)*, 2002.

[22] J. Winick and S. Jamin. Inet-3.0: Internet topology generator. Technical Report CSE-TR-456-02, University of Michigan, 2002.

[23] S. Zhuang, B. Zhao, A. Joseph, R. Katz, and J. Kubiatowicz. Bayeux: An architecture for scalable and fault-tolerant wide-area data dissemination. In *Proceedings of the Eleventh International Workshop on Network and Operating System Support for Digital Audio and Video*, 2001.

The Case for FEC-based Reliable Multicast in Wireless Mesh Networks

Dimitrios Koutsonikolas   Y. Charlie Hu
School of Electrical and Computer Engineering
Center for Wireless Systems and Applications
Purdue University, West Lafayette, IN 47907
{dkoutson, ychu}@purdue.edu

Abstract

Many important applications in wireless mesh networks require reliable multicast communication. Previously, Forward Error Correction (FEC) techniques have been proved successful for providing reliability in the Internet, as they avoid the control packet implosion and scalability problems of ARQ-based protocols. In this paper, we examine if FEC can be equally efficient in wireless mesh networks. We implement four reliable schemes initially proposed for wired networks on top of ODMRP, a popular unreliable multicast routing protocol for wireless networks. We compare the performance of the four schemes using extensive simulations. Our results show that the use of pure FEC can offer significant improvements in terms of reliability, increasing PDR up to 100% in many cases, but it can be very inefficient regarding the number of redundant packets it transmits. Moreover, a carefully designed hybrid protocol, such as RMDP, can maintain the same high level of reliability while improving the efficiency by up to 38% compared to a pure FEC scheme.

1. Introduction

An important characteristic of many multicast applications in wireless mesh networks, such as software updates or audio/video file downloads, is that they require reliable packet delivery. Many reliable multicast protocols have been proposed for multihop wireless networks (see [1] for a survey). Some of them require feedback from all receivers, leading to the well-known problem of feedback implosion, which in turn leads to congestion. Others trade off throughput for reliability, which may be acceptable for MANET applications (e.g., search-and-rescue operations), but not for commercial mesh networks. Finally, gossip-based protocols try to mitigate these problems, however they cannot guarantee 100% reliability.

All the above protocols fall into the class of Automatic

Repeat reQuest (ARQ) schemes. Forward Error Correction (FEC) has been proposed as an alternative way to provide reliable multicast in the Internet [2]. With FEC the sender sends redundant encoded packets, and the receiver can reconstruct the original data even if it receives only a fraction of the encoded packets. Hence, no feedback from the receivers is required. A carefully selected amount of redundancy can result in less overhead compared to requests and retransmissions required in ARQ schemes. However, FEC itself cannot guarantee 100% reliability. Hence, hybrid ARQ-FEC schemes, e.g., [3, 4, 5, 6, 7, 8] have been proposed to combine the advantages of both techniques.

These protocols have been evaluated in the Internet, although some of them (e.g. [4]) are claimed to work also for wireless environments. However, the wireless environment is very different from that of the wired networks. (1) In the wired Internet the main reason for losses is congestion; in wireless networks the time variability of the wireless channel is equally important. Obstacles, interference, and multipath fading lead to bursty losses, possibly decreasing the effectiveness of FEC. (2) Most wireless multicast protocols use MAC-layer broadcast to exploit the Wireless Multicast Advantage [9]. However, the commonly used 802.11 MAC protocol does not incorporate any reliability mechanism for broadcast, as opposed to for unicast, where link-layer acknowledgments and retransmissions hide some losses from the upper layer and the RTS/CTS exchange reduces the number of losses due to collisions. (3) The asymmetry of wireless links does not provide any guarantee that requests for retransmissions sent by receivers will reach the source. (4) Bandwidth is a limited resource in wireless networks, and hence a solution that provides a large amount of redundancy may not be applicable. (5) Most wireless multicast protocols use a mesh to deliver data, as opposed to the tree-based approach in the Internet. This invalidates many of the assumptions made by Internet multicast protocol design. (6) Mesh-based multicast protocols can increase reliability, since there are usually more than one paths available from the source to each of the receivers. In summary, it is entirely not obvious that the FEC-based schemes designed for the Internet will work well in wireless networks.

The above discussion argues for the need for a detailed evaluation of the existing FEC and hybrid FEC-ARQ schemes in a multihop wireless mesh network. In this paper, we compare four different reliable multicast schemes, borrowed from the wired Internet, and examine how efficiently they perform under the special characteristics of a multihop wireless mesh network. One of the four schemes is a pure-FEC based scheme, where the source just sends some amount of redundancy and no feedback is required from the receivers. Two other schemes are hybrid FEC-ARQ protocols, namely NP [3] and RMDP [4]. Finally, for completeness, we include in our comparison a pure ARQ-based scheme, ReMHoc [10], which follows the design principles of Scalable Reliable Multicast (SRM) [11], one of the most popular ARQ-based protocols for the wired Internet. ODMRP (On Demand Multicast Routing Protocol) [12], a widely used multicast protocol for wireless networks, is used as the underlying routing protocol for the four schemes.

Our results show that (1) ARQ-based protocols have a very poor performance in wireless environments, (2) the use of pure FEC can offer significant improvements in terms of reliability, increasing the PDR up to 100% in many cases, but it can be very inefficient in terms of packet transmissions, (3) a carefully designed hybrid protocol, such as RMDP, can maintain the same high level of reliability and also improve the efficiency by up to 38% compared to a pure FEC scheme.

2. Overview of Reliable Multicast Protocols

In this section we describe an ARQ-based protocol, a pure FEC-based protocol, and two hybrid protocols. All four protocols are designed to be superimposed on an unreliable multicast routing protocol.

2.1. Automatic Repeat Request

We selected ReMHoc [10] as a representative ARQ protocol for our comparison. ReMHoc follows the design principles of SRM [11], perhaps the most popular ARQ protocol for reliable multicast in the wired Internet. ReMHoc is receiver-initiated; each receiver is responsible for detecting loss, by detecting gaps in the packet sequence numbers. When a packet loss is detected, the receiver schedules a *Request* packet, asking for retransmission of the lost packet. To prevent the implosion of control packets, receivers wait for a random period of time before sending a request for a lost packet. If they receive a request for the same packet from another receiver before their timer expires, they postpone their own request by resetting the timer. This backoff

is exponential in SRM, but linear in ReMHoc (proportional to the number of times this request has already been scheduled). This is because the loss rate is much higher in wireless networks than in the Internet, and hence faster response is required.

If the timer expires, a request is sent. But there is no guarantee that the request itself will not be lost, or that the repair packet will reach this receiver. Hence, the request timer is reset. In ReMHoc there is no upper bound on the number of times a request can be sent. However, we found that by allowing infinite number of requests, the control overhead grows too fast and the PDR is reduced. Therefore, we decided to allow up to five retransmissions of the same request. After requesting a packet for five times, a receiver considers this packet permanently lost and no further action is taken for that packet in the future.

Request packets are multicast toward the whole group. Any multicast member that receives a request packet and has the requested packet, sends a *Repair* packet and does not propagate the request further. Similarly as for the request packets, a node postpones its transmission of a repair packet for a random period of time, and cancels it if in this time it hears another node retransmitting the same repair packet. Each repair packet is multicast to the whole group, so that all nodes that are missing the same data packet can recover by using the same repair packet.

2.2. Forward Error Correction

The key idea behind Forward Error Correction (FEC) [2, 13] is that k data packets are encoded at the sender to produce n encoded packets, where $n > k$, in such a way that any subset of k encoded packets suffices to reconstruct the original k data packets. Such a code is called an (n, k) FEC code and allows the receiver to recover from up to $n - k$ packet losses in a group of n encoded packets. A code is called systematic when the first k encoded packets are the original data packets. Systematic codes are much cheaper to decode and they allow partial reconstruction of data even when fewer than k encoded packets are received. In a systematic code, the $n - k$ encoded packets that are different from the original k data packets are called *parities*.

In this paper we use a particular class of FEC codes, called Reed-Solomon (RS) codes, which uses Vandermonde matrices to encode the data packets. [2] gives a description and a software implementation of RS codes which is used by many protocols, such as [3, 4]. It works for packet sizes up to 1024 bytes, and the proposed values for k and n are 32 and 255, respectively.

2.3. NP

NP [3] is a hybrid ARQ-FEC based protocol that uses systematic Reed-Solomon codes. In NP the data file at the sender is separated in transmission groups (TGs), and an (n, k) RS code is applied to each TG. Hence, each TG consists of k original data packets and $n - k$ parities.

In NP the transmission of each TG proceeds in rounds, which can be interleaved with the transmission of packets from other transmission groups. In round i the k original data packets of group TG_i are sent. Then in each following round j, $j > i$, l_i^{j-1} new parity packets are sent, where l_i^{j-1} is the maximum number of packets lost by any of the receivers in round $j - 1$ for group TG_i, until all parities are exhausted.

In more detail, the sender transmits k data packets for TG_i followed by a POLL message POLL(i, k). With POLL(i, k), the sender informs the receivers that it has sent k packets for TG_i in the current round, and it asks for feedback about the missing packets of TG_i. Then it continues by sending the data packets for group TG_{i+1}. When it receives a NACK(i, l), it interrupts sending data packets of TG_m, $m > i$, it transmits l new parity packets for group TG_i, followed by a new POLL message POLL(i, l), and it then resumes transmission for TG_m.

For TG_i, each receiver stores data packets and parities until it collects at least k packets, which allow the reconstruction of TG_i. When a POLL(i, s) is received, NACK(i, l) is scheduled to be transmitted in the interval $[(s - l)T_s, (s - l + 1)T_s]$, where l is the number of packets still missing for TG_i. When the timer for NACK(i, l) expires, NACK(i, l) is multicast to the whole group. If a NACK(i, m) is received with $m \geq l$ before the timer for NACK(i, l) expires, the timer is canceled.

Assuming an ideal environment (no NACK or POLL packets are lost) and a tree structure, the slotting and dumping mechanism of the protocol assures that the sender will receive only one NACK after every data/parity-POLL round, which will contain the maximum number of packets needed by any receiver to reconstruct TG_i.

2.4. RMDP

Reliable Multicast data Distribution Protocol (RMDP) [4] is the only protocol claimed to work in wireless environments, although it was only evaluated on the MBone. In RMDP the data file at the sender is again divided into B transmission groups of k packets each, and an (n, k) RS code is applied to each group. However, differently from in NP, in RMDP the TGs are not transmitted sequentially, but their packets are interleaved as shown in Figure 3 of [4]. The sender maintains a counter c_{s_i} for each TG_i, counting the number of packets (original plus parities) it has to send for TG_i. Similarly, each receiver maintains a counter c_{r_i} for each TG_i, counting the number of packets received for TG_i. The protocol uses only one control message type: a request $R = [f, c_{r_i}, i]$ is sent by a receiver to inform the sender that it has received c_{r_i} packets of TG_i of the file f. The sender augments each data packet p_j of TG_i with a file identifier f, the total number of original data packets constituting TG_i k, the current value of c_{s_i}, and a sequence number j. We will denote such an augmented data packet as $S = [f, k, c_{s_i}, j, p_j]$.

Whenever the sender receives a message $R \, [f, c_{r_i}, i]$, it sets $c_{s_i} = max(c_{s_i}, D(k - c_{r_i}))$ for TG_i where D is the amount of redundant data sent unconditionally ($D = 1$ means that redundant packets are only sent on demand). If $c_{s_i} > 0$ the sender has to transmit c_{s_i} packets (original plus/or parities) for TG_i. For example, in the beginning, $c_{s_i} = 0$ at the sender, and $c_{r_i} = 0$ at each receiver, hence the sender will set $c_{s_i} = D \times k$ upon receiving a message R, i.e, it has to send $D \times k$ packets for each TG. As we mentioned before, the sender sends the packets using TG interleaving, i.e., every τ seconds it transmits a packet from a different TG, where τ is the interarrival packet time imposed by the application.

Each receiver sends initially an R message with $c_r = 0$, and then it schedules a new request every T_R seconds. If it receives a data message S, it cancels any pending request. Then if the number of packets received for at least one TG is less than k, it schedules a new request after T_C seconds for the TG with the largest number of missing packets.

The largest difference between NP and RMDP, other than TG interleaving, is the way the sender reacts to the reception of request messages (NACKs or R messages, respectively). In NP, the sender responds immediately to each NACK, by sending the amount of packets requested. In RMDP, the sender takes no immediate action, but it updates the appropriate counter c_{s_i}, increasing the amount of packets it has to transmit in the future for TG_i.

3. Evaluation

3.1. Methodology

ODMRP For our comparison we used On Demand Multicast Routing Protocol (ODMRP) [12] as the underlying multicast protocol, and implemented ReMHoc, FEC, NP, and RMDP on top of it. ODMRP is a best-effort multicast protocol originally designed for mobile ad hoc networks; receivers do not attempt to recover from packet losses.

To keep the route discovery control overhead low, ODMRP does not send explicit Join Query packets (for refreshing multicast routes), but periodically incorporates this information in the header of the data packets. This implies that not all data packets are equally important; the ones that carry Join Queries are more important than the rest, since if such a packet is lost, no route is built and subsequent data packets are also lost. This creates a conflict with FEC's principle, where *any k* out of *n* packets suffice to decode the original data. Hence in this paper, we decided to decouple the tree construction/maintenance from the data transmission and use explicit Join Query packets. The original ODMRP uses short route refresh intervals (the interval between two successive route discoveries) to maintain the connectivity in the presence of node mobility. In mesh networks, routers are stationary, and hence routes are much more stable than in MANETs. Therefore, we increased the values for route refresh interval and FG timeout (the time after which a forwarding node stops forwarding packets) to reduce the control overhead.

Scenario We used the Glomosim [14] simulator in our simulation study. Glomosim is a widely used wireless network simulator with a detailed and accurate physical signal propagation model. We simulated a network of 50 static nodes placed randomly in a $1000m \times 1000m$ area. We used two multicast groups with nine receivers and one source each. In this way, the traffic for one group acts as cross-traffic for the other group. Each source sent a 4MB file, consisting of 512-byte packets at a constant rate of 5 packets/sec in a low-load scenario and 20 packets/second in a high-load scenario[1].

The radio propagation range was 250m and the channel capacity was 2Mbps (the data rate used for broadcast in 802.11 MAC protocol). The *TwoRay* propagation model was used. To make the simulations realistic, we added fading in our experiments. The Rayleigh model was used, as it is appropriate for environments with many large reflectors, e.g., walls, trees, and buildings, where the sender and the receiver are not in Line-of-Sight of each other. We envision that such environments will be common for mesh networks. We simulated each protocol on 10 different randomly generated topologies and the results for each topology as well as the average over all topologies are presented.

For the implementation of ReMHoc, FEC RS codes, NP, and RMDP, we followed [10], [2], [3] and [4], respectively. For the protocol parameters that are given specific values in these four papers, we kept the same values. For the rest of the parameters (e.g., the slot size T_s in NP), we ran simulations with different values, and we selected those that resulted in the best reliability (i.e. packet delivery ratio) without suffering too much on throughput (both metrics are defined below). These parameters along with the selected values are shown in Table 1.

Evaluation metrics The following metrics are used to evaluate the various reliable multicast protocol versions:

[1]Although the source sending rate is only 80 Kbps, the actual load on the network is much higher as taking the node density into account, the total traffic load within a transmission range is on average 800 Kbps.

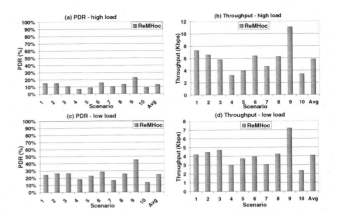

Figure 1. PDR and throughput for ReMHoc under high and low load for 10 different topologies.

Average Packet Delivery Ratio (PDR): The number of the data packets delivered to a multicast group member divided by the number of data packets transmitted by the source, averaged over all multicast group members. For FEC-based protocols, the data packets refer to the original data packets, i.e., before encoding at the source and after decoding at the destination. This metric directly measures reliability.

Average Throughput: The number of data packets (in bytes) delivered to a multicast group member divided by the total time required for this delivery, averaged over all multicast group members.

Efficiency: The number of decoded packets at a multicast group member divided by the total number of encoded packets received by that member, averaged over all multicast group members. It is a common metric in FEC-based protocols. For ARQ-based protocols there is no redundancy and efficiency is 100%, since all data/repair packets received are useful packets.

3.2. Results

ARQ We first evaluate the performance of ReMHoc, a pure ARQ protocol. Figure 1 shows the average PDR and throughput achieved by ReMHoc under high and low load.

As we observe in Figures 1(a), 1(c), the PDR is very low under both high and low load. On average, ReMHoc achieves only 13% PDR under high load, and slightly higher (23%) under low load. This PDR is much lower than that achieved by ODMRP without any reliability scheme (74% and 87%, respectively, undel high and low load). In other words, a reliable protocol achieves much lower reliability compared to a best-effort protocol which does not have any reliability characteristics. Same observations can be made for throughput which is extremely low, 5.9Kbps and 4Kbps, under high and low load, respectively.

Table 1. Parameters of the various reliable protocols and their values.

Protocol	Name - Description	Notation	Value
ReMHoc	number of times a request is sent	-	5
FEC	number of original data packets in each TG	k	32
	number of total (original + encoded) data packets in each TG	n	63,127,255
NP	number of original data packets in each TG	k	32
	number of total data packets in each TG	n	255
	slot size for NACK timers	T_s	1sec (NP), 5sec (NP_opt)
RMDP	number of original data packets in each TG	k	32
	number of total data packets in each TG	n	255
	timer for next R message after R is sent	T_R	20sec
	timer for next R message after S is received	T_C	10sec
	amount of redundant data sent unconditionally	D	1,3,5

Tang et al. observe a similarly low PDR for SRM in [15]. The poor performance of ReMHoc (or SRM) stems from the way ARQ protocols try to recover from packet losses. For each lost packet, additional request and repair packets are injected into the network, which finally leads to congestion and packet dropping. Of course request/repair suppression tries to mitigate this problem. However, suppression does not work well in wireless networks for two reasons. First, it is very possible that request packets will also be lost, like data packets. This is usually not taken into account in the wired Internet. Second, packet losses in wireless multicast are highly uncorrelated, as opposed to in the Internet. In IP multicast, a tree is built from the source to the receivers. Hence, a packet loss observed by a node is also observed by all its downstream nodes [11]. In wireless networks, most multicast protocols build a mesh instead of a tree to increase reliability. Hence, there are usually several paths from the sender to each receiver, which result in uncorrelated losses. This is true even for tree-based protocols, because of the broadcast nature of a wireless transmission.

Things get even worse due to bursty losses. We observed in ReMHoc bursty losses of up to 90 consecutive data packets. Such bursts of lost packets cause bursts of requests, and subsequently, bursts of repairs sent by the source. This results in the MAC layer queues of the nodes one hop away of the source being fully occupied by repair packets for certain periods of time, during which all new data packets are simply dropped. On average, each receiver sent 1260 requests under high load but it received only 472 repair packets. The same numbers for low load were 3564 and 1149, respectively. This shows that the request-repair mechanism does not perform well in wireless networks.

In general, the ARQ model for the Internet performs very poorly in wireless networks. The conclusion is that an efficient reliable protocol for wireless multicast should avoid or at least limit the transmission of request packets, and be able to react to bursty losses without causing congestion in the network.

FEC In this section we evaluate the performance of pure FEC, where no feedback is sent by the receivers. Rizzo in [4] proposes the use of a (255, 32) RS code as a good compromise between encoding/decoding speed and efficiency. However, this implies a large amount of redundancy (seven times the file size). In a wireless network of limited capacity, this might not be a good choice, as high traffic will compete with traffic from other sources. Hence, we examine the use of smaller values for n, while keeping the value for k equal to 32. Figure 2 shows the results for PDR, throughput, and efficiency in case of high and low load, for three different amounts of redundancy, namely for $n = 63$, 127, and 255.

As we observe in Figures 2(a), 2(d), the use of FEC significantly improves reliability. For high load, the use of (63, 32), (127, 32), and (255, 32) codes achieves on average PDRs of 89.5%, 98.4%, and 98.9%, respectively. For low load, the PDR with a (63, 32) code increases up to 97.9%, while for the other two codes it remains the same. More importantly, (127, 32) and (255, 32) codes give a 100% PDR in 5 and 8 out of 10 scenarios, respectively, under high load, and in 8 out of 10 scenarios under low load.[2]

Figures 2(b), 2(e) show that the average throughput achieved is the same for a (127, 32) and a (255, 32) code, equal to 46Kbps under high load and 15.5Kbps under low load. Taking into account the fact that the sending rate is 81.9Kbps and 20.5Kbps, under high and low load, respectively, we conclude that 100% reliability comes at the cost of reduced throughput, especially under high load. It also comes at the cost of very low efficiency, as we observe in Figures 2(c), 2(f). The efficiency of a (127, 32) code is on average 36% and 29% under high and low load, respectively. For a (255, 32) code it decreases even more – 19% and 14%, respectively. It means that a lot of packets are

---

[2] In both scenarios 5 and 6, where PDR is less than 100% even with a (255, 32) code, the reason is that one node is almost isolated from the rest of the network, due to the random placement of nodes. Such pathological cases should not happen with a planned deployment.

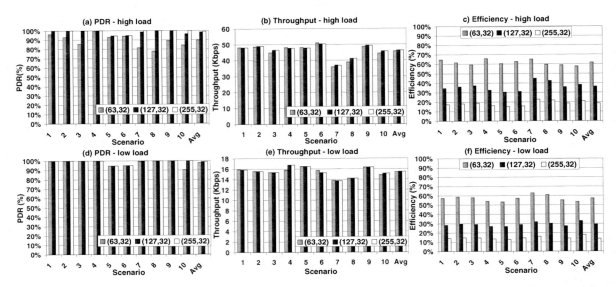

Figure 2. Comparison of RS codes of different redundancy in terms of PDR, throughput, and efficiency for 10 different topologies.

wasted in order to achieve finally 100% PDR. This is due to high uncorrelated packet losses occurring in wireless environments.

In general, a (127, 32) RS code achieves almost the same PDR as a (255, 32) RS code, but with doubled efficiency. Hence, in the overall comparison in Section 3.2, we will use this code. Since 100% PDR can be achieved in practical scenarios with a (127, 32) RS code, which sends redundant data equal to only 3 times the file size, as opposed to 7 times as proposed in [4], the use of a hybrid FEC-ARQ scheme will be preferred only if it offers higher throughput or efficiency compared to the pure FEC scheme. This is examined in the following sections.

NP In NP, redundant packets are sent only after explicit requests (NACK packets from the receivers). Hence there is no reason to keep the value of n low in the RS code. If the protocol performs well, only a part of the redundant packets is going to be sent. Hence for the NP evaluation, we used a (255, 32) RS code in all cases. Figure 3 shows the results for PDR, throughput, and efficiency in case of high and low load, for the original NP protocol (NP) and an optimized version (NP_opt) which we will describe in the following.

As Figure 3(a) shows, the average PDR under high load is only 78%, much lower than the PDR achieved by pure FEC, and only slightly better than the PDR of ODMRP (about 74%). Hence, NP in its original version fails to provide reliable data delivery in wireless networks. The reason can be explained by the way the protocol works. As we explained in Section 2.3, the sender sends a POLL message after each round, and the receivers respond to POLL messages with NACK messages containing the number of missing packets. Upon receiving a NACK, the sender sends the

appropriate amount of redundant packets. In other words, there is a chain of three types of messages, POLL, NACK, and parity packets, each of which is sent as a response to the previous one. If one of them is lost, the chain breaks. If a POLL is lost before it reaches any receiver or in the more rare case that all the NACKs generated by different receivers as a response to a specific POLL are lost, the receivers will not recover any lost packets.

Note that even if a NACK is received, it is not always the NACK with the maximum number of lost packets, since NACK suppression may not work perfectly in wireless networks, as we explained in Section 3.2. Under low load, the problem is not so intense, because there is much less contention for the channel, and the probability of collisions is lower. As Figure 3(d) shows, the PDR under low load is quite high, about 92%, but again it is worse than pure FEC.

The above discussion shows that in wireless networks this handshake mechanism (POLL - NACK) is not efficient. A second mechanism is necessary to initiate NACK messages even if POLLs are lost. On the other hand, the rationale behind this design was to keep the control overhead low. Simply sending NACK packets in response to packet losses and using no POLL messages could lead to uncontrolled bursts of NACK packets (NACK implosion), similar to what we observed in ReMHoc in Section 2.1. Our solution to the problem is as follows. We keep the POLL-NACK exchange the same as in the original NP protocol, but every time a NACK is sent, we reset the timer for that NACK. If a POLL message comes before the timer expires, we cancel it, since a new NACK will be sent in response to the POLL message. However, if the timer expires before any POLL message comes, the same NACK is re-sent. Note

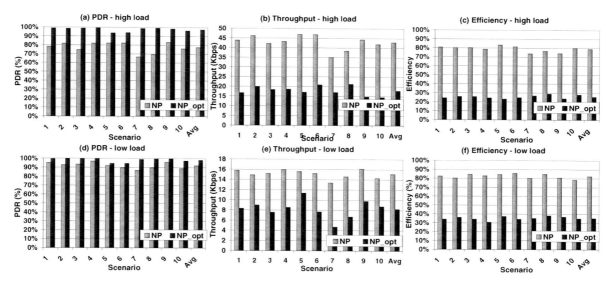

Figure 3. PDR, throughput and efficiency of the original NP protocol and an optimized version for 10 different topologies. NP and NP_opt use a (255, 32) RS code.

that we need this mechanism only as a backup mechanism, which should not interrupt the POLL-NACK exchange, and should not create more, unnecessary NACKs. Hence we set this timer to a very large value (200 sec), to make sure that it will only be activated if the basic mechanism of the protocol is not working anymore. We call this new version of NP NP_opt (optimized NP).

Figures 3(a), 3(d) show that NP_opt increases significantly the reliability compared to NP. The PDR with NP_opt is on average 97.5% under high load and 98.4% under low load, which are very close to 100%. If we look at the total number of NACK and POLL messages sent on average with NP and NP_opt, we will see that NP_opt sends on average about 7 times more NACK messages and 4 times more POLL messages compared to NP. But these extra control messages do not cause extra overhead, because they are sent in a much longer time period, compared to NP. To verify this, we look at the time the last useful data/parity packet was received. This time is on average 610 sec for NP and 3480 sec for NP_opt under high load, and 2049 sec and 8190 sec, respectively under low load.

The above values show again that increased reliability comes at the cost of low throughput. Figures 3(b), 3(e) verify this, showing that average throughput with NP and NP_opt, respectively, is 42.8Kbps and 17.8Kbps under high load, and 15.1Kbps and 8.2Kbps under low load. Similarly the efficiency drops from 79% for NP to 25% for NP_opt under high load and from 82% to 35% under low load.

Overall, the value of throughput for NP is close to that achieved by a pure (127, 32) FEC code, and the efficiency much better, but the PDR much lower. On the other hand, NP_opt achieves a PDR almost equal to that of a pure (127,

32) FEC code, but still less than 100%, with lower throughput and efficiency. A general conclusion is that in wireless environments, trying to recover from bursty losses by immediately responding to those losses is not a good solution, since it can very easily lead to congestion. Instead, a protocol that schedules future response to current requests might be a better option. This is the main design idea in RMDP, the second hybrid protocol, which we study next.

RMDP In RMDP we also used a (255, 32) RS code, as in NP, for the reasons we explained previously. Figure 4 shows the results for PDR, throughput, and efficiency in case of high and low load, for three different values of D, 1, 3, and 5, denoted as RMDP_1, RMDP_3, RMDP_5, respectively.

In Figures 4(a), 4(d), we observe that the PDR for RMDP with $D = 3$, or $D = 5$, reaches 100% with both high and low load, for all the scenarios except the two pathological scenarios we mentioned when we discussed the results of FEC. With $D=1$, the sender initially sends only the original data packets for each TG (32 packets), and extra packets are only sent after requests. This increases the protocol overhead, since many more requests (R packets) are initiated, and the probability for collisions increases, reducing the PDR. With $D > 1$, some redundancy is sent in the beginning, reducing the number of subsequent requests for more packets. We measured the number of requests sent in each case, and we found that on average each receiver sends 274 requests when $D = 1$, 45 requests when $D = 3$, and only 22 requests when $D = 5$, in case of high load, and the numbers are similar under low load.

Hence, RMDP, the only protocol designed to work in both wired and wireless environments (although previously evaluated only in the former), does achieve the goal of pro-

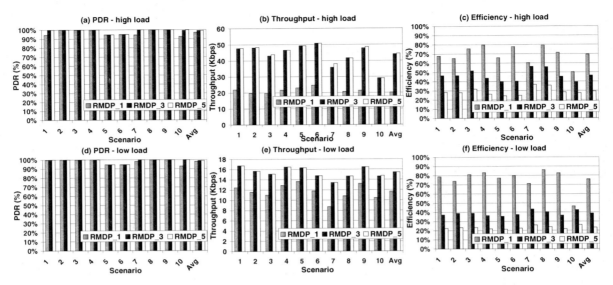

Figure 4. PDR, throughput, and efficiency of RMDP for three different values of D for 10 different topologies. RMDP uses a (255, 32) RS code.

viding reliable multicast data delivery in wireless networks. As we explained previously, RMDP does not take any action to recover from losses the moment they are observed. On the receiver side, a timer for a request for the TG with the largest number of losses is set every time a data packet is received, but in most cases this timer is reset upon reception of the next data packet. Only if a receiver experiences a large interval without receiving any packets, it initiates an R message. Also, resetting the timer after sending a request ensures that the protocol will never stop working (the mechanism is similar to that we applied in NP_opt). On the sender's side, no repair packets are sent upon the reception of a request. The only action taken is scheduling more parities for future transmission by increasing the appropriate c_s counter. This significantly reduces overhead and eliminates the problem of bursty losses, but it can potentially reduce throughput, since it may take longer for the receivers to complete the necessary number of packets to decode.

Figures 4(b), 4(e) show that throughput increases with D, since more packets are sent in advance. RMDP with $D = 1, 3$, and 5 achieves on average throughput equal to 20.2 Kbps, 43.9 Kbps, and 44.4 Kbps, respectively, under high load, and 11.7 Kbps, 15.3 Kbps, and 15.4 Kbps, under low load. For $D = 3$ or 5 these values are very close to those achieved by pure FEC in Figures 2(b), 2(e). But the great advantage of RMDP over pure FEC is efficiency. Figures 4(c), 4(f) show that the efficiency of RMDP with $D = 1, 3$, and 5, is 69%, 47%, and 29%, respectively, under high load, and 76%, 39%, and 23% under low load. For example, with $D = 3$, RMDP with a (255, 32) FEC code improves efficiency by 30% and 34% compared to a pure (127, 32) FEC code, under high and low load, while achiev-

ing the same PDR and the throughput reduced only by less than 5%.

In general, there is a tradeoff in the amount of redundancy sent unconditionally (without any request). By sending more packets unconditionally, we can increase throughput but the efficiency is reduced. $D = 3$ seems a good compromise between these two conflicting factors, and hence we will use this value in our overall comparison.

Overall Comparison In this section, we compare all five protocols, in order to give an overall picture of their relative performance. For this comparison, the best version of each protocol is used. FEC uses a (127, 32) RS code, and RMDP has $D = 3$. Figure 5 shows the PDR, throughput, and efficiency for ODMRP_static, ReMHoc, a (127, 32) FEC code, NP_opt, and RMDP with $D = 3$, for 10 different topologies.

Figures 5(a), 5(d) show that FEC and hybrid ARQ-FEC based protocols offer significant improvements in terms of reliability, increasing the PDR close or up to 100%. In contrast, pure ARQ-based protocols such as ReMHoc have a very poor performance in wireless environments, reducing the PDR to unacceptable levels, much lower than the best-effort ODMRP. As we mentioned before, ReMHoc is very vulnerable to bursty packet losses, because both the sender and the receivers try to respond immediately to each single packet loss detection. This causes the well-known request/repair implosion problem, and it finally leads to congestion. The request/repair suppression mechanism cannot mitigate the problem, because it does not work properly in wireless environments.

NP solves partly this problem, since on the receiver's side response is not immediate, but only after the reception of a POLL message. In other words, the receivers in NP

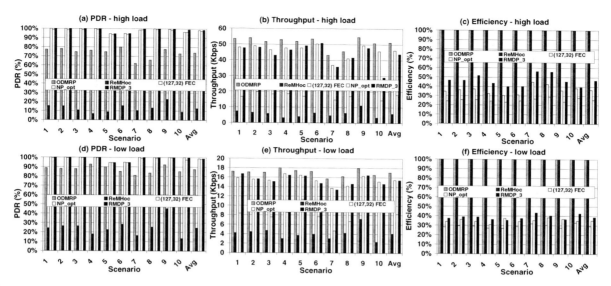

Figure 5. PDR, throughput, and efficiency for ODMRP, ReMHoc, a (127, 32) FEC code, NP_opt, and RMDP with $D = 3$, for 10 different topologies. NP_opt and RMDP use a (255, 32) RS code.

perform some kind of NACK aggregation. However, this aggregation could cause even larger problem on the sender's side and increase the burstiness of repair packets. Finally, the use of a timer for NACKs with a carefully selected value mitigates this new problem, and hence NP_opt performs almost as well as FEC and RMDP in terms of PDR.

Pure FEC and RMDP are the only two protocols that can achieve 100% PDR, because they take no immediate response in case of packet losses. Our experiments with FEC show that we can always achieve 100% PDR by increasing the amount of redundancy sent. However, FEC can be very inefficient, wasting many packets, since the amount of redundancy to be sent is decided in advance. On the other hand, RMDP sends only a fraction of redundant packets in advance, and the rest is sent only if necessary. For this reason, RMDP is the most efficient among the three protocols. As Figures 5(c), 5(f) show, the efficiencies of RMDP, NP_opt, and FEC are on average 47%, 26%, and 34%, respectively, under high load, and 37%, 35%, and 29%, under low load. Increased efficiency, especially under high load, is another advantage of RMDP over NP. For ODMRP and ReMHoc efficiency is 100%, since there are no redundant packets, but this efficiency is meaningless, since it is counterbalanced by the low PDR.

Finally, we observe in Figures 5(b), 5(e) that increased reliability comes at the cost of reduced throughput, since for all three protocols that increase reliability, i.e., FEC, NP, and RMDP, the average throughput is lower than for ODMRP. However, for FEC and RMDP, this reduction is very small – throughput is 46 Kbps for FEC and 44 Kbps for RMDP vs. 52 Kbps for ODMRP under high load, and 15 Kbps for both FEC and RMDP vs. 17 Kbps under low

load, and it can be tolerated, since the gains in reliability are much higher. On the other hand, throughput for NP is very low – 18 Kbps and 8 Kbps, under high and low load, which shows once more that the design of NP is not appropriate for wireless environments.

4. Related Work

Recently, many protocols have been proposed for reliable multicast in mobile ad hoc networks. A survey on reliable multicast protocols for ad hoc networks [16] classifies them into deterministic and probabilistic ones, depending on whether the delivery is fully reliable or not. Deterministic protocols [17, 18, 19, 20, 15, 21] provide deterministic guarantees for packet delivery ratio, but they incur high overhead when the mobility or the group size increases. In these cases, they resort to flooding, resulting in severe performance degradation. In contrast, probabilistic protocols [22, 23] do not offer hard delivery guarantees, but they incur much less overhead compared to the former. All the above protocols fall in the class of ARQ. As mentioned before, no work other than RMDP [4] has considered the use of FEC for reliable multicast in wireless networks. To our best knowledge, we are the first to study the performance of FEC for multicast in wireless mesh networks.

In our comparison we used Reed-Solomon codes in the FEC-based schemes. Reed-Solomon codes are very easy to simulate, because they are deterministic, meaning that a receiver knows in advance that it can obtain the original data if it receives *any* k out of n packets. A drawback of Reed-Solomon codes is that k and n have to be kept small (the maximum values are 64 and 255, respectively). Tornado codes [24] allow the use of very large values for k and n, but they are non-deterministic, and the receiver has to perform a partial decoding of the data stream in order to decide when it should stop receiving. Moreover, the number of packets required for decoding is $(1+\varepsilon) \times k$, but ε is different for each receiver and unknown beforehand, which complicates both the design of hybrid protocols. Finally, rateless codes is a new class of erasure codes in which an arbitrary number of encoded packets can be produced on demand. [25] uses LT codes [26], one type of rateless codes, to implement Digital Fountain, an ideal protocol that allows any number of heterogeneous receivers to acquire content with the optimal efficiency at the times of their choosing. Rateless codes are also probabilistic codes, and hence they cannot be easily incorporated into the current hybrid protocols, since receivers can not report how many parities they need.

Finally, adaptive FEC techniques that adapt the number of parities sent based on an estimation of the loss rate have been proposed for multicast in wireless LANs [27, 28]. In our future work we plan to study if these techniques can also be applied to multihop mesh networks.

5. Conclusions

In this paper we examined the applicability of FEC-based reliable multicast protocols initially proposed for the wired Internet in wireless mesh networks. We compared four different reliable multicast schemes, one ARQ-based (ReMHoc), one FEC-based (use of RS codes), and two hybrid protocols (NP and RMDP). Our simulation study shows that ARQ-based protocols perform very poorly in wireless environments, because they cannot cope with bursty packet losses. Moreover, we found that trying to respond immediately to packet losses or to requests for retransmissions is not a good design choice for wireless protocols, because it can very quickly lead to congestion. The use of FEC without any feedback from the receivers, and hence without any need for retransmissions, can offer perfect reliability in most practical scenarios, but at the cost of low efficiency. RMDP can increase the efficiency while keeping the PDR at the same level as pure FEC, by scheduling more packet transmissions in the future based on feedback from the receivers, instead of immediately responding to this feedback. In our future work, we plan to validate our simulation results on a real mesh network testbed [29].

Acknowledgment

This work was supported in part by NSF grant CNS-0626703.

References

[1] L. Huang and H. Hassanein, "A performance comparison of reliable multicast protocols over ad hoc networks," in *22nd Biennial Conference on Communications*, 2004.

[2] L. Rizzo, "Effective erasure codes for reliable computer communication protocols," *ACM Computer Communications Review*, vol. 27, no. 2, 1997.

[3] J. Nonnenmacher, E. Biersack, and D. Towsley, "Parity-based loss recovery for reliable multicast transmission," in *ACM SIGCOMM*, 1997.

[4] L. Rizzo and L. Visicano, "RMDP: an FEC-based reliable multicast protocol for wireless environments," *Mobile Computing and Communications Review*, vol. 2, no. 2, 1998.

[5] J. Yoon, A. Bestavros, and I. Matta, "Adaptive reliable multicast," in *Proc. of ICC*, 2000.

[6] E. Schooler and J. Gemmel, "Using multicast FEC to solve the midnight madness problem," Technical Report, MSR-TR-97-25, Tech. Rep., 1997.

[7] R. Kermode, "Scoped hybrid automatic repeat request with forward error correction (SHARQFEC)," in *Proc. of ACM SIGCOMM*, 1998.

[8] J. Gemmel, "Scalable reliable multicast using erasure-correcting resends," Technical Report, MSR-TR-97-20, Tech. Rep., 1997.

[9] M. Cagalj, J.-P. Hubaux, and C. Enz, "Minimum-energy broadcast in all-wireless networks: NP-Completeness and distribution," in *Proc. of ACM MobiCom*, September 2002.

[10] A. Sobeih, H. Baraka, and A. Fahmy, "ReMHoc: A reliable multicast protocol for wireless mobile multihop ad hoc networks," in *IEEE IPCCC*, 2004.

[11] S. Floyd, V. Jacobson, C.-G. Liu, S. McCanne, and L. Zhang, "A reliable framework for light-weight sessions and application level framing," *IEEE/ACM Transactions on Networking*, 1997.

[12] S.-J. Lee, M. Gerla, and C.-C. Chiang, "On-Demand Multicast Routing Protocol," in *Proc. of IEEE WCNC*, September 1999.

[13] A. J. McAuley, "Reliable broadband communication using a burst erasure correcting code," in *Proc. of ACM SIGCOMM*, 1990.

[14] X. Zeng, R. Bagrodia, and M. Gerla, "Glomosim: A library for parallel simulation of large-scale wireless networks," in *Proc. of PADS Workshop*, May 1998.

[15] K. Tang, K. Obraczka, S.-J. Lee, and M. Gerla, "Reliable adaptive lightweight multicast protocol," in *Proc. of ICC*, 2004.

[16] E. Vollset and P. Ezhilchelvan, "A survey of reliable broadcast protocols for mobile ad-hoc networks," University of Newcastle upon Tyne, Tech. Rep. CS-TR-792, 2003.

[17] E. Pagani and G. Rossi, "Reliable broadcast in mobile multihop packet networks," in *Proc. of MobiCom*, 1997.

[18] S. Gupta and P. Srimani, "An adaptive protocol for reliable multicast in mobile multi-hop radio networks," in *Proc. of IEEE Workshop on Mobile Computing Systems and Applications*, 1999.

[19] T. Gopalsamy, M. Singhal, and P. Sadayappan, "A reliable multicast algorithm for mobile ad hoc networks," in *Proc. of ICDCS*, 2002.

[20] K. Tang, K. Obraczka, S.-J. Lee, and M. Gerla, "A reliable, congestion-controlled multicast transport protocol in multimedia multi-hop networks," in *Proc. of WPMC*, 2004.

[21] V. Rajendran, Y. Yi, K. Obraczka, S.-J. Lee, K. Tang, and M. Gerla, "Combining source- and localized recovery to achieve reliable multicadt in multi-hop ad hoc networks," in *Proc. of Networking*, 2004.

[22] R. Chandra, V. Ramasubramaniam, and K. Birman, "Anonymous gossip: Improving multicast reliability in mobile ad hoc networks," in *Proc. of ICDCS*, 2001.

[23] J. Luo, P. Eugster, and J.-P. Hubaux, "Route driven gossip: Probabilistic reliable multicast in ad hoc networks," in *Proc. of IEEE Infocom*, 2003.

[24] M. Luby, M. Mitzenmacher, A. Shokrollahi, and D. Spielman, "Efficient erasure correcting codes," *IEEE Transactions on Information Theory*, vol. 47, 2001.

[25] J. Byers, M. Luby, and M. Mitzenmacher, "A digital fountain approach to asynchronous reliable multicast," *Journal on selected areas in communications*, vol. 20, 2002.

[26] M. Luby, "LT codes," in *The 43rd Annual IEEE Symposium on Foundations of Computer Science*, 2002.

[27] D. Xu, B. Li, and K. Nahrstedt, "QoS-directed error control of video multicast in wireless networks," in *Proc. of ICC*, 1999.

[28] P. Chumchu, Z. G. Zhou, and A. Seneviratne, "A model-based scalable reliable multicast transport protocol for wireless/mobile networks," *IEICE Transactions on Communications*, vol. 4E88-B, no. 4, 2005.

[29] Mesh@Purdue, "http://www.engineering.purdue.edu/MESH."

Session 8B:
Experimental Dependability
Assessment

On the Selection of Error Model(s) For OS Robustness Evaluation*

Andréas Johansson, Neeraj Suri
Dept. of CS, TU-Darmstadt, Germany
{aja,suri}@informatik.tu-darmstadt.de

Brendan Murphy
Microsoft Research, Cambridge, UK
bmurphy@microsoft.com

Abstract

The choice of error model used for robustness evaluation of Operating Systems (OSs) influences the evaluation run time, implementation complexity, as well as the evaluation precision. In order to find an "effective" error model for OS evaluation, this paper systematically compares the relative effectiveness of three prominent error models, namely bit-flips, data type errors and fuzzing errors using fault injection at the interface between device drivers OS. Bit-flips come with higher costs (time) than the other models, but allow for more detailed results. Fuzzing is cheaper to implement but is found to be less precise. A composite error model is presented where the low cost of fuzzing is combined with the higher level of details of bit-flips, resulting in high precision with moderate setup and execution costs.

1. Introduction

This paper focuses on ascertaining the robustness of OSs to errors in device drivers. While multiple OS robustness studies using fault-injection have been reported, for instance [2, 9, 13, 15], in most cases, the results are applicable mainly for the specific underlying error model. The choice of *error model* and *location* of injection directly influences the accuracy and usefulness of the obtained results.

The relative effectiveness of three distinct error models at the OS-Driver interface is compared. The OS-Driver interface was chosen as it represents an interface shared by all drivers, it is reasonably well documented and supplies the level of access needed for this type of studies. The error models are compared for efficiency (cost and coverage), implementation complexity and execution time requirements and a new *composite error model* is presented. Consequently, the paper proposes guidelines on selecting the appropriate error model for OS robustness evaluation. The results of such an evaluation are useful both in system design, i.e., where the OS and the drivers are integrated as part

of a larger system, for finding hot-spots in the system warranting refinements, and component evaluation for comparing the suitability of certain components in a system. The chosen approach makes possible a comparative study of the influence of drivers on system robustness, without requiring source code access. Experimental quantitative approaches, such as this one, complement analytical approaches (like [4]) and provide easy means for quantifying dynamic behavior of the system under study.

The chosen error models span: **a)** *bit-flips* (BF), where a bit in a data word is flipped, from 0 to 1, or vice versa. BF were used, for instance, in [9] where the robustness of the Linux kernel was evaluated. **b)** *Data type-based corruption* (DT), where the value of a parameter in a call to a function is changed, according to its data type, for instance to boundary values. This technique was used in [1] and [13]. In [3, 11] both BF and DT errors are used. **c)** *Fuzzing* (FZ), which assigns a randomly chosen value to the parameter in a function call. FZ has previously been used, for instance, in [17, 19].

Paper Contributions & Structure: Selecting an "effective" error model to use in a particular setting is not straightforward and guidelines are of value for both OS designers and evaluators. Building on previous experiences on OS robustness evaluation [13], this paper represents a step towards providing such a guideline. Using a case study based on Windows CE .NET and three different drivers (serial, network and storage card drivers) the paper specifically provides two distinct contributions, namely **i)** a comparative study of error model effectiveness in terms of coverage and cost, and **ii)** it establishes the effectiveness of using a composite error model for OS robustness evaluation.

The paper is presented detailing four main blocks:

Prerequisites: Defining the system model [Section 2]; background information on the studied error models [Section 3]; a presentation of the evaluation criteria for the error models, i.e., error propagation, failure mode analysis and execution time [Section 4].

Implementation: Presentation of the target system and the experimental technique used [Section 5].

Results: Presentation of the results from fault-injection

---

*Research supported in part by EC DECOS, ReSIST and Microsoft

experiments [Section 6] with interpretations [Section 7]. **Composite Model**: Definition and results for the *composite error model* [Section 8]; discussion and summary of the main findings [Section 9].

2. System Model

Similar to [1, 2] we use a four-layered model of the OS: Application, OS, Driver and Hardware layer. This model applies to most common monolithic OSs, such as Windows, UNIX and Linux. The *OS-Driver* interface (Figure 1) is our target of study.

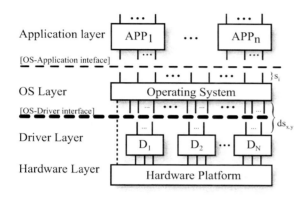

Figure 1. System model

A system containing N drivers $(D_1 \ldots D_y \ldots D_N)$ is considered. Each driver exports and imports a set of services $ds_{x.y}$ where $x.y$ is x^{th} service of driver D_y. The effects of errors are observed at the OS-Application interface by manually instrumenting a number of benchmark applications with assertions. For each system service s_i used, we study its behavior to detect deviations from the golden run.

Only the interface specifications (OS-Driver and OS-Application) are required, but no source code, neither for the drivers, nor for the OS itself. However, access is needed to the source code of the benchmark applications, for instrumenting them with assertions. The availability of interface specifications is a basic requirement for any OS open for extensions by new types of drivers/applications.

3. The Spread of Error Models

The three error models are chosen based on their appropriateness as reported in multiple previous studies and by their relation to real faults, such as those defined by Orthogonal Defect Classification (ODC) [5]. ODC is a method of classifying defects into orthogonal classes, enabling process feedback and control. As it mainly focuses on in-process

defects, it uses source code as an intrinsic basis for classification. Our decision not to require access to source code implies that we cannot directly use the ODC classification. However, an attempt is made to classify the error models depending on the defect classes they belong to. The *interface* class of ODC is a potential source for each of the models, as it deals with external interaction, such as drivers. The error models were also chosen as they represent a class of errors that previously have been reported as difficult to detect and recover from [20].

Errors are injected in service parameters. We do single injections, i.e., we do not simultaneously inject in multiple parameters. Injection is performed by intercepting calls and manipulating data at runtime.

For all three error models we use a transient error occurrence and duration model, i.e., the error appears once and then disappears. Errors are injected *on first occurrence*. This implies that the error is injected the first time a service is invoked. Previous studies have suggested that the impact of the time of injection is small [21]; however this remains to be comprehensively established.

All three error models handle pointers and structures as special cases, and inject errors in the target of a pointer and the members of a structure, when possible. Only if a pointer or structure member is already set to `NULL` an injection is not performed.

3.1. Bit-Flip Error Model

Bit-flips is an extensively used error model deriving its origins from transient hardware defects. Its ease of use and implementation has made it a candidate to also be used to simulate software (SW) defects. As it changes the value of a parameter (by manipulating one of the bits) it belongs to the *Assignment* class of ODC defects.

In the BF model, each parameter is treated as an integer (typically a 32-bit word). The model's greatest advantage is also its greatest disadvantage, namely simplicity. While it makes it very easy to implement, it suffers in expressiveness, with respect to abstract data types (strings etc.).

Each injection case flips one bit, thus resulting in 32 injection cases per parameter. However, some parameters are 16 (or 8) bit wide only, and we therefore restrict these parameters to use fewer injections.

3.2. Data Type Error Model

Data type errors are chosen depending on the data type of the targeted parameter. As the targeted interface is defined using the C language, the data types considered are all C-style. This excludes high level abstract data types supported in other high-level languages, such as classes in C++.

We follow established testing practice by choosing for each type a set of predefined (no randomness) test values, offset values and boundary values. The offset values allow us to modify the previous value (present in the intercepted call), such as adding a number to it. The number of injections defined is typically less than ten, allowing this error model to incur fewer injections (on average) than the BF model. However, there is no such inherent property and it depends on the number of cases defined for each type. This model also belongs to the *Assignment* class of ODC, though it could also be a *Checking* defect, resulting from a failing or missing check of a data value.

The number of data types for which injection cases need to be defined depends only on the data types actually used[7, 15]. Many services use the same data types for their parameters, making the approach scalable. The same observation was made in the Ballista project [15] regarding the POSIX API. In total, the three drivers targeted in this paper result in injections for 22 data types being defined. An overview is shown in Table 1. For structures (`struct`) the number of cases depends on the members (marked with * in the table). DT errors also treat pointers as special data type and reserves one injection case for the pointer, namely setting it to `NULL`. Wrong use of NULL-pointers is a common programming mistake. To further illustrate how DT errors are defined, Table 2 shows the cases for the type `int`.

Data type	C-Type	#Cases
Integers	`int`	7
	`unsigned int`	5
	`long`	7
	`unsigned long`	5
	`short`	7
	`unsigned short`	5
	`LARGE_INTEGER`	7
Misc	`* void`	3
	`HKEY`	6
	`struct {...}`	*
	Strings	4
Characters	`char`	7
	`unsigned char`	5
	`wchar_t`	5
Boolean	`bool`	1
Enums	multiple cases	#identifiers

Table 1. Overview of the data types used.

3.3. Fuzzing Error Model

Fuzzing a parameter implies assigning it a pseudo-random value from the set of legal values for the type.

Case #	New value
1	(Previous value) - 1
2	(Previous value) + 1
3	1
4	0
5	-1
6	INT_MIN
7	INT_MAX

Table 2. Error cases for type `int`.

Therefore, the result of the injection may differ across experiments, resulting in the need for multiple experiments to obtain statistically valid conclusions. A specific discussion on the number of injections needed appears in Section 6.4.

Whereas BF and DT use the parameter values, FZ differs in that it ignores these values. FZ belongs to either the *Assignment* or *Checking* classes in ODC. This model was considered in [17, 19, 10].

The pseudo-random values are chosen using the `rand()` C-runtime function. The last value produced in a round is stored in persistent storage and is used as the seed for the next round, thus ensuring that different random values are used every time.

3.4. Other Key Contemporary Models

The work in [1, 2, 3, 8, 12, 14] explored the use of various error models and injection techniques for OS robustness evaluation and benchmarking. For instance, [12] compares errors similar to the ones considered here, but injected at different levels of the Linux kernel. In [2] a mutation error model is used, in which the code segments of drivers are targeted. Further, in [18] the authors observe that effects of errors at the interface, though being useful for robustness evaluation, do not represent defects in code. As we do not inject errors at the code level we can neither verify, nor falsify this observation. We believe that our systematic comparison of error models, is a useful contribution to the community as this comparative aspect at the OS-Driver interface has not been treated in depth before.

The chosen models, even though not complete, still represent a large operational spectrum. [6] studies defects in two large OSs and almost 50% of the found defects belong to the ODC classes represented in this paper.

4. Comparative Evaluation Criteria

The chosen error models are studied based on a diverse set of commonly used evaluation criteria, namely i) error propagation (Diffusion), ii) error impact (failure class), iii) implementation complexity, and iv) execution time. Each criteria is elaborated in the following subsections.

4.1. Error Propagation Criteria (Diffusion)

In this paper, the focus of error propagation is on *Driver Error Diffusion*[1] [13]. Diffusion is defined as the degree to which a driver can spread errors in the system. It allows drivers to be compared and ranked making it possible for a system evaluator/designer to make a judgement on where to expend more resources in terms of testing/verification and quality improvement.

Diffusion considers the propagation paths from a driver, through the OS to user applications. It is the sum of the conditional probabilities for an error to propagate, given that an error exists. Diffusion is itself not a probability but a metric of sensitivity to input errors, which can be exactly estimated by code analysis, or approximated experimentally.

$$D^x = \sum_{s_i} \sum_{ds_{x.y}} PDS^i_{x.y} \qquad (1)$$

In Equation 1, $PDS^i_{x.j}$ represents the conditional probability that errors in the driver's use of OS services ($ds_{x.j}$) lead to failure (see also Figure 1).

Diffusion can be used to compare the suitability of drivers for a particular system based on to their *potential* for spreading errors. A higher diffusion value implies that a driver is more liable to spread errors. However, note that drivers are not tested per se. Consequently, we stress that the intent is *not* to give absolute values for error sensitivity, but to obtain relative rankings. A detailed discussion on diffusion and error propagation metrics is found in [13].

It is important to note that an error can propagate in the system and still remain latent (i.e., not lead to failure) without immediate detection. As the triggers for dormant faults is not known, we take an optimistic approach and consider a failure free run of the test applications to imply that the likelihood of a dormant fault is very low.

4.2. Error Impact Criteria (Failure Class)

To determine and distinguish the impact of a propagated error we use failure mode analysis. A set of four modes of increasing severity is defined including the non-propagating one representing normal or failure-free behavior.

Class NF: No discernible violation observed as outcome of an experiment, i.e., *No Failure* class. Three distinguishable explanations account for an injection resulting in this class, namely a) the error location was not activated in this execution; b) the error was injected, but

was masked by the system; or c) the fault is dormant. Section 5.3 describes how case a) can be avoided.

Class 1: The error propagated to the benchmark applications, but still satisfied the OS service specification. Examples of class 1 outcomes include unsuccessful attempts to use services where the error code returned is in the set of valid codes for this call. The propagation of data errors also fall into this category.

Class 2: This failure mode captures behaviors violating the specification of the service. It could be an unforseen hang or crash of the *application* due to the error or an incorrect error code being returned. An application is considered hung after 40 seconds of non-responsiveness, exceeding 100% of normal execution time in a golden run experiment. Note that the rest of the system is still functioning after the failure.

Class 3: The OS becomes irresponsive due to a crash or a hang. No further progress is possible.

The failure modes give rise to a partitioning of the experiment outcomes. Similar to for instance [16], when an experiment could be placed in multiple classes, e.g., when it first gives an application error code (class 1) and then the system crashes (class 3) the more severe class is assigned.

4.3. Implementation Complexity Criteria

The complexity of implementing the FI campaign is a subjective and qualitative estimation of the effort needed to implement the three different error models. A discussion on the implementation complexity appears in Section 7.

4.4. Experiment Execution Time Criteria

Experiment execution time significantly influences the usability of the chosen approach. We therefore track the execution time of all experiments. Failures requiring manual intervention (Class 3) are assigned 200 seconds. This is the standard timeout used by the system to detect if no progress is made and a reboot is required. It is set to be sufficiently large to capture any delays incurred by an error, i.e., to detect that the system is hung and is not just delayed.

5. Target Setup

The conducted experiments use Windows CE .Net 4.2. The hardware is a development board, using the Intel XScale PXA255 platform, with 64 MB RAM and 32 MB ROM (flash). The board is connected using serial and Ethernet connections. The board also provides a Compact Flash (CF) slot. We have used this setup as its structure is very similar to most other OSs and hardware. It is also small in size making it easy to work with and control.

---

[1]We use the shorter term *Diffusion* in the rest of the text.

From a SW perspective, the system comprises two main components, namely the *Interceptor* and the *Experiment Manager* (Figure 2). The Interceptor intercepts all calls to or from a specific driver, and can then inject errors on request. It interacts with the Experiment Manager, receiving commands and sending the results back in form of log messages. The Experiment Manager is responsible for setting up the needed infrastructure, sending injection commands to the Interceptor, transmitting log messages to the host computer and for monitoring the outcome of the experiments. The Experiment Manager starts the test applications and monitors their behavior, receives reports of triggered assertions, and passes them on as log messages. It is also responsible for restarting the machine after each experiment.

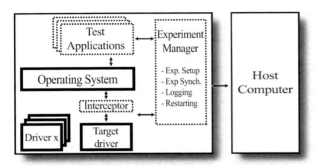

Figure 2. Experiment setup

Information on the selected experiments to perform is stored in a file in persistent storage (flash memory) on the target computer. The file is created the first time the system boots up. The injection is configured using the registry and the Interceptor automatically generates all test cases for the selected set of targeted services and the chosen error model.

Each experiment run (combination of error model and driver) uses a newly built OS image. Each experiment starts with a cold reboot where the OS image is read from ROM into RAM, ensuring that each injection is performed using a fresh, uncorrupted, OS image. Persistence between injections is limited to the error configuration file, and for FZ errors to the seed to the random number generator. Logs are stored on the host computer.

5.1. Targeted Drivers

For comparison, we target three different drivers for our experiments. Table 3 shows the number of services targeted and the total number of injection cases for the three targeted error models. The number of services reported includes both exported services, used by the OS, and imported OS services that the driver uses.

The drivers were chosen to represent three common, yet different, functional classes of drivers. The serial driver

(cerfio_serial) implements the common RS232 serial interface, a well established and commonly used interface. The Ethernet driver (91C111) represents network interface drivers. The CF driver (atadisk) represents a different class of interfaces altogether, namely filesystem drivers.

Driver	#Services	# Injection cases		
		BF	DT	FZ
cerfio_serial	60	2362	397	1410
91C111	54	1722	255	1050
atadisk	47	1658	294	1035

Table 3. Overview of the target drivers.

5.2. Benchmark Applications

The benchmark applications consist of five different processes. One application uses the driver that is currently targeted, thus there are test applications testing serial and Ethernet communication (with the host computer) as well as testing multiple reads and writes to the CF card. The general benchmark applications target a variety of general OS services, such as process creation and synchronization, file system operations and memory allocation/manipulation.

The applications are chosen to activate the system in a varied manner and to drive the experiments, i.e., function as workload for the targeted driver. For a system designer, the set of applications to be used in the target product may be known, and if so they should be used to drive the experiments. If not, then benchmark applications form the best choice, as they usually target many common features.

For each injection, all applications are used and their results tracked for deviations using assertions. Each application is written specifically for testing purposes, therefore its expected behavior is known *a priori*. This makes it possible to manually track the used services and add assertions.

5.3. System Pre-Profiling

To expedite the injection process, the system is first profiled to remove injections that will not lead to an error being injected. This is achieved by first generating all injections for a driver and then running the benchmark applications while keeping track of which services are being used. After successful execution of the benchmark applications, the list of injections is reduced to include only services actually called during profiling run. This typically reduces the number of test cases by half or more. The number of injections greatly influences the time required to execute the experiments. The more unnecessary cases identified, the more time is saved. Thus, the most time (in absolute numbers) is saved for the BF error model, since it requires the most injection cases in this study.

6. Experimental Results

A range of experiments were conducted for the three drivers. The next sections present the comparative results for the selected criteria. Due to the nature of the error models studied, BF use a significantly larger set of injection cases. Consequently, the time taken to perform the experiments is also significantly longer. The discussions in the following sections focus on class 3 failures, as these are relevant for robustness evaluation. Appropriate references to the other classes are clearly indicated. For FZ we report values for fifteen injections per parameter. Section 6.4 details a discussion on the number of injections needed.

Driver	BF	DT	FZ
cerfio_serial	1.05	1.50	1.56
91C111	0.98	0.73	0.69
atadisk	1.86	0.63	0.29

Table 4. Driver Diffusion for class 3 failures.

6.1. Comparing Drivers

Driver Diffusion (as defined in Section 4.1) is used to compare the drivers. The probability $PDS_{x,j}^i$ is approximated as the ratio of failures to the number of injections. Table 4 summarizes the results showing that DT and FZ identify the serial driver to be the most vulnerable driver (higher Diffusion value), whereas BF pin-points atadisk to be the most vulnerable.

Table 6 details the results for each driver and error type. Overall the class 3 ratio is below 5%, indicating that the OS is indeed able to handle most introduced perturbations. Furthermore, we conclude that the error model does not significantly impact the ratios for the 91C111 and cerfio_serial drivers. For class 3 failures the percentage of injections (last column) varies between 3.22% and 3.97% for the serial driver and 2.35% and 4.24% for 91C111 driver. For atadisk the differences are larger, but still within 1.26% and 3.98% with BF identifying it as more vulnerable. The results show slight differences between the drivers as well as between the error models.

While Diffusion values in Table 4 for BF indicate atadisk to have highest diffusion, the experimental results from Table 6 show that 91C111 has a higher ratio of class 3 failures. This is due to Diffusion being a "sum of probabilities". Diffusion shows that atadisk has more services with higher propagation probability than 91C111.

For class 2 failures there are some distinct differences between the drivers. 91C111 and atadisk drivers have considerably fewer class 2 failures. This is due to differ-

ences in how the drivers function, i.e., blocking vs. non-blocking. Failed blocking services are more likely to cause hangs of the system, i.e., class 2 failures. This suggests that there is, as expected, a difference between the tested drivers, which is exactly what the Diffusion metric captures. For class 1 failures, we notice the same difference with the serial driver having fewer cases due to its blocking nature.

Overall, many injections, for all drivers and all error models, end up in the NF category, i.e., no observable deviation from the expected behavior could be seen. This is in line with several previous studies, e.g., [2], [9] and [12]. It is important to note that all cases reporting the errors were in fact activated, since the pre-profiling eliminated the not used services *a priori*. Outcomes in the NF category are either masked by the system, for instance by not being used or overwritten; or handled by built-in error detection/correction mechanisms checking incoming parameter values for correctness. Another explanation could be that the fault is dormant in the system and has not yet propagated to the OS-Application interface.

Driver	Error Model	Execution Time	
		hours	minutes
cerio_serial	BF	38	14
	DT	5	15
	FZ	20	44
91C111	BF	17	20
	DT	1	56
	FZ	7	48
atadisk	BF	20	51
	DT	2	56
	FZ	11	55

Table 5. Experiment execution times.

6.2. Execution Time

Table 5 details the execution time for each experiment run. The BF model with the most injections, has the longest execution time. However, the execution time also depends on the outcome of the experiments (class 2 and 3 take longer time as they typically require timeouts to be triggered) and the nature of the test applications. There are also slight variations in the boot-up time of the target system. The serial driver and the atadisk driver both take longer time when failing, which also influences the execution time.

6.3. Comparing Error Models

Table 7 depicts services incurring class 3 failures. It shows the number of failures for each service/error model. BF clearly outperforms the other error models in terms of

Driver	Error Model	No Failure	%	Class 1	%	Class 2	%	Class 3	%
cerfio_serial	BF	1771	74.98%	209	8.85%	306	12.96%	76	**3.22%**
	DT	264	66.50%	65	16.37%	53	13.35%	15	**3.78%**
	FZ	931	66.03%	218	15.46%	205	14.54%	56	**3.97%**
91111C	BF	1166	67.71%	482	27.99%	1	0.06%	73	**4.24%**
	DT	181	70.98%	67	26.27%	1	0.39%	6	**2.35%**
	FZ	670	63.81%	350	33.33%	1	0.10%	29	**2.76%**
atadisk	BF	1246	75.15%	343	20.69%	3	0.18%	66	**3.98%**
	DT	191	64.97%	98	33.33%	1	0.34%	4	**1.36%**
	FZ	531	51.30 %	483	46.67%	7	0.67%	13	**1.26%**

Table 6. The number of experiments is shown for each driver, error model and failure class.

Service	BF	DT	FZ
SERIAL_OPEN	1	x	x
CreateThread	4	1	x
DisableThreadLibraryCalls	6		x
FreeLibrary	4		1
InitializeCriticalSection			1
LoadLibraryW	2	2	
LocalAlloc	2	4	x
MapPtrToProcess	2	1	
memcpy	77	3	32
memset	74	3	29
MmMapIoSpace	11	9	26
NDISInitializeWrapper	1	x	
NDISMSetAttributesEx	4		
NDISMSynchronizeWithInterrupt	7	1	2
QueryPerformanceCounter	2		
SetProcPermissions	1	1	7
wcscpy	6		
wcslen	11		

Table 7. Services identified by class 3 failures. "x" indicates class 2 service failures.

6.4. The Number of Injections for Fuzzing

A crucial question regarding the FZ model is how many injection cases are needed. Figure 3 shows how Diffusion changes with increasing number of injections. The X-axis shows the number of injection and the Y-axis shows the diffusion values using x injections. Diffusion stabilizes after roughly ten injections. We have injected fifteen cases for all three drivers and all of these are included in Tables 3-7.

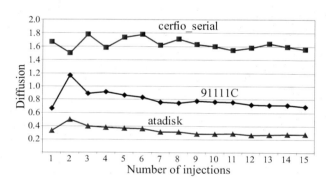

Figure 3. Stability of Diffusion for the FZ model wrt. the number of injections.

7. Interpretation & Discussion

Error Models & Error Severity: The first major finding is that the BF model causes more severe failures than the other models. Table 6 shows that BF finds by far the most class 3 failures of all error models. However, the number of injections used is also high, which comes with a cost in terms of execution time (Table 5). Therefore, when time is crucial, other error models may be considered. In terms of number of injections and execution time the DT error model performs the best, with FZ in the middle.

identifying vulnerable services, a key aspect for robustness enhancing efforts, such as using wrappers. In order to increase the identification coverage for the DT and FZ models we have indicated in the table which services exhibit class 2 failures, which increases the coverage slightly. Still there are four services identified only by BF. The DT model performs slightly better than FZ, but in two cases FZ identifies a service which DT does not. It is also important to note that one service is only found by FZ.

Comparing BF & FZ: The second major finding found in Table 7 is that BF identifies more services having class 3 failures than any of the other two models. FZ, on the other hand, identifies one service (`InitializeCriticalSection`) that none of the other two identified. So the question is: why are some of the services not identified by FZ? FZ chooses a new random value to be used in an injection, whereas the BF and DT error models modify the existing value. For services that have some basic level of checking of incoming parameters values which are well off the expected, as a random value is likely to be, are easy to find. However, values that are close to the expected value (as when only one bit is changed) are more difficult to find, and may therefore slip through and cause a failure of the system. This happens for instance when targeting different types of handles (to modules, libraries, memory areas etc.) and when targeting typical control values, such as bit-mask flags. Interestingly, FZ is traditionally regarded as not being very effective. However, our results are displaying its surprising effectiveness based on the number of injections used, especially when the intent is to identify drivers using the Diffusion metric.

Model Choice: Table 4 shows a difference in the result between the models. BF identifies `atadisk` as the most vulnerable driver and the other models identify the serial driver as most vulnerable. As described in Section 3 there are significant differences between the models. Ultimately, the choice of error model is influenced by many factors. Section 8 discusses some of the trade-offs that must be made, with respect to time, implementation complexity and more importantly the goals of the evaluation.

Implementation Complexity/Cost: Table 5 shows that BF and FZ are clearly more expensive in terms of execution time compared to DT. However, a major drawback with the DT error model is the cost for implementation. Since for every service in the interface the type of each parameter needs to be kept, it requires implementing support for this. BF and FZ on the other hand do not have this requirement, making their implementation considerably cheaper. The higher cost for the DT model could potentially be reduced by use of automatic parsing tools and/or reflection-capable programming languages. As this cost is a one-time cost for each driver, the cost might be acceptable if the experiments are to be repeated in a regression testing fashion.

Experiment Time: A factor influencing the experiment time is the degree of operator involvement. The operator is required to specify which experiment to run and for which driver. The time to do this is the same for all models. Some experiments force the system into a state where it cannot itself reboot, requiring the operator to manually reboot the system. 21.3% of the class 3 failures result in the system being left in a state where it cannot itself reboot. A consequence is that without external reboot mechanisms the execution

periment is delayed until the operator takes action, which can prolong the execution time substantially. We have not included this time in the total execution time for the experiments, since we cannot make any assumption on the presence of the operator. Each manual reboot is given a generic penalty of 200 seconds which is the timeout used to detect a hung system which automatically restarts.

Class 2/3 & Bugs: A question one might ask after seeing these results is whether the fact that class 2 and 3 failures are observed indicate that the system contains bugs? The answer is: not necessarily. It has until now been common practice to use a "gentlemen's agreement" between the OS and the drivers. This is mostly due to the fact that the costs of checking each and every call to the kernel would be too high for most systems. So the fact that the system crashes might not be due to a bug in the traditional sense. It is however from a robustness point of view a "vulnerability". All targeted drivers are deployed drivers, i.e., their producer has tested them to some extent and they do work well in our system when no errors are injected.

8. Developing the Composite Error Model

The results from Section 6 provides two major findings: a) BF pinpoints the most services for class 3 failures and b) FZ gives similar Diffusion results to BF at markedly a lower cost, but does not find as many services. This section explores these differences and use them to combine the two error models into a *composite error model* (CM) that identifies as many vulnerable services as BF but with fewer injections. We focus on the class 3 failures, as these are of highest interest when conducting robustness evaluation. The composite model combines BF & FZ by not utilizing the full bit space of the BF model. Thus a key step is to identify the subset of the BF model bits to combine with the FZ model. The following two subsections establish this basis to result in the selected composite model (CM).

8.1. CM Setup: Bit Failure Distribution

The relative inefficiency of BF in terms of execution time is a result of the number of injections. As noted in Section 3.1 the 32 bits available for flipping are not used uniformly. Figure 4 indicates that there are more services only sensitive to flips in the least significant bits than in the most significant. The bits below 10 (to the right in the figure) clearly cause failures in more services. Figure 5 shows the cumulative number of services identified, starting at bit 0 (from right to left). The figure shows that after bit 9 only bit 31 identifies a service not previously identified. Thus, the services having (class 3) failures for bits 10-31 also have failures for bits 0-9 (with `InitializeCriticalSection` being the only exception for bit 31). Thus, focus of the injections should be put on these bits.

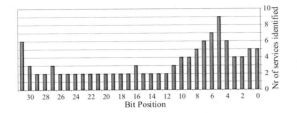

Figure 4. The number of services identified by Class 3 failures by the BF model.

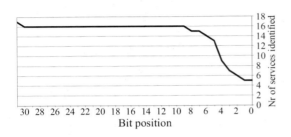

Figure 5. Moving from bit 0 and upwards the number of services increases until bit 10.

The observations made in Figures 4 and 5 allow us to modify the BF model to use fewer injections (only bits 0-9 and 31). Using only these bits reduces the number of test cases for BF by 62% (to 2164 in total), while still identifying all services. It is important to note that these results are system specific and the result of our experimental setup. Further research on methods for extracting such profiles at minimum cost is needed.

8.2. Distinguishing Control vs Data

A study of the parameters targeted for the services identified by BF, but not by FZ, reveals a prevailing trend: the parameters used are all control values, like pointers to data or handles to files, modules, functions etc. It is reasonable that these parameters are more sensitive to changes in the least significant bits (LSB) than to changes in the most significant bits (MSB). E.g., for a pointer that points to data within the process' memory region changes in the LSB will yield a new pointer within the region (but to possibly non-valid data) whereas changes of the MSB will yield a non-valid pointer which is easily detectable on modern hardware. Flipping a bit in the MSB is more likely to yield a non-valid pointer than changes to the LSB, and consequently we see a difference in the failure distribution. FZ, using random

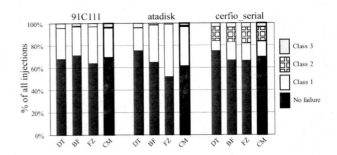

Figure 6. Failure mode distribution for CM compared to BF, DT and FZ.

Driver	Diffusion
cerfio_serial	2.9
91C111	2.0
atadisk	1.9

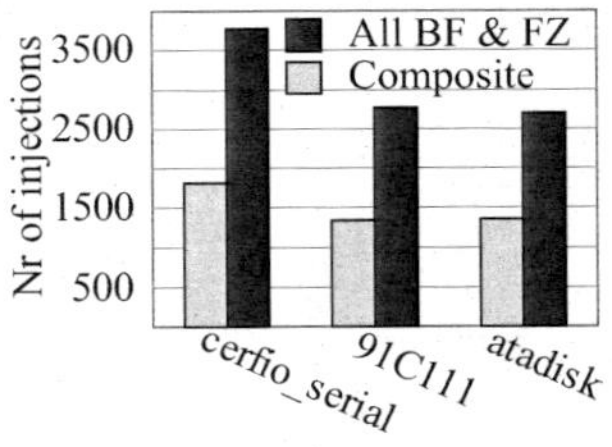

Figure 7. Diffusion and comparison of the number of injections with combined BF & FZ.

32-bit values, is also less likely to produce a valid pointer. However, since the value is random, it can also trigger failures not found by more structured injections (which is limited to changes to existing values or a small subset of special values), as shown by the fact that only FZ identifies a class 3 failure for service `InitializeCriticalSection`.

8.3. Composite Model & Effectiveness

The results in the previous sections have established the need for using multiple error models. Therefore, we recommend using **both** BF and FZ when resources are plentiful. When not, we propose to use *a composite model where the least significant bits (together with the most significant one) are targeted with BF, alongside a series of FZ experiments.* Section 6.4 established that ten FZ injections are sufficient for stabilizing the Diffusion metric. It is reasonable that more injections will increase the probability of finding "rare" cases (such as `InitializeCriticalSection`) but at the cost of increased number of injections.

A composite model, using only bits 0-9 and 31, together with ten FZ injections, identifies the same set of class 3 vulnerable services as the full set of BF and FZ injections. An overview of the results is shown in Figure 7. The table presents the Diffusion results for the composite model and it also shows how the composite model saves injection cases compared to performing all BF and fifteen FZ cases.

The Diffusion results are very similar to those presented for the individual error models in Table 4, identifying the serial driver as being the most vulnerable one, followed by the `91C111` and `atadisk`.

Figure 6 shows the results of CM alongside the other models, and it clearly show a similar trend as for the original error models, with a significant portion of the experiments ending up in the NF class. The number of injection cases is in the same range as those for BF, but higher than that for FZ with fifteen cases. Compared to performing both (BF & FZ) it *corresponds to performing only 48.7 % of the injections*, a significant reduction. Many other factors influences the actual execution time of the experiments. Assuming the execution time being proportional to the number of injections the CM gives a saving of up to 60 hours experimentation time for the combined BF & FZ.

9. Conclusions

This paper reports on extensive fault injection experiments carried out for three commonly used error models: bit-flip, data type and fuzzing. The results show bit-flips as the most acute one, but with the highest implementation cost. Based on these findings a new composite error model has been defined that compared to extensive bit-flip and fuzzing experiments achieves **a)** comparable error propagation results, and **b)** identifies the same set of vulnerable services. This is achieved using less than half the number of injections.

As this paper reports on experimental techniques the results must be viewed in this specific context, but we believe that there are some general guidelines that can be applied in the selection of the error model, namely:

- When comparing drivers on their potential to spread of errors, or evaluating the robustness of the OS to driver errors all three error models (and the composite) suffice to give guidance using the Diffusion metric. The experiments also validate the effectiveness of the Diffusion metric as an initial guideline.

- Data type errors come with a higher implementation cost, whereas bit-flips have a higher execution cost. If implementation cost (time) is a critical factor then bit-flips or fuzzing are recommended. Fuzzing gives similar Diffusion results as bit-flips with fewer injections. Thus making it the appropriate model to use when comparing drivers using Diffusion.

- When identifying services that may have serious failures, bit-flips is the most efficient error model followed by data type. However, fuzzing, being random in nature, may find cases where other models do not.

- A new composite error model, consisting of selective bit-flips with a series of fuzzing injections gives accurate results at a moderate execution/setup cost, compared to performing extensive bit-flip campaigns together with fuzzing injections.

References

[1] A. Albinet, et. al. Characterization of the Impact of Faulty Drivers on the Robustness of the Linux Kernel. *Proc. of DSN*, pp. 807–816, 2004.

[2] J. Durães and H. Madeira. Multidimensional Characterization of the Impact of Faulty Drivers on the Operating System Behavior. *IEICE Trans.*, E86-D(12):2563–2570, Dec. 2003.

[3] J. Arlat, et. al. Dependability of COTS Microkernel-Based Systems. *IEEE TOC*, 51(2):138–163, Feb. 2002.

[4] T. Ball et. al. Thorough Static Analysis of Device Drivers. *Proc. of EuroSys*, pp. 73-85, 2006.

[5] R. Chillarege, et. al. Orthogonal Defect classification-a Concept for In-Process Measurements. *IEEE TSE*, , 18(11):943–956, 1992.

[6] J. Christmansson and R. Chillarege. Generation of an Error set that Emulates Software Faults Based on Field Data. *Proc. of FTCS*, pp. 304 – 313, 1996.

[7] C. Fetzer and Z. Xiao. An Automated Approach to Increasing the Robustness of C-Libraries. *Proc. of DSN*, pp. 155-164, 2002.

[8] W. Gu, et. al. Error Sensitivity of the Linux Kernel Executing on PowerPC G4 and Pentium 4 Processors. *Proc. of DSN*, pp. 887–896, 2004.

[9] W. Gu, et. al. Characterization of Linux Kernel Behavior Under Errors. *Proc. of DSN*, pp. 459 – 468, 2003.

[10] M. Howard and S. Lipner. *The Security Development Lifecycle*. Microsoft Press, 2006.

[11] T. Jarboui, et. al. Analysis of the Effects of Real and Injected Software Faults: Linux as a Case Study. *Proc. of PRDC*, pp. 51 – 58, 2002.

[12] T. Jarboui, et. al. Experimental Analysis of the Errors Induced into Linux by Three Fault Injection Techniques. *Proc. of DSN*, pp. 331– 336, 2002.

[13] A. Johansson and N. Suri. Error Propagation in Operating Systems. *Proc. of DSN*, pp. 86–95, 2005.

[14] K. Kanoun, et. al. Benchmarking the Dependability of Windows and Linux using PostMark Workloads. *Proc. of ISSRE*, pp. 11–20, 2005.

[15] P. Koopman and J. DeVale. Comparing the Robustness of POSIX Operating Systems. *Proc. of FTCS*, pp. 30–37, 1999.

[16] E. Marsden and J.-C. Fabre. Failure Mode Analysis of CORBA Service Implementations. *Proc. of Middleware*, pp. 216–231, 2001

[17] B. P. Miller, et. al. An Empirical Study of the Reliability of Unix Utilities. *CACM*, 33(12):32–44, Dec. 1990.

[18] R. Moraes, et. al. Injection of Faults at component interfaces and inside the component code: are they equivalent? *Proc. of EDCC*, pp. 53–64, 2006.

[19] P. Oehlert. Violating Assumptions with Fuzzing. *IEEE Security & Privacy Magazine*, 3(2):58–62, 2005.

[20] M. M. Swift, et. al. Improving the Reliability of Commodity Operating Systems. *Proc. of SOSP*, pp. 207–222, 2003.

[21] T. Tsai and N. Singh. Reliability Testing of Applications on Windows NT. *Proc. of DSN*, pp. 427–436, 2000.

Experimental Risk Assessment and Comparison Using Software Fault Injection

R. Moraes[1], J. Durães[2], R. Barbosa[3], E. Martins[1], H. Madeira[2]
[1]State University of Campinas, UNICAMP, São Paulo, Brazil
[2]CISUC, University of Coimbra, Portugal
[3]Critical Software SA, Coimbra, Portugal
regina@ceset.unicamp.br, jduraes@isec.pt, rbarbosa@criticalsoftware.com,
eliane@ic.unicamp.br, henrique@dei.uc.pt

Abstract

One important question in component-based software development is how to estimate the risk of using COTS components, as the components may have hidden faults and no source code available. This question is particularly relevant in scenarios where it is necessary to choose the most reliable COTS when several alternative components of equivalent functionality are available. This paper proposes a practical approach to assess the risk of using a given software component (COTS or non-COTS). Although we focus on comparing components, the methodology can be useful to assess the risk in individual modules. The proposed approach uses the injection of realistic software faults to assess the impact of possible component failures and uses software complexity metrics to estimate the probability of residual defects in software components. The proposed approach is demonstrated and evaluated in a comparison scenario using two real off-the-shelf components (the RTEMS and the RTLinux real-time operating system) in a realistic application of a satellite data handling application used by the European Space Agency.

1. Introduction

A common practice for large scale software development is to use available general-purpose components (normally COTS components) and develop from scratch only the domain specific components and "glue" code. Given the high costs of designing and implementing software components, engineers see the reuse of general-purpose components as a way to reduce development effort and to achieve short time-to-market.

However, in spite of the advantages of COTS (and general reuse of components), their utilization introduces an unknown risk of failure, as the new operational conditions may differ substantially from those the components were initially designed for, and the new operational conditions may cause the activation of unknown residual faults. The fact that reused components have already been tested introduces a false sense of safety that may discourage additional testing. The reality has shown that new utilizations of heavily used components have exposed software faults that had not been discovered before [44]. In practice, it is necessary to test the component in the new environment to ensure high quality and reliability of the overall system.

In spite of these difficulties, component-based software development with intensive reuse of COTS components is a solid trend in the industry and it is not likely to diminish, as the alternative would be the much more expensive write-from-scratch approach. The (re)use of COTS in particular requires great care, as many COTS (e.g., operating systems, database management systems, etc) have a strong interaction with other components of the system, meaning that residual software faults in COTS components are particularly dangerous and may pose serious risk of system outage. Therefore, the software industry needs practical and effective methods to help estimate (and reduce) the risk of reusing components.

Software fault injection (i.e., injection of software faults in a given software component to emulate the activation of residual bugs that may exist in that component) can help in the experimental estimation of the risk of reusing components, although it cannot solve the problem entirely. To illustrate this point, suppose that component C is used in system S. If we perform a software fault injection campaign targeting component C we can measure the impact of failures in

512

component C in the rest of the system S. If, for example, a large percentage of the injected faults cause S to crash or to behave in an unacceptable manner, we can conclude that failures in C are particularly dangerous to S. On the contrary, if most of the faults injected in C are tolerated by S, then we can assume that S is robust to faults in C.

One important issue when using software fault injection to measure the impact of failures in a given software component is that it may produce unrealistic results if the faults injected are not realistic. To illustrate this, assume that after injecting software faults in component C we observe that most of the faults injected caused catastrophic failures in the system S. However, if the component C is small, with just a few lines of code, it is not likely to have residual bugs. Thus, the results of the fault injection campaign in C are meaningless, as they suggest that component C is potentially dangerous (because its failures have a strong impact in the system) but having a failures in C (in real use) is rather unrealistic, as C is not likely to have residual bugs.

Software fault injection can only measure impact of faults. In order to have a meaningful measure of risk we also need an estimation of the probability of fault in the target component, which can be obtained by the use of well established software complexity metrics.

Thus, the proposed approach to measure experimentally the risk of using (or reusing) a given component C in a system S is represented by the following equation:

$$Risk_C = prob(f_C) * cost(f_C) \qquad (1)$$

The term $prob(f_C)$ represents the likelihood of the existence of residual software faults in component C, estimated through well-established software complexity metrics [25, 40], and the term $cost(f_C)$ represents the impact of the activation of faults in component C measured by software fault injection [11].

Our goal is to provide a quantitative measure of the risk of system S having a failure (e.g., to produce erroneous results, or to experience a safety failure, or a timing failure, or a security failure, or become unavailable, etc.) due to a faulty behavior in component C caused by the activation of a residual software fault in that component.

The risk estimation based on an experimental approach, as proposed in this paper, is particularly very useful for the following scenarios:

- Identify software components that represent higher risk and require more testing effort or improvements.
- Help software designers and engineers to choose from alternative off-the-shelf components to be used in the system under development (i.e., choose the one that represents the lowest risk).
- Provide a quantitative evaluation of the risk reduction due to improvements introduced in components used in the system (COTS or non-COTS), such as wrapping the component to overcome robustness weakness [2]. It is worth noting that wrapping could also introduce new bugs and may change component behavior, which means that a thorough evaluation of the changed component is necessary (and it is not a trivial task).
- Help in tuning complex COTS components to minimize risk and increase the system dependability (e.g., a database management system is difficult to tune, especially in what concerns recovery features that have huge impact on whole system dependability [42]).

The use of fault injection to predict worst case scenarios and help identify weaknesses in software that could cause catastrophic disasters was proposed in [43]. However, to the best of our knowledge, this is the first time the injection of realistic software faults (based on a field study on the most common types of faults [11]) is used to experimentally estimate software risk. It is worth noting that the fault injection technique used in our method does not require the source code of the target components, which means that it can be used even in COTS for which the source code is not available. Our methodology uses software metrics, which implies either the existence of tools able to extract software metrics from executable code, or the availability of the source code itself. In the experiments presented in this paper we actually have access to the source code of all the components and we used that fact to simplify experiments, especially in what concerns the use of software complexity metrics tools, as we extract metrics based on source-code. However, for application scenarios where source-code is not available, all that is required is the use of metric assessment tools that do not require source code.

The remainder of this paper is organized as follows: the next section shows how to evaluate the risk using the proposed methodology. A case study to illustrate the actual use of the proposed methodology is presented in Section 3. Section 4 presents the related work. Section 5 concludes the paper.

2. Experimental Approach for Software Component Risk Assessment

Our main goal is to evaluate the potential risk of using a given software component in a larger system. This component is typically a COTS but the proposed technique can actually be applied to any component of the system under analysis. The risk of using a given component in a system is calculated as in equation (1).

The first term, *prob(f)*, represents the likelihood of residual faults existing in the component, i.e., corresponds to the component fault-proneness. The term *cost(f)* represents the consequence (i.e., impact in the system) of the activation of a fault *f* in the component.

Our proposal is based on three key elements:

- The estimation of *prob(f)* by using complexity metrics of the target component.
- The evaluation of *cost(f)* experimentally through the injection of software faults in the target component and measuring its impact in the system under analysis.
- The use of a real workload and operational profile during the fault injection experiments.

A very important aspect in risk assessment is the probability of the activation of the residual faults. This probability is strongly dependent on the workload, the operational profile, and the architecture of the component and cannot be easily modeled by static analysis alone (and details of the component architecture may not be available).

In our methodology the fault activation probability is actually evaluated during the fault injection experiments. This is, in fact, an intrinsic aspect of the fault injection experiments: the fault is injected and its activation/non-activation is a consequence of the workload and execution profile and the internal component architecture. The use of a real workload should not be viewed as a restriction to the methodology, as the main intended use is on fact the comparison of components for integration in a system for a well-known application scenario.

If the injection of faults in a given component shows that a large percentage of faults cause a strong impact in the system (high *cost(f)*) and the likelihood of faults in that component is high (high *prob(f)*), then that means the component represents a high risk. Note that this value resulting from the application of the methodology should not be interpreted as an absolute estimation of the probability of failure. Instead it should be understood as a *metric on risk* mainly intended for comparison.

2.1. Residual Fault Likelihood Estimation

The prediction of residual faults can be based on various methods. Some works use parametric models based on defect history [40, 12] and others use heuristics by comparing complexity metrics with a threshold [34]. Our work elaborates from previous proposals [5, 40, 31] to estimate *prob(f)* and follows a model based on logistic regression. Logistic regression

[16] was the used statistical analysis to address the relationship between metrics and the fault-proneness of modules (in this work module and component is used as having the same meaning). Logistic regression is a classification technique widely used in experimental sciences based on maximum likelihood estimation of dependent variables (e.g. the failure likelihood) in terms of independent variables (e.g. complexity metrics). Logistic regression gives to each independent variable, also called "regressor", an estimated regression coefficient β_i, which measures the regressor contribution to variations in the dependent variable. The larger the coefficient in absolute value the more important the impact of the variable on the probability of a fault to be detected in a component is. In our case, this probability *prob* represents the probability that such component has a residual fault. To be able to establish a linear relationship we need a logistic transformation and a *logit* of *prob* is taken. The *logit(prob)* is defined as *ln* (*prob* / (1 - *prob*)). The value of *prob* is given by equation (2) where α and β are the estimated logistic regression coefficients and *exp* is the inverse function of *ln*.

$$prob = \frac{\exp(\alpha + \beta x)}{1 + \exp(\alpha + \beta x)} = \frac{e^{(\alpha + \beta x)}}{1 + e^{(\alpha + \beta x)}} \quad (2)$$

Using the *logit* it is possible to obtain a simple form of a multivariate logistic regression model based on the relationship presented in equation (3) where several independent variables (in our case, static metrics) can be used.

$$logit(prob) = \ln\left(\frac{prob}{1 - prob}\right) = \alpha + \beta_1 x_1 + \beta_2 x_2 + .. + \beta_n x_n \quad (3)$$

To estimate the *prob(f)* we need to identify which metrics are relevant, since the chosen metrics strongly depend on the system characteristics, operational profile, the risk type, and the particular aspects that are being evaluated. When there is more than one metric available, we need to select which of them is best suited to the evaluation of the software complexity.

The size (in terms of lines of code - LoC) of the component was emphasized as an example of the direct relationship of measures of software complexity and measures of software quality [31] and it is one of the first and most common forms of software complexity measurement. LoC was used to compose the field observation and was combined with empirical fault density provided by Rome Laboratory [33]. We start by considering the cyclomatic complexity (Vg) as regressors for *prob(f)*. Vg measures the control flow complexity of a program and is dependent on the number of predicates (logical expression such as if, while, etc). Vg is also one of the most used software metrics and it is independent from the language.

The accuracy of the results obtained in the first experiments was evaluated through the analysis of bug reports available from open software initiatives (see [29]). Based on that study, we added the following new metrics to achieve a better approximation for the estimated fault density when compared to the bugs observed in field: number of parameters, number of returns, maximum nesting depth, program length, and vocabulary size [14]. Halstead's metrics and Vg measure two distinct program attributes [31] leading to a better fault prediction capability [24].

According to equation (3) and considering six metrics, the probability that a component has a residual fault ($prob(f(X_1, X_2, X_3, X_4, X_5, X_6))$) can then be expressed as in equation (4). This equation allows us to use any number of metrics we consider appropriate to calculate the probability of the existence of residual fault. For that purpose we only need to add one more term ($B_i X_i$) for each metric to be considered in the equation.

$$prob(f) = \frac{\exp(\alpha + \beta_1 X_1 + ... + \beta_6 X_6)}{1 + \exp(\alpha + \beta_1 X_1 + ... + \beta_6 X_6)} \quad (4)$$

In the above equation, X_i represents the product metrics (independent variables) and α and β_i the estimated logistic regression coefficients.

In order to obtain the coefficients for logistic regression [16] we proceed as follows:

- Evaluate the complexity metrics of each module.
- Adopt fault density ranges accepted by the industry community as a preliminary estimation of fault densities. In our work we use the empirical fault density reported by Rome Laboratory [33] as a starting estimation for the logistic regression. We used this preliminary estimation to replace the field observation used in any regression analysis.
- Use the binomial distribution. Taking into account $prob$ as 0.1 fault per KLoC and LoC metric for each module we get the number of lines with residual faults in the module i as a binomial random variable with parameters LoC_i and $prob$, and defines a preliminary fault density for module i. This preliminary density is then refined with the contribution of the other metrics using regression. The binomial distribution is used as we consider the existence of a fault is independent from the existence of other faults in the remaining component program lines.
- Apply the regression using the value obtained from natural logarithm of the preliminary fault density and the chosen metrics aim to obtain the coefficients.
- Estimate the probability of fault of each component by using the computed coefficients in the logistic equation presented in (4).

When necessary to estimate the probability of residual fault in a set of components (the case of a large component formed by several sub-components) we have to use the $prob(f)$ estimated for each sub-component combined with the complexity weight of each sub-component in the global component. This is obtained by equation (5), where $Metrics_i$ represents any of the available metrics for each component i. One can choose the metric that best represent the system characteristics (for example, maximum nesting depth if the system has several nested structures).

$$prob_g(f) = \sum prob_i(f) * (Metrics_i / \sum Metrics_i) \quad (5)$$

2.2. Failure Cost Estimation Through Injection of Software Faults

We use the G-SWFIT [11] technique to inject the software faults. G-SWFIT is based on a set of fault injection operators that reproduce directly in the target executable code the instruction sequences that represent most common types of high-level software faults. These fault injection operators resulted from a field study that analyzed and classified more than 500 real software faults discovered in several programs, identifying the most common (the "top-N") types of software faults [11]. Table 1 shows the 12 most frequent types of faults found in [11]. We use these 12 fault types in the present paper. The representativeness of the faults injected ensures that the fault injection experiments represent the activation of faults that are likely to exist in the component.

The locations where the injection are performed are selected by the analysis of the target code (done by the G-SWFIT tool), which allows the identification of the places where a given fault type could indeed realistically exist, and avoids using locations where faults of the intended type could not exist. For example, MIFS fault type in Table 1 can only be injected in target code locations that represent an *IF* structure. The analysis of the target code is based on the knowledge of how the high-level constructs are translated into low-level instruction sequences [11]. The distribution of the number of fault injected in each component is based in our previous proposal [29]. Furthermore, for large components with a very large number of fault locations, faults are internally distributed according to the distribution show in Table 1 (third column). For small components with a small number of fault locations is not possible to follow the distribution in Table 1. In this case, faults, inside the component, are injected using the best approximation for the distribution in Table 1.

Table 1 – Most frequent fault types found in [11]

Fault types	Description	% of total observed	ODC classes
MIFS	Missing "If (*cond*) { statement(s) }"	9.96 %	Algorithm
MFC	Missing function call	8.64 %	Algorithm
MLAC	Missing "AND EXPR" in expression used as branch condition	7.89 %	Checking
MIA	Missing "if (*cond*)" surrounding statement(s)	4.32 %	Checking
MLPC	Missing small and localized part of the algorithm	3.19 %	Algorithm
MVAE	Missing variable assignment using an expression	3.00 %	Assignment
WLEC	Wrong logical expression used as branch condition	3.00 %	Checking
WVAV	Wrong value assigned to a value	2.44 %	Assignment
MVI	Missing variable initialization	2.25 %	Assignment
MVAV	Missing variable assignment using a value	2.25 %	Assignment
WAEP	Wrong arithmetic expression used in parameter of function call	2.25 %	Interface
WPFV	Wrong variable used in parameter of function call	1.50 %	Interface
	Total faults coverage	**50.69 %**	

The evaluation of the cost of component failures is done by injecting one fault at each time. After the injection of each fault, the cost is measured as the impact of the fault injected in the component in the whole system. This impact is translated in the following failure modes: **Hang** – when the application is not able to terminate in the pre-determinate time; **Crash** – the application terminates abruptly before the workload complete; **Wrong** – the workload terminates but the results are not correct; **Correct** – there are no errors reported and the result is correct.

Considering the four failure modes proposed, only the "Correct" failure mode means that the system has delivered correct service after the injected fault. This means that we could in fact reduce the failure mode to only two: correct or incorrect behavior. However, we decide to keep the four failure modes to have more detailed information on the impact of each fault.

When a software fault is injected in a given component, that fault may or may not cause faulty behavior in the component. Furthermore, only a fraction of faults that cause erroneous behavior in the component will cause the system to fail, depending on the system architecture and the operational profile (the remaining faults are tolerated or have no visible effect). This means that the results measured by using fault injection already include two important terms:

$$cost(f) = prob(fa) * c(failure) \qquad (6)$$

where prob(*fa*) is the probability of fault activation (and consequent deviation in the component behavior) and c(*failure*) is the consequence of a failure, for example, the probability that the system crash.

3. Case Study

We present a case-study to show the experimental risk estimation as proposed in our approach. The case-study is a C application implemented for both the RTEMS and RTLinux operating systems and allows us to assess the risk for each of these alternative components. The metrics of each software component were obtained with the Resource Standard Metrics [35] and CMT++ tools [41].

The case-study is a satellite data handling system named Command and Data Management System (CDMS). A satellite data handling system is responsible for managing all data transactions between ground systems and a spacecraft. The CDMS application was developed in C and runs on top of two alternative real-time operating systems: RTEMS [36] and RTLinux [23]. This is particularly relevant as it allows us to show an interesting utilization of the proposed approach, which is to help developers in choosing between alternative off-the-shelf components (RTEMS and RTLinux in this case).

Table 2: Metrics and Logistic Regression Coefficients

Metrics	RTLinux			RTEMS		
	Global Values	Coefficients	*p-value*	Global Values	Coefficients	*p-value*
C. Complexity	39604	0.0072393	6.51 E-11	28536	0.0063537	7.09 E-05
N. Parameters	10778	-0.0051718	0.185622	8454	0.0117627	0.012413
N. Returns	13268	0.0431363	1.75 E-52	10240	0.0161907	0.000616
Progr. Length	1172521	-0.0001692	0.001896	787949	-0.0005537	7.9 E-20
Vocab. Size	171408	0.0011511	3.69 E-05	108550	0.0104020	2.48 E-47
Max. Nest. Depth	3963	0.3746203	1.0 E-140	2478	0.2354918	3.88 E-27

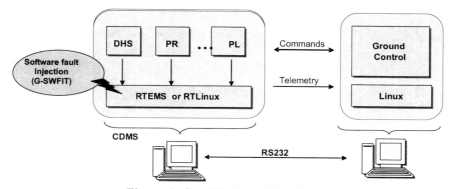

Figure 1: Satellite Data Handling System

Figure 1 shows the satellite data handling system setup. The CDMS system is composed by six subsystems (only partially shown): Packet Router (PR), Power Conditioning System (PCS), On Board Storage (OBS), Data Handling System (DHS), Reconfiguration Manager (RM), and Payload (PL).

The CDMS runs a mission scenario where a space telescope is being controlled and the data collected is sent to ground system. All data involved in this scenario is predetermined which allows deterministic experiments. The workload starts when an acknowledgement command is sent from the CDMS to the ground control. After that, the ground control sends a series of commands for the CDMS requesting telemetry information. The CDMS sends back telemetry information for each command sent. The timing of the commands and the contents of the telemetry information are used to detect the system correctness/failure during the experiments. The ground control software is hosted in a computer running Linux.

The remainder of this section describes the static and dynamic aspects of the risk assessment for the case-study.

3.1. Estimation of *prob(f)*

RTLinux is composed by 2211 modules with a total of 85108 lines of code, and the interception coefficient (α) is equal to -7.8443977 (calculated by regression as explained in section 2.1). RTEMS is composed by 1257 modules with a total of 63258 lines of code. The interception coefficient for RTEMS is -7.944308.

Table 2 presents a summary of metrics evaluation and coefficients for the two operating systems, showing the global values for each metric for both components and the coefficients (β_i) obtained. These coefficients were applied in the logistic equation (refer to equation (4)) to obtain the estimated *prob(f)* of each component. The global *prob$_g$(f)* estimated for RTLinux

is 6.50% and for RTEMS is 7.49 %. These values are calculated using equation (5) as explained in section 2.1.

A close observation of Table 2 shows that the complexity metrics of RTLinux are higher than the RTEMS metrics. It is then surprising why the *prob$_g$(f)* estimated for RTEMS is higher than the *prob$_g$(f)* estimated for RTLinux. An in depth analysis shows that RTEMS has a higher percentage of modules with high complexity when compared to RTLinux. Although the global complexity (i.e., sum of complexity metrics of all modules) of RTEMS is smaller than the global complexity for RTLinux, the large number of modules with high complexity in RTEMS is responsible for the higher *prob$_g$(f)* of RTEMS when compared to RTLinux. Table 3 shows the complexity distribution of modules for the LoC and Complexity metrics.

3.2. Estimation of *cost(f)*

The cost of the activation of residual faults is assessed through the injection of realistic faults in the components under observation (RTEMS or RTLinux) using the G-SWFIT technique as explained in section 2.2.

The identifications of the set of faults to inject in the components under evaluation is based on a simple algorithm: taking into account the fault types presented in Table 1, the target code is analyzed in an automated manner by yielding the identification of all locations were a given fault can be realistically emulated (by realistically emulated we mean that the intended fault could indeed be present at the original source-code construct relative to that location in the target executable code).

We identified 231 faults for the RTEMS setup and 341 faults for the RTLinux (the targets for the injection of fault in the code are the components used by the mission scenario, not all components in the system).

517

Table 3: Metrics Distribution and Global $prob_g(f)$

| Application | # Module | LoC | | | C. Complexity | | | Global |
		< 100	100- 400	> 400	< 25	25-40	> 40	$prob_g(f)$
RTEMS	1257	87,0%	11,0%	2,0%	80,0%	6,0%	14,0%	7,5%
RTLinux	2212	90,0%	9,0%	1,0%	84,0%	6,0%	10,0%	6,5%

Each fault is injected separately from the others. Additionally, each fault is present from the beginning of the experiment to its end. This is in accordance to the notion that a software fault is a permanent fault (i.e., it is not a transient fault). Thus, each fault implies a completely new experiment (involving the execution of the entire workload).

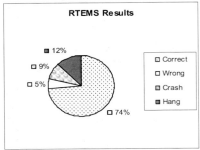

Figure 2: RTEMS Results

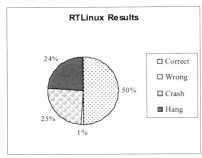

Figure 3: RTLinux Results

Figure 2 and 3 present the failure modes obtained in the fault injection campaigns in both operating systems and Table 4 shows the risk evaluation. The risk is evaluated considering each failure mode that represents erroneous and the combination of all the erroneous failure modes (Incorrect Behavior column in Table 4).

As we can see, RTLinux represents a higher risk than RTEMS for most of the failure modes considered, and RTEMS seems to be a better choice for this application.

One exception is related to the wrong results failure mode, as the CDMS version running on RTLinux represents a lower risk of wrong results when compared to the RTEMS version (i.e., the RTLinux version shows fail silent behavior more frequently). It is worth noting that, as both operating systems have Posix compliant API, the CDMS is practically the same for both operating systems. Thus, the differences observed in the measured risk do account for the operating system.

4. Related Work

Risk assessment approaches typically address risk management in software development projects [27, 19] and relate the risk estimation to quality models of software development, heuristics, and developers' experience [4, 34, 38]. In highly demanding application areas, such as avionics or nuclear power plants, the risk estimation is tightly associated to safety and reliability assessment and is regulated by strict industrial standards [15]. Modeling approaches based on architectural-level risk analysis are also quite popular, especially when applied to the early development phases [37, 32, 45].

Despite the extensive research in risk assessment, the estimation of the risk associated to the use of a given component remains a hard problem. One factor that contributes to this difficulty is the fact that the dynamic behaviour of the component is difficult to assess without experimentation using the actual component or a prototype.

The method proposed in the work at hand is based on recent software fault injection techniques [10, 11], combined with the use of well established software complexity metrics [25, 40]. We address the two classical terms of the risk equation (the probability of occurrence of an undesired event and the cost of resulting consequences) by using complexity metrics of the component under analysis to estimate the

Table 4: The Risk Evaluation – Failure Mode

| Component | prob(f) | Crash | | Wrong | | Hang | | Incorrect Behavior | |
		cost(f)	risk	cost(f)	risk	cost(f)	risk	cost(f)	risk
RTEMS	0.0749	0.09	0.67%	0.05	0.37%	0.12	0.89%	0.26	1.94%
RTLinux	0.0650	0.25	1.62%	0.01	0.06%	0.24	1.56%	0.50	3.25%

probability of residual software faults in that component, and by using software fault injection to evaluate the cost of possible component failures in the whole system (we use the term cost to refer to the impact of a component failure, as the term cost is generally used in risk works).

The approach proposed in our work is related to three main research lines: risk evaluation, the use of software metrics to estimate component fault density, and injection of software faults to evaluate cost of component failures. In this section we summarize the most relevant works for our proposal.

Software risk is often assessed based on rigorous risk analysis methods or by using heuristics [4]. Heuristic risk analysis includes a checklist of questions, suggestions or guidewords, such as "is the component unstable or new?", "does the component implements a complex business rule?", etc. Rigorous risk analysis generally apply statistical models such as software reliability modeling to estimate the component failure likelihood [25, 39], and hazard analysis to estimate the consequence of failures [22]. By combining the consequence and the likelihood of failures, it is possible to rank the risk of each individual components of a system.

Many studies have tried to mitigate the problems associated to software faults and estimate their risk with particular emphasis on studies on software testing, software reliability modelling, and software reliability risk analysis [25, 30, 17, 20]. The software risk assessment equation used in most of the literature is basically the same and reflects the probability of faulty behavior in a given software component and its impact (or cost). However, this equation is interpreted in different ways, depending on the approach used for risk assessment in each particular work.

The equation presented in [34] considers the object-oriented CK metrics [6] to estimate how error-prone the component is. The higher the metrics the more error-prone the component is. The risk is evaluated considering the probability that an undesirable event E_i occurs ($p(E_i)$) and the cost to the system if this event really occurs ($c(E_i)$), as shown in equation (7). In the context of estimating risk in software systems, an undesirable event is a component failure.

$$\text{Risk} = \sum(p(E_i) * c(E_i)) \qquad (7)$$

Sherer presents another concept of risk [38], as a function of fault activation probability in a pre-defined time, the quality of the development process and the operational profile. The work presented in [1] expands the Rosenberg's equation [34] in order to consider the component exposure from the point of view of the customer and from the point of view of the vendor.

Software complexity metrics have been widely used to estimate the probability of component faults, which are obviously related to the probability of component failure required in the typical risk equation (e.g., in equation (7)). The study presented in [5] experimentally validates object-oriented design metrics as quality indicators to predict fault-prone classes and conclude that several of these metrics appear to be useful to predict class fault-proneness during the early phases of the life-cycle.

The component failure likelihood is directly related to the complexity of that component [25]. In fact, complexity metrics have been used in many studies that show a clear link between component complexity and error proneness [21, 20, 12]. However, Fenton shows that this trend does not hold in some cases [13]. Some explanations for this apparent contradiction are provided in [28], and the use of static code metrics is recommended as predictors if these predictors are treated as probabilistic and not as categorical indicators. Menzies *et. al.* also reinforce the importance of finding good attributes set for each problem and to analyze a large amount of data sets in order to generalize the results.

Concerning the estimation of the impact of component failures (the term cost in the risk equation), the Failure Mode and Effect Analysis (FMEA) technique [22] is widely used to estimate component failure cost (in FMEA this is called severity analysis). This technique is particularly used in the development of software for highly regulated application areas such as avionics, space, and nuclear applications.

The use of fault injection to evaluate experimentally the cost (i.e., the impact) of failures in computer systems is also widely used [3, 18]. The impact of failures (equivalent to cost in the risk equation) is generally described in fault injection works as failure modes, which express the system response to the injection of each fault (e.g., crash, hang, erroneous output, etc.).

Although fault injection techniques are quite popular, their use to estimate risk has not been addressed in the literature, especially in what concerns software risk. In fact, the evaluation of the impact of software component failures would need the injection of software faults, and techniques to inject this type of faults have been largely absent from the fault injection research. Most of the fault injection works actually inject faults that emulate hardware transient faults. Very often, faults are injected using the SWIFI approach (Software Implemented Fault Injection), but this must not be confused with the injection of software faults (i.e., program defects or bugs), as SWIFI tools actually emulate hardware faults through the injection of errors by software.

The problem of injecting representative software faults was first addressed in [8]. That work was done in the context of IBM's Orthogonal Defect Classification (ODC) project [7] and the proposed method requires field data about real software faults in the target system or class of target systems. This requirement (the knowledge of previous faults in the target system) greatly reduces the usability of the method, as this information is seldom available and is simply not possible to obtain for new software. Furthermore, as shown in [26], typical fault injection tools are not able to inject a substantial part of the type of faults proposed in [8].

To the best of our knowledge, the first practical approach to inject realistic software faults without the need of the target source code was proposed in [9]. The technique is named Generic Software Fault Injection Technique (G-SWFIT) and is supported by the findings from an extensive field study (see [10]). In the work at hand we use this technique for the estimation of the cost of the activation residual faults.

5. Conclusion

This paper presents a first approach to evaluate the risk of using a given software component by software fault injection. The risk is evaluated using both software metrics and software fault injection. The faults injected are meant to represent component residual faults realistically, and provide a measure of the impact of component failures (failure of the component where the faults are injected). Several software metrics are considered such as cyclomatic complexity, number of parameters, number of returns, maximum nesting depth and Haltead's program length and vocabulary size. The complexity metrics are used to estimate the component fault proneness. Logistic regression analysis is used to fit the expression of the fault probability with these metrics. The fault injection in the experiments includes the notion probability of fault activation to model the fact that some faults are not activated or simply tolerated. The improvement that our approach brings to risk evaluation is that it assures a repeatable way of evaluating risk and removes the dependence on the evaluators that characterize classical risk evaluation approaches.

The proposed experimental risk assessment approach was illustrated using case-study of a satellite data handling real time application written in C. The risk assessment technique is illustrated in each setup at very different levels of component granularity. The risk of using two well-know off-the-shelf components (RTEMS and RTLinux operating systems) was analyzed. Results show that RTEMS represents a considerably lower risk than the RTLinux for that application.

6. Acknowledgments

The authors thank to CAPES/GRICES and FAPESP to partially support this work. We thank also to MSquared Technologies for gracefully providing the full version of RSM tool, and Testwell Oy Ltd for CMT++ and CMTjava tools.

7. References

[1] Amland, S. "Risk-based Testing: Risk analysis fundamentals and metrics for software testing including a financial application case study". The Journal of Systems and Software, 53, pp. 287-295, 2000.

[2] Anderson, T.; Feng, M.; Riddle, S.; Romanovsky, A. "Protective Wrapper Development: A Case Study". Lecture Notes in Computer Science, vol 2589, pp. 1-14, Springer Verlag, London, UK, 2003.

[3] Arlat, J. et al. "Fault Injection and Dependability Evaluation of Fault Tolerant Systems". IEEE Transaction on Computers, vol. 42, n. 8, pp.919-923, 1993.

[4] Bach, J. "Heuristic Risk-Based Testing". in Software Testing and Engineering Magazine, 1999.

[5] Basili, V.; Briand, L.; Melo, W. "Measuring the Impact of Reuse on Quality and Productivity in Object-Oriented Systems". Tech. Report, University of Maryland, Dep. Of Computer Science, Jan. 1995, CS-TR-3395.

[6] Chidamber, R.; Kemerer, F. "A Metric Suite for Object-Oriented Design". In IEEE Trans. of Software Engineering, 20 (6), 1994.

[7] Chillarege, R., "Orthogonal Defect Classification", Ch. 9 of "Handbook of Software Reliability Engineering", M. Lyu Ed., IEEE Computer Society, McGraw-Hill, 1995.

[8] Christmansson, J; Chillarege, R. "Generation of an Error Set that Emulates Software Faults-Based on Fields Data". Proc. of 26th Int. Symposium on Fault-Tolerant Computing, pp 304-13, Sendai, Japan, 1996.

[9] Durães, J.; Madeira, H. "Emulation of Software Faults by Educated Mutations at Machine-Code Level". in Proc. of The 13th Int. Symposium on Software Reliability Engineering – ISSRE'02, Annapolis, USA, 2002.

[10] Durães, J.; Madeira, H. "Definition of Software Fault Emulation Operators: A Field Data Study". In Proc. of The Int. Conf. on Dependable Systems and Networks, pp. 105-114, San Francisco, USA, 2003 (W. Carter Award).

[11] Durães, J.; Madeira, H. "Software Faults: A field data Study and a practical approach". in Trans. Of Software Engineering, Nov. 2006.

[12] El Emam, K.; Benlarbi, S.; Goel, N.; Rai, S. "Comparing Case-based Reasoning Classifiers for Predicting High Risk Software Components". Journal of Systems and Software, vol. 55, n. 3, pp. 301-320, 2001.

[13] Fenton, N.; Ohlsson, N. "Software Metrics and Risk". Proc. of The 2nd European Software Measurement Conference (FESMA'99), 1999.

[14]Halstead, M. "Elements of Software Science". Elsevier Science Inc., New York, NY, USA, 1977.

[15]Herrmann, D. "Software Safety and Reliability: Techniques, Approaches, and Standards of Key Industrial Sectors". Wiley-IEEE Computer Society Press, 1st edition, January, 2000.

[16]Hosmer, D.; Lemeshow, S. "Applied Logistic Regression". John Wiley & Sons, 1989.

[17]Hudepohl et al. "EMERALD: A Case Study in Enhancing Software Reliability". in Proc. of IEEE Eight Int. Symp. on Software Reliability Engineering - ISSRE98, pp.85-91, 1998.

[18]Iyer, R. "Experimental Evaluation". Special Issue FTCS-25 Silver Jubilee, 25th IEEE Symposium on Fault Tolerant Computing, pp. 115-132, 1995.

[19]Karolak, D. "Software Engineering Risk Management". Wiley-IEEE Computer Society Press, 1st edition, November, 1995.

[20]Khoshgoftaar et al. "Process Measures for Predicting Software Quality". in Proc of High Assurance System Engineering Workshop – HASE'97, 1997.

[21]Kitchenham, B.; Pfleeger, S.; Fenton, N. "Towards a framework for software measurement validation". IEEE Trans. on Software Eng., 21(12), pp. 929-944, 1995.

[22]Leveson, N. "Safeware, System Safety and Computers". Addison-Wesley Publishing Company, 1995.

[23]Linux kernel. www.kernel.org. Accessed on Feb/06, 2006.

[24]Lyu, M.; Chen, J.; Avizienis, A. "Experience in Metrics and Measurements for N-Version Programming". Int. Journal of Reliability, Quality and Safety Engineering, vol. 1, n. 1, pp. 41-62, 1994.

[25]Lyu, M. "Handbook of Software Reliability Engineering". IEEE Computer Society Press, McGraw-Hill, 1996.

[26]Madeira, H.; Vieira, M.; Costa, D. "On the Emulation of Software Faults by Software Fault Injection". Proc. of The Int. Conf. on Dependable Systems and Networks, NY, USA, 2000.

[27]McManus, J. "Risk Management in Software Development Projects". Butterworth-Heinemann, November, 2003.

[28]Menzies, T.; Greenwald, J.; Frank, A. "Data Mining Static Code Attributes to Learn Defect Predictors". IEEE Trans. on Software Eng., Vol.32, n. 11, pp. 1-12, 2007.

[29]Moraes, R., Durães, J., Martins, E., Madeira, H. "A field data study on the use of software metrics to define representative fault distribution". Proc. of Workshop on Empirical Evaluation of Dependability and Security – WEEDS in conjunction with DSN06, 2006.

[30] Musa, J. "Software Reliability Engineering", McGraw-Hill, 1996.

[31]Munson, J.; Khoshgoftaar, T. "Software Metrics for Reliability Assessment". in:Handbook of Software Reliability Engineering, Comp. Society Press, Michael R. Lyu editor, ch. 12, 1995.

[32]Popstojanova, G. K.; Trivedi, S. K. "Architecture Based Approach to Reliability Assessment of Software Systems". Perf. Evaluation, vol. 45, nos. 2-3, pp. 179-204, Jun/01, 2001.

[33]Rome Laboratory (RL). "Methodology for Software Reliability Prediction and Assessment". Technical Report RL-TR-92-52, vol. 1 and 2, 1992.

[34]Rosenberg, L.; Stapko, R.; Gallo, A. "Risk-based Object Oriented Testing". In Proc of. 13th Int.Software / Internet Quality Week-QW, San Francisco, USA, 2000.

[35]Resource Standard Metrics, Version 6.1, http://msquaredtechnologies.com/m2rsm/rsm.htm. Last access 2005.

[36]Real-Time Operating System for Multiprocessor Systems. www.rtems.com, accessed in Feb/06, 2006.

[37]Shaw, M.; Clements, P. "A Field Guide to Boxology: Preliminary Classification of Architectural Styles for Software Systems". Proc. 21st Int. Computer Software and Applications Conference, pp. 6-13, 1997.

[38]Sherer, S. "A Cost-Effective Approach to Testing". In IEEE Software, 8 (2), pp. 34-40, 1991.

[39] Singpurwalla, N. "Statistical Methods in Software Engineering: Reliability and Risk". Springer; 1st ed, 1999.

[40]Tang, M.; Kao, M.; Chen, M. "An Empirical Study on Object-Oriented Metrics". In: Proc. of the Sixth International Software Metrics Symp. pp. 242-249, 1999.

[41]Testwell Oy Ltd. http://www.testwell.fi. Accessed on March/06, 2006.

[42]Vieira, M.; Madeira, H. "Recovery and Performance Balance of a COTS DBMS in the Presence of Operator Faults", Int. Conf. on Dependable Systems and Networks, pp. 615-624, Washington D.C., USA, 2002.

[43]Voas, J.; Charron, F.; McGraw, G.; Miller, K.; Friedman, M. "Predicting how Badly 'Good' Software can Behave". IEEE Software, 1997.

[44]Weyuker, E. "Testing Component-Based Software: A Cautionary Tale". IEEE Software, 1998.

[45]Yacoub, S.; Ammar, H. "A Methodology for Architectural- Level Reliability Risk Analysis". IEEE Trans. Software Eng, vol. 28, no. 6, pp. 529-547, Jun/02, 2002.

Foundations of Measurement Theory Applied
to the Evaluation of Dependability Attributes

Andrea Bondavalli,
Andrea Ceccarelli, Lorenzo Falai
University of Florence
Viale Morgagni 65, I-50134 Firenze, Italy
{bondavalli; falai}@unifi.it
3697838@student.unifi.it

Michele Vadursi
Department of Technologies
University of Naples "Parthenope"
Via Medina 40, I-80133 Naples, Italy
vadursi@uniparthenope.it

Abstract

Increasing interest is being paid to quantitative evaluation based on measurements of dependability attributes and metrics of computer systems and infrastructures. Despite measurands are generally sensibly identified, different approaches make it difficult to compare different results. Moreover, measurement tools are seldom recognized for what they are: measuring instruments. In this paper, many measurement tools, present in the literature, are critically evaluated at the light of metrology concepts and rules. With no claim of being exhaustive, the paper i) *investigates if and how deeply such tools have been validated in accordance to measurement theory, and* ii) *tries to evaluate (if possible) their measurement properties. The intention is to take advantage of knowledge available in a recognized discipline such as metrology and to propose criteria and indicators taken from such discipline to improve the quality of measurements performed in evaluation of dependability attributes.*

1   Introduction

The key role of computing systems and networks in a variety of high-valued and critical applications justifies the need for reliably and quantitatively assessing their characteristics. The quantitative evaluation of performance and of dependability-related attributes is an important activity of *fault forecasting* [1], since it aims at probabilistically estimating the adequacy of a system with respect to the requirements given in its specification. Quantitative system assessment can be performed using several approaches, generally classified into three categories: *analytic*, *simulative* and *experimental*. Each of these approaches shows different peculiarities, which determine the suitableness of the method for the analysis of a specific system aspect. The most appropriate method for quantitative assessment depends on the complexity of the system, the development stage of the system, the specific aspects to be studied, the attributes to be evaluated, the accuracy required, and the resources available for the study.

Analytic and simulative approaches are generally efficient and timely, and they have proven to be useful and versatile in all the phases of the system life cycle. Analytic approach is usually cheap for manufacturers. The accuracy of the results obtained through an analytic approach is strongly dependent on the accuracy of the values assigned to the model parameters and on how realistic the assumptions the system model is based on are. The simulative approach is one of the most commonly used approaches for quantitative evaluation in practice; similarly to the analytic approach, the accuracy of the obtained evaluation depends on the accuracy of the assumptions made for the system to be analyzed as well as on the behavior of the simulation environment, and on the simulation parameters.

In the last years, increasing interest is being paid to the quantitative evaluation based on measurements, with special attention to evaluation of Quality of Service (QoS) metrics of systems and infrastructures. Experimental measurement is an attractive option for assessing an existing system or prototype. It allows monitoring the real execution of a system to obtain highly accurate measurements of the system in execution in its real usage environment. When presenting the results achieved in the experiments, the related authors usually choose parameters and indicators that appear sensible and represent the typical metrics of interests for dependability. In other words, the measurands are generally correctly and sensibly identified. It has to be noted, however, that the approach followed to quantitatively assess algorithms and systems is not univocal. It generally varies from a paper to another, making comparison among different results quite difficult, if not meaningless. Moreover, the attention is usually devoted only to the output, intended as the numerical results provided by the tool, whereas little or no attention is devoted to the (quantitative) evaluation of the quality of the measurement. This is probably a consequence of the fact that measurement tools designed and utilized to evaluate dependability attributes of computer systems and algorithms are seldom recognized for what they really are: *measuring instruments*. Hence, they are not characterized as they should, in terms of their metrological properties and parameters. Some important characteristics are not made explicit as they should, and remain hidden. The need for a common roadmap to follow when characterizing a measurement tool and the results it provides is becoming more and more urgent, as this would help a more rigorous treatment and fair comparison of the behavior of different tools.

As modern science is based on experimental evidence [2], the science of measurement, i.e. modern *metrology*, which traces its roots back to the French Revolution and even before [3], has nowadays reached an adequate level of maturity and has proved very useful in the application to several fields of science. In particular, it has developed theories as well as good practice rules to properly make measurements and evaluate measurement results, and to correctly characterize measuring instruments and assess their characteristics.

In the paper, computer systems and infrastructures are looked at with the eye of the metrologist, with the intention of highlighting the peculiarities of such modern systems, with particular regard to the quantitative assessment of dependability and QoS metrics in accordance to measurement theory. The intention is to propose a methodology based on *criteria* and *indicators* that are the foundations of a recognized discipline like metrology in order to compare the results of different measurement tools, which should now be seen as measuring instruments in all respects.

The paper is organized as follows. In Section 2, fundamentals of measurement theory are introduced, and the main metrological properties that should be analyzed to characterize measurement results and assess the characteristics of a measurement instrument are stressed. Section 3 proposes a classification of computer systems, from a metrological point of view, and singles out the most important properties to be evaluated for tools and, in general, for experimental campaigns of computing systems. In Section 4 a number of well-known measurement tools, which are currently present in computer science literature and are used with success, are taken into consideration and critically evaluated along the lines traced by metrology concepts and rules. Without expecting to be exhaustive, the idea is to investigate if and how deeply such tools have been validated in accordance to measurement theory, and try to evaluate (if possible) their properties. Finally, concluding remarks

follow in Section 5.

2 Fundamentals of measurement theory for the characterization of measurement systems

In this Section we give definitions and we describe fundamental concepts related to characterize measurement systems and methods according to metrological criteria. A complete digest of metrological terms and concepts can be found in [4].

Measuring a quantity (namely the *measurand*) consists in quantitatively characterizing it. The procedure adopted to associate quantitative information to the measurand is called *measurement*. The measurement result is expressed in terms of a measured quantity value and a related measurement uncertainty.

Accuracy is a concept that is often badly used; in metrology it must be intended only in a qualitative way. It was formerly defined as the difference between the measure and the true value of the measurand. As it is now commonly accepted that the true value of the measurand can not be exactly known, the *qualitative* concept of accuracy represents closeness of the measure to the best available estimate of the measurand value.

Uncertainty, on the contrary, provides *quantitative* information on the dispersion of the quantity values that could be reasonably attributed to the measurand. Uncertainty has to be included as part of the measurement result and represents an estimate of the degree of knowledge of the measurand. It has to be evaluated according to conventional procedures, and is usually expressed in terms of a confidence interval, that is a range of values where the measurand value is likely to fall. The probability that the measurand value falls inside the confidence interval is named confidence level. Uncertainty can also be expressed in terms of relative uncertainty, which is the ratio of uncertainty to the absolute value of the estimate of the measurand.

Indirect measurements are performed when the measurand value is not measured directly, but it is rather determined from direct measurements of other quantities, each of which is affected by uncertainty. Uncertainly of indirect measures can be obtained in principle following several ways. To give answer to the need for a univocal way of evaluating uncertainty, which offers the opportunity of comparing results from different methods and instruments, the Guide to the expression of Uncertainty in Measurements (GUM) has been published in 1993, and amended in 1995 [5], after years of discussions within, but not limited to, the scientific community. Actually, since then, some supplements to the GUM are being discussed, and some questions are still open (e.g. alternative ways of evaluating uncertainty in indirect measurements in particular cases).

According to the GUM, *standard uncertainty*, usually indicated as u, that is uncertainty expressed as a standard deviation, can be evaluated in two ways: i) statistically, as an estimate of the standard deviation of the mean of a set of independent observations, or ii) on the basis of a scientific judgement using all the relevant information available, which can include previous measurement data, knowledge of the behavior and property of relevant materials and instruments, manufacturer's specifications, data provided in calibration and other reports, and uncertainties assigned to reference data taken from handbooks. This second way of evaluating uncertainty can be as reliable as the first, especially when the independent observations are very few.

Uncertainty evaluation becomes more critical for measurand estimated through indirect measurements. Specifically, let Y be the measurand, which is determined through N other quantities $X_1, X_2, ..., X_N$, according to the functional relation

$$Y = f(X_1, X_2, ..., X_N) \qquad (1)$$

which is also called *measurement equation*. An estimate of Y, denoted by y, is achieved from (1) using input estimates $x_1, x_2, ..., x_N$ for the values of the N input quantities $X_1, X_2, ..., X_N$, that is

$$y = f(x_1, x_2, ..., x_N) \qquad (2)$$

First of all, the *standard uncertainty* (i.e. the uncertainty expressed as a standard deviation) $u(x_i)$ of each estimate x_i $(i = 1, ..N)$ involved in the measurement function has to be evaluated. Then, we have to compose such standard uncertainty to obtain the combined standard uncertainty $u_c(y)$; according to [5]:

$$u_c(y) = \sqrt{\sum_{i=1}^{N} \left(\frac{\partial f}{\partial x_i} \right)^2 u^2(x_i)} \qquad (3)$$

where the partial derivatives $\frac{\partial f}{\partial x_i}$ are equal to $\frac{\partial f}{\partial X_i}$ evaluated in $X_i = x_i$. Equation (3), referred to as the law of propagation of uncertainty, is based on a first order Taylor's approximation of (1). Actually, equation (3) is the simplified form to be used when the estimates x_i can be assumed to be not correlated. Otherwise, a further sum involving the estimated covariances associated with each pair (x_i, x_j) is needed under the square root in (3).

Singling out the most significant quantities of influence is important when we have to characterize a measurement system. These are the quantities that are not object of the measurement, but whose variation determines a modification in the relationship between measurand and instrument's output. Their presence can significantly degrade the measure, as they can represent a major cause of uncertainty. With regard to this, **selectivity** of a measurement system corresponds to its insensitiveness to quantities of influence. In other words, the less variable are measurement system's outputs due to the variability of the quantities of influence, the more selective is the system.

Resolution is the ability of a measuring system to resolve among different states of a measurand. It is the smallest variation of the measurand that can be appreciated, i.e. that determines a perceptible variation of the instrument's output.

Repeatability is the property of a measuring system to provide closely similar indications in the short period, for replicated measurements performed i) independently on the same measurand through the same measurement procedure, ii) by the same operator, and iii) in the same place and environmental conditions.

Stability is defined as the property of a measuring system to provide closely similar indications in a defined time period, for measurements performed independently on the same measurand through the same measurement procedure and under the same conditions for the quantities of influence.

To characterize a measurement system, and draw a comprehensive comparison with alternative systems, some other indicators should also be taken into account, such as measuring interval, measurement time and intrusiveness.

The **measuring interval** of a measurement system is the range of values of the measurand for which the measurement system is applicable with specified measurement uncertainty under defined conditions.

The importance of taking into consideration **measurement time** for a complete characterization is intuitive: besides being directly linked to measurement costs (in terms of resources occupation), the reciprocal of the measurement time gives an upper bound to the number of measurements that can be performed in the unit of time.

It is well known that any measurement system perturbs the measurand, determining a modification of its value. Minimizing such perturbation, that is minimizing the system's **intrusiveness**, is therefore desirable when designing a measurement system.

Finally, as measurement results are expressed in terms of ranges of values, intervals measured through different instruments ought to be compared rather than single values. Specifically, if results are expressed with the same confidence level, they are said to be **compatible** if the related intervals overlap.

3 Metrology and dependability

To adapt the concepts mentioned in the previous Section 2 to the field of computing systems is not trivial. In this Section, a classification of computing systems, and of measurements that can be of interest on such systems are drawn.

Then, on the basis of such classification, the most significant measurement properties that should characterize measurement tools designed to operate on the different kinds of systems are highlighted.

First of all, let us classify measurements that can be performed on computing systems, with special regard to dependability evaluation. They can be divided into two main classes:

- *Measurements with negligible uncertainty*. This class includes *static* quantities which depend on the static characteristics of the system under evaluation, as well as countable *dynamic* quantities, which depend on a particular execution of the system. Such measurements typically result in integer counts, either attribute counts or event counts. Many software quality measurements, typical of software engineering, such as number of source code lines of a given software element, number of system calls, and so on, belong to this class. Moreover, this class includes packet size in packet-switched networks, queue size of a particular network protocol, number of packets sent on top of a point-to-point channel, number of messages received by a network interface, maximum memory size of an application, maximum number of records in a database table, etc. Measurements belonging to this class are characterized by very low uncertainty.

- *Measurements with non-negligible uncertainty*, which generally refer to the dynamic behavior of the system under evaluation and usually involve the estimation of continuous quantities. Relevant examples of measurements belonging to this class are: delays experienced in an end-to-end connection, quality of clock synchronization, Mean Time To Failure, Mean Time Between Failures, direct and indirect measurements depending on distributed events.

It is quite obvious that this latter class includes quantities whose measurement presents more challenges than those belonging to the former one. A closer look at this class highlights the crucial role of **time intervals** measurements. Dependability-related measurements are very often based on measuring time intervals, either because the measurand is a time interval, or because the measurand is obtained through indirect measurements based on time intervals. Such measurements are often affected by non negligible uncertainty.

It can be useful to classify the computing systems whose QoS or dependability attributes are to be measured along the following dimensions:

- *Real-time*: along this paths we start from *time-free systems*, characterized by the absence of timing constraints or temporal requirements, to reach the case

of so called *hard real-time systems*, characterized by well-defined (and usually quite strict) constraints on their temporal behavior. A system is time-free when there is no deadline for its operations, whereas it is hard real-time when the correctness of its behavior is defined not only based upon the logical correctness of the operations performed but depends also upon the time frame in which such operations are performed [6].

- *Criticality*: along the criticality dimension at one extreme we find *non-critical systems*, while the other extreme is represented by *X-critical systems*, which may take many forms, e.g. *safety-critical systems*, or *mission-critical systems* or *life-critical systems*. While the failure of the former does not imply any significant damage, for the latter a failure could result in very dangerous events such as loss of life, significant property damage, or damage to the environment. There are many well-known traditional examples in different areas, such as medical devices, aircraft flight control, weapons, and nuclear systems, which fit this definition. In addition to these, many modern information systems and infrastructures are starting being considered X-critical, because the same types of damages (with even a more severe impact to their scale) can result from their failure [6].

- *Centralized/Distributed*: starting from so called centralized systems we may find several forms of distributed systems. While a centralized system is made of a unique node, which may eventually be decomposed in non autonomous and closely coupled parts, a distributed system is a set of distinct nodes, with minor and even unstable coupling constraints, interconnected by any kind of network, cooperating for common objectives [6].

The aforementioned dimensions constitute a quite simple categorization of computing systems to which the concepts of metrology introduced in Section 2 should be applied. Depending on the category a system belongs to, the metrology properties and indicators may be less or more *important* to be taken into account and less or more *difficult and costly* to apply and to assess.

Among the fundamental properties that should be taken into consideration for a significant characterization of measurement systems, those of major concern to dependability evaluation can be identified in: **uncertainty, repeatability, resolution** and **intrusiveness**.

Table 1 enlists the abbreviations used in the other tables presented in this and in the next Section.

Table 2 describes the relative importance of metrological properties for the different categories of systems. It describes the most important metrological properties that

525

should be considered to design measurement tools that can provide reliable results (X stands for important, XX for fundamental).

Some details on the arguments used to fill Table 2 are now given.

Uncertainty. A quantitative evaluation of uncertainty is necessary to appreciate the quality of the measurement. Such need is not only theoretical but has an important practical implication. Let us consider, for example, a safety critical system with hard real-time requirements; in such system there can be cases when uncertainty can be essential to state whether the system is compliant with its requirements or not. If an indicator has to be below a given threshold, and the result of measurements confirms it is below that threshold, one would be convinced that the system meets its requirements. What if after evaluating uncertainty, the interval expressing the measurement results is, even partially, over the threshold? In this case the available knowledge of the measurand does not necessarily allow to state that the system meets its requirements with enough confidence.

Uncertainty is maybe even more important (and needs to be evaluated) in the case of distributed systems. Time interval measurements carried out on such systems can, in fact, be significantly affected by offset and drift among distributed clocks. Another case in which uncertainty is very important is when indirect measurements are performed by combining results of several direct measurements. In such cases, the uncertainty of direct temporal measurements propagates on uncertainty of indirect measurements; expression (3) permits to calculate the uncertainty of an indirect measurement through the uncertainties of direct measurements utilized for its evaluation.

Intrusiveness. In general, performing measurements alters (to different extents) the state and the behavior of the system under test. More specifically, the presence of a measurement system can introduce modifications on the value of the measurand. A classical example is provided by the *load effect* of a voltmeter that can alter the voltage it is intended to measure due to its finite impedance. In computer science, we can think of a target process which acts as the measurand, and of measures collected with a process scheduled on the same CPU hosting the target process; the schedulability of the entire system might be compromised,

with consequent harmful effects on measurement results.

Performing an analysis of the intrusiveness of a measurement system is particularly important when measurements are carried out on computer systems or infrastructures, since this often implies loading the system and, ultimately, influencing its behavior in a non negligible way. The importance of intrusiveness in computer systems is clear and well understood, although it is difficult to quantify it. It should be evaluated as the impact of the measurement system on the performance of the computer system, expressed in terms of memory usage, CPU usage and/or operating system relative time. Intrusiveness is a parameter of fundamental importance for all the cases of interest of this paper. This is particularly true for real-time systems: a tool able to collect sufficiently reliable data in a non real-time environment, may behave very differently in a hard real-time environment. Intrusiveness is thus particularly critical in hard real-time systems, where timing predictability may be altered by the additional overhead of monitoring tasks, or other mechanisms, e.g. fault injection probes.

Intrusiveness and *uncertainty* are related to each other since intrusiveness has consequences on uncertainty. This explains why in Table 2 all the rows in which *Intrusiveness* is important exhibit the same importance for *Uncertainty*.

Resolution. Resolution may be critical in real-time systems since it needs to be much lower than the imposed time deadline to allow useful quantitative evaluations of time or dependability metrics. In computing systems it can be generally assumed that resolution of the measurement system for time interval evaluation is equal to the granularity of the clock used in the experiment. In a centralized context it can happen that resolution is of the same order of magnitude of the measure, and it is thus of great importance to evaluate the resolution. On the other hand, when experiments are performed on distributed systems, uncertainty is usually far greater than resolution; in such cases, the evaluation and the control of resolution may be less crucial.

Table 1. Abbreviations used in Tables 2-3

CE	Centralized	Unc	Uncertainty
DI	Distributed	Int	Intrusiveness
RT	Real-time	Res	Resolution
¬RT	Non real-time	Rep	Repeatability
CR	Critical		
¬CR	Non-critical		

Table 2. Summary on important metrological properties to consider in order to perform reliable measurements on computing systems

	Unc	Int	Res	Rep
CE-¬RT-¬CR	X	X	X	
CE-¬RT-CR	X	X	X	X
CE-RT-¬CR	XX	XX	X	
CE-RT-CR	XX	XX	XX	X
DI-¬RT-¬CR	X	X		
DI-¬RT-CR	X	X		X
DI-RT-¬CR	XX	XX	X	
DI-RT-CR	XX	XX	X	X

Repeatability. Repeatability is often not achievable when measurements are carried out on computer systems. The same environmental conditions can, in fact, hardly be guaranteed. This is especially true with regard to distributed systems, where differences among local clocks, in addition to the problems of thread scheduling and timing of events, enormously increase the difficulty of designing repeatable experiments. Critical systems are a class of systems in which repeatability is very important. In such cases, great efforts to grant the highest possible degree of repeatability are required and motivated. When performing experimental validation of a critical system, in fact, it is necessary to observe the same behavior triggered by the same trace of execution.

4 Measurements properties in tools and experiments for dependability evaluation

In this Section, tools and experiments used for experimental quantitative evaluation of computing systems are described, with the purpose of understanding if they have considered and respected the aforementioned criteria and to which extent this has been accomplished. With no intent to criticize any individual experiment or experience, the objective is to investigate the general consciousness about metrological properties addressed in the previous sections. The observations are based on an objective analysis of the considered works, and no attempt to numerically quantify measurement properties on these works is done. We do not want to question the results presented in the literature, but just to show that underestimating or neglecting factors such as uncertainty, intrusiveness, resolution and repeatability can easily reduce the trust in the achieved measures or in the developed measurement systems.

In the left part of Table 3 (columns *Tool*, *Exp* and *System classification*) the works taken into consideration are classified according to the criteria introduced in Section 3 related to the dimensions of systems. Note that the columns *tool* and *experiments* are marked depending on whether the main focus was the tool or the experiments performed (in some cases, both).

The considered works cover some very different situations in which dependability measures have been collected. Such difference stems either from the type of analysis performed or from the kind of system under study. We analyze fault-injection tools (e.g. [8], [13]) and experiments (e.g. [20]), general prototyping frameworks (e.g. [15]), an experiment in which a new total ordering protocol [24] has been tested and, finally, an experiment in which a fail-aware system is analyzed [23]. Such experiences cover a spectrum of eight different systems typologies. Note that some works belong to more than just one category of systems.

Let us now consider right part of Table 3 (columns *Rel-*

evant Properties and *Awareness*). In the column *Relevant Properties*, the most relevant metrological properties that should have been addressed, are singled out for each paper. The *Awareness* part of the table reports marks related to the measurement properties for which some concern (often with quite good observations) has been shown. Due to the very different, non-uniform, and often partial (or missing) approaches we have observed (even the name of the four measurement properties are different from a work to another), it has been actually difficult to identify these elements in the surveyed works. Therefore, in some cases the ticks in the table are the result of our own interpretation and understanding. This does not necessarily mean that measurement properties have been ignored by the related authors when designing tools and experiments, but we just note that these properties have often not been given the adequate emphasis.

Let us start analyzing *uncertainty*. Although a full consciousness of all measurement properties is not achieved in the surveyed tools, it is important to highlight that a quite exhaustive analysis of measurement parameters is, in some cases, performed. For example, in the software fault injection tool Loki ([13], [14]), a post-runtime analysis, using off-line clock synchronization, is used to place injections on a single global timeline and to determine whether the intended faults were properly injected: there is a significant attempt to evaluate the uncertainty of the time instant at which faults were injected, even though it is not referred to as *uncertainty*. Such a deep analysis is performed only for timestamping fault injection. Although the approach to uncertainty is quite informal, far from *uncertainty* as dealt with by the GUM [5], this example denotes a significant and remarkable interest in *quantitatively* evaluating the dispersion of the values that can be reasonably attributed to the measurand.

Regarding experiment papers, uncertainty issues are taken into account only in the experiments related to the testing/development of FORTRESS ([23]). FORTRESS is a support system for designing and implementing fault-tolerant distributed real-time systems that use commercial off the shelf (COTS) components. In the test case performed, when measuring the one-way delay, the FORTRESS fail-aware datagram service computes an upper bound $ub(m)$ on the transmission delay $td(m)$ of each delivered message (obviously $ub(m) > td(m)$). Due to the incapability of precisely estimating $td(m)$, an upper bound on the error $ub(m) - td(m)$ is estimated as the difference between the computed upper bound and a known lower bound for the message transmission delay δ_{min} (the error is set to $ub(m) - \delta_{min}$).

For the sake of completeness, it has to be highlighted that for some time measurements, uncertainty can be not (very) relevant. This can happen when the objective is to measure a (sufficiently) long time interval. A few examples of such sit-

Table 3. Surveyed work classification and metrological properties

Surveyed Work	Tool	Exp	System classification								Relevant Properties				Awareness			
			CE ¬RT ¬CR	CE ¬RT CR	CE RT ¬CR	CE RT CR	DI ¬RT ¬CR	DI ¬RT CR	DI RT ¬CR	DI RT CR	Unc	Int	Res	Rep	Unc	Int	Res	Rep
XCEPTION [7]	✓		✓								✓	✓	✓			✓		✓
GOOFI [8]	✓	✓	✓	✓	✓	✓					✓	✓	✓	✓		✓		
MAFALDA [9]	✓	✓		✓							✓	✓	✓	✓		✓		
MAFALDA-RT [10]	✓	✓			✓	✓					✓	✓	✓	✓		✓		
MESSALINE [11]	✓	✓		✓				✓			✓	✓	✓	✓			✓	✓
FTAPE [12]	✓	✓					✓				✓	✓				✓		
Loki [13] [14]	✓	✓					✓				✓	✓			✓	✓	✓	
Neko/NekoStat [15] [16]	✓	✓					✓				✓	✓					✓	
ORCHESTRA [17]	✓	✓							✓		✓	✓	✓			✓		
PFI Tool [18]	✓	✓					✓				✓	✓				✓		
OS dependability benchmark [19]		✓	✓								✓	✓	✓					
Impact Analysis on Real-Time Sys [20]		✓				✓					✓	✓	✓	✓				
Evaluating COTS [21]		✓				✓					✓	✓	✓	✓				
Fault-Tolerant Commercial Systems [22]		✓					✓				✓	✓					✓	✓
FORTRESS [23]		✓							✓		✓	✓	✓	✓	✓		✓	
PLATO [24]		✓						✓			✓	✓	✓				✓	

uations can be found in FTAPE [12] and in the experiment presented in [19]. In the case study presented in FTAPE, a fault injection tool, the execution time with/without faults is measured. Such a time interval is greater than one thousand seconds. In [19], a dependability benchmark for operating systems is developed and tested on Windows 2000 OS. The restart time of the operating system is measured. It is a quite long interval (dozen of seconds). Relative uncertainty here is very small, and in cases like these the absence of assumptions or concerns about uncertainty can therefore be justified.

Regarding *intrusiveness*, we have observed that a large subset of the surveyed tools show great consciousness of how important it is to design a non-intrusive measuring instrument (Loki [13], ORCHESTRA [17], XCEPTION [7], MAFALDA [9], MAFALDA-RT [10], FTAPE [12], GOOFI [8] and PFI Tool [18]).

In Loki, awareness about intrusiveness is clear, and to be as non-intrusive to the system as possible, the runtime does not block the system while notifications about the system state are in transit. A post-runtime check is made to correct possible problems due to non-compatible views of the system state.

In ORCHESTRA, a fault injection tool for distributed real-time systems, a deep analysis about intrusiveness is performed. ORCHESTRA deals with real-time systems with strict time requirements. It is designed to explicitly address the intrusiveness of fault injection on a target distributed system. This operation is performed by exploiting operating system support to quantitatively assess the intrusiveness of a fault injection experiment on the timing behavior of the target system and to compensate for it whenever possible.

In XCEPTION, a tool for software fault injection, an important attempt to evaluate tools characteristics using system performance monitoring facilities is made.

In MAFALDA, a fault injection tool for safety critical systems, the used fault injection technique is chosen with awareness of problem of intrusiveness of the tool.

In MAFALDA-RT, a tool for fault-injection in real-time systems (it is a completely new version of MAFALDA), the authors focus on the problems of temporal intrusiveness. The authors identify the main causes of intrusiveness in: i) the time related to the injection of faults, and ii) the time related to the observation of the system behavior.

In FTAPE, the authors recognize the problem of intrusiveness of the fault injection component and of the workload monitoring component, and they try to estimate the time overhead comparing the time the workload requires to execute with and without the fault injection and monitoring components.

In the fault injection Java tool GOOFI, it is recognized that logging is a time-consuming operation, thus GOOFI makes available two different logging modes: a detailed (time-consuming) mode and a normal (less time-consuming) mode.

In [18], the fault injection tool PFI Tool (Probe/Fault Injection Tool) is presented. The authors recognize that their approach can be more intrusive than others, but, despite this awareness, a metrological characterization of the tool is missing.

In the experiments we have been considering, the intrusiveness of the measurement tool used is considered only in [22]. In this experiment a dependability benchmark for commercial systems is proposed and studied on TMR-based prototype machines (using the FTAPE tool). The time overhead of the fault injection tool used is accounted, even if intrusiveness is not looked closely as in [12]. In most cases, missing observations about intrusiveness of the measurement tool may be an acceptable approach for single experiments, still allowing reliance on results, when a complete estimation of the uncertainty of the experiment results is provided (assuming that intrusiveness of the monitoring tool was already evaluated).

Resolution is usually the easiest parameter to estimate. However, it is frequently not considered at all: the reason is probably that it is often considered not important, at least if compared with intrusiveness and uncertainty. As an example on how resolution is neglected, we observe that PLATO [24] and Neko/NekoStat [15],[16] use Java system calls to collect timestamps: this way the resolution of the system is the granularity of the Java clock used, usually greater than granularity of system clock.

Finally, let us consider *repeatability*. The difficulty in reaching a satisfactory level for repeatability has been taken into account in the experiments on computer systems described in [22], even if the word *repeatability* is not explicitly used. The authors show consciousness that, due to the aforementioned limits on accurate timestamping, many executions of the same run will probably not bring exactly the same results, because the event (i.e. the injected fault) may not be signaled at the exact time instants when it is intended to occur. This explains why a second execution of the same run does not necessarily recreate a catastrophic incident that can, for instance, occur in the first execution. Among the surveyed works, the problem of creating repeatable experiments is discussed also in XCEPTION [7] and MESSALINE [11].

In XCEPTION it is highlighted that good results are achieved in experiments performed by using the spatial method for fault triggering (a spatially-defined fault is injected when the program accesses a specified memory address, either for data load/store or instruction fetch, [7]), not in the temporal trigger methods, due to execution time uncertainties. This is an obvious limit, common to all tools.

In MESSALINE it is observed that in distributed system it is really difficult to perform repeatable experiments. Moreover, the type of the architecture has usually a major impact on the difficulty to set up a reliable testbed and on the repeatability of the experiments.

To complete the review some works based on Java are briefly considered; more precisely the Neko/NekoStat tool for prototyping distributed algorithms in a Java framework, the Java tool GOOFI, and the Java implementation of the PLATO total ordering protocol. Java is actually limited by its inability to predictably control the temporal execution of applications due fundamentally to unpredictable latencies introduced by automatic memory management (the garbage collector). Because of this peculiarity, measurement tools written in Java usually have to deal with particularly relevant intrusiveness problems. Still related to Java, in [21] a comparison of the dependability of different real-time Java virtual machines in the spacecraft software context is made. Some case studies are performed to evaluate dependability of COTS components. The authors show awareness of the problems encountered in Java and they use a Real-Time Java [25], which surely fits better in real-time context. However, although the great interest shown in precise timestamping, no information about measurement properties is provided.

Finally, in [20] the behavior of a real-time system running applications under operating systems that are subject to soft-errors is studied. Although errors due to real-time problems are recognized, no estimation about the quality and trustability of the presented results is shown.

A further remark concerns comparison among measurement results provided by different tools or experiments. In the surveyed tools, result comparison is never dealt with in terms of compatibility, as introduced in Section 2. Actually while expressing measurement results as intervals of values is the practice sometimes followed in simulation studies, it is not as common in experimental dependability evaluations (with few exceptions - DBENCH). Comparison of results carried out in terms of compatibility can, in fact, be carried out only after evaluating uncertainty.

To summarize, the main findings of this brief survey on tools and experiments developed to assess dependability properties show that some consciousness about the metrology properties described in this paper is shown, but the approaches are quite intuitive, and usually quite incomplete as well. In particular, while there is a diffused consciousness about intrusiveness, there is rarely a real effort to try to estimate uncertainty and to determine solid bounds on the reliability and trustability of the measures collected with the tools. In the experiments, less attention is paid to these themes. This does not mean that experiments are badly designed, nor that the measurement systems used for the experiments are not properly constructed, but more explanations about the measurement system should have been provided in order to allow to appreciate or understand what level of uncertainty may be associated to the obtained measures.

5 Conclusion

This paper has discussed the importance of approaching quantitative evaluation, based on measurements, of dependability attributes and metrics of computer systems and infrastructures from a metrological point of view. The basic observation that has stimulated this work is that experimental quantitative evaluations of dependability attributes are *measurements* and the tools used for obtaining them are *measuring instruments*. However, as it appears from our investigations of a good sample of the available relevant literature, the former are not recognized as measurements and consequently their results are not qualified as they should, and the latter are not characterized as it is usually done for measurements tools, i.e. their fundamental metrological properties are not investigated.

Besides the pure scientific interest of applying principles and results achieved during times by metrology, the application of rigorous metrological methodologies would represent an important step forward for improving the scientific rigor and trustworthiness of the obtained measures, and for allowing to compare dependability measures collected by various tools and experiments according to rigorous and recognized criteria, i.e., to perform benchmarks.

After presenting the fundamentals of measurement theory, to set a proper framework, the paper has focused on the measurement properties which can be of major interest for dependability. It has shown that the most relevant measurement properties to take into account vary from a scenario to another (e.g. in distributed systems, resolution is often not as critical as in centralized systems). A number of works present in the literature have been analyzed and, as it could be expected, quite different approaches to the evaluation of measurement properties have been followed (when present). Some consciousness of the metrology properties has been found, still quite intuitive, and usually quite incomplete. In particular, while intrusiveness is very often recognized as a concern, a real effort to estimate uncertainty is made very rarely. Moreover, we claim that more explanations than usually done should be given about the measurement systems used in the experiments, as it is a fundamental pre-requisite to estimate uncertainty and to get real confidence and trust on the dependability measures obtained.

In conclusion, we would like to single out and recommend some basic guidelines, i.e. operative rules that should be kept in mind - and when possible put into practice - when measuring dependability attributes and properties:

- the measurand should be clearly and univocally defined;

- all the sources of uncertainty should be singled out and evaluated;

- some attributes of major concern for dependability measurements, such as intrusiveness, resolution and repeatability should be evaluated;

- measurement uncertainty should be evaluated (according to the GUM);

- comparison of measurement results provided by different tools/experiments should be made in terms of compatibility.

Acknowledgements

This work has been partially supported by the European Community through the projects IST-4-027513 (CRUTIAL - Critical Utility InfrastructurAL Resilience) and IST-FP6-STREP-26979 (HIDENETS - HIghly DEpendable ip-based NETworks and Services).

References

[1] A. Avizienis, J.C. Laprie, B. Randell, and C. Landwehr. Basic concepts and taxonomy of dependable and secure computing. *IEEE TDSC*, 1(1):Page(s): 11–33, 2004.

[2] Freeman J. Dyson. The inventor of modern science. *Nature*, 400:27, July 1999.

[3] Terry Quinn and Jean Kovalevsky. The development of modern metrology and its role today. *Philosophical Transactions of the Royal Society A: Mathematical, Physical and Engineering Sciences*, 363:2307–2327, September 2005.

[4] BIMP, IEC, IFCC, ISO, IUPAC, IUPAP, and OIML. *ISO International Vocabulary of Basic and General Terms in Metrology (VIM)*, second edition, 1993.

[5] BIMP, IEC, IFCC, ISO, IUPAC, IUPAP, and OIML. *Guide to the expression of uncertainty in measurement*, second edition, 1995.

[6] Paulo Veríssimo and Luis Rodriguez. *Distributed Systems for System Architects*. Kluwer Academic Publisher, 2001.

[7] J. Carreira, H. Madeira, and J. Silva. Xception: Software fault injection and monitoring in processor functional units. In *Pre-prints 5th Int. Working Conf. on Dependable Computing for Critical Applications (DCCA-5)*, pages pp.135–49, 1995.

[8] Joakim Aidemark, Jonny Vinter, Peter Folkesson, and Johan Karlsson. Goofi: Generic object-oriented fault injection tool. In *DSN '01: Proceedings of the 2001 International Conference on Dependable Systems and Networks (formerly: FTCS)*, pages 83–88, Washington, DC, USA, 2001. IEEE Computer Society.

[9] J.-C. Fabre, F. Salles, M. Rodriguez Moreno, and J. Arlat. Assessment of cots microkernels by fault injection. In *DCCA '99: Proceedings of the conference on Dependable Computing for Critical Applications*, page 25, Washington, DC, USA, 1999. IEEE Computer Society.

[10] Manuel Rodriguez, Arnaud Albinet, and Jean Arlat. Mafalda-rt: A tool for dependability assessment of real-time systems. In *DSN '02: Proceedings of the 2002 International Conference on Dependable Systems and Networks*, pages 267–272, Washington, DC, USA, 2002. IEEE Computer Society.

[11] Jean Arlat, Martine Aguera, Louis Amat, Yves Crouzet, Jean-Charles Fabre, Jean-Claude Laprie, Eliane Martins, and David Powell. Fault injection for dependability validation: A methodology and some applications. *IEEE Trans. Softw. Eng.*, 16(2):166–182, 1990.

[12] Timothy K. Tsai and Ravishankar K. Iyer. Ftape: A fault injection tool to measure fault tolerance. In *AIAA, Computing in Aerospace Conference, 10th, San Antonio, TX; UNITED STATES*, 1995.

[13] Ramesh Chandra, Ryan M. Lefever, Michel Cukier, and William H. Sanders. Loki: A state-driven fault injector for distributed systems. In *DSN '00: Proceedings of the 2000 International Conference on Dependable Systems and Networks (formerly FTCS-30 and DCCA-8)*, pages 237–242, Washington, DC, USA, 2000. IEEE Computer Society.

[14] Michel Cukier, Ramesh Chandra, David Henke, Jessica Pistole, and William H. Sanders. Fault injection based on a partial view of the global state of a distributed system. In *SRDS '99: Proceedings of the 18th IEEE Symposium on Reliable Distributed Systems*, page 168, Washington, DC, USA, 1999. IEEE Computer Society.

[15] Peter Urban, Andre Schiper, and Xavier Defago. Neko: A single environment to simulate and prototype distributed algorithms. In *ICOIN '01: Proceedings of the The 15th International Conference on Information Networking*, page 503, Washington, DC, USA, 2001. IEEE Computer Society.

[16] Lorenzo Falai, Andrea Bondavalli, and Felicita Di Giandomenico. Quantitative evaluation of distributed algorithms using the neko framework: The nekostat extension. In *LADC*, pages 35–51, 2005.

[17] S. Dawson, F. Jahanian, T. Mitton, and Teck-Lee Tung. Testing of fault-tolerant and real-time distributed systems via protocol fault injection. In *FTCS '96: Proceedings of the The Twenty-Sixth Annual International Symposium on Fault-Tolerant Computing (FTCS '96)*, page 404, Washington, DC, USA, 1996. IEEE Computer Society.

[18] Scott Dawson and Farnam Jahanian. Probing and fault injection of protocol implementations. In *International Conference on Distributed Computing Systems*, pages 351–359, 1995.

[19] Ali Kalakech, Tahar Jarboui, Jean Arlat, Yves Crouzet, and Karama Kanoun. Benchmarking operating system dependability: Windows 2000 as a case study. In *PRDC '04: Proceedings of the 10th IEEE Pacific Rim International Symposium on Dependable Computing (PRDC'04)*, pages 261–270, Washington, DC, USA, 2004. IEEE Computer Society.

[20] N. Ignat, B. Nicolescu, Y. Savaria, and G. Nicolescu. Soft-error classification and impact analysis on real-time operating systems. In *DATE '06: Proceedings of the conference on Design, automation and test in Europe*, pages 182–187, 3001 Leuven, Belgium, Belgium, 2006. European Design and Automation Association.

[21] Paolo Donzelli, Marvin Zelkowitz, Victor Basili, Dan Allard, and Kenneth N. Meyer. Evaluating cots component dependability in context. *IEEE Softw.*, 22(4):46–53, 2005.

[22] T. K. Tsai, R. K. Iyer, and D. Jewitt. An approach towards benchmarking of fault-tolerant commercial systems. In *FTCS '96: Proceedings of the The Twenty-Sixth Annual International Symposium on Fault-Tolerant Computing (FTCS '96)*, page 314, Washington, DC, USA, 1996. IEEE Computer Society.

[23] Christof Fetzer and Flaviu Cristian. Fortress: A system to support fail-aware real-time applications. In *IEEE Workshop on Middleware for Distributed Real-Time Systems and Services*. San Francisco, December 1997.

[24] Mahesh Balakrishnan, Ken Birman, and Amar Phanishayee. Plato: Predictive latency-aware total ordering. In *SRDS '06: Proceedings of the 25th IEEE Symposium on Reliable Distributed Systems (SRDS'06)*, pages 175–188, Washington, DC, USA, 2006. IEEE Computer Society.

[25] G. Bollella, B. Brosgol, J. Gosling, P. Dibble, S. Furr, and M. Turnbull. *The Real-Time Specification for Java*. Addison-Wesley, 2000.

PERFORMANCE AND DEPENDABILITY SYMPOSIUM (PDS)

Session 1C:
System Architecture
and Software Assessment

A Framework for Architecture-level Lifetime Reliability Modeling

Jeonghee Shin[†], Victor Zyuban, Zhigang Hu, Jude A. Rivers and Pradip Bose

IBM T. J. Watson Research Center
Yorktown Heights, NY 10598
{zyuban, zhigangh, jarivers and pbose}@us.ibm.com

Abstract

This paper tackles the issue of modeling chip lifetime reliability at the architecture level. We propose a new and robust structure-aware lifetime reliability model at the architecture-level, where devices only vulnerable to failure mechanisms and the effective stress condition of these devices are taken into account for the failure rate of microarchitecture structures. In addition, we present this reliability analysis framework based on a new concept, called the FIT of reference circuit or FORC, which allows architects to quantify failure rates without having to delve into low-level circuit- and technology-specific details of the implemented architecture. This is done through a one-time characterization of a reference circuit needed to quantify the reference FITs for each class of modeled failure mechanisms for a given technology and implementation style. With this new reliability modeling framework, architects are empowered to proceed with architecture-level reliability analysis independent of technological and environmental parameters.

1. Introduction

Lifetime reliability has become one of the major concerns in processor microarchitectures implemented with deep submicron technologies [1,2]. Extreme scaling resulting in atomic-range dimensions, inter- and intra-device variability, and escalating power densities have all contributed to this concern. At the device- and circuit-level, many reliability models have been proposed and empirically validated by academia and industry; as such, the basic mechanisms of failures at the low level have been fairly well understood and the models at that level have gained widespread acceptance. For example, Black's equation of electromigration [3] is a well-accepted model of failures applicable to on-chip wires. However, the challenge of modeling the effects of low-level failures at the architecture-level—in the context of real application workloads—continues to be a rather daunting one.

In recent work, J. Srinivasan et al. [2] and Z. Lu et al. [4] have proposed lifetime reliability models for use with single-core architecture-level, cycle-accurate simulators. These contributions focus on modeling the major failure mechanisms including electromigration (EM), negative bias temperature instability (NBTI), time dependent dielectric breakdown (TDDB), stress migration (SM) and thermal cycling (TC). However, a closer examination of how these models are put together oftentimes reveals a number of key assumptions that enable plausible abstractions at the architecture-level; yet, these assumptions have to be taken largely on faith based on intuitive reasoning. Some of these key assumptions easily defy common intuition when one tries to extend the models directly to cover the entire chip composed of many different (heterogeneous) components. For example, in RAMP [2], the baseline (target) total failure rate measured in FITs[1] is assumed to be evenly distributed across all the five modeled failure mechanisms. This is clearly a somewhat arbitrary axiom since some failure mechanisms can be more severe than others, and technology scaling affects the failure mechanisms in different ways and degrees. In addition, lifetime reliability models proposed to this point assume a uniform device density over the chip and an identical vulnerability of devices to failure mechanisms. As a result, the failure rates estimated by such models tend to be proportional to chip area, regardless of the exact component mix within that area. However, an examination of the floorplan or photo micrograph of any modern (multi-core) microprocessor chip clearly shows heterogeneity across the die area—and the consequent limitations of such an assumption.

[†] Currently, Jeonghee Shin is a PhD candidate in the computer engineering department at the University of Southern California. This work was performed while she was an intern at the IBM research center. Her email address is jeonghee@charity.usc.edu.

[1] The standard method of reporting constant failure rates for semiconductor components is Failures in Time (FITs), which is the number of failures seen in 10^9 hours. The mean time to failure (MTTF) of a component is inversely related to this constant failure rate, i.e., MTTF = 10^9/FITs.

For accurate lifetime reliability estimation, basic axioms such as those above adopted by prior architecture-level reliability models need to be improved based on a detailed understanding of the implementation of modern microarchitecture components and the characteristics of failure mechanisms. In this paper, we propose a new and robust *structure-aware* lifetime reliability model at the architecture-level, where devices only vulnerable to failure mechanisms and the effective stress condition of these devices are taken into account for the failure rate of microarchitecture structures. In addition, we separate architecture-level factors from technology- and environment-dependent parameters so as to allow architects to abstract the analysis of processor reliability from technology level effects. In particular, we propose a technology-independent unit of reliability, called the *FIT of reference circuit* or *FORC* for each failure type under study. FORC[2] is the failure rate in FITs of a specially defined circuit that is easy to model and understand while, at the same time, effective at representing the basic mechanism of a certain type of failures. The failure rate of a given structure or unit on the chip, in the context of a given failure mechanism (e.g., EM), can then be computed in relative FORC units, instead of in absolute FITs that are technology and environment dependent. In formulating our model, we show that architectural abstraction can be effected quite elegantly and accurately with *a priori*, one-time characterization of circuit-level reference models.

This paper makes the following key contributions:

- A new formalism of FORC, suitable for architecture-level quantification of FITs in a technology- and environment-independent manner for a given failure type, is proposed. We illustrate this formalism for three key failure mechanisms: EM, NBTI, and TDDB. The same methodology can be applied to formulate FORC primitives for other failure mechanisms as needed.

- We show that by defining a FORC standard for each modeled failure mechanism and by measuring the *effective defect density* and *effective stress condition* of only those devices that are subject to failures of that type, the overall FIT value can be quantified in terms of FORC for each failure type quite unambiguously and precisely.

In what follows, we provide our approach and details of the proposed reference circuits and FORC expressions for failure mechanisms in Sections 2 and

3. In Section 4, we derive expression for the failure rates of basic and widely used microarchitecture structures in terms of FORC. We discuss pervious work of lifetime reliability modeling at the device-, circuit-, and architecture-level in Section 5. Finally, we conclude the paper in Section 6.

2. Our Approach: Technology-Independent Failure Modeling and Analysis using FORC

The various failure mechanisms responsible for lifetime degradation do not contribute equally to processor core or chip failure. Moreover, the impact of failure mechanisms on different parts of the chip may vary dramatically as on-chip devices are not equally nor necessarily vulnerable even to the same failure mechanism. As a result, it is incorrect to assume a uniform device density over a chip or a subpart of the chip and an identical vulnerability of the devices to failure mechanisms, regardless of what is actually implemented over the chip area. In other words, *an accurate architectural lifetime reliability model should carefully consider the vulnerability of basic structures of the microarchitecture (e.g., arrays, register files, latches, logic, etc., composing operational units across the chip) to different types of failures by analyzing their effective defect density, taking into account their effective stress condition to specific failure mechanisms.*

Following the above approach, we define *effective defect density* as the number of devices *vulnerable* to a certain type of failure mechanisms per unit area of a structure, where the term "device" denotes the primitive physical element on which the failure can occur. For instance, for failures due to electromigration (EM), the effective defect density is given by the number of *vias* per unit area that have unidirectional current flow. *Vias* are the interconnect abutments between metal lines in different layers, e.g., between M1 and M2, M2 and M3, and so on. *Vias* constitute the weakest part of metal lines [5], but not all are vulnerable to EM; *vias* that experience bidirectional current flow are generally able to recover from deleterious EM effects as the movement of metal atoms in one direction is subsequently balanced by an equivalent movement of atoms in the opposite direction of current flow [6]. Thus, only *vias* with unidirectional current flow are counted in the effective defect density for EM failures. Similarly, for NBTI, the effective defect density is given by the number of pFET devices per unit area along the critical path as negative gate bias (i.e., $V_{gs} = -V_{dd}$) occurs only on pFET devices in digital circuits to cause increased gate

---

[2] The reader may draw an analogy to the technology independent measure of the pipeline depth of a processor, measured in terms of FO4 per stage. This abstracts away the need to delve into technology-specific parameters needed to compute the exact stage delay in nanoseconds for a given design.

delay, making only devices along the critical path vulnerable to timing violations [7]. For TDDB, the effective defect density is given by the number of pFET and nFET devices per unit area having a leakage current through gate oxide exceeding that which can be tolerated by the logic driving the devices [8].

Once the effective defect density for a certain failure mechanism is found for a given structure within the microarchitecture, an appropriate reliability model can be applied to find the FIT value for that structure and failure mechanism. In order not to overestimate the FIT value, the *effective stress condition* of the failure mechanism needs to be taken into account for the reliability model, as most CMOS devices experience discontinuous stress rather than constant stress throughout their lifetime. For instance, an EM stress condition of *vias* occurs only during a one-to-zero or zero-to-one value transition of metal lines, generating current flow through the *vias*. For NBTI, pFET devices are under stress only while their gate is low and their source is high. Similarly, for TDDB, pFET or nFET devices undergo stress condition only while their gate is low or high, and their source is high or low, respectively. We account for this effective stress condition using activity factor and/or duty cycle as described in Section 4. During the time other than stress periods, devices are either recovering from or unaffected by the failure effects [6,7,9]. In Section 4, both effective defect density and effective stress condition for structures and failure mechanisms are formulated using microarchitectural parameters.

Chip lifetime failure rate is affected not only by architectural factors such as the number of effective defects and effective stress condition of various microarchitecture structures but also by many technological and environmental parameters that are difficult to abstract for the general case. In particular, there are implementation technology differences such as device pitch, semiconductor material (bulk silicon versus SOI), manufacturing process, etc., all of which may vary from one chip maker or generation to another and strongly influence chip lifetime. For studying lifetime reliability trends among chips in the same technology and between chips of different technologies, *a more efficient and portable framework is needed that separates architecture-level factors from technology/environment-dependent parameters.*

Toward this end, we propose a technology-independent unit of reliability, called the *FIT of reference circuit* or FORC, through which the failure rate of a microarchitecture structure can be expressed for each type of failure mechanisms. That is, the appropriate reliability model for a specific failure mechanism can be applied to the microarchitecture structure of interest and describe the structure's failure rate relative to the corresponding reference circuit for that failure mechanism. By encapsulating technology/environment-dependent parameters into the FIT of the reference circuit, reliability analysis can be abstracted at the architecture level. As a result, this FORC-based approach is especially beneficial for early design reliability analysis as limited technology/environment-dependent parameters are available at that stage.

In our approach, the impact of various microarchitecture designs on lifetime reliability can be studied rather straightforwardly by parameterizing the configurations (e.g., number of entries in register files or arrays, number of ports, etc.) and quantifying activity factors (e.g., number of accesses, number of value transitions, etc.) as determined empirically through execution-driven simulation on applied workloads. From this, effective defect densities and effective stress conditions for certain failure mechanisms can be found, on which the appropriate reliability model can be applied to find the FIT value for the microarchitecture designs. Furthermore, to understand the impact of technology (e.g., scaling) and environment (e.g., temperature) on lifetime reliability of a given microarchitecture, one need only to estimate how the FORC for a given failure mechanism would scale or change and then apply this new FORC value to the architecture-level FIT expression derived relative to the reference circuit.

3. FIT of Reference Circuit (FORC) for Various Failure Mechanisms

In the following subsections, representative reference circuits for the three most concerned failure mechanisms such as EM, NBTI and TDDB [10,11,12] are described, and FORC expressions for each are derived. The same methodology can be applied to formulate FORC primitives for other failure mechanisms as needed.

3.1. FORC for EM Failures (FORC$_{EM}$)

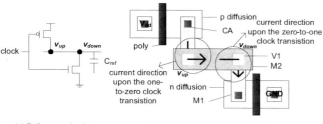

(a) Reference circuit   (b) An example layout of circuit (a)

Figure 1. The reference circuit chosen for EM. The outputs of the nFET and pFET devices are connected through a M2 metal line segment. As a result, v_{up} and v_{down} vias abut the M1 metal lines to M2 and have unidirectional current causing EM failures. Upon the one-to-zero transition of the clock, the pFET device conducts, and current flows through v_{up} upward from M1 to M2 in order to charge the wire capacitance of the M2 line, C_{ref}. On the zero-to-one transition of the clock, the nFET device conducts, and current flows through v_{down} downward from M2 to M1 in order to discharge C_{ref}.

Electromigration (EM) is a well-known and well-studied failure phenomenon that can occur on conductor lines [3,5,6]. The portions of conductor lines most vulnerable to EM are *vias* interconnecting different metal layers that experience unidirectional current flow. Figure 1 shows an example reference circuit vulnerable to EM. The outputs of the pFET and nFET devices are connected through a segment of M2 metal, as shown in Figure 1(b). As a result, v_{up} and v_{down} *vias* abut the M1 metal lines to M2, connecting the outputs of the pFET and the nFET devices[3]. When the clock transits from one to zero, the pFET device conducts, and current flows through v_{up} upward from M1 to M2 in order to charge the wire capacitance of the M2 line, given by C_{ref}. There is little current through v_{down} because the nFET device is non-conducted. Conversely, on the zero-to-one transition of the clock, the nFET device conducts, and current flows through v_{down} downward from M2 to M1 in order to discharge C_{ref}, while little current flows through v_{up}. As a result, v_{up} and v_{down} are subject to an average unidirectional current[4] of $(C_{ref} \cdot V_{dd})/t$, where t is the clock period. This causes the *vias* to be vulnerable to EM effects. Based on Black's equation [3], the FIT of our reference circuit (*vias* in this case) for EM failures is described by the following:

$$FORC_{EM} = \frac{10^9}{A_{EM}} \cdot \left(\frac{C_{ref} \cdot V_{dd}}{t} \right)^n \cdot e^{-\frac{E_{a\_EM}}{kT}},$$

where A_{EM} and n are empirical constants, E_{a_EM} is the activation energy for EM, k is Boltzmann's constant, and T is absolute temperature in degrees Kelvin. Using this notion of FORC, we can express failure rates of microarchitectural components due to EM in relative terms of FORC$_{EM}$, as described in Section 4.1, in order to isolate the architect from low-level peculiarities associated with technological and environmental parameters such as A_{EM}, V_{dd}, t, E_{a_EM}, and T.

3.2. FORC for NBTI Failures (FORC$_{NBTI}$)

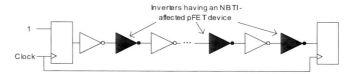

Figure 2. The reference circuit chosen for NBTI. The reference circuit consists of a series of inverters between two latches. Because the value of the signal changes between V_{dd} and GND in passing through each inverter, the pFET device in every other inverter is stressed.

NBTI occurs when the input to a gate is low while the output is high, resulting in an accumulation of positive charges at the interface between gate oxide and silicon. This accumulation causes the threshold voltage, V_T, of the pFET device to increase over time, which results in a slowdown in zero-to-one or one-to-zero transitions. Eventually, this can lead to circuit failure due to timing violations if the device is along a critical path. To capture this failure mechanism, we chose a reference circuit for NBTI that includes pFET devices under stress and limits allowable gate delay increase before timing violation occurs.

As shown in Figure 2, the reference circuit consists of a series of N_{inv} inverters between two latches. The input of one latch should propagate through the inverter chain and be latched into the other within one clock period. Because the value of the signal changes between V_{dd} and GND in passing through each inverter, the pFET device in every other inverter is stressed and the V_T of the device increases over time. This eventually can lead to a violation in the latch setup time and, ultimately, the capturing of a wrong value in the latch. In the following, we assume that microprocessors are built with a 1% timing margin. This delay margin can be converted to a maximum

---

[3] The length of the M2 line is assumed to be equal to the typical length of the wire segment between two successive wire repeaters, which is 300μm in 65nm technology.

[4] Besides occurring in the reference circuit, current also flows unidirectionally in V_{dd} and GND distribution networks.

allowable V_T increase by using the alpha power law model[5] [13]:

$$\Delta V_{T\_ref} = 0.01 \cdot N_{inv} \cdot \frac{(V_{dd} - V_T)}{\alpha}.$$

That is, a V_T shift greater than ΔV_{T_ref} can cause the failure of the reference circuit. This enables us to derive the FITs of the reference circuit by applying the NBTI V_T shift equation given in [14]:

$$FORC_{NBTI} = 10^9 \cdot \left(\frac{K}{\Delta V_{T\_ref}}\right)^{\frac{1}{n}},$$

where $K = A_{NBTI} \cdot t_{ox} \cdot \sqrt{C_{ox} \cdot (V_{gs} - V_T)} \cdot e^{\frac{E_{ox}}{E_0}} \cdot e^{-\frac{E_{a\_NBTI}}{kT}}$.

Here, A_{NBTI}, n, and E_0 are empirical constants and t_{ox}, C_{ox}, E_{ox}, E_{a_NBTI}, and V_T are oxide thickness, oxide capacitance, electric field, the activation energy for NBTI, and the original threshold voltage, respectively. In Section 4.2, we describe how to derive the failure rate of basic microarchitecture structures using $FORC_{NBTI}$.

3.3. FORC for TDDB Failures ($FORC_{TDDB}$)

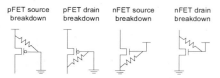

pFET source breakdown   pFET drain breakdown   nFET source breakdown   nFET drain breakdown

Figure 3. Four possible cases of TDDB. Post-breakdown behavior is modeled as 10k of resistance to determine the fatality of breakdowns [8].

TDDB is a failure mechanism causing a conductive path to form in gate oxide, which causes leakage current through the gate [15]. There can be four types of gate oxide breakdown, as illustrated in Figure 3: oxide breakdown at the pFET source, pFET drain, nFET source, and nFET drain area. The resistive path between the gate and the source or drain area leads to current flow through the gate. This can oppose the current of the logic stage that is driving the effected FET, leading to a slowdown in either zero-to-one or one-to-zero transitions, thus making the device vulnerable to timing violations. In our model, we assume that for any circuit on the critical path, a single device failure is sufficient to lead to a timing violation.

The MTTF of TDDB given in [2,15] is applicable to all four types of breakdown, assuming continuous device stress (i.e., 100% duty cycle). Thus, the FORC for TDDB assuming either a pFET or an nFET device

along the critical path with 100% duty cycle is given by

$$FORC_{TDDB} = \frac{10^9}{A_{TDDB}} \cdot V_{dd}^{a-bT} \cdot e^{\frac{X + \frac{Y}{T} + ZT}{kT}},$$

where A_{TDDB}, a, b, X, Y and Z are fitting parameters derived empirically [2]. Using this $FORC_{TDDB}$, the way to derive the FIT of microarchitecture structures is given in Section 4.3.

4. Estimating the FIT of Microarchitecture Structures Based on FORC

In the subsections below, we derive expressions for the FIT rates of several basic and widely used microarchitecture structures for the various failure mechanisms described thus far. Using these expressions, the lifetime reliability of a multi-core microprocessor is analyzed in [16] via execution-driven simulation.

4.1. FIT of Microarchitecture Structures due to EM

Using $FORC_{EM}$, we are able to estimate the FIT of a multi-port register file, such as that shown in Figure 4. In register files, *vias* having only unidirectional current are those between bitlines and pass transistors (i.e., nFETs gated by wordlines). In general, bitlines are implemented on the M2 or upper metal layers, thus requiring *vias* to connect pass transistors to bitlines. Because read bitlines are always precharged prior to cells being read, these *vias* (e.g., v_{sel}) have current flow from the bitlines toward the pass transistor upon reading out "1" to discharge the precharged capacitance of the bitlines, $C_{bitline}$, but no current flows while reading "0." Figure 4(b) depicts the current direction on the read bitline, bl_{0_k}, when cell $Cell_{ik}$ stores "1" and is being selected by asserting wordline wl_{0_i}.

As a result, the effective defect density of the register file is given by the number of *vias* between bitlines and pass transistors over the area of the structure. Each cell has one *via* between the bitline and pass transistor per read port, totaling $N_{cells} \cdot N_{readports}$ *vias* across the register file. In order to express the FIT rate of the register file relative to that of the reference circuit, we must also determine the current density through the vulnerable *vias*, which is given by $(C_{bitline} \cdot V_{dd})/t$, i.e., the amount of capacitance discharged through *vias*, where $C_{bitline} = N_{entries} \cdot C_{drain} + C_{wire}$. This current flows through the *vias* only while reading out a "1," i.e., on average, $P_1 \cdot [N_{reads}/(N_{entries} \cdot N_{readports})]$, where N_{reads} and $N_{entries}$ are

[5] α is technology-dependent, but for pFETs, the range of α is typically between 1.5 and 1.7.

the number of reads of the register file and physical registers, respectively, and P_1 is the probability of the cell storing a "1." Thus, the product of the two previous expressions gives the effective current density of the *vias*.

The following combined expression gives the FIT rate of register files due to EM based on $FORC_{EM}$:

$$FIT_{EM\_Regfile} = N_{cells} \cdot N_{readports} \cdot \left(\frac{C_{bitline}}{C_{ref}} \cdot P_1 \cdot \frac{N_{reads}}{N_{entries} \cdot N_{readports}} \right)^n \cdot FORC_{EM} \cdot$$

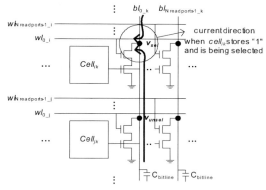

(a) Register file with $N_{readports}$ read ports

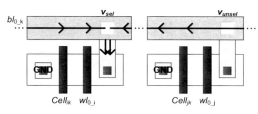

(b) An example layout of read bitline bl_{0_k}

Figure 4. Multi-port register file layout and current direction causing EM failures. Because read bitlines are always precharged prior to cells being read, *via* v_{sel} has current flow from bitline bl_{0_k} toward the pass transistor upon reading out "1" to discharge the precharged capacitance of the bitline, $C_{bitline}$, but no current flows while reading "0." In (b), an example layout is depicted for bl_{0_k} implemented on the M2 metal layer and the pass transistors of cell $Cell_{ik}$ and $Cell_{jk}$, both of which are connected to bl_{0_k} through v_{sel} and v_{unsel}, respectively. The arrows indicate the current direction on bl_{0_k} when $Cell_{ik}$ stores "1" and is being selected by asserting wordline wl_{0_i}.

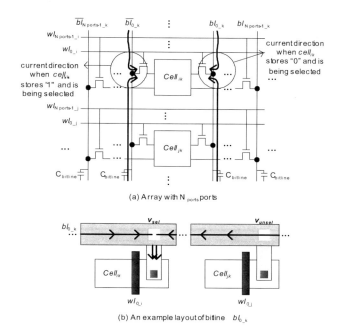

(a) Array with N_{ports} ports

(b) An example layout of bitline bl_{0_k}

Figure 5. Array structure layout and current directions causing EM failures. Arrays are similar to register files, except that the same bitlines are used for both reads and writes, and bitlines are paired for cells. The arrows depict the current direction on bl_{0_k} when $Cell_{ik}$ stores "0" and is being read and on its complementary bitline when the same cell stores "1" and is being read.

Arrays are similar to register files, except that the same bitlines are used for both reads and writes, and bitlines are paired for cells, as illustrated in Figure 5. The paired bitlines have two *vias* per cell, and the sharing of bitlines makes the computation of the average current density more complicated. For reads, the current density is the same as that computed for register files. When cells hold "0" and are being selected by asserting the wordline, this current flows through *vias* on bitlines such as bl_{0_k} in Figure 5. Likewise, the current flows with *vias* on complementary bitlines while reading "1" from cells.

For writes, current flows on the bitlines only if writes cause cells to change value. To overwrite cells holding "1" by "0," the bitline write input drivers pull down transistors in the cells, causing current flow from the cells to the bitlines. However, this current is relatively small and can be ignored since pFET transistors in the cells are generally designed to be very weak. When cells holding "0" are overwritten by "1," the write input drivers charge transistors in the cells as well as the capacitance of the bitlines, causing current similar to that of reads but only for the time needed to pull up transistors in the cells, giving $(C_{bitline} \cdot V_{dd})/(\gamma \cdot t)$, where γ is the duty cycle to pull up transistors in the cells. The complementary bitlines have the same mechanism except that current is generated when cells holding "1" are overwritten by "0."

As a result, the number of effective defects of arrays with N_{cells} cells and N_{ports} read/write ports is $N_{cells} \cdot N_{ports}$ for bitlines and for their complementary bitlines, and the average current density through these *vias* is the sum of current due to reads and writes, yielding a FIT rate for the array structure due to EM failure based on $FORC_{EM}$ given by the following:

$$FIT_{EM\_Array} = N_{cells} \cdot N_{ports} \cdot \left(\frac{C_{bitline}}{C_{ref} \cdot N_{rows} \cdot N_{ports}} \right)^n$$

$$\cdot \left[\left(N_{reads} \cdot P_1 + \frac{1}{2\gamma} \cdot N_{writes} \cdot P_{flip} \right)^n \right.$$

$$\left. + \left(N_{reads} \cdot P_0 + \frac{1}{2\gamma} \cdot N_{writes} \cdot P_{flip} \right)^n \right] \cdot FORC_{EM},$$

where P_1 and P_0 are the probability of the cell holding "1" and "0," respectively, and P_{flip} is the probability of flipping the value of the cell due to writes, either "0" to "1" or "1" to "0."

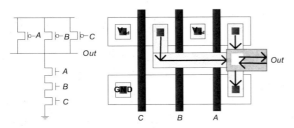

Figure 6. Logic structure layout and current direction possibly causing EM failures. The layout shows an example of an NAND gate with inputs *A*, *B*, and *C*, and output *Out*. The M1 lines connecting the drain of the three pFET devices and the upper nFET device have unidirectional current flow regardless of the value of *Out*. However, the *via* connecting the M1 lines to M2 has bidirectional current, depending on the value of *Out*.

Finally, *vias* in latches, logic gates, multiplexers, and wire repeaters are rarely affected by EM due to the balanced number of positive and negative transitions. However, metal line segments connecting the diffusions of pFET and nFET devices always have unidirectional current flow, possibly making the line segments vulnerable to EM. Figure 6 shows an example layout of a three-input NAND gate exhibiting this behavior. The M1 lines connecting the drain of the three pFET devices and the upper nFET device have unidirectional current flow regardless of value transition at the gate output, *Out*. However, according to [5], metal lines shorter than a critical length (the threshold value of the product of current density and the critical length is between 3000 and 7000A/cm) are subject to a backflow of metal atoms, called the Blech

effect, toward the cathode (i.e., the opposite direction of electron flow), resulting in an offset to the EM effect. The backflow results from an EM-induced stress gradient. The drifted metal atoms due to EM cause tensile stress by accumulating at the anode end, which results in an increase in the atomic density and compressive stress.

4.2. FIT of Microarchitecture Structures due to NBTI

While the pFET devices in the reference circuit are assumed to be under constant stress, the devices in most CMOS designs can experience stress discontinuously. When stress is removed, the NBTI effect (i.e., the shifted V_T) can undergo recovery [7], making the device less vulnerable to NBTI. Thus, NBTI lifetime is strongly affected by duty cycle, defined to be the ratio of stress time to a given period of time, i.e., the time period over which the input of pFET devices is zero, divided by the given period of time. For more accurate reliability modeling, we take this recovery effect into account by finding fitting curves of the NBTI V_T shift equation given in [14] for various duty cycles, making the exponent in the $FORC_{NBTI}$ equation given previously, n, a function of duty cycle. Assuming $n = 0.25$ with 100% duty cycle (i.e., constant stress) in accordance with the hydrogen-based NBTI model given in [7,14], $FORC_{NBTI}$ evaluates to

$$FORC_{NBTI} = 10^9 \cdot \left(\frac{K}{\Delta V_{T\_ref}} \right)^4 .$$

For pFETs along the critical path, the FIT of each pFET can be represented in terms of $FORC_{NBTI}$ as follows:

$$FIT_{NBTI\_per\_pFET} = 10^9 \cdot \left(\frac{\Delta V_{T\_ref}}{\Delta V_c} \right)^{\frac{1}{n}} \cdot \left(\frac{FORC_{NBTI}}{10^9} \right)^{\frac{0.25}{n}},$$

where ΔV_c is the upper bound of V_T shift affordable in the circuit which employs the pFET device. Now all we need for NBTI modeling is to find the number of effective defects per unit area (i.e., pFET devices of the structure that lie along critical paths) and duty cycle for the microarchitecture structure of interest. Assuming the SOFR model [2], the FIT of the structures is straightforwardly computed as the sum of the FITs of pFET devices belonging to those structures. Table 1 lists the number of effective defects and duty cycle of devices over the area of various structures composing microarchitecture operational units, from which the FIT can be found. In the table, T_0 and T_1 indicate the ratio of time when cells, latches, wire repeaters, and multiplexers store or drive "0" and "1," respectively.

P_{fatal} is the percentage of devices along the critical path. Note that precharge transistors and pFET devices in the feedback circuit of latches are not vulnerable to NBTI as they are not on the critical path, and thus should not be included in FITs.

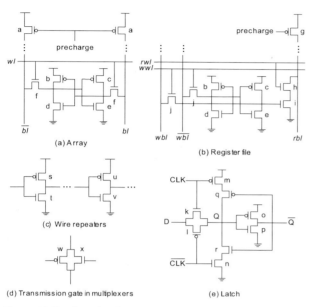

Figure 7. Devices implementing various microarchitecture structures. The number of effective defects and duty cycle of the devices for NBTI and TDDB modeling are given in Tables 1 and 2, respectively.

Table 1. The number of effective defects (EDs) and duty cycle for NBTI modeling for various microarchitecture structures. The devices in the table are indexed with letters in Figure 7.

Structure	Device	Number of EDs	Duty cycle
Array & register file	a, g	Non-fatal	
	b	N_{cells}	T_0
	c	N_{cells}	T_1
Latch	l	$N_{latches}$	$0.25^{\dagger}$
	m, q	Non-fatal	
	o	$N_{latches}$	T_0
Datapath	s, u	$0.5 \cdot N_{repeaters}$	T_0 or $T_1^{\ddagger}$
	w	$N_{mux} \cdot N_{inputs}$	$0.5/N_{inputs}^{\dagger}$
Logic gate	—	$P_{fatal} \cdot N_{pFETs}$	0.5

† Since NBTI occurs only on negatively biased pFET devices, the pFETs for transmission gates in latches and multiplexers are stressed only if the gate of the pFETs is low and the transmission gates pass high (0.5 of the probability assumed in the table).
‡ For wire repeaters, pFETs in every other repeater are under stress at a time.

4.3. FIT of Microarchitecture Structures due to TDDB

As most CMOS devices experience discontinuous stress modes, we account for this using the duty cycle of stress for the devices in order not to underestimate their lifetime. Unlike EM and NBTI, TDDB has no recovery effect on digital circuits; however, removing the stress simply suspends gate oxide breakdown [9]. Taking this into account, the FIT of each pFET or nFET due to one breakdown is as follows:

$$FIT_{TDDB\_per\_FET} = duty\ cycle \cdot FORC_{TDDB},$$

where duty cycle is the ratio of stress time to a given period of time.

Similar to NBTI, we can express failure rates of microarchitectural components due to TDDB in terms of $FORC_{TDDB}$ by finding the number of effective defects per unit area and duty cycle. That is, we need to find the number of pFETs and nFETs over the area of the structure that lie along critical paths and their duty cycle. In addition, assume that breakdown at the source and at the drain area are independent, thus counting each separately as a failure or defect if it is fatal. Assuming the SOFR model, the FIT of basic structures is straightforwardly computed as the sum of the FITs of pFET and nFET devices belonging to those structures.

Table 2 lists the number of effective defects (ED), duty cycle of devices, and the fatality of breakdown (NF: non-fatal; F: fatal) over the area of various structures, from which the FIT can be found. We assume that precharge transistors are always stressed except the time when the corresponding bitlines are accessed. We also assume that precharge takes half of the clock cycle and bitline access takes the other half of the cycle. As a result, the average duty cycle of precharge transistors is $1 - N_{reads/cycle}/(2 \cdot N_{lbls} \cdot N_{readports})$ for register files and $1 - (N_{reads/cycle} + N_{writes/cycle})/(2 \cdot N_{lbls} \cdot N_{ports})$ for arrays, where N_{lbls} is the number of local bitlines. On the other hand, pass transistors are under stress only when the corresponding bitlines are accessed.

Table 2. The number of effective defects (EDs) and duty cycle for TDDB modeling for various microarchitecture structures. The devices in the table are indexed with letters in Figure 7. The fatality of breakdown (NF: non-fatal; F: fatal) is also given for the source (Src) and drain (Drn) area. We assume that breakdown at the source and at the drain area are independent, thus counting each separately as a failure or defect if it is fatal.

Structure	Device	Fatality Src	Fatality Drn	Number of EDs	Duty cycle
Array	a	NF†	F	$2 \cdot N_{cells} \cdot N_{ports} / N_{cells/lbl}$	$1 - \dfrac{N_{reads/cycle} + N_{writes/cycle}}{2 \cdot N_{lbls} \cdot N_{ports}}$
	b	NF	F	N_{cells}	T_0
	c	NF	F	N_{cells}	T_1
	f	F	F	$4 \cdot N_{cells} \cdot N_{ports}$	$\dfrac{N_{reads\,cycle} + N_{writes\,cycle}}{2 \cdot N_{rows} \cdot N_{ports}}$
	d	F	F	$2 \cdot N_{cells}$	T_0
	e	F	F	$2 \cdot N_{cells}$	T_1
Register file (devices in the cell are the same as those in array)	g	NF†	F	$N_{cells} \cdot N_{readports} / N_{cells/lbl}$	$1 - \dfrac{N_{reads\,cycle}}{2 \cdot N_{lbls} \cdot N_{readports}}$
	h	F	F	$2 \cdot N_{cells} \cdot N_{readports}$	$\dfrac{N_{reads\,cycle}}{2 \cdot N_{entries} \cdot N_{readports}}$
	j	NF	F	$2 \cdot N_{cells} \cdot N_{writeports}$	$\dfrac{N_{writes\,cycle}}{2 \cdot N_{entries} \cdot N_{writeports}}$
	i	NF	F	$N_{cells} \cdot N_{readports}$	T_1
Latch	k, l	F	F	$2 \cdot N_{latches}$	0.25
	q	F	NF	$N_{latches}$	T_1
	r	F	NF	$N_{latches}$	T_0
	m, n	NF†	F	$N_{latches}$	0.5
	o	F	F	$2 \cdot N_{latches}$	T_0
	p	F	F	$2 \cdot N_{latches}$	T_1
Datapath	s, t, u, v	F	F	$2 \cdot N_{repeaters}$	T_0 or T_1
	w, x	F	F	$2 \cdot N_{mux} \cdot N_{inputs}$	$0.5/N_{inputs}$
Logic gate	—	F‡	F‡	$P_{fatal} \cdot N_{FETs}$	0.5

† Simultaneous multiple breakdowns may cause circuit failure.
‡ The fatality is determined by circuits where the devices belong.

4.4. Discussion

In the subsections above, we describe the FIT rate of microarchitecture structures due to each of failure mechanisms. To combine FIT rates across different failure mechanisms, the one-time quantification of FORC for the failure mechanisms needs to be done for a given technology and implementation style. Then, the total FIT rate can be computed by multiplying the FITs of the structure in terms of FORC by the value of FORC for the corresponding failure mechanism and adding the computed FIT values, assuming the SOFR model. Furthermore, to combine FIT rates across multiple structures, the total FIT rate of the structures computed in this way can be simply added.

In our reliability model, the impact of microarchitectural features to improve lifetime reliability, such as redundancy, has yet to be taken into account due to a limitation of the SOFR model [2]; the first component failure causes the microarchitecture to fail. Since redundancy features enable the microarchitecture to operate even in the presence of failures, the impact of the reliability features cannot be accurately evaluated by the SOFR model. As a result, a reliability model which improves this limitation is needed for more accurate reliability modeling.

5. Related Work

There has been enormous research to model failure mechanisms at the device level, but only some of well-accepted models for failure mechanisms under study in this paper are discussed in this section. For EM, J. R. Black proposed a mean-time-to-failure model (often called Black's equation) which has been widely used to predict the lifetime of conductor lines [3]. C.-K. Hu et al. proposed an EM model, particularly for copper conductor lines and low-k dielectric material [5]. The effect of bidirectional current on EM lifetime has been studied theoretically and experimentally in [17] and [6], respectively. For NBTI, the extensive work of modeling the NBTI failure mechanism is summarized in [7], along with fundamentals of the failure mechanism and the impact of various process and device parameters on NBTI lifetime. For TDDB, E.Y. Wu et al. proposed a mean-time-to-failure model [15] which is used in this paper. Other TDDB models proposed thus far are extensively summarized in [18].

There has also been much work to incorporate these device-level failure models into the circuit-level. UC Berkeley BERT [11] and Cadence® Virtuoso® UltraSim [19] are the most well-known lifetime reliability circuit simulators. The simulator features to predict and validate timing and reliability due to EM, NBTI, TDDB and/or HCI (hot-carrier injection) are implemented in such a way as to be compatible to the SPICE or FastSPICE circuit simulator.

Compared to that at the device- and circuit-level, lifetime reliability modeling at the architecture-level is rather a daunting one. J. Srinivasan et al. proposed an architecture-level lifetime reliability model, called RAMP [2]. Since RAMP was developed to model the lifetime of processor cores, some of its assumptions such as uniform device density and identical device vulnerability make RAMP less accurate, especially when one extends it to cover the entire chip. Z. Lu et al. proposed an EM model by accounting for dynamic thermal and current stress on conductor lines [4]. While the proposed model attempts to embrace the impact of discontinuous stress on the lifetime of conductor lines, maximum temperature across the chip and the worst-case current density specified at design time were used in the model.

6. Conclusion

In this paper, we address the issue of modeling lifetime reliability metrics at the architecture level. We propose a framework for architecture-level lifetime reliability model and present a new concept called *FITs of reference circuit* (FORC) that allows architects to quantify failure rates without having to deal with circuit- and technology-specific details of the implemented architecture. The proposed framework along with a cycle-accurate architecture simulator will allow an accurate estimation of the FIT rates of various types of microprocessor chips. In addition, the FORC-based approach allows relative performance-reliability trade-off to be evaluated to make educate design decisions, especially at the early design stage.

In addition, the impact of typical microarchitectural features to enhance chip lifetime, such as redundancy, needs to be carefully modeled to allow the exploration of area, power, and performance trade-offs. To do so, some of underlying assumptions used in this paper need to be improved in such a way that the FIT rates of redundant components can be effectively combined. Finally, the impact of technology scaling on lifetime reliability also can be revisited by using our FORC-based reliability model.

Acknowledgement

We would like to thank Professor Timothy M. Pinkston and anonymous reviewers for their useful comments. We would also like to thank Chao-Kun Hu of IBM for his help with the electromigration model. Jeonghee Shin was supported in part by an NSF grant, CCF-0541417, and an IBM internship.

References

1. S. Borkar, "Designing reliable systems from unreliable components: the challenges of transistor variability and degradation," *IEEE Micro*, vol. 25, no. 6, pp. 10-16, November/December 2005.
2. J. Srinivasan, S. V. Adve, P. Bose and J. A. Rivers, "The case for lifetime reliability-aware microprocessors," *Proceedings of International Symposium on Computer Architecture (ISCA)*, pp. 276-287, June 2004.
3. J. R. Black, "Electromigration-A brief survey and some recent results," *IEEE Transactions on Electron Devices*, Vol. 16, No. 4, pp. 338-347, April 1967.
4. Z. Lu, J. Lach, M. R. Stan and K. Skadron, "Temperature-aware modeling and banking of IC lifetime reliability," *IEEE Micro*, Vol. 25, No. 6, pp. 40-49, November/December 2005.

5. C.-K. Hu, L. Gignac and R. Rosenberg, "Electromigration of Cu/low dielectric constant interconnects," *Microelectronics and reliability*, Vol. 46, No. 2-4, pp. 213-231, February-April 2006.
6. K. P. Rodbell, A. J. Castellano and R. I. Kaufman, "AC electromigration (10MHz–1GHz) in Al metallization," *Proceedings of the fourth international workshop on stress induced phenomena in metallization*, pp. 212-223, January 1998.
7. D. K. Schroder and J. A. Babcock, "Negative bias temperature instability: Road to cross in deep submicron silicon semiconductor manufacturing," *Journal of Applied Physics*, Vol. 94, No. 1, July 2003.
8. R. Rodriguez et al., "The impact of gate-oxide breakdown on SRAM stability," *IEEE Electron Device Letters*, Vol. 23, No. 9, pp. 559-561, September 2000.
9. E. Rosenbaum, Z. Liu and C. Hu, "Silicon dioxide breakdown lifetime enhancement under bipolar bias conditions," *IEEE Transactions on Electron Devices*, Vol. 40, No. 12, pp. 2287-2295, December 1993.
10. G. La Rosa, S. Rauch and F. Guarin, "New Phenomena in the Device Reliability Physics of Advanced Submicron CMOS Technologies," *IRPS Tutorial*, 2001.
11. R. H. Tu et al., "Berkeley reliability tools-BERT," *IEEE Transactions on Computer-Aided Design of Integrated Circuits and Systems*, Vol. 12, No. 10, pp. 1524-1534, October 1993.
12. T. Kuroi et al., "Sub-Quarter-Micron Dual Gate CMOSFETs with Ultra-Thin Gate Oixde of 2nm," *Symposium on VLSI Technology*, pp.210-211, June 1999.
13. T. Sakurai and A. R. Newton, "Alpha-power law MOSFET model and its applications to CMOS inverter delay and other formulas," *IEEE Journal of Solid-State Circuit*, Vol. 25, No. 2, pp. 584-594, April 1990.
14. R. Vattikonda, W. Wang and Y. Cao, "Modeling and minimization of PMOS NBTI effect for robust nanometer design," *Proceedings of the 43rd annual conference on Design automation*, pp. 1047-1052, July 2006.
15. E.Y. Wu and E.J. Nowak and A. Vayshenker and W.L. Lai and D.L. Harmon, "CMOS scaling beyond the 100-nm node with silicon-dioxide-based gate dielectrics," *IBM Journal of Research and Development*, Vol. 46, No. 2/3, pp. 287-298, 2002.
16. J. Shin, V. Zyuban, Z. Hu, J. A. Rivers and P. Bose, "Structure-Aware Lifetime Reliability Modeling," *IBM Technical Report*, 2007 (to appear).
17. W. R. Hunter, "Self-consistent solutions for allowed interconnect current density—Part II: Application to design guidelines," IEEE Transactions on Electron Devices, Vol. 44, No. 2, pp. 310-316, February 1997.
18. J. H. Stathis, "Reliability limits for the gate insulator in CMOS technology," *IBM Journal of Research and Development*, Vol. 46, No. 2/3, pp. 265-286, 2002.
19. Cadence Design Systems, Inc., "Reliability Simulation in Integrated Circuit Design," White Paper, http://www.cadence.com.

Processor-level Selective Replication

Nithin Nakka, Karthik Pattabiraman, Ravishankar Iyer
Center for Reliable and High Performance Computing
Coordinated Science Laboratory
{nakka, pattabir, iyer}@crhc.uiuc.edu

Abstract

We propose a processor-level technique called Selective Replication, by which the application can choose where in its application stream and to what degree it requires replication. Recent work on static analysis and fault-injection-based experiments on applications reveals that certain variables in the application are critical to its crash- and hang-free execution. If it can be ensured that only the computation of these variables is error-free, then a high degree of crash/hang coverage can be achieved at a low performance overhead to the application. The Selective Replication technique provides an ideal platform for validating this claim. The technique is compared against complete duplication as provided in current architecture-level techniques. The results show that with about 59% less overhead than full duplication, selective replication detects 97% of the data errors and 87% of the instruction errors that were covered by full duplication. It also reduces the detection of errors benign to the final outcome of the application by 17.8% as compared to full duplication.

Keywords: *Application-aware, Error Detection, Redundant Hardware, Critical Variable, Duplication.*

1. Introduction

System-level replication has been widely used to detect and possibly tolerate transient errors in both commercial systems and research prototypes. Recently, processor-level replication has emerged as a viable technique [1].

The two basic approaches for processor-level replication are hardware redundancy and time redundancy. (1) Hardware redundancy [3] is achieved by carrying out the same computation on multiple, independent hardware at the same time and comparing the redundant results. (2) Time redundancy [3][5] is achieved by executing the same operation multiple times on the same or idle hardware. In both types of redundancy, all instructions of the application are replicated and checked for correct execution. However, the application cannot choose to use redundancy for a specific code section and run in a normal, unreplicated mode for the rest of the code. In other words, it is a "one size fits all" approach.

We propose hardware-based, selective replication to replicate only critical portions of the application rather than the entire application, thus reducing performance overhead. The application chooses the portions that need to be replicated and the degree of redundancy. This is done using an extension of a technique described in [8] for identifying strategic locations for placement of detectors. Critical variables and, hence, critical code sections that need to be replicated are derived from this analysis. The application is then instrumented with special CHECK instructions, which are an extension to the instruction set architecture (ISA), to invoke reconfiguration of the underlying hardware and provide the specified level of replication to the critical code sections.

Another advantage of selectively replicating an application is the reduction in detection of processor-level errors that do not affect the final outcome of the application (benign errors). Fault-injection-based experiments by Wang [6] and Saggese [7] showed that 80-85% of the errors did not manifest as errors in the application outcome. Full replication at the hardware level aims at detecting all errors in the processor, even those that are benign. This leads to false alarms, which are considered undesirable from a safety perspective. Selective replication, on the other hand, aims at detecting only the errors that result in application failure.

This work addresses the following two questions to provide selective replication:

1. Which sections of the code need to be replicated?
2. How can we modify the fetch, renaming, and commit mechanism to handle a specified level of redundancy for portions of the code?

Processor-level replication has been implemented earlier [4][5]. However, it is a non-trivial task to extend it to support selective replication of portions of the application, as it requires a reconfiguration of the fetch, rename and commit mechanisms in the processor.

In addition, to let the application to select the portions to replicate, the hardware needs to expose an API that can be used to trigger the reconfiguration of the replication mechanism.

In this paper we detail the mechanism of selective replication in a superscalar processor and present a possible implementation. The results show that Selective Replication detects about 87% of the instruction errors and 97% of the data errors detected by Full Duplication. Further, it incurs only 59% performance overhead compared to Full Duplication. Moreover, the detection of errors benign to the application outcome is reduced by about 18% as compared to full duplication.

The rest of the paper is organized as follows: Section 2 describes the analysis procedure to extract the portions of the application that need to be replicated. The basic mechanism of Selective Replication has been presented in Section 3 and the hardware implementation has been detailed in Section 4. Section 5 presents the results. Some previous work has been summarized in Section 6 and Section 7 presents the conclusions and directions for future work.

2. Application analysis

In this section, we show how the properties of the application are leveraged by selective replication in order to identify what to replicate in the application. This analysis consists of three main steps as shown in Figure 1.

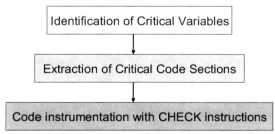

Figure 1: Steps in identifying what to replicate

These steps are carried out at compile-time prior to the application being deployed. The first two steps are carried out by an offline analysis based on the Dynamic Dependence Graph (DDG) of the application, which represents the dependencies among instructions in a real execution of the application. The third step is carried out using an enhancement made to the compiler,

using the information obtained from the first two steps. The three steps are explained in more detail as follows:

1) Identification of Critical Variables. Recent work by Pattabiraman et al. [8] has shown that it is feasible to identify critical variables in an application, which when in error are highly likely application/system failure (crashes[1] and fail silence violations). Selective replication leverages the results of this study to replicate *only those portions of the application that compute the critical variables.* In order to identify the *critical* variables we use an approach similar to the one described in [8]. The criticality of variables to error-free execution of the program has been evaluated using metrics like *lifetime*, and *fanout* (definition). It was shown that ideal detectors placed at locations with high fanout gave higher coverage, where an ideal detector is one that is able to detect any data error that propagates to the location at which it is placed. The analysis was done on the program's Dynamic Dependency Graph (DDG). For multiple inputs, faults are injected into the program variables that are being evaluated for criticality (with high fanout, lifetime etc.). For each input, the effect of each fault is traced, using the DDG for that input, to locations of the program where the program may crash. If the error led the program to a potential crash location, a detector at the critical point is said to detect an impending program crash.

Our claim is that if the computations of the critical variables are replicated, then this can enhance application dependability substantially and at the same time incur only a small performance penalty compared to that of full replication.

2) Extraction of the Critical Code Sections. Any part of the application that affects the value of a critical variable is a critical code section (consisting of *critical instructions*). A critical code section includes:

- Instructions that define *critical* variables.
- Instructions that produce a result that is subsequently consumed by *critical* instructions (i.e. backward program slice of the critical instruction [15]).

A reverse depth-first search algorithm on the DDG is used for automated identification/extraction of instructions that directly or indirectly affect the value of critical variables. The algorithm extracts the backward slice of the instruction that defines a critical variable [15]. Backward slicing using static analysis techniques is known to be imprecise [20]. Using the dynamic dependency graph, the precision of backward slicing can be improved [16]. This is important from the point of view of selective replication, as imprecise

---

[1] Program crashes must be detected preemptively to prevent error propagation and corruption of program state.

slicing algorithms can increase the number of instructions that need to be replicated..

Due to space constraints, we do not present the details of the algorithm, but these may be found in [13].

An important point to note is that when using multiple critical nodes, there may be an overlap in the instructions that affect two or more nodes. It is sufficient to replicate all such instructions that affect multiple critical nodes once for all nodes.

Formally, let Θ be the set of critical variables and I be the set of all inputs. For an input $i \in I$, let the dynamic dependency graph be $G_i = (V_i, E_i)$ where the vertices in V_i correspond to statements in the dynamic execution of the program and there is an edge (u, v) in E_i if statement u is executed before statement v and u produces a result that is used by v. For every critical variable $\theta \in \Theta$, let $H_{i,\theta} = (V_{i,\theta}, E_{i,\theta})$ be the sub-graph of G_i which is the backward slice of instructions that affect variable θ. For each dynamic instruction $w \in V_{i,\theta}$ its counterpart, s, in the static code segment is found (both of them have the same PC). The set of static instructions corresponding to the dynamic instructions in $V_{i,\theta}$ is the set of critical instructions, $S_{i,\theta}$, that need to be replicated for input i and critical variable θ. $S_i = \bigcup_{\theta \in \Theta} S_{i,\theta}$ is the set of critical instructions for input i and $S = \bigcup_{i \in I} S_i$ is the set of all instructions in the static code segment that need to be replicated for all inputs considered.

3) Insertion of CHECK Instructions. The compiler places a special CHECK instruction before and after each duplicated instruction to notify the hardware of the change in the level of replication. This is the API that the hardware exposes to the application to select the point and level of replication. Note that the critical instructions can also be consecutive to each other. In such a case, for each block of contiguous critical instructions, one CHECK instruction is placed before and one after the block of instructions to notify the replication module of entering into and exiting from replication mode. This reduces the overhead of switching between replication modes as well as the number of CHECK instructions inserted.

3. Overview of Selective Replication

This section describes the selective replication technique in detail. Instructions are fetched as in a normal pipeline. The dispatch mechanism, which allocates reorder buffer entries to the currently fetched instructions, broadly operates in two modes: the *unreplicated* mode and the *replicated* mode. In the unreplicated mode, a single copy of each instruction is dispatched, renamed, and allocated to the reorder buffer (ROB). In the replicated mode, r copies of each instruction are dispatched, where r is the degree of replication. If any instruction, i, in the replicated code consumes a value produced by a preceding unreplicated instruction, j, then all copies of i receive their input from j. If a replicated instruction i_1 is dependent on another replicated instruction i_2, then the copy of i_1 in every replica is dependent on the copy of i_2 in the same replica. The register operands of the instructions are renamed accordingly.

After instruction execution is complete the result is stored in the ROB itself. When an instruction at the head of the ROB is ready to commit, all copies of the instruction are checked to see if they are ready to commit. If all copies are ready to commit, then their results (stored in their corresponding ROB entries) are compared. If all of them match the instruction is committed. In the case of even a single mismatch appropriate recovery action is taken, such as retrying the instruction execution.

3.1. Mechanism of replication

An important contribution of this work is the mechanism for selective replication that allows the application to choose the extent and location of replication it needs. In this section the implementation of selective replication in a modern superscalar out-of-order processor is described. Implementing selective replication in a superscalar processor involves modifying the instruction fetch and dispatch, register renaming, and commit mechanisms of the processor.

The block diagram in Figure 2 shows a processor pipeline (top of the figure) with the modifications required for selective replication (shown at the bottom of the figure).

Before describing the actual mechanism of execution in the replicated mode, it is helpful to describe some key hardware data structures that would be used in the execution.

The register alias table (RAT) is used in dynamic scheduling in the rename state of pipeline. It contains as many entries as the number of architectural registers. The ith entry in the RAT contains information of the source of the most recent value of register i. If the most recent instruction producing register i has been committed to architectural state, the ith entry in the RAT contains a special sentinel value indicating that the value of a register is ready and available in the architectural register file. If the most recent instruction

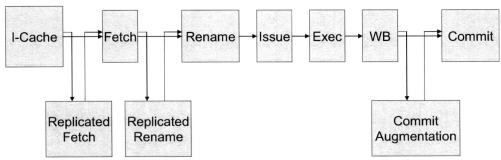

Figure 2: Modifications to pipeline for selective replication

producing register i is still executing and is in the ROB, the entry in the RAT contains the index of the ROB entry containing the instruction. Thus the RAT holds information of the (read-after-write) RAW dependencies among instructions.

The load/store queue (LSQ) contains entries for all the memory access instructions (loads and stores) that are currently in-flight. The LSQ can be used to optimize loads by forwarding the data from the immediately previous store, if both generate the same effective address and are writing the same number of bytes.

The replicated fetch mechanism shown in Figure 2 provides multiple copies of a fetched instruction to the dispatcher. The detailed hardware implementation of this mechanism is presented in Section 4.

Replicated Rename. The mechanism for renaming multiple copies of an instruction, based on the replica index, is shown in Figure 3. If a replicated instruction d reads from register x, the RAT entry for x is looked up. If the value of x is available in the architectural register file then all copies of d get the value for this source operand from the architectural register file. Otherwise, the value of x is the result of an in-flight instruction, p, that is allocated the ROB entry k. If p is an unreplicated instruction (as indicated by the REPL bit in entry k) for all replicas d_1, d_2, ..., d_r the source operand register is renamed to read from entry k. If p is a replicated instruction the register operand x of d_i is renamed to read the output from instruction p_i, where $i= 1, 2, 3..., r$.

Instructions Issue to Functional Units. With the above renaming mechanism the issue of instructions to functional units can be done without any modification to the already existing scheduling mechanism.

Execution and Storing the Result. The instructions in the unreplicated mode are always executed in a normal out-of-order fashion. The instructions in the replicated mode also execute in an out-of-order fashion. Though it complicates the mechanism to detect the completion of all copies of the instruction, it provides the benefits of superscalar out-of-order

execution by exploiting the instruction level parallelism and increasing the utilization of the multiple functional units available for instruction execution.

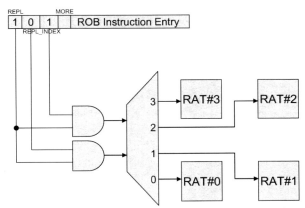

Figure 3: Mechanism for register renaming of multiple instructions

The ROB need not be empty before switching from the unreplicated mode to the replicated mode. This can be done by maintaining the information in the register alias table across the two modes. In other words, if one of the replicated instructions reads from a register that is produced by a previous unreplicated instruction (which is not committed and still holds an entry in the ROB), then all copies of the replicated instruction read from the result of the same unreplicated instruction. For dependencies among instructions within the replica, a replicated instruction that is dependent on another replicated instruction gets its input from the producing instruction in the same replica.

For switching from the replicated mode to the unreplicated mode, however, the constraint that the ROB is empty before the switch is maintained. This is because an unreplicated instruction i, that is dependent on an instruction j in the preceding replicated code, is effectively dependent on all the copies of j. Before issuing i, all copies of j must have completed execution and their results matched so as to forward the result to instruction i.

After an instruction has completed execution in the functional unit, the result is stored in the ROB entry corresponding to that instruction itself. For memory access instructions, the result of the address generation is stored in the ROB entry.

Commit Augmentation. As shown in Figure 2, the commit unit is augmented to vote on the results of multiple replicas to support selective replication. The commit stage is augmented to vote on the Each ROB entry contains a field to indicate if the instruction is ready to commit or not. Committing unreplicated instructions follows the same procedure as committing an instruction in a pipeline without support for replication.

Among replicated instructions, memory access instructions are treated separately. When a replicated memory access instruction at the head of the ROB has completed execution (generated effective address), all of its copies are checked to see if they have completed execution. If not, the commit action is postponed to the next cycle. If all r copies have generated their effective addresses (which is stored in the result field of the ROB entry), these results are compared against each other. If there is a mismatch, an error is raised and appropriate recovery action is taken. If the effective addresses of all r copies match, then a single memory access request is sent to the memory subsystem, on behalf of all the replicas. This reduces the pressure on the memory bandwidth, but loses the coverage over possible errors in memory access. When this memory access is complete, all copies of the instruction are ready to commit. In case of a load the data read is written to the architectural register file. The entries from the ROB and the LSQ for all copies are de-allocated. When any other replicated instruction is at the head of the ROB, all of its copies are checked to see if they are ready to commit. If all r copies are ready to commit, the result fields in their ROB entries are compared to verify the computation. If all r fields match, the instruction is committed and the result is committed to the architectural register file.

4. Hardware implementation

The mechanism to dispatch multiple copies of instructions is depicted in Figure 4. Instructions are fetched into a temporary fetch buffer (temp_fetch_buf in Figure 4). Depending on the degree of replication different number of copies of the instruction should be dispatched. In a processor that does not support replication the input to the dispatch mechanism would be the instructions in the temporary fetch buffer. These instructions are dispatched to the reorder buffer (ROB) based on the space available in the ROB and the dispatch width (the maximum number of instructions that can be dispatched in one clock cycle) of the processor.

Depending on the degree of replication requested by the application, the instructions that are dispatched in the current clock cycle need to be determined. The replicated instructions that can be dispatched in the current clock cycle are placed in the real fetch buffer (fetch_buf in Figure 4). The degree of replication is stored in the register REP_LVL. REP_LVL is used as an index into the combinational logic that starts with 0 when there is no replication. Consider a processor with a fetch width (maximum number of instructions fetched in a clock cycle) of 4 and a dispatch width (maximum number of instructions dispatched in a clock cycle) of 4.

The red lines show the duplicated instructions being routed from the temp_fetch_buf to the fetch_buf.

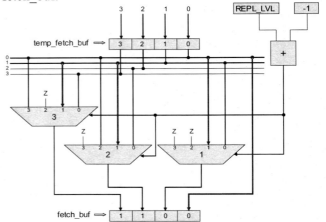

Figure 4: Mechanism for dispatching multiple copies of instructions

The ROB is augmented with a bit (referred to as the REPL bit) to indicate whether it contains a replicated or an unreplicated instruction. ROB designs are of two types: one in which the result of the instruction in the ROB entry is written to separate physical register file, and the other in which the result is written to the ROB entry itself. The replication mechanism is presented assuming an ROB design where the results are written to the ROB entry itself, though it is possible to extend the technique for the design where a separate physical register file is used to store the results of instructions. The additional hardware required in the context of Reduced Instruction Set Computer (RISC) architecture is described.[2] The RAT and commit control logic for the unreplicated mode is the same as that used in the normal superscalar out-of-order pipelines.

5. Evaluation methodology

The software-implemented functional simulator implements a MIPS-based SuperScalar processor. The *sim-outorder* processor performance simulator of the SimpleScalar Tool Set [17] has been augmented to simulate the RSE with embedded hardware modules. *sim-outorder* simulates an out-of-order pipelined processor. The main loop of the simulator is executed once for each target (simulated) machine cycle. Currently, CHECK instructions are embedded at runtime, and not at compile time. At the time of an instruction fetch, the simulator determines whether to insert a CHECK instruction before it into the instruction stream. It does this either by decoding the instruction or by monitoring the fetched instruction address. This is equivalent to the CHECK instruction being embedded in the static instruction stream of the program.

5.1. Workload for evaluation

Evaluation of the performance overhead and error coverage is based on the Siemens suite of benchmarks. These benchmark applications are representative of real-world programs and contain a few hundred lines of code [9]. The benchmarks are input-dependent and come with a rich input set with an average of 3400 inputs for each benchmark. For each benchmark, we choose the first 100 inputs from its input set. For each input i the DDG, G_i of the program is generated. For each critical variable, its backward slice in G_i is calculated. The set of nodes (instructions) in the backward slice are critical instructions that need to be replicated. In a similar manner, the set of critical instructions for each critical variable are extracted. The union of these different sets of critical instructions is calculated. This procedure is repeated for each input i in the chosen set of 100 inputs. The set of critical instructions that is replicated is the union of the sets of critical instructions for all the inputs. Table 1 gives a brief description of the Siemens suite of benchmarks.

---

[2] In a RISC architecture, load/store instructions are used to access memory and the destination of arithmetic instructions is a register.

5.2. Performance overhead

The software-level implementation evaluates the performance overhead incurred by the framework and modules in terms of additional processor cycles.

Table 1: Siemens suite of benchmarks

Benchmark	#loc	Description
schedule	412	A priority scheduler for multiple job tasks. Given a list of tasks finds an optimal schedule
schedule2	373	Same operation as Schedule but a different implementation.
print_tokens	727	Breaks the input stream into a series of lexical tokens according to pre-specified rules.
print_tokens2	569	Using the *tokenizer* interface Breaks the input stream into a series of lexical tokens according to pre-specified rules.

5.2.1. Performance overhead categories

The experiments evaluate the following two kinds of performance overheads:

1. *Framework Overhead.* This is the overhead incurred by the processor due to the presence of the framework without any modules instantiated. In such a case, the framework does not perform any checking and is decoupled from the pipeline. The overhead incurred in the performance of the application is due to the *memory arbiter* introduced to arbitrate memory accesses of the processor and the RSE [18].

2. *Performance Overhead Due to Selective Replication.* The performance overhead incurred by the application is measured in terms of the number of additional cycles taken to execute the application in comparison to the baseline processor (without the framework). In order to show the need for selective replication, a randomized replication mechanism (RANDOMREP) is also evaluated where instructions are randomly replicated. In order to make a fair comparison between the randomized and selective replication approaches the fraction of replicated instructions is maintained the same, ensuring that the overheads are approximately equal.

There can be other sources of overhead due to the additional hardware introduced in the processor. The additional circuitry will increase the capacitive load on pipeline nodes. This will in turn lead to a slight increase in the clock cycle time. Because we are doing a functional simulation this factor of overhead is not included in our experiments.

5.2.2. Results

Figure 5 shows the overheads incurred, for different applications, due to the framework with selective replication (SELREP) compared to full replication (FULLREP). The overhead of the framework with no modules instantiated is also shown (Framework). We observe that the overhead averaged over all applications and combinations of modules is 53.1% lower than the overhead due to full replication.

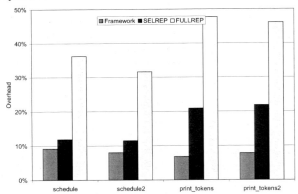

Figure 5: Performance overhead for Selective Replication

An average over all the Siemens benchmarks shows that the overhead is 16.5% for SELREP. For SELREP the overhead is due to the execution of duplicate instructions in replicated mode, and due to the switch between replicated and unreplicated modes. The overhead varied from application to application. For example, for *schedule* the overhead for SELREP was 11.9% (67.1% lower than that for FULLREP) whereas for *print_tokens2* it was 21.8% (52.7% lower than that for FULLREP).

5.3. Error analysis

In this section we describe the fault-injection analysis of the error coverage provided by Selective Replication. Firstly, the fault model is described and the classification of the outcomes of each fault-injection experiment is presented. The injection experiments are conducted for each benchmark from the Siemens suite and the results reported.

5.3.1. Fault model

An important component of the design of a fault-injection experiment to evaluate error coverage is the fault model. It describes the faults that are being targeted by the error-detection mechanisms and against which they have been evaluated. The faults considered in our experiments are as follows:

- *Instruction Errors.* Errors in the instruction binary while the instruction is being executed in the pipeline. These errors can occur during the transfer of the instruction from the cache to the pipeline or while the instruction is being decoded in the pipeline.
- *Data Errors.* Errors in the output of a functional unit that may be written to a register or used as an effective address for a memory access instruction. ECC in memory, cache, or registers does not protect against these errors. This is because the correct ECC would be calculated on the wrong data and written to registers.

This fault model also includes some software faults such as *assignment/initialization* (an uninitialized or incorrectly initialized value is used) or *checking* (a check performed on the variable fails, which is equivalent to an incorrect value of a variable being used) [19]. The error-detection mechanisms detect the symptoms of errors, irrespective of whether they occur in software or hardware.

5.3.2. Fault-injection outcomes

The SimpleScalar *sim-outorder* performance simulator simulates the timing information for instructions executing in a pipeline, i.e., it maintains the information of which instructions are present in each stage of the pipeline in any given cycle. The simulator, however, computes the results of executing the instructions in the dispatch stage, when it allocates an entry in the reorder buffer to the instruction. It detects and reports any exceptions that result from execution of the instruction at the dispatch stage itself, without waiting until the commit stage. Thus, the processor simulator does not support precise exceptions. The replication mechanism, however, performs the checks when the instruction has arrived at the commit stage and is ready for commit..

Translating the simulator behavior to that of a real processor, let us assume that the simulator does not raise an exception at the dispatch stage but allows the instruction to proceed to the commit stage. Considering this behavior of the processor the fault injection outcomes have been organized into the various categories shown in Table 2.

Table 2: Fault-injection outcomes

Outcome	Description	Error Impact
Replication Detection	Errors leading to a mismatch between the replicas.	Do not raise an exception, but are detected by the voter in the commit stage.
Exception Raised	Errors that raise a simulator exception in the same instruction (PC) as the injected PC.	Raise an exception in the commit stage of the injected instruction. Architected state would not be corrupted by these errors before the exception.
Retrospectively Detected	Errors that are not detected by replication, but are injected when the processor is in replicated mode, and raise a simulator error in a different instruction than the one that was injected into.	Can be detected by the replication if the instruction had been allowed to complete. However, the architected state might have been corrupted by then.
System Detection	Errors that are detected by the simulator but occur in a different instruction than the injected instruction.	Detected by the system, but the architected state might have been corrupted by the instruction before the system detects these errors.
Not Manifested	Errors that do not cause simulator errors and hangs, and the output files match.	Do not cause any visible effect on the outcome of the program.
Program Hang	Errors in which the simulator times out and kills the program	Cause the simulator to wait indefinitely for the program to complete
Fail-Silent Violation	Errors that do not cause simulator errors or timeouts, but result in the output files, differs from that of the golden run.	System does not detect these errors, but results in an incorrect program outcome. Potentially, most dangerous of the error categories
Benign Error Detection	Errors that are "Not Manifested" in the baseline case but are detected by the detection mechanism	Do not affect application outcome and hence need not be detected

5.3.3. Error metrics

The two metrics derived from the fault injection outcomes are the percentage of errors detected by the technique and percentage of false positives, where an error that is benign in the baseline is detected by the technique. For any technique it is desirable to have the highest detection coverage possible and as few false positives as possible, even though these are conflicting goals.

5.3.4. Error coverage for instruction errors

Errors belonging to each type mentioned in Section 5.3.1 are injected. Figure 6 presents the detection by selective replication (SELREP), averaged over the applications, when 50 critical variables are used to select the critical instructions to be replicated. The detection of selective replication is compared to the outcomes in the baseline case, when randomized replication (RANDOMREP) is used and when full duplication (FULLREP) is used.

These results show that selective replication of instructions affecting 50 critical variables *detects about 87% percent of the faults detected by FULLREP.* Yet it incurs *59.1% less overhead* and leads to *17.8% fewer benign error detection* scenarios as compared to full duplication.

In Figure 6, the y-axis shows the different outcomes from the injection of instruction errors. The x-axis shows the percentage of errors that fall into each outcome category. We can see that FULLREP detects about 71.2% of the manifested errors. The rest of the errors raise an exception at the injected instruction

itself and hence can be detected by the system and recovered easily. Even though selective replication has a much lower overhead than full duplication, it detects 62.5% of the manifested errors, whereas random replication detects only 50.9% of the errors. When random replication is used, the system detects 17% of the errors in a different instruction, which are difficult to recover from. In the case of selective replication, this contributes to only 4.2% of the errors.

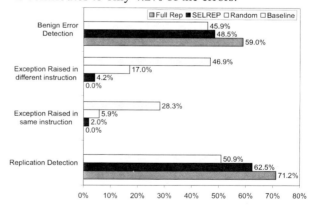

Figure 6: Instruction error injection results

Figure 7 shows the percentage of fail silence violations and program hangs that occur when instruction errors are injected and when different types of replication mechanisms are employed. Full Duplication is able to prevent most of the fail-silence violations and program hangs (Instruction and data errors are injected in one replica. The errors that make the affected replica hang are not detected by full duplication. For memory access instructions only the effective addresses computer by the two instructions are compared. Therefore, if the register field of a load instruction in one of the replicas is corrupted the data is loaded into an incorrect register, possibly leading to an error in the final application outcome. This is a fail-silence violation that is not detected by full duplication). Selective Replication is better than randomized replication but worse than full replication in detecting both fail silence violations and program hangs.

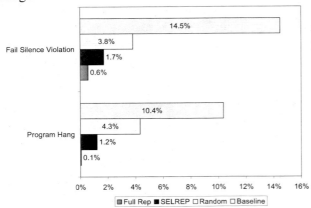

Figure 7: Fail silence violations and program hangs for instruction errors

5.3.5. Error coverage for data errors

Table 3 summarizes the results of injecting data errors (errors into the output of a functional unit when it is generating the result of an instruction). We see that FULLREP detects all the errors. This is because we inject the result of an instruction in only one of the replicas and vote on the result of each replicated instruction. Since all instructions are replicated in FULLREP it can detect all data errors. However, it is important to note that even though only less than 10% of the instructions are replicated in selective replication it detects about 97% of all data errors also. From the last row in Table 3 we see that FULLREP detects all the data errors that were Not Manifested in the Baseline case, whereas SELREP decreases this detection of errors benign to the application outcome by more than 6%.

Table 3: Fault injection results for data injection

Configuration / Outcome	Baseline	SELREP	FULLREP
Activated	490	477	477
Not Manifested	44.6%	3.0%	0.0%
Replication Detection	**0.0%**	**97.4%**	**100.0%**
Exception Raised in Different Instruction	72.2%	1.6%	0.0%
Program Hang	2.3%	0.1%	0.0%
Fail Silence Violation	25.5%	0.9%	0.0%
Benign Error Detection	0.0%	93.8%	100.0%

6. Related work

Replicated execution for fault-detection and tolerance has been investigated extensively both at the application and hardware level. *Error Detection Using Duplicated Instructions (EDDI)* [2] duplicates original instructions in the program but with different registers and variables. Duplication at the application level increases the code size of the application in memory. More importantly, it reduces the instruction supply bandwidth from the memory to the processor.

In the realm of commercial processors the IBM G5 processor [10] provides duplicate I- and E- units to provide duplicate execution of instructions. To support duplicate execution, the G5 is restricted to a single-issue processor and incurs 35% hardware overhead.

In experimental research, simultaneous multithreading (SMT) and the chip multiprocessor (CMP) architectures have been ideal bases for space and time redundant fault-tolerant designs because of their inherent redundancy. In simultaneously and redundantly threaded (SRT) processor, only instructions whose side effects are visible beyond the boundaries of the processor core are checked [11]. This was subsequently extended in SRTR to include recovery [4]. Another fault-tolerant architecture is proposed in the DIVA design [3]. DIVA comprises an aggressive out-of-order superscalar processor along with a simple in-order checker processor. *Microprocessor-based introspection (MBI)* [12] achieves time redundancy by scheduling the redundant execution of a program during idle cycles in which a long-latency cache miss is being serviced. SRTR [4] and MBI [12] have reported up to 30% performance overhead. This is contrary to the general belief that full duplication at the processor-level has little or no performance overhead.

SLICK [14] is an SRT-based approach to provide partial replication of an application. The goals of this approach are similar to ours. However, unlike this approach we do not rely on a multi-threaded architecture for the replication. Instead, this paper presents modifications to a general superscalar processor to support partial or selective replication of the application.

The basic principle of fault-tolerance employed in all the previous techniques that have been discussed is replication. This is also the focus of this paper. But a major difference is that none of the previous techniques provide a mechanism to dynamically configure the level of replication according to the application's demand. The application also does not have a choice of not replicating part of its code. This requires providing an interface to the application, either at the high-level programming language or at the assembly level, to invoke and configure the replication mechanism at run-time. It also requires extending portions of the processor pipeline to support selective replication of application execution.

7. Conclusions and future work

In this paper, we have demonstrated an approach to extract sensitive sections of code that can be selectively replicated to enhance the reliability of the application, instead of replicating the entire application. We have described a detailed design and evaluation of the mechanism to support this selective replication at the processor architecture level. The results show that with about 59% less overhead than full duplication of instructions we can detect 97% of the data errors and 87% of the instruction errors that are detected by full duplication. An important advantage of the selective replication is that it reduces the detection of errors benign to the final outcome of the application by 17.8% as compared to full duplication.

Future work will involve compiler enhancements to automatically insert the CHECK instructions. Hardware synthesis of the selective replication technique and its implementation on an FPGA is also underway.

Acknowledgements

This work was supported in part by National Science Foundation (NSF) grants CNS-0406351 and CNS-0524695, the Gigascale Systems Research Center (GSRC/MARCO), Motorola Corporation as part of the Motorola Center for Communications (UIUC), and Intel Corporation.

References

[1] R. K. Iyer, N. Nakka, Z. T. Kalbarczyk, and S. Mitra, "Recent advances and new avenues in hardware-level reliability support," *IEEE MICRO*, vol. 25, no. 6, pp. 18-29, Nov.-Dec. 2005.

[2] N. Oh, P.P. Shirvani, and E.J. McCluskey, "Error detection by duplicated instructions in super-scalar processors," *IEEE Transactions on Reliability*, vol. 51(1), pp. 63-75, Mar. 2002.

[3] C. Weaver and T. Austin. "A fault tolerant approach to microprocessor design," in *Proc. of the Intl. Conf. on Dependable Systems and Networks* 2001, pp. 411-420.

[4] T. Vijaykumar, I. Pomeranz, and K. Cheng, "Transient fault recovery using simultaneous multithreading," in *Proceedings of the 29th Intl. Symposium. on Computer Architecture (ISCA)* May 2002, pp. 87-98.

[5] J. Ray, J. C. Hoe, and B. Falsafi, "Dual use of superscalar datapath for transient-fault detection and recovery," in *Proceedings of 34th MICRO*, Austin, Texas, Dec. 2001, pp. 214-224.

[6] N. J. Wang, J. Quek, T. M. Rafacz, and S. J. Patel, "Characterizing the effects of transient faults on a high-performance processor pipeline," in *Proc. Intl. Conf. on Dependable Systems and Networks (DSN)*, 2004, pp. 61-70.

[7] G. Saggese, A. Vetteth, Z. T. Kalbarcyzk, and R. K. Iyer, "Microprocessor Sensitivity to Failures: Control vs. Execution and Combinational vs. Sequential Logic," in *Proc. Intl. Conf. Dependable Systems and Networks (DSN)*, 2005, pp. 760-769.

[8] K. Pattabiraman, Z. T. Kalbarczyk, and R. K. Iyer, "Application-based metrics for strategic placement of detectors," in *Proc. of Int. Symp. Pacific Rim Dependable Computing (PRDC)*, 2005, pp. 8-15.

[9] M. Hiller, A. Jhumka, and N. Suri, "On the placement of software mechanisms for detection of data errors," in *Proc. Intl. Conference on Dependable Systems and Networks (DSN)*, 2002, pp. 135-144.

[10] T. Slegel, et al. "IBM's S/390 G5 microprocessor design," *IEEE Micro*, vol. 19(2), pp. 12–23, 1999.

[11] S. K. Reinhardt and S. S. Mukherjee, "Transient fault detection via simultaneous multithreading," in *Proceedings of the Twenty-Seventh Inlt. Symp. on Computer Architecture (ISCA)*, June 2000, pp. 25-36.

[12] M. A. Qureshi, O. Mutlu, and Y. N. Patt, "Microarchitecture-based introspection: A technique for transient-fault tolerance in microprocessors," in *Proceedings of Intl. Conference on Dependable Systems and Networks (DSN)*, June 2005, pp. 434-443.

[13] N. Nakka. "Reliability and Security Engine: A Processor-level framework for Application-Aware detection and recovery," PhD dissertation, Department of Electrical and Computer Engineering, University of Illinois at Urban-Champaign, USA, 2006.

[14] A. Parashar, A. Sivasubramaniam, S. Gurumurthi. "SlicK: slice-based locality exploitation for efficient redundant multithreading," in *Proc. of the 12th Intl. Conf. on Architecture, Programming Lang. and Operating Systems (ASPLOS)*, 2006.

[15] Mark Weiser, "Program slicing," in 5th International Conference on Software Engineering (ICSE), 1981.

[16] H. Agrawal, and J. R. Horgan. "Dynamic program slicing," in *Proceedings of the ACM SIGPLAN Conference on Prog. Lang. Design and Impl.(PLDI)* '90, White Plains, New York, pp. 246-256

[17] D. Burger and T. M. Austin, "The SimpleScalar tool set, version 2.0," *University of Wisconsin-Madison, Technical Report CS-1342*, June 1997.

[18] N. Nakka, J. Xu, Z. Kalbarczyk, R. K. Iyer, "An Architectural Framework for Providing Reliability and Security Support," in *Proc. of Intl. Conf. Dependable Systems and Networks (DSN) 2004, pp. 585-594.*

[19] R. Chillarege. "Orthogonal defect classification," In *Handbook of Software Reliability and System Reliability, M. R. Lyu, Ed. McGraw-Hill*, NJ, 359-400.

[20] F. Tip, "A Survey of Program Slicing Techniques," *Journal of Programming Languages*, Vol.3, No.3, pp.121-189, September, 1995.

Robustness Testing of the Windows DDK[*]

Manuel Mendonça
University of Lisboa, Portugal
manuelmendonca@msn.com

Nuno Neves
University of Lisboa, Portugal
nuno@di.fc.ul.pt

Abstract

Modern computers interact with many kinds of external devices, which have lead to a state where device drivers (DD) account for a substantial part of the operating system (OS) code. Currently, most of the systems crashes can be attributed to DD because of flaws contained in their implementation. In this paper, we evaluate how well Windows protects itself from erroneous input coming from faulty drivers. Three Windows versions were considered in this study, Windows XP and 2003 Server, and the future Windows release Vista. Our results demonstrate that in general these OS are reasonably vulnerable, and that a few of the injected faults cause the system to hang or crash. Moreover, all of them handle bad inputs in a roughly equivalent manner, which is worrisome because it means that no major robustness enhancements are to be expected in the DD architecture of the next Windows Vista.

1 Introduction

Personal computers are common tools on today's modern life, not only for business, but for leisure and learning. Currently they interconnect all kinds of consumer electronic devices (e.g., cameras, MP3 players, printers, cell phones). In order to support the constant innovation of these products, operating systems (OS) had also to evolve in their architectures to become, as much as possible, independent of the hardware. Their flexibility and extensibility is achieved by the virtualization offered by device drivers (DD), which basically act as the interface between the software and the hardware. Given the typical short life cycle of chipsets and motherboards, system designers have to constantly develop new DD and/or update the existing ones. For these reasons they are the most dynamic and largest part of today's OS.

Even tough current DD are mostly written in a high level language (e.g., C), they continue to be difficult to build and verify. The development of a driver requires knowledge from a set of disparate areas, including chips, OS interfaces, compilers, and timing requirements, which are often not simultaneously mastered by the programmers, leading to both design and implementation errors. Consequently, DD are becoming one of the most important causes of system failures. A recent report showed that 89% of the Windows XP crashes are due to 3rd party DD [21]. Another analysis carried out on Linux demonstrated that a significant portion of failures can be pointed to faulty drivers [4].

As a result, commercial and open source OS are both committed in efforts to deploy more robust drivers. As an example, Microsoft has several tools to assist developers that write code in kernel-mode (e.g., Driver Verifier [16]). Other projects like [3, 6, 22, 25] also propose ways to improve the error containment capabilities of the OS.

In this paper, we want to study the behavior of three Windows versions, XP, 2003 Server and the future Windows release Vista, when they receive erroneous input from a faulty driver. We want to understand for instance if this input can frequently cause the crash of the OS, and if most functions process the input in a safe way or if they are mostly unprotected. We would like also to know the impact of the file system, FAT32 or NTFS, on the observed failure modes. This type of data is important because it helps to understand the extent of the problem, and what solutions need to be devised and applied to ameliorate the robustness of current systems.

Additionally, in the past, the origin of the bad input has been mainly from accidental nature. This situation will probably change in the future, as DD turn into the targets of the malicious attacks, especially because the most common avenues of attack are becoming increasingly difficult to exploit. If this scenario ever

---

[*] This work was partially supported by the EU through project IST-4-027513-STP (CRUTIAL) and NoE IST-4- 026764-NOE (RESIST), and by the FCT through project POSC/EIA/61643/2004 (AJECT) and the Large- Scale Informatic Systems Laboratory (LASIGE).

occurs, one might end up in a position where many drivers have vulnerabilities, and our only defense is the OS own abilities to protect itself.

The paper uses robustness testing to measure how well these OS handle the inputs from a DD [1, 5, 12]. A group of functions from the Windows interface (for kernel-mode DD, these functions are defined in the Device Driver Toolkit (DDK)) was selected and experimentally evaluated. The tests emulated a range of programming flaws, from missing function initializations to outside range parameter values.

Our results show that in general the three OS are relatively vulnerable to erroneous input, and that only a few routines made an effective checking of the parameters. A few experiments resulted in an OS hang and several caused the system to crash. When the OS installation used the FAT32 file system, some files ended up being corrupted during the crash. This problem was not observed with the NTFS file system. The minidump diagnosis mechanism was also analyzed, and it provided valuable information in most cases. Overall, the three OS versions showed a roughly equivalent behavior.

2   DDK Test Methodology

In a robustness testing campaign one wants to understand how well a certain interface withstands erroneous input to its exported functions. Each test basically consists on calling a function with a combination of good and bad parameter values, and on observing its outcome in the system execution. As expected, these campaigns can easily become too time consuming and extremely hard to perform, specially if the interface has a large number of functions with various parameters, since this leads to an explosion on the number of tests that have to be carried out. This kind of problem occurs with the Windows DDK because it exports more than a thousand functions. However, from the group of all available functions, some of them are used more often than others, and therefore these functions potentially have more impact in the system. Moreover, in most cases, (good) parameter values are often restricted to a small subset of the supported values of a given type.

Based on these observations, we have used the approach represented in Figure 1 in the tests. The DevInspect tool performs an automatic analysis of the target system to obtain a list of available DD. Then, it measures the use of each imported function from the DDK by each driver.

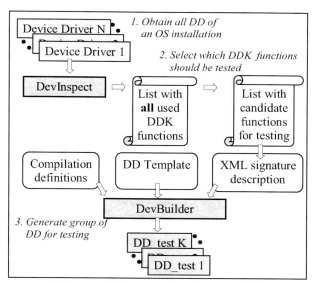

Figure 1: Generating the test DD.

Using this data, one can select a group of functions for testing, the *candidate list*. A XML file is manually written to describe the prototype of each function, which also includes the fault load (e.g., the bad values that should be tried).

Next, the DevBuilder tool takes as input the information contained in the XML file, a template of a device driver code and some compilation definitions, and generates the workload utilized to exercise the target system and to observe its behavior. The workload includes for each function test a distinct DD that injects the faulty input.

Other approaches could have been employed to implement the tests (e.g., a single DD injects all faulty data). This solution was chosen because: First, the control logic of each driver and management tool becomes quite simple. Second, the interference between experiments basically disappears since an OS reboot is performed after a driver test. Last, one can determine if the DD loading and unloading mechanisms are damaged by the injected faults.

2.1   Selecting the Candidate Functions

Windows stores drivers in the portable executable file format [15], which contains a table with the functions that are exported and imported. In the case of drivers, the imported functions are the ones provided by the DDK. Therefore, one can discover the DD currently available in a system by looking for .sys modules placed in \system32\drivers. Then, by examining the table of imported functions of the drivers, one can collect statistics about which DDK functions are utilized in practice.

We have installed Windows XP and Server 2003 with FAT32 and NTFS file systems and Windows Vista with NTFS file system in a DELL Optiplex 170L computer. Table 1 shows the number of drivers found in each Windows installation. Each line identifies the OS name and file system, the number of drivers that were found and that were running when the boot sequence completed, and the number of functions called by these drivers. It is possible to observe, for instance, that Windows Vista calls many more functions than Server 2003 for roughly the same number of drivers (2400 instead of 1463).

From the analysis of these drivers (both total and running), it was visible that a small group of functions was called by a majority of the DD, and that most of the rest of the functions were infrequently utilized (e.g., around 900 functions were only called by 1 or 2 drivers). These results indicate that if one of the most called functions unsafely treats its parameters, then almost every DD is potentially affected.

For this work, the functions that were chosen for the candidate list were the ones utilized by the majority of the drivers. We have established the following selection criterion: *the tested functions had to be present in at least 95% of all running drivers*. Table 2 displays the first group of the most used functions that satisfied this criterion. In each line, the table presents our internal identifier, the name of the function and its alias (to reduce the size of the rest of the tables). We have found out that this list changes very little when this criteria is applied to all existing drivers and not only the running ones. Table 3 displays the driver coverage by this group of functions in each OS configuration.

We considered other criteria to select the candidate list, such as the static or dynamic frequency of function calls. Static frequency picks functions that appear many times in the code without taking into account the logic under it – a function may appear repeatedly in the code but may never be executed. Dynamic frequency chooses the functions that are called most often during the execution of a given workload. Therefore, if the workload has a high file activity then disk drivers would run more, and their functions would be selected for the candidate list. This will bias the analysis towards the elected workload, which is something we wanted to avoid in these experiments.

2.2 Tested Faulty Values

The main responsibility of the DevBuilder tool is to write a number of DD based on the template code, each one carrying out a distinct function test (see Figure 1).

Table 1: Drivers in a Windows installation.

Windows	File System	Drivers Total	Drivers Run	Run Drivers Functions
XP	FAT32	259	93	1490
XP	NTFS	260	94	1494
Server 2003	FAT32	189	93	1463
Server 2003	NTFS	189	92	1463
Vista	NTFS	250	113	2400

Table 2:Top 20 called DDK functions.

ID	Name	Alias
1	ntoskrnl::RtlInitUnicodeString	InitStr
2	ntoskrnl::ExAllocatePoolWithTag	AllocPool
3	ntoskrnl::KeBugCheckEx	BugCheck
4	ntoskrnl::IofCompleteRequest	CompReq
5	ntoskrnl::IoCreateDevice	CreateDev
6	ntoskrnl::IoDeleteDevice	DeleteDev
7	ntoskrnl::KeInitializeEvent	InitEvt
8	ntoskrnl::KeWaitForSingleObject	WaitObj
9	ntoskrnl::ZwClose	ZwClose
10	ntoskrnl::IofCallDriver	CallDrv
11	ntoskrnl::ExFreePoolWithTag	FreePool
12	ntoskrnl::KeSetEvent	SetEvt
13	ntoskrnl::KeInitializeSpinLock	InitLock
14	HAL::KfAcquireSpinLock	AcqLock
15	HAL::KfReleaseSpinLock	RelLock
16	ntoskrnl::ObfDereferenceObject	DerefObj
17	ntoskrnl::ZwOpenKey	OpenKey
18	ntoskrnl::ZwQueryValueKey	QryKey
19	IoAttachDeviceToStack	AttachDev
20	ntoskrnl::memset	memset

Table 3: Top 20 Functions Driver coverage.

Windows	File System	Driver coverage
XP	FAT32	96,7%
XP	NTFS	96,8%
Server 2003	FAT32	96,7%
Server 2003	NTFS	96,7%
Vista	NTFS	97,3%

To accomplish this task, all relevant data about the functions is provided in a XML signature file, and the DD template has special marks that identify where to place the information translated from XML into code.

The signature file includes the function name, parameter type and values that should be tried out, and expected return values. In addition, for certain functions, it also contains some setup code that is inserted before the function call, to ensure that all necessary initializations are performed. Similarly, some other code can also be included, which is placed after the function call, for instance to evaluate if some parameter had its value correctly changed or to check the returned value.

In order to obtain the relevant data about the functions, we had to resort to the Windows DDK documentation. From the point of view of a DD developer, this documentation corresponds to the specification of the DDK functions. Therefore, if there are errors in documentation, then they may be translated into bugs in the drivers' implementations and also in our tests. Nevertheless, in the worst case, if a problem is observed with a test, at least it indicates that the function description contains some mistake.

The signature file defines seven types of correct and faulty inputs. These values emulate the outcomes of some of the most common programming bugs. They can be summarized as follows:

Acceptable Value: parameter is initialized with a correct value.

Missing local variable initialization: parameter with a random initial value.

Forbidden values: uses values that are explicitly identified in the DDK documentation as incorrect.

Out of bounds value: parameters that exceed the expected range of values.

Invalid pointer assignment: invalid memory locations.

NULL pointer assignment: NULL value passed to a pointer parameter.

Related function not called: this fault is produced by deliberately not calling a setup function, contrarily to what is defined in the DDK documentation.

2.3 Expected Failure Modes

The list displayed in Table 4 represents the possible scenarios that are expected to occur after a DD injects a fault into the OS. Initially we started with a much larger list of failure modes, which was derived from various sources, such as the available works in the literature and expert opinion from people that administer Windows systems. However, as the experiences progressed, we decided to reduce substantially this list because several of the original failure modes were not observed in practice.

Generally speaking there are two major possible outcome scenarios: either the faulty input produces an error (e.g., a crash) or it is handled in some manner. Since the fault handling mechanisms can also have implementation problems, the FM1 failure mode was divided in three subcategories. In order to determine which subcategory applies to a given experiment,

Table 4: Expected failure modes.

ID	Description
FM1	No problems are detected in the system execution.
FM2	The applications or even the whole system hangs.
FM3	The system crashes and then reboots; the file system is checked and NO corrupted files are found.
FM4	Same as FM3, but there are corrupted files.

the DD verifies the correctness of the return value (if it was different from void) and output parameters of the function.

Returns ERROR (RErr): The return value from the function call indicates that an error was detected possibly due to invalid parameters. This means that the bad input was detected and was handled properly.

Returns OK (ROk): The return value of the call indicates a successful execution. This category includes two cases: even with some erroneous input, the function executed correctly or did not run but returned OK; all input was correct, for instance because only good parameter values were utilized or the random parameters ended up having acceptable values.

Invalid return value (RInv): Some times several values are used to indicate a successful execution (a calculation result) or an error (reason of failure). When the return value is outside the range of possible output values (at least from what is said in the DDK documentation), this means that either the documentation or the function implementation has a problem.

Whenever crash occurs, Windows generates a minidump file that describes the execution context of the system when the failure took place. The analysis of this file is very important because it allows developers to track the origin of crashes. Although several efforts have been made to improve the capabilities of crash origin identification, still some errors remain untraceable or are detected incorrectly. Whenever an experiment caused a crash, the minidump files were inspected to evaluate their identification capabilities. Four main categories of results were considered:

Identification OK (M1): The minidump file correctly identifies the faulty driver as the source of the crash.

Identification ERROR (M2): The minidump file identifies other module as the cause of failure.

Unidentified (M3): The minidump file could not identify either the driver or other module as the source of the crash.

Memory Corruption (M4): The minidump file detected a memory corruption.

2.4 Experimental Setup

Since the experiments were likely to cause system hangs or crashes, and sometimes these crashes corrupted files, we had to utilize two machines in order to automate most of the tasks (see Figure 2). The target machine hosts the OS under test and the DD workload, and the controller machine is in charge of selecting which tests should be carried out, collecting data and rebooting the target whenever needed.

After booting the targeting machine, DevInject contacts DevController to find out which driver should be used in the next experiment. Then, DevInject loads the driver, triggers the fault, checks the outcome and, if everything went well, removes the driver. DevController is informed of each step of the experiment, so that it can tell DevInject what actions should be performed. This way, the target file system is not used to save any intermediate results or keep track of the experience, since it might end up being corrupted. The target file system is however utilized to store the minidump files and the corrupted files that were found. After a reboot, DevInject transfers to DevController this information using FTP.

3 Experimental Results

All measurements were taken on a prototype system composed by two x86 PCs linked by an Ethernet network. The target machine was a DELL Optiplex computer with 512Mb and 2 disks. Three OS versions and two distinct file systems, FAT32 and NTFS, were evaluated. The outcome was five different configurations (Vista was not tested with FAT32). The exact OS versions were: Windows XP Kernel Version 2600 (SP 2), *built*: 2600.xpsp_sp2_gdr.050301-1519, Windows Server 2003 Kernel Version 3790 (SP 1), *built*: 3790.srv03_sp1_rtm.050324-1447 and Windows Vista Kernel Version 5600, *built*: 5600.16384.x86fre.vista_rc1.060829-2230.

Microsoft provides an equivalent Device Driver Toolkit for all OS. Consequently, the same set of drivers could be used to test the various OS. In every target configuration the initial conditions were the same, the OS were configured to produce similar types

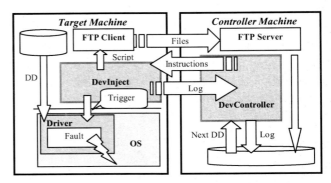

Figure 2: Injecting erroneous input.

of dump files, and the DevInject tool was basically the only user application running.

We decided to carry out the experiments without load to ensure that results were highly repeatable, and therefore to increase the accuracy to the conclusions. In the near future, we intend to complement our analysis with loaded systems, by employing some standard workload.

3.1 Observed Failure Modes

The observed failure modes are displayed in Table 5. The first three columns present the function identifier ID, its alias name and the number of experiments carried out with each function. The failure modes for the various OS configurations are represented in the next four groups of columns, under the headings FM1 to FM4. Each column group presents one value for each OS configuration.

In the 20 functions that were tested, several of them were able to deal at least with a subset of the erroneous input. There were however a few cases where results were extremely bad, indicating a high level of vulnerability. By computing the formula FM1/#DD for each FM1 entry, one can have an idea about the relative robustness of the functions (see Figure 3). Only two functions were 100% immune to the injected faults, 9-ZwClose and 18-QryKey. On the other hand, eight functions had zero or near zero capabilities to deal with the faults.

One reason for this behavior is that some of these functions are so efficiency dependent (e.g., 4-CompReq and 14-AcqLock) that developers have avoided the implementation of built in checks. Another reason is related to the nature of the function, which in the case of 3-BugCheck is to bring down the system in a controlled manner, when the caller discovers an unrecoverable inconsistency.

Table 5: Observed failure modes.

ID	Alias	#DD	FM1: Execution OK					FM2: Hangs					FM3: Crash					FM4: Crash & FCorrupt				
			XP		2003		V	XP		2003		V	XP		2003		V	XP		2003		V
			Fat	Ntfs	Fat	Ntfs	Ntfs	Fat	Ntfs	Fat	Ntfs	Ntfs	Fat	Ntfs	Fat	Ntfs	Ntfs	Fat	Ntfs	Fat	Ntfs	Ntfs
1	InitStr	12	9	9	9	9	9	0	0	0	0	0	2	3	2	3	3	1	0	1	0	0
2	AllocPool	440	416	416	416	416	420	0	0	0	0	0	14	24	13	24	20	10	0	11	0	0
3	BugCheck	12	0	0	0	0	0	0	0	0	0	0	6	12	3	12	12	6	0	9	0	0
4	CompReq	51	0	0	0	0	0	0	0	0	0	0	0	51	26	51	51	51	0	25	0	0
5	CreateDev	96	48	48	48	48	48	0	0	0	0	0	29	48	8	48	48	19	0	40	0	0
6	DeleteDev	4	0	0	0	0	0	0	0	0	0	0	0	4	2	4	4	4	0	2	0	0
7	InitEvt	18	6	6	6	6	6	0	0	0	0	0	8	12	7	12	12	4	0	5	0	0
8	WaitObj	36	18	18	18	18	18	0	0	0	0	0	15	18	2	18	18	3	0	16	0	0
9	ZwClose	3	3	3	3	3	3	0	0	0	0	0	0	0	0	0	0	0	0	0	0	0
10	CallDrv	9	0	0	0	0	0	0	0	0	0	0	0	9	4	9	9	9	0	5	0	0
11	FreePool	16	1	1	1	1	1	0	0	0	0	0	1	15	8	15	15	14	0	7	0	0
12	SetEvt	24	6	6	18	18	9	0	0	0	0	0	15	18	5	6	15	3	0	1	0	0
13	InitLock	3	2	2	2	2	2	0	0	0	0	0	0	1	0	1	1	1	0	1	0	0
14	AcqLock	8	0	0	0	0	0	2	2	2	2	2	2	6	2	6	6	4	0	4	0	0
15	RelLock	48	3	3	1	1	1	0	0	0	0	0	18	45	12	47	47	27	0	35	0	0
16	DerefObj	3	2	2	2	2	0	0	0	0	0	0	1	1	0	1	3	0	0	1	0	0
17	OpenKey	155	104	104	104	104	104	0	0	0	0	0	25	51	47	51	51	26	0	4	0	0
18	QryKey	315	315	315	315	315	315	0	0	0	0	0	0	0	0	0	0	0	0	0	0	0
19	AttachDev	9	0	0	0	0	0	1	1	1	1	1	6	8	2	8	8	2	0	6	0	0
20	memset	48	18	18	27	27	24	0	0	0	0	0	22	30	12	21	24	8	0	9	0	0
Total		1310	951	951	970	970	960	3	3	3	3	3	164	356	155	337	347	192	0	182	0	0
Total / # DD (%)			72,6	72,6	74,0	74,0	73,3	0,2	0,2	0,2	0,2	0,2	12,5	27,2	11,8	25,7	26,5	14,7	0,0	13,9	0,0	0,0

In this case, the developers probably preferred to reboot the system even if some parameters were incorrect (but notice that this reboot sometimes was not done in a completely satisfactory way since files ended up being corrupted).

From the various functions, only two caused the system to hang (FM2 ≠ 0). Functions 14-AcqLock and 19-AttachDev caused hangs in all OS configurations, when an invalid pointer was passed as argument. Most of the erroneous inputs that caused failures end up crashing the system (FM3 and FM4). From the various classes of faults that were injected, the most malicious were invalid pointer assignments and NULL values passed in pointer parameters. The first class, invalid pointers, is sometimes difficult to validate, depending on the context (e.g., a buffer pointer that was not properly allocated). On other hand, NULL pointers are easily tested and for this reason it is difficult to justify why they are left un-checked, allowing them to cause so many reliability problems.

In all experiments, we never observed any file corruption with the NTFS file system after a reboot. However, the FAT32 file system displayed in many instances cases of corruption. Traditionally, NTFS has been considered much more reliable than FAT32, and our results contribute to confirm this. The reliability capabilities integrated in NTFS, like transactional operations and logging, have proven to be quite effective in protecting the system during abnormal execution.

The overall comparison of the 3 operating systems, if we restrict ourselves to NTFS or FAT32, shows a remarkable resemblance among them. The last two rows of Table 5 present an average value for the failure modes and OS configurations. On average, OSs had an approximately equivalent number of failures in each mode, with around 73% testes with no problems detected during the system execution. Hangs were a rare event in all OSs. If a finer analysis is made on a function basis (see Figure 3), we observe a similar behavior for most functions. There were only two functions where results reasonably differ, 12-SetEvt and 20-memset. From these results, there is reasonable indication that the 3 operating systems use comparable levels of protection from faulty inputs coming from drives.

These results reinforce the idea that although the Windows NT system has undergone several name changes over the past several years, it remains entirely based on the original Windows NT code base. However, as time went by, the implementation of many internal features has changed. We expected that newer versions of the Windows OS family would become more robust; in practice we did not see this improvement at the driver's interface. Of course, this conclusion needs to be better verified with further experiments.

3.2   Return Values from Functions

As explained previously, even when the system executes without apparent problems, the checking mechanisms might not validate the faulty arguments in the most correct manner and produce fail-silent violations. Therefore, failure mode 1 can be further divided in three sub-categories to determine how well the OS handled the inputs.

Table 6 shows the analysis when the function execution returned a value in the RErr category, i.e., an error was detected by the function. Since some functions do not return any values, their corresponding table entries were filled with "-". The "# Faulty Drivers" column refers to the number of drivers produced by DevBuilder that contained at least one bad parameter. Comparing this column with the following five columns, one can realize that only two functions have a match between the number of faulty drivers and the number of RErr values. The other functions revealed a limited parameter checking capability.

To complement this analysis, Table 7 presents the results for the ROk category (i.e., the return value of the call is a successful execution). Column "Non Faulty Drivers" shows the number of drivers with only correct arguments. Comparing this column with the remaining ones, it is possible to conclude that functions return a successful execution more often then the number of non faulty drivers. However, in some cases this might not mean that there is a major problem. For instance, consider function 2-AllocPool that receives three parameters: the type of pool (P0); the pool size (P1); and a tag value (P2). Depending on the order of parameter checking, one can have the following acceptable outcome: P1 is zero, and 2-AllocPool returns a pointer to an empty buffer independently of the other parameters values.

On the other hand, by analyzing the execution log, we found out that when P1 was less than 100.000*PAGE_SIZE, Windows returned ROk even when a forbidden value was given in P0 (at least, as stated in the DDK documentation). This kind of behavior means that an error was (potentially) propagated back to the driver, since it will be using a type of memory pool different from the expected thus causing a fail silent violation. The table also reveals another phenomenon -- the three versions of Windows handle the faulty parameters differently.

Table 6: Return error (RErr) values.

Alias	# Faulty Drivers	Rerr				
		XP		2003		V
		Fat	Ntfs	Fat	Ntfs	Ntfs
InitStr	9	0	0	0	0	0
AllocPool	200	20	20	20	20	12
BugCheck	12	-	-	-	-	-
CompReq	51	-	-	-	-	-
CreateDev	76	0	0	0	0	0
DeleteDev	4	-	-	-	-	-
InitEvt	14	-	-	-	-	-
WaitObj	36	0	0	0	0	0
ZwClose	3	3	3	3	3	3
CallDrv	9	0	0	0	0	0
FreePool	15	-	-	-	-	-
SetEvt	20	0	0	0	0	0
InitLock	2	-	-	-	-	-
AcqLock	8	0	0	0	0	0
RelLock	48	-	-	-	-	-
DerefObj	3	-	-	-	-	-
OpenKey	155	104	104	104	104	104
QryKey	315	315	315	315	315	315
AttachDev	9	0	0	0	0	0
Memset	39	0	0	0	0	0

Table 7: Return OK (ROk) values.

Alias	Non Faulty Drivers	ROk				
		XP		2003		V
		Fat	Ntfs	Fat	Ntfs	Ntfs
InitStr	3	9	9	9	9	9
AllocPool	240	396	396	396	396	408
BugCheck	0	-	-	-	-	-
CompReq	0	-	-	-	-	-
CreateDev	20	48	48	48	48	48
DeleteDev	0	-	-	-	-	-
InitEvt	4	-	-	-	-	-
WaitObj	0	18	18	18	18	18
ZwClose	0	0	0	0	0	0
CallDrv	0	0	0	0	0	0
FreePool	1	-	-	-	-	-
SetEvt	4	6	6	18	18	9
InitLock	1	-	-	-	-	-
AcqLock	0	0	0	0	0	0
RelLock	0	-	-	-	-	-
DerefObj	0	-	-	-	-	-
OpenKey	0	0	0	0	0	0
QryKey	0	0	0	0	0	0
AttachDev	0	1	1	1	1	1
memset	9	18	18	27	27	22

For example, there were several cases in Vista where function 2-AllocPool succeeded while in XP and Server 2003 it caused a crash. In function 12-SetEvt, Server 2003 does not crash when TRUE was passed in one of the parameters, while the other did so (the documentation says that when this value is used, the function execution is to be followed immediately by a call to one of the KeWaitXxx routines, which was not done in either OSs).

In all experiments, we did not observe any return values belonging to the RInv category (i.e., values outside the expected return range).

3.3 Corrupted Files

The last group of results in Table 5 corresponding to FM4, displays the number of times Windows found corrupted files while booting. The Chkdsk utility is called during the booting process to detect these files. Corrupted files were found only in the configurations that used the FAT32 file system. Using the formula FM4/FM3 one can have a relative measure of how sensitive is the file system when a crash occurs. The results presented in Figure 4 shows that when using FAT32 in general, Windows Server 2003 is more sensitive than Windows XP in a majority of the cases.

3.4 Minidump Diagnosis Capabilities

The analysis of the minidump files produced during a system crash allows us to determine how well they identify a driver as the culprit of the failure. These files are fundamental tools for the Windows development teams because they help to diagnose system problems, and eventually to correct them. We have used the Microsoft's Kernel Debugger (KD) [17] to perform the analysis of these files, together with a tool, DevDump, that automates most of this task. DevDump controls the debugger, passes the minidumps under investigation, and selects a log where results should be stored. After processing all files, DevDump generates various statistics about the detection capabilities of minidumps.

In the experiments, all Windows versions correctly spotted the faulty DD in the majority of times (see Figure 5 and compare it with Table 5). The correct identification of the source of crash (M1) seams to be independent of the file system used. Only in very few cases there was a difference between the two file systems, such as for the 7-InitEvt function where Server 2003 FAT32 identified a different source of crash from Server 2003 NTFS.

In general, the results show that Windows XP is more accurate than the others OS (see 15-RelLock and 20-memset). Still there were cases where other kernel modules were incorrectly identified (functions 1-InitStr, 14-AcqLock and 15-RelLock), as displayed in Figure 6.

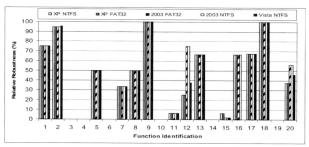

Figure 3: Relative robustness (FM1/#DD).

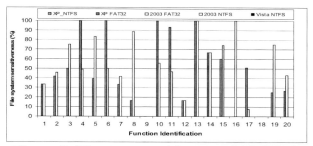

Figure 4: FSystem sensitiveness (FM4/FM3).

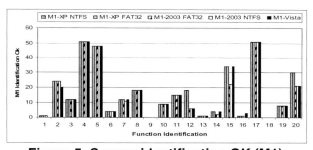

Figure 5: Source identification OK (M1).

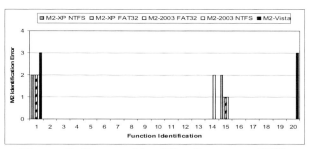

Figure 6: Source identification error (M2).

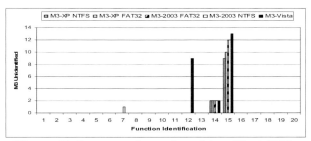

Figure 7: Source of crash unidentified (M3).

These errors are particularly unpleasant because they can lead to waist of time while looking for bugs in the wrong place, and they can reduce the confidence on the information provided by minidumps. In some other cases, Windows was unable to discover the cause of failure. This happened in Vista more frequently than the other OS configurations, for instance in functions 15-RelLock and 12-SetEvt (see Figure 7). In the last function, Vista was the only system that could not diagnose the cause of failure. Only Windows Server 2003 detected memory corruption situations (in functions 14-AcqLock and 15-RelLock). Windows Server 2003 (FAT32 and NTFS) located memory corruptions when faults were injected in functions 14-AcqLock and 15-RelLock.

4   Related Work

Robustness testing has been successfully applied to several software components to characterize their behavior when facing exceptional inputs or stressful environmental conditions. One of the main targets of these studies has been general propose OS, with erroneous inputs being injected at the application interface. Fifteen OS versions that implement the POSIX standard, including AIX, Linux, SunOS and HPUX, were assessed using the Ballista tool [12]. Shelton et al. made a comparative study of six variants of Windows, from 95 to 2000, by injecting faults at the Win 32 interface [20]. Several command line utilities of Windows NT were evaluated by Ghosh et al. [7]. Real time microkernels, such as Chorus and LynxOS, have also been the target of these studies using the MAFALDA tool [2]. Application level software can be tested using robustness techniques by, for instance, generating exceptions and returning bad values at the OS interface [8]. Middleware support systems like CORBA have been examined at the client-side interface of an ORB [19] and internally at the level of the Naming and Event services [14]. Dependability benchmarking has resorted to robustness testing in order to evaluate systems [18, 23, 24]. For example, Kalakech et al. proposed an OS benchmark which provided a comprehensive set of measures, and applied it to the Windows 2000 [11].

To our knowledge, only a few works have assessed the robustness of systems at the level of device drivers. Durães and Madeira described a way to emulate software faults by mutating the binary code of device drivers [5]. Basically, the driver executable is scanned for specific low-level instruction patterns, and mutations are performed on those patterns to emulate high-level faults. These ideas were experimented for 4 types of patterns, on 2 drivers of the Windows NT4,

2000 and XP. Albinet et al. conducted a set of experiments to evaluate the robustness of Linux systems in face of faulty drivers [1]. They intercepted the driver calls to the kernel's DPI (Drivers Programming Interface) functions, and changed the parameters on the fly with a few pre-set number faulty values. Then, the behavior of the system was observed. Johansson and Suri employed a similar methodology to evaluate a Windows CE .Net [10]. In their work, however, they focus on error propagation profiling measures, as facilitator for the selection of places to put wrappers.

Our research is complementary to these previous works, not only because we targeted different OS. The followed methodology has its roots in the original Ballista tool [13], where several test drivers are generated, containing DDK function calls with erroneous arguments. The argument values were selected specifically for each function, and they emulate seven classes of typical programming errors. Our study has looked in a comparative basis at such aspects like error containment, influence of the file system type, and the diagnosis capabilities of minidump files.

5   Conclusions

The paper describes a robustness testing experiment that evaluates Windows XP, Windows Server 2003 and the future Windows release Vista. The main objective of this study was to determine how well Windows protects itself from faulty drivers that provide erroneous input to the DDK routines. Seven classes of typical programming bugs were simulated.

The analysis of the results shows that most interface functions are unable to completely check their inputs – from the 20 selected functions, only 2 were 100% effective in their defense. We observed a small number of hangs and a reasonable number of crashes. The main reason for the crashes was invalid or NULL pointer values. Corruption of files was only observed with the FAT32 file system. The analysis of the return values demonstrates that in some cases Windows completes without generating an error for function calls with incorrect parameters; in particular, Windows Server 2003 seams to be the most permissible one. This behavior suggests a deficient error containment capability of the OS. In most cases, the examined minidump files provided valuable information about the sources of the crashes, something extremely useful for the development teams. However, Windows Vista seems to have more troubles in this identification than the other OS.

The experiments made with Windows Vista reveled that it behaves in a similar way to Windows XP and Server 2003. This probably means that Microsoft intents to continue to use the current DD architecture in its future OS, which is reasonably worrisome since Vista will be most likely the most used OS in the years to come.

6 References

[1] A. Albinet, J. Arlat, and J.-C. Fabre, "Characterization of the Impact of Faulty Drivers on the Robustness of the Linux Kernel", *Proceedings of the International Conference on Dependable Systems and Networks*, June 2004

[2] J. Arlat, J.-C. Fabre, M. Rodríguez and F. Salles, "Dependability of COTS Microkernel-Based Systems", *IEEE Transactions on Computers*, vol. 51, no. 2, 2002, pp. 138-163.

[3] A. Chou, J. Yang, B. Chelf, S. Hallem, and D. Engler, "On u-kernel construction", *Proceedings of the Symposium on Operating Systems Principles*, December 1995, pp. 237–250.

[4] A. Chou, J. Yang, B. Chelf, S. Hallem, and D. Engler, "An empirical study of operating system errors", *Proceedings of the Symposium on Operating Systems Principles*, October 2001, pp. 73–88.

[5] J. Durães and H. Madeira, "Characterization of Operating Systems Behavior in the Presence of Faulty Drivers through Software Fault Emulation", *Proceedings of the Pacific Rim International Symposium. On Dependable Computing*, December 2002, pp. 201-209.

[6] B. Ford, G. Back, G. Benson, J. Lepreau, A. Lin, and O. Shivers, "The Flux OSKit: a substrate for OS language and resource management", *Proceedings of the Symposium on Operating Systems Principles*, October 1997, pp. 38–51.

[7] A. Ghosh, M. Schmid, and V. Shah, "Testing the robustness of Windows NT software", *Proceedings of the Ninth International Symposium on Software Reliability Engineering*, November 1998, pp. 231-235.

[8] A. K. Ghosh, M. Schmid, "An Approach to Testing COTS Software for Robustness to Operating System Exceptions and Errors", *Proceedings 10th International Symposium on Software Reliability Engineering*, November 1999, pp. 166-174.

[9] R. Gruber, and M. L. Jiang, "Robustness Testing and Hardening of CORBA ORB Implementations", *Proceedings of the International Conference on Dependable Systems and Networks*, June 2001, pp. 141-150.

[10] A. Johansson, and N. Suri, "Error Propagation Profiling of Operating Systems", *Proceedings of the International Conference on Dependable Systems and Networks*, June 2005.

[11] A. Kalakech, T. Jarboui, J. Arlat, Y. Crouzet, and K. Kanoun, "Benchmarking Operating System dependability: Windows 2000 as a Case Study", *Proceedings Pacific Rim International Symposium on Dependable Computing*, March 2004, pp. 261- 270.

[12] P. Koopman, J. DeVale, "The Exception Handling Effectiveness of POSIX Operating Systems", *IEEE Transactions on Software Engineering*, vol. 26, no. 9, September 2000, pp. 837-848.

[13] N. Kropp, P. Koopman, and D. Siewiorek, "Automated Robustness Testing of Off-the-Shelf Software Components", *Proceedings of the International Symposium on Fault-Tolerant Computing*, June 1998.

[14] E. Marsden, J.-C. Fabre and J. Arlat, "Dependability of CORBA Systems: Service Characterization by Fault Injection", *Proceedings of the 21st International Symposium on Reliable Distributed Systems*, June 2002, pp. 276-285.

[15] Microsoft Corporation, "Microsoft Portable Executable and Common Object File Format Specification", February 2005.

[16] Microsoft Corporation, "Introducing Static Driver Verifier", May 2006.

[17] Microsoft Corporation, "Debugging Tools for Windows – Overview", December 2006 http://www.microsoft.com/whdc/devtools/debugging/default.mspx

[18] A. Mukherjee and D. P. Siewiorek, "Measuring Software Dependability by Robustness Benchmarking", *IEEE Transactions of Software Engineering*, vol. 23, no. 6, 1997, pp. 366-378.

[19] J. Pan, P. J. Koopman, D. P. Siewiorek, Y. Huang, R. Gruber and M. L. Jiang, "Robustness Testing and Hardening of CORBA ORB Implementations", *Proceedings of the Internatinal Conference on Dependable Systems and Networks*, June 2001, pp. 141-150.

[20] C. Shelton, P. Koopman and K. D. Vale, "Robustness Testing of the Microsoft Win32 API", *Proceedings of the International Conference on Dependable Systems and Networks*, June 2000, pp. 261-270.

[21] D. Simpson, "Windows XP Embedded with Service Pack 1 Reliability", *Tech. rep., Microsoft Corporation*, January 2003.

[22] M. Swift, B. Bershad, and H. Levy, "Improving the reliability of commodity operating systems", *Proceedings of the Symposium on Operating Systems Principles*, October 2003, pp. 207–222.

[23] T. K. Tsai, R. K. Iyer, and D. Jewitt, "An Approach Towards Benchmarking of Fault-Tolerant Commercial Systems", *Proceedings of the 26th International Symposium on Fault-Tolerant Computing*, June 1996, pp. 314-323.

[24] M. Vieira and H. Madeira, "A Dependability Benchmark for OLTP Application Environments", *Proceedings of the 29th International Conference on Very Large Data Bases*, 2003, pp. 742-753.

[25] M. Young, M. Accetta, R. Baron, W. Bolosky, D. Golub, R. Rashid, and A. Tevanian, "Mach: A new kernel foundation for UNIX development", *Proceedings of the Summer USENIX Conference*, June 1986, pp. 93–113.

Session 2C:
Measurement
and Monitoring

SLAM: Sleep-Wake Aware Local Monitoring in Sensor Networks

Issa Khalil, Saurabh Bagchi, Ness B. Shroff

Dependable Computing Systems Lab (DCSL) & Center for Wireless Systems and Applications (CWSA)
School of Electrical & Computer Engineering, Purdue University
Email: {ikhalil, sbagchi, shroff}@purdue.edu

Abstract

Sleep-wake protocols are critical in sensor networks to ensure long-lived operation. However, an open problem is how to develop efficient mechanisms that can be incorporated with sleep-wake protocols to ensure both long-lived operation and a high degree of security. Our contribution in this paper is to address this problem by using local monitoring, a powerful technique for detecting and mitigating control and data attacks in sensor networks. In local monitoring, each node oversees part of the traffic going in and out of its neighbors to determine if the behavior is suspicious, such as, unusually long delay in forwarding a packet. Here, we present a protocol called SLAM to make local monitoring parsimonious in its energy consumption and to integrate it with any extant sleep-wake protocol in the network. The challenge is to enable sleep-wake in a secure manner even in the face of nodes that may be adversarial and not wake up nodes responsible for monitoring its traffic. We prove analytically that the security coverage is not weakened by the protocol. We perform simulations in ns-2 to demonstrate that the performance of local monitoring is practically unchanged while listening energy saving of 30 to 129 times is achieved, depending on the network load.

Keywords: Sensor networks, local monitoring, sleep/wake techniques, wake-up antenna.

1. Introduction

It has been shown in the literature that sensor networks are vulnerable to a wide range of security attacks including the wormhole attack, rushing, and Sybil attacks [25]. Cryptographic mechanisms alone can not prevent these attacks since many of them such as the wormhole and the rushing attacks can be launched without needing access to cryptographic keys or violating any cryptographic check. To mitigate such attacks, many researchers have used the concept of cooperative *local monitoring* within a node's neighborhood ([17]-[24]). In local monitoring, nodes oversee part of the traffic going in and out of their neighbors. Different types of checks are done locally on the observed traffic to make a determination of malicious behavior. For the systems where arriving at a common view is important, the detecting node initiates a distributed protocol to disseminate the alarm. Many protocols have been built on top of local monitoring for intrusion detection (e.g., [16][17]), building trust and reputation among nodes (e.g. [20][21]), protecting against control and data traffic attacks (e.g. [22]-[25]) and in building secure routing protocols (e.g. [18][19][23]). Specifically, in [23] and [24] the authors have presented a technique for detection of control and data attacks in ad-hoc networks using local monitoring. Control attacks are launched by a node delaying, dropping, modifying, or fabricating control traffic that it is supposed to forward. Data attacks are similarly launched by performing these actions on data traffic. In [23] and [24], these attacks are detected by a group of nodes, called *guard nodes*, that perform local monitoring. The guard nodes are normal nodes in the network and perform the basic operations of sensing, in addition to monitoring.

Though local monitoring has been proposed by many researchers, it incurs a high energy cost since it requires the guard nodes to be awake all the time to oversee network behavior. To the best of our knowledge, no one has devised sleep-wake protocols for optimizing the energy overhead of monitoring while maintaining the quality of the monitoring service. This is the problem we address in this paper. The main challenge lies in having the sleep-wake performed securely so that an adversarial node cannot escape detection by causing its guard nodes to stay asleep.

In this paper we propose a set of mechanisms called Sleep-Wake Aware Local Monitoring (SLAM) that adapt the existing local monitoring technique to significantly reduce the time a node needs to be awake for the purpose of monitoring. The proposed mechanism adapts itself depending on the kind of sleeping protocol used in the network, henceforth referred to as the *baseline sleeping protocol* (BSP). For networks that use synchronized sleeping algorithms (e.g., [3] [8]-[10]), i.e., nodes wakeup and go to sleep in a synchronized manner, SLAM does not need to do anything since a node and its guards will be woken up by the BSP itself. There exist several application-specific sleeping algorithms, for example, to maintain a given sensing coverage (each point should be sensed by at least *k* nodes) or a given network connectivity level (each pair of nodes should have *k* disjoint paths). For these protocols (e.g., [1]-[3]), SLAM can support local monitoring by modifying an input parameter to the existing sleeping algorithm, such as the value of *k* in the connectivity or coverage preserving BSPs. Finally, we consider networks that use on-demand sleep-wake. On-demand sleep-wake means a node wakes up when it needs to communicate, and since the communication pattern can be arbitrary, the wakeup time is arbitrary in the general case. This provides the most challenging case and forms the most significant portion of the discussion in the paper.

For the third class of network, SLAM provides a generic on-demand sleeping algorithm, called On-Demand SLAM. This algorithm relies on each node having a passive or a low-power wake-up antenna in addition to the normal antenna. A node that is not involved in network activities, such as, data forwarding is ordinarily sleeping according to the BSP. However, for monitoring purposes, it is woken up on demand by a neighboring node using the wake-up antenna. The key challenge to this apparently simple scheme is that it now opens up the possibility of a new adversarial action, namely, a node not waking up a sleeping node(s) so that its own malicious action is not detectable. At a high level, our solution involves the following steps–adding to the list of behavior that a guard node needs to check and second, defining the mechanism through which the check is to be done (i.e., who checks, when, and for what).

We provide a theoretical analysis for energy saving using On-Demand SLAM compared to a baseline monitoring protocol [24]. We build a simulation model for SLAM using *ns-2* and perform a comparative evaluation of local monitoring with and without SLAM. The results show that the security of local monitoring is very close in both cases while the overhead of SLAM in terms of listening energy is between 30 to 129 times lower, depending on the network traffic. The results show the effect of the number of malicious nodes, the traffic load, and the fraction of data being monitored on the overhead of local monitoring. We summarize our contributions in this paper as follows:

1. We provide a technique for conserving energy while performing local monitoring without significantly degrading its security performance. This we believe is fundamental to deploying local monitoring in any energy conscious network.

2. We propose a generic on-demand sleep-wake algorithm for network monitoring in scenarios where either no BSP exists or the sleep-wake is based on arbitrary communication pattern.

3. We analytically prove that SLAM does not add any vulnerability to the existing local monitoring technique.

4. We show through simulations a significant reduction in monitoring cost with negligible degradation in the monitoring quality of service.

The rest of the paper is organized as follows. Section 2 presents related work in the field of sleep-wake protocols. Section 3 describes SLAM. Section 4 presents mathematical analysis of the energy overhead and security of SLAM. Section 5 presents the simulation experiments and results. Section 6 concludes the paper.

2. Related Work

Node sleeping is an important mechanism to prolong the life time of sensor networks. This topic has been discussed extensively in the literature and many protocols have been proposed for various types of applications such as object tracking ([1][2]). It has been realized that under current hardware designs, the maximum energy savings can be achieved through putting nodes to sleep—three orders of magnitude less current draw than in an idle node for the popular Mica mote platform for sensor nodes.

Primarily three different mechanisms are used to put nodes to sleep. The *first* is called *synchronized wakeup-sleep scheduling* in which the nodes in the network are put to sleep and woken up at the same time in a centralized (e.g., [10]) or a distributed manner (e.g. [3][8][9]). A disadvantage of such protocols is that the duty cycle is application dependent and not known *a priori*. Most importantly, they require the network to have an accurate time synchronization service. Furthermore, in scenarios with rare event detection, no event happens and the nodes enter sleep mode again in most of the wakeup periods. This means that nodes wake up too often resulting in wastage of energy. The *second* mechanism is based on selecting a subset of nodes to be woken up to *maintain some properties in the network*, such as sensing coverage (e.g., [4][5]), network connectivity (e.g., [3][6]), or both coverage and connectivity (e.g. [7]).

The *third* mechanism is based *on-demand sleep-wake* protocols. These on-demand sleep-wake protocols use either special purpose low-power wake-up antennas (e.g., [11]-[14]) or passive wake-up antennas [15]. These antennas are responsible for receiving an appropriate beacon from a neighbor node and waking up the node for its full operation. Thus, for environments where events of interest are relatively rare, the time for the low power operation with the wake-up antennas being on, dominates. Further details about the operation of the antennas are mentioned in Section 3.3.

To the best of our knowledge, we are the first to address local monitoring in a network where nodes may need to be put to sleep for energy conservation.

3. SLAM Protocol Description

The primary goal of SLAM is to minimize the time a node has to be awake to perform local monitoring. Local monitoring is used to make sure that packets are not dropped, delayed, modified, misrouted, or forged along the path from source to destination [23]. SLAM adds one more task to the list of events that a guard node needs to monitor—verifying whether the node being monitored wakes up the requisite guards or fails to do so due to malicious motivations.

3.1. System Model and Assumptions

SLAM assumes that the network is static and the links are bi-directional. SLAM requires a pre-distribution pair-wise key management protocol (e.g [26]) such that any two nodes can acquire a key for encryption and authentication. In

On-Demand SLAM, each node is equipped with either a passive [15] or a low-power wakeup antenna [12]. Any two nodes that need to communicate, establish a route between them using an underlying routing protocol. We assume that the source node is honest. No assumption is made about the adversary nodes following the sleep-wake protocol, only the honest nodes follow it. Each node knows its first-hop neighbors and the neighbors of each neighbor, e.g., using a technique as in [23]. The malicious behavior of fruitlessly sending a wake-up signal to a node is not addressed since this potential exists in any on-demand wake-up protocol and SLAM neither exacerbates nor solves this problem.

3.2. Different Network Models for SLAM Protocol

Depending on the BSP used in the network, SLAM has three different mechanisms for proposing sleeping for networks with local monitoring—The *No-Action-Required* SLAM protocol, the *Adapted* SLAM *protocol*, and the *On-Demand* SLAM protocol. The No-Action-Required SLAM is applicable in networks with synchronous sleep-wake mechanisms. Examples of such protocols include Span [3], S-MAC [8], and habitat monitoring [10]. The guards for the communication would also be woken up since the guards are one-hop neighbors of the two nodes that form the link on which the communication is taking place. The Adapted SLAM protocol is applicable in networks with application-specific sleep-wake protocols that can be adapted to wake up and sent to sleep guards as well. Examples of such protocols include those that maintain a k-sensing or a k-communication coverage for given values of k [4] [5] [7]. The adaptation process depends in the protocol itself, but for the connectivity or coverage problems, it involves increasing the value of k input to the protocol such that the requisite number of guards is awake in any part of the sensor field. For more details on these two kinds of networks, please refer to Sections 3.2 and 3.3 of our technical report [29].

3.3. The On-Demand SLAM Protocol

This protocol is used in a network that either has no BSP in operation or employs on-demand sleep-wake protocols. Therefore, we build a new sleep-wake protocol, called On-Demand SLAM that enables the guards to go to sleep when not required for monitoring. The approach we take is on-demand sleep-wake of the guards rather than scheduling the sleep-wake periods. The defining characteristic of on-demand sleep-wake protocols is that any node in the network may, at random, initiate communication with any other node in the network. The sleep-wake protocol does not rely on any fixed communication pattern in the network. On-Demand SLAM uses either low-power wake-up antennas (e.g., [11]-[14]) or passive antennas with circuitry that can harvest signal energy to trigger a node to wake up [15], as has been described in Section 2. These kinds of antennas are commercially available (e.g. [14]) as well as available as research prototypes in academia [15]. For example Austria Microsystems provides a low-power wake-up receiver

(AS3931) with data rate of 2.731KB/s and current consumption in standby mode of 6.6µA [14].

In On-Demand SLAM, the low-power wake-up radio remains awake all the time while the normal radio is put to sleep when it is not sending or receiving data or is not required for monitoring. If a node is to send a packet out, it simply wakes up by itself; if a neighbor node is to send a packet to this node, the sender will send a short wake-up beacon using the wake-up radio channel, and on receiving this beacon the wake-up radio triggers the normal radio to be ready for the reception. The main disadvantage of the mechanism is that it still consumes extra energy. Even though the power consumed is small compared to the normal antenna (1uW compared to 10mW in [11]), the energy is non-negligible due to long time of operation.

Hence this mechanism has been modified to use passive wake-up antennas, known as radio-triggered power management mechanisms [15]. In this mechanism a special hardware component–a radio-triggered circuit–is connected to one of the interrupt inputs of the processor. The circuit itself does not draw any current and is thus passive. The node can enter sleep mode without periodic wake-up. The wake-up mode is the usual working mode with all the functional units ready to work, and the average wake-up mode current is 20mA. In sleep mode, a node shuts down all its components except the memory, interrupt handler, and the timer. The sleep mode current is 100µA. When a network node changes from sleep mode to wake-up mode, there is a surge current of 30mA for a maximum of 5ms. When a power management message is sent by another node within a certain distance, the radio-triggered circuit collects enough energy to trigger the interrupt to wake up the node. Except for activating the wake-up interrupt, the radio-triggered circuit is independent of any other components on the node. If supported by hardware, the wake-up packet is sent at a special radio frequency. If the nodes in a one hop neighborhood have unique frequencies each listens on, then other communication at a different radio frequency does not wake up the nodes. Note that hardware cost for adding multiple-frequency support is usually fairly low. Many recent low-end radio transceivers support multiple frequency operations [30] However, the unique frequency assignment is not necessary for the correctness of On-Demand SLAM, but improves the energy efficiency. In the rest of the paper, for ease of exposition we use the term "low-power wake-up radio" to mean either the low-power wake-up hardware or the passive wake-up hardware.

3.3.1. On-Demand SLAM: Basic Approach

The basic idea in designing On-Demand SLAM is for a node to wake up the requisite guard nodes to perform local monitoring on the communication that is going out from that node. The challenge in the design comes from the fact that any of the nodes (except the source) may be malicious and therefore, may not faithfully wake up the guards. As in [23] and [24], local monitoring is used to mitigate malicious activities manifested through dropping, delaying, modifying, or forging of data/control packets. In local monitoring, the sensor node is called a *guard* when performing traffic overhearing and monitoring of neighbors. The guards of a node A over the incoming packets from a transmitter X are the common neighbors of X and A. In Figure 1, α_1 and β_1 are the guards of n_1 over the link $S \rightarrow n_1$. Information for each packet sent from X to A is saved in a *watch buffer* at each guard for a time T_w. The information maintained depends on the attack to be detected (i.e., drop, delay, modify, or forge).

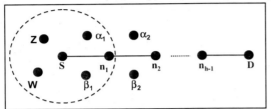

Figure 1: *h*-hop route between S and D, neighbors of S, and guards of n_1 and n_2

A malicious counter ($MalC(i,j)$) is maintained at each guard node, i, for every node, j, which i is monitoring. $MalC(i,j)$ is incremented for any suspect malicious activity of j that is detected by i. To account for intermittent natural failures, a node is determined to be misbehaving, only if the $MalC$ goes above a threshold. When $MalC(i,j)$ crosses the threshold, node i isolates node j by refraining from sending or receiving any packet from j. Node j is said to be fully isolated from the network when all its neighbors isolate it.

We use Figure 1 to explain On-Demand SLAM. A source node S is sending data to a destination node D through an h-hop route $S \rightarrow n_1 \rightarrow n_2 \rightarrow ... \rightarrow n_{h-1} \rightarrow D$. In a network where all the nodes are honest, S will wake up the next hop n_1 and the guard nodes (α_1 and β_1) before sending the packet to n_1. In turn n_1 will wake up n_2 and guard nodes α_2 and β_2 before sending the packet on the next hop and so on, till the packet reaches D. Formally, according to [24], the responsibility of a guard node α of n_{i+1} over a link $n_i \rightarrow n_{i+1}$ is to verify that:

1. n_{i+1} forwards the packet within time T_w.

2. n_{i+1} does not modify the packet it is forwarding.

3. n_{i+1} only forwards a packet if a packet is sent on the $n_i \rightarrow n_{i+1}$ link.

SLAM introduces a fourth responsibility.

4. n_{i+1} should wake up the guards for the $n_{i+1} \rightarrow n_{i+2}$ link *before* forwarding the packet on that link.

If a rule 1-3 is violated then the $MalC$ value is incremented by appropriate amount; if rule 4 is violated, the $MalC$ value increment is the maximum of the other MalC values because this rule violation may be used to mask violations of any of the rules 1-3.

In general, for any multi-hop route connecting a source node S to a destination node D, S is responsible for waking up the correct guards for n_1, and n_i is responsible for waking up the correct guards of n_{i+1} ($1 \le i \le$ h-2). The correct guards for n_1 are guaranteed to be woken up by the assumption of honest source S and whether n_i honestly wakes up the next

hop guards is monitored by the guards of n_i according to rule 4 above.

In the following we present two variations of On-Demand SLAM depending on the wake-up mechanism a node follows to wake up the guards of the next-hop.

3.3.2. Guards-Only On-Demand SLAM (*G-SLAM*)

The high level design goal in G-SLAM is to minimize the energy wasted in waking up nodes that can not serve as guards. On average half of the nodes within a single transmission range are not guards over a certain link (according to Equation I in [24]). In G-SLAM, a node wakes up a subset of its neighbors—the nodes that *can* act as guards. For this, it is assumed that the wake-up antenna of each node is tuned to receive at its own code (as in [15]), which is distinct for all one-hop neighborhood nodes.

For a guard node to verify honest wake-up, G-SLAM requires each node in the network to know, in addition to the identities of its first-hop and second-hop neighbors that are required by local monitoring, the location of each node within twice its transmission range. In Figure 1, a guard of n_1, say α_1, knows the location of its neighbor n_1 and the location of all the neighbors of n_1 (S, β_1, β_2, α_2 and n_2). Using this information, α_1 knows the common neighbors of n_1 and n_2, α_2 and β_2, which can act as the guards of n_2 over the link $n_1 \rightarrow n_2$. Therefore, α_1 can not be deceived by n_1 waking up its nodes that can not be guards for n_2 (S, β_1). A disadvantage of G-SLAM is that it requires sophisticated wakeup hardware that can be addressed using an id-attached beacon [15].

We explain the G-SLAM algorithm with the help of Figure 1. Assume that node S has some data to be sent for the destination D over the route $S \rightarrow n_1 \rightarrow n_2 \rightarrow ... \rightarrow n_{h-1} \rightarrow D$ connecting S to D. G-SLAM uses the following steps to wake up the correct guards along the route from S to D:

1. Node S sends a signal to wake up the first-hop node (n_1) and the guards for n_1 (α_1, β_1). This is a multicast signal that contains the identities of n_1, α_1, and β_1.

2. Node S sends the packets it has to n_1 following the timing schedule presented in Section 3.3.4.

3. Nodes n_1, α_1, and β_1 after being woken up continue to remain awake for T_w. T_w is a parameter of local monitoring that captures the maximum time by which an entry in the watch buffer is evicted (beyond that is evidence of malicious action). Each time a new packet is sent from S to n_1, T_w is reinitialized. After T_w expires at a node, it goes back to sleep.

4. Node n_1, after being woken up, uses the timing schedule in Section 3.3.4 and according to it sends a wake-up signal for n_2, the guards of n_2 over the link $n_1 \rightarrow n_2$ (α_2, β_2), and the guards of n_1 over the link $S \rightarrow n_1$(S, α_1, β_1). The guards of n_1 over the link $S \rightarrow n_1$ are responsible for verifying that n_1 fulfills this requirement. n_2 does not accept packets from n_1 if the wakeup signal of n_1 does not include all the necessary nodes ($S, \alpha_1, \beta_1, \alpha_2, \beta_2, n_2$).

5. If n_1 fails to send the wakeup signal, the guard of n_1 with the lowest ID sends a two-hop broadcast of the wakeup signal. If that guard fails, the guard with the next smallest ID sends the signal, and so on. This design ensures that if there is a chain of colluding malicious nodes then all the nodes will be suspected.

6. The process continues at each step up to the destination.

3.3.3. All-Neighbors On-Demand SLAM (*A-SLAM*)

The high level design goal of A-SLAM is to relax the assumption that every node knows the location of its first-hop and second-hop neighbors, and to simplify the wake-up hardware and wakeup signal. Again considering Figure 1, A-SLAM uses the following steps to wake up the guards along the route from S to D:

1. Node S broadcasts a wake-up signal to all its first-hop neighbors $(Z,W,n_1,\alpha_1,\beta_1)$. The wake-up signal includes the identity of both the current sender (S), the next-hop (n_1), and the previous-hop (empty for S).

2. Each neighbor of S, after being woken up, decides whether to stay awake or go back to sleep based on the role that it may play on the ongoing communication. If that neighbor is the next-hop (n_1), it stays awake to forward the data and to monitor the next-hop from it (n_2). If that neighbor is a guard (α_1,β_1) for the next-hop n_1 over the link $n_1 \rightarrow n_2$, it stays awake to monitor the behavior of n_1. If the node is a guard of a forwarding node over the previous-hop, it stays awake to detect fabrication by the forwarding node. A node can independently make this determination based on first- and second-hop neighbor information. If none of these cases hold, the node goes back to sleep immediately.

3. Node S sends the data packet to n_1 following the timing schedule presented in Section 3.3.4.

4. Nodes n_1, α_1, and β_1 after being woken up continue to stay awake for T_w. After that, it goes back to sleep.

5. n_1 does the same steps that S did to wake up the next-hop (n_2), n_2's guards (α_2,β_2) and n_1's guards (S,α_1,β_1).

6. If n_1 fails to send the wakeup signal, the guard of n_1 with the lowest ID sends a two-hop broadcast of the wakeup signal through. If that guard fails, the guard with the next smallest ID sends the signal, and so on. This design ensures that if there is a chain of colluding malicious nodes then all the nodes will be suspected.

7. The process continues at each step till the destination.

This scheme results in an increase in the energy consumption compared to G-SLAM due to the needless wake-up of the neighbors that are not guards.

3.3.4. Timing of the wakeup signal

In this section we generate the timing schedules for sending the wake-up signal to nodes using On-Demand SLAM. This is important because the wake-up antennas have a warm-up period that could increase the end-to-end delay of the communication. We design the schedule such that the

additional delay due to the sleep-wake protocol is not cumulative with the number of hops for Case II shown below. It is a constant independent of the number of hops. Moreover, the increase in delay with the number of hops is small for Case I. The coefficient of increase per hop is the difference between the time to send a control packet and the time to send a data packet over one hop.

Let $T_{control}$ be the time to send the signal to the wake-up antenna, T_{warmup} be the time for a node to be fully awake from the time it receives the wake-up signal (5 ms for the antenna in [15]), and T_{data} be the time to send a data packet over one hop. This time includes the transmission time and the forwarding time. Thus, within T_{data}, an intermediate node completely receives a data packet. Finally, let T_{wake} be the time a node continues to be awake after being woken up.

Consider an *isolated* flow between S and D, separated by h hops. The intermediate nodes are n_1, n_2, ..., n_{h-1}. Let g_i represents the guards of node n_i over the link $n_{i-1} \rightarrow n_i$. Let v_i represents the neighbors of n_i that are not guards of n_{i+1} over the link $n_i \rightarrow n_{i+1}$. Consider the following two disjoint cases based on the relation between ($T_{control} + T_{warmup}$) and T_{data}.

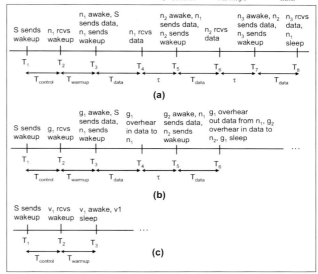

Figure 2: Case I wakeup-sleep timing schedule for (a) a node in the data route; (b) a guard node; (c) a neighbor to a node in the data route that is not valid guard (for A-SLAM only)

Case I: $(T_{control}+T_{warmup}) > T_{data}$, $\tau = (T_{control}+T_{warmup}) - T_{data}$

Figure 2 above shows the timing schedule for this case. Figure 2(a) shows the timing schedule for a node in the route between the source and the destination. The node, n_1, wakes up at T_3 and goes to sleep at T_8, where $T_8-T_3 = T_{data}$ (to receive data) + τ (wait for the next-hop to be ready to receive the data) + T_{data} (send the data to the next-hop) + {τ + T_{data}} (as a guard for n_2) = $3T_{data}+2\tau$. Figure 2(b) shows the timing schedule for a guard node. The guard, g_1, wakes up at T_3 and goes to sleep at T_6, where $T_6-T_3 = T_{data}$ (to overhear incoming data to the node being monitored, n_1) + τ (wait for the next-hop to be ready to receive the data) + T_{data} (to overhear outgoing data from the node being monitored, n_1) = $2T_{data} +\tau$. Figure 2 (c), only meaningful for A-SLAM, shows the schedule for a node that is a neighbor to a node in the route from the source to the destination but is not a guard node. The node, v_1, wakes up at T_3, determines that it can not be a guard, and thus goes back to sleep immediately.

From Figure 2, it can be seen that per hop, the delay incurred is $T_{control} + T_{warmup}$ and at the last hop, the delay due to data (T_{data}) gets exposed (see Equation (1) below).

Case II: ($T_{control}+T_{warmup})\leq T_{data}, \tau = T_{data} - (T_{control} + T_{warmup})$ Please see Case II, Section 3.4.3 of our technical report [29].

4. Security and Performance Analysis

4.1. Security Analysis

We will prove the following proposition.

Proposition: Due to the sleep-wake mechanism for guards in SLAM, no loss in detection coverage occurs w.r.t. [24].

For this we first prove the following lemma.

Lemma: For any node n_i in the path $S{\rightarrow}D$ ($i =1, ..., h-1$), the guards for n_{i+1} on the link $n_i{\rightarrow}n_{i+1}$ are woken up when the communication over the link takes place.

We prove this lemma using mathematical induction.

Let the guards of n_1 over the link $S{\rightarrow}n_1$ form the set G_1, $n_{h-1}{\rightarrow}D$ the set G_h, and $n_{i-1}{\rightarrow}n_i$ the set G_i.

Base case: The source S is honest and therefore it wakes the guard nodes in G_1.

Inductive hypothesis: For $n_1, ..., n_i$ ($i \geq 1$), $\forall G_k$ ($k \leq i$) has been woken up at the time when the communication over the link $n_{k-1}{\rightarrow}n_k$ takes place either directly or indirectly. In the later case n_{k-1} is suspected of malicious action.

To prove: G_{i+1} is woken up at the time of $n_i{\rightarrow}n_{i+1}$ communication.

Proof: If n_i is honest, it wakes up G_{i+1} (step 4 of G-SLAM/step 5 of A-SLAM).

Else, G_i wakes up G_{i+1} (step 5 of G-SLAM/step 6 of A-SLAM). In the later case n_i is suspected of malicious action (not sending the wakeup signal).

Thus, the lemma is proved by mathematical induction.

The detection of the guards according to rules 1-3 is not changed from baseline local monitoring. Combining the lemma with this observation proves that no loss of detection coverage happens due to SLAM.

4.2. Energy and End-to-End Delay Analysis

For both energy and delay we compare our scheme On-Demand Slam to bring out its worst case behavior. For end-to-end delay, we compare it with local monitoring without sleep-wake (Baseline-LM). For the energy we compare it to a protocol with on-demand sleep-wake for communication and no monitoring (Baseline-OD).

In addition to the notations defined in Section 3.3.4, let $A_{transmit}$ be the current to transmit (at the middle of the transmit range), which is 27mA for Mica2 motes [28]. Let A_{warmup} be the current consumed during the transition from sleep to wakeup (warm up), which is 30mA for Mica2 motes

[15]. Finally, let A_{active} be the current in the computationally active mode = the current in the idle listening mode = the current in receive mode (8mA for Mica2 motes).

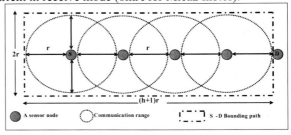

Figure 3: A bounding box over the path S $\rightarrow$ D

Let us consider a flow between S and D, separated by h hops. The intermediate nodes are $n_1, n_2, ..., n_{h-1}$. The bounding box around S and D covers all possible nodes, including forwarding and guard nodes that may be involved in the communication between S and D. The size of the bounding box is $2r(h+1)r = 2r^2(h+1)$, where r is the transmission range, Figure 3. For On-Demand SLAM, consider the wakeup-sleep scheduling cases of Section 3.3.4.

End-to-end-Delay:

Case I: ($T_{control} + T_{warmup}) > T_{data}$ with $\tau = (T_{control} + T_{warmup}) - T_{data}$

From Figure 2 it can be seen that delay at the first link ($S{\rightarrow}n_1$) is $T_{control} + T_{warmup} + T_{data}$. Over each of the succeeding links, the delay is $T_{control} + T_{warmup}$ since the delay due to data (T_{data}) gets exposed. This is due the sleep-wake schedule process that SLAM uses where the wake-up signal is sent at the earliest opportunity. Therefore, the end-to-end delay in SLAM, $\Omega_{SLAM}(h)$, for the link from S to D is

$$\Omega_{SLAM}(h) = T_{contol} + T_{warmup} + T_{data} + (h-1)(T_{control} + T_{warmup})$$
$$= h \cdot (T_{control} + T_{warmup}) + T_{data} \qquad (1)$$

The end-to-end delay in Baseline-LM is

$$\Omega_{Base-LM}(h) = h \cdot T_{data} \qquad (2)$$

In this case, the additional end-to-end delay imposed by SLAM depends on the number of hops between S and D

$$\Omega_{SLAM-Add}(h) = \Omega_{SLAM}(h) - \Omega_{Base-LM}(h) = h \cdot \tau + T_{data} \qquad (3)$$

Case II: ($T_{control} + T_{warmup}) \leq T_{data}$ with $\tau = T_{data} - (T_{control} + T_{warmup})$. The end-to-end delay of SLAM is given by

$$\Omega_{SLAM}(h) = T_{contol} + T_{warmup} + T_{data} + (h-1)(T_{data})$$
$$= h \cdot T_{data} + (T_{control} + T_{warmup}) \qquad (4)$$

For more details, please refer to Case II, Section 4.2 in our technical report.

In Figure 4, we plot the extra delay of SLAM over Baseline-LM for cases I (Equation(3)) and II (Equation (12) in the technical report [29]) above with $T_{data} = 7ms$ and $\tau = 1ms$. The figure shows that the additional delay due to SLAM increases linearly with the number of hops for Case I while it remains constant for Case II.

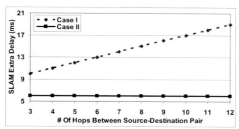

Figure 4: Extra delay due to SLAM over Baseline-LM

Energy overhead:

Case I: $(T_{control} + T_{warmup}) > T_{data}, \tau = (T_{control} + T_{warmup}) - T_{data}$

Baseline-OD: Here only the forwarding nodes are involved in the sleep-wake protocol; all other nodes are asleep. Using Figure 2(a), a forwarding node n_i ($i = 1, ..., h-1$) spends $T_{warmup} = T_3-T_2$ warming up with current consumption of A_{warmup}, $T_{data} = T_4-T_3$ receiving data with current consumption of A_{active}, $\tau = T_5-T_4$ idle waiting for the next-hop to be ready with current consumption of A_{active}, and $T_{data} = T_6-T_5$ sending data with current consumption of $A_{transmit}$. Therefore, the energy expended by a forwarding node n_i ($i = 1, ..., h-1$) is (we ignore the constant voltage term for the energy comparison since that is the same through all the cases)

$$\varepsilon_{f,base} = T_{warmup} \cdot A_{warmup} + (T_{control} + T_{warmup}) \cdot A_{active} + T_{data} \cdot A_{transmit} \quad (5)$$

Node S spends $T_{control} + T_{warmup} = T_3-T_1$ idle waiting for n_1 to wake up with A_{active} and $T_{data} = T_4-T_3$ transmitting data with $A_{transmit}$. Therefore, the energy expended by S is

$$\varepsilon_{S,base} = (T_{control} + T_{warmup}) \cdot A_{active} + T_{data} \cdot A_{transmit} \quad (6)$$

Node D spends T_{warmup} warming up with A_{warmup} and T_{data} receiving data with A_{active}. Thus, the energy expended by D is

$$\varepsilon_{D,base} = T_{warmup} \cdot A_{warmup} + T_{data} \cdot A_{active} \quad (7)$$

On-Demand SLAM: Here the sleep-wake protocol involves, in addition to S and D, the forwarding nodes, the guard nodes, the neighbors of the forwarding nodes that are not guards. We will compute separately for the three kinds of nodes (i) forwarding nodes; (ii) guard nodes that do not act as forwarders; (iii) remaining nodes. The energy of S and D is the same as that in Baseline-OD.

i. Energy expended by a forwarding node n_i ($i = 1, ..., h-1$) $\varepsilon_{f,SLAM} \le \varepsilon_{f,base} + T_w \cdot A_{active}$. The additional energy is consumed because n_i has to find if n_{i+1} forwards the packet that it was just handed by n_i. The inequality comes in because T_w is the worst-case time in case n_{i+1} is malicious.

ii. Energy expended by a guard node that is not a forwarding node $\varepsilon_{g,SLAM} \le T_{warmup} \cdot A_{warmup} + T_{data} \cdot A_{active} + T_w \cdot A_{active}$. Consider for example the guard g_1 of n_1 over the link $S \rightarrow n_1$. g_1 has to listen to the communication between S to n_1 and then has to stay listening for a maximum of T_w to see that n_1 forwarded the packet.

iii. Energy expended by a node in the bounding box around S and D that is neither a forwarding node nor a guard node (the "other node", hence the notation "o" in the

subscript). For G-SLAM where the wake-up signal is directed to the relevant guard nodes $\varepsilon_{o,G-SLAM} = 0$. For A-SLAM $\varepsilon_{o,A-SLAM} = T_{warmup} \cdot A_{warmup}$.

Case II: $(T_{control} + T_{warmup}) \le T_{data}$ with $\tau = T_{data} - (T_{control} + T_{warmup})$. Please refer to Case II, Section 4.2 in our technical report for the energy consumption of this case.

5. Simulation Results

We use the *ns-2* simulator [27] to simulate a data exchange protocol over a network with local monitoring enabled. We simulate two scenarios individually without A-SLAM (the *baseline*) and with A-SLAM. The baseline is an implementation of a state-of-the-art local monitoring protocol presented in [24]. A-SLAM scenario is built on top of the baseline scenario to provide sleep-wake service for the guards. Nodes are distributed randomly over a square area with a fixed average node density, 100 nodes over 204m×204m. Each node acts as a source and generates data according to a Poisson process with rate μ. The destination is chosen at random and is changed using an exponential distribution with rate λ. A route is evicted if unused for $TOut_{Route}$ time. The experimental parameters are in Table 1. The results are averages over 30 runs. The malicious nodes are randomly chosen so that they are more than 2 hops away.

Table 1: Default simulation parameters

Parameter	Value	Parameter	Value
Avg. number neighbors (N_B)	8	Destination change rate (λ)	0.02/sec
Tx Range (r)	30 m	# malicious nodes (M)	4
Fraction of data monitored (f_{dat})	0.6	Packet generation rate ($1/\mu$)	0.1/sec
Channel BW	40 kbps	Warm up time (T_{warmup})	5ms
Simulation time	1500 s	Watch time (T_w)	30ms
$TOut_{Route}$	50 sec	Number of nodes (N)	100

Adversary model: We are simulating a selective forwarding attack launched by a group of malicious nodes that collude and establish wormholes in the network [25]. During the wormhole attack, a malicious node captures packets from one location in the network, and "tunnels" them to another malicious node at a distant point, which replays them locally. This makes the tunneled packet arrive either sooner or with a lesser number of hops compared to the packets transmitted over normal multihop routes. This creates the illusion that the two end points of the tunnel are very close to each other. The two malicious end points of the tunnel may use it to pass routing traffic to attract routes through them and then launch a variety of attacks against the data traffic flowing on the wormhole, such as selectively dropping the data packets. Unless otherwise mentioned, each node selectively drops a packet passing through it with uniform probability of 0.6

Variable Input metrics: (i) *Fraction of data monitored* (f_{dat})—each guard node randomly monitors a given fraction of the data packets. At other times, it can be asleep from the point of view of a guard's responsibility. (ii) *Data traffic load (μ)*. (iii) *Number of malicious nodes (M)*.

Output metrics: (i) *Delivery ratio*–the ratio of the number of packets delivered to the destination to the number of packets sent out by a node averaged over all the nodes in the network. (ii) *% wakeup time*–the time a node has to wake up specifically to do monitoring averaged over all the nodes as a percentage of the simulation time; (iii) *Average end-to-end delay*–the time it takes a data packet to reach the final destination averaged over all successfully received data packets; (iv) *% True isolation*–the percentage of the total number of malicious nodes that is isolated; (v) *% False isolation*–the percentage of the total number of nodes that is isolated due to natural collisions on the wireless channel; (vi) *Isolation latency*–the time between when the node performs its first malicious action to the time by which *all* its neighbors have isolated it, averaged over all isolated malicious nodes.

Note that our goal is not to show the variation of the output metrics with the input parameters for local monitoring, since that has been covered in [23][24]. Our

goal is to study the relative effect on local monitoring with A-SLAM and without.

5.1. Effect of fraction of data monitored

The amount of data traffic is typically several orders of magnitude larger than the amount of control traffic. It may not be reasonable for a guard to monitor all the data traffic in its monitored links. Therefore, a reasonable optimization is to monitor only a fraction of the data traffic. In this set of experiments, we investigate the effect of this optimization.

Figure 5 shows the variations of delivery ratio, % true isolation, and end-to-end delay as we vary f_{dat}. Figure 5(a) shows that the delivery ratio is almost stable above 90% irrespective of the value of f_{dat}. This desirable effect is achieved by proper selection of the *MalC* increment for each value of f_{dat}. The *MalC* increment is designed with an inverse relation to the f_{dat} Figure 5(b) shows that the % of true isolation is almost stable as we vary f_{dat} due to the same reasoning as for Figure 5(a). Importantly, the delivery ratio and the % true isolation in A-SLAM are close to the baseline for all values of f_{dat}.

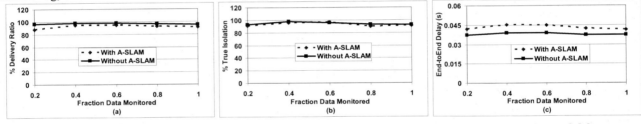

Figure 5: Effect of fraction of data monitored on (a) delivery ratio, (b) % true isolation, and (c) end-to-end delay

However, in Figure 5, the results of A-SLAM are slightly worse than those of the baseline. This is because some of the data packets are additionally dropped in A-SLAM by forwarding, destination, or guard nodes that happen to be asleep when the data packet arrives. This erroneous extra sleep may occur due to collision in the sleep-wake control channel which prevents the respective nodes from waking

up. Although the control channel is a separate channel contention still occurs, where a guard of two consecutive links are sent separate wake-up signals concurrently. Figure 5(c) shows that the end-to-end delay is slightly higher for A-SLAM due to the additional warm up time required when the source sends a packet to the first hop.

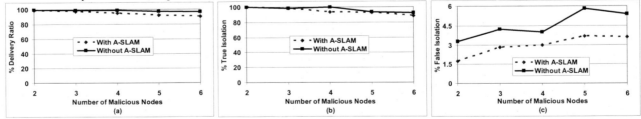

Figure 6: Effect of number of malicious nodes on (a) % delivery ratio, (b) % true isolation, and (c) % false isolation

5.2. Effect of number of malicious nodes

Figure 6 above shows the variations of % delivery ratio, % true isolation, and % false isolation as we vary the number of malicious nodes (*M*). Figure 6(a) shows that the % delivery ratio slightly decreases as *M* increases. This is due to the packets dropped before the malicious nodes are detected and isolated. As the number of malicious nodes increases, this initial drop increases and thus the delivery ratio decreases. Figure 6(b) shows that the % true isolation

also slightly decreases as we increase *M*. This is because the number of available guards in the network decreases as more and more nodes get compromised. These two metrics in A-SLAM are slightly lower than those of the base line due to the erroneous extra sleep described in Section 5.1. Figure 6(c) shows that the % false isolation increases as we increase *M*. This is because not all guard nodes come to the decision to isolate a malicious node at the same time. Thus, a guard node may suspect another guard node when the latter isolates a malicious node but the former still has not. The occurrence of this situation increases with M and hence the % of false isolation increases with M. For example, a guard node G_1 detects a malicious node Z earlier than the other guard nodes for the link to Z. G_1 subsequently drops all the traffic forwarded to Z and is therefore suspected by other guard nodes for Z. This problem can be solved by having an authenticated one-hop broadcast whenever a guard node performs a local detection. The % false isolation in A-SLAM is lower than that of the baseline. Again, this is due to some of the packets that may falsely identify a node as malicious may get lost in A-SLAM due to the erroneous extra sleep.

5.3. Wakeup time variations

In this section, we study the effect of varying the fraction of data monitored (f_{dat}), the number of malicious nodes (M),

and the data traffic load ($1/\mu$) on the percentage of time that a node needs to stay awake for monitoring using A-SLAM.

Figure 7(a) shows that the percentage of wakeup time required for monitoring increases as the fraction of monitored data increases due to the increase in the number of data packets that a node needs to overhear in its neighborhood. Figure 7(b) shows that the percentage of wakeup time decreases as we increase the number of malicious nodes. As the number of malicious nodes increases, the number of data packets in the system decreases since the malicious nodes are isolated and disallowed from generating data packets. Therefore, the number of packets that need to be monitored decreases, which results in a decrease in the average percentage of wakeup monitor time. Figure 7(c) shows that the average % of monitoring wakeup time increases as the data traffic load increases due the increase in data that needs to be monitored.

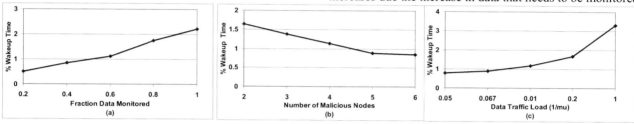

Figure 7: Variations on the percentage of monitoring wakeup time as we vary (a) the fraction of data monitored (f_{dat}); (b) number of malicious nodes (M); and (c) data traffic load (μ)

Overall, from Figure 7(c), compared to the no sleeping case, A-SLAM saves 30-129 times in listening energy for different amounts of data traffic load ($1/\mu$).

5.4. Effect of distance on delay

In this section, we evaluate the variations of the end-to-end delay with the number of hops between the source and destination pairs.

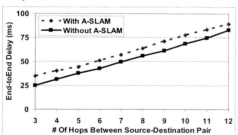

Figure 8: Variation of the end-to-end delay with the hop count

Figure 8 above shows that the end-to-end delay in A-SLAM is always higher than that of the baseline due to the warm-up time needed to wake up the nodes before sending the data. However, due the scheduling strategy in A-SLAM in which each node sends a wake-up signal at the earliest possible opportunity (Section 3.3.4), the warm-up time is only in the critical path at the first hop and therefore, the difference in delay between A-SLAM and the baseline case is not cumulative with the number of hops. The trend of the additional delay due to SLAM follows the trend obtained

analytically in Section 4.2 for the case when ($T_{control} + T_{warmup}$) < T_{data} which is true in these simulation settings.

6. Conclusion

In this paper, we have presented a protocol called SLAM to make local monitoring in sensor networks energy-efficient while maintaining the detection coverage. We classify the domain of sleep-wake protocols into three classes and SLAM correspondingly has three manifestations depending on which baseline sleeping protocol (BSP) is used in the network. For the first class (synchronized sleep-wake), local monitoring needs no modification. For the second class (connectivity or coverage preserving sleep-wake), local monitoring can call the BSP with changed parameter values. For the third class (on-demand sleep-wake), adapting local monitoring is the most challenging and requires hardware support as low-power or passive wake-up antennas. We propose a scheme whereby before communicating on a link, a node awakens the guard nodes responsible for local monitoring on its next hop. We design the scheme to work with adversarial node behavior. We prove analytically that On-Demand SLAM does not weaken the security property of local monitoring. Simulation experiments bring out that over a wide range of conditions, the performance of local monitoring with SLAM is comparable to that without SLAM, while listening energy savings of 30-129 times is realized, depending on the network load. Our ongoing work is looking at providing security guarantees in mobile ad hoc networks and building trust framework for such networks.

Acknowledgements

This work was supported in part by the National Science Foundation under grant no. ECS-0330016 and the Indiana 21st Century Fund under grant no. 512040817. Any opinions, findings and conclusions or recommendations expressed in this material are those of the authors and do not necessarily reflect those of the sponsors.

7. References

[1] W. Zhang and G. Cao, "DCTC: Dynamic Convoy Tree-Based Collaboration for Target Tracking in Sensor Networks," IEEE Trans. on Wireless Communication 3(5), pp.1689-1701, 2004.

[2] S. Pattem, S. Poduri, and B. Krishnamachari, "Energy-quality tradeoffs for target tracking in wireless sensor networks," in the second workshop on Information Processing for Sensor Networks (IPSN), pp. 32-46, 2003.

[3] B. Chen, K. Jamieson, H. Balakrishnan, and R. Morris, "Span: An energy-efficient coordination algorithm for topology maintenance in ad hoc wireless networks," in Wireless Networks, vol. 3 (5), pp. 48-494, 2002.

[4] S. Bhattacharya, G. Xing, C. Lu, G.-C. Roman, O. Chipara, and B. Harris, "Dynamic wake-up and topology maintenance protocols with spatiotemporal guarantees," in the fourth workshop on Information Processing for Sensor Networks (IPSN), pp. 28-34, 2005.

[5] S. Kumar, T. H. Lai, and J. Balogh, "On k-coverage in a mostly sleeping sensor network" in the ACM Intl. Conference on Mobile Computing and Networking (MOBICOM), pp. 144-158, 2004.

[6] W. R. Heinzelman, A. Chandrakasan, and H. Balakrishnan, "Energy-Efficient Communication Protocol for Wireless Microsensor Networks," in the 33rd Hawaii Intl. Conference on System Sciences (HICSS), pp. 3005-3014, 2004.

[7] G. Xing, X. Wang, Y. Zhang, C. Lu, R. Pless, and C. Gill, "Integrated coverage and connectivity configuration for energy conservation in sensor networks," in ACM Trans. on Sensor Networks (TOSN), Vol. 1 , Issue 1, pp. 36-72, 2005.

[8] W. Ye, J. Heidemann, and D. Estrin, "An energy efficient MAC protocol for wireless sensor Networks," in the IEEE Conference on Computer Communications (INFOCOM), pp. 1567- 1576, 2002.

[9] R. Naik, S. Biswas, and S. Datta, "Distributed Sleep-Scheduling Protocols for Energy Conservation in Wireless Networks," in the 38th HICSS, pp. 285b - 285b, 2005.

[10] A. Mainwaring, J. Polastre, R. Szewczyk, D. Culler, and J. Anderson, "Wireless sensor networks for habitat monitoring," in the ACM Intl. Workshop on Wireless Sensor Networks and Applications, pp. 88-97, 2002.

[11] C. Guo, L. C. Zhong, and J. M. Rabaey, "Low power distributed MAC for ad hoc sensor radio networks," in IEEE Global Telecommunications Conference (GLOBECOM '01), pp. 2944–2948, vol.5, 2001.

[12] J. Rabaey, J. Ammer, T. Karalar, S. Li, B. Otis, M. Sheets, and T. Tuan, "Picoradios for wireless sensor networks: The next challenge in ultra-low-power design," in the Intl. Solid-State Circuits Conference, pp. 200-201, 2002.

[13] J. Silva., J. Shamberger, M. J. Ammer, C. Guo, S. Li, R. Shah, T. Tuan, M. Sheets, J. M. Rabaey, B. Nikolic, A. S.-Vincentelli, and P. Wright, "Design methodology for picoradio networks," in Design Automation and Test in Europe (DATE), pp. 314-323, 2001.

[14] http://www.austriamicrosystems.com/03products/data/AS393 1Product_brief_0204.pdf.

[15] L. Gu and J.A Stankovic, "Radio-Triggered Wake-Up Capability for Sensor Networks," in Real-Time and Embedded Technology and Applications Symposium (RTAS), pp. 27-36, 2004.

[16] Y. Huang and W. Lee, "A cooperative intrusion detection system for ad hoc networks," in the 1st ACM workshop on Security of ad hoc and sensor networks, pp. 135-147, 2003.

[17] A. Silva, M. Martins, B. Rocha, A. Loureiro, L. Ruiz, and H. Wong, "Decentralized intrusion detection in wireless sensor networks," in the ACM Intl. workshop on Quality of service & security in wireless and mobile networks, pp. 16-23, 2005.

[18] S. Marti, T. J. Giuli, K. Lai, and M. Baker, "Mitigating routing misbehavior in mobile ad hoc networks," in MOBICOM, pp. 255-265, 2000.

[19] S.J. Lee and M. Gerla, "Split Multipath Routing with Maximally Disjoint Paths in Ad Hoc Networks," in IEEE Intl. Conference on Communications (ICC), pp. 3201-3205, 2001.

[20] A. A. Pirzada and C. McDonald, "Establishing Trust In Pure Ad-hoc Networks," in the proceedings of 27th Australasian Computer Science Conference (ACSC'04), pp. 47-54, 2004.

[21] S. Buchegger, J.-Y. Le Boudec, "Performance Analysis of the CONFIDANT Protocol: Cooperation Of Nodes - Fairness In Distributed Ad-hoc NeTworks," in the ACM Intl. Symposium on Mobile Ad Hoc Networking and Computing (MOBIHOC), pp. 80-91, 2002.

[22] I. Khalil, S. Bagchi, and N. B. Shroff, "Analysis and Evaluation of SECOS, a protocol for Energy Efficient and Secure Communication in Sensor Networks," in Elsevier Ad Hoc Networks Journal, vol. 5(3), pp. 360-391, April 2007.

[23] I. Khalil, S. Bagchi, and C. Nina-Rotaru, "DICAS: Detection, Diagnosis and Isolation of Control Attacks in Sensor Networks," in the IEEE/CreateNet Intl. Conference on Security and Privacy in Communication Networks (SecureComm), pp. 89-100, 2005.

[24] I. Khalil, S. Bagchi, and N. Shroff, "LITEWORP: A Lightweight Countermeasure for the Wormhole Attack in Multihop Wireless Networks," in the Intl. Conference on Dependable Systems and Networks (DSN '05), pp. 612-621, 2005.

[25] C. Karlof and D. Wagner, "Secure Routing in Sensor Networks: Attacks and Countermeasures," in the 1st IEEE Intl. Workshop on Sensor Network Protocols and Applications, pp. 113-127, 2003.

[26] D. Liu and P. Ning, "Establishing Pair-wise Keys in Distributed Sensor Networks," in the ACM Conf. of Computer and Communication Security, pp. 52-61, 2003.

[27] "The Network Simulator ns-2," At: www.isi.edu/nsnam/ns/

[28] http://www.xbow.com/products/Product_pdf_files/Wireless_p df/MICA2_Datasheet.pdf...

[29] I. Khalil, S. Bagchi, and N. B. Shroff, "SLAM: Sleep-Wake Aware Local Monitoring for Sensor Networks," TR ECE 06-14, Purdue University, November 2006.

[30] Chipcon   CC1000   Datasheet,   Chipcon   Inc. http://www.chipcon.com/files/CC1000DataSheet21.pdf.

What Supercomputers Say: A Study of Five System Logs

Adam Oliner[1]
Stanford University
Department of Computer Science
Palo Alto, CA 94305 USA
oliner@cs.stanford.edu

Jon Stearley[2]
Sandia National Laboratories
Albuquerque, NM 87111 USA
jrstear@sandia.gov

Abstract

If we hope to automatically detect and diagnose failures in large-scale computer systems, we must study real deployed systems and the data they generate. Progress has been hampered by the inaccessibility of empirical data. This paper addresses that dearth by examining system logs from five supercomputers, with the aim of providing useful insight and direction for future research into the use of such logs. We present details about the systems, methods of log collection, and how alerts were identified; propose a simpler and more effective filtering algorithm; and define operational context to encompass the crucial information that we found to be currently missing from most logs. The machines we consider (and the number of processors) are: Blue Gene/L (131072), Red Storm (10880), Thunderbird (9024), Spirit (1028), and Liberty (512). This is the first study of raw system logs from multiple supercomputers.

1 Introduction

The reliability and performance challenges of supercomputing systems cannot be adequately addressed until the behavior of the machines is better understood. In this paper, we study system logs from five of the world's most powerful supercomputers: Blue Gene/L (BG/L), Thunderbird, Red Storm, Spirit, and Liberty. The analysis encompasses more than 111.67 GB of data containing 178,081,459 alert messages in 77 categories. The system logs are the first place system administrators go when they are alerted to a problem, and are one of the few mechanisms available to them for gaining visibility into the behavior of the machine. Particularly as systems grow in size and complexity, there

is a pressing need for better techniques for processing, understanding, and applying these data.

We define an *alert* to be a message in the system logs that merits the attention of the system administrator, either because immediate action must be taken or because there is an indication of an underlying problem. Many alerts may be symptomatic of the same *failure*. Failures may be anything from a major filesystem malfunction to a transient connection loss that kills a job.

Using results from the analysis, we give recommendations for future research in this area. Most importantly, we discuss the following issues:

- Logs do not currently contain sufficient information to do automatic detection of failures, nor root cause diagnosis, with acceptable confidence. Although identifying candidate alerts is tractable, disambiguation in many cases requires external context that is not available. The most salient missing data is *operational context*, which captures the system's expected behavior.

- There is a chaotic effect in these systems, where small events or changes can dramatically impact the logs. For instance, an OS upgrade on Liberty instantaneously increased the average message traffic. On Spirit, a single node experiencing disk failure produced the majority of all log messages.

- Different categories of failures have different predictive signatures (if any). Event prediction efforts should produce an ensemble of predictors, each specializing in one or more categories.

- Along with the issues above, automatic identification of alerts must deal with: corrupted messages, inconsistent message structure and log formats, asymmetric alert reporting, and the evolution of systems over time.

Section 3 describes the five supercomputers, the log collection paths, and the logs themselves. Section 3.2 explains the alert tagging process and notes what challenges will be

---

[1]Work was done at Sandia National Laboratories, funded by the U.S. Department of Energy High Performance Computer Science Fellowship.

[2]Sandia is a multiprogram laboratory operated by Sandia Corporation, a Lockheed Martin Company, for the United States Department of Energy under Contract DE-AC04-94AL85000.

faced by those hoping to do such tagging (or detection) automatically. Section 4 contains graphical and textual examples of the data and a discussion of the implications for filtering and modeling. Finally, Section 5 summarizes the contributions and our recommendations.

The purpose of this paper is not to argue for a particular reliability, availability, and serviceability (RAS) architecture, nor to compare the reliability of the supercomputers. The systems we study are real, and the logs are in the form used by (and familiar to) system administrators. Our intention is to elucidate the practical challenges of log analysis for supercomputers, and to suggest fruitful research directions for work in data mining, filtering, root cause analysis, and critical event prediction. This is the first paper, to our knowledge, that has considered raw logs from multiple supercomputing systems.

2   Related Work

Work on log analysis and large-systems reliability has been hindered by a lack of data about their behavior. Recent work by Schroeder [21] studied failures in a set of cluster systems at Los Alamos National Lab (LANL) using the entries in a *remedy database*. This database was designed to account for all node downtime in these systems, and was populated via a combination of automatic procedures and the extensive effort of a full-time LANL employee, whose job was to account for these failures and to assign them a cause within a short period of time after they happened. Schroeder also examined customer-generated disk replacement databases [22], but there was no investigation into how these replacements were manifested in the system logs. Although similar derived databases exist for the supercomputers considered in this paper, our goal was to describe the behavior of the systems rather than human interpretations.

There is a series of papers on logs collected from Blue Gene/L (BG/L) systems. Liang, et al [10] studied the statistical properties of logs from an 8-rack prototype system, and explored the effects of spatio-temporal filtering algorithms. Subsequently, they studied prediction models [9] for logs collected from BG/L after its deployment at Lawrence Livermore National Labs (LLNL). The logs from that study are a subset of those used in this paper. Furthermore, they identified alerts according to the *severity* field of messages. Although it is true that there exists a correlation between the value of the severity field of the message and the actual severity, we found many messages with low severity that indicate a critical problem and vice versa. Section 3.2 elaborates on this claim and details the more intensive process we employed to identify alerts.

System logs for smaller systems have been studied for decades, focusing on statistical modeling and failure prediction. Tsao developed a *tuple* concept for data organiza-

tion and to deal with multiple reports of single events [26]. Early work at Stanford [13] observed that failures tend to be preceded by an increased rate of non-fatal errors. Using real system data from two DEC VAX-cluster multicomputer systems, Iyer found that alerts tend to be correlated, and that this has a significant impact on the behavior and modeling of these systems [25]. Lee and Iyer [8] presented a study of software faults in systems running the fault-tolerant GUARDIAN90 operating system. The task of automatically discovering alerts in log data has been explored from a pattern-learning perspective [7]. There have also been efforts at applying data mining techniques to discover trends and correlations [12, 23, 27, 28].

In order to solve the reliability and performance challenges facing supercomputer installations, we must study the machines as artifacts, characterizing and modeling what they *do* rather than what we expect them to do. By number of processor hours (~774 million), this is the most extensive system log study to date.

3   Supercomputer Logs

The broad range of supercomputers considered in this study are summarized in Table 1. All five systems are ranked on the Top500 Supercomputers List as of June 2006 [2], spanning a range from #1 to #445. They vary by two orders of magnitude in the number of processors and by one order of magnitude in the amount of main memory. The interconnects include Myrinet, Infiniband, GigEthernet, and custom or mixed solutions. The various machines are produced by IBM, Dell, Cray, and HP. All systems are installed at Sandia National Labs (SNL) in Albuquerque, NM, with the exception of BG/L, which is at Lawrence Livermore National Labs (LLNL) in Livermore, California.

3.1   Log Collection

It is standard practice to log messages and events in a supercomputing system; no special instrumentation nor monitoring was added for this study. Table 2 presents an overview of the logs. The remainder of this section focuses on the infrastructure that generated them.

On Thunderbird, Spirit, and Liberty, logs are generated on each local machine by `syslog-ng` and both stored to `/var/log/` and sent to a logging server. The logging servers (`tbird-admin1` on Thunderbird, `sadmin2` on Spirit, and `ladmin2` on Liberty) process the files with `syslog-ng` and place them in a directory structure according to the source node. We collected the logs from that directory. As is standard syslog practice, the UDP protocol is used for transmission, resulting in some messages being lost during network contention.

System	Owner	Vendor	Top500 Rank	Procs	Memory (GB)	Interconnect
Blue Gene/L	LLNL	IBM	1	131072	32768	Custom
Thunderbird	SNL	Dell	6	9024	27072	Infiniband
Red Storm	SNL	Cray	9	10880	32640	Custom
Spirit (ICC2)	SNL	HP	202	1028	1024	GigEthernet
Liberty	SNL	HP	445	512	944	Myrinet

Table 1. System characteristics at the time of collection. External system names are indicated in parentheses. Some information was obtained from the Top500 Supercomputer list [2]. The machines are representative of the design choices and scales seen in current supercomputers.

System	Start Date	Days	Size (GB)	Compressed	Rate (bytes/sec)	Messages	Alerts	Categories
Blue Gene/L	2005-06-03	215	1.207	0.118	64.976	4,747,963	348,460	41
Thunderbird	2005-11-09	244	27.367	5.721	1298.146	211,212,192	3,248,239	10
Red Storm	2006-03-19	104	29.990	1.215	3337.562	219,096,168	1,665,744	12
Spirit (ICC2)	2005-01-01	558	30.289	1.678	628.257	272,298,969	172,816,564	8
Liberty	2004-12-12	315	22.820	0.622	835.824	265,569,231	2,452	6

Table 2. Log characteristics. More alerts does not imply a less reliable system - it also reflects the redundancy of the reporting and the preferences of the system administrators. Alerts were tagged into categories according to the heuristics supplied by the administrators for the respective systems, as described in Section 3.2. Two alerts are in the same category if they were tagged by the same expert rule; the categories column indicates the number of categories that were actually observed in each log. Compression was done using the Unix utility `gzip`.

Red Storm has several logging paths [1]. Disk and RAID controller messages in the DDN subsystem pass through a 100 Megabit network to a DDN-specific RAS machine, where they are processed by `syslog-ng` and stored. Similarly, all Linux nodes (login, Lustre I/O, and management nodes) transmit syslog messages to a different `syslog-ng` collector node for storage. All other components (compute nodes, SeaStar NICs, and hierarchical management nodes) generate messages and events which are transmitted through the RAS network (using the reliable TCP protocol) to the System Management Workstation (SMW) for automated response and storage. Our study includes all of these logs.

On BG/L, logging is managed by the Machine Management Control System (MMCS), which runs on the service node, of which there are two per rack [3]. Compute chips store errors locally until they are polled, at which point the messages are collected via the JTAG-mailbox protocol. The polling frequency for our logs was set at around one millisecond. The service node MMCS process then relays the messages to a centralized DB2 database. That RAS database was the source of our data, and includes hardware and software errors at all levels, from chip SRAM parity errors to fan failures. Events in BG/L often set various RAS flags, which appear as separate lines in the log. The time granularity for BG/L logs is down to the microsecond, unlike the one-second granularity of typical syslogs. This study does not include syslogs from BG/L's Lustre I/O cluster and shared disk subsystem.

Type	Raw		Filtered	
	Count	%	Count	%
Hardware	174,586,516	98.04	1,999	18.78
Software	144,899	0.08	6,814	64.01
Indeterminate	3,350,044	1.88	1,832	17.21

Table 3. Hardware was the most common type of alert, but not the most common type of failure (as estimated by the filtered results). Filtering dramatically changes the distribution of alert types.

3.2 Identifying Alerts

For each of the systems, we worked in consultation with the respective system administrators to determine the subset of log entries that they would *tag* as being alerts. Thus, the alerts we identify in the logs are certainly alerts by our definition, but the set is (necessarily) not exhaustive. In all, we identified 178,081,459 alerts across the logs; see Table 2 for the breakdown by system and Table 4 for the alerts, themselves. Alerts were assigned *types* based on their ostensible subsystem of origin (hardware, software, or indeterminate); this is based on each administrator's best understanding of the alert, and may not necessarily be root cause. Table 3 presents the distribution of types both before and after filtering (described in Section 3.3).

Note that many of these alerts were multiply reported by one or more nodes (sometimes millions of times), requiring filtering of the kind discussed in Section 3.3. Furthermore, it means that the number of alerts we report does not neces-

Alert Type/Cat.	Raw	Filtered	Example Message Body (Anonymized)
BG/L	**348,460**	**1202**	
H / KERNDTLB	152,734	37	`data TLB error interrupt`
H / KERNSTOR	63,491	8	`data storage interrupt`
S / APPSEV	49,651	138	`ciod:  Error reading message prefix after LOGIN_MESSAGE on CioStream [...]`
S / KERNMNTF	31,531	105	`Lustre mount FAILED : bglio11 :  block_id :  location`
S / KERNTERM	23,338	99	`rts:  kernel terminated for reason 1004rts:  bad message header:  [...]`
S / KERNREC	6145	9	`Error receiving packet on tree network, expecting type 57 instead of [...]`
S / APPREAD	5983	11	`ciod:  failed to read message prefix on control stream [...]`
S / KERNRTSP	3983	260	`rts panic! - stopping execution`
S / APPRES	2370	13	`ciod:  Error reading message prefix after LOAD_MESSAGE on CioStream [...]`
I / APPUNAV	2048	3	`ciod:  Error creating node map from file [...]`
I / 31 Others	7186	519	`machine check interrupt`
Thunderbird	**3,248,239**	**2088**	
I / VAPI	3,229,194	276	`kernel:  [KERNEL_IB][...] (Fatal error (Local Catastrophic Error))`
S / PBS_CON	5318	16	`pbs_mom:  Connection refused (111) in open_demux, open_demux:  cannot [...]`
I / MPT	4583	157	`kernel:  mptscsih:  ioc0:  attempting task abort!  (sc=00000101bddee480)`
H / EXT_FS	4022	778	`kernel:  EXT3-fs error (device sda5):  [...] Detected aborted journal`
S / CPU	2741	367	`kernel:  Losing some ticks...  checking if CPU frequency changed.`
H / SCSI	2186	317	`kernel:  scsi0 (0:0):  rejecting I/O to offline device`
H / ECC	146	143	`Server Administrator:  Instrumentation Service EventID: 1404 Memory device [...]`
S / PBS_BFD	28	28	`pbs_mom:  Bad file descriptor (9) in tm_request, job [job] not running`
H / CHK_DSK	13	2	`check-disks: [node:time] , Fault Status assert [...]`
I / NMI	8	4	`kernel:  Uhhuh.  NMI received.  Dazed and confused, but trying to continue`
Red Storm	**1,665,744**	**1430**	
H / BUS_PAR	1,550,217	5	`DMT_HINT Warning:  Verify Host 2 bus parity error:  0200 Tier:5 LUN:4 [...]`
I / HBEAT	94,784	266	`ec_heartbeat_stop|src:::[node] |svc:::[node]warn|node heartbeat fault|[...]`
I / PTL_EXP	11,047	421	`kernel:  LustreError:  [...] @@@ timeout (sent at [time], 300s ago) [...]`
H / ADDR_ERR	6763	1	`DMT_102 Address error LUN:0 command:28 address:f000000 length:1 Anonymous [...]`
H / CMD_ABORT	1686	497	`DMT_310 Command Aborted:  SCSI cmd:2A LUN 2 DMT_310 Lane:3 T:299 a:  [...]`
I / PTL_ERR	631	54	`kernel:  LustreError:  [...] @@@ type == [...]`
I / TOAST	186	9	`ec_console_log|src:::[node]|svc:::[node]|PANIC_SP WE ARE TOASTED!`
I / EW	163	58	`kernel:  Lustre:[...] Expired watchdog for pid[job] disabled after [#]s`
I / WT	107	45	`kernel:  Lustre:[...] Watchdog triggered for pid[job]:  it was inactive for [#]ms`
I / RBB	105	19	`kernel:  LustreError:  [...] All mds cray_kern_nal request buffers busy (0us idle)`
H / DSK_FAIL	54	54	`DMT_DINT Failing Disk 2A`
I / OST	1	1	`kernel:  LustreError:  [...] Failure to commit OST transaction (-5)?`
Spirit	**172,816,564**	**4875**	
H / EXT_CCISS	103,818,910	29	`kernel:  cciss:  cmd 0000010000a60000 has CHECK CONDITION, sense key = 0x3`
H / EXT_FS	68,986,084	14	`kernel:  EXT3-fs error (device[device]) in ext3_reserve_inode_write:  IO failure`
S / PBS_CHK	8388	4119	`pbs_mom:  task_check, cannot tm_reply to [job] task 1`
S / GM_LANAI	1256	117	`kernel:  GM: LANai is not running.  Allowing port=0 open for debugging`
S / PBS_CON	817	25	`pbs_mom:  Connection refused (111) in open_demux, open_demux:  connect [IP:port]`
S / GM_MAP	596	180	`gm_mapper[[#]]:  assertion failed. [path]/lx_mapper.c:2112 (m->root)`
S / PBS_BFD	346	296	`pbs_mom:  Bad file descriptor (9) in tm_request, job [job] not running`
H / GM_PAR	166	95	`kernel:  GM: The NIC ISR is reporting an SRAM parity error.`
Liberty	**2452**	**1050**	
S / PBS_CHK	2231	920	`pbs_mom:  task_check, cannot tm_reply to [job] task 1`
S / PBS_BFD	115	94	`pbs_mom:  Bad file descriptor (9) in tm_request, job [job] not running`
S / PBS_CON	47	5	`pbs_mom:  Connection refused (111) in open_demux, open_demux:  connect [IP:port]`
H / GM_PAR	44	19	`kernel:  GM: LANAI[0]:  PANIC: [path]/gm_parity.c:115:parity_int():firmware`
S / GM_LANAI	13	10	`kernel:  GM: LANai is not running.  Allowing port=0 open for debugging`
S / GM_MAP	2	2	`gm_mapper[736]:  assertion failed. [path]/mi.c:541 (r == GM_SUCCESS)`

Table 4. Example alert messages from the supercomputers. System names are listed with the total number alerts before and after filtering. "Cat." is the alert category. Types are H (Hardware), S (Software), and I (Indeterminate). Indeterminate alerts can originate from both hardware and software, or have unknown cause. Due to space, we list only the most common of the 41 BG/L alert categories. Bracketed text indicates information that is omitted; a bracketed ellipsis indicates sundry text. Alert categories vary among machines as a function of system configurations, logging mechanisms, and what each system's administrators deem important.

Severity	Messages		Alerts	
	Count	%	Count	%
FATAL	855,501	18.02	348,398	99.98
FAILURE	1714	0.03	62	0.02
SEVERE	19,213	0.41	0	0
ERROR	112,355	2.37	0	0
WARNING	23,357	0.49	0	0
INFO	3,735,823	78.68	0	0

Table 5. The distribution of severity fields for BG/L among all messages and among our expert-tagged alerts. Tagging all FATAL/FAILURE severity messages as alerts would have yielded a 59% false positive rate.

Severity	Messages		Alerts	
	Count	%	Count	%
EMERG	3	0.00	0	0
ALERT	654	0.00	45	0.00
CRIT	1,552,910	6.09	1,550,217	98.69
ERR	2,027,598	7.95	11,784	0.75
WARNING	2,154,944	8.45	270	0.02
NOTICE	3,759,620	14.74	0	0
INFO	15,722,695	61.63	8,450	0.54
DEBUG	291,764	1.14	0	0

Table 6. The distribution of severity fields for Red Storm syslogs among all messages and among our expert-tagged alerts. These syslog alerts were dominated by disk failure messages with CRIT severity. Except for this failure case, these data suggest that syslog severity is not a reliable failure indicator.

sarily relate to the reliability of the systems in any meaningful way. The heuristics provided by the administrators were often in the form of regular expressions amenable for consumption by the `logsurfer` utility [18]. We performed the tagging through a combination of regular expression matching and manual intervention. The administrators with whom we consulted were responsible for their respective systems throughout the period of log collection and the publication of this work. Examples of alert-identifying rules using `awk` syntax include (from Spirit, Red Storm, and BG/L, respectively) include the following:

```
/kernel: EXT3-fs error/
/PANIC_SP WE ARE TOASTED!/
($5 ~ /KERNEL/ && /kernel panic/)
```

Previous work on BG/L log analysis used simple alert identification schemes such as the *severity* field of messages [9, 10, 20] or an external source of information [21, 25]. Because our objective was not to suggest an alert detection scheme, but rather to accurately characterize the content of the logs, we instead used the time-consuming manual process described above. We discovered, furthermore, that administrators for these machines do not use the severity field

as the singular way to detect alerts, and that many systems (Thunderbird, Spirit, and Liberty) did not even record this information.

Table 5 shows the distribution of severity fields among messages and among unfiltered alerts. If we had used the severity field instead of the expert rules to tag alerts on BG/L, tagging any message with a severity of FATAL or FAILURE as an alert, we would have a false negative rate of 0% but a false positive rate of 59.34%. Of the Sandia systems, only Red Storm is configured to store the severity of syslog messages (the Red Storm TCP log path is not syslog and has no severity analog). Table 6 gives the severity distribution, which suggests that syslog severity is of dubious value as a failure indicator. The use of message severity levels as a criterion for identifying failures be done only with considerable caution.

3.2.1 Alert Identification Challenges

Automatically identifying alerts in system logs is an open problem. To facilitate others in tackling this challenge, we offer the following account of issues we observed while manually tagging the logs that must be addressed by an automated scheme:

Insufficient Context. Many log messages are ambiguous without external context. The most salient piece of missing information was what we call *operational context*, which helps to account for the human and other external factors that influence the semantics of log messages. For example, consider the following ambiguous example message from BG/L (anonymized):

```
YY-MM-DD-HH:MM:SS NULL RAS BGLMASTER FAILURE
    ciodb exited normally with exit code 0
```

This message has a very high severity (FAILURE), but the message body suggests that the program exited cleanly. If the system administrator was doing maintenance on the machine at the time, this message is a harmless artifact of his actions. On the other hand, if it was generated during normal machine operation, this message indicates that all running jobs on the supercomputer were (undesirably) killed. The disparity between these two interpretations is tremendous. Only with additional information supplied by the system administrator could we conclude that this message was likely innocuous. In our experience, operational context is one of the most vital, but often absent, factors in deciphering system logs.

As seen in Figure 1, operational context may indicate whether a system is in engineering or production time. Sandia, Los Alamos, and Livermore National Laboratories are currently working together to define exactly what information is needed, and how to use it to quantify RAS performance [24]. It may be sufficient to record only a few bytes

579

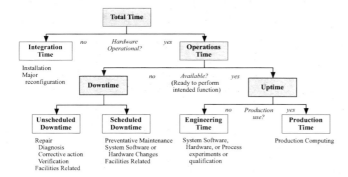

Figure 1. Operational context example. Event significance can be disambiguated if the expected state of components is known. This diagram is the current basis of Red Storm RAS metrics, and is being developed by LANL, LLNL, and SNL towards establishing standardized RAS performance metrics.

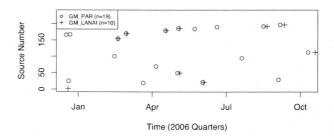

Figure 3. Two related classes of alerts from Liberty. Notice that GM_LANAI messages do not always follow GM_PAR messages, nor vice versa. However, the correlation is clear. Current tagging and filtering techniques do not adequately address this situation.

of data: the time and cause of system state changes. For example, the commencement of an OS upgrade would be accompanied by a message indicating that at time t the system entered *scheduled downtime* for a system software installation. A similar message would accompany the system's return to *production time*.

The lack of context has also affected the study of parallel workloads. Feitelson proposed removing non-production jobs from workload traces (such as workload flurries attributable to system testing [5]). Analogously, some alerts may be ignored during a scheduled downtime that would be significant during production time.

Asymmetric Reporting. Some failures leave no evidence in the logs, and the logs are fraught with messages that indicate nothing useful at all. More insidiously, even single failure types may produce varying alert signatures in the log. For example, the Red Storm DDN system generates a great variety of alert patterns that all mean "disk failure". Nodes also generate differing logs according to their function. Figure 2(b) shows the number of messages broken down by source. The chatty sources tended to be the administrative nodes or those with persistent problems, while the reticent sources were either misconfigured or improperly attributed (the result of corrupted messages).

System Evolution. Log analysis is a moving target. Over the course of a system's lifetime, anything from software upgrades to minor configuration changes can drastically alter the meaning or character of the logs. Figure 2(a) shows dramatic shifts in behavior over time. This makes machine learning difficult: learned patterns and behaviors may not be

applicable for very long. The ability to detect phase shifts in behavior would be a valuable tool for triggering relearning or for knowing which existing behavioral model to apply.

Implicit Correlation. Groups of messages are sometimes fundamentally related, but there is no explicit indication of this. See Figures 3 and 4. A common such correlation results from cascading failures.

Inconsistent Structure. Despite the noble efforts of the BSD syslog standard and others, log messages vary greatly both within and across systems. BG/L and Red Storm use custom databases and formats, and commodity syslog-based systems do not even record fields such as *severity* by default. Ultimately, understanding the entries may require parsing the unstructured message bodies, thereby reducing the problem to natural language processing on the shorthand of multiple programmers (consider Table 4). Log anonymization is also troublesome, because sensitive information like usernames is not relegated to distinct fields [6]. Our log data are not available for public study primarily because we cannot remove all sensitive information with sufficient confidence. We are working to overcome this challenge and to release the logs.

Corruption. Even on supercomputers with highly engineered RAS systems, like BG/L and Red Storm, log entries can be corrupted. We saw messages truncated, partially overwritten, and incorrectly timestamped. For example, we found many corrupted variants of the following message on Thunderbird (only the message bodies are shown):

```
kernel: VIPKL(1): [create_mr] MM_bld_hh_mr
    failed (-253:VAPI_EAGAIN)
```

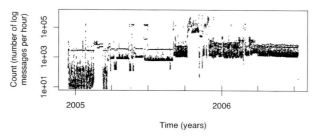

(a) The number of messages, bucketed by hour. We are told that the first major shift (end of first quarter, 2005) corresponded to an upgrade in the operating system after the machine was put into production use. The causes of the other shifts are not well understood at this time.

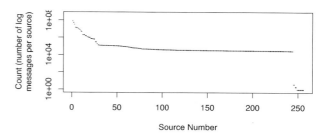

(b) The number of messages by message source, sorted by decreasing quantity. The most prolific sources were administrative nodes or those with significant problems. The cluster at the bottom is from the set of messages whose source field was corrupted, thwarting attribution.

Figure 2. The number of messages generated by Liberty.

Some corrupted versions of that line include:

```
kernel:  VIPKL(1): [create_mr] MM_bld_hh_mr
    failed (-253:VAPI_EAure = no
kernel:  VIPKL(1): [create_mr] MM_bld_hh_mr
    failed (-253:VAPI_EAGAI
kernel:  VIPKL(1): [create_mr] MM_bld_hh_mr
    failed (-253:VAPI_EAGsys/mosal_iobuf.c
    [126]: dump iobuf at 0000010188ee7880 :
```

3.3 Filtering

A single failure may generate alerts across many nodes or many alerts on a single node. Filtering is used to reduce a related set of alerts to a single initial alert per failure; that is, to make the ratio of alerts to failures nearly one. This section motivates the need for effective filtering and then describes our algorithm, which is based on previous work [9, 10] with some incremental optimizations. Briefly, the filtering removes an alert if any source had generated that category of alert within the last T seconds, for a given threshold T. Two alerts are in the same category if they were both tagged by the same expert rule.

3.3.1 Motivation for Filtering

During the first quarter of 2006, Liberty saw 2231 job-fatal alerts that were caused by a troublesome software bug in the Portable Batch System (PBS). The alerts, which read `pbs_mom:  task_check, cannot tm_reply`, indicated that the MPI rank 0 mom died. Jobs afflicted by this bug could not complete and were eventually killed, but not before generating the `task_check` message up to 74 times. We estimate that this bug killed as many as 1336 jobs before it was tracked down and fixed (see Figure 4).

Between November 10, 2005 and July 10, 2006, Thunderbird experienced 3,229,194 so-called "Local Catastrophic Errors" related to VAPI (the exact nature of many of these alerts is not well-understood by our experts). A

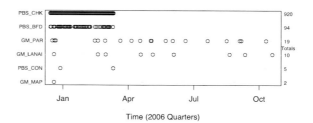

Figure 4. Categorized filtered alerts on Liberty over time. The horizontal clusters of PBS_CHK and PBS_BFD messages are not evidence of poor filtering; they are actually instances of individual failures. Specifically, they are the manifestation of the PBS bug described in Section 3.3.1. These two tags are a particularly outstanding example of correlated alerts relegated to different categories.

single node was responsible for 643,925 of them, of which filtering removes all but 246.

The Spirit logs were largest, despite the system being the second smallest. This was due almost entirely to disk-related alert messages which were repeated millions of times. For example, over a six-day period between February 28 and March 5, there was a disk problem that triggered a total of 56,793,797 alerts. These were heavily concentrated among a handful of problematic nodes. Over the complete observation period, node id sn373 logged 89,632,571 such messages, which was more than half of all Spirit alerts.

3.3.2 Filtering Algorithm

A temporal filter coalesces alerts within T seconds of each other on a given source into a single alert. For example, if a node reports a particular alert every T seconds for a week, the temporal filter keeps only the first. Similarly, a spatial filter removes an alert if some other source had previously reported that alert within T seconds. For example, if k nodes report the same alert in a round-robin fashion, each message within T seconds of the last, then only the first is kept. Previous work applied these filters serially [9, 10].

Our filtering algorithm, however, performs both temporal and spatial filtering simultaneously; an alert message generated by source s is considered redundant (and removed) if *any source*, including s, had reported that alert category within T seconds. This change reduces computational costs (16% faster on the Spirit logs), and increases conceptual simplicity. We applied this filter to the logs from the five supercomputers using $T = 5$ seconds in correspondence with previous work [4, 9, 10]. The algorithm in pseudocode is given below, where A is the sequence of N unfiltered alerts. Alert a_i happens at time t_i and has category c_i. The sequence is sorted by increasing time. The table X is used to store the last time at which a particular category of alert was reported.

Algorithm 3.1: LOGFILTER(A)

$$l \leftarrow 0$$
$$\textbf{for } i \leftarrow 1 \textbf{ to } N$$
$$\textbf{do} \begin{cases} \textbf{if } t_i - l > T \\ \quad \textbf{then } \text{clear}(X) \\ \quad l \leftarrow t_i \\ \textbf{if } c_i \in X \textbf{ and } t_i - X[c_i] < T \\ \quad \textbf{then } X[c_i] \leftarrow t_i \\ \quad \textbf{else } \begin{cases} X[c_i] \leftarrow t_i \\ \textbf{output } (a_i) \end{cases} \end{cases}$$

This filter may remove independent alerts of the same category that, by coincidence, happen near the same time on different nodes. For example, node sn373 on Spirit experienced disk problems and output tens of millions of alerts over the course of several days. Coincidentally, another node (sn325) had an independent disk failure during this time. Our filter removed the symptomatic alert, erroneously.

In some cases, serial filtering fails to remove alerts that share a root cause, and which a human would consider to be redundant. The problem arises when the temporal filter removes messages that the spatial filter would have used as cues that the failure had already been reported by another source. Alerts removed by our filter that would be left by serial filters tend to indicate failures in shared resources that were previously noticed by another node. The most common such errors in Liberty, Spirit, and Thunderbird were related to the PBS system.

At most one true positive was removed on any single machine, whereas sometimes dozens of false positives were removed by using our filter instead of the serial algorithm. Limiting false positives to an operationally-acceptable rate tends to be the critical factor in fault and intrusion detection systems, so we consider this trade-off to be justified.

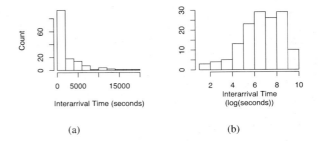

Figure 5. Critical ECC memory alerts on Thunderbird. These data are filtered, but that had little effect on the distribution. Both (a) and (b) are the same data, viewed in different ways. We conclude that these low-level failures are basically independent.

4 Analysis

Modeling the timing of failure events is a common endeavor in systems research; these models are then used to study the effects of failures on other aspects of the system, such as job scheduling or checkpointing performance. Frequently, for mathematical convenience and reference to basic physical phenomena, failures are modeled as occurring independently (exponential interarrival times). For low-level failures triggered by such physical phenomena, these models are appropriate; we found that ECC failures (memory errors that were critical, rather than single bit errors) behaved as expected. Figure 5 shows these filtered alert distributions on Thunderbird, where the distribution appears exponential and is roughly log normal with a heavy left tail.

For most other kinds of failures, however, this independence is not an appropriate assumption. Failure prediction based on time *interdependence* of events has been the subject of much research [9, 11, 13, 19], and it has been shown that such prediction can be a potent resource for improving job scheduling [17], QoS [16], and checkpointing [14, 15].

We expected CPU clocking alerts, for instance, to be similar to ECC alerts: driven by a basic physical process. We were surprised to observe clear spatial correlations, and discovered that a bug in the Linux SMP kernel sped up the system clock under heavy network load. Thus, whenever a set of nodes was running a communication-intensive job, they would collectively be more prone to encountering this bug. We investigated this message only after noticing that its occurrence was spatially correlated across nodes.

Through our attempts to model failure distributions, we are convinced that supercomputer failure types are diverse in their properties. Some clearly appear to be lognormal (Figure 5(a)), most clearly do not (Figures 6(a) and 5(b)). In even the best visual fit cases, heavy tails result in very poor statistical goodness-of-fit metrics. While the tempta-

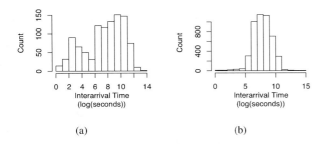

(a)   (b)

Figure 6. The log distribution of interarrival times after filtering suggests correlated alerts on BG/L (a) and largely independent categories on Spirit (b). This illustrates two weaknesses in current filtering algorithms: (1) message tags must represent independent sets of alerts to avoid timing correlations and (2) a single filtering threshold is not appropriate for all kinds of messages.

tion to select and publish best-fit models and parameters is strong, the most important observation we can make is that such modeling of this data is misguided. The mechanisms and interdependencies of failures must be better understood before statistical models of their distributions will be of significant use. The merit of a model is dependent on the context in which it is applied; one size does not fit all.

Moreover, whereas the failures in this study have widely varying signatures, previous prediction approaches focused on single features for detecting all failure types (e.g. severity levels or message bursts). Future research should consider ensembles of predictors based on multiple features, with failure categories being predicted according to their respective behavior.

Current filtering algorithms, including ours, suffer from two significant weaknesses. First, they require a mechanism for determining whether two alerts from different sources at different times are "the same" in some meaningful way. We are not aware of any method that is able to confidently state whether two messages that are labeled as different are actually correlated with one another. The second major weakness is that a filtering threshold must be selected in advance and is then applied across all kinds of alerts. In reality, each alert category may require a different threshold, which may change over time. The bimodal distribution visible in Figure 6(a) is believed to be a consequence of these shortcomings. One of the modes (the first peak) is attributed to unfiltered redundancy. Figure 3 shows an example of inter-tag correlation. On Spirit, the problems enumerated above were not as prevalent after filtering, and the result was the unimodal distribution in Figure 6(b).

5 Recommendations

In order to accurately detect, attribute, quantify, and predict failures in supercomputers, we must understand the behavior of systems, including the logs they produce. This paper presents the results of the broadest system log study to date (nearly one billion messages from five production supercomputers). We consider logs from the BG/L, Thunderbird, Red Storm, Spirit, and Liberty supercomputers (Section 3), and we identify 178,081,459 alert messages in 77 categories (Table 4). In conclusion, we describe how people want to use supercomputer logs, what obstacles they face, and our recommendations for overcoming those challenges.

Detect Faults We want to identify failures quickly. Most failures are evidenced in logs by a signature (presence or absence of certain messages), while others leave no sign. We believe such silent failures are rare. Accurate detection and disambiguation requires external information like operational context (Figure 1). We suggest logging transitions among operational states (Section 3.2.1).

Attribute Root Causes We want to respond to failures effectively, which requires knowing what failed and why. Logging mechanisms themselves may fail, resulting in corrupted or missing messages. Redundant and asymmetric alert reporting necessitates filtering (Section 3.3); we advise that future work investigate filters that are aware of correlations among messages and characteristics of different failure classes, rather than a catch-all threshold (Section 4).

Quantify RAS We want to model and improve RAS metrics. Despite the temptation to calculate values like MTTF from the system logs, doing so can be inaccurate and misleading. The content of the logs is a strong function of the specific system and logging configuration; using logs to compare machines is absurd. Even on a single system, the logs change over time, making them an unreliable measure of progress. We recommend calculating RAS metrics based on quantities of direct interest, such as the amount of useful work lost due to failures.

Predict Failures We want to predict failures in order to minimize their impact. The mapping from failures to message signatures is many-to-many. Prediction efforts must account for significant shifts in system behavior (Section 3.2.1). Just as filtering would benefit from catering to specific classes of failures, predictors should specialize in sets of failures with similar predictive behaviors (Section 4).

System logs are a rich, ubiquitous resource worth exploiting. They present many analysis challenges, however, and should not be taken lightly. Pursuing the recommendations in this paper will lead us closer to our ultimate goal: reliable computing for production users.

6 Acknowledgments

The authors would like to thank the following people for their time, expertise, and data: Sue Kelly, Bob Ballance, Ruth Klundt, Dick Dimock, Michael Davis, Jason Repik, Victor Kuhns, Matt Bohnsack, Jerry Smith, and Josh England of Sandia National Labs; Kim Cupps, Adam Bertsch, and Mike Miller of Livermore National Labs; and Ramendra Sahoo of IBM. We would also like to thank our paper shepherd, Ravishankar Iyer, for his guidance.

References

[1] Cray red storm architecture documents. http://www.cray.com/products/xt3/index.html, 2006.

[2] Top500 supercomputing sites. http://www.top500.org/, June 2006.

[3] N. R. Adiga and The BlueGene/L Team. An overview of the bluegene/l supercomputer. In *Proceedings of ACM Supercomputing*, 2002.

[4] M. F. Buckley and D. P. Siewiorek. A comparative analysis of event tupling schemes. In *FTCS-26, Intl. Symp. on Fault Tolerant Computing*, pages 294–303, June 1996.

[5] D. G. Feitelson and D. Tsafrir. Workload sanitation for performance evaluation. In *IEEE Intl. Symp. Performance Analysis Syst. & Software (ISPASS)*, pages 221–230, Mar 2006.

[6] U. Flegel. Pseudonymizing unix log files. In *Proceedings of the Infrastructure Security Conference (InfraSec)*, 2002.

[7] J. L. Hellerstein, S. Ma, and C. Perng. Discovering actionable patterns in event data. *IBM Systems Journal*, 41(3), 2002.

[8] I. Lee and R. K. Iyer. Faults, symptoms, and software fault tolerance in the tandem guardian90 operating system. In *Fault-Tolerant Computing. FTCS-23. Digest of Papers., The Twenty-Third International Symposium on*, pages 20–29, 1993.

[9] Y. Liang, Y. Zhang, M. Jette, A. Sivasubramaniam, and R. K. Sahoo. Blue gene/l failure analysis and prediction models. In *Proceedings of the Intl. Conf. on Dependable Systems and Networks (DSN)*, pages 425–434, 2006.

[10] Y. Liang, Y. Zhang, A. Sivasubramaniam, R. K. Sahoo, J. Moreira, and M. Gupta. Filtering failure logs for a bluegene/l prototype. In *Proceedings of the Intl. Conf. on Dependable Systems and Networks (DSN)*, pages 476–485, June 2005.

[11] T. T. Y. Lin and D. P. Siewiorek. Error log analysis: statistical modeling and heuristic trend analysis. *Reliability, IEEE Transactions on*, 39(4):419–432, 1990.

[12] S. Ma and J. Hellerstein. Mining partially periodic event patterns with unknown periods. In *Proceedings of the International Conference on Data Engineering (ICDE)*, pages 409–416, 2001.

[13] F. A. Nassar and D. M. Andrews. A methodology for analysis of failure prediction data. In *Real-Time Systems Symposium*, pages 160–166, December 1985.

[14] A. Oliner, L. Rudolph, and R. Sahoo. Cooperative checkpointing theory. In *Proceedings of the 20th Intl. Parallel and Distributed Processing Symposium (IPDPS)*, 2006.

[15] A. Oliner, L. Rudolph, and R. K. Sahoo. Cooperative checkpointing: A robust approach to large-scale systems reliability. In *Proceedings of the 20th Intl. Conf. on Supercomputing (ICS)*, Cairns, Australia, June 2006.

[16] A. J. Oliner, L. Rudolph, R. K. Sahoo, J. E. Moreira, and M. Gupta. Probabilistic qos guarantees for supercomputing systems. In *Proceedings of the Intl. Conf. on Dependable Systems and Networks (DSN)*, pages 634–643, 2005.

[17] A. J. Oliner, R. K. Sahoo, J. E. Moreira, M. Gupta, and A. Sivasubramaniam. Fault-aware job scheduling for bluegene/l systems. In *Proceedings of the 18th Intl. Parallel and Distributed Processing Symposium (IPDPS)*, pages 64+, 2004.

[18] J. Prewett. Analyzing cluster log files using logsurfer. In *Proceedings of the 4th Annual Conference on Linux Clusters*, 2003.

[19] R. K. Sahoo, A. J. Oliner, I. Rish, M. Gupta, J. E. Moreira, S. Ma, R. Vilalta, and A. Sivasubramaniam. Critical event prediction for proactive management in large-scale computer clusters. In *Proceedings of the 9th ACM SIGKDD, International Conference on Knowledge Discovery and Data Mining*, pages 426–435. ACM Press, 2003.

[20] R. K. Sahoo, A. Sivasubramaniam, M. S. Squillante, and Y. Zhang. Failure data analysis of a large-scale heterogeneous server environment. In *Proceedings of the Intl. Conf. on Dependable Systems and Networks (DSN)*, pages 772–781, June 2004.

[21] B. Schroeder and G. Gibson. A large-scale study of failures in high-performance-computing systems. In *Proceedings of the Intl. Conf. on Dependable Systems and Networks (DSN)*, Philadelphia, PA, June 2006.

[22] B. Schroeder and G. Gibson. Disk failures in the real world: What does an mttf of 1,000,000 hours mean to you? In *5th Usenix Conference on File and Storage Technologies (FAST 2007)*, 2007.

[23] J. Stearley. Towards informatic analysis of syslogs. In *IEEE International Conference on Cluster Computing*, pages 309–318, 2004.

[24] J. Stearley. Defining and measuring supercomputer Reliability, Availability, and Serviceability (RAS). In *Proceedings of the Linux Clusters Institute Conference*, 2005. See http://www.cs.sandia.gov/˜jrstear/ras.

[25] D. Tang and R. K. Iyer. Analysis and modeling of correlated failures in multicomputer systems. *Computers, IEEE Transactions on*, 41(5):567–577, 1992.

[26] M. M. Tsao. *Trend Analysis and Fault Prediction*. PhD dissertation, Carnegie-Mellon University, May 1983.

[27] R. Vaarandi. A breadth-first algorithm for mining frequent patterns from event logs. In *Proceedings of the 2004 IFIP International Conference on Intelligence in Communication Systems*, volume 3283, pages 293–308, 2004.

[28] K. Yamanishi and Y. Maruyama. Dynamic syslog mining for network failure monitoring. In *Proceedings of the 11th ACM SIGKDD, International Conference on Knowledge Discovery and Data Mining*, pages 499–508, New York, NY, USA, 2005. ACM Press.

How do Mobile Phones Fail?
A Failure Data Analysis of Symbian OS Smart Phones

Marcello Cinque, Domenico Cotroneo

Dipartimento di Informatica e Sistemistica
Università degli Studi di Napoli Federico II
Via Claudio 21, 80125 - Naples, Italy
{*macinque, cotroneo*}@*unina.it*

Zbigniew Kalbarczyk, Ravishankar K. Iyer

Center for Reliable and High Performance Computing
University of Illinois at Urbana-Champaign
1308 W. Main St., Urbana, IL 61801
{*kalbar, iyer*}@*crhc.uiuc.edu*

Abstract

While the new generation of hand-held devices, e.g., smart phones, support a rich set of applications, growing complexity of the hardware and runtime environment makes the devices susceptible to accidental errors and malicious attacks. Despite these concerns, very few studies have looked into the dependability of mobile phones. This paper presents measurement-based failure characterization of mobile phones. The analysis starts with a high level failure characterization of mobile phones based on data from publicly available web forums, where users post information on their experiences in using hand-held devices. This initial analysis is then used to guide the development of a failure data logger for collecting failure-related information on SymbianOS-based smart phones. Failure data is collected from 25 phones (in Italy and USA) over the period of 14 months. Key findings indicate that: (i) the majority of kernel exceptions are due to memory access violation errors (56%) and heap management problems (18%), and (ii) on average users experience a failure (freeze or self shutdown) every 11 days. While the study provide valuable insight into the failure sensitivity of smart-phones, more data and further analysis are needed before generalizing the results.

1 Introduction

New generation of mobile and embedded devices, such as smart phones and PDAs (personal digital assistants) support a rich set of applications, e.g., web browsing and entertainment software. What's more, the time-to-market pressure forces manufacturers to deliver products with new features within very short time windows (e.g., six months) often sacrificing the testing efforts. As a result, we witness an increasing susceptibility of hand-held devices to acciden-

tal errors and malicious attacks. An example is the recently reported first mobile phone virus, Cabir, affecting Symbian-OS-based smart phones.

Reliability becomes even more critical as new critical applications emerge for mobile phones, e.g., robot control [15, 10], traffic control [2] and telemedicine [4]. In such scenarios, a phone failure affecting the application could result in a significant loss or hazard, e.g., a robot performing uncontrolled actions.

Despite these concerns, very few studies have looked into the dependability of mobile phones. As a result, there is little understanding of how and why mobile phones fail.

This paper presents measurement-based failure analysis of mobile phones. The analysis starts with a high level failure characterization of mobile phones based on everyday user's experiences. Data for this study spans the four year period (between 2003 and 2006) and is obtained from publicly available web forums, where users post information on their experiences in using hand-held devices. The information collected in these forums is not well structured, and a relatively small number of entries can be considered as failure reports. However, collected data enables: (i) identification of the high level failure manifestation, (ii) categorization of the user-initiated recovery from the device failure, and (iii) characterization of the failure severity.

This initial analysis is then used to guide the development of a failure data logger for smart phones, initially introduced in [1]. The logger employs heartbeat mechanism to detect system/application failures. Upon failure detection, the logger records information about the phone activities, the list of running applications, and error conditions signaled by the system/application modules. The logger has been deployed on 25 Symbian-based smart phones in Italy and in the US since September 2005. The Symbian OS was chosen because of: (i) its open programmability features supporting C++ and Java programming languages and (ii) its relatively wide-spread use at the time of this analysis. The analysis of the collected failure data shows: (i) Majority of kernel exceptions (56%) are due to memory access violation errors and heap management problems (18%). This is despite the micro- kernel design model and advanced memory management facilities provided by the Symbian OS. (ii) System panics often occur in bursts - two or more panic events in a short succession, which indicates error propagation between applications (especially between real-time tasks and interactive applications). (iii) Users experience a failure (the phone freeze or self shutdown) every 11 days on average.

2   Background

Evolution of Mobile Phones. Mobile phone evolution can be described according to three waves, each one characterized by a specific class of mobile terminal [8]:

- *Voice-centric mobile phone* (first wave): a hand-held mobile radiotelephone for use in an area divided into small sections (cells) and supporting SMS (Short Message Service).

- *Rich-experience mobile phone* (second wave): a mobile phone with numerous advanced features, typically including the ability to handle data (web-browsing, e-mail, personal information management, images, music) through high-resolution color screens.

- *Smart phone* (third wave): a general-purpose, programmable mobile phone with enhanced processing and storing capabilities. It can be viewed as a combination of a mobile phone and a PDA, and it may have a PDA-like screen and input devices.

Recent mobile phone models on the market feature more computing and storing capabilities, new operating systems, new embedded devices (e.g., cameras, radio), and communication technologies (Bluetooth, IrDA, WAP, GPRS, UMTS). The number of units sold during the third quarter of 2005 (205 millions) doubled with respect to the third quarter of 2001 (97 millions units)[1]. In the same period, the percentage of smart phones sold has sextupled. According to industry, the time from conception to the market deployment of a new phone model is between 4 to 6 months. Clearly, the pressure to deliver a product on-time, frequently results in compromising the device reliability. The hope is that any potential reliability problems can be fixed quickly by deploying new releases of phone firmware, which can be installed on the phone by service phone centers.

---

[1] sources: http://www.itfacts.biz, http://www.theregister.co.uk

Symbian OS. Symbian [8] is a light-weight operating system developed for mobile phones and carried out by several leading mobile phone's manufacturers. The design of Symbian is based on a hard real-time, multithreaded micro-kernel. All system services are provided by *server* applications. Clients access servers using kernel supported message passing mechanisms.

Since mobile phones resources are highly constrained, special care is taken for memory management. Specific programming rules are defined to ensure freeing unused memory and avoid memory leaks even in the case of failures. In particular, the following mechanisms are provided: (i) *clean-up stack*, which is an OS resource for storing references to objects allocated on the heap memory. (ii) *trap-leave* technique, which is similar to the try-catch paradigm defined for C++ and Java languages, where upon an exception raised during the execution of a trap block, the current method "leaves" and the control returns to the caller, which handles the problem. In meantime, the operating system frees memory allocated for all objects stored on the clean-up stack during the execution of the trap block, thus avoiding potential memory leaks. (iii) *two-phase construction paradigm*, which is defined to construct objects with dynamic extensions. The mechanism assures that, when errors occur during the construction of an object, the dynamic extension is freed using the clean-up stack mechanism.

The Symbian OS defines two levels of multitasking: (i) *threads*, which execute at the lower level and are scheduled by a time-sharing, preemptive, priority-based *OS thread scheduler*, (ii) *Active Objects (AOs)*, which execute at the upper level and are scheduled by a non-preemptive, event-driven *active scheduler*. Multiple AOs can run within a thread. Use of active objects enables the light-weight OS design since the AOs eliminate need for synchronization primitives and hence, incur a lower context-switch overhead than threads.

A crucial Symbian aspect, which is of interest to us is *panic events*. A panic event represents a non-recoverable error condition signaled to the kernel by either user or system applications. Information associated with a panic (*panic category* and *panic type*) is delivered to the kernel, which decides on the recovery action, e.g., application termination or system reboot.

3   Related Research

The goal of measurement-based analysis of failure data of computer systems is to classify errors/failures, to characterize their temporal behavior, and to guide development of detection and recovery mechanisms. [17] identifies trends (*shifting error sources, explosive complexity, and global volume*) in computer industry that impact computer system dependability and security. The evolution of three research threads in experimental dependable systems (*error monitoring and failure data analysis, fault injection, and design methodology*) are traced to illustrate how research responds to or anticipates the direction of the computer industry. The authors indicate a need for more research, especially on issues of complexity, security, and reliability of current and new generation computing systems and applications. Towards this, our study proposes a method for experimental measurement-based analysis of failure mechanisms of emerging smart handheld devices.

Number of studies focus on measurement-based dependability analysis of operating systems, e.g., Windows NT [9, 20], Windows 2000 [19], and Linux [7, 18]. Other studies characterize failures of networked systems and more recently, large-scale heterogeneous server environments [11] [14].

In the field of mobile distributed systems, an architecture for gathering and analyzing failure data for the Bluetooth distributed systems is proposed in [6], whereas [12] reports on an experimental study of the drop impact on mobile devices hardware failures. [13] discusses failure data collected from the base stations of the cellular system.

All these studies exploit failure information collected in system event logs, or failure reports provided by specialized maintenance staff. In the case of smart phones devices (analyzed in this paper), logging facilities are limited and not fully exploited. In particular, the Symbian OS provides a server application (*flogger*), which allows logging the application specific information. However, in order to access the data logged by a generic system/application module, it is necessary to create (on the device) a directory with a well-defined, system specific name (e.g., Xdir). The problem is that the names of such directories are not made publicly available to developers. These directories are used by manufacturers during the development/testing. Recently, a tool called D_EXC[2] has been introduced to enable collecting panic events generated on a phone. However, the tool does not relate panic events to failure manifestations, running applications, and phone activities as we do in our study.

4 Smart Phones' High-level Failures Characterization

In order to conduct a high level failure characterization of mobile phones, we use publicly available data found on several web forums [3], where mobile phone users post information on their experience in using hand-held devices. The posted data has a free format and a relatively small number of entries report on device errors/failures. Here are two examples of user reports: *"the phone freezes whenever I try to write a text message, and stays frozen until I take the battery out"* and *"the phone exhibits random wallpaper disappearing and power cycling, due to UI memory leaks"*. Note that the latter report gives details on a potential failure cause. The posted information is filtered (to extract entries related to device failures), classified, and analyzed along several dimension as discussed further in this section.

Failure Types. Following failure categories are identified based on the extracted data. [4].

- *Freeze* (lock-up or a halting failure [3]): The device's output becomes constant, and the device does not respond to the user's input.

- *Self-shutdown* (silent failure [3]): The device shuts down itself, and no service is delivered at the user interface.

- *Unstable behavior* (erratic failure [3]): The device exhibits erratic behavior without any input inserted by the user, e.g. backlight flashing, and self-activation of applications.

- *Output failure* (value failure [5]): The device, in response to an input sequence, delivers an output sequence that deviates from the expected one. Examples include inaccuracy in charge indicator, ring or music volume different from the confgured one, and event reminders going off at wrong times.

- *Input failure* (omission value failure [5]): User inputs have no effect on device behavior, e.g. soft keys do not work.

User-Initiated Recovery. User-initiated actions to recover from a device failure can be classified according to the following categories:

- *Repeat the action*: Repeating the action is sometime sufficient to get the phone working properly, i.e., the problem was transient.

- *Wait an amount of time*: Often it is enough to wait for a certain amount of time (the exact amount is not reported by users) to let the device deliver the expected service.

- *Reboot* (power cycle or reset): The user turns off the device and then turns it on to restore the correct operation (a temporary corrupted state is cleaned up by the reboot).

---

[2]D_EXC is a Symbian project avilable at www.symbian.com/developer/downloads/tools.html

[3]*www.howardforums.com cellphoneforums.net, www.phonescoop.com,* and *www.mobiledia.com*

[4]It is possible that other failure categories, not present in the analyzed logs, exist

- *Remove battery*: Battery removal is mainly performed when the phone freezes. In this case, the phone often does not respond to the power on/off button. Battery removal can clean up a permanent corrupted state (e.g., due to a user's customized settings).

- *Service the phone*: The user has to bring the phone to a service center for assistance. Often, when the failure is firmware-related, the recovery consists of either a master reset (all the settings are reset to the factory settings and the user's content is removed from the memory) or a firmware update, i.e., uploading a new version of the firmware. Hardware problems are fixed by substituting malfunctioning components (e.g., the screen or the keypad) or replacing the entire device with a new one.

If a failure report does not contain any information about the recovery, we classify the recovery as *unreported*.

Failure Severity In introducing failure severity, this study takes the user perspective and defines severity levels corresponding to the difficulty of the recovery action(s).

- *High*: A failure is considered to be highly severe when recovery requires the assistance of service personnel.

- *Medium*: A failure is considered to be of medium severity when the recovery requires *reboot* or *battery removal*.

- *Low*: A failure is considered to be of low severity if the device operation can be reestablished by *repeating the action* or *waiting for an amount of time*.

4.1 Reports analysis

The results discussed in this section are obtained from the analysis of failure reports posted between January 2003 and March 2006. A total of 533 reports are used in this study. Phone models from all major vendors are present: Motorola, Nokia, Samsung, Sony-Ericcson, LG, besides Kyocera, Audiovox, HP, Blackbarry, Handspring, and Danger. The 22.3% of failure reports are from smart phones, although smart phones represented only 6.3% of the market share in 2005. We attribute this to the fact that smart phones: (i) have more complex architecture than voice-centric or rich-experience mobile phones and (ii) are open for users to download and install third party applications and/or develop their own applications.

Note that not all considered phones are Symbian-based smart phones. Consequently, while the discussion in this section provides high level characterization of phones failures, the reported figures may differ from the results given in section 6, which discusses failure data collected by the logger software run on the Symbian-based smart phones.

Table 1. Failure frequency distribution with respect to failure types and recovery actions; the numbers are percentages of the total number of failures

Failure Type	Recovery action					
	service phone	reboot	battery removal	wait	repeat	unrep.
freeze	3.65	2.36	9.01	4.29	0	6.01
input failure	0.64	0.64	0.21	0	0.64	0.86
output failure	6.87	8.80	0.43	0.64	5.79	13.73
self-shutdown	6.65	0	2.15	0.43	0	7.73
unstable behavior	6.87	1.72	0.21	0.21	0.64	8.80

Nevertheless, these considerations do not change our conclusions, since the purpose of this preliminary study is to gain an initial understanding of the observed phenomena, rather than conducting a detailed failure analysis.

The most frequent failure type is output failure (36.3%), followed by freeze (25.3%), unstable behavior (18.5%), self-shutdown (16.9%), and input failure (3%). Despite their high occurrence, output failures are often of low-severity since repeating the action is often sufficient to restore a correct device operation (5.8%, see Table 1). On the other hand, self-shutdown and unstable behavior can be considered as high-severity failures, because they are effectively recovered by serviceing the phone, or removing the battery. Phone freezes are usually of medium severity, since reboot (2.4% of the total number of failures; see Table 1) or the battery removal (9.0%; see Table 1) usually do the job and reestablish the proper operation. Only in about 3.7% (see Table 1) of cases must the user seek assistance.

To gain an understanding of the relationship between failure types and recovery actions, Table 1 reports failure distribution with respect to failure types and corresponding recovery actions. From the recovery action perspective, it should be noted that reboots are an effective way to recover from output failures (8.8% of the total number of failures). This indicates that output failures are often due to a temporary software corrupted state, which is cleaned up by the reboot. This is also confirmed by the fact that repeating the action is often sufficient to restore a correct device operation. Freezes are usually recovered by pulling out the battery (9.01%), even if a significant number of them (4.29%) are recovered by simply waiting an amount of time for the phone to respond. This may indicate that a certain fraction of battery removals and reboots in response to freezes are due to impatient users. In general, this lead us to observe how freezes are more annoying than output failures, where the user does not often need to pull out the battery.

Analyzed data also allows correlating failure occurrences with the user activity at the time of the failure. In particular, 13% of failures occur during the voice calls, 5.4% while creating/sending/receiving text messages, 3.6% while using Bluetooth and 2.4% when manipulating images. Finally, several reports (we guess from more sophisticated users) provide insight into the failure causes, e.g., there are indications of memory leaks, incorrect use of the device resources, bad handling (by the software) of indexes/pointers to objects, and incorrect management of buffer sizes.

5 Data Collection

In order to gain in-depth understanding of the failure behavior of handheld devices we developed a *failure data logger* for Symbian based smart phones. The logger enables: i) recording the occurrences of user-perceived application/system failures and ii) associating high-level failure events with the low-level error conditions signaled by applications and system modules in the form of panics. The collected data provide basis for analyzing the low-level causes of failures observed by users. Towards this, it is important to record the phone status at the time of failure. For example, when a phone freezes while a text message is being received, the stored failure data should enable answering the following questions:

1. Was the text message received despite of the failure?

2. Did any user/system module fail?

3. What other applications were running on the device at the time of the failure?

In order to address these questions, it is necessary to relate the failure (the freeze event in our example) with the phone activity/status at the time of the failure and with a panic event, which can be signaled by application or system modules.

In this study, we focus on *freeze* and *self-shutdown* failures, since they can be relatively easily detected without human intervention. The automated detection of value and erratic failures (output failures, input failures, and unstable behavior identified in the previous section) requires the implementation of a perfect observer, which has a complete knowledge of the system specification [5]. An alternative could be to involve the user in the detection process, by asking him/her to report the occurrence of a value or erratic failures. However, as our experience with analysis of Bluetooth failures shows [6], users are quite unreliable and often neglect or forget to post the required information, thus biasing the results. While this approach can be considered acceptable for an initial evaluation, as discussed in section 4,

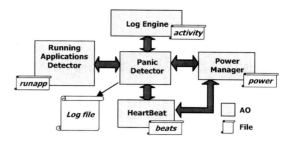

Figure 1. Overall architecture

it becomes too unreliable for a more detailed analysis. Regardless of its limited scope, the study of freezes and self-shutdowns enables us to infer valuable insight into failure behavior of Symbian-based smart phones.

5.1 Failure Logger Architecture

The high-level architecture of the failure data logger is shown in figure 1. The logger is implemented as a daemon application that starts at the phone start-up time and executes in the background. It consists of a set of Active Objects (AOs) responsible for the following tasks:

- *Heartbeat*: which is in charge of detecting both freezes and self-shutdowns (the next subsection provides more details on the heartbeat active object).

- *Running Applications Detector*: which periodically stores (in the *runapp* file) the list of IDs of the applications running on the phone. The list is obtained from the Application Architecture Server.

- *Log Engine*: which collects the smart phone activity (e.g., calls, messages, and web browsing). The information is gathered from the Database Log Server and stored into the *activity* file.

- *Power Manager*: which provides information about the battery status and enables differentiating self-shutdowns due to failures and those due to low battery. The battery status is gathered from the System Agent Server and stored into the *power* file.

- *Panic Detector*: which collects panic events as soon as they are notified. In order to gather panic related information (panic category and type), the Panic Detector exploits services provided by the RDebug object in the Symbian OS Kernel Server. The Panic Detector is also responsible collecting data produced by the other active objects into a single *Log File*. This operation is performed either when a panic is detected or when the logger application starts (i.e., when the phone starts).

5.2 Detection mechanisms

Freezes and self-shutdowns detection is accomplished by means of the heartbeat technique. This is a well known approach for crash detection. The Heartbeat AO periodically writes a heartbeat events to the *beats* file. During normal execution, the Heartbeat writes an ALIVE event. Once a shutdown is performed, the Heartbeat writes a REBOOT event. Note that before the phone reboots, the Symbian OS allows applications to complete their tasks. This is sufficient for the Heartbeat to record the REBOOT event. When the user deliberately turns off the logger application, a MAOFF (Manual OFF) event is written to the log file. Finally, if a shutdown is due to low battery (the battery status is requested to the Power Manager), a LOWBT (LOW BaTtery) event is written.

When the phone is turned on and the logger starts, the Panic Detector checks the last event logged by the Heartbeat. An ALIVE event indicates the phone has been shut down by pulling out the battery. In all other cases (i.e., a shutdown due to the low battery, the user, or the kernel) the Heartbeat would log REBOOT or LOWBT events. This means that the phone was frozen, which is consistent with the fact that pulling out the battery is the only reasonable user-initiated recovery action for a freeze. Therefore, a freeze is recorded by the Panic Detector, along with the information gathered by the Log Engine and the Running Applications Detector. On the other hand, a REBOOT event can be logged because either the phone rebooted itself or it was rebooted by the user. Hence, it becomes important to distinguish the two cases.

More details on the logger including the tuning of the heartbeat frequency and the description of the software infrastructure for automated transfer of *Log File*s from the phones used in this study, can be found in [1].

6 Experimental Results

This section reports results from the analysis of failure data collected over the period of 14 months from 25 phones, which run Symbian OS versions 6.1 to 8.0 or version 9.0. The majority of phones use the Symbian version 8.0, the most popular on the market at the time the analysis started. The targeted phones belong to students, researchers, and professors from both Italy and USA. The phones have the logger installed and have been under normal use during the period of the experiment.

Self-shutdowns Identification. As a first step in the failure data analysis, we isolate the self-shutdowns from the user triggered shutdowns. Unfortunately, it is not possible to automatically distinguish the two types of shutdowns because the generated event (i.e., the one captured by the

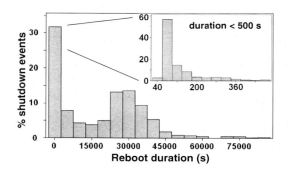

Figure 2. Distribution of reboot durations; the inner histogram zooms the external one for duration < 500 s

Heartbeat AO) is the same in both cases. We discriminate between these two events by examining the phone off-time (or the reboot duration) recorded by the Panic Detector. Figure 2 shows the distribution of reboot durations. The histogram includes all recorded shutdown events (1778 events). Two local maximums can be noticed in the figure: a first one for reboot durations shorter than 500s, which corresponds to self-shutdowns, and a second one around 30000 seconds (about eight hours and 20 minutes), corresponding to the phone off time during the night when users usually turn off their phones. The inner histogram zooms in on the data around the first local maximum (for the reboot durations less than 500 seconds) and shows a peak around 80 seconds, which corresponds to the median self-shutdown duration. Note that the number of events approaches zero seconds for durations longer than 360 seconds. We filtered-out all shutdown events with durations longer than 360 seconds. The remaining events are assumed to be self-shutdown events (471 events or 24.2% of the overall data set).

Freezes and Self-shutdowns. A total of 360 freezes and 471 self-shutdowns are reported by the logger. Based on this data we estimate the Mean Time Between Freezes (MTBFr) and the Mean Time Between Self-shutdowns (MTBS), in terms of wall-clock hours, averaged per single phone. The results show: MTBFr of 313 hours and MTBS of 250 hours. Hence, on average, a user experiences his/her phone freeze about every 13 days and the phone self-shutdown about every 10 days. These figures give an overall idea of today's mobile phones user-perceived dependability. While these values are acceptable for everyday dependability requirements [16], they indicate potential limitations in using smart phones for critical applications.

Captured Panic Events. Table 2 reports on the panic events recorded during the experiment. The panics are

Table 2. Collected panic events

Panic	Type	%	Meaning
KERN-EXEC	0	6.31	This panic is raised when the Kernel Executive cannot find an object in the object index for the current process or current thread using the specified object index number (the raw handle number).
	3	56.31	This panic is raised when an unhandled exception occurs. Exceptions have many causes, but the most common are access violations caused, for example, by dreferencing NULL. Among other possible causes are: general protection faults, executing an invalid instruction, alignment checks, etc.
	15	0.51	This panic is raised when a timer event is requested from an asynchronous timer service, an RTimer, and a timer event is already outstanding. It is caused by calling either the At(), After() or Lock() member functions after a previous call to any of these functions but before the timer event requested by those functions has completed.
E32USER-CBase	33	5.56	Raised by the destructor of a CObject. It is caused, if an attempt is made to delete the CObject when the reference count is not zero.
	46	0.76	This panic is raised by an active scheduler, a CActiveScheduler. It is caused by a stray signal.
	47	0.25	This panic is raised by the Error() virtual member function of an active scheduler, a CActiveScheduler. This function is called when an active object's RunL() function leaves. Applications always replace the Error() function in a class derived from CActiveScheduler; the default behaviour provided by CActiveScheduler raises this panic.
	69	10.10	This panic is raised if no trap handler has been installed. In practice, this occurs if CTrapCleanup::New() has not been called before using the cleanup stack.
	91	0.51	Not documented
	92	0.76	Not documented
USER	10	1.52	This panic is raised when the position value passed to a 16-bit variant descriptor member function is out of bounds. It may be raised by the Left(), Right(), Mid(), Insert(), Delete() and Replace() member functions of TDes16.
	11	5.81	This panic is raised when any operation that moves or copies data to a 16-bit variant descriptor, causes the length of that descriptor to exceed its maximum length. It may be caused by any of the copying, appending or formatting member functions and, specifically, by the Insert(), Replace(), Fill(), Fillz() and ZeroTerminate() descriptor member functions. It can also be caused by the SetLength() function.
	70	0.76	This panic is raised when attempting to complete a client/server request and the RMessagePtr is null.
KERN-SVR	0	0.25	This panic is raised by the Kernel Server when it attempts to close a Kernel object in response to an RHandleBase::Close() request. The panic occurs when the object represented by the handle cannot be found. The panic is also raised by the Kernel Server when it cannot find an object in the object index for the current process or current thread using the specified object index number (the raw handle number). The most likely cause is a corrupt handle.
ViewSrv	11	2.53	occurs when one active object's event handler monopolizes the thread's active scheduler loop and the application's ViewSrv active object cannot respond in time (the View Server monitors applications for activity/inactivity, if it thinks the application is in some kind of infinite loop state it will close it. Clever use of Active Objects should help overcome this).
EIKON-LISTBOX	3	0.25	occurs when using a listbox object from the eikon framework and no view is defined to display the object.
	5	0.76	occurs when using a listbox object from the eikon framework and an invalid Current Item Index is specified.
Phone.app	2	0.25	Not documented
EIKCOCTL	70	0.25	Corrupt edwin state for inlining editing
MSGS Client	3	6.31	Failed to write data into asynchronous call descriptor to be passed back to client
MMFAudioClient	4	0.25	it appears when the TInt value passed to SetVolume(TInt) gets 10 or more

classified according to their categories and types. The table also gives a relative frequency (with respect to the total number of panics) of occurrences of different panic types. In addition, a brief description (extracted from the Symbian OS documentation) of each panic category is given.

The data on panic events provides an overall insight into the software defects, which lead to application/system failures. The most frequent panics are due to access violations caused by dereferencing null pointers. In this case the Symbian kernel executive terminates the offending application and signals a KERN-EXEC type 3 panic. Other frequent panic causes include: invalid object indexes (KERN-EXEC type 0 panic), runtime errors related to the heap management (causing E32User-CBase panics),

and copy operations causing a descriptor to exceed its maximum length (USER type 11 panic). These findings are consistent with our observations from the analysis of failure data reported in the public web forums and discussed earlier in this paper.

Further analysis of panic events reveals that in many cases (25%), a cascade of more than one panic event is recorded in the logs (see figure 3). Since a panic generation is the last operation performed by an application or a system module (just after, the application is terminated by the kernel), multiple panic events in a short succession indicate error propagation within the operating system. The observable consequence of this phenomenon is the termination of multiple applications.

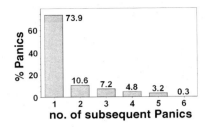

Figure 3. Distribution of subsequent panics

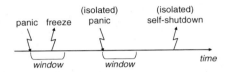

Figure 4. Panics and HL events coalescence scheme

Panics and High Level Events. From the collected data we can infer the relationship between panics and the high-level (HL) events, e.g., freezes and self-shutdowns. Towards this, we correlate panic events with freeze and self-shutdown events as depicted in Figure 4. When a panic is found in the `Log File`, we search for freeze and self-shutdown events, within a predefined temporal window. As indicated in Figure 4 there can be panic events which do not relate to HL events as well as isolated HL events. The temporal window for grouping the events must be carefully selected to avoid misinterpretation of the results. Analysis of the collected data shows that the number of coalesced events increases for window's sizes up to five minutes. A further increase in the number of the coalesced events is observed for much larger temporal windows (of the order of hours), which indicates that the coalesced events are most likely uncorrelated. For these reasons, we fix the temporal window size to be five minutes.

Figure 5 shows the results of this coalescence procedure (including the distribution of isolated panics, i.e., those panics which cannot be related to any HL event[5]).

The results show that more than a half of the recorded panics (51%) are related to HL events. If we consider a relatively small number of HL events (one every 11 days), these relationships cannot be just a coincidence. Furthermore, if we include all shutdown events recorded in the logs (hence about 300% increase in the number of events, from 471 to 1778 shutdown events), the percentage of panics related to HL events increases to 55%, i.e., only by 4%. This also confirms our previous observation that the shutdown events, which we filtered out from the data

---

[5]These panic events, most likely, relate to output failures, which our failure logger (in its current implementation) is not able to collect

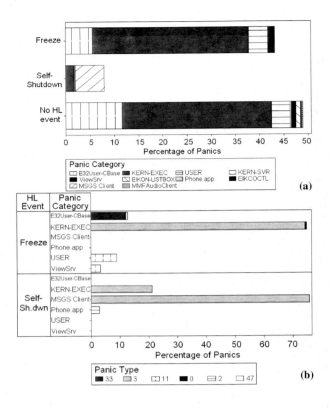

Figure 5. Panics and HL events: a) across all events, b) details with respect to freeze and self-shutdown events

analysis, are user-triggered shutdowns.

Figure 5a, also shows panic categories (EIKON-LISTBOX, EIKCOCTL, MMFAudioClient, and KERN-SVR) which do not manifest as HL events. The first three panics are typical application panics, concerning the view or the audio streaming. This indicates a good OS resilience with respect to application panics. More frequent system panics, such as KERN-EXEC, E32USER-Cbase, USER and ViewSrv, usually lead to an HL event. Depending on the component that caused the panic: (i) the phone can crash if the panic is raised by a critical system server or (ii) the phone keeps working properly once the offending application is terminated by the kernel. As a further observation, there are panics, e.g., Phone.app and MSGS Client, which always cause the self-shutdown. The two panic events correspond to the core applications provided by the phone and hence, the OS kernel always reboots the phone if any of these applications fails.

Figure 5b details the relationship between specific panic events and HL events (freezes and self-shutdowns). The data enables identifying panic categories which are symptomatic of freezes, e.g., the heap management (E32USER-Cbase), USER, and ViewSrv, and KERN-EXEC (type 0 panics). On the other hand, access violation-related panics

Table 3. Panic-activity relationship

categ. act. \ type	E32USER-CBase	KERN-EXEC	MSGS Client	Phone. app	USER	View Srv	All
	33	47	0	3	3	2	11 11
message	1.10	.	.	4.41	.	1.10	6.62
Voice call	6.62	1.10	.	17.3	9.56	4.04	38.6
unspecified	4.78	.	0.37	40.4	9.19	.	54.8

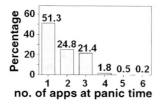

Figure 6. Distribution of the number of running applications at panic time

(KERN-EXEC type 3) can trigger both phone freeze and self-shutdowns.

Phone Activity at Panic Time. Table 3 reports the user activity at the time of the panic, in terms of voice calls and text messages (the only ones registered on the Symbian's Database Log Server). Only panics which lead to an HL event are considered in this analysis. Interestingly, about 45% of panics are recorded when the user performs real-time activities, e.g., a voice call, or sending/receiving a short message. This confirms our earlier observation (based on failure data from the web forums), which indicates presence of interferences between various applications/system modules. In other terms, this is also a symptom of the lack of sufficient (to protect error propagation) isolation between real-time and time-sharing modules. Thus, more effort should be directed to enhance the isolation between the two types of system modules. Also, there are panics, such as USER and ViewSrv, which are triggered only while a voice call is performed. Similarly, there are panics, e.g., Phone.app, which manifest only when a short message is sent/received.

The Running Application Detector allowed us to collect the set of running application at the time of the panic. It is interesting to notice that often only one user application is found to be running at the panic time, as can be observed in Figure 6. This indicates, somewhat counter intuitive, that a concurrent execution of multiple applications does not necessary lead to more frequent panics.
Table 4 summarizes panic-running applications relationship. Only cases with significant percentage are taken into account, covering 53% of the total number of panics. The

rows correspond to HL events and panic categories. The columns indicate applications which execute at the time of a panic. Numbers reported in every cell of the table represent percentages of the total number of panics, e.g., the Clock application is present in 3.2% of all recorded KERN-EXEC panics which lead to freeze. Consistently with our findings from the web forums, the Message application is one of the main panic causes. Other potential dependability bottlenecks are the camera, the Bluetoth browsing tool, and the log of incoming/outgoing calls. The table also gives an insight into the applications which, even panicking, do not cause HL events.

7 Conclusions and Lessons Learned

This work presented a measurement-based failure analysis of mobile phones. A dedicated logger has been implemented to gather failure-related information on Symbian-OS-based smart phones. Failure data has been collected from 25 phones over the period of 14 months. Key findings indicate that: (i) Majority of kernel exceptions are due to memory access violation errors and heap management problems (despite adopting the micro-kernel model in the Symbian design and providing advanced memory management facilities). This is consistent with our initial analysis of failure data on hand-held devices obtained from publicly available web forums, which pinpoints the memory leaks as one of the main causes of failures. (ii) Similarly, analysis of data collected by the logger and data from the web forums shows that the majority of failures occur when the user performs real-time tasks, e.g., a voice call or sending/receiving of a text message. This indicates the need to strength the isolation between interactive and real-time tasks. (iii)Users experience a failure (freeze or self shutdown) every 11 days, on average. Since these figures are obtained from a single study, more data and further analysis are needed before generalizing the results.

Future effort will focus on: (i) conducting experiments on a larger set of phones, including other platforms, e.g., MS Windows, (ii) enhancing the logging mechanism to enable capturing output failures (this may require involvement of users).

8 Acknowledgments

This work has been supported in part by the University of Naples Federico II - Ufficio Programmi Internazionali, by the Italian Ministry for Education,University, and Research (MIUR) in the framework of the PRIN Project "COMMUTA: Mutant hardware/software components for dynamically reconfigurable distributed systems", and by the Motorola Corporation as part of Motorola Center in the University of Illinois at Urbana-Champaign, USA. We also thank

Table 4. Panic-running applications relationship

HL event	Panic category	Messages	Messages Log	Camera Log Telephone	Log	Clock	Log Telephone	BT_ Browser Log Teleph.	Log Contacts	Contacts	battery	Messages Contacts	Telephone	FExplorer	Clock Log	TomTom
Freeze	KERN-EXEC	0.51	.	.	3.20	3.20	.	.	1.02	1.28	.	.	.	0.28	0.90	1.02
Self-Shutdown	KERN-EXEC	.	.	.	.	.	.	.	.	.	.	.	.	0.18	.	.
	MSGS Client	.	.	6.39	.	.	3.20	.	.	.	.	.	.	.	.	.
No HL event	E32USER-CBase	0.38	6.39	.	.	.	.	.	0.26	.	.	.	0.26	.	.	.
	EIKCOCTL	.	.	.	.	.	.	.	0.13	.	.	.	.	.	.	.
	EIKON-LISTBOX	.	.	0.26	.	.	.	.	.	.	.	.	.	.	.	.
	KERN-EXEC	6.78	0.26	.	1.66	1.28	.	.	1.02	1.15	2.56	1.53	1.28	0.89	0.38	0.26
	USER	.	.	.	.	.	.	3.07	.	0.38	.	.	.	.	.	.
	ViewSrv	.	.	0.13	.	.	0.13	.	.	.	.	.	.	.	.	.
	Total	8.18	6.91	6.78	5.50	4.48	3.32	3.07	3.07	2.94	2.56	1.53	1.53	1.35	1.28	1.28

Paolo Ascione for an excellent work on the implementation of the logger and Daniel Chen for help in the collection of the failure data.

References

[1] P. Ascione, M. Cinque, and D. Cotroneo. Automated Logging of Mobile Phones Failure Data. *Proc. of the 9th IEEE International Symposium on Object-oriented Real-time Distributed Computing (ISORC 2006)*, April 2006.

[2] V. Astarita and M. Florian. The use of Mobile Phones in Traffic Management and Control. *Proc. of the 2001 IEEE Intelligent Transportation Systems Conference*, August 2001.

[3] A. Avizienis, J. Laprie, B. Randell, and C. Landwehr. Basic Concepts and Taxonomy of Dependable and Secure Computing. *IEEE Transactions on Dependable and Secure Computing*, 1(1):11–33, 2004.

[4] A. A. Aziz and R. Besar. Application of Mobile Phone in Medical Image Transmission. *Proc. of the 4th National Conference on Telecommunication Technology*, January 2003.

[5] A. Bondavalli and L. Simoncini. Failures Classification with Respect to Detection. *Proc. of the 2nd IEEE Workshop on Future Trends in Distributed Computing Systems*, 1990.

[6] M. Cinque, D. Cotroneo, and S. Russo. Collecting and Analyzing Failure Data of Bluetooth Personal Area Networks. *proc. of the 2006 International Conference on Dependable Systems and Networks (DSN'06)*, June 2006.

[7] W. Gu, Z. Kalbarczyk, R. K. Iyer, and Z. Yang. Characterization of Linux Kernel Behavior under Errors. *Proc. of the 2003 International Conference on Dependable Systems and Networks (DSN'03)*, June 2003.

[8] R. Harrison. *Symbian OS C++ for Mobile Phones Volume 2*. Symbian Press, 2004.

[9] R. K. Iyer, Z. Kalbarczyk, and M. Kalyanakrishnam. Measurement-Based Analysis of Networked System Availability. *Performance Evaluation Origins and Directions, Ed. G. Haring, Ch. Lindemann, M. Reiser, Lecture Notes in Computer Science 1769, Springer Verlag*, 2000.

[10] T. Kubik and M. Sugisaka. Use of a Cellular Phone in mobile robot voice control. *Proc. of the 40th SICE Annual Conference*, July 2001.

[11] Y. Liang, Y. Zhang, A. Sivasubramaniam, R. K. Sahoo, and M. Jette. BlueGene/L Failure Analysis and Prediction Models. *proc. of the 2006 International Conference on Dependable Systems and Networks (DSN'06)*, June 2006.

[12] C. Lim. Drop Impact Study of Handheld Electronic Products. *Proc. of the 5th International Symposium on Impact Engineering*, July 2004.

[13] S. M. Matz, L. G. Votta, and M. Malkawi. Analysis of Failure Recovery Rates in a Wireless Telecommunication System. *Proc. of the 2002 International Conference on Dependable Systems and Networks (DSN'02)*, June 2002.

[14] B. Schroeder and G. Gibson. A Large-Scale Study of Failures in High-Performance Computing Systems. *Proc. of the IEEE International Conference on Dependable Systems and Networks (DSN 2006)*, June 2006.

[15] A. Sekman, A. B. Koku, and S. Z. Sabatto. Human Robot Interaction via Cellular Phones. *Proc. of the 2003 IEEE Int. Conf. on Systems, Man and Cybernetics*, October 2003.

[16] M. Shaw. Everyday Dependability for Everyday Needs. *Proc. of the 13th IEEE International Symposium on Software Reliability Engineering*, November 2002.

[17] D. P. Siewiorek, R. Chillarege, and Z. Kalbarczyk. Reflections on industry trends and experimental research in dependability. *IEEE Transactions on Dependable and Secure Computing*, 1(2), 2004.

[18] C. Simache and M. Kaâniche. Measurement-Based Availability Analysis of Unix Systems in a Distributed Environment. *Proc. of the 12th International Symposium on Software Reliability Engineering (ISSRE'01)*, November 2001.

[19] C. Simache, M. Kaâniche, and A. Saidane. Event Log based Dependability Analysis of Windows NT and 2K Systems. *Proc. of the 2002 Pacific Rim International Symposium on Dependable Computing (PRDC'02)*, December 2002.

[20] J. Xu, Z. Kalbarczyc, and R. K. Iyer. Networked Windows NT System Field Data Analysis. *Proc. of the 1999 Pacific Rim International Symposium on Dependable Computing (PRDC'99)*, December 1999.

A Real-time Network Traffic Profiling System

Kuai Xu, Feng Wang, Supratik Bhattacharyya, and Zhi-Li Zhang*

Abstract

This paper presents the design and implementation of a real-time behavior profiling system for high-speed Internet links. The profiling system uses flow-level information from continuous packet or flow monitoring systems, and uses data mining and information-theoretic techniques to automatically discover significant events based on the communication patterns of end-hosts. We demonstrate the operational feasibility of the system by implementing it and performing extensive benchmarking of CPU and memory costs using a variety of packet traces from OC-48 links in an Internet backbone network. To improve the robustness of this system against sudden traffic surges such as those caused by denial of service attacks or worm outbreaks, we propose a simple yet effective filtering algorithm. The proposed algorithm successfully reduces the CPU and memory cost while maintaining high profiling accuracy.

1 Introduction

Recent years have seen significant progress in real-time, continuous traffic monitoring and measurement systems in IP backbone networks [2]. However, *real-time* traffic summaries reported by many such systems focus mostly on volume-based heavy hitters (e.g., top N ports or IP addresses that send or receive most traffic) or aggregated metrics of interest (total packets, bytes, flows, etc) [6], which are not sufficient for finding interesting or anomalous behavior patterns. In this paper, we explore the feasibility of building a real-time traffic *behavior profiling* system that analyzes vast amount of traffic data in an IP backbone network and reports *comprehensive behavior patterns* of significant end hosts and network applications.

Towards this end, we answer a specific question in this paper: is it feasible to build a *robust* real-time traffic behavior profiling system that is capable of continuously extracting and analyzing "interesting" and "significant" traffic patterns on high-speed (OC48 or higher speed) Internet

links, even in the face of sudden surge in traffic (e.g., when the network is under a denial-of-service attack)? We address this question in the context of a traffic behavior profiling methodology we have developed for IP backbone networks [9]. The behavior profiling methodology employs a combination of data-mining and information-theoretic techniques to build comprehensive behavior profiles of Internet backbone traffic in terms of communication patterns of end hosts and applications. It consists of three key steps: significant cluster extraction, automatic behavior classification, and structural modeling for in-depth interpretive analysis. This three-step profiling methodology extracts hosts or services that generate significant traffic, classifies them into different *behavior classes* that provide a general separation of various *common* "normal" (e.g., web server and service traffic) and "abnormal" (e.g., scanning, worm or other exploit traffic) traffic as well as *rare* and anomalous traffic behavior patterns (see Section 2 for more details). The profiling methodology has been extensively validated *off-line* using packet traces collected from a variety of backbone links in an IP backbone network [9].

To demonstrate the operational feasibility of performing *on-line* traffic behavior profiling on high-speed Internet backbone links, we build a prototype system of the aforementioned profiling methodology using general-purpose commodity PCs and integrate it with an existing real-time traffic monitoring system operating in an Internet backbone network. The real-time traffic monitoring system captures packets on a high-speed link (from OC12 to OC192) and converts them into 5-tuple flows (based on source IP, destination IP, source port, destination port, protocol fields), which are then continuously fed to the real-time traffic profiling system we build. The large volume of traffic flows observed from these links creates great challenges for the profiling system to process them *quickly* on commodity PCs with *limited memory* capacity. We incorporate several optimization features in our implementation such as efficient data structures for storing and processing cluster information to address these challenges.

After designing and implementing this real-time traffic profiling system, we perform extensive benchmarking of CPU and memory costs using packet-level traces from Internet backbone links to identify the potential challenges

---

*Kuai Xu is with Yahoo! Inc, Feng Wang and Zhi-Li Zhang are with the University of Minnesota, Supratik Bhattacharyya is with SnapTell Inc.

and resource bottlenecks. We find that CPU and memory costs increase linearly with number of flows seen in a given time interval. Nevertheless, resources on a commodity PC are sufficient to continuously process flow records and build behavior profiles for high-speed links in operational networks. For example, on a dual 1.5 GHz PC with 2048 MB of memory, building behavior profiles once every 5 minutes for an 2.5 Gbps link loaded at 209 Mbps *typically* takes 45 seconds of CPU time and 96 MB of memory.

However, resource requirements are much higher under anomalous traffic patterns such as sudden traffic surges caused by denial of service attacks, when the flow arrival rate can increase by several orders of magnitude. We study this phenomenon by superposing "synthetic" packet traces containing a mix of known denial of service (DoS) attacks [1] on real backbone packet traces. To enhance the robustness of our profiling system under these stress conditions, we propose and develop sampling-based *flow filtering* algorithms and show that these algorithms are able to curb steep increase in CPU and memory costs while maintaining high profiling accuracy.

The contributions of this paper are two-fold:

- We present the design and implementation of a real-time behavior profiling system for link-level Internet traffic, and demonstrate its operational feasibility by benchmarking CPU and memory costs using packet traces from an operational backbone.

- We propose a new filtering algorithm to improve the robustness of the profiling system against traffic surges and anomalous traffic patterns, and show that the proposed algorithm successfully reduces CPU and memory costs while maintaining high profiling accuracy.

2 Behavior Profiling Methodology

In light of wide spread cyber attacks and frequent emergence of disruptive applications, we have developed a general traffic profiling methodology that automatically discovers significant behaviors with plausible interpretations from vast amount of traffic data. This methodology employs a combination of data mining and information-theoretic techniques to classify and build behavior models and structural models of communication patterns for end hosts and network applications.

The profiling methodology uses (uni-directional) 5-tuple flows, i.e., source IP address (srcIP), destination IP address (dstIP), source port number (srcPrt), destination port number (dstPrt), and protocol, collected in a time interval (e.g., 5 minutes) from Internet backbone links. Since our goal is to profile traffic based on communication patterns of end hosts and applications, we focus on the first four feature dimensions in 5-tuples, and extract clusters along

each dimension. Each cluster consists of flows with the same feature value in a given dimension. The value and its dimension are denoted as *cluster key* and *cluster dimension*. This leads to four groups of clusters, i.e., srcIP, dstIP, srcPrt and dstPrt clusters. The first two represent a collections of host behavior, while the last two yield a collection of port behaviors that aggregate flows on the corresponding ports.

2.1 Extracting Significant Clusters

Due to massive traffic data and wide diversity of end hosts and applications observed in backbone links, it is impractical to examine all end hosts and applications. Thus, we attempt to extract *significant* clusters of interest, in which the number of flows exceeds a threshold. In extracting such clusters, we have introduced an entropy-based algorithm [9] that finds adaptive thresholds along each dimension based on traffic mix and cluster size distributions.

By applying this algorithm on a variety of backbone links, we see that the number of significant clusters extracted along each dimension is far less than the total number of values. For example, in a 5-min interval on an OC-48 link, the algorithm extracts 117 significant srcIP clusters, 273 dstIP clusters, 8 srcPrt clusters and 12 dstPrt clusters from over a total of 250,000 clusters with the resulting thresholds being 0.0626%, 0.03125%, 0.25% and 1%, respectively. This observation suggests that this step is very useful and necessary in reducing traffic data for analysis while retaining most interesting behaviors.

2.2 Behavior Classification

Given the extracted significant clusters, the second step of the methodology is to classify their behaviors based on *communication patterns*. The flows in each significant cluster, e.g., a srcIP cluster, share the same feature value in srcIP dimension, thus most behavior information is contained in the other features including dstIP, srcPrt, dstPrt, which might take any possible values.

Traditional approaches mostly focus on volume-based information, e.g., unique number of dstIP's or dstPrt's in examining the patterns of such clusters. However, the traffic volume often is unable to uncover comprehensive communication patterns. For example, if two hosts communicate with 100 unique dstIP's, we cannot safely conclude that their communication patterns from dstIP feature are the same without further investigation. A simple example is that one host could be a web server talking to 100 clients, while another is an infected host randomly scanning 100 targets. More importantly, the number of flows associated with each dstIP is very likely to be different. For the case of the web server, the numbers of flows between clients and the server tend to be diverse. On the other hand, the number of probing flows between the scanner and each target is often uniform, e.g., one in most cases. This insight motivates us to use relative uncertainty [9] to measure the feature distribution of free dimensions for all significant clusters.

We use relative uncertainty to measure feature distributions of three free dimensions. As a result, we obtain a relative uncertainty vector for each cluster, e.g., [RU_{srcPrt}, RU_{dstPrt} and RU_{dstIP}] for srcIP clusters. Recall that RU is in the range of [0,1], so we could represent the RU vector of each srcIP cluster as a single point in a 3-dimensional space. Fig. 1 represents each srcIP cluster extracted in each 5-minute time slot over an 1-hour period from an OC-48 backbone link as a point in a unit cube. We see that the points are "clustered", suggesting that there are few underlying common patterns among them. Such observation holds for other dimensions as well. This leads to a behavior classification scheme which classifies all srcIP's into *behavior classes* based on their similarity/dissimilarity in the RU vector space.

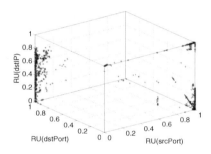

Figure 1. The distribution of relative uncertainty on free dimensions for srcIP's from an OC-48 backbone link during an 1-hour period.

By applying the behavior classification on backbone links and analyzing their temporal properties, we find this scheme is robust and consistent in capturing behavior similarities among significant clusters. Such similarities are measured on the feature distribution of free dimensions of these clusters, hence provide useful insight into communication patterns of end hosts and applications [5, 9].

2.3 Structural Modeling

To provide a plausible interpretation for behavior patterns, we adopt *dominant state analysis* technique for modeling and characterizing the interaction of various feature dimensions in a cluster. The idea of dominant state analysis comes from structural modeling or reconstructability analysis in system theory ([11]) as well as more recent graphical models in statistical learning theory [3].

The objective of dominant state analysis is to explore the interaction or dependence among the free dimensions by identifying "simpler" subsets of values or constraints (called *structural models* in the literature [7]) to represent the original data in their probability distribution. Consider a simple example, a srcIP cluster consists of 98% scans (with a fixed srcPrt 220) to over 1200 random destinations on dstPrt 6129. Then the values in the srcPrt, dstPrt and dstIP dimensions these flows take are of the form $\langle 220, 6129, * \rangle$, where $*$ (wildcard) indicates random values. Clearly this cluster is dominated by the flows of the form $\langle 220, 6129, * \rangle$. We refer to such forms as *states* of a cluster. Hence given the information about the states, we can not only *approximately* reproduce the original flow patterns, but also explain the *dominant* activities of end hosts or applications.

2.4 Properties of Behavior Profiles

We have applied the profiling methodology on traffic data collected from a variety of links at the core of the Internet through *off-line* analysis. We find that a large fraction of clusters fall into three typical behavior profiles: server/service behavior profile, heavy hitter host behavior, and scan/exploit behavior profile. These behavior profiles are built based on various aspects, including behavior classes, dominant states, and additional attributes such as average packets and bytes per flow. These behavior profiles are recorded in a database for further event analysis, such as temporal properties of behavior classes and individual clusters, or behavior change detection based on RU vectors.

The profiling methodology is able to find various interesting and anomalous events. First, it automatically detects novel or unknown exploit behaviors that match typical exploit profiles, but exhibit unusual dominant states (e.g., dstPrt's). Second, any atypical behavior is worth close examination, since they represent as "outliers" or "anomaly" among behavior profiles. Third, the methodology could point out deviant behaviors of end hosts or applications that deviate from previous patterns.

To summarize, the profiling methodology has demonstrated the applicability of the profiling methodology to critical problem of detecting anomalies or the spread of unknown security exploits, profiling unwanted traffic, and tracking the growth of new applications. However, the practical value of the profiling framework largely depends on the operational feasibility of this system in a *real-time* manner.

In the rest of this paper, we will demonstrate the feasibility of designing and implementing a real-time traffic profiling system that uses flow-level information generated from "always-on" packet monitors and reports significant online events based on communication patterns of end hosts and applications even faced with anomalous traffic patterns, e.g., denial of service attacks or worm outbreaks.

3 Real-time Profiling System

3.1 Design Guidelines

Four key considerations guide the design of our profiling system:

- **scalability:** The profiling system is targeted at high-speed (1 Gbps or more) backbone links and hence must scale to the traffic load offered by such links. Specifically, if the system has to continuously build behavior profiles of significant clusters once every time interval T (e.g, $T = 5$ minutes), then it has to take less than time T to process all the flow records aggregated in every time interval T. And this has to be accomplished on a commodity PC platform.

- **robustness:** The profiling system should be robust to anomalous traffic patterns such as those caused by denial of service attacks, flash crowds, etc. These traffic patterns can place a heavy demand on system resources. At the same time, it is vital for the profiling system to be functioning during such events since it will generate data for effective response and forensic analysis. Therefore the system must adapt gracefully to these situations and achieve a suitable balance between profiling accuracy and resource utilization.

- **modularity:** The profiling system should be designed in a modular fashion with each module encapsulating a specific function or step in the profiling methodology. Information exchange between modules should be clearly specified. In addition, the system should be designed to accept input from any packet or flow monitoring system that exports a continuous stream of flow records. However, the flow record export format has to be known to the system.

- **usability:** The profiling system should be easy to configure and customize so that a network operator can focus on specific events of interest and obtain varying levels of information about these events. At the same time, it should expose minimal details about the methodology to an average user. Finally it should generate meaningful and easy-to-interpret event reports, instead of streams of statistics.

3.2 System Architecture

Fig. 2 depicts the architecture of the profiling system that is integrated with an "always-on" monitoring system and an

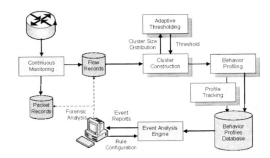

Figure 2. The architecture of real-time traffic profiling system

event analysis engine. The flow-level information used by the profiling system are generated from continuous packet or flow monitoring systems that capture packet headers on a high-speed Internet link via an optical splitter and a packet capturing device, i.e., DAG card. The monitoring system aggregates packets into 5-tuple flows and exports the flow records for a given time interval into disk files. In general, the profiling system obtains flow records through three ways: i) shared disk access, ii) file transfer over socket, and iii) flow transfer over a streaming socket. The option in practice will depend on the locations of the profiling and monitoring systems. The first way works when both systems run on the same machine, while the last two can be applied if they are located in different machines.

In order to improve the efficiency of the profiling system, we use distinct process threads to carry out multiple task in parallel. Specifically, one thread continuously reads flow records in the current time interval T_i from the monitoring systems, while another thread profiles flow records that are complete for the previous time interval T_{i-1}.

The event analysis engine analyzes a *behavior profile database*, which includes current and historical behavior profiles of end hosts and network applications reported by the *behavior profiling* and *profile tracking* modules in the profiling system.

The real-time traffic profiling system consists of four functional modules (shadowed boxes), namely, "cluster construction", "adaptive thresholding", "behavior profiling" and "profile tracking". Each of these modules implements one step in the traffic profiling methodology described in Section 2.

3.3 Key Implementation Details

3.3.1 Data Structures

High speed backbone links typically carry a large amount of traffic flows. Efficiently storing and searching these flows is critical for the *scalability* of our real-time profiling system.

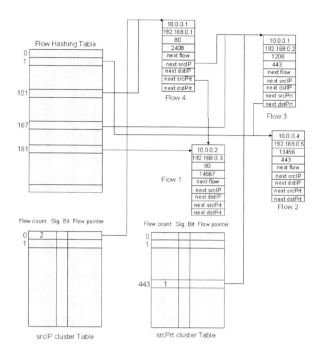

Figure 3. Data structure of flow table and cluster table

We design two efficient data structures, namely `FTable` and `CTable` for efficient storage and fast lookups during cluster extraction and behavior modeling.

Figure 3 illustrates the data structure of `FTable` and `CTable` with an example. `FTable`, an array data structure, provides an index of 5-tuple flows through a commonly-used hash function, $FH = srcip^\wedge dstip^\wedge srcport^\wedge dstport^\wedge proto \% (FTableEntries - 1)$, where $FTableEntries$ denotes the maximum entries of `FTable`. For example, in Figure 3, *flow 1* is mapped to the entry 181 in `FTable`, while *flow 2* is mapped to the entry 1. In case of hashing collision, i.e., two or more flows mapping to the same table entry, we use a linked list to manage them. In our experiments, the (average) collision rate of this flow hash function is below 5% with $FTableEntries = 2^{20}$. While constructing clusters, the naive approach would be to make four copies of 5-tuple flows, and then group each flow into four clusters along each dimension. However, this method dramatically increases the memory cost of the system since the flow table typically has hundreds or millions of flows in each time interval. Instead of duplicating flows, which is expensive, we add four flow pointers (i.e., next `srcIP`, next `dstIP`, next `srcPrt`, and next `dstPrt`) in each flow. Each flow pointer will link the flows sharing the same feature value in the given dimension. For example, the next `srcIP` pointer of *flow 4* links to `flow 3` since

they share the same `srcIP` *10.0.0.1*. Similarly, the next `srcPrt` pointer of *flow 4* links to `flow 1` since they share the same `srcPrt` *80*. However, the question is how to quickly find the "old" flows of the same clusters when adding a new flow in the flow table.

To address this problem, we create another data structure, `CTable`, which links the first flow of each cluster in `FTable`. Since there are four types of clusters, we create four instances of `CTable` for managing clusters along four dimensions. Considering `srcPrt` and `dstPrt` dimensions with 65536 possible clusters (ports), we use an array with a size of 65536 to manage the clusters for each of these two dimensions. The index of the array for each port is the same as the port number. For `srcIP` and `dstIP` dimensions, we use a simple hash function that performs a bitwise exclusive OR (XOR) operation on the first 16 bits and the last 16 bits of IP address to map each `srcIP` or `dstIP` into its `CTable` entry. When adding a new flow, e.g., `flow 3` in Fig. 3, in the given `dstPrt`, we first locate the first flow (`flow 2`) of the cluster `dstPrt` 443, and make the next `dstPrt` pointer of `flow 3` to `flow 2`. Finally the first flow of the cluster `dstPrt` 443 is updated to `flow 3`. This process is similar for the cluster `srcPrt` 1208, as well as the the clusters `srcIP` *10.0.0.1* and `dstIP` *192.168.0.2*.

In addition to pointing to the first flow in each cluster, each `CTable` entry also includes flow count for the cluster and significant bit for marking significant clusters. The former maintains flow counts for cluster keys. As discussed in Section 2, the flow count distribution will determine the adaptive threshold for extracting significant clusters.

3.3.2 Space and Time Complexity of Modules

The space and time complexity of modules essentially determines the CPU and memory cost of the profiling system. Thus, we quantify the complexity of each module in our profiling system. For convenience, Table 1 shows the definitions of the notations that will be used in the complexity analysis.

The time complexity of cluster construction is $O(|F| + \sum_{i=0}^{3} |C_i|)$ for `FTable` and `CTable` constructions. Similarly, the space complexity is $O(|F| * s_{fr} + \sum_{i=0}^{3} (|C_i| * r_v))$.

The time complexity of adaptive thresholding is $\sum_{i=0}^{3} (|C_i| * e_i)$. This module does not allocate additional memory, since its operations are mainly on the existing `CTable`. Thus, the space complexity is zero.

The time complexity of behavior profiling is $O(\sum_{i=0}^{3} \sum_{j=0}^{|S_i|} |s_j|)$, while the space complexity is $O(\sum_{i=0}^{3} [|S_i| * (r_b + r_s)])$. The output of this step are the behavior profiles of significant clusters, which are recorded into a database along with the timestamp for further analysis.

599

Table 1. Notations used in the paper

Notation	Definition
F	set of 5-tuple flows in a time interval
i	dimension id (0/1/2/3 = `srcIP`/`dstIP`/ `srcPort`/`dstPort`)
C_i	set of clusters in dimension i
S_i	set of significant clusters in dimension i
c_i	a cluster in dimension i
s_i	a significant cluster in dimension i
r_f	size of a flow record
r_v	size of the volume information of a cluster
r_b	size of behavior information of a sig. cluster
r_s	size of dominant states of a significant cluster

Table 2. Total CPU and memory cost of the real-time profiling system on 5-min flow traces

Link	Util.	CPU time (sec)			Memory (MB)		
		min	avg	max	min	avg	max
L_1	207 Mbps	25	46	65	82	96	183
L_2	86 Mbps	7	11	16	46	56	71
L_3	78 Mbps	7	12	82	45	68	842

Due to a small number of significant clusters extracted, the computation complexity of profile tracking is often less than the others in two or three orders of magnitude, so for simplicity we will not consider its time and space requirement.

3.3.3 Parallelization of Input and Profiling

In order to improve the efficiency of the profiling system, we use *thread* mechanisms for parallelizing tasks in multiple modules, such as continuously importing flow records in the current time interval T_i, and profiling flow records that are complete for the previous time interval T_{i-1}. Clearly, the parallelization could reduce the time cost of the profiling system. The disadvantage of doing so is that we have to maintain two set of `FTable` and `CTable` for two consecutive time intervals.

4 Performance Evaluation

4.1 Benchmarking

We measure CPU usage of the profiling process by using a system call, namely, *getrusage()*, which queries actual system and user CPU time of the process. The system call returns with the resource utilization including *ru_utime* and *ru_stime*, which represent the user and system time used by

the process, respectively. The sum of these two times indicates the total CPU time that the profiling process uses. Let T denote the total CPU time, and T_l, T_a, and T_p denote the CPU usage for the modules of cluster construction, adaptive thresholding and behavior profiling, respectively. Then we have

$$T = T_l + T_a + T_p \qquad (1)$$

Similarly, we collect memory usage with another system call, *mallinfo()*, which collects information of the dynamic memory allocation. Let M denote the total memory usage, and M_l, M_a, and M_p denote the memory usage in three key modules. Then we have

$$M = M_l + M_a + M_b \qquad (2)$$

In oder to track the CPU and memory usages of each module, we use these two system calls before and after the module. The difference of the output becomes the actual CPU and memory consumption of each module. Next, we show the CPU time and memory cost of profiling system on three OC-48 links during a continuous 18-hour period with an average link utilization of 209 Mbps, 86 Mbps, and 78 Mbps. For convenience, let L_1, L_2, and L_3 denote these three links, respectively.

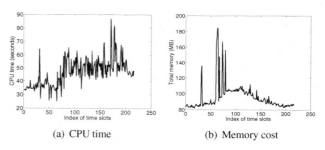

(a) CPU time   (b) Memory cost

Figure 4. CPU and memory cost of the real-time profiling system on flow records in 5-min time interval collected in L_1 for 18 consecutive hours

Table 2 shows a summary of CPU time and memory cost of the profiling system on L_1 to L_3 for 18 consecutive hours. It is not surprising to see that the average CPU and memory costs for L_1 are larger than the other two links due to a higher link utilization. Fig. 4 shows the CPU and memory cost of the profiling system on all 5-min intervals for L_1 (the link with the highest utilization). For the majority of time intervals, the profiling system requires less than 60 seconds (1 minute) of CPU time and 150MB of memory using the flow records in 5-min time intervals for L_1.

Fig. 5[a] further illustrates the number of flow records over time that ranges from 600K to 1.6M, while Fig. 5[b]

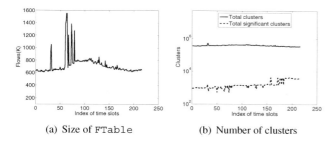

(a) Size of FTable	(b) Number of clusters

Figure 5. Input of flow traces in 5-min time interval collected in L_1 for 18 consecutive hours

shows the number of all clusters as well as the extracted significant clusters. It is very interesting to observe the similar patterns in the plot of memory cost (Fig. 4[b]) and that of the flow count over time (Fig 5[a]). This observation leads us to analyze the correlation between these two measurements. By examining the breakdown of the memory cost, we find that M_l in the cluster construction module accounts for over 98% of the total memory consumptions. Recall that the space complexity of this module is larger than the others by two or three orders of magnitude, and dominated by the size of flow table $|F|$. A deep examination on $|F|$ vs. M_l confirms the linear relationship between them. Therefore, this strong correlation suggests that the memory cost of the profiling system is mainly determined by the number of flow records collected by the monitoring system in a given time interval.

The breakdown in CPU usage suggests that cluster construction and behavior profiling account for a large fraction of CPU time. Similar to the space complexity, the time complexity in cluster construction is also determined by $|F|$. The linear relationship demonstrated by the scatter plot of $|F|$ vs. T_l confirms this complexity analysis. In addition, we observe an approximately linear relationship between the number of significant clusters and CPU time in behavior profiling. This suggests that the CPU cost in behavior profiling is largely determined by the number of significant clusters whose behavior patterns are being analyzed.

In summary, the average CPU and memory costs of the real-time profiling system on 5-min flow records collected from an OC-48 link with a 10% link utilization are 60 seconds and 100 MB, respectively. Moreover, the CPU time is largely determined by the number of flow records as well as that of significant clusters, and the memory cost is determined by the number of flow records. During these monitoring periods, these links are not fully utilized, so we can not extensively measure the performance of the real-time profiling system for a highly loaded link. Next, we will test the profiling system during sudden traffic surges such as

those caused by denial of service attacks, flash crowds, and worm outbreaks that increases the link utilization as well as the number of flow records.

4.2 Stress Test

The performance benchmarking of CPU and memory costs demonstrate the operational feasibility of our traffic profiling system during normal traffic patterns. However, the profiling system should also be robust during atypical traffic patterns, such as denial of service attacks, flash crowds, and worm outbreaks [4, 8, 10]. In order to understand the system performance during these incidents, we inject packet traces of three known denial of service attacks and simulated worm outbreaks by superposing them with backbone traffic.

We use the packet traces of three DoS attacks with varying intensity and behavior studied in [1]. All of these attacks are targeted on a single destination IP address. The first case is a multiple-source DoS attack, in which hundreds of source IP addresses send 4200 ICMP echo request packets with per second for about 5 minutes. The second case is a TCP SYN attack lasting 12 minutes from random IP addresses that send 1100 TCP SYN packets per second. In the last attack, a single source sends over 24K *ip-proto 255* packets per second for 15 minutes. In addition to DoS attacks, we simulate the SQL slammer worm on January 25th 2003 [8] with an Internet Worm Propagation Simulator used in [10]. In the simulation experiments, we adopt the same set of parameters in [10] to obtain similar worm simulation results, and collect worm traffic monitored in a 2^{20} IP space.

For each of these four anomalous traffic patterns, we replay packet traces along with backbone traffic, and aggregate synthetic packets traces into 5-tuple flows. For simplicity, we still use 5 minutes as the size of the time interval, and run the profiling system against the flow records collected in an interval. Table 3 shows a summary on flow traces of the first 5-minute interval for these four cases. The flow, packet and byte counts reflect the intensity of attacks or worm propagation, while the link utilization indicates the impact of such anomaly behaviors on Internet links. For all of these cases, the profiling system is able to successfully generate event reports in less than 5 minutes.

During the emulation process, the link utilization ranged from 314.5 Mbps to 629.2Mbps. We run the profiling system on flow traces after replaying synthetic packets and collect CPU and memory cost of each time interval, which is also shown in Table 3. The system works well for low intense DoS attacks in the first two cases. However, due to intense attacks in the last DoS case (DoS-3) and worm propagations, the CPU time of the system increases to 210 and 231 seconds, but still under the 5 minute interval. However,

Table 3. Synthetic packet traces with known denial of services attacks and worm simulations

Anomaly	Flows	Packets	Bytes	Link Utilization	CPU time	Memory	Details
DoS-1	2.08 M	18.9 M	11.8 G	314.5 Mbps	45 seconds	245.5 MB	distributed dos attacks from multiple sources
DoS-2	1.80 M	20.7 M	12.5 G	333.5 Mbps	59 seconds	266.1 MB	distributed dos attacks from random sources
DoS-3	16.5 M	39.8 M	16.1 G	430.1 Mbps	210 seconds	1.75GB	dos attacks from single source
Worm	18.9 M	43.0 M	23.6 G	629.2 Mbps	231 seconds	2.01GB	slammer worm simulations

Table 4. Reduction of CPU time and memory cost using the random sampling technique

Case	μ	Size of FTable	CPU time	memory
DoS attack	66%	10M	89 seconds	867 MB
Worm	55%	10M	97 seconds	912 MB

the memory cost jumps to 1.75GB and 2.01GB indicating a performance bottleneck. This clearly suggests that we need to provide practical solutions to improve the robustness of the system under stress. In the next section, we will discuss various approaches, including traditional sampling techniques and new profiling-aware filtering techniques towards this problem, and evaluate the tradeoff between performance benefits and profiling accuracy.

5 Sampling and Filtering

5.1 Random Sampling

Random sampling is a widely-used simple sampling technique in which each object, flow in our case, is randomly chosen based on the same probability (also known as sampling ratio μ). Clearly, the number of selected flows is entirely decided by the sampling ratio μ. During the stress test in the last section, the profiling system requires about 2GB memory when the number of flow records reach 16.5M and 18.9 during DoS attacks and worm outbreaks. Such high memory requirement is not affordable in real-time since the machine installed with the profiling system could have other tasks as well, e.g., packet and flow monitoring. As a result, we attempt to set 1GB as the upper bound of the memory cost. Recall that in the performance benchmarking, we find that memory cost is determined by the number of flow records. Based on their linear relationship we estimate that flow records with a size of 10M will require approximately 1GB memory. Thus, 10M is the desirable limit for the size of the flow records.

Using the limit of flow records, l, we could configure the sampling ratio during sudden traffic increase as $\mu = \frac{l}{|F|}$. As a result, we set the sampling ratios in the last DoS attacks and worm outbreaks as 60% and 55%, respectively, and randomly choose flows in loading flow tables in the *cluster construction* module. Table 4 shows the reduction of CPU time and memory consumptions with the sampled

flow tables for both cases.

On the other hand, random sampling has substantial impact on behavior accuracy. First, the set of significant clusters from four feature dimensions are smaller than that without sampling, which is caused by the changes of the underlying cluster size distribution after flow sampling. Table 5 shows the number of significant clusters extracted along each dimension without and with sampling for the DoS case. In total, among 309 significant clusters without sampling, 180 (58%) of the *most significant* clusters are still extracted with random sampling. Secondly, the behavior of a number of extracted clusters are altered, since flow sampling changes the feature distribution of free dimensions as well as the behavior classes for these clusters. As shown in the last column of Table 5, 161 out 180 significant clusters with random sampling are classified with the same behavior as those without sampling. In other words, the behavior of 19 (10.5%) extracted significant clusters are changed as a result of random sampling. Fig. 6 shows the feature distributions of free dimensions for 140 dstIP clusters with and without random sampling. The deviations from the diagonal line indicate the changes of feature distribution and the behavior due to flow sampling. We also perform random sampling on the synthetic flow traces in the case of worm outbreak, and the results of sampling impact on cluster extractions and behavior accuracy are very similar.

Table 5. Reduction of significant clusters and behavior accuracy

Dim.	Sig. clusters without sampling	Sig. clusters with sampling	Clusters with same behavior classes
srcPrt	23	4	3
dstPrt	6	5	4
srcIP	47	31	29
dstIP	233	140	125
Total	309	180	161

In summary, random sampling could reduce the CPU time and memory cost during sudden traffic surges caused by DoS attacks or worm outbreaks. However, random sampling reduces the number of interesting events, and also alters the behavior classes of some significant clusters. Such impact could have become worse if "lower" sampling rates are selected. Thus, it becomes necessary to develop a profiling-aware algorithm that not only reduces the size of

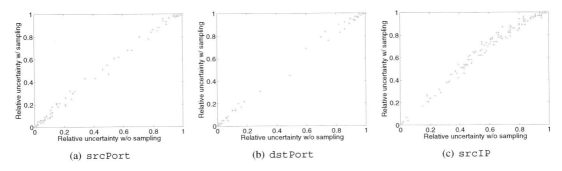

Figure 6. Feature distribution of free dimensions for 140 `dstIP` clusters with and without random sampling

flow tables, but also retains the (approximately) same set significant clusters and their behavior.

5.2 Profiling-aware Filtering

A key lesson from random sampling is that the clusters associated with denial of service attacks are usually very large in flow count, and hence consume a large amount of memory and CPU time. In addition, profiling such behavior does not require a large number of flows, since the feature distributions very likely remain the same even with a small percentage of traffic flows. Based on this insight, we develop a profiling-aware filtering solution that limits the size of very large clusters, and adaptively samples on the rest of clusters when the system is faced with sudden explosive growth in the number of flows.

The details of the profiling-aware sampling algorithm are as follow. First, we choose two *watermarks* (L and H) for the profiling system. L represents the moving average of flow tables over time, and H represents the maximum size of flow tables that system will accept. In our experiments, we set $H = 10M$, which is estimated to require 1GB memory cost. In addition, we set the maximum and minimum sampling ratios, i.g., μ_{max} and μ_{min}. The actual sampling μ will be adaptively decided based on the status of flow table size. Specifically, the sampling ratio becomes thinner as the size of flow table increases. For simplicity, let `ftable` denote the size of flow table. If `ftable` is below L, the profiling system accepts every flow. In contrary, if `ftable` is equal to H, the system will stop reading flows and exit with a warning signal.

If `ftable` is equal to L or certain marks, i.e., $L + i * D$, where D is the incremental factor and $i = 1, 2..., (H - L)/D - 1$, the system computes the relative uncertainty of each dimension and evaluates whether there is one or a few dominant feature values along each dimension. In our experiments, we set $D = 1M$ as the incremental factor. The existence of such values suggests that certain types of flows dominate current flow tables, and indicates anomalous traffic patterns. Thus, the system searches these values and

marks them as significant clusters for flow filtering. Subsequently, any flow, which contains a feature value marked with *significant*, will be filtered, since such flow will not affect the behavior of the associated clusters. On the other hand, additional flows for other small clusters have substantial contributions to their behavior. Thus, we should give preference to flows that belong to such small clusters. On the other hand, the system could not accept all of these flows with preference after `ftable` exceeds L watermark. As a result, each of these flows is added with the adaptive sampling ratio $\mu = \mu_{max} - i * \frac{\mu_{max} - \mu_{min}}{(H-L)/D - 1}$.

We run the profiling system on the flow tables in the cases of DoS attack and worm outbreaks with the profile-aware filtering algorithm. Like random sampling, *profiling-aware* sampling also reduces CPU time and memory cost by limiting the size of flow table. On the other hand, the profiling-aware sampling has two advantages over the random sampling. First, the set of clusters extracted using this algorithm is very close to the set without sampling. For example, in the case of DoS attack, the system obtains 41 `srcIP` clusters, 210 `dstIP` clusters, 21 `srcPrt` clusters and 6 `dstPrt` cluster, respectively. Compared with 58% of significant clusters extracted in random sampling, our profiling-aware algorithm could extract over 90% of 309 original clusters that are selected without any sampling. Second, the behavior accuracy of significant clusters are also improved. Specifically, among 41 `srcIP`'s, 210 `dstIP`'s, 21 `srcPrt`'s, and 6 `dstPrt`'s significant clusters, only 3 `dstIP`'s and 1 `srcPrt` clusters change to "akin" classes from their original behavior classes. These findings suggest that the *profiling-aware* profiling algorithm approximately retains the feature distributions of significant clusters and behaviors.

Fig. 7 shows the feature distribution of free dimensions of 210 `dstIP` clusters, extracted both without sampling and with profiling-aware filtering algorithm. In general, the feature distributions of all free dimensions for almost all clusters after filtering are approximately the same as those without sampling. The outliers deviant from the diagonal

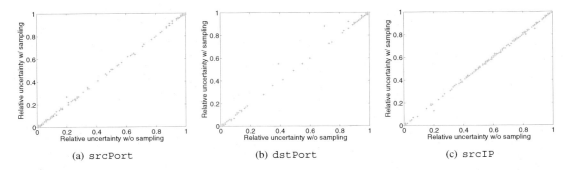

(a) srcPort   (b) dstPort   (c) srcIP

Figure 7. Feature distribution of free dimensions for 210 dstIP clusters with and without profiling-aware sampling

lines correspond to feature distributions of three clusters whose behavior has changed. Upon close examinations, we find that flows in these clusters contain a mixture of Web and ICMP traffic. The latter are the dominant flows in DoS attacks, so they are filtered after the size of flow table reaches L in the profiling-aware filtering algorithm. The filtered ICMP flows in these clusters explain the changes of the feature distributions as well as the behavior classes.

In the *worm* case, the profiling-aware filtering algorithm also successfully reduces CPU and memory cost of the profiling system, while maintaining high profiling accuracy in terms of the number of extracted significant clusters and the feature distributions of these clusters. Thus, the profiling-aware filtering algorithm can achieve a significant reduction of CPU time and memory cost during anomalous traffic patterns while obtaining accurate behavior profiles of end hosts and network applications.

6 Conclusions and Future Work

This paper explores the feasibility of designing, implementing and utilizing a real-time behavior profiling system for high-speed Internet links. We first discuss the design requirements and challenges of such a system and present an overall architecture that integrates the profiling system with always-on monitoring systems and an event analysis engine. Subsequently, we demonstrate the operational feasibility of building this system through extensive performance benchmarking of CPU and memory costs using a variety of packet traces collected from OC-48 backbone links. To improve the robustness of this system during anomalous traffic patterns such as denial of service attacks or worm outbreaks, we propose a simple yet effective filtering algorithm to reduce resource consumptions while retaining high profiling accuracy. We are currently in the process of integrating the event analysis engine into a rule-based anomaly detection system. In addition, we are extending the flow import/export protocol so that the profiling system could work with multiple continuously monitoring systems. Fi-

nally we would like to correlate anomalous and interesting events from multiple monitoring points.

Acknowledgement: This work was supported in part by the NSF grants CNS-0435444 and CNS-0626812, a University of Minnesota Digital Technology Center DTI grant and Sprint ATL gift grant.

References

[1] A. Hussain, J. Heidemann, and C. Papadopoulos. A Framework for Classifying Denial of Service Attacks. In *Proceedings of ACM SIGCOMM*, August 2003.

[2] G. Iannaccone, C. Diot, I. Graham, and N. McKeown. Monitoring Very High Speed Links. In *Proceedings of ACM SIGCOMM Internet Measurement Workshop*, November 2001.

[3] M. Jordan. Graphical models. *Statistical Science, Special Issue on Bayesian Statistics*, 19:140–155, 2004.

[4] S. Kandula, D. Katabi, M. Jacob, and A. Berger. Botz-4-Sale: Surviving Organized DDoS Attacks That Mimic Flash Crowds. In *Proceedings of Symposium on NSDI*, May 2005.

[5] T. Karagiannis, K. Papagiannaki, and M. Faloutsos. BLINC: Multilevel Traffic Classification in the Dark. In *Proceedings of ACM SIGCOMM*, August 2005.

[6] K. Keys, D. Moore, and C. Estan. A Robust System for Accurate Real-Time Summaries of Internet Traffic. In *Proceedings of ACM SIGMETRICS*, June 2005.

[7] K. Krippendorff. *Information Theory: Structural Models for Qualitative Data*. Sage Publications, 1986.

[8] D. Moore, V. Paxson, S. Savage, C. Shannon, S. Staniford, and N. Weaver. Inside the Slammer Worm. *IEEE Security and Privacy*, July 2003.

[9] K. Xu, Z.-L. Zhang, and S. Bhattacharyya. Profiling Internet Backbone Traffic: Behavior Models and Applications. In *Proceedings of ACM SIGCOMM*, August 2005.

[10] C. Zou, L. Gao, W. Gong, and D. Towsley. Monitoring and Early Warning for Internet Worms. In *Proceedings of ACM CCS*, October 2003.

[11] M. Zwick. An Overview of Reconstructability Analysis. *International Journal of Systems & Cybernetics*, 2004.

Session 3C:
Practical Experience Reports

RAS by the Yard

Alan Wood, Swami Nathan

Sun Microsystems, Inc.

alan.wood@sun.com, swami.nathan@sun.com

Abstract

Different applications require different levels of fault tolerance. Therefore, it is important to create a flexible architecture that allows a customer to choose the appropriate amount of fault tolerance, a concept we call "RAS by the yard." In this paper we describe a next generation supercomputer and the design flexibility that allows us to offer a range of alternatives for RAS (reliability, availability, serviceability). In particular we explain how checkpointing can provide an availability continuum. Design alternatives that improve RAS may be expensive, so it is important to do cost/benefit studies of the alternatives. For a fixed budget and specified system balance ratios, such as Bytes/FLOPS, we analyze the system performance impact of alternative RAS strategies. We show how to optimize the amount of RAS purchased by using a performability measure.

1. Introduction

When making a computer system purchase, customers compare system features with their requirements and budget. Features considered include functionality, performance, security, and reliability/ availability/serviceability (RAS). Some system features, such as functionality, are fairly constant while others, such as performance, are highly scalable by simply purchasing more hardware. In most current systems, RAS is a constant feature without a significant expenditure such as buying backup systems and using clustering technology. The authors propose that RAS should be scalable and that computer systems should have the architectural flexibility to permit the purchase of variable levels of RAS. We call this concept RAS "by the yard".

There are many types of systems that permit users to purchase additional RAS. RAID or mirrored disks are an example in which consumers purchase more reliable storage with built-in redundancy. However, this provides only two levels of RAS (the system either has the feature or it does not) rather than a continuum. In this paper we describe a next generation

supercomputer and evaluate discrete types of RAS improvements. In addition we describe how checkpointing can provide an availability continuum and show how this design flexibility can be used to offer a range of alternatives. For each system purchase decision of this type, there should be a cost/benefit analysis performed to determine if the improved RAS justifies the additional cost.

This paper presents examples of two types of cost/benefit analyses. The first is the standard cost/benefit analysis in which the cost required to purchase additional RAS is compared with the benefits from the RAS improvement. The second approach is to assume that the customer has a fixed budget and that purchasing additional RAS means that the customer will purchase less performance or other features. We show how consumers can use this analysis to optimize the amount of RAS purchased by combining performance and availability into a single performability measure.

2. Supercomputer Design Parameters

The "grand challenge" problems, such as simulating the birth of the universe, require a supercomputer an order of magnitude more powerful than the current supercomputers: a machine that provides PetaFLOPS[1]-scale performance [1]. Supercomputer applications often run for long periods of time, so failures can cause lengthy recomputing of results that were not preserved when the failure occurred. However, current supercomputers are not focussed on high availability [2, 3], making them a natural area in which to examine the RAS by the yard concept.

A system architecture is defined by various balance ratios, e.g., the amount of memory and I/O bandwidth per unit of compute performance. These system balance ratios are generally derived from application performance evaluations and can be changed to accommodate different workloads. An

---

1 FLOPS is floating point operations per second, a measure of peak computer performance. Current supercomputers are measured in TeraFLOPS, where Tera is a billion or 10^{12}. Peta is 10^{15}, 3 orders of magnitude larger.

example set of system balance ratios for a PetaFLOPS-scale system based on current scientific supercomputing applications is shown in Table 1. Commercial systems would have less bisection bandwidth[2], probably more I/O bandwidth, and possibly more memory or disk storage depending on the application. For example, data mining applications would require significantly more disk storage.

System balance ratios provide a way to make apples-to-apples comparisons of system design and configuration alternatives. The ratios are selected to balance the amount of resources required to support raw compute power in a cost-effective way. For example, if an application cannot fit in memory, continual reads from disk are necessary, which impacts performance. If memory or other bandwidth is not sufficient, the processors may stall, waiting for data. The ratios may represent a compromise among a set of applications, and if they change, one or more applications may be impacted. Thus, when comparing systems, it is important to keep these ratios constant.

Table 1. System Balance Ratios

System Balance Parameter	Ratio	Value for a 1 PetaFLOPS System
Peak compute performance	1 PetaFLOPS (fixed)	
Memory size	0.5 Bytes/FLOPS	0.5 PetaBytes total
Memory bandwidth	0.5 Bytes/FLOPS	0.5 PetaBytes/sec total
Bisection bandwidth	0.12 Bytes/FLOPS	0.12 PetaBytes/sec total
I/O Bandwidth	0.002 Bytes/FLOPS	2 TeraBytes/sec total
Disk Bandwidth	0.001 Bytes/FLOPS	1 TeraBytes/sec total
Disk Storage	50 Bytes/FLOPS	50 PetaBytes total

The values in Table 1 drive system cost. Table 2 shows example costs for those parameters (in percent to avoid confidentiality concerns). Processor cost is primarily driven by compute performance, which may be peak performance as shown in Table 1 or based on benchmarks. It is driven to a lesser degree by memory bandwidth and interconnect bandwidth. Memory subsystem cost is primarily driven by memory size since DRAMs are usually the most-costly single

component in a system. It is driven to a lesser extent by memory bandwidth, unless the memory size must increase to accommodate the memory bandwidth requirement. System interconnect cost is driven by bisection bandwidth. Storage and I/O subsystem cost is mainly driven by disk bandwidth because disk capacity has grown much faster than disk bandwidth and because supercomputers generally have comparatively less networking connectivity requirements than commercial systems.

Table 2. Subsystem Costs

Subsystem	Definition	Cost in %	Cost Driver
Processor	Microprocessors; cache; CPU board hardware	39%	Peak Performance
Memory	DIMMs; memory controllers	28%	Memory Size
System Interconnect	Controllers and switches; cables and connectors	14%	Bisection Bandwidth
Storage and I/O	Disks; disk and I/O controllers	19%	Disk Bandwidth

All subsystems include power, cooling, mechanical overhead

3. Cost/Benefit Analysis

The cost data in Table 2 can be combined with system RAS calculations to perform cost/benefit studies. Consider a peta-scale supercomputer with a 6 hour mean-time-to-failure (MTTF) [2, 3]. Assuming a 2 hour mean-time-to-repair (MTTR), steady-state system availability = MTTF/(MTTF+MTTR) = 6/(6+2) = 75%. A job that takes several hours might never complete, which is why application availability and checkpoints, described in the next section, are important. In this example, we consider just simple system availability to illustrate the concepts.

Our experience and calculations indicate that the memory subsystem is the main reliability inhibitor. A method for protecting against memory channel failures is memory RAID, in which an extra (fifth) memory channel is added [4,5]. Assume that memory RAID increases the system MTTF from 6 hours to 12 hours. System availability is improved from 75% to 86% (12/12+2). The cost of memory RAID is a 25% increase in the memory subsystem cost to pay for the fifth memory channel, which is a 7% increase in total system cost as shown in Column 4 of Table 3. In this example, paying an additional 7% for the system doubles the MTTF and increases system availability by 11%, which seems like a very good tradeoff. If the system MTTF only increased from 6 hours to 8 hours, system availability would only increase by 5%, and the

---

additional 7% cost could be more closely evaluated by looking at application availability, operations and administrative cost, user perception, and so forth.

Many customers have a fixed budget and could not pay for additional RAS even if it seems very beneficial as in the previous example. For those customers, it is possible to purchase the increased RAS by purchasing a slightly smaller system. Table 3 contains the appropriate calculations. Since the fifth memory channel adds 7% to the system cost, each subsystem cost is divided by 1.07 to get the rebalanced cost shown in column 5. The original system parameters are also divided by 1.07 to get the new system parameters shown in column 6. The new system parameters preserve the system balance ratios from Table 1, which is important for comparing system alternatives as described in Section 2. Also, since the new system has less processor hardware, the MTTF is 12.8 hours, 7% more than the 12 hour MTTF for the original system with a fifth memory channel. Peak system performance is lower in the rebalanced system, but the increased availability more than compensates as shown in Section 6.

The original system is a 1 PetaFLOPS system with a 6 hour MTTF and 75% system availability. The rebalanced system is a 0.93 PetaFLOPS system with a 12.8 hour MTTF and 86.5% system availability. The customer can select either system for the same total procurement cost. As shown in Section 5, the same type of analysis can also provide a range of options rather than a binary choice.

Table 3. Rebalanced System with a Fifth Memory Channel

Subsystem	System Parameters	Orig-inal Cost	Cost with 5th Memory Channel	Rebal-anced Cost	New System Parameters
Processor	1 Peta-FLOPS	39%	39%	36%	0.93 Peta-FLOPS
Memory	0.5 Peta-Bytes	28%	35%	33%	0.47 Peta-Bytes*
System Inter-connect	0.12 PB/sec	14%	14%	13%	0.11 PB/sec
Storage and I/O	2 TB/sec I/O 1 TB/sec Disk	19%	19%	18%	1.86 TB/sec I/O 0.93 TB/sec Disk
		100%	107%	100%	

*Total memory is actually 0.59 PB, but 0.12 PB is for redundancy rather than for application use

4. Checkpoints

Checkpointing [3,6] is a useful feature for both availability and minimizing human programming effort. A checkpoint is a saved application or system state from which computation can be restarted. At certain times, the system saves its entire memory and operational state (system checkpointing) or appropriate portion thereof (application checkpointing). In this paper, a simplistic model of system checkpointing is used to demonstrate performability tradeoffs. References 3 and 6 and the large body of checkpointing literature can be consulted for more complex models.

Checkpointing has two phases – (1) saving a checkpoint and (2) checkpoint recovery following a failure. To save a checkpoint, the memory and system state necessary to recovery from a failure is sent to storage. Checkpoint recovery involves restoring the system state and memory using the checkpoint and restarting the computation from the time the checkpoint was taken. The time lost to doing useful computation is the overhead time required to save a checkpoint, the time required to restore a checkpoint after a failure, and the recomputation time to replace the computation that had been performed after the checkpoint but before the failure. This lost time contributes to application unavailability, but is a much better solution than restarting the job after every failure.

The petascale supercomputer described in this paper has 0.5 PetaBytes of data that needs to be saved for a complete system checkpoint. Since the disk bandwidth of 1 TB/sec is less than the I/O bandwidth of 2 TB/sec, it is the limiting factor in the time required to take a checkpoint. The time required to dump a checkpoint to disk is 500 seconds (0.5PB at 1 TB/sec). It is possible to significantly reduce this time by saving a checkpoint to RAM. While the computation continues on the machine, the RAM checkpoint can be copied onto disk, to provide a more robust backup. Reference [6] describes this architecture in more detail and provides Markov models for determining the resulting availability and optimizing the checkpoint parameters.

5. Checkpoint Cost/Benefit Analysis

Given a set of system parameters, maximizing application availability is achieved by selecting the time between checkpoints that optimally balances the overhead of taking a checkpoint vs. the amount of recomputation required after a checkpoint recovery. The time to take a checkpoint is the most important parameter in that optimization. Ignoring checkpoint preparation time, which is usually small, time to take a disk checkpoint is a function of I/O and disk bandwidth. I/O bandwidth in Table 1 is twice the disk bandwidth in Table 1, so disk bandwidth is the limiting factor. Figure 1 shows application availability as a function of disk bandwidth for a 1 PetaFLOPS supercomputer with the system balance parameters shown in Table 1. Since disk bandwidth is the checkpoint bottleneck and is limited by spindle speed, doubling this bandwidth requires twice as many disks and disk controllers, which costs an extra 19% per Table 2. Note that varying checkpoint bandwidth provides a continuum of availability vs. cost – the RAS by the yard concept.

Disk bandwidth is increased by purchasing more disk drives and controllers. For a fixed budget, purchasing more disk resources means decreased system performance since less money is allocated to other compute resources (see Table 3 for example calculations). Thus, the increase in disk bandwidth shown in Figure 1 comes at the cost of decreased system performance as shown in Figure 2. This figure shows the increase in application availability, measured on the left axis, and the corresponding decrease in performance caused by purchasing fewer non-disk resources, measured on the right axis. In Figure 2, the application availability increase as a function of disk bandwidth is slightly higher than that shown in Figure 1 because the rebalanced system has slightly less compute hardware, and hence a slightly higher MTTF.

Figure 3 is the same graph as Figure 2 for a system that includes the fifth memory channel described in Section 3. The application availability is higher in Figure 3 since the fifth memory channel improves the MTTF, but the performance of the rebalanced system is lower due to the extra cost of the fifth memory channel. Note that the initial performance for a disk bandwidth of 1 TB/sec in Figure 3 is less than 1 PetaFLOPS because the system has been rebalanced for the fifth memory channel (see the last column in Table 3).

A similar rebalancing analysis can be performed for RAM checkpoints as shown in Table 4. A full system RAM checkpoint requires an extra 0.5 PetaByte of RAM. Application availability improves from 75% for disk checkpoints to 92% for RAM checkpoints with a 28% increase in system cost to purchase twice as much memory. The cost for the RAM checkpoint is shown in Table 4 along with the fixed budget alternative system. The increased amount of the fixed budget allocated to memory causes the performance to decrease from 1 PetaFLOPS to 0.77 PetaFLOPS.

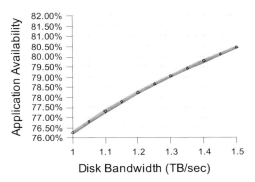

Figure 1. Application Availability vs. Disk Bandwidth

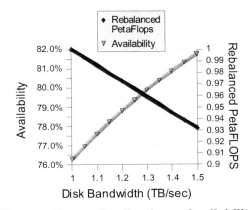

Figure 2. Application Availability and Rebalanced PetaFLOPS vs. Disk Bandwidth

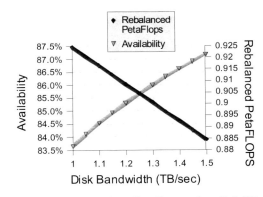

Figure 3. Application Availability and Rebalanced PetaFLOPS vs. Disk Bandwidth for a System with a Fifth Memory Channel

Figure 4 shows the same graph as Figure 3 for a system with a RAM checkpoint instead of a fifth memory channel. In this case, disk bandwidth does not have nearly as much impact on availability as in the earlier examples because the disk checkpoint is a backup to the RAM checkpoint, and most failures can be recovered using the RAM checkpoint. Increased disk bandwidth does have some effect because it allows the RAM checkpoint to be stored more quickly on disk, meaning that RAM checkpoints can be more frequent and that there will be a more current disk checkpoint if a failure occurs while a RAM checkpoint is being taken.

Table 4. Rebalanced System with a RAM Checkpoint

Sub-system	System Parameters	Orig-inal Cost	Cost with RAM Check-point	Rebal-anced Cost	New System Parameters
Processor	1 Peta-FLOPS	39%	39%	30%	0.77 PetaFLOPS
Memory	0.5 Peta-Bytes	28%	56%	45%	0.39 PetaBytes*
System Inter-connect	0.12 PB/sec	14%	14%	10%	0.09 PB/sec
Storage and I/O	2 TB/sec I/O 1 TB/sec Disk	19%	19%	15%	1.55 TB/sec I/O 0.77 TB/sec Disk
		100%	128%	100%	

*Total memory is actually 0.78 PB, but 0.39 PB is for storing a checkpoint rather than for application use

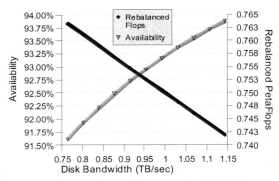

Figure 4. Application Availability and Rebalanced PetaFLOPS vs. Disk Bandwidth for a System with a RAM Checkpoint

6. Maximizing System Performability

In the previous sections, we have shown how to calculate the performance and availability for various system configurations given a fixed budget. This provides customers with a range of options, e.g., an availability/performance point on one of the curves shown in Figures 2-4. To help customers decide among the many options, it is useful to define a single availability/performance metric. In other words, we want a metric for performability [7], defined as a composite measure of a system's performance and its dependability. For the purposes of this paper, we selected a simple performability metric we call *available PetaFLOPS*, defined as

available PetaFLOPS =
application availability x peak PetaFLOPS

Available PetaFLOPS is a measure of the amount of computing a system could actually perform after accounting for failure recovery. As an example, the system configuration options from Table 3 have a available PetaFLOPS value of 0.75 (75% application availability x 1 peak PetaFLOPS) for the original system and 0.8 (86% application availability x 0.93 peak PetaFLOPS) with the fifth memory channel. In this case the fifth memory channel option would be preferred because it has the higher available PetaFLOPS even though it has a lower peak PetaFLOPS. From Table 4 the available PetaFLOPS for a system with a RAM checkpoint is 0.71 (92% application availability x 0.77 peak PetaFLOPS). Using this performability metric, this option would not be preferred over either of the others.

The available PetaFLOPS metric could be improved by using a better measure of performance e.g., performance on a benchmark suite or some kind of a utility function rather than just peak PetaFLOPS. Nevertheless, the simple metric is useful for illustrating cost/benefit trade-offs between performance and availability.

Figures 2, 3, and 4 showed the trade-off between performance and availability as a function of disk bandwidth. Figures 5, 6, and 7 show the available PetaFLOPS metric using the values from Figures 2-4. In Figure 5, as disk bandwidth is increased, application availability initially increases faster than performance decreases. Eventually, however, the performance decrease outweighs the availability increase, yielding the optimal value of 0.767 available PetaFLOPS at 1.2 TB/sec disk bandwidth. Figure 6 is similar to Figure 5, with an optimal value of 0.775 available PetaFLOPS at 1.15 TB/sec disk bandwidth. Figure 7 is interesting because the optimal value occurs when disk bandwidth is reduced rather than increased from its initial value. With a RAM checkpoint and an initial value of 1 TB/sec disk bandwidth, the availability improvement due to increased disk bandwidth has less impact on performability than the performance improvement achieved with more compute power and less disk bandwidth. The optimal value of 0.7 available PetaFLOPS occurs at 0.89 TB/sec disk bandwidth.

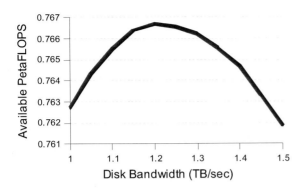

Figure 5. Available PetaFLOPS as Function of Disk Bandwidth

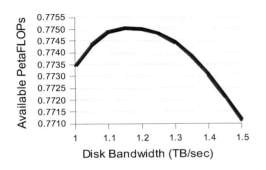

Figure 6. Available PetaFLOPS as Function of Disk Bandwidth for a System with a Fifth Memory Channel

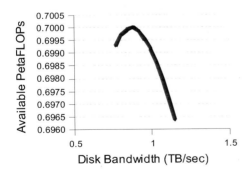

Figure 7. Available PetaFLOPS as Function of Disk Bandwidth for a System with a RAM Checkpoint

7. Summary

This paper describes RAS "by the yard" - the architectural flexibility that allows customers to purchase a range of RAS for different prices. It shows how to analyze the cost vs. RAS vs. performance

trade-offs for a system defined by a set of system balance ratios. In particular, it shows how to rebalance the system to accommodate RAS features when the system procurement budget is fixed. Using a performability metric, available PetaFLOPS, system optimization is demonstrated. The system resulting from the optimization provides the best combination of RAS and performance for a fixed cost.

The performability metric, available PetaFLOPS, described in this paper does not suitably capture all the subtleties of computer system RAS. Treating performability as linear in performance and availability does not account for all the benefits of improved RAS. Better RAS means decreased administration and maintenance cost and higher user satisfaction and productivity. At some point supercomputer users and administrators can stop waiting anxiously after submitting a job to see if it will finish. They can do useful work while trusting the supercomputer to complete the job, even in the presence of failures. The determination of a performability metric that appropriately accounts for productivity is the subject of future research.

Acknowledgments

This material is based on work supported by the US Defense Advanced Research Project Agency under contract No. NBCH3039002.

References

[1] The NITRD Program: FY2004 Interagency Coordination Report, Second Printing - October 2004, pp31-32, http://www.hpcc.gov/pubs/20041020_icr.pdf. See also http://www.highproductivity.org.

[2] M. Mueller, L. Alves, W. Fischer, M. Fair, and I Modi, "RAS Strategy for IBM S/390 G5 and G6", *IBM Journal for Research and Development*, Vol 43, No 5/6, Sept/Nov 1999, pp 875-887.

[3] J. Daly, "A Model for Predicting the Optimum Checkpoint Interval for Restart Dumps", *ICCS 2003*, LNCS 2660 Proceedings 4 (2003), pp 3-12.

[4] D.A. Patterson, P.M. Chen, G. Gibson and R.H. Katz, "Introduction to redundant arrays of inexpensive disks (RAID)", *Proc. IEEE COMPCON*, pp112-117, Spring 1989.

[5] Z. Zhang, "Recovery of Memory and Process in DSM Systems: HA Issue # 1", *Hewlett-Packard Labs Technical Report HPL-2001-76*, March, 2001. http://www.hpl.hp.com/techreports/2001/HPL-2001-76.pdf

[6] A. Wood, S. Nathan, T. Tsai, C. Vick, L. Votta, A. Vetteth, "Multi-Tier Checkpointing for Peta-Scale Systems", In *International Conference on Dependable Systems and Networking DSN2005*, Tokyo, Japan, June 28 – July 1, 2005.

[7] http://www.doc.ic.ac.uk/~nd/surprise_95/journal/vol4/eaj2/report.html

Web Services Wind Tunnel:
On Performance Testing Large-scale Stateful Web Services

Marcelo De Barros, Jing Shiau, Chen Shang, Kenton Gidewall, Hui Shi, Joe Forsmann

Microsoft Corporation

{marcelod,jshiau,cshang,kentong,huishi,josephfo}@microsoft.com

Abstract

New versions of existing large-scale web services such as Passport.com© have to go through rigorous performance evaluations in order to ensure a high degree of availability. Performance testing (such as benchmarking, scalability, and capacity tests) of large-scale stateful systems in managed test environments has many different challenges, mainly related to the reproducibility of production conditions in live data centers. One of these challenges is creating a dataset in a test environment that mimics the actual dataset in production. Other challenges involve the characterization of load patterns in production based on log analysis and proper load simulation via re-utilization of data from the existing dataset. The intent of this paper is to describe practical approaches to address some of the aforementioned challenges through the use of various novel techniques. For example, this paper discusses data sanitization, which is the alteration of large datasets in a controlled manner to obfuscate sensitive information, preserving data integrity, relationships, and data equivalence classes. This paper also provides techniques for load pattern characterization via the application of Markov Chains to custom and generic logs, as well as general guidelines for the development of cache-based load simulation tools tailored for the performance evaluation of stateful systems.

1. Introduction

Large-scale online web services are subject to very different loads and conditions when they are released on the internet. Services such as Passport.com can receive up to 300,000 user-driven transactions per second, and may contain a dataset of over 500,000,000 users. For this reason, new versions of such services have to undergo rigorous performance testing before going public. Irrespective of the tests being executed (benchmarking, load, scalability, capacity, etc), the high-level process consists of: environment (clusters, data, tools) preparation, execution, and analysis. This paper describes practical approaches for creating accurate environments for the execution of performance tests for stateful web services.

Web services are considered stateful if they contain hard-state instead of soft-state data [3]. Hard-state data is data that cannot be lost due to the unfeasibility of reconstructing it. An example is a user profile and user transactions for a bank account. Soft-state data can be reconstructed from hard-state data. An example would be aggregated financial reports. Many web services available today are stateful.

In performance test environments, pre-population of test data is a crucial step towards replicating production conditions. Traditional approaches for test data generation consist of synthesizing the data based on the application code, random and probabilistic techniques, or custom applications [4]. Other approaches make use of limited data sanitization processes based on predetermined heuristics [5]. However it is impractical to synthesize the same hard-states observed in production environments due to the unpredictability of the many ways in which the data may have been transformed based on users' activities. Performance tests are particularly sensitive to the dataset since slight differences in the test data may result in significant discrepancies in the test results.

The ideal dataset would be constructed from the same set of production data for the performance tests, but many of the items in production have restricted access. Therefore there is a need for a sustainable process of obfuscating restricted data items so that the dataset can be safely used in test laboratories. This is accomplished by the use of the *Data Sanitization* process [6], which aims to retrieve a set of databases and deterministically obfuscate restricted data, while preserving data integrity, relationships, and data equivalence classes. This process is described in section 2.

Once the right data is in place, there is still a need to simulate production behavior by duplicating the right mix of various types of transactions processed by the system and simulating the dependency between related sequences of transactions as observed in production. Many live environments contain a set of logs which can be mined to provide up-to-date statistics describing the transaction mix. By using data mining techniques, one can determine not only how APIs (Application Programming Interfaces) are being invoked, but also the relationship between invocations of the different APIs. We discuss one of these techniques based on an application of Markov Chains to generic/custom log data. This process is fully described in section 3.

Section 4 discusses approaches for writing cache-based performance test tools which can leverage the previously retrieved and sanitized production data, imported into test environments. Finally, we discuss practical results from the use of these techniques, as well as future improvements in section 5.

2. Data Sanitization

Using production data for testing new features which will operate on existing data (i.e., new search functionality that allows more fine-grained search criteria) is crucial not only for functional validation of correctness, but also for performance evaluation, since different amounts of data, dependencies, and data characteristics may have significant affects in the overall system's performance. Production data, however, contains large amounts of information regarding individuals which should be kept confidential, even if only used in restricted test laboratories. The general term to classify such confidential data is called Personally Identifiable Information (PII) [1]. The data sanitization process consists of a set of tools and methodologies to take production data and obfuscate all the pre-determined PII, preserving three key characteristics:
  i.   *Data Integrity*: Constraints applied to relational database tables, such as Primary Keys and Uniqueness are carried over after sanitization.
  ii. *Data Relationships*: Relationships between tables in a relational database persist after the sanitization process.
  iii. *Data Equivalence Classes*: Subsets of the domain input data are preserved, such that all elements in the subsets are assumed to be the same from the specification of the subsets [2].

The current process is tailored for obfuscation of data stored in relational databases. The process consists of a sequence of steps listed as:

2.1 **PII Identification**: the first step consists of identifying the data that needs to be obfuscated. Databases for large-scale systems may contain thousands of different tables and columns. A set of tools is provided along with the data sanitizer framework to assist the user with the identification of PII, although the identification process requires manual intervention and cannot be fully automated due to the

subjectivity of the data. The database schemas are modeled as XML files [7] containing all of the metadata pertinent to the tables in all of the databases.

2.2 **Sanitization Method Assignment:** The method used to sanitize a certain PII field can now be chosen in such a way to preserve (i), (ii) and (iii). Figure 1 below illustrates the PII identification and the sanitization method assignment:

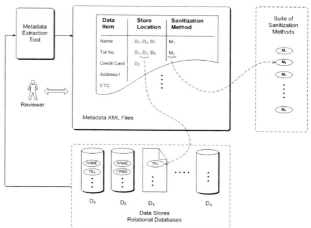

Figure 1. PII identification and method assignment

A sanitization method may have the following generic signature:

object SanitizationMethod(object OriginalValue, object[] Metadata)

The metadata may consist of the details of the particular field in question, such as data type and length. The method should perform a one-way transformation in order to avoid reverse engineering of the sanitized data. The data sanitizer framework comes with several sanitization methods, including the following ones (table 1).

Standard Sanitization Method	Description
Erase	Erases any non-binary field
EraseBinary	Erases binary fields
FillWithChar	Replaces the entire field with a random string of same length
FillWithDigit	Replaces the entire field with a random number of same length
HashString	Applies a one-way SHA1 salt-based (password) hash function
HashDigits	Applies a one-way SHA1 salt-based (password) hash function, but the result is numeric
NewGUID	Replace a GUID with a different (new) GUID

Table 1. Standard sanitization methods

New methods can be added to the framework when deemed necessary. The use of one-way SHA1 hash functions as a sanitization method is essential to ensure data integrity and relationship preservation post-sanitization: correlated data across tables/DBs can be sanitized by using one-way, salt-based SHA1 hash, ensuring the same output, thus consistency.

A crucial step is to review PII sets as well as sanitization methods and assignments with security experts and legal personnel to validate the correctness of the procedures.

2.3 **Test and Sanitization Execution**: after the proper identification of PII and sanitization methods, the overall sanitization process is tested in restricted laboratories on non-production data. Upon verification, the process is carried out in production environments. Since the sanitization is an in-place procedure, a copy of production data is made, all within secure production environments. The main sanitizer tool is multithreaded for optimal speed, thus multiple databases and tables are processed concurrently. Because of this, database constraints must be removed prior to the sanitization execution, since during the execution phase data relationships might be temporarily violated. All these constraints are saved prior to the sanitization, and are recreated upon completion of the sanitization process (figure 2).

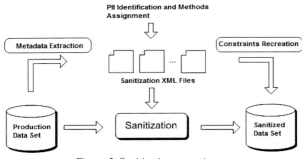

Figure 2. Sanitization execution

Table 2 below shows some results obtained running the data sanitizer on HP DL385 G1, 4xAMD 2.4GHz processors, 4GB RAM servers, against large data sets. The average percentage of PII fields identified in these data sets was ~13%, with one-way hash functions accounting for ~10% of the sanitization methods:

Databases	Data	Size	Time (h)
Subscription Service	33MM users	850GB	22
Partner Reporting Service	30MM users	600GB	16
Financial Reporting Service	32MM users	800GB	21
Customer Assistance Service	1.4MM tickets	50GB	3.5
Authentication Service	400MM users	3.5TB	100

Table 2. Sanitization runs experiments

3. Markov Chain Stress Model

The Markov Chain Stress Model includes two major components: the *knowledge retriever* component and the *knowledge exerciser* component. Both components are based on the concept of the Markov Chain dynamic stochastic process, which describes the state of systems at successive times [8]. The knowledge retriever component applies data mining on production activity logs and discovers the parameter load patterns of each API. The knowledge exerciser component uses Markov Chain Monte Carlo methods [9], which are a class of algorithms for sampling from probability distributions, based on constructing a Markov chain with the desired distribution as its stationary distribution, to manifest the former statistical knowledge to the stress test environment, and generates dynamic scenarios consistent with production load patterns.

During the *knowledge retriever* step, we assume that:

- A distributed application has a set with countable number of APIs, represented as:

$$X = \{X_0, X_1, ..., X_n\}$$

- Any API X_i is logically connected to API X_j with a probability weight, where $j = i$ is possible.

- Each API X_i has a known set of domain data as input parameters:

$$X_i = f(p_0, p_1, ..., p_{m_i})$$

Where p_j belongs to a domain set S_j,

$$p_j \in S_j, j = 0, 1, .., m_i$$

where S_j is the set of all possible values of p_j for this API X_i

- A client application makes API calls against the web service according to the Markov process. To simplify our model, we use the first-order Markov process [9] to implement the program, i.e. current API call X_i at time t depends only on the previous API call X_j at time t-1.

$$P(X_{j,t} \mid X_{i,0:t-1}) = P(X_{j,t} \mid X_{i,t-1})$$

- Client is homogenous over time, meaning that its behavior is consistent, the transition matrix can be re-built any time.

With the above assumptions, we use real production trace data as samples to estimate the Markov Transition Matrix:

$$
\begin{array}{ccccc}
 & X_0 & X_1 & X_2 \ldots X_n & \\
X_0 & p_{00} & p_{01} & p_{02} \cdots p_{0n} & \\
X_1 & p_{11} & p_{12} & p_{13} \cdots p_{1n} & \\
X_2 & p_{21} & p_{22} & p_{23} \cdots p_{2n} & \\
\vdots & & & & \\
X_n & p_{n0} & p_{n1} & p_{n2} \cdots & p_{nn}
\end{array}
$$

where:

- p_{ij} represents the transition probability
- And we have:
  For $\forall i, j \mid i = 0,1,\ldots, n;\ j = 0,1,\ldots, n$
  - $0 \le p_{ij} \le 1$
  - $\sum_{j=0}^{n} p_{ij} = 1$

During the *knowledge exerciser* step our objective is to produce load patterns that are as close as possible to those in production, using the Markov Transition Matrix we created during the Knowledge Retriever step.

An important aspect of this methodology is that the transition matrix extracted only reflects the average behavior over a certain period of time. Therefore, in order to reproduce the exact same pattern observed in production (in terms of different variables, such as CPU utilization, memory utilization, disk utilization, etc.), the matrix has to be periodically updated.

The following diagram (figure 3) describes the entire workflow:

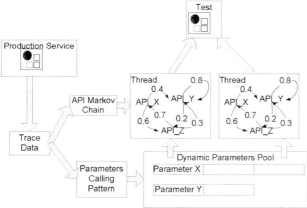

Figure 3. Markov Chain workflow

In the above workflow, we first aggregate the production activity logs by session, and order them by timestamps. Through data mining over the aggregated activity logs, we can get: (1) the Markov Transaction Matrix over the APIs, and (2) the interval between each of the APIs transacting (some authors refer to it as "Thinking Time" [10]). Through data mining over each API's parameters with aggregated statistics, we can get the parameter calling patterns of each API. At this point, we are done with the *knowledge retriever* step.

Our next step is to *exercise* the knowledge collected in previous steps in the stress testing environment. In practice, we found that it is more challenging to recover and mimic the parameter patterns of each API call than to produce the Markov transition matrix. This occurs due to the fact that the majority of input parameters are user-specific information with a high degree of randomness (i.e., user's first name). For user-specific information, we created tools or methods that would generate valid parameter values by creating them or retrieving them from our data store, and then deposit them in parameter pools.

We then use a thread to represent a client. This thread will call APIs one by one based on the Markov Transaction Matrix. We also introduce a sleep interval between two contingent API calls to make the simulation more realistic. The model will fetch needed parameters from the parameter pool for each API call.

Our model is scalable such that generation of stress load is possible. The parameter generator and threads can be distributed across machines via configurable parameters.

Figure 4 is an example of our stress load simulation during a 3 hour run. In this example, we generated load on the primary database servers in a test environment using knowledge learned from SQL profiler traces on database servers with the same role in production environments. The load profile in our test clusters was very similar to that observed in production.

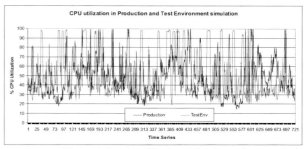

Figure 4. Load profiles in production and test

The Markov chain model not only simulates production-like stress load on test environments, but also provides important insights about system behavior, especially the correlation among APIs and among the parameters of each API. For example, highly correlated APIs might get a performance boost by improving locality, while unexpected correlations might be an indication of a potential area in need of further inspection.

4. Cache-based Load Simulation Tools

Methods described in previous sections provide a large dataset resembling production as well as a practical way to analyze and simulate real-user behaviors (i.e. scenarios). The performance tuning of a stateful system, however, often requires a particular API to be executed numerous times in isolation in order to determine the bottlenecks of the system. Web services are generally modeled after finite state machines in that the majority of APIs expect the invoking entity to be in a certain state prior to an operation [11]. The conventional test approach is to generate an entity and induce it into the required state before the actual API invocation (sometimes the state-inducement makes use of other APIs). This on-the-fly data generation and entity state inducement can hide actual system bottlenecks, since the preparation work may be the bottleneck itself. In addition, the conventional approach does not allow for taking advantage of sanitized production data.

Our solution is cache-based load simulation. This process requires pre-determination of the individual API calls to the state(s) in which the entity it operates against must be. Each defined state can be represented as a bucket. The bucket definitions are collections of Boolean conditions. When a particular entity matches the pre-defined set of conditions, the entity is said to belong to the corresponding bucket. The states are not mutually exclusive, so a given entity can potentially satisfy more than one state condition and therefore be present in more than one bucket in the cache.

Once the API state mapping and the evaluation criteria for each state have been established, the process becomes trivial. Given any API, we execute the following:

1. Determine the matching bucket for the API
2. Extract an entity from the bucket
3. Invoke the API with the selected entity
4. Re-evaluate state post API invocation
5. Re-insert the entity in the new bucket(s). If entity is no longer usable, it is discarded

Our implementation of the entity cache uses a SQL database to prevent data loss in the event of a crash, as well as allowing easy data sharing across multiple instances of the tool.

To simplify access to the database, a layer of abstraction was introduced to wrap the database calls. This layer exposes methods to modify the entities as well as the buckets. This layer exposes other methods

in addition to the normal "add", "get", and "remove" calls (table 3):

Method Type	Method
Initialization	*InitializeCache*
	LoadBuckets
	Clear
Bucket Access	*AddBucket*
	GetBucketList
	GetCountPerBucket
Entity Access	*AddEntity*
	GetEntityFromBucket
	RemoveEntity
	GetPreExistingEntity

Table 3. DB access methods for cached-based simulation

Since the operations performed on the entities will most likely change the entity state, each entity is similar to a critical section – only one thread may act on an entity at a time (however, multiple threads can still operate on different entities). To avoid corruption of entity state, we remove the entity from its matching buckets just prior to the API invocation, and after the API execution, we re-evaluate the entity state and place it back into the appropriate bucket(s).

The aforementioned process depends on a well-populated cache to work. During the cache-population stage, we utilize the database access method *"GetPreExistingEntity"* mentioned above to pick random entities from the existing dataset and use the state evaluation step to place the entities in the appropriate buckets in the cache. Population of specific buckets may only be accomplished by executing a set of pre-defined steps, which may or may not leverage existing data. Therefore, the resulting cached data would then be a combination of sanitized data and synthetic data.

In practice, we observed that the entity state can usually be determined by parsing the results from "state-retrieving" API calls (e.g. Get calls). In cases where the state-retrieving API calls do not provide sufficient information, we construct custom data access methods to query the data store.

This cache-based approach can be implemented in any of the existing commercial applications for load generation since the model is focused on interactions with the underlying system and not the load volume.

5. Results and Future Work

We have described in this paper techniques for building proper environments and performance test tools which can be used to accurately simulate the same conditions observed in production (live) environments, targeting large-scale stateful web services. The use of Data Sanitization, Markov Chain Stress Model, and Cache-based Load Simulation Tools have been successfully used for benchmark, capacity planning, and scalability tests of three major distributed web services: Subscription and Commerce Web Services, Identity Services Web Services, and Customer Assistance Web Services, all part of the Microsoft Member Platform Group. Accuracy of performance numbers collected in test laboratories have increased to a deviation of less than 5% from performance numbers observed in production environments (compared to ~9% with synthesized data). The number of real performance and functional issues found during the quality assurance process has increased by 15% with the introduction of the techniques described in this paper as part of the testing methodology.

Future work involves the enhancement and generalization of the techniques described in this paper, including:

- Extending the application of the data sanitization process to other data sources in addition to relational databases
- Real-time data sanitization
- Generalization of the application of Markov Chain Stress Model to different log sources
- Generalization of the Cache-based load simulation tools to automatically identify potential matching buckets based on the Finite State Machine for the system being tested.

6. References

[1] "Privacy in e-commerce: examining user scenarios and privacy preferences", *Proceedings of the 1st ACM conference on Electronic commerce*, ACM, 1999.

[2] W.E. Howden, "Reliability of the path analysis testing strategy", *IEEE Trans. Software Engineering*, vol SE-2, 1976 Sep

[3] Y. Saito, B.N. Bershad, H.M. Levy, "Manageability, availability, and performance in porcupine: a highly scalable, cluster-based mail service", *ACM Transactions on Computer Systems*, 2000

[4] J. Edvardsson, "A survey on automatic test data generation", *Proceedings of the Second Conference on Computer Science and Engineering*, ECSEL, October 1999.

[5] SRM Oliveira, OR Zaiane, "Protecting Sensitive Knowledge By Data Sanitization", *Third IEEE International Conference on Data Mining*, ICDM 2003

[6] O.C. McDonald, X. Wang, M. De Barros, R.K. Bonilla, Q. Ke, "Strategies for Sanitizing Data Items", US Patent Application (*patent pending*), 2004

[7] S. Abiteboul, P. Buneman, D. Suciu, "Data on the Web: From Relational to Semistructured Data and XML", *SIGMOD Record*, Vol. 32, No. 4, December 2003

[8] Stuart J. Russell, Peter Norvig, *Artificial Intelligence: A Modern Approach (2nd Edition)*, Prentice Hall, Upper Saddle River, NJ, Dec, 2003

[9] W.R. Gilks, S. Richardson, D.J. Spiegelhalter, *Markov Chain Monte Carlo in Practice*, Chapman & Hall/CRC, Dec, 1995.

[10] J.D. Meier, Srinath Vasireddy, Ashish Babbar, and Alex Mackman, *Improving .NET Application Performance and Scalability*, Microsoft Corp., Redmond, WA, April 2004

[11] B. Benatallah, F. Casati and F. Toumani, "Web service conversation modeling: A corner-stone for e-business automation," *IEEE Internet Computing, 2004.*

Application of Software Watchdog as a Dependability Software Service for Automotive Safety Relevant Systems

Xi Chen
DaimlerChrysler AG – Stuttgart, Germany

xi.chen
@daimlerchrysler.com

Juejing Feng
RWTH Aachen University – Aachen, Germany

juejing.feng
@rwth-aachen.de

Martin Hiller
Volvo Technology Corporation – Gothenburg, Sweden
martin.hiller
@volvo.com

Vera Lauer
DaimlerChrysler AG – Stuttgart, Germany

vera.lauer
@daimlerchrysler.com

Abstract

To face the challenges resulting from the increasing density of application software components and higher dependability requirements of the future safety systems in the automotive electronics, a dependability software service to monitor individual application software components in runtime is required in order to improve the overall system dependability. This paper proposes the application of a Software Watchdog service providing heartbeat monitoring and program flow checking. The Software Watchdog is integrated in a software platform for the automotive safety electronics. A model-based design with Matlab/Simulink and an evaluation of this Software Watchdog service in a hardware-in-the-loop validator are also given.

Index Terms — Software Watchdog, heartbeat monitoring, program flow checking, automotive dependable software platform and software services

1. Introduction and background

The on-board electrics and electronics (E/E) in vehicles have become subject to more demanding requirements in recent years, triggered by an ever increasing demand for safety and comfort. On the one hand, the complexity and quantity of applications implemented by electronics and software is increasing dramatically [1]. On the other hand, E/E systems and networks should exhibit at least the same dependability as state-of-the-art mechanical systems with comparable cost.

With the introduction of powerful microcontrollers and for reasons of cost, the number of ECUs (Electronic Control Unit) will be consolidated and even reduced as more and more functions will be integrated on one ECU. Facing this challenge, defining a common software platform and standardization of software services are two key approaches.

One central standardization initiative is the AUTOSAR Consortium [2], which aims to provide a standardized software platform for each in-vehicle ECU. According to the AUTOSAR vision, future embedded software will be developed independently from ECU hardware details. Application software components can be mapped onto different ECUs, where the application can be divided into code sequence components called runnables. Runnables from different applications can be mapped onto the same task, while tasks from different applications can also be mapped onto the same ECU. Therefore, it is possible, that runnables from different software components can be mapped to the same task. Considering the dependability requirements of the runnables, different time constraints can be required for two runnables. Those runnables should be treated differently in fault detection and error processing.

Taking the current trends into consideration, we need more powerful services to detect timing and program flow faults. Such services are not only required in the system integration and validation phases but also in runtime. A well-defined layered software platform [3] with flexible dependability software services for fault tolerance is a key issue for providing safety-relevant control systems in automotive applications.

The Software Watchdog service, aimed for monitoring the timing behavior and program flow, is designed in the scope of the EU project EASIS (*Electronic Architecture and System Engineering for Integrated Safety Systems*, see www.easis.org). This project is an industry consortium of 22 European leading vehicle manufacturers, system suppliers, tool producers and research institutes. Today, safety systems are mainly stand-alone systems which have little or no links across domain borders (domains in this context are e.g. powertrain, chassis, and body). So-called Integrated Safety Systems (ISS) combine active and passive safety systems across domain borders. Links to telematics services are also included in the term.

2. Related work

For automotive safety systems, satisfying real-time requirements in a deterministic manner is a critical issue. To meet timing constraints, different monitoring mechanisms have been developed, such as the ECU hardware watchdog [3][5][6], deadline monitoring [7][8] and execution time monitoring [9]. Approaches of control flow checking techniques with signatures

[10] have been developed in the IT-industry to ensure the correct execution sequence of the programs.

A hardware watchdog treats the embedded software as a whole. With the increasing density of applications on one ECU, the hardware watchdog should be supplemented with software services for the monitoring execution on a more detailed level, i.e., on the level of tasks or runnables.

Deadline monitoring of the OSEKTime [8] operating system and execution time monitoring [9] of AUTOSAR OS introduce the time monitoring of tasks, but the granularity of fault detection on the layer of tasks is not fine enough for runnables.

In the field of control flow checking, a lot of work has been made in the IT-industry to check the correctness of program flow. Most of the current methods of control flow checking are based on assigning signatures to blocks as introduced in [10]. Such a technique suffers from high performance overhead and low flexibility with regard to modification of programs.

3. Functional design

The Software Watchdog is supposed to ensure the real-time characteristics of the system. Tracing the cause of the violation of real-time requirements and an early detection of timing faults are not easy because of the complicated situations leading to the timing errors. A violation of a timing constraint can be placed into one of the following two categories:

1. An object hangs as a result of a requested resource being blocked, either by the object itself or some other object, long enough to violate the timing constraint.
2. An object is excessively dispatched for execution.

According to the categorization, the Software Watchdog identifies those two situations by monitoring the aliveness and arrival rate of the runnables. For correct execution of tasks, program flow is checked by the Software Watchdog treating runnables as basic blocks.

Before the design concept of the Software Watchdog is introduced in detail, we will briefly describe the EASIS software platform, into which the Software Watchdog is integrated.

3.1. EASIS dependable software platform

The EASIS software platform [11] focuses on ECUs for the ISS-applications which cross domain borders. It separates the safety relevant application software and the underlying ECU hardware by providing a software platform with standard interfaces.

As shown in Figure 1, the activities concerning the EASIS software platform cover layers L2 through L4. The ISS dependability software services in L3 aim to enhance the safety, reliability, availability and security of new safety functions. ISS gateway services in L3 provide secured inter-domain communication services. An OSEK-conforming operating system [7] with safety relevant services such as the Software Watchdog is integrated across L2 and L3. Device drivers, microcontroller abstraction layer and fault tolerant hardware platform reside on L2 and L1, respectively.

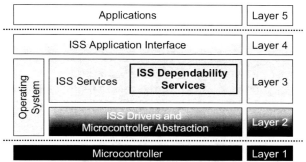

Figure 1: EASIS software topology

3.2. Design of the Software Watchdog

The design of the Software Watchdog (as depicted in Figure 2) follows the concept of heartbeat monitoring of runnables. With the information provided by the heartbeats of the runnables, it is possible to monitor periodicity and execution sequence of the runnables. Furthermore, task state, application state and global ECU state can be derived. Thus, the Software Watchdog can be designed to inform other dependability software services in the EASIS software topology, such as the Fault Management Framework [12], a general fault handling service in the platform, to undertake different fault treatments depending on the source, type and severity of the detected faults.

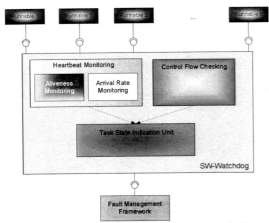

Figure 2: Functional architecture of the Software Watchdog

The Software Watchdog has three basic units: the heartbeat monitoring unit, the program flow checking unit and the task state indication unit.

- Heartbeat monitoring unit: With the help of a heartbeat indication routine, runnables report their heartbeats to the Software Watchdog.
- Program flow checking (PFC) unit: The program flow checking service monitors the execution sequence of runnables by comparing real executed successors with a predefined set of possible successors of the predecessors.
- Task state indication (TSI) unit: Errors of monitored runnables detected in the upper two blocks will be reported to the TSI unit. The TSI unit then compares the number of detected errors with some pre-defined thresholds and generates individual supervision reports on runnables. These reports can be used to derive error indication states of the tasks, which in turn can be used for determining the status of the applications.

3.2.1. Heartbeat monitoring

Heartbeat monitoring offers a mechanism for periodically monitoring the aliveness and arrival rate of independent runnables. The following fault types are handled:

- Fault type for aliveness monitoring: The runnable is blocked or preempted for some reason and its aliveness indication routine is not executed frequently enough.
- Fault type for arrival rate monitoring: Within one period, there are more aliveness indications of the monitored runnable than expected.

In EASIS, we chose a passive approach to record and monitor the runnable updates by saving the heartbeats of runnables in the Aliveness Counter (AC) and Arrival Rate Counter (ARC). These two kinds of counters are assigned to each runnable to record its heartbeats during the defined monitoring period according to the fault hypothesis and checked shortly before the next period begins. The monitoring periods are recorded in the Cycle Counter for Aliveness (CCA) and Cycle Counter for Arrival Rate (CCAR). All of those counters are reset to zero, if the periods defined in the fault hypothesis expire or an error is detected in the last cycle. In addition to the data resources used for the computation, an Activation Status (AS) is assigned to each runnable to control the heartbeat monitoring of the runnables.

3.2.2. Program flow checking

Correct program flow is a fundamental part of the correct execution of computer programs. In the embedded system, the following faults could cause program flow errors:

- Faults in the software design, implementation and/or integration.
- Transient faults in the system, e.g. memory errors.
- Corruption of the program counter.

To reduce the overhead involved during program flow checks as well as the system complexity, only the sequence of the safety-critical runnables will be monitored. With the help of aliveness indication routines, which are integrated into the runnables as automatically generated glue code, a view of which runnables are currently being executed can be derived. Compared with the widely discussed method of using embedded signatures as proposed in [10], or with the watchdog processor as discussed in [13], a simple approach with a look-up table was applied to minimize performance penalty and extensive modification requirements of applications. In the look-up table, all possible predecessor/successor relationships of the monitored runnables are stored and compared to the actual execution sequence.

3.2.3. Task state indication

In order to achieve global monitoring by integration of the results from the monitoring of runnables, the error messages of runnables are recorded by the Task State Indication Unit in an error indication vector. If one of the elements in the error indication vector reaches the threshold, the whole task will be considered faulty. Based on the mapping information of applications and tasks, corresponding fault treatments with a global view of the ECU are taken:

- If the global ECU state is "faulty", the ECU might be subjected to a software reset depending on the requirements and constraints of applications.
- If the global ECU state is "OK", the "faulty" application software components might be restarted or terminated.
- If there are other tasks, which do not belong to any of the terminated/restarted applications, these tasks might be terminated and restarted with the services provided by the operating system.

4. Validation

Before we explore the concept validation of the Software Watchdog in detail, a brief introduction to the EASIS validation activities, development process, methodology and prototyping tool chain will be given.

4.1. Brief introduction to EASIS validator

The EASIS architecture validator [14][15] focuses on the prototyping and validation of some of the most relevant properties of the EASIS architecture, including fault-tolerant hardware, dependability software architecture and services. The EASIS HIL (Hardware-in-the-Loop) validator hosts a number of ISS-applications, such as the driver assistance applications SafeLane and SafeSpeed with Steer-by-Wire technology. SafeLane is a lane departure warning application, and SafeSpeed is a system to automatically limit the vehicle speed to an externally commanded maximum value. The nodes in the architecture validator include fault-tolerant actuator and sensor nodes, driving dynamics control, environment simulation, light control node and a gateway node, which connects different vehicle domains of TCP/IP, CAN (Controller Area Network) [16] and FlexRay [16].

4.2. Brief introduction to validation process

The validation of the Software Watchdog is performed on the central node of the EASIS architecture validator. The central node is an AutoBox, a rapid prototyping platform from dSPACE [17], where the safety applications of SafeSpeed with control algorithms and dependability software services e.g. the Software Watchdog are integrated.

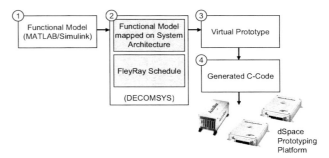

Figure 3: Tool chain and development process

As shown in Figure 3, the validation process of the Software Watchdog follows the model- and simulation based development process, in which a sub-system is developed and tested in a pure software environment with the help of simulation tools (Software-in-the-Loop test). The implementation of software on a particular hardware platform will only be initiated after a successful test of the functionalities with the help of simulation models. In the first step after requirements analysis of the applications, system functional design is initiated by building and modeling the whole system with Matlab/Simulink, in particular the modeling of runnables. The Software Watchdog is prototyped and simulated on a PC as a virtual prototype in the third step. In the next step, based on the knowledge gained from the virtual prototype and other automotive constraints such as memory and timing requirements, the AutoBox was chosen for the validation and evaluation of the concepts in the EASIS architecture validator. The virtual prototype of the Software Watchdog and the modeled safety application will be mapped onto tasks and scheduled on the system architecture. Individual hardware specific C-codes were generated, compiled and loaded onto the rapid prototyping platform.

4.3. Modeling, simulation and prototyping of the Software Watchdog

For the modeling of task dispatching and program flow of runnables in OSEK, Stateflow in Matlab/Simulink was applied. Stateflow is a design and development tool used for modeling complex system behavior based on finite state machines. Runnables are modeled with function-call subsystems and triggered by events sent by Stateflow in a defined execution sequence. A function-call subsystem is a block in Matlab/Simulink which can be invoked as a function by another block. For instance, as illustrated in Figure 4, the application SafeSpeed can be divided into three runnables: sensor value reading in *GetSensorValue*, the control algorithm in *SAFE_CC_process* and setting of the actuator in

Speed_process. These are triggered as function-call subsystems by the Stateflow chart *SafeSpeed,* in which the execution sequence of runnables is implemented. To indicate the aliveness of the runnables, further function-call subsystems to simulate the glue code are also implemented, which report the execution of the runnables.

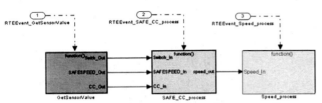

Figure 4: Modeling of runnables and program flow

The time-triggered behavior of the heartbeat monitoring unit and task state indication unit was modeled with time counters. Thus, in order to simulate the mechanism of task scheduling with different periods in the operating system, different time counters can be assigned to the Stateflow charts. On the other hand, the program flow checking unit was modeled using an event-triggered Stateflow chart.

4.4. Integration of the Software Watchdog in the EASIS software platform

Following the layered architecture of the EASIS software platform (see Figure 1), the Software Watchdog service is integrated into L3 as a separate module with defined interfaces to other software modules. There are two main interfaces to the Software Watchdog. The first interface serves for application software components in L1 to report their aliveness indications to the Software Watchdog. The other interface is used for the Software Watchdog to report the detected faults to the Fault Management Framework. Fault Management Framework is a general fault treatment system that gathers the information on the detected faults, and informs the applications about the fault detection. Lastly, coordinated fault treatment can be carried out with the help of the Operating System and Fault Management Framework.

4.5. Evaluation of the Software Watchdog in EASIS validator

The evaluation of the Software Watchdog is performed based on the fault/error definition in the design phase. Since different faults can result in the same error, error injection is applied for the evaluation of the design and prototyping of the Software

Watchdog. Such an approach has the advantage that the dependability requirements can be tested in a front-loading manner of system development. The concept can be validated independently from the specific fault-types. Faults, which are difficult to inject into the test bench or on-road test, can be relatively easily emulated with errors.

Here again Stateflow is used to manipulate the execution frequency and sequence of runnables by changing the timing parameter of runnables, manipulation of loop counters and building invalid execution branches, etc. The experiment environment ControlDesk [17] from dSPACE provides the possibility to manipulate the data assigned to the timing parameter of runnables to the condition that determine the invalid execution branches in the runtime. Therefore, it is used to trigger the error injection during the execution of the applications and visualize the results as well.

By building different evaluation cases, the three chief functionalities of the Software Watchdog, i.e. the detection of the aliveness error, the arrival rate error and the program flow error, are successfully validated. The following screenshots demonstrate some of the evaluation cases generated by injecting heartbeat or program flow errors. The x-axes of each plot in the diagram indicate the time lapse, which has a scalar of 10ms. The y-axes indicate the value of the counter and number of detected error.

In order to inject heartbeat errors, a time scalar is connected to a slider instrument to change the execution frequency, For example, Figure 5 shows the test with an injected aliveness error. Similar test with arrival rate error and control flow error were performed as well. The increase in the y-value in the last plot "AM Result" (Aliveness Monitoring Result) indicates the detection of the errors.

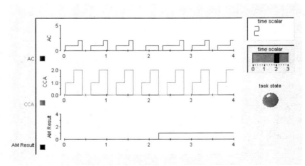

Figure 5: Test with injected aliveness error

Figure 6 shows the case in which the real cause of the erroneous state is identified through the collaboration of the units of the Software Watchdog. Here, the aliveness errors detected by the heartbeat monitoring unit are actually caused by program flow errors, which are reported with the plot "PFC Result" (Program Flow Checking Result). After the detection of three program flow errors (which here is set as the threshold), the task state is set to "faulty". Only one accumulated aliveness error is reported.

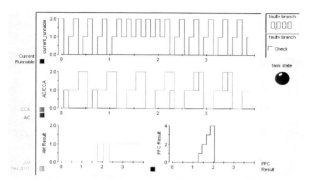

Figure 6: Collaboration of fault detection units

5. Conclusions and outlook

Conclusions

The concepts and design of the Software Watchdog proposed in this paper reflects the current trends in automotive software development.

The Software Watchdog, a software-implemented dependability service, monitors the individual timing constraints of application runnables and their program flow. It demonstrates the functional potential for improving dependability in distributed in-vehicle embedded systems. The interface of the Software Watchdog provides information for further fault treatments and variants for fault containment and tolerance.

Many valuable experiences were gained during the modeling, simulation and rapid prototyping of ISS applications and dependability software services using the concept of runnables.

Outlook

In the EASIS architecture validator, further analysis of fault detection coverage can be of interest for the mapping and application of the Software Watchdog to meet the individual dependability requirements of different safety systems. The functionalities and performance of the Software Watchdog with regard to fault handling strategies, especially concerning dynamic reconfiguration of applications and collaboration of monitoring units are further evaluated on an evaluation microcontroller S12XF from Freescale.

References

[1] M. Broy, "Automotive Software and Systems Engineering," *Proc. 25th International Conference on Software Engineering*, pp. 719 – 720, 2003

[2] AUTOSAR partnership, http://www.autosar.org/

[3] Z.T. Kalbarczyk, et al., Chameleon: A Software Infrastructure for Adaptive Fault Tolerance, *IEEE Transaction on parallel and distributed systems*, Vol. 10, No. 6, June 1999

[4] K. Tindell, F. Wolf, R. Ernst, "Safe Automotive Software Development," presented at Proceedings of the Design, Automation and Test in Europe Conference and Exhibition (DATE'03), *IEEE Computer Society*, Munich, Germany, March 2003.

[5] D. Lantrip, "General Purpose Watchdog Timer Component for a Multitasking System," *embedded world*, 1997.

[6] J. Ganssle, "Watching the Watchdog," *embedded world*, 2003.

[7] OSEK, "OSEK/VDX Operating System Specification 2.2.3," 2005, http://portal.osek-vdx.org/files/pdf/specs/os223.pdf

[8] OSEK, "OSEK/VDX time triggered operating system 1.0," 2001, http://portal.osek-vdx.org/files/pdf/specs/ttos10.pdf

[9] The AUTOSAR Consortium, "AUTOSAR Specification of Operating System," pp. 33-35, 2006 : http://www.autosar.org/download/AUTOSAR_SWS_OS.pdf

[10] Nahmsuk Oh, P. Shirvani, E. McCluskey, "Control-Flow Checking by Software Signatures," *IEEE Transaction on Reliability*, vol. 51, Mar-2002, pp. 111-121.

[11] M. Hiller, et al., "Dependability Services in the EASIS Software Platform," *DSN 2006 Workshop on Architecting Dependable Systems*, http://www.easis-online.org/wEnglish/img/pdf-files/wads_2006_easis.pdf

[12] EASIS Deliverable document D1.2-8, "Fault Management Framework", http://www.easis-online.org/wEnglish/download/Deliverables/EASIS_Deliverable_D1.2-8_V1.0.pdf

[13] T. Michel, et al., "A New Approach to Program Flow Checking without Program Modification", *Proc. 21st Symposium on Fault-Tolerant Computing*, pp. 334-341, 1991

[14] EASIS, "Specification of EASIS Validator with Telematics Gate-way, WT5.1 Deliverable," EASIS Consortium 2006.

[15] EASIS, Work Package 5 Validation, http://www.easis-online.org/wEnglish/workpackages/wp5.shtml?navid=9

[16] G. Leen, D. Heffernan, A. Dunne, "Digital Networks in the Automotive Vehicle," *IEEE Computer and Control Eng. J.*, Dec-1999, pp. 262-264.

[17] M. Eckmann, F. Mertens, "Close-to-Production Prototyping, Flexible and Cost-efficient," in ATZ electronic, vol. 01/2006, 2006, pp. 22-27.

Session 4C:
Distributed Algorithms

Evaluating the Impact of Simultaneous Round Participation and Decentralized Decision on the Performance of Consensus

Lívia Sampaio[†]   Michel Hurfin[‡]   Francisco Brasileiro[†]   Fabíola Greve[⋆]
livia@dsc.ufcg.edu.br, hurfin@irisa.fr, fubica@dsc.ufcg.edu.br, fabiola@dcc.ufba.br

[†] Universidade Federal de Campina Grande, PB, Brasil
Departamento de Sistemas e Computação

[‡] INRIA Rennes - IRISA, France

[⋆] Universidade Federal da Bahia, BA, Brasil
Departamento de Ciência da Computação

Abstract

Consensus services have been recognized as fundamental building blocks for fault-tolerant distributed systems. Many different protocols to implement such a service have been proposed, however, not a lot of effort has been placed in evaluating their performance. In particular, in the context of round-based consensus protocols for asynchronous systems augmented with failure detectors, there has been some work on evaluating how the QoS of the failure detector impacts the performance of the protocols, as well as on the trade-off between having faster decentralized decision at the expenses of generating more network load. These studies, however, focus on protocols that have no mechanism to deal with an eventual bad QoS provided by the failure detector, and have a decision pattern that is either completely centralized - only one process being able to autonomously decide - or completely decentralized - all processes being able to autonomously decide. This paper reports a thorough evaluation of the performance of a consensus protocol that has two unique features. Firstly, it mitigates the problems due to bad QoS delivered by the failure detector by allowing processes to simultaneously participate in multiple rounds. Secondly, it allows its decision pattern to be configured to have different numbers of processors allowed to autonomously decide. We have measured the decision latency of the protocol to conduct the performance analysis. The results, obtained by means of simulation, highlight the advantages and limitations of the two mechanisms and allow one to understand in a comprehensive framework how the protocol's parameters should be set, such that the best performance is achieved depending on the application's requirements.

1 Introduction

Agreement problems [4] are at the heart of fault-tolerant distributed systems and many protocols have been suggested in order to solve them in asynchronous environments subject to process crashes. The behaviors of these protocols are commonly defined by their safety and liveness properties. Moreover, given the asynchrony of the system, the liveness properties are eventual properties, in the sense that they only state what must be eventually satisfied, and make no assumptions on the actual time when the properties have to be satisfied. Therefore, although these properties are useful to precisely define the specification of the protocol, they give little help in predicting the protocol's expected performance. Nonetheless, the performance of such protocols should be a first order requirement when designing practical fault-tolerant systems. Particularly, it is of great interest to investigate characteristics of agreement protocols in order to enhance their overall performance in realistic scenarios, which must account for asynchrony and resource contention.

The consensus problem is the great common denominator among the agreement problems. In an asynchronous system prone to process crashes, consensus has no deterministic solution [7]. Failure detector oracles are an elegant abstraction proposed by Chandra and Toueg which encapsulates the extra synchrony necessary to circumvent this impossibility result [2]. They offer distributed information about failures of processes in the system. In this paper, we are interested in asynchronous systems equipped with unreliable failure detectors of the class $\diamond\mathcal{S}$. The choice is justified by the fact that this is the weakest class of failure detectors allowing to solve consensus [3]. $\diamond\mathcal{S}$ failure detectors can make an arbitrary number of mistakes, but, in spite of their inaccuracy, they will never compromise the safety properties of the consensus protocol that uses them. Such a protocol is said to be indulgent and tolerates arbitrary periods of asynchrony.

Due to the essential role played by the consensus problem, it is of utmost importance to evaluate the performance of algorithms proposed to solve it. In spite of this importance, quantitative performance evaluation of consensus protocols is normally conducted using only non-temporal metrics, such as the number of *communication steps*[1] required to reach a decision in particular runs of the protocol. Analysis using non-temporal metrics, although useful at a macro level, hide important information required for a more precise performance analysis. For instance, it is well known that the pattern and number of messages exchanged by the processes have a considerable effect on the duration (latency) of a distributed computation [1]. Since the communication pattern and the number of messages exchanged in each communication step of different consensus protocols vary widely, accounting the number of communication steps gives very little insight on how long a protocol will take to reach a decision. Moreover, these metrics are normally accounted only for restricted runs (normally named "favorable runs"); for instance, runs in which the failure detector makes no mistake.

It is only recently that efforts are being attempted towards the use of temporal metrics when analyzing the performance of consensus protocols [14, 17, 12]. While the interest in comparing the performance of these protocols using more practical metrics grows, researchers have also started to worry about designing consensus protocols that can effectively deal with the issues that impact the decision latency of these protocols [8, 12]. In particular, Hurfin *et al.* [8] have proposed an extension of the Chandra-Toueg consensus protocol which incorporates a mechanism that allows processes to simultaneously participate in several rounds, providing robustness against variability on the quality of service delivered by the failure detector, as well as a mechanism that allows flexible control on the decision pattern of the protocol. However, similar to most other works, the performance analysis conducted in [8] uses only non-temporal metrics and, therefore, is insufficient to properly

evaluate the effectiveness of the proposed mechanisms.

In this paper we fill in this gap by conducting an extensive performance evaluation of the protocol proposed by Hurfin *et al* (denoted herein the *HMMR-consensus*). We pursued a quantitative approach based on a temporal metric that gauges the latency of the protocol to reach a decision. We use a realistic simulation model, which accounts for asynchrony (denoted by wrong suspicions that are a direct consequence of the lack of timing assumptions) and resource contention (CPU and network). The results, obtained by means of simulation, give a more accurate perspective on the usefulness and limitations of the unique mechanisms incorporated within the protocol and allow one to understand in a comprehensive framework how the protocol's parameters should be set, such that the best performance is achieved depending on the application's requirements. In particular we highlight the positive effects of the simultaneous participation to several consecutive rounds. The window mechanism, which has been ignored in all previous evaluations of consensus protocols, allows to mask entirely the impact of a bad QoS of the failure detector. We also show that switching from a centralized to a decentralized decision pattern has only an interest provided that (1) simultaneous round participation is implemented and (2) the application requires that at least $k > 1$ processes decide quickly.

The remainder of this paper is structure in the following way. In Section 2 we give a brief description of the rationale behind the protocol we will study. Then, in Section 3 we present our simulation model. Section 4 brings the results of the experiments together with our analysis. We compare our work with related efforts in Section 5. Finally, Section 6 concludes the paper with our final remarks.

2 Description of the Consensus Protocol

2.1 The Problem and $\diamond\mathcal{S}$-based Solutions

In the consensus problem, each process in a group of n processes $\Pi = \{p_1, p_2, ..., p_n\}$ proposes a value and the correct processes must decide for the same value, chosen among the values initially proposed, despite the fact that up to f, $f < n$, processes may crash. Formally, the consensus is specified by the following properties: i) *Termination*, every *correct* process eventually decides some value; ii) *Validity*, if a process decides v, then v was proposed by some process; iii) *Uniform Agreement*, no two processes (*correct* or *not*) decide differently.

To circumvent the FLP impossibility result [7], Chandra and Toueg have proposed in [2] the concept of *unreliable failure detectors*. Informally, an unreliable failure detector is a distributed "oracle" that gives (possibly erroneous) hints about which processes of the system may have

---

[1]To converge towards a single decision value, a consensus protocol makes the processes engaged in the execution of the protocol exchange messages with proposed values. The number of communication steps required to converge to a decision is equal to the length of the longest communication path observed during the computation.

crashed. Chandra and Toueg characterized a failure detector in terms of two properties: *completeness* and *accuracy*. Completeness characterizes the failure detector capability of suspecting crashed processes, while accuracy characterizes the failure detector capability of not suspecting correct processes. Chandra, Hadzilacos and Toueg have also proved that a failure detector, denoted by $\Diamond S$, is the weakest failure detector for solving consensus even if such failure detectors can make an infinite number of mistakes [3]. The class $\Diamond S$ satisfies the following completeness and accuracy properties: i) *Strong Completeness*, eventually every crashed process is permanently suspected by *every* correct process; ii) *Eventual Weak Accuracy*, there is a time after which some correct process is never suspected by any correct process.

Several protocols have been proposed to solve consensus based on $\Diamond S$ failure detectors [2, 13, 9, 11]. They all rely on the rotating coordinator paradigm and follow the same basic principles. The protocol proposed by Chandra and Toueg [2] (denoted CT-consensus in this paper) is the first of them.

A $\Diamond S$ consensus protocol proceeds in a sequence of asynchronous rounds numbered 1, 2, etc. Each process manages an estimation of the decision value (equal to its initial value when the local computation starts) and updates this variable at most once per round. During each round, a single process (named the coordinator of the round) has some extra power and tries to impose a selected value as the decision value. All the processes agree on the identity of the coordinator of a round r as this identity is defined statically using a pre-defined formula. Thus a round is an attempt to converge to a decision value during which each correct process can either adopt the value suggested by the coordinator or keep its previous estimation. Following the terminology used by the authors of these protocols, the choice made by a process facing this alternative is called a vote (or also an acknowledgment).

As the communication channels are reliable and the failure detector satisfies the strong completeness property [2], any non-crashed process that starts the execution of round r eventually generates either a positive vote (when it is aware of the value proposed by the coordinator of round r) or a negative one (when it suspects the coordinator of round r to be crashed). By assumption, the maximal number of crashed processes is supposed to be less than half of the processes ($f < n/2$). Consequently, if a process p_i (for example, the coordinator) is identified as one of the recipients of all the votes generated during a round, it can wait until it gathers at least $n - f$ votes issued by a majority of distinct processes. A decision is taken by a process if it observes that a majority of processes has generated positive votes. Further, thanks to the accuracy property of the failure detector, the scenario where a decision is never reached

is impossible. A process eventually decides: indeed in the sequence of rounds, there is necessarily a round that will be coordinated by a correct process which is not (or no more) erroneously suspected to be crashed. During this round, a decision message is reliably broadcast to all the processes by the correct coordinator.

2.2 The HMMR-Consensus Protocol

The HMMR-consensus protocol proposed in [8] follows the control structure of the CT-consensus but including two interesting features aiming at improving the performance of the protocol; these features are: the *simultaneous round participation* and the *configurable decentralized decision pattern*. Both aim to speed up decisions and better circumvent uncertainties caused by asynchrony and bad QoS delivered by the failure detector.

Simultaneous Round Participation. In all the $\Diamond S$-based consensus algorithms proposed so far, messages sent during a round r have to be taken into account during round r only. Messages received earlier are logged till the process executes the right round. Messages received too late (*i.e.* after the end of round r) are ignored and discarded. Following this strict rule leads to consider that a round is definitely rotten as soon as the next round starts. The sliding round window mechanism presented in the HMMR-consensus weakens this constraint allowing processes to participate in simultaneous rounds at a time. Let w denote the number of consecutive rounds in which a process is simultaneously involved. During a round r, votes generated during the current round r, but also during the $w - 1$ previous rounds are significant and are delivered to the consensus protocol that keeps information about the last w rounds still in progress. In a run of the protocol, the window size w can vary from 1 to n. A process p_i can start round $r > w$ only if it terminates round $r - w$. Thus when round r starts, p_i can no more decide during round $r - w$.

Configurable Decentralized Decision Pattern. In any given round r, we can distinguish processes that can manage the decision and decide autonomously from those that cannot. Processes in the first set can test a decision predicate and must receive the necessary messages for this analysis; let us call this set X and its cardinality x. The second set is composed by processes that just wait for the decision, that is sent to them by processes belonging to X. In the classical CT-consensus, X is composed uniquely by the coordinator of round r, characterizing a centralized decision pattern [2]. In this case, the flow of messages is from/to the round coordinator, so that the number of messages exchanged during round r is $O(n)$. In some other protocols, we find a decentralized decision pattern in which the set X contains all the n processes in the system [13, 9], *i.e.* $X = \Pi$. Thus, the messages are exchanged from/to everybody and they attain a complexity of $O(n^2)$ in a round. The decentralization of the decision aims at having faster decisions as well as better tolerating crashes; however, at the expenses of generating a higher network load, which in turn may negatively impact the protocol's performance. The protocol in study has the noticeable feature of allowing the dynamic configuration of the set of processes belonging to the decision set X. The only constraint to be observed, in order to preserve safety, is that, giving a round r, the coordinators of r and $r + 1$ should belong to X [8]. Therefore, the protocol is able to define its proper message exchange pattern for each round, by varying the cardinality of X from 2 to n. So, in order to accomplish the best performance, the protocol must adequate the use of this feature to the network load.

3 Simulation Model

Figure 1 illustrates the design of the system by following a modular approach in which modules communicate between them through a pre-defined interface. The consensus module calls upon the failure detection module via a GET-FAULTY() interface in order to get the list of suspected processes. On the other hand, the application module starts a consensus by invoking the PROPOSE() interface and the decision value is informed to the application via a DECIDE() callback function. The modules communicate with each other by means of message passing (SEND() and RECEIVE() primitives) through a reliable network link represented by the network interface module.

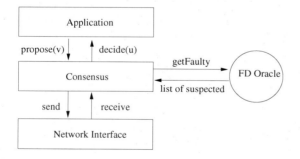

Figure 1. Design of The Consensus System

The configuration of the HMMR-consensus has two input parameters: i) the round window size (w) and ii) the number of processes able to decide during the execution of a round (x).

Failure Detection Model. To detect crash failures, a well known solution consists in using timeouts to identify processes suspected of having crashed. Usually, some monitoring mechanism based on message exchanging is used; processes that do not communicate with the others within a specific timeout are considered suspected. Particularly, in the

push-style of monitoring, every process p_i sends heartbeat messages at each η units of time to all the other processes p_j informing it is alive. If p_j does not receive a heartbeat from p_i within δ units of time after the message is expected to be sent, then p_i will be suspected by p_j. The values of η and δ can be configured in order to guarantee some QoS on the information provided by the failure detector.

QoS of failure detectors is partially defined by the restrictions imposed by their completeness and accuracy properties. Consider a failure detection service composed by independent modules. Some additional QoS metrics for the local failure detection module $FD_{i,j}$ of process p_i that monitors process p_j have been proposed in [5]. In particular, we are interested in the following accuracy QoS metrics: mistake duration (T_M), mistake recurrence time (T_{MR}) and query accuracy probability (P_A). Mistake duration and mistake recurrence time are random variables that represent, respectively, the length of a period during which a process p_i remains wrongly suspecting p_j and the time elapsed between two consecutive periods of wrong suspicions of $FD_{i,j}$. On the other hand, P_A represents the probability that a failure detector is correct at a random time. These metrics are related to each other as follows: $P_A = 1 - E(T_M)/E(T_{MR})$, where $E(V)$ is the expected value of the random variable V [5]. Our failure detection service is based on the push-style of monitoring and has a configurable QoS. However, in the simulations, the decisions on suspecting or not a process are not driven by the expiration of timeouts, but by the configuration of the QoS metrics (T_M, T_{MR} and P_A) discussed above. Yet, we use values for η and δ to configure the failure detector; these two parameters are required to determine the values of T_M and T_{MR}. Moreover the knowledge of η is also necessary to generate the message overhead corresponding to the normal activity of a push-style failure detector.

Communication Model. The communication module represents a simple Ethernet network that accounts for resource contention [15]. In this case, two resources may suffer contention: CPU (one per process) and network link. The CPU contention is related to the processing performed in each host to send and receive messages (the cost of executing the algorithm or the application itself is negligible). The network contention regards the transmission delay associated with the messages exchanged by the application. A message m transmitted from p_i to p_j will be delivered by p_j after $T_S + T_N + T_R$, where T_S and T_R represent, respectively, the CPU contention to send (source) and receive (destination) m; and T_N is the network contention. Note that, the network is shared by all processes in the system, but a mechanism is used to provide equity in the use of the network; every process has a network queue that stores messages to be transmitted, and the access to the network link is given by the use of a token that circulates among all processes. The time spent in the network resource is one unit of time (ut) and the time spent in the CPU resource is λut (the cost of processing a message is the same regardless if it is accounted in the source or in the destination). The λ parameter represents the relative speed of processing a message on a host compared to transmitting it over the network, where $\lambda = T_{CPU}/T_N$, $T_{CPU} = T_S = T_R$ and $\lambda \geq 0$ [15]. By choosing different values for λ it is possible to represent different network environments.

4 Performance Evaluation

4.1 Simulation Scenarios

The HMMR-consensus was evaluated by means of discrete event simulation with the support of the Neko framework [16]. The simulations consisted in running a number of consensus sequentially, fixing the number of processes to $n = 5$ and the maximum number of faults to $f = 2$. The performance analysis of the HMMR-consensus has been done through a number of experiments in different configuration scenarios. The configuration scenarios were defined, by varying i) the round window size ($w \in [1,5]$); ii) the decentralized decision set cardinality ($x \in [2,5]$), and (iii) the QoS of the failure detector. This last parameter was represented by the probability of wrong suspicions and denoted as P_{FD} ($1 - P_A$). Real crashes (that are rare) were not taken into account.

The failure detector was configured with three parameters: η, δ and P_{FD}. We used $\eta = 1,000ut$, $\delta = 1ut$ and four configurations for P_{FD}: 0%, 5%, 10% and 20%. As explained in Section 3, the behavior of the failure detection service is driven by the QoS metrics T_M and T_{MR} whose values are obtained from specific probability distribution functions. For T_M, it was used an uniform distribution parameterized with upper and lower bounds defined in terms of the input parameters for the service (η, δ). On the other hand, T_{MR} was obtained by means of an exponential distribution parameterized with the value of $E(T_{MR})$, which in turn is obtained from $E(T_M)$ and P_A as mentioned in Section 3.

By tuning the value of λ it is possible to represent different levels of contention in the network. Particularly, the most used values include $\lambda = 10$, $\lambda = 0.1$ and $\lambda = 1$, which represent, respectively, a LAN, WAN and an intermediate network configuration [17].

Our main performance metric was the kth-smallest decision time. By setting k to $\{1, n, f + 1\}$, we estimated the first, last and $f + 1$ smallest consensus decision times. These values represent the best ($k = 1$), worst ($k = n$) and the time required to be sure that at least one correct process has decided ($k = f + 1$).

The scenarios used in the experiments were obtained by combining w, x, the four P_{FD} configurations and the three network configurations, resulting in 240 scenarios. We executed one experiment for each scenario. Every experiment consisted in running $28,800$ sequential consensus with frequency of one consensus after each $1,000ut$. Then, the performance metrics used were related to the mean of the kth-smallest decision times of all $28,800$ consensus executed in each experiment, i.e. the mean of the 1st-smallest, the 3rd-smallest and the 5th-smallest decision times. Note that, there is one random variable in the execution of the HMMR-consensus which is related to the probabilistic behavior of the failure detection service. By running $28,800$ consensus it was possible to reach 99% of confidence level in the mean decision times calculated[2].

It was observed that the results for the three network configurations ($\lambda = 0.1, 1, 10$) follow the same pattern and lead to the same conclusions. Thus, without loss of information, we will discuss the performance of the HMMR-consensus considering the results for $\lambda = 0.1$.

4.2 Simulation Results

The analysis of the simulation results is subdivided into two parts. First we consider only the configurations where the window mechanism is not used ($w = 1$). Then we analyze the remaining configurations.

4.2.1 Impact of the Decision Pattern without Simultaneous Round Participation

The Baseline Configuration. A distinguished configuration, represented by $w = 1$ and $x = 2$, is of special interest for us. We call it the *baseline configuration*. It corresponds to a slight optimization of the CT-consensus [2].

In the classical CT-consensus, during the first phase of a round $r + 1$, all the processes send their current estimation of the decision value to the coordinator. In the code of the baseline configuration for HMMR-concensus this exchange is done at the end of the previous round r [8]: an acknowledgment message is simultaneously sent to both the coordinator of the current round and the coordinator of the next round (by construction, in the baseline configuration, this two particular processes are necessarily the two elements of the decision set X). Compared to the classical CT-consensus, this difference is barely noticeable except perhaps when one consider the coordinator of round r: the sending of its estimation done normally at the beginning of round $r + 1$ is now done during round r before it

---

[2]This confidence level were calculated considering one experiment with $w = 1$, $x = 2$ and $P_{FD} = 20\%$. Moreover, we have used the maximum error of 2% of the mean value. This scenario represents the worst one among those analyzed.

gathers acknowledgment messages related to round r. Due to this minor difference, the baseline configuration is presented as a slight variation of the CT-consensus that nevertheless exhibits similar behaviors and performances to that of the original protocol.

A study of the baseline configuration confirms that a degradation of the QoS of the failure detector has a noticeable impact on the performance of the protocol. For example, we observe a performance degradation to get the 1st-smallest decision of as much as 33.4% for the baseline configuration, when worsening P_{FD} from 0% to 20% (see line 1 of Table 1)[3]. These results are in accordance with other results presented in previous studies [6]. Moreover, the choice of a particular metric among the 3 possible ones (k^{th}-smallest decision time with $k \in \{1, f+1, n\}$) has also a non-negligible influence on the decision time. Thus, without varying the parameters x and w, we already observe that the performance of the protocol is affected by the two external factors considered during all our evaluation (*i.e.*, the selected metric and the QoS of the failure detector).

x	w	performance degradation		
		1st-smallest	3rd-smallest	5th-smallest
2	1	33.4%	26.2%	21.5%
3	1	36.8%	27.2%	23.4%
4	1	38.8%	28.8%	24.9%
5	1	41.3%	30.0%	25.3%

Table 1. Performance degradation when worsening the QoS of the failure detector from 0% **to** 20%

Other Configurations of the Decentralized Decision Pattern without Simultaneous Round Participation. While keeping the value of w equal to 1, we now increase the value of x from 2 to n. Our results show that no matter the considered metric, the performance degradation of these configurations when worsening P_{FD} from 0% to 20% are always worse than those observed in the case of the baseline configuration (see Table 1). This result is mainly due to the fact that the HMMR-consensus has been designed to be used with a window mechanism. In particular, the condition evaluated to start the next round is as weak as possible: being aware of the value proposed by the current coordinator p_c is a sufficient condition for a process $p_i \neq p_c$ to start the next round. Stating a weak condition allows to start quickly the simultaneous participation to the w first rounds. When

$w = 1$, the start of round $r + 1$ and the end of round r always coincide. Thus, adding new processes in the decision set has no interest. Indeed a new element in the set X will never receive a majority of positive acknowledgments because it is allowed to switch to the next round (and forget the current round) as soon as it receives a first positive acknowledgment. As increasing the value of x has an impact on the contention, the performance is decreasing while the value of x increases.

The adoption of a decentralized decision pattern always degrade performance when $w = 1$. In this case, the performance is always either equal or worst than the baseline configuration. In the next section, we show that, for all the remaining configurations (when $w > 1$), the performance is either equal or better.

4.2.2 Impact of the Decision Pattern with Simultaneous Round Participation

In the CT-consensus, the coordinator of round r is blocked in the last phase of round r until it gathers $n - f$ votes. In the HMMR-consensus, thanks to a window of size greater than 1, the coordinator (like any other process) can participate in the next round as soon as it has sent its own vote. The quick participation of the coordinator in the next round is positive especially when the coordinator of round r is correct but suspected by too many other processes. Additionally, all the positive votes generated in a recent past are taken into account and may allow to decide as soon as a majority of positive votes is observed by the set of coordinators, represented by X, during one of the w rounds executed in parallel. It is important to notice that the management of the window requires no additional messages. Moreover, the space cost of this mechanism is low since it requires only a single counter to be kept for each round in the window. Before analyzing the case in which simultaneous round participation and decentralized decision co-exist, we study the case in which we fix the decision pattern parameter to its smallest value ($x = 2$), while increase the size of the window ($w > 1$).

As expected, simultaneous round participation, represented by $w > 1$, is of special interest in scenarios where the failure detector provides a bad QoS. As the graphics in Figure 2 show, even considering the minimal configuration for X ($x = 2$), the performance degradation caused by wrong suspicions (variation of P_{FD} from 5% to 20%) is much smaller when simultaneous rounds are executing ($w > 1$) than for the baseline configuration ($w = 1$). As mentioned before, this is due to the fact that some processes (those belonging to X) have more chances to decide during a number of consecutive rounds in spite of the occurrence of wrong suspicions. Moreover, since the overhead incurred by the implementation of simultaneous rounds can be ne-

---

[3]Given the performance values v_1 and v_2, v_1 can be either better ($v_1 < v_2$) or worse ($v_1 > v_2$) than v_2. The corresponding percentual gains/losses are obtained by the formula: $(v_2 - v_1) * 100/max(v_2, v_1)$, where $max(v_2, v_1)$ is the maximum value between v_2 and v_1. Such formula was used to calculate the percentual performance results shown in this paper.

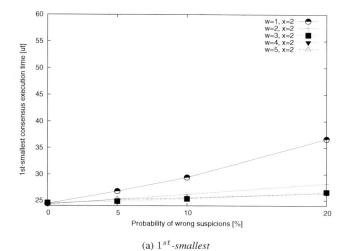

(a) 1st-smallest

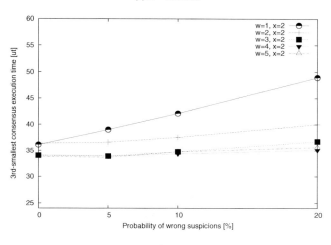

(b) 3rd-smallest

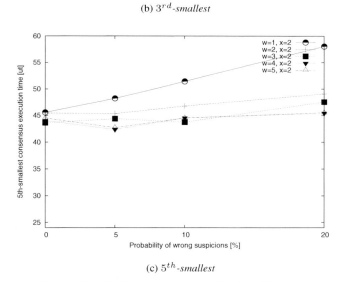

(c) 5th-smallest

Figure 2. Performance results for the baseline configuration and the one using simultaneous round participation ($w > 1$) and minimal decentralization ($x = 2$).

glected, the choice of using a window of size as large as possible contributes to achieving better performance. So, as can be attested by the graphics in Figure 2, choosing $w = n$ corresponds to the best configuration. In that case, the performances obtained when $x = 2$, $w = n$ and $P_{FD} = 20\%$, depending on the metrics of interest, can be even better than those obtained in the baseline configuration ($x = 2$ and $w = 1$) when the failure detector is perfect ($P_{FD} = 0\%$).

Figure 3 illustrates the performance results for the protocol considering the best configuration for w, $w = n$, and $2 \leq x \leq n$, against the baseline configuration. The values plotted represent the gains or losses when comparing the performance of a particular configuration with the performance of the baseline configuration. Note that, by varying the value of x, it is possible to achieve different performance gains which, usually, increase as the P_{FD} becomes worse. As mentioned before, gains exist because more processes (those belonging to X) are allowed to decide autonomously during more rounds ($w = n$).

Note that, when the P_{FD} becomes worse, the performance gains obtained when adopting a decentralized decision increase. This is due to the use of simultaneous round participation ($w > 1$) which contributes to mask the bad effects of wrong suspicions caused when processes are allowed to participate to only one ($w = 1$). The impact of decentralized decision is always positive, except for the 1st-smallest decision time when failure detectors are perfect. In this case, the choice of x has nearly no impact on the performance of the protocol because the first process to decide the consensus tends to be the coordinator of the first round. This lack of difference is due to the adoption of a homogeneous network load during the simulations. Performance gains may perhaps appear in scenarios of heterogenous workloads where processes would have different speeds. In that case the higher the value of x, the higher the chances to find a process in the deciders set that is faster than the round coordinator [12].

From the results in Figure 3, significant performance gains are obtained for the kth-decision time when $x = k$. Then, for higher values of x, the performance gains stabilize. Thus the choice of $x = k$ seems to be the best solution when one want to limit the number of messages exchanged (*i.e.* when contention in the network is also a concern at the application level). Otherwise, $x = n$ is a good choice since it contributes to attain similar performance gains.

Figure 4 allows the comparison of the best configuration ($w = n$, $x = n$) and the baseline configuration ($w = 1$, $x = 2$). In a scenario without faults nor wrong suspicions ($P_{FD} = 0\%$), the results obtained for the 1st-decision time show that the behaviors of the protocol are similar in both configurations. In the presence of wrong suspicions ($P_{FD} \geq 5\%$), the impact of a bad QoS of the failure detector is entirely masked when w and x are set to n: the

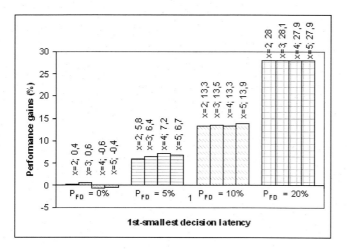

(a) 1st-smallest

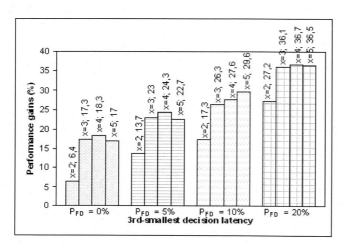

(b) 3rd-smallest

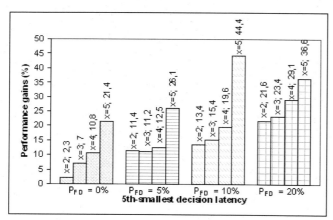

(c) 5th-smallest

Figure 3. Percentual performance results (compared to the baseline configuration) for different values for x when $w = n$.

protocol exhibits nearly the same performance results whatever the QoS of the failure detector. Very few degradation are observed (7.3% for the 1st-smallest decision). Indeed, when analyzing the curves in Figure 4 we can verify that the results exhibited for the worst QoS ($P_{FD} = 20\%$) are close to or even much better than that for the baseline configuration without wrong suspicions ($P_{FD} = 0\%$). For example, when considering the 5th-smallest decision time, the best result for the baseline configuration was $45.55ut$ and for $w = n$ and $x = n$, was $36.82ut$. So, a performance gain of 19.2% was obtained.

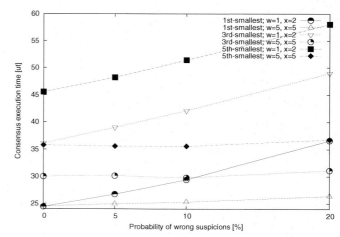

Figure 4. Comparison between the best configuration ($w = x = n$) and the baseline configuration ($w = 1, x = 2$).

5 Related Work

Previous studies on the performance of consensus protocols following a quantitative approach and using temporal metrics have been done [6, 17, 18, 12]. They analyzed the impact of external and internal factors on the performance of the protocols. While external factors are related to the characteristics of the execution environment, such as the configuration of the failure detection service, the internal factors concern characteristics of the protocol itself.

The impact of failures as well as the QoS of the failure detection service on the performance of CT-consensus have been studied in [6]. By simulating and measuring an implementation of the protocol, the authors analyzed the consensus behavior in faultloads characterized by i) no failures and no wrong suspicions; ii) no failures, with wrong suspicions and ii) failures, without wrong suspicions. The work of [17] take into account similar faultloads, but in the context of a consensus embedded in atomic broadcast protocols. Moreover, it compares the performance of consensus protocols that use failure detectors of different classes. In both works, the implementation of the failure detector does not generate any contention and its behavior is driven by some QoS metrics. Both studies conclude that the impact of wrong suspicions and failures on the performance of the protocols were negative. The studies conducted in this paper have attained the same results as [6] and [17] concerning the negative impact of wrong suspicions on the consensus protocol. Differently from these works, we did not consider a scenario with crashes. Since these are not frequent in practice, the interest on their evaluation is only recommended when a too bad performance degradation is expected for these cases, which is not the case [17]. The interesting aspect of our experiments is that they adopt an implementation of a specific failure detector which generates an amount of contention.

The impact of the characteristics of the protocol itself on its performance has not been so much explored in the literature. The work of [12] proposes an adaptive solution for consensus protocols based on process ordering. Significant performance gains can be obtained when using such a solution in heterogeneous systems. In this work, we investigate how the performance of the HMMR-consensus is impacted by the values of its two adaptive parameters x and w. By tuning these parameters it is possible to change the decision pattern from (almost) centralized ($w = 1$, $x = 2$) up to completely decentralized ($w = 1$, $x = n$).

In [18] the performance of consensus protocols is analyzed by considering the two extreme decision patterns: centralized and fully decentralized, adopted respectively by protocols CT-consensus [2] and MR-consensus [11]. More precisely, it studies the latency of a total order broadcast service implemented on top of these consensus. In this way, the performance measures obtained in that work cannot be directly compared with ours as the notion of throughput it uses does not appear in our work: we assume that a new consensus is launched every $1,000ut$. Moreover, while the baseline configuration can be considered as a slightly optimization of the classical CT-consensus (evaluated in both works), the configuration ($w = 1$, $x = n$) does not correspond to the MR-consensus. Despite all these differences, the results we obtained for the baseline configuration (see Section 4.2.1) corroborate with the conclusion of [18] which indicates that "the centralized algorithm performs better in some environments in spite of the fact that the decentralized algorithm finishes in fewer communication steps". Moreover, due to contention reasons, the gain (when it exists) is not very significant.

Our work extends the one by Urbán and Schiper [18] in two directions: i) it analyzes intermediate values of x and ii) it considers the impact of the additional parameter w. To the best of our knowledge, our work is the first one to investigate the practical interests of using simultaneous round participation, represented by w. The performance results

show that a window of size n allows to reduce significantly the latency and to entirely mask the impact of a bad QoS of the failure detector. In the related literature, the excessive attention paid to the first parameter x is mainly due to the fact that an analysis of the number of communication steps leads to predict a gain when considering this parameter. On the contrary, the lack of interest with regard to the second parameter w is partially due to the fact that no analysis regarding the interest of this parameter has been conducted at all. In fact, any analysis in terms of number of rounds and/or number of communication steps appears to be inappropriate when a process can participate to several consecutive rounds at the same time.

In [10], the authors propose a hybrid approach to analyze the performance of indulgent protocols by means of a generic framework called GIRAF. In most round-based computation models, rounds are communication-closed: a message can only be consumed in the round in which it is sent. As this requirement is not mandatory in the approach proposed in [10], it could be interesting to check if the results that we have obtained by simulation (and in particular the great interest of using a window mechanism) can also be corroborated by an analysis based on the GIRAF framework.

An important decision when conducting a performance study regards the choice of the metric. When analyzing consensus protocols, the first decision time is largely used [6, 14, 12, 17]. Other metrics can be of some interest according to the requirements of the application which uses the consensus protocol, as, for example, the last decision time [17]. The performance of the HMMR-consensus was analyzed by means of the kth-smallest decision time. By setting k to $\{1, f + 1, n\}$, we estimated the first, last and $f + 1$ smallest consensus decision times. The results obtained showed that the judicious combination of the simultaneous round execution ($w > 1$) with the decentralized pattern ($x > 2$) mechanisms had a very good impact on the decision time, in such a way that the difference among the results for each one of the metrics decreases by increasing the value of x. Interestingly, as shown in Figure 4, it is possible to set x to be sufficiently large in order to have the nth-decision time close to the 1th-decision time.

6 Conclusion

Studying and comparing the performances of consensus protocols is very important because such protocols are intensively used in many fault-tolerant distributed systems. Most protocols already published have been analyzed using metrics that provide incomplete and sometimes misleading information about their performances. In this paper we have evaluated the performance of a consensus protocol in practical settings, using a metric that gauges the time that takes for up to k processes reach a decision, with $k \in 1, f+1, n$. The protocol analyzed has two unique features. Firstly, it uses a window mechanism that allow processes to simultaneously participate to multiple rounds, mitigating the negative impacts of an eventual bad QoS delivered by the failure detector. Secondly, it allows its decision pattern to be configured to have different numbers of processors able to autonomously decide in a round.

Our results show the great importance of the window mechanism in masking wrong suspicions of the failure detector. Moreover, when $k > 1$, then the window mechanism is of interest even if the failure detector makes no mistake. As this mechanism has a fixed cost, the best configuration is obtained when the window size is equal to the number of processes. Regarding the configuration of the decision pattern, we show that this parameter is only useful when the protocol uses the window mechanism. In this case, we observed that the best performance were achieved when the number of processes allowed to autonomously decide was greater or equal to k. As a future work we intend to evaluate the behavior of the protocol when the system is subject to a background load that is heterogeneous and that varies over time. We believe that an adaptation mechanism similar to the one proposed in [12] can be used to define suitable values for the set X and maximize the performance of the protocol in such setting.

Acknowledgements. This work has been supported by grants from CNPq/Brazil, CAPES/Brazil and COFECUB/France.

References

[1] O. Bakr and I. Keidar. Evaluating the running time of a communication round over the internet. In *Proceedings of the ACM Symposium on Principles of Distributed Computing (PODC)*, pages 243–252, Monterey, California, USA, July 2002. ACM.

[2] T. Chandra and S. Toueg. Unreliable failure detectors for reliable distributed systems. *Journal of the ACM*, 43(2):225–267, Mar. 1996.

[3] T. D. Chandra, V. Hadzilacos, and S. Toueg. The weakest failure detector for solving consensus. *Journal of the ACM*, 43(4):685–722, July 1996.

[4] B. Charron-Bost. Agreement problems in fault-tolerant distributed systems. In *Proceedings of the 28th Conference on Current Trends in Theory and Practice of Informatics*, pages 10–32, Piestany, Slovak Republic, Nov. 2001.

[5] W. Chen, S. Toueg, and M. K. Aguilera. On the quality of service of failure detectors. In *International Conference on Dependable Systems and Networks (DSN'2000)*, pages 191–200, New York, USA, Jun 2000. IEEE Computer Society.

[6] A. Coccoli, P. Urbán, A. Bondavalli, and A. Schiper. Performance analysis of a consensus algorithm combining stochastic activity networks and measurements. In *International Conference on Dependable Systems and Networks (DSN'2002)*, pages 551–560, Washington, D.C., USA, June 2002. IEEE Computer Society.

[7] M. J. Fischer, N. A. Lynch, and M. D. Paterson. Impossibility of distributed consensus with one faulty process. *Journal of ACM*, 32(2):374–382, Apr. 1985.

[8] M. Hurfin, R. Macedo, A. Mostefaoui, and M. Raynal. A consensus protocol based on a weak failure detector and a sliding round window. In *Proc. of the 20th IEEE Symposium on Reliable Distributed Systems (SRDS'2001)*, pages 120–129, New-Orleans,LA,USA, Oct. 2001. IEEE Computer Society.

[9] M. Hurfin and M. Raynal. A simple and fast asynchronous consensus protocol based on a weak failure detector. *Distributed Computing*, 12(4):209–223, 1999.

[10] I. Keidar and A. Shraer. Timeliness, failure-detectors, and consensus performance. In *PODC '06: Proceedings of the twenty-fifth annual ACM symposium on Principles of distributed computing*, pages 169–178. ACM Press, 2006.

[11] A. Mostefaoui and M. Raynal. Solving consensus using chandra toueg's unreliable failure detectors: a general quorum based approach. In *Proceedings of the 13th International Symposium on Distributed Computing (DISC'99)*, pages 49–63, Bratislava, Slovaquia, Sep 1999.

[12] L. M. R. Sampaio and F. V. Brasileiro. Adaptive indulgent consensus. In *Proceedings of the International Conference on Dependable Systems and Networks (DSN'2005)*, pages 422–431, Yokohama, Japan, June 2005. IEEE Computer Society.

[13] A. Schiper. Early consensus in an asynchronous system with a weak failure detector. *Distributed Computing*, 10(3):149–157, Apr. 1997.

[14] N. Sergent, X. Défago, and A. Schiper. Impact of a failure detection mechanism on the performance of consensus. In *Proceedings of the 2001 Pacific Rim International Symposium on Dependable Computing (PRDC'2001)*, pages 137–145, Seoul, Korea, Dec. 2001. IEEE Computer Society.

[15] P. Urbán, X. Défago, and A. Schiper. Contention-aware metrics for distributed algorithms: comparison of atomic broadcast algorithms. In *Proceedings of the 9th IEEE International Conference on Computer Communications and Networks (IC3N'2000)*, pages 80–92, Las Vegas, Nevada, USA, Oct. 2000. IEEE Computer Society.

[16] P. Urbán, X. Défago, and A. Schiper. Neko: a single environment to simulate and prototype distributed algorithms. In *Proceeding of the 15th International Conference on Information Networking (ICOIN-15)*, pages 503–511, Beppu City, Japan, Feb. 2001. IEEE Computer Society.

[17] P. Urbán, N. Hayashibara, A. Schiper, and T. Katayama. Performance comparison of a rotating coordinator and a leader based consensus algorithm. In *Proceedings of the 23rd Symposium on Reliable Distributed Systems (SRDS'2004)*, pages 4–17, Florianópolis, Brazil, Oct. 2004. IEEE Computer Society.

[18] P. Urbán and A. Schiper. Comparing the performance of two consensus algorithms with centralized and decentralized communication schemes. Technical Report IS-RR-2004-009, Japan Advanced Institute of Science and Technology, Mar. 2004.

On the Cost of Modularity in Atomic Broadcast

Olivier Rütti[†]
olivier.rutti@epfl.ch

Sergio Mena[‡]
sergio.mena@cs.york.ac.uk

Richard Ekwall[†]
nilsrichard.ekwall@epfl.ch

André Schiper[†]
andre.schiper@epfl.ch

[†] *École Polytechnique Fédérale de Lausanne (EPFL), 1015 Lausanne, Switzerland*
[‡]*Department of Computer Science, University of York, York YO10 5DD, United Kingdom*

Abstract

Modularity is a desirable property of complex software systems, since it simplifies code reuse, verification, maintenance, etc. However, the use of loosely coupled modules introduces a performance overhead. This overhead is often considered negligible, but this is not always the case. This paper aims at casting some light on the cost, in terms of performance, that is incurred when designing a relevant group communication protocol with modularity in mind: atomic broadcast.

We conduct our experiments using two versions of atomic broadcast: a modular version and a monolithic one. We then measure the performance of both implementations under different system loads. Our results show that the overhead introduced by modularity is strongly related to the level of stress to which the system is subjected, and in the worst cases, reaches approximately 50%.

Keywords: atomic broadcast, modular design, microprotocols, performance cost, experimental evaluation

1 Introduction

Modularity has always been an important concern when designing complex software systems. A modular system is easier to maintain, its code being easier to debug, verify, reuse and develop in a collaborative environment. However, modularity is not a panacea and its main drawback is the performance overhead introduced by splitting the system into several independent parts. Such overhead is often deemed negligible when compared to all the good properties that modularity entails; but it is usually difficult to perform a quantitative analysis of the actual performance impact.

Group communication has been argued to be an important enabling technology to render a distributed service fault-tolerant by replicating such service at several loca-

tions [5, 8]. In this context, atomic broadcast is a well-known protocol that allows to maintain replicas consistency by ensuring a total order of message delivery. In [13, 7], Chandra and Toueg propose a reduction of this protocol to the consensus problem. This allows a modular design of atomic broadcast based on consensus and reliable broadcast. In such a design, atomic broadcast knows that it is interacting with a consensus module, but cannot make any assumption on the implementation of the consensus module (e.g., which algorithm is used). As a result, some algorithmic optimizations that make assumptions on the neighbor protocol can not take place if the system is to be modular: this is where the performance penalty is mostly located.

Is it not so easy to decide between a modular design or a monolithic one: this decision has to be made at the early stages of the software engineering process, whereas evidence of the performance cost can only be obtained later, when at least a prototype is available. Nevertheless, it is possible to foresee the performance hit at design time using an analytical method (See Sect. 5.2).

Contribution. This paper aims at shedding some light on the performance cost that modularity induces in implementation of atomic broadcast reduced to the consensus problem. For our experiments, we use Fortika [18, 19], a toolkit that includes two versions of atomic broadcast: monolithic and modular. Both versions are based on the same algorithms. In one version atomic broadcast is implemented as a set of modules, whereas in the other, these modules are merged to form a monolithic protocol. This merging allows algorithmic optimizations, since we can assume that these modules always operate together. Those optimizations aim at (a) improving the performance in *good runs* (runs where messages are timely and processes behave correctly[1]), and (b) keep algorithmic correctness in all runs. For a fair comparison, we also optimize modular version of atomic broadcast.

---
[1]Good runs are the most frequent in practice

The performance of both modular and monolithic solutions are then shown in both analytical and experimental evaluations of the two stacks.[2] Our results reveal that the performance hit can reach 50% in some cases, showing that the dilemma between a monolithic and a modular design should not be taken lightly.

2 Atomic Broadcast

This section briefly presents the system model that we consider and concisely describes the modules that constitute the atomic broadcast stack.

2.1 System Model

We consider a system with a finite set of processes $\Pi = \{p_1, p_2, \ldots, p_n\}$. The system is *asynchronous*, which means that there is no assumption on message transmission delays or relative speed of processes. The system is *static*, which means that the set Π of processes never changes after system start-up time. During system lifetime, processes can take internal steps or communicate by message exchange.

Correct, Faulty and Failure Suspicion. Processes can only fail by crashing. A process that crashes stops its operation permanently and never recovers. A process is *faulty* in a given run if it crashes in that run. A process is *correct* if it is not faulty. Every process has a local module called *failure detector* (FD) that outputs a set of processes that have crashed. This list can change over time, moreover it can be inaccurate. We say that process p *suspects* process q if q is in the output list of p's FD.

Quasi-Reliable Communication Channels. Every pair of processes is connected by a bidirectional network channel. The protocols presented later on assume *quasi-reliable channels*, which verify the following property. If process p sends message m to q, and both p and q are correct, then q eventually receives m.

2.2 Description of Modules

Our atomic broadcast implementation consists of three main protocols that are based on well-established algorithms: reliable broadcast, consensus and atomic broadcast. We now give a concise description of these protocols (see [13] for further details and formal specifications).

Reliable Broadcast. This protocol defines the primitives *rbcast* and *rdeliver*. Reliable broadcast ensures that messages are rdelivered either by all correct processes or by none, even if the sender crashes while rbcasting a message. However, it does not enforce any order in rdelivered messages.

Consensus. Consensus defines the primitives *propose* and *decide*, which mark the protocol's start and end at a given process. Consensus ensures that processes eventually reach an agreement on a value proposed by one of them, even in the presence of crashes.

Atomic Broadcast. This protocol defines the primitives *abcast* and *adeliver*. Atomic broadcast is a stronger form of reliable broadcast where all messages are adelivered in the same order at every process.

3 Modular Implementation

The current section describes the modular implementation of atomic broadcast (see Fig. 1, left). We present the implementation of all modules following a bottom-up order. These modules implement the protocols described in Sect. 2.2. Detailed knowledge of these implementations is not necessary to keep up with the rest of the paper. However, a succinct description will help the reader to better understand (1) the monolithic implementation presented in Sect. 4 and (2) the analytical evaluation presented in Sect. 5.2.

For each module, we present some optimizations that focus on good runs (runs with no suspicion, crash or unusual message delay). Our optimizations, however, do not affect the correctness of the algorithms in runs that are not good. These improvements are necessary to obtain a comparison as fair as possible, between the modular and monolithic stacks.

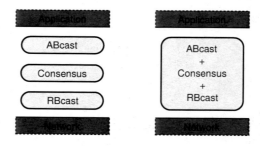

Figure 1. Modular implementation(left) and monolithic implementation(right) of Atomic Broadcast (ABcast).

---

[2]We use the terms "stack" and "implementation" interchangeably

3.1 Reliable Broadcast (RBcast)

The classical implementation of this protocol is straightforward if we can assume quasi-reliable channels (see Sect. 2.1). Here is the main idea [7]:

1. Upon broadcast of message m, send a copy of m to all processes.

2. Upon receiving m for the first time, re-send m to all processes.

Optimization. Note that this implementation sends n^2 messages over the network for each rbcast message (n denotes the number of processes to which the message is broadcast). This can be reduced by assuming that a majority of processes do not crash[3]. This optimization leads to only $(n-1) \cdot (\lfloor \frac{n-1}{2} \rfloor + 1)$ messages per rbcast message. The details of this optimization are omitted here.

3.2 Consensus

We base our implementation on the Chandra and Toueg consensus algorithm [7] due to its overall good performances [25]. Rather than presenting the full algorithm's details, we explain its principles by using a typical run, depicted in Fig. 2. The algorithm proceeds in a number of asynchronous rounds. In each round, a different process adopts the role of coordinator. A round consists of four phases:

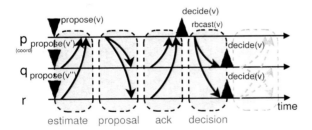

Figure 2. Example execution of consensus during good runs.

1. *Estimate* phase. All processes send their initial value as estimate to the coordinator.

2. *Propose* phase. The coordinator chooses the eldest value and sends a *propose* message with such value.

3. *Ack* phase. All processes wait for the coordinator's proposal and send an *ack* message when they receive it, or a *nack* message if they suspect the coordinator.

---

[3]The same assumption is necessary to solve consensus

4. *Decide* phase. If the coordinator gathers *ack* messages from a majority of processes, it decides and rbcasts the decision to all processes. The last phase in Fig. 2 (grayed) is the re-send part of rbcast algorithm (see reliable broadcast implementation above in this section).

If the coordinator is faulty and/or suspected, the algorithm may not be able to decide in the first round. In that case, supplementary rounds with the same phases would be needed in order to terminate. At any moment, if a running process receives a decision, it decides the received value and terminates. In runs where there are no crashes or suspicions, all processes are able to decide at the end of the first round (see dark upward triangles in Fig. 2).

Optimization. Figure 3 shows a typical run of the consensus algorithm that we implemented. Firstly, we reduce the first round by suppressing the estimate phase. Secondly, contrary to classical implementation where round $n{+}1$ begins immediately after round n terminates, a new round starts only if the coordinator is suspected to be faulty. These two improvements were previously described in [25]. Finally, we reduce the size of decision messages by sending a tag DECISION instead of the complete decision. Note that, even if this optimization works fine in good runs, additional communication steps may be required if the coordinator crashes.

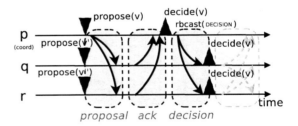

Figure 3. Example execution of optimized consensus during good runs.

3.3 Atomic Broadcast (ABcast)

We solve atomic broadcast by reduction to consensus [13, 7]. In this approach, the atomic broadcast module diffuses all messages abcast by the application. In parallel, a consensus is started to decide on the delivery order of those messages. Hence, consensus accepts a batch of messages as initial values. Figure 4 depicts an example execution where messages m (abcast by p's application) and m' (abcast by r's application) are abcast. First, both messages are disseminated to all processes; then, an instance of consensus is started to order m and m' consistently at all processes. When consensus decides, atomic broadcast adelivers the messages contained in the decision in some deterministic order. In Fig. 4 for instance, m' happens to be ordered before m, but this order is consistent everywhere. Finally, the whole mechanism is repeated as soon as further messages are abcast.

Optimization. Note that in [13, 7], reliable broadcast is used to disseminate the messages abcast by the application. In our stack, messages are simply sent using quasi-reliable channels (solid arrows in Fig. 4). This implementation is clearly equivalent to reliable broadcast when no process crashes. Otherwise, it may violate the specification of atomic broadcast. Consider for instance a message m abcast by process p. If p crashes while sending a copy of m to all processes, m may be delivered at some processes but not at others. This violates reliable broadcast's specification (see [13]). Moreover, in this example, it may also lead to a violation of atomic broadcast's specification. To avoid this in our implementation (and thus ensure correctness), if a process q does not receive messages during a period of t seconds (with t sufficiently big), q starts a consensus even if no message arrives.

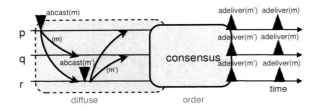

Figure 4. Example run of atomic broadcast by reduction to consensus.

4 Monolithic Implementation

In the previous sections, we have presented the algorithms (and optimizations) as they are implemented in the modular atomic broadcast stack. When we implement these algorithms as a single module in a monolithic stack, further (algorithmic) optimizations are possible. In this section, we present the optimizations that were carried out in the monolithic stack (see Fig. 1, right). Again, our optimizations focus on good runs but ensure correctness in all runs.

For each of these optimizations we explain (1) what changes are made compared to the modular version of atomic broadcast (see Section 3), (2) why these changes are possible, and (3) what (approximate) improvement in performance can be expected from these changes.

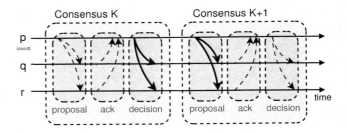

Figure 5. Consecutive consensus executions in the modular implementation of atomic broadcast.

4.1 Combining the Next Proposal with the Current Decision

In the modular implementation of atomic broadcast (see Fig. 4), atomic broadcast runs a sequence of consecutive consensus instances to order the set of undelivered messages. Due to the modular design, all consensus instances are black boxes from the point of view of atomic broadcast and are considered to be totally independent from each other. Thus, we cannot take advantage of the fact that the coordinator that sends a decision in consensus instance k is the same coordinator that sends a proposal in consensus instance $k + 1$. Figure 5 shows this. Note that in normal executions, process p does not necessarily wait until processes q and r decide to start another consensus. In other words, process p may send its proposal for consensus instance $k+1$ just after having sent the decision of consensus instance k.

In the monolithic implementation the successive consensus instances are run within the atomic broadcast module. If consensus instance k decides in the first round (which is the case in good runs), then the coordinator of consensus instances k and $k + 1$ (in its first round) are the same process. In this case, the decision of consensus k and the proposal of consensus $k + 1$ are sent together as a single message (denoted "proposal k + decision $k - 1$" in Figure 6).

This first optimization in the monolithic atomic broadcast stack allows a better use of network resources: instead of sending one small message (tag DECISION) followed by a larger message (the proposal of consensus $k+1$) the small message is piggybacked on the larger one.

4.2 Piggybacking Messages Abcast on *ack* Messages

In the modular implementation of atomic broadcast, a process abcasting a message m starts by sending m to all other processes. Whenever this message is received, it is added to the set of proposed messages for the next consensus instance. In good runs, this is inefficient for the following reason: every process delivers m, but only the coordinator of the next consensus execution actually needs m (in or-

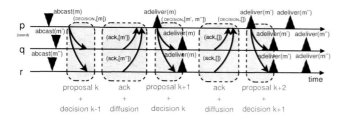

Figure 6. Consecutive consensus executions in the monolithic implementation of atomic broadcast.

der to propose m for consensus). This can not be optimized in a modular stack, since the atomic broadcast module cannot access information that is specific to the consensus module (such as the identity of the coordinator). Furthermore, to preserve modularity, atomic broadcast can not disseminate messages abcast by the application within consensus messages. This is shown in Figure 7: messages m and m' are first sent (in the diffuse step), then consensus is executed (in the order step).

A more efficient solution, which can only be implemented in the monolithic stack, is to combine *ack* messages with the sending of messages m and m' (see solid arrows in Fig. 7). This is done as follows. The sender of m *directly* sends m to the (initial) coordinator of the next consensus execution. Furthermore, instead of sending m as a standalone message to the coordinator, it can be piggybacked on the *ack* message of the consensus algorithm (denoted "ack + diffusion" in Figure 6). If the coordinator changes (i.e. if a suspicion occurs), message m is again piggybacked on the estimate sent to the new coordinator.

The gain of this optimization is twofold. Firstly, it reduces network congestion by avoiding an unnecessary diffusion of abcast messages to all processes: messages are only sent to the coordinator. Secondly, similarly to the first optimization presented above, it allows a more efficient use of network resources thanks to the aggregation of small messages with bigger ones.

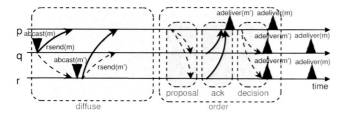

Figure 7. Diffusion of two messages m and m', followed by their ordering. The diffusion and ordering steps cannot be merged in the modular implementation of atomic broadcast.

4.3 Reducing the Message Complexity of Reliable Broadcast

Consensus decisions have to be reliably broadcast to all processes. In the modular implementation, the reliable broadcast algorithm requires $(n-1) \cdot (\lfloor \frac{n+1}{2} \rfloor)$ messages to be sent on the network for each reliable broadcast to n processes.

In the monolithic implementation, the cost of the decision diffusion is reduced to n messages: the decision is simply sent to all processes without any additional retransmissions (in good runs). The reduction relies on the knowledge that the successive consensus instances are executed on the same set Π of processes (and thus, messages in consensus $k+1$ can serve as acknowledgments for messages sent in consensus k). With this knowledge, the decision of consensus execution k is acknowledged by the messages sent by non-coordinators to the coordinator in consensus execution $k+1$.

Again, this optimization reduces the network congestion since it considerably reduces from $(n-1) \cdot (\lfloor \frac{n+1}{2} \rfloor)$ to n the number of messages sent by reliable broadcast.

5 Performance Evaluation

We now evaluate and compare the performance of our two (optimized) implementations of atomic broadcast. We specifically focus on the case of a system with three and seven processes, supporting one, respectively three, failures. This system size might seem small. However, atomic broadcast is usually used for relatively small degrees of replication. If a a larger degree of replication is needed, then alternatives that provide weaker consistency should be considered [1].

The section starts by presenting the parameters considered. An analytical evaluation of the two implementations is then presented, followed by the experimental evaluation of these implementations.

5.1 Metrics, Workload, Faultload

The following paragraphs describe the benchmarks (i.e. the performance metrics and the workloads) that were used to evaluate the performance of the atomic broadcast algorithms.

Performance Metrics. We use two performance metrics to evaluate the algorithms: *early latency* and *throughput*. For a single abcast message, the early latency L is defined as follows. Let t_0 be the time at which the $abcast(m)$ event completes and let t_i be the time at which $adeliver(m)$ occurs on process p_i, with $i \in 1, \ldots, n$. The early latency L is then defined as $L \stackrel{def}{=} (\min_i t_i) - t_0$.

The throughput T is defined as follows. Let r_i be the rate at which *adeliver* events occur on a process p_i, with $i \in 1, \ldots, n$. The throughput T is then defined as $T \stackrel{def}{=} \frac{1}{n} \sum_{i=1}^{n} r_i$ and is expressed in messages per second (or msgs/s).

In our performance evaluation, the mean for L and T is computed over many messages and for several executions. For all results, we show 95% confidence intervals.

Workloads and Faultload. The early latency L and the throughput T are measured for a certain workload, which specifies how many *abcast* events are generated per time unit. We chose a simple symmetric workload where all processes abcast messages of a fixed size s at a constant rate r (with s and r varying from experiment to experiment). The global rate of atomic broadcast events is called the *offered load* $T_{offered}$, which is expressed in messages per second. We then evaluate the dependency between, on one hand, the early latency L and the throughput T and, on the other hand, the offered load $T_{offered}$ and the size of the messages.

Furthermore, both implementations of the atomic broadcast protocol use the same flow-control mechanism that blocks further *abcast* events when necessary. More precisely, the flow-control mechanism ensures that, on average, $M = 4$ messages are ordered per consensus execution. This value of M optimizes performance of both modular and monolithic stacks. We ensure that the system stays in a stationary state by verifying that the latencies of all processes stabilize over time.

Finally, we only evaluate the performance of the algorithms in good runs, i.e. without any process failures or wrong suspicions. The latency and throughput of the implementations is measured once the system has reached a stationary state (at a sufficiently long time after the startup). The parameters that influence the latency and the throughput are n (the number of processes), the implementation (modular or monolithic) the offered load $T_{offered}$ and the size of the messages that are abcast.

5.2 Analytical Evaluation

As shown in Section 3, the Chandra-Toueg atomic broadcast algorithm reduces to a sequence of consensus executions. We assume a workload high enough so that consensus execution $k + 1$ starts directly after execution k.[4] This condition is met if the offered load $T_{offered}$ is greater than the number of consensus executions that the system can execute per second (i.e., if d is the average duration of a consensus execution, we have $T > d^{-1}$).

We now analyze two aspects of the performance of the two implementations: (1) the number of messages that are

sent and (2) the total amount of data that needs to be sent to solve atomic broadcast.

5.2.1 Number of Sent Messages

In both the modular and monolithic implementations of atomic broadcast, sets of unordered abcast messages are ordered in consensus executions. We assume that, on average, M messages are ordered per consensus execution. In the experimental evaluation, this is ensured by our flow-control mechanism. We now derive the number of messages that need to be sent in both stacks in order to adeliver these M messages.

Modular Implementation. In the modular implementation of atomic broadcast, the M unordered messages are first sent to all processes in the system, generating $M \cdot (n - 1)$ messages on the network. These messages are then received by the coordinator of the consensus algorithm that sends a proposal to all processes ($n - 1$ messages). All processes reply by sending an *ack* message to the coordinator ($n - 1$ messages), which then reliably broadcasts the decision to all processes (which necessitates an additional $(n - 1) \cdot \lfloor \frac{n+1}{2} \rfloor$ messages).

To adeliver the M abcast messages, the modular implementation thus needs to send $(n - 1)(M + 2 + \lfloor \frac{n+1}{2} \rfloor)$ messages.

Monolithic Implementation. In the monolithic implementation of atomic broadcast, the M unordered messages are not immediately sent to all processes. Instead, they are piggybacked on the *ack* messages of the previous consensus execution. The coordinator starts the consensus execution by sending both the decision of the previous consensus and a new proposal in the same message. This message is sent to all processes ($n - 1$ messages). The other processes then reply by sending an *ack* message to the coordinator ($n - 1$ messages).

To adeliver the M abcast messages, the monolithic implementation thus only needs to send $2 \cdot (n - 1)$ messages.

In the case of a system of $n = 3$ processes for example, with an average of $M = 4$ messages ordered per consensus execution[5], this means that the monolithic implementation needs 4 messages to order these 4 abcast messages (assuming of course that a previous consensus execution allows some piggybacking of messages). In the case of the modular stack, 16 messages are needed for the same result.

---

[4]Otherwise, there is no point in optimizing the algorithms.

[5]This value of M corresponds to the one that we chose for our experimental evaluation.

5.2.2 Total Amount of Sent Data

We assume that abcast messages all have a size of l bytes. We further assume that messages sent by the algorithm that have a constant size (e.g. *ack* messages and tag DECISION in the modular implementation) only represent a negligible part of the sent data. As above, we analyze how much data is sent on average per consensus execution (i.e., to adeliver M abcast messages).

Modular Implementation. In the modular implementation, abcast messages are sent to all other processes. The M messages of size l are thus sent to $n-1$ processes. The coordinator then adds these messages to a consensus proposal (sent to the $n-1$ non-coordinator processes) which thus has a size of $M \cdot l$ on average. The total amount of data exchanged per consensus in the modular stack is then $Data_{mod} = 2(n-1)M \cdot l$ bytes.

Monolithic Implementation. In the monolithic implementation, the processes do not diffuse their abcast message to everyone and instead only send them to the coordinator (by piggybacking them on *ack* messages). On average, $\frac{M}{n}$ abcast messages of size l are piggybacked by each one of the $n-1$ non-coordinator processes during a consensus execution. The coordinator then creates a proposal with the M messages ($\frac{M}{n}$ messages abcast by itself and $(n-1)\frac{M}{n}$ abcast by the other processes) of size l that is sent to the $n-1$ other processes. The total amount of data sent per consensus execution is thus on average $Data_{mono} = (n-1)(1+\frac{1}{n})M \cdot l$ bytes.

The overhead of the modular implementation with respect to the monolithic implementation is therefore

$$overhead = \frac{Data_{mod} - Data_{mono}}{Data_{mono}} = \frac{n-1}{n+1}$$

In a system with $n = 3$ processes, the modular implementation needs to send 50% more data than the monolithic one. In the case of $n = 7$, the overhead reaches 75%.

5.3 Experimental Evaluation

The paragraphs above presented an analytical evaluation of the two atomic broadcast implementations from the perspective of two performance aspects. These two aspects are however not sufficient to completely characterize the performance cost of the modular implementation versus the monolithic one. Indeed, the analysis above focuses on aspects related to the network communication of the two implementations, whereas processing times for example are not at all taken into account. The experimental evaluation of the two stacks fills this gap.

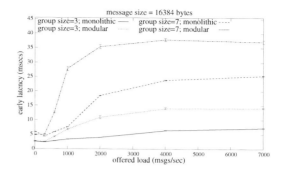

Figure 8. Early latency vs. offered load for abcast messages of size 16384 **bytes.**

The following paragraph presents the system setup used in the experiments. Then, a performance comparison is presented between the modular and monolithic stacks.

5.3.1 System Setup

The benchmarks were run on a cluster of machines running SuSE Linux (kernel 2.6.11). Each machine has a Pentium 4 processor at 3.2 GHz and 1 GB of RAM. The machines are interconnected by Gigabit Ethernet (which is exclusively used by the cluster machines) and run Sun's 1.5.0 Java Virtual Machine. The machines were dedicated to the performance benchmarks and had no other load on them.

The atomic broadcast algorithm was implemented (twice) in Fortika ver. 0.4[6] [18, 19]. Fortika is a group communication toolkit with various well-known off-the-shelf protocol modules. These protocol modules can then be composed using different protocol frameworks. The current experiments were run with the Cactus protocol framework [4, 24].

5.3.2 Performance Results

Latency of Atomic Broadcast. Figure 8 shows the evolution of the early latency (vertical axis) of atomic broadcast using the two implementations as the offered load (horizontal axis) increases. Results are shown for a system size of $n = 3$ (two bottom curves) and $n = 7$ (two top curves), with abcast messages of size 16384 bytes. Note that changing the size of messages does not significantly affect the results.

The latency of both implementations is relatively close for small offered loads. As soon as the offered load increases, however, the monolithic implementation achieves latencies that are between 30% ($n = 7$) and 50% ($n = 3$) lower than the modular implementation. Note that the latency of the two implementations remains relatively con-

---

[6]The current version of Fortika uses TCP connections rather than IP multicast facilities.

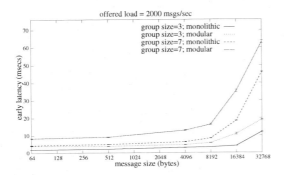

Figure 9. Early latency vs. message size for an offered load of 2000 msgs/s.

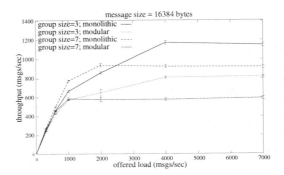

Figure 10. Throughput vs. offered load for abcast messages of size 16384 **bytes.**

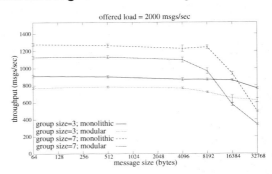

Figure 11. Throughput vs. message size for an offered load of 2000 msgs/s.

stant above a certain offered load. This is due to the flow-control mechanism that is present in both stacks: as the offered load increases, more and more abcast messages are blocked so that the network load remains more or less constant.

Figure 9 shows how the early latency of the two implementations is affected by the size of the messages that are abcast. The graph shows the early latency in a system with $n = 3$ (two bottom curves) and $n = 7$ (two top curves) processes. The offered load is fixed to 2000 msgs/s. Results are similar with other values of offered load (except with too small values where no significant differences can be observed).

Once again, the monolithic implementation achieves latencies about 50% lower than the modular implementation when the size of the messages is small (up to 4096 bytes when $n = 7$ and 8192 bytes when $n = 3$). When the size of the messages increases, the early latency also increases: here, the total amount of data that needs to be exchanged influences the latency, whereas previously the latency was determined mostly by the number of messages sent on the network (these messages all require a certain amount of processing, independently of their small size). Finally, with the largest messages considered, the monolithic implementation achieves a latency that is 25% ($n = 7$) or 35% ($n = 3$) smaller than the modular implementation.

Throughput of Atomic Broadcast. We now examine what throughput is reached by the modular and monolithic implementations of atomic broadcast. Figure 10 shows the relationship between the throughput of atomic broadcast (on the vertical axis) and the offered load (on the horizontal axis) when the size of the atomic broadcast messages is fixed at 16384 bytes. When the offered load is small (less than 500 msgs/s), the throughput is equal to the offered load. As the offered load increases, the flow-control mechanism limits the throughput that can be achieved (as in the early latency above, the throughput reaches a plateau as the offered load increases). Furthermore, for a high offered

load, the monolithic implementation sustains a throughput that is 25% ($n = 7$) to 30% ($n = 3$) higher than the modular implementation. For a low offered load, the difference between both stacks is almost negligible.

Figure 11 presents the throughput of both implementations as a function of the size of the messages that are abcast. The offered load is fixed at 2000 msgs/s. When the size of the messages is small, the monolithic implementation achieves between 10% and 15% higher throughputs than the modular one (and the throughput remains constant up to messages of size 4096 for $n = 7$ and 16384 for $n = 3$). Surprisingly, the throughput is higher when $n = 7$ processes participate in the system than when $n = 3$. This is once again due to the flow-control mechanism: each process is allowed to have a certain backlog (i.e. abcast messages that have not been delivered yet). Hence, when the number of processes grows, a larger number of abcast messages that have not been adelivered are allowed to circulate.

Finally, as the message size increases, the throughput of the system with $n = 7$ processes degrades faster than in the case of $n = 3$. This is due to the consensus proposal (which contains large messages) that needs to be sent to all processes in the system. As both the message size of and the number of processes increase, sending these large proposals results in an overall lower throughput (in msgs/s).

Discussion. From the results above, we see that the difference in performance between a modular and a monolithic implementation of the same distributed protocol is significant: the difference in latency is up to 50%, while the difference in throughput varies between 10% and 25%. This is the cost that a user must expect to pay when choosing between a modular system that is easier to maintain and update and a monolithic system that has better performance characteristics.

Furthermore, it is interesting to note that the experimental results do not always match the analysis in Section 5.2. These two results are, however, complementary. As explained earlier, the analytical evaluation of the two implementations focuses solely on the messages exchanged by the algorithm. Processing costs and resource contention, for example, are not at all considered in the analysis. On the other hand, in evaluating throughput and message latency, experimental results are strongly influenced by such elements (but do not consider explicitly number of messages exchanged). For instance, 99% of CPU resources were used with an offered load bigger than 500 msgs/s. The discrepancy between the analytical and experimental evaluations of the stacks stem from these elements (that are difficult to estimate a priori).

6 Related Work

A number of group communication toolkits have implemented atomic broadcast during the last two decades. While early implementations (Isis [5, 6], Phoenix [17] and Totem [2], among others) were designed with a monolithic architecture, more recent systems (Horus [27], Ensemble [14], Transis [11], JavaGroups [3], Eden [15], and Fortika[18, 19][7]) present a modular design. A comparison, from the architectural point of view, of most of these group communication toolkits can be found in [20]. However, the issue of performance overhead induced by modularity (i.e. comparing performance of a modular and a monolithic stack based on the same architecture) has not been covered extensively. In Ensemble, the performance was improved through several techniques [26, 14]: optimizing the interfacing code, improving the format of headers from different modules and compressing them, extracting and inlining frequently executed functions (from many modules), etc. Appia, a system inspired by Ensemble, included and furthered these techniques [21]. While these techniques significantly improved the performance of these systems (e.g., in [14], they reduce by approximately 20 the time of processing), they are rather general lower-level solutions. Their aim is not at the algorithmic level: the algorithms stayed the same

---

[7]Actually, Fortika provides both modular and monolithic implementations of atomic broadcast.

after the optimizations. On the other hand, our algorithmic improvements can not be applied to Ensemble or Appia, where atomic broadcast is not solved by reduction to consensus, but rather relies on group membership in order to avoid blocking. In [12], the authors propose to extend the specification of consensus. The new specification allows the consensus layer to share some state with the above layers (e.g. atomic broadcast) in order to reduce the amount of data sent over the network. This technique improves significantly performance (reduction by 4 of the message latency). However, this result is not comparable to current result due to significant differences in the system setup. Note that the Eden group communication toolkit [15] proposes a very similar technique.

In a more general context, there is more extensive work on protocol layer optimization. For instance, the influential x-Kernel modular system was improved with the help of various techniques like protocol multiplexing [23]. Standard compilation techniques can be combined with annotations in the code to optimize the most frequently executed functions [22]. This approach is somewhat similar to the work done in Ensemble, but for more more basic stacks like TCP/IP. Another technique to improve performance across a protocol stack is Application Level Framing [9, 10]. The intuition here is that all protocols should know the typical size of application messages, so that they are not unnecessarily fragmented on their way down the stack. Again, in all these techniques, protocols are treated as black boxes: the optimizations did not involve any modification in the protocol logic. Hence, most of these techniques can easily be combined with the ones proposed in this paper.

Modularity is a necessary property to achieve good performance in parallel computing and concurrent programming [16]. However, this is not applicable to our work, since very few tasks can be parallelized in atomic broadcast: only message diffusion and ordering can be executed concurrently.

7 Conclusion

The paper presented two versions (monolithic and modular) of a fairly complex protocol: atomic broadcast. We showed that a monolithic stack allows several algorithmic optimizations. This is principally due to (1) the fact that consensus instances are not considered independently, and (2) the possibility for different modules to share their state. We then analytically and experimentally quantified the gain obtained thanks to these optimizations. Our analytical evaluation concluded that a monolithic implementation significantly reduces the number of messages sent over the network. On the other hand, our experimental evaluation revealed an overhead incurred by the modular version that reaches 50% in the worst workload conditions.

In summary, if we are to implement atomic broadcast, it is commonly agreed that a modular design is the most sensible approach. In this paper, we have shown that we cannot be so sure of this (apparently undisputed) choice, if we care about our system's performance.

Acknowledgments

We would like to thank the anonymous reviewers for their comments and helpful suggestions.

References

[1] L. Alvisi and K. Marzullo. Waft: Support for fault-tolerance in wide-area object oriented systems. In *Proc. of the 2nd Information Survivability Workshop – ISW '98*, pages 5–10. IEEE Computer Society Press, October 1998.

[2] Y. Amir, L. E. Moser, P. M. Melliar-Smith, D. A. Agarwal, and P. Ciarfella. The Totem single-ring ordering and membership protocol. *ACM Trans. on Computer Systems*, 13(4):311–342, Nov. 1995.

[3] B. Ban. *JavaGroups 2.0 User's Guide*, Nov 2002.

[4] N. T. Bhatti, M. A. Hiltunen, R. D. Schlichting, and W. Chiu. Coyote: A system for constructing fine-grain configurable communication services. *ACM Trans. on Computer Systems*, 16(4):321–366, Nov. 1998.

[5] K. P. Birman. The process group approach to reliable distributed computing. *Comm. ACM*, 36(12):36–53, Dec. 1993.

[6] K. P. Birman and T. A. Joseph. Reliable communication in presence of failures. *ACM Trans. on Computer Systems*, 5(1):47–76, Feb. 1987.

[7] T. D. Chandra and S. Toueg. Unreliable failure detectors for reliable distributed systems. *Journal of ACM*, 43(2):225–267, Mar. 1996.

[8] G. Chockler, I. Keidar, and R. Vitenberg. Group communication specifications: A comprehensive study. *ACM Computing Surveys*, 33(4):427–469, May 2001.

[9] D. D. Clark and D. L. Tennenhouse. Architectural considerations for a new generation of protocols. In *SIGCOMM '90: Proceedings of the ACM symposium on Communications architectures & protocols*, pages 200–208, New York, NY, USA, 1990. ACM Press.

[10] J. Crowcroft, J. Wakeman, Z. Wang, and D. Sirovica. Is Layering Harmful? IEEE Network 6(1992) 1 pp. 20-24. *IEEE Network 6(1992) 1 pp. 20-24*, 1992.

[11] D. Dolev and D. Malkhi. The Transis approach to high availability cluster communication. *Comm. ACM*, 39(4):64–70, Apr. 1996.

[12] R. Ekwall and A. Schiper. Solving atomic broadcast with indirect consensus. In *2006 IEEE International Conference on Dependable Systems and Networks (DSN 2006)*, 2006.

[13] V. Hadzilacos and S. Toueg. A modular approach to fault-tolerant broadcasts and related problems. TR 94-1425, Dept. of Computer Science, Cornell University, Ithaca, NY, USA, May 1994.

[14] M. Hayden. The Ensemble system. Technical Report TR98-1662, Dept. of Computer Science, Cornell University, Jan. 8, 1998.

[15] M. Hurfin, R. Macêdo, M. Raynal, and F. Tronel. A general framework to solve agreement problems. In *Proceedings of the 18th Symposium on Reliable Distributed Systems (SRDS)*, pages 56–67, Lausanne, Switzerland, Oct. 1999.

[16] L. V. Kalé. Performance and productivity in parallel programming via processor virtualization. In *Proc. of the First Intl. Workshop on Productivity and Performance in High-End Computing (at HPCA 10)*, Madrid, Spain, February 2004.

[17] C. P. Malloth. *Conception and Implementation of a Toolkit for Building Fault-Tolerant Distributed Applications in Large Scale Networks*. PhD thesis, École Polytechnique Fédérale de Lausanne, Switzerland, Sept. 1996.

[18] S. Mena, X. Cuvellier, C. Grégoire, and A. Schiper. Appia vs. cactus: Comparing protocol composition frameworks. In *Proc. of 22th IEEE Symposium on Reliable Distributed Systems (SRDS'03)*, Florence, Italy, Oct. 2003.

[19] S. Mena, O. Rütti, and A. Schiper. *Fortika: Robust Group Communication*. EPFL, Laboratoire de Systèmes Répartis, may 2006.

[20] S. Mena, A. Schiper, and P. T. Wojciechowski. A step towards a new generation of group communication systems. In *Proc. of Conference on Middleware*, Rio de Janeiro, Brasil, June 2003.

[21] H. Miranda, A. Pinto, and L. Rodrigues. Appia: A flexible protocol kernel supporting multiple coordinated channels. In *21st Int'l Conf. on Distributed Computing Systems (ICDCS' 01)*, pages 707–710, Washington - Brussels - Tokyo, Apr.16–19 2001.

[22] D. Mosberger, L. L. Peterson, P. G. Bridges, and S. O'Malley. Analysis of techniques to improve protocol processing latency. In *SIGCOMM '96: Conference proceedings on Applications, technologies, architectures, and protocols for computer communications*, pages 73–84, New York, NY, USA, 1996. ACM Press.

[23] L. Peterson, N. Hutchinson, S. O'Malley, and M. Abbott. Rpc in the x-kernel: evaluating new design techniques. In *SOSP '89: Proceedings of the twelfth ACM symposium on Operating systems principles*, pages 91–101, New York, NY, USA, 1989. ACM Press.

[24] The University of Arizona, Computer Science Department. *The Cactus Project*. Available electronically at http://www.cs.arizona.edu/cactus/.

[25] P. Urbán. *Evaluating the Performance of Distributed Agreement Algorithms: Tools, Methodology and Case Studies*. PhD thesis, École Polytechnique Fédérale de Lausanne, Switzerland, Aug. 2003. Number 2824.

[26] R. van Renesse. Masking the overhead of protocol layering. In *SIGCOMM '96: Conference proceedings on Applications, technologies, architectures, and protocols for computer communications*, pages 96–104, New York, NY, USA, 1996. ACM Press.

[27] R. van Renesse, K. P. Birman, B. B. Glade, K. Guo, M. Hayden, T. Hickey, D. Malki, A. Vaysburd, and W. Vogels. Horus: A flexible group communications system. Technical Report TR95-1500, Dept. of Computer Science, Cornell University, Ithaca, NY, USA, Apr. 1996.

Eventually k-Bounded Wait-Free Distributed Daemons

Yantao Song and Scott M. Pike*
Department of Computer Science
Texas A&M University
College Station, TX 77843-3112, USA
{yantao,pike}@cs.tamu.edu

Abstract

Wait-free scheduling is unsolvable in asynchronous message-passing systems subject to crash faults. Given the practical importance of this problem, we examine its solvability under partial synchrony relative to the eventually perfect failure detector $\Diamond \mathcal{P}$. Specifically, we present a new oracle-based solution to the dining philosophers problem that is wait-free in the presence of arbitrarily many crash faults. Additionally, our solution satisfies eventual k-bounded waiting, which guarantees that every execution has an infinite suffix where no process can overtake any live hungry neighbor more than k consecutive times. Finally, our algorithm uses only bounded space, bounded-capacity channels, and is also quiescent with respect to crashed processes. Among other practical applications, our results support wait-free distributed daemons for fairly scheduling self-stabilizing protocols in the presence of crash faults.

Keywords: self-stabilization, daemons, wait-freedom

1. Introduction

Self-stabilization [11] is a fundamental technique for developing dependable systems. Starting from any configuration, self-stabilizing algorithms always converge to a closed set of safe states from which correct behavior follows. As such, stabilization is useful for autonomic systems that must bootstrap from arbitrary initial states. More importantly, however, stabilization is an effective technique for recovering from transient faults which, in general, can drive systems into arbitrary configurations.

A fundamental assumption for self-stabilization is that every correct process executes infinitely many steps. This assumption is necessary to guarantee convergence. For example, suppose that some live process j executes only finitely many steps, followed by a local transient fault that yields an unsafe state. If subsequent steps by j are necessary to detect and/or correct the fault, the overall system may never recover from the unsafe state.

Recent work has examined the assumption that live processes take infinitely many steps. The work in [12] shows that this requires the underlying microprocessors to be self-stabilizing as well. For example, soft errors may cause micro-code controlled processors to loop in a subset of code without the fetch-decode-execute cycle. This undermines convergence, because the microprocessor ceases to execute the subsequent instructions of its application processes.

A parallel line of work has examined self-stabilizing daemons [1, 3, 15, 19, 6]. In general, conflicting actions can impose scheduling constraints. For instance, algorithms using shared memory must coordinate access to critical sections of code that update shared variables. Concurrency control is often coordinated by a *daemon* that schedules a set of processes to execute non-conflicting actions. Distributed daemons are commonly implemented by dining philosopher algorithms, where each diner represents a process in the stabilizing protocol. As an abstraction of local mutual exclusion, processes with conflicting actions are connected as neighbors in the conflict graph, where each diner becomes hungry infinitely often. When scheduled to eat, the diner can execute any enabled action in the stabilizing protocol, because the mutual exclusion of dining guarantees that no conflicting neighbor will be scheduled to eat simultaneously.

Many dining-based daemons stabilize from transient faults to the daemon itself [1, 3, 15, 19, 6]. This is because transient corruptions to the daemon could result in deadlock, which would prevent correct processes from eating infinitely often. A limitation of these daemons, however, is that none addresses the pragmatic possibility of crash faults, whereby processes cease execution without warning and never recover. As it turns out, no purely asynchronous daemon can mask the impact of crash faults entirely; starvation of correct processes is unavoidable [8]. Since diners

*This work was supported by the Advanced Research Program of the Texas Higher Education Coordinating Board under Project Number 000512-0007-2006. The authors would also like to thank the anonymous reviewers for their many useful comments.

645

that starve are never scheduled to eat again, convergence cannot be guaranteed. The conclusion is that stabilization becomes impossible in crash-faulty environments unless we consider some recourse to crash-fault detection.

This paper explores the solvability of wait-free, eventually k-bounded distributed daemons as schedulers for self-stabilizing protocols in the presence of crash faults. We assume that only the stabilizing protocol is subject to transient faults, but that both the protocol and the daemon layers are subject to crash faults. Thus, we consider daemons that are wait-free, but not necessarily stabilizing for transient faults to daemon variables.

Our work demonstrates the solvability of wait-free scheduling in partially synchronous systems sufficient to implement the *eventually perfect failure detector* $\Diamond \mathcal{P}$ from the Chandra-Toueg hierarchy [7]. $\Diamond \mathcal{P}$ detectors always suspect crashed processes and eventually stop suspecting correct processes. As such, $\Diamond \mathcal{P}$ oracles can make finitely many false-positive mistakes during any run. Although $\Diamond \mathcal{P}$ provides unreliable information, we show that $\Diamond \mathcal{P}$ is still sufficient to solve wait-free dining under *eventual weak exclusion* $\Diamond \mathcal{WX}$. This safety model guarantees that, for every run, there exists an unknown time after which no two live neighbors eat simultaneously. As such, dining under $\Diamond \mathcal{WX}$ permits finitely many scheduling mistakes during any run.

Interestingly, wait-free dining is impossible with $\Diamond \mathcal{P}$ oracles under the slightly stronger criterion of *perpetual weak exclusion* [20]. This safety model guarantees that no two live neighbors eat simultaneously (ever). Our interest in $\Diamond \mathcal{WX}$ is motivated by two factors. First, it admits of practical wait-free implementations using only $\Diamond \mathcal{P}$, which is a modestly powerful oracle that is implementable in many realistic models of partial synchrony [7, 13, 14]. Second, $\Diamond \mathcal{WX}$ is well-suited as a scheduling model for stabilizing algorithms, insofar as each scheduling mistake can be viewed as a sharing violation that precipitates at worst a transient fault on the stabilization layer. Despite making mistakes under $\Diamond \mathcal{WX}$, a wait-free daemon guarantees that every correct process will execute infinitely many steps, which thereby guarantees convergence to safe states after finitely many transient faults.

Our distributed daemon satisfies several useful properties in addition to wait-freedom. First, it satisfies a degree of eventual fairness (eventual k-bounded waiting), which guarantees that every execution has an infinite suffix where no process overtakes any hungry neighbor more than k consecutive times. Additionally, our algorithm uses only bounded space and requires only bounded-capacity channels. Finally, our algorithm is also quiescent with respect to crashed processes, which means that correct processes eventually stop sending messages to crashed neighbors.

2. Background and Terminology

Computational Model. We consider asynchronous message-passing systems augmented with a local, eventually perfect failure detector $\Diamond \mathcal{P}_1$ (defined below). As such, message delays and relative process speeds are unbounded, but each process has access to a local oracle that provides information about crash faults in each run.

Processes can crash only as the result of a crash fault, which occurs when a process ceases execution without warning and never recovers [9]. For each run α, a process i is either *faulty* or *correct*. We say that i *is faulty in* α if i crashes at some time t in α; otherwise, i is correct in α. Additionally, process i is *live at time* t if i has not crashed by time t. Consequently, correct processes are always live, and faulty processes are live only prior to crashing.

Each system is modeled by a set of n distributed processes $\Pi = \{p_1, p_2, \ldots, p_n\}$ that communicate only by asynchronous message passing. We assume reliable FIFO channels, such that every message sent to a correct process is eventually received by that process in the order sent, and messages are neither lost, duplicated, nor corrupted.

Failure Detectors. An unreliable failure detector can be viewed as a distributed oracle that can be queried for (possibly incorrect) information about crash faults in Π. Each process has access to its own local detector module that outputs a set of processes currently suspected of having crashed.

Unreliable failure detectors are characterized by the kinds of *mistakes* they can make. Mistakes include false-negatives (i.e., not suspecting a crashed process), as well as false-positives (i.e., wrongfully suspecting a correct process). In Chandra and Toueg's original definition [7], each class of failure detectors is defined by two properties: *completeness* and *accuracy*. Completeness restricts false negatives, while accuracy restricts false positives.

We use a locally scope-restricted refinement of the eventually perfect failure detector called $\Diamond \mathcal{P}_1$ [4, 17]. This oracle satisfies the properties of $\Diamond \mathcal{P}$, but only with respect to immediate neighbors in the dining conflict graph (defined below):

- **Local Strong Completeness:** *Every crashed process is eventually and permanently suspected by all correct neighbors.*

- **Local Eventual Strong Accuracy:** *For every run, there exists a time after which no correct process is suspected by any correct neighbor.*

Therefore, $\Diamond \mathcal{P}_1$ may commit false-positive mistakes by suspecting correct neighbors for finitely many times during any run. However, $\Diamond \mathcal{P}_1$ detectors *converge* at some point after which $\Diamond \mathcal{P}_1$ detectors provide reliable information about neighbors. Unfortunately, the time of convergence is unknown and may vary from run to run.

Distributed Daemons and Dining Philosophers. The local program executed by each process i in a stabilizing protocol can be modeled as a set of actions (guarded commands). Processes i and j are connected as neighbors in a *conflict graph* if i and j cannot be scheduled independently; that is, the actions of i and j have overlapping constraints and should not be scheduled to execute simultaneously. A distributed daemon [11, 3] is a scheduler that continually selects a non-empty subset of processes to execute a set of non-conflicting actions.

Distributed daemons are often implemented as solutions to the well-known dining philosophers problem, which is a classic paradigm of process synchronization. Originally proposed by Dijkstra for a ring topology [10], dining was later generalized by Lynch for local mutual exclusion problems on arbitrary conflict graphs [18]. A dining instance is modeled by an undirected conflict graph $C = (\Pi, E)$, where each vertex $i \in \Pi$ represents a diner, and each edge $(i, j) \in E$ indicates a potential conflict between neighbors i and j. We assume that each pair of processes in the conflict graph is connected by a reliable FIFO channel.

At any time, the state of a diner is either *thinking*, *hungry*, or *eating*. These abstract states correspond to three basic phases of an ordinary process: executing independently, requesting shared resources, and utilizing shared resources in a critical section, respectively. A *hungry session* of any process i is the (inclusive) time period from when i becomes hungry until i gets scheduled to eat.

Initially, every process is thinking. Although processes may think forever, they are also permitted to become hungry at any time. By contrast, correct processes can eat for only a finite (but not necessarily bounded) period of time. Hungry neighbors are said to be in *conflict*, because they compete for shared but mutually exclusive resources. A correct dining solution under eventual weak exclusion $\Diamond \mathcal{WX}$ must satisfy the following two requirements:

- **Safety ($\Diamond \mathcal{WX}$):** *For every run, there exists a time after which no two live neighbors ever eat simultaneously.*

- **Progress (Wait-Freedom):** *Every correct hungry process eventually eats, regardless of process crashes.*

The safety criterion permits dining solutions to make at most finitely many scheduling mistakes in any run. The progress criterion prevents dining solutions from *starving* correct hungry processes by never scheduling them to eat. In the presence of arbitrarily many crash faults, a dining algorithm that satisfies progress is called *wait-free* [16].

Fairness. We say that a daemon satisfies *perpetual k-bounded waiting* ($\Box k$-$\mathcal{BW}$), if no process i can be selected more than k consecutive times, while any correct neighbor j remains continuously hungry [5, 2]. A daemon satisfies *eventually k-bounded waiting* ($\Diamond k$-$\mathcal{BW}$), if for every run,

there exists a time after which no process i can be selected more than k consecutive times, while any correct neighbor j remains continuously hungry. Thus, bounded waiting is measure of *fairness*, where $\Box k$-$\mathcal{BW}$ denotes perpetual k-*fairness* and $\Diamond k$-$\mathcal{BW}$ denotes eventual k-*fairness*.

In the context of dining-based daemons, every run of a distributed daemon that satisfies $\Diamond k$-$\mathcal{BW}$ has an infinite suffix that guarantees k-*fairness* among correct processes. That is, for every run, there exists a (potentially unknown) time after which no correct hungry process i can be overtaken more than k consecutive times by any correct neighbor j. In this paper, we present a dining-based daemon that achieves $\Diamond k$-$\mathcal{BW}$ for $k = 2$.

3. Algorithm Description

Our algorithm is related to the asynchronous doorway dining algorithm of Choy and Singh [8], insofar as we use forks for safety, an asynchronous doorway for fairness. Processes connected by an edge in conflict graph share the corresponding fork. In order to eat, a hungry process must collect and hold all of its shared forks. This provides a simple basis for safety, since at most one neighbor can hold a given fork at any time. If two neighbors compete for one fork, the conflict is solved always in favor of the neighbor with higher priority. Process priorities are static and represented by colors, which are assigned to processes at the beginning of each run. Standard node-coloring algorithms can be used to assign colors to processes, such that no two neighbors have the same color. An asynchronous doorway is used to prevent higher-priority processes from starving lower-priority neighbors.

In order to eat, every hungry process must go through two phases in the original doorway algorithm: Phase 1: outside the doorway; Phase 2: inside the doorway. In phase 1, in order to enter the doorway, every process collects acks from all of its neighbors. In phase 2, in order to eat, every process holds all of its shared forks continuously. When a process i goes to eat, i must be inside the doorway and hold all of its shared forks.

Phase 1: In the original doorway solution, when a process i becomes hungry, it tries to enter the doorway. In order to do so, the process i must receive one acknowledgment from each neighbor through the ping-ack protocol. An acknowledgment (ack) indicates that the corresponding neighbor allows i to enter the doorway. If a neighbor j is outside the doorway, then j will send the ack to process i; otherwise j will defer sending the ack to i until j exits the doorway. Provided that processes inside the doorway will eventually exit the doorway, then every hungry process must eventually enter the doorway. The doorway provides a basis for fairness, simply because a hungry process inside the doorway will prevent its neighbors from entering the doorway.

In our fault model, all crashed processes stop sending messages, including ack messages. Consequently, in the original doorway solution, if a process crashes, its neighbors will be potentially blocked outside the doorway and starve. To solve this problem, we introduce $\Diamond \mathcal{P}_1$ in our algorithm. The local strong completeness property guarantees that every crashed process will be eventually and permanently suspected by all correct neighbors. As such, these neighbors will be able to use suspicion from $\Diamond \mathcal{P}_1$ in place of the missing acks to enter the doorway.

On the other hand, in the original doorway solution, while some hungry process i waits for the ack from a neighbor j, other neighbors can enter the doorway finitely many times. To achieve *eventual 2-bounded waiting*, we introduce a modified doorway in our algorithm. Specifically, each process i grants *at most one* ack per neighbor j per hungry session of i. In addition to acks that may have been sent while i was thinking, this mechanism ensures that no neighbor of i can enter the doorway more than twice while i remains continuously hungry.

We revise the original ping-ack protocol as follows. Each hungry process i sends a ping message to each neighbor j to request the doorway ack. Upon j receiving the ping from i, j sends the ack if either (1) j is thinking, or (2) j is hungry and outside the doorway and has *not* already sent an ack to i during the current hungry session of j. Otherwise, j defers sending the ack to i until after j eats and exits the doorway.

Notice that it is possible for two neighbors to enter the doorway simultaneously. If two neighbors suspect each other (before $\Diamond \mathcal{P}_1$ converges), then both can enter the doorway regardless of ack messages. Alternatively, neighbors can receive acks from each other simultaneously while outside the doorway, and then enter together. The symmetry between hungry neighbors inside the doorway is resolved by the color-based priority scheme in phase 2.

Phase 2: In the original doorway algorithm, in order to eat, a hungry process must hold all of its shared forks continuously. After a hungry process enters the doorway, the process begins to collect all shared forks. Every fork is associated with one edge in the conflict graph. Processes connected by an edge in the conflict graph share the corresponding fork, which is used to resolve conflicts over the overlapping set of resources they both need. When two neighbors are competing for one fork, the conflict is always solved in favor of the neighbor with higher priority. This provides a simple basis for safety, since at most one neighbor can hold a given fork at any time.

In the original doorway solution, any process that crashes while holding forks will cause its corresponding hungry neighbors to starve, because the forks necessary for eating cannot be acquired. To solve this problem, we use $\Diamond \mathcal{P}_1$ in our algorithm. As such, hungry neighbors will be able to use suspicion from $\Diamond \mathcal{P}_1$ in place of the missing fork to proceed to eat.

In phase 2, we use the following fork-collection scheme. Each hungry process i that enters the doorway sends a request for each missing fork to the corresponding neighbor j. Upon receiving this request, process j sends the shared fork only if (1) j is outside the doorway, or (2) j is hungry and inside the doorway but has lower priority than i (where process priorities are represented by the static node colors). Otherwise, j defers the fork request until after j eats.

Our algorithm is shown in Algorithm 1.

3.1. Local Variables

In addition to the $\Diamond \mathcal{P}_1$ module, every process i has nine types of local variables, which are partitioned into three sets: for describing state of process i, for the ping-ack protocol, and for the fork collection scheme.

State Variables. Each process i has an integer-valued variable $color_i$. Upon initialization, we assume that each color variable is assigned a locally-unique value so that no two neighbors have the same color. Several node-coloring approximation algorithms can compute such colorings in polynomial time using only $O(\delta)$ distinct values, where δ is the maxmimum degree of the conflict graph. Color values denote process priority and are static after initialization. For each pair of neighbors i and j, process i has higher priority than j if and only if $color_i > color_j$.

Every process also has two variables describing its current state: a trivalent variable $state_i$ and a boolean variable $inside_i$. Variable $state_i$ denotes the current dining phase: *thinking, hungry, or eating*; $inside_i$ indicates whether process i is inside the doorway or not. Initially, every process is outside the doorway and thinking.

Ping-Ack Variables. Process i has four local boolean variables associated with the ping-ack protocol for each neighbor j: $pinged_{ij}$, ack_{ij}, $deferred_{ij}$ and $replied_{ij}$. Initially, all of these variables are false.

The local variable $pinged_{ij}$ is true if and only if there is a pending ping request from i to j. A *pending ping request* initiated by i to j covers the following three situations: a ping request is on its way from i to j, or is being deferred by j, or a replied ack is on its way to i. On the other hand, process i needs to remember received acks until i enters the doorway. The local variable ack_{ij} is true if and only if process i is hungry, outside the doorway, and received an ack from j during the current hungry session of i.

Variable $deferred_{ij}$ is true if and only if process i is currently deferring a ping request from j. Also, to achieve eventual 2-bounded waiting, process i needs to record which ack messages have been sent while hungry. The local variable $replied_{ij}$ is true if and only if process i has sent an ack to neighbor j during the current hungry session of i.

$1 : \{\text{state}_i = \text{thinking}\} \longrightarrow$	*Action 1*
$2 : \quad \text{state}_i := (\text{thinking } \textbf{or } \text{hungry});$	*Become Hungry*

Ping-Ack Actions

$3 : \{(\text{state}_i = \text{hungry}) \wedge \neg\text{inside}_i\} \longrightarrow$	*Action 2*
$4 : \quad \forall j \in N(i) \textbf{ where } (\neg\text{pinged}_{ij} \wedge \neg\text{ack}_{ij}) \textbf{ do}$	*Request Acks from Neighbors*
$5 : \quad\quad\quad \text{send-ping}\langle i \rangle \textbf{ to } j; \quad \text{pinged}_{ij} := \text{true};$	

$6 : \{\text{receive-ping } \textbf{from } j \in N(i)\} \longrightarrow$	*Action 3*
$7 : \quad \textbf{if } (\text{inside}_i \vee \text{replied}_{ij})$	*Inside the Doorway or Has Sent the Ack*
$8 : \quad\quad\quad \text{deferred}_{ij} := \text{true};$	*Defer Sending Ack*
$9 : \quad \textbf{else}$	*Thinking, or Hungry and Has Not Sent an Ack*
$10 : \quad\quad\quad \text{send-ack}\langle i \rangle \textbf{ to } j; \quad \text{replied}_{ij} := (\text{state}_i = \text{hungry});$	*Send an Ack*

$11 : \{\text{receive-ack } \textbf{from } j \in N(i)\} \longrightarrow$	*Action 4*
$12 : \quad \text{ack}_{ij} := ((\text{state}_i = \text{hungry}) \wedge \neg\text{inside}_i) \,;$	*Receive an Ack*
$13 : \quad \text{pinged}_{ij} := \text{false};$	

$14 : \{(\text{state}_i = \text{hungry}) \wedge (\forall j \in N(i) :: (\text{ack}_{ij} \vee (j \in \Diamond\mathcal{P}_1)))\} \longrightarrow$	*Action 5*
$15 : \quad \text{inside}_i := \text{true};$	*Enter the Doorway*
$16 : \quad \forall j \in N(i) \textbf{ do}$	
$17 : \quad\quad\quad \text{ack}_{ij} := \text{false}; \quad \text{replied}_{ij} := \text{false};$	

Fork Collection Actions

$18 : \{(\text{state}_i = \text{hungry}) \wedge \text{inside}_i\} \longrightarrow$	*Action 6*
$19 : \quad \forall j \in N(i) \textbf{ where } (\text{token}_{ij} \wedge \neg\text{fork}_{ij}) \textbf{ do}$	*Request Missing forks*
$20 : \quad\quad\quad \text{send-request}\langle \text{color}_i \rangle \textbf{ to } j; \quad \text{token}_{ij} := \text{false};$	

$21 : \{\text{receive-request}\langle \text{color}_j \rangle \textbf{ from } j \in N(i)\} \longrightarrow$	*Action 7*
$22 : \quad \text{token}_{ij} := \text{true};$	*Receive a Fork Request*
$23 : \quad \textbf{if } (\neg\text{inside}_i \vee ((\text{state}_i = \text{hungry}) \wedge (\text{color}_i < \text{color}_j)))$	
$24 : \quad\quad\quad \text{send-fork}\langle i \rangle \textbf{ to } j; \quad \text{fork}_{ij} := \text{false};$	

$25 : \{\text{receive-fork}\langle j \rangle \textbf{ from } j \in N(i)\} \longrightarrow$	*Action 8*
$26 : \quad \text{fork}_{ij} := \text{true};$	*Receive a Fork*

Other Actions

$27 : \{((\text{state}_i = \text{hungry}) \wedge \text{inside}_i \wedge (\forall j \in N(i) :: (\text{fork}_{ij} \vee (j \in \Diamond\mathcal{P}_1))))\} \longrightarrow$	*Action 9*
$28 : \quad \text{state}_i := \text{eating};$	*Enter Critical Section*

$29 : \{\text{state}_i = \text{eating}\} \longrightarrow$	*Action 10*
$30 : \quad \text{inside}_i := \text{false};$	*Exit the Doorway*
$31 : \quad \text{state}_i := \text{thinking};$	
$32 : \quad \forall j \in N(i) \textbf{ where } (\text{token}_{ij} \wedge \text{fork}_{ij}) \textbf{ do}$	
$33 : \quad\quad\quad \text{send-fork}\langle i \rangle \textbf{ to } j; \quad \text{fork}_{ij} := \text{false};$	*Send Deferred Forks*
$34 : \quad \forall j \in N(i) \textbf{ where } (\text{deferred}_{ij}) \textbf{ do}$	
$35 : \quad\quad\quad \text{send-ack}\langle i \rangle \textbf{ to } j; \quad \text{deferred}_{ij} := \text{false};$	*Send Deferred Acks*

Algorithm 1. Wait-Free, Eventual k-Bounded Waiting ($\Diamond k\text{-}\mathcal{BW}$) for Eventual Weak Exclusion ($\Diamond\mathcal{WX}$)

Each hungry process resets all of its local ack and replied variables to false upon entering the doorway. By constrast, true deferred variables remain true until the process eats and exits.

Fork Collection Variables. Process i has two local boolean variables associated with the fork collection scheme for each neighbor j: $fork_{ij}$ and $token_{ij}$. Symmetrically, j has variables $fork_{ji}$ and $token_{ji}$ for i.

The local variable $fork_{ij}$ is true if and only if process i holds the fork shared with j. Because the fork is unique and exclusive, $fork_{ij}$ and $fork_{ji}$ cannot be true simultaneously. However, both $fork_{ij}$ and $fork_{ji}$ could be false simultaneously if and only if the fork is in transit.

The local variables, $token_{ij}$ and $token_{ji}$, are introduced for fork requests between the neighboring processes i and j. In general, if a process i is hungry and holds the token $token_{ij}$, then i is permitted to request the missing fork by sending the token to the corresponding neighbor j. When both $fork_{ij}$ and $token_{ij}$ are true, process i is deferring the fork request from its neighbor j. Initially, between each pair of neighbors, the fork is at the neighbor with higher color, and the token is at the neighbor with lower color.

3.2. Algorithm Actions

A thinking process can become hungry at any time by executing Action 1. Action 1 is not an internal action of Algorithm 1 and is formalized just for completeness of process behaviors. Upon becoming hungry, processes are still outside the doorway.

Ping-Ack Actions (Action 2, 3, 4, and 5). While hungry and outside the doorway, Action 2 is always enabled. By Action 2, for each neighbor j, if the ack from j is missing and no pending ping request to j exists, then process i requests an ack from j. As a result, $pinged_{ij}$ becomes true to indicate existence of the pending ping request.

When process i receives a ping message, i decides whether to send the ack in Action 3. The ping request can be deferred for two reasons: i is inside the doorway, or i is outside the doorway but has sent an ack during its current hungry session. Otherwise, i sends the ack immediately. As a result, if i is hungry and outside the doorway, the corresponding replied variable is set to true.

Processes receive acks by Action 4. As a result, the corresponding pinged variable is set back to false to indicate that no ping request is pending with the corresponding neighbor. Action 5 determines when a hungry process enters the doorway. If for each neighbor j, a hungry process i either received the ack or suspects j continuously by $\Diamond \mathcal{P}_1$, i eventually enters the doorway. After i enters the doorway, i does not need to remember received acks. Also while inside the doorway, i always defers ping requests. Thus, after

entering the doorway, i resets its local ack and replied variables to false.

Fork Collection Actions (Action 6, 7, and 8). Process i sends fork requests for missing forks in Action 6, which is enabled while i is hungry and inside the doorway. Process i encodes its color in the request messages as a parameter.

Any process that receives a fork request in Action 7 decides whether or not to send the shared fork. If the process is outside the doorway, or hungry but with a lower color, then it sends the shared fork immediately. Otherwise, the process defers the fork request until after it eats. Action 8 simply receives a fork.

Other Actions. Action 9 determines when a hungry process goes to eat. If a hungry process i is inside the doorway, and for each neighbor j, i either holds the shared fork continuously or suspects j, then i eventually eats.

Correct processes can eat only for a finite period of time. By executing Action 10, eating processes exit eating, transit back to thinking, and exit the doorway. Also, all deferred fork requests and deferred ping requests are granted.

4. Safety Proof

This section proves that Algorithm 1 satisfies the safety property: eventual weak exclusion. The safety proof relies on two assumptions: $\Diamond \mathcal{P}_1$ can make only finitely many false-positive mistakes, and the fork between any pair of neighbors is unique and exclusive. First, we prove the uniqueness of forks in Lemmas 1.1 and 1.2. Next, we prove safety in Theorem 1.

Lemma 1.1: *In Algorithm 1, when a process receives a fork request, the process must be holding the requested fork.*

Suppose that a process j receives a request for a fork that j does not hold. If j is outside the doorway, or is hungry with a lower color, j would duplicate the fork(Action 7). As a result, uniqueness of forks and the safety property are violated. Lemma 1.1 shows that the above situation never happens and is proved based on FIFO channels.

Proof: Lemma 1.1 is proved by direct construction in two steps. The first step shows that when a process receives a fork, that process must not be holding the corresponding token. By using the result of the first step, we prove Lemma 1.1 in the second step.

Suppose that a process j receives a fork from its neighbor i. When i sent the fork, i must be holding the corresponding token (Actions 7 and 10). After i sent the fork, i may send the token to j to re-request the fork (Action 6). Because of FIFO channels, the token must arrive at j after the fork arrives. Thus, when a process j receives a fork, j must not be holding the corresponding token, which is either at the neighbor i or in transit to j.

From the above, we also can conclude that while a fork is in transit, the fork recipient can not hold the corresponding token. Hence, when a process i sends a token to its neighbor j, the fork cannot be in transit to i. Otherwise, i should not have the token. Also, j cannot send the fork away without holding the token. Thus, when i sends a fork request to j, the fork is either at j or in transit to j. Because of FIFO channels, when the token arrives at j, j must hold the fork. Lemma 1.1 holds. ☐

Lemma 1.2: *The fork is unique between each pair of neighbors.*

If two duplicated forks exist between two neighbors, both neighbors can eat simultaneously infinitely often. Thus, to prove the safety property, we must prove uniqueness of forks.

Proof: Only when processes send a fork which they do not hold, could the fork be duplicated. However, a process i sends a fork, only because i received a fork request (Actions 7 and 10). By Lemma 1.1, when i received a fork request, i must be holding the fork. Then processes cannot send a fork which they do not hold. Thus, forks cannot be duplicated. Lemma 1.2 holds. ☐

Theorem 1: *Algorithm 1 satisfies eventual weak exclusion $\Diamond\mathcal{WX}$: for each execution, there exists a time after which no two live neighbors eat simultaneously.*

Proof: The safety proof is by direct construction and depends only on the local eventually strong accuracy property of $\Diamond\mathcal{P}_1$. This property guarantees that for each run, there exists a time after which no correct process is suspected by any correct neighbor.

Faulty processes cannot prevent safety from being established. Since faulty processes eventually crash, they can eat only finitely many times in any run. Next, we focus on correct processes.

Consider any execution α of Algorithm 1. Let t denote the time in α when $\Diamond\mathcal{P}_1$ converges. Let i be any correct process that *begins* eating after time t. By Action 9, process i can go to eat only if for each neighbor j, either i holds the shared fork continuously or i suspects j. Since $\Diamond\mathcal{P}_1$ never suspects correct neighbors after time t, i must hold every fork shared with its correct neighbors to eat.

So long as i remains eating, Action 7 guarantees that i will defer all fork requests. Thus, i will not relinquish any fork while eating. Furthermore, $\Diamond\mathcal{P}_1$ has already converged in α, so no correct neighbor can suspect i either. Also by Lemma 1.2, the fork is unique between each pair of neighbors, thus no correct neighbor can hold the fork shared with i. Consequently, Action 9 remains disabled for every correct hungry neighbor of i until after i transits back to thinking. We conclude that no live neighbor can eat simultaneously after time t. ☐

5. Progress Proof

Theorem 2: *Algorithm 1 satisfies wait-free progress: every correct hungry process eventually eats.*

Proof: In order to eat, every hungry process must go through two phases: phase 1, outside the doorway; phase 2, inside the doorway. Correspondingly, our progress proof consists of two phases too. Progress proof of phase 1: every correct process outside the doorway eventually enters the doorway. Progress proof of phase 2: every correct hungry process inside the doorway eventually eats. However, progress in phase 1 relies on progress in phase 2, thus we prove progress in phases 1 and 2 in the reverse order. Next we show the progress proofs of phase 2 and 1 in Lemmas 2.3 and 2.4 respectively. ☐

Lemma 2.1: *Let processes i and j be correct neighbors, where i is hungry and inside the doorway. If $color_i > color_j$ and i does not suspect j, i eventually holds the fork shared with j continuously until after i eats.*

Proof: If process i has not sent a fork request to j and the fork is missing, i will request the fork shared with j (Action 6). When process j receives the fork request, because $color_i > color_j$, j defers the fork request only when it is eating (Action 7). Since j is correct, j eats only for a finite period of time. Thus, j eventually exits eating and sends all deferred forks, including the fork shared with i (Action 10). Thus, i eventually holds the shared fork. Next we show that i will hold the fork continuously until after i eats.

Because $color_i > color_j$, by Action 7, while i is hungry and inside the doorway, i defers any fork request from j. Consequently, i will hold the fork continuously until after i eats. Thus, Lemma 2.1 holds. ☐

Lemma 2.2: *Between each pair of neighbors i and j, there exists at most one pending ping request initiated by process i at any time.*

Proof: While there is a pending ping request from i to j, the variable $pinged_{ij}$ remains true until after i receives the ack from j. While $pinged_{ij}$ remains true, process i cannot send another ping message to j (Action 2). Lemma 2.2 holds. ☐

Lemma 2.3: *Progress in phase 2: every correct hungry process inside the doorway eventually eats.*

Proof: We prove Lemma 2.3 by complete induction on process colors. The base case shows that every correct hungry process inside the doorway with the highest color hc eventually eats. The inductive step shows that if every correct hungry process inside the doorway with a color higher than d eventually eats, then every correct hungry process inside the doorway with color d eventually eats too.

Base Case: *Every correct hungry process inside the doorway with the highest color* hc *eventually eats.*

Let i be a correct hungry process inside the doorway, where $color_i = hc$. Because no two neighboring processes have the same color, $color_i$ is higher than the colors of all neighbors. We start our proof after $\Diamond\mathcal{P}_1$ converges. Process i is guaranteed to eat after $\Diamond\mathcal{P}_1$ converges.

For process i, we partition its neighbors into two sets: *correct* or *faulty*. All faulty neighbors eventually crash. By strong completeness of $\Diamond\mathcal{P}_1$, i eventually and permanently suspects all faulty neighbors. On the other hand, i cannot suspect correct neighbors after $\Diamond\mathcal{P}_1$ converges. Since $color_i$ is higher than the color of any neighbor, by Lemma 2.1, i will hold the forks shared with its correct neighbors continuously until after i eats. Thus, eventually for each neighbor j, i either suspects j permanently or holds the fork shared with j continuously. Consequently, Action 9 is enabled continuously at i, and i eventually eats.

Inductive Step: *If every correct hungry process inside the doorway with a color higher than d eventually eats, then every correct hungry process inside the doorway with color d eventually eats too.*

Consider a correct hungry process i inside the doorway with the color d. We prove that i is guaranteed to eat after $\Diamond\mathcal{P}_1$ converges. We partition all neighbors of i into three sets: faulty neighbors, Low_i (correct neighbors with a color lower than d) and $High_i$ (correct neighbors with a color higher than d). Because no two neighbors have the same color, every correct neighbor belongs to Low_i or $High_i$.

All faulty neighbors eventually crash. By strong completeness of $\Diamond\mathcal{P}_1$, process i will suspect them eventually and permanently. For each neighbor j in Low_i, by Lemma 2.1, process i will eventually hold the fork shared with j continuously until after i eats.

For each neighbor j in $High_i$, process i will eventually hold the fork shared with j. If i does not hold the fork shared with j and has not sent the fork request to j, i sends a fork request to j (Action 6). When process j receives the fork request, j defers the fork request only when j is inside the doorway (either eating or hungry). By the inductive hypothesis, if j is hungry and inside the doorway, j eventually eats. Because j is correct, j eventually finishes eating and sends all deferred forks, including the fork shared with i.

Process i may lose forks to its neighbors in $High_i$ before i eats, but i will eventually hold all forks shared with correct neighbors continuously. Process i could lose the fork to its neighbor j only when j is hungry and inside the doorway too. Next, we show that after $\Diamond\mathcal{P}_1$ converges, i could lose the fork to j at most once before i eats.

After $\Diamond\mathcal{P}_1$ converges, j cannot suspect correct processes. Thus, in order to enter the doorway, j needs to collect all acks from all of its correct neighbors, including process i. It is possible that j receives an ack from i, which was sent before i entered the doorway. However, by Lemma 2.2, there exists at most one pending ping request from i to j at any time. Also, while i is inside the doorway, i defers any ping request. Thus, after $\Diamond\mathcal{P}_1$ converges, while i is inside

the doorway, j could receive at most one ack from i, which was sent before i entered the doorway. Consequently, j can enter the doorway at most once while i is inside the doorway. By inductive hypothesis, j eventually eats and exits the doorway. After that, j is blocked outside the doorway until after i exits the doorway. While j is blocked outside the doorway, process i cannot lose the fork to j. Thus, i holds the fork shared with j continuously until after i eats.

For each neighbor j, i either suspects j permanently or holds the fork continuously. Therefore, Action 9 is enabled continuously at i, and i eventually eats. □

Lemma 2.4: *Progress in phase 1: every correct hungry process outside the doorway eventually enters the doorway.*

Proof: We say that a process i belongs to set $H(t)$, if and only if, i is correct, hungry, and outside the doorway at time t, and at time t, no correct hungry neighbor of i has been outside the doorway longer than i. We denote t_{ih} as the time when process i started its current hungry session. Process i became hungry at time t_{ih} and remains hungry through time t. Because neighbors can become hungry at the same time, set $H(t)$ may include neighboring processes.

We only need to prove that every process in $H(t)$ eventually enters the doorway. If a correct hungry process j is outside the doorway but not in the set $H(t)$, j eventually joins in a set $H(t')$ at a later time t' and enters the doorway.

To show that every process i in $H(t)$ eventually enters the doorway, we need to prove the following: for each neighbor j, i either suspects j permanently or eventually receives an ack from j.

Every faulty neighbor eventually crashes. By strong completeness of $\Diamond\mathcal{P}_1$, process i will suspect all faulty neighbors eventually and permanently. Next, we show that i eventually receives an ack from each correct neighbor j.

After process i becomes hungry, i starts to collect acks from all neighbors (Action 2). By Lemma 2.2, after executing Action 2, for each neighbor j, if the ack from j is missing, then there exists exactly one pending ping request initiated by i. This pending ping request could be sent during the current hungry session, or perhaps a previous hungry session. Suppose that neighbor j receives the ping message at time t_{jr}. Because the ping message could be sent during a previous hungry session of i, t_{jr} may be earlier than t_{ih}. Hence, neighbor j could receive this ping message at any time. Process j will grant the ping request except two reasons as shown next(Action 3, Line 7). However, j will send the deferred ack eventually.

(1) Process j is inside the doorway (either hungry or eating). If j is hungry, by Lemma 2.3, j eventually eats. Because correct processes can eat only for a finite period of time, j eventually exits the doorway and sends the deferred ack (Action 10).

(2) $replied_{ji} = $ true. When $replied_{ji}$ is true, process j is hungry and outside the doorway at time t_{jr}. We will show

that j eventually enters the doorway before time t and will send the deferred ack to i after eating.

Suppose that $replied_{ji}$ was set to true at time t_{js} and remained true from t_{js} to t_{jr}. To set $replied_{ji}$ as true at time t_{js}, j must send an ack (denoted as ack_{js}) to i and be hungry and outside the doorway at time t_{js}. Also, j must remain hungry and stay outside the doorway from t_{js} to t_{jr}.

By Lemma 2.2, before receiving ack_{js}, process i cannot send another ping request to j. Recall that j receives a ping request from i at time t_{jr}. Thus, i must receive ack_{js} and become hungry again before time t_{jr}. In other words, i must become hungry during time period (t_{js}, t_{jr}) at least once (Action 2). Note that process i becomes hungry at time t_{ih} and remains hungry through time t. Therefore, time $t_{js} < t_{ih}$.

Process j must enter the doorway at least once during the time period (t_{js}, t). Otherwise, j would stay outside the doorway from t_{js} to time t, then j has stayed outside the doorway longer than i at time t because $t_{js} < t_{ih}$. Consequently, i cannot be in set $H(t)$, thus j must enter the doorway at least once during the time period (t_{js}, t). Furthermore, since j stayed outside the doorway from t_{js} to t_{jr}, j must enter the doorway after time t_{jr} and before time t. After j entered the doorway, by Lemma 2.3, j eventually eats. After eating, j will send the deferred ack to i.

Thus, for each neighbor j, i either suspects j permanently or eventually receives an ack from j. Hence, Action 5 is enabled continuously, process i enters doorway eventually. Lemma 2.4 holds. $\qquad\square$

6. Eventual k-Bounded Waiting Proof

Theorem 3: *Algorithm 1 satisfies eventual 2-bounded waiting: for each execution, there exists a time after which no live process i goes to eat more than twice, while any live neighbor is hungry.*

Proof: Suppose $\Diamond\mathcal{P}_1$ converges at time t_c. At time t_c, there may exist a set of live hungry processes, denoted as $Hungry(t_c)$. By Theorem 2, every correct hungry process eventually eats. Therefore, there exists a time t_1 after which all correct processes in $Hungry(t_c)$ eat, where $t_1 \geq t_c$. Thus, after time t_1, no hungry session of correct processes starts before time t_c.

Faulty processes eventually crash. Thus, there exists a time t_2 after which every live process must be correct. Let time $t_3 = max(t_1, t_2)$. Next, we will show that after time t_3, no live process i goes to eat more than twice, while any live neighbor j is hungry.

After t_3, since $\Diamond\mathcal{P}_1$ has already converged, no correct process wrongfully suspects any correct neighbor. Thus, to enter the doorway, process i must receive an ack from each correct neighbor. If process i goes to eat more than twice, then its neighbor j must send at least three acks to i. After

j sends the first ack message, $replied_{ij}$ is set to true. When j receives the second ping message, j will defer the ping message (Action 3). Thus, while j is hungry, j can send at most one ack message to i.

Although j can send at most one ack message to i while j is hungry, i still can receive two acks from j. It is possible that j sent an ack to i just before j became hungry. When j became hungry, the ack message was still in transit to i. Consequently, i could enter the doorway at most twice while j is hungry. Thus, i could go to eat at most twice while j is hungry. Theorem 3 holds. $\qquad\square$

7. Requirements on Communication Channels and Local Memory

Bounded Space Complexity. In Algorithm 1, each process i has nine types of local variables. Variables $state_i$ and $inside_i$ need a fixed size of local memory. The variable $color_i$ needs $log_2(\delta)$ bits of local memory, where δ refers to the maximal degree of the conflict graph. For each neighbor j, process i associates the remaining six boolean variables to j: $fork_{ij}$, $token_{ij}$, $pinged_{ij}$, ack_{ij}, $replied_{ij}$, $deferred_{ij}$. Putting them together, each process needs $log_2(\delta) + 6\delta + c_1$ bits of memory, where c_1 is a constant value. In the worst case (i.e, the conflict graph is clique), $\delta = n$, thus each process needs $O(n)$ bits of local memory.

Bounded Capacity of Communication Channels. At any time, the number of messages between each pair of neighbors is also bounded. Specifically, at most four messages are in transit at any time between each pair of neighbors i and j.

Algorithm 1 has four types of messages: *ping, ack, fork* and *token*. Because the fork and the token are unique between each pair of neighbors, at most one fork and one token are in transit simultaneously. By Lemma 2.2, at any time, at most one ping or ack message initiated by i is in transit. Counting the ping/ack message initiated by j, at most two ping/ack messages are in transit between each pair of neighbors at any time. Thus, at any time, at most four messages are in transit between each pair of neighbors.

On the other hand, the size of each message is bounded too. We need to encode the process id into the fork messages, and the local variable color into the fork request messages. Both process id and color need $log_2(n)$ bits. So each message needs $O(log_2(n))$ bits.

Quiescent Communication with Crashed Processes. In Algorithm 1, processes eventually stop communicating with crashed processes. For process i, after its neighbor j crashes, by Lemma 2.2, i can send at most one ping request. From the perspective of process i, this ping request is pending forever. Thus, eventually there is no ping/ack message between i and j. Similarly, by Action 6, i can send at most one fork request(token) to j, simply because i cannot get the token back. Thus, eventually there is no fork/token message between i and j. Therefore, eventually no message exists between i and j.

8. Conclusion

We have explored wait-free scheduling in environments subject to crash faults. This problem is of practical importance to stabilization, because wait-free scheduling is necessary to establish convergence in the presence of transient faults. Unfortunately, wait-free distributed daemons cannot be implemented in purely asynchronous environments subject to crash faults. As such, we have examined solvability under partial synchrony relative to the eventually perfect failure detector $\Diamond \mathcal{P}$.

Our work demonstrates that $\Diamond \mathcal{P}$ is sufficient to achieve wait-free dining philosophers under eventual weak exclusion ($\Diamond \mathcal{WX}$), even in the presence of arbitrarily many crash faults. Our algorithm uses a local refinement of the eventually perfect failure detector $\Diamond \mathcal{P}_1$, which can be implemented in sparse networks which are partitionable by crash faults. As such, our solution is also practical in the sense that it can scale to larger networks.

We have also shown that eventual k-fairness can also be achieved using $\Diamond \mathcal{P}_1$. Specifically, our algorithm satisfies eventual k-bounded waiting ($\Diamond k\text{-}\mathcal{BW}$), which guarantees that every execution has an infinite suffix where no process can overtake any live hungry neighbor more than k consecutive times. Our algorithm is efficient insofar as it requires only bounded space and bounded-capacity channels. Additionally, it is quiescent with respect to crashed processes.

A natural question is whether or not $\Diamond \mathcal{P}$ is the *weakest* failure detector to implement wait-free, eventually fair daemons. This question goes to the necessity of the oracular assumptions in this paper. Parallel work in [21] has shown that $\Diamond \mathcal{P}$ is *necessary* for wait-free, $\Diamond k\text{-}\mathcal{BW}$ daemons. Our work shows that $\Diamond \mathcal{P}$ is also *sufficient*. The composition of these two results implies that $\Diamond \mathcal{P}$ is actually the *weakest* failure detector to implement wait-free, $\Diamond k\text{-}\mathcal{BW}$ daemons. Thus, if wait-free, eventually fair scheduling is necessary for stabilization, then a corollary of our work is that $\Diamond \mathcal{P}$ is also necessary.

References

[1] G. Antonoiu and P. K. Srimani. Mutual exclusion between neighboring nodes in a tree that stabilizes using read/write atomicity. In *Proceedings of the 5th International Euro-Par Conference on Parallel Processing*, volume 1685, pages 823–830, 1999.

[2] H. Attiya and J. Welch. *Distributed Computing : Fundamentals, Simulations, and Advanced Topics*. John Wiley and Sons, Inc., 2004.

[3] J. Beauquier, A. K. Datta, M. Gradinariu, and F. Magniette. Self-stabilizing local mutual exclusion and daemon refinement. *Chicago J. Theor. Comput. Sci.*, 2002(1), July 2002.

[4] J. Beauquier and S. Kekkonen-Moneta. Fault-tolerance and self-stabilization: impossibility results and solutions using self-stabilizing failure detectors. *International Journal of Systems Science*, 28(11):1177–1187, 1997.

[5] J. E. Burns, P. Jackson, N. A. Lynch, M. J. Fischer, and G. L. Peterson. Data requirements for implementation of n-process mutual exclusion using a single shared variable. *J. ACM*, 29(1):183–205, 1982.

[6] S. Cantarell, A. K. Datta, and F. Petit. Self-stabilizing atomicity refinement allowing neighborhood concurrency. In *Proceedings of the 6th International Symposium Self-Stabilizing Systems*, pages 102–112, 2003.

[7] T. D. Chandra and S. Toueg. Unreliable failure detectors for reliable distributed systems. *J. ACM*, 43(2):225–267, 1996.

[8] M. Choy and A. K. Singh. Efficient fault-tolerant algorithms for distributed resource allocation. *ACM TOPLAS*, 17(3):535–559, 1995.

[9] F. Cristian. Understanding fault-tolerant distributed systems. *Commun. ACM*, 34(2):56–78, 1991.

[10] E. W. Dijkstra. Hierarchical ordering of sequential processes. *Acta Informatica*, 1(2):115–138, 1971.

[11] S. Dolev. *Self-Stabilization*. MIT Press, 2000.

[12] S. Dolev and Y. A. Haviv. Self-stabilizing microprocessor: Analyzing and overcoming soft errors. *IEEE Trans. Comput.*, 55(4):385–399, 2006.

[13] C. Dwork, N. A. Lynch, and L. Stockmeyer. Consensus in the presence of partial synchrony. *J. ACM*, 35(2):288–323, Apr. 1988.

[14] C. Fetzer, U. Schmid, and M. Susskraut. On the possibility of consensus in asynchronous systems with finite average response times. In *Proceedings of the 25th IEEE International Conference on Distributed Computing Systems*.

[15] M. G. Gouda and F. F. Haddix. The alternator. In *Proceedings of the 19th IEEE International Conference on Distributed Computing Systems Workshop on Self-stabilizing Systems*, pages 48–53, 1999.

[16] M. Herlihy. Wait-free synchronization. *ACM TOPLAS*, 13(1):124–149, 1991.

[17] M. Hutle and J. Widder. Self-stabilizing failure detector algorithms. In *Proceedings of the IASTED International Conference on Parallel and Distributed Computing and Networks*, pages 485–490, 2005.

[18] N. Lynch. Fast allocation of nearby resources in a distributed system. In *Proceedings of the 12th ACM Symposium on Theory of Computing*, pages 70–81, 1980.

[19] M. Mizuno and M. Nesterenko. A transformation of self-stabilizing serial model programs for asynchronous parallel computing environments. *Information Processing Letters*, 66(6):285–290, June 1998.

[20] S. M. Pike and P. A. G. Sivilotti. Dining philosophers with crash locality 1. In *Proceedings of the 24th IEEE International Conference on Distributed Computing Systems*, pages 22–29, 2004.

[21] Y. Song and S. M. Pike. The weakest failure detector for wait-free, eventually fair mutual exclusion. Technical Report tamu-cs-tr-2007-2-2, Texas A&M University, Feb 2007.

Session 5C:
Availability of
Distributed Systems

Measuring Availability in Optimistic Partition-tolerant Systems with Data Constraints

Mikael Asplund, Simin Nadjm-Tehrani
Department of Computer and Information Science,
Linköping University
SE-581 83 Linköping, Sweden
{mikas,simin}@ida.liu.se

Stefan Beyer, Pablo Galdamez
Instituto Tecnolgico Informtica
Universidad Politcnica de Valencia
Camino de Vera, s/n, 46022 Valencia, Spain
{stefan, pgaldamez}@iti.upv.es

Abstract

Replicated systems that run over partitionable environments, can exhibit increased availability if isolated partitions are allowed to optimistically continue their execution independently. This availability gain is traded against consistency, since several replicas of the same objects could be updated separately. Once partitioning terminates, divergences in the replicated state needs to be reconciled. One way to reconcile the state consists of letting the application manually solve inconsistencies. However, there are several situations where automatic reconciliation of the replicated state is meaningful. We have implemented replication and automatic reconciliation protocols that can be used as building blocks in a partition-tolerant middleware. The novelty of the protocols is the continuous service of the application even during the reconciliation process. A prototype system is experimentally evaluated to illustrate the increased availability despite network partitions.

1 Introduction

Prevalence of distributed services and networked solutions has made many enterprises critically dependent on service availability. Whereas earlier centralised solutions were made resilient to service faults by deploying redundancy, the new generation of distributed services need to show resilience to overloads and network partitions. There are many applications that require automatically managed, distributed, secure, mutable object stores. A commercial instance of this problem appears in Software distribution. According to Sun Microsystems [4], network partitions are indeed interesting to study since global corporate intranetworks are typically not richly connected. Hence, service availability of distributed data storage systems is potentially affected by denial of service attacks (DoS) that render parts

of the network as inaccessible [6].

This paper addresses support for maintaining distributed objects with integrity constraints in presence of network partitions. Providing fault tolerance in such distributed object systems requires relatively complex mechanisms to properly handle all the different fault scenarios. One solution is to relieve the application writers, and get them to rely on a middleware that provides fault tolerance services. This is a direction pursued in the European DeDiSys research project [9]. In particular, the algorithms for replication and reconciliation implemented in this paper will be deployed in an extension of CORBA middleware. However, they can be considered as general building blocks to be integrated in any middleware.

The basic problem of network partitions is that there is no way of knowing what is happening in the other parts of the system. A bank customer cannot make a payment if not enough money exists on his/her bank account, and you cannot book a flight that is already full. These kinds of integrity constraints exist in most applications either explicitly or implicitly in the operation semantics; but what happens if the bank account is used for two payments at the same time in two disconnected parts? One typically resorts to a "safe" solution that implies periods of unavailability.

Another way to deliver service in a partitioned system with integrity constraints is to act optimistically. This means to provisionally accept some operations, but allow them to be revoked or undone at a later stage, if necessary. To revoke previously accepted operations might be unacceptable in some cases, but there are also situations where it is better than general unavailability. Another possibility is to perform some kind of compensating action specific for that operation. Many applications have a mix of operations where some non-critical operations can be treated optimistically, while the critical operations must wait. We claim an application can improve its overall availability by provisionally accepting operations that may later be revoked. We propose protocols that allow for automatic reconciliation of the state of the network, by replaying the (logged) operations serviced during the partition and discarding some (revocable) operations that violate the integrity constraints in the reconstructed state. The novelty of our implemented algorithm is that it builds the new repaired network state and *at the same time* serves the new incoming operations. That is, operations arriving after network reunification but prior to installation of the new state are not denied service.

The contributions of this paper are twofold. First, we present the implementation of a previously unimplemented reconciliation protocol[1] embedded as a middleware service. The aim of the protocol is to give continuous service during network partitions. Second, we show the improved performance due to giving service during the degraded mode, and also during reconciliation phase after a network partition. The experiments thus constitute validation tests for performance of the Java implementation of the protocol. This provides a proof of concept for the algorithms prior to integration in CORBA.

To provide a repeatable experimental setting for measuring performance, we have implemented a synthetic application that simulates changes of numerical values for object states. This can, for example, be seen as an abstraction of distributed sensor-actor systems, and fusion of data based on reported measures. This application is introduced in Section 2 and is used for explaining the reconciliation process. The rest of the paper is organised as follows. Section 3 describes a partition-aware replication algorithm called P4, and Section 4 describes the continuous service reconciliation protocol. In Section 5 we propose a set of metrics that are suitable for evaluating availability in systems with optimistic replication. Using these metrics we evaluate the proposed algorithms in Section 6. Section 7 presents related work, and finally we conclude and give directions for future work.

2 Test application

A synthetic application has been developed to serve as a test bed for trade-off studies. We describe it here to reuse for illustration of the workings of the reconciliation process.

The application is composed of a set of real number objects. Possible operations are addition, multiplication and division. An operation is applied to the current value with a random constant. The constant is an integer uniformly distributed in the intervals $[-10, -1]$, and $[1, 10]$. This creates a total of 60 distinct operations. There are also integrity constraints in the system expressed as: $n_1 + c < n_2$ where n_1 and n_2 are object values and c is a constant. Although the application is very simple, it is complex enough to give an indication of how the algorithms perform. Moreover, the application allows key system parameters to be changed for

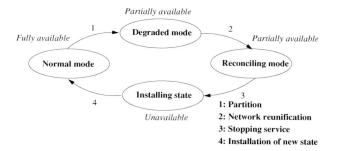

Figure 1. System modes

experimentation purposes.

3 Replication

The system modes of operation can be described as the four phases depicted in Figure 1. We proceed by describing the need for a replication protocol that allows consistency to be temporarily violated but later restored.

In the passive replication model each object has a primary copy, and the distributed replicas are updated using a replication protocol. Traditional pessimistic replication techniques that attempt to provide single-copy consistency [5] are not suitable for optimistic partitionable systems in which more than one partition continues to accept updates during partitioning. Replication protocols for such systems need to temporarily accept possible inconsistencies. Hence these protocols allow the state in different partitions to diverge. If strict consistency is to be restored when the system recovers, a reconciliation protocol is required. Replication and reconciliation protocols need to match each other, as only inconsistencies that can be removed at reconciliation time can be allowed.

An optimistic protocol might allow the degree to which inconsistencies are allowed to be configured. We have designed an optimistic replication protocol, called Primary Per Partition Protocol (P4), which uses a new approach to trade consistency for system availability. The protocol bases consistency on integrity constraints. Integrity constraints can be pre-conditions, which have to met before an operation is executed, post-conditions, which have to be met after an operation is executed or invariants, which are not associated to an operation but to a set of objects and have to be met at all times. The remainder of this section provides a short summary of the protocol that is described in detail earlier [6].

The protocol assumes the presence of a group membership service that provides all the server nodes with a single view of which nodes are part of the system or the current partition. Furthermore, a group communication service provides the nodes with reliable FIFO broadcast according to the definition by Hadzilacos and Toueg [12].

The protocol employs a relaxed passive replication model. Read-only operations are allowed on any replica, but write operations have to be directed to the primary copy of the object being accessed. If the primary copy of the object is in a different partition, a secondary copy is promoted to a temporary primary. In order to increase system availability, we allow write operations on temporary primaries in certain conditions. During partitioning, secondary copies of an object might be stale, if the primary copy resides in a different partition. During reconciliation, constraints might be violated retrospectively, when missed updates are propagated. Therefore, some operations that were performed during partitioning might have to be undone to restore consistency. This behaviour might be acceptable for the majority of the operations, but there are some operations that should never occur, if they might have to be undone later on.

These "critical operations" include operations on data that require strict consistency at all times and operations that simply cannot be undone, such as operations with irreversible side-effects. We therefore allow the labelling of integrity constraints as *critical constraints*.

A constraint labelled critical is a constraint that needs up-to-date versions of all of the participating objects. Such a constraint cannot be evaluated if a participating object is stale. Furthermore, the protocol has to take certain precautions to ensure that critical constraints are never violated "in retrospect" during reconciliation. In contrast *non-critical* constraints can be evaluated on stale objects. A non-critical invariant constraint has to be re-evaluated during the reconciliation; that is, the reconciliation protocol has to perform constraint re-evaluation.

A write operation in our replication protocol in the absence of failures can be summarised in the following steps:

1. All object write invocations have to be directed to the primary replica.
2. All the pre-condition constraints, associated with the operation are evaluated. If a constraint is not met, the invocation is aborted.
3. The operation is invoked. Nested invocations cause sub-invocations to be started.
4. Once the primary replica has updated its local state, all the post-condition and invariant constraints, associated with the operation are evaluated. If a constraint is not met, the invocation is aborted.
5. All primary replicas updated in the invocations propagate the new object states to the secondary replicas.
6. Once this update transfer has terminated, the operation result is returned to the client.

A failure might occur in the form of a node failure or a link failure. Since we cannot distinguish between a failed node and an isolated node, all failures are treated as network partitions until recovery time. A write operation in degraded mode is similar to that in normal mode with the following additions:

1. If the primary copy of an object being written to is not found, a secondary copy is chosen in some predetermined way, for example based on the replica identifier. The chosen secondary replica is promoted to a "temporary primary". This is not done, if the operation has a critical constraint as a pre- or post-condition.
2. Objects that are changed are marked as "revocable", if any of the invariant constraints associated to the operation that has been executed has been evaluated on possibly stale objects.
3. Critical constraints are not evaluated, if a participating object might be stale. If this were the case, the invocation is aborted.
4. Non-critical invariant constraints with possibly stale objects are marked for re-evaluation at reconciliation time.
5. Operations with critical constraints that include a revocable object are not permitted, so that critical constraints cannot be violated retrospectively.

Note that the above description applies both to operation in degraded mode and continuous service of incoming operations during reconciliation. In order to manage the reconciliation process (see below) the replication protocol needs to log those operations that have been serviced while in partition. These operations need to be reconsidered during the reconciliation phase.

4 Reconciliation

This section describes the implementation of a protocol that aims to continuously service client (write) requests even during the reconciliation process. A formal description of the protocol with a proof of correctness was presented earlier [1]. Here we show the architectural units that have been realised in Java and their interactions in terms of pseudo code.

Figure 2 shows the basic architectural components of our replication and reconciliation protocols. Each node contains the middleware and a number of application objects. The middleware is composed of a number of services, of which the replication support is the focus of this paper. This component is in turn composed of a replication protocol, i.e., P4, and a reconciliation protocol, i.e., the continuous service (CS) protocol. These protocols rely on additional middleware services such as Group Communication (GC) and Constraint Consistency Manager (CCM). The CCM is used to check consistency of integrity constraints. The box with

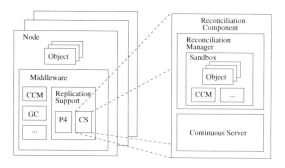

Figure 2. Architecture

"..." is an abstraction of other services in the middleware not relevant for this evaluation. Our prototype implementation that is used for evaluating the reconciliation protocol is based on this architecture.

We proceed by explaining the actions of the CS reconciliation protocol. This protocol is faced with the task of merging a number of operations that have been performed in different partitions. It must also preserve constraint consistency. Furthermore, as operations are replayed the client perceived order on operations (for operations invoked by the *same* client) is respected. In parallel with this process the protocol takes care of operations that arrive at the reunified but not fully reconciled partition.

Algorithm 1 Continuous Server

On reunify:
Send all logs to Reconciliation Manager(s)

On operation invocation:
If not stopped, apply operation
Check consistency, abort if not consistent
Send log to Reconciliation Manager
Suspend reply until later

On receive getState:
Send last stored object state (from normal mode)

On receive logAck:
Send suspended replies to client

On receive stop:
Stop accepting new operations
Send stopAck

On receive install:
Change state of local objects to received state

The reconciliation protocol is composed of two types of processes: continuous servers and reconciliation managers. Algorithms 1 and 2 show the pseudo code for the protocol running at each node. Every node will run a continuous server during the reconciliation, whereas only one elected node will run the reconciliation manager. During recon-

ciliation, the reconciliation manager will replay previously applied operations. This replay process is performed in a sandbox environment, which contains the application objects and the basic middleware components that are required for running the application on a single node.

Algorithm 2 Reconciliation Manager

On reunify:
Elect which node acts as reconciliation manager
Determine which objects to reconcile
Send *getState* request to servers

On receive log:
Add log to *opset*
Send *logAck* to server

On receive state:
Create object in sandbox environment

If opset not empty and all states received:
Replay first operation in *opset* in sandbox environment
Check consistency, abort if not consistent

If opset empty and all states received:
Send stop message to all servers

On receive stopAck:
Wait for opset to become empty
Send out new state to all servers

The responsibility of the continuous server is to accept invocations from clients and sending logs to the elected reconciliation manager during reconciliation. At the beginning of each reconciliation phase the nodes in the repaired network elect a reconciliation manager among themselves. The reconciliation manager is responsible for merging server logs that are sent during reconciling mode. Eventually, upon reaching a stable state, the reconciliation manager sends an install message with the new state to all servers (see transition 4 in Figure 1).

During reconciliation mode, the state that is being constructed by the reconciliation manager may not yet reflect all the operations that have arrived during degraded mode. Therefore, the only state in which the incoming operations can be applied to is one of the partition states from the degraded mode. In other words, we keep virtual partitions for servicing incoming operations while the reconciliation phase lasts.

Each continuous server will immediately send a log message to the reconciliation manager if it receives an invocation during the reconciliation phase. The server will then wait until it has received an acknowledge from the manager before sending a reply to the client. When the manager has finished replaying all operations, it sends a message to all nodes to stop accepting new invocations. The manager will continue accepting log messages from servers, even after a

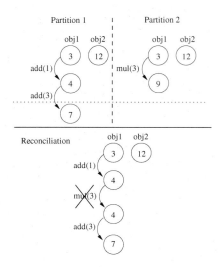

Figure 3. Reconciliation example

stop has been sent. Note also that the continuous servers keep sending the logs until they have sent their acknowledgements of the stop. However, once a stopAck message has been received from a given server, then no further log messages will arrive from it. This is to ensure that no operations are performed during the installation of a new reconciled state. This (short) period is the only interval in which the system is completely unavailable.

4.1 Example

To illustrate the potential effect of reconciliation as a result of replaying operations we show a trivial synthetic scenario with one integrity constraint in Figure 3. We use the application from Section 2, using two objects with an initial state 3 and 12 respectively. There is a constraint stating that $obj1 + 1 < obj2$. During the degraded mode one operation is performed in each partition on the first object. At the start of the reconciliation the state is (4,12) and (9,12) respectively. Just after the reconciliation starts, yet another operation is invoked in the first partition. The reconciliation revokes operation 2 since it violates the constraint but finally accepts operations 1 and 3. So the final state that is installed is (7,12). For a deeper discussion on possible operation orderings the reader is referred to [2].

5 Performance metrics

Availability is formally expressed as the probability of a system being operational at any given point of time [20]. This is to be distinguished from reliability that measures the probability of not observing any failures before a given time point. Both reliability and availability have been extensively studied in the context of computer systems with

an emphasis on hardware failures to justify a claim on a system's dependability.

In the context of this paper we are faced with a service that is to be available on a distributed (networked) platform. Measuring availability of the service is possible by performing a number of experiments on the system running over some time interval. To compute the probability of the service being available, one can measure the periods that the service is *operational* during the experiments, compute an average operational period, and then compute the probability measure by dividing the average operational period over the chosen interval. This measure is of course highly affected by the potential number of failures during the experimental period. These failures can be induced (injected) during experimentation, but their likelihood has to be supported by some empirical evidence obtained from the application domains, using the hardware and software characteristics of the real application. However, this is not the whole story. The core problem of defining metrics for consistency-dependent distributed object systems is that in presence of some degraded service, one has to identify what is exactly meant by being "operational" (which services, or which operations under which conditions).

5.1 Partially operational

Figure 4 shows the set of arriving operations during a given time interval. For a system to be considered fully operational the operations that are invoked by clients have to be performed together with checking integrity constraints. If the integrity constraints can be checked, i.e., the system is not partitioned, then the service is considered operational even though the constraint may not hold (and thus the operation not performed). If the integrity constraint cannot be checked, then we are faced with one of two situations. Either the integrity constraint is critical, in which case the operation cannot be allowed (the system is non-operational), or the constraint is non-critical. An operation with an associated non-critical constraint, which is invoked in a degraded mode, can be considered to render a system operational in the degraded mode. However, this is not the whole story either. We need to consider what happens to this operation once the degraded mode has ended. In some cases, the operation will be considered as valid after returning to the normal (fully consistent) mode of the system, and in some cases this operation has to be revoked (undone) or perhaps compensated, since the process of recovering from the earlier failure has rendered this operation as unacceptable. The new metrics thus have to consider appropriate measures that reflect these elements of partial availability and apparent availability. Another aspect in devising the set of experiments is a clear parameterisation in terms of the load; not only in terms of the volume of operations that

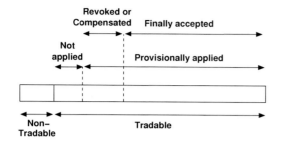

Figure 4. The set of operations during a system partition and subsets thereof

are invoked (classic throughput metrics), but also in terms of the types of operations that are invoked: those subject to critical integrity constraints and those subject to non-critical constraints.

5.2 Load profile

Operations are classified in two categories: tradable (those with associated non-critical integrity constraints), and non-tradable (those with associated critical constraints). Among those operations that are tradable we find operations that violate their integrity constraints, and would not be applied in a normal mode in similar circumstances. This is considered as a normal delivery of the service. We will denote these by "not applied operations" in Figure 4. We also find those that are provisionally applied (updating some object state). In the latter category we find operations that are later revoked (undone) when the partition failure is recovered from, and the reconciliation of states renders the application of the operation as unacceptable (due to inter-partition conflicts). Figure 4 shows these distinct load profiles.

Our evaluation metrics can be divided in two categories; time-based and operation-based metrics. The first category is typically based on the time spent in some segment of the system life time. The second category is based on the counting of the operations that pass through the system and are treated in one way or the other (subsets from Figure 4).

5.3 Time-based metrics

We consider the following metrics:

- Apparent availability: Probability of (partial) operation at a time point; that is, the average interval that the network is in partial/fully available mode divided by the length of the experiments.
- Time spent in revoking (undoing) operations within the experiment interval.

From the above, we are going to use the availability metric as a measure for improved performance. However, we need to complement this metric with other measurements in order to identify the substance of improvement (i.e., excluding the apparent availability).

The second metric is indicative of the apparent availability. That is, the higher the time spent for revocations the lower is the real availability. As far as time for revoking one operation is concerned, a real application has different values attached to different revocations (compensations). In our experimental setting, we choose to compute this time based on an estimate of an undo-time per operation (referred to as handling time in charts in Section 6, thus turning it into a parameter).

5.4 Operation-based metrics

As mentioned above measurements of apparent availability are only meaningful if they are presented together with an indication of the "loss" from revoked operations. To be specific about the level of service delivered to clients we propose two operation-based metrics:

- The number of operations finally accepted during the whole experimental interval.
- The proportion of revocations over provisionally accepted operations.

In addition, it may be interesting to study the proportion of revocations over total arrived operations in a degraded scenario for comparing different variations of reconciliation protocols.

6 Evaluation

In this section we present an experimental evaluation of the replication and continuous service reconciliation protocols. As a baseline, we consider two alternatives: first, a system that does not trade availability for consistency (using pessimistic protocols), and a second optimistic replication and reconciliation service. The second reconciliation protocol does not accept new operations during the reconciliation phase (similar to those presented in earlier work [2]).

6.1 Simulation setup

The simulations were performed with J-Sim [24] using the event-based simulation engine. A simple middleware was constructed and the test application described in Section 2 was implemented on top of it. The middleware is based on the architecture in Figure 2. However, as the main

Table 1. Simulation parameters

Number of runs	100
Number of objects	100
Number of constraints	30
Number of critical constraints	10
Simulation time	70 [s]
Number of nodes	50
Number of clients	30
Mean network delay	0.1 [s]
Normal system load	120 [ops/s]

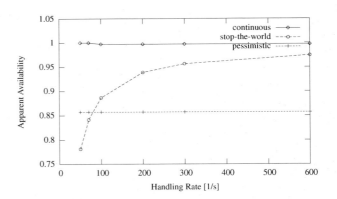

Figure 5. Apparent Availability

goal of the implementation was to evaluate the reconciliation protocol some parts of the system have been simplified. The group communication component is for example simulated using a network component that also provides a group membership service. This allows fault injection and network delays to be controlled. Faults are injected by configuring the location service component to resolve object lookups in the same way as if there had been a network partition. This is done in the beginning of each simulation run.

The simulations parameters that were constant in all experiments are shown in Table 1. We base these figures on data provided by industry partners, with real applications that can benefit from partition tolerance, in the DeDiSys project.

6.2 Results

In this section we provide the results of the performed simulations.

In all of the following curves we compare three different protocol behaviours. All three measurements are performed using the same application and random seeds. Moreover, the middleware implementations only differ in the places where the replication and reconciliation differ. The first curve ("continuous") in each graph shows a middleware that acts optimistically during the partition fault, and then uses the continuous service reconciliation (CS) protocol to merge the results. The first baseline that does not accept invocations during reconciliation is denoted as "stop-the-world". Finally, the last ("pessimistic") shows the results for a pessimistic middleware which does not accept invocations during a partitioned state.

The effect of handling rate In Figure 5 the apparent availability is plotted against the handling rate of the reconciliation manager. This rate is an estimate of the average time taken to reconsider a provisionally accepted operation, replay it, and potentially undo it. The partition lasted for 10 seconds in each run. The 95% confidence intervals are within 0.35% for all measurement points. The pessimistic approach gives just over 85% independently of

the nature of operations that are potentially revocable (since they are never run). This is natural since no operations are performed during partitions. The continuous service protocol manages to supply nearly full availability except for the small effect given by the time spent installing the new state. However, the availability of "stop-the-world" depends very much on the length of the reconciliation phase, which in turn is decided by how fast the handling rate of the reconciliation manager is.

There is an anomaly for the CS protocol for small handling rates. There is no period of unavailability for these rates. The reason is that the protocol will never reach the stop state during the simulation time, and thus never become unavailable. The termination proof from [1] gives that a condition for the termination is $H > \left(\frac{T_D + 7d}{T_F - 9d} \right) C \cdot I$ where H is the (worst case) handling rate, T_D the partition duration, d a bound on message and service time, T_F the time until next fault (in these runs the end of the simulation), C the number of clients, and I the (worst case) invocation rate for each client. If we put the (average) numbers from our simulations in this inequality we find that the handling rate must be at least 137 to *guarantee* termination. In the figure we see that termination actually occurs for rates over 100 (indicated by the fact that the CS protocol drops from full availability to just under 100%).

As the results in Figure 5 only give the apparent availability (as discussed in Section 5) we need also to compare the second availability metric, which is how many operations we have finally accepted.

In Figure 6 the relative increase of finally accepted operations compared to the pessimistic approach is plotted against the handling rate. This graph is based on the same experiment as Figure 5. The 95% confidence intervals are within 1% for all measurement points. The optimistic approaches achieve better as handling rate increases. For large enough handling rates they give significantly better results compared to the pessimistic approach. The CS reconcilia-

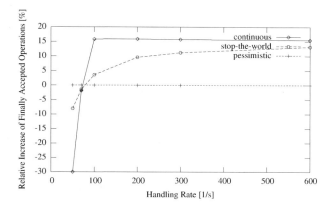

Figure 6. Increase of Finally Accepted Operations

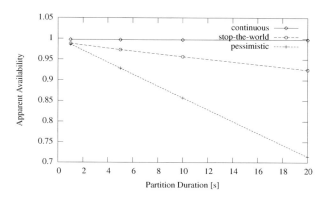

Figure 7. Apparent Availability

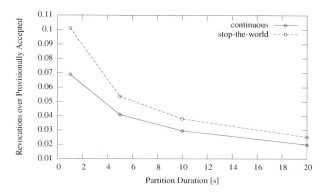

Figure 8. Revocations over Provisionally Accepted

tion protocol only gives distinctly better results than "stop the world" for handling between 100 and 300 operations per second. However, as the handling rate increases further the difference becomes marginal.

This plot indicates that an estimate of the average handling rate, based on profiling the application, is appropriate as a guideline before selecting the CS protocol in a reconfigurable middleware.

The effect of partition duration There are applications, like telecommunication, where partitions do occur but a lot of effort is spent to make them as short as possible so that acting pessimistically will not cause a big decrease in availability. In Figure 7 we see the effect that the partition duration has on the apparent availability. For long enough partitions the only approach that gives acceptable results is the continuous service reconciliation. The confidence intervals for this graph are within 0.1% for all measurement points.

Both of the optimistic reconciliation protocols considered here are operation based. That is, they use a log of operations that were performed in the degraded mode. One can also perform state-based reconciliation where only the current state of the partitions is used to construct the new state. A state based reconciliation scheme might give equally high apparent availability as the continuous service protocol but instead it might suffer in terms of finally accepted operations [2].

A very interesting metric is the number of revocations over provisionally accepted operations. This is the proportion of operations that the client thinks have been performed but which must be revoked/compensated. This is related to, but should not be confused with, the collision probability calculated by Grey et al. [11] to be proportional to the square of the number of operations. Wang et al. [23] have investigated the conflict rate for file systems. Common for these two metrics is that they consider two replicas to be

in conflict if they have been updated concurrently. In our model, on the other hand, a conflict occurs only as the result of the violation of some integrity constraint. Such violations can be caused by concurrent updates, but not necessarily.

In Figure 8 we see that as the partition duration increases the ratio of revoked operations decreases. This is a bit counter-intuitive, one would expect the opposite. However, there is an explanation to this phenomenon. The cause lies in the fact that in our synthetic application two partitions perform similar kinds of client calls. This means that an operation which has been successfully applied in one partition is likely to be compatible with changes that have occurred in the other as well. The longer the partition lasts, the more operations are performed and the risk of different types of operations in the two partitions decreases. Naturally, this behaviour depends on the nature of the integrity constraints and thus on the application. The confidence intervals are within 6.9% for all measurement points.

The effect of load So far the experiments have been performed with a constant arrival rate of 120 operations per

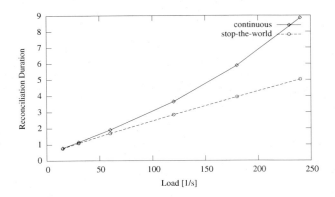

Figure 9. Reconciliation Duration

second. To see the effect of load we have plotted the reconciliation duration against load in Figure 9. Here, the 95% confidence intervalse are within 1.6% for all measurement points. The handling rate for this experiment was 300 actions per second. This figure might seem high compared to the load. However, the reconciliation process is performed at a single node which means that no network communication is needed. As can be seen in the figure the continuous service protocol suffers more than the other protocols under heavy load; especially, as it approaches the maximum load. However, this does not translate to less apparent availability as in the case of stop-the-world. The only period of unavailability for the CS protocol is during the time between the continuous servers receive a stop message from the reconciliation manager and the time to receive the installed state. The length of this period is not affected by the length of the reconciliation phase. Thus, the apparent availability of CS is not decreased (as was shown in Figure 5).

7   Related Work

In this section we will discuss how the problem of reconciliation after network partitions has been dealt with in the literature. For more references on related topics there is an excellent survey on optimistic replication by Saito and Shapiro [19]. There is also an earlier survey discussing consistency in partitioned networks by Davidson et al. [8].

The CS protocol was recently presented as a formalisation in timed I/O automata [1]. Earlier studies [2] have compared different versions of reconciliation protocols but none of them with the feature of continuously serving during reconciliation. Gray et al. [11] address the problem of update everywhere and propose a solution based on a two-tier architecture and tentative operations. However, they do not target full network partitions but individual nodes that join and leave the system (which is a special case of partition). Bayou [22] is a distributed storage system that is adapted for mobile environments. It allows updates to occur in a parti-

tioned system. Bayou can in principle deal with integrity constraints. However, there is a limitation in the sense that a primary server must be able to commit operations locally (this prevents later revocations). This makes the use of system wide integrity constraints hard or impossible.

Some work has been done on partitionable systems where integrity constraints are not considered, which simplifies reconciliation. Babaouglu et al. [3] present a method for dealing with network partitions. They propose a solution that provides primitives for dealing with shared state. They do not elaborate on dealing with writes in all partitions except suggesting tentative writes that can be undone if conflicts occur. Moser et al. [15] have designed a fault-tolerant CORBA extension that is able to deal with node crashes as well as network partitions. There is also a reconciliation scheme described in [16]. The idea is to keep a primary for each object. The states of these primaries are transferred to the secondaries on reunification. In addition, operations that are performed on the secondaries during degraded mode are reapplied during the reconciliation phase. This approach is not directly applicable with integrity constraints.

There are some systems that use more advanced optimistic replication techniques, which allow the degree to which inconsistencies are allowed to be configured. None of these protocols are aimed at operating fully in a partitioned system. They therefore do not provide the reconciliation algorithms for such a scenario. However, it is interesting to compare the way they approach configurable consistency with our integrity constraint based approach. Yu and Vahdat [25] use consistency units (conits) to specify the bounds on allowed inconsistency. A conit is a set of three values representing "numerical error", "order error" and "staleness". Numerical error defines a weight of writes on a conit that can be applied to all replicas, before update propagation has to occur. Order error defines the number of outstanding write operations that are subject to re-ordering on a single conit. Finally, staleness defines the time update propagation can be delayed. The system does not support partitioning, although the key concept of conits could be used in a partitioned context. In CoRe [10] the principle of specifying consistency is extended to allow the programmer to define consistency using a larger set of parameters. AQua [7] approaches the solution from the other direction: configuration of the allowed consistency in order to increase availability; that is, by allowing availability requirements to be specified. In AQua "quality objects" are used to specify quality of service requirements.

Most works on reconciliation algorithms dealing with constraints after network partition focus on achieving a schedule that satisfies order constraints. Lippe et al. [14] try to order operation logs to avoid conflicts with respect to a *before* relation. However, their algorithm requires a large set of operation sequences to be enumerated and then compared. The IceCube system [13, 18] also tries to order operations to achieve a consistent final state. However, they do not fully address the problem of integrity constraints that involve several objects. Phatak et al. [17] propose an algorithm that provides reconciliation by either using multiversioning to achieve snapshot isolation or using a reconciliation function given by the client. Snapshot isolation is more pessimistic than our approach and would require a lot of operations to be undone.

8 Conclusions and Future Work

In case of a network partition fault in a distributed system, there are two basic approaches: pessimistic and optimistic replication. We have shown that the optimistic solution does pay off in terms of availability even in systems with data constraints that have to be reconciled later on. Moreover, we have identified the need for additional availability metrics (e.g., number of accepted operations, proportion of revoked operations) to evaluate these systems. Using these metrics, we have evaluated an implementation of a reconciliation protocol [1] that aims at delivering continuous service during the reconciliation protocol.

The results show that for long partition durations this protocol gives the best performance in terms of apparent availability as well as number of applied operations. Moreover for longer partition durations, the risk of having to revoke a previously accepted operation can decrease for some applications.

Naturally, the gain comes with a cost. Apart from the fact that operations have to be revoked or possibly compensated during reconciliation, there will be an overhead associated with this solution. Currently, we are evaluating this protocol as a CORBA extension to make it partition-tolerant. This evaluation will include latency measurements to determine the overhead induced by the protocols. A natural continuation for this work is to extend it to more dynamic environments where partitions are more frequent and where the network topology is constantly changing.

The current implementation updates replicas with the installed state by sending the entire state. This is obviously not reasonable in a system with a large state. A relatively easy modification is to send increments, that represent changes to the state of various replicas.

9 Acknowledgments

This work has been supported by the FP6 IST project DeDiSys on Dependable Distributed Systems. The second author was partially supported by University of Luxembourg during preparation of this manuscript.

References

[1] M. Asplund and S. Nadjm-Tehrani. Formalising reconciliation in partitionable networks with distributed services. In M. Butler, C. Jones, A. Romanovsky, and E. Troubitsyna, editors, *Rigorous Development of Complex Fault-Tolerant Systems*, volume 4157 of *Lecture Notes in Computer Science*, pages 37–58. Springer-Verlag, 2006.

[2] M. Asplund and S. Nadjm-Tehrani. Post-partition reconciliation protocols for maintaining consistency. In *Proceedings of the 21st ACM/SIGAPP symposium on Applied computing*, April 2006.

[3] Ö. Babaoglu, A. Bartoli, and G. Dini. Enriched view synchrony: A programming paradigm for partitionable asynchronous distributed systems. *IEEE Trans. Comput.*, 46(6):642–658, 1997.

[4] G. Badishi, G. Caronni, I. Keidar, R. Rom, and G. Scott. Deleting files in the celeste peer-to-peer storage system. In *SRDS'06: Proceedings of the 25th IEEE Symposium on Reliable Distributed Systems*, October 2006.

[5] P. A. Bernstein, V. Hadzilacos, and N. Goodman. *Concurrency control and recovery in database systems*. Addison-Wesley Longman Publishing Co., Inc., Boston, MA, USA, 1987.

[6] S. Beyer, M. Bañuls, P. Galdámez, J. Osrael, and F. D. Muñoz-Escoí. Increasing availability in a replicated partionable distributed object system. In *Proceedings of the Fourth International Symposium on Parallel and Distributed Processing and Applications (ISPA'2006)*. Springer–Verlag, 2006.

[7] M. Cukier, J. Ren, C. Sabnis, D. Henke, J. Pistole, W. H. Sanders, D. E. Bakken, M. E. Berman, D. A. Karr, and R. E. Schantz. Aqua: An adaptive architecture that provides dependable distributed objects. In *SRDS '98: Proceedings of the The 17th IEEE Symposium on Reliable Distributed Systems*, page 245, Washington, DC, USA, 1998. IEEE Computer Society.

[8] S. B. Davidson, H. Garcia-Molina, and D. Skeen. Consistency in a partitioned network: a survey. *ACM Comput. Surv.*, 17(3):341–370, 1985.

[9] DeDiSys. European IST FP6 DeDiSys Project. http://www.dedisys.org, 2006.

[10] C. Ferdean and M. Makpangou. A generic and flexible model for replica consistency management. In *ICDCIT*, pages 204–209, 2004.

[11] J. Gray, P. Helland, P. O'Neil, and D. Shasha. The dangers of replication and a solution. In *SIGMOD '96: Proceedings of the 1996 ACM SIGMOD international conference on Management of data*, pages 173–182, New York, NY, USA, 1996. ACM Press.

[12] V. Hadzilacos and S. Toueg. Fault-tolerant broadcasts and related problems. In *Distributed systems*, chapter 5, pages 97–145. ACM Press, Addison-Wesley, 2nd edition, 1993.

[13] A.-M. Kermarrec, A. Rowstron, M. Shapiro, and P. Druschel. The icecube approach to the reconciliation of divergent replicas. In *PODC '01: Proceedings of the twentieth annual ACM symposium on Principles of distributed computing*, pages 210–218, New York, NY, USA, 2001. ACM Press.

[14] E. Lippe and N. van Oosterom. Operation-based merging. In *SDE 5: Proceedings of the fifth ACM SIGSOFT symposium on Software development environments*, pages 78–87, New York, NY, USA, 1992. ACM Press.

[15] L. E. Moser, P. M. Melliar-Smith, and P. Narasimhan. Consistent object replication in the eternal system. *Theor. Pract. Object Syst.*, 4(2):81–92, 1998.

[16] P. Narasimhan, L. E. Moser, and P. M. Melliar-Smith. Replica consistency of corba objects in partitionable distributed systems. *Distributed Systems Engineering*, 4(3):139–150, 1997.

[17] S. H. Phatak and B. Nath. Transaction-centric reconciliation in disconnected client-server databases. *Mob. Netw. Appl.*, 9(5):459–471, 2004.

[18] N. Preguica, M. Shapiro, and C. Matheson. Semantics-based reconciliation for collaborative and mobile environments. *Lecture Notes in Computer Science*, 2888:38–55, October 2003.

[19] Y. Saito and M. Shapiro. Optimistic replication. *ACM Comput. Surv.*, 37(1):42–81, 2005.

[20] D. P. Siewiorek and R. S. Swarz. *Reliable computer systems (3rd ed.): design and evaluation*. A. K. Peters, Ltd., Natick, MA, USA, 1998.

[21] D. Szentivanyi and S. Nadjm-Tehrani. Middleware support for fault tolerance. In Q. Mahmoud, editor, *Middleware for Communications*. John Wiley & Sons, 2004.

[22] D. B. Terry, M. M. Theimer, K. Petersen, A. J. Demers, M. J. Spreitzer, and C. H. Hauser. Managing update conflicts in bayou, a weakly connected replicated storage system. In *SOSP '95: Proceedings of the fifteenth ACM symposium on Operating systems principles*, pages 172–182, New York, NY, USA, 1995. ACM Press.

[23] A.-I. Wang, P. L. Reiher, R. Bagrodia, and G. H. Kuenning. Understanding the behavior of the conflict-rate metric in optimistic peer replication. In *DEXA '02: Proceedings of the 13th International Workshop on Database and Expert Systems Applications*, pages 757–764, Washington, DC, USA, 2002. IEEE Computer Society.

[24] H. ying Tyan. *Design, realization and evaluation of a component-based software architecture for network simulation*. PhD thesis, Department of Electrical Engineering, Ohio State University, 2001.

[25] H. Yu and A. Vahdat. Design and evaluation of a conit-based continuous consistency model for replicated services. *ACM Trans. Comput. Syst.*, 20(3):239–282, 2002.

Scaling and Continuous Availability in Database Server Clusters through Multiversion Replication

Kaloian Manassiev
Department of Computer Science
University of Toronto
kaloianm@cs.toronto.edu

Cristiana Amza
Department of Electrical and Computer Engineering
University of Toronto
amza@eecg.toronto.edu

Abstract

In this paper, we study replication techniques for scaling and continuous operation for a dynamic content server. Our focus is on supporting transparent and fast reconfiguration of its database tier in case of overload or failures. We show that the data persistence aspects can be decoupled from reconfiguration of the database CPU. A lightweight in-memory middleware tier captures the typically heavyweight read-only requests to ensure flexible database CPU scaling and fail-over. At the same time, updates are handled by an on-disk database back-end that is in charge of making them persistent.

Our measurements show instantaneous, seamless reconfiguration in the case of single node failures within the flexible in-memory tier for a web site running the most common, shopping, workload mix of the industry-standard e-commerce TPC-W benchmark. At the same time, a 9-node in-memory tier improves performance during normal operation over a stand-alone InnoDB on-disk database back-end. Throughput scales by factors of 14.6, 17.6 and 6.5 for the browsing, shopping and ordering mixes of the TPC-W benchmark, respectively.

1. Introduction

This paper investigates replication techniques for high-performance, self-configuring database back-end tiers in dynamic content servers. Dynamic content sites currently need to provide very high levels of availability and scalability. On-the-fly reconfiguration may be needed to either adapt to failures or bursts of traffic and should be automatic, fast and transparent. The presence of the database tier in such sites makes fast reconfiguration hard to achieve. Above all, data consistency needs to be ensured during reconfiguration, typically through complex and lengthy recovery procedures. The reconfiguration problem is exacerbated by the need to scale the database tier through asynchronous content replication solutions [5, 10, 20, 13]. Replica asynchrony has been proved absolutely necessary for scaling. On the other hand, because data is not fully consistent on all replicas at all times, asynchronous replication is at odds with fast, transparent reconfiguration. Asynchronous replication techniques thus tend to sacrifice failure transparency and data availability to performance scaling by introducing windows of vulnerability, where effects of committed transactions may be lost. Alternatively, complex failure reconfiguration protocols imply reloading transactional logs from disk and replaying them on a stale replica. Resuming servicing transaction at peak-throughput can take on the order of minutes [12] and possibly more; fail-over times are rarely formally measured and reported.

In this paper, we introduce a solution that combines transparent scaling and split-second reconfiguration. Our key idea is to interpose an *in memory* tier, consisting of lightweight database engines, providing scaling and seamless adaptation to failures on top of a traditional on-disk database back-end. Our middleware tier implements *Dynamic Multiversioning*, a database replication solution allowing both scaling and ease of self-reconfiguration of the overall system. Specifically, our replication solution has the following desirable properties:

1. provides consistency semantics identical to a 1-copy database (i.e., 1-copy serializability), thus making the underlying replication mechanism completely transparent to the user.

2. scales by distributing reads to multiple replicas without restricting concurrency at each replica in the common case.

3. provides data availability through simple and efficient techniques for reconfiguration in case of failures.

In contrast to industry solutions which rely on costly shared network-attached storage configurations [3], our solution uses only commodity software and hardware. Our focus is on achieving fast reconfiguration for scaling and data availability in the common case of single node failures, while ensuring data persistence in all cases.

An in-memory database tier with asynchronous, but strongly consistent replication offers high speed and scalability during normal operation and inherent agility in reconfiguration during common failure scenarios. An on-disk back-end database with limited replication offers data reliability for rare failure scenarios, e.g., a power outage. Our research focus on in-memory database tiers is supported by industry trends towards: i) large main-memory sizes for commodity servers, ii) the popularity of database workloads with a high degree of locality [4], such as the most common e-commerce workloads [22], which result in working sets on the order of a few Gigabytes.

Our in-memory replication scheme is asynchronous in order to provide scaling. We have previously shown that the presence of distributed versions of the same page in a transactional memory cluster with asynchronous replication can be exploited to support scaling for generic applications [16]. In this paper, our focus is on supporting both scaling and fast reconfiguration for an in-memory database cluster. In our solution, the fine-grained concurrency control of the database works synergistically with data replication to ensure high performance and ease of reconfiguration. Update transactions always occur on an in-memory master replica, which broadcasts modifications to a set of in-memory slaves. Each master update creates a version number, communicated to a scheduler that distributes requests on the in-memory cluster. The scheduler tags each read-only transaction with the newest version received from the master and sends it to one of the slaves. The appropriate version for each individual data item is then created dynamically and lazily at that slave replica, when needed by an in-progress read-only transaction. The system automatically detects data races created by different read-only transactions attempting to read conflicting versions of the same item. Conflicts and version consistency are detected and enforced at the page level. In the common case, the scheduler sends any two transactions requiring different versions of the same memory page on different replicas, where each creates the page versions it needs and the two transactions can execute in parallel.

We further concentrate on optimizing the fail-over reconfiguration path, defined as integrating a new replica (called a backup) into the active computation to compensate for a fault. The goal is to maintain a constant level of overall performance irrespective of failures. We use two key techniques for fail-over optimization. First, instead of replaying a log on a stale replica, we replicate only the changed pages with newer versions than the backup's page versions from an active slave onto the backup's memory. These pages

may have collapsed long chains of modifications to database rows registering high update activity. Thus, selective page replication is expected to be faster on average than modification log replay. Second, we warm up the buffer cache of one or more spare backups during normal operation using one of two alternative schemes: i) we schedule a small fraction of the main read-only workload on a spare backup or ii) we mimic the read access patterns of an active slave on a spare backup to bring the most-heavily accessed data in its buffer cache. With these key techniques, our in-memory tier has the flexibility to incorporate a spare backup after a fault without any noticeable impact on either throughput or latency due to reconfiguration.

Our in-memory replicated database implementation is built from two existing libraries: the Vista library that provides very fast single-machine transactions [15], and the MySQL in-memory "heap table" code that provides a very simple and efficient SQL database engine without transactional properties. We use these codes as building blocks for our fully transactional in-memory database tier because they are reported to have reasonably good performance and are widely available and used. Following this "software components" philosophy has significantly reduced the coding effort involved.

In our evaluation we use the three workload mixes of the industry standard TPC-W e-commerce benchmark [22]. The workload mixes have increasing fraction of update transactions: browsing (5%), shopping (20%) and ordering (50%).

We have implemented the TPC-W web site using three popular open source software packages: the Apache Web server [7], the PHP web-scripting/application development language [19] and the MySQL database server [2]. In our experiments we used MySQL with InnoDB tables as our on-disk database back-ends and a set of up to 9 in-memory databases running our modified version of MySQL heap tables in our lightweight reconfigurable tier.

Our results are as follows:

1. Reconfiguration is instantaneous in case of failures of any in-memory node with no difference in throughput or latency due to fault handling if spare in-memory backups are maintained warm. We found that either servicing less than 1% of the read-only requests in a regular workload at a spare backup or following an active slave's access pattern and touching its most frequently used pages on the backup is sufficient for this purpose. In contrast, with a traditional replication approach with MySQL InnoDB on-disk databases, fail-over time is on the order of minutes.

2. Using our system with up to 9 in-memory replicas as an in-memory transaction processing tier, we are able to improve on the performance of the InnoDB on-disk

667

database back-end by factors of 14.6, 17.6 and 6.5 for the browsing, shopping and ordering mixes respectively.

The rest of this paper is organized as follows. Section 2 introduces our scaling solution, based on Dynamic Multiversioning, Section 3 describes our prototype implementation and Section 4 presents its fault-tolerance and fast-reconfiguration aspects. Sections 5 and 6 describe our experimental platform, methodology and results. Section 7 discusses related work. Section 8 concludes the paper.

2. Dynamic Multiversioning

2.1. Overview

The goal of Dynamic Multiversioning is to scale the database tier through a distributed concurrency control mechanism that integrates per-page fine-grained concurrency control, consistent replication and version-aware scheduling.

The idea of isolating the execution of conflicting update and read-only transactions through multiversioning concurrency control is not new [8]. Existing stand-alone databases supporting multiversioning (e.g., Oracle) pay the price of maintaining multiple physical data copies for each database item and garbage collecting old copies.

Instead, we take advantage of the availability of distributed replicas in a database cluster to run each read-only transaction on a consistent snapshot created dynamically at a particular replica for the pages in its read set. In addition, we utilize the presence of update transactions with disjoint working sets in order to enable non-conflicting update transactions to run in parallel, thus exploiting the available hardware optimally.

We augment a simple in-memory database with a replication module implementing a scheme that is i) eager by propagating modifications from a set of master databases that determines the serialization order to a set of slave databases before the commit point, ii) lazy by delaying the application of modifications on slave replicas and creating item versions on-demand as needed for each read-only transaction.

In more detail, our fine-grained distributed multiversioning scheme works as follows. A scheduler distributes requests on the in-memory database cluster as shown in Figure 1. We require that each incoming request is preceded by its access type, e.g. read-only or update. The scheduler is pre-configured with the types of transactions used by the application and the tables each of them accesses [5]. It uses this information to categorize the incoming requests into conflict classes [18], based on the set of tables that they access. The scheduler assigns a master database to each

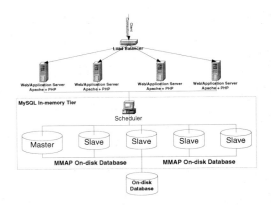

Figure 1. System design.

conflict class. It sends all queries belonging to the update transactions in each conflict class to the respective master node. If no information on conflict classes is available or if conflict classes cannot be statically determined, all update transactions are scheduled on a single node designated as master database. Read-only transactions are distributed among the slave (non-master) database replicas as shown in Figure 1. Read-only transactions can be scheduled on a master replica as well as long as the set of tables they access are not in the master's conflict class. The master database decides the order of execution of write transactions in each conflict class it manages based on its internal two-phase-locking per-page concurrency control. In our scheme, conflict classes are disjoint. Hence, there is no need for inter-master synchronization, which permits a fully parallel execution of updates.

Each update transaction committing on a master node produces a new consistent state of the database. Each database state is represented by a version vector with a single integer entry for each table of the application, called `DBVersion`. Upon transaction commit, each master database flushes its modifications to the remaining replicas. The master communicates the most recent version vector produced locally to the scheduler when confirming the commit of each update transaction. The scheduler merges incoming version vectors and it tags each read-only transaction with the version vector that it is supposed to read (i.e., the most recent version produced by all of the masters) and sends it to a slave replica. Each read-only transaction applies all fine-grain modifications received from a conflict-class master, for each of the items it is accessing, thus dynamically creating a consistent snapshot of the database version it is supposed to read.

Versions for each item are thus created dynamically when needed by a read-only transaction in progress at a particular replica. Specifically, the replica applies all local fine-grained updates received from a master on the necessary items up to and including the version vector that the read-only transaction has been tagged with. Different read-only transactions with disjoint read sets can thus run concurrently at the same replica even if they require snapshots of their items belonging to different database versions. Conversely, if two read-only transactions need two different versions of the same item(s), respectively they can only execute in parallel if sent to different database replicas.

2.2. Version-Aware Scheduling

Dynamic Multiversioning guarantees that each read-only transaction executing on a slave database reads the latest data version as if running on a single database system. The scheduler enforces the serialization order by tagging each read-only transaction sent to execute on a database replica with the latest version vector. The latest version vector contains the most recent version communicated by the master replicas on each respective table position.

The execution of read-only transactions is isolated from any concurrent updates executing on the master replicas whose write set intersects with the read set of the read-only transactions. This means that a read-only transaction will not apply and will not see modifications on items that were written later than the version it was assigned.

Assuming that the read-only transaction has been tagged with version $V(v_1, \ldots, v_n)$ by the scheduler, the slave replica creates the appropriate version on-the-fly for all items read by the transaction. Specifically, the slave replica applies all local fine-grained updates received from each master, only on the necessary items up to and including version $V(v_1, \ldots, v_n)$.

The scheduler selects a replica from the set of databases running read-only transactions with the same version vector as the one to be scheduled if such databases exist. Otherwise, it selects a replica by plain load balancing. In case of insufficient replicas, read-only transaction may need to wait for other read-only transactions using a previous version of an item, or for update transactions writing the item to finish. A read-only transaction T1 may need to be aborted if another read-only transaction T2 upgrades a shared item to a version higher than that required by T1. If T1 has already read a page with its assigned version, then reading a higher version of a different page, would result in version inconsistency. Since we do not keep old versions around, T1 would need to be aborted in this case. However, we expect these situations to be rare.

3. Implementation

Based on the standard MySQL HEAP table we have added a separate table type called REPLICATED_HEAP to MySQL. Replication is implemented at the level of physical

```
1: MasterPreCommit(PageSet[] PS):
2:     WriteSet[] WS = CreateWriteSet(PS)
3:     Increment(DBVerVector, WS)
4:     For Each Replica R Do:
5:         SendUpdate(R, WS, DBVerVector)
6:         WaitForAcknowledgment(R)
7: Return DBVerVector
```

Figure 2. Master node pre-commit actions.

memory modifications performed by the MySQL storage manager. Since MySQL heap tables are not transactional we add an undo and a redo log. The unit of transactional concurrency control is the memory page. The redo log contains a list of per-page modification encodings. Figure 2 shows the pseudo-code for pre-committing a transaction on the master node. The parameter PS (from Page Set) is a data structure maintaining all the pages that the transaction modified. At pre-commit, the master generates the *write-set* message with the modifications for each modified page. It then increments the database version and sends the write-set and the version that it would turn the database into to all other replicas. The increment of DBVersion vector on line 3 is implemented as an atomic operation to ensure that each committed transaction obtains a unique version vector. After the pre-commit step completes, the master node reports back to the scheduler that the transaction has successfully committed and piggybacks the new *DBVersion* on the reply. Finally, all page locks are released and the master commits the transaction locally. The scheduler records the new version vector and uses it to tag subsequent read-only transactions with the appropriate versions they need to read.

4. Fault Tolerance and Data Availability

In this section, we first describe our reconfiguration techniques in case of master, slave or scheduler node failures. Second, we describe our mechanisms for data persistence and availability of storage in the on-disk back-end database tier. We assume a fail-stop failure model where failures of any individual node are detected through missed heartbeat messages or broken connections.

4.1. Scheduler Failure

The scheduler node is minimal in functionality, which permits extremely fast reconfiguration in the case of single node fail-stop failure scenarios. Since the scheduler's state consists of only the current database version vector, this data can easily be replicated across multiple peer schedulers, which work in parallel. If one scheduler fails and multiple schedulers are already present, one of the peers takes over. Otherwise, a new scheduler is elected from the remaining nodes.

The new scheduler sends a message to the master databases asking them to abort all uncommitted transactions that were active at the time of failure. This may not be necessary for databases that automatically abort a transaction due to broken connections with their client. After the masters execute the abort request, they reply back with the highest database version number they produced. Then, the new scheduler broadcasts a message to all the other nodes in the system, informing them of the new topology.

4.2. Master Failure

Upon detecting a master failure, one of the schedulers takes charge of recovery. It asks all databases to discard their modification log records, which have version numbers higher than the last version number it has seen from the master. This takes care of cleaning up transactions whose pre-commit modification log flush message may have partially completed at a subset of the replicas but the master has not acknowledged the commit of the transaction before failure.

For all other failure cases, reconfiguration is trivial. The replication scheme guarantees that the effects of committed transactions will be available on all the slaves in the system. Hence, reconfiguration simply entails electing a new master from the slave replicas to replaces the failed master replica. Thereafter, the system continues to service requests. In the case of master failure during a transaction's execution, the effects of the transaction are automatically discarded since all transaction modifications are internal to the master node up to the commit point.

4.3. Slave Failure

The failure of any particular slave node is detected by all schedulers. Each scheduler examines its log of outstanding queries, and for those sent to the failed slave, the corresponding transaction is aborted and an error message is returned to the client/application server. The failed slave is then simply removed from the scheduler tables and a new topology is generated.

4.4. Data Migration for Integrating Stale Nodes

In this section, we present the **data migration** algorithm for integrating recovering or other stale replicas. New replicas are always integrated as slave nodes of the system, regardless of their rank prior to failure.

The *reintegrating node* (S_{join}) initially contacts one of the schedulers and obtains the identities of the current masters and an arbitrary slave node. We refer to this slave node as the *support slave*.

In the next step, S_{join} subscribes to the replication list of the masters, obtains the current database version vector $DBVersion$ and starts receiving modification log records. The node stores these new modifications into its local queues, as any other active slave node without applying these modifications to pages. It then requests page updates from its support node indicating the current version it has for each page and the version number that it needs to attain, according to $DBVersion$, as obtained from the master replicas upon joining. The support node then selectively transmits only the pages that changed after the joining node's version to S_{join}.

In order to minimize integration time, all nodes implement a simple fuzzy checkpoint algorithm [8], modified to suit our in-memory database. At regular intervals, each slave starts a checkpointing thread, which iterates the database pages and persists their current contents together with their current version onto local stable storage. A flush of a page and its version number is *atomic*. Dirty pages, which have been written to but not committed, are not included in the flush. However, our checkpointing scheme is flexible and efficient, because it does not require the system to be quiescent during checkpoints. Since our in-memory database normally works with its data pages having different versions at the same time, a checkpoint does not have to be synchronous either across replicas or across the pages checkpointed at each replica. Furthermore, a stale node only receives the changed pages since its last checkpointed version of each page. These pages might have collapsed long chains of modifications to database rows registering high update activity. Hence, our scheme allows for potentially faster reintegration of stale nodes into the computation compared to replaying a log of update transactions.

4.5. Fail-Over Reconfiguration Using Spare Backups

Database fail-over time consists of two phases: **data migration** for bringing the node up to date and the new node's **buffer cache warmup**. An additional phase occurs only in the case of master failure due to the need to abort unacknowledged and partially propagated updates, as described in the master failure scenario above.

The **data migration phase** proceeds as in the algorithm for stale node integration described in the previous section. In the **buffer cache warmup phase**, the backup database needs to warm up its buffer cache and other internal data structures until the state of these in-memory data structures approximates their corresponding state on the failed database replica. The backup database has its in-memory buffer cache only partially warmed up, if at all, because it is normally not executing any reads for the workload.

In order to shorten or eliminate the buffer cache warmup phase, a set of warm spare backups are maintained for a particular workload for overflow in case of failures (or potentially overload of active replicas). These nodes may be either idle e.g., previously failed nodes that have just recovered or intentionally maintained relatively unused e.g., for power savings or because they may be actively running a different workload. The spare backups subscribe to and receive the regular modification broadcasts from the master replicas just like active slave replicas. In addition, we use two alternative techniques for warming up the spare backup buffer caches during normal operation.

In the first technique, spare backups are assigned a number of read-only transactions with the sole purpose of keeping their buffer caches warm. The number of periodic read-only requests serviced by spare backups is kept at a minimum.

In the second technique, a spare backup does not receive any requests for the workload. Instead, one or more designated slave nodes collect statistics about the access pattern of their resident data set and send the set of page identifiers for pages in their buffer cache to the backup periodically. The backup simply touches the pages so that they are kept swapped into main memory. In this way, the backup's valuable CPU resource can be used to service a different workload. For spare backups running a different workload, care must be taken to avoid interference [21] in the database's buffer cache for the two workloads. This aspect is, however, beyond the scope of this paper.

4.6. Data Persistence and Availability in the Storage Database Tier

We use a back-end on-disk database tier for data persistence in the unlikely case that *all* in-memory replicas fail.

Upon each commit returned by the in-memory master database for an update transaction, the scheduler logs the update queries corresponding to this transaction and, at the same time, sends these as a batch to be executed on one or more on-disk back-end databases. Replication in the case of the on-disk databases is for data persistence and availability of data and not for CPU scaling; only a few (e.g., two) on-disk replicas are needed. Once the update queries have been successfully logged, the scheduler can return the commit response to the application server without waiting for responses from all the on-disk databases. The query logging is performed as a lightweight database insert of the corresponding query strings into a database table [21]. In case of failure, any on-disk database can be brought up to date by replaying the log of missing updates.

5. Evaluation

5.1. TPC-W Benchmark

We evaluate our solution using the TPC-W benchmark from the Transaction Processing Council (TPC) [22], that simulates an on-line bookstore.

The database contains eight tables: customer, address, orders, order_line, credit_info, item, author, and country. We implemented the fourteen different interactions specified in the TPC-W benchmark specification. The most complex read-only interactions are BestSellers, NewProducts and Search by Subject which contain complex joins.

We use the standard size with 288K customers and 100K books, which results in a database size of about 610MB. The memory-resident set of the workload is about 360MB and it consists of the most-frequently accessed sections of the database.

We use the three workload mixes of the TPC-W benchmark: browsing, shopping and ordering. These workloads are characterized by increasing fraction of writes from the browsing mix (5%) to the most commonly used workload, the shopping mix (20%) to the ordering mix (50%).

5.2. Experimental Setup

We run our experiments on a cluster of 19 dual AMD Athlons with 512MB of RAM and 1.9GHz CPU, running the RedHat Fedora Linux operating system. We run the scheduler and each of nine database replicas on separate machines. We use 10 machines to operate the Apache 1.3.31 web-server, which runs a PHP implementation of the business logic of the TPC-W benchmark and use a client emulator, which emulates client interactions as specified in the TPC-W document.

To determine the peak throughput for each cluster configuration we run a step-function workload, whereby we gradually increase the number of clients from 100 to 1000. We then report the peak throughput in web interactions per second, the standard TPC-W metric, for each configuration. At the beginning of each experiment, the master and the slave databases mmap an on-disk database. Although persistence is ensured through an InnoDB database, our prototype currently requires a translation of the database from the InnoDB table format into the MySQL heap table format before initial mmap-ing. We run each experiment for a sufficient time such that the benchmark's operating data set becomes memory resident and we exclude the initial cache warm-up time from the measurements. Our experiments focus on demonstrating the system scalability, resiliency and efficiency of failover.

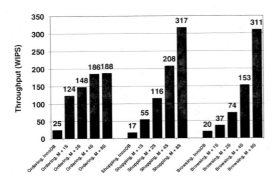

Figure 3. Comparison against InnoDB.

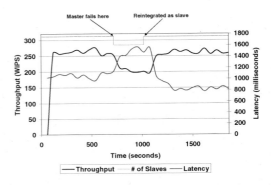

Figure 4. Node reintegration (shopping mix).

6. Experimental Results

In our experimental evaluation, we first show the performance benefits brought about by our fast in-memory transactional layer, compared to a stand-alone on-disk InnoDB database, in Section 6.1. Then, we demonstrate fast reconfiguration under failures in our in-memory tier versus a stand-alone InnoDB replicated tier in Section 6.2.

6.1. Performance Experiments

Figure 3 shows the throughput scaling we obtained over the fine-tuned single InnoDB on-disk database back-end. In the experiment InnoDB was configured for serializable concurrency control. We performed experiments with 1, 2, 4 and 8 slave replicas respectively. Overall, we improve performance over stand-alone InnoDB by factors of 6.5, 17.6 and 14.6 in our largest configuration with 8 slaves with InnoDB for the ordering, shopping and browsing mixes respectively. Furthermore, we can see that a performance jump is seen from adding the in-memory tier even in the smallest configuration due to its superior speed. Finally, system throughput scales close to linearly with increases in in-memory tier size for the browsing and shopping mixes and less well for the ordering mix. This is caused by saturation of our master database with update transactions including lock waiting on the master as a side-effect of the costly index updates in our system (due to rebalancing for inserts in the RB-tree index data structure). The read-only transactions aborted due to version inconsistency are below 2.5% out of the total number of transactions in all experiments.

6.2. Failure Reconfiguration Experiments

In this section, we first show a fault tolerance experiment with reintegration of a failed node after recovery. Next, we concentrate on fail-over onto backup nodes and we show the impact of the three components of the fail-over path on performance in our system: cleanup of partially propagated updates for aborted transactions, data migration and buffer cache warmup. For this purpose, we inject faults of either master or slaves in the in-memory tier and show reconfiguration times in the following scenarios:

i) **Stale backup case:** Master or active slave failure with reintegration of the failed node or integration of a stale backup node. ii) **Up-to-date cold backup case:** Master or active slave failure followed by integration of an up-to-date spare backup node with cold buffer cache. iii) **Up-to-date warm backup case:** Master or active slave failure followed by integration of an up-to-date and warm spare backup node. We also compare our fail-over times with the fail-over time of a stand-alone on-disk InnoDB database.

6.2.1 Fault Tolerance with Node Reintegration Experiment

In this section, we evaluate the performance of the node reintegration algorithm we introduced in section 4. The algorithm permits any failed node to be reallocated to the workload after recovery. This implies a period of node down-time (e.g., due to node reboot).

We use the master database and 4 slave replicas in the test cluster configuration, running the shopping TPC-W workload. Figure 4 shows the effect of reintegration on both throughput and latency.

We consider the most complex recovery case, that of master failure by killing the master database at 720 seconds by initiating a machines reboot. We see from the graph that the system adapts to this situation instantaneously with the throughput and latency gracefully degrading by a fraction of 20%. Since all slave databases are active and execute transactions their buffer caches are implicitly warm. Hence throughput drops no lower than the level supported by the fewer remaining slave replicas.

After 6 minutes of reboot time (depicted by the line in the upper part of the graph), the failed node is up and running again, and after it subscribes with the scheduler, the scheduler initiates its reintegration into workload processing as a slave replica. Since we used a checkpoint period of

40 minutes, this experiment shows the *worst case* scenario where all modifications since the start of the run need to be transferred to the joining node. It takes about 5 seconds for the joining node to catch up with the missed database updates. After the node has been reintegrated, it takes another 50 to 60 seconds to warm-up the in-memory buffer cache of the new node, after which the throughput is back to normal. The next section provides a more precise breakdown of the different recovery phases.

6.3. Failover Experiments

In this section we evaluate the performance of our automatic reconfiguration using fail-over on spare back-up nodes. In all of the following experiments we designate several databases as backup nodes and bring an active node down. The system immediately reconfigures by integrating a spare node into the computation immediately after the failure.

We measure the effect of the failure as the time to restore operation at peak performance. We run the TPC-W shopping mix and measure the throughput and latency that the client perceives, averaged over 20 second intervals.

Depending on the state of the spare backup, we differentiate failover scenarios into: *stale backup*, *up-to-date cold backup* and *up-to-date warm backup*. In the *stale backup* experiments, the spare node may be behind the rest of the nodes in the system, so both catch-up time and buffer warm-up time are involved on fail-over. In the *up-to-date* experiments, the spare node is in sync with the rest of the nodes in the system, but a certain amount of buffer warm-up time may be involved.

Stale Backup

As a baseline for comparison, we first show the results of fail-over in a dynamic content server using a replicated on-disk InnoDB back-end. This system is representative for state-of-the-art replicated solutions where asynchrony is used for scaling a workload to a number of replicas.

In this experiment, the InnoDB replicated tier contains two active nodes and one passive backup. The two active nodes are kept up-to-date using a conflict-aware scheduler [6] and both process read-only queries. The spare node is updated every 30 minutes. Figures 5(a) and 5(b) show the failover effect in an experiment where we kill one of the active nodes after 30 minutes of execution time. We can see from the figure that service is at half its capacity for close to 3 minutes in terms of lowered throughput, and higher latency correspondingly.

We conduct a similar experiment interposing our in-memory tier, having a master and two active slaves and one 30 minute stale backup. We used two active slaves, because

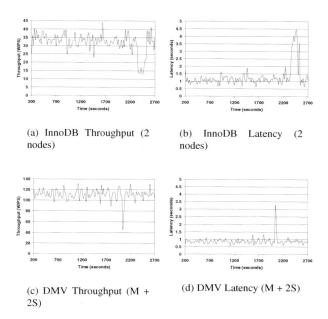

(a) InnoDB Throughput (2 nodes)

(b) InnoDB Latency (2 nodes)

(c) DMV Throughput (M + 2S)

(d) DMV Latency (M + 2S)

Figure 5. Failover onto stale backup: comparison of InnoDB and DMV databases.

in the normal operation of our scheme the master is kept lightly loaded and does not execute read-only transactions. Subsequently, we kill the master node to generate the worst-case fail-over scenario that includes master reconfiguration. The results are presented in figures 5(c) and 5(d). In this case, the total failover time is about 70 seconds, less than a third of the InnoDB fail-over time in the previous experiment.

Furthermore, from the breakdown of the time spent in the three fail-over stages presented in Figure 6, we can see that most of the fail-over time in our in-memory Dynamic Multiversioning based system is caused by the buffer-cache warm-up effect. The figure also compares the durations of the failover stages between the InnoDB and in-memory Dynamic Multiversioning cases. We can see that the database update time during which the database log is replayed onto the backup (DB Update) constitutes a significant 94 second fraction of the total fail-over time in the InnoDB case. This time reflects the cost of reading and replaying on-disk logs. In contrast, the catch up stage is considerably reduced in our in-memory tier where only in-memory pages are transfered to the backup node. The cache warm-up times are similar for both schemes. For the DMV case, there is an additional 6 second clean-up period (Recovery), during which partially committed update transactions need to be aborted due to the master failure and master reconfiguration occurs.

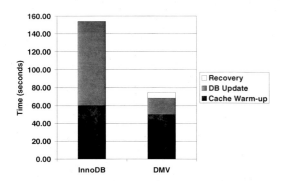

Figure 6. Failover stage weights: cleanup (Recovery), data migration (DB Update) and Buffer cache warmup (Cache Warmup)

Up-to-date Cold Backup

In this suite of experiments, the spare node is always kept in sync with the rest of the system by sending it the log of modifications.

In order to emphasize the buffer warmup phase during failover, we used a slightly larger database configuration comprised of 400K customers and 100K items. This yielded a database size of 800MB and a resident working set of approximately 460MB. We use a three-node cluster: one master, one active slave and one backup.

In this first experiment, the buffer cache of the spare node is cold, so upon fail-over the database needs to swap-in a significant amount of data, before achieving peak performance. We run the TPC-W shopping mix and after approximately 17 minutes (1030 seconds) of running time, we kill the active slave database forcing the system to start integrating the cold backup. Figure 7 shows the perceived throughput for the duration of the cold backup experiment.

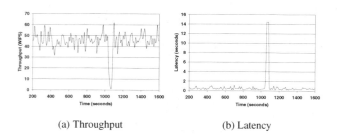

(a) Throughput (b) Latency

Figure 7. Fail-over onto cold up-to-date DMV backup.

We can see that the drop in throughput is significant in this case due to the need to warm-up the entire database cache on the cold backup. It takes more than 1 minute until

the peak throughput is restored.

Up-to-date Warm Backup

In this section, we investigate the effect on fail-over performance of our techniques for mitigating the warm-up effect.

In the first case, the scheduler sends 1% of the read-only workload to the spare backup node. We conduct the same experiment with the same configuration as above and we kill the active slave database at the same point during the run as in the previous experiment. As before, the system reconfigures to include the spare backup. Figure 8 shows the throughput for this case. The effect of the failure is almost unnoticeable due to the fact that the most frequently referenced pages are in the cache.

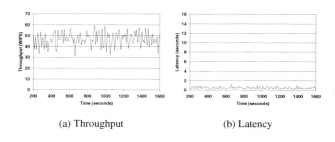

(a) Throughput (b) Latency

Figure 8. Fail-over onto warm DMV backup with 1% query-execution warm-up.

Figure 9 shows the failover effect for our alternate backup warmup scheme using page id transfers from an active slave. The active slaves transfers page ids to the backup every 100 transactions while the backup touches these pages. We see that the performance in this case is the same as that for periodic query execution allowing for seamless failure handling.

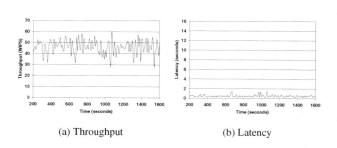

(a) Throughput (b) Latency

Figure 9. Fail-over onto warm DMV backup with page id transfer.

7. Related Work

A number of solutions exist for replication of relational databases that aim to provide both scaling and strong consistency. They range from industry-established ones, such as the Oracle RAC [3] and the IBM DB2 HADR suite [1] to research and open-source prototypes, such as MySQL Cluster [17], C-JDBC [9, 10], Postgres-R [14] and Ganymed [20].

The industry solutions provide both high availability and good scalability, but they are costly and require specialized hardware such as Shared Network Disk [3]. MySQL Cluster [17] provides very fast in-memory replicated storage engine with lazy logging of updates, similar to the one in our system prototype. However, it uses traditional two-phase locking for concurrency control which may stall readers accessing data that's being modified. In contrast, our solution resolves read/write conflicts optimistically and hence avoids thread blocking. Existing research prototypes use commodity software and hardware, but they either have limited scaling for moderately heavy write workloads [5, 10] due to their use of coarse-grained concurrency control implemented in the scheduler, or sacrifice failure transparency and data availability by introducing single points of failure [20]. Even the solutions that offer transparent fail-over and data availability [5] do so by means of complex protocols due to the crucial data that resides inside the scheduler tier. In contrast, our solution provides transparent scalability as well as fast, transparent failover. The scheduler node is minimal in functionality, which permits extremely fast reconfiguration in the case of single node fail-stop scenarios.

Previous work in the area of primary-backup replication [24] has mostly followed a "passive backup as a hot-standby" approach where the backup simply mirrors the updates of the primary. These solutions either enforce a fully synchronous application of updates to the backup or do not enforce strict consistency although the backup does maintain a copy of the database on the primary. The backup is either idle during failure free system execution [24] or could execute a different set of applications/tasks. In contrast to these classic solutions, in our replicated cluster, while backups are used for seamless fail-over, a potentially large set of active slaves are actively executing read-only transactions with strong consistency guarantees.

More recent efforts towards integration of database fine-grained concurrency control and replication techniques use snapshot isolation [11, 23, 20] to minimize consistency maintenance overheads. These solutions depend on support for multiversioning within each database replica. In contrast, our solution dynamically creates the required versions on a set of distributed replicas.

8. Conclusions

In this paper, we introduce novel lightweight reconfiguration techniques for the database tier in dynamic content web sites. Our solution is based on an in-memory replication algorithm, called Dynamic Multiversioning, which provides transparent scaling with strong consistency and ease of reconfiguration at the same time.

Dynamic Multiversioning offers high concurrency by exploiting the naturally arising versions across asynchronous database replicas. We avoid duplication of database functionality in the scheduler for consistency maintenance by integrating the replication process with the database concurrency control. Furthermore, we avoid copy-on-write overheads associated with systems that use stand-alone database multiversioning offering snapshot isolation. We show how a version-aware scheduler algorithm distributes transactions requesting different version numbers across different nodes, thus keeping aborts due to version conflicts at negligible rates.

Our evaluation shows that our system is flexible and efficient. While a primary replica is always needed in our in-memory tier, a set of active slaves can be adaptively and transparently expanded to seamlessly accommodate faults. We scale a web site using an InnoDB on-disk database back-end by factors of 14.6, 17.6 and 6.5 for the TPC-W browsing, shopping and ordering mixes, respectively when interposing our intermediate in-memory tier with 9 replicas. We also show that our in-memory tier has the flexibility to incorporate a spare backup after a fault without any noticeable impact on performance due to reconfiguration.

References

[1] IBM DB2 High Availability and Disaster Recovery. http://www.ibm.com/db2/.

[2] Mysql Database Server. http://www.mysql.com/.

[3] Oracle Real Application Clusters 10g. http://www.oracle.com/technology/products/database/clustering/.

[4] C. Amza, E. Cecchet, A. Chanda, A. Cox, S. Elnikety, R. Gil, J. Marguerite, K. Rajamani, and W. Zwaenepoel. Specification and implementation of dynamic web site benchmarks. In *5th IEEE Workshop on Workload Characterization*, November 2002.

[5] C. Amza, A. Cox, and W. Zwaenepoel. Conflict-aware scheduling for dynamic content applications. In *Proceedings of the Fifth USENIX Symposium on Internet Technologies and Systems*, pages 71–84, Mar. 2003.

[6] C. Amza, A. Cox, and W. Zwaenepoel. Distributed versioning: Consistent replication for scaling back-end databases of dynamic content web sites. In *ACM/IFIP/Usenix International Middleware Conference*, June 2003.

[7] The Apache Software Foundation. http://www.apache.org/.

[8] P. Bernstein, V. Hadzilacos, and N. Goodman. *Concurrency Control and Recovery in Database Systems*. Addison-Wesley, Reading, Massachusetts, 1987.

[9] E. Cecchet, J. Marguerite, and W. Zwaenepoel. C-jdbc: Flexible database clustering middleware. In *Proceedings of the USENIX 2004 Annual Technical Conference*, Jun 2004.

[10] E. Cecchet, J. Marguerite, and W. Zwaenepoel. RAIDb: Redundant array of inexpensive databases. In *IEEE/ACM International Symposium on Parallel and Distributed Applications (ISPA'04)*, December 2004.

[11] S. Elnikety, F. Pedone, and W. Zwaenepoel. Generalized snapshot isolation and a prefix-consistent implementation. Technical Report IC/2004/21, EPFL, 2004.

[12] IBM. High availability with DB2 UDB and Steeleye Life-keeper. IBM Center for Advanced Studies Conference (CASCON): Technology Showcase, Toronto, Canada, Oct 2003.

[13] B. Kemme and G. Alonso. A New Approach to Developing and Implementing Eager Database Replication Protocols. In *ACM Transactions on Data Base Systems*, volume 25, pages 333–379, September 2000.

[14] B. Kemme and G. Alonso. Don't be lazy, be consistent: Postgres-R, a new way to implement database replication. In *The VLDB Journal*, pages 134–143, 2000.

[15] D. Lowell and P. Chen. Free transactions with Rio Vista. In *Proceedings of the 16th ACM Symposium on Operating Systems Principles*, Oct. 1997.

[16] K. Manassiev, M. Mihailescu, and C. Amza. Exploiting distributed version concurrency in a transactional memory cluster. In *PPOPP*, pages 198–208, 2006.

[17] MySQL Cluster. `http://www.mysql.com/products/database/cluster/`.

[18] M. Patino-Martinez, R. Jimenez-Peris, B. Kemme, and G. Alonso. Scalable replication in database clusters. In *DISC '00: Proceedings of the 14th International Conference on Distributed Computing*, pages 315–329. Springer-Verlag, 2000.

[19] PHP Hypertext Preprocessor. http://www.php.net.

[20] C. Plattner and G. Alonso. Ganymed: Scalable replication for transactional web applications. In *Proceedings of the 5th ACM/IFIP/USENIX International Middleware Conference, Toronto, Canada*, October 18-22 2004.

[21] G. Soundararajan, C. Amza, and A. Goel. Database replication policies for dynamic content applications. In *EuroSys'06: Proceedings of the EuroSys 2006 Conference*, pages 89–102. ACM, 2006.

[22] Transaction Processing Council. http://www.tpc.org/.

[23] S. Wu and B. Kemme. Postgres-r(si): Combining replica control with concurrency controlbased on snapshot isolation. In *Proceedings of the 21st International Conference on Data Engineering*, Apr 2005.

[24] Y. Zhou, P. Chen, and K. Li. Fast cluster failover using virtual memory-mapped communication. In *Proc. of the Int'l Conference on Supercomputing*, June 1999.

Improving recoverability in multi-tier storage systems

Marcos K. Aguilera*, Kimberly Keeton*, Arif Merchant*,
Kiran-Kumar Muniswamy-Reddy+, Mustafa Uysal*
*HP Labs, Palo Alto, CA, USA and +Harvard University, Cambridge, MA, USA

Abstract

Enterprise storage systems typically contain multiple storage tiers, each having its own performance, reliability, and recoverability. The primary motivation for this multi-tier organization is cost, as storage tier costs vary considerably. In this paper, we describe a file system called TierFS that stores files at multiple storage tiers while providing high recoverability at all tiers. To achieve this goal, TierFS uses several novel techniques that leverage coupling between multiple tiers to reduce data loss, take consistent snapshots across tiers, provide continuous data protection, and improve recovery time. We evaluate TierFS with analytical models, showing that TierFS can provide better recoverability than a conventional design of similar cost.

1 Introduction

The explosive growth of digital data prompts us to rethink the way we design and use storage systems to keep enormous volumes of data at a reasonable cost. Current enterprise systems comprise multiple online storage *tiers*, each with its own features and cost: high-end tiers use expensive, highly reliable disk arrays and typically provide remote mirrors, snapshots, and daily backups; middle storage tiers may use cheaper mid-range disk arrays and might only provide snapshots and daily backups; and low-end tiers might use inexpensive disk appliances protected by weekly backups to decrease operational cost. Administrators place data on each of these tiers according to the business value and access characteristics of the data. Thus, business-critical data is placed on the highest tier, while less-important information is placed on lower tiers. However, when the administrator is constrained by limited space in the highest, most expensive tiers, data may be placed in a lower tier than is desirable.

Different storage tiers provide different levels of performance, reliability, and recoverability. Recoverability is the ability to recover data when there are problems, such as operator mistakes, disk crashes, site failures, or disasters, which are likely to occur within the lifetime of a system. Better recoverability can be achieved through remote mirroring, snapshots, and frequent backups, which all come at

a cost.

In this paper, our goal is to improve the recoverability-cost trade-off of storage systems, that is, to provide better recoverability at a lower cost. We propose a multi-tier file system called *TierFS* that employs a *recoverability log* to boost the recoverability of lower tiers by using the highest tier. The recoverability log stores an extra copy of updates destined for a lower tier until the lower tier is protected by a backup. In a conventional multi-tier storage system, data stored in a lower tier typically suffers from a considerable loss of recent updates if a recovery from backup is needed (say, due to a failure), since the backups may be infrequent. The recoverability log eliminates the backup-window data loss, because recent updates can be recovered from the log copy on the highest tier. By logging updates to all tiers and keeping them around, the recoverability log can also provide *continuous data protection*, which offers users a fine-grained set of recovery points—finer than the backup frequency of each tier. Finally, the recoverability log enables TierFS to take *consistent snapshots of all tiers* (to produce a consistent backup of the file system) without blocking file system writes. TierFS also provides a new mechanism to *improve recovery time*, by applying the recovery log in the background after restoring a backup copy and by using the recovery log to facilitate coordinated recovery using both a local, fast, but less up-to-date backup copy and a relatively slow, but more up-to-date remote mirror. To the best of our knowledge, TierFS is the first system that couples multiple storage tiers to improve recoverability.

We evaluate TierFS with analytical models to determine the overheads and benefits of using the recoverability log and the parallel recovery technique. We find that TierFS can provide a system with better recoverability than a conventional system of similar cost.

The remainder of the paper is organized as follows. Section 2 provides background on storage recoverability and multi-tier storage systems. Section 3 outlines the design of TierFS and introduces several mechanisms for coupling tiers to enhance recoverability. Section 4 describes our evaluation methodology, and Section 5 presents results. We describe related work in Section 6, and conclude in Section 7.

677

2 Background

In this section, we first explain storage recoverability, and provide background on the data protection techniques used to provide recoverability. We then explain how these techniques are used in tiered storage systems.

2.1 Recoverability metrics and techniques

Recoverability is the ability to recover from problems, like user mistakes, disk crashes, or disasters. Recoverability is measured using two metrics: *recent data loss* and *recovery time*. *Recent data loss* measures how much recent data (measured in time) is lost when recovery is performed. For example, if a disk gets backed up every day and the disk fails, then recovery can result in loss of data of up to one day. The best value of this metric is zero, which means that all updates are recovered. *Recovery time* measures how long the recovery process takes until data is available again.

Storage systems are designed to provide recoverability of the *primary copy* of the application's evolving dataset, using techniques like backups, snapshots, continuous data protection (CDP) and remote mirroring. A storage system will typically have multiple *point-in-time copies* of the same dataset, which capture the state of the data at different points in its evolution. Techniques are often configured to create point-in-time copies with varying frequency, which is referred to as *recovery point granularity*. Snapshots and backups create discrete recovery points, while CDP creates continuous recovery points. Recovery point granularity determines the ability to restore to an earlier point-in-time copy, often referred to as *time-travel recoverability*.

Backups are used to make relatively infrequent point-in-time copies by copying the full dataset (*full backups*) or the updates since the last backup (*incremental backups*). Backups have been traditionally stored on tape; more recently, decreasing disk costs have resulted in disk-based backup systems, as well. To protect against site disasters, backup copies must be transported to an offsite vault.

Snapshots capture the state of storage at a given point in time, typically in a very space efficient way by using copy-on-write and similar techniques. Like backups, snapshots are useful to undo user mistakes and software errors. However, snapshots are less useful to recover from disk failures or disasters because they share data with the primary copy; so if the primary copy is lost, the snapshot is affected, too. Snapshots are also useful to produce consistent online backups: the system first takes a snapshot and then derives the backup from the snapshot.

Continuous data protection (CDP) creates a continuous set of recovery points, rather than just one every hour or day, to permit finer grained time-travel recovery. A simple way to provide CDP is to create a copy of a file as it is modified (e.g., using VMS file versioning or VersionFS [10]). A more space-efficient way to provide CDP is to use copy-on-write (e.g., Elephant [12] and CVFS [14]): when a file is overwritten, the new data blocks are written at a new location, but the old and new versions share all unmodified blocks.

Storage devices may also have the capability to maintain *remote mirror* copies at multiple geographic locations, typically at one or more remote sites. The geographic dispersion capability allows a storage tier to survive larger failure scopes (e.g., a site disaster). *Synchronous mirroring* ensures that both copies are always in sync, while with *asynchronous mirroring*, the remote copy may lag behind by a few seconds. Remote mirroring is provided by high-end and some mid-range disk arrays.

2.2 Tiers of storage

Enterprises keep a huge amount of online data, ranging from critical data required to run the business to emails kept according to regulations to derived or historical information for trend analysis. A variety of online storage alternatives exist for storing these vast quantities of data, ranging from high-end disk arrays with snapshot and remote mirroring capabilities, to small disk appliances used to aggregate a few disks together, which offer only limited data protection (e.g., RAID). These alternatives differ in cost by as much as an order of magnitude. As a result, enterprises use high-end disk arrays very sparingly, only to keep the most important data. They set up storage systems comprising multiple tiers of storage, and allocate their online datasets to these storage tiers based on the data's business value and access characteristics.

A sample multi-tier storage system might have three tiers. At the highest (most expensive) tier, there are high-end disk arrays with remote mirroring and frequent point-in-time snapshot capabilities. At the middle tier, there are mid-range disk arrays with less frequent point-in-time snapshots and without remote mirroring. And at the lowest tier, there are inexpensive disks managed by software or firmware RAID. Lower tiers with large capacity and/or small update rates may be backed up less frequently than higher tiers, to reduce operational costs.

Leveraging distinct capabilities of multiple storage tiers dates back to *hierarchical storage systems (HSM)*, which coupled disk systems with tape storage to transparently increase the apparent storage capacity. For example, HPSS [5] automatically moves infrequently-accessed files from a higher tier (disk) to a lower tier (tape) or another archival device, and then automatically moves data back to disk when access is requested. HPSS allows files be read or written only at the highest tier, and so if a file has been migrated to a lower tier, it needs to be migrated back before it is accessed. This restriction exists for historical reasons, because early HSM systems treated lower tiers as offline devices.

More recently, the VxFS file system introduced greater flexibility in dealing with multiple storage tiers [6]. VxFS allows users or administrators to define placement rules to

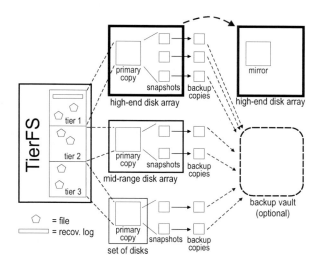

Figure 1. *TierFS uses multiple storage tiers to provide high recoverability at low relative cost. It leverages the highest tier—one with good recoverability—to boost the recoverability of lower tiers.*

indicate in which tier new files are created, and migration rules to indicate when a file in one tier should be moved to another tier. These policies can be based on a file's name, extension, creator, timestamps, and/or frequency of access.

3 TierFS design

TierFS, illustrated in Figure 1, couples multiple storage tiers to provide a high level of recoverability across all storage tiers. TierFS uses the tier with the highest recoverability and performance to store a *recoverability log*, which contains a copy of updates destined for a lower tier until the lower tier is protected by a backup. TierFS uses the recoverability log, along with the snapshot and backup facilities of the individual tiers, to provide improved recent data loss and faster recovery time for files stored in lower tiers, consistent multi-tier file system backups, and continuous data protection.

Each file or directory in TierFS has a *home tier*, where the contents of the file are stored. The home of any file can be any tier, and users are not required to know the home tier of a file to access it (i.e., there is a single namespace). TierFS can transparently migrate a file to a different tier if desired, based on user or administrator control. Similar to VxFS [6], in TierFS a file's initial home tier and any subsequent migration can be controlled by simple rules based on file attributes such as owner, extension, and modification and access time. The details of these mapping and migration rules are outside the scope of this paper.

The improved recoverability provided by TierFS enables allocation of files to tiers to be based on considerations other

than recoverability, such as cost and performance. For example, a cost-driven design might choose to place no files at the highest tier, which reduces its size to what is needed by the internal logs of TierFS. Another design might use the highest tier (which is typically the fastest) to store files that are frequently used in an application's critical path to boost performance. However, these files are not necessarily the ones that need the highest recoverability.

The following sections explain several techniques that TierFS uses to provide good recoverability for lower tiers.

3.1 Improving recent data loss

TierFS uses the highest tier to maintain a *recoverability log*, which contains an extra copy of updates destined for a lower tier until the lower tier is protected by a backup. This technique, similar to file system journaling, improves the recent data loss characteristics of lower tiers. When we recover a lower tier from its most recent backup (or snapshot) copy, we can replay the most recent entries in the recovery log that are not reflected in the backup, in order to prevent data loss. For this technique to work, we must ensure that log entries are garbage collected only after (1) the updates have been applied to the appropriate tier, and (2) since then, the tier has been backed up.

If protection against site disaster is desired, TierFS further delays garbage collection of the recovery log until the backup has arrived at a remote vault, which can take a long time. If the highest tier employs remote mirroring (as shown in Figure 1), TierFS can take periodic snapshots of the mirrored log at the remote site, as an optimization. We can then relax the above requirement and garbage collect the recovery log when it has been snapshotted at the remote mirror. The remote site serves as protection against disasters, in lieu of the vault. The reason for the snapshot is to keep data at the remote site after the log gets garbage collected. Only the log (not the entire highest tier) needs to be snapshotted, which is achieved by keeping the log in its own logical volume. Once the backup arrives at the vault, the log snapshot at the remote site can be deleted.

We use a *block-level* log, which refers to operations on physical blocks rather than files, to make the log *idempotent*, so that it can be replayed without destroying data. Idempotency is important because TierFS does not always have perfect control of the copying mechanisms in each tier. For example, if a disk array at a lower tier keeps an asynchronous remote mirror, the mirror may lag behind by a bounded amount of time that is unknown by TierFS. If TierFS had to recover using this mirror and the log were not idempotent, it would have to replay the log from the first entry not yet applied to the mirror, which is unknown. With an idempotent log, TierFS can replay the log conservatively, by starting at the point corresponding to the largest lag allowed by the disk array.

The benefit of the recoverability log is that the recent

data loss of all tiers becomes equal to the recent data loss of the highest tier. However, there are some overheads. First, each update is written twice: once to the log and then again to the appropriate tier. TierFS partly offsets this overhead by performing both updates in parallel, where the log update is synchronous and the other update is asynchronous. Second, the log takes up space. In theory, the log can become arbitrarily large before it is garbage collected; however, our evaluations show that the log size under real workloads is reasonable.

3.2 Improving recovery time

We now turn our attention to recovery from failures. TierFS uses two techniques to improve the time to recover a tier (e.g., in the event of a disk array failure).

The first technique reduces the overhead of applying the updates in the recoverability log. Recall that recovery of a tier in TierFS comprises two steps: populating the tier with the latest available backup and applying the changes in the recoverability log that are not reflected in the backup. With TierFS, only the first step contributes to recovery time: after the first step, the tier is ready for use in TierFS (without any recent data loss), because TierFS remaps reads from that tier to the recovery log for the blocks that are in the log. Therefore, replaying the recovery log can be done online as a background task.

The second technique applies to a tier that has a remote mirror as well as local backups (e.g., the highest tier). Recovery from a remote mirror requires copying the entire remote volume into the local volume. Because the connection to the remote site is provisioned to only carry recent data updates, its bandwidth is typically small compared to that of an archival device (such as disk or tape), sometimes by orders of magnitude. Thus, transferring an entire volume from the remote site to the local site can take a long time. Recovering from a backup is faster, but the backup has less recent data than the remote mirror copy. Thus, there is a trade-off between recovery time and recent data loss. TierFS breaks this trade-off by recovering the tier from backup and then only transferring the most recent updates from the remote site. TierFS uses the recoverability log to determine the blocks that are changed but might not be reflected in the latest backup. To do so, TierFS puts markers in the recoverability log to indicate when backups are made.

3.3 Consistent full-system backups

The recoverability log can also enable consistent full-system backups of all tiers. While tiers are backed up at different rates based on cost considerations, there is also a desire to periodically perform full-system backups of all tiers, for archival purposes. The challenge is to ensure that the backup is *consistent*.

In a traditional, single-tier file system, backup consistency comes from snapshots: a snapshot preserves the state of the whole file system at a single time, which is then used to populate the backup, even as the file system is changing. In TierFS, creating consistent backups poses an additional challenge: how to synchronize snapshots between tiers when each tier might implement its own snapshots. The problem is that snapshots of different tiers could be taken at slightly different times, even if they are requested simultaneously, and a backup made from such snapshots might be inconsistent.

If the recoverability log is extended to log updates to all tiers, rather than just the lower tiers, it can help solve the consistent backup problem. Before taking snapshots, TierFS pauses the block-level writes to each tier at a point when they form a consistent file system image (e.g., there are no unattached inodes). TierFS can continue to accept file system writes without blocking, though, because they are logged in the recoverability log, even though the block-level writes to each tier are paused. Once writes are paused, TierFS takes a snapshot of each tier, without fear of inconsistency, even if the snapshots are taken at slightly different times. TierFS uses standard techniques like copy-on-write to implement snapshot capabilities for tiers that do not provide them natively.

3.4 Providing CDP

TierFS uses its recoverability log for yet another purpose: to provide continuous data protection (CDP) by using the recoverability log and appropriate prior point-in-time copies of each tier. The basic idea is to store updates to all tiers in the recoverability log, and to retain and protect them rather than garbage collecting them as soon as a backup and/or offsite copy of the data is created, as described in Section 3.1. To ensure log entries are available for CDP, we modify the garbage collection mechanism of Section 3.1 in the obvious way: a log entry is discarded only after the lower tier has been updated, and both the log and the lower tier have been backed up. In addition, if protection against site disasters is desired, both the log and lower tier updates must have arrived at the vault or have been remotely snapshotted.

TierFS's approach to CDP provides two advantages over previous approaches. First, it makes it efficient to move the voluminous amount of CDP information to backup tiers, by simply copying the sequential log. Second, because log entries are ordered by time, it is easier to manage CDP information stored online or in a backup; for example, one can delete CDP data for uninteresting periods by simply erasing the appropriate log segments (if stored online) or by getting rid of the appropriate backup archive (if stored in a backup). As a result, it becomes feasible to preserve CDP information for archival purposes.

However, using logs to provide CDP poses a difficulty: if a block has not been modified for a long time then its last log entry will be far in the past. This scenario creates a problem for garbage collection and recovery, which we call the *10-year log problem*: if a file has not been modified for 10 years and a user overwrites it, then going back just a few seconds before the overwrite requires a log that is 10 years long! This problem could be avoided by keeping an undo log in addition to the recoverability log of TierFS, but we would prefer to maintain just one log. Furthermore, undo logs have their own drawbacks: they are more expensive to maintain, as writing new entries to the undo log requires reading of the old information, and they are inefficient for restoring to points far in the past, as they require all intervening operations to be undone.

TierFS solves the 10-year log problem by using backup or other point-in-time copies of each tier, which provide a starting point from which to replay the log. Thus, to recover the file system to some time t we first use a backup or other point-in-time copy to recover the system to the latest available time t_0 before time t. We then replay the log entries from t_0 to t. In other words, the log entries between two backup copies enable CDP in that time range.

3.5 Availability and performance of tiers

Availability refers to the ability to mask failures, that is, to continue normal operation as if failures never occurred. While TierFS improves the recoverability of all tiers, each tier keeps its original availability. Thus, in the period between a failure and its recovery, some of the tiers may be available, while others are not. Because TierFS places all information needed to access a file in the same tier (including its inode and data blocks), files in available tiers will continue to be available. For other files, TierFS will block accesses until they have been recovered. This provides a form of graceful degradation, similar to the DGRAID [13] system. TierFS also places the root directory and other top-level directories at the highest tier as an additional precaution to make the top level of the name space accessible.

TierFS may improve performance of a tier when there are bursts of writes, since writes are acknowledged as soon as they are placed in the log at the highest tier. TierFS's total write bandwidth is limited by the maximum write bandwidth of the highest tier (e.g., high-end disk array bandwidth or remote mirroring interconnect bandwidth). But note that TierFS writes updates to the log sequentially, so it uses write bandwidth at the highest tier efficiently. In addition, instead of a single log, TierFS can keep several logs—one for each tier—which are stored on separate volumes and/or devices at the highest tier for greater bandwidth. As for read bandwidth, TierFS will typically read data from its home tier, unless a more up-to-date copy exists in the recoverability log. Thus, TierFS tends to preserve the read bandwidth of each tier.

Category	Metric	Description
Recoverability	recent data loss	data loss on recovery
	recovery time	duration of recovery
Operational requirements	storage bandwidth	under normal operation
	tape bandwidth	under normal operation
	remote bandwidth	under normal operation
	storage capacity	data stored after a month
	tape capacity	data on tapes after a month
	remote capacity	remote site data after a month
	vault capacity	data at vault after a month

Table 1. *Metrics for evaluation.*

4 Evaluation

We evaluate TierFS's recoverability, bandwidth requirements and capacity requirements under several workloads. We compare TierFS against two alternative approaches: a system that stores all its data on a single high-end storage tier, and a conventional multi-tier file system that does not employ our mechanisms to improve recoverability. We provide the details of our evaluation methodology (Section 4.1), the metrics and the faults we consider (Section 4.2), the alternative approaches (Section 4.3), and our experimental setup (Section 4.4).

4.1 Methodology

We evaluate the recoverability of TierFS and the alternatives we consider through analytical models. We extend the dependability models of Keeton and Merchant [8] to derive the data loss upon recovery for multi-tier systems. These extensions model the behavior and overheads of the techniques that TierFS uses to improve recoverability. We combine these models with a recovery graph representation [7] of the schedule of recovery operations to compute the recovery time under several failure scenarios and workloads, as well as normal mode capacity and bandwidth utilization. We use this model framework to evaluate the recovery time, data loss upon recovery, and capacity and bandwidth utilizations for all of the alternative approaches we consider.

4.2 Metrics and failure types

Our evaluation consists of two parts. The first part measures recoverability under different failure scenarios, and the second part measures operational requirements under normal system operation. Table 1 presents the metrics we use for our evaluation.

The recovery metrics—recent data loss and recovery time—are described in Section 2. We evaluate recovery under three different types of failures. A *storage device failure* causes complete data loss at one of the tiers. We assume that the highest tier has sufficient redundancy that it is unlikely to fail. A *site failure* causes complete data loss at all tiers. A *human error* requires a recovery from a past point in time, rather than the most recent version.

The meaning of *recent data loss* for a recovery from hu-

Parameter	Tier 1	Tier 2	Tier 3
Online Bandwidth	13 GB/s	675 MB/s	256 MB/s
Remote Mirror	Synchronous	None	None
Snapshot frequency	Every 4 hours	Daily	None
Snapshots retained	Last 12	Last 2	N/A
Backup frequency (full)	Daily	Weekly	Weekly
Backup frequency (incr)	None	Daily	None
Backups retained	Last 28 days	Last 28 days	Last 28 days
Shipment to remote vault	Weekly	Weekly	Weekly
Backups in vault	Last 52 weeks	Last 52 weeks	Last 52 weeks
CDP backups retained[†]	Last 28 days	Last 28 days	Last 28 days
CDP backups in vault[†]	Last 52 weeks	Last 52 weeks	Last 52 weeks

[†] for TierFS+CDP system only

Table 2. *Data protection techniques for the three storage tiers in our evaluation.*

man error is the difference between the time to which the user *wants* to recover the system and the time to which recovery is possible.

We measure operational requirements through the resources utilized by each system. We consider bandwidth and capacity at each storage tier, as well as for the remote site. We also consider capacity used at the vault.

4.3 Systems

We evaluate four different systems:

- *Single-tier*: This system stores all data in a single high-end storage tier. This system is our benchmark system; its drawback is its high cost.
- *Basic multi-tier*: This system stores data in multiple tiers, but does not couple tiers together to improve recoverability.
- *TierFS*: Our TierFS system couples multiple tiers to improve recoverability. The recoverability log contains updates to all but the highest tier, and the log is garbage collected aggressively, as described in Section 3.1.
- *TierFS+CDP*: In this TierFS variant, the recoverability log contains and preserves updates to all tiers, to enable CDP, as described in Section 3.4.

4.4 Experimental setup

We use a three-tier storage system for our evaluation, as shown in Table 2. Tier 1, the highest tier in our setup, consists of two high-end disk arrays that are remote mirrors of each other and connected using four OC3 links (155 Mbps each). This tier uses remote mirroring, snapshots, local backups, and tape vaults for data protection. Tier 2 consists of mid-range disk arrays that provide snapshots, local backups, and tape vaults; but no remote mirrors for data protection. Tier 3 consists of a disk appliance and uses only infrequent backups and tape vaults. All three tiers employ RAID-protected online storage. Additionally, all three tiers share a single remote vault, which is located at the same site as tier 1's remote mirror.

We use two workgroup file server workloads for our eval-

Parameter	Harvard trace	Cello trace
Dates of trace	9-11/2001	9/2002
Capacity (GB)	450	1360
Avg. Access Rate (KB/s)	161	1028
Avg. Update Rate (KB/s)	103	799
Unique Update Rate (KB/s)	60	317
Peak:Avg. Update Ratio	1000	10
Peak:Avg. Access Ratio	1000	10

Table 3. *Summary of the workload characteristics used in our evaluation.*

System	Tier-2 failure	Tier-3 failure	Site failure
Single Tier	—	—	0
Basic multi-tier	48 hrs	192 hrs	384 hrs
TierFS	0	0	0
TierFS+CDP	0	0	0

Table 4. *Recent data loss for the Harvard workload under various failures.*

uation representing research and software development workloads in an industrial research lab (Cello workload) and a university (Harvard workload [3]). The Cello trace contains I/O activity from a departmental server for a total of 254 users and the Harvard trace contains NFS activity of a Network Appliance Filer for a total of 416 users. Table 3 summarizes the characteristics of these two workloads.

The multi-tier storage system is used differently by each system we evaluate. The single-tier system places all of its data onto the highest tier. The remaining systems use all three tiers to store file system data. They place 10% of all data from a given file system on tier 1, the next 30% onto tier 2, and the remaining 60% of the data on tier 3. This allocation represents the importance and the expected use of the data within the file system.

5 Experimental results

In this section, we present our results. First we evaluate all systems for recoverability; both to recover to the most recent version of the data and to recover to a past version, i.e., time travel. We then look at the bandwidth and capacity requirements of TierFS and the other alternatives. We conclude this section with a discussion.

5.1 Recoverability

TierFS is designed to have zero recent data loss when the system is recovered to its latest version. Table 4 shows the data loss for failures of tiers 2 and 3, and a site failure for the Harvard workload; results for the Cello workload are very similar. As can be seen, Single-tier, TierFS, and TierFS+CDP have zero loss, whereas the loss for the Basic multi-tier system is considerable.

Figure 2 shows the recovery time for various systems on the y-axis, under three types of failures, represented by the x-axis. As can be seen, in both the Harvard and Cello work-loads, recovery time for TierFS and TierFS+CDP is essentially the same as for a Basic multi-tier file system, because replaying the recoverability log occurs in the background. For site failures, Single-tier performs much better than all other systems, because with the other systems, recovery of tiers 2 and 3 needs to wait for the arrival of backup tapes from the vault (which takes 24 hours in our setup). Single-tier can recover from the mirror over the network.

5.2 Time travel recoverability

In this section, we explore the time travel recoverability of the various systems. Certain classes of failures, including human errors, software bugs, and virus infections, require the ability to recover the system to a point in the past. This time travel recoverability is possible in systems that support point-in-time copies and continuous data protection.

Figure 3(a) quantifies the recent data loss that the systems incur when recovering to a recovery target in the past for the Harvard workload. We observed similar results for the Cello workload. Where multiple tiers exhibit different recent data loss values, we present the maximum value.

The Single-tier system experiences different amounts of recent data loss, depending on how far in the past the recovery target is. Snapshots can recover the recent past with minimal data loss (up to four hours, the granularity of the snapshots); daily backups can recover the moderate past, with data loss of up to a day; and the weekly vault copies can recover the distant past, with up to a week of data loss. Both the Basic multi-tier system and TierFS provide a uniform recent data loss of up to a week, due to the weekly backup policy for tier 3. TierFS+CDP provides complete recoverability, with zero data loss. We note that none of the systems can recover to a point older than the retention period of the vault (one year).

Figure 3(b) quantifies the time to recover to a point in the past for the Harvard workload. We observed similar results for the Cello workload. The Single-tier system achieves very fast recovery for a snapshot, but takes several hours to restore a backup copy, and over a day to restore a vaulted copy (due to the delay to retrieve the vaulted tapes). The remaining systems (Basic multi-tier, TierFS, and TierFS+CDP) take several hours to recover recent and moderately recent targets; this recovery time is limited by the need to recover a tape backup for tier 3. As with the Single-tier system, recovery of the distant past takes over a day.

5.3 Bandwidth usage

Figure 4 shows the peak operational bandwidth of TierFS compared to the alternatives. We focus on the tier 1 bandwidth, since it is the most expensive. First, we observe that the Single-tier system has a substantially higher peak bandwidth at tier 1 than any other alternative. The Basic multi-tier system has the lowest peak bandwidth at tier

1, as we expect. The peak bandwidth of the TierFS and TierFS+CDP systems ranges between a quarter and a third of the Single-tier peak bandwidth. We note that these alternatives have similar recoverabilities. The bandwidth requirements of TierFS and TierFS+CDP are significantly higher than that of the Basic multi-tier system, due to the bandwidth requirements of maintaining the recoverability log.

5.4 Capacity usage

We now consider the storage space used by TierFS and alternatives after one month of normal system operation, as shown in Figure 5. The Single-tier system has the highest capacity requirement in tier 1, because it stores all the data there. In addition, it requires a large number of point-in-time copies in order to preserve recoverability. The Basic multi-tier design, on the other hand, uses the lowest capacity in tier 1, but the total capacity over all tiers is similar to the capacity usage of the Single-tier system. TierFS and TierFS+CDP require tier 1 storage capacity that is intermediate between the Single-tier and the Basic multi-tier systems. The precise amount of storage required depends on the workload, but we find that it is much smaller than the Single tier system requires, in most cases. On the other hand, as seen in the capacity requirements for the Cello workload, the capacity requirements at the remote site can be considerable for TierFS+CDP, approaching that of the Single tier system. Note, however, that the TierFS+CDP system offers lower time travel data loss than the Single tier system, particularly if the desired recovery target is well in the past.

The archival capacity requirements of the four alternatives are shown in Figure 6. The Single-tier system has a high capacity requirement at the tape library because it keeps all its data in tier 1, which gets backed up frequently to maintain recoverability of the data. The other alternatives have similar (and lower) tape library requirements. The Single-tier, Basic multi-tier and TierFS systems have similar vault capacity requirements; however, the TierFS+CDP system has a slightly higher vaulting requirement since it vaults CDP data.

5.5 Discussion

We have compared four systems, the Single-tier system that stores all the data on a single, highly recoverable storage tier; the Basic multi-tier system that distributes data over disk arrays with varying levels of recoverability, without an attempt to give the data in low-recoverability tiers additional protection; TierFS, which stores data in multiple disk arrays, but adds mechanisms to protect the data stored in low-recoverability tiers; and, finally, TierFS+CDP, a system that additionally provides the ability to recover to any point in time, in order to recover from software and human errors. We find that the Single-tier system can provide high recoverability, but the cost of such a system is very high,

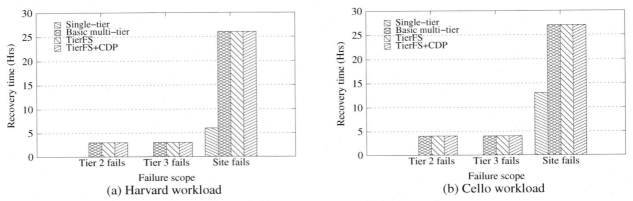

Figure 2. *Time to recover to the latest version.*

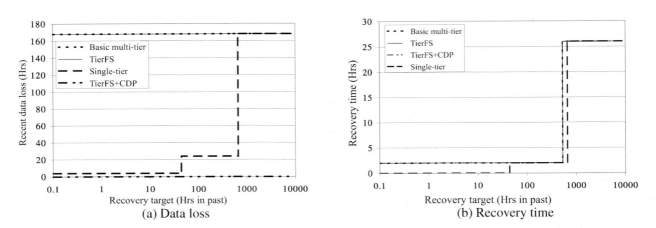

Figure 3. *Data loss and recovery time to travel to past version for the Harvard workload. Results for the Cello workload are similar.*

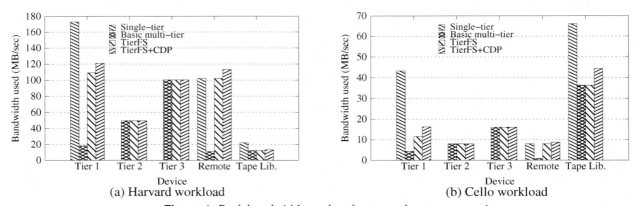

Figure 4. *Peak bandwidth used under normal system operation.*

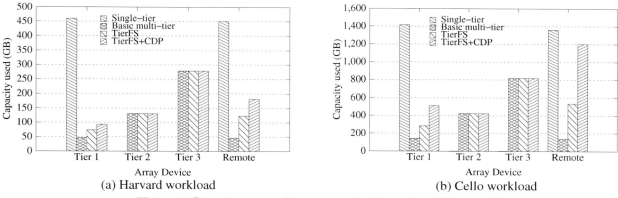

Figure 5. *Capacity usage after one month of normal system operation.*

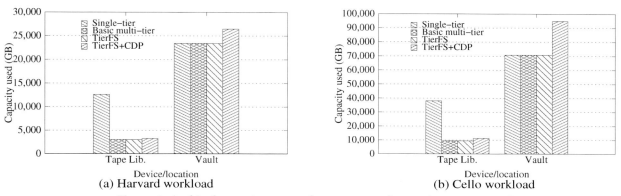

Figure 6. *Archival capacity usage after one year of normal system operation.*

because it stores all its data on an expensive medium. The Basic multi-tier system is much less expensive, but it is subject to substantial data loss in case of failures in the lower tiers. TierFS enables us to store data in multiple tiers, and enables recoverability comparable to the Single- tier system, but requires a fraction of the capacity that Single-tier uses on the highest storage tier. The only significant downside of TierFS compared to the Single-tier system is that, in case of a site failure, the recovery time of TierFS is substantially higher because of the time to recover data from a vault. TierFS+CDP goes a step further in recoverability, by allowing recovery to arbitrary points in time, again with a much lower cost than a Single-tier system.

We also evaluated scenarios where the bandwidth and capacity requirements are increased by a factor of ten for both workloads. We observed the same trends across the systems in recovery behavior for the various failure scenarios, and in bandwidth and capacity usage.

6 Related work

The VxFS file system places files on multiple tiers and uses user-defined rules to place and migrate files [6]. Unlike TierFS, VxFS provides no mechanisms to improve recoverability of storage tiers.

There are many file systems that use logs, for purposes other than improving recoverability. The log-structured file system of Rosenblum and Ousterhout [11] uses sequential logs to avoid scattered writes to disk, hence improving write performance. Journaling file systems record file system changes in a log, called the journal, before applying them to the file system structures, to speed up file system recovery after a crash. Upon recovery, replaying the journal obviates the need for a full file system scan for inconsistencies. In contrast, TierFS uses the log for improving recoverability and providing continuous data protection for a less recoverable tier. Unlike a log-structured file system, which stores updates in the log as their final destination, with TierFS updates must eventually be sent to the appropriate storage tier. Thus, the recoverability log in TierFS is more similar to a write-ahead log.

Versioning file systems allow users to recover older versions of files (e.g., VMS, AFS [9], Elephant [12], and WAFL [4]). None of these file systems span multiple tiers, and many of them do not provide continuous data protection, either because they only snapshot at specific points in time (WAFL) or upon request (AFS), or because they do not track metadata operations such as renames (VMS). The only file systems that provide continuous versioning, as far as we know, are Elephant [12], CVFS [14], VersionFS [10], and the Wayback file system [2]. Of these, Elephant, CVFS, and VersionFS use specialized data structures to keep track of the common and distinct information of each version, rather than using logs to keep old versions of data. Thus, the old version's data is scattered, which makes it inefficient to transfer to archives or other tiers; data transfer, however, is not a goal of these systems. In contrast, TierFS uses a log to store the update history, which can be read sequentially and transferred efficiently. The Wayback file system [2] also uses logs, to store versioning information. TierFS is different from Wayback in three aspects: (1) Wayback uses undo logs, not redo logs; so, to create a log entry, Wayback needs to read a file's old data, which imposes extra overhead, (2) Wayback uses a separate log for each file, and logs are not stored sequentially one after the other, (3) in Wayback, log entries are permanent, without any proposed mechanisms for garbage collection, whereas in TierFS, old log entries are optionally archived and eventually removed.

Continuous data protection is also available in products from many companies [1]. These products operate either at the block level (typically block devices on a storage area network), file level (integrated with a file system), or application level (e.g., integrated with an email server or a database system). The idea is to tap into the stream of updates, and then store those updates to allow subsequent recovery of arbitrary points in time within a protection window. In this respect, TierFS is similar to file-level CDP products. The difference is that TierFS makes use of point-in-time copies to improve the efficiency and flexibility of CDP. For example, existing products can only provide CDP within a recent time window, typically a few days, and there is no way to archive CDP information.

AutoRAID [15] provides block-storage comprising two tiers: the first one uses data mirroring for high performance, and the second uses RAID-5 for space efficiency. The system automatically migrates frequently-written blocks to the higher tier and less frequently written blocks to the lower tier to optimize performance. Unlike TierFS, AutoRAID does not provide mechanisms to bridge the reliability levels of its backing storage tiers, and couples tiers only for performance and capacity trade-offs.

7 Conclusions

We present the design and evaluation of TierFS, a file system that takes advantage of different storage tiers in an enterprise system. TierFS maintains a recoverability log at the highest tier to increase the recoverability of lower tiers. The result is a multi-tier system that reduces recent data loss to that of a single-tier system that uses only the highest tier, while using significantly fewer resources at the highest tier. TierFS uses the recoverability log in conjunction with snapshots and backups at the tiers to improve recovery time. The

recoverability log also enables consistent multi-tier backups and CDP. Our results show that coupling the tiers can yield substantial benefits over a conventional multi-tier system.

Acknowledgments. We thank Xiaozhou Li and the anonymous reviewers for many useful comments.

References

[1] CDP buyers guide, 2005. Available at http://www.snia.org/tech_activities/dmf/docs/CDP_Buyers_Guide_20050822.pdf.

[2] B. Cornell, P. A. Dinda, and F. E. Bustamante. Wayback: a user-level versioning file system for Linux. In *Proceedings of Usenix Annual Technical Conference, FREENIX Track*, pages 19–28, June 2004.

[3] D. Ellard, J. Ledlie, P. Malkani, and M. Seltzer. Passive NFS tracing of email and research workloads. In *Proceedings of the Conference on File and Storage Technologies*, pages 203–16, Mar. 2003.

[4] D. Hitz, J. Lau, and M. Malcolm. File system design for an NFS file server appliance. In *Proceedings of the USENIX Winter Technical Conference*, pages 235–246, Jan. 1994.

[5] HPSS user's guide, 1992. http://www.hpss-collaboration.org.

[6] G. Karche, M. Mamidi, and P. Massiglia. Using dynamic storage tiering, Apr. 2006. Available at http://www.symantec.com/enterprise/yellowbooks/index.jsp.

[7] K. Keeton, D. Beyer, E. Brau, A. Merchant, C. Santos, and A. Zhang. On the road to recovery: restoring data after disasters. In *Proceedings of the European Systems Conference*, pages 235–48, Apr. 2006.

[8] K. Keeton and A. Merchant. A framework for evaluating storage system dependability. In *Proceedings of the International Conference on Dependable Systems and Networks*, pages 877–886, June 2004.

[9] J. J. Kistler and M. Satyanarayanan. Disconnected operation in the Coda File System. *ACM Transactions on Computer Systems*, 10(1):3–25, Feb. 1992.

[10] K.-K. Muniswamy-Reddy, C. P. Wright, A. Himmer, and E. Zadok. A versatile and user-oriented versioning file system. In *Proceedings of the Conference on File and Storage Technologies*, pages 115–128, Mar. 2004.

[11] M. Rosenblum and J. K. Ousterhout. The design and implementation of a log-structured file system. *ACM Transactions on Computer Systems*, 10(1):26–52, Feb. 1992.

[12] D. S. Santry, M. J. Feeley, N. C. Hutchinson, A. C. Veitch, R. W. Carton, and J. Ofir. Deciding when to forget in the Elephant file system. In *Proceedings of the ACM Symposium on Operating Systems Principles*, pages 110–123, Dec. 1999.

[13] M. Sivathanu, V. Prabhakaran, A. C. Arpaci-Dusseau, and R. H. Arpaci-Dusseau. Improving storage system availability with D-GRAID. *ACM Transactions on Storage*, 1(2):133–170, May 2005.

[14] C. A. N. Soules, G. R. Goodson, J. D. Strunk, and G. Ganger. Metadata efficiency in versioning file systems. In *Proceedings of the Conference on File and Storage Technologies*, pages 43–58, Mar. 2003.

[15] J. Wilkes, R. Golding, C. Staelin, and T. Sullivan. The HP AutoRAID hierarchical storage system. *ACM Transactions on Computer Systems*, 14(1):108–136, Feb. 1996.

Portable and Efficient Continuous Data Protection for Network File Servers

Ningning Zhu   Tzi-cker Chiueh

Computer Science Department
Stony Brook University

Abstract

Continuous data protection, which logs every update to a file system, is an enabling technology to protect file systems against malicious attacks and/or user mistakes, because it allows each file update to be undoable. Existing implementations of continuous data protection work either at disk access interface or within the file system. Despite the implementation complexity, their performance overhead is significant when compared with file systems that do not support continuous data protection. Moreover, such kernel-level file update logging implementation is complex and cannot be easily ported to other operating systems. This paper describes the design and implementation of four user-level continuous data protection implementations for NFS servers, all of which work on top of the NFS protocol and thus can be easily ported to any operating systems that support NFS. Measurements obtained from running standard benchmarks and real-world NFS traces on these user-level continuous data protection systems demonstrate a surprising result: Performance of NFS servers protected by pure user-level continuous data protection schemes is comparable to that of unprotected vanilla NFS servers.

1 Introduction

Data in a file system could be lost or corrupted in the face of natural disasters, hardware/software failures, human mistakes or malicious attacks. While replication and mirroring represent effective defenses against hardware and site failures, they cannot protect file system data from human mistakes, software failures and malicious attacks, against which conventional data backup systems provide limited protection. Advanced multi-snapshots backup systems [12] decrease the amount of potential data loss, but still cannot completely prevent data loss. The most effective way to prevent these types of data losses is *continuous data protection* (CDP) or *comprehensive versioning*, which logs every modification to the file system and enables each file update operation to be undoable. CDP allows a user to rollback

his file system to any point in time in the past. As per-byte disk storage cost continues to drop precipitously and the financial penalty of data loss and system downtime increases significantly over time, CDP has emerged as a critical file system feature.

The key technical challenge for CDP is how to minimize the bandwidth and latency penalty associated with the file update logging it requires. Because file update logs are mainly for repair purpose, they are not expected to be accessed frequently. Therefore, it is possible to minimize the run-time performance overhead of CDP at the expense of increased access delay at repair time.

Previous versioning file systems [16, 11, 21] are based on kernel-level implementation, and thus are both complex and non-portable. Wayback [8] is a user-level versioning system and requires only a small kernel module. All of these systems incur non-trivial performance overhead. Some commercial products [3, 4] support continuous snapshotting at the user level but are tailored to specific applications such as Microsoft Exchange and Microsoft SQL rather than a general CDP solution for the entire file system.

The goal of this research is to develop user-level CDP implementations that incur minimal performance overhead and are portable across multiple platforms. Reparable File Service (RFS) [23] is designed to transparently augment existing NFS servers with user-level file update logging and automatic data repair upon detection of user mistakes or malicious attacks. RFS logs file updates in terms of NFS commands/responses, and can inter-operate with the existing IT infrastructure without requiring any modifications. In addition to the portability advantage, logging NFS commands/responses also leads to more compact log and simpler design, because one NFS operation can result in multiple inode/indirect-block/data-block updates. For example, an NFS request `create` involves the following local file system operations on the NFS server: (1) a new inode for the created file is generated, (2) an entry for the created file is added to the current directory, (3) the current directory file may be expanded with a new block, (4) the block pointer of the current directory file is updated to point to the new block, and (5) the inode of the directory file is updated

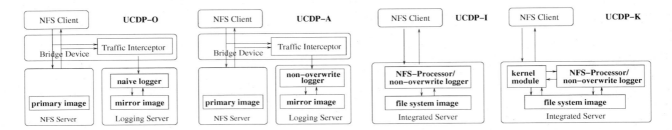

Figure 1. *Comparison among the system architectures of the four user-level CDP schemes studied in this paper. Both UCDP-O and UCDP-A require a Traffic Interceptor to intercept NFS commands and responses, process them and log them asynchronously. They differ in how they log write requests to disk. UCDP-I integrates NFS packet processing and file update logging into the protected NFS server and eliminates the need for a separate logging server. UCDP-K includes an in-kernel packet interception module to reduce context switching and memory copying overhead.*

with new attributes. As a consequence, a `create` operation may generate multiple log records at the inode/block level but only one NFS-level log record.

The file update logging scheme in RFS, called UCDP-O (user-level continuous data protection using overwriting) requires a separate logging server that contains a mirror file system of the protected NFS server, and thus could log each file update asynchronously to minimize the performance impact on the protected NFS server. UCDP-O only incurs non-negligible performance overhead in the face of a long burst of file write operations place. For each file write, UCDP-O (1) reads the before-image of the written block to compose an undo operation, (2) applies the write operation in place to the mirror file system, and (3) flushes the undo record onto disk. The target file block is overwritten in step (2), thus the name UCDP-O.

Although in-place update preserves on-disk data proximity, it requires an expensive three-step procedure for each file write: reading the before-image, writing the current image, and writing the before-image. One way to solve this problem is to use an append strategy to log file updates, where a new version is written to a different disk location than the old version. The append approach to file update logging, while more efficient, requires significant modification to file system metadata, as is the case with existing kernel-level versioning file systems [13, 11]. UCDP-A is a user-level continuous data protection scheme that uses an append approach but does not require any OS modification.

UCDP-I improves upon UCDP-A by integrating the file update logging functionality directly into the protected NFS server and thus doing away with a separate logging server. In both UCDP-O and UCDP-A, the file update logging module only needs to process write requests, but not read requests. In contrast, the logging module in UCDP-I needs to process both read and write requests and send their replies to NFS clients. Even though user-level file update logging is more portable, it also incurs additional performance overhead in the form of additional data copying and context switch. UCDP-K improves upon UCDP-I by incorporating kernel-level optimizations that can eliminate most of these overheads at the expense of portability. Figure 1 compares

the system architectures used by these four CDP schemes.

A complete CDP consists of a run-time logging component and a repair-time restoration component. Due to space constraints, this paper mainly focuses only on the efficiency of the logging component as it is the dominant factor in run-time performance. More specifically, this work makes the following three research contributions:

- The first known user-level continuous data protection system that uses an append approach to file update logging and is portable across multiple platforms,
- A comprehensive comparison among four user-level continuous data protection implementations based on empirical measurements of their performance under various workloads, and
- A fully operational prototype that demonstrates the feasibility of portable and efficient user-level continuous data protection systems that can provide point-in-time rollback while incurring minimal performance overhead, and thus can be readily incorporated into mainstream file servers.

The rest of this paper is organized as follows. Section 2 provides a comprehensive survey on previous file versioning and continuous data protection systems. Section 3 describes the design and implementation of the four user-level continuous data protection schemes studied in this work. Section 4 presents the results of a comprehensive performance evaluation study of these CDP implementations and their analysis. Section 5 concludes this paper with a summary of its major research results.

2 User-Level Continuous Data Protection

2.1 UCDP-O: Overwriting Before Image

RFS [23] uses a *mirror file system* that is an exact replica of the protected file server. The mirror file system is accessed using NFS commands over a loop-back interface. RFS's undo log consists of a list of undo records, each of which is essentially an NFS command, and contains all the necessary information to undo a file update operation, e.g., the before-image (or a link to it) of an updated file block. Undo records also contain a timestamp and are kept for a period of time called the *logging window*.

RFS classifies update requests into three categories: file block updates, directory updates, and file attribute updates. To log a file block update, RFS first reads the before-image of the target block, updates the target block, and then appends the before-image to the undo log. For directory updates, RFS does not need to save the old directory explicitly. For example, the undo operation for `create` is `remove`, which RFS can directly put into the undo log without reading any before-image. The same holds for `mkdir`, `rmdir`, `symlink`, `link` where the corresponding undo operations are `rmdir`, `mkdir`, and `remove`, respectively. The only exception is `remove`, whose undo operation depends on the object being deleted. If the object is a hard link, the undo operation is `link`. If the object is a symbolic link, the undo operation is `symlink`. If the object is a regular file, the undo operation is to create a new file, and write it to the full length; hence the logging system needs to read the whole file and appends the content into undo log entry. For a file attribute update, i.e., `set attribute`, RFS saves the old attribute value to the undo log and updates the attribute accordingly. Because the NFS protocol already includes the old attribute value in the NFS reply, RFS does not need to issue another `getattr` request to get the before-image. For a file truncate operation, RFS needs to read the truncated data and write it into the undo log before truncating the file. File block update, file truncate and regular file delete are the most expensive NFS commands in terms of logging overhead and thus represent promising targets for performance optimization. Figure 3 shows the four data structures used in UCDP-O:

- *Protected file system* stores the current file system image, which is managed by the underlying kernel file system.
- *Mirror file system* stores the mirrored file system image, which is also managed by underlying kernel file system.
- *Undo log* is managed by a user-level file update logging daemon and consists of a list of time-stamped undo records, each of which stores the old image necessary to perform an undo operation, including old data blocks, directory entries or and attributes.
- *File handle map* associates the file system objects in the protected file system to those in the mirror file system.

2.2 UCDP-A: Leaving Before Image Intact

2.2.1 Overview

UCDP-A uses a *non-overwrite* or *append-only* file update logging strategy to reduce the three-step file update logging procedure used in UCDP-O to one step. When a file block is updated, UCDP-A allocates a new file block to hold the new version, and stores a pointer to the old version in the corresponding undo record. Unlike kernel-level versioning file systems, which can directly modify file metadata (such as inode) to point to the new version, UCDP-A needs to maintain a separate user-level metadata called *block map* to achieve the same purpose. Old data is kept intact during the logging window and recycled only when the corresponding undo record expires.

The *first* version of every file block is stored in UCDP-A's *base image*, which is similar to the mirror file system in UCDP-O. It has the same directory hierarchy and inode attribute values (except the file length attribute) as the protected file system, but is *not* an exact replica of the protected file system. UCDP-A uses a separate disk block pool, called *overwrite pool*, to hold the second and later versions of each file block. Each file block in the *overwrite pool* is a virtual block that is uniquely identified by a *vblkno*. The pool is physically organized into multiple regular files in the local file system. UCDP-A uses a *block usage map* to keep track of the *overwrite pool*'s usage, and store the `obsolete time` of each virtual block.

Each virtual block becomes obsolete when its associated logical file block is overwritten. Each virtual block in the overwrite pool can be free, contain the newest version of some file block or contain an older version of some file block. The obsolete time of a free virtual block is 0. The obsolete time of a virtual block containing the newest version is infinity. If a virtual block contains an older version, its obsolete time corresponds to the timestamp of the undo record of the file update operation that obsoletes it. Any block with obsolete time smaller than the lower bound of the logging window can be reused. For each block in the *base image* that contains an old version, there is an entry in the *block map* of the form <timestamp, fid, blkno, vblkno>, which indicates that the newest version of the block `blkno` of file `fid` is stored at the virtual block `vblkno`. If `vblkno` is -1, it means the target file block has been truncated.

In summary, when a logical file block is created, it is created in the *base image*. When a logical file block is overwritten for the first time, a virtual block is allocated from the *overwrite pool*, and a mapping entry is added to the *block map* to maintain the mapping between the logical file block and its location in the *overwrite pool*. When a logical file block is overwritten for the second time, the `vblkno` number currently in its *block map* entry is stored in an undo log record, a new virtual block from the *overwrite pool* is allocated, and the *block map* entry is updated with the newly allocated block's virtual block number.

Essentially, UCDP-A distinguishes between write-once file blocks and overwritten file blocks. When a file contains only write-once file blocks, all its blocks are stored in the *base image*. However, as soon as some of them are overwritten, they will be stored in the *overwrite pool*. As a result, this design reduces the *block map*'s size and im-

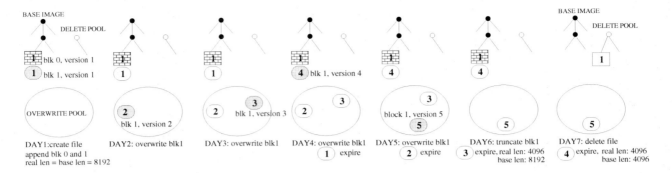

Figure 2. *This figure illustrates the design of UCDP-A by showing the evolution of a two-block file in a period of 7 days with a logging window of 3 days. Block 0 (sharp corner box) of the file is never overwritten. Block 1 (arcbox) is written fives times. Shaded boxes represent newest versions. Since the logging window is 3 days, the first version of Block 1 is created at day 1 and expires at day 4. At day 6, the file's* userlen *attribute in the file length map is modified due to a truncate operation, but the file in the base image remains intact. The file in the base image is physically truncated at day 7 when the fourth version of Block 1 expires. Due to a delete operation, the file is moved to the delete pool and physically deleted at day 10.*

proves its access performance because of improved hashing and caching efficiency. For write-once file blocks, this scheme also preserves the disk proximity among adjacent file blocks.

For a file truncate operation, UCDP-A leaves the truncated data alone in the base image and decreases only the file's length attribute. Because UCDP-A does not physically truncate files in the *base image*, it needs to maintain a *file length map* to distinguish the file length of a logical file and that of the corresponding physical file in the *base image*. Each *file length map* entry is of the form <fid, userlen, baselen>. The truncate operation is executed as an update to the userlen field. Note that with non-overwrite logging, whether a write operation is an "append" or an "overwrite" is based on baselen and not userlen. Although the baselen is available from the *base image*, it is stored in this map because it's frequently accessed. All other file attributes in the *base image* except file length are correct. The undo record for a file truncate operation again contains only a pointer to the truncated data.

A file delete operation is replaced by a rename operation followed by moving the deleted file to a special directory called *delete pool*, which has a flat structure, and assigns each new file inserted into it a unique name that is generated based on the file's inode number. Accordingly, the undo operation for a file delete operation is another rename operation that brings the file back to the original directory. The change time attribute of a deleted file serves as the obsolete time and determines when the file will be deleted from the *delete pool*.

Figure 2 illustrates the lifetime of a two-block file, starting from the time when it is created, appended, overwritten and truncated, until it is eventually deleted. UCDP-A's undo log is much smaller than UCDP-O because its undo log contains pointers to old versions rather than the actual data. Finally, just like UCDP-O, UCDP-A also needs a *file handle map* to maintain the mapping between the file handles in the *base image* and those in the protected file system.

Figure 3 shows the data structures used in UCDP-A:

- *Protected file system* is the same as that in UCDP-O.
- *Base image* contains the current file directory hierarchy and most file attributes except *file length*, but its blocks could be current or obsolete.
- *Overwrite pool* is an extension of the base image that could also hold both current and obsolete blocks.
- *Delete pool* holds deleted files, i.e., old data and attributes.
- *Block map* contains the location of each file block and their timestamps, which are for storage reclamation.
- *Block usage map* is used for allocation of virtual blocks in the overwrite pool.
- *File length map* stores the file length attribute of every logical file.
- *Undo log* is similar to UCDP-O except that each undo record contains a pointer to an old data block rather the data block itself.
- *File handle map* is the same as that in UCDP-O.

2.2.2 Storage Reclamation

Each deleted file, truncated file block and overwritten file block is pointed to by some undo record. The obsolete time of these blocks and files is the timestamp of the corresponding undo records. These timestamps allow UCDP-A to reclaim these blocks after they fall off the logging window. The obsolete time of each block in the overwrite pool is stored in its corresponding entry in the block usage map. Because allocation of new virtual blocks is also based on the block usage map, it is straightforward to integrate virtual block reclamation with new block allocation by examining each block's obsolete time when scanning through the block usage map. This way, the expired virtual blocks can be re-allocated.

Figure 3. *This figure compares the data structures of UCDP-O, UCDP-A and UCDP-I. There is no difference between UCDP-I and UCDP-K in their data structures. There are three kinds of data structures: data, kernel-level metadata and user-level metadata. Data refers to the regular file block data. Kernel-level metadata includes super-block, inode, indirect block and directory, and is maintained inside the kernel. User-level metadata refers to the auxiliary data structures maintained by the user-level CDP system.*

The obsolete time of a base image file block is kept in the corresponding block map entry, if it exists. When a file block is overwritten, UCDP-A checks the corresponding block map entry to see if the associated file block in the base image has already expired, and overwrites the base image block if that is the case, essentially reclaiming this base image block. However, this approach cannot reclaim an old file block in the base image if it never gets overwritten after it expires. One way to reclaim blocks that never get overwritten is to have a background cleaner periodically check whether any block in the base image has expired, and move an expired block that holds the current version of some logical block from the overwrite pool to the base image. This block migration incurs extra overhead, and therefore should be done only when the system load is light and when the file block is not going to be be overwritten any time soon.

The background cleaner also checks the last update time attribute of files in the delete pool. Expired files are physically deleted and the corresponding entries in the file handle map and file length map are freed. Finally the background cleaner periodically scans through the block map to look for any entry with a virtual block number of −1, which indicates that the associated block has been logically truncated. If a truncated virtual block is a file's last logical block according to the file's *baselen* attribute, the file's base image is physically truncated and its *baselen* is modified accordingly.

The undo log is itself is recycled in a cyclic fashion. Because undo log entries contain old versions of file attributes, they are also reclaimed together with the recycling of the undo log entries.

2.2.3 File System Consistency and Fault Tolerance

After a machine crashes, UCDP-A restores the following three types of consistency: (a) consistency of the local file system on the logging server and on the protected NFS server, (b) consistency of user-level metadata, and (c) consistency between a logging server and the NFS server it protects. After restart, first the standard local file system recovery (fsck) is performed to guarantee (a), and then user-level

file system recovery is performed for (b) and (c).

Similar to the standard file system journaling technique, an operation journal recorded by the *traffic interceptor* and the undo log on the logging server facilitate the user-level file system recovery. The "fsck" algorithm of UCDP-A works as follows:

1. Traverse the base image, and check (1) whether for each file system object on the logging server, there is an object on the protected NFS server, an entry in the file handle map, and an entry in the file length map; (2) whether the size of each object on the protected NFS server is equal to the `userlen` field of its corresponding file length map entry, and the size of an object's base image is equal to the `baselen` attribute in the corresponding *file length map* entry.

2. Examine each `<timestamp, fid, blkno, vblkno>` entry in the block map. If `vblkno` is not -1, check that `blkno` is within the `userlen` of the file `fid`, and the block usage map entry for the virtual block number `vblkno` has an obsolete time of infinity. If the virtual block number is -1, check if the file block is a truncated file block according to the `userlen` of the file.

3. Check that for each entry in the block usage map with an obsolete time of infinity, there is a corresponding entry in the block map.

The "fsck" algorithms for UCDP-O, UCDP-I and UCDP-K are simpler and can be easily derived from the UCDP-A's "fsck" algorithm. UCDP-O only needs to maintain consistency among the protected file system, the mirror file system and the file handle map. The "fsck" algorithm for UCDP-I and UCDP-K are largely the same as UCDP-A's except that there is no logging server and file handle map, therefore there is no need to maintain the consistency related to them.

With a separate logging server, UCDP-A not only provides file update logging, but also serves as a mirroring system that can tolerate single node failure. Upon a system failure, if the disks on both the protected NFS server and

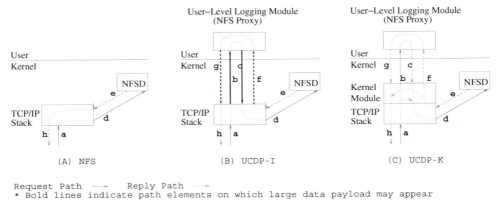

Figure 4. *This figure illustrates the NFS packet processing path in UCDP-I and its overhead due to context switch, memory copy and user-level processing. In UCDP-K, a kernel packet interception module reduces the overhead by providing short-cut path and eliminating the copy of large data payload.*

the logging server fail, data is lost; if the disk on the protected NFS server fails, data can be copied from the logging server; if the disk on the logging server fails, current data can be copied from the protected NFS server but the old data is lost; if both disks are working but they lost synchronization with each other, they need to run "fsck" to guarantee local file system consistency.

2.3 UCDP-I: Integrating Logging with Protected File Server

Both UCDP-O and UCDP-A log file updates on a dedicated logging server, and thus are more transparent to the protected file server in terms of performance impact and deployment simplicity. In contrast, UCDP-I integrates file update logging to an existing network file server without requiring additional hardware. There are three design changes in the transition from UCDP-A to UCDP-I: (1) UCDP-I does not need the file handle map because there is only one copy of the protected file system in the UCDP-I architecture. (2) UCDP-I needs to process both read and write requests as well as their responses, because the protected network file server is logically built on top of the file update logging module of UCDP-I. In contrast, UCDP-O and UCDP-A only need to process write requests, and do not need to touch the replies to read or write requests. (3) The undo logging in UCDP-I has to be done *synchronously*, because a request cannot be serviced before its before-image is saved. As a result, the logging overhead is added to the latency of normal request processing.

Logically, each incoming NFS request first goes to UCDP-I's user-level file update logging module or NFS proxy, which modifies the request properly and sends it to the local NFS daemon in the kernel, which in turn sends a reply back. The file update logging module converts the reply into a response packet and sends it back to the requesting NFS client. In this design, as shown in Figure 4(B), the file update logging module acts like an NFS proxy.

If an NFS request involves only one data block, UCDP-I needs to determine whether the request should be directed to the base image or to the overwrite pool. If it should go to the overwrite pool, the request's parameters (file handle, offset, count) need to be modified first. If the request involves more than one block, UCDP-I needs to check each block and if necessary, splits the request into multiple requests. After receiving a reply, UCDP-I may need to modify the file handle and attribute information if the request has been directed to the overwrite pool. If an incoming request is split into multiple requests, UCDP-I reassembles their replies into one reply and sends the whole reply back to the requesting NFS client. In case some of these replies are successful and some are not, UCDP-I resolves the inconsistency and returns a coherent reply.

Figure 3 shows the data structures used in UCDP-I, which are similar to those in UCDP-A except it does not need a mirror file system or file handle map.

2.4 UCDP-K: Reducing Context Switching and Memory Copying overhead

With user-level implementation, an NFS request and its reply are passed between the kernel and the user-level file update logging module multiple times in UCDP-I. UCDP-K introduces a special kernel module to reduce this context switching and memory copying overhead. Figure 4 illustrates the difference in packet processing path between UCDP-I and UCDP-K. When the kernel module receives an NFS request/reply, UCDP-K processes it in one of the following three ways:

- **Path-0:** Forwarding the request/reply to the in-kernel NFS daemon/NFS-client directly (a→d/e→h in Figure 4(C)), if the user-level NFS proxy does not need to modify the request/reply, e.g., the `readdir` command.

- **Path-1:** Forwarding the request/reply to the in-kernel NFS daemon as well as the user-level NFS proxy (a→b

692

and a→d in parallel /e→f and e→h in parallel in Figure 4(C)) if the request/reply does not need to be modified, but needs to be recorded, e.g., the `create` command.

- **Path-2:** Forwarding the request/reply to the user-level NFS proxy if the request/reply potentially needs to be modified (a→b→c→ d →e→f→g→h in Figure 4 (C)), e.g., the `read` or `write` command.

Path-0 represents the zero-overhead path, which is as fast as normal kernel-level NFS processing. Path-2 involves two context switches/memory copies because the original request and reply have to be sent to the user-level NFS proxy, and after user-level processing, the modified request or reply has to be sent back to kernel and forwarded to the NFS daemon or requesting NFS client. The additional overhead affects not only the CPU utilization but also the end-to-end latency experienced by the NFS requests. Path-1 incurs only one additional context switching/memory copying for sending a packet to the user-level daemon. The overhead affects only the CPU utilization but not the end-to-end latency because the user-level processing is not on the critical path of NFS packet processing.

The *intelligent demultiplexing* scheme directly moves to the NFS daemon those NFS requests and replies that are not at all related to continuous data protection. However, in many cases an NFS reply only requires very simple modification. For example, the `getattr` reply has complete correct content except that file length, which needs to be changed from `baselen` to `userlen` according to the file length map. It is the same for many of the replies to `read` and `write` where the requests are directed to the *base image*. Therefore we introduce another optimization into UCDP-K called *in-kernel reply modification*. When a user-level CDP system sends a request to the NFS daemon (step c in Figure 4(C)), whenever possible it also gives the kernel module specific instructions on how to perform the simple modification when the corresponding reply arrives (step e). With this optimization, many NFS replies that used to take Path-2 can now take the less expensive Path-0 or Path-1. This optimization is particularly effective for `read reply` that contains large data payload.

The last optimization in UCDP-K is *write payload decoupling*, which reduces the memory copying overhead of `write` requests. A `write request` always needs to be processed by the user-level NFS proxy. However, because usually the user-level processing does not touch the payload, the kernel module can save a write request inside the kernel and forward only the request header to the user-level module (step b). When the NFS proxy sends the modified header back, the kernel module replaces the old header with the new header. In case the NFS proxy does need the payload because the request needs to be split, it will make another system call to explicitly retrieve the request's data payload.

3   Performance Evaluation

In this section, we evaluate and compare the run-time performance overheads of the four user-level continuous data protection schemes using micro benchmarks, the Harvard NFS traces [9], the SPECsfs 3.0 benchmark [5]. By default all the machines are equipped with the same hardware configuration (1.4GHz Pentium IV CPU, 500 MB memory, 100Mbps Ethernet card) and OS platform (Redhat 7.2 with Linux kernel 2.4.7-10). The base case for performance comparison is the vanilla NFS server on the same platform, which sets the lower bound on the performance overhead of all CDP implementations.

3.1   Effects of Non-Overwrite Logging

A vanilla NFS server services write requests using in-place updates, whereas UCDP-A, UCDP-I and UCDP-K use the non-overwrite strategy. Under the non-overwrite strategy, random overwrite operations are turned into sequential writes to the *overwrite pool* if there are enough contiguous free virtual blocks. At the same time, sequential reads may become random reads if the file blocks have been overwritten randomly and dispersed in the *overwrite pool*. As a result, the non-overwrite strategy may perform better than in-place updates for workload dominated by random writes, but perform worse for workload dominated by sequential reads after random writes.

To quantify the performance impact of non-overwrite logging strategy, we constructed the following micro benchmark for the vanilla NFS and UCDP-K. The experiments use a server with 256MB RAM and a client with 128MB RAM. The server may run vanilla NFS or UCDP-K. The client is a generic NFS client. First we created a 500MB file on the server through sequential write from the client. In this setup, there is no cache hit on either the client side or the server side. The sequential write throughput for both vanilla NFS and UCDP-K is 11MB/sec.

Then we performed a sequence of overwrite operations of the size of 4096 bytes at random file offset of the 500MB file until the size of *overwrite pool* reaches 2GB, which produces sufficient disk layout difference between vanilla NFS and UCDP-K. Under vanilla NFS the disk utilization is 100% and the write throughput is 1.54MB/sec. Under UCDP-K, the disk utilization is 22.5% and the write throughput is 10.23MB/sec. Overall, the disk access efficiency of UCDP-K is 30 times *higher* than the vanilla NFS. This result shows that the non-overwrite strategy behaves similarly to log-structured file system [20], which is designed specifically to convert random writes into sequential writes.

Finally, we performed a sequence of sequential read operations against the same 500MB file with a request size of 4096 bytes. Under vanilla NFS, the disk utilization is 18.6% and the read throughput is 4.76 MB/sec. Under UCDP-K, the disk utilization is 94.4% and the read throughput is 0.87 MB/sec. Overall, the disk access efficiency of UCDP-K is

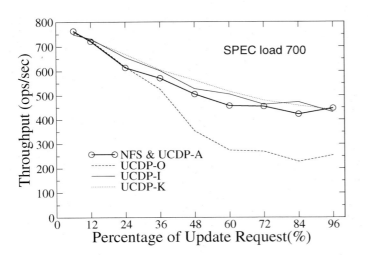

Figure 5. *Throughput comparison as the percentage of write requests in the input workload varies.*

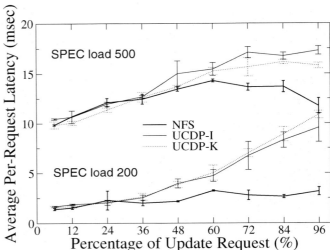

Figure 6. *Average request processing latency comparison as the percentage of write requests in the input workload varies.*

28 times *worse* than the vanilla NFS server. Periodic cleaning can mitigate the loss of sequential read locality by moving the current versions of those file blocks that have become read-only from the *overwrite pool* to the *base image*.

3.2 Comparison among Continuous Data Protection Schemes

SPECsfs has a default NFS request mix, where 12% of the requests update the file system and the remaining requests are read-only. The file update logging overhead is more pronounced when the proportion of write requests is high. To stress-test the CDP schemes, we varied the write request percentage from 12% to 96%. The distribution among different types of write requests, and the distribution among different types of read-only requests remain fixed throughout the experiments. We also varied the input load, and set the initial working set size to be proportional to the input load, for example, 7GB for the load of 700 ops/sec and 5GB for the load of 500 ops/sec.

The measured peak throughput of a vanilla unprotected NFS server under SPECsfs decreases as the write percentage increases. At 12%, it is about 700 ops/sec and goes down to 500 ops/sec at 96%. Figure 5 shows that all four continuous data protection schemes yield almost the same throughput when the percentage of write requests in the input workload is less than 12%. UCDP-A performs the same as the vanilla NFS server because the logging server in UCDP-A is not the system bottleneck, and the protected NFS server in UCDP-A is identical to the vanilla NFS server. As the write request percentage increases, UCDP-O is limited by the logging server due to the expensive three-step file update logging procedure (Section 1). Surprisingly, even with all the extra processing due to version-

ing, UCDP-I and UCDP-K actually out-perform the vanilla NFS server in throughput by around 7%. In this case, the disk is the system bottleneck, and the advantage of the non-overwrite strategy in processing random write requests, as discussed in Section 3.1, is significant enough that it results in a small but distinct overall performance improvement. Another block-level versioning system, Clotho [17], reported similar performance gain due to the use of a non-overwrite strategy. Because the kernel module in UCDP-K has no effects on disk access efficiency, UCDP-K performs roughly the same as UCDP-I in all cases.

Figure 6 shows the average per-request latency of the vanilla NFS server, UCDP-I, and UCDP-K. Each latency number represents the average of ten measurements. The upper three curves correspond to a SPEC load of 500 ops/sec, while the lower three curves correspond to a SPEC load of 200 ops/sec. The latencies of UCDP-O and UCDP-A are similar to that of the vanilla NFS because the reply to each NFS request actually comes from their primary NFS server. The results for UCDP-I and UCDP-K are similar, because the kernel module has no significant impact on latency. When the write request percentage is no more than 36%, the average per-request latency of UCDP-I/UCDP-K is similar to that of the vanilla NFS server. As the write request percentage increases further, the per-request latency of UCDP-I/UCDP-K becomes higher than that of vanilla NFS server, and the latency gap also increases. In the worst case, when the write request percentage is at 96% of the SPEC load of 200 ops/sec, the gap is about 7 msec, which represents a 200% latency overhead. However, this latency gap decreases as the load increases. For example, the additional latency overhead is reduced to 10% to 30% at load 500.

The latency overhead of UCDP-I/UCDP-K when com-

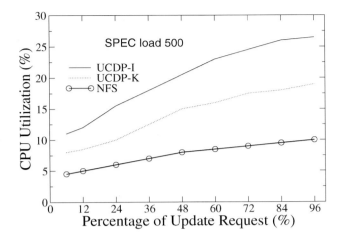

Figure 7. *CPU utilization comparison as the percentage of write requests in the input workload varies.*

pared with the vanilla NFS server comes from the extra processing associated with file update logging. With the non-overwrite strategy, to serve a client request, multiple requests may need to be issued to the local NFS daemon, such as reassembling read/write requests, reading the before image when a `write` request is not aligned, checking out the file type of an object to be deleted, etc. These requests do not impose much additional disk bandwidth requirements, but they do increase the request processing latency. As the write request percentage grows, more and more blocks are overwritten and reside in *overwrite pool*, more reassembling of `read` or `write` requests is needed, the probability of issuing multiple local requests per client request becomes higher, and eventually the per-request latency of UCDP-I/UCDP-K increases.

Figure 7 compares the CPU utilization of NFS, UCDP-I and UCDP-K. UCDP-O and UCDP-A are excluded because both of them require a separate server. When the input SPECsfs load is 500 ops/sec, the throughputs of vanilla NFS, UCDP-I and UCDP-K are comparable, but the CPU utilization of UCDP-I and UCDP-K is about 170% and 85%, respectively, higher than that of vanilla NFS. These results suggest that file update logging processing indeed consumes additional CPU resource, and the kernel module in UCDP-K effectively reduces the CPU consumption by eliminating a large portion of context switching and memory copying overhead. When CPU is the system bottleneck, UCDP-K should out-perform UCDP-I in terms of overall throughput. To substantiate this claim, we modify the SPEC workload so that it is read-only and has high buffer hit ratio, and upgrade the network connection from a 100 Mbps to a 1000 Mbps network. As a result, disk and network are no longer the system bottleneck. With an initial working set size of 300MB and a SPECsfs input load of 7000 ops/sec, the measured throughput of NFS, UCDP-I and UCDP-K are 6560, 4166, 5441 respectively. UCDP-K indeed out-performs UCDP-I by 30%.

4 Related Work

WAFL [12] is a general-purpose high performance file system with snapshot support developed by Network Appliance. WAFL is not optimized for fine file update logging, and allows only a limited number (32 originally) of snapshots. Each snapshot is taken at a coarse granularity and the cost is amortized over hundreds of file updates.

Wayback [8] is a user-level comprehensive versioning file system for Linux. For each data update, Wayback uses an undo logging scheme similar to UCDP-O. For each metadata update, Wayback incurs a higher overhead than all of our logging schemes. For normal file system update, the performance of Wayback is quite poor compared with traditional file systems. When compared with EXT3, the data read/write overhead ranges from -2% to 70%, and the metadata update overhead ranges from 100% to 400%. In contrast, the performance of UCDP-I and UCDP-K are comparable to generic NFS server running on top of EXT3.

CVFS [11] is a kernel-level comprehensive versioning file system that is optimized for metadata logging efficiency. *Journal-based meta-data* is used for inode/indirect-block update and *multiversion B-tree* [10] is used for directory update. S4 [16] is a secure network-attached object store against malicious attacks. S4 logs every update and minimizes the space explosion. S4 uses a log-structured design to avoid overwriting of old data. S4 improves the inode/indirect-block logging efficiency by encoding their changes in a logging record. Although the overhead of S4's logging scheme is low, its cleaning cost can be as high as 50%.

Log structured file system [20] has been used to reduce the disk access penalty of random small writes. Yet it shares one common feature of non-overwrite with file update logging. Logging systems do not overwrite to save old data. Log structured file system writes data into new location in big batch to improve write performance. In LFS, cleaning is essential to keep the disk locality of file but the overhead is often high. This issue is not pronounced in the proposed user-level file update logging system because we use a *base image* (Section 4.3.1) to maintain the disk locality and our cleaning cycle is much longer hence the cost is amortized.

Elephant [13] is a kernel-level versioning file system that creates a new version only when a file is closed. Therefore, it does not distinguish updates between a file open and file close operation. VersionFS [19] is a versioning file system implemented using stackable file system technique [22]. Similar to Elephant [13], the version is based on open-close session and the versioning policy is flexible. VersionFS also provides friendly interface for user to access old versions and to customize the versioning policies. VersionFS still incurs non-negligible performance overhead - about 100% when measured by Postmark benchmark.

Clotho [17] is a versioning system at the disk block level. Compared with file system versioning, block-level versioning is less complex due to its simpler interface. However, it is more difficult for users to directly manage versions of disk blocks. Usually another layer on top of block-level versioning is required to provide easy version access. Clotho aggregates updates that take place within a period of time (e.g. a minute) and create new versions for them, and therefore does not support CDP.

5 Conclusion

Continuous data protection is a critical building block for quickly repairing damage to a file system due to malicious attacks or innocent human errors. So far it has not been incorporated into mainstream file servers because of the concern of additional storage requirements, performance overhead, and the implementation complexity. Given the dramatic improvements in the per-byte cost of magnetic disk technology, disk cost is no longer an issue. Measurements on a real-world NFS trace shows that a $200 200GB disk can easily support a one-month logging window for a large NFS server whose size is 400GB and whose average load is 34 requests/sec [23]. The performance overhead and implementation complexity associated with continuous data protection, however, remain significant barriers to its deployment in practice. This paper describes a user-level continuous data protection architecture that is both efficient and portable, and thus completely eliminates these barriers. We have implemented four variants of this user-level CDP architecture, and compared their latency, throughput, and CPU usage characteristics using standard benchmarks, NFS traces, and synthetic workloads. The main lessons from this implementation effort and performance study are

- User-level continuous data protection based on the NFS protocol that is portable across multiple operating system platforms is feasible and relatively simple to implement.

- UCDP-A incurs close to zero latency and throughput penalty compared with an unprotected vanilla NFS server, and is thus the best choice for IT environments where performance is the main concern, mirroring file system image is desirable, and minimum disruption to the primary NFS server is important.

- User-level continuous data protection, when embedded into an NFS server, can have comparable throughput as the unprotected NFS server although it does incur 3∼5 msec of latency penalty when the write request percentage is above 36%. The write request percentage in typical NFS sites, as specified in the SPECsfs benchmark, is less than 12%.

- If portability can be slightly compromised, simple in-kernel optimizations could significantly decrease the CPU overhead due to context switching and memory copying associated with user-level CDP. But they do not produce noticeable latency and throughput improvement when the write request percentage in the input workload is lower than 12%.

- Logging updates at a higher level of abstraction, such as NFS requests and replies, tends to produce a much more compact log than logging at a lower level of abstraction, such as disk accesses and responses, and is also more portable and flexible.

Acknowledgement

This research is supported by NSF awards SCI-0401777, CNS-0410694 and CNS-0435373.

References

[1] *The Advanced Maryland Automatic Network Disk Archiver.* (http://www.amanda.org/).

[2] *Concurrent Versions System.* (http://www.cvshome.org/).

[3] *Enterprise Rewinder: Product Suite for Continuous Data Protection (CDP).* (http://www.xosoft.com/).

[4] *RealTime - Near-Instant Recovery to Any Point in Time.* (http://www.mendocinosoft.com/).

[5] *System File Server Benchmark SPEC SFS97_R1 V3.0.* Standard Performance Evaluation Corporation. (http://www.specbench.org/sfs97r1/).

[6] *NFS: Network file system protocol specification.* Sun Microsystems, Mar 1989.

[7] A. Chervenak, V. Vellanki, and Z. Kurmas. Protecting file systems: A survey of backup techniques. In *Proceedings Joint NASA and IEEE Mass Storage Conference*, March 1998.

[8] Brian Cornell, Peter A. Dinda, and Fabin E. Bustamante. Wayback: A user-level versioning file system for linux. In *USENIX 2004 Annual Technical Conference (Freenix)*.

[9] D. Ellard, J. Ledlie, P. Malkani, and M. Seltzer. Passive nfs tracing of email and research workloads. In *2nd USENIX Conference on File and Storage Technologies*, Mar 2003.

[10] B. Becker et al. *An asymptotically optimal multiversion b-tree.* Very Large Data Bases Journal, 1996.

[11] C.A.N. Soules et al. Metadata efficiency in a comprehensive versioning file system. In *2nd USENIX Conference on File and Storage Technologies*, Mar 2003.

[12] D. Hitz et al. File system design for an nfs file server appliance. In *USENIX winter 1994 conference*, pages 235–246, Chateau Lake Louise, Banff, Canada, 1994.

[13] D. S. Santry et al. Deciding when to forget in the elephant file system. In *Proceedings of the Seventeenth ACM Symposium on Operating Systems Principles*, pages 110–123, December 12-15, 1999.

[14] G. W. Dunlap et al. Revirt: Enabling intrusion analysis through virtual-machine logging and replay. In *Proceedings of 5th Symposium on Operating Systems Design and Implementation*, Dec 2002.

[15] Hugo Patterson et al. Snapmirror: file system based asynchronous mirroring for disaster recovery. In *Conference on File and Storage Technologies*, pages 28–30, Monterey, CA, January 2002.

[16] J. Strunk et al. Self-securing storage: Protecting data in compromised systems. In *Proceedings of the 2000 OSDI Conference*, October 2000.

[17] Michail D. Flouris and Angelos Bilas. Clotho: Transparent data versioning at the block i/o level. In *21st IEEE Conference on Mass Storage Systems and Technologies*, April 2004.

[18] D. Mazires. A toolkit for user-level file systems. In *Proceedings of the 2001 USENIX Technical Conference*, pages 261–274, June 2001.

[19] K. Muniswamy-Reddy, C. P. Wright, A. Himmer, and E. Zadok. A Versatile and User-Oriented Versioning File System. In *Proceedings of the Third USENIX Conference on File and Storage Technologies (FAST 2004)*, pages 115–128, San Francisco, CA, March/April 2004.

[20] M. Rosenblum and J. K. Ousterhout. The design and implementation of a log-structured file system. In *ACM Transactions on Computer Systems*, 1991.

[21] Michael Rowan. Continuous data protection: A technical overview. In *http://www.revivio.com/index.asp?p=tech_white_papers*, 2004.

[22] E. Zadok and J. Nieh. FiST: A Language for Stackable File Systems. In *Proceedings of the Annual USENIX Technical Conference*, pages 55–70, June 2000.

[23] N. Zhu and T. Chiueh. Design, implementation, and evaluation of repairable file service. In *The International Conference on Dependable Systems and Networks*, June 2003.

Session 6C:
Modeling and Evaluation

Variational Bayesian Approach for Interval Estimation of NHPP-based Software Reliability Models

Hiroyuki Okamura,[‡] Michael Grottke,[♯] Tadashi Dohi,[‡] and Kishor S. Trivedi[♯]
[‡]Department of Information Engineering
Graduate School of Engineering, Hiroshima University
1–4–1 Kagamiyama, Higashi-Hiroshima, 739–8527, Japan
{okamu, dohi}@rel.hiroshima-u.ac.jp
[♯]Department of Electrical & Computer Engineering
Duke University, Durham, NC 27708-0291, USA
{grottke, kst}@ee.duke.edu

Abstract

In this paper, we present a variational Bayesian (VB) approach to computing the interval estimates for non-homogeneous Poisson process (NHPP) software reliability models. This approach is an approximate method that can produce analytically tractable posterior distributions. We present simple iterative algorithms to compute the approximate posterior distributions for the parameters of the gamma-type NHPP-based software reliability model using either individual failure time data or grouped data. In numerical examples, the accuracy of this VB approach is compared with the interval estimates based on conventional Bayesian approaches, i.e., Laplace approximation, Markov chain Monte Carlo (MCMC) method, and numerical integration. The proposed VB approach provides almost the same accuracy as MCMC, while its computational burden is much lower.

Keywords: Software reliability, non-homogeneous Poisson process, interval estimation, variational Bayes

1. Introduction

Software reliability is one of the most important metrics of software quality. During the last three decades, many software reliability models (SRMs) have been proposed [10]. In particular, SRMs based on the non-homogeneous Poisson process (NHPP) have gained much popularity for describing the stochastic development of the number of failures experienced over time.

Much of the past research in software reliability modeling has focused on the point estimation of the model parameters as well as the reliability itself. How to take into account the uncertainty of the estimates by using interval estimation has not been fully discussed. The most commonly applied interval estimation technique is based on the central limit theorem, assuming the availability of a large number of samples [12]. However, in real-world testing the number of software failures observed is usually not large enough to justify the application of the central limit theorem.

On the other hand, Bayesian approaches can produce interval estimates even in the case of small sample sizes, by utilizing prior knowledge [15]. Since the posterior distribution is derived from both the prior distribution of the parameters and the likelihood of the observed data, Bayesian statistics contains the likelihood-based statistical analysis (such as maximum likelihood estimation) from a mathematical point of view. In the Bayesian framework, interval estimates are derived from the quantiles of the posterior distribution. The calculation is based on the analytical expression for the posterior distribution, if such an expression is feasible. For example, Meinhold and Singpurwalla [11] present the explicit form for the posterior distribution in the Jelinski-Moranda model [6].

However, for almost all SRMs the posterior distribution is mathematically complicated; therefore, it usually needs to be either simulated or approximated. Kuo and Yang [8, 9] propose the application of the Markov chain Monte Carlo (MCMC) approach to compute the posterior distributions in several types of NHPP-based SRMs. This approach can provide very accurate results if a large number of parameter samples is generated. However, the time required for computing such large samples can get very long. Yin and Trivedi [20] use direct numerical integration in the context of Bayesian analysis of the Goel-Okumoto model [5] and the delayed S-shaped model [18]. While direct numerical integration can produce very accurate results, it is vulner-

698

able to round-off and truncation errors. Multiple-precision arithmetic can partially reduce the round-off errors, but the problem of truncation errors remains. To overcome these computational problems, Okamura *et al.* [13] propose a variational Bayesian (VB) approach for the Goel-Okumoto model [5]. While this VB approach leads to a simple algorithm, its underlying assumptions are too restrictive for achieving a good approximation of the posterior distribution.

In this paper, we improve upon the previous work related to the VB approach [13] in three ways: Firstly, we relax the central assumption in the VB approach, which enhances the accuracy of the approximation. While the computation time required by the proposed method is still less than for the MCMC approach, its accuracy is comparable to the one attained by MCMC. An additional advantage over MCMC is that the posterior distribution resulting from our approach is analytically tractable. Secondly, we increase the set of applicable models by presenting a VB algorithm for the gamma-type NHPP-based SRM, which contains the Goel-Okumoto model and the delayed S-shaped model as special cases. Thirdly, we extend the applicability of the VB approach to the grouped data case. While almost all previous results for the Bayesian estimation of SRMs have relied on failure time data, grouped data are easier to collect and thus more widely available. The derivation of methods for the analysis of grouped data is therefore important from a practical point of view.

The rest of this paper is organized as follows: Section 2 describes NHPP-based SRMs of the finite failures category. In Section 3, we discuss the point estimation of NHPP-based SRMs, which is fundamental to the interval estimation. Section 4 is devoted to conventional Bayesian interval estimation. In Section 5, we propose a new VB approach for estimating NHPP-based SRMs. In Section 6, we carry out numerical experiments to compare the application of this VB approach to the estimation of the Goel-Okumoto model with the results obtained by conventional Bayesian approaches; these comparisons are conducted for both failure time data and grouped data. Finally, the paper concludes with a brief summary of the results and an outlook on our future research in Section 7.

2. NHPP-based software reliability models

Consider NHPP-based SRMs of the finite failures category. According to this model class, the number of faults present in the software at the beginning of testing, N, follows a Poisson probability mass function with expected value ω_0:

$$P(N = n) = \frac{\omega_0^n}{n!} \exp(-\omega_0) \qquad \text{for } n = 0, 1, \ldots. \quad (1)$$

Moreover, the failure times $Y_1, Y_2, \ldots, Y_N$ of all N faults are assumed to be independent and identically distributed (i.i.d.), following a general distribution with parameter vector $\boldsymbol{\theta}_0$, $G(\cdot; \boldsymbol{\theta}_0)$. These assumptions imply that $M(t)$, the number of failure occurrences experienced in the time interval $(0, t]$, has a Poisson probability mass function,

$$P(M(t) = m) = \frac{\Lambda(t)^m}{m!} \exp(-\Lambda(t)), \quad (2)$$

with expected value $\Lambda(t) = \omega_0 G(t; \boldsymbol{\theta}_0)$. Hence, the mean value function in the NHPP-based SRMs can be completely characterized by only the failure time distribution $G(t; \boldsymbol{\theta}_0)$. For example, an exponential failure time distribution leads to the Goel-Okumoto model [5], while the delayed S-shaped model [18] is obtained by assuming that $G(t; \boldsymbol{\theta}_0)$ is the distribution function of a 2-stage Erlang distribution.

Software reliability is defined as the probability that no failure occurs in a prefixed time interval. In the NHPP-based SRMs, the software reliability $R(t + u \mid t)$ for time period $(t, t + u]$ is given by

$$R(t + u \mid t) = P(M(t + u) - M(t) = 0) \quad (3)$$
$$= \exp\big(-\omega_0 G(t + u; \boldsymbol{\theta}_0) + \omega_0 G(t; \boldsymbol{\theta}_0)\big).$$

3. Point estimation

Usually, when NHPP-based SRMs are applied, point estimates for the model parameters are determined based on the observed failure data. The most commonly used technique is maximum likelihood estimation. The maximum likelihood estimates (MLEs) of the model parameters are those parameter values for which the likelihood function attains its maximum. Since the likelihood function depends on the data structure, our discussion of the MLEs distinguishes between two kinds of data: failure time data, and grouped data.

Let $\mathcal{D}_T = \{T_1, \ldots, T_{M(t_e)}\}$ be the ordered set of failure times experienced before time t_e; i.e., $0 < T_1 < \cdots < T_{M(t_e)} \leq t_e$ are the first $M(t_e)$ order statistics of the failure times $Y_1, \ldots, Y_N$. Given the parameters ω_0 and $\boldsymbol{\theta}_0$, the log-likelihood for the failure time data $\mathcal{D}_T$ is

$$\log P(\mathcal{D}_T | \omega_0, \boldsymbol{\theta}_0) = \sum_{i=1}^{M(t_e)} \log g(T_i; \boldsymbol{\theta}_0) + M(t_e) \log \omega_0$$
$$- \omega_0 G(t_e; \boldsymbol{\theta}_0), \quad (4)$$

where $g(t; \boldsymbol{\theta}_0)$ is the probability density function connected to the failure time distribution $G(t; \boldsymbol{\theta}_0)$. We use the probability measure $P(\cdot)$ to indicate the probability density function in the case of a continuous random variable and the probability mass function in the case of a discrete random variable.

Let $\mathcal{D}_G = \{X_1, \ldots, X_k\}$ denote the grouped data for a time sequence $s_0 \equiv 0 < s_1 < \cdots < s_k$, where X_i represents the number of failures experienced during the time interval $(s_{i-1}, s_i]$. For the grouped data $\mathcal{D}_G$, the log-likelihood is given by

$$\log P(\mathcal{D}_G | \omega_0, \boldsymbol{\theta}_0) \tag{5}$$
$$= \sum_{i=1}^{k} X_i \log \left(G(s_i; \boldsymbol{\theta}_0) - G(s_{i-1}; \boldsymbol{\theta}_0) \right)$$
$$+ \sum_{i=1}^{k} X_i \log \omega_0 - \sum_{i=1}^{k} \log X_i! - \omega_0 G(s_k; \boldsymbol{\theta}_0).$$

Based on the observed data $\mathcal{D}_T = \{T_1 = t_1, \ldots, T_{M(t_e)} = t_{m_e}\}$ or $\mathcal{D}_G = \{X_1 = x_1, \ldots, X_k = x_k\}$, we can compute the log-likelihood and find the maximum likelihood estimates $\hat{\omega}_{MLE}$ and $\hat{\boldsymbol{\theta}}_{MLE}$. Since Eqs. (4) and (5) are non-linear, Newton or quasi-Newton method is traditionally applied to derive the MLEs. Recently, Okamura et al. [14] proposed a powerful iteration scheme based on the EM (Expectation-Maximization) algorithm to compute the MLEs for almost all NHPP-based SRMs. This technique is especially suitable for use in automated reliability prediction tools.

The framework of Bayesian statistics produces somewhat different point estimates. Bayesian estimation is employed to make use of prior knowledge. The key idea is to regard the parameters as random variables and to embody the prior knowledge via so-called prior distributions for these parameters. So far, we have used ω_0 and $\boldsymbol{\theta}_0$ to denote the fixed but unknown parameter values. Let ω and $\boldsymbol{\theta}$ denote the corresponding random variables. According to Bayes' theorem, the relationship between the prior density $P(\omega, \boldsymbol{\theta})$, the likelihood $P(\mathcal{D} | \omega, \boldsymbol{\theta})$ and the posterior density $P(\omega, \boldsymbol{\theta} | \mathcal{D})$ is as follows:

$$P(\omega, \boldsymbol{\theta} | \mathcal{D}) = \frac{1}{C} \cdot P(\mathcal{D} | \omega, \boldsymbol{\theta}) P(\omega, \boldsymbol{\theta})$$
$$\propto P(\mathcal{D} | \omega, \boldsymbol{\theta}) P(\omega, \boldsymbol{\theta}), \tag{6}$$

where C is a normalizing constant ensuring that the total probability is one. This equation shows how the prior knowledge is updated via the information $\mathcal{D}$. Although the Bayesian estimation produces a complete posterior density instead of single parameter estimates, point estimates can easily be derived. For example, the maximum a posterior (MAP) estimates are those parameter values for which the posterior density - or its logarithm - is maximized; i.e.,

$$(\hat{\omega}_{MAP}, \hat{\boldsymbol{\theta}}_{MAP}) = \underset{\omega_0, \boldsymbol{\theta}_0}{\mathrm{argmax}} \left\{ \log P(\mathcal{D} | \omega = \omega_0, \boldsymbol{\theta} = \boldsymbol{\theta}_0) \right.$$
$$\left. + \log P(\omega = \omega_0, \boldsymbol{\theta} = \boldsymbol{\theta}_0) \right\}. \tag{7}$$

Alternatively, the first moments of the posterior distribution can also be used as point estimates.

4. Bayesian interval estimation

For many software products, only a small number of failure data points are available. In such cases, Bayesian estimation is a more effective method than MLE-based approaches for deriving interval estimates in SRMs. The main challenge in Bayesian estimation is to derive the posterior distribution. If the posterior distribution is explicitly given, the interval estimates are obtained by evaluating the quantile of posterior distribution. However, the posterior density is usually expressed in proportional form, like in Eq. (6). Therefore, except for some specific cases, the calculation of the posterior distribution is quite difficult both analytically and from the computational standpoint.

4.1. Direct methods

The simplest approach is to evaluate Eq. (6) analytically or numerically. Suppose that the failure times $Y_1, \ldots, Y_N$ follow an exponential distribution with probability density function $g(t; \beta) = \beta e^{-\beta t}$. Given the failure time data $\mathcal{D}_T = \{T_1 = t_1, \ldots, T_{M(t_e)} = t_{m_e}\}$, the joint posterior density for the parameters ω and β can be written as

$$P(\omega, \beta | \mathcal{D}_T) \propto P(\omega, \beta) \omega^{M(t_e)} \beta^{M(t_e)}$$
$$\times \exp \left(-\beta \sum_{i=1}^{M(t_e)} T_i - \omega(1 - e^{-\beta t_e}) \right). \tag{8}$$

To derive an interval estimate from this expression, we have to determine the normalizing constant in the equation. Yin and Trivedi [20] discuss the interval estimation based on numerical integration. When using this method, the upper and lower limits chosen for the area of integration strongly affect the interval estimates. Choosing too wide a range can cause numerical exceptions like underflows; a too narrow range, on the other hand, leads to an underestimation of the normalizing constant.

4.2. Laplace approximation

The idea behind the Laplace approximation is to approximate the joint posterior distribution of the parameters by a multivariate normal distribution. In general, the MAP estimates and the second derivatives of the posterior distribution evaluated at the MAP estimates are used as the mean vector and the variance-covariance matrix of the approximating multivariate normal distribution, respectively. If a flat prior density (i.e., a constant density over the entire joint parameter domain) is used, the Laplace approximation is reduced to the MLE-based derivation of confidence intervals discussed in [19]. The Laplace approximation does not require complicated computational procedures. However, since the multivariate normal distribution cannot account for skewness, the accuracy of the approximation is low in many cases.

4.3. Markov chain Monte Carlo

The Markov chain Monte Carlo (MCMC) approach is the most popular and versatile method to evaluate the posterior distribution. Instead of an analytical expression for the posterior distribution, the method uses sampling data generated from this posterior distribution. The main idea behind the MCMC approach is to derive samples from the joint posterior distribution of the model parameters by alternatingly applying conditional marginal densities related to the joint posterior distribution.

MCMC methods for NHPP-based SRMs are discussed by Kuo and Yang [8, 9]. For example, suppose that the failure times follow an exponential distribution, and that the prior distribution is the non-informative flat density. Let the random variable $\overline{N} = N - M(t_e)$ denote the residual number of faults at the end of testing. Given the failure time data $\mathcal{D}_T = \{T_1 = t_1, \ldots, T_{M(t_e)} = m_e\}$, Kuo and Yang [8] propose the following Gibbs sampling scheme:

$$\overline{N} \mid \omega, \beta \sim \text{Poisson}(\omega e^{-\beta t_e}), \quad (9)$$

$$\omega \mid \overline{N} \sim \text{Gamma}(m_e + \overline{N}, 1), \quad (10)$$

$$\beta \mid \overline{N} \sim \text{Gamma}(m_e, \textstyle\sum_{i=1}^{m_e} t_i + \overline{N} t_e), \quad (11)$$

where $\sim$ indicates the probability distribution. Also, 'Poisson(a)' and 'Gamma(b, c)' represent the Poisson distribution with mean a and the Gamma distribution with shape parameter b and scale parameter c. In the MCMC approach, we start from provisional values for ω and β and generate new samples based on the above sampling scheme, using the current parameter values. Repeating this procedure, we obtain samples from the joint posterior distribution of the parameters.

By introducing the residual number of faults, $\overline{N}$, Kuo and Yang are able to reduce the computational cost of sampling. However, to derive interval estimates, we have to determine quantile points from the sampling data. Unlike the computation of moments, the computation of quantiles from samples usually requires a large sample size [2]. From a computational point of view, the derivation of interval estimates via the MCMC approach is therefore not efficient. Moreover, the MCMC methods developed in [8, 9] require failure time data. The application of MCMC to grouped data requires general-purpose sampling methods such as the Metropolis-Hastings algorithm [3], which is even more computationally intensive.

5. Variational Bayesian approach

5.1. Variational posterior for NHPP-based SRMs

The variational Bayesian (VB) approach is based on the variational approximation to the posterior distribution. Unlike MCMC methods, it derives closed analytical forms for the posterior distributions.

Consider the two data sets $\mathcal{D}$ and $\mathcal{U}$, corresponding to observed and unobserved information, respectively. Note that the data sets $\mathcal{D}$, $\mathcal{U}$ together contain the complete information on the ordered software failure times $T_1 < \cdots < T_N$, where N is again the total number of faults. Denoting the set of model parameters by $\boldsymbol{\mu} = \{\omega, \boldsymbol{\theta}\}$, the marginal log-likelihood of $\mathcal{D}$ can be obtained from the complete likelihood $P(\mathcal{D}, \mathcal{U}|\boldsymbol{\mu})$ and the prior density $P(\boldsymbol{\mu})$:

$$\log P(\mathcal{D}) = \log \int \int P(\mathcal{D}, \mathcal{U}, \boldsymbol{\mu}) d\mathcal{U} d\boldsymbol{\mu}$$
$$= \log \int \int P(\mathcal{D}, \mathcal{U}|\boldsymbol{\mu}) P(\boldsymbol{\mu}) d\mathcal{U} d\boldsymbol{\mu}. \quad (12)$$

Here we use $\int P(A, B) dA$ to represent the calculation of the marginal probability measure for the random variable B. That is, if A is a discrete random variable, the corresponding operation is the summation of $P(A, B)$ over all possible values of A. Otherwise, if A is a continuous random variable, the operation reduces to the integral of $P(A, B)$ over the domain of A.

Let $P_v(\cdot)$ be an arbitrary probability measure. From Jensen's inequality, we have

$$\log P(\mathcal{D}) = \log \int \int P_v(\mathcal{U}, \boldsymbol{\mu}) \frac{P(\mathcal{D}, \mathcal{U}, \boldsymbol{\mu})}{P_v(\mathcal{U}, \boldsymbol{\mu})} d\mathcal{U} d\boldsymbol{\mu}$$
$$\geq \int \int P_v(\mathcal{U}, \boldsymbol{\mu}) \log \frac{P(\mathcal{D}, \mathcal{U}, \boldsymbol{\mu})}{P_v(\mathcal{U}, \boldsymbol{\mu})} d\mathcal{U} d\boldsymbol{\mu} \equiv \mathcal{F}[P_v], \quad (13)$$

where $\mathcal{F}[P_v]$ is a functional of $P_v(\mathcal{U}, \boldsymbol{\mu})$. From Eq. (13), the difference between the marginal log-likelihood of $\mathcal{D}$ and the functional $\mathcal{F}$ can be obtained as follows:

$$\log P(\mathcal{D}) - \mathcal{F}[P_v]$$
$$= \int \int P_v(\mathcal{U}, \boldsymbol{\mu}) \log \frac{P_v(\mathcal{U}, \boldsymbol{\mu})}{P(\mathcal{U}, \boldsymbol{\mu}|\mathcal{D})} d\mathcal{U} d\boldsymbol{\mu}. \quad (14)$$

The right-hand side of Eq. (14) represents the Kullback-Leibler distance between $P_v(\mathcal{U}, \boldsymbol{\mu})$ and the posterior density $P(\mathcal{U}, \boldsymbol{\mu}|\mathcal{D})$. Hence the problem of minimizing the difference $\log P(\mathcal{D}) - \mathcal{F}[P_v]$ with respect to $P_v(\mathcal{U}, \boldsymbol{\mu})$ amounts to approximating the posterior density $P(\mathcal{U}, \boldsymbol{\mu}|\mathcal{D})$ with $P_v(\mathcal{U}, \boldsymbol{\mu})$ as closely as possible. The probability measure P_v is often called a *variational posterior*.

In the most general application of variational Bayes, the following assumption is made about the approximating variational posterior density:

$$P_v(\mathcal{U}, \boldsymbol{\mu}) = P_v(\mathcal{U}) P_v(\boldsymbol{\mu}). \quad (15)$$

In fact, this is also the assumption used in [13]. However, Eq. (15) implies that the unobserved data is independent of the parameters. This assumption imposes a hard restriction on the variational posterior density. The unobserved data $\mathcal{U}$ contains information about the total number of faults N. This information influences the posterior distribution. We therefore refine the assumption in Eq. (15) by separating the unobserved data $\mathcal{U}$ into the total number of faults N and the other information $\mathcal{T}$; i.e., $\mathcal{U} = \{\mathcal{T}, N\}$:

$$P_v(\mathcal{U}, \boldsymbol{\mu}) = P_v(\mathcal{T}, N, \boldsymbol{\mu}) = P_v(\mathcal{T}|N)P_v(\boldsymbol{\mu}|N)P_v(N). \tag{16}$$

This equation represents the conditional independence relationship between $\mathcal{T}$ and the model parameters, given that N is fixed. From this assumption, the optimal variational posterior densities maximizing the functional $\mathcal{F}[P_v]$ are

$$P_v(\mathcal{T}|N) \propto \exp\left(\int P_v(\boldsymbol{\mu}|N)\log P(\mathcal{D}, \mathcal{T}, N|\boldsymbol{\mu})d\boldsymbol{\mu}\right)$$
$$= \exp\left(E_{\boldsymbol{\mu}|N}\left[\log P(\mathcal{D}, \mathcal{T}, N|\boldsymbol{\mu})\right]\right), \tag{17}$$

$$P_v(\boldsymbol{\mu}|N)$$
$$\propto P(\boldsymbol{\mu})\exp\left(\int P_v(\mathcal{T}|N)\log P(\mathcal{D}, \mathcal{T}, N|\boldsymbol{\mu})d\mathcal{T}\right)$$
$$= P(\boldsymbol{\mu})\exp\left(E_{\mathcal{T}|N}\left[\log P(\mathcal{D}, \mathcal{T}, N|\boldsymbol{\mu})\right]\right), \tag{18}$$

and

$$P_v(N) \propto \exp\left(\int\int P_v(\mathcal{T}|N)P_v(\boldsymbol{\mu}|N)\right.$$
$$\left.\times \log \frac{P(\mathcal{D}, \mathcal{T}, N|\boldsymbol{\mu})P(\boldsymbol{\mu})}{P_v(\mathcal{T}|N)P_v(\boldsymbol{\mu}|N)}d\mathcal{T}d\boldsymbol{\mu}\right)$$
$$= \exp\left(E_{\mathcal{T}, \boldsymbol{\mu}|N}\left[\log \frac{P(\mathcal{D}, \mathcal{T}, N|\boldsymbol{\mu})P(\boldsymbol{\mu})}{P_v(\mathcal{T}|N)P_v(\boldsymbol{\mu}|N)}\right]\right)$$
$$=: \tilde{P}_v(N), \tag{19}$$

where $E_{\boldsymbol{\mu}|N}[\cdot]$ and $E_{\mathcal{T}|N}[\cdot]$ are the conditional expectations with respect to $\boldsymbol{\mu}$ and $\mathcal{T}$ under the variational posterior densities, provided that N is given. Also, $E_{\mathcal{T}, \boldsymbol{\mu}|N}[\cdot] = E_{\mathcal{T}|N}[E_{\boldsymbol{\mu}|N}[\cdot]]$. The variational posterior distribution of the parameter vector becomes the mixture-type distribution of the conditional variational posterior distributions of $\boldsymbol{\mu}$: $P_v(\boldsymbol{\mu}) = \sum_N P_v(\boldsymbol{\mu}|N)P_v(N)$.

Based on this scheme, we propose the following general VB algorithm:

Step 1: Set the range of the total number of faults N to $[m_e, n_{max}]$, where m_e (≥ 0) is the number of previously observed failures, and n_{max} is a sufficiently large number.

Step 2: Compute the conditional variational posterior densities of $\mathcal{T}$ and $\boldsymbol{\mu}$, Eqs. (17) and (18), for each $N \in [m_e, n_{max}]$.

Step 3: Evaluate $\tilde{P}_v(N)$, the unnormalized form of the variational posterior density $P_v(N)$, at each $N \in [m_e, n_{max}]$, and approximate the probability mass function $P_v(N)$ by $\tilde{P}_v(N)/\sum_{i=m_e}^{n_{max}}\tilde{P}_v(i)$.

Step 4: If the probability mass allocated to the value n_{max} by this approximated probability mass function $P_v(N)$ is smaller than the tolerance ε, i.e., if $P_v(n_{max}) < \varepsilon$, go to Step 5. Otherwise, increase n_{max} and go to Step 2.

Step 5: Return $P_v(\boldsymbol{\mu}) = \sum_N P_v(\boldsymbol{\mu}|N)P_v(N)$ as the optimal variational posterior density.

This algorithm approximates the variational posterior density while simultaneously trying to determine an adequate upper bound n_{max} for the value of N. As shown later, $P_v(N)$ is not a closed form of N. Therefore, in Step 3 the appropriateness of n_{max} is checked via the (approximated) probability mass $P_v(N)$. The approach taken here is a heuristic and has the potential for further improvement.

5.2. Computational steps in the VB algorithm

We now assume that the failure times $Y_1, \ldots, Y_N$ are i.i.d., each following a gamma distribution with scale parameter β and fixed shape parameter α_0; i.e., their common marginal probability density function is given by

$$g_{Gam}(t; \alpha_0, \beta) = \frac{\beta^{\alpha_0}t^{\alpha_0-1}}{\Gamma(\alpha_0)}e^{-\beta t}, \tag{20}$$

where $\Gamma(\cdot)$ denotes the standard gamma function. This class of gamma-type NHPP-based SRMs contains both the Goel-Okumoto model [5] and the delayed S-shaped model [18]. The model parameters to be estimated are ω and β. To simplify the computations, the independent prior distributions for the parameters ω and β are chosen to be gamma distributions with parameters (m_ω, ϕ_ω) and (m_β, ϕ_β), respectively.

For the complete data $\{\mathcal{D}, \mathcal{T}, N\} = \{T_1 < \cdots < T_N\}$, the complete log-likelihood under the given ω and β is

$$\log P(\mathcal{D}, \mathcal{T}, N \mid \omega, \beta) \tag{21}$$
$$= -\omega + N\log\omega + N\alpha_0\log\beta$$
$$+ (\alpha_0 - 1)\sum_{i=1}^{N}\log T_i - \beta\sum_{i=1}^{N}T_i - N\log\Gamma(\alpha_0).$$

From Eq. (18), we have the following variational posterior density for the parameters ω and β:

$$P_v(\omega, \beta \mid N) \propto P(\omega)P(\beta)\omega^N\beta^N e^{-\omega-\zeta_{\mathcal{T}|N}}, \tag{22}$$

where $\zeta_{\mathcal{T}|N} = E_{\mathcal{T}|N}\left[\sum_{i=1}^{N}T_i\right]$. Based on the conjugate gamma prior distributions for ω and β, the variational posterior distributions of these parameters are obtained as gamma distributions with parameters $(m_\omega + N, \phi_\omega + 1)$ and $(m_\beta + N\alpha_0, \phi_\beta + \zeta_{T|N})$, respectively. Moreover, from Eq. (17), the general form of the variational posterior density of $\mathcal{T}$ is obtained as

$$P_v(\mathcal{T}|N) \quad \propto \quad \prod_{i=1}^{N} g_{Gam}(T_i; \alpha_0, \xi_{\beta|N}), \quad (23)$$

where $\xi_{\beta|N} = \mathrm{E}_{\mu|N}[\beta]$. Note that the concrete form of the variational posterior density is determined after $\mathcal{D}$ and $\mathcal{T}$ are specified.

Given the total number of faults N, the computational step for deriving the variational posterior densities mainly consists of the computation of the expected values $\zeta_{T|N}$ and $\xi_{\beta|N}$. Basically, these expected values can be computed from non-linear equations. Since the variational posterior density of $\mathcal{T}$ depends on the data structure, this paper provides the non-linear equations of $\zeta_{T|N}$ and $\xi_{\beta|N}$ for both failure time data and grouped data under the gamma prior distribution for β.

Consider the failure time data $\mathcal{D}_T = \{T_1 = t_1, \ldots, T_{M(t_e)} = t_{m_e}\}$ collected until time t_e. Then $\zeta_{T|N}$ and $\xi_{\beta|N}$ can be calculated via the following equations:

$$\zeta_{T|N} = \sum_{i=1}^{m_e} t_i + \frac{(N - m_e)\alpha_0}{\xi_{\beta|N}} \frac{\overline{G}_{Gam}(t_e; \alpha_0 + 1, \xi_{\beta|N})}{\overline{G}_{Gam}(t_e; \alpha_0, \xi_{\beta|N})}, \quad (24)$$

and

$$\xi_{\beta|N} = \frac{m_\beta + N}{\phi_\beta + \zeta_{T|N}}. \quad (25)$$

On the other hand, given the grouped data $\mathcal{D}_G = \{X_1 = x_1, \ldots, X_k = x_k\}$ for the time sequence $s_0 \equiv 0 < s_1 < \cdots < s_k$, the expected values $\zeta_{T|N}$ and $\xi_{\beta|N}$ are given by

$$\zeta_{T|N} = \sum_{i=1}^{k} \frac{x_i \alpha_0}{\xi_{\beta|N}} \frac{\Delta G_{Gam}(s_i, s_{i-1}; \alpha_0 + 1, \xi_{\beta|N})}{\Delta G_{Gam}(s_i, s_{i-1}; \alpha_0, \xi_{\beta|N})}$$
$$+ \frac{(N - \sum_{i=1}^{k} x_i)\alpha_0}{\xi_{\beta|N}} \frac{\overline{G}_{Gam}(s_k; \alpha_0 + 1, \xi_{\beta|N})}{\overline{G}_{Gam}(s_k; \alpha_0, \xi_{\beta|N})}, \quad (26)$$

and

$$\xi_{\beta|N} = \frac{m_\beta + N}{\phi_\beta + \zeta_{T|N}}, \quad (27)$$

where $\Delta G_{Gam}(s_i, s_{i-1}; \alpha_0, \xi_{\beta|N})$ is the increment of $G_{Gam}(t; \alpha_0, \xi_{\beta|N})$ for time period $(s_{i-1}, s_i]$.

In the case of the Goel-Okumoto model (i.e., $\alpha_0 = 1$) and the availability of failure time data, the non-linear equation can explicitly be solved. For the other cases, we need to apply numerical techniques to solve the simultaneous equations. The simplest way is successive substitution. Such a method is guaranteed to have the global convergence property [1].

The variational posterior density $P_v(N)$ can also be derived from the complete log-likelihood. Based on the expected operations $\mathrm{E}_\mu[\cdot]$ and $\mathrm{E}_{T|N}[\cdot]$, we obtain

$$P_v(N) \propto \frac{\Gamma(m_\omega + N)\Gamma(m_\beta + N\alpha_0)}{(\phi_\omega + 1)^{m_\omega + N}(\phi_\beta + \zeta_{T|N})^{m_\beta + N\alpha_0}}$$
$$\times C(N) \cdot \frac{1}{\xi_{\beta|N}^{N\alpha_0} \exp(-\xi_{\beta|N}\zeta_{T|N})}, \quad (28)$$

where $C(N)$ is the normalizing constant appearing in the denominator of the conditional variational posterior density $P_v(\mathcal{T}|N)$. The form of $C(N)$ depends on the data structure. In the case of failure time data, we get

$$C(N) = \prod_{i=1}^{m_e} g_{Gam}(t_i; \alpha_0, \xi_{\beta|N})$$
$$\times \overline{G}_{Gam}(t_e; \alpha_0, \xi_{\beta|N})^{N - m_e} / (N - m_e)!. \quad (29)$$

For grouped data, the normalizing factor is given by

$$C(N) = \prod_{i=1}^{k} \Delta G_{Gam}(s_i, s_{i-1}; \alpha_0, \xi_{\beta|N})^{x_i} \quad (30)$$
$$\times \overline{G}_{Gam}(s_k; \alpha_0, \xi_{\beta|N})^{N - \sum_{i=1}^{k} x_i} / (N - \sum_{i=1}^{k} x_i)!.$$

6. Numerical experiments

In this section, we investigate the efficacy of our variational Bayesian approach. To this end, we use the System 17 data collected during the system test phase of a military application [4]. The data is available in two forms:

$\mathcal{D}_T$: failure time data consisting of the failure times (measured in wall-clock seconds) for all 38 failures experienced during the system test phase.

$\mathcal{D}_G$: grouped data consisting of the number of failure occurrences for each of the 64 working days of the system test phase.

The Goel-Okumoto model is applied to the above data sets. Moreover, we assume the following two scenarios about prior information:

Info: The prior information consists of good guesses of parameters. In the failure time data case, the mean and standard deviation of the prior distributions are (50, 15.8) for ω and (1.0e-5, 3.2e-6) for β. In the grouped data case, the prior distribution of β is different; its mean and standard deviation are given by (3.3e-2, 1.1e-2).

NoInfo: No informative prior information about the parameters is available. Therefore, flat prior densities on the parameters are used. The estimates are thus only based on the likelihood resulting from the observed data.

Table 1. Moments of approximate posterior distributions for $\mathcal{D}_T$ and $\mathcal{D}_G$.

	$\mathcal{D}_T$ and Info						$\mathcal{D}_G$ and Info				
	$E[\omega]$	$E[\beta]$	$Var(\omega)$	$Var(\beta)$	$Cov(\omega,\beta)$		$E[\omega]$	$E[\beta]$	$Var(\omega)$	$Var(\beta)$	$Cov(\omega,\beta)$
NINT	41.78	1.11E-05	37.69	4.26E-12	-2.13E-06	NINT	48.63	2.57E-02	65.35	3.51E-05	-2.20E-02
LAPL	40.69	1.10E-05	36.07	4.20E-12	-1.88E-06	LAPL	47.08	2.50E-02	60.21	3.53E-05	-2.15E-02
	-2.6%	-1.6%	-4.3%	-1.5%	-11.6%		-3.2%	-2.6%	-7.9%	0.4%	-2.5%
MCMC	41.82	1.11E-05	37.50	4.27E-12	-2.21E-06	MCMC	48.68	2.56E-02	65.49	3.46E-05	-2.18E-02
	0.1%	-0.2%	-0.5%	0.3%	3.8%		0.1%	-0.4%	0.2%	-1.6%	-1.1%
VB1	41.37	1.14E-05	34.47	2.60E-12	0	VB1	47.11	2.64E-02	39.26	1.23E-05	0
	-1.0%	1.8%	-8.5%	-39.0%	100.0%		-3.1%	2.8%	-39.9%	-64.9%	-100.0%
VB2	41.75	1.12E-05	37.57	4.15E-12	-2.08E-06	VB2	48.39	2.59E-02	63.90	3.31E-05	-2.13E-02
	-0.1%	0.2%	-0.3%	-2.5%	-2.3%		-0.5%	0.8%	-2.2%	-5.9%	-3.1%

	$\mathcal{D}_T$ and NoInfo						$\mathcal{D}_G$ and NoInfo				
	$E[\omega]$	$E[\beta]$	$Var(\omega)$	$Var(\beta)$	$Cov(\omega,\beta)$		$E[\omega]$	$E[\beta]$	$Var(\omega)$	$Var(\beta)$	$Cov(\omega,\beta)$
NINT	40.66	1.23E-05	44.62	6.83E-12	-3.23E-06	NINT	116.04	1.62E-02	2.65E+04	9.40E-05	-8.86E-01
LAPL	39.26	1.22E-05	41.44	6.56E-12	-2.41E-06	LAPL	53.48	1.94E-02	2.37E+02	8.31E-05	-1.16E-01
	-3.5%	-1.3%	-7.1%	-4.0%	-25.5%		-53.9%	19.4%	-99.1%	-11.6%	-86.9%
MCMC	39.80	1.18E-05	44.11	6.84E-12	-3.78E-06	MCMC	1.56E+03	1.03E-02	1.13E+07	9.88E-05	-1.53E+01
	-2.1%	-4.1%	-1.1%	0.2%	17.0%		1245.8%	-36.3%	42653.5%	5.1%	1627.8%
VB1	39.20	1.22E-05	39.20	3.82E-12	0	VB1	50.82	2.12E-02	5.08E+01	8.86E-06	0
	-3.6%	-0.8%	-12.1%	-44.0%	-100.0%		-56.2%	30.8%	-99.8%	-90.6%	-100.0%
VB2	39.83	1.19E-05	44.61	6.62E-12	-3.56E-06	VB2	90.50	1.64E-02	1.09E+04	7.77E-05	-5.15E-01
	-2.0%	-3.7%	0.0%	-3.1%	10.1%		-22.0%	1.1%	-59.1%	-17.3%	-41.8%

In the following, we compare the inteval estimation results for numerical integration (NINT), Laplace approximation (LAPL), Markov chain Monte Carlo (MCMC), the variational Bayesian approach proposed in [13] (VB1), and the variational Bayesian approach proposed here (VB2).

We implement all of these methods using Mathematica[1]. As noted before, one issue in numerical integration is the adequate choice of the area of integration. In our implementation of NINT, for each parameter the upper and lower limits of integration are determined based on the 0.5%- and 99.5%-quantiles of the respective marginal distribution derived for VB2: While each lower limit is chosen as the corresponding 0.5%-quantile divided by two, the upper limit is chosen as the respective 99.5%-quantile multiplied by 1.5. The numerical integration uses the multiple-precision arithmetic provided by Mathematica.

Under the MCMC method, we generate samples of the posterior distribution from one long-range MCMC series. In order to prevent dependence on the starting values of the parameters, the first 10000 samples (so-called "burn-in samples") are discarded. Moreover, at only every 10th MCMC iteration a sample is collected, to avoid autocorrelation between the samples taken. The quantiles of the posterior distribution are estimated by the corresponding order statistics. For instance, the lower bound of the two-sided 95% confidence interval for ω is estimated by the 500th smallest value of ω in all 20000 samples collected, i.e., by the empirical 2.5%-quantile. The accuracy of these estimates depends on the sample size. In our example, the sample size of 20000 gives us 95% confidence that the empirical 2.5%-quantile lies between the theoretical 2.4%- and 2.6%-quantiles [2].

Analyzing the results for all methods, we first investigate their approximation accuracy from the viewpoint of the entire posterior distribution. Table 1 presents the means, variances and covariances of the approximate joint posterior distributions of ω and β, obtained for failure time data $\mathcal{D}_T$ or grouped data $\mathcal{D}_G$. Although there can be numerical errors in the application of NINT (such as those connected to the truncation of the area of integration), we assume that NINT provides the most accurate approximation. Therefore, for all other methods we show the relative deviations from the results obtained by NINT. Except for the $\mathcal{D}_G$-NoInfo case, the first two moments calculated for NINT, MCMC and VB2 are similar. For higher moments - not shown in Table 1 - the results of NINT, MCMC and VB2 are also almost same; for example, the relative deviations of the third centralized moment $E[(\omega - E[\omega])^3]$ in the $\mathcal{D}_T$-Info case are 0.3% for MCMC and -0.9% for VB2. These results suggest that NINT, MCMC and VB2 provide similarly good approximations for the actual posterior distribution. On the other hand, LAPL and VB1 produce considerably worse results. For example, both methods seem to consistently underestimate the mean and the variance of ω. An important reason for the bad performance of VB1 seems to be its inability to model the correlation between ω and β. While LAPL can account for this correlation, its joint posterior density is necessarily symmetric. Why this restriction leads to biased means for ω and β, can be explained with the help

---
[1]Wolfram Research, Inc. http://www.wolfram.com/

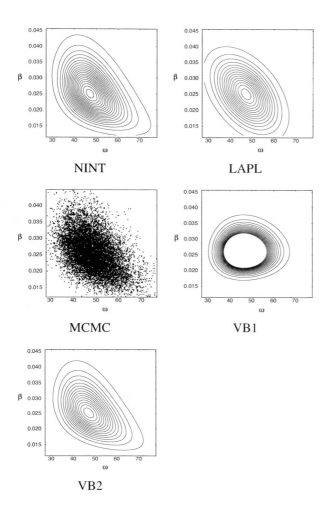

Table 2. Two-sided 99% confidence intervals ($\mathcal{D}_T$).

		ω_{lower}	ω_{upper}	β_{lower}	β_{upper}
Info	NINT	27.74	59.45	6.27E-06	1.69E-05
	LAPL	25.22	56.16	5.70E-06	1.63E-05
		-9.1%	-5.5%	-9.1%	-3.7%
	MCMC	27.81	59.28	6.20E-06	1.67E-05
		0.2%	-0.3%	-1.1%	-1.0%
	VB1	27.81	58.05	7.63E-06	1.59E-05
		0.2%	-2.4%	21.7%	-5.6%
	VB2	27.73	59.38	6.41E-06	1.69E-05
		-0.1%	-0.1%	2.2%	0.0%
NoInfo	NINT	25.68	60.35	5.98E-06	1.95E-05
	LAPL	22.68	55.84	5.58E-06	1.88E-05
		-11.7%	-7.5%	-6.6%	-3.8%
	MCMC	24.88	59.59	5.53E-06	1.90E-05
		-3.1%	-1.3%	-7.4%	-2.9%
	VB1	24.95	57.20	6.92E-06	1.56E-05
		-2.8%	-5.2%	15.7%	-20.0%
	VB2	24.95	59.68	5.68E-06	1.90E-05
		-2.8%	-1.1%	-5.0%	-2.7%

Figure 1. Approximate posterior distribution for $\mathcal{D}_G$ and Info.

of Figure 1. This figure shows the contour plots for the joint posterior densities approximated by NINT, LAPL, VB1 and VB2, as well as the scatter plot using 10000 MCMC samples in the $\mathcal{D}_G$-Info case. The results for NINT, MCMC and VB2 indicate that the marginal posterior densities of ω and β are in fact right-skewed. Therefore, the MAP estimates, around which the LAPL method centers its approximate posterior distribution, tend to be smaller than the true expected parameter values. Like Table 1, the diagrams in Figure 1 suggest that NINT, MCMC and VB2 produce similar results, while LAPL and VB1 cannot approximate the joint posterior distribution as accurately as the other methods.

According to Table 1, the $\mathcal{D}_G$-NoInfo case seems to be special, because NINT, MCMC and VB2 (as well as LAPL and VB1) produce highly different results. As pointed out by several authors [7, 17, 20], in the absence of prior information accurate parameter estimates can only obtained if the failure time data itself contains enough information about the parameters. If this is not the case, the posterior distribution becomes a long-tailed distribution with large variances and covariances. Since the grouped data $\mathcal{D}_G$ of System 17 cannot be fitted by the Goel-Okumoto model as well as the failure time data $\mathcal{D}_T$, it contains less information about the parameters than $\mathcal{D}_T$. Therefore, in the absence of an informative prior distribution, none of the Bayesian methods provides accurate estimates.

The interval estimates for the parameters ω and β obtained by the different approaches confirm our findings. Tables 2 and 3 present the two-sided 99% confidence intervals for $\mathcal{D}_T$ and $\mathcal{D}_G$, respectively. As before, for LAPL, MCMC, VB1 and VB2, we compute the relative deviations from the results obtained for NINT. Again, with the exception of the $\mathcal{D}_G$-NoInfo case, the results calculated by MCMC and VB2 are close to the ones derived by NINT. The fact that the interval estimates calculated by LAPL are usually shifted to the left is explained by the bias in the estimated expected values discussed earlier. On the other hand, because VB1 underestimates the variances of the parameters, it tends to derive interval estimates that are too narrow.

Since none of the methods produces reliable results in the $\mathcal{D}_G$-NoInfo case, we focus our attention on the Info case for the rest of this paper.

We now discuss the statistical inference on the software reliability. Tables 4 and 5 present the point estimates and two-sided 99% confidence intervals of software reliability for $\mathcal{D}_T$ and $\mathcal{D}_G$. The reliability is estimated for the time intervals $(t_e, t_e + u]$, where $u \in \{1000, 10000\}$ for $\mathcal{D}_T$ and

Table 3. Two-sided 99% confidence intervals ($\mathcal{D}_G$).

		ω_{lower}	ω_{upper}	β_{lower}	β_{upper}
Info	NINT	31.20	73.80	1.27E-02	4.29E-02
	LAPL	27.09	67.06	9.72E-03	4.03E-02
		-13.2%	-9.1%	-23.7%	-6.0%
	MCMC	31.15	73.46	1.29E-02	4.23E-02
		-0.2%	-0.5%	1.3%	-1.3%
	VB1	32.54	64.81	9.93E-03	1.84E-02
		4.3%	-12.2%	-22.1%	-57.1%
	VB2	31.10	73.18	1.35E-02	4.28E-02
		-0.3%	-0.8%	5.6%	-0.3%
NoInfo	NINT	31.86	788.14	7.59E-04	4.25E-02
	LAPL	13.84	93.12	<-4.11E-03>	4.29E-02
		-56.6%	-88.2%	-641.9%	0.9%
	MCMC	32.51	1.85E+04	3.06E-05	3.83E-02
		2.1%	2242.6%	-96.0%	-9.8%
	VB1	34.33	71.05	1.43E-02	2.97E-02
		7.8%	-91.0%	1788.1%	-30.1%
	VB2	31.11	583.35	1.06E-03	4.09E-02
		-2.4%	-26.0%	39.3%	-3.7%

$u \in \{1, 5\}$ for $\mathcal{D}_G$.

For NINT, the point estimate $\hat{R}(t_e + u | t_e)$ and the p-quantile $\hat{R}_p^{-1}(t_e + u | t_e)$ of software reliability are computed via the following equations:

$$\hat{R}(t_e + u | t_e) = \int_0^\infty \int_0^\infty \exp\{-\omega(e^{-\beta t_e}$$
$$- e^{-\beta(t_e + u)})\} P(\omega, \beta | \mathcal{D}) d\omega d\beta, \quad (31)$$

$$\int_0^\infty \int_{\frac{-\log \hat{R}_p^{-1}(t_e + u | t_e)}{e^{-\beta t_e} - e^{-\beta(t_e + u)}}}^\infty P(\omega, \beta | \mathcal{D}) d\omega_0 d\beta = p. \quad (32)$$

Since Eq. (32) is non-linear, we use the bisection method to derive $\hat{R}_p^{-1}(t_e + u | t_e)$. For VB1 and VB2, $P(\omega, \beta | \mathcal{D})$ is replaced by the respective variational posterior density. The point estimate in LAPL is obtained by directly plugging $\hat{\omega}_{MAP}$ and $\hat{\beta}_{MAP}$ into Eq. (3), and the confidence interval is computed from the first derivatives of software reliability with respect to ω and β. For MCMC, we calculate the software reliability for all 20000 parameter samples and derive the point estimate and the interval estimate as the sample mean and the respective order statistics of all reliability values computed.

The results for NINT, MCMC and VB2 shown in Tables 4 and 5 are almost the same for both point estimation and interval estimation. Thus the accuracies of the software reliability estimates can be considered high. The other two methods produce considerably worse results. Especially, since VB1 underestimates the variance of the model parameters, the estimated intervals of software reliability derived by this method tend to be too narrow.

Finally, we discuss computational speed. Since the computation of NINT relies on VB2 to detect the area of in-

Table 4. Interval estimation for software reliability ($\mathcal{D}_T$ and Info).

		reliability	lower bound	upper bound
$u = 1000$	NINT	0.9791	0.9483	0.9946
	LAPL	0.9802	0.9580	<1.0024>
	MCMC	0.9790	0.9474	0.9945
	VB1	0.9806	0.9607	0.9933
	VB2	0.9792	0.9492	0.9946
$u = 10000$	NINT	0.8200	0.5974	0.9513
	LAPL	0.8268	0.6448	<1.0087>
	MCMC	0.8192	0.5919	0.9502
	VB1	0.8314	0.6795	0.9391
	VB2	0.8210	0.6029	0.9513

Table 5. Interval estimation for software reliability ($\mathcal{D}_G$ and Info).

		reliability	lower bound	upper bound
$u = 1$	NINT	0.7907	0.6618	0.9015
	LAPL	0.7678	0.6281	0.9075
	MCMC	0.7901	0.6629	0.8998
	VB1	0.7987	0.7202	0.8688
	VB2	0.7923	0.6637	0.9015
$u = 5$	NINT	0.3382	0.1353	0.6198
	LAPL	0.2829	0.0283	0.5374
	MCMC	0.3369	0.1359	0.6149
	VB1	0.3480	0.2080	0.5173
	VB2	0.3413	0.1374	0.6197

tegration, we focus only on MCMC and VB2. The computational speed of MCMC and VB2 directly depends on the number of samples and the truncation point n_{max}, respectively. Tables 6 and 7 show the computation times for the MCMC and VB2 algorithms we implemented using Mathematica. In MCMC, we measure the computation time to collect 20000 samples; taking into account the burn-in samples and the fact that a sample is only collected at every tenth iteration, the total number of Poisson and gamma random variates to be generated is 630000 ($=3 \cdot (10000+10 \cdot 20000)$). In the grouped data case, in which we additionally use data augmentation [16] at each stage, to generate the 38 failure times, the total number of Poisson, gamma and exponential random variates to be computed is 8610000 ($=(3+38) \cdot (10000+10 \cdot 20000)$). The computation time for VB2 is measured for the truncation points $n_{max} \in \{100, 200, 500, 1000\}$. Here we use successive substitution to solve the non-linear equations (24)–(27). Even for $n_{max} = 1000$, the computation time of VB2 is considerably smaller than the one for MCMC. However, such a large value of n_{max} is not necessary, as can be seen from the respective probability masses $P_v(n_{max})$ shown in Table 7. For example, given a tolerance of $\varepsilon = 5e-15$, the criterion $P_v(n_{max}) < \varepsilon$ is already fulfilled for $n_{max} = 200$. The values in Table 7 suggest that the computation time of

Table 6. Computation time for MCMC.

Data	random variates	time (sec)
$\mathcal{D}_T$ and Info	630000	541.97
$\mathcal{D}_G$ and Info	8610000	4036.38

Table 7. Computation time for VB2.

Data	n_{max}	$P_v(n_{max})$	time (sec)
$\mathcal{D}_T$ and Info	100	2.35e-11	0.56
	200	4.48e-21	1.44
	500	3.67e-46	6.59
	1000	1.94e-86	23.22
$\mathcal{D}_G$ and Info	100	1.49e-06	13.28
	200	2.66e-15	58.32
	500	6.56e-40	369.53
	1000	4.85e-80	1429.41

our current VB2 algorithm increases disproportionally with n_{max}. This is because the complexity of the problem to solve the non-linear equations becomes larger as n_{max} increases. If we use fast convergence methods like the Newton method to solve the non-linear equations, then the computation time can be expected to be proportional to n_{max}.

7. Conclusions

This paper proposes a new VB approach to approximate the posterior distribution in the Bayesian estimation of NHPP-based SRMs. In particular, we have presented a concrete numerical procedure to compute the variational posterior distributions for gamma-type NHPP-based SRMs, for both failure time data and grouped data. In numerical experiments, we have compared our VB approach with conventional approximate methods. Our results indicate that the proposed method provides almost the same accuracy as MCMC, while its computational burden is much lower. For the future, we are planning to develop methods for the computation of confidence intervals using analytical expansion techniques.

Acknowledgments

This research was partially supported by the Ministry of Education, Science, Sports and Culture, Grant-in-Aid for Scientific Research (B), Grant No. 1631011600 (2004-2006) and Scientific Research (C), Grant No. 18510138 (2006-2008).

References

[1] H. Attias. Inferring parameters and structure of latent variable models by variational Bayes. In *Proc. 15th Conf. on Uncertainty in Artificial Intelligence*, pages 21–30, 1999.

[2] E. J. Chen and W. D. Kelton. Simulation-based estimation of quantiles. In *Proc. of the 1999 Winter Simulation Conference*, pages 428–434, 1999.

[3] S. Chib and E. Greenberg. Understanding the Metropolis-Hastings algorithm. *American Statistician*, 49(4):327–335, 1995.

[4] Data & Analysis Center for Software. The software reliability dataset. http://www.dacs.dtic.mil/databases/sled/swrel.shtml.

[5] A. L. Goel and K. Okumoto. Time-dependent error-detection rate model for software reliability and other performance measures. *IEEE Trans. Reliab.*, R-28:206–211, 1979.

[6] Z. Jelinski and P. B. Moranda. Software reliability research. In W. Freiberger, editor, *Statistical Computer Performance Evaluation*, pages 465–484. Academic Press, New York, 1972.

[7] H. Joe. Statistical inference for general-order-statistics and nonhomogeneous-Poisson-process software reliability models. *IEEE Trans. Software Eng.*, SE-15:1485–1490, 1989.

[8] L. Kuo and T. Y. Yang. Bayesian computation of software reliability. *J. Comput. Graphical Statist.*, 4:65–82, 1995.

[9] L. Kuo and T. Y. Yang. Bayesian computation for nonhomogeneous Poisson processes in software reliability. *J. Amer. Statist. Assoc.*, 91:763–773, 1996.

[10] M. R. Lyu, editor. *Handbook of Software Reliability Engineering*. McGraw-Hill, New York, 1996.

[11] R. J. Meinhold and N. D. Singpurwalla. Bayesian analysis of commonly used model for describing software failures. *The Statistician*, 32:168–173, 1983.

[12] J. D. Musa, A. Iannino, and K. Okumoto. *Software Reliability - Measurement, Prediction, Application*. McGraw-Hill, New York, 1987.

[13] H. Okamura, T. Sakoh, and T. Dohi. Variational Bayesian approach for exponential software reliability model. In *Proc. 10th IASTED Int'l Conf. on Software Eng. and Applications*, pages 82–87, 2006.

[14] H. Okamura, Y. Watanabe, and T. Dohi. An iterative scheme for maximum likelihood estimation in software reliability modeling. In *Proc. 14th Int'l Symp. on Software Reliab. Eng.*, pages 246–256, 2003.

[15] N. D. Singpurwalla and S. P. Wilson. *Statistical Methods in Software Engineering*. Springer-Verlag, New York, 1997.

[16] M. A. Tanner and W. H. Wong. The calculation of posterior distributions by data augmentation. *J. Amer. Statist. Assoc.*, 82:528–540, 1987.

[17] M. C. van Pul. Asymptotic properties of a class of statistical models in software reliability. *Scand. J. Statist.*, 19:235–253, 1992.

[18] S. Yamada, M. Ohba, and S. Osaki. S-shaped reliability growth modeling for software error detection. *IEEE Trans. Reliab.*, R-32:475–478, 1983.

[19] S. Yamada and S. Osaki. Software reliability growth modeling: Models and applications. *IEEE Trans. Software Eng.*, SE-11:1431–1437, 1985.

[20] L. Yin and K. S. Trivedi. Confidence interval estimation of NHPP-based software reliability models. In *Proc. 10th Int'l Symp. Software Reliab. Eng.*, pages 6–11, 1999.

Dynamic Fault Tree analysis using Input/Output Interactive Markov Chains[*]

Hichem Boudali
hboudali@cs.utwente.nl

Pepijn Crouzen[§,†]
crouzen@alan.cs.uni-sb.de

Mariëlle Stoelinga
marielle@cs.utwente.nl

University of Twente, Department of Computer Science,
P.O. Box 217, 7500 AE Enschede, the Netherlands.

[§]Saarland University, Department of Computer Science,
D-66123 Saarbrücken, Germany.

Abstract

Dynamic Fault Trees (DFT) extend standard fault trees by allowing the modeling of complex system components' behaviors and interactions. Being a high level model and easy to use, DFT are experiencing a growing success among reliability engineers. Unfortunately, a number of issues still remains when using DFT. Briefly, these issues are (1) a lack of formality (syntax and semantics), (2) limitations in modular analysis and thus vulnerability to the state-space explosion problem, and (3) lack in modular model-building. We use the input/output interactive Markov chain (I/O-IMC) formalism to analyse DFT. I/O-IMC have a precise semantics and are an extension of continuous-time Markov chains with input and output actions. In this paper, using the I/O-IMC framework, we address and resolve issues (2) and (3) mentioned above. We also show, through some examples, how one can readily extend the DFT modeling capabilities using the I/O-IMC framework.

KEYWORDS: Fault tree, Interactive process, Markov chain, compositional aggregation, modularity.

1. Introduction

Dynamic fault trees (DFT) [10, 7, 19] extend standard (or static) fault trees (FT) [20] by defining additional gates called dynamic gates. These gates allow the modeling of complex system components' behaviors and interactions which is far superior to the modeling capabilities of standard FT. Like standard FT, dynamic fault trees are a high-level formalism for computing reliability measures of computer-based systems, such as the probability that the system fails during its mission time. For over a decade now, DFT have been experiencing a growing success among reliability engineers. Unfortunately, a number of issues still remains when using DFT. Most notably the following three issues are a matter of concern: (1) the DFT semantics is rather imprecise and the lack of formality has, in some cases, led to undefined behavior and misinterpretation of the DFT model. (2) DFT lack modular analysis. That is, even though stochastically-independent sub-modules exist in a certain DFT module (specifically those whose top-node is a dynamic gate), these sub-modules cannot be solved separately and still get an exact solution. Consequently, a DFT model, which is typically analyzed by first converting it into a Markov chain (MC), becomes vulnerable to the state space explosion problem. (3) DFT also lack modular model-building, i.e. there are some rather severe restrictions on the type of allowed inputs to certain gates (e.g. inputs to spare gates and dependent events of functional dependency gates have to be basic events), which greatly diminish the modeling flexibility and power of DFT.

DFT are comprised of various elements[1]: Basic events, static gates (AND, OR, and K/M gates), and dynamic gates (functional dependency, priority AND, and spare gates). Each of these elements is viewed as a process moving from one state to another. States denote either the operation or the failure of the element. Each element, or process, also interacts (communicates) with its environment by responding to certain input signals and producing output signals. These elements[2] could also possess a purely stochastic behavior by allowing (in a probabilistic fashion) the passage of time prior to moving to another state. In the remainder

---

[*]This research has been partially funded by the Netherlands Organisation for Scientific Research (NWO) under FOCUS/BRICKS grant number 642.000.505 (MOQS); the EU under grant number IST-004527 (ARTIST2); and by the DFG/NWO bilateral cooperation programme under project number DN 62-600 (VOSS2).

[†]The majority of this work was done while the author was at the University of Twente.

[1]Also called components.
[2]At this point only the basic events.

of the paper, we assume this passage of time to be governed by an exponential probability distribution (thus behaving as a Markovian process). Moving from one state to another is therefore caused by either an input or output transition or due to a Markovian transition.

Given the nature of DFT elements we have used the input/output interactive Markov chain (I/O-IMC) formalism [4] to model the semantics of DFT. In fact, I/O-IMC augment continuous-time Markov chains with input and output actions and a clear separation between Markovian transitions and interactive (involving input or output actions) transitions is made. Furthermore, I/O-IMC have a precise and formal semantics and have proved to be a suitable and natural way to model DFT elements.

I/O-IMC are an example of a stochastic extension to a process algebra. These stochastic process algebras have recently gained popularity in performance modeling and analysis due to their *compositional aggregation* approach. We refer the reader to [14] for case studies on the application of the compositional aggregation approach to the modeling and analysis of real systems. Compositional aggregation is a technique to build an I/O-IMC by composing, in successive iterations, a number of elementary and smaller I/O-IMC and reducing (i.e. aggregating) the state-space of the generated I/O-IMC as the composition takes place (cf. Section 3).

Issue (1), mentioned above, has been addressed in [4] where a formal syntax and semantics for DFT have been defined. The formal syntax is derived by characterizing the DFT as a directed acyclic graph. The formal DFT semantics is described in terms of I/O-IMC, and provides a rigorous basis for the analysis of DFT. In fact, each DFT element has a corresponding elementary I/O-IMC. This semantics is fully compositional, that is, the semantics of a DFT is expressed in terms of the semantics of its elements. This enables an efficient analysis of DFT through compositional aggregation to produce a single I/O-IMC, on which we can then carry out performance analysis. Earlier work on formalizing DFT can be found in [8], where DFT are specified using the Z formal specification language. The main difference between the formal specification in [8] and the formal specification used in this paper is that in our framework we use a process algebra-like formalism (i.e. I/O-IMC) which allows us to use the well-defined concept of compositional aggregation which helps us to combat the state-space explosion problem. In fact, this notion of compositional aggregation is not present in [8] and the state-space explosion problem is not addressed or mitigated whatsoever.

We address issue (2) by showing, using the I/O-IMC framework, how the DFT analysis becomes greatly modular compared to current state of the art DFT analysis techniques. In particular, we demonstrate, through an example system, how an I/O-IMC corresponding to a certain (independent) dynamic module[3] can be reused in any larger DFT model.

We also tackle issue (3) and lift two previously enforced restrictions on DFT; namely, the restriction on spares and functional dependency gates' dependent events to be basic events. In fact, in our framework it becomes possible to, for instance, model a spare as a complex sub-system comprised of several basic events and gates. The use of (shared) spares in DFT has always been somehow problematic [8]. In this paper, we carefully examine, clarify, and generalize the concept of *spare activation*.

To summarize, we make the following contributions:

1. Illustrate, through a case study, the use of the I/O-IMC framework for the analysis of DFT, and in particular we show the benefits of the compositional aggregation approach.

2. Show the increased DFT modular analysis and the concept of reuse of dynamic modules.

3. Extend the DFT modeling capabilities by allowing complex spares (through the generalization of the concept of activation) and complex functionally dependent events.

4. Illustrate how readily one can define new DFT elements and provide 3 examples.

The remainder of the paper is organized as follows: In Section 2 and Section 3, we introduce DFT and I/O-IMC respectively. In Section 4, we show how a DFT is automatically converted into a community of I/O-IMC and discuss non-determinism. In Section 5, we illustrate the DFT modular analysis. In Section 6, we lift the restrictions on the spare and functional dependency (FDEP) gates. Finally, in Section 7, we illustrate how one can readily extend the modeling capabilities of DFT by augmenting or modifying the set of elementary I/O-IMC models. Some of these extensions include *mutually exclusive events* and *repair*. We conclude the paper and suggest future work in Section 8.

2. Dynamic fault trees

A fault tree model describes the system failure in terms of the failure of its components. Standard FT are combinatorial models and are built using static gates (the AND, the OR, and the K/M gates) and basic events (BE). A combinatorial model only captures the combination of events and not the order of their occurrence. Combinatorial models become, therefore, inadequate to model today's complex dynamic systems. DFT introduce three novel modeling capabilities: (1) spare component management and allocation,

---

[3]Also called sub-system or sub-tree.

709

(2) functional dependency, and (3) failure sequence dependency. These modeling capabilities are realized using three main dynamic gates[4]: The spare gate, the functional dependency (FDEP) gate, and the priority AND (PAND) gate. Figure 1 depicts the three dynamic gates.

The PAND gate fails when all its inputs fail and fail from left to right (as depicted on the figure) order. The spare gate has one primary input and one or more alternate inputs (i.e. the spares). The primary input is initially powered on and when it fails, it is replaced by an alternate input. The spare gate fails when the primary and all the alternate inputs fail (or are unavailable). A spare could also be shared among multiple spare gates. In this configuration, when a spare is taken by a spare gate, it becomes unavailable (i.e. essentially seen as failed) to the rest of the spare gates. The FDEP gate is comprised of a trigger event and a set of dependent components. When the trigger event occurs, it causes the dependent components to become inaccessible or unusable (i.e. essentially failed). The FDEP gate's output is a 'dummy' output (i.e. it is not taken into account during the calculation of the system's failure probability). Along with

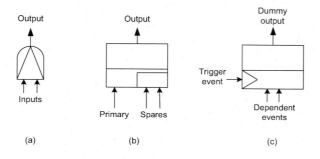

Figure 1. Dynamic gates: (a) PAND, (b) spare, (c) FDEP.

static and dynamic gates, DFT also possess basic events, which are leaves of the tree. A basic event usually represents a physical component having a certain failure probability distribution (e.g. exponential). A DFT element has a number of operational or failed states. In the case of a BE[5], operational states could be further classified as *dormant* or *active* states. A dormant state is a state where the BE failure rate is reduced by a factor called the dormancy factor α. An active state is a state where the BE failure rate λ is unchanged. Depending on the value of α, we classify BE as: cold BE ($\alpha = 0$), hot BE ($\alpha = 1$), and warm BE ($0 < \alpha < 1$). The dormant and active states of a BE correspond to dormant and active modes of the physical component. For instance, a spare tire of a car is initially in a dormant mode and switches to an active mode when it is fixed on the car for use.

---

[4]A fourth gate called 'Sequence Enforcing' gate has also been defined in [10]; however, it turns out that this gate can be emulated using a cold spare gate.

[5]Also a spare gate as we will see in Section 6.

Galileo DIFTree [11] was the first package to introduce, use, and analyze DFT. DIFTree uses a modular approach to analyze a DFT. Indeed, the DFT is first split into independent static and dynamic modules, the modules are then solved separately and each of them is replaced by a BE with a constant failure probability. The modules' solutions are then combined to find the overall system reliability. This process is iterative as independent modules could be nested. An independent module is dynamic if it contains at least one dynamic gate, otherwise it is static. Static modules are solved using binary decision diagrams and dynamic modules are solved by converting them into Markov chains.

Note that when an independent module is replaced by a BE with a constant failure probability, some information (i.e. the shape) of the module's failure distribution is lost since it is replaced by a single failure probability value. Moreover, since any dynamic gate requires the knowledge of the entire failure probability density functions of their inputs, solving an independent module and replacing it by a BE with a constant failure probability is only possible if the module is part of a larger static (and not dynamic) module. This constraint, which is linked to issue (2) mentioned in the Introduction, makes DFT far less modular (cf. Section 5).

3. Input/output interactive Markov chains

Input/output interactive Markov chains [4] are an integration of input/output automata [16] and CTMC [15, 18]. I/O-IMC are closely related to Interactive Markov Chains [12] (IMC) which are an integration of interactive processes [17] and CTMC.

Figure 2.a shows two examples of input/output interactive Markov chains. Circles denote states in the model and transitions are depicted as arrows. The starting state is identified by a black dot. There are two different kinds of transitions in an I/O-IMC model: *Markovian transitions*, denoted by a small rectangle on the arrow and *interactive transitions*, denoted by a line on the arrow. Each I/O-IMC has an *action signature*, written next to its starting state, which shows how it communicates with the environment. I/O-IMC B, for instance, has an input action $a?$, an output action $b!$ and no internal actions. When each of the I/O-IMC's actions has at least one associated transition, the action signature can be (and often is) omitted. The difference between inputs, outputs and internal actions will be discussed later in this section.

I/O-IMC B has a Markovian transition from state 1 to state 2. This transition has a *rate* of λ. Markovian transitions in I/O-IMC behave exactly the same way as Markovian transitions in CTMC: the I/O-IMC moves from state 1 to state 2 after an exponentially distributed delay. An I/O-IMC with only Markovian transitions can thus be interpreted as a CTMC. I/O-IMC B also has an interactive transition from state 1 to state 3 labeled $a?$. This denotes that the move from 1 to 3 is an *input action* named a. Input actions are denoted with a question mark (i.e. $a?$). If some other I/O-IMC performs an *output action* named a while I/O-IMC B is in state 1 then B will move to state 3 immediately. It is important to note that every state of I/O-IMC B has an outgoing input transition named a. This means that B is always ready to respond to an output-action a, even if this does not result in a state-change (when B is in state 3, 4, or 5). For clarity we will omit these transitions (input-actions from a state to itself) from now on. We say that I/O-IMC B is *input-enabled* with respect to action a. Note that input actions are delayable, i.e. they must wait until another I/O-IMC performs the corresponding output-action.

A different kind of interactive transition from state 4 to state 5 is also present in B. This transition is labeled $b!$ and is an output action. Output actions are denoted with an exclamation mark (i.e. $b!$). When I/O-IMC B performs this output action all I/O-IMC which have b as an input action must perform this input action. Unlike input actions, output actions are immediate; i.e. when I/O-IMC B moves to state 4 no *time* passes before it moves to state 5. It is however possible that another interactive transition is taken immediately. Specifically, if two or more different output actions are possible in a state, then the choice between the transitions is *non-deterministic*. One of the transitions is taken immediately, but it is not known how this choice is made.

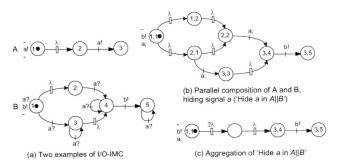

(a) Two examples of I/O-IMC

(b) Parallel composition of A and B, hiding signal a ('Hide a in A||B')

(c) Aggregation of 'Hide a in A||B'

Figure 2. Composition, hiding, and aggregation.

Besides input and output actions there are also internal actions. Internal actions are denoted with a semi-colon (;) and model internal computation steps of the system they represent. Thus, internal actions do not influence other I/O-IMC and are not influenced by other I/O-IMC. Similar to output actions, internal actions are immediate.

The reason it is interesting to combine Markovian and interactive transitions is that interactive transitions enable the construction of large I/O-IMC by composition of several smaller I/O-IMC [12]. The subject at hand (the analysis of dynamic fault trees) is a good example. Instead of transforming the entire DFT into one large CTMC we transform the basic events and gates of the DFT first and then cre-

ate a single I/O-IMC by combining the smaller ones (see Section 5). The I/O-IMC formalism is one such approach to combining Markovian and interactive transitions. A discussion on different approaches to combining Markovian and interactive transitions in one formalism can be found in [12]. An I/O-IMC can also be transformed into a smaller *aggregated* I/O-IMC that is equivalent (i.e. preserving the system reliability measure) to the original I/O-IMC. This state space aggregation, which generalizes the notion of *lumping* in CTMC, can very effectively reduce the resources necessary to create a model of a real-life system [14]. In this work we have used *weak bisimulation* to aggregate the I/O-IMC. For the definition of weak bisimulation for I/O-IMC we refer the reader to [4] and for details on the complexity of the minimization algorithm we refer to [12]. Figure 2 shows an example of how two I/O-IMC A and B can be composed (and hiding signal a with which they communicate) and how the resulting I/O-IMC can then be aggregated. When composing I/O-IMC A and B we *synchronize* on signal a, because it is in both their action signatures. Since B has a as an input, it has to wait for A's output action $a!$. This explains the absence of an input transition $a?$ from state $(1, 1)$ in the composed model. However, in state $(2, 1)$, for instance, A outputs its signal a (and moves to state 3) and B simultaneously makes the corresponding input transition and moves from state 1 to 3. All Markovian transitions and non-synchronizing signals are essentially interleaved during composition. Since weak bisimulation abstracts from internal (unobserved) actions; states $(1,2)$, $(2,1)$, $(2,2)$, and $(3,3)$ are equivalent given that they essentially all move with a rate λ to the same state $(3,4)$. Indeed, these 4 states are aggregated into a single (unlabeled) state in Figure 2.c.

4. DFT to I/O-IMC conversion

During the conversion of a DFT to a MC, the DIFTree algorithm [11] proceeds as follow: First, the MC's initial state is created, listing the states of all basic events contained in the DFT as operational [6]. From the initial state, every BE is being failed (according to its failure rate) one at a time and the corresponding transition and next state are created where the state information (i.e. operational or failed) of the basic event is updated. For every newly created state, the DFT model (i.e. system state) is evaluated to determine whether the state corresponds to an operational or a failed system state[7]. As long as a state is an operational state, every operational BE contained in that state is being failed, and a corresponding new transition (and optionally a new state) is created. Note that each MC state has a vector list-

---

[6]Some extra information, such as which spare gate is using a given spare, is also appended to the state.

[7]This operation is unnecessary in the I/O-IMC framework.

ing the state of all basic events contained in the DFT; consequently, this makes the state-space grow exponentially with the number of basic events.

This DIFTree MC generation approach, where the model of a dynamic system is generated at once and as a whole, is to be contrasted with our compositional aggregation approach. paper In our I/O-IMC framework, each DFT element (i.e. basic event and gates) has a corresponding I/O-IMC precisely defining its behavior (i.e. semantics). Every I/O-IMC has an initial operational state (i.e. with no incoming transition), some intermediate operational (dormant or active) states, a *firing* (i.e. about to output a failure signal) state, and an absorbing *fired* state. The firing and fired states are both failed states and are drawn as gray circles and double circles respectively. There are two main signals (or actions): a *firing signal* and an *activation signal*. The firing signal of element A is denoted by f_A and it signals the failure of a BE or a gate. The activation signal refers to the activation (i.e. switching from dormant to active mode) of a spare A and is denoted by a_A. An activation signal is only output by spare gates, and $a_{A,B}$ denotes the activation of spare A by spare gate B. Indeed, since a spare A can be shared, and thus activated, by multiple spare gates, an activation signal is needed for each of the spare gates. These activation signals are then translated by an auxiliary I/O-IMC model[8] called activation auxiliary (AA) into a single activation signal a_A which acts as an input to the spare A. In the original DIFTree methodology, only BE can act as spares, and thus BE are the only elements that exhibit a dormant as well as an active behavior. However, in our framework we lift this restriction by allowing any independent sub-system to act as a spare. As a consequence, spare gates also exhibit dormant and active behaviors (see Section 6 for further details).

In the following, we show the I/O-IMC of the basic event, the PAND gate, the FDEP gate, and the spare gate (the full details on all the gates can be found in [4]). We postpone the discussion on the spare gate model until Section 6.

4.1. Basic event I/O-IMC model

As pointed out in Section 2, a basic event has a different failing behavior depending on its dormancy factor. For this reason we identify three types of basic events and correspondingly three types of I/O-IMC. Figure 3 shows the I/O-IMC corresponding to a cold, warm, and hot basic events (all called A). The I/O-IMC clearly captures the behavior of the basic event described in Section 2.

[8]The AA model is essentially an OR gate having as inputs the various activations signals coming from the spare gates, and as an output a spare activation signal rather than a firing signal.

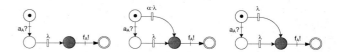

Figure 3. I/O-IMC models of cold, warm, and hot BE.

4.2. PAND gate I/O-IMC model

The PAND gate fires if all its inputs fail and fail from left to right order. If the inputs fire in the wrong order, the PAND gate moves to an operational absorbing state (denoted with an X on Figure 4). Figure 4 shows the I/O-IMC

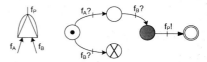

Figure 4. I/O-IMC of the PAND gate.

of the PAND gate P with two inputs A and B (A being the leftmost input).

4.3. FDEP gate I/O-IMC model

A functional dependency is modeled using a firing auxiliary (FA). The FA governs when a dependent DFT element fires, i.e. either when the element fails by itself or when its failure is triggered by the FDEP gate trigger. There exists a different FA for each dependent event. Figure 5 shows the FA of element A, which is functionally dependent upon B. The signal f_A^* corresponds to the failure of element A by itself without factoring in its functional dependency (i.e. in isolation), and the signal f_A corresponds to the failure of A when also considering its functional dependency upon B. In order to get the correct behavior of the element A, one has to compose the three I/O-IMC corresponding to A in isolation, to its FA, and to the trigger B. Note that any element which has A as input has to now interface with A's FA rather than directly with A. Note also that the firing auxil-

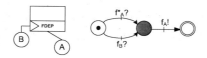

Figure 5. I/O-IMC of the firing auxiliary.

iary I/O-IMC is similar to the OR gate I/O-IMC with two input signals f_A^* and f_A.

In the original DIFTree methodology, only BE can be dependent events. However, in our framework we lift this restriction by allowing any sub-system to be an FDEP gate dependent event (Section 6).

The I/O-IMC models discussed above have been generalized (cf. [9] for details) to deal with any number of inputs.

4.4. Simultaneity and non-determinism

In earlier development of the DFT modeling formalism, the semantics (i.e. the model interpretation) of some DFT configurations where FDEP gates are used remained unclear. For instance, in Figure 6, the FDEP gate triggers (in both configurations) the failures of two basic events. Does this mean that the dependent events fail simultaneously and, if so, what is the state of the PAND gate (in configuration a) and which spare gate gets the shared spare S (in configuration b)? These examples were also discussed in [8], and we believe that this is an inherent non-determinism in these models. In [8], these special cases are dealt with by systematically removing the non-determinism by transforming it into a probabilistic (or deterministic) choice. In our framework, we allow non-determinism and naturally provide a mechanism for detecting it should this arise in a particular DFT configuration. Moreover, if the non-determinism was not intended, then its detection indicates that an error occurred during the model specification. Non-determinism could also be an inherent characteristic of the system being analyzed, and should therefore be explicitly modeled. An example of such a system would be a repairman following a first failed first repaired policy and being in charge of two components. Now, if both components fail at the same time, then we might decide to model the choice of which one to pick first for repair to be a non-deterministic choice made by the repairman.

In the I/O-IMC formalism, the DFT configurations depicted in Figure 6 will be interpreted as follows: Whenever the dependent events failure has been triggered, then the trigger event (the cause) happened first and was then immediately (with no time elapsing) followed by the failure of the dependent events (the effect). This adheres to the classical *notion of causality*. Moreover, the dependent events

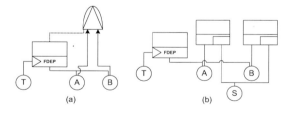

Figure 6. The occurrence of non-determinism.

fail in a non-deterministic order (i.e. essentially consider all combinations of ordering). In this case, the final I/O-IMC model is not a continuous-time Markov chain (CTMC) but rather a continuous-time Markov decision process (CTMDP), which can be analysed by computing bounds of the

performance measure of interest (see [2] for an efficient algorithm on analysing CTMDP).

4.5. Conversion of a DFT into a community of I/O-IMC

We have defined the individual I/O-IMC models for each of the DFT elements and some were described in the previous sub-sections. We can now convert any given DFT into a corresponding set of I/O-IMC models. Moreover, we need to match the inputs and outputs of all the models. The mapping between the DFT and the I/O-IMC community is a *one-to-one mapping*, except for some cases (e.g. spare activation and functional dependency) where extra auxiliary I/O-IMC are also used.

5. DFT analysis

Once the DFT has been converted into an I/O-IMC community, the compositional aggregation methodology can be applied on the I/O-IMC community to reduce the community to a single I/O-IMC. The final I/O-IMC reduces in many cases to a CTMC[9]. This CTMC can be then solved using standard methods [18] to compute performance measures such as system unreliability. The full conversion/analysis algorithm[10] is as follows:

1. Map each DFT element to its corresponding (aggregated) I/O-IMC and match all inputs and outputs. The result of this step is an I/O-IMC community.

2. Pick two I/O-IMC and parallel compose them.

3. Hide output signals that won't be subsequently used (i.e. synchronized on).

4. Aggregate (using weak bisimulation as mentioned in Section 3) the I/O-IMC obtained from the composition of the two I/O-IMC picked in Step 2 and the hiding of the output signals in Step 3.

5. Go to Step 2 if more than 1 I/O-IMC is left, otherwise go to Step 6.

6. Analyse the aggregated CTMC (or CTMDP).

5.1. Example: The cardiac assist system

The cardiac assist system (CAS) model is taken from [3] and is based on a real system. The DFT is shown in Figure 7. The CAS consists of three separate and distinct modules: The CPU unit, the motor unit and the pump unit.

---

[9]Occasionally to a CTMDP if some non-determinism remains.
[10]Note that this algorithm is amenable to parallelization.

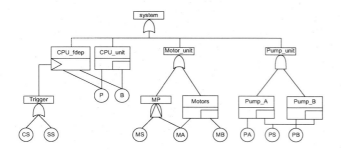

Figure 7. The cardiac assist system DFT.

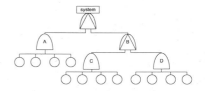

Figure 8. The cascaded PAND system.

There are two CPUs: a primary (P, $\lambda = 0.5$) and a warm spare (B, $\lambda = 0.5$) with $\alpha = 0.5$. Both are functionally dependent on a cross switch (CS, $\lambda = 0.2$) and a system supervision (SS, $\lambda = 0.2$), which means that the failure of either these components will trigger the failure of both CPUs. There are also two motors: a primary (MA, $\lambda = 1$) and a cold spare (MB, $\lambda = 1$). The switching component (MS, $\lambda = 0.01$) turns on the spare motor when the primary fails. The MS is also subject to failure, but this failure is only relevant if it occurs before the failure of the primary motor. Finally, there are three pumps: two primary pumps (PA and PB with $\lambda = 1$ for both) running in parallel and a cold shared spare pump (PS, $\lambda = 1$). All three pumps must fail for the pump unit to fail.

We have developed our own conversion tool which takes as input a DFT specified in the Galileo DFT format [11], and translates the DFT into its corresponding community of I/O-IMC models in the format of the TIPP tool [13]. The I/O-IMC models are then composed and aggregated using the TIPP tool. Finally, the system unreliability is computed also using the TIPP tool. Each of the aggregated I/O-IMC models of the three modules had 6 states. This result was comparable to the Galileo tool results, where the biggest generated CTMC (the pump unit) had 8 states. The system unreliability obtained using the TIPP tool was 0.6579 for a mission time equals to 1 time unit. The result provided by the Galileo DIFTree tool was identical. In the next section, we show, through a second example, the enhanced modular analysis that we attain using the I/O-IMC framework.

5.2. Modular analysis

In this section, we illustrate the lack of modularity (already pointed out in [1, 5] and which leads to a worsening of the state-space explosion problem) in the DIFTree methodology with respect to dynamic modules. The example at hand, shown in Figure 8, is called the cascaded PAND system (CPS) for which a variation can be found in [5]. The CPS consists of two PAND gates and three AND gates each having four identical BE with a failure rate equals to 1. In fact, the three AND gates constitute independent and identi-

cal modules. However, since the top gate is a dynamic gate, the DIFTree methodology does not modularize the tree into five[11] distinct modules; but it rather considers the whole tree as a single module. The reason that DIFTree does not consider, for instance, module A as an independent module is because its parent gate (i.e. the PAND gate *System*) is a dynamic gate (cf. Section 2).

Thanks to the interactivity of I/O-IMC, we are able to further modularize the CPS and generate the corresponding I/O-IMC for each of the five modules. Moreover, since A, C, and D are identical, we only need to generate the I/O-IMC for one of these modules and reuse it by renaming some of the activation and firing signals. Figure 9 shows the I/O-IMC of module A after parallel composition and aggregation. The I/O-IMC is particularly small because all basic events have the same failure rate and the order in which they fail is irrelevant. Solving the CPS following this mod-

Figure 9. I/O-IMC of module A.

ular compositional aggregation analysis technique resulted in 156 states and 490 transitions for the biggest generated I/O-IMC. This result is to be contrasted with the DIFTree solution which resulted in 4113 states and 24608 transitions. The system unreliability, for a mission time equals to 1 time unit, is the same in both cases and equals 0.00135. The reason DIFTree performs so poorly is because the corresponding CTMC is generated for the whole tree (i.e. with 12 basic events) and at once, and in which even irrelevant failure orders (such as for the BE belonging to module A) are accounted for. The compositional aggregation approach performs particularly well for this example due to the high modularity of the system. However, the approach does not perform as well for some examples we have worked on where the DFT elements are highly connected (i.e. numerous interdependencies/interactions between DFT elements), which leads to the incapacity to effectively divide the system into independent small modules.

---

[11]Each gate acts as an independent module.

6. Modular model-building

Static fault trees are highly modular, i.e., any sub-tree can be used as an input to another static gate. Unfortunately, this modularity does not currently apply to dynamic trees. Indeed, only BE are allowed as inputs to spare gates and as dependent events of FDEP gates. In the I/O-IMC framework, we increase the modularity of DFT by allowing: (1) independent sub-trees to act as primary and spare components and (2) FDEP gates to trigger any arbitrary element (BE and gates).

This section and the CPS example of the previous section show the enhanced modularity obtained in our framework and the ability to reuse, without restrictions, independent sub-modules within larger dynamic modules. Such reusability, which was previously only fully implementable in static FT, is a very powerful and useful concept in large FT. Indeed, being able to 'plug-in' modules is a practical feature when designing very large systems where the model is build incrementally and/or various teams are working on different parts of the system.

6.1. Spare modules extension

The system depicted in Figure 10.a is a typical system we would like to be able to model using the DFT formalism. The primary and spare components are not BE, but rather more complex sub-systems. In the I/O-IMC framework, we allow primary and spare components to be any independent sub-system[12]. We enforce the independence restriction because otherwise the activation of these components becomes unclear.

This extension of primary and spare components requires the reexamination of the concept of activation. The intuition is as follows: In Figure 10.a, the activation of module 'spare' simply means the activation of the two BE C and D. The module's (represented by its top-node AND gate) dormancy is defined by the dormancy of its BE. The AND gate I/O-IMC model is not changed and has the same behavior whether 'spare' is dormant or active. In fact, whenever an activation signal is received by module 'spare', this same activation signal is simply passed on to the next components (which happen to be BE in this example), one level down the tree. The behavior of all the gates (i.e. I/O-IMC models) is unchanged whether they are used as spares or not. However, the spare gate is an exception to this rule and does behave differently when used as a spare. Figure 10.b illustrates this: When 'spare' is not activated (i.e. 'primary' has not failed), BE C and D are dormant; and even if C (being a warm

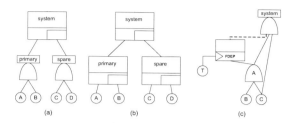

Figure 10. Complex spares and FDEP gate extension.

spare) fails, D remains dormant. This is the same behavior as with the 'spare' AND gate in Figure 10.a. If 'spare' is activated, the activation signal is only passed to the primary C and D remains dormant (this is clearly different from the AND gate where both BE are activated). Should C fail and 'spare' being in its active state, then D is activated. Based on the above explanation, Figure 11 shows the behavior of the spare gate A[13]. Signals $a_{S,A}$ and $a_{S,C}$ are actions out-

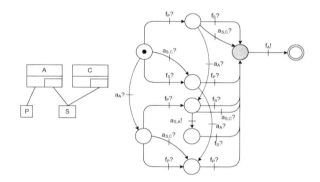

Figure 11. The spare gate I/O-IMC model.

put respectively by A and C signaling that the spare S has been taken[14]. The spare gate I/O-IMC model has been, of course, generalized to handle multiple spare gates sharing multiple spares (i.e. the most general case).

6.2. FDEP gate extension

In this framework, the FDEP gate can trigger the failure of any gate (representing a sub-system) and not only BE. Indeed, this extension comes at no extra cost, and the I/O-IMC used in this case is still the same as the one shown in Figure 5. Figure 10.c shows such a configuration where T triggers the failure of the sub-tree A. Note that sub-system A does not need to be an independent module. Note also that the trigger T only affects the failure of the gate A and none of its elements below it such as the basic event C.

---

[12]A sub-system is usually named after its top-node and is independent if (1) all the elements in the tree have inputs from only elements within the same tree and (2) all the outputs, except for the top-node, are also within the tree and therefore hidden to the rest of the system

[13]For clarity, the activation signal is drawn as a dashed line.

[14]This solution is not very scalable since it suggests that all spare gates sharing a spare communicate with each other. A better solution has been found where a 'spare granting' auxiliary is used.

7. DFT elements extension

In this section, we show, through some examples, how readily one can extend the DFT elements within the I/O-IMC framework. In fact, adding/modifying elements is done at the level of the elementary I/O-IMC models. Moreover, adding/modifying one element does not affect the remainder of the elements (i.e. their corresponding I/O-IMC models). This is indeed a desirable property of the I/O-IMC framework, where the behavioral details and interactions of any element is kept as local as possible. These extensions only affect Step 1 of the DFT conversion/analysis algorithm laid out in Section 5. The remaining five steps, including the composition, the aggregation and the analysis remain unchanged. The first extension concerns the modeling of *inhibition* and *mutually exclusive events*. The second extension is somewhat more involved and concerns the modeling of repair.

7.1. Inhibition and mutual exclusivity

We say that event A inhibits the failure of B if the failure of B is prevented when A fails before B. Following the idea of the firing auxiliary (cf. Section 4.3), this could be modeled by simply adding an *inhibition auxiliary* (IA). Figure 12 shows the configuration of such inhibition and the corresponding I/O-IMC model of the IA of B. Signal f_B^* corresponds to the failure signal of B taken in isolation, i.e. without A's inhibition. Note that, as with the FA, any element which has B as input has to now interface with B's IA rather than directly with B.

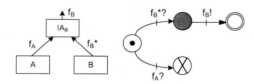

Figure 12. The I/O-IMC model of the IA.

If event B also inhibits the failure of A, then we need to add an IA for A as well. In this way, the failure of A and the failure of B become two mutually exclusive events. Mutual exclusivity is very useful when modeling a component exhibiting various failure modes. A typical example is a switch with two failure modes: 'failing to close' and 'failing to open'. These failures have normally different probabilities of occurrence and different consequences on the overall system. The switch failure modes have to be modeled as two mutually exclusive BE since the switch can either fail open or fail closed, but not both.

7.2. Repair

Adding a notion of repair is somewhat more complicated as every DFT element can now fail or be repaired. Thus, no longer only a 'failed event' should be signaled but also a 'repaired event'. However, as mentioned above, we only need to modify 'locally' the elementary I/O-IMC corresponding to each DFT element behavior. Due to the lack of space, we will only discuss the new I/O-IMC for the BE and the AND gate (other elements are treated in the same fashion). The repairable cold BE's I/O-IMC is shown on Figure 13. Here, μ denotes the BE repair rate and $r!$ is a signal output by the BE notifying, to the rest of the elements, that it has been repaired. Note that the fired state is not absorbing anymore. As an alternative model, one can of course think of the BE interacting with a repair station (RS); in which case, the repair process[15] would be part of the RS I/O-IMC model and f would also be an input to the RS. An extra signal (input to the BE and an output of the RS) would also be needed for communication between the BE and RS and signaling that the RS has finished the repair. The repairable AND

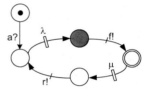

Figure 13. The repairable BE I/O-IMC model.

gate I/O-IMC model is shown on Figure 14. The AND gate has its own repair output signal (i.e. $r!$) and needs to consider both failure ($f_A?$ and $f_B?$) and repair ($r_A?$ and $r_B?$) signals coming from its inputs A and B. Compared to the unrepairable AND gate, Figure 14 has 3 extra states. If we

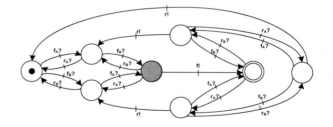

Figure 14. The repairable AND gate I/O-IMC model.

consider a very simple repairable system composed of an AND gate with two BE A and B (Figure 15.a), then the resulting I/O-IMC after automatic composition and aggregation[16] is, as expected, a CTMC shown on Figure 15.b.

---

[15]Which could be more complicated than a single Markovian transition with repair rate μ.

[16]And abstraction of the AND gate's activation and failure signals.

At this point, one can perform some analysis on the CTMC

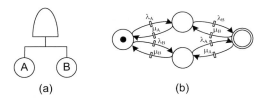

(a)   (b)

Figure 15. A simple repairable system.

such as computing the system unavailability.

8. Conclusion and future work

In this paper, we have illustrated the use of the I/O-IMC framework for the analysis of DFT and showed, through some examples, the increase of the DFT modularity both at the analysis level and the model-building level. We have also demonstrated the ease with which one can define new DFT elements and provided examples of such extensions.

Areas of future research include: (1) From a process algebra point of view, we would like to achieve even more drastic state-space reduction using more suitable aggregation techniques. (2) Generalize the concept of activation to any type of mode switch[17]; this is similar to the notion of 'triggered Markov processes' defined in [6]. (3) In this paper, we have only considered exponential failure distributions for BE; it would be worthwhile investigating the use of phase-type distributions, which naturally integrate into the I/O-IMC framework, to approximate any BE failure probability distribution.

References

[1] S. Amari, G. Dill, and E. Howald. A new approach to solve dynamic fault trees. In *Annual Reliability and Maintainability Symposium*, pages 374–379, January 2003.

[2] C. Baier, H. Hermanns, J.-P. Katoen, and B. R. Haverkort. Efficient computation of time-bounded reachability probabilities in uniform continuous-time Markov decision processes. *Theor. Comput. Sci.*, 345(1):2–26, 2005.

[3] H. Boudali. *A Bayesian network reliability modeling and analysis framework*. Phd dissertation, University of Virginia, Charlottesville, VA, May 2005.

[4] H. Boudali, P. Crouzen, and M. I. A. Stoelinga. A compositional semantics for Dynamic Fault Trees in terms of Interactive Markov Chains. Technical report, University of Twente, Enschede, the Netherlands, to appear.

[5] H. Boudali and J. B. Dugan. A new Bayesian network approach to solve dynamic fault trees. In *Reliability and Maintainability Symposium*, Jan 2005.

[6] M. Bouissou and J.-L. Bon. A new formalism that combines advantages of fault-trees and Markov models: Boolean logic driven Markov processes. *Reliability Engineering and System Safety*, 82(2):149–163, 2003.

[7] M. A. Boyd. *Dynamic fault tree models: techniques for analyses of advanced fault tolerant computer systems*. Phd dissertation, Dept. of Computer Science, Duke University, 1991.

[8] D. Coppit, K. J. Sullivan, and J. B. Dugan. Formal semantics of models for computational engineering: A case study on dynamic fault trees. In *Proceedings of the International Symposium on Software Reliability Engineering*, pages 270–282. IEEE, Oct 2000.

[9] P. Crouzen. Compositional analysis of dynamic fault trees. MSc thesis, University of Twente, Enschede, the Netherlands, 2006.

[10] J. B. Dugan, S. J. Bavuso, and M. A. Boyd. Dynamic fault-tree models for fault-tolerant computer systems. *IEEE Transactions on Reliability*, 41(3):363–377, September 1992.

[11] J. B. Dugan, B. Venkataraman, and R. Gulati. DIFTree: a software package for the analysis of dynamic fault tree models. In *Reliability and Maintainability Symposium*, pages 64–70, Jan 1997.

[12] H. Hermanns. *Interactive Markov Chains*, volume 2428 of *Lecture Notes in Computer Science*. Springer-Verlag, 2002.

[13] H. Hermanns, U. Herzog, U. Klehmet, V. Mertsiotakis, and M. Siegle. Compositional performance modelling with the TIPPtool. *Lecture Notes in Computer Science*, 1469:51–62, 1998.

[14] H. Hermanns and J.-P. Katoen. Automated compositional Markov chain generation for a plain-old telephone system. *Science of Computer Programming*, 36(1):97–127, 2000.

[15] R. A. Howard. *Dynamic probability systems. Volume 1: Markov models*. Decision and Control. John Wiley & Sons, Inc., 1971.

[16] N. A. Lynch and M. R. Tuttle. An introduction to input/output automata. *CWI Quarterly*, 2(3):219–246, 1988.

[17] R. Milner. *Communication and Concurrency*. Prentice Hall Inc., 1989.

[18] W. J. Stewart. *Introduction to the Numerical Solution of Markov Chains*. Princeton University Press, 1994.

[19] K. K. Vemuri, J. B. Dugan, and K. J. Sullivan. Automatic synthesis of fault trees for computer-based systems. *IEEE Transactions on Reliability*, 48(4):394–402, December 1999.

[20] W. E. Veseley, F. F. Goldberg, N. H. Roberts, and D. F. Haasl. *Fault Tree Handbook, NUREG-0492*. United States Nuclear Regulatory Commission, NASA, 1981.

---

[17]In this respect, inhibition can be viewed as a mode switch where the inhibited event moves to a permanent operational state upon the receipt of the failure signal from the inhibitor.

Uniformity by Construction in the Analysis of Nondeterministic Stochastic Systems

Holger Hermanns   Sven Johr

Universität des Saarlandes, FR 6.2 Informatik
D-66123 Saarbrücken, Germany

Abstract

Continuous-time Markov decision processes (CTMDPs) are behavioral models with continuous-time, nondeterminism and memoryless stochastics. Recently, an efficient timed reachability algorithm for CTMDPs has been presented [2], allowing one to quantify, e. g., the worst-case probability to hit an unsafe system state within a safety critical mission time. This algorithm works only for uniform CTMDPs – CTMDPs in which the sojourn time distribution is unique across all states. In this paper we develop a compositional theory for generating CTMDPs which are uniform by construction. To analyze the scalability of the method, this theory is applied to the construction of a fault-tolerant workstation cluster example, and experimentally evaluated using an innovative implementation of the timed reachability algorithm. All previous attempts to model-check this seemingly well-studied example needed to ignore the presence of nondeterminism, because of lacking support for modelling and analysis.

1 Motivation

Nondeterministic stochastic systems combine the behavior of classical labeled transition systems (LTSs), with classical stochastic processes, Markov chains in particular. The most widely known model is that of Markov decision processes in discrete time (DTMDPs) which combines LTS and discrete-time Markov chains (DTMCs). This model originates from the operations research (OR) and planning context. In the setting of concurrency theory, that model is often called probabilistic automata [27, 28], and has been the subject of many studies [24, 22]. Model checking algorithms for DTMDPs are available [3, 7], have been implemented and applied [18].

Continuous-time Markov chains (CTMCs) extend DTMCs with memoryless continuous time. These models have a very rich spectrum of applications, ranging from disk storage dimensioning [26] to signalling transduction networks [6]. In the context of concurrency theory, the extension of CTMCs with nondeterminism has lead to different models, including stochastic transition systems [8] and interactive Markov chains (IMC) [14]. The latter is an orthogonal superposition of LTSs and CTMCs with convenient compositional properties.

On the other hand, continuous-time Markov decision processes (CTMDPs) have been proposed in OR [25], but not many results are available, and model checking of CTMDP has not been addressed successfully thus far. A core ingredient to model check timed safety and liveness properties has been developed in [2] by an algorithm addressing timed-bounded reachability probabilities in a CTMDP. The algorithm computes the maximal probability to reach a set of goal states within a given time bound, among all CTMCs induced by time-abstract schedulers. Unfortunately, the algorithm is of limited generality, since it is restricted to so-called uniform CTMDPs (uCTMDPs), CTMDPs in which the sojourn time distribution is unique across all states.

Nevertheless we have recently made use of this algorithm in the verification of large STATEMATE [4] models of train control systems. The algorithm allowed us to verify properties like: *"The probability to hit a safety-critical system configuration within a mission time of 3 hours is at most 0.01."* for very large systems with about 10^6 states and 10^7 transitions.

The main goal in [4] has been to show how we can generate models (LTSs) from STATEMATE, incorporate timing behavior in a compositional way into them, and finally obtain a uCTMDP, amenable to timed reachability analysis. The LTSs have *huge* intermediate state spaces which required us to develop special symbolic data structures and minimizers to make this trajectory possible. Our tool chain therefore consists of a series of symbolic steps, followed by another series of explicit steps. The main contribution of the present paper is the theoretical foundation for the explicit part of that trajectory, (Section IV(b) and IV(c1) of [4]), namely *uniformity preservation* along the explicit part of the tool chain. Additionally, we describe the construction and transformation steps formally, and prove that uniformity is indeed preserved and that timed reachability properties are preserved as well. A second contribution which goes beyond the work reported in [4] is that we provide insight into the construction and timed reachability analysis algorithm, using a more academic but easily scalable case study. This case study allows us to provide a detailed analysis of the time and memory behavior of our implementation of the algorithm in [2]. It turns out that the implementation is quite efficient, albeit being only prototypical.

As a case study, we focus on the *fault-tolerant workstation cluster* (FTWC). This modeling problem has earlier been studied [13, 18] using CTMCs, although the system is nondeterministic in nature. As an interesting side result, our analysis results are compared to the results obtained in the past using that less faithful modelling style.

The paper is organized as follows. Section 2 introduces the necessary background. Section 3 discusses our compositional uIMC construction approach, while Section 4 describes the transformation to uCTMDPs and the implementation details for the timed reachability algorithm. In Section 5 we apply the discussed steps to the FTWC. Finally, Section 6 concludes the paper.

2 Background

This section introduces the necessary background concerning CTMDPs and IMCs. Disjoint union is denoted $A \mathrel{\dot{\cup}} B$. $Distr(\Omega)$ denotes the set of all probability distributions over Ω, and given $\mu \in Distr(\Omega)$ the *support* of μ is the smallest closed measurable set A such that $\mu(\Omega \setminus A) = 0$.

Continuous-time Markov decision processes. We introduce a mild variation of continuous-time Markov decision processes [25] where states may have multiple transitions labeled with the same action. As will be evident later, the transformation procedure yields this mild variation of continuous-time Markov decision processes.

Definition 1 (CTMDP) *A continuous-time Markov decision process (CTMDP) is a tuple $(S, L, \mathbf{R}, s_0)$ where S is a finite non-empty set of states, L is a finite non-empty set of transition labels also called actions, $\mathbf{R} \subseteq S \times L \times (S \longrightarrow \mathbb{R}^+)$ is the transition relation, $s_0 \in S$ is the initial state.*

Given a transition $(s, a, R) \in \mathbf{R}$ and set $Q \subseteq S$ we denote by $R(Q) := \sum_{s' \in Q} R(s')$ the cumulative rate to reach set Q from state s under transition (s, a, R), R is the *rate function* of (s, a, R). In $\mathbf{R}(s) := \{(s, a, R) \in \{s\} \times L \times (S \longrightarrow \mathbb{R}^+) \mid (s, a, R) \in \mathbf{R}\}$ we collect all transitions emanating from s.

Behavior. The behavior of a CTMDP is as follows. Suppose $(s, a, R) \in \mathbf{R}$ for some $R : S \longrightarrow \mathbb{R}^+$. Then $R(s') > 0$ indicates the existence of an a-transition emanating from s and leading to s'. If there are distinct outgoing transitions of s, one of them is selected nondeterministically. This nondeterminism is resolved by a *scheduler*, see below. Given that a transition labeled a has been selected, the probability of triggering that a-transition from s to s' within t time units equals the outcome of a negative exponential distribution with rate $R(s')$, i.e., $1 - e^{-R(s') \cdot t}$. If $R(s') > 0$ for more than one s' the transition (s, a, R) can be viewed as a hyperedge [10] labeled with a, connecting s with target states s', and possibly different rates for each of the s'. In this case there is a race between the relevant transitions. The probability to reach state s' from state s within t time units given that $(s, a, R) \in \mathbf{R}$ is taken is given by $Pr_R(s, s') \cdot (1 - e^{-E_R \cdot t})$ where $E_R = \sum_{s \in S} R(s)$ denotes the total rate of leaving state s under transition (s, a, R)

and $Pr_R(s, s') := \frac{R(s')}{E_R}$. The first factor of the product denotes the discrete branching probability to reach s' from s under transition (s, a, R), the second factor denotes the sojourn time in s, i.e., a negative exponential distribution with rate E_R. Note, that the sojourn time only depends on the rate function R. We extend the notation for discrete branching probabilities to sets of states by standard summation, i.e., $Pr_R(s, Q) = \sum_{q \in Q} Pr_R(s, q)$.

Whenever all of the E_R are equal to each other we call the CTMDP *uniform*, for short uCTMDP. Intuitively, this means that the sojourn time distribution in each state s is the same, independently of the transition chosen.

Paths. A *(timed) path* σ in CTMDP $\mathcal{C} = (S, L, \mathbf{R}, s_0)$ is a possibly infinite sequence of states, labels and time points, i.e.,
$$\sigma \in \left(S \times (L \times \mathbb{R}^+ \times S)^*\right) \mathrel{\dot{\cup}} \left(S \times (L \times \mathbb{R}^+ \times S)^\omega\right).$$
By $first(\sigma) = s_0$ we denote the first state of path σ. A finite path $\sigma' = s_0 a_1 t_1 s_1 \ldots a_k t_k s_k$ has *length* k, denoted as $|\sigma'| = k$ and its last state equals $last(\sigma') = s_k$.

Scheduler. A scheduler resolves the nondeterminism inherent in a CTMDP. Most generally, schedulers can be considered as functions from finite paths to probability distributions over transitions. We can distinguish essentially three dimensions: randomization, time dependence and history dependence. Motivated by the availability of the timed reachability algorithm presented in [2], we restrict ourselves to randomized time-abstract history-dependent schedulers.

Definition 2 (CTMDP scheduler) *Let $\mathcal{C}$ be a CTMDP with transition set $\mathbf{R}$. A scheduler D over $\mathcal{C}$ is a function $D : (S \times L)^* \times S \to Distr(\mathbf{R})$ such that each support of $D(\sigma)$ is a subset of $\mathbf{R}(last(\sigma))$.*

The support condition ensures that the scheduler distributes its whole probability mass among the outgoing transitions of $last(\sigma)$.

σ-algebra and probability measure for CTMDP. The σ-algebra over infinite paths and the probability measure $Pr_D^\mathcal{C}$ over infinite paths induced by some scheduler D is given by a standard construction [1]. We need to omit it due to space constraints. We refer to [31] for more details concerning measurability of the induced timed path probabilities.

Interactive Markov chains. We recall the model of interactive Markov chains from [14] and give here only the most relevant definitions.

Definition 3 (Interactive Markov Chain) *An interactive Markov chain, IMC, is a tuple $(S, Act, \longrightarrow, \dashrightarrow, s_0)$ where S is a nonempty, finite set of states, Act is a finite set of actions, $\longrightarrow \subseteq S \times Act \times S$ is the set of interactive transitions, $\dashrightarrow \subseteq S \times \mathbb{R}^+ \times S$ is the set of Markov transitions and $s_0 \in S$ is the initial state.*

As usual, we assume a distinguished internal action τ. We assume $\tau \in Act$, and let $Act_{\setminus \tau}$ denote $Act \setminus \{\tau\}$. All

719

other actions are called visible. **Rate**(s, s') denotes the cumulative[1] transition rate from s to s'. We let $\mathbf{r}(s, C) := \sum_{s' \in C} \mathbf{Rate}(s, s')$ and let $E_s = \mathbf{r}(s, S)$ denote the exit rate of state s. We call state s *stable*, written $s \not\xrightarrow{\tau}$, whenever no $s' \in S$ exists such that $s \xrightarrow{\tau} s'$. Otherwise it is called *unstable*.

Behavior. An IMC can be viewed as a usual labeled transition system that additionally supports stochastic behavior. The usual behavior of labeled transition systems is present via interactive transitions leading from state s to s' via some action $a \in Act$. Stochastic behavior is included via Markov transitions. A Markov transition leads from state s to s' with a particular rate $\lambda \in \mathbb{R}^+$. The delay of this transition is governed by a negative exponential distribution with rate λ, i.e., the probability of triggering this transition within t time units is given by $1 - e^{-\lambda \cdot t}$. When all transitions emanating from state s are Markov transitions, the next state is selected according to the *race condition* between these transitions. The probability to move from state s to state s' within t time units is then given as $\Pr(s, s', t) = \mathbf{P}_s(s') \cdot \left(1 - e^{-E_s \cdot t}\right)$, where $\mathbf{P}_s(s') := \frac{\mathbf{Rate}(s, s')}{E_s}$ is the discrete branching probability to reach s' from s.

Definition 4 (Uniform IMC) *We call IMC* $\mathcal{M} = (S, Act, \longrightarrow, \dashrightarrow, s_0)$ *uniform iff there exists an* $E \in \mathbb{R}^+$ *such that for all* $s \in S$ *it holds that if* $s \not\xrightarrow{\tau}$ *then* $E_s = E$. *The class of uniform IMCs is denoted by* uIMC.

Due to the maximal progress assumption, rates of Markov transitions at unstable states do not play a role in this definition. This will become important later.

Special cases. LTSs and CTMCs are special cases of IMCs. For LTS the set of Markov transitions is empty. By definition, LTSs are uniform with rate $E = 0$. If, on the other hand the interactive transition relation is empty, the IMC reduces to a CTMC. The definition of uniform IMCs is a conservative extension of uniformity in CTMCs: A CTMC is uniform if there exists a rate $E \in \mathbb{R}^+$ such that $E_s = E$ for all states s. Intuitively, this means that the probability of taking a transition within t time units is the same regardless of the state currently occupied.

Nonuniform CTMCs can be *uniformized* [19], without affecting the probabilistic behavior (in terms of state probabilities). Uniformization is often considered as a mapping from a CTMC to a DTMC, but it is better to view it as a twist on the CTMC level [25]. To uniformize a non-uniform CTMC, one chooses a rate E at least as large as the largest exit rate of any of the states. Suppose in state s the cumulative rate E_s in the CTMC is smaller than E, then s is equipped with an additional self-loop with rate $E - E_s$. Intuitively, this ensures that all state changes occur with the same (average) frequency in the resulting uniform CTMC. The probability that n state changes occur within t time units in a uCTMC is given by a

Poisson distribution with parameter $E \cdot t$, $\psi(n, E \cdot t)$, denoted by $\psi(n)$ whenever parameter $E \cdot t$ is clear.

State partitioning. It will be instrumental to partition the states of an IMC according to the outgoing transitions of each state. We use this partitioning when discussing the transformation from IMCs to CTMDPs later on. A distinction is made between *Markov states* (S_M) with at least one emanating Markov and no interactive transition; *interactive states* (S_I) with at least one emanating interactive transition and no Markov transitions; *hybrid states* (S_H) with both Markov and interactive outgoing transitions; *absorbing states* (S_A) without outgoing transitions. S can thus be written as $S = S_M \mathbin{\dot\cup} S_I \mathbin{\dot\cup} S_H \mathbin{\dot\cup} S_A$. As an abbreviation we use $S_{IH} := S_I \mathbin{\dot\cup} S_H$.

Open vs. closed system view. We distinguish two different views on a given IMC $\mathcal{M}$. Usually, we consider $\mathcal{M}$ as being *open* which means that $\mathcal{M}$ can interact with the environment. In particular, it can be composed with other IMCs (e. g. via parallel composition). In this case we impose the *maximal progress* assumption [14] which embodies the precedence of τ-actions (but not of visible actions) over Markov transitions. The intuition is that visible actions can be subject to composition, and are hence delayable, while internal actions are not. The maximal progress condition is central to the compositional theory of IMC.

In contrast the *closed system view* only exhibits its actions to the environment but closes the IMC for interaction. We assume that models we are going to analyze are closed, and impose an *urgency assumption* which means that any action (visible or not) has precedence over Markov transitions, since it can no longer be delayed by composition. This urgency assumption, is not compatible with composition of IMCs [14]. But this does not influence our modeling trajectory, since the closed system view is applied only on *complete* models, which are no longer subject to composition.

Paths. A *path label* is a pair comprising an action $a \in Act \mathbin{\dot\cup} \{\top\}$ and a time point $t \in \mathbb{R}^+$. The distinguished action $\top$ is used to uniquely identify a path label which belongs to a Markov transition. For given IMC $\mathcal{M}$ the set of all path labels is given by $L_{Path_\mathcal{M}} = (Act \mathbin{\dot\cup} \{\top\}) \times \mathbb{R}^+$. Intuitively, whenever in a given path σ a state change from s to s' is possible via (a, t) this means that in s a transition labeled a and leading to s' was taken at time t. Whenever a state change occurs w.r.t. a Markov transition at time t this is indicated by $(\top, t)$.

A *timed path* in IMC $\mathcal{M}$ is a possibly infinite alternating sequence $\sigma = v_0(a_0, t_0)v_1(a_1, t_1)\ldots$ of states and path labels. We use the same notation as introduced for CTMDPs. The subscript $\mathcal{M}$ indicates that we refer to paths in IMC $\mathcal{M}$.

Scheduler. The inherent nondeterminism in a closed IMC is, as for CTMDPs, resolved by a scheduler. In its most general form schedulers are functions from decision paths to probability distributions over interactive transitions. Note, that so far, schedulers over IMCs have not been considered in the literature. We restrict to the class randomized time-abstract history dependent schedulers, which matches the class of schedulers we use for CTMDPs.

Definition 5 (IMC scheduler) *Let* $\mathcal{M}$ *be an IMC with inter-*

---

[1] Since Markov transitions form a relation they may have multiple outgoing Markov transitions from s to s' with possibly different rates.

active transition relation $\rightarrow$. *A scheduler over* $\mathcal{M}$ *is a function* $D : (S \times Act)^* \times S_{IH} \longrightarrow Distr(\rightarrow)$ *such that each support of* $D(\sigma)$ *is a subset of* $(\{s\} \times Act \times S) \cap \longrightarrow$.

Note, that there is a difference in the domain on which a scheduler in an IMC and a CTMDP bases its decision for the next step. Since finite paths in IMCs can end in Markov states, in which a scheduler decision is simply not possible, these paths are not included in the domain.

σ-algebra and probability measure for IMC. The σ-algebra over infinite paths follows a standard cylinder set construction as, e. g., given in [31] for CTMDPs. The scheduler dependent probability measure $Pr_D^{\mathcal{M}}$ over infinite paths can easily be defined but is not in the scope of this paper. For details we refer to [16].

Phase-type distributions. A phase-type distribution is usually defined as the distribution of the time until absorption in a finite and absorbing[2] CTMC [23]. In principle, any probability distribution on $[0, \infty)$ can be approximated arbitrarily closely by a phase-type distribution given enough phases, i. e., states. In order to derive uniformity by construction it is important that the absorbing CTMC of a phase-type distribution can be uniformized, just like any CTMC. The result will no longer have an absorbing state, but a state which is reentered from itself according to a Poisson distribution. It is, after all, a special IMC.

3 Uniformity in composition and minimization of uIMCs

In [4] we constructed uniform IMCs by composition out of smaller uIMCs. The strategy is based on the nowadays classical compositional minimization principle (see, e.g., [12]) which has its roots in process algebra, and has been implemented in an exemplary way in the CADP toolkit [5] together with convenient scripting support [29]. We make use of this toolkit in our studies.

In this section we first present the formal properties of our specific construction, focussing on hiding, parallel composition and minimization of uIMC. In particular, we prove for each of these concepts that it preserves uniformity. Thus we can ensure that constructing larger IMCs out of smaller uniform IMCs yields again uniform IMCs.

Hiding. Hiding, also called abstraction, is used to internalize particular actions of a given IMC. Hiding of action a in IMC $\mathcal{M}$ turns this particular action a into the unobservable action τ. The structural operational semantic rules for hiding in IMCs are as follows [14]:

$$\frac{s \xrightarrow{b} s' \quad a \neq b}{\text{hide } a \text{ in } (s) \xrightarrow{b} \text{hide } a \text{ in } (s')} \qquad \frac{s \xrightarrow{a} s'}{\text{hide } a \text{ in } (s) \xrightarrow{\tau} \text{hide } a \text{ in } (s')}$$

$$\frac{s \dashrightarrow^{\lambda} s'}{\text{hide } a \text{ in } (s) \dashrightarrow^{\lambda} \text{hide } a \text{ in } (s')}$$

IMC hide a in $(\mathcal{M})$ is obtained by applying these rules to the initial state of $\mathcal{M}$. The first two rules are as expected, the third rule gives the definition of hide for Markov transitions, which remain untouched by the operator semantics.

Lemma 1 hide a in $(\mathcal{M})$ *is uniform whenever* $\mathcal{M}$ *is uniform.*

The proof is based on the observation that the uniformity definition manifests itself in conditions for stable states, and that hiding does not introduce more stable states, but introduces instable ones. The converse is not necessarily true: A non-uniform IMC $\mathcal{N}$ might give rise to a uniform IMC hide a in $(\mathcal{N})$.

Parallel composition. The structural operational rules of parallel composition $|[A]|$ [14], with *synchronization set* $A \subseteq Act_{\backslash \tau}$, are defined on the state-level of IMCs.

$$\frac{s \xrightarrow{a} s' \quad a \notin \{a_1, \dots, a_n\}}{s|[\{a_1, \dots, a_n\}]|v \xrightarrow{a} s'|[\{a_1, \dots, a_n\}]|v} \qquad \frac{v \xrightarrow{a} v' \quad a \notin \{a_1, \dots, a_n\}}{s|[\{a_1, \dots, a_n\}]|v \xrightarrow{a} s|[\{a_1, \dots, a_n\}]|v'}$$

$$\frac{s \xrightarrow{a} s' \quad v \xrightarrow{a} v' \quad a \in \{a_1, \dots, a_n\}}{s|[\{a_1, \dots, a_n\}]|v \xrightarrow{a} s'|[\{a_1, \dots, a_n\}]|v'}$$

$$\frac{s \dashrightarrow^{\lambda} s'}{s|[\{a_1, \dots, a_n\}]|v \dashrightarrow^{\lambda} s'|[\{a_1, \dots, a_n\}]|v} \qquad \frac{v \dashrightarrow^{\lambda} v'}{s|[a_1, \dots, a_n]|v \dashrightarrow^{\lambda} s|[\{a_1, \dots, a_n\}]|v'}$$

The upper rules are common for CSP- (or LOTOS-) style calculi. The two rules at the bottom leave the Markov behavior in both states untouched: The transitions are just interleaved (which is justified by the memoryless property of exponential distributions). The parallel composition of two IMCs $\mathcal{M}$ and $\mathcal{N}$ on synchronization set A is defined as $s_0^{\mathcal{M}}|[A]|s_0^{\mathcal{N}}$, where $s_0^{\mathcal{M}}$ denotes the initial state of $\mathcal{M}$ and $s_0^{\mathcal{N}}$ is the initial state of $\mathcal{N}$. The resulting IMC is referred to as $\mathcal{M}|[A]|\mathcal{N}$. Given the structural operational semantics, we can establish the following lemma.

Lemma 2 $\mathcal{M}|[A]|\mathcal{N}$ *is uniform whenever* $\mathcal{M}$ *and* $\mathcal{N}$ *are uniform.*

The proof uses that Markov transitions are just interleaved by the operational rules, which implies that the uniform rates of $\mathcal{N}$ and $\mathcal{M}$ just add up in $\mathcal{M}|[A]|\mathcal{N}$. Again the converse direction is not valid, i. e., whenever a uIMC is the result of a parallel composition of two IMCs $\mathcal{M}$ and $\mathcal{N}$ this does not imply that $\mathcal{M}$ and $\mathcal{N}$ are uniform.

Minimization. We will follow a compositional minimization strategy, where we minimize intermediate graphs according to an equivalence relation which (1) abstracts from internal computation, similar to weak or branching bisimulation, (2) employs lumping [21] of Markov transitions, and (3) leaves the branching structure otherwise untouched. There are many candidates for such an equivalence notion. The equivalence relation we focus on here is *stochastic branching bisimulation* which is a variant of branching bisimulation [30] and stochastic weak bisimulation [14]. Among various possible notions, branching bisimulation and its stochastic counterpart have been proven useful, and are implemented efficiently in the

---

[2] An absorbing CTMC has a single absorbing state.

CADP toolkit [11]. The uniformity preservation result we establish below can also be established for other variations (such as weak bisimulation [14]). In the sequel, when we talk about uniform IMCs, we mean uniform with respect to its reachable states. The restriction to reachable states allows us to handle models with unreachable states having arbitrary rates. This contradicts the original uniformity condition, but is irrelevant for the behavior of the IMC.

Definition 6 (Stochastic branching bisimulation) *For a given IMC* $\mathcal{M} = (S, Act, \longrightarrow, \dashrightarrow, s_0)$, *an equivalence relation* $B \subseteq S \times S$ *is a* stochastic branching bisimulation *iff for all* $s_1, s_2, t_1 \in S$ *the following holds: If* $(s_1, t_1) \in B$ *then*

1. $s_1 \xrightarrow{a} s_2$ *implies*
   either $a = \tau$ and $(s_2, t_1) \in B$, or
   $\exists t_1', t_2 \in S : t_1 \xrightarrow{\tau^*} t_1' \xrightarrow{a} t_2 \wedge (s_1, t_1') \in B \wedge (s_2, t_2) \in B$, and

2. $s_1 \not\rightarrow$ *implies* $\exists t_1' : t_1 \xrightarrow{\tau^*} t_1' \not\rightarrow: \forall C \in S/B : \mathbf{Rate}(s_1, C) = \mathbf{Rate}(t_1', C)$.

Two states are stochastic branching bisimilar, *iff they are contained in some stochastic branching bisimulation* B.

Given IMC $\mathcal{M}$, $StoBraBi(\mathcal{M})$ denotes the stochastic branching bisimilarity quotient IMC of $\mathcal{M}$. For two IMCs $\mathcal{M}$ and $\mathcal{N}$ we say that $\mathcal{M}$ and $\mathcal{N}$ are stochastic branching bisimilar iff $s_0^{\mathcal{M}}$ and $s_0^{\mathcal{N}}$ are branching bisimilar. We can prove the following lemma, using that the uniformity condition for IMCs is imposed for stable states only.

Lemma 3 *Given IMCs* $\mathcal{M}$ *and* $\mathcal{N}$, *it holds that if* $\mathcal{M}$ *and* $\mathcal{N}$ *are stochastic branching bisimilar then:* $\mathcal{M}$ *is uniform iff* $\mathcal{N}$ *is uniform.*

We can directly derive the following corollary from the above lemma.

Corollary 1 *An IMC* $\mathcal{M}$ *is uniform iff* $StoBraBi(\mathcal{M})$ *is uniform.*

Elapse. We use phase-type distributions to specify the timed probabilistic behavior of a system under study. Recall that, structurally, a phase-type distribution Ph is a CTMC (S, A, R) with a distinguished initial state i and absorbing state a. In the composition context, the distribution Ph can be viewed as describing the time up to which the occurrence of an event f has to be delayed, since the occurrence of some other event r. This interpretation is a special case of what is called a *time constraint* in [15], where an *elapse* operator is introduced. This operator enriches Ph with "synchronization potential" needed to effectively incorporate the Markov chain of Ph into the behavior described by some LTS or IMC. Since Ph is a CTMC we can assume that it is uniformized without making any restrictions [19].

We will use this operator below, so we give its semantics here, simplified to what is actually used later. We denote the operator by $El(Ph, f, r)$. It takes as parameters a distribution Ph (given as a uCTMC (S, A, R) with distinguished states i and a and uniform rate E), an action f which should only occur once the Ph distributed delay is over, and an action r governing when that delay should start. With these parameters, $El(Ph, f, r)$ generates IMC $(S \dot\cup \{s'\}, A, \{a \xrightarrow{f} s', s' \xrightarrow{r} i\}, R \dot\cup \{s' \xrightarrow{E} s'\}, s')$. Here s' is a fresh initial state of the resulting IMC where we have added two interactive transitions. The freshly inserted state s' gets a Markov self-loop with rate E assigned. This assures uniformity of the resulting IMC. We will also use a variant of this operator, referred to as El', where the initial state remains unchanged at i, but otherwise the construction is the same.

In $El(Ph, f, r)$, between the occurrences of r and f, there must be a delay which is given by Ph. To enforce this also for the LTS of our system under study, we incorporate this IMC into the system model using parallel composition with appropriate synchronization sets.

4 Transformation and uCTMDP analysis

In this section we describe a transformation procedure from closed uIMCs to uCTMDPs and discuss in what sense it preserves the properties we are interested in. We then recall from [2] how to analyze the resulting CTMDP, explain how we implemented this algorithm, and apply both steps to the FTWC case study.

4.1 From uIMC to uCTMDP

In the following description we assume that uIMC $\mathcal{M} = (S, Act, \longrightarrow, \dashrightarrow, s_0)$ is given and that we aim to transform $\mathcal{M}$ into a CTMDP, say $\mathcal{C}_{\mathcal{M}}$. We present a transformation from a (u)IMC under consideration to a *strictly alternating* (u)IMC. The latter is a (u)IMC in which interactive and Markov states occur strictly alternating, and where hybrid states are not present anymore. Each strictly alternating IMC corresponds to a CTMDP such that the timed behavior of both systems is the same.

We do not allow for Zeno-behavior in the model under consideration, Zenoness manifests itself as cycles of interactive transitions, which owed to the closed system view can happen in zero time. The model may in general contain absorbing states, but for the sake of simplicity, we will not consider them, and thus assume $S_A = \emptyset$. In the uniform setting absorbing states are absent (for non-zero uniform rates).

An IMC $\mathcal{M}$ with state space S is called *alternating* iff for all $s \in S$, $(\{s\} \times \mathbb{R}^+ \times S) \cap \dashrightarrow \neq \emptyset$ implies $(\{s\} \times Act \times S) \cap \longrightarrow = \emptyset$. If in addition *(i.)* $(S_M \times \mathbb{R}^+ \times S_M) \cap \dashrightarrow = \emptyset$ and *(ii.)* $(S_I \times Act \times S_I) \cap \longrightarrow = \emptyset$, we call $\mathcal{M}$ *strictly alternating*. An IMC satisfying the condition *(i.)* (respectively *(ii.)*) is called *Markov (interactive) alternating* IMC.

Technically, the transformation procedure comprises the following steps, which will be shown to preserve the probabilistic behavior of the model, and which result in a strictly alternating IMC: (1) ensure that S contains interactive and

Markov states only (alternating IMC); (2) make the target state of each Markov transition an interactive state (Markov alternating IMC); (3) make the target state of each interactive transition a Markov state (interactive alternating IMC). While (1) has to be done first, steps (2) and (3) can also be interchanged.

Step (1): Alternating. An alternating IMC does not posses hybrid states while the original IMC may do. Thus let $s \in S_H$. Owed to the *urgency* assumption which is due to our closed system view, all Markov transitions are cut off and s is added to S_I. For the corresponding *alternating* IMC $\mathbf{a}(\mathcal{M})$ we change the Markov transition relation to $(S_M \times \mathbb{R}^+ \times S) \cap \dashrightarrow$.

Step (2): Markov alternating. We need to split all occurring sequences of Markov transitions and states. In summary this ensures that each Markov transition always ends in an interactive state. This is achieved as follows. Suppose $s \in S_M$ with $s \overset{\lambda}{\dashrightarrow} s'$ and $s' \in S_M$. In order to break this sequence of Markov states we introduce a fresh interactive state (s, s') which is connected to s via $s \overset{\lambda}{\dashrightarrow} (s, s')$. State (s, s') in turn is connected via $(s, s') \overset{\tau}{\longrightarrow} s'$ to s'. This yields the following transformation step. For a given alternating IMC $\mathcal{M}$, we define the *Markov alternating* IMC:

$\mathbf{mA}(\mathcal{M}) := (S', Act, \longrightarrow_{\mathbf{mA}(\mathcal{M})}, \dashrightarrow_{\mathbf{mA}(\mathcal{M})}, s_0)$ with

- $S' = S \,\dot{\cup}\, \{(s, s') \in S_M \times S_M \mid \exists \lambda \in \mathbb{R}^+ : s \overset{\lambda}{\dashrightarrow} s'\}$,
- $\longrightarrow_{\mathbf{mA}(\mathcal{M})} = \longrightarrow \dot{\cup} \, \{((s, s'), \tau, s') \in S' \times \{\tau\} \times S_M \mid \exists \lambda \in \mathbb{R}^+ : s \overset{\lambda}{\dashrightarrow} s'\}$,
- $\dashrightarrow_{\mathbf{mA}(\mathcal{M})} = \dashrightarrow \cap (S_M \times \mathbb{R}^+ \times S_I) \, \dot{\cup} \, \{(s, \lambda, (s, s')) \in S_M \times \mathbb{R}^+ \times S' \mid s \overset{\lambda}{\dashrightarrow} s'\}$.

Step (3): Interactive alternating. We now handle sequences of interactive transitions ending in a Markov state. To compress these sequences, we calculate the transitive closure of interactive transitions for each interactive state s that (is either the initial state of the uIMC or) has at least one Markov predecessor. The computation is carried out in a way such that we get all Markov successors of s that terminate these sequences. We label the resulting compressed transitions with words over the alphabet $Act_{\backslash\tau}^+ \,\dot{\cup}\, \{\tau\}$ (also denoted *Words*). Note, that interactive states that do not have any Markov state as predecessor will not be contained in the resulting interactive (or strictly) alternating uIMC any more. These states violate the strict alternation of interactive and Markov states and therefore will not be contained in the CTMDP.

For a Markov alternating IMC $\mathcal{M}$ we define $\mathbf{iA}(\mathcal{M}) := (S', \textit{Words}, \longrightarrow_{\mathbf{iA}(\cdot)}, \dashrightarrow, s_0)$ by

- $S' = S_M \,\dot{\cup}\, S'_I$ where $S'_I = \{s \in S_I \mid \exists t \in S_M : t \overset{\lambda}{\dashrightarrow} s, \text{ for some } \lambda \in \mathbb{R}^+\} \cup \{s_0\}$,
- $\longrightarrow_{\mathbf{iA}(\cdot)} := \{(s, W, t) \in S'_I \times \textit{Words} \times S_M \mid s \overset{W}{\Longrightarrow} t\}$.

This yields a strictly alternating IMC. So, after applying steps (1)–(3) to uIMC $\mathcal{M}$ we obtain uIMC $\mathcal{M}'$ which is strictly alternating and where interactive transitions are labeled by words over the alphabet $Act_{\backslash\tau}^+ \,\dot{\cup}\, \{\tau\}$. The resulting uIMC

$\mathcal{M}' = (S = S_I \,\dot{\cup}\, S_M, \textit{Words}, \longrightarrow, \dashrightarrow, s_0)$ can now be interpreted as CTMDP $\mathcal{C}_\mathcal{M} = (S_I, \textit{Words}, \mathbf{R}, s_0)$ where $\mathbf{R} := \{(s, A, R) \mid R(s') = \sum_{i=1}^n \lambda_i \text{ iff } \exists u \in S_M, \lambda_i \in \mathbb{R}_{\geq 0} \text{ such that } s \overset{A}{\longrightarrow} u \wedge u \overset{\lambda_i}{\dashrightarrow} s', i = 1, 2 \ldots, n\}$.

Property preservation. Given a path σ in $\mathcal{M}$ we know that there exists a path σ' in CTMDP $\mathcal{C}_\mathcal{M}$ that corresponds to σ due to the transformation. On the other hand, for each path σ in $\mathcal{C}_\mathcal{M}$ there exists a set of paths in $\mathcal{M}$ that corresponds to σ. For a given σ in $\mathcal{M}$ let $\Psi(\sigma)$ denote the corresponding path in $\mathcal{C}_\mathcal{M}$ and, for given σ in $\mathcal{C}_\mathcal{M}$ let $\Phi(\sigma)$ be the set of corresponding paths in $\mathcal{M}$. We extend this notation to sets of paths.

Theorem 1 *Given IMC* $\mathcal{M} = (S_\mathcal{M}, Act, \longrightarrow, \dashrightarrow, s_0)$ *and CTMDP* $\mathcal{C}_\mathcal{M} = (S_\mathcal{C}, \textit{Words}, \mathbf{R}, s_0)$ *as result of the transformation. (1) For each scheduler D in $\mathcal{M}$ there exists a scheduler D' in $\mathcal{C}_\mathcal{M}$ such that for all measurable sets A of paths (in $\mathcal{M}$)*
$$Pr_D^\mathcal{M}(A) = Pr_{D'}^{\mathcal{C}_\mathcal{M}}(\Psi(A)).$$
(2) For each scheduler D in $\mathcal{C}_\mathcal{M}$ there exists a scheduler D' in $\mathcal{M}$ such that for all measurable sets A of paths (in $\mathcal{C}_\mathcal{M}$)
$$Pr_D^{\mathcal{C}_\mathcal{M}}(A) = Pr_{D'}^\mathcal{M}(\Phi(A)).$$

Note that this theorem does not require uniformity. The proof of this theorem uses the path measures induced by a scheduler in the original system (uIMC or uCTMDP) to construct the scheduler in the goal system (uCTMDP or uIMC). For (1) it can be shown that there exists a set of paths Λ in $\mathcal{M}$ for each path σ in $\mathcal{C}_\mathcal{M}$ such that Λ comprises all paths (of $\mathcal{M}$) that share the same *trace* information as σ and the same stochastic behavior. Assume that D is the scheduler in $\mathcal{M}$ and D' denotes the scheduler we intend to construct for $\mathcal{C}_\mathcal{M}$. Now, $D'(\sigma')(s, a, R)$ is then defined as the sum over $D(\sigma')(\sigma'')$ for all $\sigma' \in \Lambda$ and σ'' that correspond to (s, a, R) (in $\mathcal{C}_\mathcal{M}$). Each of the summands has to be weighted by the probability of its occurrence in $\mathcal{M}$. To show (2) we need to reconstruct scheduler D' in $\mathcal{M}$ from scheduler D in $\mathcal{C}_\mathcal{M}$. This is the more difficult case. For a σ in $\mathcal{M}$ there is not necessarily a path σ' in $\mathcal{C}_\mathcal{M}$ that corresponds to σ, because $last(\sigma)$ may end in an interactive state without Markov predecessors. Thus, for the construction of D' we have to take prefixes of σ into account for which a corresponding path in $\mathcal{C}_\mathcal{M}$ exists. For details we refer to [16].

4.2 Timed reachability in uCTMDPs

In this section we briefly recall the algorithm for timed reachability analysis in uCTMDPs [2]. Note, that the slight variant considered here (in which we allow for nondeterministic choices among the same action $a \in L$) implies only a slight change in the algorithm given in [2] where we have to range over all emanating transitions (instead of all actions) of a given state s.

For a uCTMDP $\mathcal{C}$ with uniform rate E we aim to calculate the maximal probability to reach a given set of states B within t time units from a particular state s in $\mathcal{C}$ w.r.t. all schedulers D according to Definition 2. We denote this by

Algorithm 1 (c.f. [2]) Computing $\sup_D Pr_D^{\mathcal{C}}(s, \overset{\leq t}{\leadsto} B)$

$k := k(\varepsilon, E, t); \forall s \in S : q_{k+1} := 0;$
for all $i = k, k-1, \ldots, 1$ **do**
    for all $s \in S \backslash B$ **do** m := -1;
        for all $(s, a, R) \in \mathbf{R}(s)$ **do**
            $m := \max\{m, \psi(i) \cdot Pr_R(s, B) + \sum_{s' \in S} Pr_R(s, s') \cdot$
        $q_{i+1}(s')\};$
        $q_i(s) = m;$
    for all $s \in B$ **do** $q_i(s) := \psi(i) + q_{i+1}(s);$
    for all $s \in S$ **do**
        if $s \notin B$ **then** $q(s) := q_1(s);$ **else** $q(s) := 1;$
    return q;

$\sup_D Pr_D^{\mathcal{C}}(s, \overset{\leq t}{\leadsto} B)$, where $Pr_D^{\mathcal{C}}$ is the scheduler dependent probability measure on $\mathcal{C}$. $Pr_D^{\mathcal{C}}$ is defined on infinite paths, and thus we have to map the timed reachability probability $s, \overset{\leq t}{\leadsto} B$ to the set of all infinite paths in which it is fulfilled.

In [2] the problem of approximating this probability is tackled. It it is shown that it is sufficient to consider non-randomized step-dependent schedulers $D : S \times \{0, \ldots, k\} \mapsto L$ and that in order to derive the maximal value of $Pr_D^{\mathcal{C}}(s, \overset{\leq t}{\leadsto} B)$, the transitions to be selected by a scheduler D can be computed by a greedy backward strategy up to a specific depth k which can be precomputed on the basis of E, t and the accuracy ε of the approximation. In particular, k is the smallest index such that $\sum_{n=k+1}^{\infty} \psi(n) \leq \varepsilon$. Note, that this is the *right truncation point* as defined in [9].

Algorithm 1 shows the pseudo-code of the timed reachability algorithm. For $i = k$ the transition that has to be scheduled is chosen such that the one-step probability to reach B is maximized. Since this is the kth step in evolution of the CTMDP, this probability is weighted with the Poisson probability for realizing k steps within t time units ($\psi(i)$). In [2] it is shown that $q_i(s) = \sum_{n=i}^{k} \psi(n) \cdot Pr_{R_i}(s, B) \cdot Pr_{R_{i+1}}(s, B) \cdot \ldots \cdot Pr_{R_n}(s, B)$ has to be computed such that it is optimal under all $\sum_{n=i}^{k} \psi(n) \cdot Pr_{R_*}(s, B) \cdot Pr_{R_{i+1}}(s, B) \cdot \ldots \cdot Pr_{R_n}(s, B)$. Where R_j is the rate function that belongs to the transition selected by scheduler D_0 at step j and R_* ranges over all rate functions that could be selected at step i. Scheduler D_0 is the scheduler that is constructed to maximize the reachability probability.

The algorithm returns for each state the maximal probability to reach a state $s \in B$ within time t.

We have implemented Algorithm 1 in JAVA and integrated it into the ETMCC model checker [17]. The transition relation is stored as sparse matrices storing action and rate information separately. This means that we partitioned the state space in interactive and Markov states (as for strictly alternating IMCs). The Markov states are in one-to-one correspondence to the rate functions of the CTMDP transitions. The implementation is prototypical and so far we have not put efforts in implementing more advanced techniques, e.g., more efficient state space representations of the CTMDP. However, the performance of this prototypical implementation is quite promising as can be seen in the next paragraph.

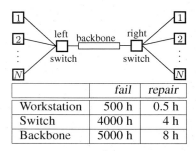

	fail	repair
Workstation	500 h	0.5 h
Switch	4000 h	4 h
Backbone	5000 h	8 h

Figure 1. FTWC with mean fail and repair times.

5 Fault-tolerant work station cluster

We are now in the position to construct a model of the fault-tolerant workstation cluster (FTWC) example. This example has first been studied in [13], and is also one of the PRISM benchmarks. Remarkably, these studies treated the model as a CTMC, which is not easy to justify, as we will argue below. The general design of the workstation cluster is depicted on the top of Figure 1. The overall system consists of two sub-clusters which are connected via a backbone. There are N workstations in each sub-cluster which are connected together in a star topology with a switch as central node that additionally provides the interface to the backbone.

Each of the components in the fault-tolerant workstation cluster can break down (fail) and then needs to be repaired before becoming available again. The mean time to failure and the mean repair time for each component in isolation are depicted on the bottom of Figure 1. They correspond to mean durations of exponential distributions.

There is a single repairunit for the entire cluster, not depicted in Figure 1, which is only capable of repairing one failed component at a time. Essentially, this means that when multiple components are failed, they must be handled in sequence, and there is a decision to be taken which of the failed components the repairunit is assigned first (or next). Notably, this nondeterminism which is inherent in the specification has been ignored in the original model [13] and subsequent work. It has been approximated by using a very fast, but probabilistic decision, encoded via the use of very high rates (of exponential distributions) assigned to the decisive transitions. These high rates are absent in the original problem statement where the repairunit is assigned nondeterministically.

Labeled transition systems. We now construct a uIMC modeling the behavior of the FTWC example. We do so in a compositional manner. There are six basic ingredients, namely the workstations (left and right), the switches (left and right), the backbone and the repairunit. Their behavior is modeled as simple LTSs. In Figure 2 we depict two different LTSs, where a white circle is used to represent the initial state of the respective LTS. The LTS of the repairunit (RU) is shown on the left hand side, where we depicted for sake of readability only two transitions. In fact, there are five parallel transitions emanating the initial state labeled with, e.g., g_wsL, and five transitions ending in the initial state labeled with, e. g., *r_wsL*. The LTSs for workstations (WS), switches (SW) and the backbone (BA) are very similar in nature, their general structure is given on the right hand side of the figure. Each of them can *fail* and has to grab the repairunit afterwards. Only when the repairunit is assigned to that particular component, a *repair* can be performed. Once the component is repaired, the repairunit will be released and can be assigned to another failed component. For a particular component, e. g., the left workstations, the actions *g* and *r* in Figure 2 have to be replaced by the according actions, e. g., by *g_wsL* and *r_wsL*, respectively (this is an instance of process algebraic relabelling).

Time constraints. For each of the components, except for the repairunit, the occurence of *fail* and *repair* is governed by delays. These delays have to be incorporated in the model by composition.

We exemplify the construction of time constraints and the incorporation of these time constraints into the LTS for the (left) workstations as follows: The LTS of a workstation is shown rightmost in Figure 2. The belonging time constraints are depicted on the left hand side of Figure 3. They are obtained by applying $El'(\circ \overset{0.002}{\longrightarrow} \overset{}{\bullet} \overset{}{\dashrightarrow} 0.002$, *fail*, *r_wsL*) and $El(\circ \overset{2}{\longrightarrow} \overset{}{\bullet} \overset{}{\dashrightarrow} 2$, *repair*, *g_wsL*), respectively. The *elapse* operator preserves uniformity and thus these time constraints are uIMCs.

On the right hand side of Figure 3 we have depicted the IMC describing the timed behavior of a (left) workstation. This IMC is obtained by fully interleaving the time constraints and subsequently synchronizing with *WS* on synchronization set {*fail*, *repair*, *g_wsL*, *r_wsL*}. Parallel composition of uIMCs preserves uniformity and thus the resulting IMCs are uniform, too.

System model. The FTWC is composed out of the components for the workstations, switches, the backbone and the repairunit. First, the workstations, switches and the backbone are constructed as exemplified above and, after hiding actions *fail*, *repair* they are composed in parallel (with empty synchronization set).

The resulting uIMCs are then minimized, and composed with the repairunit on the synchronization alphabet {*g_i*, *r_i*}, for $i \in$ {*wsL*, *wsR*, *swL*, *swR*, *bb*}, which yields the overall system description of the FTWC (modulo another hiding and minimization step) as an IMC, which, *by construction*, is still uniform.

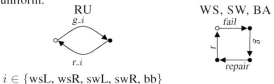

$i \in$ {wsL, wsR, swL, swR, bb}

Figure 2. LTSs for the FTWC.

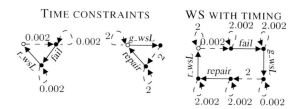

Figure 3. Time constraints and Workstation.

Technicalities. The compositional construction of the FTWC has been carried out using the CADP toolbox [5], and here especially the SVL scripting language and the BCG_MIN tool. For $N = 14$ we obtained an intermediate state space with $5 \cdot 10^6$ states and $6 \cdot 10^7$ transitions. This model then reduces to a uIMC with $6 \cdot 10^4$ states and $5 \cdot 10^5$ transitions. For $N = 16$ we were not able to construct the FTWC in a compositional way. The intermediate state space generation stopped with an incomplete system description that already took 2 GB of hard disk memory.

Larger models were generated with PRISM [18]. PRISM generates a CTMC of the FTWC example in which the nondeterminism is replaced by uniform probability distributions using a fixed large rate Γ. In order to retain the original nondeterminism, we replaced this particular Γ by an interactive transition and applied afterwards the transformation. We made sure that for $N \leq 14$ equivalent models were obtained via CADP and PRISM – up to uniformity.

Results. In this section we report on the results and statistics we obtained when analyzing the FTWC. We focus on the performance of the transformation and of the analysis algorithm.

As in [13] we say that our system operates in *premium* quality when there are at least N workstations operational. These workstations have to be connected to each other via operational switches. When the number of operational workstations in one sub-cluster is below N the premium quality can be ensured by an operational backbone under the condition that there are N operational workstations in total. We are interested in the following property: *"What is the worst case probability to hit a state in which premium service is not guaranteed within t time units?"* for which we report results and statistics.

In Table 1 we have collected different statistics of the transformation and reachability analysis for different N. Columns 2-6 display the number of states, number of transitions and the memory usage of the CTMDP representation of the FTWC. The depicted numbers are given for the strictly alternating IMCs (which comprises precisely what needs to be stored for the corresponding CTMDP), and thus are differentiated in interactive states/transitions and Markov states/transitions. In column 7 the time for the transformation (from uIMC to uCTMDP) is shown. We highlight, that the prototypical implementation of the transformation procedure works quite efficiently also for large systems ($N = 128$). In columns 8 and 9 we collect statistics of the implementation of the reachability algorithm. The runtime results for a time bound of $100h$ are given in column 8 and the results for a time bound of $30000h$

are shown in the column 9. In the last two columns we show the required number of iterations taken by the reachability algorithm in order to have a precision of 0.000001. Readers familiar with CTMC analysis time and space requirements will appreciate the efficiency apparent in these figures, given that we report about a JAVA prototype, and need to deal with nondeterminism.

Finally, we show in Figure 4 graphs for $N = 4$ and $N = 128$ in which we compare the worst case probabilities obtained by the CTMDP algorithm with the probabilities obtained from CTMC analysis. As evident in the plot, the CTMC analysis consistently overestimates the true probabilities (computed with ETMCC, confirmed with CADP). This is quite remarkable, because the CTMDP algorithm accounts for the worst-case. Nothing worse is possible in the model, and we would thus expect, that this probability will be higher than in a corresponding CTMC model of the system. This overestimation, which indicates a modeling flaw in the CTMC approach, can be explained as follows. When replacing a nondeterministic selection by high rates, certain paths become possible (though with low probability), that in a nondeterministic interpretation would be absent, and thus not contribute to the reachability probability. Concretely, in the CTMC implementation, there are sometimes races between very high rates and ordinary rates, which are entirely artificial and do not exist in the more faithful interpretation we use.

6 Conclusion

This paper has introduced a compositional approach to the generation of nondeterministic stochastic systems, and their analysis. More precisely, the paper has made the following contributions: (1) we have devised a sound compositional trajectory to construct *uniform* interactive Markov Chains. This model is transformed into a *uniform* continuous-time Markov decision process, and this transformation is shown to preserve path probability measures. (2) We have presented convincing experimental results for the first implementation of the uniform CTMDP analysis algorithm of [2]. (3) We have discussed that nondeterminism lets certain systems look different, in particular the fault-tolerant workstation cluster example. Surprisingly, the previous studies of this model overestimated the worst-case reachability probabilities which we, for the first time, were able to compute accurately.

The experiments show that the transformation and the analysis algorithm scale very well. Especially compared to the simpler CTMC case, the time and space requirements are of similar order (for models of similar size). Even though our prototypical JAVA implementation is performing remarkably well on this example, we are currently porting the algorithm to C++ in order to integrate it with the MRMC tool [20].

References

[1] R. B. Ash and C. A. Doléans-Dade. *Probability & Measure Theory*. Academic Press, second edition, 2000.

[2] C. Baier, B. R. Haverkort, H. Hermanns, and J.-P. Katoen. Efficient Computation of Time-Bounded Reachability Probabilities in Uniform Continuous-Time Markov Decision Processes. *Theor. Comput. Sci.*, 345(1):2–26, 2005.

[3] A. Bianco and L. de Alfaro. Model Checking of Probabilistic and Nondeterministic Systems. *FSTTCS*, 15, 1995.

[4] E. Böde, M. Herbstritt, H. Hermanns S. Johr, T. Peikenkamp, R. Pulungan R. Wimmer, and B. Becker. Compositional Performability Evaluation for Statemate. In *International Conference on Quantitative Evaluation of Systems (QEST)*, pages 167–176. IEEE Computer Society, 2006.

[5] CADP. Project Website, Aug 2006. http://www.inrialpes.fr/vasy/cadp/demos.html.

[6] M. Calder, V. Vyshemirsky, D. Gilbert, and R. Orton. Analysis of signalling pathways using continuous time Markov chains. *Transactions on Computational Systems Biology*, 2006. To appear.

[7] R. Cleaveland, S. P. Iyer, and M. Narasimha. Probabilistic temporal logics via the modal mu-calculus. *Theor. Comput. Sci.*, 342(2-3):316–350, 2005.

[8] L. de Alfaro. Stochastic Transition Systems. In *International Conference on Concurrency Theory (CONCUR)*, pages 423–438, 1998.

[9] B. L. Fox and P. W. Glynn. Computing Poisson probabilities. *Communications of the ACM*, 31(4):440–445, 1988.

[10] G. Gallo, G. Longo, S. Pallottino, and S. Nguyen. Directed hypergraphs and applications. *Discrete Appl. Math.*, 42(2-3):177–201, 1993.

[11] H. Garavel and H. Hermanns. On Combining Functional Verification and Performance Evaluation Using CADP. In *Formal Methods Europe (FME)*, pages 410–429, 2002.

[12] S. Graf, B. Steffen, and G. Lüttgen. Compositional Minimisation of Finite State Systems Using Interface Specifications. *Formal Asp. Comput.*, 8(5):607–616, 1996.

[13] B.R. Haverkort, H. Hermanns, and J.-P. Katoen. On the Use of Model Checking Techniques for Dependability Evaluation. In *Symposium on Reliable Distributed Systems (SRDS'00)*, pages 228–237. IEEE Computer Society, 2000.

[14] H. Hermanns. *Interactive Markov Chains and the Quest for Quantified Quality*, volume 2428 of *LNCS*. Springer, 2002.

[15] H. Hermanns and J.-P.Katoen. Automated compositional Markov chain generation for a plain-old telephone system. *Science of Comp. Programming*, 36:97–127, 2000.

[16] H. Hermanns and S. Johr. Uniformity by Construction in the Analysis of Nondeterministic Stochastic Systems, 2006. Long version of submission. Available at http://depend.cs.uni-sb.de/~johr/PDS/longV.pdf.

N	# States		# Transitions		Mem	Transf. time (s)	Runtime (s)		# Iterations	
	Inter.	Markov	Inter.	Markov			100 h	30000 h	100 h	30000 h
1	110	81	155	324	14.2 KB	5.37	0.01	6.04	372	62161
2	274	205	403	920	38.6 KB	4.32	0.01	12.33	372	62284
4	818	621	1235	3000	122 KB	5.25	0.04	37.28	373	62528
8	2770	2125	4243	10712	428 KB	5.83	0.13	47.77	375	63016
16	10130	7821	15635	40344	1.56 MB	6.61	0.52	294.97	378	63993
32	38674	29965	59923	156440	6.01 MB	9.44	3.23	877.52	384	65945
64	151058	117261	234515	615960	23.6 MB	20.58	37.42	3044.72	397	69849
128	597010	463885	927763	2444312	93.6 MB	57.31	557.52	20867.06	423	77651

Table 1. Model sizes, memory usage and runtime for strictly alternating IMCs

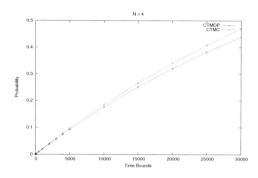
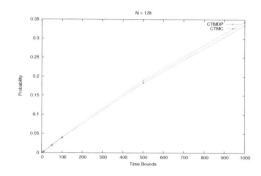

Figure 4. Different probabilities

[17] H. Hermanns, J.-P. Katoen, J. Meyer-Kayser, and M. Siegle. A tool for model-checking Markov chains. *Journal on Software Tools for Technology Transfer (STTT)*, 4(2):153–172, 2003.

[18] A. Hinton, M. Kwiatkowska, G. Norman, and D. Parker. PRISM: A Tool for Automatic Verification of Probabilistic Systems. In *TACAS*, pages 441–444. Springer, 2006.

[19] A. Jensen. Markoff Chains as an Aid in the Study of Markoff Processes. *Skandinavisk Aktuarietidsskrift*, pages 87–91, March 1953.

[20] J.-P. Katoen, M. Khattri, and I. S. Zapreev. A Markov Reward Model Checker. In *Quantitative Evaluation of Systems (QEST)*, pages 243–244. IEEE Computer Society, 2005.

[21] J. G. Kemeny and J. L. Snell. *Finite Markov Chains*. Van Nostrand, 1960.

[22] N.A. Lynch, I. Saias, and R. Segala. Proving Time Bounds for Randomized Distributed Algorithms. In *Symposium on the Principles of Distributed Computing*, pages 314–323, 1994.

[23] M. F. Neuts. *Matrix-Geometric Solutions in Stochastic Models: An Algorithmis Approach*. Dover, 1981.

[24] A. Pogosyants, R. Segala, and N. A. Lynch. Verification of the Randomized Consensus Algorithm of Aspnes and Herlihy: a Case Study. In *Workshop on Distributed Algorithms (WDAG'97)*, volume 1320, pages 111–125. Springer-Verlag, 1997.

[25] M. L. Puterman. *Markov Decision Processes: Discrete Stochastic Dynamic Programming*. Wiley, 1994.

[26] M. A. Salsburg, D. Lifka, and R. S. Mitchell. A Management Framework For Petabyte-Scale Disk Storage. In *Int. CMG Conference*, pages 767–782, 2005.

[27] R. Segala. *Modeling and Verification of Randomized Distributed Real-Time Systems*. PhD thesis, Department of Electrical Engineering and Computer Science, MIT, 1995.

[28] R. Segala and N. Lynch. Probabilistic simulations for probabilistic processes. *Nordic Journal of Computing*, 2(2):250–273, 1995.

[29] SVL. Project Website, March 2006. http://www.inrialpes.fr/vasy/cadp/man/svl.html.

[30] R. J. van Glabbeek and W. P. Weijland. Branching time and abstraction in bisimulation semantics. *J. ACM*, 43(3):555–600, 1996.

[31] N. Wolovick and S. Johr. A Characterization of Meaningful Schedulers for Continuous-time Markov Decision Processes. In *Formal Modeling and Analysis of Times Systems (FORMATS)*, pages 352–367. Springer, 2006.

Session 7C:
Quality of Service
and Error Recovery

A Reinforcement Learning Approach to Automatic Error Recovery

Qijun Zhu
Artificial Intelligence Lab
Tianjin University
Tianjin, China
zhuqijun@tju.edu.cn

Chun Yuan
Microsoft Research Asia
No.49, Zhichun Road
Beijing, China
cyuan@microsoft.com

Abstract

The increasing complexity of modern computer systems makes fault detection and localization prohibitively expensive, and therefore fast recovery from failures is becoming more and more important. A significant fraction of failures can be cured by executing specific repair actions, e.g. rebooting, even when the exact root causes are unknown. However, designing reasonable recovery policies to effectively schedule potential repair actions could be difficult and error prone. In this paper, we present a novel approach to automate recovery policy generation with Reinforcement Learning techniques. Based on the recovery history of the original user-defined policy, our method can learn a new, locally optimal policy that outperforms the original one. In our experimental work on data from a real cluster environment, we found that the automatically generated policy can save 10% of machine downtime.

1. Introduction

Maintaining high dependability has always been a critical topic for computer systems. Doing so usually is implemented in two ways: increasing reliability or availability. Reliability characterizes the ability of a system to perform services correctly, which can be measured by the meantime between failures (MTBF). Availability means that the system is available to perform services, which can be characterized by the meantime to repair (MTTR). Despite great improvements in research and practice in software engineering, latent bugs in complex software systems persist, and often it is just too difficult to improve system reliability by recognizing faults or fixing bugs. Actually, as the complexity of the software systems increases dramatically, analyzing system problems and finding root causes has become costly and time-consuming work even for skilled operators and diagnosticians [13][18]. Making computer systems more consistently available is indeed practical and can increase effectiveness and productivity.

Traditional fault tolerant techniques rely on some form of redundancy to achieve high availability, which can come in the form of function or data redundancy. However, such methods usually sacrifice system performance and can cause high hardware costs and increase complexity. For example, process pairs [3] utilize good processors taking over the functionality of failed processors in which non-stop processing is at the cost of hardware redundancy and performance. Auragen [4] also applies a similar scheme to the UNIX environment.

Another important way to achieve high availability is through recovery schemes that restore systems to a valid state after a failure. One of these recovery schemes is based on check-pointing, which periodically creates a valid snapshot of a system's state and, in the case of a failure, returns the system to a valid state. Often this method is system-specific and may create great burdens on system designers and operators. Baker *et al.* [1] utilized Recovery Box to realize quick recovery in which operating systems and application programs need to use the interface provided by Recovery Box to implement data insertion and retrieval. Moreover, it is difficult to determine the right time to create a checkpoint and ensure its validity.

A more popular recovery scheme is simple rebooting technique, which can be applied at various levels and is employed by many nontrivial systems today. Actually, a significant fraction [5][10][14][22] of failures are cured by simple recovery mechanisms such as rebooting even when exact causes are unknown. Candea *et al.* [6] built crash-only programs to crash safely and recover quickly, and then improved this approach by introducing a fine-grained mechanism called microreboot [7] which can provide better recovery performance and cause less disruption or downtime.

However, to achieve efficient error recovery, potential repair actions need to be scheduled reasonably based on policies like state-action rules. An example of such policies includes recursively attempting the remaining cheapest action [7]. This simple policy may not be sufficient in real environments because of imprecise fault localization, recurring failures, or failed repair actions [8]. The overall cost of cheap actions, including the time for observing recovery effects, is actually not that negligible either. Due to similar difficulties in root cause analysis, as mentioned above, generating recovery policies automatically could be important in effective error recovery. Joshi *et al.* [16][17] attempt to tackle the problem with a model-based approach that enables automatic recovery in distributed systems. Though their method works well in simulated experiments, there are still problems. First, the method needs detailed information on the system model, which is often too complex to obtain for large-scale systems. Second, it can locate faults well along the recovery process, but may have difficulties in determining how to deal with the faults since some faults may need the combination of several actions to complete a recovery in real systems.

In this paper, we also utilize application-independent techniques to achieve automatic recovery. However, we are focusing on recovery policy generation when system models are not available. To the best of our knowledge, this has not been fully studied before. We have investigated how to make proper decisions on which repair action to choose when the actual root cause is only localized at a coarse level. Particularly, we propose a novel approach based on reinforcement learning (RL) to automatically find the locally optimal policy, and show that it can achieve better recovery performance. Another benefit of our learning-based approach is that it can adapt to the change of the environment without human involvement.

Our contributions are as follows:

1. An offline reinforcement learning method to automatically generate optimal recovery rules. We should point out that the generated rules are locally optimal since the learning is restricted by the original, user-defined rules to be optimized.

2. A hybrid approach to handle noisy states that cannot be cured by generated rules. The results show that our approach cannot only maintain nearly the same performance as using the generated rules in isolation, but also can cover all possible states.

3. A new type-oriented model of automatic error recovery. Each rule corresponds to a potential error type induced from the recovery log.

4. Some experience in reducing rule-training time. By using a selection tree, we can guarantee discovery of optimal rules within much less time than the standard RL process.

The rest of the paper is organized as follows. Section 2 defines the automatic recovery problem and provides an overview of our approach. Section 3 gives additional details on the training method, and presents some assumptions based on how a reasonable evaluation cab be conducted. Section 4 describes our experimental data and evaluation framework. Section 5 presents experimental results. Section 6 discusses related work and Section 7 serves as our conclusion.

2. Overview

An automatic recovery framework typically consists of three functions: event monitoring, fault detection, and error recovery, as shown in the upper part of Figure 1. A recovery process may run like the following: Event monitoring collects various information and events for further analysis, such as symptoms of error states corresponding to different faults that occur in the target system. Then, fault detection recognizes failures and informs error recovery so that it can decide which repair action should be used based on the given recovery policy and the failure information. The chosen action is applied to the corresponding component and the result of the recovery will be monitored, which may lead to another round of recovery.

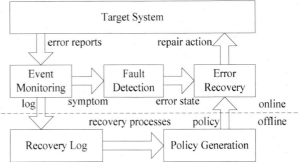

Figure 1: Automatic recovery framework.

Usually, recovery policies are user-defined by system developers or operators. The issues with this approach are manifold. First, policies are often difficult to build and evaluate for large-scale, complex systems in which detailed system models may not always be available or up to date. Second, an ideal policy should be able to target each fault. However, due to the limitation of fault localization, people often have to build coarse-grained policies to cover all possible error states. This sometimes may be too inaccurate to guarantee the desired result. Third, unanticipated errors and varying symptoms may appear throughout the running of systems, which requires policies evolve over time.

In our recovery framework we have two additional offline components for automatically generating recovery policies, as shown in the lower part of Figure 1. Recovery log keep a history of error recovery via the event monitoring component. Policy generation components learn recovery policies from the recovery history with statistical induction techniques to instruct error recovery. Specifically, we use reinforcement learning to generate error type-oriented policies. Our simulated experiments show that the policies learned by our method outperform manual ones.

2.1. Problem formalization

If we consider the recovery process as selecting a repair action according to current state and then getting a reward (e.g. recovery time) after taking the action, we can naturally formalize it as a sequential decision-making process, or particularly a Markov decision process (MDP) [15].

A Markov decision process can be represented as a tuple (S, A, δ, c, S_0), where S is the set of possible error states, each of which consists of some related features; In particular, S_0 is all possible starting states; A is the available repair actions; δ is the state transition function, which decides the next state s_{t+1} based on the current state s_t and the selected action a_t; c is the cost function, which determines the cost for executing an action under an error state. In our experiments, we use Meantime to Repair (MTTR) as the metric for evaluation, so c is based on recovery time (downtime). Therefore our goal is to minimize the expected cost V,

$$V = E[\sum_{t=0}^{\infty} c(s_t, a_t)] \tag{1}$$

that is, to achieve the shortest recovery time. We will give more detailed explanation in Section 3.2.

2.2. Reinforcement learning and Q-learning

As further background of our method, we give a brief introduction to reinforcement learning, an unsupervised learning method for sequential decision making. In this learning paradigm, the learning agent receives reinforcement (reward) after each action execution. The objective of learning is to construct a control policy so as to minimize the discounted cumulative reinforcement in the future or, for short, utility:

$$V_t = \sum_{k=0}^{\infty} \gamma^k c_{t+k} \tag{2}$$

which is a generalized form of equation (1). γ is the discount factor. In this paper, we simply set it to 1.0 to make sure the expected cost is equal to MTTR.

Q-learning is a widely used reinforcement learning algorithm. The idea of Q-learning is to construct an evaluation function called Q-function,

$$Q(state, action) \rightarrow utility$$

to predict the utility when the agent is executing some action in certain state. Given an optimal Q-function

and a state s, the optimal control policy is simply to choose the action a such that $Q(s, a)$ is minimal over all actions. Often the Q-function can be represented in a generalized way like multi-layer neural networks and incrementally learned through temporal difference (TD) methods [23]. Given a sequence of state transitions, the Q-function can be computed by iteratively applying the learning procedure to each two successive states along the sequence. Note that this procedure is actually the simplest form of TD methods, $TD(0)$. More details and discussions on Q-learning algorithm can be found in standard machine learning textbooks or related papers [20][21].

2.3. Automated policy generation

In this section, we will present the motivation for offline training and a brief description of the policy generation process.

2.3.1. Offline training. There are a few issues in applying reinforcement learning to learn recovery policies online.
1. Before finding out the optimal policy, the RL training process may explore many bad policies, which, once applied, might seriously degrade normal system performance.
2. The training process may start with an arbitrarily bad policy.
3. The training process requires tens of thousands of observations. For error recovery, several years may be required to converge for infrequent errors.

To address these limitations, we devised an offline training method that enables RL to take advantage of user-defined policies. Although it is at the cost of missing the globally optimal policy and only producing the locally optimal one, the obvious improvement it can bring to original policies and the avoidance of online training overhead still makes it a reasonable choice.

2.3.2. RL approach. We use the error types induced from failure symptoms to approximate the real faults. An induced error type represents the errors that share the same symptoms, which ideally corresponds to a unique fault, though different faults may be inferred as the same error type. Specifically, we simply use the error types and the previously tried actions to form the states. The learning algorithm analyzes a real-world recovery log generated by a user-defined policy and computes the value of the Q-function $Q(s, a)$, which satisfies the following equation

$$Q(s, a) = E[c(s, a)] + \sum_{s'} P(s'|s, a) min_{a'} Q(s', a')$$
$$, where \ s' = \delta(s, a) \tag{3}$$

Here, the Q-function $Q(s, a)$ stands for the minimal time cost for state s beginning with action a. The generated recovery policy may be restricted by two factors, the error types and the original recovery policy, so it can only achieve local optimum.

3. Approach

This section gives details on the RL approach to automatic recovery policy generation, and discusses some difficulties and our solutions.

```
function Q-learning
input
        Pr   recovery processes (in the recovery log)
        Q    initial Q-function values
return
        updated Q-function values
begin
        // select one recovery process from Pr
        p = SelectProcess(Pr)
        // induce error type based on recovery process
        t = InduceErrorType(p)
        // build initial state
        s = InitialState(t)
        // explore different recovery actions
        while(!Healthy(s)){
            a = SelectRecoveryAction(Q, s)
            c = UpdateState(Pr, s, a, s')
            Record(s, a, c, s')
            s = s'
        }
        // update Q-function values
        for every two successive states s, s' in record
            UpdateQfunction(Q, s, s')
        return Q
end
```

Figure 2: Q-learning algorithm for optimal policy generation

As stated in the previous section, we use Q-learning algorithm to obtain repair policy. The training process is implemented by applying Q-learning algorithm to each error type, which can be inferred from error symptoms in the recovery log. The procedure described in Figure 2 is iteratively used on the recovery log to get an optimal Q-function. In the following sections, we provide a closer look at each key step.

3.1. Error type inference and noise filtering

In this paper, we attempt to extract potential faults based on the error symptoms in the recovery log.

To get a rough idea of how symptoms are distributed, we generate a number of symptom sets from a real-world recovery log (to be introduced in section 4.1). In each set, the symptoms are highly related based on the ratio of the number of recovery processes in which they appear together out of all the recovery processes in which one symptom appears. Due to the fact that some symptoms may occur quite infrequently, we use m-pattern algorithm [19], which is capable of finding infrequent but highly correlated items, to mine mutually dependent symptoms in the log. The strength of mutual dependence is measured by parameter *minp*.

We summarize the percentage of the recovery processes with only highly dependent symptoms for various dependence strength in Figure 3. We can observe that the whole log is mainly made up of a number of highly cohesive symptom sets. Additionally, we find different sets share few intersections. This motivates us to generate policy at symptom level since we do not have any knowledge about real faults. Actually, we think the symptom sets may have strong correlation with the faults in the system. Based on these observations, we define *error type* as the initial symptom of a recovery process to approximate the real fault. For example, if the sequence of symptoms occurring during a recovery process is "A; B; C", then we use symptom "A" to represent its error type. We choose the initial symptom since it is usually representative enough of the symptom set to which it belongs and the other symptoms in the recovery process often co-occur with it. Based on this definition, we employ the error type as the unit in building recovery policies.

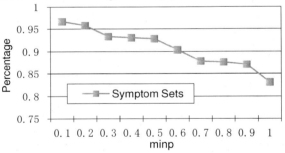

Figure 3: Symptom sets extracted from recovery log

Moreover, we still need do some noise filtering based on the above results because the evaluation is based on a simulation platform in our experiments and those noise data are often too difficult to simulate and may impact the precision of the evaluation. Actually we choose *minp* = 0.1 in m-pattern algorithm, and ultimately get 119 symptom clusters covering 96.67 % of the total logs. The left 3.33% are regarded as noisy cases that may contain more than one error. The noise data only take up a trivial part within the logs, so the filtering process does not influence the conclusions much. Although our RL approach can also be applied to these noisy cases, we still ignore them to get a precise evaluation.

3.2. State transition

We use error types (beginning symptoms) and previously tried repair actions to define states. A state s_t is represented by a tuple $(e, r, (a_o, a_1, \dots, a_{t-1}))$, where e is error type, r is the recovery result (failure or health) before time t, and a_i, $i = 0, 1, \dots, t-1$, are all repair actions executed before. From this definition, it is obvious that before the last repair action the recovery result r of any state will be f (failure) and after that it will become h (health). This definition also makes automatic error recovery a Markov decision process.

Transition function, δ, here is partially known, since the state s_{t+1} produced by the acts on $s_t = (e, f, (a_0, a_1, \dots, a_{t-1}))$ and a_t could only be two types, $s_{t+1}^f = (e, f, (a_0, a_1, \dots, a_{t-1}, a_t))$ or $s_{t+1}^h = (e, h, (a_0, a_1, \dots, a_{t-1}, a_t))$, the probabilities of which depend on the environment and properties of the errors. So the equation (3) could be rewritten as

$$Q(s_t, a_t) = E[c(s_t, a_t)] + q(s_t, a_t) \min_{a_{t+1}} Q(s_{t+1}^f, a_{t+1})$$

$$\text{,where } s_{t+1}^f = \delta(s_t, a_t) \qquad (4)$$

Figure 4 illustrates the decisions and possible sequences in a recovery process after an error is detected.

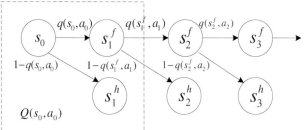

Figure 4: Error recovery process. The Q-function Q(s, a) is the expected time cost for both two directions (failure or health).

We restrict the count of the repair actions to a finite number N for each recovery process (in the experiment we set N = 20). It means that if the preceding N-1 repair actions fail to cure the problem, we will end the process by requesting a manual repair (the recovery action which is to be conducted by human). Since all policies produced with this limitation are proper, according to the theorem of value contraction in [14], our RL method will converge with probability 1.

3.3. Explore strategy and table update

To explore different repair actions, we first need to infer the state transitions based on the existing recovery processes. This amounts to finding the correct repair actions for each recovery process. The easiest method is to choose the last repair action as the correct one. However, it may not always be safe to make such assumptions and sometimes some stronger repair actions also play an important role in the recovery process. A more realistic assumption is to regard both the last action and other stronger actions as the correct repair actions. Besides, since a stronger action includes the processes of the weaker ones, it can at least cause the same effect as the weaker ones. Based on this analysis, our hypotheses about the recovery process is as follows:

1. For any successful recovery process, we need at least the same correct repair actions (including the last action and the stronger ones in the process) to achieve the same recovery result.

2. Stronger actions can replace weaker ones in a successful recovery process.

3. Recovery processes for different errors are independent of each other.

With these hypotheses, we can carry out the explore strategy and estimate the time cost for each possible policy.

Starting from some initial states of recovery processes, we have to explore a large enough state space first and then find the optimal policy. We can roughly divide the learning course into two phases, one for exploration and the other for search. Like the simulated annealing algorithm, we use a temperature T to control the learning course from exploration to search.

Actually, at time t for certain error e, we will utilize the following probability distribution (Boltzmann distribution) to select a repair action stochastically,

$$P(a_i|s_t) = \frac{e^{-\frac{Q(s_t, a_i)}{T}}}{\sum_j e^{-\frac{Q(s_t, a_i)}{T}}}, \quad a_i \in A \qquad (5)$$

Here, the temperature T will decrease with more and more recovery processes analyzed, so the repair action will eventually be selected completely based on Q values, thus generating the policy.

When a repair action is selected, its time cost will be estimated based on the recovery log. Specifically, one of the following values will be chosen: actual time cost in the recovery process average success time cost, or average failing time cost. Based on these values, we can further update the Q-function and reasonably evaluate the policy. As we show in Section 4.2, this approach works well in our experiments.

Another important step in the whole training course is how to update the Q values. In our method, we chose to use a table look-up representation of the Q-function and update the Q values based on the following equation,

$$Q_n(s, a) \leftarrow (1 - \partial_n)Q_{n-1}(s, a)$$
$$+ \partial_n \left[c(s, a) + \min_{a'} Q_{n-1}(s', a') \right]$$
$$\text{and, } \partial_n = \frac{1}{Visits_n(s,a)} \qquad (6)$$

where $Q(s,a)$ records the expected value of the Q-function, and $Visits(s,a)$ represents how many times (s,a) pair is explored. It is easy to prove that this updating method is contracted and Q values will eventually converge to the optimal ones [20].

3.4. Hybrid approach

Occasionally, the RL-trained policy might fail to repair some exceptional error cases. To get beyond this issue, we provide a hybrid approach that combines the trained policy with the user-defined one. In particular, if an error still exists after the last action selected according to the trained policy, we will automatically revert to the user-defined policy. Since these noisy cases do not happen frequently, the hybrid policy cannot only guarantee to repair all errors as well as the user-defined policy does, but also can maintain the advantage of automatic policy generation with RL, as we show in Section 5.2.

4. Experimental setup

This section introduces the data used in our experiments and the simulation platform that outputs feedback of a repair action on a state -based on the hypotheses.

4.1. Experimental data

Our experimental data are based on the recovery log collected from a large-scale cluster system with thousands of servers that contained more than 2 million entries of error symptoms and repair actions over nearly half a year of operations. The recovery policy used in the real system is user-defined, which mainly tries the cheapest action enabled by the state. There are four actions for repairing a machine: TRYNOP (simply watch and do not try any operation), REBOOT, REIMAGE (rebuild the operating system), and RMA (let human repair).

Table 1: Example of recovery process (machine name is omitted).

Time	Description (details omitted)
3:07:12 am	error:IFM-ISNWatchdog: …
3:10:58 am	errorHardware:EventLog: …
3:23:26 am	TRYNOP
3:25:37 am	errorHardware:EventLog: …
3:27:34 am	errorHardware:EventLog: …
3:42:10 am	REBOOT
4:13:07 am	Success

The log entries can be represented in the format of <time, machine name, description>, in which the description can be the repair action, symptom of an error,

or report of a successful recovery that occurs at the recorded time on the monitored machine. Therefore, the logs can be divided into an ensemble of recovery processes. The processes start with the advent of a new error, experience a series of repair actions, and end with successful recovery. Table 1 gives an example of recovery process.

After noise filtering, we get 97 error types from the recovery log with the error type inference method mentioned in Section 3.1. To guarantee enough training data, we choose the 40 most frequent error types, which constitute 98.68% of the total recovery processes.

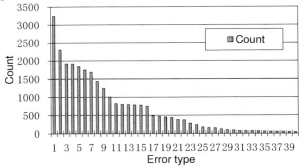

Figure 5: Count of 40 most frequent error types

Figure 5 shows the count of the selected error types. The remaining error types, since they are much less frequent, still need more time to accumulate enough training samples by monitoring the real system. The total downtime of each error type in the recovery processes controlled by the user-defined policy is given in Figure 6.

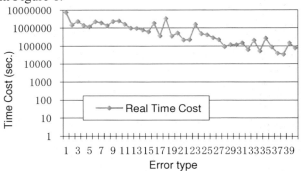

Figure 6: Total downtime of 40 most frequent error types under user-defined policy

4.2. Simulation platform

Our simulation platform is built to compute time cost for a repair action on a state based on the assumptions mentioned in Section 3.3 and the recovery log.

To verify our assumptions and the settings of the simulation platform, we run the platform under the user-defined recovery policy of the real system. Because we could not refer to all the information considered by the user-defined policy from the log, we could only expect an approximate result. Figure 7 shows the results for the 40 most frequent error types. The relative time cost here is the ratio of the estimated time cost compared to the real one for each error type, which is also used as the evaluation measure in the following experiments.

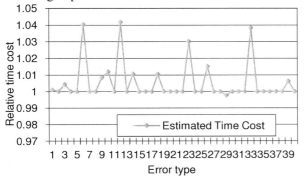

Figure 7: Relative cost for 40 most frequent errors compared to real ones. Biggest deviation is less than 5%.

We can see that the time costs computed by the simulation platform are close to the real ones and only one computed cost (error type 29) is slightly less than the real one. Therefore, by using this platform we can expect a conservative evaluation for most cases and thus make a fair comparison between the trained policy and the original policy.

5. Experimental results

In this section, we first evaluate the policy originally trained by RL, then the performance of the hybrid approach. In each experiment we will apply the learning algorithm to a portion of the log to train a policy, and then test the performance of the policy on the remaining log. The training set and the test set are divided according to time order. We choose 20%, 40%, 60% and 80% of the recovery log for used in the training, thus forming four tests (test 1, test 2, test 3, and test 4).

5.1. Results of RL-trained policy

Figure 8 shows the fractions of the estimated time cost of the trained policy with respect to the actual time cost for each error type. The time cost of the unhandled cases is not counted in the total cost.

In Figure 8, the four plots show the results of the four policies trained with 20, 40, 60 and 80 percent of the whole log. For most error types, the trained policy performs almost the same as the original policy. Through our observation of the corresponding recovery

log, we find that the original policy has already achieved good enough recovery steps. This is hard to optimize any more based only on the existing log. On the other hand, we find that for some error types such as 1, 35, and 39, the trained policy gains a significant improvement over the original policy, reducing the cost to nearly half. When looking at the policy more closely, we find that the trained policy for most error types is nearly the same as the original one. The deviation of the time cost for some error types (e.g. 6, 10, and 23) comes from simulation error (see Section 3.1). For error type 1, 35, and 39, the trained policy will try a stronger repair action at the beginning instead of the weakest one as done by the original policy. Since the stronger action is more effective in recovering the system from the error, it gains a big savings in recovery time without trying the weaker actions first and waiting to find out that they do not work.

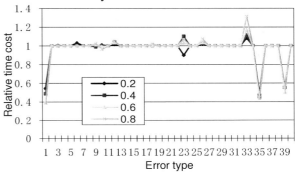

Figure 8: Relative time cost for trained policy compared to real one

The overall absolute time cost for the different test sets is shown in Figure 9. We can see that the trained policy can always gain over 10% time savings in the four tests. In particular, the policy trained from 40% of the log results in only 89.02% of the original downtime on the remaining log. Here, we only summarize the total time cost of the cases that could be handled by our trained policy. Since some unhandled cases exist that will be discussed in the next paragraph, the total time cost is a little less than the following experiment.

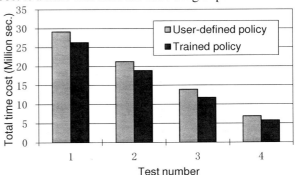

Figure 9: Total time cost of trained policy under different tests

Finally, we present the *coverage* of the trained policy in Figure 10, that is, the percentage of the errors it can handle. For each test, only a small number of error types cannot be handled and even in these cases the coverage is still more than 90%. Besides, the unhandled cases decrease dramatically with the more training data used.

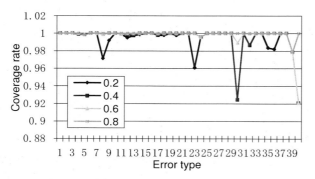

Figure 10: Coverage of the trained policy.

5.2. Results of hybrid approach

To solve the noisy cases not covered by the RL-trained policy, we combine it with the original user-defined defined policy. Figure 11 shows two results comparing the pure RL approach and the hybrid approach.

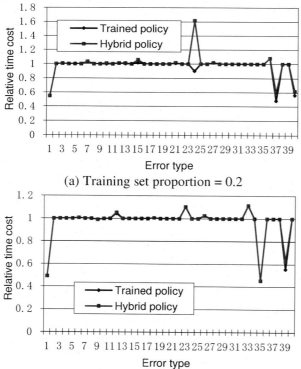

(a) Training set proportion = 0.2

(b) Training set proportion = 0.4

Figure 11: Performance comparison between trained policy and hybrid policy

For the policy trained with 20% of the log, the performance of the hybrid approach is almost the same as the RL-trained policy except for several exceptions, such as error type 23 (Figure 11(a)). However, when we take a closer look at the training data of error type 23, we find that some new patterns that appear in the test set are not covered by the training set, so the trained policy is suboptimal and may not perform stably. As the size of the training data increases, more precise policy is generated and the hybrid approach performs nearly the same as the trained policy, as presented in Figure 11(b).

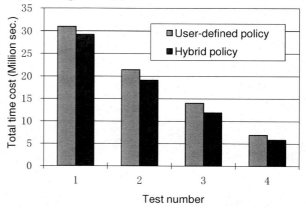

Figure 12: Total time cost of hybrid approach under different tests

Figure 12 summarizes the total cost for the original user-defined policy and the hybrid policy. Like the trained policy, the hybrid policy can also achieve more than 10% improvement over the original policy, on average. Corresponding to the policy trained with 40% of the log, the hybrid approach only costs 89.18% of the original downtime.

5.3. Learning rate experience

In this section, we introduce our effort in improving the learning process to shorten the training time. To this end, we use a technique called selection tree in the learning process. To build the selection tree, we consider the best two repair actions each time when generating the policy from the Q values. If the expected total cost of the second best action is close enough (based on a threshold) to that of the best one, we will choose both actions as candidates. Otherwise we will only choose the best one. Then, the selection tree can be built by iteratively putting these candidate actions as the children of the previous repair action, and the optimal policy can be generated by scanning the tree. Figure 13 shows the training time of this method (with selection tree) compared to the standard RL training course (without selection tree) with a maximum of 160 thousand sweeps (training set proportion = 0.4).

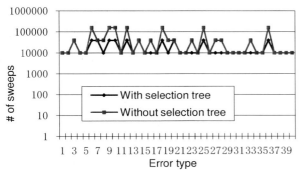

Figure 13: Training time comparison. Vertical axis stands for sweep number before convergence of training process for each error type.

Moreover, the performance of the policies trained by these two methods is shown in Figure 14. We can find that, using standard RL method, some training courses do not converge to the optimal policies even after 160 thousand sweeps. In contrast, with a selection tree, we can speed up the learning rate and successfully find the optimal policy within 40 thousand sweeps in our experiment.

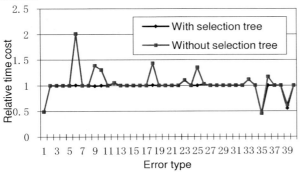

Figure 14: Performance comparison between optimized training method and standard method

6. Related work

Gray's classic text on failure analysis [14] surveys a range of failure statistics of a commercially available fault-tolerant system. He also discusses various approaches to software fault-tolerance, which mainly focus on how to prevent the occurrence of failures or reduce their frequency.

More recent work attempted to employ statistical learning techniques in automated fault diagnosis and performance management. An early work by Ma and Hellerstein [19] presented an efficient algorithm to discover all infrequent Mutually Dependent Patterns (*m-pattern*) for system management, for example, isolating problems in computer networks. Some statistical tools were developed for diagnosing configuration errors that cause a system to function incorrectly. Whi-

taker et al. presented the *Chronus* tool [26], which automates the task of searching for a failure-inducing state change. A similar work was completed by Wang et al. [25]. They presented the PeerPressure troubleshooting system that uses statistics from a set of sample machines to diagnose misconfiguration on a sick machine. There are still many projects focusing on performance analysis and debugging or bottleneck detection. Examples that include Magpie [2] and Pinpoint [9] make efforts to associate failures or performance problems with possible components via request traces. On failure diagnosis, Cohen *et al.* proposed to correlate the low-level system metrics with high-level performance states using Tree-Augmented Naïve Bayesian networks [11]. Based on this work, they construct *signatures* for clustering and retrieving, which could yield insights into the causes of observed performance effects and provide a way to leverage past diagnostic efforts [12][28]. Yuan et al. [27] proposed to correlate known faults to system behaviors with pattern classification techniques so as to recognize future occurrences of the faults automatically. Compared to these research efforts, our approach focuses on automated error recovery instead of performance diagnosis. Recently, Tesauro *et al.* [24] completed a similar work that employed a hybrid reinforcement learning approach to performance management.

In the area of error recovery, the common approaches rely on a priori knowledge from human experts to build policies for systems. Often, these repair actions can be expensive, causing nontrivial service disruption or downtime. Some recent research seeks to improve this method by introducing fine-grained recovery mechanisms. Microreboot [7], for example, provides a way for recovering faulty application components in an Internet auction system, without disturbing the rest of the application. We believe this work is complement to our work since we do not set any limitations on the set of repair actions. Additionally, with more potential repair actions, authoring or generating reasonable recovery policy will become evermore critical.

7. Conclusion

In this paper, we proposed a novel reinforcement learning approach to improve the framework of automatic error recovery. Specifically, we focus on recovery policy generation when a system model is not available, which we believe has not yet been fully studied. We have investigated how to make proper decisions on which repair actions to choose when the actual root cause is only localized at a coarse level. With our method, a locally optimal policy is guaranteed to be found, and it can adapt to changes in environment without human involvement. Finally, experimental results on data from a real cluster environment show that automatically generated policy achieved more than 10% savings in machine downtime on average. Several possible extensions of the approach include using generalization functions to approximate the Q-learning values, introducing more complicated relationships among actions, and designing initial policies that can be improved. In addition, we believe the approach provide greater benefits when we gain more information from event monitoring or fault detection.

8. Acknowledgments

We would like to thank Ken Cao, Peirong Liu and Yi Li for clarifying the details of the user-defined policy and the recovery log. We also thank the anonymous reviewers for their helpful comments and Dwight Daniels for proofreading the paper.

References

[1] M. Baker and M. Sullivan. The Recovery Box: Using fast recovery to provide high availability in the UNIX environment. In Proc. Summer USENIX Technical Conference, San Antonio, TX, 1992

[2] P. Barham, A. Donnelly, R. Isaacs and R. Mortier. Using Magpie for request extraction and workload modeling. In Proc. 6th Symposium on Operating Systems Design and Implementation (OSDI), Dec. 2004.

[3] J.F. Bartlett. A NonStop kernel. In Proc. 8th ACM Symposium on Operating Systems Principles, Pacific Grove, CA, 1981.

[4] A. Borg, W. Blau, W. Graetsch, F. Herrman and W. Oberle. Fault Tolerance under UNIX. ACM Transactions on Computer Systems, 7(1): 1–24, Feb 1989.

[5] E. Brewer. Lessons from giant-scale services. IEEE Internet Computing, 5(4):46–55, July 2001.

[6] G. Candea and A. Fox. Crash-only software. In Proc. 9th Workshop on Hot Topics in Operating Systems, Lihue, Hawaii, 2003.

[7] G. Candea, S. Kawamoto, Y. Fujiki, G. Friedman and A. Fox. Microreboot – A Technique for Cheap Recovery. In Proc. 6th Symposium on Operating Systems Design and Implementation (OSDI), Dec 2004.

[8] G. Candea, E. Kiciman, S. Kawamoto and A. Fox, Autonomous Recovery in Componentized Internet Applications. Cluster Computing Journal, 9(1), Feb 2006

[9] M. Chen, E. Kiciman, E. Fratkin, A. Fox and E. Brewer. Pinpoint: Problem determination in large, dynamic systems. In Proc. 2002 Intl. Conf. on Dependable Systems and Networks, Washington, DC, June 2002.

[10] T.C. Chou. Beyond fault tolerance. IEEE Computer, 30(4):31–36, 1997.

[11] I. Cohen, M. Goldszmidt, T. Kelly, J. Symons and J.S. Chase. Correlating instrumentation data to system states: A building block for automated diagnosis and control. In Proc. 6th Symposium on Operating Systems Design and Implementation, Dec. 2004.

[12] I. Cohen, S. Zhang, M. Goldszmidt, J. Symons, T. Kelly and A. Fox. Capturing, Indexing, Clustering, and Retrieving System History. In Proceedings of the ACM Symposium on Operating Systems Principles (SOSP), Oct. 2005.

[13] A. Fox and D. Patterson. Self-repairing computers. Scientific American, June 2003.

[14] J. Gray. Why Do Computers Stop and What Can Be Done About It? 6th International Conference on Reliability and Distributed Databases, June 1987.

[15] G.J. Gordon. Stable Function Approximation in Dynamic Programming, tech report CMU-CS-95-103, 1995.

[16] K.R. Joshi, W.H. Sanders, M.A. Hiltunen and R.D. Schlichting. Automatic Model-Driven Recovery in Distributed Systems. SRDS 2005: 25-38

[17] K.R. Joshi, W.H. Sanders, M.A. Hiltunen and R.D. Schlichting. Automatic Recovery Using Bounded Partially Observable Markov Decision Processes. In Proc. of the 2006 International Conference on Dependable Systems and Networks (DSN'06): 445-456

[18] J.O. Kephart and D.M. Chess. The vision of autonomic computing. Computer, 36(1):41–50, 2003.

[19] S. Ma and J.L. Hellerstein. Mining Mutually Dependent Patterns for System Management. IEEE Journal on Selected Areas in Communications, VOL. 20, NO. 4, May 2002.

[20] T.M. Mitchell. Machine Learning. McGraw-Hill, 1997.

[21] S.A. Murphy. A Generalization Error for Q-Learning. Journal of Machine Learning Research, 6 (2005) 1073–1097.

[22] B. Murphy and T. Gent. Measuring system and software reliability using an automated data collection process. Quality and Reliability Engineering Intl., 11:341–353, 1995.

[23] R.S. Sutton. Learning to Predict by the Methods of Temporal Differences. Machine Learning 3: 9-44, 1988.

[24] G. Tesauro, R. Das and N. Jong. Online Performance Management Using Hybrid Reinforcement Learning. First Workshop on Tackling Computer Systems Problems with Machine Learning Techniques (SysML'06), June 2006.

[25] H.J. Wang, J.C. Platt, Y. Chen, R. Zhang and Y.M. Wang. Automatic Misconfiguration Troubleshooting with PeerPressure. In Proc. 6th Symposium on Operating Systems Design and Implementation, Dec. 2004.

[26] A. Whitaker, R.S. Cox and S.D. Gribble. Configuration Debugging as Search: Finding the Needle in the Haystack. In Proc. 6th Symposium on Operating Systems Design and Implementation, Dec. 2004.

[27] C. Yuan, N. Lao, J.-R. Wen, J. Li, Z. Zhang, Y.-M. Wang and W.-Y. Ma. Automated Known Problem Diagnosis with Event Traces. 1st EuroSys Conference, April 2006

[28] S. Zhang, I. Cohen, M. Goldszmidt, J. Symons and A. Fox. Ensembles of Models for Automated Diagnosis of System Performance Problems. In Proc. of the 2005 International Conference on Dependable Systems and Networks (DSN'05).

On the Quality of Service of Crash-Recovery Failure Detectors

Tiejun Ma, Jane Hillston and Stuart Anderson
LFCS, School of Informatics, University of Edinburgh
Edinburgh, UK
t.j.ma@ed.ac.uk, jeh@inf.ed.ac.uk, soa@inf.ed.ac.uk

Abstract

In this paper, we study and model a crash-recovery target and its failure detector's probabilistic behavior. We extend Quality of Service (QoS) metrics to measure the recovery detection speed and the proportion of the detected failures of a crash-recovery failure detector. Then the impact of the dependability of the crash-recovery target on the QoS bounds for such a crash-recovery failure detector is analysed by adopting general dependability metrics such as MTTF and MTTR. In addition, we analyse how to estimate the failure detector's parameters to achieve the QoS from a requirement based on Chen's NFD-S algorithm. We also demonstrate how to execute the configuration procedure of this crash-recovery failure detector. The simulations are based on the revised NFD-S algorithm with various MTTF and MTTR. The simulation results show that the dependability of a recoverable monitored target could have significant impact on the QoS of such a failure detector and match our analysis results.

Keywords: Failure Detectors, Crash-Recovery, Quality of Service, Dependability, Monitoring.

1. Introduction

The Quality of Service of crash failure detection is a widely studied topic [3, 4, 6, 7, 11, 14]. Most of the previous work on this topic is based on the *crash-stop* or *fail-free* assumption and focus on how to estimate the probabilistic message arrival time and a suitable timeout length for such failure detectors. In this paper, we investigate and model a *crash-recovery* target service (CR-TS), which has the ability to recover from the crash state. We assume that the survival time and crash time of such a target follow some probability distribution. We extend the previous QoS metrics [3] to measure the QoS of a *crash-recovery* failure detection service (FDS) and analyse the QoS bounds for such a FDS. We show how to estimate the FDS's parameters from a given QoS set of requirements and indicate how to esti-

mate the inputs for the FDS's parameters estimation. Our analysis and simulation results show that the crash and recovery of the monitored target will have impact on the QoS of the FDS. For monitoring a recoverable target, especially for the recoverable target with low reliability, our analysis is more realistic and the FDS's parameters estimation is more strict.

2. Related Work

In [3] Chen *et al.* proposed a set of QoS metrics to measure the *accuracy* and *speed* of a failure detector. Their model contains a pair of processes — the monitor process and the monitored process — and there is only one crash during the monitoring period. The analysis work is based on two distinct stages of failure detection: the pre-crash stage, which is a *fail-free* run; and the post-crash stage, which is a *crash-stop* run and terminates the monitoring procedure. In order formally to define the QoS metrics, Chen *et al.* defined the state transitions of a failure detector monitoring a target process under the *fail-free* assumption [3]. At any time, the failure detector's state is either *trust* or *suspect* with respect to the monitored process's liveness. If a failure detector moves from a trust state to a suspect state then an *S-transition* occurs; if the failure detector moves from a suspect state to a trust state then a *T-transition* occurs. Chen *et al.* define the following QoS metrics for a failure detectors in a *crash-stop* run in [3]:

Detection time (T_D): the elapsed time from when the monitored process crashes until the monitoring process permanently suspects the monitored process: the final *S-transition* occurs.

Mistake recurrence time (T_{MR}): the time between occurrence of the i-th and $(i + 1)$-th mistakes: *S-transition i* to *S-transition $i + 1$*, where $i \geq 1$.

Mistake duration (T_M): the time to correct a mistaken suspect state: *S-transition* to *T-transition*.

Query accuracy probability (P_A): the probability that the state information from the failure detector is correct at an arbitrary time: $P_A = 1 - \frac{E(T_M)}{E(T_{MR})}$.

Additionally in [3], three *push-style* algorithms, one for clock synchronized systems (NFD-S) and the other two for clock unsynchronized systems (NFD-U and NFD-E) are defined. The authors show how to estimate the failure detector parameters (heartbeat interval η and shift of freshness point δ^1) according to a given QoS specification for each of the above algorithms.

Some recent research has extended the QoS work of [3] in a number of ways. For example, [4, 11, 14] refine the model with different probabilistic message delay and loss estimation methods. Meanwhile, others, such as [5, 6, 7, 13] focus on the scalability and adaptivity of crash failure detection. But all of this work is based on eventual *crash-stop* behavior of the monitored process or the *fail-free* assumption.

Crash-recovery failure detectors have been considered by several groups, e.g. [1, 8, 12]. However, each of these papers propose failure detectors to solve consensus or group membership problems rather than focusing on the QoS of the failure detector itself. In [1], the monitored process is characterised as *always-up*, *eventually-up*, *eventually-down* or *unstable*. A process which crashes and recovers infinitely many times is regarded as unstable. But *crash-recovery* looping behavior exists for most systems. From the perspective of stochastic theory, *crash-recovery* behavior can be regarded as a regenerative process, in which the probabilistic live and recovery time are not zero. For example, a web service system, in which the deployed service might crash but can be recovered by some recovery techniques, such as reboot or restart from the last available checkpoint, can be regarded as a typical *crash-recovery* system. From the system designer's perspective, the recovery should be as quick as possible. However, from the failure detection perspective, in order to detect the occurrence of such a failure, the failure detector expects that the recovery has a reasonable duration.

In [10], a preliminary study of the QoS of the *crash-recovery* failure detector (FDS) is presented. A *crash-recovery* target service (CR-TS) is modeled as a stochastic process, which can be regarded as an alternating renewal process with the random variable $X_a(t)$ presenting the elapsed time from a recovery time to the next crash time and the random variable $X_c(t)$ presenting the elapsed time from a crash time to the next recovery time (see Fig 1). General dependability metrics such as reliability, availability and consistency are adopted to characterize the behaviors of the CR-TS. In [10], the reliability is captured by the Mean Time To Failure (MTTF), the availability is captured by the Mean Time To Failure over the Mean Time Between Failure ($\frac{MTTF}{MTBF}$), the consistency is captured by the Mean Time To Repair (MTTR). Note that $E(X_a(t)) = \text{MTTF}$, $E(X_c(t)) = \text{MTTR}$ and $E(X_a(t) + X_c(t)) = \text{MTBF}$.

$^1\delta$ is replaced by *timeout* in this paper.

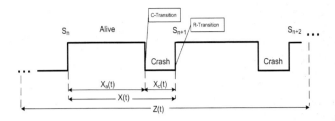

Figure 1. Crash-Recovery Service Modeling

In [10] it is concluded that in steady state, observing one MTBF period is enough to capture the *crash-recovery* failure detection characteristics of a failure detection pair.

3. QoS of the Crash-Recovery FDS

3.1. Analysis of the Crash-Recovery FDS

Let $\mathcal{S}_A \in \mathcal{S}_a$ represent the accuracy of the FDS's current output value, where $\mathcal{S}_a := \{Accurate, Mistake\}$. Here *Accurate* means the current FDS's output value presents the CR-TS's current state accurately. *Mistake* means the FDS's output value presents the CR-TS's current state inaccurately. Let $\mathcal{S}_{CR\text{-}TS} \in \mathcal{S}$ represent the current state of the CR-TS, where $\mathcal{S} := \{Alive, Crash\}$. $\mathcal{S}_{FDS\text{-}O} \in \mathcal{S}_s$ represents the current output value of the FDS, where $\mathcal{S}_s := \{Trust, Suspect\}$ is the state space of the suspicion levels of the FDS. If each of *Trust*, *Alive* and *Accurate* is regarded as True and each of *Suspect*, *Crash*, and *Mistake* as False, the FDS's current accuracy can be derived from the following deduction:

$$\mathcal{S}_{FDS\text{-}O} \; (XNOR) \; \mathcal{S}_{CR\text{-}TS} \Rightarrow \mathcal{S}_A$$

This deduction can be justified by observing the fact that if the value of $\mathcal{S}_{FDS\text{-}O}$ and $\mathcal{S}_{CR\text{-}TS}$ are the same then the value of $\mathcal{S}_A$ is True, because the FDS's output value presents the CR-TS's state accurately. If the value of $\mathcal{S}_{FDS\text{-}O}$ and $\mathcal{S}_{CR\text{-}TS}$ are different then the value of $\mathcal{S}_A$ will be False. Thus the value of $\mathcal{S}_A$ is the result of an Exclusive-NOR operation between the value of $\mathcal{S}_{FDS\text{-}O}$ and $\mathcal{S}_{CR\text{-}TS}$.

For a *fail-free* run (MTTF $\rightarrow +\infty$) or a *crash-stop* run (MTTR $\rightarrow +\infty$), the CR-TS's current state $\mathcal{S}_{CR\text{-}TS}$ is always *Alive* (for the time up to the crash) and it is easy to deduce the FDS's accuracy $\mathcal{S}_A$ directly from the FDS's current state $\mathcal{S}_{FDS\text{-}O}$. However, for a *crash-recovery* run, since the CR-TS could fail or recover at arbitrary time, $\mathcal{S}_A$ cannot be deduced solely from $\mathcal{S}_{FDS\text{-}O}$. Therefore, measuring the accuracy of a FDS for a CR-TS is more complex. In addition, compared with a *fail-free* or *crash-stop* run, there are more mistake types in a *crash-recovery* run. In previous work, such as [3, 7, 11, 13, 14], only the mistakes caused by the message transmission behaviors (message delay and

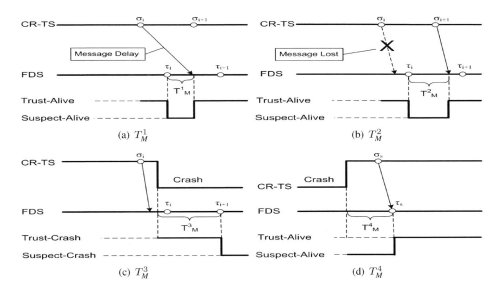

Figure 2. The Analysis of Possible T_M in a Crash-Recovery Run

loss) are considered. Fig. 2 shows the four types of mistakes which could occur within a *crash-recovery* run, and their associated durations. T_M^1 (Fig 2(a)) represents the duration of a mistake caused by a message delay. T_M^2 (Fig 2(b)) represents the duration of a mistake caused by a message loss. T_M^3 (Fig 2(c)) represents the duration of a mistake caused by CR-TS's crash and T_M^4 (Fig 2(d)) represents the duration of mistakes caused by CR-TS's recovery. Moreover, since the errors that may occur in a *crash-recovery* run are more complex, the QoS of such systems may exhibit quite different characteristics.

3.2. QoS Metrics Extension for the Crash-Recovery FDS

For a *crash-recovery* FDS, in addition to the QoS metrics introduced in [3] (T_D, T_M, T_{MR}, P_A), we propose some new QoS metrics. In order to measure the speed with which a FDS can discover a recovery of the CR-TS, we define:

Recovery detection time (T_{DR}): represents the time that elapses from CR-TS's recovery time to the time when the FDS discovers the recovery. If the recovery is not detected, then $T_{DR} = +\infty$.

Since in a *crash-recovery* run there is no eventual behavior of a CR-TS, a fast recovery could make a failure undetectable by a FDS. Under such circumstances, the *completeness* property of a failure detector proposed in [2] cannot be always satisfied. In order to reflect this situation, we refine the definition of *completeness* as follows:

- *Strong completeness*: every crash failure of a recoverable process will be detected.

- *Weak completeness*: a proportion of crash failures of recoverable process will be detected, satisfying a specified requirement.

Thus, in order to measure the *completeness* of a *crash-recovery* failure detector, we propose another new QoS metric:

Detected failure proportion (R_{DF}): the ratio of the detected failures over the occurred failures ($0 \leq R_{DF} \leq 1$). When no crash failure is detected, $R_{DF} = 0$. When all crash failures occurrences are detected, $R_{DF} = 1$. The *strong completeness* property of a FDS's requires that $E(R_{DF}) = 1$. The *weak completeness* property requires $E(R_{DF}) \geq R_{DF}^L$, where R_{DF}^L is the required lower bound on the detected failure proportion and $0 < R_{DF}^L < 1$.

Overall, the QoS for a *crash-recovery* FDS, can be captured by P_A, T_M, T_{MR}, T_D, T_{DR}, R_{DF}.

4. The Analysis of the NFD-S Algorithm in a Crash-Recovery Run

4.1. System Model

We consider a distributed system model with two services, one FDS and one CR-TS, distributed over a wide-area network. The FDS and the CR-TS are connected by an unreliable communication channel. Liveness messages are transmitted from the CR-TS to the FDS through the channel. The QoS of the communication through a channel can be measured by the average message delay ($E(D)$), the probability of message loss (p_L) and the average consecutive message loss-length ($E(X_L(t))$) (i.e. the average num-

741

ber of consecutive messages lost). We assume the communication channel will not create or duplicate liveness messages, but the messages might be lost or infinitely delayed during transmission (the same as the probabilistic network model in [3]). The CR-TS can fail by crashing but can be repaired and restart to run again after some repair time, behaving as a *crash-recovery* model. The drift of the local clocks of the FDS and the CR-TS are small enough to be ignored and their local clocks are synchronized to be regarded as a clock synchronized system (e.g., using the Network Time Protocol as in [4]). The failure detection algorithm we adopt is therefore the NFD-S algorithm proposed in [3].

4.2. QoS Bounds Analysis

In [10], it is shown that in order to study the steady state behavior of a CR-TS throughout its lifetime, we only need to observe the time period between two consecutive regeneration points. Fig. 3 shows the relationship between a FDS and a CR-TS on the interval $t \in [t_0, t_3)$, where both t_0 and t_3 are regeneration points. Obviously, the mean time between t_0 and t_3 is MTBF. We split $[t_0, t_3)$ into $[t_0, t_1)$, $[t_1, t_2)$, $[t_2, t_3)$. Here t_0 and t_3, are the time at which the CR-TS recovers; t_1 is the time when the FDS detects the recovery; t_2 is the time of the next CR-TS's crash. With respect to messages, σ_s is the liveness message sending time, i.e. the sending time of the first message received by the FDS after a recovery; σ_i is the sending time of a liveness message after σ_s before the CR-TS's crash; η is the message sending interval; τ_s is the first decision time (the first liveness message receiving time) after recovery; τ_d is the failure detection time.

In a *crash-recovery* run, the state of a CR-TS can switch between *Alive* and *Crash*. Let t_r^m be the recovery time of the m-th MTBF period (m is a positive integer). The following definitions are extensions of [3] Definition 1.

Definition 4.1. *For the fail-free duration $[t_1, t_2)$ within each MTBF period:*

1. *k: For any $i \geq 1$, let k be the smallest integer such that, for all $j \geq i + k$, m_j is sent at or after time τ_i.*

2. *For any $i \geq 1$, let $p'_j(x)$ be the probability that the FDS does not receive message m_{i+j} by time $\tau_i + x$, for every $j \geq 0$ and every $x \geq 0$; let $p'_0 = p'_0(0)$.*

3. *For any $i \geq 2$, let q'_0 be the probability that the FDS receives message m_{i-1} before time τ_i.*

4. *For any $i \geq 1$, let $u'(x)$ be the probability that the FDS suspects the CR-TS at time $\tau_i + x$, for every $x \in [0, \eta)$.*

5. *p'_s: for any $i \geq 2$, let p'_s be the probability that an S-transition occurs at time τ_i.*

According to the QoS analysis of the NFD-S algorithm in [3] (Proposition 3), we now analyze the QoS metrics of the NFD-S algorithm in a *crash-recovery* run and show the following relations hold:

Proposition 4.1. *Within the period $[t_1, t_2)$ for each MTBF period:*

1. *$k = \lceil timeout/\eta \rceil$.*

2. *for all $j \geq 0$ and for all $x \geq 0$,*

$$p'_j(x) = (p_L + (1-p_L) \cdot Pr(D(t) > timeout + x - j\eta))$$
$$\times Pr(X_a(t) > \tau_i + x - t_r^m).$$

3. *$q'_0 = (1 - p_L) \cdot Pr(D(t) < timeout + \eta)$*
$$\times Pr(X_a(t) > \tau_i - t_r^m).$$

4. *For all $x \in [0, \eta)$, $u'(x) = \prod_{j=0}^{k} p'_j(x)$.*

5. *$p'_s = q'_0 \cdot u'(0)$.*

Theorem 4.1. *The crash-recovery FDS based on the NFD-S algorithm has the following properties:*

$$\text{MTBF} \geq E(T_{MR})$$

$$\geq \frac{\text{MTBF}}{(\lfloor \frac{\text{MTTF} - E(T_{DR})}{\eta} \rfloor + 1) \cdot p'_s + \lceil \frac{E(D)}{\eta} \rceil + 2} \quad (1)$$

If the recovery duration is larger than $\eta + timeout$, then

$$\frac{\text{MTBF}}{2} \geq E(T_{MR})$$

$$\geq \frac{\text{MTBF}}{(\lfloor \frac{\text{MTTF} - E(T_{DR})}{\eta} \rfloor + 1) \cdot p'_s + \lceil \frac{E(D)}{\eta} \rceil + 2} \quad (2)$$

$$E(T_M) \leq$$

$$\frac{E(T_{DR}) + \frac{\text{MTTF} - E(T_{DR})}{\eta} \cdot \int_0^\eta u'(x)dx + E(T_D)}{(\lfloor \frac{\text{MTTF} - E(T_{DR})}{\eta} \rfloor + 1) \cdot p'_s + 1} \quad (3)$$

$$P_A \geq 1-$$

$$\frac{E(T_D) + E(T_{DR}) + \frac{\text{MTTF} - E(T_{DR})}{\eta} \cdot \int_0^\eta u'(x)dx}{\text{MTBF}} \quad (4)$$

$$E(T_{DR}) = E(D) + \eta E(X_L(t)) \quad (5)$$

$$E(R_{DF}) \geq Pr(X_c(t) > \eta + timeout) \quad (6)$$

The proof of Theorem 4.1 is based on the analysis of the average number of possible mistakes within the distinct intervals $[t_0, t_1)$, $[t_1, t_2)$ $[t_2, t_3)$, respectively. Since the proof of the whole theorem is long,[2] here we give only a brief sketch of the proof.

---

[2]The details of the proof is in [9].

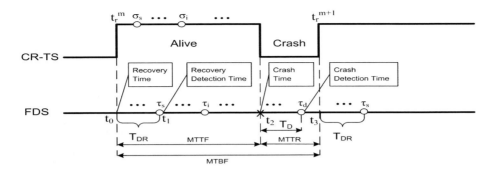

Figure 3. Analysis of the Crash-Recovery NFD-S Algorithm

Even if the FDS always trusts or suspects the CR-TS, due to state changes of the CR-TS within each MTBF period, there will be at least one mistake when the CR-TS crashes or recovers. If the failure can be detected before the recovery, both the crash and the recovery of the CR-TS can generate mistakes. If the FDS has already suspected the CR-TS before it crashes, it means there is at least one mistake caused by message delay or loss. If the FDS trusts the CR-TS before it recovers, it means there is at least one *false positive* mistake. Thus when the recovery duration is larger than $\eta + timeout$, there will be at least two mistakes for each MTBF period.

For the *fail-free* duration $[t_1, t_2)$, the average number of mistakes can be derived from the fact that if an S-transition occurs then a mistake will happen. Within $[t_1, t_2)$, the average number of mistakes will depend on the number of decision time points (τ_i) and the probability that a valid liveness message is not received by the decision time. From Fig. 3, we can see that the average duration of $[t_1, t_2)$ is $MTTF - E(T_{DR})$. Thus the average number of τ_i is less than $\lfloor \frac{MTTF - E(T_{DR})}{\eta} \rfloor + 1$. Since according to Proposition 4.1 the probability that the FDS suspects the CR-TS within $[t_1, t_2)$ is p'_s, then the average number of mistakes within $[t_1, t_2)$ can be estimated as $(\lfloor \frac{MTTF - E(T_{DR})}{\eta} \rfloor + 1) \cdot p'_s$. In addition, after the CR-TS has crashed, on average there are $\lceil \frac{E(D)}{\eta} \rceil$ messages still on the way to the FDS, which might also generate mistakes. Therefore the overall average number of mistakes within each MTBF is less than $(\lfloor \frac{MTTF - E(T_{DR})}{\eta} \rfloor + 1) p'_s + \lceil \frac{E(D)}{\eta} \rceil + 2$.

For $E(T_{MR})$, inequalities (1) and (2) can be easily derived by using the observation duration (MTBF) divided by the mean number of mistakes within that period.

$E(T_M)$ is less than the total mistake duration within the period divided by the minimum number of mistakes within that duration. The average mistake duration within $[t_0, t_1)$, $[t_1, t_2)$, $[t_2, t_3)$ is $E(T'_M), E(T''_M), E(T'''_M)$ respectively. $E(T'_M) = E(T_{DR})$. $E(T''_M)$, which is in the *fail-free* period, can be estimated using equation (3.3) of Theorem 5 in

[3]. Thus $E(T''_M) \leq \frac{1}{p'_s} \cdot \int_0^\eta u'(x)dx$. $E(T'''_M) \leq E(T_D)$. The total mistake duration within $[t_1, t_2)$ can be obtained by using the number of mistakes within this period multiplied by $E(T''_M)$. Thus the total mistake duration can be estimated by $E(T_{DR}) + \frac{MTTF - E(T_{DR})}{\eta} \cdot \int_0^\eta u'(x)dx + E(T_D)$. The minimum number of mistakes for each MTBF period is $(\lfloor \frac{MTTF - E(T_{DR})}{\eta} \rfloor + 1) \cdot p'_s + 1$. Therefore inequality (3) can be derived.

P_A, the probability that the FDS is accurate, can be derived from the total time that the FDS has an accurate output divided by the total observation period (MTBF). The total time that the FDS is accurate can be estimated using $MTBF - \left(E(T_D) + E(T_{DR}) + \frac{MTTF - E(T_{DR})}{\eta} \cdot \int_0^\eta u'(x)dx \right)$. Thus the inequality (4) can be obtained.

$E(T_{DR})$, is obtained directly from the average consecutive message loss number ($E(X_L(t))$) multiplied by the liveness message sending interval (η), plus the average message delay ($E(D)$), because, if a failure is detectable, after the recovery, when the first valid liveness message is received by the FDS, the recovery is detected (see Fig. 2(d)).

$E(R_{DF})$ can be estimated using the fact that if the recovery duration is larger than the failure detection time, then the occurred failure can be detected. Thus the proportion of the detectable failures can be estimated using $E(R_{DF}) \geq Pr(X_c(t) > \eta + timeout)$.

From the above analysis, Theorem 4.1 can be used to estimate the FDS's parameters and QoS bounds. Particularly, when the monitoring target is *fail-free*, for the QoS metrics in [3] (see inequalities (1)-(4) in Theorem 4.1), we can easily deduce that $E(T_{MR}) \geq \frac{\eta}{p'_s}$; $P_A \geq 1 - \frac{1}{\eta} \cdot \int_0^\eta u'(x)dx$; $E(T_M) \leq \frac{1}{p'_s} \cdot \int_0^\eta u'(x)dx$. As $MTTF \to +\infty$, $Pr(X_a(t) > \tau_i + x - t_r^m)$ approaches one. Therefore, p'_s, $u'(x)$ and q'_0 in the Definition 4.1 are reduced to p_s, $u(x)$ and q_0 in the Definition 1 in [3]. Thus $E(T_{MR})$, $E(T_M)$ and P_A are exactly reduced to the QoS analysis results in [3]. Therefore, we can conclude that in terms of the QoS of failure detection, a *fail-free* run or a *crash-stop* run with $MTTF \to +\infty$ is a particular case of a *crash-recovery* run.

743

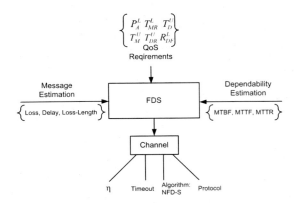

Figure 4. The Extended NFD-S Algorithm Configuration

If the monitored target's MTTF is not sufficiently long and the monitored target is recoverable, then the impact of its dependability should be taken into consideration.

4.3. The Revised NFD-S Algorithm for the Crash-Recovery FDS

For the NFD-S algorithm in a *crash-recovery* run, the assumption that the sequence numbers of the heartbeat messages are continually increasing after every recovery of the CR-TS is needed to ensure that the NFD-S algorithm is still valid after each recovery. However, without persistent storage to snapshot the runtime information frequently, when a crash failure occurs, all of the current runtime information might be lost. In such a situation, increasing heartbeat message numbers cannot be guaranteed. In addition, resetting the heartbeat sequence number can indicate the occurrence of a recovery and simplify the parameter computation as well. Since for the NFD-S algorithm, the local clocks of the FDS and the CR-TS are synchronized, we can use the comparison of the sending time of each heartbeat message instead of the comparison of the heartbeat sequence number. Then, for a *crash-recovery* FDS, given the QoS requirements of the FDS, the configuration procedure is illustrated in Fig. 4.

For given QoS requirements, expressed as bounds, the following inequalities need to be satisfied:

$$T_D \leq T_D^U, \ E(T_{MR}) \geq T_{MR}^L, \ P_A \geq P_A^L,$$
$$E(T_M) \leq T_M^U, \ E(T_{DR}) \leq T_{DR}^U, \ E(R_{DF}) \geq R_{DF}^L. \quad (7)$$

From Theorem 4.1, we can estimate the parameters (η and *timeout*) of the NFD-S algorithm according to the following inequalities:

$$\eta + timeout \leq T_D^U, \ \eta > 0 \quad (8)$$

$$\frac{\text{MTBF}}{(\lfloor \frac{\text{MTTF} - E(T_{DR})}{\eta} \rfloor + 1) \cdot p'_s + \lceil \frac{E(D)}{\eta} \rceil + 2} \geq T_{MR}^L \quad (9)$$

$$1 - \frac{E(T_{DR}) + \frac{\text{MTTF} - E(T_{DR})}{\eta} \cdot \int_0^\eta u'(x)dx + E(T_D)}{\text{MTBF}} \geq P_A^L \quad (10)$$

$$\frac{E(T_{DR}) + \frac{\text{MTTF} - E(T_{DR})}{\eta} \cdot \int_0^\eta u'(x)dx + E(T_D)}{(\lfloor \frac{\text{MTTF} - E(T_{DR})}{\eta} \rfloor + 1) \cdot p'_s + 1} \leq T_M^U \quad (11)$$

$$E(D) + \eta E(X_L(t)) \leq T_{DR}^U \quad (12)$$

$$Pr(X_c(t) > \eta + timeout) \geq R_{DF}^L \quad (13)$$

Then, the configuration of the NFD-S algorithm becomes the problem to find the largest η satisfying inequalities (9)-(12) and if such η exists, find the largest *timeout* that satisfies $\eta + timeout \leq T_D^U$ and $Pr(X_c(t) > \eta + timeout) \geq R_{DF}^L$. The configuration procedure can be done in the following steps:

Step I If $T_{MR}^L <$ MTBF continue, else the QoS of the FDS cannot be achieved.

Step II Find the largest η that satisfies the inequalities (9)-(12), otherwise cannot find appropriate η.

Step III If $\eta > 0$, find the largest $timeout \leq T_D^U - \eta$ and $Pr(X_c(t) > \eta + timeout) \geq R_{DF}^L$.

From the above steps, the estimation of η and *timeout* for a *crash-recovery* FDS based on the NFD-S algorithm amounts to finding a numerical solution for the inequalities (8)-(13). This can be done using binary search similarly to [3]. But the estimation of the input parameters of the configuration become more difficult because parameters, such as $E(X_L(t))$, MTTF, MTTR etc., are needed for such a FDS. We will introduce input parameter estimation shortly in Section 5. Note that for this configuration procedure, choosing a different message transmission protocol (e.g. TCP, UDP) can achieve different QoS for message communication. Thus, this new configuration can be more adaptive to the message transmission. For example, if the message loss probability or message delay is high for a certain protocol, then the FDS can switch to a more reliable protocol to achieve a better QoS without increasing the communication frequency or the *timeout* length.

4.4. Discussion

In Section 4.2 we introduced how to estimate the QoS bounds for a *crash-recovery* FDS based on the NFD-S algorithm. However, there are several facts which need to be taken into consideration.

In reality, the MTTF and MTTR are non-deterministic values, governed by random distributions. The proportion of detected failures is dependent on the probability distribution of $X_c(t)$, the length of η and *timeout*. If it is required to detect most failures before recovery, in practice $\eta + timeout$ should be much smaller than MTTR. For example, for exponentially distributed $X_c(t)$, if $\eta + timeout =$

MTTR, then $E(R_{DF}) \geq 36.8\%$. If $\eta + timeout = \frac{\text{MTTR}}{2}$, then $E(R_{DF}) \geq 60.7\%$. If $\eta + timeout = \frac{\text{MTTR}}{10}$, $E(R_{DF}) \geq 90.5\%$.

Theorem 4.1 gives the bounds of $E(T_{MR})$ and $E(T_M)$. However, from Fig. 3 we can see that the characteristics of $E(T_{MR})$ and $E(T_M)$ in the durations of $[t_0, t_1]$ $(E(T'_{MR}), E(T'_M))$, $[t_1, t_2]$ $(E(T''_{MR}), E(T''_M))$, $[t_2, t_3]$ $(E(T'''_{MR}), E(T'''_M))$ are quite different. Estimating η and $timeout$ using the mean of the dependability measurements might not satisfy the QoS requirement all the time. A stricter bound can be achieved by using the maximum value in the set $\{E(T'_M), E(T''_M), E(T'''_M)\}$, which must be smaller than T_M^U and the minimum value in $\{E(T'_{MR}), E(T''_{MR}), E(T'''_{MR})\}$, which must be larger than T_{MR}^L.

For T_M, $E(T'_M)$ is $E(T_{DR})$; $E(T'''_M)$ is less than $E(T_D)$; $E(T''_M)$, which is the *fail-free* duration, can be estimated by using the equation (3.3) of Theorem 5 in [3]. Thus $E(T''_M) \leq \frac{1}{p'_s} \cdot \int_0^\eta u'(x)dx \leq \frac{\eta}{q'_0}$. Then the mistake duration within each MTBF can be as follows:

$$\max\left(E(T_{DR}), \frac{\eta}{q'_0}, E(T_D)\right) \leq T_M^U \qquad (14)$$

More strictly, $E(T_{DR})$ can be substituted by the maximum recovery detection time to have been recorded and $E(T_D)$ can be substituted by T_D^U.

For T_{MR}, the possible mistake recurrence of the FDS is affected by the message delays, and losses, and the CR-TS's crashes and recoveries. The impact of the CR-TS's crash and recovery is governed by MTTF and MTTR, which mainly occur during $[t_0, t_1)$ and $[t_2, t_3)$. The impact of message delays and losses on T_{MR} mainly happen within $[t_1, t_2)$. From the analysis of Theorem 4.1 in Section 4.2, we know that $E(T''_{MR}) \geq \frac{\text{MTTF} - E(T_{DR})}{(\lfloor \frac{\text{MTTF} - E(T_{DR})}{\eta} \rfloor + 1) \cdot p'_s}$. Therefore, $E(T_{MR})$ can be estimated by using the minimum value in the set $\{\text{MTTF}, E(T''_{MR}), \text{MTTR}\}$. When $\text{MTTF} - E(T_{DR}) >> \eta$, $E(T''_{MR}) \geq \frac{\eta}{p'_s}$, the bound estimation of $E(T_{MR})$ can be reduced as follows:

$$\min\left(\text{MTTF}, \frac{\eta}{p'_s}, \text{MTTR}\right) \geq T_{MR}^L \qquad (15)$$

Inequality (15) gives a stricter constraint for the QoS estimation. However, the drawback of this method is obvious. For a highly consistent CR-TS, due to small MTTR, T_{MR} could be too small to satisfy a given QoS requirement. In this situation, using $E(T_{MR})$ instead could be a reasonable solution because the recovery of the CR-TS only happens once per MTBF period. Furthermore, if $timeout$ is scaled up or even becomes larger than MTTR, from Theorem 4.1 we can know that the $E(T_{MR})$ can increase, but more failures will become undetectable. For such a highly consistent

CR-TS, some new algorithm is needed to tackle this problem.[3]

5. Parameter Estimation

For a *crash-recovery* run, there are more input parameters than the *fail-free* run, e.g. parameters such as MTBF, MTTF, MTTR, p_L, $E(D)$ and $E(X_L(t))$, are used for the FDS configuration. For such a *crash-recovery* FDS's configuration, the following strategies are used. During the first MTBF period (at the very beginning), we can assume that the QoS of the message communication is perfect ($p_L = 0$, $E(D)$ is small and $E(X_L(t)) = 0$), and the CR-TS is *fail-free* ($\text{MTTF} \to +\infty$). For the following MTBF periods, initially, the previous period's estimations can be used. As the monitoring procedure continues, the estimation of the QoS of the message communication and the dependability metrics of the CR-TS will become more and more accurate. Thus the FDS can be reconfigured to adapt to the changing input parameters achieving better η and $timeout$ values. The following gives a brief description of how to estimate the FDS's inputs.

QoS of Message Transmission Estimation: the estimation of p_L and $E(D)$ can proceed similarly to [3]. However the estimation of p_L and $E(D)$ should now be for each MTBF period. In addition, the average message loss-length $E(X_L(t))$ is used for the recovery detection speed $E(T_{DR})$ estimation. In our model, each message's transmission and loss behaviors are assumed to be independent (as in [3]). Thus the mean number of consecutive message losses $E(X_L(t)) = 1 \times p_L + 2 \times p_L^2 + 3 \times p_L^3 + 4 \times p_L^4 + \cdots + m \times p_L^m = \sum_{n=1}^m n p_L^n$. Hence after arithmetic manipulation, it can be simplified to:

$$E(X_L(t)) = \frac{p_L(1 - p_L^m)}{(1 - p_L)^2} - \frac{m p_L^{m+1}}{1 - p_L} \qquad (16)$$

where m is the maximum number of consecutive messages lost and p_L is the probability that each message is lost during the transmission. When $m \to +\infty$ and $p_L < 1$, $p_L^m \to 0$ and $m p_L^m \to 0$. Therefore equation (16) can be simplified further:

$$\lim_{m \to +\infty} E(X_L(t)) = \frac{p_L}{(1 - p_L)^2} \qquad (17)$$

If dependencies between message transmissions exist, then adopting the empirical probability distribution of $X_L(t)$ for estimation of $E(X_L(t))$ is needed (c.f. [14]).

Crash-Recovery Service's Dependability Metrics Estimation: let t_r^1 be the CR-TS's first start time, then for $m \geq 1$, t_r^m represents the m-th recovery time; t_{dr}^m (τ_s in

---

[3]The recovery detection protocols are presented in [9] to discover a failure after the recovery and estimate the recovery time, which can improve the $E(R_{DF})$ without reducing other QoS aspects.

Fig. 3) represents the m-th recovery detection time; t_c^m (t_2 in Fig. 3) represents the m-th crash time; t_d^m (τ_d in Fig. 3) presents the m-th crash detection time, all of which can be recorded by the FDS's local clock. Since the FDS can detect the crash and the recovery of the CR-TS, therefore the dependability characteristics of the CR-TS can estimated by the FDS itself as follows:

Estimated MTBF: estimating MTBF depends on the estimation of the recovery time (t_r^m). If t_r^m can be obtained (see footnote 3), then MTBF can be estimated using:

$$\text{MTBF} = E(t_r^{m+1} - t_r^m) = \frac{1}{n}\sum_{m=1}^{n}(t_r^{m+1} - t_r^m) \quad (18)$$

Estimated MTTF: MTTF can be estimated using the recovery time (t_r^m) and the crash detection time (t_d^m):

$$
\begin{aligned}
E(t_d^m - t_r^m) &= \text{MTTF} + E(T_D)\\
\text{MTTF} &= E(t_d^m - t_r^m) - E(T_D)\\
&= \frac{1}{n}\sum_{m=1}^{n}(t_d^m - t_r^m) - E(T_D)
\end{aligned}
\quad (19)
$$

Estimated MTTR: MTTR can be estimated directly using MTBF and MTTF: MTTR = MTBF − MTTF, or using t_r^{m+1} and t_d^m. Hence MTTR can be estimated using the following equation:

$$
\begin{aligned}
E(t_r^{m+1} - t_d^m) &= \text{MTTR} - E(T_D)\\
\text{MTTR} &= E(t_r^{m+1} - t_d^m) + E(T_D)\\
&= \frac{1}{n}\sum_{m=1}^{n}(t_r^{m+1} - t_d^m) + E(T_D)
\end{aligned}
\quad (20)
$$

Estimated $Pr(X_a(t) > \tau_i + x - t_r^m)$: the probability that the CR-TS does not crash until $\tau_i + x$ after its last recovery, can be estimated as follows:

$$
\begin{aligned}
Pr(X_a(t) > \tau_i + x - t_r^m) &= 1 - \int_0^{\tau_i + x - t_r^m} f_a(x)dx\\
&\geq 1 - F_a(x)\big|_0^{\tau_i - t_r^m}
\end{aligned}
\quad (21)
$$

When the probability density function $f_a(x)$ or distribution function $F_a(x)$ is unknown, an empirical distribution function (EDF) estimation can be adopted to estimate $f_a(x)$ or $F_a(x)$. Similarly, for $Pr(X_c(t) > \eta + timeout)$ estimation, an empirical probability distribution can be used.

6. Simulation and Evaluation

For the simulation studies, we fix the heartbeat interval at $\eta = 1$ and increase the *timeout* length gradually. The message transmission parameters are $p_L=0.01$, $E(D) = 0.02$, both exponentially distributed random variables. All of

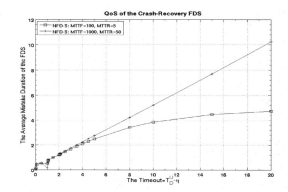

Figure 5. The NFD-S Algorithm: $E(T_M)$

these settings are similar to the simulations in [3]. The CR-TS is defined as a recoverable process with various MTTF and MTTR as exponentially distributed random variables. We choose the exponential distribution for the non-deterministic MTTF and MTTR for the following reasons. First, exponential failures are widely adopted for reliability analysis in many practical systems; second, unlike some heavy tail distributions such as the log-normal distribution, crash and recovery with an exponential distribution will occur with reasonable inter-arrival times, avoiding the CR-TS behaving like a *fail-free* or *crash-stop* process. Furthermore, some reasonable durations of MTTF and MTTR are provided as simulation cases. Such *crash-recovery* targets are highly available and consistent, but not highly reliable, targets. We implement the revised NFD-S algorithm to evaluate the QoS of the algorithm. Figs. 5-7 demonstrate the algorithm from different perspectives.

Fig. 5 shows that in a *crash-recovery* run, the mistakes caused by the CR-TS's crash and recovery have impact on $E(T_M)$. For the same *timeout* length, there are four aspects which have impact on T_M: the message delay and loss, the CR-TS's crash and recovery (see Fig. 2). T_M caused by a message delay is governed by the ratio between $E(D)$ and *timeout*. For the same $E(D)$, as *timeout* increases, a larger delay can be tolerated. Thus T_M caused by message delay (T_M^1) will decrease and occur less frequently. T_M caused by a message loss (T_M^2) is related to η, p_L, $E(D)$ and the *timeout* length. For constant QoS of message communication (i.e. the same p_L and $E(D)$), T_M caused by message loss is governed by the ratio between η and *timeout*. Since as the *timeout* length increases more consecutive message losses can be tolerated, the average duration of T_M^2 will decrease and T_M^2 will occur less frequently. T_M caused by a crash (T_M^3) is mainly governed by the *timeout* length (see Fig. 2(c)) and bounded by the CR-TS's recovery duration, because if a crash occurs, a *false positive* mistake will last until the failure detection time or until the CR-TS recovers. For detectable crashes, as the *timeout* length increases, T_M^3 will increase. T_M caused by a recovery (T_M^4) is mainly governed by p_L and $E(D)$ (see Fig. 2(d)), since after CR-TS's recovery, the recovery can be detected when a valid liveness message is received.

From the above analysis we know, for the same η, p_L, $E(D)$, MTTF and MTTR (as set in each simulation case), when $timeout$ increases, the mistake duration caused by the message delay and loss will decrease ($T_M^1 \downarrow$ and $T_M^2 \downarrow$), the mistake duration caused by the CR-TS's crash increases ($T_M^3 \uparrow$), and the mistake caused by the recovery for the detectable crashes is not affected by the $timeout$ length ($\overline{T_M^4}$), but less crashes and recoveries will be detected. In the first simulation, p_L=0.01 and MTBF $= 105$, when $timeout$ length is small, T_M^2 and T_M^3 occur with similar frequency. When $timeout$ is increased from 0.5 to 1.0, (the FDS can tolerate zero message loss and most message delays), the $E(T_M)$ increases slowly because $T_M^1 \downarrow$, $T_M^2 \downarrow$, $T_M^3 \uparrow$ and $\overline{T_M^4}$. Thus their impacts counterbalance. Overall $E(T_M)$ is stable within this duration. As the $timeout$ length increases, T_M^2 will occur less frequently. But T_M^3 occurs every MTBF period. Thus, as the $timeout$ length increases, T_M^3 will become dominant and $E(T_M)$ will increase gradually.

In the second simulation, p_L=0.01 and MTBF $= 1050$. When $timeout$ is small, T_M^2 will have more impact than T_M^3, because T_M^2 occurs more frequently than crash and recovery. Therefore, as the $timeout$ length increases, the average duration of T_M^2 decreases and T_M^2 occurs less frequently; $E(T_M)$ will increase slower or even decrease since more message losses are tolerated. But if $timeout$ continues to increase, T_M^3 will become dominant, and $E(T_M)$ will later increase gradually.

Overall, Fig. 5 shows that in a *crash-recovery* run, $E(T_M)$ exhibits quite different characteristics from a *fail-free* or *crash-stop* run. If the message delay and the probability of message loss are not very large, $E(T_M)$ is bounded by MTTR. From Fig. 5 we also observe that $E(T_M)$ can possibly be decreased when some $timeout$ value is chosen. In a *crash-recovery* run, continually increasing the $timeout$ length cannot achieve a better T_M as in a *fail-free* run.

Fig. 6 demonstrates the $E(T_{MR})$ of the NFD-S algorithm with exponential MTTF and MTTR with various values. We can see that as MTBF increases, for the same $timeout$ length, $E(T_{MR})$ increases. This implies that $E(T_{MR})$ is greatly impacted by the dependability of the CR-TS. We can also see that, for both the simulation cases, $E(T_{MR})$ increases exponentially fast at the beginning but after $E(T_{MR})$ reaches $\frac{\text{MTBF}}{2}$, it will stop increasing exponentially. If the CR-TS has a deterministic recovery duration, $E(T_{MR})$ will stop at $\frac{\text{MTBF}}{2}$ when failures are detectable. This is because when $timeout + \eta$ is smaller than MTTR, all of the crashes are detectable. Even if all of the message delays and losses are tolerated, for every MTBF period there are still two mistakes (T_M^3, T_M^4) which will certainly occur. Thus $E(T_{MR}) \leq$

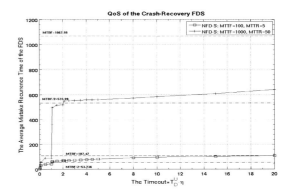

Figure 6. The NFD-S Algorithm: $E(T_{MR})$

$\frac{\text{MTBF}}{2}$ within this period (see inequality (2) in Theorem 4.1). If $timeout + \eta$ is larger than the recovery duration, all of the crashes might become undetectable. When mistakes caused by the message delays and message losses occur less frequently than the crash and recovery of the CR-TS, $E(T_{MR})$ will become stable at MTBF. In our simulation, the recovery duration of the CR-TS is an exponentially distributed random variable. Therefore, $E(T_{MR})$ will increase gradually and approach MTBF, rather than stop at $\frac{\text{MTBF}}{2}$, until all of the crashes become undetectable since for non-deterministic recovery duration, as the $timeout$ length increases, the proportion of the detectable crashes decreases. For the detectable crashes, $T_{MR} \leq \frac{\text{MTBF}}{2}$ and for the undetectable crashes, $T_{MR} \leq$ MTBF. Thus $E(T_{MR})$ will increase gradually between $[\frac{\text{MTBF}}{2}, \text{MTBF}]$ and finally stabilize at MTBF. All of these results match our analysis of inequalities (1)-(2) in Theorem 4.1 well and indicate that if a CR-TS is not *fail-free* or *crash-stop*, $E(T_{MR})$ will be bounded by MTBF when failures are undetectable and $\frac{\text{MTBF}}{2}$ when failures are detectable.

Fig. 7 shows the proportion of the detected failures of the NFD-S algorithm with different CR-TS dependability.

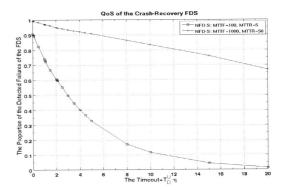

Figure 7. The NFD-S Algorithm: $E(R_{DF})$

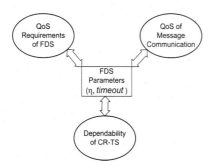

Figure 8. The QoS Relationship for the FDS's Parameters Estimation

Notice that as the *timeout* length increases, $E(R_{DF})$ of the NFD-S algorithm decreases. When MTTR becomes shorter, $E(R_{DF})$ will decrease faster. This is because the smaller MTTR is, the faster *timeout* + η crosses MTTR ($T_D^U >$ MTTR). Therefore, more crashes remain undetected. Thus we can conclude that NFD-S algorithm can achieve a *weak completeness* in a *crash-recovery* run. If a *strong completeness* is required for a *crash-recovery* failure detector, then new solutions are needed to achieve such a goal (see footnote 3).

Overall, from Figs. 5-7, we can see that, $E(T_{MR})$ and $E(T_M)$ have bounds; continually increasing the *timeout* length might not be a reasonable way to achieve better P_A, $E(T_{MR})$ and $E(T_M)$. It might in fact decrease $E(R_{DF})$. A trade-off exists between the QoS metrics. For instance, according to our simulation settings, for the NFD-S algorithm, *timeout* $\in [1, 1.1]$ ($T_D^U = $ *timeout* + $\eta \in [2, 2.1]$) might achieve the best overall QoS for a highly available, highly consistent but not highly reliable CR-TS.

7. Conclusions

In this paper, we have extended previously proposed QoS metrics to adapt to the behavior of a *crash-recovery* target to measure the recovery detection speed and the *completeness* property of a failure detector. In addition to the QoS of message transmission, the dependability characteristics of the *crash-recovery* target are involved in the analysis of failure detector's QoS bounds. Our analysis results show that the QoS analysis in [3] is a particular case of a *crash-recovery* run. The dependability of the *crash-recovery* target could have significant impact on the QoS of a failure detector when the target is not *fail-free* or *crash-stop*. We have shown that when MTTF and MTTR do not approach infinity, the dependability metrics must also be used as inputs for the estimation of η and *timeout*, rather than only considering the impact of the liveness message transmission measurements (see Fig. 8). Furthermore we have given

a method to estimate the FDS's parameters according to the QoS of message communication, the dependability of the CR-TS and the QoS requirements of the FDS based on Chen's NFD-S algorithm.

References

[1] M. K. Aguilera, W. Chen, and S. Toueg. Failure Detection and Consensus in the Crash-Recovery Model. *Distributed Computing*, 13(2):99 – 125, Apr. 2000.

[2] T. D. Chandra and S. Toueg. Unreliable Failure Detectors for Asynchronous Distributed Systems. Technical Report TR93 - 1377, Department of Computer Science, Cornell University, 1993.

[3] W. Chen, S. Toueg, and M. K. Aguilera. On the Quality of Service of Failure Detectors. *IEEE Tran. on Computers*, 51(5):561 – 580, 2002.

[4] L. Falai and A. Bondavalli. Experimental Evaluation of the QoS of Failure Detectors on Wide Area Network. In *Proc. of Int. Conf. on Dependable Systems and Networks (DSN2005)*, pages 624 – 633, Jul. 2005.

[5] I. Gupta, T. D. Chandra, and G. S. Goldszmidt. On Scalable and Efficient Distributed Failure Detectors. In *Proc. of the Twentieth Annual ACM Symp. on Principles of Distributed Computing*, pages 170 – 179, 2001.

[6] N. Hayashibara, A. Cherif, and T. Katayama. Failure Detectors for Large-Scale Distributed Systems. In *Proc. of the 21st IEEE Symp. on Reliable Distributed Systems*, pages 404 – 409, 2002.

[7] N. Hayashibara, X. Defago, R. Yared, and T. Katayama. The Accrual Failure Detector. In *Proc. of 23rd IEEE Int. Symp. on Reliable Distributed Systems*, pages 66 – 78, 2004.

[8] M. Hurfin, A. Mostefaoui, and M. Raynal. Consensus in Asynchronous Systems Where Processes Can Crash and Recover. In *Proc. of the 17th IEEE Symp. on Reliable Distributed Systems (SRDS)*, pages 280 – 286, 20-23 Oct 1998.

[9] T. Ma. *Quality of Service of Crash-Recovery Failure Detectors*. PhD thesis, The University of Edinburgh, March 2007.

[10] T. Ma, J. Hillston, and S. Anderson. Evaluation of the QoS of Crash-Recovery Failure Detection. In *SAC'07: Proc. of the ACM Symp. on Applied Computing (DADS Track)*, pages 538 – 542. ACM, 2007.

[11] R. C. Nunes and I. Jansch-Pôrto. QoS of Timeout-Based Self-Tuned Failure Detectors: The Effects of the Communication Delay Predictor and the Safety Margin. In *Proc. of the Int. Conf. on Dependable Systems and Networks*, pages 753 – 761, 2004.

[12] R. Oliveira, R. Guerraoui, and A. Schiper. Consensus in the Crash-Recover Model. Technical Report TR-97/239, Départment d'Informatique, Ecole Polytechnique Federale de Lausanne (EPFL), 1997.

[13] R. V. Renesse, Y. Minsky, and M. Hayden. A Gossip-Style Failure Detection Service. *Proc. of Middleware*, 98:55–70, 1998.

[14] I. Sotoma and E. R. M. Madeira. A Markov Model for Quality of Service of Failure Detectors in the Pressure of Loss Bursts. In *AINA '04: Proc. of the 18th Int. Conf. on Advanced Information Networking and Applications*, volume 2, pages 62 – 67, 2004.

E2EProf: Automated End-to-End Performance Management for Enterprise Systems

Sandip Agarwala, Fernando Alegre, Karsten Schwan, Jegannathan Mehalingham[†]

College of Computing	Delta Technology Inc.[†]
Georgia Institute of Technology	Delta Air Lines
Atlanta, GA 30332	Atlanta, GA 30354
{sandip, fernando, schwan}@cc.gatech.edu	Jegannathan.Mehalingham@delta.com

Abstract

Distributed systems are becoming increasingly complex, caused by the prevalent use of web services, multi-tier architectures, and grid computing, where dynamic sets of components interact with each other across distributed and heterogeneous computing infrastructures. For these applications to be able to predictably and efficiently deliver services to end users, it is therefore, critical to understand and control their runtime behavior. In a datacenter environment, for instance, understanding the end-to-end dynamic behavior of certain IT subsystems, from the time requests are made to when responses are generated and finally, received, is a key prerequisite for improving application response, to provide required levels of performance, or to meet service level agreements (SLAs).

The E2EProf toolkit enables the efficient and non-intrusive capture and analysis of end-to-end program behavior for complex enterprise applications. E2EProf permits an enterprise to recognize and analyze performance problems when they occur – online, to take corrective actions as soon as possible and wherever necessary along the paths currently taken by user requests – end-to-end, and to do so without the need to instrument applications – non-intrusively. Online analysis exploits a novel signal analysis algorithm, termed pathmap, *which dynamically detects the causal paths taken by client requests through application and backend servers and annotates these paths with end-to-end latencies and with the contributions to these latencies from different path components. Thus, with pathmap, it is possible to dynamically identify the bottlenecks present in selected servers or services and to detect the abnormal or unusual performance behaviors indicative of potential problems or overloads. Pathmap and the E2EProf toolkit successfully detect causal request paths and associated performance bottlenecks in the RUBiS ebay-like multi-tier web application and in one of the datacenter of our industry partner, Delta Air Lines.*

1 Introduction

Modern distributed systems are becoming increasingly complex, in part because of the prevalent use of web services, multi-tier architectures, and grid computing, where dynamic sets of machines interact via dynamically selected application components. A key problem in this domain is to understand the runtime behavior of these highly distributed, networked applications and systems, in order to better manage system assets or application response and/or to reduce undesired effects. In fact, sometimes, the processing of a single request can generate intricate interactions between different components across many machines, making it hard even for experts to understand system behaviors. A concrete example are the '*poison messages*' experienced in the IT infrastructure run by one of our industry partners [19]. Rapid problem detection, diagnosis [10], and resolution in cases like these are critical, since the potential business impact of problematic behaviors (e.g., inordinate request delays, request losses, or service outages), can be substantial. A recent study found, for example, that for a typical enterprise, the average cost of downtime either due to outright outage or due to service degradation is about US$125,000 per hour [1].

Online behavior understanding is also important under normal operating conditions. A case in point is runtime management to meet application-specific Service Level Agreements (SLAs), by classifying requests and then ensuring different service levels for different request classes, or by managing systems to meet certain utility goals [18, 26]. Additional examples are management tasks like job scheduling [15] or resource allocation [23]. For instance, a front-end web request scheduler making online scheduling and dispatching decisions in a multi-tier web service [5] requires continuous updates about the execution of the client's requests at the backend servers.

This paper presents the *E2EProf* toolkit for online per-

---

[1] IDC #31513, July 2004

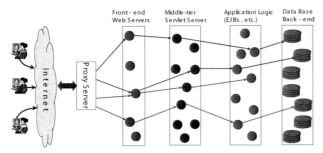

Figure 1: Example ServicePath in a multi-tier web service

formance understanding. E2EProf can be used to diagnose the performance problems that arise from complex interactions across multiple subsystems and machines. First, its methods for *end-to-end* performance understanding can capture the entire life-cycles of requests as they are being processed by an enterprise application's many hardware and software components. Second, E2EProf analysis enables *online* problem diagnosis, because of its optimzations and compact trace representations. Third, since E2EProf uses *non-intrusive* kernel-level network tracing for application monitoring, it can operate across the large diversity of applications routinely used in the enterprise domain, without the need to assume the existence of common, clean, and perhaps most importantly, without requiring uptodate monitoring instrumentation. Fourth, E2EProf operates without requiring access to source code, since it is not likely readily available for all of the applications being evaluated and managed by an organization. In fact, even if sources were accessible, the lack of proper documentation often makes it a daunting task to analyze these extensive codes.

The *E2Eprof* toolkit uses an incremental approach to performing *end-to-end* analyses of request behaviors. Specifically, it encapsulates different request interactions across distributed program components with different '*service paths*', where each such path describes a set of dynamic dependencies across distributed components formed because of the services they provide and the requests they service. Figure 1 shows the multiple service paths used by three different types of clients in a multi-tier web service, for example, where paths are differentiated by the kinds of requests being submitted.

Online service path encapsulation is done by correlating the timestamps of the messages exchanged between interacting components. E2EProf's cross-correlation analyses can capture application-relevant performance metrics, such as the end-to-end latencies experienced by requests, and they can determine the contributions of specific application-level services and network communications to such latencies. The choice of requests, components, and service paths to be analyzed can be changed at any time, without the need to recompile, re-link, or re-edit programs.

While the idea of path-based analysis been used by other

researchers to discover faults and performance problems in distributed systems [1, 8, 4, 25, 24], E2EProf makes the following unique contributions:

- Its *service path* abstraction can be used to encapsulate the causal paths of different requests (or services), capture end-to-end request delays, and the components of those delays due to each individual software component.

- Its time-series analysis algorithm, termed *pathmap*, discovers the causal request paths from network packet traces non-intrusively, which means pathmap neither requires access to application source code, nor modifications to deployed application services.

- Its ability to understand the performance of complex distributed applications is demonstrated by carrying out detailed online performance analyses for the RUBiS multi-tier auctioning web application.

- The low latency, efficient analyses performed by E2EProf permit it to be used for online management, using a black-box scheduling algorithm to manage Service Level Agreements (SLA) in RUBiS.

- E2EProf has gone beyond in-lab concept demonstrations, by using its pathmap algorithm to evaluate the performance of an enterprise application deployed in one of our industry partner's datacenters, the 'Revenue Pipeline' used in Delta Air Line's Atlanta datacenter.

E2EProf is the outcome of a multi-year effort to develop efficient mechanisms and methods for runtime performance understanding. E2EProf's online analysis permits it to capture and deal with the dynamic behaviors of complex enterprise applications. A specific target class of applications addressed by E2EProf are the *Operational Information Systems*(OIS) [13] used by large organizations for controlling day-to-day operations, an example being the OIS run by one of our industrial partners, Delta Air Lines. In order to function properly, these systems must operate and adapt to changes within well-defined constraints derived from their SLAs and dependent on the business values or utilities associated with their various services. If a SLA is violated, system administrators usually analyze large complex logs in order to isolate faulty components. E2EProf can be used to automate performance diagnosis, thereby reducing such maintenance costs.

In the remainder of this paper, we describe the service path abstraction and various components of E2EProf toolkit. The next section surveys the related work. Section 3 describes the pathmap algorithm and analyzes it in detail. Experimental evaluation is presented in Section 4 together with some realistic test cases of performance diagnosis and management. Conclusions appear in Section 5.

2 Related Work

The large number of tools available for distributed system performance diagnosis may be categorized based on three broad features: online/offline, level of intrusiveness, and quality of analysis.

Single web server system performance has been studied extensively. EtE [12] and Certes [22] measure client-perceived response time at the server side. The former does offline analysis of the packets sent and received at the server side, while the latter does online analysis by observing the states of TCP connections.

Tracing tools for single systems like the Linux Trace Toolkit [27] and Dtrace [6] provide mechanisms for logging events by inserting instrumentation code. Compiler-level instrumentation is commonly used to understand program behaviors (e.g. gprof.) However, source code may not always be available, and the sizes and complexities of sources are disincentives for software engineers engaged in post-development instrumentation or evaluation. Even binary instrumentation requires some level of understanding of application details.

Path-level analysis of distributed systems tracks the causal relationship between different components and has recently been an area of active research. ETE [14] uses application-specific instrumentation to measure the latencies between component interactions and relates them to end-to-end response times to detect performance problems. Pinpoint [9] detects system components where requests fail, by tagging (and propagating) a globally unique request ID with each request. Magpie [4], on the other hand, requires no global ID, and it can capture not only the causal paths, but also monitor the resource consumption of each request. Industry standards like ARM [3] used by HP's Openview, IBM's Tivoli, and BEA's Weblogic require middleware-level instrumentation to measure end-to-end application performance. In contrast, E2Eprof does not require any modification to applications and therefore, can also be used with legacy components. However, unlike Magpie, it does not measure general resource usage.

The work by Aguilera *et al.* [1] is most closely related to E2Eprof. They propose two algorithms to determine causally dependent paths and the associated delays from the message-level traces in a distributed system. While their *nesting* algorithm assumes 'RPC-style' (call-returns) communication, their *convolution* algorithm is more general and does not assume a particular messaging protocol. Our pathmap algorithm is similar to the *convolution* algorithm, in that both uses time series analysis and can handle non-RPC-style messages. While the convolution algorithm is primarily intended for offline analysis, pathmap uses compact trace representations and a series of optimizations, which jointly, make it suitable for online performance diagnosis.

3 Service Paths

3.1 Basic Abstractions, Methods, and Assumptions

In modern enterprise systems, different client requests may belong to one or more *service class(es)*, which are defined on the basis of simple request types, clients IDs, or more generally, SLAs. These requests may take different paths through the enterprise software, invoking different and multiple software components before responses are generated. We term the ensemble of paths taken by client requests in different service classes as '*Service Paths*'.

Service paths form the basis of E2EProf's online end-to-end performance analyses, because they characterize the end-to-end properties sought by the enterprise and capture the complex dependencies that exist across the different software components involved in service provision. For each path, E2EProf's analyses can describe not only the path's end-to-end latency but also the latencies incurred across different path edges, which can be used to pinpoint the bottleneck components in a request path.

The *pathmap* algorithm uses time-series analysis to discover the service paths of different service classes, making the following assumptions:

- Each client's requests belong to a unique *service class*, which is known to the front end (i.e., the first nodes in the distributed system that receives the request). Pathmap assumes that requests belonging to the same service class have similar resource requirements.

- A request path can either be unidirectional (as in streaming media applications) or bidirectional as in the request-response conduits used in multi-tier web services. In the latter case, responses traverse the same set of nodes as the corresponding requests, but in reverse order.

- Pathmap assumes that the distributed application and system are operating in steady state during the analysis 'time window', where deviations are due to internal anomalies or external drastic changes in system usage. Such anomalies occur when a node malfunctions, when a network link goes down, or when a buggy application overloads the system, for example.

- At small time scales, there may be large variability in the processing of individual requests, but in steady state, the system is assumed to be adequately provisioned so that the queuing and processing delays at each of its nodes don't significantly change the distribution of the intermediate responses (generated as a result of partial processing of the requests at the intermediate nodes in the path), as compared to the arrival distribution at the front-end. Pathmap can, however, accommodate changes in rate across nodes (e.g., an EJB server issuing multiple data base queries for a single client requests).

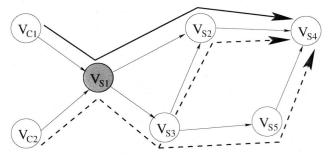

Figure 2: Example Service Graph: V_{c1} and V_{c2} are the client nodes and V_{sn} are service nodes.

3.2 System Representation

Formally, a distributed application or system may be described as a directed graph G(V,E), where the vertices in the graph represent application components and the edges represent their logical communication links. The *service graphs* considered in this paper are comprised of nodes that may be processes, threads, or machines, communicating with each other via network links.

Each service graph has two type of nodes: client nodes(V_C) and service nodes (V_S). Requests originate in client nodes, where we assume that the requests issued by each particular client node belong to the same service class. A physical client issues multiple classes of requests will be modelled as multiple client nodes, one per request class. Service nodes house software components that operate on requests. They are labelled by their IP addresses or by a combination of their IP addresses and process IDs, depending on whether there is one or more service node per physical machine node (e.g., an application server and database server being located on the same physical machine).

Edges denote logical communication link between service nodes. These logical connections are characterized by source and destination address pairs. They may be transient, which will usually be the case in front-end servers, or persistent, which is typical for middle and back-end servers. Furthermore, a single connection may consist of aggregated traffic from separate clients. Figure 2 depicts a sample service graph. For this graph, the goal of the *pathmap* algorithm is to compute the paths of requests from each client node through the service graph, along with the delays incurred in traversing the edges and nodes in those paths.

3.3 Pathmap Algorithm

The pathmap algorithm relies on the E2EProf tracing subsystem, which uses standard operating system facilities to collect timestamp traces for every (*src*, *dest*) pair of inter-component messages at each service node. Traces are not collected from client nodes, since those are usually beyond the reach of enterprises. The key idea of the pathmap algorithm is to convert these traces to per-edge time series signals and then compute the cross-correlations of these sig-

nals. Specifically, if a signal f contains a copy of the signal g, then their cross-correlation signal ($f \star g$) has a distinguishable spike at position d, where d is equal to the time that the copy of g in f has shifted from g. This kind of correlation analysis is commonly used in digital signal processing to compute the level of similarity between two signals.

First introduced by Aguilera *et al.* [1] in a similar context, pathmap uses cross-correlation analysis to discover the most probable request paths in a distributed system. Consider the request path ($V_{C1} \rightarrow V_{S1} \rightarrow V_{S2} \rightarrow V_{S4}$) shown in Figure 2. Let $T^x_{x \rightarrow y}$ be the time series signal of the messages from x to y collected at the node x, and $T^y_{x \rightarrow y}$ be the time series signal for the same set of messages collected at node y. The cross-correlation plot of $T^{s1}_{c1 \rightarrow s1}$ and $T^{s1}_{s1 \rightarrow s2}$ (denoted by $corr(T^{s1}_{c1 \rightarrow s1}, T^{s1}_{s1 \rightarrow s2})$) has a spike at position d, where d is the time that V_{s1} takes to process V_{c1}'s request. This implies that there is a causal relationship between messages on edge $V_{c1} \rightarrow V_{s1}$ and messages on edge $V_{s1} \rightarrow V_{s2}$. Similarly, the cross correlation plot $corr(T^{s1}_{c1 \rightarrow s1}, T^{s2}_{s2 \rightarrow s4})$ also has a spike, and its position is the sum of the communication latencies at the two edges ($V_{C1} \rightarrow V_{S1}$ and $V_{S1} \rightarrow V_{S2}$) and of the computation latencies at the two vertices (V_{s1} and V_{s2}). The presence of the spike also indicates a causal relationship between messages on edge $V_{c1} \rightarrow V_{s1}$ and messages on edge $V_{s2} \rightarrow V_{s4}$. The cross-correlation plot $corr(T^{s1}_{c1 \rightarrow s1}, T^{s1}_{s1 \rightarrow s3})$, however, has no distinguishable spike as no requests from V_{c1} pass through V_{s3}.

The above example illustrates how correlation can be used to establish causality between different edges. Given this background, Algorithm 1, outlines the actual pathmap algorithm. It takes as input the time-series data streams computed from the message timestamps collected at different service nodes. The most recent *sliding window* of size W is maintained for each of these streams. After every time interval ΔW, the '*ServiceRoot*' function is invoked to update the service graphs for all *clients* belonging to different service classes. The algorithm starts tracking the path at the front-end service nodes, which become the roots of service graphs. In addition, it adds an edge between the client node and the root vertex and then calls *ComputePath* to calculate rest of the graph.

ComputePath's parameters are a partial service graph G_c, a time-series signal (T_c) of the incoming requests of the service class (say C) at the front-end for which the service graph G_c is being determined, and the service node (S_i) to be processed next. ComputePath finds the next set of service nodes used by the request class represented by the time-series T_c. This is done by the process of correlation described above. Basically, T_c is cross-correlated with the time-series signal from the nodes(d_s) adjacent to S_i. If the correlation is high (as indicated by the presence of the spikes), then there exists a path from S_i to d_s taken by the

Algorithm 1 Pathmap

Let W = Length of sliding window
Let ΔW = Service Graph refresh interval
Input: Online time series data streams from service nodes
function ServiceRoot()
for all Service node S_i that are at the front-end **do**
  for all Client nodes V_c connected to S_i **do**
    Service Graph $G_c = \{\}$
    Add S_i in Graph G_c
    Add an edge $E_c(V_c \rightarrow S_i)$
    ComputePath($G_c, T_{V_c \rightarrow S_i}^{S_i}, S_i$)
  end for
end for

function ComputePath(G_c, T_c, S_i)
Mark S_i as visited
Let S_d = List of destination nodes S_i is connected to
for all d_s in S_d **do**
  $corr$ = ComputeCrossCorrelation($T_c, T_{S_i \rightarrow d_s}^{d_s}$)
  P = List of spike's position in $corr$
  if P is not empty **then**
    if vertex d_s not in G_c **then**
      Add vertex d_s in G_c
    end if
    Add an edge $E_s(S_i \rightarrow d_s)$ and label it with P
    if d_s not visited **then**
      ComputePath(G_c, T_c, d_s)
    end if
  end if
end for

---

requests belonging to service class C. This is recorded by adding vertex d_s into the graph G_c (if such a vertex does not yet exist) and by adding an edge from S_i to d_s. The edge is labelled with the *delay*(s) as denoted by the spikes' position in the cross-correlation test. This delay is the sum of the time taken by the request to arrive at node S_i, the processing delay at node S_i, and the communication delay in the path from S_i to d_s. The computing delay at node S_i is the difference of the delays corresponding to its incoming and outgoing edges. The existence of more than one spike indicates that the request may have taken different paths to S_i (e.g., $S_1 \rightarrow S_2 \rightarrow S_i \rightarrow S_4$ and $S_1 \rightarrow S_3 \rightarrow S_i \rightarrow S_4$). Once the path to d_s is established, the algorithm proceeds further by performing a recursive depth-first search and exploring other edges in the service graph.

Spikes in the cross-correlation series are detected by finding *points* that are local maximas and exceed a threshold ($mean + 3 \times Std.Dev.$). In traces with some noise, there may exist spikes that are very close to each other. To address this issue, we define a resolution threshold window that chooses only the tallest spike in a particular window.

3.4 Computing Cross-Correlation

The most expensive step in the pathmap algorithm is computing the cross-correlation. The basic formulation of the discrete cross-correlation shown in Eq. 1 can be computed in $O(n^2)$ time.

$$Corr_d(x, y) = \frac{\sum_{i=0}^{n-1} (x_i - \overline{x})(y_{(i+d)} - \overline{y})}{\sqrt{\sum_{i=0}^{n-1} (x_i - \overline{x})^2}\sqrt{\sum_{i=0}^{n-1} (y_{(i+d)} - \overline{y})^2}} \quad (1)$$

$where, \quad d = 0,1,...,(n-2),(n-1)$

The *cross-correlation theorem* (Eq. 2) provides an efficient alternative to compute cross-correlation. The *Fourier transform* can be computed using FFT(*Fast Fourier Transform*), which reduces the time to calulate cross-correlation from $O(n^2)$ to $O(n \log n)$.

$$x \star y = \mathcal{F}^{-1}\left[\mathcal{F}[x]\mathcal{F}[y]^*\right] \quad (2)$$

$where, \quad \mathcal{F}$ denotes Fourier transform, and

z^* denotes the complex conjugate of z.

For our analysis, we choose the direct cross-correlation method (Eqn. 1), because it can be adapted easily for incremental computation of correlation metrics, in addition to other optimizations. The first optimization is based on the fact that most transactions in a distributed system are just a small fraction of the *sliding window*. Since our goal is to find the service transaction delays and not the full range of cross-correlation series, by assuming an upper bound (say T_u) on the transaction delay, the time complexity of computing cross-correlation directly (i.e., without FFT) is drastically reduced from $O\left(\lceil\frac{W}{\tau}\rceil^2\right)$ to $O\left(\frac{T_u}{\tau} \cdot \frac{W}{\tau}\right)$. τ is the time quanta or the smallest delay of interest. In comparison, the time complexity of FFT-based cross-correlation (Eqn. 2) is $O\left(\frac{W}{\tau} \log \frac{W}{\tau}\right)$, which is less than the $O\left(\frac{T_u}{\tau} \cdot \frac{W}{\tau}\right)$ even for small values of T_u. Fortunately, direct cross-correlation is incremental (as discussed earlier), and therefore, it can be computed over only the newly appended trace of size ΔW. This reduces the time complexity of direct cross-correlation further, to $O\left(\frac{T_u}{\tau} \cdot \frac{\Delta W}{\tau}\right)$.

A third important optimization is based on the fact that the network packet traffic in the Internet and in most enterprise systems is inherently bursty. This burstiness can be due to system or user behavior [11, 2], or it can be due to the lower level network protocol (e.g., TCP) behavior and network queueing [17]. In addition, a single transaction may be composed of multiple packets sent back-to-back. Bursty behavior results in dense network packet traffic intermixed with 'long' quiet zones. Our optimization takes advantage of this fact by simply omitting to compute correlation in the 'quiet' region, without compromising the accuracy of the result. This is done by computing the *time series* in such a way that the entries with value 0 (i.e., zero packets seen at the time corresponding to that entry) are discarded. As a result, the length of the *time series* trace is reduced by a large margin (more than 10 times for some of our enterprise traces). This not only decreases the computation time of the direct cross-correlation, but also increases the efficiency (both in time and space) of collecting the trace at each service node, as we shall see in the next section. In summary, assuming that the average factor of *time series* reduction is 'k', the time complexity of direct cross-correlation drops to $O\left(\frac{T_u}{\tau} \cdot \frac{(\Delta W)/k}{\tau}\right)$.

3.5 Computing Time Series

The message traces collected at service nodes are converted to time-series data using a *density function* $d(i)$, which is based on two parameters: time quanta (τ) and the size of *rectangular sampling window* (ω), an integral multiple of τ.

$d_{x \to y}^x(i) = $ square root of number of messages at service node x transmitted to y in time interval $\left[i \cdot \tau - \frac{\omega}{2},\ i \cdot \tau + \frac{\omega}{2}\right]$

Figure 3 shows a pictorial representation of time series computation. The message arrivals are shown as small rectangular boxes. Both W (size of sampling window) and ΔW (refresh interval) are also integer multiples of τ. Note the entry $d_i = (t_i, n_i)$ in the time-series computation in Figure 3. No packet was received during the ith sampling window, and therefore, as discussed in the previous section, d_i is not recorded in the time-series. The size of time quanta τ determines the resolution of the analysis. For a given sliding window size (W), a small τ results in longer time-series ($\frac{W}{\tau}$) and a proportional increase in the cost of servicepath analysis. Its value, therefore, should not be arbitrary small, but equal to the shortest service delay of interest. The purpose of the rectangular sampling window is to reduce the effect of variance in delay and suppress infrequent paths that occur due to the noise in the trace. A very small ω may produce many spikes during cross-correlation analysis resulting in false delays/paths. On the other hand, a large value of ω may over-generalize the result (collapsing two spike into one, for example). For the systems we have analyzed, $\omega = 50 \cdot \tau$ gave the best set of results.

The process of time-series computation is further optimized using run-length encoding (RLE). Upon close examination of the time-series of actual enterprise traces, we found that there are many repeatable sequences, which provide substantial room for compression. RLE is particularly appropriate for this purpose, because it can be computed online, with negligible compression and decompression overheads. This not only reduces the network transmission overhead (when the time-series data is streamed to the remote node for analysis), but it also decreases the cost of cross-correlation analysis because the correlation of overlapping sequences in the series (Eqn 1) can be computed in a single step. The resultant time-series becomes a 3-tuple series

(t, c, n) (one tuple for each *run*), where t is the timestamp of the first density function entry in the *run*, c is the length of the *run* and n is the value of density function.

3.6 Trace Collection

One of the requirements of service path analysis is that no application components should be modified or restarted. Also, the system should experience as little perturbation as possible. Our analysis requires timestamps and (source, destination) identification of the inter-component messages. These messages may be collected at various levels: at the application level (e.g., apache web server's access logs), at the middleware level (e.g., J2EE-level tracing [8]) or at the system and network level. The problem with tracing transactions at the application- or middleware-level is that there is not a single and widely deployed standard.

Passive network tracing provides a convenient way of listening to the interactions between different *service nodes*, without the need to modify any system components. Network packet traces may be collected from ethernet switch with *port mirroring* support or directly from service nodes by running *tcpdump*. The traces obtained can be streamed to some central location for analysis. Although, this looks like a simple and attractive approach, it limits the scalability of our overall servicepath analysis. This is because the analysis node has to first compute the time series and then the service paths. Offloading the time-series computation to the service nodes decreases the work on central node. Also, the time-series can be calculated directly from the network activity at the service nodes instead of first logging the raw packet traces (using tcpdump) and then converting it to time-series signals. Towards this end, we implemented a linux kernel module called *tracer*, which uses the '*netfilter*' hooks to listen to the packets in the network stack and streams *REL*-encoded time series data.

3.7 Complexity Analysis

The overall time complexity of our pathmap algorithm is $O\left(E \cdot \left[\frac{W}{\tau}\right]^2\right)$, where E is the total number of edges in the service graph, W is the sliding window size and τ is the *time quanta*. After applying all optimizations discussed in previous sub-sections, the time complexity is reduced to:

$$O\left(E \cdot \frac{T_u}{\tau} \cdot \frac{(\Delta W)/(k \cdot r)}{\tau}\right),$$

where T_u is the maximum possible transaction delay and ΔW is the service graph update interval. k is the optimization factor achieved by skipping quiet intervals in the packet traces and r is RLE compression factor. Assuming $W = m \cdot \Delta W$, the above can be rewritten as:

$$c_1 \cdot \left[\frac{1}{k \cdot r \cdot m} \cdot \frac{T_u}{\tau} \cdot E \cdot \frac{W}{\tau}\right],$$

where c_1 is a constant.

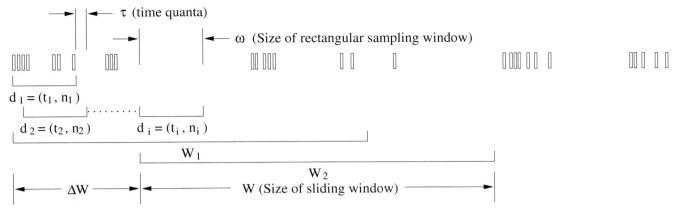

Figure 3: Time series computation

The pathmap algorithm receives a total $2 \cdot E$ number of time-series signal streams from the service nodes, two from the two nodes connected by an edge. It stores the cross-correlation vectors (of size $\frac{T_u}{\tau}$) and a history of time-series (of the size of sliding window $\frac{W}{\tau}$) for each of these edges. The total space complexity, therefore, turns out to be

$$O\left(2 \cdot E \cdot (c' \cdot \frac{T_u}{\tau} + c'' \cdot \frac{W/(k \cdot r)}{\tau})\right).$$

The pathmap algorithm can easily be made more scalable by parallelly computing the service graph of each client nodes (i.e., parrallelizing the inner loop of *ServiceRoot*). The results reported in this paper use a single central analyser.

3.8 Other Considerations

We have implicitly assumed that the clocks of all service nodes are time-synchronized. Pathmap can tolerate small clock skews (i.e., equal to few times of the time quanta τ) when determining service paths, but will exhibit some inaccuracy (equal to the amount of skew) when computing service delays. Fortunately, most of today's machines are synchronized using NTP, which has an RMS errors of less than 0.1 ms on LANs and of less than 5 ms on Internet (except during rare disruptions) [20]. If the skew is large, cross-correlation results will not be accurate. We can, however, estimate time skew between two service nodes (say x and y) by cross-correlating the time series $T_{x \to y}^{x}$ and $T_{x \to y}^{y}$ streamed from x and y respectively. The resultant cross-correlation series will have a spike at position 'd', where d is equal to the sum of the time by which x lags behind y and the network delay. The latter can be computed easily by one of the various passive network measurement techniques [16].

4 Evaluation

The E2Eprof toolkit has been implemented in C and tested extensively on Linux-based platform for both artificial traces and actual enterprise applications. For lack of space, we will present results from just two enterprise-scale

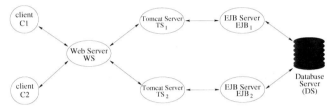

Figure 4: Multi-tier RUBiS application setup

multi-tier applications. The first is an open source multi-tier online auction benchmark, called *RUBiS*, from Rice University [7], and the second is the *Revenue Pipeline* application used by Delta Air Lines. We evaluate the overhead and accuracy of E2Eprof and demonstrate how it can be used for online performance debugging in these applications.

4.1 Multi-tier Application: RUBiS

RUBiS implements the core functionalities of an auction site like selling, browsing, and bidding. RUBiS is available in three different flavors: PHP, Java HTTP Servlets and Enterprise Java Beans (EJB). We use the EJB's stateless session beans implementation with the configuration shown in Figure 4. The *Tracer* kernel module runs on all six server nodes and streams time series data to a remote analyzer (not shown in the figure). The two client nodes run *httperf* [21] to generate requests belonging to two service classes (i.e., *bidding* and *comment*). The httperf workload generator in the client nodes emulates 30 clients by initiating 30 client sessions each. Web service requests generated by these client sessions have a *Poisson* arrival distribution. We experiment with two different path configurations:

- *Affinity-based*: the web server forwards all bidding requests to Tomcat server 1 (TS_1) and all comment requests to Tomcat server 2 (TS_2). The path of the bid request becomes $C_1 \to WS \to TS_1 \to EJB_1 \to DS$. Similarly, the path of the comment request is $C_2 \to WS \to TS_2 \to EJB_2 \to DS$.

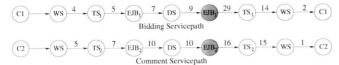

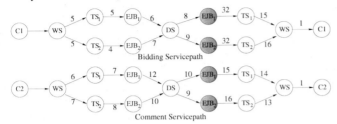

Figure 5: Service Graph for affinity-based server selection. (All delays in milliseconds)

Figure 6: Service Graph for round-robin server selection (All delays in milliseconds)

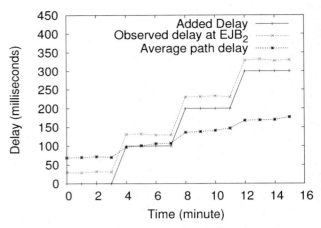

Figure 7: Performance change detection

- *Round-Robin*: the web server dispatches requests to the two tomcat servers in a round-robin fashion. Here, the bid requests take two different paths: $C_1 \rightarrow WS \rightarrow TS_1 \rightarrow EJB_1 \rightarrow DS$ and $C_1 \rightarrow WS \rightarrow TS_2 \rightarrow EJB_2 \rightarrow DS$. Similarly, comment requests has two paths: $C_2 \rightarrow WS \rightarrow TS_2 \rightarrow EJB_2 \rightarrow DS$ and $C_2 \rightarrow WS \rightarrow TS_1 \rightarrow EJB_1 \rightarrow DS$.

For RUBiS experiments, the pathmap algorithm parameters are configured as follows: Sliding Window (W) = 3 minutes, refresh interval (ΔW) = 1 minute, time quanta (τ) = 1ms and sampling window size (ω) = 50ms. The upper bound on transaction delay (T_u) is set to 1 minute. These values are chosen based on the guidelines discussed in section 3.4.

4.1.1 Service Path Detection

Figure 5 shows the service graph for affinity-based server selection. Here, E2Eprof correctly discover the paths of the two type of client requests. The vertices indicate the different servers, which are hosted on different physical machines. The label on the edge indicates the sum of the computation delay at the source node and of the communication delay from source to destination node. The paths of two types of requests are structurally similar, except for the difference in the service nodes they traverse and the delays incurred. The major sources of delay are automatically detected by E2Eprof and marked in grey (i.e., the EJB servers in the figure). Note the duplicate vertex label in the service path. This is due to the return path taken by the response. For clarity, we avoid using cycles in the figure.

Figure 6 shows the service graph for round-robin server selection approach. The two paths taken by each type of requests are shown, and the major source of delay are marked in grey.

In order to verify the correctness of our results, we add code to RUBiS' servlets and EJB components to keep track

of transaction latency at different servers, by piggybagging performance delay information in requests and responses. The resulting performance data coupled with the access logs from the web server and the response time observed at the clients are compared against the service path results generated by E2Eprof. The difference of the processing delays computed at each server is within 10%. The latency observed at the client is about 16% more than that obtained from E2Eprof.

4.1.2 Change Detection

One of the goals of online service path analysis is to detect changes in path performance. We are interested not only in cumulative end-to-end delays, but also in fluctuations in *per-edge* performance. This is useful for isolating bottlenecks, re-routing request traffic, debug anomalies, etc. In order to demonstrate this capability of E2Eprof, we vary the performance of one of the EJB servers (EJB_2) in the round-robin server selection setup, by artificially introducing some amount of delay in the bid request processing and increasing it after every 3 minutes. The length of the sliding window (W) is set to 1 minute. The other parameters of the pathmap algorithm are the same as in the previous experiments. Figure 7 shows the actual delay introduced and the bid request processing delay at EJB_2 captured by E2Eprof. The algorithm correctly tracks the change in performance. The difference between the observed and added delay is due to the fact that the former includes the actual time spent by EJB_2 in processing the requests in addition to the artificial delay introduced in the experiment. The delay patterns of other edges remain unchanged. The figure also shows the average processing delay observed at the front-end web server. Since more than half of the requests take the low latency path (via EJB_1), the average delay does not change by the same amount. In cases like these, E2Eprof can help diagnose bottlenecks faster, because it can separately track the performance of each service node.

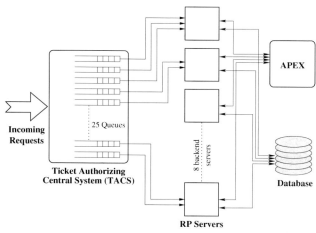

Figure 8: Delta Airlines' Revenue Pipeline Application

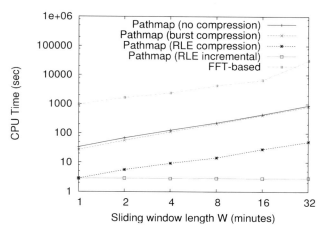

Figure 9: Execution time of service path analysis

4.2 Delta's Revenue Pipeline Application

The "*Revenue Pipeline System*" is a subsystem of Delta's OIS (Operational Information System) that keeps track of operational revenue from worldwide flight operations. It is composed of multiple black-box components (including legacy components) purchased from many different software vendors. About 40K events per hour arrive in one of 25 queues in the front-end control system and are then forwarded to the back-end servers, as shown in Figure 8. Each event/request has strict SLAs. If an SLA is violated, system administrators have to analyze complex logs in order to isolate the faulty components. This process is quite time-consuming, in part because of complex dependencies across multiple black-box components.

E2EProf is used to analyse a week long trace collected from this subsystem. This trace consists of *access logs* from different servers and contains timestamps, server IDs, and request IDs for every application-level transactional event processed by the system (as opposed to the network-level packet events analysed in earlier experiments).

Several limitations of the existing pathmap algorithm are exposed by this use case. First, this subsystem's queuing delays can be large (much larger than the actual processing time). This changes the arrival pattern of the requests at different stages of request processing. Second, there can be wide variations in request traffic. For example, a batch process consisting of all of Delta Air Lines' paper tickets processed all over the world in the last 24 hours is submitted at 4 AM EST, due to which the queue length goes as high as 4000. These facts break the 'steady state' assumption made by the algorithm. Thus, although the pathmap algorithm is able to compute the service path correctly, the computed delays are far from accurate. In response, we have to carefully set the sliding window length (1 hour), the time quanta (1 second) and the sample window (50 seconds), thereby eliminating the error due to traffic variation. The analysis error due to the large queue length could not be eliminated.

Despite inaccurate delay computation, the service paths computed above are still useful in detecting causal dependencies across different components. For instance, E2EProf was able to successfully diagnose a slow database server connection that resulted in large response time for a moderate workload.

4.3 Micro-Benchmarks

Micro-benchmarks are used to examine the costs of E2Eprof analysis for RUBiS traces. We evaluate the cost of E2Eprof analysis with the different optimizations discussed in earlier sections and compare it with the FFT-based analysis. Figure 9 shows the time required to compute the service graphs shown in Figure 6 for different sliding window sizes (W). Other parameters of the pathmap algorithm are the same as in earlier experiments with RUBiS: τ = 1ms, ω = 50ms, T_u= 1 minute. The plot labelled '*no compression*' just assumes an upper bound on transactional delay with no other optimizations. The '*burst compression*' plot only considers non-zero time series entries. '*RLE compression*' uses run-length encoded time series data.

From the results, it is clear that the RLE-based pathmap algorithm outperforms other methods by orders of magnitude. The cost of pathmap analysis increases linearly with W. For a sliding window of length 32 minutes, the RLE-based algorithm takes just 50 seconds. FFT-based analysis does not have linear cost and thus, takes an order of magnitude more time than pathmap to compute the same service graphs. Note that the cost of '*incremental*' pathmap analysis is almost constant for refresh interval (ΔW) set to 1 minute. This makes pathmap suitable for online analysis. The *burst compression* technique does not show much improvement over normal pathmap for RUBiS traces, but it decreases the length of time series (and therefore space overhead) significantly, as shown next.

Trace size: Figure 10 shows the compression achieved by different pathmap's optimizations for the time-series data of the connection between one of the tomcat servers

757

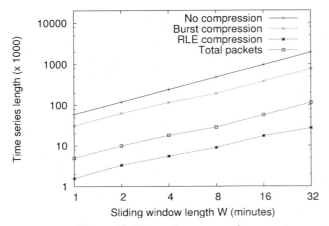

Figure 10: Time series compression

and the web server. The plot labelled '*total packets*' shows the number of packets captured from which these time-series was computed. The time series length increases linearly with window size W, and the plot labelled '*no compression*' is the upper bound $(\frac{W}{\tau})$ on the time series length for a given W and τ. Once again, RLE compression achieves the best results and decreases the length of time series by an order of magnitude as compared to other optimizations. It is also much smaller than the raw timestamped data (indicated by the total number of packets).

5 Conclusions and Future Work

The complexity of distributed systems have been increasing rapidly. To address this complexity, our research has developed a toolkit for online, end-to-end performance diagnosis of distributed systems, called E2EProf. The toolkit uses a modified form of time-series analysis (commonly used in Digital Signal Processing or DSP), to detect the paths taken by requests and delays incurred due to different path components. Since the toolkit does not require applications to be modified, it can also handle legacy components. Experimental evaluations show that E2EProf can detect performance bottlenecks in realistic enterprise applications, while at the same time, reducing the analysis time by an order of magnitude compared to similar techniques presented in the literature.

Our near term future work will explore other areas and applications to which the techniques presented in this paper can be applied. These include network overlays and publish-subscribe systems. Further, we have recently been able to start a collaboration with another group at Delta Air Lines that manages the Delta.com infrastructure, which is much more complex than the revenue pipeline system. Analyzing these new traces will provide us with new insights into the challenges posed by complex enterprise applications. We are also building visualization interfaces that would highlight interesting performance behaviors of service paths.

References

[1] M. K. Aguilera et al. Performance debugging for distributed systems of black boxes. In *SOSP*, 2003.

[2] M. Arlitt et al. A workload characterization study of the 1998 World Cup site. *IEEE Network*, 14(3):30–37, 2000.

[3] Systems Management: Application Response Measurement (ARM). http://www.opengroup.org/products/publications/catalog/c807.htm.

[4] P. T. Barham et al. Using Magpie for Request Extraction and Workload Modelling. In *OSDI*, 2004.

[5] N. Bhatti and R. Friedrich. Web server support for tiered services. *IEEE Network*, 13(5):64–71, September 1999.

[6] B. Cantrill et al. Dynamic Instrumentation of Production Systems. In *USENIX ATC*, 2004.

[7] E. Cecchet et al. Performance and Scalability of EJB Applications. In *OOPSLA*, 2002.

[8] M. Y. Chen et al. Pinpoint: Problem determination in large, dynamic internet services. In *DSN*, 2002.

[9] M. Y. Chen et al. Path-based failure and evolution management. In *NSDI*, 2004.

[10] I. Cohen et al. Correlating instrumentation data to system states: A building block for automated diagnosis and control. In *OSDI*, 2004.

[11] M. Crovella et al. Self-Similarity in World Wide Web Traffic: Evidence and Possible Causes. *TON*, 5(6):835–846, '97.

[12] Y. Fu et al. Ete: Passive end-to-end internet service performance monitoring. In *USENIX ATC*, 2002.

[13] A. Gavrilovska et al. A Practical Approach for Zero Downtime in an Operational Info System. In *ICDCS*, 2002.

[14] J. L. Hellerstein et al. ETE: A Customizable Approach to Measuring End-to-End Response Times and Their Components in Distributed Systems. In *ICDCS*, 1999.

[15] J. L. Hellerstein et al., editors. *Feedback Control of Computing Systems*. Wiley-Interscience, 2004.

[16] S. Jaiswal et al. Inferring TCP connection characteristics through passive measurements. In *Infocom*, 2004.

[17] H. Jiang and C. Dovrolis. Why is the internet traffic bursty in short time scales? In *Sigmetrics*, 2005.

[18] J. O. Kephart and D. M. Chess. The vision of autonomic computing. *IEEE Computer*, 36(1):41 – 50, January 2003.

[19] M. Mansour et al. I_RMI: Performance Isolation in Service Oriented Architectures. In *ACM Middleware*, 2005.

[20] D. L. Mills. The network computer as precision timekeeper. In *PTTI*, 1996.

[21] D. Mosberger et al. httperf: A Tool for Measuring Web Server Performance. *Performance Evaluation Review*, 26(3):31–37, 1998.

[22] D. P. Olshefski, J. Nieh, and D. Agrawal. Inferring client response time at the web server. In *Sigmetrics*, 2002.

[23] R. Rajkumar et al. A resource allocation model for QoS management. In *IEEE RTSS*, 1997.

[24] P. Reynolds et al. WAP5: black-box performance debugging for wide-area systems. In *WWW*, 2006.

[25] E. Thereska et al. Stardust: tracking activity in a distributed storage system. In *Sigmetrics*, 2006.

[26] J. Wilkes, J. Mogul, and J. Suermondt. Utilification. In *SIGOPS European Workshop*, 2004.

[27] K. Yaghmour et al. Measuring and Characterizing System Behavior Using Kernel-Level Event Logging. In *ATC '00*.

Bounding Peer-to-Peer Upload Traffic in Client Networks[*]

Chun-Ying Huang
National Taiwan University
huangant@fractal.ee.ntu.edu.tw

Chin-Laung Lei
National Taiwan University
lei@cc.ee.ntu.edu.tw

Abstract

Peer-to-peer technique has now become one of the major techniques to exchange digital content between peers of the same interest. However, as the amount of peer-to-peer traffic increases, a network administrator would like to control the network resources consumed by peer-to-peer applications. Due to the use of random ports and protocol encryption, it is hard to identify and apply proper control policies to peer-to-peer traffic. How do we properly bound the peer-to-peer traffic and prevent it from consuming all the available network resources?

In this paper, we propose an algorithm that tries to approximately bound the network resources consumed by peer-to-peer traffic without examining packet payloads. Our methodology especially focuses on upload traffic for that the upload bandwidth for an ISP are usually more precious than download bandwidth. The method is constructed in two stages. First, we observe several traffic characteristics of peer-to-peer applications and traditional client-server based Internet services. We also observe the generic traffic properties in a client network. Then, based on the symmetry of network traffic in both temporal and spatial domains, we propose to use a bitmap filter to bound the network resources consumed by peer-to-peer applications. The proposed algorithm takes only constant storage and computation time. The evaluation also shows that with a small amount of memory, the peer-to-peer traffic can be properly bounded close to a predefined amount.

1 Introduction

The behavior of traditional Internet applications is simple. That is, a client sends a request to an Internet server and then receives replies from the server. Network re-source management for these applications is also simple. To manage the network traffic of a specific network service, a network administrator can easily apply traffic control policies to traffic that communicates using corresponding server ports. However, as the emerging of peer-to-peer technologies, modern popular services like file sharing and video streaming now leverage peer-to-peer technologies to increase the availability and the performance of the services. Therefore, it also brings new challenges to network resource management. The major reason is that the peer-to-peer traffic is more difficult to identify. First, peer-to-peer applications tend to communicate using random ports and thus it is hard to define port-based control policies for such network traffic. Second, as any one can develop their own protocols, even if network administrators are able to identify network traffic by analyzing packet payloads, it is impossible to know all peer-to-peer protocols beforehand. Besides, the use of "protocol encryption" (PE), "message stream encryption" (MSE), and "protocol header encryption" (PHE) also complicates the problem. Since the PE, MSE, and PHE encrypts the parts of peer-to-peer protocol messages in payloads, it also increases the difficulties to identify peer-to-peer traffic.

Recent studies have shown that the peer-to-peer traffic has gradually dominated the Internet traffic. While ISPs are usually charged based on the traffic they send upstream to their providers, they would like to keep traffic generated by their customers within the boundaries of their own administrative domains. However, this conflicts with the core spirit of peer-to-peer applications, which encourages clients to *share* what they possess to the public. The more the clients share, the more the uplink bandwidth are consumed for the share. From the view point of network administrators, the precious uplink bandwidth *should be used for client requests, not for the shares*. To reserve the uplink bandwidth for the right purposes, peer-to-peer upload traffic should be properly controlled in a client network. As we already knew that peer-to-peer traffic is hard to identify, how do we control these unknown uplink traffic in a client networks?

An effective method to achieve this goal is adopting a

---

[*]This work is supported in part by the National Science Council under the Grants NSC 95-3114-P-001-001-Y02 and NSC 95-2218-E-002-038, and by the Taiwan Information Security Center (TWISC), National Science Council under the Grants No. NSC 95-2218-E-001-001 and NSC 95-2218-E-011-015.

positive listing strategy. That is, the client network allows only outbound requests initiated by clients in the network. At the same time, to keep peer-to-peer applications working, a limited amount of the uplink bandwidth could still be allowed for those applications. While peer-to-peer upload traffic are mostly triggered by inbound requests, by limiting the inbound requests, the upload traffic can be constrained to a given bounds. To do this, a stateful packet inspection (SPI) filter can be installed at the entry points of a client network to maintain the per-flow state of each outbound connection. The SPI filter tracks the states of network flows that pass it. It allows all outbound requests and the corresponding inbound responses. However, on receipt of inbound requests, the SPI filter decides to accept or reject the request according to the uplink bandwidth throughput. Applying such a mechanism in an ISP-like scale network may incur a high computational cost as the required storage space and computation complexity depends linearly on the number of concurrent active connections, which may be in the order of tens of thousands or even millions.

In this paper, we try to solve the above problem with an efficient and effective method. An *bitmap filter* algorithm is proposed to maintain outbound connection states and permit inbound connections according to monitored bandwidth throughput. The effectiveness of the bitmap filter is similar to that of an SPI filter, but it requires only constant storage space and computational resources.

The remainder of this paper is organized as follows. In Section 2, we review some previous works that are related to our solution. In Section 3, we observe several client network traffic characteristics that are useful to construct our solution. In Section 4, we discuss the usage model and the detailed design of the proposed solution. In Section 5, we then evaluate the effectiveness and the performance of the solution. Finally, in Section 6, we present our conclusions.

2 Related Works

A great deal of research effort has been devoted to peer-to-peer networks. In [1], the authors investigate several characteristics of peer-to-peer traffic, which includes the bottleneck bandwidths, latencies, the degree of peer cooperations, etc. In [2], the authors analyze the peer-to-peer traffic by measuring flow level information and show that the high volume and good stability properties of peer-to-peer traffic makes it a good candidate for being managed in an ISP network. Authors of [3] and [4] also show that the amount of peer-to-peer traffic keeps growing and now it has now become one of the major Internet applications.

In contrast to our solution, authors of [5] purpose to save the download bandwidth by caching those shared data. The cache system works only when it can identify and understand the peer-to-peer protocols. To identify peer-to-peer

traffic, besides counting on well-known ports, Sen et al. [6] developed a signature-based methodology to identify peer-to-peer traffic. However, the use of "protocol encryption" (PE) makes it difficult to detect peer-to-peer traffic using payload identification. In [4], Karagiannis et al. try to identify peer-to-peer traffic without examining the payloads. The proposed PTP algorithm performs well on identification of unknown peer-to-peer traffic. Nevertheless, the algorithm use a table to records flow states, which may be not suitable to operate in a real-time and large-scale environment.

To limit the peer-to-peer upload traffic, we believe that an SPI-based filter is a possible solution for client networks. However, since SPI-based filters have to keep all per-flow states in detail, adopting it incurs high cost for an ISP. Take a popular SPI implementation in the Linux open-source operating system as an example. The required storage space grows linearly according to the number of kept flows. Besides, the data structures used to maintain these states are basically link-lists with an indexed hash table. It is obvious that both the storage and computation complexities are $O(n)$, which is not affordable for a larger ISP containing several client networks.

3 The Client Network Traffic Characteristics

3.1 Network Setup

Our packet traces are collected in a subnet of our campus network. Most of hosts in the subnetwork are clients. The trace collection environment is illustrated in Figure 1. A traffic monitor is used to receive and analyze both inbound and outbound traffic of the subnetwork. The traffic monitor is a Fedora Core 5 Linux equipped with dual-processor Intel Xeon 3.2G and a Broadcom BCM95721 gigabit network interface. To save the storage space for packet traces, the traces are collected in three different stages. First, we collect *full packet traces* (including both packet headers and full payloads) using the well-known `tcpdump` [7] program. The full packet traces are then used to verify the correctness of our customized traffic analyzer. The verified analyzer is finally used to extract useful information from packet payloads on-line and simultaneously collect *header packet traces*, which contains only layer 2 to layer 4 packet headers, for future use. The design of the customized traffic analyzer is introduced later in Section 3.2.

3.2 The Traffic Analyzer

One purpose of the traffic analyzer is to identify *network applications* from current network connections. A network connection is identified by a five tuple socket pair, which includes the layer 4 protocol (TCP or UDP), the

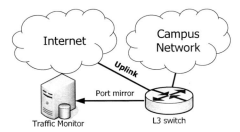

Figure 1. The network setup for packet trace collection. The traffic sent to the campus network is inbound traffic while traffic in the other direction is outbound traffic.

source address, the source port, the destination address, and the destination port. An example of a socket pair s is $\{TCP, A, x, B, y\}$. Since packets of the same connection are transmitted in different directions between two end hosts, the inverse of a socket pair, $\bar{s} = \{TCP, B, y, A, x\}$, also identifies the same connection. In our traffic analyzer, it first classifies packets into connections and then try to identify the application of each connection.

Two methods are used to identify the applications. As we know that many modern applications, for example, peer-to-peer applications, do not use fixed ports to communicate, we first try to identify application by matching the packet payloads against several predefined patterns. To do so, the analyzer must have the ability to examine the payloads either by reading the full packet traces collected by the tcpdump program or by accessing packets directly through the network interface. The analyzer focuses only on TCP and UDP traffic for that these two are the major data transmission protocols used over Internet. Packets with incorrect checksum values are not considered for examination.

The payload of each UDP packet is always examined. However, to guarantee the completeness of payloads in a TCP connection, we only examine TCP connections with an explicitly TCP-SYN packet, which indicates the beginning of a TCP connection. Unlike the examination for UDP data packets, the pattern matching algorithm does not match for a single TCP data packet. Instead, it matches a concatenated TCP data stream against the patterns. For a TCP connection, we have to concatenate payloads of several very first data packets[1] to form a short TCP stream. The algorithm then matches the concatenated data stream against all the patterns. The patterns used for pattern matching are written in the form of regular expressions. Most of these patterns are adopted from the L7-filter project [8]. Examples

---
[1]In our program, we concatenate at most four TCP data packets. This is because most of the patterns used to check the connection type are short and thus it is not necessary to store and check the full TCP data stream.

of some of these patterns are listed in Table 1. If it is failed to identify an application by pattern matching, the analyzer then tries to identify by matching the port numbers of the connection against well-known port numbers.

To focus more on file exchanging applications, we use two alternative strategies to identify peer-to-peer and FTP applications, respectively. For the ease of explanations, a network connection c is denoted by $c = \{A : x \rightarrow B : y\}$, where A is a client that connects to a service provider B on port y using port x. In the first strategy, if c is identified as one of the peer-to-peer applications, all future connections to $B : y$ are also identified as the same application. In the second strategy, since we know that the FTP command and the FTP data are transmitted in separated connections, if c is identified as an FTP application, all payloads of the identified connection are examined to identify the corresponding FTP data connections specified in a FTP command connection.

Another purpose of the analyzer is to measure and log some fundamental properties of network connections for further traffic analyses. These properties include the direction (inbound or outbound) of a network connection, the number of packets and bytes transmitted in each direction, the lifetime of a connection, and the out-in packet delays. To keep the original traffic patterns and save the storage spaces, payloads of all processed packets are stripped and then stored using the same format as the tcpdump program.

3.3 Traffic Characteristics

Based on the information collected by the traffic analyzer, we make several observations on these traffic. The observations are done on a 7.5-hour TCP and UDP packet trace, which was collected in the environment introduced in Section 3.1. In the 7.5-hour packet trace, there were 6739733 collected connections. Among all the connections, 29.8% were TCP connections and 70.1% were UDP connections. Although there are more UDP connections, 99.5% bandwidth are contributed by TCP traffic. The average bandwidth throughput of this trace was 146.7 Mbps, where 10.2% were download traffic and 89.8% were upload traffic. The first observation is the distributions of each observed applications. Among the observed applications, 5% are HTTP/HTTP-PROXY traffic, 55% are peer-to-peer traffic (including bittorrent, edonkey, and gnutella), 5% are other traditional internet services, and most of traffic (35%) are still unidentified. A brief summary of the protocol distribution can be found in Table 2.

The second observation focuses on the port number distributions of network connections. We classify all the port numbers into four different classes, namely "ALL", "P2P", "Non-P2P", and "UNKNOWN". For each TCP connec-

Table 1. Patterns and ports used to identify network applications.

Application	Regular Expressions	Ports
bittorrent	\x13bittorrent protocol|d1:ad2:id20:|\x08'7P\)[RP]|^azver\x01$|^get /scrape?info_hash=	N/A
edonkey	^[\xc5\xd4\xe3-\xe5].?.?.?([\x01\x02\x05\x14\x15\x16\x18\x19\x1a\x1b\x1c\x20\x21\x32\ x33\x34\x35\x36\x38\x40\x41\x42\x43\x46\x47\x48\x49\x4a\x4b\x4c\x4d\x4e\x4f\x50\x51\x52\ x53\x54\x55\x56\x57\x58[\x60\x81\x82\x90\x91\x93\x96\x97\x98\x99\x9a\x9b\x9c\x9e\xa0\ xa1\xa2\xa3\xa4]|\x59................?[-~]|\x96....$)	TCP/UDP: 4662
fasttrack	^get (/.download/[-~]*|/.supernode[-~]|/.status[-~]|/.network[-~]*|/.files|/.hash=[0-9a-f]*/ [-~]*) http/1.1|user-agent: kazaa|x-kazaa(-username|-network|-ip|-supernodeip|-xferid| -xferuid|tag)|^give [0-9][0-9][0-9][0-9][0-9][0-9][0-9][0-9]?[0-9]?[0-9]?	N/A
gnutella	^(gnd[\x01\x02]?.?.?\x01|gnutella connect/[012]\.[0-9]\x0d\x0a|get /uri-res/n2r\ ?urn:sha1:|get /.*user-agent: (gtk-gnutella|bearshare|mactella|gnucleus|gnotella|limewire| imesh)|get /.*content-type: application/x-gnutella-packets|giv [0-9]*:[0-9a-f]*/|queue [0-9a-f]* [1-9][0-9]?[0-9]?\.[1-9][0-9]?[0-9]?\.[1-9][0-9]?[0-9]?\.[1-9][0-9]?[0-9]?:[1-9][0-9]?[0-9]?[0- 9]?|gnutella.*content-type: application/x-gnutella|..................?lime)	N/A
http/http-proxy	http/(0\.9|1\.0|1\.1) [1-5][0-9][0-9] [\x09-\x0d -~]*(connection:|content-type:|content- length:|date:)|post [\x09-\x0d -~]* http/[01]\.[019]	TCP: 80, 3128, 8080
ftp	^220[\x09-\x0d -~]*ftp	TCP: 21

Table 2. Summary of Protocol Distributions in the Trace Data

Protocol	Connections	Utilizations
HTTP	2.17%	5%
bittorrent	47.90%	18%
gnutella	7.56%	16%
edonkey	22.00%	21%
UNKNOWN	17.55%	35%
Others	2.82%	5%

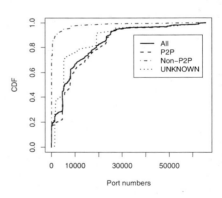

Figure 2. The port number CDF plot of TCP connections. Only ports that used to accept TCP connections are counted.

tion, we only count the port number that is used by the service provider, i.e. the destination port of the corresponding TCP-SYN packet. This is because the source ports of TCP connections are usually randomly generated. We also gather the same statistics for UDP connections. However, since there is no explicitly signals to determine the direction of an UDP connection, for UDP connections, both source ports and destination ports are counted. Figure 2 and Figure 3 show the cumulative distributions of TCP and UDP port numbers, respectively. In Figure 2, we can find that most of the "Non-P2P" connections use several well-know ports. We also found that besides these well-known peer-to-peer ports, a great deal of random ports between port 10000 and port 40000 are also used for peer-to-peer communications. Although there are many unidentified connections in our trace, we found that the port distributions of these "UNKNOWN" connections are close to "P2P" applications. As the development of proprietary peer-to-peer protocols and the use of "protocol encryption" technologies, we believe that many of those unidentified connections have a high probability to also be peer-to-peer traffic.

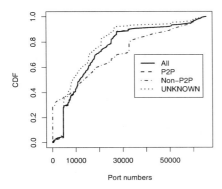

Figure 3. The port number CDF plot of UDP connections. Both source ports and destination ports of UDP connections are counted.

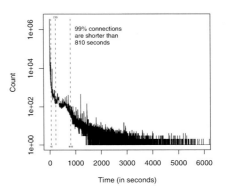

Figure 4. Statistics for connection lifetime. The average connection lifetime is 45.84 seconds.

Figure 3 shows the results of UDP connections. While we count both source ports and destination ports for UDP connections, the result also reflects that the port numbers are almost uniformly distributed. However, we can still identify several frequently used ports, like DNS (port 53) and the edonkey ports (port 4661, 4662, 4672, etc.).

We have mentioned that 89.8% of the throughput was contributed by outbound traffic. Among all the outbound traffic, it should be noticed that 80% are sent along with inbound connections while the other 20% are actively sent out by inner clients. In general, the design of data transmission protocols can be classified into two categories. Data can be delivered either within the same connection to the request or using a different connections. This statistics show that most applications prefer the former design.

We also examine the lifetime of connections from the packet trace. The lifetime of TCP connections are counted from the first TCP-SYN packet to the appearance of a valid TCP-FIN or TCP-RST packet. The connection lifetime varies widely from a minimum of several milliseconds to a maximum of six hours, as shown in Figure 4 (data exceeding the 6000th second are removed, since there are no more peaks). However, the lifetime of most connections is short. The statistics show that 90% of connections are under 45 seconds, 95% are under 4 minutes, and less than one percent last for more then 810 seconds.

Although the lifetime for each connection varies greatly, an interesting phenomenon is that *the out-in packet delay is always short*. Before introducing out-in packet delay, we define two types of packet. An *outbound packet* is a packet sent from a client network, while *inbound packet* is a packet received by a client network. A packet always contains a socket pair σ of $\{protocol, source\text{-}$

$address, source\text{-}port, destination\text{-}address, destination\text{-}port\}$. Thus, for an outbound packet with a socket pair of $\sigma_{out} = \{protocol, saddr, sport, daddr, dport\}$, the socket pair of its corresponding inbound packet should be in an inverse form, that is $\sigma_{in} = \{protocol, daddr, dport, saddr, sport\}$. Note that for an outbound packet and its corresponding inbound packet, $\overline{\sigma_{in}}$, which is the inverse of the socket pair σ_{in}, and σ_{out} should be the same. Based on these definitions, the out-in packet delay is then obtained as follows:

1. On receipt of an outbound packet with a socket pair $\sigma_{out} = \{protocol, saddr, sport, daddr, dport\}$ on an edge router at time t, the router checks if the socket pair has been recorded previously. If the socket pair is new, it is associated with a timestamp of time t and stored in the edge router's memory. Otherwise, the timestamp of the existed socket pair is updated with the time t.

2. On receipt of an inbound packet with a socket pair $\sigma_{in} = \{protocol, daddr, dport, saddr, sport\}$ at time t, the edge router checks if the inverse socket pair $\overline{\sigma_{in}}$ has been recorded before. If it already exists, the timestamp associated with the inverse socket pair $\overline{\sigma_{in}}$ is read as t_0 and the out-in packet delay is computed as $t - t_0$.

3. To avoid the problem of port-reuse, which affects the accuracy of computing the out-in packet delay, an expiry timer T_e deletes existing socket pairs when $t - t_0 > T_e$.

The out-in packet delay may be caused by network propagation delay, processing delay, queueing delay, or mechanisms

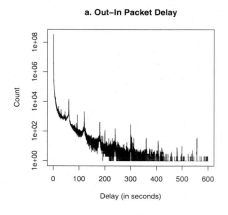

a. Out-In Packet Delay

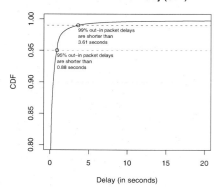

b. Out-In Packet Delay (CDF)

99% out-in packet delays are shorter than 3.61 seconds

95% out-in packet delays are shorter than 0.88 seconds

Figure 5. The measured out-in packet delay in the trace data. Part-(a) shows the raw data with observed port-reuse effects on peaks. Part-(b) shows the CDF of the out-in packet delays.

4 The Bitmap Filter

By definition, a client network should have only client hosts, such as a business enterprise customer, a group of

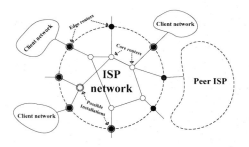

Figure 6. An ISP network with bitmap filters.

DSL users, a wireless network, or buildings in a campus. Usually client hosts only initiate requests and seldom receive requests from the Internet. However, as the peer-to-peer softwares become more and more popular, client hosts now also wait for inbound connections from other peers and thus generate huge volumes of upload traffic. The bitmap filter is a lightweight and efficient algorithm that can be used to bounding upload traffic from client networks. In this section, we first illustrate the usage model of our solution and then introduce the detailed design of the algorithm.

4.1 The Usage Model

Bitmap filters should be installed in an ISP network. As shown in Figure 6, an ISP usually has edge routers (black nodes) and core routers (white nodes). The bitmap filter can be installed on an edge router directly connected to a client network or on a core router, which is an aggregate of two or more client networks. In Figure 6, the nodes with an outlined circle are possible locations to install the bitmap filter. Actually, the bitmap filter can be installed at any location through which traffic from client networks must pass.

4.2 Construct the Bitmap Filter

The design of the bitmap filter leverages certain client network traffic characteristics to improve the filter performance. Based on the observations that 1) the client network traffic is bi-directional, 2) most out-in packet delays are short, and 3) most of the outbound traffic are triggered by inbound requests, a naïve solution is proposed to limit the upload traffic. The solution basically keeps only the outbound requests initiated by inner clients. When the upload bandwidth throughput is low, all the inbound packets, either responses to previous outbound requests or inbound requests to the client network, are permitted. However, if the upload bandwidth throughput is high, only the inbound packets that are responses to previous outbound requests are permitted. The solution works as follows: Suppose that a timer with an initial value of T is associated with the socket pair $\sigma_{out} = \{protocol, source\text{-}address, source\text{-}$

like delayed-ACK. However, they should not be too long. The statistics of out-in packet delay are shown in Figure 5-b. Since we use a large expiry timer, $T_e = 600$ seconds, to handle expired socket pairs, in Figure 5-b, the effect of port-reuse can be observed roughly at the peaks. Although the port-reuse timer varies in different implementations, we find that most of them are in multiples of 60 seconds. The statistics also show that most out-in packet delays are very short. In Figure 5-c, 99% of out-in packet delays are under 2.8 seconds. The result also implies that the most Internet traffic is bi-directional and has high locality in the temporal domain.

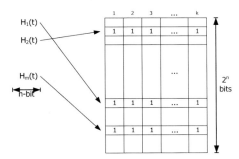

Figure 7. An example of a $\{k \times n\}$-bitmap, the core architecture for a bitmap filter.

port, destination-address, destination-port} of each outbound packet that is new to an edge router. If the socket pair σ_{out} is not new to the router, the value of the associated timer is simply reset to T. The timer reduces every time unit Δt. When the timer expires (reaches zero), the associated socket pair is deleted. For each inbound packet, the router extracts the socket pair σ_{in} and checks if its inverse $\overline{\sigma_{in}}$ exists. If it exists, the packet is bypassed; otherwise, it is dropped under certain probability P_d. The dropping probability P_d in our algorithm varies according to the uplink bandwidth throughput. It can be lower when the throughput is low and higher when the uplink is fully utilized.

The problem of the above solution is that the complexities for both storage and computations make it infeasible to deploy in a large scale network. Thus, a bitmap filter, which is a composite of k bloom filters [9] of equal size $N = 2^n$ bits, denoted as a $\{k \times N\}$-bitmap filter, is used instead. An example of a bitmap is illustrated in Figure 7. Each column in the bitmap represents a bit-vector of a bloom filter. For the convenient of explanation, in the algorithm, the bit-vector of the ith bloom filter is written as $bit\text{-}vector[i]$.

At the initialization phase, all the bits on the $\{k \times n\}$-bitmap are set to zero and an index of the current bit vector idx is set to the first bit-vector. All the bloom filters in the bitmap share the same m hash functions, each of which should only output an n-bit value. An output that exceeds n-bit should be truncated. The bitmap filter comprises two algorithms, the $b.rotate$ algorithm, which clears expired bits from the bitmap, and the $b.filter$ algorithm, which marks and looks up bits in the bitmap. The algorithms are detailed in Algorithm 1 and Algorithm 2, respectively. The $b.rotate$ algorithm is quite simple. The algorithm runs every time unit Δt. When it is activated, the index of the current bit vector idx is set to the next bit vector and all bits in the previous bit vector are set to zero. For example, assume there are k bit vectors in a bitmap filter indexed from $\{1, \cdots, k\}$. If the current index is set to the 1st bit vector, then the last bit vector will be the kth bit-vector; however, if the current index is set to the jth ($1 < j \leq k$) bit vector, then the last bit vector will be the $(j-1)^{th}$ bit-vector.

Algorithm 1 The Timer Handler - $b.rotate()$

Require: An initialized $\{k \times n\}$-bitmap and an index to current bit vector idx.

1: $last = idx$
2: $idx = (idx + 1) \pmod{k}$
3: set all bits in $bit\text{-}vector[last]$ to zero
4: **return** idx

The bitmap is marked and looked up using the $b.filter$ algorithm, as shown in Algorithm 2. When a packet is received by an edge router, the $b.filter$ algorithm is applied to determine whether the packet should be bypassed or dropped. For an outbound packet, the $b.filter$ iteratively applies all the m hash functions on the socket pair σ_{out} and marks the corresponding bits in all bit vectors to a value of 1. Outbound packets are always bypassed. On the other hand, when an inbound packet is received, the $b.filter$ iteratively applies all the hash functions on the socket pair $\overline{\sigma_{in}}$ and checks if the corresponding bit in the current bit vector indicated by the index idx is marked or not. If a bit is not marked, then the packet will be dropped under a probability of P_d. The value of P_d can be dynamically adjusted according to the upload bandwidth throughput. An example of generating P_d is a similar form to the random early detection (RED) algorithm [10]. Given two threshold L, H ($L < H$), and an indicator of upload bandwidth throughput b, the P_d is computed by Equation 1.

$$P_d = \begin{cases} 0 & \text{, if } b \leq L \\ \frac{b-L}{H-L} & \text{, if } L < b < H \\ 1 & \text{, if } b \geq H \end{cases} \quad (1)$$

Note that the bitmap filter is not necessary to use all fields in the socket pair σ to compute the hash value. Instead, for an outbound packet, the hash functions can be applied only to the parts of {*protocol, source-address, source-port, destination-address*}. In contrast, for an inbound packet, only {*protocol, destination-address, destination-port, source-address*} are used to compute the hash value. The reason not to use all fields is to support the "hole-punching" [11] technique, which is usually used for a client host to create bypass rules on the network address translation (NAT) or firewall device for future inbound connections. The support to "hole-punching" can be enabled or disabled depending on the network administrator's choice.

In summary, the "mark" action is always performed on all bit vectors, the "look up" and the "clean up" actions are only performed for the current bit vector and the last bit vector, respectively. The combination of these operations achieves the same purpose as the naïve solution described

Algorithm 2 The Filtering Function - $b.filter()$

Require: An initialized $\{k \times n\}$-bitmap, an index of current bit vector idx, a conditional dropping probability P_d, and a packet pkt to be inspected.

1: **if** pkt is an outbound packet **then**
2:     **for** $h \in$ *hash-function list* **do**
3:         $j = h(\sigma_{out})$
4:         mark the jth bit in all bit vectors as 1
5:     **end for**
6: **else if** pkt is an inbound packet **then**
7:     **for** $h \in$ *hash-function list* **do**
8:         $j = h(\overline{\sigma_{in}})$
9:         **if** the jth bit in $bit\text{-}vector[idx]$ is 0 **then**
10:           p = a randomly generated number in $[0, 1]$
11:           **if** $p < P_d$ **then**
12:             **return** DROP
13:           **end if**
14:         **end if**
15:     **end for**
16: **end if**
17: **return** PASS

at the beginning of this sub-section, which effectively limits the upload traffic sent from a client network.

4.3 Choose Proper Parameters

As stated in Section 4.2, several parameters for the bitmap filter must be decided. They are the k - the number of bit vectors in a bitmap, the N - the size of a bit vector, the Δt - the time unit to clean up a bit vector, and the m - the number of hash functions used in the bitmap filter. The k and N parameters decide how much storage space is required for the bitmap filter; and the k and Δt parameters decide the countdown time of the timer T_e mentioned in Section 3.3. Thus, given a moderate expiry timer T_e and a proper time unit Δt, the value k can be decided by $\lfloor \frac{T_e}{\Delta t} \rfloor$.

Recall the result in Section 3.3. T_e should not be too long, since the port-reuse effect may incur more false positives[2], which decrease the precision of the bandwidth limiter. In other words, a packet that should be dropped may be accepted by the limiter. However, to prevent overkilling connections with longer delays, T_e should not be too short either. A value below 60 seconds, such as 20 or 30 seconds, would be acceptable. On the other hand, the time unit Δt need not to be too short. Although a shorter Δt improves the timer's granularity, a Δt that is too short may raise the frequency of running bitmap clean-ups too much and thus reduce the overall performance of the system. A value of 4 or 5 seconds would be appropriate.

---

[2]The definition of false positives is defined in Section 5

The n is a flexible parameter. A network administrator can decide the value according to the number of concurrently active connections and the memory space that they are willing to devote to the system. Note that a small n will raise the possibility of false positives and reduce the effectiveness of traffic limiter. To avoid the problem, more hash functions (i.e., m) may be used to reduce false positives. When deploying such a system, administrators should consider a trade-off between storage space and computation power to decide the value of n and m. We further evaluate the effects of different sets of parameters in the next section.

5 Evaluations

In this section, we evaluate several aspects of the proposed solution by analyses and simulations.

5.1 False Positives and False Negatives

As our solution adopts an approximate algorithm to maintain outbound connection states, it may incur false positives and false negatives. The definition of a false positives is similar to that used in the original bloom filter paper [9]. That is, an inbound packet that should be dropped is accepted by the filter. In contrast, a false negative is an inbound packet that should be accepted is dropped. Since the bitmap filter works in flavor of a positive listing, only inbound packets with an out-in packet delay longer than the expiry timer T_e are filtered out. Thus, the number of false negatives is very low. As the result in Section 3.3 shows, false negatives should be lower than 1% when T_e is greater than 3.61 seconds.

However, we should focus more on false positives. Assume m hash functions are applied to a single inbound packet and the utilization of the current bit vector is $U = \frac{b}{N}$, where b is the number of marked bits in a bit vector. The probability p that a random inbound socket pair σ will penetrate the bitmap filter is

$$p = U^m = \left(\frac{b}{N}\right)^m. \qquad (2)$$

The number of marked bits on the bit vector should be proportional to the number of active connections c inside a time unit of T_e. If we assume that the results of the hash functions seldom collide when the utilization of the bit vector is low, Equation 2 can be rewritten as

$$p \simeq \left(\frac{c \cdot m}{N}\right)^m. \qquad (3)$$

Given a bit vector size N and the expected max number of active connections c, then to minimize the desired penetration probability p, we differentiate Equation 3 and get

$$p' = \left(\frac{c}{N} \cdot m\right)^m \left(1 + \ln\left(\frac{c}{N} \cdot m\right)\right). \qquad (4)$$

Thus, m that minimizes the penetration probability p can be obtained by solving $1 + \ln(\frac{c}{N} \cdot m) = 0$, which is

$$m = \frac{e^{-1} \cdot N}{c}, \qquad (5)$$

where e is the base for the natural logarithm. By replacing m in Equation 3 with $\frac{e^{-1} \cdot N}{c}$ when m minimizes the penetration probability p, the ratio of the expected max number of active connections c should satisfy

$$\frac{c}{N} \leq -\frac{1}{e \ln p}. \qquad (6)$$

For example, if we adopt a bitmap filter of size $N = 2^{20}$ (about 1-million bits) with $k = 4$, and $\Delta t = 5$ seconds, and set the desired penetration probability to be roughly 10%, 5%, and 1%, the number of active connections inside a time unit $T_e = 20$ seconds should be less than 167K, 125K, and 83K, respectively. Compared with our trace data, which has only average 15K active connections inside a time unit of 20 seconds, these upper bounds are much higher than the actual traffic. The number of used hash functions m in the setup can be 3, and the memory space required by the bitmap filter is only $(k \times N)/8 = 512K$ bytes.

5.2 Performance

The bitmap filter is efficient because almost all operations can be performed in constant time. The processing time for an outbound packet is $O(m \times t_h) + O(m \cdot k \times t_m)$, where m is the number of used hash functions, t_h is the time taken to execute a hash function, k is the number of bit vectors to be marked, and t_m is the processing time to mark a bit. Processing inbound packets is simpler than for outbound packets. The required processing time is $O(m \times t_h) + O(m \times t_c)$ where t_c is the processing time need to check whether a bit on a bit vector is marked or not. Inbound packet processing is also a constant time operation. When an inbound packet is considered to be dropped, the bitmap filter drops the packet according to the dropping probability P_d. Computing the P_d requires only the knowledge of current bandwidth throughput, which is an essential component in off-the-shelf network devices.

The most time consuming operation may be the $b.rotate$ algorithm, which executes every Δt seconds. The algorithm first advances the current index idx to set to the next bit vector, and then resets all bits in the last bit vector to zero. Thus, the operation is proportional to the size of a bit vector, which is $O(n)$. However, since the memory space of a bit vector is fixed and continuous, implementing such an algorithm in software is simple and efficient. As all the components used in the algorithm already have corresponding hardware implementations, it is also easy to accelerate the algorithm by using hardware coprocessors.

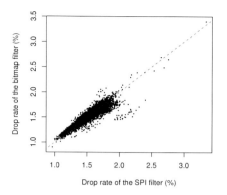

Figure 8. Comparison of the packet drop rates of the SPI and the bitmap filters. The gray-dashed line has a slope of 1.0.

5.3 Simulation with the Packet Trace

We also perform several simulations to verify the effectiveness of the bitmap filter. A bitmap filter and an SPI-based filter are both implemented. The input to both filters is the packet trace used in Section 3.3. First, we compare the packet drop rate of the two filters. The SPI filter is set to delete idle connections after 240 seconds, which is the default **TIME_WAIT** timeout used in the Microsoft windows operating system The bitmap filter is configured as follows: $N = 2^{20}$, $k = 4$, $T_e = 20$, $\Delta t = 5$, and drop all inbound packets without states. This constructs a 512K-byte bitmap filter that handles the out-in packet latency shorter than 20 seconds. As Figure 8 shows, the filters have similar packet drop rates, and the gray-dashed line has a slope of 1.0. The SPI filter has an average drop rate of 1.56% compared to 1.51% for the bitmap filter. This is because that the SPI filter knows the exact time of closed connections and can therefore drop packets precisely than the bitmap filter.

The second simulation is to show the effectiveness of the bitmap filter on the same packet trace data. The bitmap filter now monitors the bandwidth throughput of upstream traffic and blocks incoming connections when the uplink bandwidth throughput is high. The dropping probability P_d is generated by Equation 1 with a upper bound bandwidth limit H of 100Mbps and a lower bound bandwidth limit L of 50Mbps. To simulate a blocked connection, when an inbound packet is decided to be dropped by the bitmap filter, the socket pair σ of that packet is stored and all the future packets that match any stored σ or $\bar{\sigma}$ are all dropped without checking the bitmap. The configuration of the bitmap filter tries to control peer-to-peer upload traffic below an upper bound of 100Mbps. Figure 9-a and Figure 9-b show the

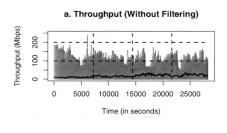

a. Throughput (Without Filtering)

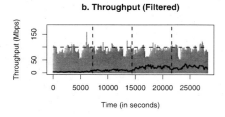

b. Throughput (Filtered)

Figure 9. The performance of the bitmap filter to limit upload traffic.

original and the filtered bandwidth throughput, respectively. In the two figures, the black line indicates the downlink throughput and the gray part indicates the uplink throughput. It should be noted that both parts of the downlink and uplink traffic are limited. This is because some download peer-to-peer traffic are transfered in different inbound connections. Since the simulation is done with replayed packet trace, as the simulation is unable to block the outbound connections that may triggered by previously blocked inbound requests, the effect of the traffic filtering is limited. We believe that the filter can perform better in a real network environment. The result of simulation also shows that the 512K bytes $\{4 \times 2^{20}\}$-bitmap filter with 3 hash functions can properly limit uplink traffic for the small- or medium-scale client network.

6 Conclusions

The core spirit of peer-to-peer applications is to share with the public. Thus, a client host that running peer-to-peer applications always generates a considerable amount of upload traffic, which should be limited in a client network. However, with randomly selected port numbers and the use of protocol encryption, peer-to-peer traffic is hard to identify and manage. As the upload traffic are usually triggered by inbound request, in this paper, we propose a bitmap filter to bound the peer-to-peer upload traffic by controlling inbound requests. The proposed algorithm requires only constant storage and computation power. Analyses and simulations show that with a small amount of resources, an ISP can efficiently prevent the peer-to-peer traffic from affecting the normal operations of traditional Internet services.

References

[1] S. Saroiu, P. K. Gummadi, and S. D. Gribble, "A measurement study of peer-to-peer file sharing systems," in *Proceedings of the SPIE/ACM Conference on Multimedia Computing and Networking (MMCN)*, Jan. 2002.

[2] S. Sen and J. Wang, "Analyzing peer-to-peer traffic across large networks," *IEEE Transactions on Networking*, vol. 12, no. 2, pp. 219–232, Apr. 2004.

[3] T. Karagiannis, A. Broido, N. Brownlee, K. Claffy, and M. Faloutsos, "Is P2P dying or just hiding?" in *Proceedings of IEEE Global Telecommunications Conference*, vol. 3. IEEE, Nov. 2004, pp. 1532–1538.

[4] T. Karagiannis, A. Broido, M. Faloutsos, and K. claffy, "Transport layer identification of P2P traffic," in *IMC '04: Proceedings of the 4th ACM SIGCOMM conference on Internet measurement*. New York, NY, USA: ACM Press, 2004, pp. 121–134.

[5] N. Leibowitz, A. Bergman, R. Ben-Shaul, and A. Shavit, "Are file swapping networks cacheable? characterizing P2P traffic," in *Proceedings of the 7th International Workshop on Web Content Caching and Distribution (WCW)*, Aug. 2002, pp. 121–134.

[6] S. Sen, O. Spatscheck, and D. Wang, "Accurate, scalable in-network identification of P2P traffic using application signatures," in *WWW '04: Proceedings of the 13th international conference on World Wide Web*. New York, NY, USA: ACM Press, 2004, pp. 512–521.

[7] V. Jacobson, C. Leres, and S. McCanne, *TCP-DUMP public repository*. [Online]. Available: http://www.tcpdump.org/

[8] J. Levandoski, E. Sommer, and M. Strait, *Application Layer Packet Classifier for Linux*. [Online]. Available: http://l7-filter.sourceforge.net/

[9] B. H. Bloom, "Space/time trade-offs in hash coding with allowable errors," *Communication of ACM*, vol. 13, no. 7, pp. 422–426, 1970.

[10] S. Floyd and V. Jacobson, "Random early detection gateways for congestion avoidance," *IEEE/ACM Transactions on Networking*, vol. 1, no. 4, pp. 397–413, 1993.

[11] B. Ford, P. Srisuresh, and D. Kegel, "Peer-to-peer communication across network address translators," in *USENIX Annual Technical Conference*, Apr. 2005.

Session 8C:
Stochastic Modeling

Performability Models for Multi-Server Systems with High-Variance Repair Durations

Hans-Peter Schwefel
Center for Teleinfrastruktur
Aalborg University
Email: hps@kom.aau.dk

Imad Antonios
Dept. of Computer Science
Southern Connecticut State University
Email: antoniosi1@southernct.edu

Abstract

We consider cluster systems with multiple nodes where each server is prone to run tasks at a degraded level of service due to some software or hardware fault. The cluster serves tasks generated by remote clients, which are potentially queued at a dispatcher. We present an analytic queueing model of such systems, represented as an M/MMPP/1 queue, and derive and analyze exact numerical solutions for the mean and tail-probabilities of the queue-length distribution. The analysis shows that the distribution of the repair time is critical for these performability metrics. Additionally, in the case of high-variance repair times, the model reveals so-called blow-up points, at which the performance characteristics change dramatically. Since this blowup behavior is sensitive to a change in model parameters, it is critical for system designers to be aware of the conditions under which it occurs. Finally, we present simulation results that demonstrate the robustness of this qualitative blow-up behavior towards several model variations.

1. Introduction and Motivation

Performability modeling seeks to capture the behavior of systems that exhibit degradable performance. In recent years, as both the size and the pervasiveness of distributed systems have increased in support of mission-critical and high performance applications, the need to assess the performance of such systems has become more important. In this paper, we consider a model of a cluster with a small number of N nodes, where each node is prone to degradation in service, which in the limit also include crash failures. We assume and argue for that servers recover from their degraded state after a period of time that shows high variance in most practical scenarios. For such high-variance distributions however, performability metrics of such cluster systems show very peculiar behavior that has previously only been observed in recent telecommunication models.

Within the body of research on performability, Mitrani in [12] surveyed several queueing models where tasks are fed into unreliable servers, and [8] had studied the completion time of tasks in a fault-prone queueing environment for various failure handling strategies. Solutions to such models are presented with the assumptions that task service time, up and breakdown durations are exponentially distributed. More recently, a study provided evidence that hyperexponential distributions provide a better fit for the repair times associated with crash failure [13]. Under certain parameter settings, this repair behavior can lead to power-tail distributed durations. Since in practice repair times are bounded, a truncated power-tail (TPT) distribution introduced in [6] is used. Put in a queueing context, long breakdown periods that are symptoms of high variance inevitably lead to long queue backups, making the study of systems with such behavior worthwhile.

In developing a queueing model for the system laid out above, it is easy to recognize is that each server can be represented as an ON/OFF model. Our model extends to allow for an aggregation of servers being fed by a single queue with a Poisson arrival rate. This can thus be represented as an M/MAP/1 queueing system, for which analytical solutions are provided in [9]. The model construction makes the assumption of load independence, that is the task processing rate is independent of the number of tasks in the system. We show through simulation that this approximation of the physical system is of little bearing on our analysis results. We highlight the symmetry between the multi-server model and an MAP/M/1 traffic model termed N-Burst, and the applicability of results from the latter to understand the performance characteristics of the degradable system. With our analytic results as a baseline, we explore using simulation failure-handling strategies for systems that allow for node crash failures. Additionally, we consider such systems with nonexponential task service times and look at how these affect queueing performance.

The contributions of this paper are as follows: 1) The development of an analytic queueing model with variations amenable to exact solutions of queue-length distributions, 2) a characterization of blow-up points denoting a change in the qualitative behavior of the mean queue-length at specific parameter settings, and 3) simulation results showing that the qualitative behavior is robust towards small model variations including failure handling strategies.

2. System Model

The type of system modeled in this paper is a cluster of N servers fed by a FIFO queue at which tasks arrive according to some process with average rate λ. A fail-safe dispatcher assigns a task to the first available server where, given the server is in its fully operational state, it executes for an exponential service time with mean $1/\nu_p$. The exponential task service time allows to model the N server cluster system by a single server with an MMPP for the service times. However, we will show via simulations in Section 4 that the qualitative performance results in most scenarios are insensitive to it.

A server alternates between two states: the UP state denoting an operational server at full capacity with a mean duration corresponding to MTTF, and the DOWN state representing a degraded level of service lasting for a mean duration corresponding to MTTR. The level of service degradation is captured by a fixed degradation factor δ, where $\delta = 0$ represents a crash failure, and $1 > \delta > 0$ may be viewed as a non-catastrophic fault at the server, which slows down the execution of a task, such as in the case when some erratic process consumes a large amount of CPU time. We assume that faults causing the service degradation are independent of the current processed tasks, of faults on other servers, and of faults in subsequent UP-DOWN cycles at the same node. We also assume that the dispatcher has instantaneous and always correct information about the nodes in case of crash faults (ideal failure detection). Consistent with convention, we express the server's availability as

$$A := \frac{MTTF}{MTTR + MTTF}. \qquad (1)$$

This definition of A does not depend on the fault type, meaning that it is independent of δ.

With respect to the recovery behavior of tasks interrupted by crash failures, a case that only occurs for $\delta = 0$, we consider three strategies:

- Discard: The interrupted task is removed from the cluster. Such an approach can be applicable in soft real-time systems, where the utility of the result of computation decreases with time.

- Restart: The identical task is restarted at either the original node after it is repaired, or at a different node. This is different from the case considered in [14] where the task completion time can benefit from restarting it. The restart strategy adopted here would require that the dispatcher maintain the necessary task activation information until it is completed. A restarted task can be handled using two approaches: 1) add it to the head of the queue, or (2) add the failed task to the end of the queue.

- Resume: The server nodes apply ideal checkpointing to the task execution with the consequence that the dispatcher can ask another node to resume the execution of the task at the point where it stopped. Compared to Restart, this has the advantage that the remaining processing time is the task residual time, which for exponential task times is also exponential with the same mean. However, the disadvantage of Resume is that the checkpointing is rather costly and may only be applied in limited cases. Same as in Restart, a resumed task may be placed at either the front or the tail of the queue.

Note that with respect to the influence on the queue length process, Discard is the best strategy, Resume second, and Restart worst; the price for the former is the increased cost of checkpointing, and for the discard strategy, that some tasks are not successfully completed (even when there is no QoS/delay bound). For the queue-length process in case of exponential task times, it is irrelevant whether the resumed task is stored at the head of the queue or at the tail due to the properties of residual times of exponential distributions. However, there is an impact on system time distribution, which is defined as the sum of queueing delay and total service time including potentially multiple restarts. The impact on system time distribution is even more pronounced for the two restart cases, which are not equivalent for the queue-length based metrics.

In summary, the basic system assumptions are:

- Cluster consisting of fixed number N of statistically identical nodes.

- Independent failures and repairs of each node, failures lead to either performance degradation (slowdown by factor $1 > \delta > 0$) or to complete crash ($\delta = 0$).

- A dispatcher maintains the queue of tasks to be executed in a transaction manner on one of the cluster nodes. The dispatcher never fails. In case of crash failures (not in main focus of this paper though), the dispatcher has instantaneous and always correct fault-detection implemented.

- Tasks are generated by clients according to some general process with rate λ.

- Task time in principle can also be general, see Section 4, but the analytic model is based on exponential task times.

- Time to failure (TTF) and time to repair (TTR) can be generally distributed.

We will however, for the ease of description of the analytic model, include more limiting assumptions that can easily be removed, and are shown to be performance-wise not relevant in Section 4. Most of these assumptions can be circumvented by utilizing matrix-exponential dirstibutions [10] or Markovian Arrival Processes (MAP) [15] at the cost of increased model state-space, with typically also impact on the accuracy of the numerical evaluation of the anlytic model. Furthermore, complex distribution types increase the parameter space of the model which makes the numerical analysis more cumbersome. Finally, in order to gain understanding of the causes of certain performance behavior, it is in most cases advisable to use the most parsimonious model by which such behavior can be created.

2.1. Distribution of UP and DOWN Periods of the Servers

The model presented in the next section will allow for general, matrix exponential [10] UP and DOWN times. We use the latter interchangeably with repair time to refer to a server being in either a degraded or crashed state.

Using analogies from teletraffic models, see Section 2.3 and [21], we will show later that the actual distribution of UP times only has marginal influence on queue performance other than by its mean, and as such the analytic results in Section 3 will be presented using exponential UP times for convenience. As the goal of analytic modeling is to focus the model on the aspects that are influential for the considered metrics, here mean queue length and probability that a task with QoS/delay bound finishes successfully, using exponential assumptions here is not only useful for modeling convenience, but also helpful in determining clear evidence of performability relevant aspects of the cluster system.

Regarding the repair/DOWN time, the results in Section 3 will show a dramatic impact, both on average queue-length and on tail probabilities of the queue-length distribution. Since this is closely related to probabilities of exceeding a certain system time, it can be used to approximate the fraction of successfully completed tasks under certain delay constraints.

The DOWN period corresponds to the fault detection time and repair time of an individual server. Depending on the type of fault, a repair time can range from a few seconds for a restart of a small process, to the order of minutes for a system reboot, or hours for hardware faults with spare parts in stock, up to even days and weeks for the replacement of the faulty machine or hardware component.

Assuming that these different fault-types each lead to exponential repair times, but with different rates, the repair-time distribution can be represented as hyperexponential distribution with increasing average holding time for the different fault severity (in terms of effort for repair). For certain parameter settings, namely geometric decay of the entrance probability with geometric growth of mean state holding times, these hyperexponentials can exhibit power-tail behavior until the reliability function finally drops off exponentially (see [6] for details). This exponential drop off denotes a truncation in the tail, and it corresponds to the longest repair time.

Regardless of whether a hyperexponential distribution with high variance, or as a special case a truncated power-tail distribution is assumed for the repair times, the performability metrics of the cluster system will show very peculiar behavior. Section 3 analyzes and explains this behavior first for the example of truncated Power-Tal distributions (in resemblance to teletraffic models [17, 19]) and then for 2-state hyperexponential distributions with large variance.

2.2. Matrix Representation of Server Model

With exponential task times, the proposed multi-node cluster system is equivalent to a single server system with modulated service rate, namely the number of servers that are UP and the number of tasks in the system influence the instantaneous service rate as follows:

$$\nu(t) = \nu_p * \text{SourcesUP}_t + \delta * \nu_p(N - \text{SourcesUP}_t) \quad (2)$$

given that the number of tasks in the system is larger or equal to N. Otherwise, the number of tasks in the system has a limiting impact, since not all servers can be utilized.

In order to simplify the model specification, we make the following assumptions, see Sect. 2.4 for more discussion on them:

- We do not consider the limiting influence that occurs, when the number of tasks in the system is smaller than N, i.e. Eq. (2) is always assumed to be exactly true. As such, the analytic model will lead a lower bound on the performance behavior, but Section 4 demonstrates that for the scenario in our interest, this lower bound is very close to the actual exact result. The analytic model below can be extended to include this load-dependence utilizing the same approach as in [7, 20]. The model extension however makes the numerical analysis computationally more expensive and also numerically much less stable.

- We assume that task arrivals are Poisson (despite other distributions can be easily included, see Sect. 2.4).

- Task execution times are exponential, as stated already at the beginning of this section.

- The number of servers, N, is a low integer, e.g. between 2 and 10 or 20. There are three main reasons for this assumption. (1) computational effort and numerical accuracy: The size of the state space of the model as introduced below grows exponentially with N. (2) High-availability clusters with redundantly stored processing states typically consist of only a few, closely coupled (within the same IP-subnet) nodes. (3) The performance and dependability impact that we identify in this paper is particularly pronounced for the settings of low N.

- the dispatcher queue is infinite.

Utilizing the first assumption/approximation together with the exponential task times, the collective N nodes in the cluster system can be represented as a single-server Markov Modulated Poisson Process (MMPP). We assume that all servers are independent and identical, namely with Matrix-Exponential DOWN(repair)/UP periods, represented by the vector-matrix pairs, $< \mathbf{p}_{down}, \mathbf{B}_{down} >$ and $< \mathbf{p}_{up}, \mathbf{B}_{up} >$, respectively, following the notation of [10]. Consequently, the modulating Markov process for the service rate of a single server then has the following generator matrix:

$$\mathcal{Q}_1 = \left[\begin{array}{c|c} -\mathbf{B}_{down} & \mathbf{B}_{down}\varepsilon'_{down}\,\mathbf{p}_{up} \\ \hline \mathbf{B}_{up}\varepsilon'_{up}\mathbf{p}_{down} & -\mathbf{B}_{up} \end{array} \right],$$

and the corresponding Poisson service rates on the diagonal of the following matrix:

$$\mathcal{L}_1 = \left[\begin{array}{c|c} \delta\nu_p\mathbf{I}_{down} & \\ \hline & \nu_p\mathbf{I}_{up} \end{array} \right].$$

Note that the individual blocks may have different dimensions. $\mathbf{I}$ is the identity matrix, and ε' is a column vector with all elements equal to 1, both of the corresponding dimension as indicated by the subscript.

For multiple independent servers, the service process can be expressed by multiple Kronecker sums of the matrices $\mathcal{Q}_1$ and $\mathcal{L}_1$,

$$\mathcal{Q}_N = \mathcal{Q}_1^{\oplus N}, \quad \mathcal{L}_N = \mathcal{L}_1^{\oplus N},$$

but more efficient representations can be used since some of the states are redundant, if the servers do not need to be distinguished.

The cluster model therefore can be represented as a M/MMPP/1 queueing system with a standard Quasi-Birth Death representation, for which a matrix geometric solution can be numerically obtained, see [15, 9].

Note that in principle QBDs can also be described with other methods, such as infinite stochastic Petri Nets [16], but as we had mapped the cluster system to a simple M/MMPP/1 queueing system, where the MMPP has a structured form when using matrix-exponential distributions, the use of high-level description tools is not necessary. Alternatively, the heavy-tailed repair periods can be modeled as occasional heavy-tailed services, where the repair and the consecutive re-service are viewed as one long service, and in which case the model would lend itself to an M/G/1 or M/G/c type analysis, see [2, 10].

The matrix-geometric solution allows to compute explicit formulas for the mean queue length and for the tail probabilities of the queue-length distribution. The tail probability of the queue-length distribution, $Pr(Q > k)$ is equivalent to the probability that the queue-length as seen by an arriving customer is exceeding k, which for large k is closely related to system time, i.e. the following approximation links queue-length tail probabilities to system time S:

$$Pr(S > d) \approx Pr(Q > d\bar{\nu}).$$

Thereby $\bar{\nu} = N\nu_p(A + \delta(1 - A))$ is the average service rate. In the case that tasks have to meet some delay requirement d, the equation above allows to determine the probability of violating this requirement.

2.3. Resemblance to Bursty Teletraffic Models

The MMPP model that has been developed in Section 2.2 as a single-server approximation of the cluster service process, very closely resembles a class of models well known in communication network performance analysis, although there the MMPP models have been used for arrival processes. Packet-based network traffic in many cases shows burstiness, i.e. fluctuating arrival rates, which can be modeled by MMPPs, see [11]. In particular, ON/OFF behavior of traffic sources has a long history, and more recently, also matrix-exponential distributions have been utilized [17, 19] to reflect burstiness on multiple time-scales, or even self-similar or long-range dependent traffic models, see e.g. [22, 3].

When using ON/OFF traffic sources, the aggregated arrival rate is modulated by the number of sources in an ON period, hence closely resembles the scenarios for the service times in the cluster model of this paper. In fact, the MMPP model in Sect. 2.2 is equivalent to the aggregated traffic model, proposed first in [17].

Those traffic models represent a set of N statistically identical and independent sources that intermittently emit data. Each of the sources is an ON/OFF model with a peak rate of λ_p (during an ON period), and a mean rate of κ, leading to the aggregate arrival rate of $\lambda = N \times \kappa$. The burstiness of the traffic is expressed by the burst parameter, b, which is the fraction of the time that a source is OFF.

The following table illustrates the resemblance of the two models by comparing the parameters:

Telco Model MMPP/M/1 queue	Cluster Model M/MMPP/1 queue
number of sources N	number of servers N
arrival rate during ON λ_p	service during UP ν_p
$b = \frac{OFF}{ON+OFF}$	avail. $A = \frac{MTTF}{MTTF+MTTR}$
average arrival rate =	avg svc rate =
$\lambda = N\lambda_p(1-b)$	$\bar{\nu} = N\nu_p A$

Note that the average service rate for the cluster model is given in the table for the case of $\delta = 0$ (crash faults). A somewhat similar notion to a degraded service rate $\delta\nu_p$ in the cluster model exists in traffic models by assuming a background Poisson process for the aggregation of other, non-bursty traffic.

As the queueing analysis in Section 3 will show, the performance behavior of the cluster model also has many similarities to the observed performance behavior in network performance models. Also, the mechanisms that lead to poor performance in case of high variance DOWN times (corresponding to high-variance ON periods in the traffic models) are very similar.

2.4. Variations of the Analytic Model

Most of the assumptions on the analytic model can be easily removed within the matrix-analytic framework, leading however to more complex matrices and possibly more complexity in the queueing analysis. We do not implement these model modifications here, but in order to show the power of the modeling approach, we highlight how the extensions can be incorporated:

- Nonexponential task arrival processes: Any finite-dimensional matrix exponential renewal process, or even any MAP can be included in the analytic model. The state space of the arrival process then has to be included in the overall state space of the queue-length process.

- Finite task queue at the dispatcher: The finite QBD representing a ME/MMPP/1/K queue also has a matrix-geometric solution. For large buffer sizes however, qualitative results are expected to be unchanged, see [18] for arguments in a comparable setting.

- Nonexponential TTF: The model in Section 2.2 already includes matrix-exponential TTF. However, the

analysis results in the subsequent section will be based on exponential TTFs, since earlier results from the corresponding teletraffic models indicate that high-variance distributions are most significant performance-wise in what now corresponds to the TTR, see [21].

- Including queue-size dependence when less than N tasks are present: This modification of the queue length dependence would require a modification in the service events in the first N block-rows of its QBD matrix representation, see [20] for an example.

- Hyperexponential task times: By some extension of the state space, namely by keeping track of the selected phase for the (residual) times of the tasks that are being processed at one of the nodes, nonexponential task times can also be modeled.

Furthermore, in the scenario of crash faults, discard strategies for the task under execution at the failing server can also be represented by using a MAP for the service process, namely transitions corresponding to failures of a node would then lead to a reduction of the queue size by 1 (one specific instance of a 'service' event, although unsuccessful here).

3. Discussion of Analytic Results

We will first present and discuss queue performance results from the analytic model, more specifically the behavior of the mean queue-length and of tail-probabilities of the queue-length distribution. All participating processes (task arrivals, task service time, UP time) except for the repair time are thereby assumed to be exponential. First, we look at the case of truncated power-tail distributions for the repair time, since those resemble closely recently used models for teletraffic.

3.1. Task queue behavior for TPT repair times

We illustrate the behavior of the mean size of the task-queue (also counting the tasks in service) using a cluster with $N = 2$ nodes with a degradation factor $\delta = 0.2$ while varying the task arrival rate λ and thereby varying the utilization $\rho := \lambda/\bar{\nu}$. Figure 1 shows the resulting normalized mean queue length; normalization is thereby performed with respect to an M/M/1 Queue at same utilization, mainly in order to avoid the vertical asymptote of the mean queue-length for $\rho \to 1$. For an exponential repair time (solid line in the bottom), the normalized mean queue-length shows no surprising behavior, but it grows monotonously and steadily

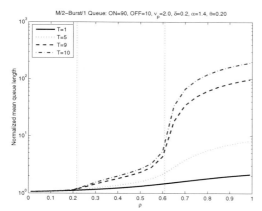

Figure 1. Normalized mean queue-length for a 2-node cluster under varying task-arrival rate: For TPT distributions with larger range ($T = 9, 10$), the mean queue-length shows peculiar blow-up behavior at the points marked by the dotted vertical lines, see text. Note that for $\rho \to 1$, the normalized mean queue-length of all models converges, i.e. the mean queue-length shows the same vertical growth as $1/(1-\rho)$ as the M/M/1 queue.

with ρ. The growth is a consequence of the fluctuations in the service rates due to failures of the servers.

However, when truncated Power-tail distributions with large range are used ($T = 9, 10$), the three different regions with respect to ρ have to be distinguished, namely:

- For small ρ (approximately $\rho < 21.7\%$ for the chosen example), the mean queue-length is rather insensitive to the repair time distribution.

- For the intermediate range $21.7\% < \rho < 60.9\%$, the normalized mean queue-length is significantly higher than for exponential repair times, and with longer tails of the repair time distribution, this difference grows slowly.

- For large $\rho > 60.9\%$, the mean queue-length jumps to huge values, 100 times larger than for an M/M/1 model. Note the log-scale on the y-axis in the figure. With increasing Power-tail range, the mean queue-length rapidly increases.

Figure 2 shows the probability mass function of the queue-length distributions that correspond to utilization values in the three different regions, and, for comparison, that of an M/M/1 queue at the largest of these utilization values. The queue-length distributions show (truncated) power law behavior, which in the utilized log-log plot appears as straight line, for the two parameter settings belonging to the intermediate and worst performance region in Figure 1. The slope of the linear part, corresponding to the Power-tail exponent, however is different between the two curves. In the

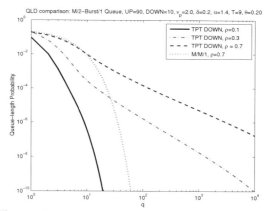

Figure 2. Probability mass function (pmf) of queue lengths for 2-node cluster model with TPT distributed repair times: The shape of the distribution is changing significantly for different utilization values, $\rho = 0.1, 0.3, 0.7$. Shown is also in comparison the queue-length distribution of a M/M/1 queue.

region of small ρ (solid curve), the queue-length distribution decays exponentially, as for an M/M/1 model.

Similar behavior was observed first in [17] and then later analyzed in more detail for teletraffic models in [19]. The underlying mechanism that causes this remarkable behavior of the mean queue-length of the task queue in the cluster model is the same as for teletraffic models: truncated Power-tail distribution for the repair time allow for large repair times to occur with non-negligible probability. Temporarily, during time-intervals in which i servers simultaneously are in a LONG repair time, the mean service rate of the cluster degrades to

$$\overline{\nu_i} = (N-i)(\nu_p A + \delta \nu_p (1-A)) + i \delta \nu_p, i=1,2,...,N. \quad (3)$$

Note that $0 < \overline{\nu_N} < ... < \overline{\nu_2} < \overline{\nu_1} < \bar{\nu}$, for $N > 2$ and $0 < \delta < 1$. Hereby, $\bar{\nu} =: \overline{\nu_0}$ is the overall long-term average service rate.

Hence, if the task arrival rate λ is smaller than ν_N, even a simultaneous long repair time of all N server does not cause any oversaturation period since the degraded modes of the servers can still handle the average arrival rate. This setting corresponds to the leftmost region in Figure 1 and the queue-length distribution decays geometrically. For the case of crash faults, $\delta = 0$, $\overline{\nu_N} = 0$ and the model thus always operates in a setting for which (truncated) power-tailed queue-length probability mass functions are observed. If and only if the condition

$$\overline{\nu_i} < \lambda < \overline{\nu_{i-1}}, \quad i = 1, ..., N, \quad (4)$$

holds, at least i servers have to be in a long repair period in order to create an oversaturation period, and using equivalent residual time arguments as in [19], it can

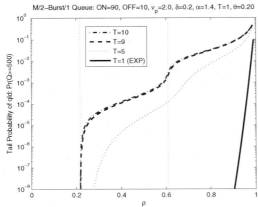

Figure 3. Tail distribution of length of task-queue for 2-node cluster with different repair-time distributions for varying utilization: The blow-up behavior as observed for mean queue-length also occurs for these tail probabilities, which can be translated into probabilities of violating delay bounds.

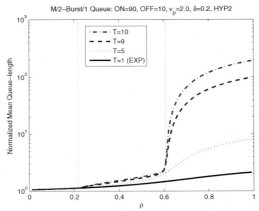

Figure 4. Blow-up point for 2-node cluster model using HYP-2 distributed repair times: The parameters are chosen such that the first 3 moments of the HYP-2 distribution match the moments of the TPT distribution used earlier.

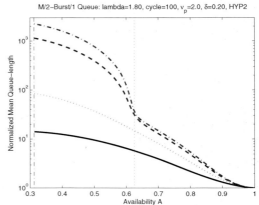

Figure 5. Blow-up point for two-node cluster model while varying the availability A of the individual nodes: high-variance HYP-2 distributions are used for the repair times.

be shown that the probability mass function of the queue-length distribution shows a (truncated) power-tail with exponent $\beta_i = i(\alpha - 1) + 1$, where α is the tail exponent of the DOWN distribution for each server. The condition in Eq. (4) can be reformulated in terms of the utilization ρ as $\overline{\nu_i}/\bar{\nu} < \rho < \overline{\nu_{i-1}}/\bar{\nu}$, or in terms of any of the other parameters N, A, ν_p and δ that influence the blow-up behavior. Note that the mean TTF and mean TTR do not have any impact on the location of the blow-up points.

To shed some light on how these results extend to a QoS analysis setting, we consider the tail probabilities of the queue length distribution, which are shown in Figure 3 for varying values of the TPT parameter T. In particular we compute the probability that an arriving task sees more than 500 customers in the queue. For larger values of T, the blowup points can be distinguished quite clearly on the plot, and correspond to those from Figure 1. The case of exponential repair time ($T = 1$, solid curve) is qualitatively comparable to that of the M/M/1 queue, and only shows non-negligible tail probabilities for ρ close to 1.

3.2. Hyperexponential Repair Times with High Variance

In our analysis thus far we employed TPT distributions to describe the repair time durations, and have argued that they serve as good descriptors for degradation periods spanning multiple time scales. Here we show that under weaker assumptions, mamely with a high-variance hyperexponential-2 DOWN time distribution, that the blowup behavior still holds, even in some cases is more pronounced. As only two states are required to represent a hyperexponential distribution, this reduces computation time and in many cases

increases numerical accuracy as compared to a T state TPT distribution, hence allowing to obtain numerical results for a larger number of servers, N.

To illustrate the blowup behavior, we use a 2-stage hyperexponential distributions (HYP-2) for the repair time, for which we set the three parameters such that it has the same first three moments as the correpording TPT distributions used in Figure 1. Figure 4 shows the resulting normalized mean queue-length, which is subject to the same blow-up behavior as for TPT distributions. In the worst blow-up region at the right-hand side, even the actual values closely match the ones from Figure 1, while in the intermediate region, the normalized mean queue-length is slightly lower in this case.

Finally, we use the model setting with HYP-2 distributions to illustrate the blow-up behavior when varying the

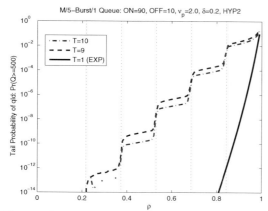

Figure 6. **Tail probabilities for 5-node cluster model with high variance HYP-2 repair times:** The five blow-up points are clearly visible.

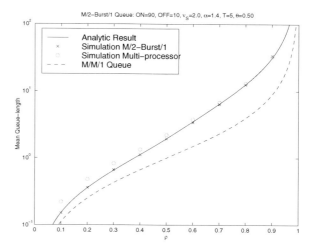

Figure 7. **Simulation of a 2-server system:** The plot marked with circles shows that the effect of load independence assumption can only be observed for short queue lengths. The one marked by crosses corresponds to a simulation of exactly the analytical model and is used to validate our numerical results.

availability of the individual server in Fig. 5. A decrease of the availability is thereby achieved by a reduction of the mean UP duration, while at the same time increasing the mean repair time accordingly, such that the average duration of an UP-DOWN cycle is kept constant. Note that not the whole range of A between 0 and 1 can be covered, since for the fixed arrival rate $\lambda = 1.8$, the cluster becomes instable for values of A below approximately 31%, marked by the vertical dashed-dotted line. Note also that for the used choice of $\lambda = 1.8$ in Figure 5, and for the given settings of $\delta = 0.2$ and $\nu_p = 2$, the mean service rate during long repair times of both nodes simultaneously is $\overline{\nu_2} = 0.72$, hence for any $A < 1$, the model immediately is at least in the inter-mediate blow-up region. Hence, the region of operation with insensitivity towards the repair time distribution is here reduced to a single point at $A = 1$, at which the model reduces to a plain M/M/1 queue, since repair times are infinitely small.

In the general case, the reformulation of Eq. (4) in terms of the availability A leads to the following condition for blow-up region $i = 1, 2, ..., N-1$:

$$\frac{\lambda - N\nu_p\delta}{\nu_p(1-\delta)(N-i+1)} < A < \frac{\lambda - N\nu_p\delta}{\nu_p(1-\delta)(N-i)}.$$

Note that the lower bound on A for blow-up region $i = 1$ is in fact the stability condition for the queueing system, $\rho < 1$. The last blow-up region $i = N$ for

$$A > \frac{\lambda - N\nu_p\delta}{\nu_p(1-\delta)}$$

is only present, if and only if $\lambda > N\nu_p\delta$.

Although the discussion of blow-up points has been general for any $N \geq 1$, the numerical examples so far focused on the case $N = 2$. Since for Hyperexponential distributions with 2 states, larger settings of N can be easily

computed even without reduced state space representations, we conclude this section by demonstrating that the blow-up points in terms of tail probabilities of the queue-length distribution can be also clearly seen for larger N; in the case of Figure 6 for $N = 5$, all five blow-up points are very pronounced.

4. Simulation Experiments

With the analytic results as a baseline for comparison, simulation experiments served two purposes: first to evaluate the effect of the load-independence assumption in the analytic model, and second to explore our model under more general assumptions. In particular, we perform experiments that simulate the failure handling strategies presented in Section 2.

Before we present these results, we discuss the difficulties inherent in creating simulations experiments that sample the TPT distribution.

As discussed in Section 2, the repair time distribution can show power-tail like behavior over a wide range of time-scales, but eventually the repair-time distribution is expected to drop off exponentially corresponding to a truncated tail. Truncated tails can also be an artifact of the finiteness of sample sets in measurements or simulation experiments. For instance, taking a large set of K samples from inter-arrival times of the TPT-DOWN model with infinite tail, corresponds to on average sampling $L := K/(\lambda E(UP + DOWN))$ DOWN periods, or L power-tail

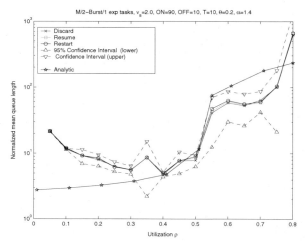

Figure 8. **Comparison between calculations from analytic model and simulation results:** The latter show that the failure handling strategies behave almost identically with respect to mean queue length when task times are exponentially distributed. 95% The confidence interval plotted is for Discard.

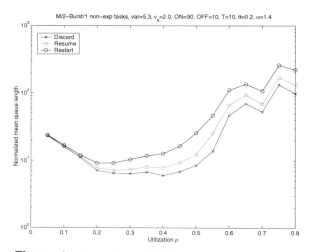

Figure 9. Simulation of M/2-Burst/1 system with hyperexponential task service times for varying fault handling mechanisms.

samples. Since for high quality components the UP periods can be very long (days to months), the number of power-tail samples is rather small $L := N \cdot simultime/(UP + DOWN)$. Simulation experiments would therefore require immensely long simulated virtual time in order to assure adequate sampling of the tails.

Figure 7 compares the exact analytic result of a M/2-Burst/1 Queue with a simulation of the same system as well as a simulation of the actual corresponding multi-processor system. Since it is difficult to obtain stable results for large values of T, we limited our test case to $T = 5$. The main difference of the multi-processor system is that $i \leq N$ operational servers can only be fully utilized if at least i tasks are at the queue. Hence, the service rate is not only modulated by the number of active servers but also by the queue length. This impact is however only visible for small queue lengths, as Figure 7 shows.

In Figure 8, we compare the simulation results of the three failure handling strategies for varying values of ρ against the analytic computations. Each sample point in the figure represents the mean of 10 indepedent runs that each uses 2×10^5 UP/DOWN cycles. The results show that the failure handling strategies behave almost identically, with Restart being the worst and Discard the best. The choice of parameter values for the UP and DOWN periods, namely 90 and 10, relative to that of the mean task service time 1, was to allow us to obtain results within reasonable simulation times. To improve the stability of the simulation results and to provide for a more realistic choice of parameter values, the application of certain rare-event techniques, such as importance sampling, may be investigated. Such a tech-

nique, as applied to systems with heavy-tailed properties is, however, still a subject of ongoing research [1].

Another variation that we considered is that of the task service time being nonexponential. Intuitively, the Restart strategy can be expected to be worst performing since a restarted task's duration is biased in that it must take at least as long to execute as its elapsed execution duration when the server failed. In fact, it is shown in [4] that the completion time of a restarted task exhibits power-tail behavior. In Figure 9, we use a HYP-2 distribution with variance = 5.3 to model the task service time distribution. The simulation results in that figure show that the ordering in which the strategies perform holds, although the difference in mean queue length has grown significantly compared to that in Figure 8. The blowup behavior, however, can still be observed for all three variations. Other simulation experiments, not shown here due to space limitations, show that for the Resume and Restart recovery models, placing the interrupted task in the back of the queue is better than placing it in the front.

5. Summary

This paper presents an analytic model of a cluster of N nodes, which are subject to failure and repair. We formulate the analytic model for general matrix-exponential repair and failure times but then focus in the analysis on high-variance repair times, due to their practical relevance. Under certain assumptions, most of them can be easily removed and also are shown to be not of major performance influence, the cluster model can be expressed as a single server M/MMPP/1 queue, which bears resemblance to earlier teletraffic models.

The analysis of performability metrics mainly focuses

on the mean queue length and on tail probabilities of the queue-length distributions, since the latter can be mapped to successful task completion probabilities under delay constraints. Parameter variations of any of the model parameters, i.e. the number of server nodes N, the availability of the server nodes, A, the degradation factor of service rate during DOWN periods, δ, the service rate during UP, ν_p, and the task arrival rate λ, can lead to a dramatic change of all performance metrics, referred to as blowup-up points, if high-variance repair time distributions are present. The exact placement of the blowup boundaries in the parameter space is obtained Section 3.

The analytic results are confirmed by simulation experiments which show that the main qualitative result, namely the existence of the blow-up points for such systems, is robust to model variations, in particular the type of participating distributions, and the failure handling strategy employed.

ACKNOWLEDGEMENTS: This research was partially supported by the EU IST FP6 project 'HIghly DEpendable ip-based NETworks and Services – HIDENETS', see www.hidenets.aau.dk. The authors would like to thank the HIDENETS consortium, in particular Felicita Di Giandomenica, ISTI-CNR Italy, and Andrea Bondavalli, University of Florence, Italy, for their helpful comments. Furthermore, the authors would like to thank Michael Clark for the implementation of the simulation, Lester Lipsky at the University of Connecticut for the discussions, and the anonymous reviewers for their helpful comments.

References

[1] Asmussen, S., Fuckerieder, P., Jobmann, M., Schwefel, H.-P.: *Large Deviations and Fast Simulation in the Presence of Boundaries*. Stochastic Processes and Applications, 102, pp. 1–23, 2002.

[2] Borst, S.C. Boxma, O.J., and Nunez-Queija, R.: *Heavy Tails: The Effect of the Service Discipline*. Proceedings of Performance Tools 2002, pp. 1–30, London, 2002.

[3] Crovella, M. and Bestavros, A.: *Self-Similarity in World Wide Web Traffic: Evidence and Possible Causes*. Proceedings of the ACM Sigmetrics, pp.160–169, Philadelphia, PA, 1996.

[4] Fiorini, P., Sheahan, R., Lipsky, L., and Asmussen, S.: *On the Completion Time Distribution for Tasks that Must Restart from the Beginning if a Failure Occurs*. Proceedings of SPECTS 2006, Calgary, Canada.

[5] Gaver, D. P., Jacobs, P. A., and Latouche, G.: *Finite Birth-and-Death Models in Randomly Changing Environments*. Advances in Applied Probability, 16, pp. 715–731, 1984.

[6] Greiner, M., Jobmann, M., and Lipsky, L.: *The Importance of Power-tail Distributions for Telecommunication Traffic Models*. Operations Research, 47, No. 2, pp 313-326, March 1999.

[7] Krieger, U., and Naumov, V.: *Analysis of a Delay-Loss System with a Superimposed Markovian Arrival Process and State-Dependent Service Times*, Proceedings of MMB converence, University Trier, September 1999.

[8] Kulkarni, V.G., Nicola, V.F., and Trivedi, K.S.: *The Completion Time of a Job on Multimode Systems*. Advances in Applied Probability, 19, No. 4, pp. 932–954, 1987.

[9] Latouche, G., and Ramaswami, V.: *INTRODUCTION TO MATRIX ANALYTIC METHODS IN STOCHASTIC MODELING*. ASA-SIAM Series on Statistics and Applied Probability, 5, 1999.

[10] Lipsky, L.: *QUEUEING THEORY: A Linear Algebraic Approach*. MacMillan Publishing Company, New York, 1992.

[11] Meier-Hellstern, K. and Fischer, W.: *MMPP Cookbook*. Performance Evaluation **18**, pp. 149–171, 1992.

[12] Mitrani, I.: *Queues with Breakdowns*. Performability Modelling: Techniques and Tools, Haverkort, B.R., et al. (eds.). Wiley, 2001.

[13] Palmer, J., and Mitrani, I.: *Empirical and Analytical Evaluation of Systems with Multiple Unreliable Servers*. Technical Report CS-TR-936, University of New Castle, 2005.

[14] van Moorsel, A., and Wolter, K., *Analysis and Algorithms for Restart*. Proceedings of the First International Conference on the Quantitative Evaluation of Systems (QEST), pp. 195–204, 2004.

[15] Neuts, M.: *MATRIX-GEOMETRIC SOLUTIONS IN STOCHASTIC MODELS*. John Hopkins University Press, London, 1981.

[16] Ost, A., and Haverkort, B., *Evaluating Computer-Communication Systems using Infinite State Petri Nets*. Proceedings of 3rd International Conference on Matrix Analytic Methods, pp. 295–314, 2000.

[17] Schwefel, H.-P. and Lipsky, L.: *Performance Results For Analytic Models of Traffic In Telecommunication Systems, Based on Multiple ON-OFF Sources with Self-Similar Behavior*. In P. Key and D. Smith (eds.), 'Teletraffic Engineering in a Competitive World, Vol 3A', pp. 55–66. Elsevier, 1999.

[18] Schwefel, H.P.: *Performance Analysis of Intermediate Systems Serving Aggregated ON/OFF Traffic with Long-Range Dependent Properties*. PhD Dissertation, Technische Universität München, 2000.

[19] Schwefel, H.-P. and Lipsky, L.: *Impact of Aggregated, Self-Similar ON/OFF Traffic on Delay in Stationary Queueing Models (extended version)*. Performance Evaluation, No. 41, pp. 203–221, 2001.

[20] Schwefel, H.-P.: *Behavior of TCP-like Elastic Traffic at a Buffered Bottleneck Router*. Proceedings of IEEE Infocom, 2001.

[21] Schwefel, H.-P., Antonios, I., and Lipsky, L.: *Performance-Relevant Network Traffic Correlation*, submitted to ASMTA 2007, Prague, Czech Republic.

[22] Willinger, W., Taqqu, M., Sherman, R., and Wilson, D.: *Self-Similarity Through High-Variability: Statistical Analysis of Ethernet LAN Traffic at the Source Level (Extended Version)*. Proceedings of the ACM Sigcomm, 1995.

Computing Battery Lifetime Distributions

Lucia Cloth, Marijn R. Jongerden, Boudewijn R. Haverkort
University of Twente
Design and Analysis of Communication Systems
[lucia,brh,jongerdenmr]@ewi.utwente.nl
http://dacs.ewi.utwente.nl/

Abstract

The usage of mobile devices like cell phones, navigation systems, or laptop computers, is limited by the lifetime of the included batteries. This lifetime depends naturally on the rate at which energy is consumed, however, it also depends on the usage pattern of the battery. Continuous drawing of a high current results in an excessive drop of residual capacity. However, during intervals with no or very small currents, batteries do recover to a certain extend. We model this complex behaviour with an inhomogeneous Markov reward model, following the approach of the so-called Kinetic battery Model (KiBaM). The state-dependent reward rates thereby correspond to the power consumption of the attached device and to the available charge, respectively. We develop a tailored numerical algorithm for the computation of the distribution of the consumed energy and show how different workload patterns influence the overall lifetime of a battery.

1 Introduction

With the proliferation of cheap wireless access technologies, such as wireless LAN, Bluetooth as well as GSM, the number of wireless devices an average citizen is using has been steadily increasing since a few years. Such devices not only add to the flexibility with which we can do our work, but also add to our reachability and our security. Next to these personal wireless devices, an ever growing number of wireless devices is used for surveillance purposes, most notably in sensor-type networks. A common issue to be dealt with in the design of all of these devices is power consumption. Since all of these devices use batteries of some sort, mostly rechargeable, achieving low power consumption for wireless devices has become a key design issue. This fact is witnessed by many recent publications on this topic, and even a special issue of *IEEE Computer* (November 2005) devoted to it [1].

Low-power design is a very broad area in itself, with so-called "battery-driven system design" a special branch of it,

that becomes, due to the reasons mentioned, more and more important. A key issue to be addressed is to find the right tradeoff between battery usage and required performance: how can we design a (wireless) system such that with a given battery, good performance (throughput, reachability, and so on) is obtained, for a long-enough period. Stated differently, how should the processes in the wireless device be organised such that the battery lifetime (which determines the system lifetime) will be as high as possible. Indeed, it has been observed recently that due to the specific physical nature of batteries, achieving the longest battery lifetime is not always achieved by "just" trying to minimise the power consumption at any point in time. Instead, also the way in which the power is consumed, that is, the current-extraction patterns and the employed current levels play a role in the battery lifetime.

In order to obtain a better insight in the lifetime of batteries, a wide variety of models has been developed. We will discuss some of these models in the next section, thereby focusing on the Kinetic Battery Model (KiBaM). What has not been done, however, is the combination of such power consumption models in a versatile way with performance models for mobile communication systems, thereby taking into account typical physical aspects of battery operation. *It is exactly this issue that we address in the current paper.*

Our approach will be to describe the operation of a system with an abstract workload model, describing the various states the wireless device can be in, together with the energy consumption rates in those states. Also, the transition possibilities between these states will be represented in the workload model. Such a description can be interpreted as a Markov-reward model in which accumulated reward stands for the amount of energy consumed. The system or battery lifetime would then be equal to the time until a certain level of consumption (the available charge of the battery) is reached. Determining this time, or better, its distribution, could be done with well-known techniques for performability evaluation. However, such an approach does not well take into account the physical aspect of battery operation. Indeed, studies on batteries reveal that the battery depletion rate in general is non-linear in time, and, moreover, also depends on the amount of energy still in the battery. Furthermore, in periods when a battery is not used, subtle but important battery-restoration effects are in place, that apparently refill the battery. Translating such effects to a Markov reward model context, this would amount to models in which, possibly, the reward and transition rates depend on time and/or on the amount of reward accumulated so far, and in which both positive and negative reward rates are in place.

In this paper we take the analytical KiBaM as a starting point and combine it with performance models. We also present a tailored algorithm for evaluating battery lifetime distributions for the so-called KiBaMRM (Kinetic Battery Markov reward model).

The rest of the paper is organised as follows. We introduce into the world of batteries in Section 2. Section 3 refers to battery models and describes the KiBaM in detail. We then fix some notation for inhomogeneous Markov reward models and present the Markov reward models for batteries used in the rest of the paper in Section 4. In Section 5 we describe the algorithm for the computation of the battery lifetime. Section 6 discusses the results obtained for the models and in Section 7 we conclude this paper.

2 Batteries

The two most important properties of a battery are its voltage (expressed in volts V) and its capacity (mostly expressed in Ampere-hour, Ah); the product of these two quantities gives the energy stored in the battery. For an ideal battery the voltage stays constant over time until the moment it is completely discharged, then the voltage drops to zero. The capacity in the ideal case is the same for every load for the battery. Reality is different, though: the voltage drops during discharge and the effectively perceived capacity is lower under a higher load.

In the ideal case it would be easy to calculate the lifetime of a battery. The lifetime (L) in the case of a constant load is the capacity (C) over the load current (I (Ampere)), $L = C/I$. Due to various nonlinear effects this relation does not hold for real batteries. A simple approximation for the lifetime under constant load can be made with Peukert's law [2]:

$$L = \frac{a}{I^b},$$

where $a > 0$ and $b > 1$ are constants which depend on the battery. This relation does not hold for a variable load. Following Peukert's law, all load profiles with the same average would have the same lifetime. Experimentally it can be shown that this is not the case. One of the effects playing an important role here is the recovery effect of the battery, as follows.

All batteries are driven by electro-chemical reactions. During the discharge, an oxidation reaction at the anode takes place. In this reaction electrons are produced, which are released into the (connected) circuit. At the cathode a reduction reaction takes place. Here electrons are accepted from the circuit and consumed in the reaction:

$$O_1 + ne^- \rightarrow R_1, \qquad \text{cathode}$$
$$R_2 \rightarrow O_2 + me^-. \qquad \text{anode}$$

As an example of a chemical reaction, this is what happens in the highly-used Lithium-ion batteries [3]:

$$Li_{1-x}CoO_2 + xLi^+ + xe^- \rightarrow LiCoO_2,$$
$$CLi_x \rightarrow C + xLi^+ + xe^-.$$

These are the reactions for discharging the battery. For charging the battery the arrows in the reaction equations are directed to the left.

In a lithium ion battery, the Li^+ ions made at the anode have to diffuse to the cathode when a current is drawn from the battery. When the current is too high the internal diffusion cannot keep up with the rate the ions react at the cathode. As a result, the positive charge at the cathode drops and rises at the anode. This causes a drop in the output voltage of the battery. However, when the battery is less loaded for a while, the ions have time enough to diffuse again and charge recovery takes place.

Another effect that occurs when high currents are drawn is that no reaction sites (molecules) are available in the cathode. At small load (low currents) the reaction sites are uniformly distributed over the cathode. But at high currents the reduction takes place only at the surface of the cathode. Due to this, the reaction sites in the internal of the cathode become unreachable. This also results in a drop of the effective capacity of the battery.

3 Battery models

In an attempt to get a grip on the above physical battery processes, a variety of models has been proposed. The simplest models are purely analytical and similar to Peukert's law. With more detail, so-called equivalent electrical circuit models have been introduced, that can be evaluated (simulated) using a package such as Spice [4]. With even more detail, electro-chemical models have been developed; although these models can be very accurate for predicting battery lifetime under concrete loads, these models are often too large and complicated to be used as part of high-level system models [5]. Recently, also stochastic models have been proposed, in which the battery charge is discretised and in which probabilistic transitions between charge levels are included to account for the above presented effects [6]. With these, in essence, Markovian models, also the effect of workload variations (around a given mean) has been studied [7].

The Kinetic Battery Model (KiBaM) [8] is an intuitive analytical battery model. It is called kinetic because it uses a chemical kinetics process as its basis. The battery

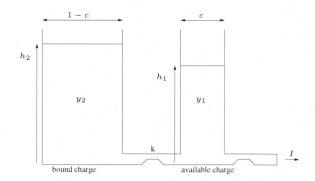

Figure 1. Two well model of the Kinetic Battery Model

charge is distributed over two wells, the available-charge well and the bound-charge well, see Figure 1. The available charge well supplies electrons directly to the load, the bound-charge well supplies electrons only to the available-charge well. The rate at which charge flows between the wells depends on the difference in heights of the two wells, and on a parameter k. The parameter c gives the fraction of the total charge in the battery that is part of the available-charge well. The change of the charge in both wells is given by the following system of differential equations:

$$\begin{cases} \frac{dy_1}{dt} = -I + k(h_2 - h_1), \\ \frac{dy_2}{dt} = -k(h_2 - h_1), \end{cases} \quad (1)$$

with initial conditions $y_1(0) = c \cdot C$ and $y_2(0) = (1-c) \cdot C$, where C is the total battery capacity. For h_1 and h_2 we have: $h_1 = y_1/c$ and $h_2 = y_2/(1-c)$. When a load I is applied to the battery, the available charge reduces, and the difference in heights between the two wells grows. Now, when the load is removed, charge flows from the bounded-charge well to the available-charge well until h_1 and h_2 are equal again. So, during an idle period, more charge becomes available effectively and the battery lasts longer than when the load is applied continuously.

A special case arises if $c = 1$, that is, all charge is readily available. The pair of differential equations (1) then reduces to a single equation $\frac{dy_1}{dt} = -I$, because $y_2 = 0$ at any time.

The system of differential equations can be solved analytically when the load current I is constant. This solution can be used to calculate the battery lifetime for any given workload with piecewise constant currents. We calculated the battery lifetime for simple workloads consisting of a square wave with fixed frequency. In Figure 2 the charges in the available-charge and bound-charge well are given as a function of the time for such a workload with a frequency of $f = 0.001$Hz. The current drawn during the on periods was set to 0.96A. We see the charge in the available-charge well decreasing when the current is drawn from the battery and rising again during the idle periods. The flow of charge from the bound-charge well starts slowly and gets faster over time, because of the increasing difference of the heights $h_2 - h_1$ of the two wells.

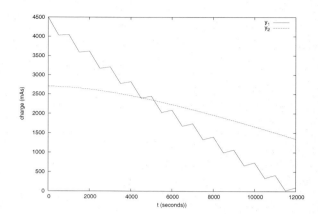

Figure 2. Evolution of the available-charge and the bound-charge for f = 0.001Hz

Frequency	Exp. lifetime	KiBaM lifetime	Modified KiBaM lifetime	
			stochastic	numerical
(Hz)	(min)	(min)	(min)	(min)
Continuous	90	91	90	89
1	193	203	193	193
0.2	230	203	226	193

Table 1. Experimental and computed lifetimes

To be able to do these calculations, the parameters c and k have to be determined. The parameter c can be calculated from the capacity delivered under very large and very small loads. At very large loads the battery lifetime is short, and there is no time for the charge to move from the bound-charge well to the available-charge well. The capacity delivered equals the amount of charge in the available-charge well. At very small loads, however, all the charge from both the bound and available-charge well is delivered. The quotient of these two numbers is exactly c, from [9] we take $c = 0.625$. We set the parameter k in such a way that the calculated lifetime for a continuous load of $0.96A$ corresponded to the experimental value given in [9].

In Table 1 we see the battery lifetimes according to the KiBaM and some experimental results given in [9]. We see that for KiBaM the lifetime is constant for both frequencies. However, the experimental results show a longer lifetime for the slower frequency. To overcome this problem Rao et al. have developed a modified Kinetic Battery Model [9]. In the modified model the recovery rate has an additional dependence on the height of the bound-charge well, making the recovery slower when less charge is left in the battery. With a stochastic simulation of this model they obtain very good results for the battery lifetimes. However, we numerically evaluated the modified KiBaM with a deterministic workload and saw that the lifetime still does not depend on the frequency (see Table 1). Personal correspondence with the authors of [9] has not shed light on the discrepancy.

4 Inhomogeneous MRMs for Batteries

We first introduce the notation for inhomogeneous Markov reward models and their measures of interest. We then show how the KiBaM can be integrated into a CTMC workload model. Finally we present several small example workload models.

4.1 Inhomogeneous MRMs

Homogeneous case. A (homogeneous) Markov reward model (MRM) consists of a finite state space $S = \{1, \ldots, N\}$, the transition rate matrix $\mathbf{Q} \in \mathbb{R}^{N \times N}$ and a reward vector $\underline{r} \in \mathbb{R}^N$.

The matrix $\mathbf{Q}$ is an infinitesimal generator matrix, i.e., with entries $q_{i,j} \geqslant 0$, $j \neq i$, and $q_{i,i} = -\sum_{j \in S, j \neq i} q_{i,j}$. The diagonal entry $q_{i,i}$, which is often denoted as $-q_i$, describes the rate at which state i is left. This rate is to be interpreted as the rate of a negative exponential distribution, i.e., the probability that state i is left within s seconds is given as $1 - e^{-q_i \cdot s}$. The next state then is j with probability $q_{i,j}/q_i$. The initial distribution of states at time $t = 0$ is denoted as $\underline{\alpha}$. The generator matrix $\mathbf{Q}$ together with $\underline{\alpha}$ determines the CTMC $X(t)$.

When in state i, reward is accumulated with rate r_i which might be positive or negative. The total reward accumulated when residing in state i from time t_1 until time $t_2 \geqslant t_1$ is denoted $y_i(t_1, t_2)$ and equals

$$y_i(t_1, t_2) = r_i \cdot (t_2 - t_1).$$

Given the state process $X(t)$, the accumulated reward at time t, $Y(t)$, is defined as

$$Y(t) = \int_0^t r_{X(s)} ds.$$

The distribution of $Y(t)$, the so-called performability distribution [10, 11], equals $F^Y(t, y) = \Pr\{Y(t) \leqslant y\}$. The corresponding density (with respect to y) equals

$$
\begin{aligned}
f^Y(t, y) &= \frac{\partial F^Y(t, y)}{\partial y} \\
&= \lim_{h \downarrow 0} \frac{1}{h} \Pr\{y \leqslant Y(t) \leqslant y + h\}.
\end{aligned}
$$

Inhomogeneous case. In the inhomogeneous case, the transition rate matrix $\mathbf{Q}$ and the reward vector $\underline{r}$ can depend on the time t (time-inhomogeneous) and the accumulated reward y (reward-inhomogeneous). We then have $\mathbf{Q}(t, y)$ and $\underline{r}(t, y)$, where y is the current level of accumulated reward. The reward accumulated between time t_1 and $t_2 \geqslant t_1$ when residing completely in state i is described by the following differential equation with initial value $y_i(t_1, t_1) = 0$:

$$\frac{dy_i(t_1, t_2)}{dt_2} = r_i(t_2, y_i(t_1, t_2)).$$

The equation describes the rate of change at the end of the interval $[t_1, t_2]$ and so the reward rate depends on t_2. The accumulated reward until time t in this case is defined as

$$Y(t) = \int_0^t r_{X(s)}(s, Y(s)) ds.$$

An MRM can easily have more than one reward structure. State i is then equipped with reward rates $r_{i,1}$ through $r_{i,K}$, i.e., we have a reward matrix $\mathbf{R}(t, \underline{y}) \in \mathbb{R}^{N \times K}$ for $\underline{y} \in \mathbb{R}^K$. The accumulated reward is then a vector of random variables $\underline{Y}(t) = (Y_1(t), \ldots, Y_K(t))$ and its distribution is defined as

$$F^{\underline{Y}}(t, (y_1, \ldots, y_K)) = \Pr\{Y_1(t) \leqslant y_1, \ldots, Y_K(t) \leqslant y_K\}.$$

Battery case. For the KiBaM we need an MRM that is time-homogeneous but reward-inhomogeneous and has two types of rewards. We therefore denote the generator matrix as $\mathbf{Q}(y_1, y_2)$ and the reward rates as $\mathbf{R}(y_1, y_2) \in \mathbf{R}^{N \times 2}$. The reward accumulated in a state i between time t_1 and time t_2 is described by the following differential equations with initial values $y_{i,1}(t_1, t_1) = y_{i,2}(t_1, t_1) = 0$:

$$
\begin{cases}
\frac{dy_{i,1}(t_1, t_2)}{dt_2} = r_{i,1}\left(y_{i,1}(t_1, t_2), y_{i,2}(t_1, t_2)\right), \\
\frac{dy_{i,2}(t_1, t_2)}{dt_2} = r_{i,2}\left(y_{i,1}(t_1, t_2), y_{i,2}(t_1, t_2)\right).
\end{cases}
$$

The accumulated reward is then defined as

$$
\begin{aligned}
\underline{Y}(t) &= (Y_1(t), Y_2(t)) \\
&= \int_0^t \underline{r}_{X(s)}(\underline{Y}(s)) ds \\
&= \int_0^t \left(r_{X(s),1}(Y_1(s), Y_2(s)), r_{X(s),2}(Y_1(s), Y_2(s))\right) ds,
\end{aligned}
$$

and its distribution equals

$$F^{(Y_1, Y_2)}(t, y_1, y_2) = \Pr\{Y_1(t) \leqslant y_1, Y_2(t) \leqslant y_2\}. \quad (2)$$

We assume that the accumulated rewards have to be non-negative and are bounded by a minimum $\underline{l} = (l_1, l_2)$ and a maximum $\underline{u} = (u_1, u_2)$. This is absolutely reasonable when considering batteries because their charge is always between 0 and a predefined capacity C. We then have

$$f^{(Y_1, Y_2)}(t, y_1, y_2) = 0, \quad \text{for } y_1 < l_1 \text{ or } y_2 < l_2 \\ \text{or } y_1 > u_1 \text{ or } y_2 > u_2. \quad (3)$$

In the following we often consider the joint distribution of state and accumulated rewards, that is,

$$F_i(t, y_1, y_2) = \Pr\{X(t) = i, Y_1(t) \leqslant y_1, Y_2(t) \leqslant y_2\},$$

with density $f_i(t, y_1, y_2)$. The distribution of the accumulated rewards can then be calculated using

$$F^{(Y_1, Y_2)}(t, y_1, y_2) = \sum_{i \in S} F_i(t, y_1, y_2).$$

4.2 The KiBaMRM

We state the KiBaMRM as an MRM with two reward types. The CTMC states $\{1, \ldots, N\}$ of the MRM reflect the different operating modes of the device. The first accumulated reward $Y_1(t)$ represents the available-charge well, the second accumulated reward $Y_2(t)$ represents the bound-charge well. The corresponding rates are derived from the KiBaM differential equations (1), using the constants k and c and the equations $h_1 = y_1/c$ and $h_2 = y_2/(1-c)$. Let I_i be the energy consumption rate in a state $i \in S$. The first reward rate then is

$$r_{i,1}(y_1, y_2) = \begin{cases} -I_i + k \cdot (h_2 - h_1), & h_2 > h_1 > 0, \\ 0, & \text{otherwise}, \end{cases}$$

and the second reward rate is

$$r_{i,2}(y_1, y_2) = \begin{cases} -k \cdot (h_2 - h_1), & h_2 > h_1 > 0, \\ 0, & \text{otherwise}. \end{cases}$$

The interesting question for battery-powered devices is "When does the battery get empty?" For the KiBaMRM model, the battery is empty at time t if the available-charge well $Y_1(t)$ is empty. Since the accumulated rewards $Y_1(t)$ and $Y_2(t)$ are random variables, we can only indicate the *probability* that the battery is empty at time t:

$$\Pr\{\text{battery empty at time } t\} = \Pr\{Y_1(t) = 0\} \quad (4)$$

The *lifetime* L of a battery is the instant the battery gets empty for the first time,

$$L = \min\{t \mid Y_1(t) = 0\}.$$

4.3 Stochastic Workload Models

In the following we consider three stochastic workload models. First we concentrate on simple on/off models like the ones used in [9] with the only difference that those were not stochastic. For a given frequency f, the workload toggles between the off-state (no energy consumed) and the on-state (energy consumed at a fixed rate $I = 0.96A$). We model the on/off times as Erlang-K distributions such that with increasing K they become close to deterministic.

Figure 3 shows the state-transition diagram for this simple model. For frequency f, all transitions have rate

$$\lambda = 2 \cdot f \cdot K.$$

The expected on and off times, respectively, are then $K/(2fK)$ which leads exactly to a frequency f.

We furthermore consider two workload models of a small battery-powered device. The first, simple one consists of three states as depicted in Figure 4. At the beginning the model is in idle state. With rate $\lambda = 2$ per hour there is the necessity to send data over the wireless interface. If such data is present, the model moves into the send state. The

sending of data is complete in 10 minutes on average (resulting in a sending rate of $\mu = 6$ per hour). From the idle state the device can also move into a power-saving sleep state, this is done – on average – once per hour ($\tau = 1$). The power-consumption rate is low when idling ($I_0 = 8$mA), it is high when sending data ($I_1 = 200$mA) and negligible in the sleep state ($I_2 = 0$mA). With a typical battery capacity $C = 800$mAh (check your cell phone!), this means that theoretically the device can be 4 hours in send mode or 100 hours in idle mode.

To extend the overall battery lifetime it seems to be beneficial to have short periods of high sending activity (bursts) and long periods without sending activity. In the modelled wireless device this could be achieved by accumulating the data to be transmitted and then send all in a row instead of transmitting lower amounts of data more frequently. This can be modelled by buffering the flow of arriving data. When the flow is active, data arrives with a very high rate. If the flow is inactive, the device can safely go to sleep. Figure 5 shows a state-transition diagram for such a burst model. It has the same sending rate μ and timeout rate τ as the simple model. Bursts start with rate switch_on=1 per hour and stop with rate switch_off=6 per hour. To make any results of the latter two models comparable, we have chosen $\lambda_{\text{burst}} = 182$ per hour such that the steady-state probability to be in off $-$ send or on $-$ send in the burst model is the same as the probability to be in send in the simple model. As could be expected, the steady-state probability to be in sleep is higher in the burst model than in the simple model.

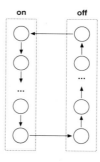

Figure 3. Simple on/off model

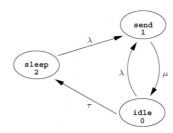

Figure 4. State transition diagram for the simple model

784

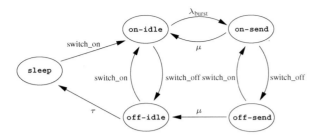

Figure 5. State transition diagram for the burst model

5 Markovian Approximation

In this section we present a numerical algorithm for the computation of the distribution of the accumulated reward (performability) in an inhomogeneous Markov reward model. It uses a Markovian approximation, in which the computation is reduced to the transient solution of a pure CTMC via uniformisation. The underlying idea already appeared in [12] and is also used in [13] and [14] (steady-state solution). We described the algorithm for homogeneous MRMs with positive reward rates in the CSRL context [15, 16], then extended it to reward-inhomogeneous models with positive reward rates [17]. We also explored the applicability of a discretisation algorithm like the one presented in [18]. However, this algorithm requires integer reward rates to work efficiently. In the case of rational reward rates these have to be scaled which in turn substantially increases the number of required discretisation steps, thus making the algorithm unattractive and often even infeasible. Techniques for the reduction of the space complexity like the one presented in [19] have still to be explored. Nevertheless, a detailed description of the discretisation algorithm can be found in [20].

There is also other work that addresses performability-like measures in an inhomogeneous context. In the 1990's some work has been published on the computation of transient state probabilities for inhomogeneous Markovian models without rewards were addressed there [21, 22, 23]. A more recent paper [24] characterises the performability distribution in inhomogeneous MRMs through a coupled system of partial differential equations that is solved through discretisation, and used to derive systems of ordinary differential equations to determine moments of accumulated reward.

In what follows we approximate the joint distribution of state process and accumulated reward by the transient solution of a derived homogeneous CTMC, that is, by a PH-distribution. The approximation is applicable if the generator matrix and the reward rates depend on the current accumulated reward and not on the current time. This is exactly the case with our battery model and we therefore restrict the presentation to a two dimensional reward structure, even though the approach applies for three or more reward types equally well.

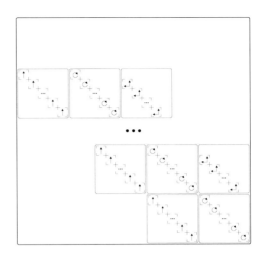

Figure 6. Structure of the new generator matrix Q^*.

The joint distribution of state and accumulated reward (2) can be rewritten by summing over evenly-sized subintervals of the reward intervals $[l_1, y_1]$ and $[l_2, y_2]$:

$$F_i(t, y_1, y_2) = \sum_{j_1 = \frac{l_1}{\Delta}}^{\frac{y_1}{\Delta}-1} \sum_{j_2 = \frac{l_2}{\Delta}}^{\frac{y_2}{\Delta}-1} \Pr \left\{ \begin{array}{l} X_t = i, \\ Y_1(t) \in (j_1\Delta, (j_1+1)\Delta], \\ Y_2(t) \in (j_2\Delta, (j_2+1)\Delta] \end{array} \right\}.$$

Here, Δ is the stepsize at which the state space is discretised.

5.1 Discretisation of the state space

We want to approximate the terms $\Pr\{X_t = i, Y_1(t) \in [j_1\Delta, (j_1+1)\Delta], Y_2(t) \in [j_2\Delta, (j_2+1)\Delta]\}$ in such a way that the computation is done for a pure CTMC (without rewards). This is accomplished as follows. An MRM modelling a battery can be seen as having an infinite and uncountable state space $S \times [l_1, u_1] \times [l_2, u_2]$, where state (s, y_1, y_2) indicates that the "CTMC part" of the MRM is in state s and the accumulated reward of the first type is y_1 and of the second type is y_2. For our approximation we break down the uncountable state space to a finite one. Let

$$S^* = S \times \left\{ \frac{l_1}{\Delta}, \dots, \frac{u_1}{\Delta} \right\} \times \left\{ \frac{l_2}{\Delta}, \dots, \frac{u_2}{\Delta} \right\}$$

be the state space of the new CTMC. A state (s, j_1, j_2) then indicates that the MRM is in state s and has accumulated rewards in the intervals $(j_1\Delta, (j_1+1)\Delta]$ and $(j_2\Delta, (j_2+1)\Delta]$, respectively (for $j_1 = 0$ or $j_2 = 0$ these intervals are left-closed). In the special case where $c = 1$ ($y_2 = 0$) only the first accumulated reward y_1 has to be discretised.

The initial distribution $\underline{\alpha}^*$ depends on the original initial distribution α and the initial values for the accumulated rewards a_1 and a_2:

$$\alpha^*_{(i,j_1,j_2)} = \begin{cases} \alpha_i, & a_1 \in (j_1\Delta, (j_1+1)\Delta] \text{ and} \\ & a_2 \in (j_2\Delta, (j_2+1)\Delta], \\ 0, & \text{otherwise.} \end{cases}$$

The distribution of the accumulated rewards is then approximated as

$$F^{(Y_1,Y_2)}(t, y_1, y_2) \approx \sum_{i \in S} \sum_{j_1 = \frac{l_1}{\Delta}}^{\frac{y_1}{\Delta}-1} \sum_{j_2 = \frac{l_2}{\Delta}}^{\frac{y_2}{\Delta}-1} \pi_{(i,j_1,j_2)}(t),$$

where $\pi_{(i,j_1,j_2)}(t)$ is the transient probability of residing in state (i, j_1, j_2) at time t in the derived CTMC.

For battery models, the probability that the battery is already empty at time t, cf. (4), is approximated as:

$$\Pr\{\text{battery empty at time } t\} \approx \sum_{i \in S} \sum_{j_2 = \frac{l_2}{\Delta}}^{\frac{u_2}{\Delta}} \pi_{(i,0,j_2)}(t).$$

5.2 Transitions in the new generator

In the following we restrict the presentation to the solution of KiBa models. However, the approach is easily applicable to general inhomogeneous MRMs with multiple rewards.

Two types of transitions are possible in the new CTMC with generator $\mathbf{Q}^*$: transitions taken from the original CTMC and transitions between different reward levels (for each of the two reward types). An entry in the new generator matrix $\mathbf{Q}^*$ is defined depending on the type of transition it represents. Figure 6 shows the structure of the generator matrix $\mathbf{Q}^*$. Each small block corresponds to a fixed j_1 and j_2 and has dimension $N \times N$, each of the big block corresponds to one value of j_1.

Transitions from the original generator. If the original CTMC part of two states (i, j_1, j_2) and (i', j_1, j_2) are different $(i \neq i')$ but the reward levels are identical, the entry is taken from the original generator. Since it is a reward-inhomogeneous MRM, the current reward level $(j_1\Delta, j_2\Delta)$ must be taken into account, that is,

$$Q^*_{(i,j_1,j_2),(i',j_1,j_2)} = Q_{i,i'}(j_1\Delta, j_2\Delta).$$

In Figure 6 these entries are found in the blocks $\boxed{\text{c}}$.

Transitions indicating the consumption of energy. If the CTMC states are identical, the levels of the first accumulated reward are different and the levels of the second accumulated reward are again identical, the entry indicates a change in the first accumulated reward, the available charge well. Such a change can only happen between neighbouring levels, hence, between j_1 and $j_1 - 1$ (entries in blocks $\boxed{\uparrow}$).

$$Q^*_{(i,j_1,j_2),(i,j_1-1,j_2)} = \frac{I_i}{\Delta}, j_1 > 0$$

Transitions indicating the transfer from the bound-charge well to the available-charge well. When charge is transferred between the two wells the level of the first reward has to increase while simultaneously the level of the second reward decreases. This corresponds to a transition between state (i, j_1, j_2) and $(i, j_1 + 1, j_2 - 1)$ for $j_1 < u_1/\Delta, j_2 > 0$ and $h_2 \geqslant h_1$:

$$Q^*_{(i,j_1,j_2),(i,j_1+1,j_2-1)} = \frac{k(h_2 - h_1)}{\Delta} = k\left(\frac{j_2}{1-c} - \frac{j_1}{c}\right),$$

where $h_1 = (j_1\Delta)/c$ and $h_2 = (j_2\Delta)/(1-c)$. These entries can be found in the blocks $\boxed{\nwarrow}$.

The entries in the first row of big blocks correspond to $j_1 = 0$, which means that the battery is empty. These states are made absorbing, because the lifetime of a battery is defined to be the first time at which its get empty, so we do not allow recovery in this case. However, the recovery transitions could easily be included. All other off-diagonal entries of $\mathbf{Q}^*$ are zero, the diagonal entries are defined as the negative row sums.

5.3 Complexity

The time complexity is $\mathcal{O}\left(N^2 \cdot qt \cdot \frac{y_1}{\Delta} \cdot \frac{y_2}{\Delta}\right)$. The algorithm is quadratic in the number of states and linear in time and in each of the reward bounds. The step size Δ enters as Δ^{-2}. However, the step size is also coded into the generator matrix of the new CTMC by multiplying the reward rates with $\frac{1}{\Delta}$ (see the definition of $\mathbf{Q}^*$). The transient solution of the CTMC has a time complexity linear in the *uniformisation constant* q. For small Δ, this uniformisation constant gets linear in $\frac{1}{\Delta}$ and we thus obtain a time complexity in Δ^{-3}.

6 Results

In this section we evaluate the battery lifetime distribution of the systems described in Section 4 using simulations of the stochastic workload on the analytical KiBaM and the Markovian approximation algorithm for the KiBaMRM.

6.1 On/Off Model

We start with a degenerate case of the KiBaM, where the bound-charge well is empty from the beginning and the complete charge is in the available-charge well. There is no transfer of charge between the two wells. We choose the simplest Erlang model (see Figure 3) for frequency $f = 1$Hz with $K = 1$, that is, on- and off-times follow a negative exponential distribution with rate $\lambda = 2$. The battery capacity is $C = 2000$mAh$= 7200$As; the KiBaM constants are $c = 1$ and $k = 0$/s.

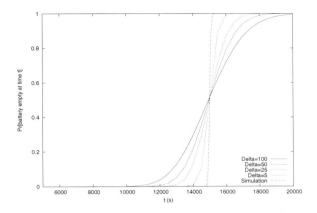

Figure 7. Battery lifetime distribution for the on/off-model (f = 1Hz, K = 1, C = 7200As, c = 1, k = 0/s)

Figure 7 shows the resulting lifetime distribution calculated by simulation and using the approximation algorithm using different stepsizes Δ.

The simulation results are obtained by 1000 independent runs. They suggest that the battery lifetime is close to deterministic with a mean of about 15000 seconds. This is reasonable since the overall time spent in the on-state in one of the runs has approximately an Erlang$_{15000}$(2 s) distribution, which is a good approximation to a deterministic distribution with mean 7500 seconds. In 7500 seconds the consumed energy is 7500s $\cdot$ 0.96A = 7200As $= C$. For pure deterministic on- and off-times, the analytical KiBaM also yields a lifetime of 15000 seconds.

As an example of the computational complexity, the CTMC for $\Delta = 5$ has 2882 states and a generator with more than $3.2 \cdot 10^6$ nonzero transition rates. To compute the transient state probabilities for $t = 17000$ seconds more than 36000 iterations are needed.

For decreasing stepsize Δ the curves from the approximation algorithm approach the simulation curve. This an indication for the correct operation of the algorithm. However, even for $\Delta = 5$ the approximation is not really a good one, since it is in general difficult to closely approximate an almost deterministic value through a phase-type distribution.

We also evaluated the battery lifetime of the on/off-model for better approximations to the deterministic on- and off-times, that is, for $K > 1$ in the Erlang model (we do not show curves here). While the lifetime distribution obtained from simulation gets even closer to a deterministic one for increasing K, the values computed by the approximation algorithm do not change visibly. This is due to the fact that the approximation is not good enough to capture the relatively small differences.

Figure 8 shows the lifetime distribution of the on/off model with $K = 1$ for $c = 0.625$, that is, at the beginning 62.5% of the charge are in the available-charge well and 37.5% are in the bound-charge well. The constant for the

flow between the two wells is $k = 4.5 \cdot 10^{-5}$/s. The curves

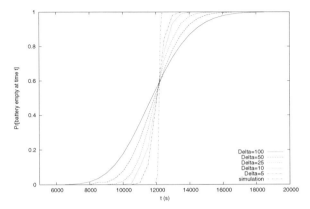

Figure 8. Battery lifetime distribution for the on/off model (f = 1Hz, K = 1, C = 7200As, c = 0.625, k = 4.5 $\cdot$ 10^{-5}/s)

for the approximation algorithm are quite far away from the one obtained by simulation. Unfortunately it is not feasible to consider a substantially smaller Δ for this example. For $\Delta = 5$ we have about $3.2 \cdot 10^6$ non-zeroes in the generator matrix Q^*. For $t = 10000$, uniformisation requires more than $2.3 \cdot 10^4$ iterations, each with $3.2 \cdot 10^6$ multiplications. For $t = 20000$, more than $4.6 \cdot 10^4$ iterations are needed.

In Figure 9 we compare the lifetime distribution of the two cases already described with a third scenario, where the initial capacity of the battery is only 4500As$= 0.625 \cdot$ 7200As and completely in the available-charge well. In the first case ($C = 7200$As, $c = 1$) the battery lasts generally longer than in the second case ($C = 7200$As, $c = 0.925$), because all charge is available. In the third case ($C = 4500$As, $c = 1$), the battery lifetime is in general shorter, because there is no bound-charge to be transferred to the available-charge well.

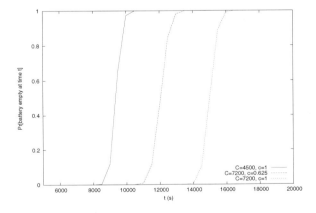

Figure 9. On/off model with different initial capacities ($\Delta = 5$).

787

6.2 Simple & burst model

We now evaluate and compare the battery lifetime distributions for the simple and the burst model.

Figure 10 shows the lifetime distribution for the simple model (see Figure 4) for three different battery settings. The left set of curves is calculated for a capacity $C = 500$mAh and $c = 1$, that is, all capacity sits in the available-charge well. The rightmost curve is for $C = 800$mAh and $c = 1$. It is computed by a uniformisation-based algorithm [25] which is applicable for this special case and the small number of states. The middle set of curves corresponds to the actual KiBaMRM with $C = 800$mAh, $c = 1$ and $k = 4.5 \cdot 10^{-5}/$s$= 1.96 \cdot 10^{-2}/$h.

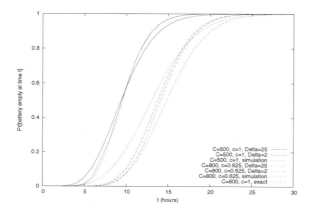

Figure 10. Battery lifetime distribution for the simple model

For the simple model, it is possible to compute good approximations using the Markovian approximation algorithm. For the leftmost set of curves, only the available-charge well is discretised while for the middle set of curves both wells have to be discretised. This results in a better approximation for the left curves in comparison to the middle curves.

From Figure 10 one can see that if only 62.5% of the capacity becomes available at all (leftmost curves) the battery is most certainly empty (with probability $> 99\%$) after about 17 hours. If the rest of the charge is initially in the bound charge well, the battery gets surely empty after about 23 hours, if all capacity is readily available (rightmost curve), after about 25 hours. Hence, for this workload model it is in general not possible to make use of the total capacity of 800mAh, if it is distributed between the bound-charge well and the available-charge well. However, a large fraction of the total capacity becomes available, which is shown by the fact that the middle curves are closer to the right curve than to the left set of curves.

In Figure 11 we finally compare the battery lifetime distribution of the simple and the burst model. The burst model condenses the send activity and consequently spends more time in sleep mode. This lets the battery last longer, that

is, its lifetime distribution curve lies right from the one for the simple model. For example, after 20 hours the battery is empty with a probability of about 95% when using the simple model while it is empty with probability only about 89% in case of the burst model.

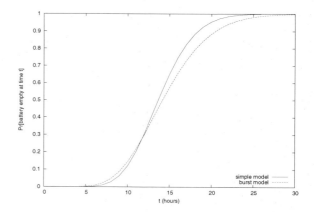

Figure 11. Battery lifetime distribution for the simple and the burst model ($C = 800$mAh, $c = 0.625$, $\Delta = 5$)

7 Conclusion

The aim of this paper has been twofold. First of all we have discussed the increasing importance of the incorporation of battery aspects into system models. In particular, we stressed the need for considering the nonlinear aspects of the battery models. Using the analytical KiBaM as a starting point, we developed the KiBaMRM, a reward-inhomogeneous Markov reward model for batteries. With this model we can assess the battery lifetime distribution for a stochastic workload model. We would like to mention that the KiBaM does not cover all aspects of battery behaviour (see Section 2). However, the class of time- and reward-inhomogeneous MRMs is flexible enough to describe more realistic battery models.

For the actual computation of the battery lifetime distribution we provided an efficient approximation algorithm where the accumulated rewards are discretised. The computation then boils down to the transient solution of a CTMC. With an implementation of this algorithm we evaluated the lifetime of some small workload models, thereby also comparing to simulation results. Trying to approximate the almost deterministic lifetime for the on/off model resulted in a poor accuracy. In contrast, for the simple and burst mode of a wireless device, the algorithm gave good results. Using the computed lifetime distributions we could show that in general the battery lasts longer for the burst model than for the simple model.

Future work will include the exploration of more realistic MRMs for batteries and the evaluation of real world power-aware devices.

References

[1] *IEEE Computer*, vol. 38, no. 11. IEEE Press, 2005.

[2] D. Rakhmatov and S. Vrudhula, "An analytical high-level battery model for use in energy management of portable electronic systems," in *Proceedings of the International Conference on Computer Aided Design (ICCAD'01)*, 2001, pp. 488–493.

[3] Overview of lithium ion batteries. [Online]. Available: `http://www.panasonic.com/industrial/battery/oem/images/pdf/Panasonic_LiIon_Overview.pdf`

[4] The spice page. [Online]. Available: `http://bwrc.eecs.berkeley.edu/Classes/IcBook/SPICE/`

[5] K. Lahiri, A. Raghunathan, S. Dey, and D. Panigrahi, "Battery-driven system design: a new frontier in low power design," in *7th Asia and South Pacific Design Automation Conference (ASP-DA'02)*, 2002, pp. 261–267.

[6] C. Chiasserini and R. Rao, "Pulsed battery discharge in communication devices," in *Proceedings of the 5th International Conference on Mobile Computing and Networking*, 1999, pp. 88 – 95.

[7] D. Panigrahi, C. Chiasserini, S. Dey, R. Rao, A. Raghunathan, and K. Lahiri, "Battery life estimation of mobile embedded systems," in *Proceedings of the 14th International Conference on VLSI Design*, 2001, pp. 57 – 63.

[8] J. Manwell and J. McGowan, "Lead acid battery storage model for hybrid energy systems," *Solar Energy*, vol. 50, pp. 399–405, 1993.

[9] V. Rao, G. Singhal, A. Kumar, and N. Navet, "Battery model for embedded systems," in *VLSID '05*. Washington, DC, USA: IEEE Computer Society, 2005, pp. 105–110.

[10] J. F. Meyer, "On evaluating the performability of degradable computing systems," *IEEE Transactions on Computers*, vol. 29, no. 8, pp. 720–731, 1980.

[11] ——, "Performability: a retrospective and some pointers to the future," *Performance Evaluation*, vol. 14, no. 3, pp. 139–156, 1992.

[12] A. Bobbio and L. Roberti, "Distribution of the minimal completion time of parallel tasks in multi-reward semi-Markov models," *Performance Evaluation*, vol. 14, pp. 239–256, 1992.

[13] G. Horton, V. G. Kulkarni, D. M. Nicol, and K. S. Trivedi, "Fluid stochastic Petri nets: Theory, applications, and solution techniques," *European Journal of Operational Research*, vol. 105, pp. 184–201, 1998.

[14] A. Horvath and M. Gribaudo, "Matrix geometric solution of fluid stochastic Petri nets," in *Proceedings of the 4th International Conference on Matrix Analytic Methods in Stochastic Models*. World Scientific, 2002.

[15] B. R. Haverkort, H. Hermanns, J.-P. Katoen, and C. Baier, "Model checking CSRL-specified performability properties," in *Proceedings of the 5th International Workshop on Performability Modeling of Computer and Communications Systems (PMCCS'01)*, 2001, pp. 105–109.

[16] B. R. Haverkort, L. Cloth, H. Hermanns, J.-P. Katoen, and C. Baier, "Model checking performability properties," in *Proceedings of the International Conference on Dependable Systems and Networks (DSN'02)*. IEEE Press, 2002, pp. 102–112.

[17] L. Cloth, "Model Checking Algorithms for Markov Reward Models," Ph.D. dissertation, University of Twente, 2006.

[18] B. Haverkort and J. Katoen, "The performability distribution for nonhomogeneous Markov-reward models," in *Proceedings 7th Performability Workshop (PMCCS'05)*, 2005, pp. 38–42.

[19] M. Gribaudo and A. Horvath, "Fluid stochastic Petri nets augmented with flush-out arcs: A transient analysis technique," *IEEE Transactions on Software Engineering*, vol. 28, no. 10, pp. 944–955, 2002.

[20] L. Cloth, B. Haverkort, and M. Jongerden, "Evaluation of battery lifetimes using inhomogeneous Markov reward models," CTIT, University of Twente, Tech. Rep. 06-58, 2006.

[21] N. van Dijk, "Uniformisation for nonhomogeneous Markov chains," *Operations Research Letters*, vol. 12, 1992.

[22] A. Rindos, S. Woolet, I. Viniotis, and K. Trivedi, "Exact methods for the transient analysis of nonhomogeneous continuous time Markov chains," in *2nd International Workshop on the Numerical Solution of Markov Chains*, 1995, pp. 121–133.

[23] A. van Moorsel and K. Wolter, "Numerical solution of non-homogeneous Markov processes through uniformisation," in *Proceedings of the 12th European Simulation Multiconference*, 1998, pp. 710–717.

[24] M. Telek, A. Horváth, and G. Horváth, "Analysis of inhomogeneous Markov reward models," *Linear Algebra and its Applications*, vol. 386, pp. 383–405, 2004.

[25] B. Sericola, "Occupation times in Markov processes," *Communications in Statistics — Stochastic Models*, vol. 16, no. 5, pp. 479–510, 2000.

Quantifying the Effectiveness of Mobile Phone Virus Response Mechanisms

Elizabeth Van Ruitenbeek,
Tod Courtney, and William H. Sanders
Coordinated Science Laboratory
University of Illinois at Urbana-Champaign
Urbana, IL, USA
evanrui2, tcourtne, whs@uiuc.edu

Fabrice Stevens
France Telecom Research and Development
Network and Services Security
92794 Issy les Moulineaux Cedex 9, France
fabrice1.stevens@orange-ftgroup.com

Abstract

Viruses that infect smartphones are emerging as a new front in the fight against computer viruses. In this paper, we model the propagation of mobile phone viruses in order to study their impact on the dependability of mobile phones. We propose response mechanisms and use the models to obtain insight on the effectiveness of these virus mitigation techniques. In particular, we consider the effects of multimedia messaging system (MMS) viruses that spread by sending infected messages to other phones. The virus model is implemented using the Möbius software tool and is highly parameterized, enabling representation of a wide range of potential MMS virus behavior. Using the model, we present the results of four illustrative MMS virus scenarios simulated with and without response mechanisms. By measuring the propagation rate and the extent of virus penetration in the simulation phone population, we quantitatively compare the effectiveness of mobile phone virus response mechanisms.

1. Introduction

The enhanced computational and communication capabilities of smartphones are beginning to attract viruses targeted at these increasingly sophisticated mobile phones [12]. The problem is expected to worsen as smartphones become more prevalent and as virus writers become more proficient in working with mobile phones [11].

Attacks from mobile phone viruses can compromise personal information, delete data, drain the battery [9], and steal phone services by using expensive features [3]. The impact of mobile phone viruses on phone service providers includes increased customer complaints concerning infected phones and extra network congestion due to the virus-related traffic [12]. It is imperative that the mobile phone industry anticipate and act now against these looming threats to dependable and secure mobile phone services.

Because mobile phones are communications devices with many connectivity options, there exist many possible infection vectors [11]. Mobile phones can become infected by downloading infected files using the phone Internet browser, by transferring files between phones using the Bluetooth interface, by synchronizing with an infected computer, by accessing an infected physical memory card, or by opening infected files attached to multimedia message service (MMS) messages. MMS messages are similar to text messages between mobile phones, but MMS messages are capable of including attached files, much like email with attached files.

The most threatening propagation vectors permit rapid and widespread virus penetration throughout a network of phones. Based on this criterion, one of the most significant threats is propagation by MMS message attachments [11], [12], [7]. Thus, we choose to focus on mobile phone viruses spreading via MMS messages.

Mobile phone security measures can leverage existing antivirus efforts against traditional computer viruses, but the effectiveness of these measures must be evaluated in the context of the mobile phone network environment. Mobile phone viruses are expected to follow an evolution similar to that of computer viruses, only at an accelerated pace [12].

Our model of mobile phone virus propagation leverages related work in computer virus modeling. Kephart and White introduced epidemiological models to the study of computer viruses [6]. More recent work utilizes Markov models to incorporate the probability distributions of model behavior [1]. Some other related work on models of email viruses has influenced our work on models of mobile phone viruses. In much the same way that models of email virus propagation incorporate user behavior [14], our model of mobile phone viruses considers factors such as how quickly a phone user reads a new MMS message and how likely a phone user is to open an infected attachment. In addition, our development of mobile phone response mechanisms is related to research on defenses against computer network worms [8]. Some researchers have proposed mobile phone defense measures [5], but they perform no quantitative evaluation on their proposed measures.

In this paper we present research quantifying the impact of virus propagation on the dependability of mobile phone systems. We also quantify the effectiveness of a range of potential virus mitigation techniques. Section 2 describes the general attack process of a mobile phone virus, and Section 3 describes the six response mechanisms to be evaluated. In Section 4, we discuss the implementation of the model used to generate the results presented in Section 5. Four test case virus scenarios are defined. We analyze the simulation results by comparing the virus propagation with and without response mechanisms.

2. Mobile Phone Virus Attack Process

For the mobile phone virus propagation that we model, the infection starts with a single infected phone. The virus on this phone sends MMS messages with an infected attachment file to other phones. These targeted phones are either selected from the contact list of the infected phone or selected by dialing a random phone number.

Each infected MMS message is delivered to its target phone. After the user of the target phone notices this new MMS message, the user must choose whether to accept the accompanying attachment. If the unsuspecting user accepts the infected attachment file using a phone susceptible to the virus, then the virus is installed, the target phone becomes infected, and the target phone begins to function as an attacker phone.

3. Mobile Phone Virus Response Mechanisms

In response to the mobile phone viruses spreading via MMS messages, we present mechanisms intended to slow or stop the infection dissemination. In contrast to the situation with email viruses, where the antivirus vendor is typically separate from the Internet service provider, mobile phone service providers have expressed an interest in developing and deploying antivirus measures. As a consequence, these response mechanisms can incorporate the network infrastructure hardware owned by the mobile phone service provider, as well as the information already collected by the phone service provider for billing purposes.

In this section, we propose six response mechanisms for mobile phone viruses. We categorize the response mechanisms as actions taken at one of three response points during the virus propagation process: the point of reception by target phones, the point of infection on target phones, and the point of dissemination from infected phones.

3.1. Virus Response Mechanisms at the Point of Reception

The first two response mechanisms focus on preventing infected MMS messages from reaching their intended targets. These response mechanisms use the infrastructure owned by the mobile phone service provider.

Virus scan of all MMS attachments in an MMS gateway. During the normal delivery process for an MMS message, the mobile phone service provider routes the MMS message through its MMS gateway hardware. As each MMS message passes through a gateway, this virus scan response mechanism examines the MMS attachment for known virus signatures. Attachments identified as infected are prevented from reaching their intended recipients. Admittedly, when a new virus appears, there is lag time between the initial appearance and when the new virus signature can be added to the list of known viruses. Our experimental results illustrate how the length of that delay affects the relative effectiveness of this response mechanism.

Virus detection algorithm in an MMS gateway. While the virus scan response mechanism identifies specific known virus signatures, the virus detection algorithm approach is more universal and can detect previously unidentified viruses. The algorithm identifies infected MMS messages by looking for suspicious traits characteristic of a virus. When a virus is first detected, the virus detection algorithm in the MMS gateway analyzes the infected messages to determine the best way to recognize the presence of this virus in subsequent MMS messages. After the analysis period is complete, the MMS gateway detection algorithm successfully recognizes and stops each subsequent virus-infected MMS with some probability. We study how high this probability must be in order for the detection algorithm to be effective.

Both the virus scan and the virus detection algorithm operate within the MMS gateway infrastructure of the phone service provider. These response mechanisms at the point of reception stop the infected message in transit before the message reaches the target phone. The next line of defense involves stopping the virus at the point of infection.

3.2. Virus Response Mechanisms at the Point of Infection

The next two response mechanisms focus on the infected MMS messages that have already passed through the MMS gateways and have arrived in the inboxes of target phones. The goal here is to stop the virus from actually infecting the target phone. This can be accomplished by stopping the user from accepting the infected MMS attachment or by immunizing the phone against the virus attack.

Phone user education. Educating phone users about the risks associated with accepting and installing unsolicited MMS message attachments can help reduce the probability that users will choose to accept infected messages [3]. Since the user acceptance of the virus is a vital link in the virus propagation, reducing the probability of acceptance has a direct impact on the ability of a virus to spread. Many people are still unaware of the existence of mobile phone viruses, and educating those phone users would encourage them to be more cautious concerning suspicious MMS messages. Phone user education can also include warning messages when the user attempts to perform actions that would potentially compromise the security of the phone. For example, the installation of digitally unsigned executable files could trigger a warning message to the user.

Our experimental results illustrate how decreasing the probability that a phone user will accept a virus to only one-half or one-fourth of the baseline acceptance rate can limit the virus spread.

Immunization using software patches. Although the phone user education response mechanism strives to dissuade the user from accepting infected messages, other response mechanisms, such as immunization, can prevent infection even if the user accepts the MMS message attachment. The immunization response mechanism operates using software placed directly on each mobile phone.

After the service provider detects a virus that exploits a vulnerability, the service provider begins developing a patch to fix that vulnerability. Once the patch is developed, the immunization software resident on each mobile phone automatically installs any immunization patches available. Due to bandwidth constraints, all the phones cannot receive the patch simultaneously, so the patch is rolled out to the entire phone population uniformly over a period of time. The more servers that are dedicated to distributing these patches, the faster the deployment to all susceptible phones in the network. After the deployed patch arrives at a particular phone, that phone becomes immunized from the virus if not already infected, or the patch stops further propagation attempts from the phone if the phone is already infected.

Our experimental results show how both the time to develop the patch and the time to distribute the patch to the entire population of susceptible phones can influence the effectiveness of this response mechanism. Varying the patch distribution time is equivalent to varying the number of servers dedicated to deploying the patch.

Immunization and phone user education are both defensive response mechanisms to protect uninfected phones from becoming infected. However, after a phone has already been compromised, the response mechanism must act offensively to stop further dissemination of the virus.

3.3. Virus Response Mechanisms at the Point of Dissemination

The final two response mechanisms focus on containing the virus spread by preventing infected phones from disseminating more infected messages. Virus spread can be contained if propagation efforts by infected phones are detected and suppressed.

Monitoring for anomalous behavior. Some anomaly detection algorithms for mobile phones already exist [10], [2]. Before the monitoring response mechanism can detect anomalous virus behavior, the monitoring mechanism must first be trained to recognize normal user behavior. Our monitoring mechanism is a count of the number of MMS messages sent from a particular phone during a period of time. When the monitor detects an excessive number of outgoing MMS messages (above a threshold based on normal expected usage), the behavior is flagged as suspicious.

When a phone is suspected of being infected, there are several possible responses, including simply alerting the phone user, completely blocking subsequent outgoing messages from the phone, or adding a forced waiting time between outgoing messages. For the monitoring response mechanism in our experiments, the forced delay between outgoing messages is imposed on phones that exceed the specified threshold. Our studies compare the effectiveness of the monitoring response mechanism while varying the length of the enforced minimum time between outgoing messages.

Blacklist phones suspected of infection. In contrast to the monitoring response mechanism that counts all outgoing MMS messages (infected or not), the blacklisting response mechanism counts only messages suspected of being infected. Then, when the number of suspected infected messages for a phone reaches some threshold value, the service provider places that phone on a blacklist and completely stops MMS service for that phone (until the phone is proven to be uninfected). Our experiments determine how low the threshold must be for blacklisting to be effective against different types of viruses.

In summary, the six proposed response mechanisms are categorized based on the three response points in the propagation process: the point of reception by target phones, the point of infection on target phones, and the point of dissemination from infected phones. The effectiveness of these six response mechanisms is evaluated using a model of virus propagation in a mobile phone system.

4. Model Implementation

To quantify mobile phone virus spread and evaluate the effectiveness of the response mechanisms, we perform simulations using a parameterized stochastic model of a network of mobile phones. Some parameters control virus behavior and are varied to produce different virus scenarios. Other parameters control specific characteristics of the response mechanisms.

The scope of the model includes only mobile phone viruses that spread between phones via infected MMS message attachments. The model only simulates the MMS traffic due to the virus and does not track the delivery of legitimate messages between the phones. The mobile phone viruses that are simulated here infect only the phones themselves, not the phone network infrastructure. It is also assumed that the phone network infrastructure can support the extra volume of MMS messages generated by the viruses.

In this section, we describe how the model construction facilitates evaluating the effectiveness of response mechanisms. Using the general parameterized model, we show how four specific virus scenarios are defined. These four viruses are the test cases for evaluating the response mechanisms. The section concludes with brief discussions of the topology of contact list connections and the role of phone user consent in virus propagation.

4.1. Modeling Phones and Phone Networks

To simulate virus propagation, we first develop a model representing the mobile phone system in which the virus operates. The entire phone system model is developed in the Möbius software tool [4] and is composed of 1000 individual phone submodels, of which 800 are randomly designated as susceptible to infection. We assume that there is enough homogeneity in the population of mobile phones—the same operating system platform or the same application software—that 80% of the mobile phone population could be vulnerable to the same virus.

Each phone submodel represents a single phone and is initialized and assigned a unique identification number. Then the phone is given a contact list containing the identification numbers of other phones. The contact lists are reciprocal; if phone 22 is in the contact list of phone 83, then phone 83 is in the contact list of phone 22. The contact lists connect phones so that MMS messages can be sent between them.

The submodel for each phone contains two functionalities: receiving and sending infected messages. The portion of the model that receives messages is the only active part of the model for phones that are still uninfected. The incoming infected MMS messages wait in the inbox until the phone user makes a decision whether to accept (open) the MMS message attachment. The decision to accept the MMS message occurs with some defined probability. If the user rejects (deletes) the MMS message attachment, then the infection attempt was unsuccessful. However, if the user

chooses to accept the MMS message attachment, then that phone becomes newly infected.

After a phone becomes infected, the portion of the phone submodel that sends out infected messages becomes enabled. Several parameters control the frequency at which outgoing infected messages are dispersed. The virus may restrict the total number of infected messages sent from a particular phone within a certain time period (e.g., 30 messages per day).

Because the model is implemented in a parameterized fashion, many different virus behaviors can be simulated. For example, the propagation process can identify new target phones either by using the contact lists of infected phones or by randomly selecting mobile phone numbers. Another example of the parameterized options is that each infected message can be addressed to single or multiple recipients.

4.2. Four Illustrative Virus Scenarios

The flexibility of our parameterized phone virus propagation model enables the study of a large variety of possible viruses. However, to perform any meaningful analysis, we must choose feasible sets of input parameters that characterize potential viruses. We define four example virus scenarios that demonstrate a range of attack approaches based on real mobile phone viruses such as CommWarrior.

Virus 1. When a mobile phone is infected with Virus 1, the phone immediately begins to send infected MMS messages to the phones in its contact list. To avoid alerting the phone user that something is amiss, the virus waits at least 30 minutes between consecutive infected messages, and each message is sent to a single recipient.

Virus 1 also limits itself to sending 30 messages between reboots of the phone. This limit is based on behavior seen in the mobile phone virus CommWarrior. The time between phone reboots is on average approximately 24 hours.

Virus 2. Compared with Virus 1, Virus 2 attempts to spread much more aggressively, engaging in behavior that a phone user might more readily recognize as suspicious. As with Virus 1, a phone infected with Virus 2 immediately begins to send infected MMS messages to the phones in its contact list; however, Virus 2 waits a minimum of only one minute between consecutive infected messages instead of the minimum 30-minute wait for Virus 1. In addition, Virus 2 addresses each infected MMS message to multiple recipients (up to 100 recipients per message). These factors dramatically increase the speed at which Virus 2 can reach all the contacts in the contact list of an infected phone.

The main throttle on the number of messages that Virus 2 spawns is that only 30 infected MMS messages can be sent from each infected phone per 24-hour period. Because the minimum wait between infected messages is so short for Virus 2, those 30 messages are all sent very near the start of each 24-hour period. This non-uniform nature of the active infection spread of Virus 2 will be evident in the simulation results.

Virus 3. Virus 3 propagates by dialing random mobile phone numbers. In France, all mobile phone numbers start with the same prefix, and approximately one third of the possible phone numbers with the mobile phone prefix are valid mobile phone numbers. This parameter—the fraction of valid random mobile phone numbers—can be adjusted to reflect other circumstances.

When a phone becomes infected with Virus 3, the phone immediately begins to send MMS messages to random mobile phone numbers. One-third of the attempted phone numbers are valid. The minimum wait between these infected messages is one minute, and each message is sent to only one phone number. This virus imposes no daily limits on the number of infected messages sent, so the spread of Virus 3 is very rapid.

Virus 4. The final example virus is the most stealthy virus of the four. When a phone is infected with Virus 4, the phone does not immediately begin sending out infected messages as the other viruses do. After an initial one-hour dormancy period, this stealthy virus waits until the phone user sends or receives a legitimate MMS message and then automatically either appends the infection to outgoing MMS messages or sends infected reply messages in response to incoming MMS messages. Although the model implementation does not include legitimate message traffic, the model still simulates sending infected messages in conjunction with legitimate incoming and outgoing traffic. The model does so by sending out infected messages at the same rate that a phone might expect to send and receive legitimate messages. The virus is less likely to be noticed by the phone user because the user already expects some data transmission to occur while sending or receiving legitimate messages.

To perform a quantitative analysis of virus spread, we choose combinations of parameter values to simulate the four specific virus scenarios described above. Some response mechanisms are more effective against some types of viruses than others, so this suite of virus test cases can demonstrate the strengths and weaknesses of each response mechanism.

4.3. Phone Contact List Network Topology

Since the contact lists define the connections over which three of the four example viruses spread, the MMS contact lists should appropriately reflect the structure of connectivity within a real phone network.

Although the structure of connectivity through mobile phone contact lists is unknown, email address books can be represented by a power law network [14]. Since a contact list is populated based on the same general social network principles as an email address book, it is not unreasonable to use a power-law random graph to represent the contact list connections within a phone population.

To generate a random graph to represent realistic contact list connections between phones, we utilize the software package Network Graphs for Computer Epidemiologists (NGCE) [13], which is an open source software package for generating network graphs. We modify this graph generation software to produce a contact list output file to be read as input by our Möbius model. Since we expect the sizes of the contact lists for a population of 1000 to conform to a certain distribution, we are able to manipulate the graph package input parameters to produce contact lists with an average contact list size of 80.

4.4. Probability of User Consent

Although the topology of the contact list network can influence the penetration and speed of a mobile phone virus, the virus propagation is also affected by the probability that a phone user will consent to the installation of an infected attachment file. Since users are likely to become more suspicious (and less likely to accept the attachment) as they receive more and more infected MMS messages, the model uses a dynamic probability of acceptance that is dependent on the total number of infected messages that the phone user has previously received.

The decreasing probability of acceptance curve is defined as some initial quantity called the Acceptance Factor divided by the quantity two to the power of the number of infected messages received by that phone. Thus, when the Acceptance Factor is 0.468, as it is in our simulations, the probability of acceptance for the nth received message is $0.468 \div 2^n$. Thus, given that the user receives a large number of infected messages, the probability that a user will eventually give consent to accept an infected file is 0.40.

5. Experimental Results

To evaluate the relative effectiveness of the six proposed response mechanisms, we have defined four test-case virus scenarios using feasible combinations of input parameters. Baseline experiments simulate virus propagation unconstrained by any response mechanism. Experimental results from simulations of the model then demonstrate how effective each response mechanism is against each of the four virus scenarios.

One measure to gauge the effectiveness of a response mechanism is a count of the total number of infected phones

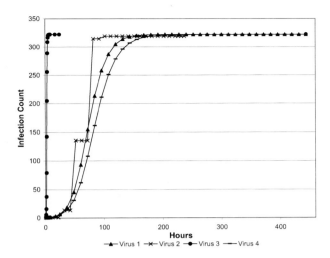

Figure 1. Baseline Infection Curves without Response Mechanisms

in the simulation population. The simulation population contains 800 phones that are susceptible to infection, and the total probability that any given phone user will eventually accept an infected message and become infected is 0.40. Therefore, given enough time, all the unrestrained viruses (without any active response mechanisms) can be expected to infect approximately $800 \times 0.40 = 320$ phones, assuming each susceptible phone receives enough infected messages.

Before we can evaluate the effectiveness of any response mechanism, we must first examine the baseline virus spread without any response mechanisms.

5.1. Baseline Studies

All four of the virus scenarios produce classic virus infection curves, although Virus 2 displays a more jagged curve. As shown in all four curves in Figure 1, the infected population grows at a rate that is first increasing and then decreasing as the number of infected phones reaches a plateau. The virus propagation occurs on different time scales for different viruses. The progression of Virus 2 is tracked over 10 days, and Viruses 1 and 4 are examined over an 18-day period. In contrast, Virus 3 travels so quickly that the simulations only record the infection spread over a 24-hour period. (For that reason, the baseline infection spread for Virus 3 is better observed in Figure 6, which also includes the monitoring response mechanism results for Virus 3.)

The baseline infection curve for Virus 2 resembles a step function more than a smooth curve due to the definition of the virus. The minimum waiting time between infected messages being sent from an infected phone is only one minute (contrasted with a 30-minute wait for Viruses 1 and 4), so the virus sends its whole allotment of 30 messages allowed per day within the first hour of each 24-hour period. This results in a step-like infection curve.

Because of the model parameters held constant, the peak number of infected phones is 320 for all four virus scenarios without response mechanisms. In all four scenarios, 800 phones are susceptible, and each phone user has a 0.40 probability of eventually accepting the virus and becoming infected (provided the phone receives enough opportunities to accept the virus). However, the reaction mechanisms affect the propagation of different viruses in different ways.

5.2. Response Mechanism Studies

Some response mechanisms completely stop further virus propagation, but others simply slow the propagation rate of the virus. Both types of response can be useful. Ideally, the response mechanism would always quickly and completely stop the propagation of a mobile phone virus. However, some viruses spread so quickly that a first response mechanism that slows the spread could buy time to enable activation of a secondary response mechanism that completely halts the propagation process. In the following studies, each response mechanism is evaluated independently.

Virus scan of all MMS attachments in MMS gateways. A virus scan of all MMS attachments as they pass through an MMS gateway is completely effective against viruses with known virus signatures. For that reason, after the new virus signature is added to the list of known viruses, the gateway virus scan is able to completely halt virus propagation.

The gateway virus scan response mechanism is evaluated for three cases. The time required to identify and add the new virus signature to the list (after the virus reaches a detectable level) is varied from 6 hours to 12 hours to 24 hours. As Figure 2 illustrates for Virus 1, a prompt response is most effective because the infection is contained before the virus spread reaches the rapid propagation portion of the curve. When the activation delay is only six hours, the infection only reaches 5% of the infection level in the baseline. Even for an activation delay as large as 24 hours, the virus spread is still contained to 25% of the baseline infection level.

For Viruses 1, 2, and 4, the results with the gateway virus scan look similar because the response mechanism is able to respond while the virus spread is still in its early stages. In contrast, the gateway virus scan is completely ineffectual against rapid viruses like Virus 3 because the virus has already completely penetrated the entire susceptible population before the new virus signature is added to the watch list.

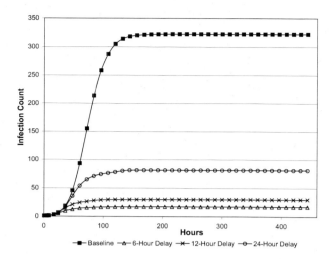

Figure 2. Virus Scan: Varying the Activation Time Delay (Virus 1 shown)

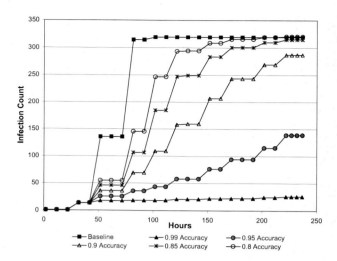

Figure 3. Virus Detection Algorithm: Varying Detection Accuracy (Virus 2 shown)

Thus, the relationship between the speed of the virus propagation and the response mechanism deployment is critical to the success of this response mechanism.

Virus detection algorithm in MMS gateways. In contrast to the gateway virus scan response mechanism, the gateway virus detection algorithm is able only to slow the virus spread, not stop it. Because the detection algorithm attempts to identify infected MMS messages by looking for suspicious traits characteristic of a virus, the algorithm does not catch 100% of the infected MMS messages sent through the MMS gateways. Thus, a small percentage of infected messages still reach target recipients, so the potential for some virus spread remains.

The accuracy of the detection algorithm is a critical factor in the effectiveness of this response mechanism. Therefore, the detection algorithm is evaluated at different levels of accuracy based on the percentage of infected messages that are successfully detected and stopped: 80%, 85%, 90%, 95%, and 99% accuracy. Figure 3 displays how the infection spread of Virus 2 is slowed by the detection algorithm. When the detection algorithm accurately stops 95% of the infected messages, the number of infected phones reaches 135 after nine days of propagation. However, without this reaction mechanism, Virus 2 has infected 135 phones after only two days of propagation. The difference between two and nine days is significant because the extra time could enable the phone service provider to find a more permanent fix to the problem that could completely halt the virus spread.

Like the gateway virus scan, the gateway detection algorithm produces similar results for Viruses 1, 2, and 4. The gateway detection algorithm is ineffective against rapid-spreading Virus 3 for the same reason that the gateway virus

scan is ineffective: the response mechanism cannot react fast enough.

Phone user education. Since all four of the illustrative virus scenarios require the consent of the phone user to accept the message and infect the phone, changing the probability that a user will accept an infected message has a direct effect on virus propagation.

In the baseline virus scenarios, the total probability that a user will accept an infected message is 0.40. When the phone user education response mechanism is evaluated, the virus spread is examined for the cases in which the total probability of acceptance has been reduced to 0.20 or 0.10. In each case, the 0.20 total probability of acceptance produced a final infection level at one-half the baseline level. Similarly, the 0.10 total probability of acceptance produced a final infection level at one-quarter the baseline level. Figure 4 shows the baseline spread for each virus scenario (with total probability of acceptance equal to 0.40), as well as the phone user education response mechanism (with the total probability of acceptance reduced to 0.20). When the user education response mechanism is enabled, the total number of infected phones plateaus at approximately 80, which is 25% of the number of infected phones in the baseline case. This reduced plateau at 80 infected phones is observed in the infection curve for all four viruses with user education enabled.

Because reducing the probability that a phone user will accept infected MMS messages is the most consistent defense against any type of mobile phone virus requiring user consent, phone user education should be part of any long-term virus response effort. Decreasing the probability of acceptance both slows and eventually stops the virus spread.

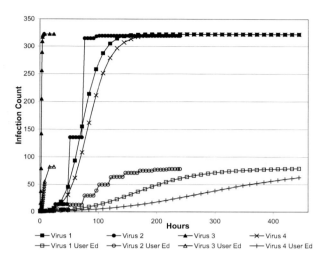

Figure 4. Phone User Education: Effective for All Viruses

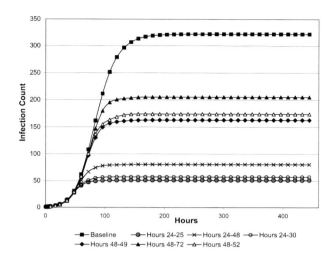

Figure 5. Immunization Using Patches: Varying the Deployment Times (Virus 4 shown)

The caveat is that education is an ongoing effort due to the constant influx of new users.

Immunization using software patches. Mobile phone immunization involves the installation of patches to fix vulnerabilities that a virus could otherwise exploit. Both the time to develop the patch and the time to install the patch on every susceptible phone contribute to the delay in fully activating this response mechanism. As the analysis of other response mechanisms has demonstrated, the time required to fully deploy a response mechanism can have a large bearing on its effectiveness, especially concerning rapidly spreading viruses such as Virus 3.

Of the six tested variations of the immunization response mechanism, three require 24 hours to develop the patch after the virus becomes detectable, and the other three require 48 hours. Within each set of three, the length of time to deploy the patch to all susceptible phones varies from 1 hour to 6 hours to 24 hours. As shown by the results for Virus 4 in Figure 5, the patch development time determines how long the virus is permitted to spread unrestrained. Each curve is identified by the hours during which the deployment is in progress. For example, the "Hours 24-30" curve displays the results when patch development requires 24 hours and distribution requires an additional 6 hours. The three most effective cases, in which the patch is developed in only 24 hours, start limiting the virus spread earlier in the propagation curve than do those cases that require 48 hours to develop the patch.

Regardless of the patch development time, the length of time to fully distribute the immunization patch (1, 6, or 24 hours) influences how much more the virus can spread during the patch distribution process. When patch deployment

begins 24 hours after the initial virus detection and occurs uniformly over a 24-hour period, approximately 60% more phones become infected than if the patch deployment had occurred over only one hour. However, the trade-off to a fast deployment is that many servers are necessary to handle the large amount of bandwidth, which can be expensive.

Viruses 1 and 2 once again show results comparable with Virus 4, and Virus 3 once again resists the efforts of a response mechanism. Virus 3 moves too fast for a patch to be developed and deployed in time to be effective.

Monitoring for anomalous behavior. The final two response mechanisms are responsible for limiting the attempts of infected phones to send outgoing infected MMS messages. Since monitoring detects sharp peaks in activity, monitoring for anomalous behavior is most effective against aggressive viruses that attempt to send an extremely large number of messages within a short time period. Once activated, the monitoring response mechanism introduces a forced waiting period between any two consecutive messages, which greatly slows the pace of virus propagation.

The monitoring response mechanism is evaluated while the length of the enforced waiting period is varied from 15 to 30 to 60 minutes. Figure 6 displays the effect of the monitoring response mechanism on fast-moving Virus 3. The speed of Virus 3 makes it resistant to response mechanisms with long activation times, but that same aggressive nature is what enables the monitoring response mechanism to identify its suspicious behavior. Even when the imposed waiting time between all outgoing messages from a suspected infected phone is only 15 minutes, this response mechanism can still constrain the infection level to under 150 phones for up to 20 hours. In contrast, the baseline Virus 3 can in-

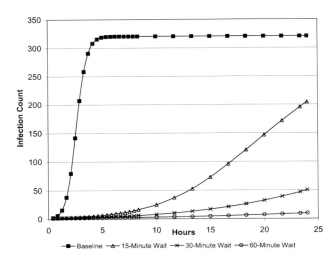

Figure 6. Monitoring: Varying the Wait Time for Suspicious Phones (Virus 3 shown)

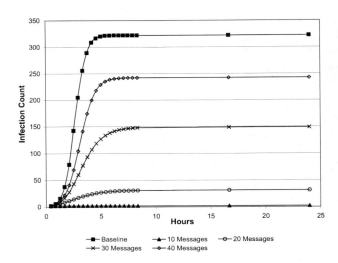

Figure 7. Blacklisting: Varying the Activation Threshold (Virus 3 shown)

fect 150 phones in only about two and one-half hours. The monitoring response mechanism buys time for a secondary response mechanism to be implemented and stop a rapidly-spreading virus.

Although very effective against Virus 3, the monitoring response mechanism is ineffectual against Viruses 1, 2, and 4 because the self-imposed constraints of those viruses limit the total number of messages sent from each phone per unit time. As a result, the volume of infected messages sent from any one infected phone within a monitoring observation period is not radically different from the volume of normal message traffic. Thus, the monitoring response mechanism does not effectively detect Viruses 1, 2, or 4.

Blacklist phones suspected of infection. The blacklist response mechanism blocks all outgoing messages from a phone after the number of suspected infected messages exceeds some threshold. The threshold should ideally be as high as possible to avoid false positive activation of the blacklist response, but the threshold must be low enough to effectively restrict the dissemination of infected messages. To study the effectiveness of the blacklist response mechanism, infected phones are blacklisted after 10, 20, 30, or 40 infected messages.

Blacklisting at a threshold level of 10 infected messages is somewhat effective for Viruses 1 and 4. The infection penetration is restricted to approximately 60% of the baseline infection penetration. However, blacklisting at higher thresholds is ineffective for these viruses.

Blacklisting is completely ineffective for Virus 2 at any threshold level because Virus 2 sends each infected message to many recipients, so the number of infected messages sent from a phone does not accurately capture the amount

of virus propagation activity.

The blacklist response mechanism is most effective against Virus 3 (Figure 7) because Virus 3 propagates to random phones without using contact lists. Only one-third of the randomly-addressed infected messages are sent to valid recipients, but all of those infected messages count toward the threshold limit of suspected infected messages. Therefore, blacklisting with a threshold level of 30 infected messages implemented against a virus with random propagation is equivalent, in terms of effectiveness, to blacklisting with a threshold level of 10 against a virus with contact list propagation (where all contact phone numbers are assumed to be valid).

5.3. Optimal Response Strategy

Each response mechanism is designed to slow or stop the propagation of mobile phone viruses, but different response mechanisms are needed to fight different types of viruses.

For rapidly propagating viruses like Virus 3, the most effective response mechanisms are based on monitoring for anomalous behavior, such as the excessive volume of outgoing messages generated by an infected phone. The specific response strategy implemented after the virus is detected determines whether the response mechanism merely slows the virus spread (as monitoring did) or completely stops infected messages from being sent from the infected phone (as blacklisting did).

For more slowly propagating viruses, a more discriminating response mechanism is necessary to identify the presence of a mobile phone virus. This response can occur in the MMS gateway infrastructure owned by the phone service provider or in individual mobile phones. The advantage to stopping infected messages in MMS gateways is that the mechanism is controlled by the phone service provider and is largely hidden from phone users. Also, response mechanisms in the MMS gateways could mitigate some traffic congestion due to infected messages.

Though possibly less straightforward to implement, educating phone users about the risks of mobile phone viruses should not be neglected. Since user education has universal effectiveness, this response mechanism could enhance the overall effectiveness of any virus mitigation strategy.

Because mobile phone viruses have the potential to attack in many different ways, an optimal response strategy must incorporate mechanisms to counteract a wide variety of virus behaviors. Although the results presented here use a population size of 1000 phones, additional experiments with a 2000-phone population demonstrate that our results scale nicely to larger population sizes.

Our results would also be valuable in conjunction with implementation cost data for each response mechanism. Since the implementation costs could vary greatly depending on the implementation details and the existing infrastructure of an individual service provider, broad cost-based comparisons between response mechanisms without company-specific cost data would be difficult to justify. However, we can still assume that there are increasing costs associated with implementing a stronger version of the same response mechanism. Given this, the results of our experiments are useful for locating the point of diminishing returns for each individual response mechanism, the point where implementing a faster or more accurate response mechanism does not much improve the success rate of the response mechanism.

6. Conclusions

Mobile phone viruses present an emerging problem that threatens the dependability and security of mobile phone communications. We proposed six response mechanisms that respond to this threat at three response points in the propagation process: the point of reception by target phones, the point of infection on target phones, and the point of dissemination from infected phones. To quantify the effectiveness of these response mechanisms, we developed a model to simulate virus propagation with and without response mechanisms. Within the model, four specific virus test cases were used to evaluate the effectiveness of the response mechanisms. The experimental results revealed that response mechanisms must be agile enough to respond quickly to rapidly propagating viruses and discriminating enough to detect more stealthy, slowly propagating viruses. An optimal virus response strategy must be able to address many different types of virus behavior.

This work can be extended with an evaluation of com-

binations of reaction mechanisms, particularly when a response mechanism that only slows virus propagation requires a secondary mechanism to completely halt virus spread. This same virus propagation modeling approach can also be used to evaluate response mechanisms for mobile phone viruses that spread through means other than MMS messages, such as viruses that spread using the Bluetooth interface on a phone.

Acknowledgments The authors would like to thank Olivier Billet of France Telecom and Sankalp Singh of the University of Illinois at Urbana-Champaign for useful technical discussions and Jenny Applequist for her editorial comments. The authors thank France Telecom for funding support for this research.

References

[1] L. Billings, W. Spears, and I. Schwartz. A unified prediction of computer virus spread in connected networks. *Physics Letters Review*, pages 261–266, May 2002.

[2] A. Boukerche and M. Notare. Behavior-based intrusion detection in mobile phone systems. *Parallel and Distributed Computing*, (9):1476–1490, 2002.

[3] D. Dagon, T. Martin, and T. Starner. Mobile phones as computing devices: The viruses are coming! *Pervasive Computing, IEEE*, 3(4):11–15, Oct.-Dec. 2004.

[4] D. Deavours, G. Clark, T. Courtney, D. Daly, S. Derisavi, J. M. Doyle, W. H. Sanders, and P. G. Webster. The Möbius framework and its implementation. *IEEE Trans. on Software Engineering*, 28(10):956–969, Oct. 2002.

[5] C. Guo, H. Wang, and W. Zhu. Smart-phone attacks and defenses. *HotNets III*, Nov. 2004.

[6] J. Kephart and S. White. Directed-graph epidemiological models of computer viruses. In *IEEE Comp. Soc. Symp. on Research in Security and Privacy*, pages 343–359, 1991.

[7] N. Leavitt. Mobile phones: The next frontier for hackers? *Computer, IEEE Computer Society*, 38(4):20–23, Apr. 2005.

[8] M. Liljenstam and D. Nicol. Comparing passive and active worm defenses. *Conf. on Quant. Eval. of Sys.*, Sept. 2004.

[9] R. Racicm, D. Ma, and H. Chen. Exploiting MMS vulnerabilities to stealthily exhaust mobile phone's battery. *SECURECOMM*, 2006.

[10] B. Sun, F. Yu, K. Wu, and V. Leung. Mobility-based anomaly detection in cellular mobile networks. *ACM Workshop on Wireless Security*, 2004.

[11] Trend Micro. *Security for Mobile Devices: Protecting and Preserving Productivity*, Dec. 2005.

[12] S. Viveros. The economic impact of malicious code in wireless mobile networks. *4th Intl. Conf. on 3G Mobile Communication Technologies*, pages 1–6, Jun. 2003.

[13] V. Vlachos, V. Vouzi, D. Chatziantoniou, and D. Spinellis. NGCE — network graphs for computer epidemiologists. In *Advances in Informatics: 10th Panhellenic Conf. on Informatics*, pages 672–683, Berlin, Nov 2005. Springer-Verlag.

[14] C. C. Zou, D. Towsley, and W. Gong. Email worm modeling and defense. *Computer Communications and Networks*, pages 409–414, Oct. 2004.

SPECIAL TRACKS

DSN 2007 Tutorials

Luís Rodrigues
Universidade de Lisboa
ler@di.fc.ul.pt

Message from the Tutorials Chair

Tutorials are an important part of the DSN program. They provide an opportunity for attendees to acquire a basic understanding of, and familiarity with, several state of the art topics related to the dependability, security and resilience of systems and networks. Tutorial proposals providing guidance on how technology can be applied successfully in practical systems were particularly encouraged.

This year, nine tutorial proposals were submitted. From these, five tutorials were selected using a two-phase procedure. In the first phase, all proposals were carefully evaluated by a scientific panel composed of Anish Arora, Danny Dolev, Shivakant Mishra, Michel Raynal, Neil Speirs and myself. The panel prepared a recommendation that was discussed, in a second phase, by the DSN steering committee in cooperation with the DSN organizers. The final selection considered many different issues such as, but not limited to, the relevance to the DSN attendees of the subject addressed, the quality of the tutorial structure, the merit and qualification of the speakers, but also practical aspects such as logistic constraints.

Due to the high quality of the submissions received, DSN 2007 is able to offer an excellent set of tutorials on very timely and relevant topics. On behalf of the tutorial scientific panel, I wish to thank all of the authors that submitted proposals and made it possible to assemble such a strong tutorial program. I would also like to thank the members of the scientific panel for their insightful contribution to the selection process. Finally, I would like to thank the DSN 2007 organization, and in particular Tom Anderson and Mohamed Kaâniche, for all the support provided to our panel.

Scientific Panel

A. Arora Ohio State U., USA.

D. Dolev Hebrew U. of Jerusalem, Israel.

L. Rodrigues U. de Lisboa, Portugal. (chair)

M. Raynal IRISA, France.

N. Speirs Newcastle U., UK.

S. Mishra U. Colorado at Boulder, USA.

List of Selected Tutorials

Tutorial 1 *Surviving Large Scale Failures in the Internet.* K. Kant, Intel Corp.

Tutorial 2 *Model-Based Engineering of Dependable Systems with AADL.* D. Gluch, SEI/Embry-Riddle Aeronautical U. and B. Lewis, Army AMCOM SED.

Tutorial 3 *Dependable E-Voting Systems.* P. Ryan, Newcastle U.

Tutorial 4 *Software Architectures for Dependable Systems.* R. de Lemos, U. of Kent, C. Gacek, Newcastle U. and A-E. Rugina, LAAS-CNRS

Tutorial 5 *Robustness Patterns: coping with software bugs at run-time.* P. Felber, U. of Neuchatel and C. Fetzer, Dresden U.

DSN 2007 Workshops

Christof Fetzer
Chair of Systems Engineering
Computer Science Department
TU Dresden
christof.fetzer@tu-dresden.de

Workshops at DSN provide a forum for a group of participants (typically 20 to 50 in size) to interact and exchange opinions on topics related to any of the many facets of dependable systems and networks. We welcome participation by professionals from a range of diverse backgrounds who can contribute to advancing the technology and understanding of the workshop subject.

This year we received 11 workshop submission. All submissions were reviewed by the DSN Workshop PC which consisted of:

- Christof Fetzer (Chair, Technische Universität, Dresden, Germany)

- Phil Koopman (CMU, USA)

- Shivakant Mishra (University of Colorado, USA)

- Neeraj Suri (Technische Universität, Darmstadt, Germany)

Acceptance of workshop proposals was based on an evaluation of the workshops potential for generating useful results, the timeliness of and expected interest in the topic and the proposers ability to lead a successful workshop.

From the 11 submissions the DSN Workshop PC selected – in coordination with the DSN Steering Committee – 5 workshop proposals:

- Dependable Application Support for Self-Organizing Networks

- Hot Topics in System Dependability

- Assurance Cases for Security: The Metrics Challenge

- Dependable and Secure Nanocomputing

- Architecting Dependable Systems

I would like to take this opportunity to thank all PC members for their work, all workshop proposers for their submissions and all workshop organizers for their hard work of organizing a workshop.

Workshop on Dependable Application Support for Self-Organizing Networks (DASSON 2007)

Paul Ezhilchelvan
Newcastle University, UK
paul.ezhilchelvan@ncl.ac.uk

Michel Raynal
ASAP, IRISA, France
raynal@irisa.fr

Ajoy Datta
Univ of Nevada, Las Vegas, US
datta@cs.unlv.edu

Abstract

This report gives an overview of the workshop on "Dependable Application Support for Self-Organising Networks" held in conjunction with DSN 2007. The principal objective of the workshop is to facilitate a forum for researchers to explore, examine and address dependability related challenges in hosting distributed applications in self-organised networks such as MANETs, sensor and P2P networks.

Workshop Objectives

As self-organising networks, such as mobile ad-hoc networks (MANETs), sensor networks, Peer-to-Peer (P2P) get established through the consolidation of efficient routing and information dissemination schemes, an aspiration will emerge, sooner rather than later, to host sophisticated distributed applications on these networks. Such an aspiration will also be underpinned by advances in hardware technology continually rendering devices more capable in terms of information storage, processing and dissemination. Meeting this aspiration however poses several challenges. For example, MANETs are the only viable technology for conducting mobile multi-party collaborations in terrains void of communication infrastructures. Collaborations in their sophisticated form cannot simply be achieved through the use of reliable multicasts alone; support for maintaining shared state (e.g., group membership) in a dependably consistent manner becomes essential. Though related problems are comprehensively addressed in wired distributed computing, MANET specific solutions are still in the development stage. Similarly, sensor networking is the only fast and effective way to host certain applications such as deep underwater sensing and monitoring the propagation of major oil leaks. However, managing a programmable sensor network comprising several nodes – to a scale typically not encountered in wired distributed computing – will require novel solutions. This proposed workshop will form a forum for researchers to focus on challenges in hosting sophisticated distributed applications in the emerging class of self-organised networks such as MANETs, sensor and P2P networks.

The topics of interest covered mainly are:

- Novel applications and their dependability requirements
- Consensus in MANETs and P2P networks
- Self-stabilisation in Sensor networks
- Algorithms for sensor coverage
- Protocol evaluation and 3-D Simulations
- Data Dissemination and aggregation, and
- Security Issues in Self-Organised Networking Contexts

Keynote

Professor Jon Crowcroft will be the workshop keynote speaker. He is the Marconi Professor of Networked Systems in the Computer Laboratory, the University of Cambridge. Prior to that, he was a Professor of Networked Systems at the University College London (UCL) in the Computer Science Department. Jon is also the Principle Investigator of the prestigious multi-disciplinary project, Communications Research Network, funded to the tune of £3M by the UK government as well as industry to automate the successful exploitations of disruptive communications technologies. He intends to share some of the outcomes of this work during his talk.

Programme Committee

The following members constituted the workshop PC together with the authors of this report. Sajal K. Das (*USA*), Patrick Eugster (*USA*), Roy Friedman (*Israel*), Maria Gradinariu (*France*), Luigi Mancini (*Italy*) Manoj Misra (*India*), Ravi Prakash (*USA*) François Taïani (*UK*) and Alan Tully (*UK*).

Volker Turau (*Germany*) helped us in the review process.

Third Workshop on Hot Topics in System Dependability
HotDep'07

Miguel Castro
Microsoft Research
Cambridge, UK

John Wilkes
Hewlett Packard Laboratories
Palo Alto, CA, USA

1. Introduction

The goals of HotDep are to bring forth cutting-edge research ideas spanning the domains of fault tolerance/reliability and systems, and to build linkages between the two communities (e.g., between people who attend traditional "dependability" conferences such as DSN and IS-SRE, and those who attend "systems" conferences such as OSDI, SOSP, and EuroSys). Previous HotDep workshop programs are available at

`http://hotdep.org/`

To achieve these goals, we selected a program committee for HotDep'07 with a mix of people from both communities. The program committee for this year's workshop was composed of:

Marcos K. Aguilera, Hewlett-Packard Labs
Lorenzo Alvisi, University of Texas at Austin
Paul Barham, Microsoft Research, Cambridge
Garth Gibson, Carnegie Mellon University
Anne-Marie Kermarrec, INRIA, Rennes
Petros Maniatis, Intel Research
Armando Fox, University of California, Berkeley
Ashvin Goel, University of Toronto
Rick Schlichting, AT&T Labs
Paulo Verissimo, University of Lisboa, Portugal
Yuanyuan Zhou, UIUC
Willy Zwaenepoel, EPFL, Lausanne

We received 22 submissions. The program committee wrote a total of 118 reviews and each paper was reviewed by at least 5 program committee members. After a meeting in Lisbon on March 23, we decided to accept 6 papers and to accept 16 of the other submissions as posters to be presented at the workshop. The 6 accepted papers were:

Delta Execution for Software Reliability Yuanyuan Zhou, Darkov Marinov, Craig Zilles, William Sanders, Joe Tucek, Marcelo D'Amorim, and Steven Lauterburg (University of

Illinois at Urbana Champaign)

Reliable Device Drivers Require Well-Defined Protocols Leonid Ryzhyk, Timothy Bourke, and Ihor Kuz (NICTA and the University of New South Wales)

Large-Scale Byzantine Fault Tolerance: Safe but Not Always Live Rodrigo Rodrigues (INESC-ID and Tech. Univ. Lisbon), Petr Kouznetsov (MPI-SWS), and Bobby Bhattacharjee (Univ. of Maryland)

Data Sanitization: Improving the Forensic Utility of Anomaly Detection Systems Gabriela F. Cretu, Angelos Stavrou, Salvatore J. Stolfo and Angelos D. Keromytis(Columbia University)

Improving Dependability by Revisiting Operating System Design Francis David, Jeffrey Carlyle, Roy Campbell, Ellick Chan, and Philip Reames (University of Illinois at Urbana Champaign)

Classic Paxos vs. Fast Paxos: Caveat Emptor Flavio Junqueira (Yahoo! Research), Yanhua Mao, and Keith Marzullo (UC San Diego)

The posters span many subjects: operating systems, hardware, networking, security, and distributed systems. The papers and posters will be published in a supplement to the DSN proceedings and also online at

`http://hotdep.org/2007`

We thank all the authors, the program committee, and George Candea (the chair of the steering committee) for helping us put this fun program together.

Workshop on Architecting Dependable Systems (WADS 2007)

Rogério de Lemos
University of Kent, UK
r.delemos@kent.ac.uk

Felicita Di Giandomenico
ISTI-CNR, Italy
f.digiandomenico@isti.cnr.it

Cristina Gacek
Newcastle University, UK
cristina.gacek@ncl.ac.uk

Abstract

This workshop summary gives a brief overview of the workshop on "Architecting Dependable Systems" held in conjunction with DSN 2007. The main aim of this workshop is to promote cross-fertilization between the software architecture and dependability communities. We believe that both of them will benefit from clarifying approaches that have been previously tested and have succeeded as well as those that have been tried but have not yet been shown to be successful.

1. Introduction

This workshop will continue the initiative, which started five years ago, of bringing together the international communities of dependability and software architectures. The first workshop on Architecting Dependable Systems was organised during the International Conference on Software Engineering (ICSE) 2002. Since then six workshops were organised and three books were published [1]. This series of workshops have shown to be a fertile ground for both communities to clarify previous approaches, thus helping to promote new topical areas where the most promising research may lie, while avoiding the reinvention of the wheel.

The main focus of this series of workshops is to address at the architectural level the structuring, modelling, and analysis of dependable software systems. During DSN 2007 WADS the underlying theme will be Architecting Critical Infrastructures.

2. Architecting Dependable Systems

A major challenge lying ahead is how to build dependable systems from existing undependable components and systems that were not originally designed to interact with each other. These components and systems might not provide access to their internal designs and implementations, and they can evolve independently of the overall system. Based on these limitations, the delivery of correct service, and the justification of this ability, has to be obtained from the interfaces and interactions of these components and systems. Architectural representations of systems are effective in understanding broader system concerns by abstracting away from system details, hence the trend of addressing dependability at the architectural level, rather than late in the development process.

The reasoning about dependability at the architectural level can be addressed from different perspectives:

- Architectural description languages, or a combination of different notations, can be employed for modelling systems' architectures in terms of their components and connectors, which might also include adaptors for preventing architectural mismatches.
- For the provision of assurances that indeed faults have been removed from the architectural representation, techniques like model checking and theorem provers are employed together with more traditional approaches, such as architectural inspections. Tests and fault injection are also performed to check whether the implementation fulfils the architectural specification.
- Since it is difficult to remove all the faults from a system, provisions have to be made at the architectural level to tolerate residual faults. Efforts for this are in the form of structuring rules, as well as incorporating existing fault-tolerance techniques into architectural abstractions.
- Architectural evaluation of systems should analyse the impact that architectural decisions might have upon system failure. Architectural fault injection and stochastic modeling are some of the means that have been used and are being developed.

3. Workshop Objectives and Topics

The aim of the workshop is to bring together the communities of software architectures and dependability to discuss the state of research and practice when dealing with dependability issues at the architecture level. We are interested in submissions from both industry and academia on all topics related to software architectures for dependable systems. These include, but are not limited to:

- *Rigorous design*: architectural description languages; architectural patterns; formal development; architectural views; architectural support for evolution; integrators (wrappers) for dependability; representation of fault assumptions;
- *Verification & validation*: architectural inspection techniques; theorem proving; type checking; model checking; architecture-based fault injection; architecture-based conformance testing; simulation;
- *Fault tolerance*: redundancy and diversity at the architectural level; error confinement; architectural monitoring; dynamically adaptable architectures; exception handling in software architectures; tolerating architectural mismatches; architectural support for self-healing, self-repairing, self-stabilizing systems; support for adaptable fault tolerance;
- *System evaluation*: assurance based development; dependability modeling and analysis in software architectures; run-time checks of dependability models at the architectural level; tradeoff between dependability and cost;
- *Enabling technologies*: model driven architectures; component based development; aspects oriented development; middleware;
- *Application areas*: safety-critical systems; critical infrastructures; mobile systems; service oriented architectures; embedded systems.

4. Workshop Program

4.1. Keynote Speaker

Professor Wolfgang Emmerich will be our keynote speaker. He is the head of the Software Systems Engineering group (Department of Computer Science) at the University College London. He is well known for his work on middleware-based distributed software architectures, and will be talking about the Dependability of Web Service Architectures.

4.2. Architecting Critical Infrastructures

This year we are building on the theme of *critical infrastructures*. Nowadays, public health, economy, security and quality of life heavily depend on the resiliency of a number of critical infrastructures, including electrical power, telecommunications, transportation and many others. Therefore, addressing the current and future problems in these various critical infrastructure sectors is of paramount importance. With that in mind, a considerable amount of time will be devoted to this topic, with discussions being focused around that area.

For more program details please refer to the DSN 2007 WADS web site [http://www.cs.kent.ac.uk/wads].

5. Committees

5.1 Workshop Organisers

Rogério de Lemos (UK), Felicita Di Giandomenico (Italy), Cristina Gacek (UK).

5.2 Programme Committee

Ivica Crnkovic (Sweden), Holger Giese (Germany), Swapna S. Gokhale (USA), Lars Grunske (Australia), Karama Kanoun (France), Istvan Majzik (Hungary), Eliane Martins (Brazil), Nenad Medvidovic (USA), Henry Muccini (Italy), Priya Narasimhan (USA), Roshanak Roshandel (USA), Rick Schlichting (USA), Elisabeth Strunk (USA), Paulo Verissimo (Portugal)

References

[1] Architecting Dependable Systems. http://www.cs.kent.ac.uk/people/staff/rdl/ADSFuture/index.htm.

Assurance Cases for Security: The Metrics Challenge

Robin Bloomfield[1], Marcelo Masera[2], Ann Miller[3], O. Sami Saydjari[4], Charles B. Weinstock[5]
[1]Center for Software Reliability, [2]Joint Research Center of the European Commission,
[3]University of Missouri at Rolla, [4]Cyber Defense Agency, [5]Software Engineering Institute
reb@csr.city.ac.uk, marcelo.masera@jrc.it, milleran@umr.edu,
ssaydjari@CyberDefenseAgency.com, weinstock@sei.cmu.edu

Abstract

For critical systems it is important to know whether the system is trustworthy and to be able to communicate, review and debate the level of trust achieved. In the safety domain, explicit Safety Cases are increasingly required by law, regulations and standards. Yet the need to understand risks is not just a safety issue and the type of argumentation used for safety cases is not specific to safety alone.

Prior workshops, beginning with one held at DSN 2004, have identified a number of technical, policy and research challenges. The focus of this workshop is on one of these challenges: metrics for assurance cases for security.

1. Introduction

For critical systems it is important to know whether the system is trustworthy and to be able to communicate, review and debate the level of trust achieved. In the safety domain, explicit Safety Cases are increasingly required by law, regulations and standards. It has become common for the case to be made using a goal-based approach, where claims (or goals) are made about the system and arguments and evidence are presented to support those claims.

The need to understand risks is not just a safety issue: more and more organizations need to know their risks and to be able to communicate and address them to multiple stakeholders. The type of argumentation used for safety cases is not specific to safety alone, but it can be used to justify the adequacy of systems with respect to other attributes of interest including security, reliability, etc.

An international community has begun to form around this issue of generalized assurance cases and the challenge of moving from the rhetoric to the reality of being able to implement convincing and valid cases. In a recent article in IEEE Security and Privacy [1] we

outline what we have been doing so far in the security area, what we hope to achieve and where we go next.

Prior workshops, beginning with one held at DSN 2004, have identified a number of technical, policy and research challenges. This workshop will focus on one of these challenges: metrics for assurance cases for security.

2. The Importance of Metrics

Metrics can be essential for supporting decisions regarding the resources provided to develop the assurance case, and the efficacy of the resulting case. However, there is no commonly accepted approach to this topic. The purpose of this workshop is to identify the state of the practice in metrics for assurance cases in the specific context of security, identify promising ways forward and research directions.

We expect that the workshop will produce the following outputs:
1. Identification of the candidate metrics for assurance cases for security and the characteristics which those metrics must posses.
2. A listing of the major classes of evidence for assurance cases for security and a mapping of classes of evidence to metrics.
3. Candidate methods for combining the various classes of evidence toward the desired system security properties.

3. Questions to be Answered

In the context of security the workshop will answer questions such as:
1. What makes an argument compelling?
2. Are there standard patterns for arguments?
3. What arguments should be compelling? What arguments do people actually find compelling?
4. How do additional arguments or evidence serve to increase the compelling nature of a case?

5. If there are accepted notions of what makes a case compelling, to what extent do we know that these accepted notions are correct or incorrect?

6. Is there a measure of compellingness that could be used to compare alternative argumentation structures?

7. How can assurance cases be composed? If they are composed, is it also possible to compose the metrics associated with the individual cases?

8. How can arguments with different compelling force be compounded for supporting the case claims?

9. What new types of evidence are needed to create arguments which are more sound and how will we measure that they are more sound?

10. By what metrics do we assess the effectiveness of evidence?

11. What is the cost/benefit justification for developing an assurance case?

12. Are there different levels of effort depending on the motivation? Can these levels be quantified?

13. Can it be shown that a well-defined and executed assurance case process will cost less than current assurance processes?

14. Given two cases, one that costs more and, by some metric, is more compelling than the other, how does one make the trade?

4. Format and Expected Output

The one day workshop will be held on Wednesday, June 27, 2007. An invited talk will be followed by brief presentations by those who have previously submitted position papers. The "toy" example developed at the June 2005 workshop referenced in [1] will be presented and used to motivate and focus the ensuing discussions. A breakout session will be formed if appropriate and at the end of the day a consolidated report and conclusions will be presented.

5. References

[1] Robin E. Bloomfield, Sofia Guerra, Ann Miller, Marcelo Masera, and Charles B. Weinstock, "International Working Group on Assurance Cases (for Security)," *IEEE Security & Privacy*, vol. 4, no. 3, May/June 2006, pp. 66-68.

Workshop on Dependable and Secure Nanocomputing

Jean Arlat
LAAS-CNRS, University of Toulouse
7, Avenue du Colonel Roche
31077 Toulouse Cedex 04 – France
jean.arlat@laas.fr

Ravishankar K. Iyer
Coordinated Science Laboratory
1308 West Main Street
Urbana, IL 61801 – USA
iyer@crhc.uiuc.edu

Michael Nicolaïdis
TIMA and iRoc Technologies
46, Avenue Felix Viallet
38031 Grenoble – France
michael.nicolaidis@imag.fr

1 Motivation and Topics

The continuous advances and progress made in hardware technology makes it possible to foresee a realm of unprecedented performance levels and new application-driven architectural designs, as evidenced by the recent announcement of a 80-core chip [1]. Nevertheless, the evolution of nanotechnologies raises serious challenges with respect to both dependability and security viewpoints. Issues at stake go far beyond developing protections with respect to accidental disturbances in operation, they also relate to the unreliability and variability that will characterize emerging nanoscale devices. Accounting for malicious threats targeting hardware circuits will constitute another increasing concern.

1.1 Transient Faults in Operation

One classical issue to cope with is related to mitigating the impact of disturbances (e.g., the so called "soft errors") that are increasingly affecting the operation of computing systems [2]. Such a problem, well known in aerospace applications, is currently an issue in networking, servers and medical electronics and is expected to affect also cell phones and automotive systems, due to the impact of ground-based radiation. Indeed, this problem will only worsen as future deep submicron manufacturing processes will create substantial challenges for designers of automotive electronics who are considering turning to programmable logic devices, such as FPGAs, as a flexible, low-cost solution for their next-generation electronics designs. An even wider issue than the one related to scaling, is the impact of power, current and voltage fluctuations. These effects are expected to lead to not only a larger level of transients, but also to a larger defect rate.

Solutions for hardened technologies exist and have been intensively used in the past. However, the high (and often excessive) cost attached to the fabrication lines for such realizations have restricted their usage and obstructed their continuation. Hence, the increasingly need to rely on various forms of fault tolerance techniques [3]. For example, [4] proposes a low-cost time redundancy scheme to cope with soft errors and timing faults. It consists in duplicating the functional flip-flops, driving the duplicate flip-flops by delayed clocks, and then comparing the results of functional and duplicate flip-flops. The Razor architecture [5] uses a similar approach also featuring redundant flip-flops (referred to as "shadow latches") and extends it to achieve lower power dissipation by i) reducing aggressively power supply and ii) using the contents of shadow latches to replace those of the functional ones upon error detection.

1.2 Chips with Massively Defective Devices

The relentless advances made in semiconductor technologies make it possible to envision chips that will incorporate several hundred billions of nanoscale transistor devices in a near future. Two paths are envisioned [6] along this route: either an evolutionary path (reduction of dimensions of silicon microelectronics [7]), or a revolutionary one (design of atomic assemblies investigated in molecular electronics) [8]. In any case, due to small geometrical dimensions and low signal strength, nanoelectronic devices are inherently unreliable and moreover, unpredictable [9, 10].

Accordingly, beyond memory chips, for which reconfiguration of faulty cells at production time is now common practice [11], it is anticipated that general-purpose large-scale processor architectures will also suffer from low-fabrication yield resulting in an increasing number of defective components at delivery. Indeed, the increased circuit sensitivity to small spot defects, the growing sensitivity of long buses (Network on Chips) to cross talk, and in a larger extent the dramatic increase of statistical variation of process parameters in upcoming nanometric process nodes is expected to become the nightmare for yield and reliability engineers. Another important issue concerns control logic in processors, which is growing in size and complexity, and is basically unprotected. The generalization of multicore architectures, and potentially another layer of control, could well exacerbate this problem.

This calls for new paradigms in nanochip design, manufacturing and operation. Actually, resilience enhancement methods (temporal, spatial, as well as adaptive) are needed at various stages of chip lifecycle (production and run-time). Recently, novel fault tolerance approaches have been proposed, beyond device-level and coding techniques, for processor chips, e.g., see [12].

1.3 Hardware Vulnerabilities and Security Threats

Besides accidental faults, one should consider the risks faced by modern integrated circuits with respect to hacking and malicious threats. Of course, smart chips and crypto-processors are the most sensitive targets.

Intrusions may be performed via a wide variety of side channel attacks (e.g., differential power analysis or electromagnetic analysis). Embedded testing devices (such as scan-chains) that are meant to obtain high controllability and observability for test engineers constitute also a weakness from the security viewpoint; indeed, the properties of the scan chain architecture can be used for

809

other kinds of side channel attacks via malevolent "fault injections" exploiting the related "leakage". Indeed, the likelihood of a successful attack depends on both the information leakage of the implementation and the strength/skill of the hacker to make the most of it [13].

To circumvent such attacks, enhanced mechanisms have been proposed beyond the more classical tamper resistant designs or irreversible disconnections; they are either based on asynchronous logic designs [14], signature checks [15] or a mix of reliability and security mechanisms (e.g., see [16]).

2 Objectives and Aims

The aim of the Workshop is to analyze the current status, report on recent advances and forecast the trends for the next decade. Due to the large size of the architectures planned and of the huge number of complex components being involved, the solutions to be investigated gather many facets of the computing discipline: semiconductor technology, chip (processor and memory) architecting, interconnection bandwidth and high speed communication, networking protocols, basic software, fault tolerance, risk assessment, validation, testing, etc.

The Workshop is aimed at characterizing the various impairments and threats as well as distinguishing possible alternative design approaches and operation control paradigms that have to be enforced and/or favored in order to keep achieving dependable and secure computing. Three main goals were identified for the Workshop:

- Review the state-of-knowledge concerning the issues at stake in nanoscale technologies: manufacturing faults, accidental operational faults, malicious attacks.
- Identify existing solutions attached to various design options for mitigating faults and implementing secure and resilient computing devices and systems.
- Assess the risks induced by emerging technologies and foster new trends for cooperative work combining various skills to increase the pace of progress and solutions.

Acknowledgement

The organizers would like to thank the members of the Program Committee for their dedication and support in the set up and organization of this Workshop:
- Jacob A. Abraham, University of Texas, Austin, USA
- Jacques Collet, LAAS-CNRS, Toulouse, France
- Jiri Gaisler, Gaisler Research, Gothenburg, Sweden
- Christian Landrault, LIRMM, Montpellier, France
- Régis Leveugle, TIMA, Grenoble, France
- Subhasish Mitra, Stanford University, CA, USA
- Shubhendu S. Mukherjee, Intel, Hudson, MA, USA
- Nithin M. Nakka, Motorola, Urbana, IL, USA
- Takashi Nanya, University of Tokyo, Japan
- Rubin A. Parekhji, Texas Instruments, Bangalore, India
- Michel Pignol, CNES, Toulouse, France
- Jean-Jacques Quisquater, UCL, Louvain, Belgium
- Pia Sanda, IBM, Poughkeepsie, NY, USA
- Shiuhpyng W. Shieh, Nat. Chiao Tung U. Hsinchu, Taiwan
- Matteo Sonza Reorda, Politecnico di Torino, Italy
- Alex Yakovlev, University of Newcastle upon Tyne, UK
- Vivian Zhu, Texas Instruments, Dallas, TX, USA

References

[1] S. Vangal et al., "An 80-Tile 1.28TFLOPS Network-on-Chip in 65nm CMOS," in Proc. IEEE Int. Solid-State Circuits Conf. (ISSCS-2007), San Francisco, CA, USA, 2007..

[2] Y. Crouzet, J.-H. Collet and J. Arlat, "Mitigating Soft Errors to Prevent a Hard Threat to Dependable Computing," in Proc. 11th IEEE Int. On-Line Testing Symp. (IOLTS-2005), Saint Raphaël, France, 2005, pp. 295-298.

[3] R. K. Iyer, N. M. Nakka, Z. T. Kalbarczyk and S. Mitra, "Recent Advances and New Avenues in Hardware-level Reliability Support," IEEE Micro, vol. 25, no. 6, pp. 18-29, June 2005.

[4] M. Nicolaïdis, "Time Redundancy Based Soft-Error Tolerance to Rescue Nanometer Technologies," in Proc. 17th IEEE VLSI Test Symp. (VTS'99), San Diego, CA, USA, 1999, pp. 86-94.

[5] D. Ernst, S. Das, S. Lee, D. Blaauw, T. Austin, T. Mudge, N. S. Kim and K. Flautner, "Razor: Circuit-Level Correction of Timing Errors for Low-Power Operation," IEEE Micro, vol. 24, no. 6, pp. 10-20, November-December 2004.

[6] R. I. Bahar, D. Hammerstrom, J. Harlow, W. H. Joyner, C. Lau, D. Marculescu, A. Orailoglu and M. Pedram, "Architectures for Silicon Nanoelectronics and Beyond," Computer, vol. 40, no. 1, pp. 25-33, January 2007.

[7] D. A. Antoniadis, I. Aberg, C. N. Chléirigh, O. M. Nayfeh, A. Khakifirooz and J. L. Hoyt, "Continuous MOSFET Performance Increase with Device Scaling: The Role of Strain and Channel Material Innovations," IBM J. Research & Development, vol. 50, no. 4/5, pp. 363-376A, July/Sept. 2006.

[8] M. T. Nienmier, R. Ravichandran and P. M. Kogge, "Using Circuits and Systems-level Research do Drive Nanotechnology," in Proc. IEEE Int. Conf. on Computer Design: VLSI in Computers and Processors (ICCD-2004), San Jose, CA, USA, 2004, pp. 302-309.

[9] G. Roy, A. R. Brown, F. Adamu-Lema, S. Roy and A. Asenov, "Simulation Study of Individual and Combined Sources of Intrinsic Parameter Fluctuations in Conventional Nano-MOSFETs " IEEE Trans. on Electron Devices, vol. 53, no. 12, pp. 3063-3070, December 2006.

[10] W. Haensch et al., "Silicon CMOS Devices Beyond Scaling," IBM J. Research & Development, vol. 50, no. 4/5, pp. 339-361A, July/Sept. 2006.

[11] M. Nicolaïdis, N. Achouri and L. Anghel, "A Diversified Memory Built-In Self-Repair Approach for Nanotechnologies," in Proc. 22nd IEEE VLSI Test Symp (VTS'2004), Napa Valley, CA, USA, 2004, pp. 313-318.

[12] T. Nakura, K. Nose and M. Mizuno, "Fine-Grain Redundant Logic Using Defect-Prediction Flip-Flops," in Proc. IEEE Int. Solid-State Circuits Conf. (ISSCS-2007), San Francisco, CA, USA, 2007.

[13] F.-X. Standaert, E. Peeters, C. Archambeau and J.-J. Quisquater, "Towards Security Limits in Side-Channel Attacks (With an Application to Block Ciphers)," in Proc. Cryptographic Hardware and Embedded Systems (CHES 2006), (L. Goubin and M. Matsui, Eds.), LNCS 4249, pp. 30-45, Yokohama, Japan: Springer, 2006.

[14] Y. Monnet, M. Renaudin and R. Leveugle, "Designing Resistant Circuits against Malicious Faults Injection Using Asynchronous Logic," IEEE Trans. on Computers, vol. 55, no. 9, pp. 1104-1115, September 2006.

[15] D. Hely, M.-L. Flottes, F. Bancel, B. Rouzeyre, N. Bérard and M. Renovell, "Scan Design and Secure Chip," in Proc. 10th IEEE On-Line Testing Symp. (IOLTS-2004), Madeira Island, Portugal, 2004, pp. 219-224.

[16] N. Nakka, Z. T. Kalbarczyk, R. K. Iyer and J. Xu, "An Architectural Framework for Providing Reliability and Security Support," in Proc. IEEE/IFIP Int. Conf. on Dependable Systems and Networks (DSN-2004), Florence, Italy, 2004, pp. 585-594.

Student Forum

Farnam Jahanian
Department of EECS, University of Michigan
farnam@umich.edu

The Student Forum at DSN provides an opportunity for students currently working in the area of dependable computing to present and discuss their research objectives, approach and preliminary results. The Forum is centered on a conference track during which the selected student research papers are presented. Student Forum research papers are brief three-page single-authored presentations of ongoing research by graduate students.

Papers were selected according to their originality, relevance and interest to the dependability community. The submitted papers were reviewed by a selection committee that included: Andrea Bondavalli (University of Florence, Italy), Michel Cukier (University of Maryland, USA), William Sanders (University of Illinois, USA) and the Student Forum Chair.

This year, the DSN technical program includes two sessions on the accepted Student Forum papers, gathering stimulating and enriching contributions from doctoral student from across the world.

Fast Abstracts

Chair
Hiroshi Nakamura

Research Center for Advanced Science and Technology, The University of Tokyo, JAPAN
nakamura@hal.rcast.u-tokyo.ac.jp

Fast Abstracts are brief two page presentations, either on new ideas, opinion pieces, or a project update. They cover wide variety of issues within the field of dependable systems and networks. They are also designed to offer an opportunity for late-breaking results, partial results, or work in progress to be reported in a timely fashion. As such, they are lightly reviewed by the Fast Abstracts Program Committee and are not subjected to the rigorous referee process for regular DSN papers. The late submission deadline and expedited screening, along with the corresponding 5-minute talk during DSN, allow for very rapid dissemination and timely feedback from the community.

This year's program features 45 papers from university and industry spanning 14 countries. Accepted Fast Abstracts will be published in the supplementary volume of the 2007 International Conference on Dependable Systems and Networks. We are particularly pleased to have presentations from scientists and engineers in industry that would not normally have the time to produce a full DSN paper. Their contribution mirrors the goal of Fast Abstracts to provide a greater diversity of participation and corresponding exchange of ideas than is possible with regular paper presentation alone.

We hope that this year's presentations stimulate much thought and make exchange of views enjoyable.

Fast Abstracts Program Committee

Hiroshi Nakamura, The University of Tokyo, Japan
Antonio Casimiro Costa, University of Lisboa, Portugal
Michel Cukier, University of Maryland, USA
Elias Procopio Duarte Jr., Federal University of Parana, Brazil

The National Programme for Information Technology in the UK Health Service

Dependability Challenges and Strategies

Brian Randell

Newcastle University

The National Health Service (NHS) provides the majority of health-care in the UK. Its main section, that for England, serves a population of over 50 million, employs 40,000 general practitioners (family physicians), 80,000 other doctors, and 350,000 nurses, and includes over 300 hospitals. Its National Programme for Information Technology (NPfIT) is the largest civil IT project in the world. (Estimates of its total cost have ranged from £6.2 billion up to £20 billion.) This project, which was launched in 2002, aims to implement electronic care records for all patients and to provide a reliable and secure information service, for medical records, radiography, patient administration, etc., for all the hospitals, and all general practitioners' premises, to which all the NHS health professionals in England will have strictly-controlled access. This Special Plenary Session will provide an overview of NPfIT, and its dependability challenges and strategies. Speakers will, it is hoped, include representatives of Connecting for Health (the NHS Agency responsible for NPfIT), the medical profession, and the dependability research community.

Industry Session

Lisa Spainhower
IBM, USA

Author Index

IEEE Computer Society
Conference Publications
Operations Committee

CPOC Chair
Phillip Laplante
Professor, Penn State University

Board Members
Thomas Baldwin, *Manager, Conference Publishing Services* (CPS)
Mike Hinchey, *Director, Software Engineering Lab, NASA Goddard*
Paolo Montuschi, *Professor, Politecnico di Torino*
Linda Shafer, *Professor Emeritus, University of Texas at Austin*
Jeffrey Voas, *Director, Systems Assurance Technologies, SAIC*
Wenping Wang, *Associate Professor, University of Hong Kong*

IEEE Computer Society Executive Staff
Angela Burgess, *Publisher*

IEEE Computer Society Publications
The world-renowned IEEE Computer Society publishes, promotes, and distributes a wide variety of authoritative computer science and engineering texts. These books are available from most retail outlets. Visit the CS Store at *http://www.computer.org/portal/site/store/index.jsp* for a list of products.

Revised: 16 March 2007

An IEEE Online Collaborative Publishing Environment

CPS Online is a new IEEE online collaborative conference publishing environment designed to speed the delivery of price quotations and provide conferences with real-time access to all of a project's publication materials during production, including the final papers. The *CPS Online* workspace gives a conference the opportunity to upload files through any Web browser, check status and scheduling on their project, make changes to the Table of Contents and Front Matter, approve editorial changes and proofs, and communicate with their CPS editor through discussion forums, chat tools, commenting tools and e-mail.

The following is the URL link to the CPS Online Publishing Inquiry Form:
http://www.ieeeconfpublishing.org/cpir/inquiry/cps_inquiry.html